The first Latin dictionary ever to be compiled on the basis of modern lexicographical principles.

THE NEW COLLEGE
LATIN & ENGLISH DICTIONARY

COMPREHENSIVE: More than 63,000 words and phrases.

DEFINITIVE: Based on the foremost Classical authorities and organized to achieve the utmost clarity, precision, and convenience.

MODERN: Obsolete definitions have been replaced by fresh translations that correspond to current English usage.

A NEW LANDMARK
IN LATIN-ENGLISH DICTIONARIES
FOR THE MODERN STUDENT!

THE BANTAM NEW
COLLEGE DICTIONARY SERIES

John C. Traupman, Author

JOHN C. TRAUPMAN received his B.A. in Latin and in German at Moravian College and his M.A. and Ph.D. in Classics at Princeton University. He is chairman of the Department of Classical Languages at St. Joseph's University (Philadelphia). He served as president of the Philadelphia Classical Society, of the Pennsylvania Classical Association, and of the Classical and Modern Language League. He has published widely in learned journals and is the author of *The Bantam New College German & English Dictionary* (Bantam Books, 1981) and an associate editor of *The Scribner-Bantam English Dictionary* (Scribner's, 1977; Bantam Books, 1979)

Edwin B. Williams, General Editor

EDWIN B. WILLIAMS (1891–1975), A.B., A.M., Ph.D., Doct. d'Univ., LL.D., L.H.D., was chairman of the Department of Romance Languages, dean of the Graduate School, and provost of the University of Pennsylvania. He was a member of the American Philosophical Society and the Hispanic Society of America. Among his many lexicographical works are *The Williams Spanish and English Dictionary* (Scribner's, formerly Holt and *The Bantam New College Spanish and English Dictionary*. He created and coordinated the Bantam series of original dictionaries—English, French, German, Italian, Latin, and Spanish. The University of Pennsylvania named "Williams Hall" in honor of Edwin B. Williams and his wife, Leonore, and is establishing the "Williams Chair in Lexicography," as the first chair in lexicography in an English-speaking country.

THE NEW COLLEGE
LATIN & ENGLISH
DICTIONARY

JOHN C. TRAUPMAN, Ph.D.
St. Joseph's University, Philadelphia

BANTAM BOOKS
TORONTO · NEW YORK · LONDON · SYDNEY

THE NEW COLLEGE LATIN & ENGLISH DICTIONARY
Bantam Language Library edition / April 1966

2nd printing .... *May 1966*	10th printing .... *June 1973*
3rd printing .. *September 1967*	11th printing .... *April 1974*
4th printing .. *September 1968*	12th printing .... *July 1975*
5th printing .. *December 1968*	13th printing .. *February 1977*
6th printing .... *August 1969*	14th printing .... *May 1978*
7th printing .... *May 1970*	15th printing .... *June 1979*
8th printing .... *August 1970*	16th printing .... *March 1980*
9th printing .... *August 1971*	17th printing .... *May 1981*

Library of Congress Catalog Card Number: 66-12159

ISBN 0–553–20255–3

Published simultaneously in the United States and Canada

Bantam Books are published by Bantam Books, Inc. Its trade-mark, consisting of the words "Bantam Books" and the por-trayal of a bantam, is Registered in U.S. Patent and Trademark Office and in other countries. Marca Registrada. Bantam Books, Inc., 666 Fifth Avenue, New York, New York 10103.

PRINTED IN THE UNITED STATES OF AMERICA

26 25 24 23 22 21 20 19 18

INTRODUCTION

Both Latin and English entry words, as well as illustrative phrases under entry words, are treated in strictly alphabetical order.

Adverbs on the Latin-English side are inserted as separate entries and translated in that position without cross-reference to the corresponding adjective.

Adverbs on the English-Latin side ending in -ly are listed under their adjectives

Compound words are generally given in their assimilated forms, e.g., accurrō rather than adcurrō. Cross-references are provided as guides for those using texts which employ the unassimilated forms.

The letter j has been used in place of consonantal i because some recent texts have begun to use the former again and because students can thus more readily distinguish the consonant from the vowel.

If a feminine substantive, singular or plural, of the first declension, a neuter substantive, singular or plural, of the second declension, or a masculine substantive of the second declension falls alphabetically more than one word before or after the corresponding adjective, it is inserted as a separate entry and translated in that position, and a cross-reference to it is given under the adjective; for example, nāt·a -ae *f* occurs fifteen entries before nāt·us -a -um *adj* ... ; *f* see nata.

If such a substantive does not fall alphabetically more than one word before or after the corresponding adjective, it is treated under the adjective.

Many of the variations in spelling of Latin words are indicated by means of cross-references, e.g., sēpiō see saepio.

Only those past participles are listed as separate entries whose difference in form from the first person singular present indicative warrants such listing, provided they fall alphabetically more than one word before or after the first person singular present indicative.

Only the first person singular present indicative and the present infinitive of regular active verbs of the first conjugation are given; in the case of deponent verbs, the perfect is added. For the other three conjugations and for irregular and defective verbs, all principal parts in use are given.

Discriminations between two or more meanings of the entry word are often shown by means of English words in parentheses.

Transitive and intransitive verbs, with their dependent

constructions, are clearly differentiated and are presented in a fixed order of transitive first and intransitive second.

Centered periods within entry words indicate division points at which inflectional elements are to be added.

All source words and phrases are printed in boldface type.

On the English-Latin side a boldface dash represents the vocabulary entry.

On the Latin-English side, the twofold purpose in marking the quantity of vowels is (1) to indicate accentuation of words and (2) to provide the basis for scansion of Classical Latin verse. Thus, all vowels that are long by nature and occur in open syllables are marked, whereas vowels in closed syllables, whether long or short by nature, are not marked, since the syllable in either case is long. However, since a vowel followed by a mute and a liquid can be open or closed, its quantity is marked when it is long. As a further aid to pronunciation, in words of three or more syllables, the short vowel of the penult is marked.

On the English-Latin side, Latin vowels have been marked to distinguish:

(a) words otherwise spelled alike: **lēvis, levis**

(b) the genitive singular and the nominative and accusative plural from the nominative singular of the fourth declension

(c) the ablative singular from the nominative singular of nouns of the first declension whenever the distinction is not clear from the context

(d) the nominative and genitive singular from the accusative plural of *i*-stem words of the third declension

(e) the infinitive of verbs of the second conjugation from the infinitive of verbs of the third conjugation.

On the English-Latin side, the genitive of the nouns of the fourth declension is provided in order to distinguish these nouns from nouns of the second declension ending in -us.

John C. Traupman

vi

PRONUNCIATION

Vowels

	CLASSICAL METHOD	ECCLESIASTICAL METHOD
ă	Like *a* in *ago*: compărō	(Generally as in the Classical Method.
ā	Like *a* in *father*: imāgō	However, in practice the different
ĕ	Like *e* in *pet*: propĕrō	values of the vowels are frequently
ē	Like *a* in *late*: lēnis	not rigidly adhered to.)
ĭ	Like *i* in *hit*: ĭdem	
ī	Like *ee* in *keen*: amīcus	
ŏ	Like *o* in *often*: mŏdus	
ō	Like *o* in *hope*: nōmen	
ŭ	Like *u* in *put*: ŭt	
ū	Like *u* in *rude*: ūtor	
ў	Like *ü* in German *Hütte*: mўrica	
ȳ	Like *ü* in German *über*: Tȳdeus	

Diphthongs

	CLASSICAL METHOD	ECCLESIASTICAL METHOD
ae	Like *y* in *by*: caecus	Like *a* in *late*: caecus
au	Like *ow* in *now*: nauta	As in the Classical Method
ei	Like *ey* in *grey*: deinde	As in the Classical Method
eu	Like *eu* in *feud*: Orpheus	Like *eu* in Italian *neutro*: euge
oe	Like *oi* in *oil*: coepit	Like *a* in *late*: coepit
ui	Like *uey* in *gluey*: cui	As in the Classical Method
	After **q**, like *wee* in *week*: qui	

Consonants

	CLASSICAL METHOD	ECCLESIASTICAL METHOD
b	As in English	As in English
c	Always like *c* in *can*: cīvis, cantō, actus	Before **e, i, ae,** or **oe** like *ch* in *cherry*: excelsis, cīvis, caelum, coepit, but before other letters like *c* in *can*: cantō, actus
d	As in English	As in English
f	As in English	As in English
g	Always like *g* in *go*: genus, gula, gallīna, grātus	Before **e** or **i** like *g* in *gentle*: genus, regīna, but before other letters except **g** and **n** (see under Consonant Groups) like *g* in *go*: gula, gallīna, fugō, grātus
h	As in English	As in English
j	Like *y* in *yes*: jungō, jam	As in the Classical Method
k	As in English	As in English
l	As in English	As in English
m	As in English, but in verse final **m** before an initial vowel in the following word was presumably not pronounced	As in English
n	As in English	As in English
p	As in English	As in English
q	As in English and used only before consonantal **u**	As in the Classical Method
r	Trilled as in the Romance languages	
s	Always like *s* in *sing*: miser, mors	Like *s* in *sing*: salūs, but when standing between two vowels or when final and preceded by a voiced consonant, like *z* in *dozen*: miser, mors
t	Like English *t*, but unaspirated	As in the Classical Method

vii

	CLASSICAL METHOD	ECCLESIASTICAL METHOD
u	Like *w* in *w*ine, when un-accented, preceded by **q,** sometimes by **s,** and sometimes by **g,** and fol-lowed by a vowel: **qui·a, suā·vis (but su·ō·rum), dis·tin·guŏ (but ex·i-gŭ·us)**	As in the Classical Method
v	Like *w* in *w*ine: **vīvŏ**	As in English
x	Like *x* (= ks) in si*x*: **exactus**	Like *x* (=ks) in si*x*: **pax;** but in words beginning with **ex** and followed by a vowel, **h,** or **s,** like *x* (= gz) in e*x*haust: **exaudī, exhālŏ, exsolvŏ**
z	*Like dz in adze:* **zōna**	As in the Classical Method

Consonant Groups

	CLASSICAL METHOD	ECCLESIASTICAL METHOD
bs	Like *ps* in a*pse*: **obsidĕŏ, urbs**	Like *bs* in o*bs*ession: **obsidĕŏ,** but in the final position, like *bs* in o*bs*erve: **urbs**
bt	Like *pt* in ca*pt*ain: **obtinēre**	Like *bt* in o*bt*ain: **obtinēre**
cc	Like *kk* in boo*kk*eeper: **ecce, occīdŏ, occāsum, occlūdŏ**	Before **e** or **i** like *tch* in ca*tch*: **ecce, occīdŏ;** but before other letters, like *kk* in boo*kk*eeper: **occāsum, occlū-dŏ**
ch	Like *ch* in *ch*aotic: **pulcher**	As in the Classical Method
gg	Like *gg* in le*g g*uard: **agger**	Before **e** or **i** like *dj* in a*dj*ourn: **agger;** but before other letters, like *gg* in le*g g*uard: **aggrĕgŏ**
gn	As in English	Like *ny* in ca*ny*on: **dignus**
gu	See consonant **u**	As in the Classical Method
ph	Like *p-h* in to*p-h*eavy: **phōca**	Like *ph* in *ph*oenix: **phōca**
qu	See consonant *u*	As in the Classical Method
sc	Like *sc* in *sc*ope; **sciŏ, scūtum**	Before **e** or **i** like *sh* in *sh*in: **ascendŏ, sciŏ;** but before other letters, like *sc* in *sc*ope: **scandŏ, scūtum**
su	See consonant **u**	As in the Classical Method
th	Like *t* in *t*ake: **theātrum**	As in the Classical Method
ti	Like *ti* in English pa*ti*o: **nātiŏ**	When preceded by **s, t,** or **x** or when followed by a consonant, like *ti* in English pa*ti*o: **hostia, admixtiŏ, fortĭter;** but when unaccented, fol-lowed by a vowel, and preceded by any letter except **s, t,** or **x,** like *tzy* in ri*tzy*: **nātiŏ, pretium**

SYLLABIFICATION

1. Every Latin word has as many syllables as it has vowels or diphthongs: **ae·ger, fī·lĭ·us, Bai·ae**

2. When a word is divided into syllables:
   a) a single consonant between two vowels goes with the following syllable: (**h** is regarded as a consonant; **ch, ph, th, qu,** and sometimes **gu** and **su** are regarded as single consonants)*: **a·ger, ni·hil, a·qua, ci·cho·rē·um**
   b) the first consonant of a combination of two or more consonants goes with the preceding vowel: **tor·men·tum, mit·tō, mon·strum**
   c) a consonant group consisting of a mute (**b, d, g, p, t, c**) followed by **l** or **r** is generally left undivided and goes with the following vowel: **pa·trēs, a·cris, du·plex.** In Classical poetry this combination is often treated like any other pair of consonants: **pat·rēs, ac·ris, dup·lex**
   d) prefixes form separate syllables even if the division is contrary to above rules: **ab·est, ob·lā·tus, abs·ti·nĕ·ō, ab·stō**

3. A syllable ending in a vowel or diphthong is called *open*; all others are called *closed*

4. The last syllable of a word is called the *ultima*; the next to last is called the *penult*; the one before the penult is called the *antepenult*

---

* The double consonant **x** goes with the preceding vowel: **dix·it**

QUANTITY OF VOWELS

1. A vowel is *long* (**lēvis**) or *short* (**lĕvis**) according to the length of time required for its pronunciation

2. A vowel is long:
   a) before **ns, nf,** (and perhaps **gn**): **ingēns, īnfāns, (māgnus)**
   b) when resulting from a contraction: **nīl = nihil, cōgō = cŏăgō, inīquus = inaequus**

3. A vowel is short:
   a) before another vowel or **h**: **dĕa, trăhō**
   b) generally before **nd** and **nt**: **amăndus, amănt**

4. Diphthongs are long: **causae**

QUANTITY OF SYLLABLES

1. Syllables are distinguished as *long* or *short* according to the length of time required for their pronunciation

2. A syllable is long:
   a) if it contains a long vowel or a diphthong: **vē·nī, scrī·bō, cau·sae** (such a syllable is said to be *long by nature*)
   b) if it contains a short vowel followed by **x, z,** or any two consonants except a mute (**b, d, g, p, t, c**) followed by **l** or **r**: **sax·um, gaz·a, mit·tō, cur·sor** (such a syllable is said to be *long by position,* but the vowel is pronounced *short*)

3. A syllable is short:
   a) if it contains a short vowel followed by a vowel or by a single consonant (**h** is regarded as a consonant; **ch, ph, th, qu,** and sometimes **gu** and **su** are regarded as single consonants): **me·us, ni·hil, ge·rit, a·qua**
   b) if it contains a short vowel followed by a mute (**b, d, g, p, t, c**) plus **l** or **r,** but it is sometimes long in verse: **flă·grans, ba·ră·thrum, ce·lĕ·brō** (such a syllable is said to be *common*)

NOTE: In this dictionary, long vowels are marked except before **x, z,** or two or more consonants unless the two consonants are a mute plus a liquid. Only the short penult of words of three or more syllables is marked.

ACCENT

1. Words of two syllables are accented on the first syllable: om′nēs, tan′gō, ge′rit

2. Words of more than two syllables are accented on the penult if it is long: a·mī′cus, re·gun′tur and on the antepenult if the penult is short: fa·mi′lĭ·a, ge′rĭ·tur

3. These rules apply to words with enclitics appended (-ce, -dum, -met, -ne, -que, -ve): vos′met, lau·dat′ne, de′ă·que (nominative), de·ā′que (ablative)

4. In the second declension, the contracted genitive and the contracted vocative of nouns in -ius and the contracted genitive of those in -ium retain the accent of the nominative: Vir·gĭ′lī, in·gĕ′nī

5. Certain words which have lost a final -e retain the accent of the complete forms: il·līc′ for il·lĭ′ce, tan·tōn′ for tan·tō′ne

6. Certain compounds of faciō, in which a feeling for the individuality of the components was preserved, retain the accent of the simple verb: be·ne·fā′cit

---

ABBREVIATIONS

abbr	abbreviation	*interrog*	interrogative
abl	ablative	*loc*	locative
acc	accusative	*m*	masculine noun
adj	adjective	*masc*	masculine
adv	adverb	*math*	mathematics
astr	astronomy	*med*	medicine
bot	botany	*mil*	military
c.	circa, about	*m pl*	masculine plural noun
cent.	century	*mus*	music
coll	colloquial	*n*	neuter noun
com	commercial	*neut*	neuter
comp	comparative	*nom*	nominative
conj	conjunction	*n pl*	neuter plural noun
d.	died	*p*	participle
dat	dative	*phil*	philosophy
defect	defective	*pl*	plural
eccl	ecclesiastical	*pol*	politics
esp.	especially	*pp*	past participle
f	feminine noun	*prep*	preposition
fem	feminine	*pres*	present
fig	figurative	*pron*	pronoun
fl	floruit	*reflex*	reflexive
f pl	feminine plural noun	*rel*	relative
fut	future	*rhet*	rhetoric
genit	genitive	*s*	substantive
gram	grammar	*singl*	singular
impers	impersonal	*subj*	subjunctive
impv	imperative	*superl*	superlative
indecl	indeclinable	*v defect*	defective verb
indef	indefinite	*vi*	intransitive verb
inf	infinitive	*v impers*	impersonal verb
interj	interjection	*vt*	transitive verb

LATIN–ENGLISH

A

ā *interj* ah!

ā or **ab** *prep* (with *abl*) (of agency) by; (of time) since, after, from; (of space) from, away from; at, on, in; **a latere** on the side; **a tergo** in the rear

abactus *pp* of abigo

abăc·us -ī *m* cupboard; game board; abacus, counting board; panel; tray

abaliēnāti·ō -ōnis *f* transfer of property

abaliēn·ō -āre *vt* to alienate, estrange; to sell; to separate

Abantiăd·ēs -ae *m* descendant of Abas

Ab·ās -antis *m* king of Argos, father of Acrisius and grandfather of Perseus

abăv·us -ī *m* great-great-grandfather

abdicāti·ō -ōnis *f* abdication, renunciation, resignation

abdīc·ō -āre *vt* to abdicate, renounce, resign; to disinherit; **se magistrātu abdicāre** to resign from office

ab·dīcō -dīcĕre -dixī -dictum *vt* (in augury) to disapprove of, forbid

abdītē *adv* secretly, privately

abdīt·us -a -um *adj* hidden, secret

ab·dō -dĕre -didī -ditum *vt* to hide; to remove, withdraw; to plunge (*e.g., a sword*)

abdōm·en -inis *n* abdomen, belly; (fig) gluttony, greed

ab·dūcō -dūcĕre -duxī -ductum *vt* to lead away, take away; to seduce; to alienate

ab·eō -īre -iī -itum *vi* to go away, depart; to vanish, disappear; to pass away, die; (of time) to pass, elapse; to change, be changed; to retire

abequit·ō -āre *vi* to ride off

aberrāti·ō -ōnis *f* wandering, escape, relief

aberr·ō -āre *vi* to wander, go astray; to deviate, differ

abesse *inf* of absum

abhinc *adv* ago

abhorr·eō -ēre -uī *vi* to shrink back; (with **ab** + *abl*) **a** to be averse to; **b** to be inconsistent with, differ from; **c** to be free from

abiegn·us -a -um *adj* fir

abi·ēs -ĕtis *f* fir; ship; spear; writing tablet

ab·igō -igĕre -ēgī -actum *vt* to drive away, get rid of; to banish, expel

abit·us -ūs *m* departure; outlet; end

abjectē *adv* abjectly, meanly

abject·us -a -um *adj* abject, mean; downhearted

ab·jiciō -jicĕre -jēcī -jectum *vt* to throw away, throw down; to slight; to give up; to humble, debase

abjūdĭc·ō -āre *vt* to take away (*by judicial decree*)

ab·jungō -jungĕre -junxī -junctum *vt* to unyoke; to detach

abjūr·ō -āre *vt* to deny on oath

ablātīv·us -a -um *adj & m* ablative

ablātus *pp* of aufero

ablēgāti·ō -ōnis *f* sending away, sending off; banishment

ablēg·ō -āre *vt* to send away; to remove, banish; to dismiss

abligurr·iō or **abligūr·iō -īre -īvī** or **-iī -ītum** *vt* to squander, waste

ablŏc·ō -āre *vt* to lease, rent out

ab·lūdō -lūdĕre -lūsī -lūsum *vi* to be unlike; (with **ab** + *abl*) to differ from

ab·lŭō -luĕre -luī -lūtum *vt* to wash away, cleanse, remove

ablūti·ō -ōnis *f* washing, cleansing

abnĕg·ō -āre *vt* to refuse, turn down

abnĕp·ōs -ōtis *m* great-great-grandson

abnept·is -is *f* great-great-granddaughter

abnoct·ō -āre *vi* to stay out all night, sleep out

abnorm·is -e *adj* irregular, unorthodox

ab·nŭō -nuĕre -nuī -nūtum *vt* to refuse, deny

abol·eō -ēre -ēvī -itum *vt* to abolish, destroy, annihilate

abol·escō -escĕre -ēvī *vi* to decay, vanish, die out

abolīti·ō -ōnis *f* abolition

abōmĭn·or -ārī -ātus sum *vt* to detest

aborīgin·ēs -um *m pl* aborigines, original inhabitants

ab·orior -orīrī -ortus sum *vi* to miscarry; to fail; (of stars, etc.) to set

abortī·ō -ōnis *f* miscarriage

abortīv·us -a -um *adj* prematurely born

abort·us -ūs *m* miscarriage

ab·rādō -rādĕre -rāsī -rāsum *vt* to scrape off, shave; (fig) to squeeze out, rob

ab·ripiō -ripĕre -ripŭī -reptum *vt* to take away by force, carry off; to squander

ab·rōdō -rōdĕre -rōsī -rōsum *vt* to gnaw off

1

abrogāti·ō -ōnis *f* repeal

abrŏg·ō -āre *vt* to repeal, annul

abrotŏn·um -ī *n* southernwood (*aromatic, medicinal plant*)

ab·rumpō -rumpĕre -rūpī -ruptum *vt* to break off; to tear, sever

abruptē *adv* abruptly, rashly

abrupti·ō -ōnis *f* breaking off; divorce

abrupt·us -a -um *pp* of **abrumpo**; *adj* abrupt, steep; *n* precipice

abs *prep* (with *abl*, confined almost exclusively to the combination **abs te**) by, from

abs·cēdō -cēdĕre -cessī -cessum *vi* to go away, depart; to retire; to desist

abscessi·ō -ōnis *f* diminution

abscess·us -ūs *m* departure, absence, remoteness

abs·cīdō -cīdĕre -cīdī -cīsum *vt* to cut off, chop off; to cut short

ab·scindō -scindĕre -scīdī -scissum *vt* to tear off, break off; to divide

abscīs·us -a -um *pp* of **abscido**; *adj* steep, precipitous; concise; abrupt

absconditē *adv* secretly; obscurely; profoundly

abscondit·us -a -um *adj* concealed, secret

abs·condō -condĕre -condī or -condīdī -condītum *vt* to hide; to lose sight of, leave behind; to bury (*weapon*)

abs·ens -entis *pres p* of **absum**; *adj* absent

absenti·a -ae *f* absence

absil·iō -īre -īī or -ūī *vi* to jump away

absimil·is -e *adj* unlike; (with *dat*) unlike

absinth·ium -īī or -ī *n* wormwood

abs·is -īdis *f* vault, arch; orbit (*of a star*)

ab·sistō -sistĕre -stitī *vi* to withdraw, depart; to cease, lay off

absolūtē *adv* perfectly

absolūti·ō -ōnis *f* acquittal; perfection, completeness

absolūtōri·us -a -um *adj* of acquittal, granting acquittal

absolūt·us -a -um *adj* perfect, complete, unqualified

ab·solvō -solvĕre -solvī -solūtum *vt* to release, set free, detach; to acquit; to finish off; to pay off, discharge

absŏn·us -a -um *adj* discordant, incongruous, incompatible

absorb·ĕō -ēre -ūī *vt* to swallow, devour; to engross

absque *prep* (with *abl*) without, apart from, but for; **absque me foret** if it had not been for me

abstēmi·us -a -um *adj* abstemious, temperate, sober

abs·tergĕō -tergēre -tersī -tersum *vt* to wipe off, wipe dry; to expel, banish

absterr·ĕō -ēre -ūī -ĭtum *vt* to scare away, deter

abstin·ens -entis *adj* temperate, forbearing; continent, chaste

abstinenter *adv* with restraint

abstinenti·a -ae *f* abstinence, self-control

abs·tinĕō -tinēre -tinŭī -tentum *vt* to withhold, keep away; *vi* to abstain, refrain; (with *genit*, *abl*, or with **ab** + *abl*, with *inf*, with **quin** or **quominus**) to refrain from

abst·ō -āre *vi* to stand at a distance, stand aloof

abs·trāhō -trahĕre -traxī -tractum *vt* to pull away, drag away, remove, detach

abs·trūdō -trūdĕre -trūsī -trūsum *vt* to push away; to conceal

abstrūs·us -a -um *adj* hidden, deep, abstruse; reserved

absum abesse afŭī *vi* to be away, be absent, be distant; (with *abl* or **ab** + *abl*) to be removed from, keep aloof from, be disinclined to; (with **ab** + *abl*) **a** to be different from, be inconsistent with; **b** to be free from; **c** to be unsuitable to, be unfit for; (with *dat*) to be no help to

ab·sūmō -sūmĕre -sumpsī -sumptum *vt* to take away, diminish; to consume, use up, waste; to destroy, ruin

absurdē *adv* out of tune; absurdly

absurd·us -a -um *adj* out of tune; absurd, illogical, senseless, silly

Absyrt·us -ī *m* son of Aeëtes, king of Colchis, killed by his sister Medea when she eloped with Jason

abund·ans -antis *adj* overflowing, abundant; rich, affluent

abundanter *adv* copiously

abundanti·a -ae *f* abundance, wealth

abundē *adv* abundantly, amply

abund·ō -āre *vi* to overflow; to abound; to be rich

abūsi·ō -ōnis *f* incorrect use (*of figure of speech*)

abusque *prep* (with *abl*) all the way from

ab·ūtor -ūtī -ūsus sum *vi* (with *abl*) **a** to use up; **b** to misuse, abuse

Abȳd·os or **Abȳd·us** -ī *f* town on Hellespont, opposite Sestos

ăc *conj* (usually used before consonants) and, and also, and moreover, and in particular; (in comparisons) than, as

Acadēmi·a -ae *f* Academy (*where Plato taught*); Platonic philosophy; Cicero's villa near Puteoli

Acadēmic·us -a -um *adj* Academic; *m* Academic philosopher; *n pl* Cicero's treatise on Academic philosophy

acalanth·is -īdis *f* thistlefinch

acanth·us -ī *m* acanthus

Acarnāni·a -ae *f* district of N.W. Greece

Acast·us -ī *m* son of Pelias

ac·cēdō -cēdĕre -cessī -cessum *vi* to come near, approach; (with *dat* or **ad** + *acc*) to assent to, agree with, approve of; **b** to come near in resemblance, be like, resemble; **c** to be added to; (with **ad** or **in** + *acc*) to enter upon, undertake; **accedit ut** or **quod** there is the additional fact that

accelĕr·ō -āre *vt* to speed, quicken; *vi* to hurry

ac·cendō -cendĕre -cendī -censum *vt* to light up, set on fire; (fig) to kindle, inflame, excite, awaken

accens·ĕō -ēre -ŭī -um *vt* to reckon, regard

accens·us -ī *m* attendant, orderly; *m pl* rear-echelon troops

accent·us -ūs *m* accent

acceptĭ·ō -ōnis *f* accepting, receiving

accept·ō -āre *vt* to accept, receive

accept·or -ōris *m* recipient, approver

acceptr·ix -īcis *f* recipient (*female*)

accept·us -a -um *pp* of **accipio**; *adj* welcome, pleasing; *n* receipt; credit side (*in account books*)

accers·ō -ĕre -īvī -ītum *vt* to call, summon; to bring, procure

accessĭ·ō -ōnis *f* approach; passage, entrance; admittance

ac·cīdō -cīdĕre -cīdī -cīsum *vt* to cut down; to impair, weaken; to eat up

ac·cĭdō -cidĕre -cĭdī *vi* to fall; to happen, occur; (with *dat*) to happen to, befall; (with **in** + *acc*) to fall on, fall upon; (with *dat* or **ad** + *acc*) to fall before, fall at (*e.g., someone's feet*); **aures** or **auribus** or **ad aures accidere** to reach or strike the ears

ac·cingō -cingĕre -cinxī -cinctum *vt* to gird; to arm, equip, furnish; to make ready; **accingi** or **se accingere** (with *dat* or with **ad** or **in** + *acc*) to prepare oneself for, to enter upon, to undertake

ac·ciō -cīre -cīvī -cītum *vt* to call, send for, invite

ac·cipiō -cipĕre -cēpī -ceptum *vt* to take, receive, accept; to admit, let in; to welcome, entertain; to hear, learn, understand; to interpret, explain; to undertake, assume, undergo; to approve of, assent to

accipĭt·er -ris *m* hawk, falcon

accīs·us -a -um *pp* of **accīdo**; *adj* impaired, ruined; to troubled, disordered

accīt·us -ūs *m* summons, call

Acc·ĭus -ĭī or **-ī** *m* Roman tragic poet (170-85? B.C.)

acclāmātĭ·ō -ōnis *f* shout, acclamation

acclām·ō -āre *vt* to hail, acclaim; *vi* to shout, cry out; (with *dat*) to shout at

acclār·ō -āre *vt* to make clear, make known

acclīnāt·us -a -um *adj* prostrate; sloping; (with *dat*) sloping toward

acclīn·is -e *adj* (with *dat*) **a** leaning on or against; **b** inclined toward, disposed to

acclīn·ō -āre *vt* (with *dat* or **in** + *acc*) to lean or rest (*something*) against; **se acclinare** (with **ad** + *acc*), (fig) to be inclined toward

acclīv·is -e *adj* sloping upwards, uphill, steep

acclīvĭt·ās -ātis *f* slope, ascent

accŏl·a -ae *m* neighbor

ac·cŏlō -colĕre -colŭī -cultum *vt* to dwell near

accommŏdātē *adv* suitably, fittingly

accommŏdātĭ·ō -ōnis *f* adjustment, compliance, accommodation

accommŏdāt·us -a -um *adj* (with *dat* or **ad** + *acc*) fit for, adapted to, suitable to

accommŏd·ō -āre *vt* (with *dat* or **ad** + *acc*) to adjust or adapt or apply (*something*) to; **se accommodare** (with **ad** + *acc*) to apply or devote oneself to

accommŏd·us -a -um *adj* fit, suitable; (with *dat*) fit for, adapted to, suitable to

ac·crēdō -crēdĕre -crēdidī -crēditum *vi* (with *dat*) to believe, give credence to

ac·crescō -crescĕre -crēvī -crētum *vi* to grow larger, increase, be added

accrētĭ·ō -ōnis *f* increase

accubitĭ·ō -ōnis *f* reclining at table

accŭb·ō -āre *vi* to lie nearby; to recline at table; (with *dat*) to lie near

accūd·ō -ĕre *vt* to coin

ac·cumbō -cumbĕre -cubŭī -cubĭtum *vi* to take one's place at table

accumulātē *adv* abundantly

accumulāt·or -ōris *m* hoarder

accumŭl·ō -āre *vt* to heap up, amass; to load, overwhelm

accūrātē *adv* carefully, accurately, exactly

accūrātĭ·ō -ōnis *f* carefulness, accuracy

accūrāt·us -a -um *adj* careful, accurate, exact, studied

accūr·ō -āre *vt* to take care of, attend to

ac·currō -currĕre -currī -cursum *vi* to run up; (with **ad** or **in** + *acc*) to run to

accurs·us -ūs *m* running, concourse

accūsābĭl·is -e *adj* blameworthy

accūsātĭ·ō -ōnis *f* accusation; indictment, bill of indictment

accūsātīv·us -a -um *adj* & *m* accusative

accūsāt·or -ōris *m* accuser, prosecutor; informer

accūsātōrĭē *adv* like an accuser or prosecutor

accūsātōrĭ·us -a -um *adj* accuser's, prosecutor's

accūsātr·ix -īcis *f* accuser (*female*)

accūsĭt·ō -āre *vt* to keep on accusing

accūs·ō -āre vt to accuse, prosecute; to reproach, blame

ac·er -ēris n maple tree

āc·er -ris -re adj sharp, pointed; pungent, stinging, penetrating, piercing, shrill; sagacious, keen, judicious; energetic, enthusiastic, ardent, brave; passionate, fierce, violent; severe, vigorous

acerbē adv bitterly, harshly

acerbĭt·ās -ātis f bitterness, harshness, sharpness, sourness; distress

acerb·ō -āre vt to embitter, aggravate

acerb·us -a -um adj bitter, harsh, sour; unripe; severe; morose, rough; untimely, premature; painful, troublesome; sad

acern·us -a -um adj maple

acerr·a -ae f incense box

acersecōm·ēs -ae m young man, youth

acervātim adv in heaps; briefly

acerv·ō -āre vt to heap or pile up

acerv·us -ī m heap, pile; multitude; (in logic) sorites

acescō acescĕre acŭī vi to turn sour

Acest·ēs -ae m mythical king of Sicily

acētābŭl·um -ī n vinegar bottle

acēt·um -ī n sour wine, vinegar; (fig) pungent wit, shrewdness

Achaemĕn·ēs -is m first king of Persia, grandfather of Cyrus

Achaemenĭ·us -a -um adj Persian

Achae·us -a -um adj & m Achaean; Greek

Achai·a or **Achāï·a -ae** f province in northern part of the Peloponnesus on Gulf of Corinth; Greece

Achāïc·us -a -um adj & m Achaean; Greek

Achāt·ēs -ae m companion of Aeneas; river in Sicily

Achelō·üs -ī m river in N.W. Greece; river god

Achĕr·ōn -ontis or **Achĕr·os -ī** m river in Hades

Achill·ēs -is m Greek warrior, son of Peleus and Thetis

Achillē·us -a -um adj of Achilles

Achillīd·ēs -ae m descendant of Achilles

Achīv·us -a -um adj Achaean, Greek

Acīdalĭ·a -ae f Venus

acĭd·us -a -um adj sour, tart; (of sound) harsh, shrill; sharp, keen, pungent; unpleasant, disagreeable

acĭ·ēs -ēī f sharpness, sharp edge; keenness of vision, glance; eyesight, eye, pupil; mental power; battle line, battle array, battlefield, battle; debate

acīnāc·ēs -is m scimitar

acĭn·um -ī n or **acĭn·us -ī** m berry, grape; seed in berry

acipens·er -ĕris or **acipens·is -is** m sturgeon

Ac·is -īdis m son of Faunus, loved by Galatea, changed into a river

acl·ys -ўdis f small javelin

aconīt·um -ī n wolf's-bane; strong poison

ac·or -ōris m sour taste, sourness

acqui·escō -escĕre -ēvī -ētum vi to become quiet; to rest; to die; (with abl, dat, or with in + abl) to find rest in, acquiesce in, be content with, find pleasure in, rejoice in

ac·quīrō -quīrĕre -quīsīvī -quīsītum vt to acquire, obtain, gain, win

Acrāg·ās -antis m town on S.W. coast of Sicily

acrēdŭl·a -ae f bird (perhaps owl or nightingale)

ācricŭl·us -a -um adj irritable, peevish

ācrimōnĭ·a -ae f sharpness, pungency; irritation; energy

Ācrisiōnĭăd·ēs -ae m descendant of Acrisius; Perseus

Ācris·ĭus -ĭī or **-ī** m king of Argos, father of Danaë

ācrĭter adv sharply, keenly, vehemently, severely

acroām·a -ătis n entertainment; entertainer

Ācrocĕraunĭ·a -ōrum n pl promontory on the Adriatic Sea in Epirus

Ācrocorinth·us -ī f citadel of Corinth

act·a -ae f seashore, beach

act·a -ōrum n pl deeds, actions; public acts; proceedings of the senate; records, minutes; journal

Actae·ōn -ōnis m grandson of Cadmus, changed into a stag

Actae·us -a -um adj Attic, Athenian

actĭ·ō -ōnis f doing, performance, action, activity; proceedings; (law) suit, process, action, permission for a suit; delivery, gesticulation; plot, action (of play)

actĭt·ō -āre vt to plead (cases) often; to perform (plays) often

Act·ĭum -ĭī or **-ī** n promontory in Epirus (where Octavian defeated Antony and Cleopatra in 31 B.C.)

actīv·us -a -um adj (gram) active; practical (opposite of contemplative)

act·or -ōris m doer, performer; (law) plaintiff, pleader, advocate; agent, manager; player, actor; **actor summarum** cashier, accountant

Act·or -ōris m companion of Aeneas

actuārĭŏl·um -ī n small barge

actuārĭ·us -a -um adj swift; m stenographer; f swift ship; n swift ship

actuōsē adv energetically

actuōs·us -a -um adj energetic, very active

actus pp of **ago**

act·us -ūs m act, performance; driving, motion, impulse; right of way; public business; presentation, delivery, gesture, recital; act (of play)

actūtum adv instantly, immediately

acŭl·a -ae f rivulet

aculeāt·us -a -um *adj* prickly; (fig) stinging, sharp, subtle

aculē·us -ī *m* barb, sting; point; sarcasm

acūm·en -inis *n* point, sharpness; sting (*of insect*); pungency; shrewdness, ingenuity, cunning

acuō acuēre acuī acūtum *vt* to make sharp or pointed, to whet; to exercise; to stimulate; to give an edge to, enhance; to tease

ac·us -ūs *f* needle, pin; **acu rem tangere** to hit the nail on the head

acūtē *adv* acutely, sharply, keenly

acūtŭl·us -a -um *adj* somewhat sharp, rather subtle

acūt·us -a -um *pp* of **acuo**; *adj* sharp, pointed; shrill; intelligent

ad *prep* (with *acc*) (of space) to, towards, near, at; (of time) toward, about, until, at, on, by; (with numbers) about, almost; for the purpose of, to; according to, in consequence of; with respect to; compared with

adactī·ō -ōnis *f* enforcing

adactus *pp* of **adigo**

adact·us -ūs *m* bringing together; snapping (*of jaws*)

adaequē *adv* equally

adaequ·ō -āre *vt* to make level; to equal, match; (fig) to put on the same level; *vi* to be on the same level, be equal; (with *dat*) to be level with

adamantē·us -a -um *adj* made of steel

adamantin·us -a -um *adj* hard as steel, adamantine

adăm·ās -antis *m* adamant; steel; diamond

adambŭl·ō -āre *vi* (with **ad** + *acc*) to walk about near

adăm·ō -āre *vt* to fall in love with

ad·aperiō -aperīre -aperuī -apertum *vt* to uncover, throw open

adăqu·ō -āre *vt* to water; *vi* to fetch water

adauct·us -ūs *m* growth

ad·augeō -augēre -auxī -auctum *vt* to increase, aggravate

adaugesc·ō -ēre *vi* to begin to grow

ad·bibō -bibĕre -bĭbī -bĭbitum *vt* to drink in; to listen attentively

adbīt·ō -ĕre *vi* to come near, approach

adc- = **acc-**

ad·dĕcet -decĕre *v impers* it becomes

addens·eō -ēre or **addens·ō -āre** *vt* to close (*ranks*)

ad·dīcō -dīcĕre -dixī -dictum *vt* to assign; to doom; to dedicate, devote; *vi* (in augury) to be favorable

ad·discō -discĕre -didĭcī *vt* to learn in addition

additāment·um -ī *n* addition

ad·dō -dĕre -dĭdī -dĭtum *vt* to add, increase; to impart, bestow

ad·doceō -docēre -docŭī -doctum *vt* to teach in addition

addubĭt·ō -āre *vt* to call into doubt; *vi* to begin to feel doubt; to hesitate

ad·dūcō -dūcĕre -duxī -ductum *vt* to lead up, bring up; to draw together, wrinkle; to prompt, induce, persuade, move

adduct·us -a -um *adj* drawn tight, strained; narrow, tight (*place*); strict, serious, stern (*character*)

ad·ĕdō -esse -ēdī -ēsum *vt* to nibble at; to eat up, consume; to waste

ademptĭ·ō -ōnis *f* taking away

ad·eō -īre -iī or **-īvī -ĭtum** *vt* to approach; to attack; to consult, apply to; to visit; to undertake, set about, undergo; *vi* to go up, come up; (with **ad** + *acc*) **a** to go to, approach; **b** to enter upon, undertake, set about, submit to

adĕō *adv* to such a degree, so; (following pronouns and numerals, to give emphasis) precisely, exactly, quite, just, chiefly; (at the beginning of sentence) thus far, to such an extent; even, indeed, truly

ad·eps -ipis *m* or *f* fat; corpulence

adeptĭ·ō -ōnis *f* obtaining, attainment

adeptus *pp* of **adipiscor**

adequĭt·ō -āre *vi* to ride up; (with *dat* or **ad** + *acc*) to ride up to, ride towards

adesse *inf* of **adedo** or of **adsum**

adēsurĭ·ō -īre -īvī *vi* to be very hungry

adēsus *pp* of **adedo**

ad·haereō -haerēre -haesī -haesum *vi* (with *dat* or *abl* or with **in** + *abl*) **a** to cling to, stick to; **b** to keep close to, hang on to

ad·haerescō -haerescĕre -haesī -haesum *vi* to stick; to falter; (with *dat* or *abl*, with **ad** + *acc*, or with **in** + *abl*) **a** to stick to, cling to; **b** to be devoted to; **c** to correspond to, accord with

adhaesī·ō -ōnis *f* clinging, adhesion

adhaes·us -ūs *m* adhering, adherence

adhib·ĕō -ēre -ŭī -ĭtum *vt* to bring, put, add; to summon, invite; to apply; to use, employ; to consult; to handle, treat

adhinn·iō -īre -iī or **īvī -ītum** *vt* to whinny after, lust after; *vi* (with *dat* or with **ad** or **in** + *acc*) **a** to whinny after, lust after, crave; **b** to whinny in delight at

adhortātĭ·ō -ōnis *f* exhortation, encouragement

adhortāt·or -ōris *m* cheerer, supporter

adhort·or -ārī -ātus sum *vt* to cheer on, encourage

adhūc *adv* thus far, hitherto; till now; as yet, still; besides, in addition, moreover

ad·igō -igĕre -ēgī -actum *vt* to drive; to drive home, thrust; to compel; to inflict; to bind (*by oath*)

ad·imō -imĕre -ēmī -emptum *vt* to withdraw, take away; to carry off

adipāt·us -a -um *adj* fatty, greasy; gross, bombastic; *n* pastry (*made in fat*) ad·ipiscor -ipiscī -eptus sum vt to reach, get, obtain, win

aditiāl·is -e adj inaugural

aditĭ·ō -ōnis f approach

adĭt·us -ūs m approach, access; entrance; admittance, audience, interview; beginning, commencement; chance, opportunity

adjac·ĕō -ēre -ŭī vt to adjoin; vi (with dat or ad + acc) a to lie near or at; b to border on, be contiguous with

adjectĭ·ō -ōnis f addition, annexation

adjectīv·us -a -um adj adjectival

ad·jiciō -jicĕre -jēcī -jectum vt to add, increase; (with dat or ad + acc) a to throw (weapon) at; b to add (something) to; c to turn or direct (eyes, mind, etc.) to; (with in + acc) to hurl (weapon) at

adjūdĭc·ō -āre vt to adjudge, award; to ascribe, assign

adjūment·um -ī n aid, help, support

adjunct·a -ōrum n pl accessory circumstances

adjunctĭ·ō -ōnis f joining, union; addition; (rhet) repetition

ad·jungō -jungĕre -junxī -junctum vt (with dat) to yoke or harness (animal) to; (with dat or ad + acc) a to add, attach, join (something) to; b to apply, direct (mind, attention, etc.) to

adjūr·ō -āre vt to swear to, confirm by oath; vi to swear

adjūtābĭl·is -e adj helpful

adjŭt·ō -āre vt to help, assist; vi (with dat) to be of assistance to

adjūt·or -ōris m helper, assistant, promoter; aide, adjutant, deputy, secretary; supporting actor

adjūtōr·ium -iī or -ī n help, support

adjūtr·ix -īcis f helper, assistant (female)

ad·jŭvō -juvāre -jūvī -jūtum vt to help, encourage, sustain; vi to be of use, be profitable

adl- = all-

admātūr·ō -āre vt to bring to maturity; to hasten, expedite

ad·mētĭor -mētīrī -mensus sum vt to measure out

Admēt·us -ī m king of Pherae in Thessaly, husband of Alcestis

admīgr·ō -āre vi (with ad + acc) a to go to; b to be added to

adminicŭl·ō -āre or adminicŭl·or -ārī -ātus sum vt to prop, support

adminicŭl·um -ī n prop, support, stake, pole; rudder; aid; assistant

administ·er -rī m assistant, attendant

administr·a -ae f assistant, attendant (female)

administrātĭ·ō -ōnis f help, aid; administration, management, government

administrāt·or -ōris m administrator, manager, director

administr·ō -āre vt to administer, manage, direct

admīrābĭl·is -e adj admirable, wonderful; strange, surprising, paradoxical

admīrābilĭt·ās -ātis f admiration, wonder, wonderfulness

admīrābĭlĭter adv admirably; astonishingly, paradoxically

admīrātĭ·ō -ōnis f admiration, wonder, surprise

admīrāt·or -ōris m admirer

admīr·or -ārī -ātus sum vt to admire, wonder at, be surprised at

ad·misceō -miscēre -miscŭī -mixtum vt to mix, add; to involve, implicate; to join, mingle; (with dat, with ad or in + acc, or with cum + abl) to add (something) to, to mix or mix up (something) with; se admiscere to get involved, to meddle

admissār·ius -iī or -ī m stallion, stud; lecherer

admissĭ·ō -ōnis f interview, audience

admiss·um -ī n crime

ad·mittō -mittĕre -mīsī -missum vt to let in, admit; to let go, let loose; to put at a gallop; to allow; to commit (crime)

admixtĭ·ō -ōnis f admixture

admixtus pp of admisceo

admoderātē adv appropriately

admŏdum adv to the limit; very, quite, fully; (with numbers) just about; (with negatives) at all; (in answers) quite so, yes

admoen·ĭō -īre vt to besiege, blockade

admōl·ior -īrī -ītus sum vt to bring up, move up; admoliri (with inf) to strive to, struggle to

admon·ĕō -ēre -ŭī -ĭtum vt to admonish, remind, suggest; to warn; to urge

admonitĭ·ō -ōnis f admonition, reminder, suggestion

admonĭt·or -ōris m admonisher, reminder

admonĭtr·ix -īcis f admonisher, reminder (female)

admonĭt·um -ī n admonition

admonĭt·us -ūs m suggestion; reproof

ad·mordĕō -mordēre -momordī -morsum vt to bite at, gnaw at; (fig) to fleece

admōtĭ·ō -ōnis f moving, movement

ad·movĕō -movēre -mōvī -mōtum vt to move up, bring up, bring near; to lead on, conduct; (with dat or ad + acc) a to move or bring (something) to; b to apply (something) to; c to direct (attention, etc.) to; vi to draw near, approach

admūg·ĭō -īre vi (with dat) to low to, bellow to

admurmurātĭ·ō -ōnis f murmuring

admurmŭr·ō -āre vi to murmur (in approval or disapproval)

admutĭl·ō -āre vt to clip close; (fig) to clip, cheat

adn- = ann-

ad·olĕō -olēre -olŭī -ultum vt to magnify; to honor, worship; to sacrifice, burn; to pile up (altars); to sprinkle (altars)

adol·ĕō -ēre vi to smell

adolesc·ens -entis m young man; f young woman

adol·escō -escĕre -ēvī vi to grow, grow up; to be kindled, burn

Adōn·is -is or -īdis m son of Cinyras, king of Cyprus, loved by Venus

adoper·iō -īre -ŭī -tum vt to cover up; to close

adopīn·or -ārī vi to suppose, conjecture

adoptātī·ō -ōnis f adopting (of child)

adopti·ō -ōnis f adoption (of child)

adoptīv·us -a -um adj adoptive, by adoption

adopt·ō -āre vt to adopt; to select; to graft (plants)

ad·or -ōris or -ōris n spelt

adōrātī·ō -ōnis f adoration, worship

adōrĕ·a -ae f reward for valor; praise, glory

adōrĕ·us -a -um adj of spelt

ad·orior -orīrī -ortus sum vt to rise up against, attack, assault; to attempt; to undertake

adorn·ō -āre vt to equip, get ready; to adorn

adōr·ō -āre vt to implore, entreat; to ask for; to adore, worship

adp- = app-

ad·rādō -rādĕre -rāsī -rāsum vt to scrape, shave; to lop off

Adrast·us -ī m king of Argos, father-in-law of Tydeus and Polynices

adr- = arr-

adsc- = asc-

adse- = ass-

adsi- = assi-

adso- = asso-

adsp- = asp-

adst- = ast-

adsu- = assu-

ad·sum -esse -fŭī vi to be near, be present; to appear; to be at hand; to be of assistance; (with dat) to share in, participate in, stand by, assist; animo or animis adesse to pay attention; to cheer up

adt- = att-

adūlātī·ō -ōnis f fawning, cringing, servility, flattery

adūlāt·or -ōris m flatterer

adūlātōrī·us -a -um adj flattering

adulesc·ens -entis adj young

adulesc·ens -entis m young man; f young woman

adulescenti·a -ae f youth, young people

adulescentŭl·a -ae f little girl

adulescentŭl·us -ī m young man

adūl·ō -āre vi to fawn

adūl·or -ārī -ātus sum vt to flatter (in a servile manner); vi (with dat) to kowtow to

adult·er -ĕra -ĕrum adj adulterous,

unchaste; m adulterer; f adulteress

adulterīn·us -a -um adj adulterous; forged, counterfeit

adulter·ium -iī or -ī n adultery; adulteration

adultĕr·ō -āre vt to defile, corrupt; to falsify; vi to commit adultery

adult·us -a -um adj grown, mature, adult

adumbrātim adv in outline

adumbrātī·ō -ōnis f sketch, outline

adumbrāt·us -a -um adj shadowy, sketchy, unreal, fictitious, dim, imperfect

adumbr·ō -āre vt to shade, overshadow; to sketch; to represent

aduncit·ās -ātis f curvature

adunc·us -a -um adj curved, hooked

adurg·ĕō -ēre vt to pursue closely

ad·ūrō -ūrĕre -ussī -ustum vt to set on fire; to scorch; to nip, freeze; (fig) to inflame

adusque adv entirely, throughout

adusque prep (with acc) all the way to, as far as, right up to

adustī·ō -ōnis f burning

adust·us -a -um pp of aduro; adj scorched; sunburned

advectīcī·us -a -um adj imported, foreign

advectī·ō -ōnis f transportation

advect·ō -āre vt to keep on conveying

advect·us -ūs m conveyance

ad·vēhō -vehĕre -vexī -vectum vt to carry, convey, transport; (equo) advehi (with ad or in + acc) to ride to; (nave) advehi (with ad + acc) to sail to

advēl·ō -āre vt to veil; to wreathe

advĕn·a -ae m or f stranger, foreigner

ad·veniō -venīre -vēnī -ventum vi to arrive; (with ad or in + acc or with acc of limit of motion) to arrive at, come to, reach

adventīcī·us -a -um adj foreign, strange, extraneous; unusual, extraordinary; unearned

advent·ō -āre vi to keep coming closer, approach

advent·or -ōris m visitor, guest; customer

advent·us -ūs m arrival, approach

adversārī·us -a -um adj (with dat) turned towards, opposed to, opposite; m & f adversary, enemy, rival; n pl journal, notebook, memoranda, assertions (of opponent)

adversātr·ix -īcis f opponent (female)

adversī·ō -ōnis f directing, direction

advers·ō -āre vt to direct (attention)

advers·or -ārī -ātus sum vi (with dat) to oppose, resist

adversum or adversus adv in the opposite direction; prep (with acc) facing, opposite, towards; compared with, contrary to

advers·us -a -um adj opposite, in front; facing; unfavorable, hostile;

adverso flumine upstream; **n** misfortune; opposite

ad·vertō or **ad·vortō -vertĕre -vertī -versum** vt (with *dat* or in + *acc*) **a** to turn or direct (*something*) to; **b** to steer (*ship*) to; **animum** or **animos advertere** to pay attention; **animum** or **animos advertere** (with *dat* or ad + *acc*) to give attention to, attend to, heed, observe; **vi** to land; (with **in** + *acc*) to punish

advesper·ascit -ascĕre -āvit v *impers* evening approaches

advigil·ō -āre vi to be vigilant, keep watch; (with *dat*) to keep watch over, bestow attention on; (with **pro** + *abl*) to watch out for

advocātī·ō -ōnis f legal assistance; legal counsel; the bar; period of time allowed to procure legal assistance; delay, adjournment

advocāt·us -ī m witness; advocate, counsel; helper, friend

advŏc·ō -āre vt to call, summon; to consult

advŏl·ō -āre vi (with *dat* or with ad or in + *acc*) **a** to fly to; **b** to dash to

ad·volvō -volvĕre -volvī -volūtum vt (with *dat* or ad + *acc*) to roll (*something*) to or toward; **advolvi** or **se advolvere genua** or **genibus** (*with genit*) to fall prostrate before

advor- = adver-

adȳt·um -ī n sanctuary; tomb

Aeacĭd·ēs -ae m descendant of Aeacus

Aeāc·us -ī m king of Aegina, father of Peleus, Telamon, and Phocus, and judge of the dead

aed·ēs or **aed·is -is** f shrine, temple; building; f pl rooms, apartments; house

aedĭcŭl·a -ae f chapel, shrine; small room, closet; small house; f pl small house

aedificātī·ō -ōnis f constructing, building; structure, building

aedificātiuncŭl·a -ae f tiny building

aedificāt·or -ōris m builder, architect

aedific·ĭum -iī or **-ī** n building

aedific·ō -āre vt to build, construct, establish

aedīlĭcĭ·us -a -um adj aedile's; m ex-aedile

aedīl·is -is m aedile

aedīlĭt·ās -ātis f aedileship

aedis see **aedes**

aedĭtŭ·us or **aedĭtĭm·us** or **aedĭtŭm·us -ī** m temple attendant, sacristan

Aeēt·ēs -ae m king of Colchis and father of Medea

Aegae·us -a -um adj Aegean; n Aegean Sea

Aegāt·ēs -um f pl three islands W. of Sicily

aeg·er -ra -rum adj sick, infirm,

unsound; dejected; painful

Aeg·eus -ĕi m king of Athens, father of Theseus

Aegīd·ēs -ae m Theseus

Aegīn·a -ae f island off Attica; mother of Aeacus

aeg·is -ĭdis f shield of Minerva and of Jupiter; aegis, protection

Aegisth·us -ī m son of Thyestes, seducer of Clytemnestra, and murderer of Agamemnon

aegrē adv painfully; with difficulty; reluctantly; hardly, scarcely

aegr·ĕō -ēre vi to be sick

aegr·escō -escĕre vi to become sick; to be aggravated, get worse; to be troubled

aegrimōnĭ·a -ae f sorrow, anxiety, trouble

aegritūd·ō -ĭnis f sickness; sorrow

aegr·or -ōris m illness

aegrōtātī·ō -ōnis f sickness, disease

aegrŏt·ō -āre vi to be sick; to languish

aegrŏt·us -a -um adj sick

Aegypt·us -ī f Egypt; m mythical king of Egypt, whose 50 sons married the 50 daughters of his brother Danaüs

aelīn·os -ī m dirge

aemŭl·a -ae f rival (*female*)

aemulātī·ō -ōnis f emulation, rivalry

aemulāt·or -ōris m rival, imitator

aemulāt·us -ūs m rivalry

aemŭl·or -ārī -ātus sum vt to emulate, rival; vi (with *dat*) to be envious of, be jealous of

aemŭl·us -a -um adj (with *genit* or *dat*) emulous of, envious of, jealous of, striving after; m rival

Aeneăd·ēs -ae m descendant of Aeneas; Trojan; Roman; Augustus

Aenē·ās -ae m son of Venus and Anchises, and hero of Virgil's epic

Aenē·is -ĭdis or **-ĭdos** f Aeneid (*Virgil's epic*)

aenĕ·us or **ahēnĕ·us -a -um** adj bronze

aenigm·a -ătis n riddle, mystery

aenĭp·ēs -ĕdis adj bronze-footed

aēn·us or **ahēn·us -a -um** adj bronze; (fig) firm, invincible; n cauldron

Aeolĭ·a -ae f realm of Aeolus, king of winds; group of islands near Sicily

Aeolĭ·ī -ōrum or **Aeŏl·ēs -um** m pl Aeolians (*inhabitants of N.W. Asia Minor*)

Aeŏl·is -ĭdis f Aeolia, N.W. part of Asia Minor

Aeŏl·us -ī m god of winds

aequābil·is -e adj equal, alike; consistent, uniform; fair, impartial

aequābilĭt·ās -ātis f equality; uniformity; impartiality

aequābilĭter adv equally; uniformly

aequaev·us -a -um adj of the same age

aequāl·is -e adj equal; even, level; of the same age, contemporary

aequāl·is -is *m* or *f* comrade; contemporary

aequālit·ās -ātis *f* equality; evenness; smoothness

aequāliter *adv* equally; evenly

aequanimit·ās -ātis *f* calmness, patience; kindness; impartiality

aequāti·ō -ōnis *f* equal distribution; **aequatio bonorum** communism

aequē *adv* equally; justly, fairly; **aeque . . . ac** or **atque** or **et** just as, as much as, as; **aeque . . . ac si** just as if; **aeque . . . quam** as . . . as, in the same way as

Aequ·ī -ōrum *m pl* people of central Italy

aequilibrit·ās -ātis *f* balance

aequilibr·ium -iī or **-ī** *n* horizontal position; equilibrium

aequinoctiāl·is -e *adj* equinoctial

aequinoct·ium -iī or **-ī** *n* equinox

aequiperābil·is -e *adj* (with *dat* or **cum** + *abl*) comparable to

aequiper·ō or **aequipăr·ō -āre** *vt* to compare; to equal, rival, come up to; (with *dat*, with **ad**+ *acc*, or **cum** + *abl*) to compare (*something*) to; *vi* (with *dat*) a to become equal to, be equal to; b to attain to

aequit·ās -ātis *f* evenness, conformity, symmetry, equity; calmness

aequ·or -ŏris *n* level surface; sea, ocean

aequorĕ·us -a -um *adj* of the sea, marine

aequ·us -a -um *adj* level, even, flat; favorable, friendly; fair, just; calm; *n* level, plain; justice, fairness

ā·ēr -ĕris *m* air, atmosphere, sky; weather; mist

aerāment·um -ī *n* bronze vessel or utensil

aerāri·us -a -um *adj* copper, bronze; of mines; financial, fiscal; *m* coppersmith; low-class Roman citizen; *f* mine; smelting furnace; *n* treasury

aerāt·us -a -um *adj* bronze; rich

āěrě·us -a -um *adj* aerial, airy, lofty, high

aerě·us -a -um *adj* bronze

aerif·er -ěra -ěrum *adj* carrying cymbals

aerip·ēs -ĕdis *adj* bronze-footed

āěri·us -a -um *adj* aerial, airy, lofty, high

Āěrŏp·ē -ēs or **Āěrŏp·a -ae** *f* wife of Atreus, mother of Agamemnon and Menelaus

aerūginōs·us -a -um *adj* rusty

aerūg·ō -inis *f* copper rust, verdigris; corroding passion, envy, greed

aerumn·a -ae *f* need, want, trouble, hardship, calamity

aerumnābil·is -e *adj* full of troubles, calamitous

aerumnōs·us -a -um *adj* full of troubles, wretched, distressed

aes aeris *n* crude metal, copper, bronze; bronze object; armor, statue, utensil, trumpet; money; payment; reward; *n pl* wages, soldier's pay; **aes alienum** debt

Aeschўl·us -ī *m* Athenian tragic poet (525-456 B.C.)

Aesculāp·ius -iī or **-ī** *m* god of medicine, son of Apollo and Coronis

aescul·ēt·um -ī *n* oak forest

aesculĕ·us -a -um *adj* oak

aescŭl·us -ī *f* Italian oak

Aes·ōn -ŏnis *m* Thessalian prince, father of Jason, restored to youth by Medea

aest·ās -ātis *f* summer; summer heat

aestif·er -ěra -ěrum *adj* heatbearing, sultry

aestimābil·is -e *adj* valuable

aestimāti·ō -ōnis *f* appraisal, assessment; esteem

aestimāt·or -ōris *m* appraiser

aestim·ō -āre *vt* to appraise, rate, value, estimate; to esteem, judge, hold

aestīv·a -ōrum *n pl* summer camp; campaign season, campaign; summer pastures

aestīv·ō -āre *vi* to pass the summer

aestīv·us -a -um *adj* summer

aestuār·ium -iī or **ī** *n* tidal waters, lagoon, estuary, marsh; air shaft

aestŭ·ō -āre *vi* to boil, seethe; to burn, glow; to undulate, swell, be tossed, heave; to waver, hesitate; to be excited

aestuōsē *adv* hotly, impetuously

aestuōs·us -a -um *adj* sultry; billowy

aest·us -ūs *m* agitation; glow, heat, sultriness; surge, billows, ebb and flow; tide; raging, seething, passion; uncertainty, irresolution

aet·ās -ātis *f* lifetime, age, generation

aetātŭl·a -ae *f* tender age

aeternit·ās -ātis *f* eternity, immortality

aetern·ō -āre *vt* to perpetuate, immortalize

aeternum *adv* forever; constantly, perpetually

aetern·us -a -um *adj* eternal, everlasting, immortal, imperishable

aeth·ēr -ěris or **-ěros** *m* upper air, sky, heaven

aetheri·us -a -um *adj* ethereal, heavenly, celestial; of the upper world

Aethi·ops -ŏpis *m* Ethiopian; Negro; blockhead

aethr·a -ae *f* ether, pure air, serene sky; air, sky, heavens

Aetn·a -ae or **Aetn·ē -ēs** *f* volcano in Sicily

Aetōli·a -ae *f* district in N. Greece

aevit·ās -ātis *f* age, lifetime

aev·um -ī *n* or **aev·us -ī** *m* age, lifetime, life; time, period; generation; eternity

Āf·er -ra -rum *adj & m* African

affābil·is -e *adj* affable, courteous, kind

affābilit·ās -ātis *f* affability, courtesy**

affăbrē *adv* in a workmanlike manner, cunningly

affătim *adv* sufficiently, enough, satisfactorily

affāt·us -ūs *m* address, discourse

affectātĭ·ō -ōnis *f* eager desire; affectation, conceit

affectāt·or -ōris *m* affected person

affectāt·us -a -um *adj* choice, select; farfetched, studied

affectĭ·ō -ōnis *f* disposition, state of mind; inclination, partiality; affection, love

affect·ō -āre *vt* to grasp, seize; to pursue, strive after, aim at; to try to win over; to affect, feign

affect·us -a -um *adj* furnished, provided, gifted; weakened, impaired, sick; affected, moved, touched

affect·us -ūs *m* state, disposition, mood; feeling, passion, emotion; affection

affĕrō afferre attŭlī allātum *vt* to bring, carry, convey; to report, announce; to introduce, apply, employ, exert, exercise; to produce, cause, occasion, impart; to allege, assign; to contribute, help; **manus afferre** (with *dat*) to lay hands on, attack, do violence to, rob, plunder

af·ficĭō -ficĕre -fēcī -fectum *vt* to treat, handle, manage; to affect, move, influence, impress; to attack, afflict; to impair, weaken; (*abl* and verb may be rendered by the verb corresponding to the *abl*): **cruce afficere** to crucify; **honoribus afficere** to honor; **supplicio afficere** to punish

af·fīgō -fīgĕre -fīxī -fīxum *vt* (with *dat* or **ad** + *acc*) to fasten, attach, affix, annex (*something*) to; (with *dat*) to impress (*something*) upon (*mind*)

af·fingō -fingĕre -fīnxī -fictum *vt* to form, fashion besides; to make up, invent; (with *dat*) to attach, affix, add, join, contribute (*something*)

affīn·is -e *adj* adjoining, neighboring; related by marriage; (with *dat* or **ad** + *acc*) taking part in, privy to, associated with

affīn·is -is *m* or *f* in-law

affīnit·ās -ātis *f* relationship by marriage

affirmātē *adv* with solemn assurance, positively, certainly

affirmātĭ·ō -ōnis *f* affirmation, assertion, declaration

affirm·ō -āre *vt* to strengthen; to confirm, encourage; to aver, assert

afflāt·us -ūs *m* breeze, blast, breath; inspiration

aflĭ·ĕō -ēre *vi* to weep

afflictātĭ·ō -ōnis *f* physical pain, torture

afflictō -āre *vt* to shatter, damage, harass, injure; to trouble, vex, distress, torment

afflict·or -ōris *m* destroyer, subverter

afflict·us -a -um *adj* damaged, shattered; cast down, downhearted; vile

af·flīgō -flīgĕre -flīxī -flictum *vt* to knock, strike down; (fig) to crush

afflŭ·ō -āre *vt* (with *dat*) a to breathe (*something*) upon; b to impart (*something*) to; *vi* (with *dat*) a to breathe upon; b to be favorable to

afflŭ·ens -entis *adj* flowing; rich, affluent; abounding, numerous

affluenter *adv* lavishly, abundantly

affluentĭ·a -ae *f* abundance

af·fŭō -flŭēre -flūxī -flūxum *vi* (with *dat* or **ad** + *acc*) a to flow to, flow towards, glide by; b to hasten to, flock to; (with *abl*) to abound in

af·for -fārī -fātus sum *vt* to address, accost, pray to

affŏre = **adfuturus esse**

affŏrem = **adessem**

afformīd·ō -āre *vi* to be afraid

af·fulgĕō -fulgēre -fulsī *vi* to shine, beam, dawn, appear; (with *dat*) to shine on

af·fundō -fundĕre -fūdī -fūsum *vt* (with *dat*) a to pour, sprinkle, scatter (*something*) on; b to send or despatch (*someone*) to; **affundī** *or* **se affundere** (with *dat*) to throw oneself at, prostrate oneself before

Afric·us -a -um *adj* African; *m* S.W. Wind; *f* originally the district of Carthage, made a Roman province in 146 B.C.; continent of Africa

Agamemn·ōn -ŏnis *m* king of Mycenae, son of Atreus and of Aërope, brother of Menelaus, and commander in chief of Greek forces at Troy

Aganipp·ē -ēs *f* fountain on Mount Helicon, sacred to the Muses

agās·ō -ōnis *m* driver, groom; lackey

agĕdum *interj* come on!; well!

agell·us -ī *m* little field, plot

agēm·a -ătis *n* corps or division (*of soldiers*)

Agēn·or -ŏris *m* son of Belus, king of Phoenicia, father of Cadmus and Europa, and ancestor of Dido

Agēnorīd·ēs -ae *m* descendant of Agenor; Cadmus; Perseus

ag·er -rī *m* field, ground, arable land, farm, estate; territory, district

agg·er -ĕris *m* fill dirt, rubbish, soil, mound; rampart, dike, dam, pier; fortification; causeway; funeral pile

aggĕr·ō -āre *vt* to pile up, fill up, amass, increase; to stimulate

ag·gĕrō -gĕrĕre -gessī -gestum *vt* to bring forward, utter; (with *dat* or **ad** + *acc*) to bring, convey (*something*)

aggest·us -ūs *m* accumulation

agglomĕr·ō -āre *vt* to wind up (*as on a ball*); to annex; **se agglomare** (with *dat*) to attach oneself to, join

agglūtĭn·ō -āre *vt* to glue, paste, solder, cement

aggravesc·ō -ĕre *vi* to grow heavy

aggrăv·ō -āre *vt* to make heavier; to make worse, aggravate

ag·gredĭor -grĕdī -gressus sum *vt* to approach; to address; to attack; to undertake, begin

aggrĕg·ō -āre vt to assemble, collect; to attach, join, include, implicate

aggressī·ō -ōnis f attack, assault; introduction

agil·is -e adj easily moved, agile, nimble, quick; busy, active

agilit·ās -ātis f mobility, agility, nimbleness, quickness, activity

agitābil·is -e adj easily moved, light

agitāti·ō -ōnis f motion, movement, agitation; activity, pursuit; prosecution

agitāt·or -ōris m driver, charioteer

agit·ō -āre vt to set in motion, drive on, impel; to hunt, chase, pursue; to drive, urge, support, insist on; to practice, exercise; to observe, keep, celebrate; to obey, carry out; to spend, pass (time); to shake, toss, disturb; to vex, distress; to stimulate, excite; to deride, insult; to criticize; to consider, deliberate on; to discuss, debate; vi to live, dwell, be

Aglaur·ŏs -ī f daughter of Cecrops, changed by Mercury into a stone

agm·en -ĭnis n herd, flock, troop, crowd; body, mass; army (on march), procession, train

agn·a -ae f ewe, lamb (female)

ag·nascor -nascī -nātus sum vi to be born (after the father has made his will)

agnāti·ō -ōnis f blood relationship (on father's side)

agnāt·us -ī m relative (on father's side)

agnell·us -ī m little lamb

agnīn·a -ae f mutton

agnīti·ō -ōnis f recognition, acknowledgment, admission; knowledge

ag·noscō -noscĕre -nōvī -nĭtum vt to recognize, identify, acknowledge

agn·us -ī m lamb

agō agĕre ēgī actum vt to drive, lead, conduct; to chase, hunt; to drive away, steal; to spend (time); to do, act, perform; to manage, administer, carry on; to plead, transact, discuss, propose; to play, act the part of; to accuse, impeach; to exercise, practice, perform, deliver, pronounce; to treat; **agī** to be at stake; **se agere** to behave, deport oneself

ag·ōn -ōnis m contest, combat (in public games)

agrāri·us -a -um adj agrarian; m pl land-reform party

agrest·is -e adj rustic; boorish, wild, savage

agricŏl·a -ae m farmer, peasant

Agricŏl·a -ae m father-in-law of Tacitus

agricultūr·a -ae f agriculture

Agrigent·um -ī n city on south coast of Sicily (sometimes called Acragas)

agripĕt·a -ae m colonist, settler

Agripp·a -ae m son-in-law of Au-

gustus, husband of Julia, and father of Agrippina

Agrippīn·a -ae f wife of Tiberius; daughter of Agrippa and Julia, and mother of Caligula

āh interj ah!, ha!, oh!

aha interj aha!

ai interj (denoting grief) alas!

āin = **aisne** (see **aio**)

aiō vt & vi (used mainly in present and imperfect indicative) I say; I say yes, I say so; I affirm, assert, tell, relate; **ain** (= **aisne**) **tandem?, ain tu?, ain tute?**, or **ain vero?** (colloquial phrase, expressing surprise) do you really mean it?, you don't say!, really?

Aj·ax -ācis m son of Telamon, king of Salamis; son of Oileus, king of the Locri

āl·a -ae f wing; armpit; squadron (of cavalry); flank (of battle line)

alăc·er -ris -re adj lively, brisk, quick, eager, active, cheerful

alacrĭt·ās -ātis f liveliness, briskness, eagerness, cheerfulness

alăp·a -ae f slap; emancipation (of slave)

ālāri·ī -ōrum m pl auxiliaries, allies

ālār·is -e adj (mil) on the flank, of the flank

ālāri·us -a -um adj (mil) on the flank, of the flank

ālāt·us -a -um adj winged

alaud·a -ae f lark

alāz·ōn -ōnis m boaster

Alb·a -ae f town, also called Alba Longa, mother city of Rome, founded by Ascanius, son of Aeneas

albāt·us -a -um adj dressed in white

alb·ĕō -ēre -ŭī vi to be white

albesc·ō -ĕre vi to become white, whiten; to dawn

albic·ō -āre vt to make white, whiten vi to be white

albĭd·us -a -um adj white, whitish

Albī·ōn -ōnis f Britain

albitūd·ō -ĭnis f whiteness

Albŭl·a -ae f Tiber River

albŭl·us -a -um adj whitish

alb·um -ī n white; white tablet, record, list, register

Albunĕ·a or **Albūn·a -ae** f fountain at Tibur; nymph of the fountain

alb·us -a -um adj dead white, white, bright; favorable

Alcae·us -ī m Greek lyric poet of Lesbos, contemporary with Sappho (610 B.C.)

alcēd·ō -ĭnis f kingfisher, halcyon

alcēdŏni·a -ōrum n pl halcyon days; (fig) deep calm, tranquillity

alc·ēs -is f elk

Alcibiăd·ēs -is m Athenian politician, disciple of Socrates (450?-404 B.C.)

Alcīd·ēs -ae m Hercules

Alcimĕd·ē -ēs f wife of Aeson and mother of Jason

Alcinŏ·ŭs -ī m king of the Phaeacians, by whom Ulysses was entertained

Alcmēn·a or **Alcumēn·a** -ae or **Alcmēn·ē** -ēs *f* wife of Amphitryon and mother of Hercules by Jupiter

āle·a -ae *f* dice game; chance, risk, venture

āleāt·or -ōris *m* dice player, gambler

āleātōri·us -a -um *adj* of dice, gambling

ālē·ō -ōnis *m* gambler

āl·es -ītis *adj* winged; swift

āl·es -ītis *m* or *f* winged creature, fowl, bird; *m* poet; *f* augury, omen, sign

al·escō -escĕre *vi* to grow up, increase

Alexand·er -rī *m* Paris, son of Priam and Hecuba; Alexander the Great, king of Macedon

Alexandrē·a or **Alexandrī·a** -ae *f* city in Egypt, founded by Alexander the Great

alg·a -ae *f* seaweed

al·geō -gēre -sī *vi* to be cold, feel cold

al·gescō -gescĕre -sī *vi* to catch cold; to become cold

algĭd·us -a -um *adj* cold

alg·or -ōris *m* cold, chilliness

alg·us -ūs *m* cold

aliā *adv* by another way

aliās *adv* at another time; **alias ... alias** at one time ... at another, sometimes ... sometimes

alibī *adv* elsewhere; otherwise, in other respects; **alibi ... alibi** in one place ... in another, here ... there

alicŭbī *adv* at any place, somewhere, anywhere

alicunde *adv* from somewhere, from any place, from someone else

aliēnātĭ·ō -ōnis *f* transfer (*of property*); separation, alienation; aversion, dislike

aliēnigĕn·a -ae *m* foreigner, alien, stranger

aliēn·ō -āre *vt* to make strange, transfer, sell; to alienate, set at variance; to remove, separate; to make insane, drive mad

aliēn·us -a -um *adj* another's; foreign; contrary, hostile; strange, unsuitable, incongruous, inconsistent, inconvenient; *m* stranger, foreigner

āli·ger -gĕra -gĕrum *adj* wearing wings, winged

alimentārĭ·us -a -um *adj* alimentary

aliment·um -ī *n* nourishment, food, provisions; fuel

alimōnĭ·a -ae *f* or **alimōn·ĭum** -ĭī or -ī *n* nourishment, food, support

aliō *adv* to another place, elsewhere

aliōquī or **aliōquīn** *adv* otherwise, in other respects, for the rest; besides; in general; in any case

aliorsum or **aliorsus** *adv* in another direction; in another manner, in a different sense

ālĭp·ēs -ĕdis *adj* wing-footed, swift-footed

alipt·ēs or **alipt·a** -ae *m* wrestling trainer

aliquā *adv* somehow, in any direction

aliquam *adv* in some degree

aliquamdĭū *adv* for some time

aliquandō *adv* sometime or other, once; at any time, ever; sometimes, now and then; for once, now; finally, now at last

aliquantisper *adv* for a while, for a time

aliquantō *adv* somewhat, a little, rather

aliquantŭlum *adv* somewhat

aliquantŭl·us -a -um *adj* little, small

aliquantum *adv* somewhat, a little, rather

aliquant·us -a -um *adj* considerable

aliquātĕnus *adv* for some distance, to a certain extent, somewhat; in some respects, partly

ali·quī -qua -quod *adj* some, any

aliquid *adv* to some extent, at all

ali·quid -cūjus *pron* something, anything; something important

ali·quis -cūjus *pron* someone, somebody, anyone; someone important

aliquō *adv* to some place, somewhere

aliquot (indecl) *adj* some, several, a few

aliquotiens *adv* several times

aliquōvorsum *adv* to some place, one way or another

aliter *adv* otherwise, else, differently

aliŭbī *adv* elsewhere; **aliubi ... aliubi** here ... there

āl·ĭum -ĭī or -ī *n* garlic

aliunde *adv* from another source, from elsewhere

ali·us -a -ud *adj* another, other, different; *pron* another; **alii ... alii** some ... others; **alius ... alius** one ... another, the one ... the other; **alius ex alio** one after another

al·lābor -lābī -lapsus sum *vi* to glide, slide, slip; to flow

allabōr·ō -āre *vi* to work hard

allacrĭmō -āre *vi* to weep, shed tears

allaps·us -ūs *m* stealthy approach

allātr·ō -āre *vt* to revile; (*of sea*) to break against, dash against

allātus *pp* of **affero**

allaud·ō -āre *vt* to praise highly

all·ēc -ēcis *n* fish sauce

Allectō (indecl) *f* one of the three Furies

allect·ō -āre *vt* to allure, entice

allēgātĭ·ō -ōnis *f* sending, despatching

allēg·ō -āre *vt* to commission, deputize, despatch; to allege; to instigate

al·lĕgō -legĕre -lēgī -lectum *vt* to select, elect

allevāment·um -ī *n* alleviation, relief

allevātĭ·ō -ōnis f raising, elevating; easing

allĕv·ō -āre vt to lift up, raise; to alleviate; to comfort; to lighten

all·ex -ĭcis m (the) big toe; midget

al·lĭcĭō -lĭcĕre -lexī -lectum vt to attract

al·līdō -līdĕre -līsī -līsum vt (with dat or with ad or in + acc) to dash (something) against; **allidi** to be wrecked

allĭg·ō -āre vt to bind, fetter; to bandage; to hinder, detain; to impugn, accuse; (with ad + acc) to bind (something) to

al·lĭnō -lĭnĕre -lēvī -lĭtum vt to smudge; (with dat) to smear (something) on

all·ĭum -ĭī or **-ī** n garlic

Allobrŏg·ēs -um m pl Gallic tribe living between the Rhone and the Isère

allocūtĭ·ō -ōnis f address; consoling, comforting

alloqu·ĭum -ĭī or **-ī** n address, conversation; encouragement, consolation

al·lŏquor -lŏquī -locūtus sum vt to speak to, address; to exhort, rouse; to console, comfort

allūdĭ·ō -āre vi to play, jest

al·lūdō -lūdĕre -lūsī -lūsum vi to play, joke; (of waves) (with dat) to play against

al·lŭō -lŭĕre -lŭī vt to wash

alluvĭ·ēs -ēī f inundation, pool (left by flood waters); alluvial land

alluvĭ·ō -ōnis f inundation; alluvial land

alm·us -a -um adj nourishing; genial, kind, propitious, indulgent, bountiful

aln·us -ī f alder tree; ship

al·ō -ĕre -ŭī -tum or **-ĭtum** vt to feed, nourish, rear; to support, maintain; to promote; to increase, strengthen

alŏ·ē -ēs f aloe; bitterness

alogĭ·a -ae f folly

Alp·ēs -ĭum f pl Alps

alpha (indecl) n alpha (first letter of Greek alphabet)

Alphē·us or **Alphē·os -ī** m chief river of the Peloponnesus

Alpĭc·us -a -um adj Alpine

Alpīn·us -a -um adj Alpine

alsĭ·us or **als·us -a -um** adj chilly, cool, cold

altār·ĭa -ĭum n pl altar top, altar, high altar

altē adv high, on high, highly, deeply, far, remotely; loftily, profoundly

alt·er -ĕra -ĕrum adj one (of two); a second, the second, the next; pron one (of two), the one, the other; a second one, the second one, the next one; another (one's fellow man); **alter . . . alter** the one . . . the other, the former . . . the latter

altercātĭ·ō -ōnis f debate, dispute, discussion

alterc·ō -āre or **alterc·or -ārī**

-ātus sum vi to quarrel, wrangle, bicker

alternīs adv by turns, alternately

altern·ō -āre vt to do by turns; to exchange; vi to alternate

altern·us -a -um adj one after another, alternate, mutual, every other

alterŭt·er -ra -rum (f also: **altĕra utra**; n also: **altĕrum utrum**) adj one (of two), either, one or the other; pron one, either one, one or the other

Althae·a -ae f daughter of Thestius, wife of Oeneus, king of Calydon, and mother of Meleager

alticinct·us -a -um adj active, busy, energetic

altĭl·is -e adj fattened, fat, full; rich

altĭsŏn·us -a -um adj high-sounding; sounding from on high

altĭtŏn·ans -antis adj thundering on high

altĭtūd·ō -ĭnis f height; depth; (fig) depth, reserve, secrecy

altĭvŏl·ans -antis adj high-flying

alt·or -ōris m foster father

altrinsĕcus adv on the other side

altr·ix -ĭcis f nourisher, foster mother

altrōvorsum adv on the other side

alt·us -a -um adj high; deep, profound; ancient, remote (lineage); n high seas, the deep; heaven; **ab alto** from on high, from heaven; **ex alto** farfetched

ālūcĭn·or -ārī vi to indulge in small talk, ramble

alumn·a -ae f foster daughter; pupil

alumn·us -ī m foster son; pupil

alūt·a -ae f soft leather; shoe; purse

alveār·ĭum -ĭī or **ī** n beehive

alveŏl·us -ī m tray, basin; bed of a stream; game board

alvĕ·us -ī m hollow, cavity; tub; bathtub; riverbed; hull of boat, boat; game board; beehive

alv·us -ī m belly, bowels, stomach; womb; boat; beehive

amābĭl·is -e adj lovable, lovely, attractive, pleasant

amābĭlĭt·ās -ātis f charm

amābĭlĭter adv lovingly, delightfully

Amalthē·a -ae f nymph who fed infant Jupiter with goat's milk; sibyl at Cumae

āmandātĭ·ō -ōnis f sending away

āmand·ō -āre vt to send away, remove

am·ans -antis adj loving, affectionate; **amans patriae** patriotic; m lover

amanter adv lovingly, affectionately

amārāc·us -ī m or f marjoram

amarant·us -ī m amaranth

amārē adv bitterly

amārĭtĭ·ēs -ēī f bitterness

amārĭtūd·ō -ĭnis f bitterness; sadness, sorrow, trouble

amār·or -ōris m bitterness

amār·us -a -um adj bitter; n pl disappointments

amās·ĭus -ĭī or **-ī** m lover

amāti·ō -ōnis f love affair

amāt·or -ōris m lover, friend; **amator patriae** patriot

amātorcŭl·us -ī m poor little lover

amātōri·us -a -um adj erotic, love; n love charm

amātr·ix -īcis f mistress, girl friend

Amāz·ōn -ōnis or **Amāzŏn·is -ĭdis** f Amazon (member of mythical female warrior tribe dwelling in the Caucasus)

ambact·us -ī m vassal

ambāg·ēs -is f winding, labyrinth; double-talk, evasion, digression; ambiguity, obscurity; **per ambages** enigmatically

amb·ĕdō -esse -ēdī -ēsum vt to eat up; (of fire) to char; to waste

ambĭg·ō -ĕre vt to go around, avoid; vi to waver, hesitate, be undecided; to argue, debate, wrangle; **ambigitur** it is uncertain

ambiguē adv doubtfully, indecisively

ambigŭit·ās -ātis f ambiguity, double meaning

ambigŭ·us -a -um adj wavering, changeable; uncertain, doubtful; disputed; unreliable, untrustworthy; ambiguous, dark, obscure; n doubt, uncertainty, paradox

amb·ĭō -īre vt to go around, encircle; (pol) or canvass; to entreat, solicit, court

ambĭti·ō -ōnis f (pol) campaigning (by lawful means); popularity, flattery; ambition (in good or bad sense); partiality, favortism; pomp, ostentation

ambĭtiōsē adv ostentatiously; from a desire to please

ambĭtiōs·us -a -um adj winding, entwining; publicity-conscious, eager for popularity, ambitious; ostentatious

ambĭt·us -ūs m winding, revolution; circuit, circumference, border, orbit; (pol) illegal campaigning, bribery; pomp, ostentation; circumlocution; (rhet) period

amb·ō -ae -ō adj both, two; pron both, the two

Ambraci·a -ae f district of Epirus in N.W. Greece

ambrosi·us -a -um adj ambrosial, divine, immortal; f food of the gods

ambūbāi·a -ae f Syrian flute player

ambulācr·um -ī n walk, avenue

ambulāti·ō -ōnis f (act) walk; (place) walk

ambulātiuncŭl·a -ae f short walk; (place) small promenade

ambulāt·or -ōris m peddler; idler

ambŭl·ō -āre vt to traverse, travel; vi to walk, take a walk; to march, travel; to strut

amb·ūrō -ūrĕre -ussī -ustum vt to burn up, scorch, singe; to consume; to numb, nip

amell·us -ī m wild aster

ām·ens -entis adj out of one's mind, mad; foolish, stupid

āmenti·a -ae f madness; folly

āment·ō -āre vt to fit (a javelin) with a strap

āment·um -ī n strap

am·es -ĭtis m pole for fowler's net

amethystin·us -a -um adj dressed in purple; n pl purple garments

amethyst·us -ī f amethyst

amīc·a -ae f girl friend, lady friend

amīcē adv in a friendly manner

amīc·ĭō -īre -ŭī -tum vt to wrap around; to cover, clothe, wrap

amīcĭter adv in a friendly way

amīcĭti·a -ae f friendship

amīct·us -ūs m wrap, cloak; style, fashion (in dress)

amīcŭl·a -ae f girl friend

amĭcŭl·um -ī n wrap, mantle

amīcŭl·us -ī m pal, buddy

amīc·us -a -um adj friendly; m friend; patron

āmigr·ō -āre vi to move away, emigrate

āmissi·ō -ōnis f loss

amĭt·a -ae f aunt (father's sister)

ā·mittō -mittĕre -mīsī -missum vt to lose, let slip; **fidem amittĕre** to break one's word

amnicŏl·a -ae m or f riverside plant (e.g., willow tree)

amnicŭl·us -ī m brook

amn·is -is m river; **secundo amni** downstream

am·ō -āre vt to love, like, be fond of; to fall in love with; **amabo** or **amabo te** (coll) please

amoenē adv charmingly

amoenĭt·ās -ātis f charm

amoen·us -a -um adj charming, pleasant; n pl charming sights

amōl·ior -īrī vt to remove; to put aside, put away; **se amolīrī** to remove oneself, clear out

amŏm·um -ī n amomum plant (aromatic shrub)

am·or or **am·ōs -ōris** m love, affection; object of affection, love; Cupid; m pl love affair

āmōti·ō -ōnis f removal

ā·movĕō -movēre -mōvī -mōtum vt to remove, withdraw, put away, put aside; to steal; **se amovere** to retire, withdraw

Amphiarā·ūs -ī m famous Greek seer

amphibolĭ·a -ae f (rhet) ambiguity

Amphĭ·ōn -ōnis m son of Antiope by Jupiter, twin brother of Zethus, king of Thebes, and husband of Niobe

amphitheātr·um -ī n amphitheater

Amphitrȳ·ō or **Amphitrȳ·ōn -ōnis** m husband of Alcmena

Amphitryōniăd·ēs -is m Hercules

amphŏr·a -ae f amphora; liquid measure (about 7 gallons)

amplē adv largely, abundantly, broadly, spaciously; splendidly

am·plector -plectī -plexus sum vt to embrace, entwine, enclose, encircle; to grab, get hold of; to understand, comprehend; to embrace, include, comprise; to sum up; to embrace affectionately, esteem, cling to; (mil) to occupy, cover

amplex·ō -āre *or* **amplex·or -ārī -ātus sum** *vt* to embrace; to honor, esteem

amplex·us -ūs *m* circuit; embrace, caress

amplificātī·ō -ōnis *f* extension, enlargement; (rhet) amplification, development

amplificāt·or -ōris *m* enlarger, amplifier

amplificē *adv* splendidly

amplific·ō -āre *vt* to enlarge, extend, widen; to increase; (rhet) to enlarge upon, develop

amplī·ō -āre *vt* to widen, enlarge; to enhance; to postpone (*judgment*), adjourn (*court, in order to gather further evidence*); to remand

ampliter *adv* splendidly

amplitūd·ō -inis *f* width, size, bulk, extent; greatness, dignity, importance, high rank; (rhet) development, amplification

amplius *adv* any further, any more, any longer, besides; further, more, longer; **amplius uno die** one day longer; longer than one day; **nec amplius** no longer

amplius *adj* (neuter comparative of **amplus**) more, further, else; (with numerals) more than; **hoc amplius** this further point; **nihil amplius** nothing further, no more; **quid amplius** what more, what else; *n* more, a larger amount; **amplius negoti** more trouble

ampl·us -a -um *adj* ample, large, wide, spacious; strong, great, powerful; grand, imposing, splendid; eminent, prominent, illustrious, distinguished

ampull·a -ae *f* bottle, jar, flask; bombast

ampullār·ius -iī *or* **-ī** *m* flask maker

ampull·or -ārī -ātus sum *vi* to be bombastic

amputātī·ō -ōnis *f* pruning

amput·ō -āre *vt* to lop off, prune; to curtail, shorten; **amputata loqui** to speak disconnectedly

Amūl·ius -iī *or* **-ī** *m* king of Alba Longa, brother of Numitor, and granduncle of Romulus and Remus

amurc·a -ae *f* dregs of oil

amygdăl·a -ae *f* almond tree

amygdăl·um -ī *n* almond

amyst·is -ĭdis *f* drinking bottoms up

an *conj* (introducing the latter clause of a disjunctive direct or indirect question) or

anabăthr·a -ōrum *n pl* bleachers

Anăcrě·ōn -ontis *m* famous lyric poet of Teos (*fl* 540 B.C.)

anadēm·a -ătis *n* fillet, headband

anagnost·ēs -ae *m* reader, reciter

analectr·is -ĭdis *f* shoulder pad (*to improve the figure*)

anapaest·us -a -um *adj* anapestic; *m* anapest; *n* poem in anapestic meter

an·as -ătis *f* duck; **anas fluvialis** wild duck

anaticŭl·a -ae *f* duckling

anatīn·us -a -um *adj* duck's

anatocism·us -ī *m* compound interest

Anaxagŏr·ās -ae *m* Greek philosopher of Clazomenae, teacher of Pericles and Euripides (500?-428 B.C.)

Anaximand·er -rī *m* Greek philosopher of Miletus (610-547 B.C.)

Anaximĕn·ēs -is *m* Greek philosopher of Miletus (*fl* 544 B.C.)

an·ceps -cipitis *adj* two-headed; two-edged; twin-peaked; amphibious; double, twofold; doubtful, undecided, ambiguous; hazardous, critical; *n* danger, peril

Anchīs·ēs -ae *m* son of Capys and father of Aeneas

Anchīsiăd·ēs -ae *m* son of Anchises, Aeneas

ancīl·e -is *n* oval shield said to have fallen from heaven in reign of Numa, second king of Rome

ancill·a -ae *f* maidservant

ancillār·is -e *adj* maidservant's

ancillŭl·a -ae *f* young slave (*female*)

ancŏr·a -ae *f* anchor

ancorāl·e -is *n* cable

ancorāri·us -a -um *adj* of an anchor

Ancyr·a -ae *f* Ankara, capital of Galatia

andabăt·a -ae *m* blindfold gladiator

And·ēs -ium *f pl* village near Mantua, birthplace of Virgil

androgyn·us -ī *m* *or* **androgyn·ē -ēs** *f* hermaphrodite

Andromăch·a -ae *or* **Andromăch·ē -ēs** *f* Hector's wife

Andromĕd·a -ae *f* daughter of Cepheus and Cassiope, rescued from a sea monster by Perseus

andr·ōn -ōnis *m* corridor

Andronic·us -ī *m* Lucius Livius Andronicus (*fl* 241 B.C., *first epic and dramatic poet of the Romans*)

Andr·os -ī *f* Aegean island

ānell·us -ī *m* little ring

anēth·um -ī *n* anise, dill

anfract·us -ūs *m* curve, bend (*of road*); orbit; digression, prolixity

angell·us -ī *m* small corner

angīn·a -ae *f* tonsillitis, inflamation of the throat

angiport·us -ūs *m* *or* **angiport·um -ī** *n* alley

ang·ō -ěre *vt* to choke, throttle; to distress, tease, trouble

ang·or -ōris *m* strangling, suffocation; anguish

anguicŏm·us -a -um *adj* snake-haired

anguicŭl·us -ī *m* small snake

anguif·er -ěra -ěrum *adj* snaky

anguigĕn·a -ae *m* offspring of a dragon; Theban

anguill·a -ae *f* eel

anguině·us -a -um *adj* snaky; serpent-like

anguīn·us -a -um *adj* snaky

anguíp·ēs -ĕdis *adj* serpent-footed

angu·is -is *m* or *f* snake, serpent

Angu·is -is *m* or *f* Dragon, Hydra (*constellation*)

Anguitĕn·ens -entis *m* Ophiuchus (*constellation*)

angulár·is -e *adj* angular

angulāt·us -a -um *adj* angular

angŭl·us -ī *m* angle, corner; nook, recess; **ad paris angulos** at right angles

angustē *adv* within narrow limits, closely, hardly, scarcely; briefly, concisely

angusti·ae -ārum *f pl* narrow place, defile; narrow passage, strait; (fig) shortness; scarcity, want, deficiency; difficulty, tight spot, perplexity, distress, straits; narrow-mindedness

angusticlāvi·us -a -um *adj* wearing a narrow purple stripe

angust·ō -āre *vt* to make narrow

angust·us -a -um *adj* narrow, close, short, brief (*time*); scanty (*means*); difficult, critical; narrow-minded; base, mean; *n* narrowness; critical condition, danger

anhēlit·us -ūs *m* panting, difficulty in breathing, puffing; breath, breathing; vapor

anhēl·ō -āre *vt* to breathe out; to pant after; *vi* to pant, puff; to exhale; (of fire) to roar

anhēl·us -a -um *adj* panting, puffing

anicŭl·a -ae *f* little old woman, silly old woman

Aniēns·is -e or **Aniēn·us -a -um** *adj* of the Anio (*tributary of the Tiber*)

anīl·is -e *adj* of an old woman

anīlit·ās -ātis *f* old age (*of women*)

anīliter *adv* like an old woman

anĭm·a -ae *f* air, wind, breeze; breath; breath of life, life; soul (*as the principle of life, opposed to* **animus** *as the principle of thought and feelings*); spirit, ghost

animadversĭ·ō -ōnis *f* attention, observation; reproach, criticism; punishment

animadvers·or -ōris *m* observer

animad·vertō or **animad·vortō -vertĕre -vertī -versum** *vt* to pay attention to, attend to; to notice, observe, realize; to reproach, criticize; to punish

anĭm·al -ālis *n* animal; living creature

animāl·is -e *adj* consisting of air; animate, living

anĭm·ans -antis *adj* living, animate; *m* & *f* & *n* living being; animal

animātĭ·ō -ōnis *f* living being

animāt·us -a -um *adj* courageous; inclined, disposed; (with **erga** or **in** + *acc*) disposed toward

anĭm·ō -āre *vt* to make alive, to animate; to encourage

animōsē *adv* courageously; eagerly

animōs·us -a -um *adj* full of air,

airy; full of life, living, animate; blowing violently; full of courage, bold, spirited, undaunted; proud

animŭl·a -ae *f* little soul, life

animŭl·us -ī *m* darling

anĭm·us -ī *m* soul (*as principle of intellection and sensation, whereas* **anima** *is soul as principle of life*); intellect, understanding, mind, thought, reason; memory; knowledge; sense, consciousness; judgment, opinion; imagination; heart, feelings, passions; spirit, courage, morale; disposition, character; pride, haughtiness; will, purpose, desire, inclination; pleasure, delight; confident hope; **aequo animo** patiently, calmly; **animi causā** for amusement; **bono animo esse** to take heart; **ex animo** from the bottom of the heart, sincerely; **ex animo effluere** to slip one's mind; **in animo habere** (*with inf*) to intend to; **meo animo** in my opinion

Aniĕ·ō -ēnis *m* tributary of the Tiber

An·ĭus -ĭī or **-ī** *m* king and priest on Delos who welcomed Aeneas

annāl·is -e *adj* lasting a year, annual; **lex annalis** law fixing minimum age for holding public offices; *m pl* annals, chronicle

annāt·ō -āre *vi* (with *dat* or **ad** + *acc*) to swim to

anne *conj* (pleonastic form of **an**) or

an·nectō -nectĕre -nexŭī -nexum *vt* (with *dat* or **ad** + *acc*) to tie, connect, annex (*something*) to; (with *dat*) to apply (*something*) to

annex·us -ūs *m* connection

annicŭl·us -a -um *adj* one year old, yearling

an·nītor -nītī -nīsus sum or **nixus sum** *vi* (with *dat* or **ad** + *acc*) to press against, lean on; (with **ut** or **inf**) to strive to

anniversārĭ·us -a -um *adj* annual, yearly

ann·ō -āre *vi* (with *dat*, with **ad** + *acc*, or with *acc* of limit of motion) to swim to or towards; (with *dat*) to swim with or along with

annōn *conj* or not

annōn·a -ae *f* year's crop; grain; price of grain; cost of living; high price

annōs·us -a -um *adj* aged, old

annotātĭ·ō -ōnis *f* notation, remark

annotīn·us -a -um *adj* last year's

annŏt·ō -āre *vt* to write down, note down; to comment on; to observe, perceive

annumĕr·ō -āre *vt* (with *dat*) to count out (*money*) to; (with *dat* or **in** + *acc*) to add (*something*) to, to include (*someone*) among

annuntĭ·ō -āre *vt* to announce, make known, proclaim

an·nŭō -nuĕre -nŭī -nūtum *vt* to designate by a nod; to indicate, declare; (with *dat*) to promise, grant (*something*) to; *vi* to nod, nod assent; (with *dat*) to nod assent to, to be favorable to, to smile on

ann·us -ī *m* year; season; age, time of life; year of office; **ad annum** for the coming year, a year hence; **annum** or **in annum** for a year; **per annos** year to year

annŭ·us -a -um *adj* lasting a year; annual, yearly; *n pl* yearly pay, pension

an·quīrō -quīrĕre -quīsīvī -quīsītum *vt* to search carefully; to examine, inquire into; (with *genit* or *abl* of the charge) to accuse (*someone*) of; *vi* to hold an inquest

ans·a -ae *f* handle; opportunity

ansāt·us -a -um *adj* having handles; **homo ansatus** man with arms akimbo

ans·er -ĕris *m* gander

ante *adv* before, previously; in front, forwards

ante *prep* (with *acc*) before; more than, above

anteā *adv* before, previously, formerly

ante·capiŏ -capĕre -cēpī -ceptum *vt* to receive beforehand; to take possession of beforehand, preoccupy; to anticipate

ante·cēdō -cēdĕre -cessī -cessum *vt* to precede; to excel, surpass; *vi* (with *dat*) **a** to have precedence over; **b** to excel, surpass

antecessi·ō -ōnis *f* antecedent cause

antecess·or -ōris *m* (mil) scout; *m pl* advance guard

antecurs·or -ōris *m* (mil) scout; *m pl* advance guard

ante·ĕō -īre -iī *vt* to precede; to excel, surpass; to anticipate, prevent; *vi* to precede; to take the lead; (with *dat*) **a** to go before; **b** to excel, surpass

ante·fĕrō -ferre -tŭlī -lātum *vt* to prefer; to anticipate

antefix·us -a -um *pp* of **antefigo**; *n pl* images, statues, etc., affixed to roofs and gutters of homes or temples

ante·gredior -grĕdī -gressus sum *vt* to precede

antehab·ĕō -ēre *vt* to prefer

antehāc *adv* before this time, before now, formerly

antelātus *pp* of **antefero**

antelūcān·us -a -um *adj* before dawn

antemerīdiān·us -a -um *adj* before noon

ante·mittō -mittĕre -mīsī -missum *vt* to send out ahead

antenn·a -ae *f* yardarm, sail yard

Antēn·or -ŏris *m* Trojan who after the fall of Troy went to Italy and founded Patavium

antepīlān·ī -ōrum *m pl* front ranks, front line

ante·pōnō -pōnĕre -posŭī -posĭtum *vt* to prefer; to serve (*food*)

antepŏt·ens -entis *adj* very wealthy

antĕquam or **ante . . . quam** *conj* before

Antēr·ōs -ōtis *m* avenger of unrequited love

ant·ēs -ium *m pl* rows (*e.g., of vines*)

antesignān·us -ī *m* soldier who fought in front of the standards to defend them; leader, commander

ante·stō or **anti·stō -stāre -stĕtī** *vi* to excel, be distinguished; (with *dat*) to be superior to

antest·or -ārī -ātus sum *vt* to call as witness

ante·veniō -venīre -vēnī -ventum *vt* to anticipate, thwart; to surpass, excel; *vi* to become more distinguished; (with *dat*) **a** to anticipate; **b** to surpass, excel

ante·vertō -vertĕre -vertī -versum *vt* to go or come before, precede; to anticipate; to prefer

antevŏl·ō -āre *vi* to dash out ahead

anticipātĭ·ō -ōnis *f* preconception, foreknowledge

anticĭp·ō -āre *vt* to anticipate

antīc·us -a -um *adj* front, foremost

Antigŏn·ē -ēs *f* daughter of Theban king Oedipus; daughter of Trojan king Laomedon

Antilŏch·us -ī *m* son of Nestor, killed by Hector at Troy

Antiphāt·ēs -ae *m* king of the Laestrygones, who sank the fleet of Greeks returning from Troy with Ulysses

antīquārĭ·us -a -um *adj* & *m* antiquarian

antīquē *adv* in former times; in the good old style

antīquit·ās -ātis *f* antiquity; men of former times, the ancients; the good old days

antīquitus *adv* in former times, of old; from ancient times; in the old style

antīqu·ō -āre *vt* to reject (*law, bill*)

antīqu·us -a -um *adj* old, ancient; oldfashioned, venerable; *m pl* ancients, ancient authors; *n* antiquity; old custom

antist·es -ĭtis *m* priest presiding over temple, high priest

antist·es -ĭtis or **antistĭt·a -ae** *f* priestess presiding over temple, high priestess

Antisthĕn·ēs -is or **-ae** *m* pupil of Socrates and founder of Cynic philosophy

antithĕt·on -ī *n* (rhet) antithesis

antr·um -ī *n* cave, cavern

ānulār·ĭus -ĭī or **-ī** *m* ring maker

ānulāt·us -a -um *adj* wearing a ring

ānŭl·us -ī *m* ring, signet ring

ān·us -ī *m* anus, rectum; ring

an·us -ūs *f* old woman; hag

anxiē *adv* uneasily

anxiĕt·ās -ātis *f* anxiety, trouble

anxif·er -ĕra -ĕrum *adj* causing anxiety

anxi·us -a -um *adj* worried, troubled; disquieting

apăge *interj* go on!; scram!

apēliōt·ēs -ae *m* east wind

Apell·ēs -is *m* famous Greek painter (*fl 4th cent.* B.C.)

ap·er -rī *m* boar

aper·iŏ -īre -uī -tum *vt* to uncover, open, lay bare, disclose, reveal; to prove, demonstrate; to explain, recount

apertē *adv* openly, frankly, candidly

apert·ŏ -āre *vt* to keep on laying bare

apert·us -a -um *pp of* **aperio**; *adj* bare, uncovered, exposed; without decks; clear (*style*); frank, candid (*character*); manifest, plain, evident; accessible, unobstructed; *n* open space; **in aperto** in the open; **in aperto esse** to be clear, evident, well known, notorious

ap·ex -ĭcis *m* point, top, summit; hat, cap, crown; crowning glory

aphract·us -ī *f or* **aphract·um -ī** *n* ship without deck

apiār·ius -iī *or* **-ī** *m* beekeeper

apicŭl·a -ae *f* little bee

ap·is -is *f* bee

ap·iscor -iscī -tus sum *vt* to pursue; to take, reach, gain, get

ap·ium -iī *or* **-ī** *n* celery

aplustr·e -is *n* stern

apoclēt·ī -ōrum *m pl* select committee (*of Aetolian League*)

apodytēr·ium -iī *or* **-ī** *n* dressing room (*at a bath*)

apolactiz·ŏ -āre *vt* to kick aside, scorn

Apoll·ŏ -ĭnis *m* son of Jupiter and Latona, twin brother of Diana, god of the sun, divination, archery, healing, poetry, and music

Apollodōr·us -ī *m* famous rhetorician, teacher of Augustus; famous Athenian grammarian and author of an extant work on mythology (*fl 140* B.C.)

apolŏg·us -ī *m* story, fable

apophorēt·a -ōrum *n pl* presents for house guests

aposphrāgism·a -ătis *n* device on signet ring, seal

apothēc·a -ae *f* warehouse, storehouse, magazine

apparātē *adv* with much preparation, sumptuously

apparātĭ·ŏ -ōnis *f* preparation

apparāt·us -a -um *adj* prepared, well prepared; sumptuous

apparāt·us -ūs *m* getting or making ready, preparing, providing; equipment, apparatus, paraphernalia; pomp, magnificence

appăr·ĕŏ -ēre -uī -itum *vi* to appear, become visible; to be seen, show oneself; (*with dat*) to wait on, serve; **apparet** it is evident, clear, certain

appārĭtĭ·ŏ -ōnis *f* attendance, service; *f pl* household servants

appārĭt·or -ōris *m* servant; attendant of public official (*e.g.,* aide, lictor, secretary)

appăr·ŏ -āre *vt* to prepare, make ready, provide

appellātĭ·ŏ -ōnis *f* addressing; appeal; naming, calling by name; name, title; pronunciation

ap·pellō -pellĕre -pŭlī -pulsum *vt* (*with dat or* ad + *acc*) to drive (*something*) to, steer (*ship*) to; *vi* (*of ship*) to land

appell·ŏ -āre *vt* to accost, address; to appeal to; (*law*) to sue; to name, call; to mention by name; to pronounce

appendicŭl·a -ae *f* small addition

append·ix -ĭcis *f* addition, supplement

ap·pendō -pendĕre -pendī -pensum *vt* to weigh; to pay out; (*fig*) to weigh, consider

appĕt·ens -entis *adj* greedy, avaricious; (*with genit*) eager for, craving

appetenter *adv* eagerly, greedily

appetentĭ·a -ae *f* craving, desire; (*with genit*) craving for, desire for

appetītĭ·ŏ -ōnis *f* grasping, craving; (*with genit*) grasping at, craving for

appetīt·us -ūs *m* craving, desire; *m pl* appetites, passions

appĕt·ŏ -ĕre -īvī -ītum *vt* to try to reach; to lay hold of; to make for, head for; to attack, assail, assault; *vi* to approach, draw near

apping·ŏ -ĕre *vt* to paint; to write

ap·plaudō -plaudĕre -plausī -plausum *vt* (*with dat*) to strike (*something*) against; *vi* to applaud

applicātĭ·ŏ -ōnis *f* applying, application

applicāt·us -a -um *adj* (*with* ad + *acc*) inclined to; (*with dat*) lying close to, attached to

applicĭt·us -a -um *adj* (*with dat*) applied or joined to, attached to

applic·ŏ -āre -āvī *or* **-uī -ātum** *or* **ĭtum** *vt* to bring in close contact; (*with dat or* ad + *acc*) **a** to apply, attach, add, join (*something*) to; **b** to steer (*ship*) toward; **c** to devote (*attention, mind*) to

applōr·ŏ -āre *vt* to deplore, lament

ap·pōnō -pōnĕre -posuī -posĭtum *vt* to serve (*food*); (*with dat or* ad + *acc*) to put or lay (*something*) near, at, or beside; (*with dat*) **a** to set (*food*) before; **b** to appoint or designate (*someone*) to (*a duty, task*); **c** to reckon (*something*) as

apporrect·us -a -um *adj* stretched out

apport·ŏ -āre *vt* to carry or bring up; to cause; (*with dat*) to carry (*something*)

apposc·ŏ -ĕre *vt* to demand in addition

appositē *adv* appropriately, pertinently

apposĭt·us -a -um *pp of* **appono**; *adj* fit, suitable, appropriate; (*with dat*) situated near, contiguous with, bordering on; (*with* ad + *acc*) suited to, fit for

appōt·us -a -um *adj* drunk

apprĕc·or -ārī -ātus sum vt to pray to, worship

appre·hendō -hendĕre -hendī -hensum vt to seize, take hold of; (mil) to occupy

apprīmē adv chiefly, especially

ap·prĭmō -prĭmĕre -pressī -pressum vt (with dat) to press (something) close to

approbātĭ·ō -ōnis f approbation, approval; proof

approbāt·or -ōris m one who seconds or approves

approbē adv very well

approb·ō -āre vt to approve; to prove

appromitt·ō -ĕre vt to promise in addition

approper·ō -āre vt to hasten, speed up; vi to hurry

appropinquātĭ·ō -ōnis f approach

appropinqu·ō -āre vi to approach; (with dat or ad + acc) to come near to, approach

appugn·ō -āre vt to fight, attack

appuls·us -ūs m landing, approach

aprĭcātĭ·ō -ōnis f basking in the sun

aprīc·or -ārī vi to bask, sun oneself

aprīc·us -a -um adj sunny; n sunny spot

Aprīl·is adj of April; **mensis Aprīlis** April, month of April

aprugn·us -a -um adj of a wild boar

aps- = abs-

apsūmēd·ō -īnis f devouring

aptē adv closely; suitably

apt·ō -āre vt to fasten, fit, adjust; to make ready, equip

apt·us -a -um adj suitable, adapted, appropriate, proper

apŭd prep (with acc) at, by, near, among; at the house of; before, in the presence of; in the writings of; over, (with influence) over

Āpūlĭ·a -ae f district in S.W. Italy

aqu·a -ae f water; f pl baths, spa; **aquā et igni interdicere** to outlaw; **aquam praebere** (with dat) to entertain (guests)

aquaeduct·us -ūs m aqueduct

aquālicŭl·us -ī m belly, stomach

aquāl·is -e adj of water; m & f washbasin

aquārĭ·us -a -um adj of water; m water-conduit inspector

Aquār·ĭus -ĭī or -ī m Aquarius (constellation; sign of the Zodiac)

aquātĭc·us -a -um adj growing in water; watery, moist, humid

aquātĭl·is -e adj living or growing in water, aquatic

aquātĭ·ō -ōnis f fetching water; water hole

aquāt·or -ōris m water carrier

aquĭl·a -ae f eagle (bird; Roman legionary standard); (fig) legion; gable of house

aquĭl·ex -ĕgis m water finder, douser; water-conduit inspector

aquilĭf·er -ĕrī m standard-bearer

aquilīn·us -a -um adj eagle's

aquĭl·ō -ōnis m north wind; north

aquilōnĭ·us -a -um adj northerly

aquĭl·us -a -um adj swarthy

Aquīn·um -ī n town of the Volsci, birthplace of Juvenal

Aquītānĭ·a -ae f province in S.W. Gaul

aqu·or -ārī -ātus sum vi to fetch water

aquōs·us -a -um adj rainy, humid, full of water

aquŭl·a -ae f small stream, brook

ār·a -ae f altar

Ār·a -ae f Altar (constellation)

arabarch·ēs -ae m customs officer in Egypt

Arabĭ·a -ae f Arabia

Arabĭc·us or **Arabĭ·us** or **Arăb·us -a -um** adj Arabian

Arachn·ē -ēs f Lydian girl whom Minerva changed into a spider

arānĕ·a -ae f spider; cobweb

arānĕŏl·a -ae f small spider

arānĕŏl·us -ī m small spider

arānĕōs·us -a -um adj full of cobwebs

arānĕ·us -a -um adj spider's; m spider; n spider web

Ar·ar -āris m tributary of the Rhone

arātĭ·ō -ōnis f cultivation, tilling, agriculture; arable land

arātiuncŭl·a -ae f small plot, small farm

arāt·or -ōris m farmer; m pl farmers on state-owned land

arātr·um -ī n plow

Arāt·us -ī m Greek author of poem on astronomy (fl 270 B.C.)

arbĭt·er -rī m eyewitness; arbiter, judge, umpire; ruler, director, controller

arbĭtr·a -ae f eyewitness (female)

arbĭtrārĭō adv uncertainly

arbĭtrārĭ·us -a -um adj uncertain

arbĭtrāt·us -ūs m decision; inclination, pleasure; direction, guidance

arbĭtr·ĭum -ĭī or -ī n decision, judgment; mastery, power, control, authority

arbĭtr·or -ārī -ātus sum vt & vi to decide or judge (as an arbiter); to testify; to think, suppose

arb·or or **arb·ōs -ōris** f tree; mast, oar, ship; gallows

arborĕ·us -a -um adj of a tree; treelike

arbust·us -a -um adj wooded, planted with trees; n orchard; vineyard planted with trees; n pl trees

arbutĕ·us -a -um adj of arbutus

arbŭt·um -ī n fruit of arbutus

arbŭt·us -ī f arbutus, strawberry tree

arc·a -ae f chest, box, safe; coffin; prison cell

Arcadĭ·a -ae f district of central Peloponnesus

arcānō adv in secret, privately

arcān·us -a -um adj secret, concealed, private; n secret; sacred mystery

arc·ĕō -ēre -ŭī vt to shut up, enclose; to keep at a distance, keep off; to hinder, prevent; (with *abl* or **ab** + *abl*) to keep (*someone*) off, away from

arcessīt·us -a -um *pp* of **arcesso**; *adj* farfetched

arcessīt·us -ūs *m* summons

arcess·ō -ĕre -īvī -ītum *vt* to send for, fetch, summon; (law) to arraign; to derive

archetȳp·us -a -um *adj* & *n* original

Archilŏch·us -ī Greek iambic poet of Paros (c. 714-676 B.C.)

archimagīr·us -ī *m* chief cook

Archīmēd·ēs -is *m* scientist and mathematician of Syracuse (287-212 B.C.)

archipīrāt·a -ae *m* pirate captain

architect·ŏn -ŏnis *m* architect, master builder; master in cunning

architect·or -ārī -ātus sum *vt* to build, construct

architectūr·a -ae *f* architecture

architect·us -ī *m* architect; deviser, author, inventor, contriver

arch·ŏn -ŏntis *m* archon (*chief magistrate in Athens*)

arcitĕn·ens -entis *adj* holding a bow, wearing a bow

Arcitĕn·ens -entis *m* Archer (*constellation*)

Arctophȳl·ax -ăcis *m* Boötes (*constellation*)

Arct·os -ī *m* the Great and Little Bear (*double constellation*)

arct·os -ī *m* North Pole; North; north wind; night

Arctūr·us -ī *m* brightest star in Boötes

arcŭl·a -ae *f* small box, jewelry box; (rhet) ornament

arcŭ·ō -āre *vt* to curve

arc·us -ūs *m* bow; rainbow; curve; arch, triumphal arch

Ardĕ·a -ae *f* town in Latium

ardĕ·a -ae *f* heron

ardelī·ō -ōnis *m* busybody

ard·ens -entis *adj* blazing, burning, hot, fiery; gleaming, glittering; smarting, burning; (of emotions) glowing, hot, ardent

ardenter *adv* ardently, eagerly, passionately

ardĕō **ardēre** **arsī** *vi* to be on fire, burn, blaze; to flash, glow; to smart, burn

ardesc·ō -ĕre *vi* to catch fire; to gleam, glitter; (of passions) to become more intense, increase in violence

ard·or -ōris *m* heat, flame; flashing, brightness; heat (*of passions*); loved one, flame

ardŭ·us -a -um *adj* steep, high; difficult; in difficulty

ārĕ·a -ae *f* open space; park, playground; building site; threshing floor

arēna see **harena**

ār·eō -ēre *vi* to be dry; to be thirsty

āreŏl·a *f* small open space

Areŏpăg·us -ī *m* criminal court in Athens; hill where criminal court met

Ar·ēs -is *m* Greek god of war

āresc·ō -ĕre *vi* to become dry; to wither

aretālŏg·us -ī *m* braggart

Arethūs·a -ae *f* nymph pursued by river god Alpheus in Peloponnesus and changed by Diana into a fountain; fountain near Syracuse

Argē·ī -ōrum *m pl* consecrated places in Rome ascribed to Numa; figures of men, made of rushes and thrown annually into the Tiber

argentārī·us -a -um *adj* silver; financial, pecuniary; *m* banker; *f* banking; bank; silver mine

argentāt·us -a -um *adj* plated or ornamented with silver

argenteŏl·us -a -um *adj* made of pretty silver

argentĕ·us -a -um *adj* silver, silvery

argent·um -ī *n* silver; silver plate; money

Argē·us or **Argīv·us** or **Argolĭc·us** -a -um *adj* Argive; Greek

Arg·ī -ōrum *m pl* Argos, town in N.E. Peloponnesus

Argīlēt·um -ī *n* district in Rome between the Quirinal and Capitoline

argill·a -ae *f* clay

Arg·ō -ūs *f* Jason's ship

Argŏl·is -idis *f* district around Argos

Argonaut·ae -ārum *m pl* argonauts

Argos *n* (only *nom* and *acc*) Argos

argūmentātī·ō -ōnis *f* argumentation; proof

argūment·or -ārī -ātus sum *vt* to adduce as proof; (with de + *abl*) to conclude from; *vi* to bring evidence

argūment·um -ī *n* evidence, proof, argument; theme, plot; topic; subject, motif (*of artistic representation*)

arg·uŏ -uĕre -uī -ūtum *vt* to prove; to reveal, betray; to accuse, charge, impeach (*person*), find fault with (*thing*)

Arg·us -ī *n* many-eyed monster set over Io and killed by Mercury

argūtē *adv* subtly; craftily

argūtĭ·ae -ārum *f pl* subtlety; brightness, genius, cunning, shrewdness

argūtŭl·us -a -um *adj* somewhat subtle

argūt·us -a -um *adj* clearcut, clear, bright, distinct; penetrating, piercing; chatty; acute, subtle; bright, smart, witty; cunning, sly

argyrasp·is -idis *adj* wearing a silver shield

Ariadn·a -ae *f* daughter of Minos, king of Crete, who extricated Theseus from the labyrinth

Arīcĭ·a -ae *f* town in Latium on the Via Appia

āridŭl·us -a -um *adj* somewhat dry

ārĭd·us -a -um *adj* dry, parched, withered; meager; (of style) dry, dull

arĭ·ēs -ētis *m* ram; battering ram; beam (*used as breakwater*)

Arĭ·ēs -ētis *m* Aries (*sign of the Zodiac*)

arĭĕt·ō -āre *vt & vi* to butt, ram

Ariobarzān·ēs -is *m* king of Cappadocia

Arĭ·ōn -ōnis *m* early Greek poet and musician, rescued from drowning by dolphin

arist·a -ae *f* ear of grain

Aristarch·us -ī *m* Alexandrine critic and scholar (*fl* 156 B.C.); stern critic

aristolochĭ·a -ae *f* birthwort

Aristophăn·ēs -is *m* the most famous Greek comic poet (*c.* 444-380 B.C.)

Aristotĕl·ēs -is *m* Aristotle (384-322 B.C.)

arithmētĭc·a -ōrum *n pl* arithmetic

ārĭtūd·ō -ĭnis *f* dryness

arm·a -ōrum *n pl* armor, defensive arms, arms; warfare; camp life; armed men; equipment, tools

armāment·a -ōrum *n pl* ship's gear

armāmentār·ĭum -ĭī or **-ī** *n* arsenal, armory

armārĭŏl·um -ī *n* little chest, little closet

armār·ĭum -ĭī or **-ī** *n* cupboard, chest

armātūr·a -ae *f* outfit, equipment, armor; light-armed troops

armāt·us -a -um *adj* armed, equipped; *m* armed man

Armenĭ·a *f* country in N.E. Asia Minor

armenĭăc·um -ī *n* apricot

armenĭăc·us -ī *f* apricot tree

armentāl·is -e *adj* of a herd

armentār·ĭus -ĭī or **-ī** *m* herdsman

arment·um -ī *n* herd

armĭf·er -ĕra -ĕrum *adj* armed

armĭg·er -ĕra -ĕrum *adj* armed; producing warriors; *m* armed person; armor-bearer

armill·a -ae *f* armlet, bracelet

armillāt·us -a -um *adj* wearing a bracelet

armĭpŏt·ens -entis *adj* powerful in arms, warlike

armĭsŏn·us -a -um *adj* reverberating with arms

arm·ō -āre *vt* to furnish with arms, to arm; to rouse to arms

arm·us -ī *m* shoulder, shoulder blade, upper arm; flank (*of animal*)

ar·ō -āre *vt* to plow, till

Arpīn·um -ī *n* town in Latium, birthplace of Marius and Cicero

arquāt·us -a -um *adj* jaundiced

arrect·us -a -um *pp* of **arrigo**; *adj* upright; steep, precipitous

arrēp·ō -ĕre -sī *vi* (with *dat* or *ad* + *acc*) to creep towards, steal up on

arrhăb·ō -ōnis *m* deposit (*of money*)

ar·rīdĕō -rīdēre -rīsī -rīsum *vt* to smile at; *vi* (with *dat*) **a** to smile at

or on, laugh with; **b** to be favorable to; **c** to be pleasing to, please

ar·rĭgō -rĭgĕre -rexī -rectum *vt* to erect, raise; to rouse, excite

ar·rĭpĭō -rĭpĕre -rĭpŭī -reptum *vt* to snatch, seize; (fig) to grasp quickly; (law) to arrest, arraign; to satirize

ar·rōdō -rōdĕre -rōsī -rōsum *vt* to gnaw at

arrŏg·ans -antis *adj* arrogant

arroganter *adv* arrogantly

arrogantĭ·a -ae *f* assumption, presumption; arrogance

arrŏg·ō -āre *vt* to question; to associate; to assume for oneself, claim

ars artis *f* skill; craft, trade; method, way, manner, means; artificial means; work of art; science, theory; manual, textbook; *f pl* cunning; moral qualities, character

artē *adv* closely, tightly; (to love) deeply, dearly; (to sleep) soundly

Artĕm·is -ĭdis *f* Greek counterpart of Diana

artērĭ·a -ae *f* artery; windpipe

arthrītĭc·us -a -um *adj* arthritic

articŭlātim *adv* piecemeal; (to speak) articulately, distinctly

articŭl·ō -āre *vt* to utter distinctly, articulate

articŭl·us -ī *m* joint, knuckle; finger; limb; (gram) clause; turning point; **in ipso articulo temporis** in the nick of time

artĭf·ex -ĭcis *adj* skillful, ingenious; artistic; broken, trained (*horse*); *m* craftsman, artist, master; originator, contriver, author

artificĭōsē *adv* skillfully

artificĭōs·us -a -um *adj* skillful, ingenious, accomplished; artificial

artifĭc·ĭum -ĭī or **-ī** *n* skill, workmanship; artistic work, work of art; art, profession; cleverness, cunning; theory

art·ō -āre *vt* to pack closely; to compress, contract; to limit

artolagăn·us -ī *m* cake

artŏpt·a -ae *m* baker; bread pan (*to bake in*)

art·us -a -um *adj* close, tight; confined, restricted; dense, firm; scanty, small, needy; strict, severe; sound, deep (*sleep*); stingy; *n* narrow space; **art·us -ūs** *m* joint; *m pl* joints, limbs

ārŭl·a -ae *f* small altar

arund·ō -ĭnis *f* reed; shaft, arrow; pipe, flute; pen; fishing rod; hobbyhorse; (in weaving) comb

arvīn·a -ae *f* grease

arv·us -a -um *adj* arable; *n* arable land, soil, land, plain, region; grain

arx arcis *f* fortress, stronghold, citadel, castle, protection, refuge, mainstay; height, summit; **arcem facere e cloaca** to make a mountain out of a molehill

ās assis *m* pound (*divisible into twelve ounces*); bronze coin; **heres ex asse** sole heir

Ascăn·ius -iī or **-ī** *m* son of Aeneas and Creusa and founder of Alba Longa

ascendō ascendĕre ascendī ascensum *vt* to climb; to mount (*horse*); to board (*ship*); *vi* to climb up, ascend; (of voice) to rise; (with **ad** or **in** + *acc*) to climb, climb up to; (with **super** or **supra** + *acc*) to rise above, surpass

ascensi·ō -ōnis *f* climbing up, ascent

ascens·us -ūs *m* climbing up, ascent; means of ascending, approach; step, degree; (fig) climb, rise

asci·a -ae *f* ax; mason's trowel

asc·iō -īre *vt* to associate with oneself, admit

asc·iscō -iscĕre -īvī -ītum *vt* to adopt, approve (*bill*); to adopt (*custom*); to assume, claim, arrogate; to receive, admit (*e.g., as ally, citizen, etc.*); (with **in** + *acc*) to admit (*someone*) to

ascīt·us -a -um *adj* acquired (*as opposed to innate*)

Ascr·a -ae *f* birthplace of Hesiod in Boeotia

a·scrībō -scrībĕre -scripsī -scriptum *vt* to add (*by writing*); to impute, ascribe, attribute; to enroll, register; to reckon, number, class

ascripticī·us -a -um *adj* enrolled, registered

ascriptī·ō -ōnis *f* addition (*in writing*)

ascriptīv·us -ī *m* (mil) reserve

ascript·or -ōris *m* supporter

asell·a -ae *f* little ass

asell·us -ī *m* little ass

Āsi·a -ae *f* Roman province; Asia Minor; Asia

asīl·us -ī *m* gadfly

asĭn·us -ī *m* ass; fool

Ās·is -ĭdis *f* Asia

asōt·us -ī *m* playboy

asparăg·us -ī *m* asparagus

aspargō see **aspergo**

aspectābĭl·is -e *adj* visible

aspect·ō -āre *vt* to look at, gaze at; to look with respect at; to face, lie in the direction of; to observe

aspect·us -ūs *m* look, sight, glance; sense of sight; manner of appearance, appearance, countenance

aspell·ō -ĕre *vt* to drive away

asp·er -ĕra -ĕrum *adj* rough, uneven; harsh, severe, stormy (*climate*); harsh, grating, hoarse (*sound*); pungent, strong (*smell*); rough, hard, unkind, rude (*character*); austere, rigid (*person*); wild, fierce, savage (*animal*); rough, annoying, adverse (*circumstances*) rugged (*style*)

aspĕrē *adv* roughly; (fig) harshly, sternly, severely

a·spergō -spergĕre -spersī -spersum *vt* to sprinkle, scatter, taint; (with *dat*) to sprinkle (*something*) on

asperg·ō -ĭnis *f* sprinkling; spray

asperĭt·ās -ātis *f* unevenness, roughness; severity, fierceness; difficulty, trouble

aspernātĭ·ō -ōnis *f* disdain, contempt

aspern·or -ārī -ātus sum *vt* to disdain, despise, reject

aspĕr·ō -āre *vt* to make rough or uneven, roughen; to make fierce, exasperate; to excite

aspersĭ·ō -ōnis *f* sprinkling; laying on of colors

a·spiciō -spicĕre -spexī -spectum *vt* to catch sight of, spot; to look at; to examine closely, inspect; to observe, consider

aspīrātĭ·ō -ōnis *f* breathing, blowing; evaporation, exhalation; (gram) aspiration

aspīr·ō -āre *vi* to breathe, blow; (with *dat* or with **ad** or **in** + *acc*) to aspire to, desire to reach or obtain, come near to obtaining; (with *dat*) to favor

asp·is -ĭdis *f* asp

asportātĭ·ō -ōnis *f* removal

asport·ō -āre *vt* to carry away

asprēt·a -ōrum *n pl* rough terrain

assĕcl·a -ae *m* hanger-on

assectātĭ·ō -ōnis *f* (respectful) attendance

assectāt·or -ōris *m* attendant, escort; disciple

assect·or -ārī *vt* to follow, tail after

assecŭl·a -ae *m* hanger-on

assensĭ·ō -ōnis *f* assent, approval; *m pl* expressions of approval; (phil) realism

assens·or -ōris *m* backer, supporter

assens·us -ūs *m* assent, approval; *m pl* expressions of approval; (phil) realism; echo

assentātĭ·ō -ōnis *f* assent, agreement; flattery

assentātiuncŭl·a -ae *f* base flattery

assentāt·or -ōris *m* flatterer

assentātōrĭē *adv* flatteringly

assentātr·ix -īcis *f* flatterer (*female*)

as·sentiō -sentīre -sensī -sensum *vi* to agree; (with *dat*) to assent to, agree with, approve

as·sentĭor -sentīrī -sensus sum *vi* to agree; (with *dat*) to assent to, agree with, approve

assent·or -ārī -ātus sum *vi* to agree always; (with *dat*) to agree with always, to flatter

as·sĕquor -sĕquī -secūtus sum *vt* to pursue, catch up to, reach; to gain, obtain, procure; to come up to, equal, match; to comprehend, understand

ass·er -ĕris *m* pole, stake, post

as·sĕrō -serĕre -sēvī -situm *vt* (with *dat*) to plant (*something*) near

assĕr·ō -ĕre -uī -tum *vt* to set free, liberate (*slave*); to protect, defend; to claim, appropriate; **in servitutem asserere** to claim (*someone*) as one's slave

assertĭ·ō -ōnis f declaration of civil status

assert·or -ōris m defender, champion

asserv·ĭō -īre vi (with dat) to serve, assist

asserv·ō -āre vt to preserve, keep, watch over, guard

assessĭ·ō -ōnis f company, companionship

assess·or -ōris m companion, assistant; (law) assistant to a judge, counselor

assess·us -ūs m company, companionship

asseveranter adv emphatically

asseverātĭ·ō -ōnis f assertion, protestation; firmness, earnestness

assever·ō -āre vt to assert strongly, affirm, insist on

as·sidĕō -sidēre -sēdī -sessum vi to seat nearby; (with dat) **a** to sit near, stand by, attend upon, take care of, keep (someone) company; **b** to be busily engaged in; **c** to attend to, mind; **d** to be near (in some respect), be like, resemble

as·sīdō -sīdĕre -sēdī vi to sit down; (with acc) to sit down beside

assĭdŭē adv assiduously, continually, incessantly

assĭdŭĭt·ās -ātis f constant presence or attendance; persistence; frequent recurrence

assĭdŭō adv continually

assĭdŭ·us -a -um adj continually present; persistent, tireless, incessant, busy; m taxpayer; rich man

assignātĭ·ō -ōnis f allotment (of land)

assign·ō -āre vt to mark out, allot, assign (land); to assign, confer; to ascribe, attribute; to consign; to seal

as·silĭō -silīre -silŭī -sultum vi to jump; (with dat) to jump upon, leap at; (with ad + acc) **a** to jump to; **b** to have recourse to

assimiliter adv in like manner

assimĭl·is -e adj similar; (with dat) like

assimulātĭ·ō -ōnis f likeness, similarity

assimulāt·us -a -um adj similar; counterfeit

assimŭl·ō -āre vt to consider as similar, compare; to imitate, counterfeit

as·sistō -sistĕre -stĭtī vi to stand nearby; (with ad + acc) to stand at or by; (with dat) to assist, defend

assĭtus pp of **assero**

assol·ĕō -ēre vi to be usual

assŏn·ō -āre vi to echo; (with dat) to sound in response to, to echo (a sound)

assuē·facĭō -facĕre -fēcī -factum vt to train; (with dat, with ad + acc, or with inf) to accustom (someone) to

assu·escō -escĕre -ēvī -ētum vt (with dat) to accustom (someone) to, make (someone) familiar with, familiarize (someone) with; vi (with dat, with ad + acc, or with inf) to become used to

assuētūd·ō -ĭnis f habit, custom

assuēt·us -a -um pp of **assuesco**; adj accustomed, customary, usual; (with abl) trained in; (with dat, with ad or in + acc, or with inf) accustomed to, used to

as·sūgō -ĕre — -suctum vt to suck in

assŭl·a -ae f splinter, chip, shaving

assulātim adv in splinters, in fragments, piecemeal

assult·ō -āre vt to assault, attack; vi to jump; (with dat) to jump to, jump at

assult·us -ūs m assault, attack

as·sūmō -ĕre -sumpsī -sumptum vt to take up, adopt, accept; to usurp, claim, assume; to receive, obtain, derive

assumptĭ·ō -ōnis f taking, receiving, assumption; adoption; (in logic) minor premise

assumptīv·us -a -um adj resting on external evidence, extrinsic

assŭ·ō -ĕre vt (with dat) to sew (e.g., patch) on (e.g., clothes)

as·surgō -surgĕre -surrexī -surrectum vi to rise up, rise, stand up; to mount up, increase, swell; (with dat) to yield to, stand up for (out of respect)

ass·us -a -um adj roasted; n roast; n pl steam bath, sweat bath

ast conj (older form of **at**) but

Astart·ē -ēs f Syro-Phoenician goddess, counterpart of Venus

a·sternō -sternĕre vt (with dat) to strew (something) on; **asterni** (with dat) to throw oneself down upon

astipulāt·or -ōris m legal assistant; supporter

astipŭl·or -ārī -ātus sum vi (with dat) to agree with

a·stō -stāre vi to stand erect, stand up, stand nearby; (with dat) to assist

Astrae·a -ae f goddess of justice

astrĕp·ō -ĕre -ŭī -ĭtum vi to roar; to make a noise; to applaud; (with dat) to assent loudly to, applaud

astrictē adv concisely; strictly

astrict·us -a -um pp of **astringo**; drawn together, tight; stingy, tight; concise

a·stringō -stringĕre -strinxī -strictum vt to tighten, bind fast; to put under obligation, obligate, oblige; (fig) to draw closer; to compress, abridge; to occupy (attention); to embarrass

astrologĭ·a -ae f astronomy

astrolŏg·us -ī m astronomer; astrologer

astr·um -ī n star; constellation; n pl stars, sky, heaven; immortality

astŭ (indecl) n city

astup·ĕō -ēre vi (with dat) to be amazed at

ast·us -ūs m cunning, cleverness

astūtē *adv* slyly

astūtĭ·a -ae *f* skill, dexterity; cunning, astuteness

astūt·us -a -um *adj* clever; sly, cunning

Astyăn·ax -actis *m* son of Hector and Andromache

asȳl·um -ī *n* refuge, sanctuary, asylum

at *conj* but; (in a transition) but, but on the other hand; (in anticipation of an opponent's objection) but, it may be objected; (in an ironical objection) but really, but after all; (after a negative clause, to introduce a qualification) but at least; **at contra** but on the contrary; **at tamen** and yet, but at least

Atăbŭl·us -ī *m* sirocco, southeast wind

Atalant·a -ae *f* daughter of King Schoeneus, defeated by Hippomenes in a famous footrace; daughter of Iasius and participant in the Calydonian boar hunt

atat *interj* (expressing surprise, pain, warning) oh!

atăv·us -ī *m* great-great-great-grandfather; ancestor

Ătell·a -ae *f* Oscan town in Campania

Atellān·us -a -um *adj* Atellan; **Atellana** or **fabula Atellana** comic farce which originated in Atella

āt·er -ra -rum *adj* (opposed to **niger** glossy black) dead black, black; dark, gloomy, eerie; black, unlucky; malicious; poisonous

Athăm·ās -antis *m* king of Thessaly, father of Helle and Phrixus by Nephele, and of Learchus and Melecerta by Ino

Athēn·ae -ārum *f pl* Athens

athĕ·os -ī *m* atheist

athlēt·a -ae *m* athlete, wrestler

athlēticē *adv* athletically

athlētic·us -a -um *adj* athletic

Atl·ās -antis *m* giant supporting the sky, son of Iapetus and Clymene

atŏm·os -ī *f* indivisible particle, atom

atque *conj* (denotes closer internal connection than is implied by **et** and gives prominence to what follows) and, as well as, together with, and even, and . . . too; (after words of comparison) as, than; **atque . . . atque** both . . . and; **atque adeo** and in fact

atquī *conj* but yet, but anyhow, however, rather, and yet

ātrāment·um -ī *n* ink

ātrāt·us -a -um *adj* clothed in black

Atr·eus -eī *m* son of Pelops, brother of Thyestes, father of Agamemnon and Menelaus

Atrīd·ēs -ae *m* descendant of Atreus

ātriēns·is -is *m* butler

ātriŏl·um -ī *n* small hall, anteroom

ātrit·ās -ātis *f* blackness

ātrĭum -ĭī or **-ī** *n* main room, entrance room (*of Roman house*); hall (*of temples or public buildings*)

atrōcit·ās -ātis *f* hideousness, repulsiveness (*of form, appearance*); fierceness, brutality, cruelty (*of character*); severity, rigidity (*of law*)

atrōcĭter *adv* horribly, fiercely, cruelly, grimly

Ātrŏp·os -ī *f* one of the three Fates

atr·ox -ōcis *adj* horrible, hideous, frightful; savage, cruel, fierce; harsh, stern, unyielding, grim

attactus *pp* of **attingo**

attact·us -ūs *m* touch, contact

attăg·ēn -ēnis *m* woodcock

attagēn·a -ae *f* woodcock

Attalic·us -a -um *adj* of Attalus; Pergamean; rich, splendid; *n pl* gold-brocaded garments

Attăl·us -ī *m* king of Pergamum in Asia Minor, who bequeathed his kingdom to Rome

attāmen *conj* but still, but yet

attat or **attătae** *interj* (indicating surprise, joy, dismay) oh!

attegĭ·a -ae *f* hut, cottage

attemperātē *adv* on time, in the nick of time

attempt·ō -āre *vt* to try, attempt; to test; to tempt, try to corrupt; to attack

at·tendō -tendĕre -tendī -tentum *vt* to notice, mark; to pay attention to, mind, consider; (with *dat* or **ad** + *acc*) to direct (*mind, attention*) to; *vi* to pay attention, listen

attentē *adv* attentively

attentĭ·ō -ōnis *f* attention, attentiveness

attentō see **attempto**

attent·us -a -um *pp* of **attendo**; *adj* attentive; careful, frugal, industrious

attenuātē *adv* (rhet) without flowery language, simply

attenuāt·us -a -um *adj* weak, weakened; shortened, brief; over-refined, affected; plain, bald (*style*)

attenŭ·ō -āre *vt* to make weak, weaken; to thin, attenuate; to lessen, diminish; to humble

at·tĕrō -terĕre -trīvī -trītum *vt* to rub, wear away, wear out, weaken, exhaust; to waste, destroy

attest·or -ārī -ātus sum *vt* to attest, confirm, corroborate, prove

attex·ō -ĕre -uī -tum *vt* to weave; to add

Atth·is -ĭdis *f* Attica

Attic·a -ae *f* district of Greece, of which Athens was the capital

atticē *adv* in the Attic or Athenian style

atticiss·ō -āre *vi* to speak in the Athenian manner

Attic·us -a -um *adj* Attic, Athenian; *m* T. Pomponius Atticus (*friend of Cicero, 109-32 B.C.*)

attigō see **attingo**

at·tinĕō -tinēre -tinŭī -tentum *vt* to hold tight, hold on to, hold, detain, hold back; to reach for; *vi* (with **ad** + *acc*) to pertain to, relate to, refer to, concern; **quod ad me attinet** as far as I am concerned

at·tingō -tingĕre -tĭgī -tactum *vt* to touch, come in contact with; to reach, arrive at; to touch (*food*), taste; to touch, lie near, border; to touch upon, mention lightly; to touch, strike, attack; to touch, affect; to undertake, engage in, take in hand, manage; to resemble; to concern, belong to

Att·is -ĭdis *m* priest of Phrygian goddess Cybele

attoll·ō -ĕre *vt* to lift up, raise; to exalt, extol

at·tondĕō -tondēre -tondī -tonsum *vt* to clip, shave, shear; to prune; to crop; to clip, fleece, cheat

attonĭt·us -a -um *adj* thunderstruck, stunned, amazed, dazed, astonished; inspired; frantic

attorqu·ĕō -ēre *vt* to hurl up

at·trăhō -trahĕre -traxī -tractum *vt* to attract, draw, drag by force

attrect·ō -āre *vt* to touch, handle; to appropriate to oneself

attrepĭd·ō -āre *vi* to hobble along

attrib·ŭō -uĕre -uī -ūtum *vt* to allot, assign, bestow, give, annex; to impose (*taxes*)

attribūtĭ·ō -ōnis *f* payment of a debt; (gram) predicate

attribūt·us -a -um *pp* of **attribuo**; *n* (gram) predicate

attrīt·us -a -um *pp* of **attero**; *adj* worn away, wasted; shameless

au *interj* ouch!

au·ceps -cŭpis *m* fowler, bird catcher; spy, eavesdropper

auctār·ium -ĭī or **-ī** *n* addition

auctific·us -a -um *adj* increasing

auctĭ·ō -ōnis *f* increase; auction

auctiōnārĭ·us -a -um *adj* auction

auctiōn·or -ārī -ātus sum *vi* to hold an auction

auctĭt·ō -āre *vt* to increase greatly

auct·ō -āre *vt* to increase, augment

auct·or -ōris *m* originator, author; writer, historian; reporter, informant (*of news*); authority (*for statement or theory*); proposer, backer, supporter; progenitor (*of race*); founder (*of city*); model, example; adviser, counselor; teacher; guarantor, security; leader, statesman

auctōrāment·um -ī *n* contract; pay, wages

auctōrĭt·ās -ātis *f* origination, source, cause; view, opinion, judgment; advice, counsel, encouragement; might, power, authority, weight, influence, leadership; importance, significance, worth, consequence; example, model, precedent; authority (*for establishing a fact*); document, record; decree (*of senate*); right of possession

auctōr·ō -āre *vt* to bind; **auctorari** or **se auctorare** to hire oneself out

auctus *pp* of **augeo**

auct·us -ūs *m* increase, growth, abundance

aucup·ium -ĭī or **-ī** *n* fowling; trap; eavesdropping; **aucupia verborum** quibbling

aucup·ō -āre or **aucŭp·or -ārī -ātus sum** *vt* to lie in wait for, watch for, chase, strive after, catch; *vi* to catch birds

audācĭ·a -ae *f* (in good sense) boldness, courage, daring; (in bad sense) recklessness, effrontery, audacity; bold deed; *f pl* adventures

audacter *adv* boldly, audaciously

aud·ax -ācis *adj* (in good sense) bold, daring; (in bad sense) reckless, rash, foolhardy

aud·ens -entis *adj* bold, daring, courageous

audentĭ·a -ae *f* daring, boldness

audĕō audēre ausus sum *vt* to dare, venture, risk; **vix ausim** (*old perf subj*) **credere** I could scarcely dare to believe; *vi* to dare, be bold

audĭ·ens -entis *m* hearer, listener; *m pl* audience

audientĭ·a -ae *f* hearing, attention; **audientiam facere** to command attention, to command silence

aud.ĭō -īre -īvī or **-ĭī ītum** *vt* to hear, listen to, give attention to; to hear, be taught by, learn from; to hear, listen to, grant; to accept, agree with, approve, yield to, grant, allow; to listen to, obey; to be called, be named, be reported, be regarded

audītĭ·ō -ōnis *f* hearsay, rumor, report, news

audītōr·ium -ĭī or **-ī** *n* lecture hall; the audience

audīt·us -ūs *m* sense of hearing; a hearing; report, rumor

aufĕrō auferre abstŭlī ablātum *vt* to bear or take away, bear off, remove, withdraw; to snatch away, steal, rob; to sweep away, kill, destroy; to gain, obtain, receive, get; to learn, understand; to mislead, lead into a digression; **auferri e conspectu** to disappear from sight

Aufīd·us -ī *m* river in Apulia

au·fugĭō -fugĕre -fūgī *vt* to escape, flee from; *vi* to escape, run away

Augē·ās -ae *m* king of Elis whose stables Hercules cleaned by diverting the River Alpheus through them

augĕō augēre auxī auctum *vt* to increase, enlarge, augment, spread; to magnify, extol, exalt; to exaggerate; to enrich; to honor, advance, promote; to feed (*flame*)

augesc·ō -ĕre *vi* to begin to grow; to become larger, increase

aug·ur -ŭris *m* or *f* augur (*priest who foretold the future by observing the flight of birds, lightning, etc.*), prophet, seer

augurāl·is -e *adj* of divination; augur's; *n* area in Roman camp where the general took auspices

augurāti·ō -ōnis *f* prophesying

augurātō *adv* after taking the auguries

augurāt·us -ūs *m* office of augur

augur·ium -iī or **-ī** *n* observation of omens, interpretation of omen, augury; sign, omen; prophesy, prediction, forecast; foreboding

auguri·us -a -um *adj* of augurs; **jus augurium** the right to take auguries

augur·ō -āre or **augur·or -ārī -ātus sum** *vt* to consult by augury; to consecrate by augury; to conjecture, imagine; to foretell, predict, prophesy; *vi* to act as augur; to take auspices; to play augur

August·a -ae *f* (in imperial period) mother, wife, daughter, or sister of the emperor

Augustāl·is -e *adj* of Augustus; *n pl* games in honor of Augustus; **sodales Augustales** priests of deified Augustus

Augustān·us -a -um *adj* Augustan; imperial

augustē *adv* reverently

august·us -a -um *adj* august, sacred, venerable; majestic, magnificent

August·us -a -um *adj* Augustan, imperial; cognomen of Octavius Caesar and of subsequent emperors; **mensis Augustus** August

aul·a -ae *f* inner court, hall (*of house*); palace; royal court; people of the royal court, the court

aulae·um -ī *n* curtain, canopy; theater curtain; bed cover, sofa cover, tapestry

aulic·us -a -um *adj* courtly, princely; *n pl* courtiers

Aul·is -is or **-idis** *f* port in Boeotia from which the Greeks sailed for Troy

auloed·us -ī *m* singer (*accompanied by flute*)

aur·a -ae *f* breeze, breath of air, wind; air, atmosphere; heights, heaven; upper world; odor, exhalation; daylight, publicity; **ad auras ferre** to make known, publicize; **ad auras venire** to come to the upper world; **auram captare** to sniff the air; **aura popularis** popular favor; **auras fugere** to hide; **aura spei** breath of hope

aurāri·us -a -um *adj* of gold, golden, gold; *f* gold mine

aurāt·us -a -um *adj* decorated with gold, made of gold, gold-plated, golden; glittering

aureōl·us -a -um *adj* gold; splendid

aurě·us -a -um *adj* of gold, golden; gilded; beautiful, magnificent, splendid; *m* gold coin

auricōm·us -a -um *adj* golden-haired; with golden foliage

auricŭl·a *f* external ear, ear

aurīf·er -ěra -ěrum *adj* producing

or containing gold; (of tree) bearing golden apples

aurif·ex -icis *m* goldsmith

aurīg·a -ae *m* or *f* charioteer, driver; (fig) pilot

Aurīg·a -ae *m* Auriga, Wagoner (*constellation*)

aurigěn·a -ae *m* offspring of gold (*i.e., Perseus*)

aurig·er -ěra -ěrum *adj* gold-bearing; gilded

aurīg·ō -āre *vi* to drive a chariot, compete in chariot race

aur·is -is *f* ear; *f pl* listeners; critical ears; **aurem admovere** to listen; **auribus servire** to flatter; **auris adhibere** to be attentive, pay attention; **in aurem dextram** or **in aurem utramvis dormire** to sleep soundly, i.e., to be unconcerned

aurītŭl·us -ī *m* ass

aurīt·us -a -um *adj* long-eared; attentive; nosey; **testis aurītus** witness by hearsay only; *m* rabbit

aurōr·a -ae *f* morning, dawn, daybreak; the Orient, the East

Aurōr·a -ae *f* goddess of dawn

aur·um -ī *n* gold; color of gold, golden luster; gold cup; gold necklace; gold jewelry; gold plate; golden fleece; gold money; Golden Age

auscultāti·ō -ōnis *f* obedience

auscultāt·or -ōris *m* listener

auscult·ō -āre *vt* to hear (*with attention*), listen to; to overhear; *vi* (*with dat*) to obey, listen to

ausim see **audeo**

Ausōn·ēs -um *m pl* Ausonians (*ancient inhabitants of central Italy*)

Ausonĭd·ae -ārum *m pl* Italians

Ausonĭ·us -a -um *adj* Ausonian, Italian; *m pl* Ausonians, Italians; *f* Ausonia, Italy

ausp·ex -icis *m* augur, soothsayer; author, founder, leader, director, protector; *m pl* witnesses (*at marriage ceremony*)

auspicātō *adv* after taking the auspices; under good omens, at a fortunate moment

auspicāt·us -a -um *adj* consecrated (*by auguries*); auspicious, favorable, lucky

auspic·ium -iī or **-ī** *n* divination (*through observation of flight of birds*), auspices; sign, omen, premonition; command, leadership, guidance, authority; right, power, will, inclination; **auspicium habere** to have the right to take auspices; **auspicium facere** (of birds) to give a sign, to yield an omen

auspic·or -ārī -ātus sum *vt* to begin, take up; *vi* to take auspices; to make a start

aust·er -rī *m* south wind; the South

austērē *adv* austerely, severely

austērīt·ās -ātis *f* austerity

austēr·us -a -um *adj* austere, stern, harsh (*person*); pungent (*smell*); harsh (*taste*); drab, dark (*color*); serious (*talk*); gloomy, sad, hard (*circumstances*)

austrāl·is -e *adj* southern; cingulus, regio, or ora australis torrid zone

austrīn·us -a -um *adj* from the south, southerly; southern

aus·us -a -um *pp* of audeo; *n* daring attempt, enterprise, adventure

aut *conj* or; (correcting what precedes) or, or rather, or else; (adding emphatic alternative) or at least; aut ... aut either ... or

autem *conj* (regularly follows an emphatic word) but, on the other hand, however; (in a transition) but, and now

autheps·a -ae *f* cooker, boiler (*utensil*)

autogrāph·us -a -um *adj* written with one's own hand, autograph

Autolyc·us -ī *m* father of Anticlea, maternal grandfather of Ulysses, and famous robber

automat·on -ī *n* automaton

automāt·us -a -um *adj* automatic, spontaneous, voluntary

Automēd·ōn -ontis *m* charioteer of Achilles

Autonŏ·ē -ēs *f* daughter of Cadmus, wife of Aristaeus, and mother of Actaeon

autumnāl·is -e *adj* autumn, autumnal

autumn·us -a -um *adj* autumn, autumnal; *m* autumn

autŭm·ō -āre *vt* to assert, affirm, say

auxiliār·ēs -ium *m pl* auxiliary troops

auxiliār·is -e *adj* auxiliary

auxiliāri·us -a -um *adj* auxiliary

auxiliāt·or -ōris *m* helper, assistant

auxiliāt·us -ūs *m* aid

auxil·or -ārī -ātus sum *vi* (with *dat*) a to help, aid, assist; b to relieve, heal, cure

auxil·ium -iī or -ī *n* help, aid, assistance; *n pl* auxiliary troops, auxiliaries; military force, military power; auxilio esse (with *dat*) to be of assistance to

avārē *adv* greedily

avārĭter *adv* greedily

avāriti·a -ae *f* greed, selfishness, avarice; gluttony

avāriti·ēs -ēī *f* avarice

avār·us -a -um *adj* greedy, covetous, avaricious; (with *genit*) desirous of, eager for

avē see aveo

ā·vĕhō -vehĕre -vexī -vectum *vt* to carry away; avehi to ride away, sail away

ā·vellō -vellĕre -vellī (or -vulsī or -volsī) -vulsum (or -volsum) *vt* to pull or pluck away; to tear off; to separate, remove; avelli or se avellere (with ab + *abl*) to tear oneself away from, withdraw from

avēn·a -ae *f* oats; reed, stalk, a straw; shepherd's pipe

Aventīn·us -a -um *adj* Aventine; *m* & *n* Aventine Hill (*one of the seven hills of Rome*)

av·ĕō -ēre *vt* to wish, desire, long for, crave; (with *inf*) to wish to, long to; *vi* to say good-bye; ave! or avete! hail!, hello!; good morning!; farewell!, good-bye!

Avernāl·is -e *adj* of Lake Avernus

Avern·us -a -um *adj* without birds; of Lake Avernus; *m* Lake Avernus (*near Cumae, said to be an entrance to the lower world*)

āverrunc·ō -āre *vt* to avert

āversābil·is -e *adj* abominable

āvers·or -ārī -ātus sum *vt* to repulse, reject, refuse, decline, shun, avoid, send away; *vi* to turn away (*in displeasure, contempt, shame, etc.*)

āvers·or -ōris *m* embezzler

āvers·us -a -um *adj* turned away (*in flight*); rear, in the rear; disinclined, alienated, unfavorable, hostile; (with *dat* or *abl* + *abl*) averse to, hostile to, opposed to, estranged from; *n* the back part, the back; *n pl* the back parts, the back; hinterland; in adversum backwards

ā·vertō (or ā·vortō) -vertĕre -vertī -versum *vt* to turn away, avert; to embezzle, misappropriate; to divert; to alienate; se avertere to retire; *vi* to withdraw, retire

avi·a -ae *f* grandmother; old wives' tale

avi·a -ōrum *n pl* pathless, lonely places

aviāri·us -a -um *adj* of birds, bird; *n* aviary; haunt of wild birds

avidē *adv* eagerly, greedily

avidit·ās -ātis *f* eagerness, longing, great desire; avarice

avid·us -a -um *adj* eager, earnest, greedy; hungry, greedy, voracious, gluttonous, insatiable; (with *genit* or *dat* or with in + *acc*) desirous of, eager for

av·is -is *f* bird; sign, omen; avis alba rarity

avīt·us -a -um *adj* grandfather's, ancestral; old

āvi·us -a -um *adj* out-of-the-way, lonely; trackless, pathless, untrodden; wandering, straying; going astray

āvocāment·um -ī *n* diversion, recreation

āvocāti·ō -ōnis *f* distraction, diversion

āvŏc·ō -āre *vt* to call away; to divert, remove, withdraw; to divert, amuse

āvŏl·ō -āre *vi* to fly away; to hasten away, dash off

āvulsus *pp* of avello

avuncul·us -ī *m* mother's brother, maternal uncle; avunculus magnus great-uncle; avunculus major great-great-uncle

av·us -ī *m* grandfather; forefather, ancestor

Axěn·us -ī *m* Black Sea

axici·a -ae *f* scissors

axill·a -ae *f* armpit

ax·is -is *m* axle; chariot, wagon; axis, pole; North Pole; sky; the heavens; region, country; board, plank

B

babae *interj* wonderful!, strange!

Babȳl·ōn -ōnis *f* city on Euphrates

Babylōni·a -ae *f* country between Tigris and Euphrates

bāc·a -ae *f* berry; olive; fruit; pearl

bācāt·us -a -um *adj* adorned with pearls

bacc·ar -ǎris *n* cyclamen (*plant whose root yields fragrant oil*)

Bacch·a -ae *f* bacchante, maenad

bacchābund·us -a -um *adj* raving, riotous

Bacchān·al -ālis *n* place sacred to Bacchus; *n pl* bacchanalian orgies

bacchāti·ō -ōnis *f* orgy; revelry

bacch·or -ārī -ātus sum *vi* to celebrate the festival of Bacchus; to revel, rave, rage

Bacch·us -ī *m* god of wine; (fig) vine; (fig) wine

bācif·er -ěra -ěrum *adj* bearing berries or olives

bacill·um -ī *n* small staff, wand; lictor's staff

bacŭl·um -ī *n* or **bacŭl·us -ī** *m* stick; staff; scepter

badiss·ō -āre *vi* to go, walk

Baetic·us -a -um *adj* of the Baetis; *f* Baetica (*Roman province*)

Baet·is -is *m* river in Spain

Bāi·ae -ārum *f pl* resort town at northern extremity of Bay of Naples

bājŭl·ō -āre *vt* to carry, bear

bājŭl·us -ī *m* porter; day laborer

bālaen·a -ae *f* whale

balanāt·us -a -um *adj* anointed with balsam; embalmed

balǎn·us -ī *m* or *f* acorn; date; balsam; shell-fish

balātr·ō -ōnis *m* jester, buffoon

bālāt·us -ūs *m* bleating

balb·us -a -um *adj* stammering

balbūti·ō -īre *vt & vi* to stammer, stutter

balně·um -ī *n* bath

ballist·a -ae *f* large military device for hurling stones; heavy artillery

ballistār·ium -iī or **-ī** *n* artillery emplacement

balně·ae -ārum *f pl* baths

balneāri·us -a -um *adj* of a bath; *n pl* baths

balneāt·or -ōris *m* bath superintendent

balneŏl·ae -ārum *f pl* baths

balneŏl·um -ī *n* small bath

balně·um -ī *n* bath

bāl·ō -āre *vi* to bleat

balsam·um -ī *n* balsam; balsam tree

baltě·us -ī *m* belt; baldric; girdle

baptister·ium -iī or **-ī** *m* bath; swimming pool

barǎthr·um -ī *n* abyss, chasm, pit; lower world

barb·a -ae *f* beard

barbǎrē *adv* in a foreign language; barbarously, cruelly

barbari·a -ae or **barbari·ēs -ēī** *f* foreign country, strange land; rudeness, want of culture

barbaric·us -a -um *adj* foreign, outlandish

barbariēs see **barbaria**

barbǎr·us -a -um *adj* foreign; barbarous, savage, uncivilized, rude; *m* foreigner; barbarian

barbātŭl·us -a -um *adj* wearing a small beard

barbāt·us -a -um *adj* bearded; adult; old-time; *m* old-timer; philosopher, longhair; goat

barbig·er -ěra -ěrum *adj* wearing a beard, bearded

barbit·os -ī *m* lyre; lute

barbŭl·a -ae *f* small beard

bard·us -a -um *adj* stupid, dull

bard·us -ī *m* bard

bār·ō -ōnis *m* dunce, blockhead

barr·us -ī *m* elephant

bāsiāti·ō -ōnis *f* kissing; kiss

basilic·us -a -um *adj* royal; splendid; *f* public building, basilica (*used as law court and exchange*); portico

bāsi·ō -āre *vt* to kiss

bas·is -is *f* base, foundation, support; pedestal

bās·ium -iī or **-ī** kiss

Bassǎr·eus -ěī *m* Bacchus

batill·um -ī *n* brazier

battŭ·ō -ěre -ī *vt* to beat, pound

beātē *adv* happily

beātit·ās -ātis *f* happiness

beātitūd·ō -ĭnis *f* happiness

beāt·us -a -um *adj* happy; prosperous, rich; fertile; abundant; *n* happiness

Bēlid·ēs -um *f pl* descendants of Belus, the Danaids, who killed their husbands on their wedding night

bellāri·a -ōrum *m pl* dessert

bellāt·or -ōris *adj* warlike; valorous; spirited; *m* warrior

bellāt·rix -īcis *adj* warlike, skilled in war; *f* warrior (*female*)

bellē *adv* prettily, neatly, nicely, well

Bellerŏph·ōn -ontis *m* slayer of Chimaera and rider of Pegasus

bellicōs·us -a -um *adj* warlike, martial, valorous

bellĭc·us -a -um *adj* war, military; warlike, fierce; *n* bugle; bugle call

bellĭger·er -ĕra -ĕrum *adj* belligerent, warlike, aggressive; martial; valiant

belligĕr·ō -āre or belligĕr·or -ārī -ātus sum *vi* to wage war, fight

bellĭpŏt·ens -entis *adj* mighty or valiant in war; *m* Mars

bell·ō -āre or bell·or -ārī -ātus sum *vi* to wage war, fight

Bellōn·a -ae *f* Roman goddess of war

bellŭl·us -a -um *adj* pretty, lovely, cute, fine

bell·um -ī *n* war; battle

bēlŭ·a -ae *f* beast, monster, brute

bēluōs·us -a -um *adj* full of monsters

Bēl·us -ī *m* Baal; king of Tyre and father of Dido; king of Egypt, father of Danaus and Aegyptus

bene *adv* well; thoroughly; very, quite

bene·dīcō -dīcĕre -dixī -dictum *vt* to speak well of, praise; (eccl) to bless

beneficenti·a -ae *f* beneficence, kindness

beneficiārī·ī -ōrum *m pl* soldiers exempt from menial tasks

benefĭc·ium -iī or -ī *n* kindness, favor, benefit, service; help, support; promotion; right, privilege

benefĭc·us -a -um *adj* generous, liberal, obliging

Benevent·um -ī *n* town in Samnium in S. Italy

benevŏlē *adv* kindly

benevŏl·ens -entis *adj* kindhearted, obliging

benevolenti·a -ae *f* benevolence, kindness, goodwill; favor

benevŏl·us -a -um *adj* kind, friendly; devoted, faithful

benignē *adv* in a friendly manner, kindly, courteously; mildly, indulgently; liberally, generously

benignĭt·ās -ātis *f* kindness, friendliness, courtesy; liberality, bounty

benign·us -a -um *adj* kind-hearted; mild, affable; liberal; favorable; bounteous, fruitful

be·ō -āre *vt* to make happy; to bless; to enrich; to refresh

Berecynt·us -ī *m* mountain in Phrygia sacred to Cybele

bēryll·us -ī *m* precious stone, beryl

bēs bessis *m* two thirds

besti·a -ae *f* beast, wild beast

bestiārĭ·us -a -um *adj* of wild beasts; *m* wild-beast fighter

bestĭŏl·a -ae *f* little beast

bēt·a -ae *f* beet

bēta (indecl) *n* second letter of Greek alphabet

bibliopŏl·a -ae *m* bookseller

bibliothēc·a -ae *f* library

bibliothēcār·ius -iī or -ī *m* librarian

bib·ō -ĕre -ī *vt* to drink; to visit, reach, live near (*river*); (fig) to take in, absorb, listen eagerly to

bibŭl·us -a -um *adj* fond of drinking; absorbent; thirsty

bi·ceps -cipĭtis *adj* two-headed; twin-peaked

biclīn·ium -iī or -ī *n* table for two

bicŏl·or -ōris *adj* two-colored

bicorn·is -e *adj* two-horned; two-pronged

bid·ens -entis *adj* with two teeth; with two points; two-pronged; *m* hoe, mattock; sacrificial animal; sheep

bident·al -ālis *n* place struck by lightning

bīdŭ·um -ī *n* period of two days; two days

bienn·ium -iī or -ī *n* period of two years; two years

bifārĭam *adv* on both sides, twofold, double, in two parts, in two directions

bifārĭ·us -a -um *adj* double, twofold

bif·er -ĕra -ĕrum *adj* bearing fruit twice a year; of twofold form

bifĭd·us -a -um *adj* split in two, forked, cloven

bifŏr·is -e *adj* having two doors; having two holes or openings; double

biformāt·us -a -um *adj* double, having two forms

biform·is -e *adj* double, having two forms

bifr·ons -ontis *adj* two-headed; two-faced

bifurc·us -a -um *adj* two-pronged, forked

bīg·a -ae *f* or **bīg·ae -ārum** *f pl* span of horses; team; two-horse chariot

bijŭg·ī -ōrum *m pl* team of horses; two-horse chariot

bijŭg·is -e *adj* yoked two together; drawn by a pair of horses

bijŭg·us -a -um *adj* yoked two together; two-horse

bilĭbr·is -e *adj* two-pound

bilingu·is -e *adj* two-tongued; bilingual; hypercritical, deceitful, false

bīl·is -is *f* gall, bile; wrath, anger; **bilis atra** melancholy; madness

bimăr·is -e *adj* situated between two seas

bimarīt·us -ī *m* bigamist

bimāt·er -ris *adj* having two mothers

bimembr·is -e *adj* half man, half beast

bimembr·is -is *m* centaur

bimestr·is -e *adj* two-month-old; lasting two months

bimŭl·us -a -um *adj* two-year-old

bīm·us -a -um *adj* two-year-old; for two years

bīn·ī -ae -a *adj* two by two; two to each, two each; two at a time; a pair of

binoct·ium -iī or -ī *n* two nights

binōmĭn·is -e *adj* having two names

bipalm·is -e *adj* two spans long

bipart·iō -īre — -ītum *vt* to divide into two parts; to bisect

bipartītō *adv* in two parts

bipăt·ens -entis *adj* open in two directions

bipedāl·is -e *adj* two feet long, broad, thick, or high

bipennĭf·er -ĕra -ĕrum *adj* wielding a two-edged ax

bipenn·is -e *adj* two-edged; *f* two-edged ax

bip·ēs -ĕdis *adj* two-footed, biped

birēm·is -e *adj* two-oared; with two banks of oars; *f* ship with two banks of oars

bis *adv* twice

Bistŏn·ēs -um *m pl* fierce tribesmen in Thessaly

bisulc·us -a -um *adj* split, cloven; forked

bīt·ō -ĕre *vi* to go

bitūm·en -ĭnis *n* bitumen, asphalt

bivĭ·us -a -um *adj* two-way; *n* crossroads, intersection

blaes·us -a -um *adj* lisping; indistinct

blandē *adv* flatteringly: courteously

blandĭloquentĭ·a -ae *f* flattery

blandĭloquentŭl·us -a -um *adj* smooth-tongued

blandĭment·um -ī *n* flattery, compliment; charm

bland·ĭor -īrī -ītus sum *vt* to flatter; to coax; to allure; to please

blandĭter *adv* flatteringly

blandĭtĭ·a -ae *f* caress, flattery, compliment; charm

blandītim *adv* flatteringly

bland·us -a -um *adj* smooth; flattering, fawning; alluring, charming, winsome, pleasant

blatĕr·ō -āre *vi* to talk foolishly, to babble

blatt·a -ae *f* cockroach; moth

blenn·us -ī *m* idiot, blockhead

blĭtĕ·us -a -um *adj* silly; tasteless

blĭt·um -ī *n* tasteless vegetable, kind of spinach

boārĭ·us -a -um *adj* cattle

Boeotĭ·a -ae *f* district north of Attica in central Greece, the capital of which was Thebes

bōlēt·us -ī *n* mushroom

bol·us -ī *m* throw (*of the dice*); cast (*of the net*); haul, piece of good luck, gain; choice morsel

bombax *interj* strange!; indeed!

bomb·us -ī *m* booming; buzzing, humming

bombўcĭn·us -a -um *adj* silk, silken

bomb·ўx -ўcis *m* silkworm; silk; silk garment

Bon·a De·a (*genit:* **Bon·ae De·ae**) *f* goddess of chastity and fertility

bonĭt·ās -ātis *f* goodness, integrity; kindness, benevolence

bon·us -a -um *adj* good; honest, virtuous; faithful, patriotic; fit, suitable; able, clever; brave; noble; auspicious, favorable; useful, advantageous; *n* good; profit, advantage; *n pl* goods, property

bo·ō -āre *vi* to cry aloud; to roar

Boöt·ēs -ae *m* constellation containing the bright star Arcturus

borĕ·as -ae *m* north wind

borĕ·us -a -um *adj* north, northern

bōs bovis *m or f* ox, bull; cow

Bospŏr·us -ī *m* strait between Thrace and Asia Minor, connecting Propontis and Black Sea

botŭl·us -ī *m* sausage

bovīl·e -is *n* ox stall

bovīl·us -a -um *adj* cattle

brāc·ae -ārum *f pl* pants, trousers

brācāt·us -a -um *adj* wearing trousers; foreign, barbarian; effeminate

bracchĭāl·is -ē *adj* of the arm

bracchĭŏl·um -ī *n* dainty arm

bracch·ĭum -ĭī or -ī *n* arm, lower arm; claw; bough; tendril; arm of the sea; sail yard

bractĕ·a -ae *f* gold leaf; gold foil

bractĕŏl·a -ae *f* very thin gold leaf

brassĭc·a -ae *f* cabbage

breviār·ĭum -ĭī or -ī *n* summary, abridgement; statistics

brevĭcŭl·us -a -um *adj* rather short

brevĭlŏqu·ens -entis *adj* brief (*in speech*)

brevĭloquentĭ·a -ae *f* brevity

brevī *adv* briefly, in a few words; shortly, in a short time

brĕv·is -e *adj* short, little, brief; concise; small; shallow; narrow; *n pl* shoals, shallows

brevĭt·ās -ātis *f* brevity; smallness; shortness

brevĭter *adv* shortly, briefly

Britannĭ·a -ae *f* Britain; British Isles

Brom·ĭus -ĭī or -ī *m* Bacchus

brūm·a -ae *f* winter solstice; winter; winter's cold

brūmāl·is -e *adj* wintry

Brundĭs·ĭum -ĭī or -ī *n* port in S.E. Italy on Adriatic Sea

Bruttĭ·ī -ōrum *m pl* inhabitants of toe of Italy

Brūt·us -ī *m* Lucius Junius Brutus (*credited with having driven out the last Roman king, Tarquinius Superbus*); Marcus Junius Brutus (*one of the murderers of Julius Caesar*)

brūt·us -a -um *adj* heavy, unwieldy; dull, stupid

būbīl·e -is *n* ox stall

būb·ō -ōnis *m* owl

būbŭl·a -ae *f* beef

bubulcĭt·or -ārī -ātus sum *vi* to be a herdsman; to ride herd

bubulc·us -ī *m* cowherd; plowman

būbŭl·us -a -um *adj* of cows or oxen

būcaed·a -ae *m* flogged slave

bucc·a -ae *f* cheek; loudmouthed person; trumpeter; parasite; mouthful

buccell·a -ae *f* small mouthful; morsel

buccŭl·a -ae *f.* little cheek; visor

bucculent·us -a -um *adj* loudmouthed

būcĕr·(ĭ)·us -a -um *adj* horned

būcĭn·a -ae *f* (curved) trumpet; war trumpet; shepherd's horn

būcĭnāt·or -ōris *m* trumpeter

būcolĭc·us -a -um *adj* pastoral, bucolic

būcŭl·a -ae *f* heifer

būf·ō -ōnis *m* toad

bulb·us -ī *m* onion

būl·ē -ēs *f* (Greek) council, senate

būleut·a -ae *m* councilor

būleuter·ium -iī *or* **-ī** *n* meeting place of Greek council

bull·a -ae *f* bubble; boss, stud, knob; amulet; badge (*symbol of boyhood*)

bullāt·us -a -um *adj* inflated, bombastic; studded; wearing a bulla, i.e., still a child

būmast·us -ī *f* species of grape with large clusters

būr·is -is *m* curved handle of plow

bustirāp·us -ī *m* ghoul, grave robber

bustuārī·us -a -um *adj* of a tomb or pyre

bust·um -ī *n* pyre; tomb, sepulcher

buxif·er -ĕra -ĕrum *adj* producing boxwood trees

bux·um -ī *n* boxwood; (spinning) top; comb; writing tablet (*made of boxwood*)

bux·us -ī *f* boxwood tree

Byzant·ium -iī *or* **-ī** *n* city on the Bosporus, later named Constantinople

C

caball·us -ī *m* pack horse, nag, hack

cachinnātī·ō -ōnis *f* loud or immoderate laughter

cachinn·ō -āre *vi* to laugh loud; to roar (*with laughter*)

cachinn·ō -ōnis *m* scoffer

cachinn·us -ī *m* loud laugh; jeering; rippling, roaring

cac·ō -āre *vt* to defile; *vi* to defecate

cacoëth·es -is *n* malignant disease; itch

cacūm·en -inis *n* point, tip, top, peak

cacūmin·ō -āre *vt* to make pointed; to sharpen

Cāc·us -ī *m* son of Vulcan, a giant who lived on the Aventine Hill, killed by Hercules

cadāv·er -ĕris *n* corpse, carcass

cadāverōs·us -a -um *adj* cadaverous, ghastly

Cadmē·us -a -um *adj* Cadmean; Theban; *f* citadel of Thebes

Cadm·us -ī *m* son of Phoenician king Agenor, brother of Europa, and founder of Thebes

cadō cadĕre cecidī cāsum *vi* to fall, sink, drop; to be slain, die, be sacrificed; to happen; to belong, refer, be suitable, apply; to abate, subside, flag, decline, decay, vanish, fail, cease; to end, close

cadūceāt·or -ōris *m* herald

cadūc·us -ī *m* herald's staff, caduceus

cadūcif·er -ĕra -ĕrum *adj* with herald's staff

cadūc·us -a -um *adj* falling, fallen; inclined to fall; frail, perishable, transitory; vain, futile, ineffectual; (law) lapsed, without heir

cad·us -ī *m* jar, flask, jug

caecigĕn·us -a -um *adj* born blind

caecit·ās -ātis *f* blindness

caec·ō -āre *vt* to make blind; to make obscure

Caecŭb·um -ī *n* famous wine from S. Latium

caec·us -a -um *adj* blind; invisible; vague, random, aimless, uncertain, unknown; making invisible, blind-

ing; dark, gloomy, obscure

caed·ēs -is *f* murder, slaughter, massacre; bloodshed, gore; the slain

caed·ō caedĕre cecīdī caesum *vt* to hack at, chop; to strike, beat; to fell, cut down, cut off, cut to pieces; to kill, murder

caelām·en -inis *n* engraving, bas-relief

caelāt·or -ōris *m* engraver

caelātūr·a -ae *f* engraving

cael·ebs -ibis *adj* unmarried, single (*whether bachelor or widower*)

cael·es -itis *adj* heavenly, celestial

caelest·ia -ium *n pl* heavenly bodies

caelest·is -e *adj* heavenly, celestial; divine, supernatural

caelest·is -is *m* deity

caelibāt·us -ūs *m* celibacy

caelicŏl·a -ae *m* god

caelif·er -ĕra -ĕrum *adj* supporting the sky

caelipŏt·ens -entis *adj* powerful in heaven

caelit·ēs -um *m pl* inhabitants of heaven, gods

Cael·ius Mon·s (*genit:* **Cael·iī** *or* **-ī Mon·tis**) *m* Caelian Hill in Rome

cael·ō -āre *vt* to engrave in relief, to emboss, to carve; to cast; to fashion, compose; to adorn

cael·um -ī *n* sky, heaven, heavens; air, climate, weather; engraver's chisel, burin

caement·um -ī *n* quarry stone; rubble; cement

caenōs·us -a -um *adj* dirty, filthy, muddy

caen·um -ī *n* dirt, filth, mud, mire

caep·a -ae *f* or **caep·e -is** *n* onion

Caere (indecl) *n* city in Etruria

caerimōnī·a -ae *f* rite; ritual, religious ceremony; sanctity, sacredness; awe, reverence, veneration

caerŭl·a -ōrum *n pl* sea

caerŭlĕ·us *or* **caerŭl·us -a -um** *adj* blue, azure, dark-blue, green, dark-green; dark, gloomy

Caes·ar -ăris *m* C. Julius Caesar (102?-44 B.C.)

caesariāt·us -a -um *adj* long-haired

caesarī·ēs -ēī *f* hair

caesicī·us -a -um *adj* bluish, dark blue

caesim *adv* by cutting; in short clauses, in a clipped style

caesī·us -a -um *adj* bluish-grey; blue-eyed; gray-eyed; cat-eyed

caesp·es -ĭtis *m* sod, turf, grass; altar of sod

caest·us -ūs *m* boxing glove

caetr·a -ae *f* short Spanish shield

caetrāt·us -a -um *adj* armed with a shield

Caiēt·a -ae *f* nurse of Aeneas; town on coast of Latium

Caius see Gaius

Calăb·er -ra -rum *adj* Calabrian

Calabri·a -ae *f* S.W. peninsula of Italy

Cală·is -is *m* son of Boreas and Orithyia, and brother of Zetes

calamist·er -rī *m* hair curler, curling iron; (rhet) flowery language

calamistrāt·us -a -um *adj* curled (*with a hair curler*)

calamistr·um -ī *n* curling iron

calamit·ās -ātis *f* loss, injury, damage; misfortune, calamity, disaster; military defeat

calamitōsē *adv* unfortunately

calamitōs·us -a -um *adj* disastrous, ruinous, destructive; exposed to injury, suffering great damage, unfortunate

calăm·us -ī *m* reed, stalk; pen; arrow; fishing rod; pipe

calathisc·us -ī *m* small wicker basket

calăth·us -ī *m* wicker basket; milk pail; wine cup

calāt·or -ōris *m* servant, attendant

calc·ar -āris *n* spur; stimulus

calcāre·um -ī *n* heel

calceāment·um -ī *n* shoe

calceāt·us -ūs *m* sandal, shoe

calcě·ō -āre *vt* to furnish with shoes, to shoe

calceolār·ius -iī or -ī *m* shoemaker

calceŏl·us -ī *m* small shoe, half-boot

calcě·us -ī *m* shoe, half-boot

Calch·ās -antis *m* Greek prophet at Troy

calcitr·ō -āre *vi* to kick; to resist; to be stubborn; to kick up one's heels

calcitr·ō -ōnis *m* blusterer

calc·ō -āre *vt* to tread, tread under foot; to trample on, oppress; to scorn, abuse

calculāt·or -ōris *m* arithmetic teacher; accountant, bookkeeper

calcŭl·us -ī *m* pebble, stone; kidney stone; counter of an abacus; stone used in games; stone used in voting; vote, sentence, decision

caldāri·us -a -um *adj* warm-water; *n* hot bath

caldus see calidus

Caledōni·a -ae *f* Highlands of Scotland

cale·faciŏ or cal·faciŏ -facĕre -fēcī -factum *vt* to warm, heat; to rouse up, excite, make angry

calefact·ō -āre *vt* to warm, heat

Calend·ae -ārum *f pl* first day of Roman month, calends

calendār·ium -iī or -ī *n* account book

cal·eŏ -ēre -ŭī *vi* to be warm, hot; to feel warm; to glow; to be hot with passion; to be troubled; to be perplexed; to be zealously pursued; to be new or fresh

Cal·ēs -ium *f pl* Campanian town famous for its wine

cal·escŏ -escĕre -ŭī *vi* to get warm or hot; to become excited, be inflamed

calĭd·a or cald·a -ae *f* warm water

calĭdē *adv* quickly, promptly

calĭd·us or cald·us -a -um *adj* warm, hot; eager, rash, hasty, hotheaded, vehement; quick, ready, prompt; *n* warm drink; *f* see calida

caliendr·um -ī *n* wig (*for women*)

calĭg·a -ae *f* shoe, soldier's boot; soldier

caligāt·us -a -um *adj* wearing soldier's boots; (of a peasant) wearing clodhoppers

calīg·ō -ĭnis *f* mist, vapor, fog; gloom, darkness, obscurity; mental blindness; calamity, affliction

calīg·ō -āre *vt* to veil in darkness, to obscure; to make dizzy; *vi* to steam, reek; to be wrapped in mist or darkness; to be blind, grope

caligŭl·a -ae *f* small military boot

Caligŭl·a -ae *m* pet name given by the soldiers to Gaius Caesar when he was a small boy

cal·ix -ĭcis *m* cup; pot; (fig) wine

callaïn·us -a -um *adj* turquoise

call·eŏ -ēre -ŭī *vt* to know by experience or practice, to understand; (with *inf*) to know how to; *vi* to be callous, to be thick-skinned; to be insensible; to be experienced, clever, skillful

calliditāt·ās -ātis *f* skill; shrewdness; cunning, craft

callĭdē *adv* skillfully, expertly, shrewdly; well; cunningly

callĭd·us -a -um *adj* expert, adroit, skillful; ingenious, prudent, dexterous; clever, shrewd; sly, cunning, crafty, calculating

Callimăch·us -ī *m* famous Alexandrine poet and grammarian (c. 270 B.C.)

Calliŏp·ē -ēs or Calliopē·a -ae *f* Calliope (*muse of epic poetry*)

call·is -is *m* stony, uneven footpath; mountain path; cattle trail; mountain pasture; mountain pass, defile

Callist·ō -ūs *f* daughter of Lycaon, king of Arcadia, who was changed into the constellation Helice or Ursa Major

callōs·us -a -um *adj* hard-skinned; thick-skinned, callous; solid, hard, thick

call·um -ī m hard or thick skin; insensibility, stupidity

cal·ō -āre vt to call out, proclaim; to convoke

cāl·ō -ōnis m soldier's servant; menial servant, drudge

cal·or -ōris m warmth, heat, glow; passion, love; fire, zeal, impetuosity, vehemence

calth·a -ae f marigold

calthŭl·a -ae f yellow robe

calumni·a -ae f trickery; pretense, evasion; false statement, misrepresentation; false accusation, fallacy; malicious charge; conviction for malicious prosecution

calumniāt·or -ōris m malicious prosecutor, perverter of the law, pettifogger

calumni·or -ārī -ātus sum vt to accuse falsely; to misrepresent, calumniate; to blame unjustly; to put in a false light

calv·a -ae f scalp, bald head

calvit·ium -iī or **-ī** n baldness

calv·us -a -um adj bald

cal·x -cis f heel; (fig) foot, kick; **calcibus caedere** to kick

cal·x -cis f pebble; limestone, lime; finish line (marked with lime), goal; **ad calcem pervenire** to reach the goal; **ad carceres a calce revocari** to be recalled from the finish line to the starting gate; to have to start all over again

Calȳd·ōn -ōnis f town in Aetolia, scene of the famous boar hunt led by Meleager

Calȳps·ō -ūs f nymph, daughter of Atlas, who entertained Ulysses on the island of Ogygia

camell·a -ae f drinking cup

camēl·us -ī m camel

Camēn·a -ae f Muse; poem; poetry

camĕr·a -ae f vault, arched roof, arch; houseboat

Camerīn·um -ī n town in Umbria

Camill·a -ae f Volscian female warrior who assisted Turnus against Aeneas

Camill·us -ī m M. Furius Camillus, who freed Rome from the Gauls

camīn·us -ī m fireplace; furnace; forge; **oleum addere camino** to pour oil on the fire

cammăr·us -ī m lobster

Campāni·a -ae f district on E. coast of central Italy

campest·er -ris -re adj flat, level; overland (march); (of city) situated in a plain; (of army) fighting in a plain; (of sports, elections, etc.) held in the Campus Martius; n shorts (worn in sports); n pl flat lands

camp·us -ī m flat space, plain; sports field; level surface, surface (of sea); **Campus Martius** field near the Tiber used for sports, elections, military exercises, etc.

cam·ur -ūra -ŭrum adj crooked, concave

canāl·is -is m pipe, conduit, gutter

cancell·ī -ōrum m pl railing, grating; barrier (at sports, public events); boundaries, limits

canc·er -rī m crab; the South; tropical heat; cancer (disease)

Canc·er -rī m Cancer (northern zodiacal constellation; sign of the zodiac)

cande·faciō -facĕre -fēcī -factum vt to make dazzling white; to make glow, make red-hot

candēl·a -ae f candle, torch, taper; waxed cord; **candelam apponere valvis** to set the house on fire

candēlābr·um -ī n candlestick, candelabrum, chandelier; lamp stand

cand·ens -entis adj shining white, glittering, dazzling, glowing

cand·ĕō -ēre vi to be shining white, glitter, shine; to be white-hot

cand·escō -escĕre -ŭī vi to become white, begin to glisten; to get red-hot

candidātōri·us -a -um adj of a candidate, candidate's

candidāt·us -a -um adj clothed in white; m candidate for office

candidē adv in dazzling white; clearly, simply, sincerely

candidŭl·us -a -um adj pretty white

candid·us -a -um adj (cf **albus**) shiny white, white, bright, dazzling, gleaming, sparkling; fair, radiant (complexion); candid, open, sincere, frank (person); bright, cheerful (circumstances); clear, bright (day); (of winds) bringing clear weather; white, silvery (poplar, hair, etc.); clear, unaffected (style); clothed in white; **candida sententia** vote of acquittal

cand·or -ōris m glossy whiteness, brightness, radiance; candor, sincerity; naturalness (of style); brilliance (of discourse)

cān·ens -entis adj grey, white

cān·ĕō -ēre -ŭī vi to be grey, be white

cānescō -ĕre vi to grow white, become grey; to grow old; (of discourse) to lose force, grow dull

can·ī -ōrum m pl grey hair

canicŭl·a -ae f small dog, pup; (as term of abuse) little bitch

Canicŭl·a -ae f Canicula, Sirius, Dog Star (brightest star in Canis Major)

canīn·us -a -um adj canine; snarling, spiteful, caustic; **canina littera** letter R

can·is -is m or f dog, hound; (term of reproach to denote vile person, enraged person, hanger-on, etc.) dog; worst throw (in dice)

Can·is -is m Canis Major (constellation, of which the brightest star is Canicula)

canistr·um -ī n wicker basket (for bread, fruit, flowers, etc.)

cānitĭ·ēs (genit not in use) f greyness; grey hair; old age cann·a -ae f reed; reed pipe, flute

cannăb·is -ae f or cannăb·um -ī n hemp

Cann·ae -ārum f pl village in Apulia where Hannibal won great victory over Romans in 216 B.C.

canō canĕre cecīnī cantum vt to sing; to play; to speak in a singsong tone; to sing the praises of, celebrate; to prophesy, predict, foretell; (mil) to blow, sound; **signa canere** to sound the signal for battle; vi to sing; to play; (of birds) to sing; (of roosters) to crow; (of frogs) to croak; **receptuī canere** to sound retreat; **tibiā canere** to play the flute

can·or -ōris m tune, sound, melody, song; tone (of instruments)

canōr·us -a -um adj melodious, musical; singsong, jingling; n melody, charm (in speaking)

Cantăbri·a -ae f district in N.W. Spain

cantăm·en -ĭnis n incantation, spell

cantăt·or -ōris m singer

canthăr·is -ĭdis f beetle; Spanish fly

canthăr·us -ī m wide-bellied drinking vessel with handles, tankard

canthēr·ĭus or cantēr·ĭus -ĭī or -ī m gelding; eunuch

canth·us -ī m iron tire; wheel

cantĭc·um -ī n song; aria in Roman comedy; (in delivery of speech) singsong

cantĭlēn·a -ae f old song, gossip; **cantilenam eandem canere** to sing the same old song, harp on the same theme

cantĭ·ō -ōnis f singing; incantation, charm, spell

cantĭt·ō -āre vt to keep on singing or playing, to sing or play repeatedly

cantiuncŭl·a -ae f catchy tune

cant·ō -āre vt to sing; to play; to sing of, celebrate, praise in song; to harp on, keep repeating; to predict; to drawl out; (of actor) to play the part of; vi to sing, to play; (of instruments) to sound; to drawl; (of rooster) to crow; **ad surdas aures cantare** to preach to deaf ears

cant·or -ōris m singer, poet; eulogist; actor, player; musician

cantr·ix -īcis f musician, singer (female)

cant·us -ūs m tune, melody, song, playing; incantation; prediction; magic spell

cān·us -a -um adj white, grey; aged, old venerable

capācĭt·ās -ātis f capacity

cap·ax -ācis adj capacious, spacious, wide, roomy; (of mind) able to grasp, receptive, capable

capĕd·ō -ĭnis f cup or bowl used in sacrifices

capĕduncŭl·a -ae f small cup or bowl used in sacrifices

capell·a -ae f she-goat, nanny goat

Capell·a -ae f Capella (star of the

first magnitude in Auriga)

Capēn·a -ae f Porta Capena (a gate in the Servian Wall which marked the start of the Via Appia)

cap·er -rī m he-goat, billy goat

caperr·ō -āre vt & vi to wrinkle

capess·ō -ĕre -īvī or -ĭī -ītum vt to try to reach, make for, seize, get hold of, snatch at; to take up, undertake, engage in; **capessere rem publicam** to be engaged in politics

capillāt·us -a -um adj having hair, hairy; **bene capillatus** having a fine head of hair

capill·us -ī m hair

capĭ·ō capĕre cēpī captum vt (archaic fut: capso) to take hold of, grasp, seize; to occupy; to take up, assume (office); to catch, capture; to captivate, charm; to cheat, seduce, mislead, delude; to defeat, overcome (in suite); to convince (in a dispute); to reach, arrive at, land at; to exact, extort, accept as a bribe; to take, obtain, get, enjoy, reap (profit, advantage); to acquire, cherish, cultivate, adopt (habits, etc.); to form, conceive, come to, reach (conclusions, plans, thoughts, resolutions, purposes); to take, derive, draw, obtain (examples, proofs, instances); to entertain, conceive, receive, experience (impressions, feelings); (of feelings, experiences) to seize, overcome, occupy, take possession of; to suffer, be subjected to (injury); to hold, contain, be large enough for; to comprehend, grasp

cap·is -ĭdis f bowl (with one handle, used in sacrifices)

capistr·ō -āre vt to muzzle

capistr·um -ī n halter, muzzle

capĭt·al or capĭt·āle -ālis n capital offense

capĭtāl·is -e adj relating to the head or life; (law) affecting a man's life or civil status; (of crime) punishable by death, punishable by loss of civil rights, capital; dangerous, deadly, mortal; chief, preeminent, distinguished, of first rank

capĭt·ō -ōnis m big-head

Capĭtōlin·us -a -um adj Capitoline; m Capitoline Hill; m pl persons in charge of the Capitoline games

Capĭtōl·ĭum -ĭī or -ī n the Capitol (temple of Jupiter on the summit of Mons Tarpeius); the Capitoline Hill (including temple and citadel); citadel (of any city)

capĭtulātim adv briefly, summarily

capĭtŭl·um -ī n small head; (as term of endearment) dear fellow

Cappadoci·a -ae f country in Asia Minor between the Taurus and Pontus

capr·a -ae f she-goat, nanny goat; body odor of armpits

caprĕ·a -ae f wild goat, roe

Caprĕ·ae -ārum f pl island at S. end of Bay of Naples off Sorrento

capreŏl·us -ī *m* roebuck, chamois; prop, support

Capricorn·us -ī *m* Capricorn (*sign of the zodiac*)

caprifīc·us -ī *f* wild fig tree

caprigĕn·us -a -um *adj* of goats; **caprigenum pecus** herd of goats

caprimulg·us -ī *m* rustic

caprīn·us -a -um *adj* of goats, goat; **de lana caprina rixari** to argue over nothing

caprĭp·ēs -ĕdis *adj* goat-footed

caps·a -ae *f* holder, container, box, case (*esp. for book rolls*)

capsō see **capio**

capsŭl·a -ae *f* small box

capt·a -ae *f* captive, prisoner (*female*)

captātĭ·ō -ōnis *f* hunt, quest; **captatio verborum** verbalism, sophistry

captāt·or -ōris *m* (fig) hound; **aurae popularis captator** publicity hound

captĭ·ō -ōnis *f* taking, catching; fraud; loss, disadvantage; sophism

captiōsē *adv* slyly, insidiously, deceptively

captiōs·us -a -um *adj* deceitful; captious, sophistical; dangerous, harmful

captiuncŭl·a -ae *f* quibble, sophism

captīvĭt·ās -ātis *f* captivity; conquest, capture

captīv·us -a -um *adj* caught, taken captive; prisoner's; captured, conquered; *mf* prisoner of war, captive

capt·ō -āre *vt* to catch at eagerly; to keep reaching for; to try to catch, chase after; to strive after, long for, desire earnestly; to try to hear; to try to trap, entice, allure; to adopt (*plan*); to try to cause (*laughter*); to watch for (*opportunity*); to begin (*conversation*)

captūr·a -ae *f* capture; quarry

capt·us -a -um *pp* of **capio**; *adj* **oculis et auribus captus** blind and deaf; **mente captus** mad, crazy; *m* captive, prisoner

capt·us -ūs *m* mental grasp, mental capacity; notion

Capŭ·a -ae *f* chief city of Campania

capŭlār·is -e *adj* with one foot in the grave

capŭl·us -ī *m* coffin; hilt, handle

cap·ut -ĭtis *n* head; top, summit, point, extremity; source (*of river*); root (*of plant*); top (*of tree*); head, leader; capital (*of country*); main point (*of discourse*); chapter, principal division, heading; substance, summary; (com) capital; main course; life, civil status; **capitis accusare** to accuse of a capital offense; **capitis damnare** to condemn to death; **capitis res** matter of life and death; **diminutio capitis** loss of civil rights; **diminutio capitis maxima** condemnation to death or slavery; **diminutio capitis media** loss of citizenship; **di-minutio capitis minima** change of status (*as by adoption or, in the case of women, by marriage*)

Cap·ys -yos *m* son of Assaracus and father of Anchises; companion of Aeneas; eighth king of Alba Longa

carbasĕ·us -a -um *adj* linen, canvas

carbăs·us -ī *f* (*pl:* **carbăs·a -ōrum** *n*) fine Spanish flax; linen garment; sail, canvas; awning

carb·ō -ōnis *m* charcoal

carbōnār·ius -iī or **-ī** *m* charcoal burner, collier

carbuncŭl·us -ī *m* small piece of coal; grief, sorrow; precious stone, garnet

carc·er -ĕris *m* prison, jail; prisoner; (term of reproach) jailbird; *m pl* starting gate (*at racetrack*); **ad carceres a calce revocari** to have to start all over again

carcerārĭ·us -a -um *adj* prison

carchēs·ium -iī or **-ī** *n* drinking cup (*slightly contracted in the middle*); upper part of mast (*similarly formed*)

cardiāc·us -ī *m* dyspeptic

card·ō -ĭnis *m* hinge; turning point, crisis; (astr) axis, pole; **cardo re-rum** critical juncture, crisis

cardŭ·us -ī *m* thistle

cārē *adv* at a high price, dearly; highly

cārect·um -ī *m* sedge

cār·ĕō -ēre -uī *vi* (with *abl* or *genit*) **a** to be without; **b** to miss; **c** to be free from; **d** to keep away from, be absent from; **e** to abstain from

cār·ex -ĭcis *f* sedge

Cārĭ·a -ae *f* province in S.W. Asia Minor

carĭ·ēs (*genit* not in use) *f* decay, rot

carīn·a -ae *f* bottom of ship, keel; ship

Carīn·ae -ārum *f pl* the Keels (*district in Rome Between the Caelian and Esquiline Hills*)

carīnār·ius -iī or **-ī** *m* dyer of yellow

cariōs·us -a -um *adj* rotten, decayed, crumbled; wrinkled

cār·is -ĭdis *f* crab

cārĭt·ās -ātis *f* dearness, costliness, high price, high cost of living; affection, love

carm·en -ĭnis *n* song, tune; lyric poetry, poetry; incantation, charm; oracular utterance; ritual formula, legal formula; adage

Carment·a -ae or **Carment·is -is** *f* Roman goddess of prophecy, the mother of Evander, who came with him from Arcadia to Latium

Carmentāl·is -e *adj* of Carmenta; **Porta Carmentalis** gate at Rome near temple of Carmenta (*also called* **Porta Scelerata**, *i.e., ominous gate*)

cacnār·ium -iī or **-ī** *n* meat hook; pantry

Carneăd·ēs -is *m* famous philosopher, born at Cyrene, and founder of the New Academy (215-130 B.C.)

carnif·ex -ĭcis *m* hangman, executioner; murderer, butcher; scoundrel

carnificĭn·a -ae *f* execution; torture, torment

carnific·ō -āre *vt* to mutilate, cut to pieces, behead

car·ō -nis or **carn·is -is** *f* flesh, meat; **caro ferīna** venison; **caro putĭda** carrion; (fig) rotten egg

car·ō -ēre *vt* to card (*wool*)

Carpăth·us -ī *f* island between Crete and Rhodes

carpatĭn·us -a -um *adj* of rough leather; *f* crude shoe

carpent·um -ī *n* two-wheeled covered carriage (*esp. used by women on holidays*)

carp·ō -ēre -sī -tum *vt* to pluck, pick, cull; to carp at, criticize, take apart; to enjoy, make use of; to crop, browse on (*grass*); to pick, gather (*fruit*); to separate into parts, divide; (mil) to harass, weaken (*esp. by repeated attacks*); **auras vitales carpere** to breathe the breath of life; **diem carpere** to make the most of the present; **gyrum carpere** to go in a circle; **iter** or **viam carpere** to make one's way, pick one's way, travel; **vellera carpere** to spin

carptim *adv* piecemeal, separately, in parts; at different times; at different points; gradually

carpt·or -ōris *m* carver (*of food*)

Carrh·ae -ārum *f pl* town in Mesopotamia where Crassus was defeated and killed by the Parthians (53 B.C.)

carrūc·a -ae *f* four-wheeled carriage

carr·us -ī *m* four-wheeled wagon

Carthāginiens·is -e *adj & mf* Carthaginian

Carthāg·ō -ĭnis *f* Carthage (*city in N. Africa, founded as a Phoenician colony in 9th cent. B.C.*)

caruncŭl·a -ae *f* little piece of meat

cār·us -a -um *adj* dear, high-priced, expensive, costly; dear, beloved, esteemed; loving, affectionate

cas·a -ae *f* cottage, cabin, hut

casc·us -a -um *adj* old, primitive

căseŏl·us -ī *m* small piece of cheese

căse·us -ī *m* cheese

casĭ·a -ae *f* mezereon (*fragrant plant with purple flowers*)

Cassandr·a -ae *f* daughter of Priam and Hecuba who had the gift of prophecy but was believed by no one

cass·ēs -ĭum *m pl* hunting net, snare; spider web

cassĭd·a -ae *f* metal helmet

Cassiŏp·ē -ēs or **Cassiopē·a -ae** *f* wife of Cepheus and mother of Andromeda, afterwards made a constellation

Cass·ĭus -ĭī or **-ī** *m* C. Cassius Longinus (*one of the murderers of Caesar*)

cass·is -ĭdis *f* metal helmet

cass·ō -āre *vi* to totter, trip

cass·us -a -um *adj* empty, hollow; (fig) empty, groundless, vain, pointless; (with *abl*) deprived of, devoid of, without; **cassus lumine** without life, dead; **in cassum** to no purpose, pointlessly

Castăl·is -ĭdis *adj* Castalian; **sorores Castalides** Muses; *f* Muse

Castalĭ·us -a -um *adj* Castalian; *f* fountain on Mt. Parnassus, sacred to Apollo and the Muses

castanĕ·a -ae *f* chestnut tree; chestnut

castē *adv* purely, chastely, spotlessly; virtuously; devoutly, piously

castellān·us -a -um *adj* of a fort, of a castle; *m* occupant of a castle or fortress; *m pl* garrison (*of a fortress*)

castellātim *adv* one fortress after another; **castellatim dissipati** (troops) stationed in various fortresses

castell·um -ī *n* fort, fortress, stronghold, castle; (fig) defense, shelter, refuge

castērĭ·a -ae *f* rowers' quarters

castigābĭl·is -e *adj* punishable

castigātĭ·ō -ōnis *f* correction, punishment; censure, reproof

castigāt·or -ōris *m* corrector, critic

castigātŏrĭ·us -a -um *adj* reproving

castigāt·us -a -um *adj* small, contracted, slender

castīg·ō -āre *vt* to correct, make right, blame, reprove, censure, chide, find fault with, punish; to correct, amend; to hold in check, restrain

castimōnĭ·a -ae *f* purity, morality; chastity, abstinence

castit·ās -ātis *f* purity, chastity

cast·or -ōris *m* beaver

Cast·or -ōris *m* son of Tyndareus, twin brother of Pollux, brother of Helen and Clytemnestra, and patron of sailors

castorĕ·um -ī *m* bitter, strong-smelling secretion of beavers

castrens·is -e *adj* camp, military

castr·ō -āre *vt* to castrate

castr·um -ī *n* fort, fortress, castle; *n pl* military camp; day's march; the service, army life; (pol) party; (phil) school; **bina castra** two camps; **castra facere** or **habere** to encamp; **castra movere** to break camp; **castra munire** to construct a camp; **castra ponere** to pitch camp; **castra una** one camp

cast·us -a -um *adj* (morally) pure, chaste, spotless, guiltless, virtuous; religious, pious, holy, sacred

casŭl·a -ae *f* little hut, little cottage

cās·us -ūs *m* falling; (fig) fall, downfall, overthrow, end; chance, event, happening, occurrence, emergency; occasion, opportunity; misfortune, mishap, accident, calamity; fall,

death; fate; (gram) case; **non consulto sed casu** not on purpose
but by chance

catagelasim·us -a -um adj bantering, jeering; exposed to ridicule

catagraph·us -a -um adj painted,
colored

cataphract·ēs -ae m coat of mail

cataphract·us -a -um adj mail-clad

catāpl·us -ī m arrival of ship; ar-
riving ship or fleet

catapult·a -ae f catapult; (fig) missile

catapultāri·us -a -um adj cata-
pulted, shot (from catapult)

**cataract·a or catarract·a or ca-
tarract·ēs -ae** f waterfall, cataract (esp. on the Nile); floodgate;
drawbridge

cataractri·a -ae f spice

catast·a -ae f stage on which slaves
were displayed for sale

catē adv skillfully, wisely

catēi·a -ae f javelin

catell·a -ae f puppy (female); small
chain

catell·us -ī m puppy; small chain

catēn·a -ae f chain; series; barrier,
restraint, bond

catēnāt·us -a -um adj chained

caterv·a -ae f crowd, throng, band,
mob; troop (of actors); (mil) troop,
horde

catervātim adv in companies, by
troops; in crowds or flocks (of
plague-stricken people)

cathēdr·a -ae f armchair, cushioned
seat; litter, sedan; professional
chair

Catilin·a -ae m L. Sergius Catiline
(Roman patrician whose conspiracy
was exposed by Cicero in 63 B.C.)

catill·ō -āre vi to lick the plate

catill·us -ī m plate

catīn·us -ī m plate, pot, bowl

Cat·ō -ōnis m M. Porcius Cato (model of Roman aristocratic conserva-
tism, 239-149 B.C.); M. Porcius Cato
Uticensis (grandson of Porcius Cato, inveterate enemy of Caesar, 95-
45 B.C.)

catōn·ium -iī or **-ī** n lower world

Catull·us -ī m C. Valerius Catullus
(lyric and elegiac poet of Verona,
86-54 B.C.)

catūl·us -ī m puppy; whelp, cub

cat·us -a -um adj sharp, shrewd,
keen; sly, cunning

Caucas·us -ī m Caucasus mountains

caud·a -ae f tail (of animal); penis;
caudam jactare (with dat) to flatter; **caudam trahere** to be mocked

caudĕ·us -a -um adj of wood,
wooden

caud·ex or cōd·ex -icis m trunk (of
tree); block (of wood to which one
was tied for punishment); book,
ledger; blockhead

caudicāl·is -e adj of wood cutting

Caud·ium -iī or **-ī** n town in Samnium

caul·ae -ārum f pl hole, opening
passage; sheepfold, pen

caul·is -is f stalk, stem; cabbage
stalk, cabbage

caup·ō -ōnis m innkeeper

caupōn·a -ae f inn, tavern; retail
shop

caupōni·us -a -um adj of a shop or
tavern

caupōn·or -ārī -ātus sum vt to
trade in or traffic in

caupōnul·a -ae f small inn or tavern

caus·a or causs·a -ae f (law) lawsuit, case; grounds, cause, motive,
purpose, reason; good reason, just
cause; pretext, pretense; inducement, occasion, opportunity; side,
party, faction, cause; condition,
situation, position; (rhet) matter of
discussion, subject matter; matter,
business, concern; commission,
charge; personal relationship, con-
nexion; **causā** (with genit) for the
sake of, on account of; **causā cadere** to lose a case; **causam agere,
causam dicere,** or **causam orare**
to plead a case; **causam cognos-
cere** to examine a case (as judge);
vestrā causā in your interests;
per causam (with genit) under the
pretext of; **sine causa** without
good reason

causāri·us -a -um adj sick; m (mil)
malingerer, goldbrick

causi·a -ae f Macedonian hat (with
wide brim)

causidic·us -ī m pleader, lawyer;
shyster

causific·or -ārī -ātus sum vi to
make excuses

caus·or -ārī -ātus sum vt to pretend, give as a reason

caussa see **causa**

causul·a -ae f petty lawsuit; minor
cause

cautē adv cautiously, carefully; with
security

cautēl·a -ae f precaution

caut·ēs -is f rock, crag

cautim adv warily, cautiously

caut·iō -ōnis f caution, wariness;
guarantee, provision; (law) bond,
security, bail, warranty; **mea cautio est I** must see to it; **mihi cautio est I** must take care

caut·or -ōris m wary person; bondsman, surety

caut·us -a -um adj cautious, careful; safe, secure

cavaed·ium -iī or **-ī** n inner court
of Roman house

cavē·a -ae f cavity; enclosure for
animals; cage, den, stall, beehive,
bird cage; auditorium, theater; **prima cavea** section of auditorium
for nobility; **ultima cavea** section
for lower classes

caveō cavēre cāvī cautum vt to
guard against, beware of; to keep
clear of; to stipulate, decree, order;
to guarantee; vi to be careful, look
out, be on one's guard; (with abl or

ab + abl) to be on one's guard against; (with ab + abl) to get a guarantee from; (with dat) a to guarantee, give a guarantee to; b to provide for, take care of; cave tangere (= noli tangere) do not touch

cavern.a -ae f hollow, cavity, cave, cavern; vault; hold (of ship)

cavill.a -ae f jeering, scoffing

cavillāti.ō -ōnis f banter, scoffing, raillery; sophistry, quibbling

cavillāt.or -ōris m scoffer; quibbler, sophist

cavill.or -ārī -ātus sum vt to scoff at, mock, criticize, satirize; vi to scoff, jeer; to quibble

cav.ō -āre vt to hollow out, excavate; to pierce, run through

cav.us -a -um adj hollow, hollowed; concave, vaulted; deep-channeled (river); m & n hole, cavity, hollow

-ce demonstrative enclitic appended to pronouns and adverbs (like colloquial English here, there, with this or that); hice (for hicce) this (here); hujusce of this (here); (when followed by the enclytic -ne, the form becomes -ci: hicine, sicine)

Cecropid.ae -ārum m pl descendants of Cecrops, Athenians

Cecrōp.is -ĭdis f female descendant of Cecrops (esp. Aglauros); Procne; Philomela; Athenian woman

Cecr.ops -ŏpis m first king of Athens

cēdō cēdĕre cessī cessum vt to grant, concede, yield, give up; vi to go, move, walk, walk along; to go away, depart, withdraw; (of time) to pass; (of events) to turn out; to pass away, die; (mil) to retreat; (with dat) a to befall, fall to the lot of, accrue to; b to yield to, submit to, give in to; c to yield (in rank) to, be inferior to; d to comply with, conform to, obey; (with in + acc) to be changed into, become; (with pro + abl) to pass for, be the equivalent of, be the price of; bonis or possessiōnibus alicui cedere to give up or cede one's property to someone; foro cedere to go bankrupt

cedo (pl: cette) (old impv) here with, bring here, give here; let's hear, tell, out with; look at; cedo dum! all right!; come now!; cedo ut inspiciam let me look

cedr.us -ī f cedar, juniper; cedar wood; cedar oil

Celaen.ō -ūs f daughter of Atlas and one of the Pleiades; one of the Harpies; greedy woman

cēlāt.um -ī n secret

celĕb.er -ris -re adj crowded, populous, frequented; well-attended; famous; well-known, common, usual; solemn, festive; numerous, repeated, frequent

celebrāti.ō -ōnis f large assembly; festival, celebration; f pl throngs

celebrāt.us -a -um adj much-frequented, much-visited, crowded, populous; celebrated, famous, renowned; customary, usual, frequent; solemn, festive; trite, familiar, often-repeated

celebrĭt.ās -ātis f throng, crowd, multitude, large assembly; publicity; repetition, frequency; fame, renown; celebration

celĕbr.ō -āre vt to frequent, crowd, fill, visit in crowds; to repeat, practice, exercise; to publicize, advertise, honor, glorify; to escort, attend; to cause to resound

cel.er -ĕris -ĕre adj swift, speedy, quick, rapid, hurried; rash, hasty

celĕrĕ adv quickly

Celĕr.ēs -um m pl mounted bodyguards of Roman kings

celerĭp.ēs -ĕdis adj swift-footed

celerĭt.ās -ātis f speed, quickness, rapidity

celerĭter adv quickly, speedily

celĕr.ō -āre vt to quicken, speed up, accelerate; vi to be quick, rush, speed

cell.a -ae f storeroom, storehouse, grain elevator, silo; cheap apartment, garret; sanctuary (of temple, where the cult image stood); cell (of beehive)

cellāri.us -a -um adj of a storeroom; m storekeeper, butler

cellŭl.a -ae f small storeroom, small apartment

cēl.ō -āre vt to hide, conceal; to veil (feelings); to keep (something) secret, keep quiet about; (with acc of thing and acc of person from whom one conceals) to keep (someone) in the dark about, hide (something) from (someone); celari (with dē + abl) to be kept in ignorance of

cel.ox -ōcis adj swift, quick; f swift-sailing ship, cutter, speedboat

cels.us -a -um adj high, lofty, towering, prominent, erect; lofty, elevated (thoughts); high (rank); proud, haughty

Celt.ae -ārum m pl Celts (who occupied most of W. Europe); (in more restricted sense) inhabitants of central Gaul

Celtibēr.ī -ōrum m pl Celtiberians (early people of Central Spain)

cēn.a -ae f principal meal, dinner; dish, course; company at dinner

cēnācŭl.um -ī n dining room (usually on an upper floor); attic

cēnātĭc.us -a -um adj dinner

cēnātĭ.ō -ōnis f dining room

cēnāt.us -a -um adj having dined; spent in feasting

cēnĭt.ō -āre vi to dine habitually, dine often

cēn.ō -āre vt to make a meal of, dine on, eat; vi to dine, eat dinner

cens.ĕō -ēre -ŭī -um vt to assess, rate, estimate, tax; to esteem, appreciate, value; (of senate) to decree, resolve; to propose, move, vote, argue, suggest, advise; to think, believe, hold, suppose, imagine, expect

censi·ō -ōnis *f* rating, assessment, taxation; opinion

cens·or -ōris *m* censor (*one of two Roman magistrates who took the census and exercised general control over morals, etc.*); severe judge of morals, critic

censōri·us -a -um *adj* of the censors; subject to censure; rigid, stern, austere; **homo censorius** ex-censor; **lex censoria** contract (*drawn up by censors*) for leasing buildings

censūr·a -ae *f* office of censor, censorship; criticism

cens·us -ūs *m* census; register of the census; income bracket; wealth, property; rich presents, gifts; **censum agere** or **habere** to hold a census; **censu prohibere** to exclude from citizenship, disenfranchise

centaurē·um -ī *n* centaury (*medical herb*)

Centaur·us -ī *m* centaur (*creature fabled to be half man and half horse*); **Centaurus** (*southern constellation between the Southern Cross and Hydra*)

centēn·ī -ae -a *adj* one hundred each; **deciens centena milia passum** ten hundred thousand paces, one million paces

centēsim·us -a -um *adj* hundredth; *f* hundredth part, one percent; (com) 1% monthly (12% per annum)

centī·ceps -cipĭtis *adj* hundred-headed

centiēs or **centiens** *adv* a hundred times; (fig) a great many times

centimān·us -a -um *adj* hundred-handed

cent·ō -ōnis *m* patchwork, quilt

centum (*indecl*) *adj* hundred

centumgemĭn·us -a -um *adj* hundredfold

centumpl·ex -ĭcis *adj* hundredfold

centumpond·ium -iī or **-ī** *n* hundred pounds, hundred-pound weight

centumvirāl·is -e *adj* of the centumviri

centumvir·ī -ōrum *m pl* panel of one hundred (*jurors chosen annually to try civil suits under a quaestor, esp. concerning inheritances*)

centuriātim *adv* by companies, by centuries

centuriāt·us -a -um *adj* divided into companies or centuries; **comitia centuriata** centuriate assembly

(*legislative body which met in the Campus Martius to elect high magistrates, decree war, etc.*)

centurĭ·ō -ōnis *m* centurion (*commander of an infantry company*)

centurĭ·ō -āre *vt* to divide into centuries

centuriōnāt·us -ūs *m* election of centurions

centuss·is -is *m* a hundred aces (*bronze coins*)

cēnŭl·a -ae *f* little dinner

Cephăl·us -ī *m* husband of Procris, whom he unintentionally shot

Cēph·eus -ĕī *m* king of Ethiopia, husband of Cassiope and father of Andromeda

Cēphīs·us -ī *m* river in Attica; river in Phocis and Boeotia

cēr·a -ae *f* wax; writing tablet (*covered with wax*); wax seal; wax bust of an ancestor; cell (*of beehive*)

Cerāmīc·us -ī *m* cemetery of Athens

cērār·ium -iī or **-ī** *n* fee for affixing a seal

cerast·ēs -ae *m* horned serpent

ceră̆s·us -ī *f* cherry tree; cherry

cērāt·us -a -um *adj* waxed

Cerbĕr·us -ī *m* three-headed dog which guarded the entrance to the lower world

cercopithēc·us -ī *m* long-tailed monkey

cercūr·us -ī *m* swift-sailing ship, cutter

cerd·ō -ōnis *m* workman, laborer

Cereāl·ia -ium *n pl* festival of Ceres (*April 10th*)

Cereāl·is -e *adj* of Ceres; of grain; **arma Cerealia** utensils for grinding and baking

cerebrōs·us -a -um *adj* hot-headed

cerĕbr·um -ī *n* brain; head, skull; understanding; hot temper

Cer·ēs -ĕris *f* goddess of agriculture and mother of Proserpine; grain bread, food

cērĕ·us -a -um *adj* of wax, waxen; wax-colored; soft, pliant; *m* candle

cērinth·a -ae *f* wax flower

cērīn·us -a -um *adj* wax-colored; *n pl* wax-colored clothes

cernō cernĕre crēvī crētum *vt* (of sight) to discern, distinguish, make out, see; (of mind) to discern, see, understand; to decide, decree, determine; **hereditatem cernere** to formally declare oneself heir to an inheritance, accept an inheritance

cernŭ·us -a -um *adj* with face turned toward the earth, stooping forwards

cērōm·a -ătis *n* wrestler's oil

cērōmatĭc·us -a -um *adj* smeared with oil, oily, greasy

cerrīt·us -a -um *adj* crazy, frantic

certām·en -ĭnis *n* contest, match; rivalry; (mil) battle, combat

certātim *adv* with a struggle, in rivalry

certātĭ·ō -ōnis *f* contest; rivalry, discussion, debate

certē *adv* surely, certainly, unquestionably, undoubtedly, of course; (in answers) yes, certainly; (to restrict an assertion) at least, at any rate

certō *adv* for certain, for sure; surely, in fact, really

cert·ō -āre *vi* to fight, contend, struggle, do battle; to compete; (law) to debate; (with *inf*) to strive to

cert·us -a -um *adj* certain, determined, resolved, fixed, settled; specific, particular, certain, precise, definite; faithful, trusty, dependable; sure of aim, unerring; unwavering, inexorable; **certiorem facere** to inform; **certum est mihi** (with *inf*) I am determined to; **certum habere** to regard as certain; **pro certo** for sure; **pro certo habere** to be assured

cērūl·a -ae *f* piece of wax; **cerula miniata** red pencil (*of a critic*)

cēruss·a -ae *f* ceruse, white paint

cērussāt·us -a -um *adj* painted white

cerv·a -ae *f* hind, deer

cervīc·al -ālis *n* pillow, cushion

cervīcul·a -ae *f* slender neck

cervīn·us -a -um *adj* of a stag or deer

cerv·īx -īcis *f* neck; nape of the neck; **in cervicibus nostris esse** to be on our necks., i.e., to have (*something or someone unpleasant*) on our hands; **a cervicibus nostris avertere** to get (*someone*) off our neck, get rid of (*someone*); **cervicibus sustinere** to shoulder (*responsibility*)

cerv·us -ī *m* stag, deer; (mil) palisade

cessātī·ō -ōnis *f* letup, delay; inactivity, idleness, cessation

cessāt·or -ōris *m* idler, loafer

cessi·ō -ōnis *f* surrendering, relinquishment

cess·ō -āre *vi* to let up, slack off, become remiss, stop; to be inactive, be idle, do nothing; to lie fallow

cestrosphendon·ē -ēs *f* artillery piece for hurling stones

cest·us or **cest·os -ī** *m* girdle (*esp. of Venus*)

cētār·ium -ī or **-ī** *n* fish pond

cētār·ius -ī or **-ī** *m* fish dealer

cētēra *adv* otherwise, in all other respects, for the rest

cētērōquī or **cēterōquin** *adv* otherwise, in all other respects, for the rest

cētērum *adv* otherwise, in all other respects, for the rest; but, yet, still, on the other hand

cētēr·us -a -um *adj* the other, the remaining, the rest of; *pron m pl & f pl* the others, all the rest, everybody; *n* the rest

Cethēg·us -ī *m* C. Cornelius Cethegus (*fellow conspirator of Catiline*)

cette see **cedo**

cēt·us -ī (*pl:* cēt·ē) *m* sea monster: whale, shark, seal, dolphin

ceu *conj* (in comparisons) as, just as; (in comparative conditions) as if, just as if; **ceu cum** as when

cēv·eō -ēre *vi* (*cf* **criso**) (of a male) to move the haunches

Cē·yx -ўcis *m* king of Trachis, who was changed into a kingfisher, as was his wife Alcyone

Chaldae·us -a -um *adj* Chaldaean; *m* astrologer, fortune-teller

chalybēi·us -a -um *adj* steel

Chalyb·es -um *m pl* people of Pontus in Asia Minor noted as steel-workers

chal·ybs -ybis *m* steel

Chāon·es -um *m pl* a tribe in Epirus

Chāoni·us -a -um *adj* Chaonian; of Epirus; *f* Chaonia (*district of Epirus*)

Cha·os -ī *n* chaos, the unformed world, empty space, shapeless mass from which the world was formed; **a Chao** from the beginning of the world

char·a -ae *f* wild cabbage

charistī·a -ōrum *n pl* Roman family festival

Charīt·es -um *f pl* the Graces

Char·ōn -ontis *m* ferryman of the lower world

chart·a -ae *f* sheet of papyrus; sheet of paper; writing, letter, poem; book; record

chartūl·a -ae *f* sheet of paper; letter, note

Charybd·is -is *f* whirlpool between Italy and Sicily, personified as a female monster

Chatt·ī -ōrum *m pl* people of central Germany

Chēl·ae -ārum *f pl* the Claws (*of Scorpio*); Libra (*constellation into which Scorpio extends*)

chelydr·us -ī *m* water snake

chely·s (*genit* not in use; *acc:* chelyn) *f* tortoise; lyre

cheragr·a -ae *f* arthritis in the hand

chīliarch·ēs -ae or **chīliarch·us -ī** *m* commander of 1000 men; Persian chancellor (*highest office next to the king*)

Chimaer·a -ae *f* fire-breathing monster, with lion's head, goat's body, and dragon's tail

Chi·os -ī *f* island off coast of Asia Minor, famous for its wine

chīrogrāph·um -ī *n* handwriting; autography; document; **falsa chirographa** forgeries

Chīr·ōn -ōnis *m* Chiron (*centaur, tutor of Aesculapius, Hercules, and Achilles, and famous for his knowledge of medicine and prophecy*)

chīronŏm·os -ī or **chironŏm·ōn -untis** *m* pantomimist

chīrurgī·a -ae *f* surgery

Chi·us -a -um *adj & mf* Chian; *n* Chian wine; *n pl* Chian cloth

chlamydāt·us -a -um *adj* wearing a military uniform

chlam·ys -ўdis *f* military cloak; gold-brocaded mantle

Choerīl·us -ī *m* incompetent Greek panegyrist of Alexander the Great

chorāg·ium -iī or **-ī** *n* choreography

chorāg·us -ī *m* choragus (*man who finances the chorus*)

choraul·ēs -ae *m* flute player who accompanied the choral dance

chord·a -ae *f* gut string, string (*of musical instrument*); cord, rope

chorē·a -ae *f* dance

chorē·us -ī *m* trochee

chor·us -ī *m* chorus; choir

Chrem·ēs -ētis or **-is** or **-ī** *m* miserly old man (*in Roman comedy*)

Christiān·us -ī *m* Christian

Christ·us -ī *m* Christ

Chrȳsē·is -ĭdis *f* Agamemnon's slave girl, daughter of Chryses

Chrȳs·ēs -ae *m* priest of Apollo

Chrysipp·us -ī *m* famous Stoic philosopher (290-210 B.C.)

chrȳsolĭth·os -ī *m* chrysolite, topaz

chrȳs·os -ī *m* gold

cibāri·us -a -um *adj* of food; common, coarse (*food of slaves*); *n pl* rations, provisions, food allowance

cibāt·us -ūs *m* food

cib·ō -āre *vt* to feed

cibōr·ium -iī or **-ī** *n* drinking cup

cib·us -ī *m* food; feed; (fig) food, nourishment

cicād·a -ae *f* locust, harvest fly

cicātrīcōs·us -a -um *adj* scarred, covered with scars

cicātr·ix -īcis *f* scar

cicc·us -ī *m* core of pomegranate; something worthless, trifle

cic·er -ĕris *n* chick-pea

Cicĕr·ō -ōnis *m* M. Tullius Cicero (*orator and statesman*, 106-43 B.C.)

cīchorē·um -ī *n* endive

Cicŏn·es -um *m pl* Thracian tribe

cicōni·a -ae *f* stork

cic·ur -ŭris *adj* tame

cicūt·a -ae *f* hemlock tree; hemlock poison; pipe, flute (*carved from hemlock tree*)

ciĕō ciēre cīvī citum *vt* to set in motion, move; to stir, agitate; to call for, send for; to summon for help; to invoke, appeal to; to call on by name, mention by name; to start, bring about; to renew (*combat*)

Cilici·a -ae *f* country in S. Asia Minor

Cilici·us -a -um *adj* Cilician; *n* garment of goat's hair

Cil·ix -īcis *adj & m* Cilician

Cimbr·ī -ōrum *m pl* Germanic tribe (*defeated by Marius in 101 B.C.*)

cīm·ex -īcis *m* bug

Cimmeri·ī -ōrum *m pl* people in the Crimea; mythical people living in perpetual darkness in caves at Cumae

cinaedic·us -a -um *adj* lewd

cinaed·us -ī *m* sodomite; lewd dancer

cincinnāt·us -a -um *adj* curly-haired

Cincinnāt·us -ī *m* L. Quinctius Cincinnatus (*famous Roman hero, dictator in 458 B.C.*)

cincinn·us -ī *m* curled hair, artificial curl (*of hair*); (rhet) highly artificial expression

cincticŭl·us -ī *m* small belt or sash

cinctūr·a -ae *f* belt, sash

cinct·us -ūs *m* tucking up; belt, sash; **cinctus Gabinius** Gabinian style of wearing toga (*usually employed at religious festivals*)

cinctūt·us -a -um *adj* wearing a belt or sash; old-fashioned

cinefact·us -a -um *adj* reduced to ashes

cinerār·ius -iī or **-ī** *m* curling iron, hair curler

cingō cingĕre cinxī cinctum *vt* to surround, encircle; to wreathe (*head*); to tuck up (*garment*); (mil) to beleaguer, invest; to cover, protect; **cingi in proelia** to prepare oneself for battle, get ready for battle; **ferrum cingi** to put on one's sword

cingŭl·a -ae *f* belt; sash (*worn by women*); girth (*worn by horses, etc.*); sword belt; chastity belt

cingŭl·um -ī *m* belt; sword belt; sash (*worn by women*); girdle, chastity belt

cingŭl·us -ī *m* zone (*of the earth*)

cinifl·ō -ōnis *m* hair curler

cin·is -ĕris *m/nom*; ruin, death

Cinn·a -ae *m* L. Cornelius Cinna (*consul 87-84 B.C. and supporter of Marius, d. 84 B.C.*)

cinnamōm·um or **cinnăm·um -ī** *n* cinnamon; *n pl* cinnamon sticks

Cinȳr·ās -ae *m* father of Myrrha and Adonis

cipp·us -ī *m* stake, post, pillar; gravestone; (mil) palisade

circā *adv* around, round about, all around, in the vicinity; *prep* (with *acc*) (of place) around, surrounding, about, among, through, in the neighborhood of, near; attending, escorting (*persons*); (of time) at about, around, towards; (with numerals) about, nearly, almost; concerning, in respect to

circamoer·ium -iī or **-ī** *n* area on both sides of a city wall

Circ·ē -ēs or **-ae** *f* daughter of Helios and Perse, famous for her witchcraft

circens·is -e *adj* of the racetrack; *m pl* races

circin·ō -āre *vt* to make round; to circle

circin·us -ī *m* (geometer's) compass, pair of compasses

circĭter *adv* (of time and number) nearly, about, approximately; *prep* (with *acc*) about, near

circlus see **circulus**

circŭeō see **circumeo**

circuitiō see **circumitio**

circuĭt·us or **circumĭt·us -ūs** *m* circuit; going round, revolution; de-

tour; circumference; circumlocution; (rhet) period

circulāt·or -ōris *m* peddler, vendor

circŭl·or -ārī -ātus sum *vi* to
gather around *(for conversation)*;
to stroll about

circŭl·us or **circl·us -ī** *m* circle, circuit; ring, hoop; social circle; (astr)
orbit

circum *adv* about, all around; *prep*
(with *acc*) around, about; in the
neighborhood of

circum·ăgō -agĕre -ēgī -actum *vt*
to turn around; to sway *(emotionally)*; **circumagi** or **se circumage-
re** to go out of one's way, go in a
round about way; (of time) to pass
away, roll around

circumăr·ō -āre *vt* to plow around

circumcaesŭr·ă -ae *f* contour, outline

circum·cīdo -cīdĕre -cīdī -cīsum
vt to cut around, trim; to cut short,
cut down on; to abridge, shorten;
to circumcise

circumcircă *adv* all around

circumcīs·us -a -um *pp* of **cir-
cumcīdo;** *adj* steep; inaccessible;
abridged, short

**circum·clūdō -clūdĕre -clūsī -clū-
sum** *vt* to shut in, hem in, enclose,
surround

circumcŏl·ō -ĕre *vt* to live near

circumcurs·ō -āre *vt* & *vi* to run
around

circum·dō -dare -dĕdī -dătum *vt*
to surround, enclose, encircle; (with
dat) to place or put *(something)*
around

**circum·dūcō -dūcĕre -duxī -duc-
tum** *vt* to lead around, draw
around; (with double *acc*) to lead
(someone) around to; **aliquem omnia praesidia circumducere** to
take someone around to all the gar-
risons

circum·ĕō or **circu·ĕō -īre -īvī** or
īī -ĭtum *vt* to go around, go around
to, visit, make the rounds of; to
surround, encircle, enclose, encompass; to get around, circumvent, deceive, cheat; *vi* to go around, make
a circuit

circumequĭt·ō -āre *vt* to ride
around

circum·fĕrō -ferre -tŭlī -lātum
vt to carry around, hand around; to
publicize, spread abroad; to purify;
circumferri to revolve; **oculos
circumferre** to look around,
glance about

**circum·flectō -flectĕre -flexī -flex-
um** *vt* to turn around, wheel about

circumflō -āre *vt* to blow around;
(fig) to buffet

circum·flŭō -flŭĕre -fluxī *vt* to flow
around; to surround; to overflow;
vi to be overflowing, abound

circumflŭ·us -a -um *adj* flowing
around; surrounded *(by water)*

circumforānĕ·us -a -um *adj* strolling about from market to market,

itinerant; around the forum

**circum·fundō -fundĕre -fūdī -fū-
sum** *vt* to pour around; to surround, cover, envelop; **circumfundi** or **se circumfundere** to crowd
around; **circumfundi** (with *dat*) to
cling to

circumgĕm·ō -ĕre *vt* to growl
around *(e.g., a sheepfold)*

circumgest·ō -āre *vt* to carry
around

**circum·gredior -grĕdī -gressus
sum** *vt* to surround

circumitĭ·ō or **circuitĭ·ō -ōnis** *f*
going round; patrolling; circumlocution

circumītus see **circuitus**

circumjac·ĕō -ēre *vi* (with *dat*) to
lie near, border on, be adjacent to

circum·jiciō -jicĕre -jēcī -jectum
vt to throw or place around; to surround; (with *dat*) to throw *(something)* around *(someone or something)*; **fossam circumjicere** to
dig a trench all around

circumject·us -a -um *adj* surrounding, adjacent; (with *dat*) adjacent
to; *n pl* neighborhood

circumject·us -ūs *m* surrounding;
embrace

circumlātus *pp* of **circumfero**

circumlĭg·ō -āre *vt* to bind; (with
dat) to bind or fasten *(something)*
to

circum·lĭnō -lĭnĕre — -lĭtum *vt* to
smear all over; to anoint

circumlŭ·ō -ĕre *vt* to flow around

circumluvĭ·ō -ōnis *f* island *(formed
by a river flowing in a new channel)*

**circum·mittō -mittĕre -mīsī
-missum** *vt* to send around

circummūn·ĭō or **circummoen·ĭō
-īre** *vt* to fortify

circummūnītĭ·ō -ōnis *f* investment
(of town); circumvallation

circumpadān·us -a -um *adj* situated along the Po River

circumpend·ĕō -ēre *vi* to hang
around

circumplaud·ō -ĕre *vt* to applaud
from every direction

**circum·plector -plectī -plexus
sum** *vt* to clasp, embrace, surround

circumplic·ō -āre *vt* to wind; (with
dat) to wind *(something)* around

**circum·pōnō -pōnĕre -posŭī -po-
situm** *vt* (with *dat*) to place or set
(something) around

circumpōtātĭ·ō -ōnis *f* round of
drinks

circumrēt·ĭō -īre -īvī -ītum *vt* to
snare

circum·rōdō -rōdĕre -rōsī *vt* to
nibble all around; to hesitate to say;
to slander, backbite

circumsaep·ĭō or **circumsēp·ĭō
-īre -sī -tum** *vt* to fence in, enclose

circumscind·ō -ĕre *vt* to strip off

**circum·scrībō -scrībĕre -scripsī
-scriptum** *vt* to draw a line
around, mark the boundary of; to

limit, restrict; to set aside; to defeat the purpose of; to trap, defraud

circumscriptē *adv* comprehensively; (rhet) in periods

circumscriptī·ō -ōnis *f* encircling; circle; circuit, limit, boundary; comprehensive statement; cheating, deceiving; (rhet) period

circumscript·or -ōris *m* cheat

circumscript·us -a -um *pp* of **circumscrībo**; *adj* restricted, limited; (rhet) periodic

circumsēc·ō -āre *vt* to cut around

circum·sedēō -sedēre -sēdī -sessum *vt* to beset, besiege, invest, blockade

circumsēpiō see **circumsaepio**

circumsessī·ō -ōnis *f* besieging, blockading

circumsīd·ō -ere *vt* to besiege

circumsil·iō -īre *vi* to hop around, dance around

circum·sistō -sistēre -stētī *vt* to stand around, surround

circumsŏn·ō -āre *vt* to make resound, fill with sound; *vi* to resound everywhere; (with *dat*) to resound to

circumsŏn·us -a -um *adj* noisy

circumspectātr·ix -īcis *f* spy (female)

circumspectī·ō -ōnis *f* looking around; circumspection, caution

circumspect·ō -āre *vt* to search attentively, watch for; *vi* to keep looking around, look around anxiously

circumspect·us -a -um *pp* of **circumspicio**; *adj* well-considered; guarded (*words*); circumspect, cautious (*person*)

circumspect·us -ūs *m* consideration; view

circum·spiciō -spicēre -spexī -spectum *vt* to look around for, survey, see; to consider, examine; *vi* to be circumspect, be cautious, be on the watch; **se circumspicere** to think highly of oneself

circumstant·ēs -ium *m pl* bystanders

circum·stō -stāre -stētī *vt* to surround, envelop; (of terror, etc.) to grip, confront, overwhelm; *vi* to stand around

circumstrĕp·ō -ere *vt* to surround with noise or shouts

circumsurg·ō -ere *vi* (of mountains) to rise all around

circumtent·us -a -um *adj* tightly covered

circumtĕr·ō -ere *vt* to rub shoulders with, crowd around

circumtext·us -a -um *adj* with embroidered border

circumtŏn·ō -āre -ŭī *vt* to crash around (*someone*)

circumtons·us -a -um *adj* clipped

circum·vādō -vādere -vāsī *vt* to attack on every side; (of terror, etc.) to grip, confront

circumvăg·us -a -um *adj* flowing around, encircling

circumvall·ō -āre *vt* to blockade, invest

circumvectī·ō -ōnis *f* carting around (*of merchandise*); revolution (*of sun*)

circumvect·ō -āre *vt* to carry around

circumvect·or -ārī -ātus sum *vt* to ride or cruise around; to describe; *vi* to ride about, cruise about

circum·vĕhor -vĕhī -vectus sum *vt* to ride or cruise around; to describe, express by circumlocution; *vi* to ride about, cruise about

circumvēl·ō -āre *vt* to veil, envelop, cover

circum·veniō -venīre -vēnī -ventum *vt* to encircle, surround; to go around to; to surround (*in a hostile manner*), invest; to distress, afflict, oppress; to circumvent, cheat, deceive

circumvert·ō -ere *vt* to turn (*something*) around; **circumverti** to turn oneself around, turn around; **circumverti axem** to turn around an axle

circumvest·iō -īre *vt* to clothe, wrap

circumvinc·iō -īre *vt* to bind, tie up

circumvīs·ō -ere *vt* to look around, glare around at

circumvolit·ō -āre *vt & vi* to fly around, dash about, rove around; to hover around

circumvŏl·ō -āre *vt* to fly around, hover about, flit about

circum·volvō -volvēre — -volūtum *vt* to wind, roll around; **circumvolvi** or **se circumvolvere** (with *dat* or *acc*) to revolve around, wind oneself around

circ·us -ī *m* circle; racetrack; (astr) orbit

Circ·us Maxĭm·us (genit: **Circ·ī Maxĭm·ī**) *m* oldest racetrack in Rome, between the Palatine and Aventine, alleged to have been built by Tarquinius Priscus

cirrāt·us -a -um *adj* curly-haired

Cirrh·a -ae *f* town near Delphi, sacred to Apollo

cirr·us -ī *m* lock, curl; forelock; fringe

cis *prep* (with *acc*) on this side of; within

Cisalpīn·us -a -um *adj* Cisalpine, on the Roman side of the Alps

cis·ium -iī or **-ī** *n* light two-wheeled carriage

Cissē·is -ĭdis *f* Hecuba

Ciss·eus -ĕī *m* king of Thrace and father of Hecuba

cist·a -ae *f* box, chest

cistell·a -ae *f* small box

cistellātr·ix -īcis *f* female slave in charge of a money box

cistellŭl·a -ae *f* small box

cistern·a -ae *f* cistern, reservoir

cistophŏr·us -ī *m* Asiatic coin

cistŭl·a -ae *f* small box

citātim *adv* quickly, hastily

citāt·us -a -um *adj* quick, speedy, rapid; citato equo at full gallop

citeri·or -us *adj* on this side; nearer to earth, more down to earth, more mundane

Cithaer·ōn -ōnis *m* mountain range dividing Attica from Boeotia

cithăr·a -ae *f* zither, lyre, lute; art of playing the zither, lyre, or lute

citharist·a -ae *m* zither player, lute player

citharistrĭ·a -ae *f* zither player, lutist (*female*)

citharĭz·ō -āre *vt* to play the zither, lyre, or lute

citharoed·us -ī *m* singer accompanied by zither, lyre, or lute

citĭm·us -a -um *adj* nearest

citĭus *adv* sooner, rather; dicto citĭus no sooner said than done; serĭus aut citĭus sooner or later

cito *adv* quickly; soon

cit·ō -āre *vt* to excite, rouse; to call, summon, cite; to call to witness, appeal to

citrā *adv* on this side, on the near side; citra cadere to fall short; *prep* (with *acc*) on this side of, on the near side of; (of time) since, before; short of, less than

citrĕ·us -a -um *adj* of citrus wood

citrō *adv* to this side, this way; ultro citro, ultro citroque, or ultro et citro to and fro, up and down; mutually

citr·us -ī *f* citrous tree; citron tree

cit·us -a -um *pp* of cieo; *adj* quick, rapid, swift

cīvĭc·us -a -um *adj* civil; civic; corona civica oak-leaf crown awarded for saving a fellow soldier's life

cīvĭl·is -e *adj* civil; civic; political; civilian; democratic; polite; jus cīvīle rights as a citizen, civil rights; civil law; ratio civīlis political science

cīvilit·ās -ātis *f* politics; courtesy

cīvīliter *adv* like a citizen; as an ordinary citizen would; politely

cīv·is -is *m* or *f* citizen; fellow citizen; private citizen

cīvit·ās -ātis *f* citizenship; state, commonwealth, community

clăd·ēs -is *f* disaster, ruin, damage, loss; (mil) defeat; (fig) scourge

clam *adv* secretly, privately, in secret; stealthily; *prep* (with *abl* or *acc*) without the knowledge of, unknown to; clam habere aliquem to keep someone in the dark; neque clam me est nor is it unknown to me

clāmāt·or -ōris *m* loudmouth

clāmitātĭ·ō -ōnis *f* bawling, noise, racket

clāmĭt·ō -āre *vt* & *vi* to cry out, yell

clām·ō -āre *vt* to call out, call upon; to proclaim, declare; to invoke; *vi* to cry out, yell, shout

clām·or -ōris *m* shout, cry, call; acclamation, applause; outcry, complaint; war cry; noise, sound, echo

clāmōs·us -a -um *adj* clamorous, noisy

clancŭlum *adv* secretly, privately; *prep* (with *acc*) unknown to

clandestīnō *adv* secretly

clandestīn·us -a -um *adj* clandestine, secret, hidden

clang·or -ōris *m* clang, din, shrill cry

clārē *adv* distinctly, clearly; brightly; with distinction

clār·ĕō -ēre *vi* to be clear, be bright, be distinct; to be evident; to be famous

clār·escō -escĕre -ŭī *vi* to become clear, become distinct, become bright; to become obvious; to become famous

clārigātĭ·ō -ōnis *f* demand for satisfaction, ultimatum; fine

clārĭg·ō -āre *vi* to give an ultimatum

clārisŏn·us -a -um *adj* clear-sounding, loud

clārĭt·ās -ātis *f* clarity, distinctness; clearness (of style); celebrity, distinction

clārĭtūd·ō -ĭnis *f* brightness; distinction, fame

clār·ō -āre *vt* to make clear, explain, illustrate; to make famous; to illuminate

Clar·os -ī *f* town in Asia Minor near Colophon, famous for a temple and an oracle of Apollo

clār·us -a -um *adj* clear, distinct, bright; plain, manifest; famous, renowned; notorious

classĭārĭ·us -a -um *adj* naval; *m pl* marines

classĭcŭl·a -ae *f* flotilla

classĭc·us -a -um *adj* first-class; naval; *m pl* marines; *n* battle signal; bugle

class·is -is *f* fleet; army; (pol) class

clāthr·ī or clātr·ī -ōrum *m pl* bars, cage, lattice

clātrāt·us -a -um *adj* barred

claud·ĕō -ēre or claud·ō -ĕre *vi* to limp; to falter, hesitate, waver

claudĭcātĭ·ō -ōnis *f* limping

claudĭc·ō -āre *vi* to be lame, limp; to waver; to be defective

Claud·ĭus -ĭī or -ī *m* Appius Claudius Claudius Caecus (censor in 312 B.C. and builder of the Appian aqueduct and the Appian Way); Roman emperor, 41-54 A.D.

claudō claudĕre clausī clausum *vt* to bolt, bar, shut, close; to bring to a close, conclude; to lock up, imprison; to blockade, hem in; to limit, restrict; to cut off, block; agmen claudere to bring up the rear; numeris or pedibus claudere to put into verse; transitum claudere to block traffic

claud·us -a -um *adj* lame, limping; crippled, imperfect, defective; wavering, untrustworthy

claustr·a -ōrum *n pl* lock, bar, bolt; gate, dam, dike; barrier, barricade; cage, den; fortress, defenses

clausŭl·a -ae f close, conclusion, end; (rhet) close of a period

claus·us -a -um pp of **claudo**; n enclosure

clāv·a -ae f cudgel, club, knotty branch

clāvār·ium -ī or **-ī** n allowance to soldiers for shoe nails

clāvicŭl·a -ae f tendril

clāvĭg·er -ĕra -ĕrum adj carrying a club; carrying keys; m club bearer (Hercules); key bearer (Janus)

clāv·is -is f key; **clavīs adimere uxori** to take the keys away from a wife, get a divorce

clāv·us -ī m nail; rudder, helm; purple stripe (on a tunic, broad for senators, narrow for knights); **clavus anni** beginning of the year; **clavus trabalis** spike; **trabali clavo figere** to nail down, clinch

Cleanth·ēs -is m Stoic philosopher, pupil of Zeno (300?-220 B.C.)

clēm·ens -entis adj gentle, mild, merciful, kind, compassionate; mitigated, qualified, toned down

clēmenter adv gently, mildly, mercifully, kindly, compassionately; by degrees, gradually

clēmenti·a -ae f mildness, mercy, clemency, compassion

Cle·ōn -ōnis m Athenian demagogue after death of Pericles in 429 B.C.

Cleopātr·a -ae f queen of Egypt (68-31 B.C.)

clep·ō -ĕre -sī -tum vt to steal

clepsȳdr·a -ae f water clock; (fig) time (allotted to speakers); **clepsydram dare** (with dat) to give (someone) the floor; **clepsydram petere** to ask for the floor

clept·a -ae m thief

cli·ens -entis m client, dependant (freeman protected by a patron); follower, retainer; companion, favorite; vassal

client·a -ae f client (female)

clientēl·a -ae f clientele; patronage, protection; f pl allies, dependants; clienteles

clientŭl·us -ī m poor client

clīnām·en -inis n swerve

clīnāt·us -a -um adj bent, inclined

Clī·ō -ūs f Muse of history

clipeāt·us -a -um adj armed with a shield

clipĕ·um -ī n or **clipĕ·us -ī** m round bronze Roman shield; medallion; disc (of sun)

clītell·a -ae f saddlebag; f pl packsaddle

clītellāri·us -a -um adj carrying a packsaddle

olivōs·us -a -um adj hilly, full of hills; steep

clīv·us -ī m slope, ascent, hill; slope, pitch; **adversus clivum** uphill; **primi clivi** foothills

Clīv·us Sac·er (genit: **Clīv·ī Sac·rī**) m part of the Via Sacra ascending the Capitoline Hill, also called Clivus Capitolinus

cloāc·a -ae f sewer, drain; **cloaca maxima** main sewer (draining the valley between the Capitoline, Palatine, and Esquiline)

Cloācīn·a -ae f Venus

Clōdi·a -ae f sister of Publius Clodius Pulcher and thought to be the person called Lesbia in Catullus' poems

Clōd·ius -iī or **-ī** m Publius Clodius Pulcher (notorious enemy of Cicero who caused the latter to be exiled in 58 B.C. and was himself killed by Milo in 52 B.C.)

Cloeli·a -ae f Roman girl who was given as hostage to Porsenna and escaped by swimming the Tiber

Clōth·ō (genit not in use; acc: -ō) f one of the three Fates

clu·ĕō -ēre or **clu·ĕor -ērī** vi to be named, be spoken of, be reputed, be famous

clūn·is -is m or f buttock

clūrīn·us -a -um adj of apes

Clūs·ium -iī or **-ī** n ancient Etruscan town

Clūs·ius -iī or **-ī** m Janus

Clymĕn·ē -ēs f wife of Merops and mother of Phaëthon

Clytaemnestr·a -ae f wife of Agamemnon, sister of Helen, Castor, and Pollux, and mother of Electra, Iphigenia, and Orestes, the latter of whom killed her

Cnid·us -ī f town in Caria, famous for worship of Venus

coacervāti·ō -ōnis f piling up, accumulation

coacerv·ō -āre vt to pile up, accumulate

coac·escō -escĕre -ŭī vi to become sour

coact·ō -āre vt to force

coact·or -ōris m collector (of money); **agminis coactores** rearguard elements

coactus pp of **cogo**; adj forced, unnatural, hypocritical; n felt

coact·us -ūs m coercion, compulsion

coaedific·ō -āre vt to build up (an area), fill with buildings; **loci coaedificati** built-up areas

coaequ·ō -āre vt to level off, make level, bring down to the same level

coagmentāti·ō -ōnis f combination, union

coagment·ō -āre vt to join, glue, cement

coagment·um -ī n joint

coāgŭl·um -ī n rennet

coal·escō -escĕre -ŭī -itum vi to grow firm, take root; to increase, become strong, become established, thrive

coangust·ō -āre vt to contract, compress; to limit, restrict

coarct· = coart·

coargu·ō -ĕre -ī vt to prove conclusively, demonstrate; to refute, prove wrong or guilty; (with genit of the charge) to prove (someone) guilty of

coartātī·ō -ōnis f crowding together

coart·ō -āre vt to crowd together, confine; to shorten, abridge

coccināt·us -a -um adj clothed in scarlet

coccine·us or **coccĭn·us -a -um** adj scarlet

cocc·um -ī n scarlet

coclě·a or **cochlě·a -ae** f snail

cocleār·e -is n spoon

cocl·es -ĭtis m person blind in one eye

Cocl·es -ĭtis m Horatius Cocles (famous for defending the Pons Sublicius against Porsenna's army)

coctĭl·is -e adj baked; brick

coct·us -a -um pp of **coquo**; adj well-considered

Cōcyt·us -ī m river of the lower world

cōdex see **caudex**

cōdicill·ī -ōrum m pl small trunks of trees, fire logs; note; petition; codicil

Codr·us -ī m last king of Athens, who sacrificed his life for an Athenian victory (1160-1132 B.C.)

coel- = cael-

co·ēmō -emēre -ēmī -emptum vt to buy up

coēmptĭ·ō -ōnis f marriage (contracted by fictitious sale of contracting parties); fictitious sale of an estate (to relieve it of religious obligations)

coēmptiōnāl·is -e adj of a fictitious marriage; used in a mock sale; worthless

coen- = caen-

co·eō -īre -īvī or **-iī -ĭtum** vt societatem coire to enter an agreement, form an alliance; vi to come or go together; to meet, assemble; to be united, combine; to copulate; to congeal, curdle; to agree; to conspire; to clash (in combat); (of wounds) to close, heal up

coep·iō -ĕre -ī -tum vt & vi to begin

coept·ō -āre vt to begin eagerly; to try; (with inf) to try to; vi to begin, make a beginning

coept·us -a -um pp of **coepio**; n beginning; undertaking

coept·us -ūs m beginning

coēpulōn·us -ī m dinner guest

coërc·eō -ēre -uī -ĭtum vt to enclose, confine, hem in; to limit; to restrain, check, control

coërcitĭ·ō -ōnis f coercion; right to punish

coët·us -ūs m coming together, meeting; crowd, company

Coe·us -ī m Titan, father of Latona

cōgitātē adv deliberately

cōgitātĭ·ō -ōnis f thinking, deliberating; reflection, meditation; thought, plan, design; reasoning power, imagination

cōgit·ō -āre vt to consider, ponder, reflect on; to imagine; (with inf) to intend to; vi to think, reflect, meditate

cōgitāt·us -a -um adj well-considered, deliberate; n pl thoughts, ideas

cōgnātĭ·ō -ōnis f relationship by birth; agreement, resemblance, affinity; relatives, family

cōgnāt·us -a -um adj related by birth; related, similar, connected; mf relative

cōgnitĭ·ō -ōnis f learning, acquiring knowledge; notion, idea, knowledge; recognition; (law) inquiry, investigation, trial; (with genit) knowledge of, acquaintance with

cōgnĭt·or -ōris m advocate, attorney; defender, protector; witness

cōgnĭtus pp of **cognosco**; adj acknowledged

cōgnōm·en -ĭnis n surname, family name (e.g., Caesar); nickname

cōgnōment·um -ī n surname; name

cōgnōmĭnāt·us -a -um adj synonymous

cōgnōmĭn·is -e adj like-named, of the same name

co·gnōscō -gnōscĕre -gnōvī -gnĭtum vt to become acquainted with, get to know, learn; to recognize, identify; to inquire into, investigate; to criticize, appreciate; to reconnoiter; **cognovisse** to know

cō·gō -gĕre -ēgī -actum vt to gather together, collect, convene; to thicken, condense, curdle; to pressure, bring pressure upon; to compel, force; to coax; to exact, extort; to infer, conclude; **agmen cogere** to bring up the rear

cohaer·ens -entis adj adjoining, continuous; consistent; harmonious

cohaerentĭ·a -ae f coherence, connection

co·haerĕō -haerēre -haesī -haesum vi to stick or cling together, cohere; to be consistent, be in agreement; (with abl) to consist of, be composed of; (with cum + abl) to be closely connected with, be in harmony with, be consistent with; **inter se cohaerere** to be consistent

co·haerescō -haerescĕre -haesī vi to cling together, cohere

cohēr·ēs -ēdis m or f coheir

cohĭb·eō -ēre -uī vt to hold together, hold close, confine; to hold back, repress, check, stop

cohonest·ō -āre vt to do honor to, celebrate

cohorr·escō -escĕre -uī vi to shiver all over

cohor·s -tis f yard (esp. for cattle or chickens); train, retinue, escort; (mil) cohort (comprising 3 maniples or 6 centuries and forming one tenth of a legion)

cohortātĭ·ō -ōnis f encouragement

cohortĭcŭl·a -ae f small cohort

cohort·or -ārī -ātus sum vt to encourage, cheer up, urge on

coïtĭ·ō -ōnis f conspiracy, coalition; agreement

coït·us -ūs m meeting; sexual union

colăph·us -ī m slap, blow with a fist

Colch·is -ĭdis f country on E. end of the Black Sea; Medea

cōlĕ·us -ī m sack, scrotum

cōl·is -is m stalk, cabbage

collabasc·ō -ĕre vi to waver, totter

collabefact·ō -āre vt to shake hard

collabe·fīō -fĭĕrī -factus sum vi to collapse, be ruined, fall to pieces

col·lābor -lābī -lapsus sum vi to collapse, fall to pieces

collacerāt·us -a -um adj torn to pieces

collacrĭmātĭ·ō -ōnis f weeping

collacrĭm·ō -āre vt to cry bitterly over; vi to cry together

collactĕ·a -ae f foster sister

collār·e -is n collar

Collātĭ·a -ae f old town in Latium

Collātīn·us -ī m husband of Lucretia

collātĭ·ō -ōnis f bringing together; contribution of money, collection; comparison, analogy; **signorum collatio** clash of troops

collāt·or -ōris m contributor

collātus pp of **confero**

collaudātĭ·ō -ōnis f warm praise

collaud·ō -āre vt to praise highly

collax·ō -āre vt to make loose

collect·a -ae f contribution of money

collectīcĭ·us -a -um adj hastily-gathered

collectĭ·ō -ōnis f gathering; summing up, recapitulation; inference

collectus pp of **colligo**

collect·us -ūs m collection

collēg·a -ae m colleague, partner (in office); associate, companion; fellow member (of a club)

collēg·ĭum -ĭī or -ī n association in office; official body, board, college, guild, company, corporation, society

collībert·us -ī m fellow freedman

collĭb·et or **collŭb·et** -ēre -ŭit -ĭtum v impers it pleases

col·līdō -līdĕre -līsī -līsum vt to smash to pieces, shatter, crush; to cause to clash, set at variance

colligātĭ·ō -ōnis f binding together; connection

collĭg·ō -āre vt to tie together, connect; to unite, combine; to fasten, chain; to stop, hinder

col·lĭgō -lĭgĕre -lēgī -lectum vt to pick up, gather together, collect; to contract, compress, concentrate; to acquire gradually; to infer, conclude, gather; to assemble, bring together; to enumerate; to gather, repair; to check, control (horse); **animum colligere, mentem colligere,** or **se colligere** to collect or compose oneself, muster one's courage, rally, come to, come around; **vasa colligere** to pack up (for the march)

Collīn·a Port·a (genit: **Collīn·ae Port·ae**) f Colline Gate (near the Quirinal Hill)

collĭnĕ·ō -āre vt to aim straight; vi to hit the mark

col·līnō -linĕre -lēvī -lĭtum vt to smear; to defile

colliquefact·us -a -um adj dissolved, melted

coll·is -is m hill

collocātĭ·ō -ōnis f arrangement; giving in marriage

collŏc·ō -āre vt to place, put in order, arrange; to station, deploy; to give in marriage; to lodge, quarter; to occupy, employ; **se collocare** to settle, settle down (in a place)

colloouplēt·ō -āre vt to enrich, make quite rich

collocūtĭ·ō -ōnis f conversation, conference

colloqu·ĭum -ĭī or -ī n conversation, conference

col·lŏquor -lŏquī -locūtus sum vt to talk to; vi to talk together, converse, hold a conference

collŭbet see **collĭbet**

collūc·ĕō -ēre vi to shine brightly, be entirely illuminated; (fig) to be resplendent

col·lūdō -lūdĕre -lūsī -lūsum vi to play together; to be in collusion; (with dat) to play with

coll·um -ī n neck

col·lŭō -luĕre -lŭī -lūtum vt to wash out, rinse, moisten; **ora colluere** to wet the mouth, quench the thirst

collūsĭ·ō -ōnis f collusion

collūs·or -ōris m playmate; fellow-gambler

collustr·ō -āre vt to light up; to survey, inspect; (in painting) to represent in bright colors

collutulent·ō -āre vt to soil, defile

colluvĭ·ō -ōnis or **colluvĭ·ēs** (genit not in use) f dregs, impurities, filth; rabble

collȳb·us -ī m conversion of currency; rate of exchange

collȳr·a -ae f noodles, macaroni

collȳr·ĭum -ĭī or -ī n eyewash

colō colĕre colŭī cultum vt to till, cultivate, work; to live in (a place); to guard, protect; to honor, cherish, revere, worship; to adorn, dress; to practice, follow; to experience, live through, spend

colocāsĭ·a -ae f lotus, water lily

colōn·a -ae f peasant woman

colōnĭ·a -ae f colony, settlement; colonists, settlers

colōnĭc·us -a -um adj colonial

colōn·us -ī m settler; farmer

col·or or **col·ōs** -ōris m color, hue, tint; external condition; complexion; tone, style; luster; grace; colorful pretext

colōrāt·us -a -um adj colored, tinted; healthily tanned

colōr·ō -āre vt to color, tan; (fig) to give a certain tone to

colossĕ·us -a -um adj colossal

coloss·us -ī m gigantic statue, colossus

colostr·a -ae f or **colostr·um** -ī n first milk after delivery, colostrum

col·ŭb·er -rī m snake, adder

colŭbr·a -ae f snake, adder (female)

colubrĭf·er -ĕra -ĕrum adj snaky

colubrīn·us -a -um adj snaky; wily, sly

cōl·um -ī n strainer

columb·a -ae f pigeon, dove (female)

columb·ar -āris n collar

columbār·ĭum -iī or -i n pigeonhole; (fig) vault with niches for cinerary urns

columbīn·us -a -um adj of a dove or pigeon; m little dove

columb·us -ī m pigeon, dove

columell·a -ae f small column

colŭm·en -ĭnis n height, summit, peak; gable; pillar; head, leader; support, prop

column·a -ae f column, pillar, post; (fig) pillar, support; waterspout; **ad columnam** (i.e., **Maeniam**) **pervenire** or **ad columnam adhaerescere** to be brought to punishment (because at the Columna Maenia in the Roman forum criminals and debtors were tried); f pl display columns (in bookshop); bookshop

Column·a Maenĭ·a (genit: **Column·ae Maenĭ·ae**) f column in the Roman forum, possibly of the Basilica Porcia supporting a projecting balcony (maenianum), at which thieves and slaves were whipped and to which debtors were summoned for trial; whipping post

columnār·ĭum -iī or -i n tax on house pillars

columnār·ĭus -iī or -i m criminal debtor (punished at the Columna Maenia)

colurn·us -a -um adj made of hazel wood

col·us -ī or -ūs m or f distaff

cōlўphĭ·a -ōrum n pl choice cuts of meat, loin cuts

com·a -ae f hair (of the head); mane (of horse or lion); fleece; foliage; grass; sunbeams

com·ans -antis adj hairy, longhaired; plumed (helmet); leafy; **comans stella** comet

cōmarch·us -ī m chief burgess

comāt·us -a -um adj long-haired; leafy

combĭb·ō -ĕre -ī vt to drink up; to absorb; to swallow, engulf; to repress, conceal (tears); to imbibe, acquire (knowledge)

combĭb·ō -ōnis m drinking partner

comb·ūrō -ūrĕre -ussī -ustum vt to burn up, consume; (fig) to ruin

com·ĕdō -edĕre (or -esse) -ēdī -ēsum (or -estum) vt to eat up, consume, devour; to waste, squander, dissipate, spend; **se comedere** to pine away

com·es -ĭtis m or f companion, fellow traveler; associate, comrade; attendant, retainer, dependant; concomitant, consequence

comēt·ēs -ae m comet

cōmĭcē adv like a comedy

cōmĭc·us -a -um adj of comedy, comic; **comicum aurum** stage money; m actor (of comedy); playwright (of comedy)

cōm·is -e adj courteous, polite; kind, friendly; (with dat or with **erga** or **in** + acc) friendly toward

cōmissābund·us -a -um adj parading in a riotous bacchanalian procession; carousing

cōmissātĭ·ō -ōnis f riotous bacchanalian procession; wild drinking party

cōmissāt·or -ōris m drinking partner, reveler, guzzler

cōmiss·or or **cōmis·or -ārī -ātus sum** vi to join in a bacchanalian procession; to revel, guzzle

cōmĭt·ās -ātis f politeness, courteousness; kindness, friendliness

comĭtāt·us -ūs m escort, retinue; imperial retinue, court; company (traveling together), caravan

cōmĭter adv politely, courteously; kindly

comĭtĭ·a -ōrum n pl comitia, popular assembly; elections; **comitia consularia** or **comitia consulum** election of consuls; **comitia praetoria** election of praetors

comitĭāl·is -e adj of the assembly; of the elections, election

comitĭāt·us -ūs m assembly of the people in the comitia

comĭt·ĭum -iī or -i n comitium, assembly place

comĭt·ō -āre or **comĭt·or -ārī -ātus sum** vt to accompany, attend, follow

commacŭl·ō -āre vt to spot, stain; to defile

commanipulār·is -is m comrade in the same brigade

commarīt·us -ī m fellow husband

commeāt·us -ūs m passage, thoroughfare; leave of absence, furlough; transport, passage, convoy; (mil) lines of communication; (mil) supplies; **in commeatu esse** to be on a furlough

commedĭt·or -ārī -ātus sum vt to practice; to imitate

commemin·ī -isse vt & vi to remember well

commemorābĭl·is -e adj memorable, worth mentioning

commemorātĭ·ō -ōnis f recollection, remembrance; mentioning, reminding

commemŏr·ō -āre vt to keep in mind, remember; to bring up (in conversation), to mention, recount, relate; vi (with **de** + abl) to be mindful of

commendābĭl·is -e adj commendable, praiseworthy

commendātĭcĭ·us -a -um adj of recommendation, of introduction; **litterae commendaticiae** letter of introduction or of recommendation

commendātǐ·ō -ōnis f recommendation, recommending; commendation, praise; excellence, worth

commendāt·or -ōris m backer, supporter

commendātr·ix -īcis f backer, supporter (female)

commendāt·us -a -um adj commended, recommended, acceptable, approved

commend·ō -āre vt to entrust, commit; to recommend; to render acceptable

commentārǐŏl·um -ī n short treatise

commentār·ǐum -ǐī or **-ī** n or **commentār·ǐus -ǐī** or **-ī** m notebook, journal, diary, notes, memorandum; (law) brief; pl memoirs

commentātǐ·ō -ōnis f careful study, deep reflection; preparation; essay, treatise

commentīcǐ·us -a -um adj thought out; invented, fictitious, imaginary; ideal; forged, false; legendary

comment·or -ārī -ātus sum vt to think over, consider well, study; to invent, contrive, make up; to prepare, produce (writings); to discuss, write about; to imitate, adopt the language of; vi to meditate, deliberate, reflect; to experiment in speaking, attempt to speak

comment·or -ōris m inventor

comment·us -a -um pp of **comminiscor**; adj fictitious, feigned, invented, pretended; n invention, fiction, fabrication; device, contrivance

commě·ō -āre vi to come and go; to go back and forth; to travel repeatedly; to make frequent visits

commerc·ǐum -ǐī or **-ī** n trade, commerce; right to trade; dealings, business; communication, correspondence; **belli commercia** ransom

commerc·or -ārī vt to deal in, purchase

commer·ěō -ēre -ǔī -ǐtum or **commer·ěor -ērī -ǐtus sum** vt to earn, merit, deserve fully; to be guilty of

com·mētǐor -mētīrī -mensus sum vt to measure; (with **cum + abl**) to measure (something) in terms of

commēt·ō -āre vi to go often

commigr·ō -āre vi to move, migrate

commīlit·ǐum -ǐī or **-ī** n comradeship, companionship, fellowship

commīlit·ō -ōnis m fellow soldier, army buddy

comminātǐ·ō -ōnis f threatening, menacing; f pl violent threats

com·mingō -mingěre -minxī -mictum vt to urinate on; to wet (bed); to defile, pollute; **commictum caenum** (term of reproach) dirty skunk

com·miniscor -miniscī -mentus sum vt to contrive, invent, devise

commin·or -ārī -ātus sum vt to threaten violently

commin·ǔō -uěre -ǔī -ūtum vt to lessen considerably, diminish; to break up, shatter; to weaken, impair; to humble, crush, humiliate

commǐnus adv hand to hand, at close quarters; near at hand, near; **comminus conferre signa** to engage in hand-to-hand fighting

com·miscěō -miscēre -miscǔī -mixtum vt to mix together, mix up, join together; to unite, bring together, mingle

commiserātǐ·ō -ōnis f pitying; (rhet) appeal to compassion

commiseresc·ō -ěre vi (with genit) to feel pity for; v impers (with genit) **me commiserescit ejus** I pity him

commisěr·or -ārī -ātus sum vt to feel sympathy for; vi (rhet) to try to evoke sympathy

commissǐ·ō -ōnis f beginning (of fight, game, etc.)

commissūr·a -ae f connection; joint

commiss·us -a -um pp of **committo**; n offense, crime; secret; undertaking

commītǐg·ō -āre vt to soften up

com·mittō -mittěre -mīsī -missum vt to connect, unite; to match (for a fight, etc.); to start, commence; to undertake; to commit, perpetrate; to entrust, commit; to engage in (battle); to incur (penalty); **se committere** (with dat or in + acc) to venture into

commodǐt·ās -ātis f proportion, symmetry; aptness of expression; convenience, comfort; right time; pleasantness (of personality); courtesy, kindness

commŏd·ō -āre vt to adjust, adapt; to bestow, supply, lend, give; vi to be obliging; (with dat) to adapt oneself to, be obliging to

commodūlē or **commodǔlum** adv nicely, conveniently

commŏdum adv at a good time, in the nick of time; **commodum cum** just at the time when

commŏd·us -a -um adj adapted, suitable, fit, convenient; opportune (time); convenient, comfortable, advantageous; agreeable, obliging, pleasant (person); **quod commodum est** just as you please; n convenience, opportunity; profit, advantage; privilege, favor; loan; pay, reward; **commodo tuo** at your convenience

commŏl·ior -īrī -ītus sum vt to set in motion

commone·facǐō -facěre -fēcī -factum vt to recall, call to mind; (with acc of person and genit of thing) to remind (someone) of

common·ěō -ēre -ǔī -ǐtum vt to remind, warn; (with genit or de + abl) to remind (someone) of

commonstr·ō -āre vt to point out clearly

commorātǐ·ō -ōnis f delaying, staying; residence, sojourn; (rhet) dwelling (on some point)

com·morior -mōrī -mortŭus sum vi (with dat or with cum + abl) to die with, die at the same time as

commŏr·or -ārī -ātus sum vt to stop, detain; vi to linger, stay, stop off; (with apud + acc) to stay at the house of; in sententia commorari to stick to an opinion

commōtĭ·ō -ōnis f commotion; animi commotio excitement

commōtiuncŭl·a -ae f minor inconvenience

commōt·us -a -um adj excited, angry; deranged, insane; impassioned, lively (style)

com·movĕō -movēre -mōvī -mōtum vt to stir up, agitate, shake; to disturb, unsettle, disquiet, excite, shake up; to arouse, provoke; to stir up, generate, produce; to start, introduce (novelties); to displace, dislodge (enemy); to refute

commūn·e -is n community, state; in commune for general use, for all; in general

commūnicātĭ·ō -ōnis f imparting, communicating

commūnic·ō -āre or commūnic·or -ārī vt to make common; to communicate, impart, share; to share in, take part in; to unite, connect, join

commūnĭ·ō -ōnis f sharing in common

commūn·ĭō -īre -īvī or -ĭī -ītum vt to fortify, strengthen, barricade

commūn·is -e adj common, public, universal, general; familiar; courteous, affable; democratic; loca communia public places; loci communes commonplaces, general topics; sensus communis common sense; n see commune

commūnĭter adv in common, together

commūnītĭ·ō -ōnis f road building; (rhet) introduction

commurmŭr·ō -āre or commurmŭr·or -ārī vi to murmur, grumble

commūtābĭl·is -e adj changeable, subject to change; interchangeable

commūtātĭ·ō -ōnis f changing, change, alteration

commūtāt·us -ūs m change, alteration

commūt·ō -āre vt to change, alter; to interchange, exchange; (with abl or cum + abl) to exchange (something) for

cōm·ō -ĕre -psī -ptum vt to comb, arrange, braid; to adorn, deck out

cōmoedĭ·a -ae f comedy

cōmoedĭcē adv as in comedy

cōmoed·us -ī m comic actor

cōmōs·us -a -um adj with long hair, hairy; leafy

compact·us -a -um pp of compingo; adj compact, well built; n agreement

compāg·ēs -is f joining together, joint, structure, framework

compāg·ō -ĭnis f connection

comp·ar -ăris adj equal, on an equal level; (with dat) matching

comp·ar -ăris m or f comrade; playmate; perfect match; spouse

comparābĭl·is -e adj comparable

comparātĭ·ō -ōnis f comparison; arrangement; acquisition; preparation, provision; relative position (of planets)

comparātīv·us -a -um adj comparative

compār·ĕō -ēre -ŭī vi to be visible, be plain, be evident, appear; to be at hand, be present

compăr·ō -āre vt to put together, get together, provide; to prepare, arrange; to match; to compare; to procure, get, obtain, collect; to appoint, establish, constitute; se comparare (with ad or in + acc) to prepare oneself for, get ready for

comp·ascō -ascĕre — -astum vt & vi to feed together

compascŭ·us -a -um adj of public grazing

compec·iscor -iscī -tus sum vi to come to an agreement

compect·us -a -um adj in agreement, agreed; n agreement; compecto by agreement, according to the agreement

comped·ĭō -īre — -ītum vt to shackle

compellātĭ·ō -ōnis f rebuke, reprimand

compell·ō -āre vt to summon, call; to call to account, bring to book; to reproach; (law) to arraign

com·pellō -pellĕre -pŭlī -pulsum vt to drive together; to crowd, concentrate; to compel, force, urge, drive on

compendiārĭ·us -a -um adj short, abridged; via compendiaria shortcut

compend·ium -ĭī or -ī n careful weighing; saving (of money); profit; shortening, abridging; shortcut; compendi facere to save; compendi fieri to be brief; suo privato compendio servire to serve one's own private interests

compensātĭ·ō -ōnis f compensation, recompense

compens·ō -āre vt to compensate, make up for

com·percō -percĕre -persī vt to save, hoard up

comperendinātĭ·ō -ōnis f or comperendināt·us -ūs m (law) two-day adjournment

comperendin·ō -āre vt to adjourn (court) for two days; to put off (defendant) for two days

comper·ĭō -īre -ī -tum or comper·ĭor -īrī -tus sum vt to find out, ascertain, learn; compertum habeo or compertum mihi est

I have ascertained, I know for certain

compert·us -a -um _adj_ discovered, well authenticated; (with _genit_) convicted of

comp·ēs -ĕdis _f_ shackle (_for the feet_); (fig) bond

compesc·ō -ĕre -ŭī _vt_ to confine, restrain, suppress, check, chain down

competīt·or -ōris _m_ competitor, rival

competītr·ix -īcis _f_ competitor, rival (_female_)

compĕt·ō -ĕre -īvī or **-ĭī -ītum** _vi_ to coincide, come together, meet; to be adequate, to be suitable; (with **ad** + _acc_) to be capable of

compīlātĭ·ō -ōnis _f_ pillaging, plundering; (contemptuously said of a collection of documents) compilation

compīl·ō -āre _vt_ to pillage, plunder

com·pingō -pingĕre -pēgī -pactum _vt_ to put together, frame, compose; to confine, lock up, put (_in jail_)

compitāl·ĭa -ĭum or **-ĭōrum** _n pl_ festival celebrated annually at the crossroads in honor of the Lares of the crossroads on a day appointed by the praetor

compitālicĭ·us -a -um _adj_ of the crossroads

compitāl·is -e _adj_ of the crossroads

compĭt·um -ī _n_ crossroads, intersection

complac·ĕō -ēre -ŭī or **-ĭtus sum** _vi_ (with _dat_) to be quite pleasing to, suit just fine

complān·ō -āre _vt_ to make even or level; to raze to the ground, pull down

com·plector -plectī -plexus sum _vt_ to embrace, clasp; to comprise; (_of writings_) to include; to grasp, understand; to display affection for, display esteem for; to enclose (_an area_); to seize, take possession of

complēment·um -ī _n_ complement

complĕ·ĕō -ēre -ēvī -ētum _vt_ to fill, fill up; (mil) to bring (_legion, etc._) to full strength; (mil) to man; to complete; to impregnate; to fill with sound, make resound; to supply fully, furnish

complēt·us -a -um _adj_ complete; perfect

complexĭ·ō -ōnis _f_ combination, connection; conclusion in a syllogism; dilemma; (rhet) period

complex·us -ūs _m_ embrace; (fig) love, affection; close combat; **in complexum alicujus venīre** to come to close grips with someone

complicāt·us -a -um _adj_ complicated, involved

complĭc·ō -āre _vt_ to fold up

complōrātĭ·ō -ōnis _f_ or **complōrāt·us -ūs** _m_ groaning, lamentation, wailing

complōr·ō -āre _vt_ to mourn for

complūr·ēs -ĭum _adj_ several; a good many

complūrĭens or **complūrĭēs** _adv_ several times, a good many times

compluscŭl·ī -ae -a _adj_ a fair number of

compluv·ĭum -ĭī or **-ī** _n_ rain trap (_quadrangular open space in middle of Roman house towards which the roof sloped so as to direct the rain into a basin, called impluvium, built into the floor_)

com·pōnō -pōnĕre -posŭī -posĭtum _vt_ to put together, join; to construct, build; to compose, write; to arrange, settle, agree upon, fix, set; to match, pair, couple; to compare, contrast; to put away; take down, lay aside; to lay out, bury (_the dead_); to compose, pacify, allay, calm, appease, quiet, reconcile; to feign, invent, concoct, contrive

comport·ō -āre _vt_ to carry together, bring in, collect, gather, accumulate

comp·os -ŏtis _adj_ (with _genit_ or _abl_) in possession of, master of, having control over; having a share in, participating in; **compos animi** or **compos mentis** sane; **compos sui** self-controlled; **compos voti** having one's prayer answered

composĭtē _adv_ in an orderly manner, orderly, regularly; **composite dicere** to speak logically

composĭtĭ·ō -ōnis _f_ putting together, connecting, arranging, composition; matching (_of gladiators, etc._); reconciliation (_of friends_); orderly arrangement (_of words_)

composĭt·or -ōris _m_ composer, author

composĭtūr·a -ae _f_ connection

composĭt·us -a -um _pp_ of **compono**; _adj_ compound (_words, etc._); prepared, well arranged, orderly; made-up, feigned, false; adapted; composed, calm, settled; _n_ agreement, compact; **composito** or **ex composito** by agreement, as agreed, as had been arranged

compotātĭ·ō -ōnis _f_ drinking party

compot·ĭō -īre -īvī -ītum _vt_ (with _acc_ of person and _abl_ of thing) to make (_someone_) master of, put (_someone_) in possession of

compōt·or -ōris _m_ drinking partner

compōtr·ix -īcis _f_ drinking partner (_female_)

comprans·or -ōris _m_ dinner companion, fellow guest

comprecātĭ·ō -ōnis _f_ public supplication

comprĕc·or -ārī -ātus sum _vt_ to pray earnestly to, implore, supplicate

compre·hendō -hendĕre -hendī -hensum or **compren·dō -dĕre -dī -sum** _vt_ to bind together, unite; to take hold of, grasp, seize, catch, apprehend; to attack, seize, arrest, capture, apprehend; to detect, discover; to occupy (_places_); to grasp, perceive, comprehend, take in; to express, describe, narrate, recount; **ignem comprehendere** to catch fire; **memoriā comprehendere** to remember; **numerō comprehendere** to enumerate, count

comprehensibil·is -e *adj* comprehensible, conceivable, intelligible

comprehensi·ō -ōnis *f* seizing, laying hold of; arrest; comprehension, perception; combining; (rhet) period

comprendō see **comprehendō**

compressi·ō -ōnis *f* pressing closely; embrace; (rhet) compression

compress·us -ūs *m* compression; embrace

com·primō -primĕre -pressī -pressum *vt* to press together, bring together, compress, close; to embrace; to check, curb, restrain; to keep back, suppress, withhold, conceal; **animam comprimere** to hold the breath; **compressis manibus sedere** to sit on folded hands, to not lift a hand; **ordines comprimere** to close ranks

comprobāti·ō -ōnis *f* approbation, approval

comprobāt·or -ōris *m* enthusiastic backer

comprob·ō -āre *vt* to approve, sanction, acknowledge; to prove, establish, make good, confirm, verify

comprōmiss·um -ī *n* mutual agreement to abide by arbiter's decision

comprō-mittō -mittĕre -mīsī -missum *vi* to agree to abide by an arbiter's decision

compt·us -a -um *pp* of **como**; *adj* neat, elegant

compt·us -ūs *m* hairdo

com·pungō -pungĕre -punxī -punctum *vt* to puncture, prick; to tattoo; to prod

comput·ō -āre *vt* to compute, count

computresc·ō -ĕre *vi* to become putrid, rot

Cōm·um -ī *n* Como (*town N. of the Po and birthplace of Pliny the Younger*)

cōnām·en -inis *n* effort, struggle; support, prop; **conamen mortis** attempt at suicide

cōnāt·um -ī *n* effort, exertion; attempt, undertaking, venture

cōnāt·us -ūs *m* effort; endeavor; impulse, inclination, tendency; undertaking

concāc·ō -āre *vt* to defile with excrement

concaed·ēs -ium *f pl* log barricade

concale·faciō -facĕre -fēcī -factum *vt* to warm up

concall·escō -escĕre -uī *vi* to grow hard; to become insensible; to become shrewd

concastīg·ō -āre *vt* to punish severely

concăv·ō -āre *vt* to curve, bend

concăv·us -a -um *adj* concave, hollow; curved, arched, bent, vaulted; deep (*valley*)

con·cēdō -cēdĕre -cessī -cessum *vt* to give up, relinquish, cede; to pardon, overlook; to allow, grant; *vi* to go away, give way, depart, withdraw, retire; (with *dat*) **a** to yield to, submit to, give way to, succumb to; **b** to submit to, comply with; **c** to make allowance for, pardon; **d** to be inferior to; (with **in** + *acc*) to pass over to, be merged in; **fato concedere, naturae concedere,** or **vitā concedere** to die

concelĕbr·ō -āre *vt* to frequent, fill; to pursue (*studies*); to fill with life, enliven; to celebrate; to make widely known, proclaim, publish

concēnāti·ō -ōnis *f* dining together

concenti·ō -ōnis *f* singing together, harmony

concenturi·ō -āre *vt* to marshal by the hundreds; (with *dat*) to bring (*fear*) to

concent·us -ūs *m* concert, symphony; harmony; choir; concord, agreement, harmony

concepti·ō -ōnis *f* conception (*becoming pregnant*); (law) composing legal formulas

conceptīv·us -a -um *adj* movable (*holidays*)

concept·us -ūs *m* conception (*becoming pregnant*), pregnancy

concerp·ō -ĕre -sī -tum *vt* to tear up, tear to shreds; (fig) to cut up, abuse, revile

concertāti·ō -ōnis *f* controversy, dispute

concertāt·or -ōris *m* rival

concertātōri·us -a -um *adj* controversial

concert·ō -āre *vi* to fight it out; to quarrel, debate

concessi·ō -ōnis *f* concession; admission (*of guilt with plea for mercy*)

concess·ō -āre *vt* (with *inf*) to stop (*doing something*)

concess·us -a -um *pp* of **concedo**; *n* concession (*thing allowed*)

concess·us -ūs *m* permission, leave

conch·a -ae *f* clam, oyster, mussel, murex; clam shell, oyster shell, mussel shell; pearl; purple dye; trumpet (*of Triton*); vessel (*containing ointments, etc.*); vulva

conch·is -is *f* bean

conchīt·a -ae *m* clam digger, conch digger

conchȳliāt·us -a -um *adj* purple

conchȳl·ium -iī or **-ī** *n* shellfish, clam, oyster; murex; purple dye, purple; purple garments

concīd·ō -ĕre -ī *vi* to collapse; to fall (*in battle*); (fig) to decline, fail, fall, decay, perish, go to ruin; (of winds) to subside

con·cīdō -cīdĕre -cīdī -cīsum *vt* to cut up, cut to pieces, kill; to beat severely; (fig) to crush (*with arguments*); (rhet) to chop up (*sentences*)

con·cieō -ciēre -cīvī -cītum or **-ciō**

-cīre -cīvī -cītum vt to assemble; to shake, stir up; (fig) to rouse, stir up, provoke

conciliābŭl·um -ī n public meeting place

conciliāti·ō -ōnis f union, bond; conciliating, winning over; inclination, bent, desire

conciliāt·or -ōris m mediator, promoter

conciliātrīcŭl·a -ae f procuress, madame

conciliātr·īx -īcis f mediator, promoter, match maker (female)

conciliāt·us -a -um adj (with ad + acc) endeared to, favorable to

conciliāt·us -ūs m union, connection, combination

concilĭ·ō -āre vt to bring together, unite, connect; to unite (in feeling), make friendly, win over; to bring about (by mediation); to acquire, win

concil·ium -iī or -ī n gathering, meeting, assembly; council; combination, union

concinnē adv nicely, elegantly

concinnit·ās -ātis or concinnitūd·ō -ĭnis f finish, elegance, symmetry (of style)

concinn·ō -āre vt to make symmetrical, get right, adjust; to bring about, produce, cause; to make (e.g., insane)

concinn·us -a -um adj symmetrical; neat, elegant; courteous, agreeable, nice; polished (style)

concĭn·ō -ēre -ŭī vt to sing, celebrate; to prophesy; vi to sing or play together, harmonize; (fig) to agree, harmonize

concĭō see concieo

concĭō see contio

concipĭl·ō -āre vt to carry off

con·cipĭō -cipĕre -cēpī -ceptum vt to take hold of, take up, take, receive; to take in, absorb; to imagine, conceive, think; to understand, comprehend, perceive; to catch (fire); to entertain (hope); to draw up in formal language; to announce in formal language

concīsē adv concisely

concīsĭ·ō -ōnis f (rhet) dividing a sentence into short phrases

concīs·us -a -um pp of concido; adj cut up, short, concise

concitātē adv vigorously, vividly

concitāti·ō -ōnis f rapid movement; excitement; sedition, agitation

concitāt·or -ōris m instigator, ringleader; rabble-rouser

concitāt·us -a -um adj rapid, swift; excited

concĭt·ō -āre vt to stir up, rouse, urge; to cause, occasion

concĭt·or -ōris m instigator, ringleader; rabble-rouser

conclāmāti·ō -ōnis f loud shouting, yell; acclamation

conclāmĭt·ō -āre vi to keep on shouting, keep on yelling

conclām·ō -āre vt to shout, yell; to call to (for help); to call repeatedly by name, bewail (the dead); to exclaim; jam conclamatum est all's lost; vasa conclamare to give the signal to pack up (for the march); vi to shout, yell, cry out; ad arma conclamare to sound the alarm (for an attack)

conclāv·e -is n room; bedroom; dining room; cage, stall, coop

con·clūdō -clūdĕre -clūsī -clūsum vt to shut up, enclose; to include, comprise; to round off, conclude (letter, speech); to end rhythmically; to deduce, infer, conclude

conclūsē adv (rhet) in rhythmical cadence

conclūsĭ·ō -ōnis f blockade; end, conclusion; conclusion (of a speech), peroration; conclusion (of syllogism); (rhet) period

conclūsiuncŭl·a -ae f false conclusion

conclūs·us -a -um pp of concludo; adj confined; n logical conclusion

concŏl·or -ōris adj of the same color

concomitāt·us -a -um adj escorted

con·cŏquō -coquĕre -coxī -coctum vt to cook thoroughly; to boil down; to digest; to stomach, put up with; to cook up, concoct (plans); to weigh seriously, reflect upon, consider well; to prepare, ripen

concordĭ·a -ae f concord, harmony, good rapport; union

concordĭter adv harmoniously

concord·ō -āre vi to be of one mind, be in harmony, agree

concor·s -dis adj of the same mind, concordant, agreeing, harmonious

concrēbr·escō -escĕre -ŭī vi to grow strong

concrēd·ō -ĕre -ĭdī -ĭtum vi to entrust, commit, consign

concrĕm·ō -āre vt to burn to ashes, burn up

concrĕp·ō -āre -ŭī -ĭtum vi to rattle, creak, grate, clash, sound, make noise; digitis concrepare to snap the fingers

con·crescō -crescĕre -crēvī -crētum vi to grow together; to congeal, curdle, clot; to stiffen; to take shape, grow, increase

concrētĭ·ō -ōnis f condensing, congealing; matter, substance

concrēt·us -a -um pp of concresco; adj grown together, compounded; condensed, congealed, curdled, thick, stiff, hard; frozen; inveterate; dim (light); n hardness, solid matter

concrīmĭn·or -ārī vi to make bitter charges

concrucĭ·ō -āre vt to torture

concubīn·a -ae f concubine

concubīnāt·us -ūs m concubinage, free love

concubīn·us -ī m adulterer

concubĭt·us -ūs m reclining together (at table); sexual intercourse

concubĭ·us -a -um adj used only in

the expression **concubiā nocte** early in the night, at bedtime; *n* bedtime

conculc·ō -āre *vt* to trample under foot, despise, treat with contempt

con·cumbō -cumbĕre -cubŭī -cubĭtum *vi* to lie together; (with **cum** + *abl*) to sleep with, have intercourse with

concup·iscō -iscĕre -īvī -ītum *vt* to long for, covet; to aspire to, strive after

concūr·ō -āre *vt* to take good care of

con·currō -currĕre -curri or **-curri -cursum** *vi* to run together, flock together; to unite; to strike one another, crash; (mil) to clash, engage in combat; to happen at the same time, coincide; (with **ad** + *acc*) to have recourse to, run for help to; **concurritur** the armies meet, there is a clash

concursāti·ō -ōnis *f* running together; rushing about; (mil) skirmishing

concursāt·or -ōris *m* (mil) skirmisher

concursi·ō -ōnis *f* meeting, concurrence; (rhet) repetition for emphasis

concurs·ō -āre *vt* to run around to; **domos concursare** to run from house to house; *vi* to rush about excitedly, dash up and down; (mil) to skirmish

concurs·us -ūs *m* running together, concourse, assembly; union, combination; collision; (mil) rush, charge, clash

concuss·us -ūs *m* shaking, concussion

con·cutiō -cutĕre -cussī -cussum *vt* to strike together, bang together; to convulse; to strike, shake, shatter; to shock; to wave (*the hand*); to brandish (*weapon*); to shake out, ransack, examine; to shake, alarm, trouble, terrify

condal·ium -iī or **-ī** *n* slave's ring

condĕc·et -ēre *v impers* it befits, it becomes

condecōr·ō -āre *vt* to grace, honor, adorn

condemnāt·or -ōris *m* accuser, prosecutor

condemn·ō -āre *vt* to condemn, convict, find guilty, sentence, doom; to blame, condemn; to prosecute successfully, bring a conviction against

condens·ō -āre *vt* to press close together, condense

condens·us -a -um *adj* close together, thick, crowded

condici·ō -ōnis *f* arrangement, settlement, agreement; stipulation, terms, condition; state, situation; circumstances, rank, place; marriage contract, marriage; **ea condicione ut** on condition that; **sub condicione** conditionally; **vitae condicio** way of life, living conditions

con·dīcō -dīcĕre -dīxī -dictum *vt*

to talk over, arrange together; to promise; **cenam condicere** (with *dat*) or **ad cenam condicere** (with *dat*) to make a dinner engagement with (*someone*)

condignē *adv* very worthily

condign·us -a -um *adj* fully deserving; (with *abl*) fully worthy of

condiment·um -ī *n* seasoning, spice

cond·iō -īre -īvī or **-ĭī -ītum** *vt* to preserve, pickle (*fruits, vegetables*); to season; to embalm (*the dead*); (fig) to spice, give spice to

condiscipulāt·us -ūs *m* companionship at school

condiscipŭl·us -ī *m* schoolmate, school companion, fellow student

con·discō -discĕre -didicī *vt* to learn by heart

conditĭō see **condicio**

conditī·ō -ōnis *f* preserving (*of fruits, etc.*); seasoning, spicing

condĭt·or -ōris *m* founder, builder; author, composer

conditōr·ium -iī or **-ī** *n* coffin, cinerary urn; tomb

condĭt·us -a -um *pp* of **condio**; *adj* seasoned, spicy; polished (*style*)

con·dō -dĕre -dĭdī -dĭtum *vt* to build, found; to write, compose (*poetry*); to establish (*an institution*); to store, treasure, hoard; to preserve, pickle; to bury; to conceal, hide, suppress; to shut (*eyes*); to sheathe (*sword*); to place (*soldiers*) in ambush; to plunge, bury (*sword*); to imprison; to memorize; to store up

condoce·faciō -facĕre -fēcī -factum *vt* to train well

condoc·ĕō -ēre -ŭī -tum *vt* to teach, instruct thoroughly

condol·escō -escĕre -ŭī *vi* to begin to ache, get very sore

condōnāti·ō -ōnis *f* donating, donation

condōn·ō -āre *vt* to give, present, deliver, abandon, surrender; to adjudge; (with double *acc*) to make (*someone*) a present of; (with *acc* of thing and *dat* of person) to forgive, pardon (*someone an offense*); **condonare alicui pecunias creditas** to remit someone's debt

condorm·iō -īre *vi* to sleep soundly

condorm·iscō -iscĕre -īvī *vi* to fall sound asleep

condūcĭbĭl·is -e *adj* advantageous, profitable; (with **ad** + *acc*) just right for

con·dūcō -dūcĕre -dŭxī -ductum *vt* to draw together, collect, assemble; to connect, unite; to hire, rent, borrow; to bribe; to employ; to induce; to contract for; *vi* to be of use; (with *dat*) to be useful to, profitable to; (with **ad** or **in** + *acc*) to be conducive to

conductĭcĭ·us -a -um *adj* hired, mercenary

conductĭ·ō -ōnis *f* bringing together; recapitulation; hiring, renting

conduct·or -ōris *m* contractor; lessee, tenant

conduct·us -a -um *pp* of **conduco**; *m pl* hired men; (mil) mercenaries; *n* rented apartment, rented house

conduplicātĭ·ō -ōnis *f* doubling; (humorously) embrace

conduplĭc·ō -āre *vt* to double; **corpora conduplicare** (humorously) to embrace

condūr·ō -āre *vt* to harden, make very hard

cond·us -ī *m* storeroom manager

cō·nectō -nectĕre -nexŭī -nexum *vt* to tie; to connect, join, link; to state as a conclusion; (with *dat*) to implicate (*someone or something*) in; (with *dat* or **cum** + *abl*) to join (*something*) to, connect (*something*) with

cōnexĭ·ō -ōnis *f* logical conclusion

cōnex·us -a -um *pp* of **conecto**; *adj* connected, joined; **per affinitatem conexus** (with *dat*) related by marriage to; *n* necessary inference, logical connection, necessary consequence

cōnex·us -ūs *m* combination

confābŭl·or -ārī -ātus sum *vt* to discuss; *vi* to converse, have a talk

confarreātĭ·ō -ōnis *f* solemn marriage ceremony in the presence of the Pontifex Maximus and ten witnesses

confarrĕ·ō -āre *vt* to marry with solemn rites

confātāl·is -e *adj* bound by the same fate

confectĭ·ō -ōnis *f* completion, successful completion; chewing, mastication

confect·or -ōris *m* finisher, executor; destroyer, consumer

con·fercĭō -fercīre — -fertum *vt* to stuff, cram, pack together; to stuff full

con·fĕrō -ferre -tŭlī -lātum *vt* to bring together; to contribute (*money, etc.*); to condense, compress; to bring together (*plans, ideas, etc.*), discuss, talk over; to bear, convey, direct; to devote, apply, confer, bestow, give, lend, grant; to ascribe, attribute, impute, assign; to put off, defer, postpone; (with **in** + *acc*) to change or transform (*someone or something*) into; to compare, contrast; **capita conferre** to put heads together, confer; **gradum conferre** (with **cum** + *abl*) to walk together with; **lites conferre** to quarrel; **pedem cum pede conferre** to fight toe to toe; **se conferre** (with **in** + *acc*) a to go to, head for; **b** to have recourse to; **c** to join (*a group, etc.*); **sermones conferre** (with **cum** + *abl*) to engage in conversation with, to engage (*someone*) in conversation; **signa conferre** to engage in combat, begin fighting

confertim *adv* (mil) shoulder to shoulder

confert·us -a -um *pp* of **confercio**; *adj* crowded, packed, thick, dense; (mil) shoulder to shoulder

confervĕfac·ĭō -ĕre *vt* to make glow, make melt

con·fervescō -fervescĕre -ferbŭī *vi* to begin to boil, grow hot

confessĭ·ō -ōnis *f* confession, acknowledgment

confess·us -a -um *pp* of **confiteor**; *adj* acknowledged, incontrovertible, certain; *m* self-acknowledged criminal; *n* admission; **ex confesso** admittedly, beyond doubt; **in confessum venire** to be generally admitted

confestim *adv* immediately, without delay, suddenly

confic·ens -entis *adj* productive, efficient; (with *genit*) productive of; efficient in; *n pl* (with *genit*) sources of

con·ficĭō -ficĕre -fēcī -fectum *vt* to make, manufacture, construct; to make ready, prepare, bring about, complete, accomplish, execute, fulfill; to bring about, cause; to bring together, collect; to get together, secure, obtain; to use up, wear out, exhaust; to finish off, weaken, sweep away, destroy, kill; to run through (*money, inheritance*); to chew (*food*); to complete, finish, spend, pass (*time*)

conficti·ō -ōnis *f* fabrication, invention (*of an accusation*)

confīd·ens -entis *adj* trustful; self-confident; presumptuous, smug

confīdenter *adv* confidently; smugly

confīdentĭ·a -ae *f* confidence; self-confidence, smugness

confīdentĭlŏqu·us -a -um *adj* speaking confidently

con·fīdō -fīdĕre -fīsus sum *vi* to have confidence, be confident, be sure; (with *dat*) to confide in, rely on, trust, believe; **sibi confidere** to rely on oneself, have self-confidence

con·fīgō -fīgĕre -fīxī -fīxum *vt* to fasten, join together; to pierce, transfix; (fig) to paralyze

con·fingō -fingĕre -fīnxī -fictum *vt* to make up, invent, fabricate

confīn·is -e *adj* having common boundaries, adjoining; (fig) closely related, akin

confīn·ium -ĭī or **-ī** *n* common boundary, frontier; (fig) borderline; *n pl* neighbors; confines

confirmātĭ·ō -ōnis *f* confirmation, encouragement; affirmation, verification, corroboration; (rhet) presentation of evidence

confirmāt·or -ōris *m* guarantor, surety

confirmāt·us -a -um *adj* resolute, confident, courageous; established, certain

confirmit·ās -ātis *f* firmness; stubbornness

confirm·ō -āre vt to strengthen, reinforce; to confirm, sanction, ratify; to encourage; to corroborate; to assert positively; **se confirmare** to recover, get back one's strength

confisc·ō -āre vt to deposit in a bank; to confiscate

confisī·ō -ōnis f confidence, assurance

con·fitĕor -fitērī -fessus sum vt to confess, acknowledge, admit; to reveal; vi to confess

conflāgr·ō -āre vi to burn, be on fire; (fig) to burn

conflicti·ō -ōnis f conflict

conflict·ō -āre vt to beat down, strike down; to ruin; **conflictari** to be afflicted, be tormented; vi to contend, struggle, fight

conflict·or -ārī -ātus sum vi to struggle, wrestle

conflict·us -ūs m striking together; wrestling, struggle

con·flīgō -flīgĕre -flīxī -flictum vt to throw or knock together; (with **cum** + abl) to contrast (something) with, compare (something) with; vi to come into conflict, clash, fight, battle; (with **cum** + abl) to come into conflict with, clash with; (with **adversus** + acc or **contra** + acc) to fight against; **inter se confligere** to collide, collide with one another

conflō -āre vt to kindle, ignite; to inflame (passions); to melt down (metals); to bring together, get up, raise (army, money, etc.); to forge, invent (accusation); to bring about, cause, occasion, produce

conflŭ·ens -entis m confluence, junction (of rivers); m pl confluence

con·flŭō -flŭĕre -flūxī vi to flow or run together; (fig) to pour in together, come together in crowds

con·fodiō -fodĕre -fōdī -fossum vt to dig up (soil); to stab; (fig) to stab

conformāti·ō -ōnis f shape, form, fashion; idea, notion; arrangement (of words); expression (in the voice); (rhet) figure of speech

conform·ō -āre vt to shape, fashion, put together; to modify, educate

confoss·us -a -um pp of confodio; adj full of holes

confractus pp of confringo

confragōs·us -a -um adj rough, rugged (terrain); n pl rough terrain

confrĕm·ō -ĕre -ŭī vi to grumble

confric·ō -āre vt to rub vigorously, rub in; **genua confricare** to nag, pester

con·fringō -fringĕre -frēgī -fractum vt to smash, crush; to break down, destroy

con·fugiō -fugĕre -fūgī vi to flee, take refuge, run for help; (with **ad** + acc) (fig) **a** to resort to, have recourse to; **b** to appeal to

confug·ium -iī or **-ī** n place of refuge, shelter

confulg·ĕō -ēre vi to glitter, sparkle

con·fundō -fundĕre -fūdī -fūsum vt to pour together, blend, mingle; to mix up, jumble together, confuse, bewilder, perplex; to spread, diffuse

confūsē adv in disorder, in confusion

confūsi·ō -ōnis f mixing, blending; confusion, mixup, trouble; **confusio oris** blush

confūs·us -a -um pp of confundo; adj confused, perplexed; troubled, confused (look)

confut·ō -āre vt to prevent (water, etc.) from boiling over; to repress, stop; to silence, confute

congĕl·ō -āre vt to cause to freeze up, freeze, harden; **in lapidem congelare** to petrify; vi to freeze, freeze up

congemināti·ō -ōnis f doubling

congemin·ō -āre vt to double

congĕm·ō -ĕre -ŭī vt to deplore deeply; vi to gasp, sigh, or groan deeply

cong·er -rī m eel

congeri·ēs -ēī f heap, pile, mass; funeral pile; accumulation

con·gĕrō -gĕrĕre -gessī -gestum vt to bring together; to heap up, build up; to keep up, multiply, repeat (arguments); (with **in** + acc) **a** to shower (weapons) upon, send a barrage of (weapons) upon; **b** to heap (curses, favors, etc.) upon

congĕr·ō -ōnis m thief

congerr·ō -ōnis m playmate

congestĭcĭ·us -a -um adj piled up

congest·us -ūs m heap, mass, accumulation

congiāl·is -e adj holding a gallon

congiāri·us -a -um adj holding a gallon; n gift of one gallon (e. g., of oil) apiece to the people; bonus to the army; gift of money to the Roman people; gift of money among private friends

cong·ius -iī or **-ī** m Roman liquid measure equaling six sextarii, i.e., about six pints

conglaci·ō -āre vi to freeze up

conglisc·ō -ĕre vi to blaze up

conglobāti·ō -ōnis f massing together

conglŏb·ō -āre vt to make round, form into a ball, roll up

conglomĕr·ō -āre vt to roll up, group together, crowd together; **se in forum conglomerare** to crowd into the forum

conglūtināti·ō -ōnis f gluing together; (fig) combining (of words)

conglūtin·ō -āre vt to glue, cement; (fig) to weld together, cement

congraec·ō -āre vt to squander like the Greeks

congrātŭl·or -ārī -ātus sum vi to offer congratulations

con·gredior -grĕdī -gressus sum vt to meet, accost, address, associate with; to fight; vi to come together, meet; to fight; (with **cum** + abl) **a**

to meet with; **b** to associate with; **c** to fight against

congregābĭl·is -e *adj* gregarious

congregātĭ·ō -ōnis *f* flocking together, congregation, union, association

congrĕg·ō -āre *vt* to herd together; to unite, associate

congressĭ·ō -ōnis *f* meeting, conference

congressus *pp* of **congredior**

congress·us -ūs *m* meeting, association, society, union; hostile encounter, contest, fight

congru·ens -entis *adj* coinciding, corresponding; suitable, consistent; self-consistent, uniform, harmonious

congruenter *adv* consistently; (with *dat* or **ad** + *acc*) in conformity with; **congruenter naturae vivere** to live in conformity with nature

congruentĭ·a -ae *f* consistency, symmetry

congru·ō -ĕre -ŭī *vi* to coincide; to correspond, agree, be consistent; (with **ad** + *acc* or with **cum** + *abl*) to coincide with; (with *dat* or **cum** + *abl*) to correspond to, agree with, be consistent with; (with *dat* or **in** + *acc*) to agree (*in feeling, opinion*) with

congru·us -a -um *adj* agreeing, agreeable

cōnicĭo or **cōĭcĭō** see **conjicio**

cōnif·er -ĕra -ĕrum *adj* coniferous

cōnĭg·er -ĕra -ĕrum *adj* coniferous

cō·nitor -nītī -nixus sum or **-nīsus sum** *vi* to make a great effort, struggle, exert oneself; (with **in** + *acc*) to struggle toward, press on toward, try to reach

cōnīv·ĕō -ēre -ī *vi* to close the eyes (*in sleep, from light, from fear, etc.*), to blink; (of sun or moon) to be darkened, be eclipsed; (fig) to be drowsy; (with **in** + *abl*) to connive at, wink at, overlook

conjectĭ·ō -ōnis *f* throwing, barrage (*of missiles*); conjecture, interpretation

conject·ō -āre *vt* to conjecture, infer, conclude, guess

conject·or -ōris *m* interpreter of dreams, seer

conjectr·ix -īcis *f* interpreter of dreams, seer (*female*)

conjectūr·a -ae *f* conjecture, guess, inference; interpretation

conjectūrāl·is -e *adj* conjectural

conject·us -ūs *m* throwing together; crowding together; connecting; heap, crowd, pile; throwing, casting, hurling; turning, directing (*eyes*); casting (*a glance*); barrage (*of stones, weapons*); **ad** or **intra teli conjectum venire** to come within range of a weapon

con·jĭcĭō -jĭcĕre -jēcī -jectum *vt* to pile together (*e.g., baggage*); to

conclude, infer, conjecture; to interpret (*omen*); to throw, fling, cast; to throw in (*e.g., words in a letter or speech*); **se in fugam** or **se in pedes conjicere** to take to one's heels

conjugāl·is -e *adj* conjugal

conjugātĭ·ō -ōnis *f* etymological relationship (*of words*)

conjugāt·or -ōris *m* uniter (*said of Hymen, god of marriage*)

conjugiāl·is -e *adj* marriage

conjug·ĭum -ĭī or **-ī** *n* union (*e.g., of body and soul*); marriage, wedlock; mating (*of animals*); (fig) husband, wife, spouse

conjŭg·ō -āre *vt* to form (*friendship*); **verba conjugata** cognates

conjunctē *adv* conjointly; at the same time; (in logic) conditionally, hypothetically; **conjuncte vivere** to live intimately together

conjunctim *adv* jointly

conjunctĭ·ō -ōnis *f* combination, union; association, connection; friendship; intimacy; marriage; relationship (*by blood or by marriage*); sympathy, affinity; (gram) conjunction

conjunct·us -a -um *adj* (with *dat* or *abl*) bordering upon, near; (with *dat* or *abl*, or with **cum** + *abl*) a connected with; **b** agreeing with, conforming with; *n* connection

con·jungō -jungĕre -junxī -junctum *vt* to join together, connect, unite; to unite in making (*war*); to unite or join in marriage; to unite (*by bonds of friendship*); (with *dat*) to add (*e.g., words*) to (*e.g., a letter*)

con·junx or **con·jux -jŭgis** *m* married person, spouse, husband; *m pl* married couple; *f* married person, spouse, wife; fiancee; bride; the female (*of animals*)

conjūrātĭ·ō -ōnis *f* conspiracy, plot; alliance

conjūrāt·us -a -um *adj* bound together by an oath, allied, associate; (mil) sworn in; *m pl* conspirators

conjūr·ō -āre *vi* to take an oath together; to plot, conspire

conjux see **conjunx**

conl- = coll-

conm- = comm-

Con·ōn -ōnis *m* famous Athenian admiral (*fl 400 B.C.*); famous mathematician and astronomer of Samos (283-222 B.C.)

cōnōpē·um or **cōnōpĕ·um -ī** *n* mosquito net

cōn·or -ārī -ātus sum *vt* to try, endeavor, venture, attempt

conquassātĭ·ō -ōnis *f* severe shaking; disturbance

conquass·ō -āre *vt* to shake hard; (fig) to shatter, upset, disturb

con·quĕror -quĕrī -questus sum *vt* to complain bitterly about, deplore; *vi* to complain, complain bitterly

conquestĭ·ō -ōnis *f* complaining, complaint; (rhet) appeal for sympathy; (with *genit*, with **de** + *abl*, or with **adversus** + *acc*) complaint about

conquest·us -ūs *m* loud complaint

conqui·escō -escĕre -ēvī -ētum *vi* to rest, take a rest; to find rest, find recreation; to keep quiet, remain inactive; to slacken, flag; to lie dormant; to take a nap; to stop, pause

conquinisc·ō -ĕre *vi* to squat, stoop down

con·quīrō -quīrĕre -quīsīvī -quīsitum *vt* to search for, look for; to procure, bring together, collect; (fig) to search for, go after (*pleasures, etc.*)

conquīsītī·ō -ōnis *f* search; procuring, collection; (mil) conscription, draft, recruitment

conquīsīt·or -ōris *m* recruiting officer

conquīsīt·us -a -um *pp* of **conquīrō**; *adj* chosen, select

conr- = corr-

consaep·iō or **consēp·iō -īre -sī -tum** *vt* to fence in, hedge in, enclose

consaept·um -ī *n* enclosure

consalūtāti·ō -ōnis *f* exchange of greetings

consalūt·ō -āre *vt* to greet (*as a group*), greet cordially; *vi* **inter se consalūtāre** to greet one another, exchange greetings

consān·escō -escĕre -ŭī *vi* to heal up; to recover

consanguinĕ·us -a -um *adj* related by blood; *m* brother; *m pl* relatives; *f* sister

consanguinīt·ās -ātis *f* blood relationship; **consanguinitāte propinquus** closely related

consauci·ō -āre *vt* to wound severely

conscelerāt·us -a -um *adj* wicked, depraved, criminal; (fig) rotten to the core

conscelĕr·ō -āre *vt* to stain with guilt, dishonor, disgrace

con·scendō -scendĕre -scendī -scensum *vt* to climb up, mount, ascend; to board (*ship*); **aequor navibus conscendere** to go to sea; *vi* to climb; to go aboard, board; (with **in** + *acc*) to go aboard (*ship*)

conscensi·ō -ōnis *f* embarkation; **in navīs conscensio** boarding the ships

conscienti·a -ae *f* joint knowledge; consciousness, knowledge; moral sense, conscience; good conscience; bad conscience; scruple; sense of guilt, remorse

con·scindō -scindĕre -scīdī -scissum *vt* to tear up, tear to pieces; (fig) to tear to pieces, abuse

consc·iō -īre *vt* to become conscious of (*wrong*)

consc·īscō -īscĕre -īvī or **-iī -ītum** *vt* to approve or decide upon; (**sibi**) **mortem consciscere** to decide

upon death for oneself, commit suicide

consci·us -a -um *adj* sharing knowledge with another; cognizant, conscious, aware; (with *genit* or *dat*) having knowledge of, aware of, privy to; *mf* partner, accomplice, confidant(e), confederate

conscrĕ·or -ārī -ātus sum *vi* to clear the throat

con·scrībō -scrībĕre -scripsī -scriptum *vt* to enlist, enroll; to write, write up, compose; to prescribe

conscriptī·ō -ōnis *f* document, draft; record, report

conscript·us -a -um *pp* of **conscribo**; *m* senator; **patres conscripti** members of the senate

consĕc·ō -āre -ŭī -tum *vt* to cut up into small pieces, dismember

consecrātī·ō -ōnis *f* consecration; deification (*of emperors*)

consĕcr·ō -āre *vt* to make holy, consecrate, dedicate to a god; to dedicate to the gods below, doom to destruction, execrate; to immortalize, deify

consectāri·us -a -um *adj* logic; *n pl* conclusions, inferences

consectātī·ō -ōnis *f* eager pursuit

consectātr·ix -īcis *f* pursuer (*female*)

consecti·ō -ōnis *f* cutting up

consect·or -ārī -ātus sum *vt* to follow eagerly, go after; to follow up, pursue, chase, hunt; to overtake; to imitate, follow

consecūtī·ō -ōnis *f* effect, consequences; (rhet) order, sequence

consen·escō -escĕre -ŭī *vi* to grow old, grow old together; to become gray; to become obsolete; to waste away, fade, decline; to degenerate, sink

consensi·ō -ōnis *f* agreement, unanimity; harmony; plot, conspiracy

consens·us -ūs *m* agreement, unanimity; agreement, harmony; plot, conspiracy; **consensū** with one accord; **in consensum vertere** to become a general custom; **omnium vestrum consensu** with the agreement of all of you, as you all agree

consentānĕ·us -a -um *adj* (with *dat* or **cum** + *abl*) agreeing with, according to, in accord with, proper for; **consentaneum est** it is reasonable; *n pl* concurrent circumstances

consenti·ens -entis *adj* unanimous

con·sentiō -sentīre -sensī -sensum *vt* **bellum consentire** to agree to war, vote for war; *vi* to agree; (with *inf*) to agree, plot, conspire to; (with **cum** + *abl*) to harmonize with, fit in with, be consistent with

consēp- = consaep-

consēqu·ens -entis *adj* reasonable;

corresponding, logical, fit, suitable; *n* consequence, conclusion

consequenti·a -ae *f* consequence, natural sequence

con·sĕquor -sĕquī -secūtus sum *vt* to follow, follow up, pursue, go after; to catch up with, catch, reach, attain to, arrive at; (fig) to follow, copy, imitate; to obtain, get, acquire; to understand, perceive, learn; (of speech) to be equal to, do justice to; (of time) to come after, follow; to result from, be the consequence of, arise from

con·sĕrō -serĕre -seruī -sertum *vt* to entwine, tie, join, string together; **manum** or **manūs conserere** to fight hand to hand, engage in close combat; **proelium conserere** to begin fighting

con·sĕrō -serĕre -sēvī -situm *vt* to sow, plant

consertē *adv* in close connection, connectedly

conserv·a -ae *f* fellow slave (*female*)

conservātī·ō -ōnis *f* keeping, preserving

conservāt·or -ōris *m* preserver, defender

conservit·ium -iī or **-ī** *n* servitude

conserv·ō -āre *vt* to keep safe, preserve, maintain; (fig) to keep intact

conserv·us -ī *m* fellow slave

consess·or -ōris *m* table companion; fellow spectator; (law) assessor

consess·us -ūs *m* assembly, court

considerātē *adv* with caution, deliberately

considerātī·ō -ōnis *f* contemplation, consideration

considerāt·us -a -um *adj* circumspect, cautious; well considered, deliberate

considĕr·ō -āre *vt* to look at closely, inspect, examine, survey; to consider, contemplate; reflect upon

con·sīdō -sīdĕre -sēdī -sessum *vi* to sit down, be seated, settle; (of assemblies) to hold sessions, be in session; (mil) to encamp, take up a position; to settle, stay (*in residence*); to settle, sink down, subside; (fig) to settle, sink, be buried; to diminish, subside, abate, die out

consign·ō -āre *vt* to seal, sign; to certify, attest, vouch for; to note, register, record

consil·escō -escĕre -uī *vi* to become still, calm down

consiliāri·us -a -um *adj* counseling; *m* counselor, adviser; interpreter, spokesman

consiliāt·or -ōris *m* counselor

consiliō *adv* intentionally, purposely

consil·ior -ārī -ātus sum *vi* to take counsel, consult; (with *dat*) to give counsel to, advise

consil·ium -iī or **-ī** *n* consultation, deliberation; deliberative body, council; council of war; plan, measure, stratagem; decision; purpose, intention, design, policy; judgment, wisdom, prudence, discretion, sense;

cabinet; advice, counsel; **consilium capere** or **consilium inire** or **consilium suscipere** to form a plan, come to a decision, decide, determine; **consilium est mihi** (with *inf*) I intend to; **non est consilium mihi** (with *inf*) I don't mean to; **privato consilio** for one's own purposes

consimil·is -e *adj* quite similar; (with *genit* or *dat*) completely similar to, just like

consip·iō -ĕre *vi* to be sane

con·sistō -sistĕre -stitī -stitum *vi* to come to a stop, come to rest, stop, pause, halt, take a stand, stand still; to grow hard, become solid, set; (mil) to take up a position, be posted, make a stand; (of ships) to come to anchorage, to ground; (of travelers) to halt on a journey; to be firm, be steadfast, continue, endure; to be, exist, occur, take place; (with *abl* or with **in +** *abl*) to consist of, depend on

consitī·ō -ōnis *f* sowing, planting

consit·or -ōris *m* sower, planter

consitūr·a -ae *f* sowing, planting

consōbrīn·a -ae *f* first cousin (*daughter of a mother's sister*)

consōbrīn·us -ī *m* first cousin (*son of mother's sister*)

consociātī·ō -ōnis *f* association, society

consociāt·us -a -um *adj* held in common, shared

consoci·ō -āre *vt* to associate, join, unite, connect, share

consōlābil·is -e *adj* consolable

consōlātī·ō -ōnis *f* consolation, comfort; encouragement; alleviation

consōlāt·or -ōris *m* comforter

consōlātōri·us -a -um *adj* comforting; **litterae consolatoriae** letter of condolence

consōl·or -ārī -ātus sum *vt* to console, comfort, reassure, soothe, encourage, cheer up; to relieve, alleviate, mitigate

consomni·ō -āre *vt* to dream about

consōn·ō -āre -uī *vi* to sound together, ring, resound, reecho; (with *dat* or with **cum +** *abl*) to harmonize with, agree with; **inter se consonare** to agree, harmonize

consŏn·us -a -um *adj* harmonious; (fig) fit, suitable

consōp·iō -īre *vt* to put to sleep

consor·s -tis *adj* having a common lot, of the same fortune; common; shared in common; *mf* partner, associate; *m* brother; *f* wife; sister

consortī·ō -ōnis *f* partnership, association, fellowship

consort·ium -iī or **-ī** *n* partnership; participation; (with *genit*) partnership in

conspect·us -a -um *pp* of **conspicio**; *adj* visible; in full sight; conspicuous, striking

conspect·us -ūs *m* look, sight, view; sight (*power of seeing*); mental view;

being seen, appearance on the scene; **conspectu in medio** before all eyes

con·spergō -spergĕre -spersī -spersum *vt* to sprinkle, splatter

conspiciend·us -a -um *adj* worth seeing; distinguished

conspicill·um -ī *n* (with *genit*) keeping an eye on

con·spiciō -spicĕre -spexī -spectum *vt* to look at attentively, observe, fix the eyes upon; to catch sight of, spot; to look at with admiration; to face (*e.g., the forum*); to perceive, see, discern; **conspici** to be conspicuous, be noticed, be admired, attract attention

conspic·or -ārī -ātus sum *vt* to catch sight of, spot, see

conspicŭ·us -a -um *adj* visible, in sight; conspicuous, striking, remarkable, distinguished

conspīrātĭ·ō -ōnis *f* agreement, unanimity, harmony, concord; plot, conspiracy

conspīrāt·us -a -um *adj* conspiring, in conspiracy

conspīr·ō -āre *vi* to breathe together, blow together, sound together; to act in unison, to agree; to plot together, conspire

conspons·or -ōris *m* coguarantor

con·spŭō -spuĕre — -spūtum *vt* to spit on; **nive conspuere** to sprinkle with snow

conspurc·ō -āre *vt* to defile, mess up

conspūt·ō -āre *vt* to spit on in contempt

constabilĭ·ō -īre -īvī -ītum *vt* to establish, confirm

const·ans -antis *adj* constant, uniform, steady, fixed, stable, regular, invariable, persistent; consistent, harmonious; (fig) faithful, constant, trustworthy

constanter *adv* constantly, steadily, uniformly, invariably; consistently; calmly

constantĭ·a -ae *f* steadiness, firmness, constancy, perseverance; harmony, symmetry, consistency; steadfastness; self-possession

consternātĭ·ō -ōnis *f* consternation, dismay, alarm; disorder, disturbance; mutiny; wild rush, stampede

con·sternō -sternĕre -strāvī -strātum *vt* to spread, cover; to pave; to thatch; **constrata navis** ship with deck

constīp·ō -āre *vt* to crowd together

constit·ŭō -uĕre -uī -ūtum *vt* to set up, erect, establish; to settle (*e.g., a people in a place*); to set up, establish (*authority*); to settle, determine, fix (*date, price, penalty*); to arrange, set in order, organize; to construct, erect; to designate, select, assign, appoint; to decide, arbitrate, decree, judge; (mil) to station, post, deploy

constitūtĭ·ō -ōnis *f* constitution, nature; disposition; regulation, or-

dinance, order; definition; (rhet) issue, point of discussion

constitūt·us -a -um *pp* of **constituo**; *adj* ordered, arranged; **bene constitutum corpus** good constitution; *n* agreement, arrangement

con·stō -stāre -stĭtī -stātum *vi* to stand together; to agree, correspond; to stand firm, remain unchanged, be constant; to stand still, stand firm; to be in existence; (of facts) to be established, be undisputed, be well known; (com) to tally, be correct; (with *abl* of price) to cost; **non mihi satis constat** I have not quite made up my mind; **ratio constat** the account tallies, is correct

constrāt·us -a -um *pp* of **consterno**; *n* flooring

con·stringō -stringĕre -strinxī -strictum *vt* to tie up; to shackle, chain; (fig) to bind, restrain; (rhet) to condense, compress

constructĭ·ō -ōnis *f* building, construction; arrangement (*of words*)

con·strŭō -strŭĕre -struxī -structum *vt* to heap up, pile up; to construct, build up; (gram) to construct

constuprāt·or -ōris *m* rapist

constŭpr·ō -āre *vt* to rape

consŭăd·ĕō -ēre *vi* (with *dat*) to advise strongly

Consŭāl·ĭa -ĭum *n pl* feast of Consus, ancient Italian god of fertility, celebrated on August 21st

consŭās·or -ōris *m* adviser

consūcĭd·us -a -um *adj* very juicy

consūd·ō -āre *vi* to sweat profusely

consŭē·faciō -facĕre -fēcī -factum *vt* to accustom, inure

consŭ·escō -escĕre -ēvī -ētum *vt* to accustom, inure; *vi* to become accustomed; (with *inf*) to become accustomed to; (with **cum** + *abl*) to cohabit with

consŭētĭ·ō -ōnis *f* sexual intercourse

consŭētūd·ō -ĭnis *f* custom, habit; usage, idiom; social intercourse, social ties; sexual intercourse; **ad consuetudinem** (with *genit*) according to the custom of; **consuetudine** or **ex consuetudine** according to custom, from habit; **pro consuetudine mea** according to my habit, as is my habit; **ut fert consuetudo** as is usual

consŭēt·us -a -um *pp* of **consuesco**; *adj* usual, regular, customary

con·sul -sŭlis *m* consul (*one of the two highest magistrates of the Roman republic*); **consul designatus** consul-elect; **consulem creare, dicere,** or **facere** to elect a consul; **consul ordinarius** consul who entered office on the first of January; **consul suffectus** consul chosen in the course of the year to fill a vacancy in the consulship

consŭlār·is -e *adj* consular; **aetas**

consularis minimum legal age for election to consular office; **comitia consularia** consular elections; *m* ex-consul

consulāriter *adv* like a consul, in a manner worthy of a consul

consulāt·us -ūs *m* consulship; **consulatum petere** to run for the consulship; **se consulatu abdicare** to resign from the consulship

consŭl·ō -ĕre -ŭī -tum *vt* to consult, ask advice of; to consider; to advise (*something*), offer as advice; **boni consulere** to regard favorably; *vi* to deliberate, reflect; (with **ad** or **in** + *acc*) to reflect on, take into consideration; (with *dat*) to look after; (with **in** + *acc*) to take measures against; (with **de** + *abl*) to pass sentence on

consultāti·ō -ōnis *f* mature deliberation, consideration; consulting, inquiry; subject of consultation, case

consultē *adv* deliberately, after due consideration

consultō *adv* deliberately, on purpose

consult·ō -āre *vt* to reflect on, consider maturely; to ask (*someone*) for advice, consult; *vi* to deliberate, reflect; (with *dat*) to take into consideration, look after, care for; **in medium consultare** to look after the common good

consult·or -ōris *m* counselor, adviser; advisee, client

consultr·ix -īcis *f* protectress

consult·us -a -um *pp* of **consulo**; *adj* skilled, experienced; *m* expert; **juris consultus** legal expert, lawyer; *n* deliberation, consideration; decree, decision, resolution; response (*from an oracle*)

consummāt·us -a -um *adj* consummate, perfect

consumm·ō -āre *vt* to sum up; to finish, complete, accomplish, perfect

con·sūmō -sūmĕre -sūmpsī -sūmptum *vt* to use up, consume, exhaust; to devour; to squander; to wear out, destroy; to spend, waste (*money, time, effort*)

consumpti·ō -ōnis *f* consumption, wasting

consumpt·or -ōris *m* destroyer

con·sŭō -sŭĕre -sŭī -sūtum *vt* to stitch together, sew up

con·surgō -surgĕre -surrexī -surrectum *vi* to stand up; to rise in a body; (with **ad** or **in** + *acc*) to aspire to

consurrecti·ō -ōnis *f* rising up, standing up in a body

Cons·us -ī *m* ancient Italian deity of agriculture and fertility

consusurr·ō -āre *vi* to whisper together

contābefac·iō -ĕre *vt* to wear out completely, consume, waste

contāb·escō -escĕre -ŭī *vi* to waste away

contabulāti·ō -ōnis *f* flooring; story

contabŭl·ō -āre *vt* to cover with boards; to build with (*several*) stories

contact·us -ūs *m* touch, contact; contagion; (fig) contagion, infection

contāg·ēs -is *f* touch, contact

contāgi·ō -ōnis *f* touching; touch; contact; contagion, infection; moral contagion, bad example

contāg·ium -iī or **-ī** *n* touch, contact; contagion; moral contamination

contāmināt·us -a -um *adj* polluted, contaminated, impure, vile, degraded; *m pl* perverted youths

contāmin·ō -āre *vt* to bring into contact, mingle, blend; to corrupt, defile; (fig) to corrupt, stain, taint, spoil

contechn·or -ārī -ātus sum *vi* to devise plots, think up tricks

con·tĕgō -tegĕre -texī -tectum *vt* to cover up; to hide; to protect

contemĕr·ō -āre *vt* to defile

con·temnō -temnĕre -tempsī -temptum *vt* to think little of, depreciate, slight, belittle, disregard; to despise, defy

contemplāti·ō -ōnis *f* viewing, surveying, contemplation

contemplāt·or -ōris *m* contemplator, observer

contemplāt·us -ūs *m* contemplation

contempl·ō -āre or **contempl·or -ārī -ātus sum** *vt* to observe, survey, gaze upon, contemplate

contemptim *adv* contemptuously

contempti·ō -ōnis *f* belittling, despising; **in contemptionem venire** (with *dat*) to become an object of contempt to

contempt·or -ōris *m* or **contemptr·ix -īcis** *f* scorner, despiser

contempt·us -a -um *pp* of **contemno**; *adj* contemptible, despicable

contempt·us -ūs *m* belittling, despising, scorn; **contemptui esse** to be an object of contempt

con·tendō -tendĕre -tendī -tentum *vt* to stretch, draw tight; to tune (*instrument*); to aim, shoot, hurl; (fig) to strain, stretch, exert; to hold, assert, maintain; to compare, contrast; to direct (*course*); *vi* to exert oneself; to compete, contend, fight; to travel, march; (with *inf*) to be in a hurry to; (with **in** + *acc*) to rush to, head for; (with **ad** + *acc*) to strive for, aspire to

contentē *adv* with great effort, earnestly; closely, scantily, sparingly

contenti·ō -ōnis *f* competition, struggle, dispute; straining, exertion, effort; contrast, comparison, antithesis

content·us -a -um *pp* of **contendo**; *adj* tense, tight, taut, strained; eager, intense

content·us -a -um *pp* of **contineo**; *adj* content, satisfied

contermĭn·us -a -um adj (with dat) bordering upon

con·tĕrō -terĕre -trīvī -trītum vt to grind to powder, pulverize, crumble; (fig) to wear away, wear out, use up; to consume, waste (time)

conterr·ĕō -ēre -ŭī -ĭtum vt to frighten, scare the life out of

contest·or -ārī -ātus sum vt to call to witness; (fig) to prove, attest; **lītem contestari** to open a lawsuit by calling witnesses

contex·ō -ĕre -ŭī -tum vt to weave together; to brace together; to connect; to devise, build; to compose (writings); to dream up (a charge)

contextē adv in a coherent manner

context·us -a -um pp of contexo; adj connected

context·us -ūs m connection, coherence

contic·escō or **contic·iscō -escĕre -ŭī** vi to become quite still, fall completely silent, hush; to keep silence; (fig) to cease, abate

conticinnō adv in the evening

contignātĭ·ō -ōnis f floor, story

contign·ō -āre vt to lay a floor on

contigŭ·us -a -um adj touching, adjoining; within reach; (with dat) bordering on, near

contĭn·ens -entis adj contiguous, adjacent; unbroken, uninterrupted; self-controlled, continent; (with dat) bordering on, contiguous with, adjacent to

contĭn·ens -entis f continent, mainland

contĭn·ens -entis n chief point, main point (of a speech)

continenter adv in unbroken succession; without interruption; (sitting) close together; moderately, temperately

continentĭ·a -ae f self-control; continence

con·tĭneō -tĭnēre -tĭnŭī -tentum vt to hold or keep together; to keep within bounds, confine; to contain, comprise, include; to control, repress

con·tingō -tingĕre -tĭgī -tactum vt to come into contact with; (fig) to touch, affect; to touch, border on; to reach, reach to; to contaminate; vi to happen, turn out, come to pass; (with dat) **a** to touch, border on; **b** to happen, to befall

continuātĭ·ō -ōnis f unbroken series, succession; (rhet) period

continŭ·ō -āre vt to make continuous, join together, connect; to extend; to continue, carry on, draw out, prolong; to pass, occupy (time); **continŭari** (with dat) **a** to be contiguous with, adjacent to; **b** to follow closely upon

continŭō adv immediately, without delay; as a necessary consequence, necessarily

continŭ·us -a -um adj continuous, unbroken; successive; **dies con-**

tinuos quinque for five successive days

contĭ·ō -ōnis f meeting, rally; public meeting (of the people or of soldiers); speech, pep talk, harangue

contiōnābund·us -a -um adj haranguing

contiōnāl·is -e adj typical of a public assembly; demagogic

contiōnāri·us -a -um adj mob-like

contiōnāt·or -ōris m demagogue, public agitator, rabble-rouser

contiōn·or -ārī -ātus sum vi to hold forth at a rally, to harangue; to come to a rally; to make a statement at a rally

contiuncŭl·a -ae f short harangue, trifling speech

contoll·ō -ĕre vt to bring together

contōn·at -āre v impers it is thundering hard

contor·quĕō -quēre -sī -tum vt to whirl, twist; to throw hard; to twist (words) around

contortē adv intricately

contortiōn·ēs -um f pl intricacies (of language)

contort·or -ōris m perverter; **contortor legum** pettifogger

contortŭl·us -a -um adj rather complicated

contortuplicāt·us -a -um adj all twisted up

contort·us -a -um pp of contorqueo; adj involved, intricate; vehement (speech)

contrā adv in opposition, opposite, in front, face to face; in turn, in return, on the other hand, on the other side; reversely, in the opposite way, the other way; on the contrary, conversely; **contra atque** or **ac** contrary to, otherwise than; **contra dicere** to reply, say in reply; to raise objections; **contra dicitur** the objection is raised; **contra ferire** to make a counterattack; **contra qua fas est** contrary to divine law; **contra quam senatus consuluisset** contrary to what the senate would have decided, contrary to the senate resolution; **quin contra** nay on the contrary, in fact it's just the opposite

contrā prep (with acc) opposite, opposite to, facing, towards, against; in answer to, in reply to; (in hostile sense) against, with, in opposition to, as the opponent of; against, injurious to, unfavorable to; contrary to, the reverse of; in violation of; against, in defiance of; **contra ea putare** to think otherwise; **quod contra** whereas, while; **valere contra** to counterbalance

contractĭ·ō -ōnis f drawing together, contraction; shortening (of syllable); despondency

contractiuncŭl·a -ae f slight mental depression

contract·us -a -um pp of contraho; adj contracted; narrow, limited (*place*); brief; pinching (*poverty*); in seclusion; **res contracta** contract

contract·us -ūs *m* shrinking

contrā·dīcō -dīcĕre -dīxī -dictum *vi* (with *dat*) to contradict, speak against

contrādictī·ō -ōnis *f* objection, refutation

con·trăhō -trahĕre -traxī -tractum *vt* to draw together, collect, assemble; to contract, shorten, narrow, abridge, lessen, diminish; to wrinkle; (fig) to bring about, accomplish, cause, produce, incur; to conclude (*bargain*); to transact (*business*); to settle (*an account*); to complete (*business arrangements*)

contrāriē *adv* in opposite ways, in a different way

contrāri·us -a -um *adj* opposite; contrary, conflicting; hostile, antagonistic; from the opposite direction; (with *dat*) opposed to, contrary to; *n* the opposite, the contrary, the reverse; antithesis; **ex contrario** on the contrary, on the other hand; **in contraria** in opposite directions; **in contraria versus** changed into its opposite

contrectābĭlĭter *adv* appreciably, tangibly

contrectātĭ·ō -ōnis *f* handling, touching

contrect·ō -āre *vt* to touch, handle; (fig) to defile; (fig) to dwell upon, consider

contrem·iscō -iscĕre -ŭī *vt* to shudder at; *vi* to tremble all over; to waver

contrĕm·ō -ĕre -ŭī *vi* to tremble all over; to quake

contrib·ŭō -uĕre -ŭī -ūtum *vt* to bring together, reunite, enroll together, associate, unite, incorporate; to contribute, add

contrist·ō -āre *vt* to sadden, cover with gloom; (fig) to darken, cloud

contrīt·us -a -um *pp* of **contero**; *adj* worn out, common, trite

controversi·a -ae *f* controversy, quarrel, dispute, debate; civil lawsuit, litigation; subject of litigation; contradiction; question; **sine controversia** indisputably

controversiōs·us -a -um *adj* much disputed, controversial

controvers·us -a -um *adj* disputed, controversial, questionable, undecided

contrucīd·ō -āre *vt* to cut down, cut to pieces, massacre; (fig) to wreck, make a mess of

con·trūdō -trūdĕre -trūsī -trūsum *vt* to crowd together

contrunc·ō -āre *vt* to hack to pieces

contubernāl·is -is *m* army comrade, army buddy; junior staff officer; (coll) husband (*of slave*); personal attendant; comrade, companion, associate; colleague; *f* (coll) wife (*of slave*)

contubern·ĭum -ĭī or **-ĭ** *n* military companionship; common war tent; concubinage; marriage (*of slaves*); hovel (*of slaves*)

con·tuĕor -tuērī -tuĭtus sum *vt* to look at attentively, regard, survey

contuĭt·us or **contūt·us -ūs** *m* sight, observation

contumācĭ·a -ae *f* stubbornness, defiance, willfulness; constancy, firmness

contumācĭter *adv* stubbornly, defiantly

contūm·ax -ācis *adj* stubborn, defiant

contumēlĭ·a -ae *f* mistreatment, rough treatment; outrage, insult, abuse, affront

contumēliōsē *adv* abusively

contumēliōs·us -a -um *adj* bringing dishonor; insulting, abusive; reproachful, insolent

contumŭl·ō -āre *vt* to bury

con·tundō -tundĕre -tŭdī -tūsum *vt* to crush, grind, pound, bruise; (fig) to crush, destroy, break, subdue; to baffle

conturbātĭ·ō -ōnis *f* confusion, consternation

conturbāt·us -a -um *adj* confused, distracted, disordered, in confusion

conturb·ō -āre *vt* to confuse, throw into confusion; to disquiet, disturb; to upset (*plans*); **rationes** or **rationem conturbare** to be bankrupt; *vi* to be bankrupt

cont·us -ī *m* pole

cōnūbĭāl·is -e *adj* marriage, connubial

cōnūb·ĭum -ĭī or **-ĭ** *n* intermarriage; right to intermarry according to Roman law; marriage; sexual intercourse; **jus conubi** right to intermarry

cōn·us -ī *m* cone; apex (*of helmet*)

convād·or -ārī -ātus sum *vt* to subpoena

conval·escō -escĕre -ŭī *vi* to grow strong; to regain strength, convalesce; (fig) to improve

convall·is -is *f* valley

convās·ō -āre *vt* to pack up, pack

convect·ō -āre *vt* to heap together; to bring home

convect·or -ōris *m* fellow passenger

con·vĕhō -vehĕre -vexī -vectum *vt* to collect, bring in (*esp. the harvest*)

con·vellō -vellĕre -vellī -vulsum *vt* to tear away, pull off, pluck, wrest; to tear to pieces, dismember; to break, shatter; (fig) to turn upside down, subvert, overthrow; **convellere signa** to break camp

convĕn·ae -ārum *m pl* or *f pl* strangers; refugees, vagabonds

convenĭ·ens -entis *adj* agreeing, harmonious, consistent; appropriate; (with *dat* or with **cum** + *abl*) consistent with, appropriate to; (with **ad** + *acc*) appropriate for, suitable for

convenienter *adv* consistently; suitably; (with **cum** + *abl* or with **ad** + *acc*) in conformity with

convenienti·a -ae *f* agreement, accord, harmony; conformity

con·veniō -venire -vēnī -ventum *vt* to meet, go to meet; to interview; *vi* to come together, meet, gather, come in a body; to coincide; to unite, combine; to come to an agreement, agree; (with + *acc*) to fit (*as a shoe fits the foot*); (with *dat*, with **ad** or **in** + *acc*, or with **cum** + *abl*) to be applicable to, appropriate to, fit; **convenit** it is fitting, proper; **convenit inter se** (with *dat*) there is harmony among

conventīcī·us -a -um *adj* coming together, gathering together; *n* fee for attending the assembly

conventīcul·um -ī *n* small gathering; meeting place

conventī·ō -ōnis *f* agreement, contract

convent·us -a -um *pp* of **convenio**; *n* agreement, contract

convent·us -ūs *m* gathering, assembly; congress; district court; company, corporation; agreement; **ex conventu** by agreement; of one accord; **conventum agere** to hold court

con·verrō or **con·vorrō -verrĕre -verrī -versum** *vt* to sweep together, sweep up; to brush thoroughly; (fig) to scoop up (*e.g., an inheritance*)

conversātī·ō -ōnis *f* social intercourse; conversation

conversī·ō -ōnis *f* revolving, revolution; (fig) alteration, change; (rhet) repetition of word at end of clause; (rhet) balancing of phrases

convers·ō -āre *vt* to turn around; **se conversare** to revolve

con·vertō or **con·vortō -vertĕre -vertī -versum** *vt* to cause to turn, turn back, reverse; (fig) to turn, direct (*laughter, attention*); to convert, transform; to translate; to attract (*attention*); (mil) **sese convertere** to retreat; *vi* to return; to change, be changed, turn; (with **in** + *acc*) to be changed into, turn into

convest·iō -īre *vt* to clothe, cover

convex·us -a -um *pp* of **conveho**; *adj* rounded off; arched, convex; concave; sloping down; *n* vault, arch

convīciāt·or -ōris *m* reviler

convīcī·or -ārī -ātus sum *vt* to revile

convīc·ium -iī or **-ī** *n* noise, chatter; wrangling; jeers, invective, abuse; cry of protest; reprimand; **conviciis consectari aliquem** to keep after someone with abuses

convictī·ō -ōnis *f* companionship; companions

convict·or -ōris *m* bosom friend

convict·us -ūs *m* association, socializing; close friends; feast, banquet

con·vincō -vincĕre -vīcī -victum *vt* to refute, prove wrong; to convict, prove guilty; to prove true, demonstrate clearly

convīs·ō -ĕre *vt* to examine, search; to shine on

convīv·a -ae *m* guest, table companion

convīvāl·is -e *adj* convivial, festive

convīvāt·or -ōris *m* master of ceremonies; host

convīv·ium -iī or **-ī** *n* banquet, dinner; dinner party; *n pl* dinner guests; **convivium agitare** to throw a party

con·vīvō -vīvĕre -vixī *vi* to live together; (with **cum** + *abl*) to feast with

convīv·or -ārī -ātus sum *vi* to feast together, have a party

convocātī·ō -ōnis *f* calling together

convŏc·ō -āre *vt* to call together, assemble

convŏl·ō -āre *vi* to flock together; (fig) to flock together, gather hastily

con·volvō -volvĕre -volvī -volūtum *vt* to roll together; to roll up (*a scroll*); to fasten together, interweave; to wrap; **se convolvere** to roll along; to go in a circle

convŏm·ō -ĕre *vt* to vomit on, vomit all over

convortō see **converto**

convulnĕr·ō -āre *vt* to wound seriously

convulsus *pp* of **convello**

coöper·iō -īre -ŭī -tum *vt* to cover; to overwhelm

coöptātī·ō -ōnis *f* cooption, election of a colleague by vote of incumbent members

coöpt·ō -āre *vt* to coopt

coör·ior -īrī -tus sum *vi* to rise, rise suddenly; (fig) (of war) to break out; (of wind) to arise

coört·us -ūs *m* rising, originating

cōp·a -ae *f* barmaid

cophĭn·us -ī *m* basket

cōpi·a -ae *f* abundance, supply, store, plenty; multitude, large number; wealth, prosperity; opportunity, means; command of language, fluency, richness of expression; (with *genit*) power over; (with *dat*) access to; **pro copia** according to opportunity, according to ability; *f pl* troops, armed forces; provisions, supplies

cōpiŏl·ae -ārum *f pl* small contingent of troops

cōpiōsē *adv* abundantly, plentifully; (rhet) fully, at length

cōpiōs·us -a -um *adj* plentiful; well supplied, rich, wealthy; eloquent, fluent (*speech*); (with *abl*) abounding in, rich in

cōp·is -e *adj* rich, well supplied

cōpŭl·a -ae *f* cord, string, rope, leash; (fig) tie, bond

cōpŭlātĭ·ō -ōnis f coupling, joining, union; combining (of words)

cōpŭl·ō -āre vt to couple, join; (fig) to unite; (with dat or with **cum +** abl) to couple with, join to, combine with

cōpŭl·or -ārī -ātus sum vt to join, clasp; **dexterās copulari** to shake hands

coqu·a -ae f cook (female)

coquīn·ō -āre vi to be a cook

co·quō -quěre -xī -ctum vt to cook; to fry, roast, bake, boil; to prepare (a meal); to burn, parch; to ripen, mature; to digest; to disturb, worry, disquiet; to plan, concoct, dream up

coqu·us or **coc·us -ī** m cook

cor cordis n heart; mind, judgment; (as seat of feelings) heart, soul; dear friend; n pl persons, souls; **cordi esse** (with dat) to please, be dear to, be agreeable to

cōram adv in person, personally; publically, openly; in someone's presence, face to face; prep (coming before or after abl) before, in the presence of, face to face with

corb·is -is m or f wicker basket

corbīt·a -ae f slow-sailing merchant ship

corbŭl·a -ae f small basket

corcŭl·um -ī n little heart; sweetheart; poor fellow

Corcȳr·a -ae f island off the coast of Epirus, identified with Scheria, the island of Alcinous

cordātē adv wisely, prudently

cordol·ĭum -ĭī or **-ī** n heartache

Corfīn·ĭum -ĭī or **-ī** n town in Central Italy which served as headquarters of Italian allies during the Social War against Rome in 90-89 B.C.

coriandr·um -ī n coriander

Corinthĭ·us -a -um adj Corinthian; **aes Corinthium** alloy of gold, silver, and copper, used in making expensive jewelry, etc.; m pl Corinthians; n pl costly Corinthian products

Corinth·us -ī f Corinth

Coriŏl·ī -ōrum m pl town in Latium, capital of the Volsci, from the capture of which, in 493 B.C., C. Marcius received the surname of Coriolanus

cor·ĭum -ĭī or **-ī** n or **cor·ĭus -ĭī** or **-ī** m skin, hide; bark; leather

Cornēlĭ·us -a -um adj Cornelian; gens **Cornelia** Cornelian tribe (famous Roman tribe, especially for the Scipios, the Gracchi, and Sulla); f Cornelia (daughter of Scipio Africanus Major and mother of the Gracchi)

corneŏl·us -a -um adj horny

corně·us -a -um adj horny; of the cornel tree; of cornel wood

cornĭc·en -inis m horn blower

cornĭc·or -ārī -ātus sum vi to caw

cornĭcŭl·a -ae f poor little crow

cornĭculār·ĭus -ĭī or **-ī** m soldier decorated with a horn-shaped medal for bravery; adjutant to a centurion

cornĭcŭl·um -ī n little horn; horn-shaped decoration, awarded for bravery

cornĭg·er -ěra -ěrum adj horn-bearing, horned

cornĭp·ēs -ědis adj hoofed

corn·ix -īcis f crow (whose appearance on one's left side was considered a favorable omen and whose cries were regarded as a sign of rain)

corn·ū -ūs or **corn·um -ī** n horn; horn, trumpet; lantern; funnel; oil cruet; hoof; bill (of bird); horn (of moon); branch (of river); arm (of bay); tongue (of land); crest socket (of helmet); roller end (of book); (mil) wing, flank; **cornua addere** (with dat) to give courage to, add strength to; **cornua sumere** to gain strength

corn·um -ī n cornel cherry

corn·us -ī f cornel cherry tree; dogwood tree; spear, shaft, javelin

coroll·a -ae f small garland

corollar·ĭum -ĭī or **-ī** n garland; gilt wreath given as reward to actors; gift, gratuity

corōn·a -ae f crown, garland; circle of bystanders; (mil) cordon of besiegers; ring of defense; **corona civica** decoration for saving a life; **corona muralis** decoration for being the first to scale an enemy wall; **corona navalis** decoration for naval victory; **sub corona vendere** to sell (captives) as slaves; **sub corona venire** (of captives) to be sold at public auction

Corōn·a -ae f Ariadne's crown, Corona Borealis (constellation)

corōnārĭ·us -a -um adj for a crown; **aurum coronarium** gold collected in the provinces for a victorious general

Corōnē·ă -ae f town in Boeotia

Corōn·eus -ěī m king of Phocis whose daughter was changed into a crow

Corōnīd·ēs -ae m Aesculapius, the son of Coronis

Corōn·is -ĭdis f daughter of Phylegyas and mother of Aesculapius

corōn·ō -āre vt to crown, wreathe; to enclose, encircle, shut in

corporě·us -a -um adj physical, of the body; corporeal, substantial; of flesh

corpulent·us -a -um adj corpulent

corp·us -ŏris n body; matter, substance; flesh; trunk; corpse; person, individual; body, frame, structure; framework; community; corporation; particle, grain

corpuscŭl·um -ī n puny body; particle, atom; (as term of endearment) little fellow

cor·rādō -rāděre -rāsī -rāsum vt to scrape together, rake up; (fig) to scrape (e.g., money) together

correctī·ō -ōnis f correction, improvement, amendment; rhetorical restatement

correct·or -ōris m reformer; censor, critic

correctus pp of **corrigo**

cor·rēpō -rēpĕre -repsī vi to creep, slink; **in dumeta correpere** (fig) to beat around the bush, indulge in jargon

correptius adv more briefly; **correptius exire** to end in a short vowel, have a short vowel

correptus pp of **corripio**

corrīd·ĕō -ēre vi to laugh out loud

corrigī·a -ae f shoelace

cor·rĭgō -rigĕre -rexī -rectum vt to make straight, straighten out; to smooth out; to correct, improve, reform; to make up for (delay); to make the best of

cor·ripiō -ripĕre -ripŭī -reptum vt to seize, snatch up, carry off; to speed up, rush; to steal, carry off; to attack; to shorten, contract; to reprove, accuse, reproach; to cut (a period of time) short

corrōbŏr·ō -āre vt to strengthen, invigorate, corroborate; (fig) to fortify, encourage

cor·rōdo -rōdĕre -rōsī -rōsum vt to gnaw, chew up

corrōg·ō -āre vt to go asking for, collect, drum up, solicit

corrōsus pp of **corrodo**

corrūg·ō -āre vt to wrinkle, corrugate; **nares corrugare** (with dat) to cause (someone) disgust

cor·rumpō -rumpĕre -rūpī -ruptum vt to burst; to break to pieces, smash; to destroy completely, ruin, waste; to mar, corrupt, adulterate; to falsify, tamper with (documents); to bribe; to seduce, corrupt

corrŭ·ō -ĕre -ī vt to shatter, wreck, ruin; vi to fall down, tumble, sink; (fig) to fall, fail, sink, go down

corruptē adv corruptly, perversely; in a lax manner

corruptēl·a -ae f corruption, seduction; bribery; seducer, misleader

corruptī·ō -ōnis f corrupting, ruining, breaking up; corrupt condition

cŏrrupt·or -ōris m or **corruptr·ix -īcis** f corrupter, seducer, briber

corrupt·us -a -um pp of **corrumpo**; adj corrupt, spoiled, bad, ruined

cort·ex -īcis m or f bark, shell, hull, rind; cork; **nare sine cortice** to swim without a cork life preserver; to be on one's own

cortīn·a -ae f kettle, caldron; tripod; (fig) vault of heaven

corŭlus see **corylus**

corusc·ō -āre vt to shake, brandish; vi to flit, flutter, to oscillate; to tremble; to flash, gleam

corusc·us -a -um adj oscillating, vibrating, tremulous; flashing, gleaming, glittering

corv·us -ī m raven; (mil) grapnel

Corybant·ēs -ĭum m pl Corybantes (priests of Cybele)

Corybanti·us -a -um adj of the Corybantes

cŏrȳc·us -ī m punching bag

corylēt·um -ī n cluster of hazel trees

corȳl·us or **corŭl·us -ī** f hazel tree

corymbĭf·er -ĕra -ĕrum adj wearing or bearing clusters of ivy berries; m Bacchus

corymb·us -ī m cluster (esp. of ivy berries)

coryphae·us -ī m leader, head

cŏrȳt·os or **cŏrȳt·us -ī** m quiver (for arrows)

cōs cōtis f flint; grindstone, whetstone

Cō·s or **Co·ūs -ī** f small island in the Aegean Sea, famous for its wine and fine linen

cosmēt·a -ae m slave in charge of the wardrobe

cost·a -ae f rib; (fig) side, wall

cost·um -ī n perfume

cothurnāt·us -a -um adj wearing the tragic buskin; suitable to tragedy; tragic, of tragedy

cothurn·us -ī m high boot; hunting boot; buskin (worn by tragic actors); subject of tragedy; tragedy; lofty style of Greek tragedy

cōtĭd- = cottid-

cottăb·us -ī m game which consisted in flicking drops of wine on a bronze vessel

cottăn·a or **cottŏn·a -ōrum** n pl Syrian figs

cottīdiānō adv daily

cottīdiān·us or **cotīdiān·us -a -um** adj daily; everyday, ordinary

cottīdiē or **cōtīdiē** adv daily, every day

coturn·ix -īcis f quail

Cotyttĭ·a -ōrum n pl festival of Cotytto

Cotytt·ō -ūs f Thracian goddess of lewdness

Coüs see **Cos**

Cō·us -a -um adj Coan; n Coan wine; n pl Coan garments

covinnār·ĭus -ĭī or -ī m soldier who fought from a chariot

covinn·us -ī m war chariot of the Britons and the Belgae; coach

cox·a -ae f hipbone

coxend·ix -īcis f hip

crăbr·ō -ōnis m hornet; **irritare crabrones** (fig) to stir up a hornet's nest

cramb·ē -ēs f cabbage; **crambe repetita** warmed-over cabbage; same old story

Crant·or -ōris m Greek Academic philosopher of Soli in Cilicia (fl 300 B.C.)

crāpŭl·a -ae f drunkenness; hangover

crāpŭlārĭ·us -a -um adj for (i.e., to prevent) a hangover

crās adv tomorrow; (fig) in the future

crassē *adv* thickly; rudely; confusedly; dimly

crassitūd·ō -inis *f* thickness, density; dregs

crass·us -a -um *adj* thick, dense; dense, dull, stupid

Cras·us -ī *m* L. Licinius Crassus (*famous orator, d* 90 B.C.); M. Licinius Crassus (*triumvir, together with Caesar and Pompey*, 112?-53 B.C.)

crastin·us -a -um *adj* tomorrow's; (old *abl* form) **die crastini** tomorrow; *n* tomorrow; **in crastinum differre** to put off till tomorrow

crāt·ēr -ēris *m* or **crātēr·a -ae** *f* mixing bowl; bowl; crater

Crāt·ēr -ēris *m* Bowl (*constellation*)

crāt·is -is *f* wickerwork; harrow; ribs of shield; (mil) faggots (*for filling trenches*); joint, rib (*of body*); honeycomb

creāti·ō -ōnis *f* election

creāt·or -ōris *m* creator; procreator, father; founder

creātr·ix -icis *f* creatress; mother

crēb·er -ra -rum *adj* luxuriant, prolific (*growth*); numerous, crowded; repeated; frequent

crēbr·escō or **crēb·escō -escēre -ūī** *vi* to increase, become frequent; to gain strength

crēbrit·ās -ātis *f* frequency

crēbrō *adv* repeatedly, frequently, again and again

crēdibil·is -e *adj* credible, trustworthy

crēdibiliter *adv* credibly

crēdit·or -ōris *m* creditor, lender

crēd·ō -ēre -idī -itum *vt* to lend, loan; to entrust, consign; to believe; to think, believe, suppose, imagine; *vi* (with *dat*) to believe, put faith in, have trust or confidence in; **credas** one would image; **satis creditum est** it is believed on good evidence

crēdulit·ās -ātis *f* credulity, trustfulness

crēdul·us -a -um *adj* credulous, trustful; gullible; (with *dat* or **in** with *acc*) trusting in

crem·ō -āre *vt* to burn to ashes; to cremate

Cremōn·a -ae *f* town in N. Italy, which became a Roman colony in 209 B.C.

crem·or -ōris *m* juice obtained from animal or vegetable substances; broth

cre·ō -āre *vt* to create, produce; to elect to office; to cause, occasion; to beget, bear

Cre·ō or **Cre·ōn -ontis** *m* brother of Jocaste and brother-in-law of Oedipus; king of Corinth who gave his daughter in marriage to Jason

crep·er -era -erum *adj* dark; (fig) uncertain, doubtful

crepid·a -ae *f* slipper, sandal

crepidāt·us -a -um *adj* sandal-wearing

crepīd·ō -inis *f* base, pedestal; quay, pier; dam, dike, causeway

crepidul·a -ae *f* small sandal

crepit·ō -āre *vi* to make noise, rattle, crackle, creak, chatter, rumble, rustle

crepit·us -ūs *m* noise, rattle, creak, chatter, rumble, rustle

crep·ō -āre -ūī -itum *vt* to make rattle; to talk noisily about, chatter about; *vi* to make noise, rattle, crackle, creak, chatter, rumble, rustle

crepundī·a -ōrum *n pl* rattle; toys

crepuscul·um -ī *n* dusk, twilight; dimness, obscurity; *n pl* darkness

crescō crescēre crēvī crētum *vi* to come into being, arise; to grow, grow up; to increase, swell; to prosper, thrive; to become great, attain honor

crēt·a -ae *f* chalk; white clay; cosmetic

Crēt·a -ae *f* Crete

crētāt·us -a -um *adj* chalked; dressed in white (*as candidate for office*)

crētē·us -a -um *adj* of chalk, of clay

crēti·ō -ōnis *f* (law) formal acceptance of an inheritance

crētōs·us -a -um *adj* abounding in chalk or clay

crētul·a -ae *f* white clay (*used for seals*)

crētus *pp* of **cerno**; *pp* of **cresco**

Creūs·a -ae *f* daughter of Priam and wife of Aeneas; daughter of Creon, king of Corinth and wife of Jason

cribr·um -ī *n* sieve; **imbrem in cribrum gerere** to carry coals to Newcastle

crim·en -inis *n* charge, accusation; reproach; guilt, crime; **esse in crimine** to be accused

crīmināti·ō -ōnis *f* accusation; slander, false charge

crīmināt·or -ōris *m* accuser

crīmin·ō -āre or **crīmin·or -ārī -ātus sum** *vt* to accuse; to slander; to complain of, denounce

crīminōsē *adv* by way of accusation, accusingly, reproachfully

crīminōs·us -a -um *adj* accusing, reproachful, slanderous

crīnāl·is -e *adj* for the hair; *n* hairpin

crīn·is -is *m* hair; (fig) tail of a comet

crīnīt·us -a -um *adj* long-haired; **stella crinita** comet

crīs·ō -āre *vi* (of women) to wiggle the buttocks

crisp·ans -antis *adj* curled, wrinkled

crisp·ō -āre *vt* to curl, wave (*hair*); to swing, brandish (*a weapon*)

crisp·us -a -um *adj* curled, waved (*hair*); curly-headed; curled, wrinkled; tremulous, quivering

crist·a -ae *f* cock's comb; crest, plume

cristāt·us -a -um *adj* crested, plumed

critic·us -ī *m* critic

crocē·us -a -um *adj* of saffron; saffron-colored, yellow, golden

crocīn·um -ī *n* saffron

crōc·iō -īre *vi* to croak

crocodīl·us -ī *m* crocodile

crocōtāri·us -a -um *adj* of saffron-colored clothes

crocōtŭl·a -ae *f* saffron-colored dress

croc·us -ī *m* or croc·um -ī *n* crocus; saffron; saffron color

Croes·us -ī *m* king of Lydia, famous for his wealth (590?-546 B.C.)

crotalistri·a -ae *f* castanet dancer

crotăl·um -ī *n* castanet

cruciābilitāt·ēs -um *f pl* torments

cruciābiliter *adv* with torture

cruciāment·um -ī *n* torture

cruciāt·us -ūs *m* torture; mental torment; instrument of torture; (humorously) calamity

cruci·ō -āre *vt* to put to wrack, torture, torment; (fig) to grieve, torment

crūdēl·is -e *adj* cruel, hardhearted; (with in + *acc*) cruel toward

crūdēlit·ās -ātis *f* cruelty

crūdēliter *adv* cruelly

crūd·escō -escĕre -ŭī *vi* to grow violent, grow worse

crūdit·ās -ātis *f* indigestion

crūd·us -a -um *adj* bloody, bleeding; uncooked, raw; unripe, green; undressed (*hide*); undigested; suffering from indigestion; hoarse; fresh, vigorous (*old age*); cruel, merciless

cruent·ō -āre *vt* to bloody, stain with blood; (fig) to wound

cruent·us -a -um *adj* gory, bloodstained; bloodthirsty, cruel; blood-red

crumēn·a or crumīn·a -ae *f* purse, pouch; (fig) money

crumill·a -ae *f* purse

cru·or -ōris *n* gore, blood; *m pl* bloodshed, murder

cruppellāri·ī -ōrum *m pl* mail-clad combatants

crūrifrag·ius -iī or -ī *m* slave with broken shins

crūs crūris *n* leg, shin

crust·a -ae *f* crust, shell, rind, bark; inlaid work, mosaic; stucco

crustŭl·um -ī *n* cooky

crust·um -ī *n* pastry

crux crucis *f* cross, gallows; trouble, misery; gallows bird; tormentor; i in malam crucem (coll) go hang yourself

crypt·a -ae *f* underground passage, covered gallery

cryptoportic·us -ūs *f* covered walk

crystallīn·us -a -um *adj* made of crystal; *n pl* crystal vases

crystall·us -ī *f* or crystall·um -ī *n* crystal

cubiculār·is -e *adj* bedroom

cubiculāri·us -a -um *adj* bedroom; *m* chamberlain

cubicŭl·um -ī *n* bedroom; emperor's box in the theater

cubīl·e -is *n* bed, couch; marriage bed; lair, nest, hole; kennel; avaritiae cubilia (fig) den of greediness

cubit·al -ālis *n* elbow cushion

cubitāl·is -e *adj* of the elbow; one cubit long

cubit·ō -āre *vi* to be in the habit of lying down; (with cum + *abl*) to go to bed with, have intercourse with

cubĭt·um -ī *n* elbow; cubit

cubĭt·us -ūs *m* lying down; intercourse

cub·ō -āre -ŭī or -āvī -ĭtum *vi* to lie, lie down; to recline at table; to lie in bed; to lie sick; (of roof) to slope; (of towns, etc.) to lie on a slope

cucull·us -ī *m* cowl, hood

cucŭl·us -ī *m* cuckoo; lazy farmer

cucŭm·is -ĕris *m* cucumber

cucurbĭt·a -ae *f* gourd; (med) cupping glass

cūd·ō -ĕre *vt* to strike, beat, pound; thresh; to forge; to coin, stamp

cuicuimŏdī or quoiquoimŏdī *adj* any kind of

cuj·ās -ātis *pron* from what country

culcĭt·a -ae *f* mattress, feather tick; cushion, pillow

culcitell·a -ae *f* little cushion

cūlĕus see culleus

cul·ex -ĭcis *m* or *f* gnat

culīn·a -ae *f* kitchen; cuisine

cullĕ·us or cūlĕ·us -ī *m* leather bag (*for holding liquids*); scrotum

culm·en -ĭnis *n* stalk; top, summit; roof; (fig) height, pinnacle, zenith

culm·us -ī *m* stalk, stem; straw, thatch

culp·a -ae *f* fault, blame; immorality; in culpa esse or in culpa versari to be at fault

culpĭt·ō -āre *vt* to blame, find fault with

culp·ō -āre *vt* to blame, reproach, censure, find fault with, complain of

cult·a -ōrum *n pl* plantation; grain fields

cultē *adv* elegantly, sophisticatedly, with refinement

cultell·us -ī *m* small knife

cult·er -rī *m* knife; razor; plowshare

cultī·ō -ōnis *f* cultivation; tilling of the ground, agriculture

cult·or -ōris *m* tiller, planter, cultivator, farmer; inhabitant; supporter; worshiper

cultr·ix -īcis *f* cultivator (*female*); inhabitant (*female*); (fig) nurse

cultūr·a -ae *f* tilling, cultivating; agriculture; care, cultivation (*of the mind*); (with *genit*) playing up to (*e.g., influential friends*)

cult·us -a -um *pp* of colo; *adj* tilled, cultivated; neat, well dressed, prim; cultivated, refined, civilized (*person*); cultured, refined (*mind*)

cult·us -ūs *m* tilling, cultivation (*of land*); care, tending, keeping (*of flocks, etc.*); care (*of body*); training, education; culture, refinement, civilization; high style of living; luxury;

style of dress, fancy clothes; fancy outfit; worship, reverence, veneration

culull·us -ī *m* drinking cup

cūl·us -ī *m* buttock

cum *prep* (with *abl*) (accompaniment) with, together with, in company with; (time) at the same time with, at the time of, at, with; (circumstance, manner, etc.) with, under, in, in the midst of, among, in connection with; **cum eo quod** or **cum eo ut** on condition that; **cum pace** peacefully; **cum prima luce** at dawn; **cum primis** especially, particularly; **mecum** at my house

cum, quum, or **quom** *conj* when, at the time when; whenever; when, while, as; since, now that, because; although; **cum maxime** just when; especially when, just while; just then, just now; **cum primum** as soon as; **cum ... tum** both ... and, not only ... but also, while ... so too; **praesertim cum** or **cum praesertim** especially since, especially as; **quippe cum** since of course; **utpote cum** seeing that

Cūm·ae -ārum *f pl* town on coast of Campania and oldest Greek colony in Italy, famous as the residence of its Sibyl

Cūmān·us -a -um *adj* Cumaean; *n* Cicero's estate near Cumae

cumb·a or **cymb·a** -ae *f* boat, skiff

cumēr·a -ae *f* bin

cumīn·um -ī *n* cumin (*medicinal plant, said to produce paleness*)

cumque, cunque, or **quomque** *adv* at any time

cumulātē *adv* fully, completely, abundantly, copiously

cumulāt·us -a -um *adj* increased, augmented; filled, full, perfect, complete

cumul·ō -āre *vt* to heap up, pile up; to amass, accumulate; to overload; to make complete, make perfect, crown

cumul·us -ī *m* heap, pile; increase, addition

cūnābul·a -ōrum *n pl* cradle

cūn·ae -ārum *f pl* cradle; nest

cunctābund·us -a -um *adj* hesitant, loitering, delaying

cunct·ans -antis *adj* hesitant, reluctant, dilatory

cunctanter *adv* hesitantly, slowly

cunctāti·ō -ōnis *f* hesitation, reluctance, delay

cunctāt·or -ōris *m* dawdler, slowpoke

cunct·or -ārī -ātus sum *vi* to hesitate, delay, linger, be in doubt; **cunctatus brevi** after a moment's hesitation

cunct·us -a -um *adj* all together, the whole, all, entire

cuneātim *adv* in the form of a wedge

cuneāt·us -a -um *adj* wedge-shaped

cunē·ō -āre *vt* to fasten with a wedge; (fig) to wedge in, squeeze in

cunĕ·us -ī *m* wedge; wedge-form sections of seats in the theater; (mil) troops formed up in the shape of a wedge

cunīcul·us -ī *m* rabbit; burrowing underground; (mil) mine

cunque see **cumque**

cūp·a -ae *f* vat

cuped· = **cupped-**

cupīdē *adv* eagerly

cupīdit·ās -ātis *f* eagerness, enthusiasm, desire; passion, lust; ambition; greed, avarice; partisanship

cupīd·ō -īnis *m* eagerness, desire, longing; passion, lust; greed, avarice

Cupīd·ō -īnis *m* Cupid (*son of Venus*)

Cupīdinĕ·us -a -um *adj* Cupid's

cupīd·us -a -um *adj* eager, enthusiastic, desirous, longing; ambitious; (with *genit*) desirous of, longing for, fond of, attached to

cupi·ens -entis *adj* eager, enthusiastic; (with *genit*) desirous of, longing for, fond of, enthusiastic about

cupienter *adv* eagerly, enthusiastically

cup·iō -ĕre -īvī or iī -ītum *vt* to wish, be eager for, long for, desire

cupīt·or -ōris *m* daydreamer

cuppēdi·a -ōrum *n pl* or **cupēdi·a** -ae *f* delicacies; sweet tooth

cuppēdinār·ius or **cupēdinār·ius** -iī or -ī *m* confectioner

cuppēd·ō -īnis *f* desire, longing

cupp·ēs -ēdis *adj* fond of delicacies

cupress·ēt·um -ī *n* cypress grove

cupress·e·us -a -um *adj* cypress

cupressif·er -ēra -ērum *adj* cypress-bearing

cupress·us -ī or -ūs *f* cypress tree; box of cypress

cūr or **quor** *adv* why

cūr·a -ae *f* care, concern, worry; care, pains, attention; heartache; object of concern; sweetheart; administration, management, charge; trusteeship, guardianship; means of healing, cure, treatment; guardian, keeper; study, reflection; literary effort, literary work; **curae esse** (with *dat*) to be of concern to

cūrābil·is -e *adj* troublesome

cūral·ium -iī or -ī *n* coral

cūrāti·ō -ōnis *f* management, administration; office; treatment, cure

cūrātius *adv* more carefully

cūrāt·or -ōris *m* superintendent, manager; (law) guardian, keeper

cūrātūr·a -ae *f* care, attention; dieting

cūrāt·us -a -um *adj* cared-for, attended-to; anxious, earnest

curcul·iō -ōnis *m* weevil

curculiuncul·us -ī *m* little weevil; (fig) trifle

Cur·ēs -ium *m pl* ancient Sabine town

Cūrēt·ēs -um *m pl* mythical people of Crete who attended Jupiter at his birth

cūrĭ·a -ae *f* curia, ward (*one of the thirty parts into which Romulus divided the Roman people*); meeting place of a curia; senate building

cūrĭāl·is -is *m* member of a curia or ward

cūrĭātim *adv* by curiae, by wards

cūrĭāt·us -a -um *adj* composed of curiae or wards; passed by the assembly of curiae; **comitia curiata** assembly of the curiae

cūrĭ·ō -ōnis *m* ward boss; **curio maximus** chief ward boss

cūrĭ·ō -ōnis *adj* lean, emaciated

cūrĭōsē *adv* carefully; curiously; (of style) affectedly

cūrĭōsĭt·ās -ātis *f* curiosity

cūrĭōs·us -a -um *adj* careful, diligent; curious, prying, inquisitive; careworn

cur·is or **quir·is -ĭtis** *f* spear

cūr·ō -āre *vt* to take care of, look after, attend to, trouble oneself about; to take charge of, see to; to provide for the payment of, settle up; to attend to (*the body with food, washing, etc.*); to cure; to worry about; **cura ut** see to it that; (*at the end of a letter*) **cura ut valeas** take care of yourself

curricŭlō *adv* at full speed, quickly

curricŭl·um -ī *n* race; lap (*of race*); racetrack; racing chariot; (fig) career

currō currĕre cucurrī cursum *vt* to run over, skim over, traverse; *vi* to run, dash, hurry; to sail; to move quickly, flow along; to fly; (of a speech) to move along; (of night, day) to pass away

curr·us -ūs *m* chariot, car; war chariot; triumphal car; triumph; racing chariot; plow wheel; ship

cursim *adv* on the double

cursĭt·ō -āre *vi* to keep running around, run up and down; to vibrate

curs·ō -āre *vi* to run around, run up and down

curs·or -ōris *m* runner, racer; courier; errand boy

cursūr·a -ae *f* running; haste, speed

curs·us -ūs *m* running, speeding, speed; trip; course, direction; suitable time or weather for travel; rapid movement, speed, flow; flow, progress; **magno cursu** at top speed; **cursus honorum** political career

curt·ō -āre *vt* to shorten; to circumcise

curt·us -a -um *adj* shortened; gelded, castrated; circumcised; broken; defective

curūl·is -e *adj* official, curule; **aedilis curulis** patrician aedile; **sella curulis** curule chair, official chair (*used by consuls, praetors, and patrician aediles*)

curvām·en -ĭnis *n* curve, bend

curvātūr·a -ae *f* curvature; **curvatura rotae** rim of a wheel

curv·ō -āre *vt* to curve, bend, arch; (fig) to affect, move, stir

curv·us -a -um *adj* curved, bent; crooked; concave, arched, hollow; winding (*stream, shore*); (fig) crooked; *n* wrong, crookedness

cusp·is -ĭdis *f* point, pointed end; bayonet; spearhead; spear, javelin; trident; scepter; sting (*of scorpion*)

custōdĕl·a -ae *f* watch, guard, care

custōdĭ·a -ae *f* watch, guard, care; sentry, guard; sentry post; custody, prison; **custodiam agitare** to keep guard, be on guard; **in libera custodia** under surveillance, under house arrest

custōd·iō -īre -īvī or **-ĭī -ītum** *vt* to guard, watch over, protect, defend; to hold in custody; to keep an eye on; to keep carefully, preserve; **memoriā custodire** to keep in mind, remember well

cust·ōs -ōdis *m* guard, guardian, watchman; protector, bodyguard; jailer, warden; (mil) sentinel; spy; *m pl* garrison; *f* guardian; protectress; box, container

cutĭcŭl·a -ae *f* skin, cuticle

cut·is -is *f* skin; **cutem curare** (fig) to look after one's own skin

Cyăn·ē -ēs *f* nymph who was changed into a fountain

cyathiss·ō -āre *vi* to serve wine

cyăth·us -ī *m* ladle; liquid measure (*one-twelfth of a sextarius, i.e., a half pint*)

cybae·a -ae *f* merchant ship

Cybĕl·e or **Cybēl·ē -ēs** *f* originally a Phrygian goddess of fertility, later worshiped in Rome as Ops or Mater Magna

Cyclăd·es -um *f pl* Cyclades (*group of islands in Aegean Sea*)

cycl·as -ădis *f* woman's formal gown

cyclĭc·us -a -um *adj* cyclic; **poeta cyclicus** cyclic poet (*one of a group of poets treating the epic sagas revolving around the Trojan War*)

Cycl·ops -ōpis *m* mythical one-eyed giant of Sicily, esp. Polyphemus

cycnē·us -a -um *adj* swan's

cycn·us or **cygn·us -ī** *m* swan; (fig) poet

Cycn·us or **Cygn·us -ī** *m* king of the Ligurians, son of Sthenelus, changed into a swan, and placed among the stars; son of Neptune, changed into a swan

Cydōnĭ·us -a -um *adj* Cretan; *n* quince

cygnus see **cyonus**

cylindr·us -ī *m* cylinder; roller (*for rolling ground*)

Cyllēn·ē -ēs or **-ae** *f* mountain in Arcadia where Mercury was born

Cyllēnĭ·us -a -um *adj* of Mt. Cyllene; *m* Mercury

cymb·a -ae *f* boat, skiff

cymbăl·um -ī *n* cymbal

cymb·ĭum -ĭī or **-ī** *n* small cup

Cynĭcē *adv* like the Cynics

Cynĭc·us -a -um *adj* Cynic, relating to the Cynic philosophy; *m* Cynic philosopher, esp. Diogenes, its founder (412-323 B.C.)

cynocephăl·us -ī *m* dog-headed ape

Cynosūr·a -ae *f* Cynosure (*the northern constellation Ursa Minor*)

Cynthĭ·us -a -um *adj* of Mt. Cynthus; Cynthian; *m* Apollo; *f* Diana

Cynth·us -ī *m* mountain of Delos, famous as the birthplace of Apollo and Diana

cypariss·us -ī *f* cypress tree

Cyprĭ·us -a -um *adj* Cypriote; *f* Venus

Cypr·us or **Cypr·os -ī** *f* Cyprus (*island off the coast of Asia Minor*)

Cypsĕl·us -ī *m* despot of Corinth (655-625 B.C.)

Cyrēn·ē -ēs *f* or **Cyrēn·ae -ārum** *f pl* chief city of Greek settlement in N.E. Africa

Cyr·us -ī *m* founder of the Persian monarchy in 559 B.C. (*d.* 529 B.C.); Cyrus the Younger (*under whom Xenophon served, d.* 401 B.C.)

Cyt·ae -ārum *f pl* town in Colchis, birthplace of Medea

Cytae·is -ĭdis *f* Medea

Cythēr·a -ōrum *n pl* island off the S. coast of the Peloponnesus, famous for worship of Venus

Cytherē·is -ĭdis *f* Venus

Cytherēĭ·us -a -um *adj* Cytherean; **heros Cythereius** Aeneas; *f* Venus

Cytherē·us -a -um *adj* Cytherean; *f* Venus

cytĭs·us -ī *m* or *f* clover

Cytōrĭăc·us -a -um *adj* of Cytorus, Cytorian; **pecten Cytoriacus** comb made of boxwood

Cytōr·us or **Cytōr·os -ī** *m* mountain of Paphlagonia, famous for its boxwood

Cyzĭc·um -ī *n* or **Cyzĭc·us** or **Cyzĭc·os -ī** *f* town on Sea of Marmora

D

Dāc·ī -ōrum *m pl* Dacians (*people of the lower Danube*)

dactylĭc·us -a -um *adj* dactylic

dactȳl·us -ī *m* dactyl

daedăl·us -a -um *adj* skillful, artistic, artfully constructed

Daedăl·us -ī *m* mythical builder of the labyrinth in Crete and the first to build wings and fly

Damascēn·us -a -um *adj* of Damascus

Damasc·us -ī *f* Damascus (*capital of Coele-Syria*)

damm·a or **dām·a -ae** *f* deer; venison

damnātĭ·ō -ōnis *f* condemnation

damnātŏrĭ·us -a -um *adj* guilty (*verdict*)

damnāt·us -a -um *adj* criminal; hateful

damnĭfĭc·us -a -um *adj* harmful, injurious, pernicious

damnĭgerŭl·us -a -um *adj* harmful, injurious

damn·ō -āre *vt* to find guilty, sentence, condemn; to disapprove of, reject, blame; to consecrate, offer as a sacrifice, doom to the gods below; (with *genit* or *abl* of charge or punishment) to find (*someone*) guilty of; **capite** or **capitis damnare** to condemn to death; **de majestate damnare** to find guilty of treason; **voti damnare** to oblige (*someone*) to fulfill a vow

damnōsē *adv* destructively, so as to bring ruin

damnōs·us -a -um *adj* damaging, injurious, destructive, pernicious; prodigal; **canes damnosi** crap (*worst throw of the dice*); *m* spendthrift

damn·um -ī *n* loss, damage, harm, injury; misfortune; fine, penalty; fault; defect

Dană·ē -ēs *f* daughter of Acrisius and mother of Perseus

Danaĭd·ēs -um *f pl* daughters of Danaus who killed their husbands on their wedding night, with the exception of Hypermnestra, and as punishment were made to carry water in the lower world

Dană·us -ī *m* king of Argos and father of fifty daughters; *m pl* Greeks

danist·a -ae *m* money lender, banker

danistĭc·us -a -um *adj* money-lending, banking, of bankers

danō see **dō**

Dānuv·ĭus -ĭī or **-ī** *m* Danube

Daphn·ē -ēs *f* nymph pursued by Apollo and changed into a laurel tree

Daphn·is -ĭdis *m* handsome young Sicilian shepherd, the inventor of pastoral song

dapĭn·ō -āre *vt* to serve (*food*)

dap·s -is *f* ceremonial feast; sumptuous meal, banquet; simple food, poor meal

dapsĭl·is -e *adj* sumptuous, costly

Dardăn·us -a -um *adj* Dardanian, Trojan; Roman (*descendant of Aeneas*); *m* son of Jupiter and Electra and ancestor of the Trojan race; *m pl* people of Upper Moesia (*on Danube*)

Darē·us -ī *m* Darius (*king of Persia,* 521-485 B.C.); Darius Ochus or

Nothus (*king of Persia,* 424-405 B.C.); Darius Codomanus (*last king of Persia,* 336-331 B.C.)

datāri·us -a -um *adj* to be handed out, to give away

datātim *adv* giving in turn, passing from one to another

datī·ō -ōnis *f* giving, alloting; (law) right of alienation

datīv·us -a -um *adj & m* dative

dat·ō -āre *vt* to keep giving away, be in the habit of giving

dat·or -ōris *m* giver

dat·us -ūs *m* giving

Daul·is -ĭdis *f* town in Phocis, famous for the fable of Procne and Philomela

Daun·us -ī *m* king of Apulia and ancestor of Turnus, the opponent of Aeneas

dē *prep* (with *abl*) (of space) down from, from, away from, out of; (of origin) from, of, descended from, derived from; (of separation) from among, out of; (of time) immediately after; about, concerning, of, in respect to; for, on account of, because of; according to, in imitation of; de improviso unexpectedly; de industria on purpose; de integro afresh, all over again; de novo anew

de·a -ae *f* goddess

dealb·ō -āre *vt* to whiten, whitewash, plaster

deambulātī·ō -ōnis *f* strolling, walking about, stroll, walk

deambŭl·ō -āre *vi* to go for a walk, take a stroll

deăm·ō -āre *vt* to be in love with; to be much obliged to

dearm·ō -āre *vt* to disarm

deartŭ·ō -āre *vt* to tear limb from limb, dismember; (fig) to waste, wreck

deascĭ·ō -āre *vt* to smooth with an ax; (coll) to cheat, con

dēbacch·or -ārī -ātus sum *vi* to rant and rave

dēbellāt·or -ōris *m* conqueror

dēbell·ō -āre *vt* to fight it out with, wear down, subdue; *vi* to fight it out to the end; to bring a war to an end

dēb·ĕō -ēre -ŭī -ĭtum *vt* to owe; to be responsible for; (with *inf*) a to have to, be bound to, be obliged to; b to be destined to, be fated to; (with *dat*) to owe (*e.g., a favor*) to, be indebted to (*someone*) for; dēbeērī (with *dat*) to be due to

dēbil·is -e *adj* lame, crippled, frail, feeble, paralyzed

dēbilit·ās -ātis *f* lameness, debility, weakness, helplessness

dēbilitātĭ·ō -ōnis *f* disabling, paralyzing

dēbilit·ō -āre *vt* to lame; to disable, debilitate, weaken; to unnerve; to paralyze

dēbitĭ·ō -ōnis *f* debt

dēbĭt·or -ōris *m* debtor; person under obligation

dēbĭt·um -ī *n* debt; obligation

dēblatĕr·ō -āre *vt* to blurt out

dēcant·ō -āre *vt* to repeat monotonously; *vi* to sing on to the end; to stop singing

dē·cēdō -cēdĕre -cessī -cessum *vi* to withdraw, clear out, depart; to retire, retreat, fall back, abandon a position; to give place, make way, make room, yield; to depart, disappear, die; to abate, subside, cease; to go wrong, go awry; (with *dat*) to yield to, give in to; (with de + *abl*) to give up, relinquish, abandon

decem (indecl) *adj* ten; (fig) large number of

Decemb·er -ris *adj & m* December

decemjŭg·is -is *m* ten-horse chariot

decempĕd·a -ae *f* ten-foot measuring rod, ten-foot rule

decempedāt·or -ōris *m* surveyor

decempl·ex -ĭcis *adj* tenfold

decemprīm·ī or decem prīm·ī -ōrum *m pl* board of ten (*governing Italian towns*)

decemscalm·us -a -um *adj* ten-oared

decemvirāl·is -e *adj* decemviral; leges decemvirales laws passed by the decemviri

decemvirāt·us -ūs *m* decemvirate

decemvir·ī -ōrum *m pl* decemviri, ten-man commission (*appointed in Rome at different times and for various purposes*); decemviri legibus scribundis commission to codify the laws (451 B.C.); decemviri sacris faciundis commission for attending to religious matters

decenn·is -e *adj* ten-year, lasting ten years

dec·ens -entis *adj* proper, becoming; handsome, pretty; decent, proper

decenter *adv* becomingly, decently, properly, with propriety

decentĭ·a -ae *f* propriety, decency

dē·cernō -cernĕre -crēvī -crētum *vt* to sift, separate; to decide, settle, determine, decree, resolve, vote; to decide by combat, fight out; to fight, combat; *vi* to contend, compete, struggle; to put forward a proposal; (with de or pro + *abl*) to fight over, fight for (*in court*)

dēcerp·ō -ĕre -sī -tum *vt* to pluck off, tear away, break off, gather, crop; to derive, enjoy (*e.g., benefits, satisfaction*); aliquid de gravitate decerpere to detract somewhat from the dignity

dēcertātĭ·ō -ōnis *f* decision, decisive struggle

dēcert·ō -āre *vi* to fight it out, decide the issue

dēcessĭ·ō -ōnis *f* withdrawing; retirement, departure (*from a province*); decrease; disappearance

dēcess·or -ōris *m* retiring official, predecessor in office

dēcess·us -ūs *m* withdrawal; retirement (*of official from a province*); decease, death

dec·et -ēre -ŭit (used only in 3d sing & pl) vt to befit, be becoming to; (with inf) it is fitting to (someone) to, it is proper for (someone) to; vi to be fitting, be proper; (with dat & inf) it is fitting to (someone) to, it is proper for (someone) to

dēcid·ō -ēre -ī vi to fall down; to fall dead, die; to fall, drop, sink, fail, perish

dē-cīdō -cīdĕre -cīsī -cīsum vt to cut off, cut away; to cut short, terminate, put an end to, decide, settle; **pennas decidere** (fig) to clip (someone's) wings

deciens or **deciēs** adv ten times; **deciens centena milia** or **deciens** million

decimānus see **decumanus**

decim·us or **decŭm·us -a -um** adj the tenth; **cum decimo** tenfold; **cum decimo effecit ager** the field produced a tenfold return; **decimum** for the tenth time

dē-cipiō -cipĕre -cēpī -ceptum vt to deceive, cheat; to snare, mislead, beguile; to escape the notice of; **aliquem laborum decipere** to make one forget his troubles; **laborum decipi** to be freed of troubles, forget one's troubles

dēcisi·ō -ōnis f decision, settlement

decīsum pp of **dēcīdō**

Dec·ius -iī or **-ī** m P. Decius Mus (Roman hero who voluntarily gave his life in battle during the Latin War in 340 B.C. to bring victory to the Roman army; his son who likewise gave his life in Samnite War in 295 B.C.)

dēclāmāti·ō -ōnis f practice in public speaking; theme or subject matter in rhetorical exercise; loud talking, shouting, hubbub

dēclāmāt·or -ōris m elocutionist, declaimer; ranter

dēclāmātōri·us -a -um adj rhetorical

dēclāmit·ō -āre vt to plead (cases); vi to practice public speaking; to bluster

dēclām·ō -āre vt to recite; vi to practice public speaking

dēclārāti·ō -ōnis f disclosure, declaration

dēclār·ō -āre vt to make clear, make evident, disclose; to proclaim, announce officially; to show, prove, demonstrate; to mean, express, signify; to declare (as chosen for office)

dēclināti·ō -ōnis f leaning away, bending aside, swerving; shunning, avoiding; digression; (gram) declension

dēclīn·ō -āre vt to deflect; to parry, avoid; to decline, conjugate; vi to deviate; to digress

dēcliv·e -is n declivity, slope

dēcliv·is -e adj sloping, steep, downhill

dēclivit·ās -ātis f sloping terrain

dēcoct·a -ae f cold drink

dēcoct·or -ōris m bankrupt; (coll) old rake

dēcoct·us -a -um pp of **decoquo**; adj boiled down; mellow (style)

dēcoll·ō -āre vt to behead

dēcŏl·ō -āre vi to trickle away, come to naught, fail

dēcŏl·or -ōris adj off-color, faded; dark, tanned; degenerate

dēcolōrāti·ō -ōnis f discoloring

dēcolōr·ō -āre vt to discolor, stain, deface

dē-cŏquō -cŏquĕre -coxī -coctum vt to boil down, boil thoroughly; to bring to ruin; vi to go bankrupt

dec·or -ōris m beauty, grace, elegance, charm; ornament

decōrē adv beautifully, gracefully; suitably, properly

decŏr·ō -āre vt to beautify, adorn, embellish; to decorate, honor

decŏr·us -a -um adj beautiful, graceful, adorned; decorous, proper, suitable; fine, handsome; noble; n grace, propriety

dēcrepit·us -a -um adj decrepit, broken down, worn out

dē-crescō -crescĕre -crēvī -crētum vi to grow less, become fewer, diminish, subside, wane

dēcrēt·us -a -um pp of **decerno**; n decision, decree; principle, doctrine

decŭm·a or **decĭm·a -ae** f tenth part, tithe, land tax; largess to the people

decumān·us or **decimān·us -a -um** adj paying tithes; of the tenth cohort, of the tenth legion; m tax collector; m pl men of the tenth legion; f tax collector's wife; **porta decumana** main gate of a Roman camp on the side turned away from the enemy

decumāt·ēs -ium adj subject to tithes

dē-cumbō -cumbĕre -cubŭī vi to lie down; to recline at table; to fall (in battle)

decŭm·ō or **decĭm·ō -āre** vt to decimate

decŭri·a -ae f decuria, group of ten; tenth part (of a curia); division, class (without reference to number); panel (of judges); social club

decuriāti·ō -ōnis f dividing into decuries

decuriāt·us -ūs m dividing into decuries

decŭri·ō -āre vt (pol) to divide into groups of ten; (fig) to divide into groups

decuri·ō -ōnis m decurion (head of a decuria); (mil) cavalry officer (in charge of ten men); senator of a municipality or colony

dē-currō -currĕre -cucurrī or **-currī -cursum** vt to pass over, run over, traverse; to pass through (life); to get over (troubles); to discuss, treat; vi to run down; (mil) to parade, maneuver; (of river, ship) to run down to the sea; to run for help; to sail; to land; **eo decursum est ut** it got to the point where

dēcursi·ō -ōnis *f* (mil) dress parade; maneuvers; raid, descent

dēcurs·us -ūs *m* running down; downward course; (mil) dress parade; (mil) maneuvers; (mil) raid; end of course, completion; **decursus honorum** completion of political career

dēcurtāt·us -a -um *adj* cut down, cut off short, mutilated; clipped (*style*)

dec·us -ŏris *n* beauty, glory, honor, dignity; virtue, worth; source of glory; *n pl* great deeds, distinctions

dēcuss·ō -āre *vt* to divide crosswise (*in the form of an* X)

dē·cutiō -cutĕre -cussī -cussum *vt* to shake off, beat off, strike down; to chop off (*head*); to break down (*wall with battering ram*)

dē·decet -decēre -decŭit (used only in 3d *sing & pl*) *vt* it ill becomes, ill befits; (with *inf*) it is a disgrace to

dēdecŏr·ō -āre *vt* to disgrace, dishonor, bring shame to; to make a sham of

dēdecŏr·us -a -um *adj* disgraceful, dishonorable, unbecoming

dēdec·us -ŏris *n* disgrace, dishonor, shame; vice, crime, outrage; (mil) disgraceful defeat; **dedecori esse** (with *dat*) to be a source of disgrace to; **dedecus admittere** to incur disgrace; **per dedecus** disgracefully

dēdicāti·ō -ōnis *f* dedication, consecration

dēdic·ō -āre *vt* to dedicate, consecrate, set aside; to declare (*property in a census return*)

dēdign·or -ārī -ātus sum *vt* to scorn, disdain, look down on; (with double *acc*)▸to scorn (*someone*) as; **aliquem maritum dedignari** to regard someone as an unworthy husband

dē·discō -discĕre -didicī *vt* to forget

dēditīc·ĭus -iī or **-ī** *m* captive; *m pl* prisoners of war

dēditi·ō -ōnis *f* surrender, capitulation

dēdĭt·us -a -um *pp* of **dedo**; *adj* (with *dat*) given to, devoted to, addicted to; (with **in** + *abl*) absorbed in; *m pl* prisoners of war, captives

dē·dō -dĕre -dĭdī -dĭtum *vt* to give up, surrender; to devote; to apply; to abandon; **aliquem hostibus in cruciatum dedere** to hand someone over to the enemy to be tortured; **deditā operā** on purpose, intentionally; **neci** or **ad necem dedere** to put to death

dēdoc·ĕō -ēre -uī -tum *vt* to cause to forget; (with *inf*) to teach (*someone*) not to

dēdol·ĕō -ēre -uī *vi* to grieve no more

dēdŏl·ō -āre *vt* to chop away; to chop smooth

dē·dūcō -dūcĕre -duxī -ductum *vt* to lead or draw down; to launch (*ship*); to accompany, escort; to lead out (*colonists to new colony*); to conduct (*bride to her husband*), give away (*bride*); to evict; to subtract, deduct, diminish; to summon (*as witness*); to divert, mislead; to derive (*name*); to compose (*poetry*); to dissuade; to spin out (*thread*); to comb out (*hair*)

dēducti·ō -ōnis *f* leading or drawing off; settling (*of colonists*); (law) eviction; reduction; inference; **rationis deductio** train of reasoning

dēduct·us -a -um *pp* of **deduco**; *adj* drawn down; bent inwards, concave; lowered, modest; subtle, well wrought (*poem*)

deerr·ō -āre *vi* to go astray, wander away; **a vero deerrare** (fig) to stray from the truth

dēfaec·ō -āre *vt* to cleanse of dregs; to wash; (fig) to clear up, make clear

dēfatigāti·ō -ōnis *f* exhaustion

dēfatīg·ō -āre *vt* to wear out, exhaust

dēfatiscor see **defetiscor**

dēfecti·ō -ōnis *f* failure; defection, desertion; weakening, exhaustion; eclipse; **defectio animi** mental breakdown; **in defectione esse** to be up in revolt

dēfect·or -ōris *m* defector, deserter; rebel

dēfect·us -a -um *pp* of **deficio**; *adj* weak, worn out

dēfect·us -ūs *m* failing, failure; desertion; revolt; eclipse

dē·fendō -fendĕre -fendī -fensum *vt* to repel, beat off, avert; to defend, protect, guard; to keep off (*the cold*); to answer (*a charge*); to champion (*a cause*); to support, uphold, maintain (*an argument*); to play the part of (*a character*); (law) to defend

dēfensi·ō -ōnis *f* defense

dēfensit·ō -āre *vt* to defend often; **causas defensitare** to be a lawyer

dēfens·ō -āre *vt* to defend, protect

dēfens·or -ōris *m* defender, protector; (law) defense lawyer; (law) guardian; champion (*of people*); *m pl* garrison

dēfensus *pp* of **defendo**

dē·ferō -ferre -tŭlī -lātum *vt* to bring or carry down; to bear off, carry away; to throw (*ship*) off course; to offer, confer, grant; to inform against, indict; to give an account of, announce, report; to recommend; to register; **ad aerarium deferre** to recommend (*someone*) for a monetary reward (*because of outstanding service to the State*); **ad consilium deferre** to take into consideration

dē·fervescō -fervescĕre -fervī or **-ferbŭī** *vt & vi* to cool off, calm down; (of a speech) to lose momentum; (of passions) to die out

dēfess·us -a -um *adj* weary, worn out, exhausted

dē·fetīscor or **dē·fatīscor -fe-tīscī -fessus sum** *vi* to become weary, tired

dē·ficiō -ficĕre -fēcī -fectum *vt* to fail, disappoint; to desert, abandon; *vi* to fail, be a failure; to defect, desert; to secede; (of arms, food, etc.) to run short, run out; (of strength, morale, etc.) to fail, grow weak, droop, sink; (of sun, moon) to be eclipsed; (of fire) to die out; (com) to be bankrupt

dē·figō -figĕre -fixī -fixum *vt* to fix, fasten down; to drive down; to fix, concentrate (*eyes, attention*); to root to the spot, astound, stupefy; to bewitch, enchant; **in terra dēfigere** to stick, plant, set up (*something*) in the ground

dē·fingō -fingĕre -finxī *vt* to form, mold; to portray; to disfigure, deface

dēfin·iō -īre -īvī -ītum *vt* to set bounds to, limit; (fig) to limit, define, explain; to fix, determine, appoint; to delimit, bring to a finish, end; to assign, prescribe

dēfinītē *adv* precisely

dēfinīti·ō -ōnis *f* boundary; (fig) marking out, prescribing; definition

dēfinītīv·us -a -um *adj* explanatory

dēfinīt·us -a -um *adj* definite, precise

dē·fīō -fiĕrī *vi* to fail, be lacking

dēflagrāti·ō -ōnis *f* conflagration

dēflagr·ō -āre *vt* to burn down; *vi* to burn down, go up in flames; to perish, be destroyed; (of passions) to cool off, be allayed, subside

dē·flectō -flectĕre -flexī -flexum *vt* to deflect, bend aside, turn away, divert; (fig) to turn away, lead astray; *vi* to turn away, digress, deviate

defl·eō -ēre -ēvī -ētum *vt* to cry bitterly for; to mourn as lost; *vi* to cry bitterly

dēfloccāt·us -a -um *adj* stripped of wool, shorn; bald (*head*)

dēflōr·escō -escĕre -ūī *vi* to shed blossoms; (fig) to fade, droop

dēflu·ō -ĕre -xī *vi* to flow or float down; to glide down, slide, fall; to flow out, run dry; to vanish, pass away, disappear, cease; to go out of style, become obsolete

dē·fodiō -fodĕre -fōdī -fossum *vt* to dig down; to hollow out; to bury, hide, conceal

dēfōre = **dēfutūrum esse**

dēformāti·ō -ōnis *f* disfiguring, defacing

dēform·is -e *adj* shapeless, amorphous; misshapen, disfigured, ugly; degrading; degraded; unbecoming, humiliating

dēformit·ās -ātis *f* deformity, ugliness, hideousness; vileness, turpitude

dēformiter *adv* without grace, without beauty

dēform·ō -āre *vt* to form from a pattern; to sketch, delineate; to deform, disfigure, mar

dēfossus *pp* of **dēfodio**

dēfraud·ō or **dēfrūd·ō -āre** *vt* to defraud, rob; to cheat; **genium suum dēfraudāre** to deny oneself some pleasure

dēfrēnāt·us -a -um *adj* unbridled, uncontrolled

dēfric·ō -āre -ūī -ātum *vt* to rub down; to brush (*teeth*); (fig) to satirize

dē·fringō -fringĕre -frēgī -fractum *vt* to break off, break to pieces

dēfrūdō see **dēfraudo**

dēfrūt·um -ī *n* new wine

dē·fugiō -fugĕre -fūgī *vt* to run away from, avoid, shirk; to evade (*e.g., authority, law*); *vi* to run off, escape

dēfunct·us -a -um *pp* of **dēfungor**; *adj* finished; dead

dē·fundō -fundĕre -fūdī -fūsum *vt* to pour out; to empty (*e.g., bucket*)

dē·fungor -fungī -functus sum *vi* (with *abl*) to perform, finish, be done with; **b** to have done with, get rid of; **dēfunctus jam sum** I'm safe now; **defungī vītā** or **dēfungī** to die; **parvo victu dēfungī** to do with or be content with little food

dēfūsus *pp* of **dēfundo**

dēgĕn·er -ĕris *adj* degenerate; unworthy; ignoble

dēgenēr·ō -āre *vt* to disgrace, dishonor, fall short of; *vi* to be inferior to one's ancestors, be degenerate; (fig) to fall off, degenerate, decline

dēgĕr·ō -ĕre *vt* to carry off, carry away

dēg·ō -ĕre -ī *vt* to spend, pass (*time, life*); **aetātem degere** to live; *vi* to live

dēgrandīnat *v impers* it is hailing hard

dēgrăv·ō '-āre *vt* to weigh down; (fig) to burden, distress, inconvenience, overpower

dē·gredior -grĕdī -gressus sum *vi* to march down, go down, walk down, descend; **ad pedes degredi** to dismount

dēgrunn·iō -īre *vi* to grunt hard, grunt out loud

dēgust·ō -āre *vt* to taste; (fig) to taste, sample, try, experience; (of weapon) to graze

dehinc *adv* from here; from now on; then; next; hereafter

dehisc·ō -ĕre *vi* to part, divide, open, yawn

dehonestāment·um -ī *n* blemish, disfigurement, dishonor, disgrace

dehonest·ō -āre *vt* to dishonor, disgrace

dehort·or -ārī -ātus sum *vt* to advise to the contrary, dissuade

Dēianīr·a -ae *f* daughter of Oeneus and wife of Hercules

dein see **deinde**

deinceps *adv* one after another, in succession, in order; in regular order, without interruption

deinde or **dein** *adv* (of place) from that place, from there; (of time) then, thereafter, thereupon, afterwards; (in enumerating facts, presenting arguments) secondly, next in order, in the next place

Dēiotărus -ī *m* king of Galatia (*defended by Cicero before Caesar in the latter's house*)

Dēiphŏbus -ī *m* son of Priam and Hecuba, and husband of Helen after Paris' death

dējectiō -ōnis *f* (law) eviction

dēject·us -a -um *pp* of **dejicio**; *adj* low, depressed, sunken (*place*); discouraged, downhearted, despondent

dēject·us -ūs *m* felling (*of trees*); steep slope

dējĕr·ō or **dējūrō -āre** *vi* to swear solemnly

dē·jiciō -jicĕre -jēcī -jectum *vt* to throw down, fling down; to fell, bring low, kill; to depose (*from office*); to lower (*eyes*); to drive off course; (law) to evict; (mil) to dislodge, drive out; to deprive; (with *abl* or *de* + *abl*) to deprive (*someone*) of, prevent (*someone*) from obtaining, rob (*someone*) of; **oculos dejicere** (with *ab* + *abl*) to divert the eyes from; to turn away from

dējung·ō -ĕre *vt* to unyoke; to sever

dējūrō see **dejero**

dējŭv·ō -āre *vt* to fail to help

dē·lābor -lābī -lapsus sum *vi* to slip down, fall down, sink down; to glide down, float down; (fig) to come down, sink; (fig) to stoop, condescend; (with **ad** + *acc*) to be inclined toward, be partial to, tend toward; (with **in** + *acc*) to sneak in among

dēlacĕr·ō -āre *vt* to tear to pieces

dēlāment·or -ārī -ātus sum *vt* to grieve deeply for

dēlass·ō -āre *vt* to tire out, weary

dēlātĭ·ō -ōnis *f* reporting; informing, denouncing; **nominis delatio** indicting of a person

dēlāt·or -ōris *m* reporter; informer, denouncer

dēlātus *pp* of **defero**

dēlectābĭl·is -e *adj* delightful, enjoyable

dēlectāment·um -ī *n* delight, amusement, pastime

dēlectātĭ·ō -ōnis *f* delight, pleasure, charm, amusement, satisfaction

dēlect·ō -āre *vt* to delight, amuse, charm; to attract, allure; **delectari** (with *abl*) to be delighted by, delight in; *v impers* **me ire delectat** I like to go, I enjoy going

dēlect·us -a -um *pp* of **deligo**; *adj* picked, choice, select

dēlect·us -ūs *m* choosing, choice

dēlēgātĭ·ō -ōnis *f* substitution, delegation (*of one person for another*); payment (*of debt*)

dēlēg·ō -āre *vt* to assign, transfer; to attribute, impute, ascribe

dēlēnĭfĭc·us -a -um *adj* soothing, seductive

dēlēnīment·um -ī *n* palliative, solace, comfort; allurement, bait

dēlēn·iō or **dēlīn·iō -īre -īvī -ītum** *vt* to soothe, calm down, console, appease; to allure, seduce, win over

dēlēnīt·or -ōris *m* charmer, cajoler

dēl·ĕō -ēre -ēvī -ētum *vt* to destroy, annihilate, overthrow, extinguish, raze; to blot out, erase, obliterate (*writing*); to annul, put an end to, abolish, finish

dēlētr·ix -īcis *f* destroyer

Dēlĭăc·us -a -um *adj* Delian, of or from Delos

dēlīberābund·us -a -um *adj* deliberating maturely

dēlīberātĭ·ō -ōnis *f* considering, weighing; deliberation, consultation; **habet res deliberationem** the matter requires thought, needs consideration

dēlīberātīv·us -a -um *adj* deliberative; requiring deliberation

dēlīberāt·or -ōris *m* thoughtful person

dēlīberāt·us -a -um *adj* resolved upon, determined

dēlīber·ō -āre *vt* to weigh well, ponder; to resolve, determine; to consult (*oracle*); *vi* to reflect, deliberate; (with *de* + *abl*) to think seriously about, think over well

dēlīb·ō -āre *vt* to sip, take a sip of; to taste, take a taste of, nibble at; to take away, detract, subtract, remove

dēlibr·ō -āre *vt* to strip the bark off (*trees*); to peel

dēlibūt·us -a -um *adj* anointed; defiled, stained, smeared; steeped

dēlicātē *adv* delicately, softly, luxuriously

dēlicāt·us -a -um *adj* delicate, dainty, tender, soft; pampered, spoiled; dainty, fastidious

dēlicĭ·ae -ārum *f pl* allurements, enticements, delights; whims, pet ideas, fanciful ideas; voluptuousness; favorite, sweetheart, darling; **delicias facere** to play tricks; **delicias facere** (with *dat*) to play around with (*a girl*); **esse in deliciis** (with *dat*) to be the pet or favorite of; **habere in deliciis** to have as a pet or favorite

dēlicĭŏl·ae -ārum *f pl* darling

delic·ĭum -ĭī or **-ī** *n* sweetheart; favorite

dēlĭc·ō -āre *vt* to make clear, explain

dēlict·um -ī *n* fault, offense, wrong, transgression, defect

dēlĭcŭ·us -a -um *adj* lacking, wanting

dēlĭg·ō -āre *vt* to tie up, bind together, bind fast

dē·lĭgō -lĭgĕre -lēgī -lectum *vt* to

choose, select, pick out, single out, elect; to gather, gather in

dē·lingō -lingĕre -linxī vt to lick off; to have a lick of

dēlini- = deleni-

dē·linquō -linquĕre -līquī -lictum vi to fail, be wanting, fall short; to do wrong, commit a fault or crime

dē·liquescō -liquescĕre -licŭī vi to melt, melt away, dissolve; to pine away

dēliquī·ō -ōnis f failure; (with genit) failure to get

dēliqu·ium -iī or -ī n failure

dēliqu·ō or dēlic·ō -āre vt to clear up, explain

dēlīrāment·um -ī n nonsense, absurdity

dēlīrāti·ō -ōnis f silliness, folly, madness; infatuation; dotage

dēlīr·ō -āre vi to be off the beam, be crazy, be mad; to drivel

dēlīr·us -a -um adj crazy, demented, silly; in dotage

dēlit·escō -escĕre -ŭī vi to conceal oneself, lie hidden, lurk

dēlītig·ō -āre vi to rant

Dēl·ĭus -a -um adj Delian, of Delos

Dēl·os -ī f sacred island in the Cyclades, where Apollo was born

Delph·ī -ōrum m pl town in Phocis, in Central Greece, famous for the shrine and oracle of Apollo; inhabitants of Delphi

delphīn·us -ī or delph·ĭn -ĭnis m dolphin

Delphīn·us -ī m Dolphin (constellation)

Deltōt·on -ī n Triangulum (constellation)

dēlūbr·um -ī n shrine, temple, sanctuary

dēluct·ō -āre or dēluct·or -ārī -ātus sum vi to wrestle

dēlūdĭfic·ō -āre vt to make fun of

dē·lūdō -lūdĕre -lūsī -lūsum vt to dupe, mock, deceive, delude

dēlumb·ĭs -e adj enervated, enfeebled, weakened

dēmad·escō -escĕre -ŭī vi to become drenched; to be moistened

dēmand·ō -āre vt to hand over, entrust

dēmarch·us -ī m demarch (chief of a village in Attica); (fig) tribune of the people

dēm·ens -entis adj out of one's mind, demented, distracted, mad; senseless, wild, reckless

dēmensus pp of demetior; n ration, allowance

dēmenter adv insanely

dēmenti·a -ae f insanity, madness; f pl follies

dement·iō -īre vi to be mad

dēmer·ĕō -ēre -ŭī -ĭtum or dēmer·ĕor -ērī -ĭtus sum vt to earn, merit, deserve; to serve well, do a service to

dē·mergō -mergĕre -mersī -mersum vt to sink, plunge, submerge; (fig) to plunge, cast down, overwhelm

dēmessus pp of dēmeto

dē·mētĭor -mētīrī -mensus sum vt to measure off, measure out

dē·mētō -metĕre -messŭī -messum vt to mow, reap, cut off, cut down, harvest

dēmigrāti·ō -ōnis f emigration

dēmigr·ō -āre vi to migrate, emigrate, move, depart; (fig) to depart, die

dēmin·ŭō -uĕre -ŭī -ūtum vt to make smaller, lessen, diminish; (fig) to remit, reduce, lessen; capite deminuere to deprive of citizenship

dēminūtĭ·ō -ōnis f lessening, diminution, abridging; (law) right of disposing of property; capitis diminutio loss of civil rights; provinciae diminutio shortening of term of office

dēmīr·or -ārī -ātus sum vt to be surprised at, to be amazed at

dēmissē adv low; humbly, modestly; abjectly, meanly

dēmissĭcĭ·us -a -um adj allowed to hang down, flowing

dēmissĭ·ō -ōnis f letting down, sinking, lowering; demissio animi low morale

demiss·us -a -um pp of demitto; adj low, low-lying (place); drooping (lips, etc.); bent (head); allowed to hang down, flowing, loose (hair); downhearted, dejected; shy, unassuming, retiring, humble; poor, humble

dēmītig·ō -āre vt to make mild; dēmitigari to grow more lenient

dē·mittō -mittĕre -mīsī -missum vt to drop, let drop, let sink, lower; to bring downstream; to land (ship); to grow (beard); to move down (troops from higher place); se demittere to descend; to stoop, bend down

dēmiurg·us or dāmiurg·us -ī m chief magistrate in a Greek state

dēm·ō -ĕre -psī -ptum vt to take away, remove, withdraw, subtract; (with dat or with dē + abl) to take away from, subtract from, withhold from

Dēmocrĭt·us -ī m famous philosopher of Abdera, in Thrace, founder of the atomic theory (460-361 B.C.)

dēmōl·ĭor -īrī -ītus sum vt to demolish, pull down

dēmōlītĭ·ō -ōnis f pulling down (of statues)

dēmonstrātĭ·ō -ōnis f pointing out; explanation

dēmonstrātīv·us -a -um adj showy

dēmonstrāt·or -ōris m indicator

dēmonstr·ō -āre vt to point out clearly; to state precisely, explain, describe; to mention, speak of; to demonstrate, prove, establish

dē·morĭor -mŏrī -mortŭus sum vi to die, die off

dēmŏr·or -ārī -ātus sum vt to delay, detain; to hinder, block; vi to wait

Dēmosthĕn·ēs -is *m* greatest Greek orator (384-322 B.C.)

dē·movĕō -movēre -mōvī -mōtum *vt* to remove, move away, dispossess, expel; to remove, discharge (*from office*); (fig) to divert, turn away

demptus *pp* of **demo**

dēmūgīt·us -a -um *adj* bellowing, lowing

dē·mulcĕō -mulcēre -mulsī *vt* to stroke lovingly, to caress

dēmum *adv* at last, finally; not till then; (to give emphasis) precisely, exactly, just; (to give assurance) in fact, certainly, to be sure, as a matter of fact; **decimo demum anno** not till the tenth year; **modo demum** only now, not till now; **nunc demum** now at last, not till now; **post demum** not till after; **sic demum** thus finally; **tum demum** then at length, not till then

dēmurmŭr·ō -āre *vt* to grumble right through (*e.g., a performance*)

dēmūtātĭ·ō -ōnis *f* changing, perversion, degeneracy

dēmūt·ō -āre *vt* to change, alter; to make worse; *vi* to change one's mind

dēnār·ĭus -ĭī or **-ī** *m* Roman silver coin, originally containing ten aces, later eighteen, approximately equivalent to twenty-five cents; money

dēnarr·ō -āre *vt* to recount in detail

dēnās·ō -āre *vt* to bite the nose off (*the face*)

dēnăt·ō -āre *vi* to swim downstream

dēnĕg·ō -āre *vt* to deny, refuse, turn down; *vi* to say no, give a flat refusal

dēn·ī -ae -a *adj* in sets of ten, ten each, in tens; ten; tenth

dēnĭcāl·ĭs -e *adj* purifying from death; **feriae denicales** purification service (*after death in the household*)

dēnĭque *adv* finally, at last; in short, in a word, briefly; (for emphasis) just, precisely; (ironical) of course; **octavo denique mense** not till after the eighth month; **tum denique** then at last, only then, not till then

dēnōmĭn·ō -āre *vt* to name, designate

dēnorm·ō -āre *vt* to make crooked or irregular; to disfigure, spoil

dēnŏt·ō -āre *vt* to mark down, specify; to take careful note of, observe closely

den·s -tis *m* tooth; ivory; point, prong, fluke; (fig) tooth (*of envy, hatred, time, etc.*); **albis dentibus deridere aliquem** to laugh heartily at someone; **dens Indus** elephant's tusk

densē *adv* closely, thickly; in quick succession, repeatedly

densĭt·ās -ātis *f* closeness, thickness

dens·ō -āre or **dens·ĕō -ēre — -ētum** *vt* to make thick, thicken; to press close together; to close

(*ranks*); to condense (*a speech*)

dens·us -a -um *adj* dense, close, crowded, thick; frequent, continuous; intense (*love, cold*); concise (*style*)

dentāl·ĭa -ĭum *n pl* plow beam

dentāt·us -a -um *adj* toothed, having teeth; serrated; polished (*paper*)

dentifrangĭbŭl·us -a -um *adj* tooth-breaking; *m* thug; *n* fist

dentilĕg·us -ī *m* toothpicker (*one who picks up teeth after they have been knocked out*)

dent·ĭō -īre *vi* to teethe, cut one's teeth

dē·nūbō -nūbĕre -nupsī -nuptum *vi* (of a woman) to marry beneath one's rank

dēnūd·ō -āre *vt* to denude, strip naked, strip bare; (fig) to lay bare (*facts*)

dēnuntĭātĭ·ō -ōnis *f* intimation, warning, threat; announcement, proclamation; **senātūs denuntiatio** senate ordinance; **testimoni denuntiatio** summons to testify

dēnuntĭ·ō -āre *vt* to intimate; to give notice of; to announce officially; to give official warning to; (mil) to report to, give an official report to; to warn, threaten; **denuntiare testimonium** (with *dat*) to give (*someone*) a summons to testify

dēnŭō *adv* anew, afresh, once more, all over again

deonĕr·ō -āre *vt* to unload

deorsum or **deorsus** *adv* downwards, down; (of position) down, below

deoscŭl·or -ārī -ātus sum *vt* to kiss warmly, kiss up and down

dēpacīscor see **depeciscor**

dēpact·us -a -um *adj* lashed down; driven tight

dēparc·us -a -um *adj* very stingy

dē·pascō -pascĕre -pāvī -pastum or **dē·pascor -pasci -pastus sum** *vt* to feed off, graze on; to consume; to destroy, waste; (fig) to prune off (*excesses of style*)

dēpec·ĭscor or **dēpac·ĭscor -iscī -tus sum** *vt* to agree upon, bargain for, settle by bargaining

dē·pectō -pectĕre — -pexum *vt* to comb, curry; to curry (*one's hide*), flog

dēpecŭlāt·or -ōris *m* embezzler, plunderer

dēpecŭl·or -ārī -ātus sum *vt* to embezzle, plunder

dē·pellō -pellĕre -pŭlī -pulsum *vt* to drive off, drive away, drive out, expel; to avert; (mil) to dislodge; (with **quin** or with **de** or **ab** + *abl*) to avert, deter, dissuade, wean from; (with *abl*) to dislodge from; *vi* to deviate

dēpend·ĕō -ēre *vi* to hang down; (with *abl*) to be derived from; (with **de** + *abl*) to depend upon; (with **ex** + *abl*) to hang down from

dē·pendō -pendĕre -pendī -pen-

sum *vt* to pay up; **poenam depen-dere** (with *dat*) to pay the penalty to

dēper·dō -**děre** -**dĭdī** -**dĭtum** *vt* to lose completely; to ruin, destroy

dēper·ĕō -**īre** -**ĭī** *vt* to be hopelessly in love with; *vi* to go to ruin, perish; to be lost, finished

dē·pingō -**pingĕre** -**pinxī** -**pictum** *vt* to paint, portray; to embroider; to portray, describe, represent (*in words or thoughts*)

dē·plangō -**plangĕre** -**planxī** *vt* to grieve over, cry one's heart out over

dēplex·us -**a** -**um** *adj* gripping firm-ly, grasping

dēplōrābund·us -**a** -**um** *adj* weep-ing bitterly, sobbing

dēplōr·ō -**āre** *vt* to cry over, mourn; to despair of; *vi* to take it hard, cry bitterly

dēplŭ·it -**ĕre** -**it** *v impers* it is rain-ing hard, pouring down

dē·pōnō -**pōnĕre** -**posŭī** -**posĭtum** *vt* to lay down; to put down, put aside, get rid of; to bet, wager; to deposit; (with **apud** + *acc*) to en-trust to, commit to the care of; **bellum deponere** to give up war; **imperium deponere** to relinquish power, renounce power

dēpopulātĭ·ō -**ōnis** *f* ravaging, pil-laging

dēpopulāt·or -**ōris** *m* pillager, ma-rauder

dēpopŭl·ō -**āre** *vt* or **dēpopŭl·or** -**ārī** -**ātus sum** *vt* to ravage, pillage, lay waste; to depopulate; (fig) to waste, destroy, wreck

dēport·ō -**āre** *vt* to carry down; to carry away; to bring home (*vic-tory*); to transport; to banish; (fig) to win

dē·poscō -**poscĕre** -**poposcī** *vt* to demand, require; to request earn-estly; to challenge; **sibi deposcere** to claim (*something*) for oneself

dēposĭt·us -**a** -**um** *pp* of **depono**; *adj* despaired of; *n* deposit (*of money as first payment*); deposit (*for safe keeping*)

dēprāvātē *adv* perversely

dēprāvātĭ·ō -**ōnis** *f* distorting; (fig) distortion

dēprāv·ō -**āre** *vt* to make crooked, distort; to pervert, corrupt, seduce; to misrepresent

dēprecābund·us -**a** -**um** *adj* im-ploring

dēprecātĭ·ō -**ōnis** *f* supplication; deprecation, averting by prayer; in-vocation, earnest entreaty; (with *genit*) intercession against (*danger, etc.*)

dēprecāt·or -**ōris** *m* intercessor (*generally against rather than for*)

dēprěc·or -**ārī** -**ātus sum** *vt* to pray against, avert by prayer; to pray for, beg for; to intercede in behalf of; to plead in excuse

dēpre·hendō -**hendĕre** -**hendī** -**hensum** or **dēpren·dō** -**děre** -**dī**

-**sum** *vt* to get hold of; to arrest, intercept; to surprise, catch in the act; to detect, discover, find out; to perceive, understand; to embarrass

dēprehensĭ·ō -**ōnis** *f* detection

dēpress·us -**a** -**um** *pp* of **deprimo**; *adj* low, suppressed (*voice*); low (*land*)

dē·primō -**primĕre** -**pressī** -**pres-sum** *vt* to depress, press down, weigh down; to plant deep; to dig (*e.g., a trench*) deep; to sink (*a ship*)

dēproelĭ·or -**ārī** -**ātus sum** *vi* to fight it out, battle fiercely

dē·prōmō -**prōměre** -**prompsī** -**promptum** *vt* to take down; to bring out, produce

dēproper·ō -**āre** *vt* to make in a hurry; *vi* to hurry

deps·ō -**ěre** -**ŭī** -**tum** *vt* to knead

dēpŭd·et -**ēre** -**ŭit** *v impers* **eum depudet** he has no sense of shame

dēpŭg·is or **dēpŷg·is** -**is** *adj* with-out buttocks, with thin buttocks

dēpugn·ō -**āre** *vi* to fight hard; to fight it out; (with **cum** + *abl*) to be in a death struggle with

dēpulsĭ·ō -**ōnis** *f* averting; (rhet) defense

dēpuls·ō -**āre** *vt* to push aside; **de via depulsare** to push out of the way

dēpuls·or -**ōris** *m* averter

dēpulsus *pp* of **depello**

dēpung·ō -**ěre** *vt* to mark off, desig-nate

dēpurg·ō -**āre** *vt* to clean

dēpŭt·ō -**āre** *vt* to prune; to reckon, consider

dēpŷgis see **depugis**

dēque *adv* down, downwards

dērect·us -**a** -**um** *pp* of **derigo**; *adj* straight, direct, level, upright, per-pendicular; (fig) straightforward, direct, simple, right

dērelictĭ·ō -**ōnis** *f* dereliction, disre-garding, neglecting

dēre·linquō -**linquĕre** -**līquī** -**lic-tum** *vt* to leave behind, forsake, abandon

dērepente *adv* suddenly

dērēp·ō -**ěre** -**sī** *vi* to creep down

dēreptus *pp* of **deripio**

dē·rīdĕō -**rīdēre** -**rīsī** -**rīsum** *vt* to deride

dērīdicŭl·us -**a** -**um** *adj* quite ridic-ulous; *n* derision, mockery; absurd-ity; **deridiculo esse** to be the ob-ject of derision, be the butt of ridi-cule

dērig·escō -**escĕre** -**ŭī** *vi* to grow stiff, grow rigid; to curdle

dē·rigō -**rigĕre** -**rexī** -**rectum** *vt* to direct, aim; to steer (*ship*); to draw up in battle line; (fig) to di-rect, guide, regulate; (with *dat* or with **ad** or **in** + *acc*) to direct or aim at, guide to; (with **ad** + *acc*) to regulate (*e.g., life*) according to

dē·ripĭō -**ripĕre** -**ripŭī** -**reptum** *vt* to tear down, tear off, pull down

dērīs·or -**ōris** *m* scoffer, cynic

dērīs·us -ūs m derision

dērīvātī·ō -ōnis f diversion, diverting (of river from its course)

dērīv·ō -āre vt to draw off, divert; to derive

dērŏg·ō -āre vt to propose to repeal in part; to restrict, modify; to take away, diminish, impair

dērōs·us -a -um adj gnawed away, nibbled

dēruncĭn·ō -āre vt to plane off; to cheat

dērŭ·ō -ĕre -ŭī vt to throw down, overthrow, demolish; to detract

dērupt·us -a -um adj rough, steep, broken; n pl crevasses

dēsaev·ĭō -īre -ĭī vi to rage furiously; to run wild

dēsalt·ō -āre vi to dance

de·scendō -scendĕre -scendī -scensum vi to climb down, descend, come or go down; to dismount; to fall, sink, sink down, penetrate; (fig) to go down, sink, sink down, penetrate; (fig) to lower oneself, stoop, yield; (mil) to march down

descensĭ·ō -ōnis f going down; **descensio Tiberina** sailing down the Tiber

descens·us -ūs m climbing down, descent; slope, descent

desc·iscō -iscĕre -īvī or **-ĭī -ītum** vi to revolt, desert; (fig) to depart, deviate, fall off; (with **ab** + abl) **a** to revolt from, break allegiance with; **b** to deviate from, fall away from

de·scrībō -scrībĕre -scrīpsī -scrīptum vt to write out, transcribe, copy; to describe, represent, portray, draw, design, sketch

descriptē see **discripte**

descriptĭ·ō -ōnis f copy; representation, diagram, sketch, map; description

descriptus pp of **describo**

dēsĕc·ō -āre -ŭī -tum vt to cut off

dēsĕr·ō -ĕre -ŭī -tum vt to desert, abandon, forsake; (law) to forfeit

dēsert·or -ōris m deserter

dēsert·us -a -um pp of **desero**; adj deserted; unpopulated, uninhabited; n pl wilderness, desert

dēserv·ĭō -īre vi (with dat) to be a slave to, serve devotedly

dēs·es -ĭdis adj sitting down, sitting at ease; lazy, apathetic, lifeless, idle

dēsicc·ō -āre vt to dry up; to drain

dē·sidĕō -sidĕre -sēdī vi to sit idle, remain inactive

dēsīderābĭl·is -e adj desirable

dēsīderātĭ·ō -ōnis f missing, feeling the absence; **desideratio voluptatum** the missing of pleasures, yearning for pleasures

dēsīder·ĭum -ĭī or **-ī** n longing, missing, feeling of loss; want, need, necessity; request, petition; **ex desiderio laborare** to be homesick; **me desiderium tenet** (with genit)

I miss, am homesick for

dēsīdĕr·ō -āre vt to miss, long for, feel the want of; (mil) to lose (men) as casualties; **desiderari** (mil) to be missing, be lost, be a casualty

dēsidĭ·a -ae f idleness, inactivity; laziness; apathy

dēsidĭābŭl·um -ī n place to lounge, hangout

dēsidĭōsē adv idly

dēsidĭōs·us -a -um adj idle, indolent, lazy; causing idleness or laziness; spent in idleness

dē·sīdō -sīdĕre -sēdī vi to sink, settle down; (fig) to sink, deteriorate

dēsignātĭ·ō -ōnis f specification; designation, election to office

dēsignātor see **dissignator**

dēsign·ō -āre vt to mark out, point out, designate, define, trace; to denote, describe, represent; to appoint, choose, elect; **consul designatus** consul-elect

dē·silĭō -silīre -silŭī -sultum vi to jump down, alight; **ab equo desilire** to dismount; **de nave desilire** to jump overboard; (fig) to venture forth

dē·sĭnō -sinĕre -sĭī -situm vt to give up, abandon; **furere desinere** to stop raging; vi to stop, come to a stop, end; (with **in** + acc) to end in; **similiter desinere** to have similar endings

dēsipĭ·ens -entis adj foolish, silly

dēsipientĭ·a -ae f folly, foolishness

dēsip·ĭō -ĕre vi to be silly, act foolishly

dē·sistō -sistĕre -stĭtī -stĭtum vi to stop, desist; to get stuck, stick; (with abl or with **ab** or **de** + abl) to desist from, abandon, give up (an action begun); **desistere a defensione** to give up the defense

dēsitus pp of **desino**

dēsōl·ō -āre vt to leave desolate, leave alone, forsake, abandon; **desolatus** (with abl) deprived of

despect·ō -āre vt to look down on, overlook, command a view of; to look down on, despise

despect·us -a -um pp of **despicio**; adj contemptible

despect·us -ūs m commanding view, view

despēranter adv hopelessly

despērātĭ·ō -ōnis f desperation, despair

despērāt·us -a -um adj despaired of; hopeless; desperate, hopeless

despēr·ō -āre vt to despair of; vi to despair, give up hope; (with **de** + abl) to despair of

despicātĭ·ō -ōnis f contempt; f pl feelings of contempt

despicāt·us -a -um adj despicable; **aliquem despicatum habere** to hold someone in contempt

despic·ĭens -entis adj contemptuous; (with genit) contemptuous of

despicientĭ·a -ae f despising, contempt

de·spiciō -spicĕre -spexī -spectum vt to despise, look down on, express contempt for; vi to look down; (with **in** + acc) to look down on, have a view of

despic·or -ārī -ātus sum vt to despise, disdain

despoliāt·or -ōris m robber, plunderer, marauder

despoli·ō -āre vt to strip, rob, plunder

de·spondĕō -spondēre -spondī -sponsum vt to pledge, promise solemnly; to promise in marriage; to give up, lose; **animum despondere** or **animos despondere** to lose heart

despūm·ō -āre vt to skim off, skim; vi to stop foaming

despŭ·ō -ĕre vt to spit upon, show contempt for; vi to spit (on the ground)

desquăm·ō -āre vt to take the scales off, to scale (fish); (fig) to peel off

destill·ō -āre vt to drip, distil; vi to trickle down, drip

destimŭl·ō -āre vt to goad on, stimulate

destināti·ō -ōnis f establishing; resolution, determination, purpose, design

destināt·us -a -um adj fixed, determined; **destinatum est mihi** (with inf) I have made up my mind to; n pl designs, intentions

destin·ō -āre vt to lash down, secure; (fig) to fix, determine, resolve; to design, destine; to appoint, designate; to take aim at

destit·ŭō -ŭĕre -ŭī -ūtum vt to set apart; to set down, place; to forsake, abandon; to leave in the lurch, leave high and dry, betray, desert; (with **ab** + abl) to rob of, leave destitute of

destitūti·ō -ōnis f forsaking, abandonment; disappointment

district·us -a -um adj severe, rigid

de·stringō -stringĕre -strinxī -strictum vt to strip; to unsheathe; to give (someone) a rubdown; to brush gently against, skim; (of weapon) to graze; (fig) to criticize, satirize

destructi·ō -ōnis f pulling down (e.g., of walls); destruction, demolition; refutation

de·strŭō -strŭĕre -struxī -structum vt to pull down, demolish, destroy; (fig) to ruin

dēsubitō or **dē subitō** adv suddenly

dēsūdasc·ō -ĕre vi to begin to sweat all over

dēsūd·ō -āre vi to sweat; (with dat) (fig) to sweat over, work hard at

dēsuē·fīō -fĭĕrī -factus sum vi to become unused or unaccustomed

dēsu·escō -escĕre -ēvī -ētum vi to become unaccustomed

dēsuētūd·ō -inis f disuse, lack of use

dēsuēt·us -a -um pp of desuesco; adj unused, out of use, obsolete; out of practice; (with dat) unused to, unfamiliar with

dēsult·or -ōris m circus rider who leaps from one horse to another; **amoris desultor** (fig) fickle lover

dēsultōrĭ·us -a -um adj of a circus rider; **equus desultorius** show horse

dēsultūr·a -ae f leaping down (from horse), dismounting

dē·sum -esse -fŭī -futūrus vi to fall short, fail; to fail in one's duty; to be absent, be missing; (with dat) to be absent from, be missing from, be lacking from; **sibi deesse** to cheat oneself, sell oneself short; **tempori deesse** or **occasioni temporis deesse** to pass up the opportunity, pass up the chance

dē·sūmō -sūmĕre -sumpsī -sumptum vt to pick out, choose; to assume, undertake; **sibi hostem desumere** to take on an enemy

dēsŭper adv from above, from overhead

dēsurg·ō -ĕre vi to rise; **cenā desurgere** to get up from the table

dē·tĕgō -tegĕre -texī -tectum vt to detect, uncover, expose, lay bare; to reveal, disclose, betray; **formidine detegi** to be betrayed by fear

dē·tendō -tendĕre - **-tensum** vt to unstretch; to take down (tent)

dētentus pp of detineo

dē·tergĕō -tergēre -tersī -tersum vt to wipe off, wipe away, wipe clean; (fig) to wipe clean; **mensam detergere** to eat up everything on the table

dēterĭ·or -us adj inferior, worse, poorer, meaner; less favorable, worse (time); degenerate (person); (mil) weaker (e.g., in cavalry)

dēterius adv worse

dētermināti·ō -ōnis f boundary; conclusion, end; end (of speech)

dētermin·ō -āre vt to bound, limit, prescribe; to determine, settle

dē·tĕrō -terĕre -trīvī -trītum vt to rub away, wear away; to wear out; to lessen, weaken, detract from; **calces alicujus deterere** to tread on someone's heels

dēterr·ĕō -ēre -ŭī -ĭtum vt to deter, frighten away, discourage; (with abl, or with ab or de + abl, or with ne, quin, or quominus) to deter or discourage from; **deterruit quominus hostes persequerentur** he discouraged them from pursuing the enemy

dētersus pp of detergeo

dētestābil·is -e adj detestable, abominable

dētestāti·ō -ōnis f execration, curse; averting (by sacrifices or prayers)

dētest·or -ārī -ātus sum vt to curse, execrate; to invoke (the gods); to avert; to plead against; to detest, loathe, abhor; (with **in** + acc) to call down (*e.g.*, *vengeance*) upon; **invidiam detestari** to avert envy, avoid unpopularity

dētex·ō -ĕre -ŭī -tum *vt* to weave, finish weaving; (fig) to finish, finish off

dē·tĭneō -tinēre -tinŭī -tentum *vt* to hold back, keep back; to hold up, detain; to occupy, keep occupied; (with **ab** or **de** + *abl*) to keep back from; (with *abl* or with **in** + *abl*) to occupy (*e.g.*, *day*, *mind*) with, keep (*someone*) busied with

dē·tondĕō -tondēre -totondī or **-tondī -tonsum** *vt* to cut off, clip off, shear off (*hair*, *wool*); (fig) to strip

dĕtŏn·ō -āre -ŭī *vi* to stop thundering; (of Jupiter) to thunder down

dĕtonsus *pp* of **detondeo**

dē·torquĕō -torquēre -torsī -tortum *vt* to twist or bend aside; to twist out of shape; to turn aside; to turn, direct; to avert (*eyes*); to divert, pervert; to distort, misrepresent (*words*)

dētractĭ·ō -ōnis *f* taking away, wresting; removal; (rhet) ellipsis

detractō see **detrecto**

detract·or -ōris *m* detractor

dē·trāhō -trahĕre -traxī -tractum *vt* to drag down, drag away, pull down, pull away; to remove, withdraw; to take away, deprive, rob, strip; to induce to come down, draw down (*e.g.*, *an enemy from a strong position*); to disparage, detract, slander; (with *dat* or **de** + *abl*) to take away from (*someone*), rob (*someone*) of

dētrectātĭ·ō -ōnis *f* drawing back, avoidance; **militiae detrectatio** draft dodging

dētrectāt·or -ōris *m* detractor, disparager

dētrect·ō or **detract·ō -āre** *vt* to draw back from, shirk, decline, reject, refuse; to disparage, depreciate; to demean; **militiam detrectare** to dodge the draft

dētrīmentōs·us -a -um *adj* detrimental, harmful

dētrīment·um -ī *n* detriment, loss, damage; **detrimentum accipere** or **detrimentum capere** to incur or suffer harm; **detrimentum inferre** or **detrimentum afferre** to cause harm

dētrītus *pp* of **detero**

dē·trūdō -trūdĕre -trūsī -trūsum *vt* to push down, push away, push off; (mil) to dislodge; (law) to evict; to postpone, put off; **aliquem de sua sententia detrudere** to force someone to change his mind

detrunc·ō -āre *vt* to cut off, chop off; (fig) to mutilate, behead

dēturb·ō -āre *vt* to beat down, expel, tear down, strike down; (mil) to dislodge, force to come down; to eject, dispossess; **aliquem de sani-**

tate deturbare to drive a person mad

Deucalĭ·ōn -ōnis *m* son of Prometheus, who, together with his wife Pyrrha, was the sole survivor of the Deluge

de·unx -uncis *m* eleven twelfths; **heres ex deunce** heir to eleven twelfths

dē·ūrō -ūrĕre -ussī -ustum *vt* to burn up, destroy; (of frost) to nip

de·us -ī (*nom pl:* **deī** or **dī**; *genit pl:* **deōrum** or **deum**) *m* god, deity; (of a person) god, divine being; *m pl* (of persons in high places) the powers that be; **dī boni!** good heavens!; **di hominesque** all the world; **di meliora!** Heaven forbid!; **dis volentibus** with the help of the gods; **di te ament!** bless your little heart!

deustus *pp* of **deuro**

dē·ūtor -ūtī -ūsus sum *vi* (with *abl*) to mistreat

dēvast·ō -āre *vt* to devastate, lay waste

dē·vĕhō -vehĕre -vexī -vectum *vt* to carry down, carry away, carry off; **devehi** to ride down, sail down

dē·vellō -vellĕre -vellī or **-volsī -vulsum** *vt* to pluck out

dēvēl·ō -āre *vt* to unveil

dēvenĕr·or -ārī -ātus sum *vt* to reverence, worship; to avert by prayer

dē·veniō -venīre -vēnī -ventum *vi* to come down, arrive; (with *acc* of extent of motion or with **ad** or **in** + *acc*) to arrive at, reach; (with **ad** + *acc*) to happen to, befall

dēverbĕr·ō -āre *vt* to thrash soundly

dēvers·or -ārī -ātus sum *vi* to stay as a guest; (with **apud** + *acc*) to stay at the house of

dēvers·or -ōris *m* guest

dēversōrĭŏl·um -ī *n* small inn, motel

dēversōrĭ·us or **dēvorsorĭ·us -a -um** *adj* of an inn; fit to stay at; **taberna deversoria** inn; *n* inn, hotel

dēverticŭl·um or **dēvorticŭl·um -ī** *n* side road, detour; digression; inn, hotel, tavern; low haunt, dive; refuge

dē·vertō (or **dē·vortō) -vertĕre -vertī -versum** or **dē·vertor -vertī -versus sum** *vi* to turn aside, turn away; to stay as guest, spend the night; (with **ad** or **apud** + *acc*) to stay with or at the house of; (with **ad** + *acc*) to have recourse to, resort to

dēvex·us -a -um *adj* inclining, sloping, steep; (with **ad** + *acc*) prone to, inclined to

dē·vinciō -vincīre -vinxī -vinctum *vt* to tie up, clamp; (fig) to bind fast, obligate, unite closely; **se vino devincire** (coll) to get tight

dē·vincō -vincĕre -vīcī -victum *vt* to conquer, subdue

dēvinct·us -a -um *pp* of **devincio;** *adj* (with *dat*) strongly attached to
dēvītātī·ō -ōnis *f* avoidance
dēvīt·ō -āre *vt* to avoid
dēvĭ·us -a -um *adj* out of the way, off the beaten track; devious; living apart, solitary, sequestered; inconsistent
dēvŏc·ō -āre *vt* to call down; to call off, recall, call away; to allure, seduce; **deos ad auxilium devocare** to invoke the gods for help
dēvŏl·ō -āre *vi* to fly down; to fly away; to hasten down, hasten away
dē·volvō -volvĕre -volvī -volūtum *vt* to roll down; **ad spem inanem pacis devolvi** to fall back on false hopes of peace; **devolvi** to roll down, go tumbling down, sink down
dēvŏr·ō -āre *vt* to devour, gulp down; to consume, waste, squander (*money, etc.*); (*of the sea*) to engulf, swallow up; to swallow, mumble (*words*); to repress (*tears*); to bear with patience
dēvor- = dever-
dēvortĭ·a -ōrum *n pl* side roads, detour
dēvŏtĭ·ō -ōnis *f* self-sacrifice; cursing, outlawing; incantation, spell; **capitis devotio** or **vitae devotio** sacrifice of one's life
dēvŏt·ō -āre *vt* to lay a spell on, bewitch, jinx
dēvŏt·us -a -um *pp* of **devoveo;** *adj* devoted, faithful; accursed; (with *dat*) **a** devoted to, faithful to; **b** addicted to, given to (*wine, drinking*)
dē·voveō -vovēre -vōvī -vōtum *vt* to devote, vow, sacrifice, dedicate; to mark out, doom, destine; to curse, execrate; to bewitch; **se devovere dis** to devote oneself to death
dēvulsus *pp* of **devello**
dext·ans -antis *m* five sixths
dextell·a -ae *f* little right hand; right-hand man
dext·er -ĕra -ĕrum or **-ra -rum** *adj* right, on the right side; handy, dexterous; lucky, propitious, favorable; opportune, right; *f* right hand; right side, the right; **a dextra laevaque** to the right and left, right and left, everywhere; **dextrā** with the right hand; (fig) with valor; **dextrā** (with *acc*) to the right of; **dextram dare** or **dextram tendere** to give a pledge of friendship; **dextram renovare** to renew a solemn pledge
dextĕrē or **dextrē** *adv* dexterously, skillfully; **dextre fortunā uti** (fig) to play the cards right
dexterĭt·ās -ātis *f* dexterity, adroitness; readiness
dextrorsum or **dextrorsus** or **dextrōvorsum** *adv* to the right, towards the right side
dī see **deus**

Dī·a -ae *f* ancient name of the island of Naxos; mother of Mercury
diabathrār·ius -iī or **-ī** *m* shoemaker
diadēm·a -ātis *n* diadem
diaet·a -ae *f* diet; living room
dialectĭcē *adv* logically
dialectĭc·us -a -um *adj* dialectical; *m* dialectician; *f* dialectics, logic; *n pl* dialectics, logical discussions
dialect·os -ī *f* dialect
Diāl·is -e *adj* of Jupiter; of Jupiter's high priest; **apex Dialis** high priest's miter; **conjux Dialis** high priest's wife; **flamen Dialis** high priest of Jupiter
dialŏg·us -ī *m* dialogue, conversation
Diān·a or **Diān·a -ae** *f* Diana (*goddess of hunting, patroness of virginity, of the moon as Luna, of childbirth as Lucina, and of incantations and magic as Hecate*); (fig) Diana's temple; (fig) moon; **iracunda Diana** lunacy
diārĭ·a -ōrum *n pl* daily ration
dibăph·us -ī *f* crimson robe; official robe of magistrate
dic·a -ae *f* lawsuit, case, judicial process, judicial proceedings; **dicam scribere** (with *dat*) to sue (*someone*); **sortiri dicas** to select a jury
dicācĭt·ās -ātis *f* wittiness, sarcasm
dicācŭl·us -a -um *adj* quick-witted, sharp
dicātĭ·ō -ōnis *f* declaration of intent of becoming a citizen
dic·ax -ācis *adj* witty, sharp, sarcastic, caustic; pert
dichorē·us -ī *m* double trochee
dicĭ·ō -ōnis *f* jurisdiction, sway, authority, control, rule, dominion, sovereignty; **in dicione esse** (with *genit*) or **sub dicione esse** (with *genit*) to be under the control of, be subject to, be under the jurisdiction of; **in dicionem redigere** (with *genit*) or **dicioni subjicere** (with *genit*) to bring (*someone*) under the control of
dicis causā or **grātiā** *adv* for show, for the sake of appearances
dic·ō -āre *vt* to dedicate, consecrate; to deify; to inaugurate; to set apart, devote; (with *dat*) to devote (*e.g., time, energy*) to; **se dicare** (with *dat* or **in** + *acc*) to dedicate oneself to
dicō dīcĕre dixī dictum *vt* to say, tell; to indicate, mention, specify, point out; to nominate, appoint; to fix, set, appoint (*day or date*); to speak, deliver, recite; to pronounce, utter, articulate; to call, name; to assert, affirm; to describe, relate, celebrate; to tell, predict; (with double *acc*) to appoint (*someone*) as; **causam dicere** to plead or defend a case; **diem dicere** (with *dat*) to set a date for; **facete dictum!** well put!; **sententiam dicere** to

express an opinion; **testimonium dicere** to give evidence

dicrŏt·um -ī n bireme

dictamn·us -ī f dittany (wild marjoram, growing in abundance on Mt. Dicte in Crete)

dictāt·a -ōrum n pl lessons, rules; dictation

dictāt·or -ōris m dictator (emergency magistrate in Rome with absolute authority, legally appointed for a maximum six-month term); chief magistrate (of Italic town)

dictātōri·us -a -um adj dictatorial

dictātr·ix -īcis f mistress of ceremonies

dictātūr·a -ae f dictatorship

Dict·ē -ēs f mountain in Crete where Jupiter was hidden in a cave from his father Saturn

dicti·ō -ōnis f saying, speaking, uttering; diction, style; conversation; oracular response, prediction; **dictio causae** defense of a case; **dictio testimoni** right to give testimony; **juris dictio** administration of justice; jurisdiction

dictit·ō -āre vt to keep saying, to state emphatically; **causas dictitare** to practice law; **ut dictitabat** as he used to say, as he continually alleged

dict·ō -āre vt to say repeatedly, reiterate; to dictate; to compose; to suggest, remind

dict·us -a -um pp of **dīco**; n saying word, statement; witticism; maxim, proverb; prediction, prophecy; order, command, instruction; promise, assurance

Dictynn·a -ae f Diana

dī·dō or **dis·dō -děre -dĭdī -dĭtum** vt to publicize, broadcast, disseminate; to distribute, hand out

Dīd·ō -ūs (acc: **Dīdō**) f daughter of Tyrian king Belus, sister of Pygmalion, foundress and queen of Carthage, also called Elissa

dī·dūcō -dūcěre -duxī -ductum vt to draw apart, part, sever, separate, split; to undo, untie; to divide, distribute; to scatter, disperse; (in mathematics) to divide; **animus dīductus** (with abl) the mind torn between (alternatives)

diēcŭl·a -ae f little while

diērect·us -a -um adj (coll) finished, done for; **i dierectus** or **abi dierectus!** go to the devil!

di·ēs -ēī m or f day; time, period, space of time, interval; daylight, light of day; anniversary; daybreak; season; **dicere diem** (with dat) to impeach, bring an accusation against; **diem ex die** from day to day, day after day; **diem noctemque** day and night, uninterruptedly; **dies meus** my birthday; **in diem** for the moment; for a future day; **in dies** (more and more) every day; **multo denique die** not till

late in the day; **postridie ejus diei** the day after that; **post tertium ejus diei** two days after that

Diespĭt·er -ris m Jupiter

diffām·ō -āre vt to divulge (something); to defame (someone)

differenti·a -ae f difference, diversity; specific difference, species

differĭt·ās -ātis f difference

differō differre distŭlī dīlātum vt to carry in different directions; to scatter, disperse; to publicize, spread around, divulge; to defer, postpone, delay; to humor; to get rid of, put off; to distract, disquiet; vi to differ, be different, be distinguished; (with **ab** + abl) to differ from

differt·us -a -um adj stuffed, crowded, overcrowded

difficĭl·is -e adj difficult, hard; surly, cantankerous; hard to manage, hard to please

difficiliter adv with difficulty, barely

difficult·ās -ātis f difficulty, hardship, trouble, distress; surliness; poverty, financial embarrassment

difficulter adv with difficulty, barely

diffīd·ens -entis adj diffident, anxious, nervous

diffīdenter adv without confidence, distrustfully

diffīdenti·a -ae f diffidence, mistrust, distrust

dif·fīdō -fīděre -fīsus sum vi (with dat) to distrust, despair of

dif·findō -finděre -fīdī -fissum vt to split, split apart, divide; (law) **diem diffindere** to cut short the business day; (fig) to detract

dif·fingō -ěre vt to form differently, remodel; to alter

diffissus pp of **diffindo**

diffĭt·ěor -ērī vt to disavow, disown

diffl·ō -āre vi to blow away; to disperse

difflŭ·ō -ěre vi to flow in different directions, flow away; to dissolve, melt away, disappear; (with abl) to wallow in (luxury, vice)

dif·fringō -fringěre — -fractum vt to shatter, break apart, smash

dif·fugiō -fugěre -fūgī vi to flee in different directions; to disperse; to disappear

diffug·ium -ī or -**ī** n dispersion

diffundit·ō -āre vt to pour out, scatter; to waste

dif·fundō -funděre -fūdī -fūsum vt to pour, pour out; to scatter, diffuse, spread, extend; to give vent to; to cheer up, gladden

diffūsē adv diffusely; fully, at length, in detail

diffūsĭl·is -e adj diffusive, expanding

diffūs·us -a -um pp of **diffundo**; adj spread out, spread abroad; wide; prolix; protracted

diffutūt·us -a -um adj exhausted by excessive sexual indulgence

Dīgentĭ·a -ae *f* small stream on Horace's Sabine farm

dī·gĕrō -gerĕre -gessī -gestum *vt* to spread about, distribute, divide; to arrange, assort, catalogue; to interpret; to digest

dīgestĭ·ō -ōnis *f* arrangement; (rhet) enumeration

dīgestus *pp* of **dīgero**

dīgĭtŭl·us -ī *m* little finger

dĭgĭt·us -ī *m* finger; inch (*one sixteenth of a Roman foot*); toe; **cae-lum digito attingere** to reach the heights of happiness, be thrilled; **digitis concrepare** to snap the fingers; **digito uno attingere** to touch lightly, touch tenderly; **digi-tum intendere** (with **ad** + *acc*) to point the finger at; **digitus pollex** thumb; **in digitos arrectus** on tip-toe; **minimus digitus** little finger

dīgladĭ·or -ārī -ātus sum *vi* to fight hard

dīgnātĭ·ō -ōnis *f* esteem, respect, dignity, honor

dīgnē *adv* worthily, fitly

dīgnĭt·ās -ātis *f* worth, worthiness; dignity; authority, rank, reputation, distinction, majesty; self-respect; dignitary; political office; dignity (*of style*)

dīgn·ō -āre or **dīgn·or -ārī -ātus sum** *vt* to think worthy; (with *abl*) to think worthy of; (with double *acc*) to think (*someone*) worthy of being (*e.g., a son*)

dīgnosc·ō or **dīnosc·ō -ĕre** *vt* to distinguish; (with *abl*) to distinguish (*someone*) from; **dominum ac servum dignoscere** to know the difference between master and slave

dīgn·us -a -um *adj* worthy, deserving (*person*); fit, adequate, suitable, deserved, proper; (with *abl*) worthy of

dī·gredĭor -grĕdī -gressus sum *vi* to move apart, separate; to deviate; to digress

dīgressĭ·ō -ōnis *f* parting, separation; deviation; digression

dīgressus *pp* of **dīgredior**

dīgress·us -ūs *m* departure; digression

dījūdĭcātĭ·ō -ōnis *f* decision

dījūdĭc·ō -āre *vt* to decide, settle; **vera et falsa dijudicare** or **vera a falsis dijudicare** to distinguish between truth and falsehood

dījun = disjun

dī·lābor -lābī -lapsus sum *vi* to fall apart, break up; (of ice, etc.) to break up, dissolve; to disperse; to break up, decay; (of time) to slip away; (of water) to flow in different directions

dīlacĕr·ō -āre *vt* to tear to pieces

dīlāmĭn·ō -āre *vt* to split in two; **nuces dilaminare** to crack nuts

dīlanĭ·ō -āre *vt* to tear to pieces

dīlapĭd·ō -āre *vt* to demolish (*a*

structure of stone); to squander

dīlapsus *pp* of **dilabor**

dīlarg·ĭor -īrī -ītus sum *vt* to hand out generously, lavish

dīlātĭ·ō -ōnis *f* postponement, delay

dīlāt·ō -āre *vt* to dilate, stretch, broaden, extend, enlarge; (fig) to amplify, spread, extend; to drawl out

dīlāt·or -ōris *m* procrastinator, slowpoke

dīlātus *pp* of **differo**

dīlaud·ō -āre *vt* to praise enthusiastically

dīlect·us -a -um *pp* of **diligo**; *adj* beloved

dīlect·us -ūs *m* selection; (mil) selective service, draft; draftees; recruitment; **dilectum habere** to conduct a draft; **legiones ex novo dilectu conficere** to bring the legions to full strength with new draftees

dīlĭg·ens -entis *adj* careful, conscientious, accurate; exacting, strict; thrifty, industrious; (with *genit*) observant of; (with **ad** + *acc* or with **in** + *abl*) careful in, careful to, conscientious about

dīligenter *adv* carefully, diligently, industriously

dīligentĭ·a -ae *f* diligence, care, industry, attentiveness, faithfulness; economy, frugality; (with *genit*) regard for

dī·lĭgō -ligĕre -lexī -lectum *vt* to single out; to esteem, love, value, prize; to approve, be content with, appreciate

dīlōrĭc·ō -āre *vt* to tear open

dīlūc·ĕō -ēre *vi* to be clear, be evident; (with *dat*) to be obvious to

dī·lūcescō -lūcescĕre -luxī *vi* to grow light, dawn

dīlūcĭdē *adv* clearly, distinctly, plainly

dīlūcĭd·us -a -um *adj* clear, distinct, plain, evident

dīlūcŭl·um -ī *n* daybreak, dawn

dīlūd·ĭum -ĭī or **-ī** *n* intermission

dī·luō -luĕre -ŭī -ūtum *vt* to wash away, break up, separate; to dilute; to get rid of (*worries, annoyances*); to atone for; to explain, solve

dīluvĭ·ēs -ēī *f* inundation, flood, deluge

dīluvĭ·ō -āre *vt* to inundate, flood, deluge

dīluv·ĭum -ĭī or **-ī** *n* flood, deluge; (fig) destruction

dīmān·ō -āre *vi* to flow in different directions; (fig) to spread around

dīmensĭ·ō -ōnis *f* measurement

dī·mētĭor -mētīrī -mensus sum *vt* to measure out, measure off; to count off

dīmēt·ō -āre or **dīmēt·or -ārī -ātus sum** *vt* to measure out, mark out (*area*)

dīmĭcātĭ·ō -ōnis *f* fight, combat, struggle; contest, rivalry dīmĭc·ō -āre *vi* to fight, struggle; to be in conflict, run a risk, be in peril; (with **cum** + *abl*) to fight against; **de capite dimicare** or **de vita dimicare** to fight for one's life

dīmĭdĭāt·us -a -um *adj* half, in half

dīmĭdĭ·us -a -um *adj* half; broken in two, broken; **dimidius patrum, dimidius plebis** half patrician, half plebeian; *n* half; **dimidium militum quam** half as many soldiers as

dīmissĭ·ō -ōnis *f* dismissal, discharging, sending out

dī·mittō -mittĕre -mīsī -missum *vt* to send away, send around, send out, scatter, distribute; to break up, dismiss, disband; (mil) to discharge; to let loose; to divorce (*wife*); to leave, desert, abandon, give up, relinquish; to let go, let slip, forgo, forsake, renounce; to remit

dimminŭ·ō or dīmĭnŭ·ō -ĕre *vt* to break to pieces, smash, shatter

dī·movĕō -movēre -mōvī -mōtum *vt* to move apart, part, separate; to disperse, dismiss, scatter; to lure away

Dindymēn·ē -ēs *f* Cybele (*also called Magna Mater by the Romans*)

Dindȳm·us -ī *m* or Dindȳm·a -ōrum *n pl* mountain in Asia Minor, sacred to Cybele

dīnoscō see dignosco

dīnŭmĕrātĭ·ō -ōnis *f* enumeration, counting up

dīnŭmĕr·ō -āre *vt* to enumerate, count up, compute; to count out, pay

dĭōbŏlār·is -e *adj* costing two obols

Dĭŏdŏt·us -ī *m* Stoic philosopher and tutor of Cicero (d. 59 B.C.)

diŏcēs·is -is *f* district, governor's jurisdiction

diŏcēt·ēs -ae *m* treasurer; secretary of revenue

Dĭŏgĕn·ēs -is *m* famous Ionic philosopher and pupil of Anaximenes (5th cent. B.C.); Cynic philosopher, born at Sinope, in Pontus (412?-323 B.C.)

Dĭŏmēd·ēs -is *m* son of Tydeus and king of Argos; hero at Troy

Dĭōn·ē -ēs or Dĭōn·a -ae *f* mother of Venus

Dĭŏnȳsĭ·a -ōrum *n pl* Greek festival of Bacchus

Dĭŏnȳsĭ·us -ī *m* tyrant of Syracuse (430-367 B.C.); Dionysus the Younger (397-330?)

Dĭŏnȳs·us or Dĭŏnȳs·os -ī *m* Bacchus

dĭōt·a -ae *f* two-handled wine jar

dĭplōm·a -ătis *n* official letter of recommendation

Dĭpȳl·on -ī *n* N.W. gate at Athens

Dīr·a -ae *f* a Fury; *f pl* the Furies (*goddesses of revenge and remorse*)

dīr·ae -ārum *f pl* curse, execration

Dircae·us -a -um *adj* Dircean, Boeotian; **cycnus Dircaeus Dir-**

cean or Boeotian swan (*i.e., Pindar, famous lyric poet from Boeotia, 522?-442 B.C.*)

Dirc·ē -ēs *f* famous fountain in Boeotia

dīrect·us -a -um *pp* of dirigo; *adj* straight, direct; straightforward

dīremptus *pp* of dirimo

dīrempt·us -ūs *m* separation

dīreptĭ·ō -ōnis *f* plundering, pillaging; *f pl* acts of pillage

dīrept·or -ōris *m* plunderer

dīreptus *pp* of diripio

dīrĭb·ĕō -ēre — -ĭtum *vt* to sort (*votes taken out of the ballot box*)

dīrĭbĭtĭ·ō -ōnis *f* sorting

dīrĭbĭt·or -ōris *m* sorter (*of ballots*)

dīrĭbĭtōr·ĭum -ĭī or -ĭ *n* sorting room

dī·rĭgō -rĭgĕre -rēxī -rectum *vt* to put in order, arrange, line up, deploy

dir·ĭmō -imĕre -ēmī -emptum *vt* to take apart, part, separate, divide; to break off, disturb, interrupt; to separate, dissolve; to put off, delay; to break off, end, bring to an end; to nullify, bring to naught

dī·rĭpĭō -rĭpĕre -rĭpŭī -reptum *vt* to tear apart, tear to pieces; to lay waste, pillage, plunder, ravage; to snatch away, tear away; to whip out (*sword*); to steal

dīrĭt·ās -ātis *f* mischief; misfortune; cruelty

dī·rumpō or dis·rumpō -rumpĕre -rūpī -ruptum *vt* to break to pieces, smash, shatter; to break off (*friendship*); to sever (*ties*); **dirumpi** to burst (*with laughter, envy, indignation, etc.*)

dīrŭ·ō -ĕre -ī -tum *vt* to pull apart, demolish, destroy, overthrow; to scatter, disperse; (mil) to break up (*enemy formation*); to bankrupt

dīr·us -a -um *adj* fearful, awful; ominous, ill-omened; dreadful, awful, abominable; cruel, relentless, fierce; **temporibus diris** in the reign of terror; **venena dira** deadly poisons

dī·s -tis *adj* rich, wealthy; rich, fertile (*land*); rich, generous, expensive (*offerings*); (with *abl*) abounding in

Dī·s -tis *m* Pluto (*king of the lower world*)

dis·cēdō -cēdĕre -cessī -cessum *vi* to go away, depart; to separate, be severed; to disperse, scatter, be dissipated, disappear; (mil) to march off, break camp; to come off (*victorious, etc.*); to deviate; to swerve; to pass away, vanish, cease; (with **ab** + *abl*) to forsake (*e.g., friends*); **b** to deviate from, swerve from; **c** to abandon, give up; (with **ex** or **de** + *abl*) to go away from, depart from; (with **ad** + *acc*) to depart for; (with **in** + *acc*) to vote for; **discedere in Catonis sen-**

tentiam to vote for Cato's proposal

disceptātǐ·ō -ōnis f dispute, difference of opinion; discussion, debate

disceptāt·or -ōris m or **disceptā-trīx·īcis** f arbitrator

discept·ō -āre vt to debate, dispute, discuss, treat; to decide, settle (controversies, wars); vi to act as umpire; to be at stake

dis·cernō -cernĕre -crēvī -crētum vt to separate, mark off, divide; to keep apart; to distinguish between; to discern, make out, distinguish

dis·cerpō -cerpĕre -cerpsī -cerptum vt to tear to pieces, mangle, mutilate; (fig) to tear apart (with words, arguments)

discessǐ·ō -ōnis f separation, division; separation, divorce; (in the senate) division, formal vote; **discessio sine ulla varietate** unanimous vote

discess·us -ūs m separation, parting; going away, departure; banishment; marching away, marching off

discid·ǐum -ǐī or **-ī** n parting, separation; discord, dissension, disagreement; divorce

discīd·ō -ĕre vt to cut to pieces, cut up

discinct·us -a -um pp of **discingo**; adj without a girdle; dissolute, loose; effeminate, voluptuous

di·scindō -scindĕre -scīdī -scissum vt to tear apart, tear open, rend, tear; **amicitias discindere** to break off ties of friendship

dis·cingō -cingĕre -cinxī -cinctum vt to take off, ungird; to loose; (fig) to relax

disciplīn·a -ae f instruction, training, teaching, education; learning, knowledge, science; discipline; custom, habit; system; **militaris disciplina** basic training; **rei publicae disciplina** statesmanship

discipǔl·us -ī m or **discipǔl·a -ae** f pupil, student; disciple, follower

discissus pp of **discindo**

dis·clūdō -clūdĕre -clūsī -clūsum vt to keep apart, divide, shut off; **iram et cupiditatem locis discludere** to assign anger and passion to their proper places

discō discĕre didǐcī vt to learn, learn to know, become acquainted with; to be told (e.g., the truth); (with inf) to learn how to

discobǒl·us -ī m discus thrower

discǒl·or -ōris adj of a different color; different; (with dat) different from

discondūc·ō -ĕre vi to be unprofitable

disconvenǐ·ō -īre vi to disagree; to be inconsistent

discordābǐl·is -e adj discordant, disagreeing

discordǐ·a -ae f discord, dissension, disagreement; mutiny

discordiōs·us -a -um adj prone to discord, seditious

discord·ō -āre vi to quarrel, disagree; (with dat or ab + abl) to be out of harmony with, be opposed to

discor·s -dis adj discordant, inharmonious; disagreeing, at variance; contradictory, inconsistent; warring (winds, etc.); (with abl) inconsistent with, at variance with, different from

discrepantǐ·a -ae f discrepancy, dissimilarity, difference

discrepātǐ·ō -ōnis f disagreement, dispute

discrepǐt·ō -āre vi to be completely different

discrep·ō -āre -ǔī vi to be different in sound, sound different; to be out of tune; to disagree, be different, be inconsistent, vary, differ; to be disputed; (with dat or abl or with ab or cum + abl) to disagree with, be different from, be inconsistent with; v impers there is a difference of opinion, it is undecided, it is a matter of dispute; **discrepat inter scriptores rerum** there is a difference of opinion among historians

di·scrībō -scrībĕre -scripsī -scriptum vt to distribute, classify, divide; to assign, apportion; (with in + acc) to distribute among, divide among

discrīm·en -ǐnis n dividing line; interval, intervening space, division, distance, separation; discrimination, difference, distinction; critical moment, turning point; decision, determination; crisis, jeopardy, peril, danger, risk; decisive battle

discrīmin·ō -āre vt to divide, separate; to apportion

discriptē adv orderly, lucidly, distinctly

discriptǐ·ō -ōnis f distribution, classification

discript·us -a -um pp of **discribo**; adj well arranged; secluded

discrucǐ·ō -āre vt to torture; to distress, torment

dis·cumbō -cumbĕre -cubǔī -cubitum vi to take their places at the table; (of several) to go to bed

discup·ǐō -ĕre vt (coll) to want badly; (with inf) (coll) to be dying to

dis·currō -currĕre -cucurrī or **-currī -cursum** vi to run in different directions, scamper about, run up and down, dash around

discurs·us -ūs m running up and down, running about; (mil) pincer movement

disc·us -ī m discus

dis·cutǐō -cutĕre -cussī -cussum vt to knock apart; to smash to pieces, shatter; to break up, disperse, scatter, dispel; to frustrate, bring to naught; to suppress, destroy

disertē or **disertim** adv eloquently

disert·us -a -um adj fluent, well-spoken; clear, articulate

disject·ō -āre vt to toss about

disject·us -a -um pp of **disjicio**; adj scattered; dilapidated

disject·us -ūs m scattering

dis·jiciō -jicĕre -jēcī -jectum vt to drive apart, scatter, break up; to tear to pieces; to ruin, destroy; to thwart, frustrate, wreck; (mil) to break up (enemy formation)

disjunctĭ·ō or **dījunctĭ·ō -ōnis** f separation, alienation; diviation, variation; dilemma; asyndeton (succession of clauses without conjunctions)

disjunct·us -a -um adj separate, distinct; distant, remote; disjointed, disconnected, incoherent (speech); logically opposed; n pl opposites

dis·jungō or **dī·jungo -jungĕre -junxī -junctum** vt to unyoke; to sever, divide, part, remove; to separate, part, estrange, disunite, alienate

dispalesc·ō -ĕre vi to be divulged, spread

dispāl·or -ārī -ātus sum vi to wander about, straggle

dis·pandō (or **dis·pendō**) **-pandĕre — -pansum** (or **dis·pennō -pennĕre — -pessum**) vt to stretch out, extend; to spread out, expand

dis·pār -pāris adj different, unlike; unequal, ill-matched; unequal, of different lengths

disparĭl·is -e adj different, dissimilar

disparilĭter adv differently

dispăr·ō -āre vt to separate, segregate

dispartĭō or **dispartĭor** see **dispertio**

dispectus pp of **dispicio**

dis·pellō -pellĕre -pŭlī -pulsum vt to disperse, scatter; to drive away, dispel

dispend·ĭum -ĭī or **-ī** n expense, cost; loss

dispendō see **dispando**

dispennō see **dispando**

dispensātĭ·ō -ōnis f weighing out, doling out; management, superintendence, direction, administration; position of superintendent or treasurer

dispensāt·or -ōris m household manager, chief butler; cashier, treasurer

dispens·ō -āre vt to weigh out, pay out; to distribute, manage (household stores); to regulate, manage, superintend

dispercut·ĭō -ĕre vt to knock out; cerebrum dispercutĕre (with dat) (coll) to knock out (someone's) brains

disper·dō -dĕre -dĭdī -dĭtum vt to spoil, ruin; to squander

disper·ĕō -īre -ĭī vi to go to ruin; to go to waste; to be undone, perish; **disperiī** (coll) I'm finished; **dispeream si** (coll) I'll be darned if

di·spergō -spergĕre -spersī -spersum vt to scatter about, disperse; to splatter; to distribute, scatter (e.g., men) without organization; to spread, extend (war, rumor, etc.)

dispersē adv here and there; occasionally

dispersus pp of **dispergo**

dispert·ĭō -īre -īvī or **-ĭī -ītum** or **dispert·ĭor** or **dispart·ĭor -īrī -ītus sum** vt to distribute, divide; to assign (e.g., gates, areas) as posts to be guarded

dispessus pp of **dispando**

di·spiciō -spicĕre -spexī -spectum vt to see clearly, make out, distinguish, detect; to consider carefully, perceive, detect, discern, discover, reflect on

displic·ĕō -ēre -ŭī -ĭtum vi to be unpleasant, be displeasing; (with dat) to displease; **sibi displicere** to be dissatisfied with oneself; to be in a bad humor

dis·plōdō -plōdĕre — -plōsum vi to explode

dis·pōnō -pōnĕre -posŭī -posĭtum vt to place here and there; to distribute, arrange, set in order; to station, post, assign; to adjust, order, dispose; **diem disponere** to arrange the day's schedule

disposĭtē adv orderly, methodically

disposĭtĭ·ō -ōnis f orderly arrangement, development (of theme, essay)

disposĭtūr·a -ae f orderly arrangement

disposĭt·us -a -um pp of **dispono**; adj well arranged; methodical, orderly

disposĭt·us -ūs m orderly arrangement

dispŭd·et -ēre -ŭit v impers (with inf) it is a great shame to

dispulsus pp of **dispello**

dis·pungō -pungĕre -punxī -punctum vt to check, balance, audit (an account)

disputātĭ·ō -ōnis f arguing; argument, debate

disputāt·or -ōris m disputant, debater

disput·ō -āre vt to dispute, discuss; (com) to estimate, compute; to examine, treat, explain

disquīr·ō -ĕre vt to examine in detail

disquīsitĭ·ō -ōnis f inquiry, investigation

disrumpō see **dirumpo**

dissaep·ĭō -īre -sī -tum vt to separate, wall off, fence off

dissaept·um -ī n partition, barrier

dissāvĭ·or or **dissuāvĭ·or -ārī -ātus sum** vt to kiss passionately

dissĕc·ō -āre -ŭī -tum vt to cut apart, dissect

dissēmĭn·ō -āre vt to disseminate

dissensĭ·ō -ōnis f difference of opinion, disagreement; dissension; conflict, incompatibility

dissens·us -ūs m dissension, discord

dissentānĕ·us -a -um *adj* disagreeing, contrary

dis·sentĭō -sentīre -sensī -sensum *vi* to differ in opinion, disagree, dissent; to differ, be in conflict, be inconsistent; (with *dat* or with **ab** or **cum** + *abl*) to differ with, disagree with; (with **ab** + *abl*) to differ from, be opposed to

disserēn·at -āre *v impers* it is clearing up

dis·sĕrō -serĕre -sēvī -situm *vt* to scatter; to sow here and there; to stick in the ground at intervals

dissĕr·ō -ĕre -ŭī -tum *vt* to arrange; to examine; to discuss, argue, treat

disserp·ō -ĕre *vi* to creep about; to spread gradually

dissertĭ·ō -ōnis *f* gradual abolition, severance

dissert·ō -āre *vt* to discuss, treat

dissertus *pp* of **dissero** (to arrange)

dis·sĭdĕō -sĭdēre -sēdī -sessum *vi* to be located far apart, be distant, be remote; to disagree, be at variance; to differ, be unlike; (of a garment) to be on crooked; (with **ab** or **cum** + *abl*) to disagree with

dissignātĭ·ō -ōnis *f* arrangement

dissignāt·or -ōris *m* master of ceremonies; usher (*at the theater*); undertaker

dissign·ō -āre *vt* to regulate, arrange; to contrive

dissil·ĭō -īre -ŭī *vi* to fly apart, split, break up, burst; to be dissolved

dissimĭl·is -e *adj* dissimilar, unlike, different; (with *genit* or *dat* or with **atque** or **ac**) to be dissimilar to, different from

dissimilĭter *adv* differently

dissimilitūd·ō -ĭnis *f* difference

dissimulanter *adv* secretly, slyly

dissimulanti·a -ae *f* faking, hiding, dissembling

dissimulātĭ·ō -ōnis *f* concealing, disguising; Socratic irony

dissimulāt·or -ōris *m* dissembler, faker

dissimŭl·ō -āre *vt* to dissemble, conceal, disguise; to keep secret; to pretend not to see, ignore

dissipābĭl·is -e *adj* diffusible, dispersible

dissipātĭ·ō -ōnis *f* scattering, dispersal, dissipation; destruction

dissĭp·ō or **dissŭp·ō -āre** to scatter, disperse; to break up (*enemy formation*); to demolish, overthrow; to squander, dissipate; to circulate, spread; to drive away (*worries*)

dissĭt·us *pp* of **dissero** (to scatter)

dissociābĭl·is -e *adj* separating, estranging; incompatible

dissociātĭ·ō -ōnis *f* separation

dissocĭ·ō -āre *vt* to dissociate, separate; to ostracize; to set at variance, estrange; to divide into factions; to detach

dissolūbĭl·is -e *adj* dissoluble, separable

dissolūtē *adv* disconnectedly, loosely; carelessly

dissolūtĭ·ō -ōnis *f* dissolution, dissolving, breaking up; abolishing, destruction; refutation; looseness, dissoluteness; asyndeton (*succession of clauses without conjunctions*)

dissolūt·us -a -um *adj* disconnected, loose; careless, negligent, remiss; loose, licentious, dissolute; *n* asyndeton (*succession of clauses without conjunctions*)

dis·solvō -solvĕre -solvī -solūtum *vt* to dissolve, break up, loosen; to free, release; (fig) to break up; to pay; to refute; to untie; **animam dissolvere** to die; **legem dissolvere** to abrogate or annul a law; **poenam dissolvere** to pay the penalty

dissŏn·us -a -um *adj* dissonant, discordant, jarring, confused (*sounds, voices*); different; (with *abl*) differing from, different from

dissor·s -tis *adj* having a different fate; unshared

dis·suādĕō -suādēre -suāsī -suāsum *vt* to advise against, dissuade, object to, oppose

dissuāsĭ·ō -ōnis *f* dissuasion; (with *genit*) opposition to, objection to

dissuās·or -ōris *m* objector, opponent

dissuāvĭor see **dissavior**

dissult·ō -āre *vi* to fly apart, burst

dis·sŭō -sŭĕre — -sūtum *vt* to unstitch; to untie, undo, unfasten

dissūpō see **dissipo**

distaed·et -ēre *v impers* it makes (*one*) tired; (with *genit*) it makes (*one*) tired of; **me distaedet loqui** I'm sick and tired of speaking

distanti·a -ae *f* distance, remoteness; difference, diversity

dis·tendō (or **dis·tennō**) **-tendĕre -tendī -tentum** *vt* to stretch apart, stretch out; to distend, swell; to distract, perplex

distent·us -a -um *pp* of **distendo**; *adj* distended; *pp* of **distineo**; *adj* busy, occupied, distracted

distermĭn·ō -āre *vt* to separate by a boundary, divide, limit

distĭch·on -ī *n* couplet

distinctē *adv* distinctly, clearly, with precision

distinctĭ·ō -ōnis *f* distinction, differentiation, discrimination; difference; (gram) punctuation

distinct·us -a -um *pp* of **distinguo**; *adj* distinct, separate; studded, adorned; varied, diversified; lucid (*speaker*); eminent

distinct·us -ūs *m* difference, distinction

dis·tĭnĕō -tĭnēre -tĭnŭī -tentum *vt* to keep apart, separate; to detain, hold back, hinder; to employ, engage, divert; to put off, delay; (mil) to keep (*troops*) from meeting; to keep divided; to stand in the way of (*peace, victory, etc.*); to distract

di·stinguō -stinguĕre -stinxī -stinctum *vt* to mark off; to separate, part; to set off (*with colors, gold, etc.*); to distinguish, specify; to punctuate

dist·ō -āre *vi* to stand apart, be separate, be distant; to differ, be different; (with *dat* or **ab** + *abl*) to differ from; *v impers* there is a difference, it is important, makes a difference

dis·torqueō -torquĕre -torsī -tortum *vt* to twist, distort; to curl (*lips*); to roll (*eyes*)

distortī·ō -ōnis *f* twisting; contortion

distort·us -a -um *pp* of **distorqueo**; *adj* distorted, misshapen, deformed; perverse

distracti·ō -ōnis *f* pulling apart; dividing; discord, dissension

distract·us -a -um *adj* severed, separate

dis·trahō -trahĕre -traxī -tractum *vt* to pull or drag apart, separate forcibly; to tear away, drag away, remove; to distract; to sever, break up; to estrange, alienate; to prevent, frustrate; to end, settle (*e.g., disputes*); to sell at retail, sell (*e.g., land*) in lots

distrib·uō -uĕre -uī -utum *vt* to distribute

distribūtē *adv* methodically

distribūti·ō -ōnis *f* distribution, apportionment, division

district·us -a -um *adj* drawn in opposite directions; distracted, busied, engaged

di·stringō -stringĕre -strinxī -strictum *vt* to draw apart; to distract, draw the attention of

distrunc·ō -āre *vt* to cut in two, hack apart

disturbāti·ō -ōnis *f* destruction

disturb·ō -āre *vt* to throw into confusion; to smash up, demolish; to break up (*a marriage*); to frustrate

ditesc·ō -ĕre *vi* to grow rich

dīthyrambic·us -a -um *adj* dithyrambic; *m* dithyramb (*song in honor of Bacchus*)

dīthyramb·us -ī *m* dithyramb

dīti·ae -ārum *f pl* wealth

dit·ō -āre *vt* to make rich, enrich; **ditari** to get rich

diū *adv* by day, in the daytime; long, for a long time; in a long time; **diu noctuque** by day and by night, continually; **iam diu** this long; **satis diu** long enough

diurn·us -a -um *adj* of the day, by day, day, daytime; daily, of each day; day's, of one day; **acta diurna** daily newspaper; **merum diurnum** daytime drinking; *n* account book; *n pl* record, journal, diary

dī·us -a -um *adj* godlike, divine, noble

diūtīnē *adv* for a long time

diūtīn·us -a -um *adj* long, lasting

diūtissĭmē *adv* for a very long time; longest; **iam diutissime** long, long ago

diūtius *adv* longer, still longer; **paulum diutius** a little too long

diūturnĭt·ās -ātis *f* length of time, long duration; durability

diūturn·us -a -um *adj* long, longlasting

dīv·a -ae *f* goddess

dīvārĭc·ō -āre *vt* to stretch out, spread

dī·vellō -vellĕre -vellī -vulsum *vt* to tear apart, tear to pieces; to tear away; to untie; to wrest, remove, separate; to estrange

dī·vendō -vendĕre — -vendĭtum *vt* to sell piecemeal, retail

dīverbĕr·ō -āre *vt* to zip through, fly through

diverb·ium -iī *or* **-ī** *n* dialogue, verbal exchange

dīversē *or* **dīvorsē** *adv* in different directions; differently

dīversĭt·ās -ātis *f* diversity, difference; contradiction, direct opposite

dīvers·us *or* **dīvors·us -a -um** *pp* of **diverto**; *adj* in different directions; apart, separate; different; remote, opposite, diametrically opposed; hostile; unsettled, irresolute; dissimilar, distinct; *m pl* individuals; *n* opposite direction, different quarter, opposite side, opposite view

dī·vertō *or* **dī·vortō -vertĕre -vertī -versum** *vi* to go different ways; to turn off; to stop off, stay

dīv·es -ĭtis *adj* rich, wealthy; costly, precious, sumptuous; plentiful, abundant; (with *genit* or *abl*) rich in, abounding in

dīvex·ō -āre *vt* to plunder; to violate

dīvidĭ·a -ae *f* worry, trouble, nuisance; dissension, antagonism

dī·vidō -vidĕre -vīsī -vīsum *vt* to divide, force apart; to divide, distribute, share; to break up, destroy; to arrange, apportion; to separate, distinguish; to separate, segregate, keep apart; to accompany (*songs with music*); **sententiam dividere** to break down a proposal (*so as to vote on each part separately*)

dīvidŭ·us -a -um *adj* divisible; divided, separated

dīvīnāti·ō -ōnis *f* clairvoyance; forecasting, predicting, divination; (law) selection of the most suitable prosecutor

dīvīnē *adv* through divine power; prophetically, by divine inspiration; divinely, gorgeously

dīvīnĭt·ās -ātis *f* divinity, godhead; prophetic power, clairvoyance; excellence

dīvīnĭtus *adv* from heaven, from god; providentially; prophetically; divinely, in a godlike manner; excellently

dīvīn·ō -āre vt to divine, predict, prophesy, foresee, dread

dīvīn·us -a -um adj divine, heavenly; divinely inspired, prophetic; godlike, superhuman, excellent, gorgeous; dīvīnum jus natural law; dīvīnum jus et hūmānum natural and positive law; dīvīnum scelus sacrilege; rērum dīvīnārum et hūmānārum scientia physics and ethics; rem dīvīnam facere to worship; to sacrifice; rēs dīvīna worship; sacrifice; rēs dīvīnae religious affairs, religion; m prophet; n offering; n pl divine matters; religious duties; agere dīvīna hūmānaque to perform religious and secular duties; dīvīna hūmānaque things divine and human, the whole world

dīvīsi·ō -ōnis f division, distribution

dīvīs·or -ōris m distributer; person hired by a candidate to distribute bribes

dīvīs·us -a -um pp of dīvidō; adj separate, distinct

dīvīs·us -ūs m distribution; dīvīsuī facilis easily divided, easy to divide

dīvitī·ae -ārum f pl riches, wealth; richness (of soil); costly things

dīvolg- = dīvulg-

dīvor- = dīver-

dīvort·ium -iī or -ī n separation; divorce; fork (of road or river); dīvortium facere cum aliquā to divorce some woman

dīvulgāt·us -a -um adj common, widespread

dīvulg·ō -āre vt to divulge, spread among the people; to publish (a book); to spread, publicize, advertise

dīvulsus pp of dīvellō

dīv·us -a -um adj divine; deified; m god, deity; n sky; the open; sub dīvo out in the open, under the open sky; sub dīvum rapere to bring out in the open

dō dare dedī datum (danit = dat; danunt = dant; dane = dasne; duim = dem) vt to give; to offer, dedicate; to give out, pay (money); to bestow, confer; to permit, grant, concede, allow; to give up, hand over; to communicate, tell; to ascribe, impute, assign; to cause, produce, make; to furnish, afford, present; to grant, admit; to administer (medicine); to utter, give expression to, announce; legem dare to enact a law; locum dare (with dat) to make way for; nomen dare to enlist; operam dare to pay attention; operam dare (with dat) to pay attention to, give or devote attention to, look out for; poenam or poenas dare to pay the penalty; se dare to present oneself; to plunge, rush; velum dare to set sail; veniam dare to grant pardon

doc·eō -ēre -uī -tum vt to teach, instruct; to instruct, give instructions

to; (with double acc) to teach (some-one something); fabulam docere to teach a play (to the actors), produce a play, put on a play

dochm·ius -iī or -ī m dochmaic foot (consisting of a trochee and a cretic)

docil·is -e adj docile, easily taught, teachable; docile, tractable

docilit·ās -ātis f docility, aptitude for learning

doctē adv learnedly, skillfully; shrewdly, cleverly

doct·or -ōris m teacher

doctrin·a -ae f teaching, instruction, education, training; lesson; erudition, learning; science

doct·us -a -um pp of doceo; adj learned, skilled, experienced, clever, trained; cunning, shrewd; (with abl, with ad + acc, or in + abl) skilled in, experienced in, clever at

document·um -ī or docūm·en -inis n example, model, pattern; object lesson, warning; evidence, proof

Dōdōn·a -ae f town in Epirus, famous for the oracular oak tree sacred to Jupiter

Dōdōnae·us -a -um adj of Dodona

dōdr·āns -antis m three fourths; hērēs ex dodrante heir entitled to three fourths of the estate

dogm·a -ātis n doctrine, tenet

dolābr·a -ae f pickax, mattock

dol·ēns -entis adj painful, smarting; distressing

dolenter adv painfully; with sorrow

dol·eō -ēre -uī -itum vt to give pain to, hurt; vi to feel pain, be sore, ache, smart; to grieve, be sorry, be hurt; take offense; (with dat) to give pain to, afflict, hurt; caput mihi dolet I have a headache

dōliār·is -e adj fat, tubby

dōliōl·um -ī n small barrel

dōl·ium -iī or -ī n large wine jar

dol·ō -āre vt to chop; to beat, beat up, drub; (fig) to hack out (e.g., a poem)

dol·ō or dol·ōn -ōnis m pike; string; fore topsail

Dol·ō -ōnis m Dolon (Trojan spy)

Dolop·es -um m pl a people of Thessaly

dol·or -ōris m pain, ache, smart; pain, grief, distress, anguish; indignation, resentment, chagrin; pathos; object of grief; capitis dolor headache; dentis dolor toothache; esse dolorī (with dat) to be a cause of grief or resentment to

dolōsē adv shrewdly, slyly

dolōs·us -a -um adj wily, cunning, deceitful

dol·us -ī m trick, device; deceit, cunning, trickery; dolus malus (law) intentional deceit, willful wrong, fraud, malice

domābil·is -e adj tameable

domesticātim adv at home

domestic·us -a -um adj of the house or home; domestic, household;

familiar, private, personal; domestic, native, of one's own country; **bellum domesticum** civil war; *m pl* members of the household or family

domī *adv* at home

domicil·ium -iī or **-ī** *n* residence, home

domin·a or **domn·a -ae** *f* lady of the house; mistress, owner; lady; sweetheart; wife

domin·ans -antis *adj* ruling, holding sway; **nomen dominans** word in its literal sense; *m* ruler

dominātĭ·ō -ōnis *f* mastery; tyranny, despotism, absolute power; *f pl* control, supremacy; rulers

domināt·or -ōris *m* ruler, lord

dominātr·ix -īcis *f* ruler, mistress

domināt·us -ūs *m* absolute rule, sovereignty, tyranny; control, mastery

dominĭc·us -a -um *adj* of a lord, lord's, master's

Dominĭc·us -a -um *adj* (eccl) the Lord's

domin·ium -iī or **-ī** *n* absolute ownership; banquet, feast

domin·or -ārī -ātus sum *vi* to be master, be lord, have dominion; to play the master, domineer; (with **in** + *acc* or **in** + *abl*) to lord it over, tyrannize

domin·us -ī *m* owner, proprietor, possessor, master, ruler, lord; ruler, despot, tyrant; commander, chief; entertainer, host

Domin·us -ī *m* (eccl) Lord, Master

domiport·a -ae *f* snail

Domitiān·us -ī *m* T. Flavius Domitianus (*son of Vespasian, brother of Titus, and Roman emperor, 81-96 A.D.*)

domĭt·ō -āre *vt* to train, break in

domĭt·or -ōris *m* or **domĭtr·ix -īcis** *f* tamer

domĭt·us -ūs *m* taming

dom·ō -āre -uī -ĭtum *vt* to tame, break in; to domesticate; to master, subdue, vanquish, conquer

dom·us -ūs or **-ī** (*dat:* **domuī** or **domō;** *abl:* **domō** or **domū;** *locat:* **domī** rarely **domō** or **domuī;** *genit pl:* **domŭum** or **domōrum**) *f* house, building, mansion, palace; home, residence, family; native country; philosophical sect; **domī** at home; **domī militiaeque** at home and in the field, in peace and in war; **domum** homewards, home

dōnābĭl·is -e *adj* worthy of a gift

dōnār·ium -iī or **-ī** *n* gift repository of a temple; sanctuary; altar; votive offering

dōnātĭ·ō -ōnis *f* donation

dōnātīv·um -ī *n* (mil) bonus

dōnec *conj* while; as long as; until

dōn·ō -āre *vt* to present, bestow, grant, confer; to forgive, pardon; to give up, sacrifice; **aliquem civitate donare** to present someone with citizenship; **civitatem ali-**

cui donare to bestow citizenship on someone

dōn·um -ī *n* gift, present; votive offering, sacrifice; **ultima dona** funeral rites, obsequies

dorc·as -ādis *f* gazelle

Dōr·ēs -um *m pl* Dorians (*one of the four Hellenic tribes*)

Dōrĭc·us or **Dōrĭcĭ·us -a -um** *adj* Dorian; Greek

Dōr·is -idis *f* daughter of Oceanus, wife of Nereus, and mother of fifty sea nymphs

dorm·ĭō -īre -īvī or **-iī -ītum** *vi* to sleep; to be inactive, be idle, be lazy

dormītāt·or -ōris *m* dreamer

dormĭt·ō -āre *vi* to be sleepy, be drowsy; to nod, fall asleep

dormītōrĭ·us -a -um *adj* for sleeping; **cubiculum dormitorium** bedroom

dors·um -ī *n* back; ridge; reef

dōs dōtis *f* dowry

Dossenn·us -ī *m* hunchback, clown (*well-known character in early Italic comedy*)

dōtāl·is -e *adj* of a dowry, given as a dowry, dotal

dōt·ō -āre *vt* to endow

drachm·a or **drachŭm·a -ae** *f* drachma (*Greek coin approximately the value of a denarius*)

drac·ō -ōnis *m* dragon; huge serpent

Drac·ō -ōnis *m* Dragon (*constellation*); Draco (*Athenian lawgiver, notorious for his severity, c. 621 B.C.*)

dracōnĭgĕn·us -a -um *adj* sprung from a dragon; **urbs draconigena** Thebes

drāpĕt·a -ae *m* runaway slave

drom·as -ādis *m* dromedary, camel

drom·os -ī *m* Spartan racetrack

Druĭd·ēs -um or **Druĭd·ae -ārum** *m pl* Druids (*priests and sages of the Gauls and Britons*)

Drūsill·a -ae *f* Livia Drusilla (*second wife of Augustus and mother of Tiberius, 63 B.C.-29 A.D.*)

Drūs·us -ī *m* Livius Drusus (*tribune of the people with C. Gracchus in 122 B.C.*); M. Livius Drusus (*former's son, famous orator and tribune of the people in 91 B.C.*); Nero Claudius Drusus (*son of Livia, brother of Tiberius, 38-9 B.C.*)

Dry·ad -ădis *f* dryad (*wood nymph*)

Dryŏp·es -um *m pl* people of Epirus

dubĭē *adv* doubtfully; **haud dubie** undoubtedly, indubitably

dubitābĭl·is -e *adj* doubtful

dubitanter *adv* doubtingly, hesitantly

dubitātĭ·ō -ōnis *f* doubt, uncertainty; wavering, hesitancy, irresolution; hesitation, delay; (rhet) pretended embarrassment (*to win over the sympathy of the audience*)

dubĭt·ō -āre *vt* to doubt; to consider, ponder; *vi* to be doubtful, be in doubt, be uncertain, be perplexed;

to deliberate; to waver, hesitate, delay

dubi·us -a -um *adj* wavering, doubtful, dubious, uncertain, irresolute; dubious, undermined; precarious, critical, adverse, difficult; dim (*light*); overcast (*sky*); indecisive (*battle*); *n* doubt, question; **haud pro dubio habere** to regard as beyond doubt; **in dubium venire** to come in question; **in dubium vocare** to call in question; **procul dubio** beyond doubt, undoubtedly

ducēnāri·us -a -um *adj* receiving a salary of 200,000 sesterces

ducēn·ī -ae -a *adj* two hundred each

ducentēsim·a -ae *f* half percent

ducent·ī -ae -a *adj* two hundred

ducentiens or **ducentiēs** *adv* two hundred times

dūcō dūcĕre duxī ductum *vt* to lead, guide, direct, conduct; to lead, command; to lead, march; to draw, pull, haul; to draw out, protract, prolong; to put off, stall (*someone*); to pass, spend (*time*); to pull at (*oars*); to mislead, take in, fool, trick; to draw, attract; to draw (*lots*); to draw in, breathe in, inhale; to suck in, drink; to draw, trace; to construct, form, fashion, shape; to run (*a wall from one point to another*); to assume, get (*name*); to lead home, marry (*a woman*); to calculate, compute; to regard, consider, hold, account; to derive, trace (*lineage*); to spin (*wool*); (of a road) to lead, take (*someone*)

ductim *adv* in a continuous stream

ductit·ō -āre *vt* to take home, marry (*a woman*); to lead on, trick, deceive, cheat

duct·ō -āre *vt* to lead; to draw; to accompany, escort

duct·or -ōris *m* leader, commander, general; guide, pilot

duct·us -ūs *m* drawing, conducting; line, row; leadership, command; **oris ductus** facial expression

dūdum *adv* a short time ago, a little while ago; just now; once, formerly; **cum dudum** just as; **haud dudum** not long ago, just now; **jam dudum** for some time; **jam dudum eum expecto** I have been expecting him; **quam dudum** how long; **ut dudum** just as

Duīli·us or **Duīl·ius -iī** or **-ī** *m* Roman consul who won Rome's first naval engagement against the Carthaginians off Sicily in 260 B.C.

dūm see **do**

dulcēd·ō -inis *f* sweetness; pleasantness, charm, delightfulness

dulc·escō -escĕre -uī *vi* to become sweet

dulcicŭl·us -a -um *adj* rather sweet

dulcif·er -ĕra -ĕrum *adj* full of sweetness, sweet

dulc·is -e *adj* pleasant, charming,

delightful; dear, friendly, kind; sweet

dulcĭter *adv* agreeably, pleasantly, sweetly

dulcitūd·ō -inis *f* sweetness

dūlĭcē *adv* like a slave

Dūlich·ium -iī or **-ī** *n* or **Dīlichǐ·a -ae** *f* island in the Ionian Sea, belonging to the realm of Ulysses

dum *adv* up to now, yet, as yet; now; **age dum!** or **agite dum!** come now!; all right!; **nemo dum** no one yet, no one as yet; **non dum** not yet, not as yet

dum *conj* while, during the time in which; as long as; until; provided that, if only; **dum modo** or **dummodo** provided that, if only; **expectabam dum rediret** I was waiting for him to return

dūmēt·um -ī *n* thicket, underbrush

dummŏdo *conj* provided that, if only

dūmōs·us -a -um *adj* overgrown with bushes, bushy

dumtaxat *adv* strictly speaking, at least; only, simply, merely

dūm·us -ī *m* bush, bramble

du·o -ae -o *adj* two

duodeciēns or **duodeciēs** *adv* twelve times

duodĕcim (indecl) *adj* twelve

duodecĭm·us -a -um *adj* twelfth

duodēn·ī -ae -a *adj* twelve each, twelve apiece, twelve; a dozen; **duodenis assibus** at twelve percent

duodēquadrāgēsĭm·us -a -um *adj* thirty-eighth

duodēquadrāgintā (indecl) *adj* thirty-eighth

duodēquinquāgēsĭm·us -a -um *adj* forty-eighth

duodētrīcĭēns or **duodētrīcĭēs** *adv* twenty-eight times

duodētrīgintā (indecl) *adj* twenty-eight

duodēvīcēn·ī -ae -a *adj* eighteen each

duodēvīgintī (indecl) *adj* eighteen

duoetvīcēsimān·ī -ōrum *n pl* soldiers of the twenty-second legion

duoetvīcēsĭm·us -a -um *adj* twenty-second

duovirī see **duumvirī**

dupl·a -ae *f* double the price

dupl·ex -icis *adj* twofold, double; divided into two; in double rows; double, twice as big, twice as long; complex, compound; two-faced, double-dealing, false

duplicār·ius -iī or **-ī** *m* soldier receiving double pay

duplĭcĭter *adv* doubly, on two accounts

duplĭc·ō -āre *vt* to double; to bend double; to enlarge, lengthen, increase

dupl·us -a -um *adj* double, twice as much, twice as large; *n* double price; **in duplum** twice the amount, double; **in duplum ire** to pay twice as much, pay double

dupond·ius -iī or -ī m or dupond·ium -iī or -ī n two-ace coin, worth about five cents

dūrābil·is -e adj durable, lasting

dūrām·en -ĭnis n hardness

dūratē·us -a -um adj wooden

dūrē or dūriter adv hard, sternly, rigorously, roughly; stiffly, awkwardly

dūr·escō -escĕre -ŭī vi to grow hard, harden

dūrĭt·ās -ātis f hardness, toughness, harshness

dūriter see dure

dūritĭ·a or dūritĭ·ēs -ēī f hardness; austerity; strictness, harshness, rigor; oppressiveness; insensibility, callousness

dūriuscŭl·us -a -um adj somewhat hard, rather harsh

dūr·ō -āre vt to make hard, harden, solidify; (fig) to harden, inure, toughen up; to make insensible, to dull, blunt; to bear, endure; vi to be inured, be tough; to endure, last, remain, continue, hold out; (of hills) to continue unbroken, extend

dūr·us -a -um adj hard; lasting; rough (to the senses); tough, hardy, hale; rough, rude, uncouth; shameless, brazen; harsh, cruel, callous,

insensible; severe, oppressive; parsimonious, miserly

duum·vir -vĭrī m member of a commission or board of two

duumvirāt·us -ūs m duumvirate, office of a duumvir

duumvir·ī -ōrum or duovĭr·ī -ōrum m pl two-man commission; duumviri ad aedem faciendam two-man commission for the construction of a temple; duumviri juri dicundo two-man board of colonial magistrates; pair of judges; duumviri navales two-man commission to equip the navy; duumviri perduellionis criminal court; duumviri sacrorum two-man commission in charge of the Sibylline books

dux ducis m or f conductor, guide; leader, head, author, ringleader; general

Dym·ās -antis m father of Hecuba, the queen of Troy

dynăm·is -is f store, plenty

dynast·ēs -ae m ruler, prince, petty monarch

Dyrrach·ĭum -ĭī or -ī n Adriatic port in Illyria which served as landing place for those who sailed from Italy

---

E

ē see ex

eā adv there, that way

ea ejus f pron she

eādem adv by the same way, the same way; at the same time; likewise, by the same token

eāpropter adv therefore

eapse see ipse

eātĕnus adv to such a degree, so far

ebēnus see hebenus

ēbĭb·ō -ĕre -ī vt to drink up, drain; to absorb; to spend in drinks, squander

ēbland·ĭor -īrī -ītus sum vt to coax out, obtain by flattery

Eborac·um or Eburāc·um -ī n town of the Brigantes in Britain, York

ēbriĕt·ās -ātis f drunkenness

ēbrĭŏl·us -a -um adj tipsy

ēbriōsĭt·ās -ātis f habitual drunkenness, heavy drinking

ēbriōs·us -a -um adj & m drunk

ēbrĭ·us -a -um adj drunk; drunken (acts, words), of a drunk; (fig) intoxicated (e.g., with love, power)

ēbull·ĭō -īre vt to brag about; vi to bubble up, boil over

ebŭl·um -ī n or ebŭl·us -ī m danewort, dwarf elder

eb·ur -ŏris n ivory; ivory objects; statue, flute, scabbard; elephant

eburāt·us -a -um adj inlaid with ivory

eburneŏl·us -a -um adj ivory

eburnĕ·us or eburn·us -a -um adj ivory; white as ivory; ensis eburneus sword with ivory hilt; dentes eburnei tusks (of elephant)

ēcastor interj by Castor!

ecca see ecce

eccam see ecce

ecce interj see!, look!, look here!, here!; ecce me here I am; (colloquially combined with the pronouns is, ille, and iste): ecca (i.e., ecce + ea) or eccam (i.e., ecce + eam) here she is; eccilla or eccistam there she is; eccillum or eccum here he is; eccos here they are

eccĕrē interj there!

eccheum·a -ătis n pouring out

ecclēsĭ·a -ae f Greek assembly of people; (eccl) church, congregation

ecdĭc·us -ī m legal representative of a community

ecf- = eff-

echidn·a -ae f viper

Echidn·a -ae f hydra; Echidna Lernaea Lernaean hydra; monstrous mother of Cerberus, half woman and half serpent

Echinăd·es -um f pl cluster of small islands off Acarnania

echīn·us -ī m sea urchin; dishpan

Echĭ·ōn -ŏnis m hero who sprang from the dragon's teeth sown by

Cadmus, married Agave, and became father of Pentheus

Ech·ō -ūs *f* nymph who was changed by Hera into an echo

eclŏg·a -ae *f* literary selection; eclogue

eclogāri·ī -ōrum *m pl* excerpted literary passages

ecquandō *adv* ever, at any time; (in indirect questions) whether ever

ecquī *conj* whether

ecqu·ī -ae or **-od** *adj* any

ec·quid -cūjus *pron* anything; (in indirect questions) whether, if at all

ec·quis -cūjus *pron* any, anyone; (in indirect questions) whether anyone

ecquō *adv* anywhere

ecul·eus -ī *m* foal, colt; small equestrian statue; wooden torture rack

edācit·ās -ātis *f* gluttony

ed·ax -ācis *adj* gluttonous; (fig) devouring, destructive

ēdent·ō -āre *vt* to knock the teeth out of

ēdentŭl·us -a -um *adj* toothless, old

edēpol *interj* by Pollux!, gad!

edēra see **hedera**

ē-dīcō -dīcĕre -dīxī -dictum *vt* to proclaim, announce, decree, ordain, appoint

ēdictī·ō -ōnis *f* edict, order

ēdict·ō -āre *vt* to proclaim, publish

ēdict·um -ī *n* decree, edict, proclamation; edict of a praetor listing rules he would follow in his capacity as judge; order, command

ē-discō -discĕre -didīcī *vt* to learn by heart, learn thoroughly

ēdissĕr·ō -ĕre -uī -tum *vt* to explain in detail, analyze fully

ēdissert·ō -āre *vt* to explain fully, explain in all details

ēditīcī·us -a -um *adj* set forth, proposed; **judices editicii** panel of jurors (*subject to challenge by the defendant*)

ēditī·ō -ōnis *f* statement, account, published statement; publishing, publication; edition (*of a book*); (law) declaration (*of the form of judicial procedure to be followed*)

ēdit·us -a -um *adj* high; (with *abl*) descended from; *n* height; command, order

e·dō -dĕre -didī -ditum *vt* to give out, put forth, bring forth, emit; to give birth to, bear; to publish; to tell, announce, declare, disclose; to show, display, produce, perform; to bring about, cause; to promulgate

edō edĕre (or **esse**) **ēdī ēsum** *vt* to eat; (fig) to devour, consume, destroy; **pugnos edere** to eat fists, to get a good beating

ēdoc·eō -ēre -uī -tum *vt* to teach thoroughly; to instruct clearly; to inform; to show clearly; (with double *acc*) to teach (*someone something*) well

ēdŏl·ō -āre *vt* to chop out, hack out; to finish, prepare

ēdŏm·ō -āre -uī -itum *vt* to conquer, subdue

Ēdŏn·ī -ōrum *m pl* Thracian tribe noted for its heavy drinking

Ēdŏn·is -idis *adj* Edonian; *f* bacchante

ēdorm·iō -īre -īvī or **iī** *vt* to sleep off; **crapulam edormire** to sleep off a hangover; *vi* to sleep soundly

ēdormisc·ō -ĕre *vt* to sleep off; **crapulam edormiscere** to sleep off a hangover

ēducātī·ō -ōnis *f* rearing; education

ēducāt·or -ōris *m* foster father; tutor, instructor

ēducātr·ix -īcis *f* nurse

ēdŭc·ō -āre *vt* to bring up; to train, educate, develop; to produce

ē-dūcō -dūcĕre -duxī -ductum *vt* to draw out; to take away; to draw (*sword*); to draw out, spend (*time*); to lead out, march out (*army*); to summon (*to court*); to hatch; to rear, bring up, educate, train; to raise, erect

edūl·is -e *adj* edible

ēdūr·ō -āre *vi* to last, continue

ēdūr·us -a -um *adj* hard, tough; (fig) tough

Ēëtī·ōn -ōnis *m* father of Andromache and king of Thebe in Cilicia

effarciō see **effercio**

effāt·us -a -um *pp* of **effor**; *adj* solemnly pronounced; solemnly dedicated; *n* axiom; prediction

effectī·ō -ōnis *f* accomplishment, performing; efficient cause

effectīv·us -a -um *adj* producing, practical

effect·or -ōris *m* or **effectr·ix -īcis** *f* producer, author

effect·us -a -um *pp* of **efficio**; *adj* finished, complete; *n* effect

effect·us -ūs *m* effecting, completion; operation; effect, result, consequence

effēminātē *adv* effeminately, like a woman

effēmināt·us -a -um *adj* effeminate

effēmin·ō -āre *vt* to make a woman of; to represent as a woman; to effeminate, enervate

efferāt·us -a -um *adj* wild, brutal, savage

ef·ferciō or **ec·ferciō** or **ef·farciō -fercīre — -fertum** *vt* to stuff; to fill in (*e.g., a ditch*)

efferit·ās -ātis *f* wildness, barbarism

effĕr·ō -āre *vt* to make wild, brutalize; to exasperate

effĕrō or **ecfĕrō efferre extŭlī ēlātum** *vt* to carry out, bring out, bring forth; to utter, express; to publish, spread (*news*); to carry out for burial, bury; to produce, bear; to name, designate; to lift up, raise; to promote, advance; to bring out, expose; to praise, extol; to sweep off one's feet; **efferri** (fig) to be carried away; **se efferre** to be haughty, be proud, be conceited

effert·us -a -um *pp* of **effercio;** *adj* full, crammed, bulging

effer·us -a -um *adj* wild, fierce, savage

ef·fervescō -fervescĕre -fervī *vi* to boil, boil over; to burst forth

efferv·ō -ēre *vi* to boil over; (of bees) to swarm out; (of volcano) to erupt

effēt·us -a -um *adj* effete, spent; vain, delusive; (with *genit*) incapable of

efficācĭt·ās -ātis *f* efficiency

efficācĭter *adv* efficiently, effectively

effic·ax -ācis *adj* efficient, effective, efficacious

effici·ens -entis *adj* efficient, effective; **res efficientes** causes

efficienter *adv* efficiently

efficienti·a -ae *f* efficiency, efficacy, influence

ef·ficiō -ficĕre -fēcī -fectum *vt* to bring about, bring to pass, effect, cause, produce; to make, form; to finish, complete, accomplish; (of a field) to yield, produce; (of numbers) to amount to; to prove, show; **ita efficitur ut** thus it follows that

efflictus *pp* of **effingo**

effigĭ·ēs -ēī or **effigĭ·a -ae** *f* effigy, likeness, semblance; opposite number; copy, imitation; image; statue, figure, portrait; ghost, phantom

ef·fingō -fingĕre -finxī -fictum *vt* to mold, form, fashion; to imitate; to wipe out, wipe clean; to represent, portray; to imagine

effĭō passive of **efficio**

efflāgĭtātĭ·ō -ōnis *f* urgent demand

efflāgĭtāt·us -ūs *m* urgent request; **efflagitatu meo** at my insistence

efflāgĭt·ō -āre *vt* to demand, insist upon

efflictim *adv* (to love, desire) desperately

efflict·ō -āre *vt* to strike dead

ef·flīgō or **ecf·flīgō -flīgĕre -flixī -flictum** *vt* to strike dead, exterminate

effl\·ō or **ecfl·ō -āre** *vt* to breathe out; **animam efflare** to expire

efflōr·escō -escĕre -ŭī *vi* to bloom, blossom, flourish

efflŭ·ō or **ecflŭ·ō -ĕre -xī** *vi* to flow out, flow forth, run out; to slip away, drop out, disappear; (of a rumor) to get out, circulate; **ex pectore effluere** to be forgotten

efflŭ·ĭum -ĭī or **-ĭ** *n* outlet; **effluvium lacūs** outlet of a lake

ef·fodĭō or **ecf·fodĭō -fodĕre -fōdī -fossum** *vt* to dig up; to gouge out (*eyes*); to root out, gut; to excavate

ef·for or **ecf·for -fārī -fātus sum** *vt* to speak out, say out loud, tell; (in augury) to mark off, consecrate (*area*); *vi* to state a proposition

effossus *pp* of **effodio**

effrēnātē *adv* without restraint, out of control

effrēnātĭ·ō -ōnis *f* impetuosity

effrēnāt·us -a -um *adj* unbridled; (fig) unbridled, unrestrained

ef·fringō or **ec·fringō -fringĕre -frēgī -fractum** *vt* to break open, smash, break off; to break in (*door*)

ef·fugĭō -fugĕre -fūgī *vt* to escape; to escape the notice of; *vi* to escape; (with *abl* or with **ab** or **ex** + *abl*) to escape from

effug·ĭum -ĭī or **-ĭ** *n* escape, flight; means of escape; avoidance

ef·fulgĕō -fulgēre -fulsī *vi* to shine forth, gleam, glitter

effult·us -a -um *pp* of **effulcio**

ef·fundō or **ec·fundō -fundĕre -fūdī -fūsum** *vt* to pour out, pour forth; to fling (*weapon*); to give up, let go, abandon, resign; to throw down; to produce in abundance; to lavish, waste, squander, run through; to empty out (*bags, etc.*); to given vent to, pour out; **effundi** or **se effundere** to pour out, rush out; to yield, indulge

effūsē *adv* far and wide; at random, in disorder; lavishly; immoderately

effūsĭ·ō -ōnis *f* outpouring, rushing out; shedding; effusion; profusion, lavishness, extravagance; *f pl* excesses

effūs·us -a -um *pp* of **effundo;** *adj* spread out, extensive, broad, wide; relaxed, loose; disheveled; lavish; straggly, disorderly; loose, dissolute

effūt·ĭō -īre — -ītum *vt* & *vi* to blab, babble, chatter

ef·futŭō or **ec·futŭō -futuĕre -futuī -futūtum** *vt* to exhaust through excesses

ēgelĭd·us -a -um *adj* chilly, cool; lukewarm

eg·ens -entis *adj* needy, poor; (with *genit*) in need of

egēn·us -a -um *adj* needy, destitute; (with *genit* or *abl*) in need of

eg·ĕō -ēre -ŭī *vi* to be needy, suffer want; (with *genit* or *abl*) **a** to be in need of; **b** to lack, be without; **c** to want, desire, miss

Ēgerĭ·a -ae *f* nymph whom King Numa visited at night for advice

ē·gerō -gerĕre -gessī -gestum *vt* to carry out, take away, remove; to discharge, vomit, emit

egest·ās -ātis *f* need, want, poverty; (with *genit*) lack of

ēgestĭ·ō -ōnis *f* squandering

ēgestus *pp* of **egero**

ego *pron* I

egŏmet *pron* I personally, I and nobody else

ē·gredĭor -grĕdī -gressus sum *vt* to go beyond, pass; to quit; (fig) to go beyond, surpass; *vi* to go out, come out; to march out; to set sail, put out to sea; to disembark, land; to go up, climb; to digress

ēgregĭē *adv* exceptionally, singularly, uncommonly, splendidly ēgregĭ·us -a -um *adj* exceptional, singular, uncommon; distinguished, illustrious; *n* honor, distinction

ēgressus *pp* of egredior

ēgress·us -ūs *m* departure; way out, exit; disembarking, landing; mouth (*of river*); digression; *m pl* comings and goings

ēgurgĭt·ō -āre *vt* to pour out, lavish

ehem *interj* (expressing pleasant surprise) ha!, aha!

eheu *interj* (expressing pain) oh!

eho *interj* (expressing rebuke) look here!, see here!; **eho dum!** look here now!

ei *interj* (expressing fear or dismay) golly!

ēĭa or hēĭa *interj* (expressing joy or surprise) ah!, ah ha!; good!; (expressing haste) quick!, come on!

ējacŭl·or -ārī -ātus sum *vt* to squirt (*e.g., water*); **sē ejaculari** to squirt

ējectāment·a -ōrum *n pl* refuse; jetsam

ējectĭ·ō -ōnis *f* ejection; banishment, exile

ēject·ō -āre *vt* to spout forth; to keep throwing up (*e.g., blood*)

eject·us -ūs *m* emission

ējēr·ō or ējūr·ō -āre *vt* to refuse upon oath, abjure, forswear; to deny on oath; to resign, abdicate; to disown, abandon

ē·jiciō -jicĕre -jēcĭ -jectum *vt* to throw out, drive out, put out, eject, expel; to banish, drive into exile; to utter; to run aground; to reject, disapprove; to boo (*someone*) off the stage; **ejĭcī** to be stranded; **sē ejicere** (of passions) to break out, come to the fore

ējulātĭ·ō -ōnis *f* wailing, lamenting

ējūl·ō -āre *vi* to wail, lament

ējūrō see ejero

ē·lābor -lābī -lapsus sum *vi* to glide off; to slip away, escape; to pass away, disappear; (with *abl* or with **super** + *acc*) to glance off

ēlabōrāt·us -a -um *adj* studied, overdone; elaborate, finished

ēlabōr·ō -āre *vt* to work out, elaborate; to produce; *vi* to make a great effort, take great pains; (with *inf*) to strive to

ēlāmentābĭl·is -e *adj* pathetic

ēlangu·escō -escĕre -ī *vi* to slow down, slacken, let up

ēlapsus *pp* of elabor

ēlātē *adv* proudly

ēlātĭ·ō -ōnis *f* elation, ecstasy

ēlātr·ō -āre *vt* to bark out

ēlāt·us -a -um *pp* of effero; *adj* high, elevated; exalted; haughty, proud

ē·lăvō -lavāre -lāvī -lautum or -lōtum *vt* to wash out; (coll) to clean out, rob

Elĕ·a -ae *f* town in Lucania in S. Italy, birthplace of Eleatic philosophy

Eleātĭc·ī -ōrum *m pl* Eleatics, Eleatic philosophers

ēlecēbr·a -ae *f* snare; seductress

ēlectē *adv* tastefully

ēlectĭl·is -e *adj* choice, dainty

ēlectĭ·ō -ōnis *f* choice; *f pl* selection

ēlect·ō -āre *vt* to select, choose; to wheedle out, coax out (*a secret*)

Ēlectr·a -ae *f* Pleiad, daughter of Atlas and Pleione and the mother of Dardanus by Jupiter; daughter of Agamemnon and Clytemnestra

ēlectr·um -ī *n* amber; electrum (*alloy of gold and silver*); *f pl* amber beads

ēlect·us -a -um *pp* of eligo; *adj* select, picked, choice; (mil) elite

ēlect·us -ūs *m* choice

ēlēg·ans -antis *adj* fine, elegant, refined; choosy; fine, choice, select

ēleganter *adv* tastefully, neatly, elegantly

ēlegantĭ·a -ae *f* elegance, refinement, taste, propriety

ēlēg·ī -ōrum *m pl* elegiac verses

elegī·a or elegē·a -ae *f* elegy

Elēl·ĕus -ĕī *m* (epithet of) Bacchus

elementārĭ·us -a -um *adj* elementary; **senex elementarius** old schoolteacher

element·um -ī *n* first principle, element; *n pl* elements, rudiments; beginnings; ABC's

elench·us -ī *m* pearl

elephantomăch·a -ae *m* fighter mounted on an elephant

elephant·us -ī or elĕph·ās -antis *m* elephant; (fig) ivory

Eleus·īn -īnis *f* Eleusis (*sacred city in Attica, famous for its cult of Demeter*)

Eleusīn·us -a -um *adj* Eleusinian; **Eleusina mater** Ceres

ēlĕv·ō -āre *vt* to lift up, raise; to alleviate; to lessen, diminish; to make light of, disparage

ē·liciō -licĕre -licŭī -licĭtum *vt* to elicit, draw out; to lure out, entice; to conjure up

Ēlĭc·ĭus -ĭī or -ī *m* (epithet of) Jupiter

ē·līdō -līdĕre -līsī -līsum *vt* to knock out, strike out, tear out, force out; to shatter, smash to pieces, crush; to force out, stamp out; (fig) to stamp out

ē·līgō -ligĕre -lēgī -lectum *vt* to pluck out; to pick out, choose

ēlīmĭn·ō -āre *vt* to carry outside; to spread abroad

ēlīm·ō -āre *vt* to file; to finish off, perfect

ēlingu·is -e *adj* without tongue, speechless; (fig) inarticulate

ēlingu·ō -āre *vt* (coll) to tear out the tongue of

Ēl·is or Āl·is -ĭdis *f* district and town on the W. coast of the Peloponnesus in which Olympia is located

Eliss·a or Ēlĭs·a -ae *f* Dido

ēlīsus *pp* of elido

ēlix·us -a -um *adj* wet through and through, soaked

ellam = ecce + illam

elleborōs·us -a -um *adj* crazy

ellebŏr·us or hellebŏr·us -ī *m* or ellebŏr·um -ī *n* hellebore (*plant used for mental illness*)

ellips·is -is *f* ellipsis

ellum = ecce + illum

ēlŏc·ō -āre *vt* to lease out, rent out

ēlocūtī·ō -ōnis *f* style of speaking, delivery

ēlog·ium -iī or -ī *n* saying, maxim; inscription, epitaph; clause (*in a will*)

ēlŏqu·ens -entis *adj* eloquent

ēloquenter *adv* eloquently

ēloquenti·a -ae *f* eloquence

ēlŏqu·ium -iī or -ī *n* eloquence

ē·lŏquor -lŏquī ·locūtus sum *vt* to speak out, declare; *vi* to give a speech

ēlōtus *pp* of elavo

ē·lūcĕō -lūcēre -luxī *vi* to shine forth; to glitter

ēluct·or -ārī -ātus sum *vt* to struggle out of, struggle through (*e.g., deep snow*); to surmount; *vi* to force a way out

ēlūcŭbr·ō -āre or ēlūcŭbr·or -ārī -ātus sum *vt* to compose by lamp light

ē·lūdō -lūdĕre -lūsī -lūsum *vt* to elude, parry, avoid; to escape, shun; to delude, deceive; to make fun of; to get the better of, outmaneuver; *vi* to end the game

ē·lūgĕō -lūgēre -luxī *vt* to mourn for; to cease to mourn

ēlumb·is -e *adj* loinless; bland (*style*)

ē·lŭō -luĕre -lŭī -lūtum *vt* to wash off, wash clean; to wash away; (fig) to wash away, remove, get rid of

ēlūsus *pp* of eludo

ēlūt·us -a -um *pp* of eluo; *adj* washed out, watery, insipid

ēluvi·ēs -ēī *f* inundation, overflow; sewage

ēluvi·ō -ōnis *f* deluge

Ēlys·ium -iī or -ī *n* realm of the blessed in the lower world

em *interj* (expressing wonder or emphasis) there!

emācit·ās -ātis *f* fondness for shopping

ēmancĭpātī·ō or ēmancŭpātī·ō -ōnis *f* emancipation; transfer of property

ēmancĭpāt·us -a -um *adj* made over, sold

ēmancĭp·ō or ēmancŭp·ō -āre *vt* to transfer; to declare (*a son*) free and independent, emancipate; to surrender, abandon

ēmān·ō -āre *vi* to flow out; to trickle out, leak out; to become known

Ēmathī·a -ae *f* Macedonia

Ēmăth·is -ĭdis *adj* Macedonian; *f pl* the Pierides (*daughters of the Macedonian king Pierus*)

ēmātūr·escō -escĕre -ŭī *vi* to begin to ripen; to soften; (fig) to soften

em·ax -ācis *adj* fond of shopping

emblēm·a -ătis *n* mosaic, inlaid wood

embol·ium -iī or -ī *n* interlude

ēmendābil·is -e *adj* capable of correction

ēmendātē *adv* faultlessly

ēmendātī·ō -ōnis *f* emendation, correction

ēmendāt·or -ōris *m* or ēmendātr·ix -īcis *f* corrector

ēmendāt·us -a -um *adj* faultless

ēmendīc·ō -āre *vt* to obtain by begging

ēmend·ō -āre *vt* to emend, correct; to reform, improve, revise; to atone for

ēmensus *pp* of emetior

ēment·ior -īrī -ītus sum *vt* to falsify, fabricate, feign; *vi* to tell a lie

ēmerc·or -ārī -ātus sum *vt* to buy up; to bribe

ēmer·ĕō -ēre or ēmer·ĕor -ērī -ĭtus sum *vt* to merit fully; to lay under obligation; (mil) to serve out (*term of service*); aliquem emerere to do someone a favor or favors

ē·mergō -mergĕre -mersī -mersum *vt* to raise (*from the water*); emergi or se emergere to raise oneself up, rise; *vi* to emerge; to rise (*in power*); to extricate oneself; (with ex + *abl*) to get clear of

ēmerĭt·us -a -um *pp* of emereor; *adj* worn out, unfit for service; *m* veteran

ēmersus *pp* of emergo

emetĭc·a -ae *f* emetic

ē·mētĭor -mētīrī -mensus sum *vt* to measure out; to traverse, travel over; to live through; to impart, bestow

ēmēt·ō -ĕre *vt* to mow down

ēmĭc·ō -āre -ŭī -ātum *vi* to dart out, shoot out, dash out; to flash out; (fig) to shine, be prominent

ēmĭgr·ō -āre *vi* to move out, depart; e vita migrare to pass on, die

ēmĭn·ens -entis *adj* projecting out, prominent, high; eminent

ēminenti·a -ae *f* projection, prominence; (in painting) highlights

ēmĭn·ĕō -ēre -ŭī *vi* to stand out, project; to be conspicuous, stand out; (in painting) to be highlighted

ēmĭn·or -ārī -ātus sum *vt* to threaten

ēmĭnus *adv* out of range, at a distance; from afar

ēmīr·or -ārī -ātus sum *vt* to be greatly surprised at, stand aghast at

ēmissār·ium -iī or -ī *n* drain, outlet

ēmissār·ius -iī or -ī *m* scout, spy

ēmissīcī·us -a -um *adj* prying, spying

ēmissī·ō -ōnis *f* discharge, hurling, shooting; releasing; letting off

ēmissus *pp* of emitto

ēmiss·us -ūs *m* emission

ē·mittō -mittĕre -mīsī -missum *vt* to sound out; to hurl, discharge, shoot; to let go, let slip, let loose, drop, release, let out; to send out, publish; to allow to escape; to emancipate, set at liberty; to utter; to pass up (*an opportunity*); **animam emittere** to give up the ghost; **emitti** or **se emittere** (with **ex** + *abl*) to break out of (*e.g., jail*)

emō -ĕmĕre ēmī emptum *vt* to buy; to pay for; to gain, obtain, acquire; to bribe; **bene emere** to buy cheap; **in diem emere** to buy on credit; **male emere** to pay dearly for

ē·modĕr·or -ārī -ātus sum *vt* to moderate

ē·modŭl·or -ārī -ātus sum *vt* to sing the praises of, celebrate in seng

ēmōl·ior -īrī -ītus sum *vt* to accomplish

ēmollĭ·ĭō -īre -īvī or **-lĭ -ītum** *vt* to soften; to make mild; to enervate

ēmōl·ō -ĕre — -ĭtum *vt* to grind up; to consume

ēmolument·um -ī *n* profit, gain, advantage

ēmon·ĕō -ēre *vt* to advise, admonish

ē·morior -mŏrī -mortŭus sum *vi* to die, die off; (fig) to die out

ēmortuāl·is -e *adj* of death; **dies emortualis** day of one's death

ēmortŭus *pp* of **emorior**

ē·movĕō -movēre -mōvī -mōtum *vt* to move out, remove, expel; to dislodge; to shake (*e.g., foundations of wall*)

Empedŏcl·ēs -is *m* philosopher of Sicily who is said to have jumped into the crater of Mt. Aetna (*fl* 444 B.C.)

emphăs·is -is *f* emphasis, stress

empīric·us -ī *m* self-trained physician

empor·ĭum -ĭī or **-ĭ** *n* market town, market, mart

emptĭ·ō -ōnis *f* buying, purchase; thing purchased, purchase

emptĭt·ō -āre *vt* to be in the habit of buying

empt·or -ōris *m* buyer, purchaser

emptus *pp* of **emo**

ēmūg·ĭō -īre *vt* to bellow out

ē·mulgĕō -mulgēre — -mulsum *vt* to drain out; to exhaust

ēmunct·us -a -um *adj* discriminating; **naris emunctae esse** to have discriminating tastes

ē·mungō -mungĕre -munxī -munctum *vt* to blow the nose of; to swindle; (with *abl*) to cheat (*someone*) of; **emungi** to blow one's nose

ēmūn·ĭō -īre -īvī or **-ĭī -ītum** *vt* to build up; to fortify; to make a road through (*woods*)

ēn *interj* (in questions) really?; (in commands) come on!; (to call attention) look!, see!

ēnarrābil·is -e *adj* describable, intelligible

ēnarrātĭ·ō -ōnis *f* description; analysis

ēnarr·ō -āre *vt* to explain in detail, describe; to interpret

ē·nascor -nascī -nātus sum *vi* to grow out, sprout, arise

ēnăt·ō -āre *vi* to swim away, escape by swimming; (fig) to get away with it

ēnātus *pp* of **enascor**

ēnāvig·ō -āre *vt* to sail over, traverse; *vi* to sail away; (fig) to escape

Encelăd·us -ī *m* one of the giants whom Jupiter buried under Aetna

endrŏm·is -ĭdis *f* athlete's bathrobe

Endymĭ·ōn -ōnis *m* handsome young man with whom Luna fell in love and who was doomed to everlasting sleep on Mt. Patmos in Caria

ē·nĕcō (or **ē·nĭcō**), **-necāre -necŭī** (or **-nicāvī**) **-nectum** (or **-necātum**) *vt* to kill, kill off; to exhaust, wear out; (coll) to kill, pester to death

ēnervāt·us -a -um *adj* without sinews; without energy or force

ēnerv·is -e *adj* weak, feeble

ēnerv·ō -āre *vt* to weaken, enervate, render impotent

ēnĭcō see **eneco**

enim *conj* namely, for instance; yes, indeed, certainly; in fact, to be sure; (in replies) of course, no doubt; for, because

enimvērō *adv* yes indeed, to be sure, certainly; (ironical) of course

Enīp·eus -ĕī *m* tributary of the Peneus in Thessaly

ēnīsus *pp* of **enitor**

ēnĭt·ĕō -ēre -ŭī *vi* to shine out, sparkle; to be distinguished or conspicuous

ēnĭtesc·ō -ĕre *vi* to begin to shine, begin to brighten, become conspicuous

ē·nītor -nītī -nīsus or **nixus sum** *vt* to work one's way up, climb; to give birth to; *vi* to exert oneself, make an effort; (with *inf*) to struggle to, strive to

ēnixē *adv* strenuously, earnestly

ēnix·us -a -um *pp* of **enitor**; *adj* strenuous, earnest

Enni·us -ī *m* father of Latin literature, writer of tragedy, comedy, epic, and satire, born at Rudiae in Calabria (239-169 B.C.)

Ennosigae·us -ī *m* (epithet of Neptune) Earthshaker

ēn·ō -āre *vi* to swim out, swim away, escape by swimming

ēnōdātē *adv* without knots; plainly, clearly

ēnōdātĭ·ō -ōnis *f* solution, explanation

ēnōd·is -e *adj* without knots; plain, clear

ēnōd·ō -āre *vt* to explain, clarify

ēnorm·is -e *adj* irregular; enormous

ēnormĭt·ās -ātis *f* irregular shape

ēnōt·escō -escĕre -ŭī *vi* to become known

ēnōt·ō -āre *vt* to take notes of, note down

ensĭcŭl·us -ī *m* small sword

ensĭf·er -ĕra -ĕrum *adj* with a sword, wearing a sword

ensĭg·er -ĕra -ĕrum *adj* with a sword, wearing a sword

ens·is -is *m* sword

enthȳmēm·a -ătis *n* thought, reflection; condensed syllogism

ē·nūbō -nūbĕre -nupsī *vi* (said of a woman) to marry out of one's rank

ēnucleātē *adv* plainly

ēnucleāt·us -a -um *adj* pure, clean; straightforward; simple, clear (*style*)

ēnuclĕ·ō -āre *vt* (fig) to give in a nutshell, explain to the point

ēnumerātĭ·ō -ōnis *f* enumeration

ēnumĕr·ō -āre *vt* to count up; to pay; to recount, relate, detail, describe

ēnuntiātĭ·ō -ōnis *f* (in logic) proposition

ēnuntĭ·ō -āre *vt* to disclose, reveal, betray; to say, assert, express

ēnuptĭ·ō -ōnis *f* right to marry outside the clan

ēnŭtr·iō -īre -īvī *or* **-ĭī -ītum** *vt* to nourish, raise, bring up (*children*)

eō īre īvī *or* **iī ĭtum** *vi* to go: to go, walk, sail, ride; (mil) to march; (of time) to pass; (of events) to go on, happen, turn out; **in sententiam ire** to vote for a bill

eō *adv* there, to that place; to that end, to that purpose; so far, to such an extent; to such a pitch; on that account, for that reason, with that in view; **eo ero brevior** I will be all the briefer; **eo magis** all the more; **eo maxime quod** especially because; **eo quo** to the place to which; **eo ... quo the ... the ...; eo quod** because; **eo ... ut** to such an extent ... that

eōdem *adv* to the same place, purpose, or person

Ēōs (*nom only*) *f* Dawn

Ēō·us -ī *m* morning star; inhabitant of the East, Oriental; one of the horses of the sun

Epamīnond·ās -ae *m* famous Theban general who fought against the Spartans (*d.* 362 B.C.)

Epăph·us -ī *m* son of Jupiter and Io

ēpast·us -a -um *adj* eaten up

Epē·us *or* **Epī·us -ī** *m* builder of the Trojan horse

ephēb·us -ī *m* young man (18 *to* 20 *years of age*)

ephēmĕr·is -ĭdis *f* diary, journal

Ephĕs·us -ī *f* city in Asia Minor with famous temple of Diana

ephippĭāt·us -a -um *adj* riding a saddled horse

ephipp·ĭum -ĭī *or* **-ī** *n* saddle

ephŏr·us -ī *m* ephor (*Spartan magistrate*)

Ephȳr·a -ae *or* **Ephȳr·ē -ēs** *f* ancient name of Corinth

Epicharm·us -ī *m* Greek philosopher and writer of early comedy (540-450 B.C.)

epichȳs·is -is *f* jug

epicrŏc·us -a -um *adj* transparent, thin

Epicŭr·us -ī *m* Greek philosopher, born on Samos (342-270 B.C.)

epĭc·us -a -um *adj* epic

epidictĭc·us -a -um *adj* for display

epidĭpn·is -ĭdis *f* dessert

epigramm·a -ătis *n* inscription; short poem, epigram

epĭlŏg·us -ī *m* epilogue, peroration

epimēnĭ·a -ōrum *n pl* month's rations

Epimēth·eus -ĕī *m* son of Iapetus and brother of Prometheus

epirēd·ĭum -ĭī *or* **-ī** *n* trace

epistol·ĭum -ĭī *or* **-ī** *n* note

epistŭl·a -ae *f* letter

epitaph·ĭum -ĭī *or* **-ī** *n* eulogy

epithalam·ĭum -ĭī *or* **-ī** *n* wedding song

epithēc·a -ae *f* addition, increase

epitŏm·a -ae *or* **epitŏm·ē -ēs** *f* epitome, abridgment

epitȳr·um -ī *n* olive salad

epŏd·es -um *m pl* seafish

ep·ops -ŏpis *m* hoopoe

epos (*nom & acc only*) *n* epic

ēpōt·us *or* **expōt·us -a -um** *adj* drained to the dregs; drunk dry

epŭl·ae -ārum *f pl* courses, dishes; sumptuous meal, banquet; **epulae regum** dinner fit for a king

epulār·is -e *adj* at dinner, of a dinner; **sermo epularis** talk at dinner

epŭl·ō -ōnis *m* dinner guest, guest at a banquet; **Tresvirī** *or* **Septemvirī Epulones** college of priests who superintended the state dinner to the gods

epŭl·or -ārī -ātus sum *vt* to feast on; *vi* to attend a dinner; (with *abl*) to feast on

epŭl·um -ī *n* banquet, feast

equ·a -ae *f* mare

equ·es -ĭtis *m* rider; (mil) trooper, cavalryman; cavalry; *m pl* cavalry

Equ·es -ĭtis *m* knight; capitalist (*member of Roman middle class*); equestrian order, bourgeoisie

equest·er -ris -re *adj* cavalry; equestrian; middle class, bourgeois, capitalist

equĭdem *adv* truly, indeed, in any event; (with *first person*) for my part, as far as I am concerned; of course, to be sure

equīn·us -a -um *adj* horse's

equīrĭ·a -ōrum *n pl* horse race

equĭtāt·us -ūs *m* cavalry

equĭt·ō -āre *vi* to ride, ride a horse

equŭlĕ·us -ī *m* foal, colt; small equestrian statue; torture rack

equ·us -ī *m* horse; **equis virisque** *or* **equis viris** (fig) with might and main; **equo merere** to serve in the cavalry; **equo vehi** to ride, to ride a horse; **equus bipes** sea horse; **in equo** mounted; *m pl* (fig) chariot

er·a -ae *f* mistress of the house

ērādīc·ō or **exrādīc·ō -āre** *vt* to root out, uproot, destroy

ē·rādō -rādĕre -rāsī -rāsum *vt* to scratch out, erase, obliterate

erăn·us -ī *m* mutual insurance society

Ĕrātō (*nom* only) *f* Muse of erotic poetry; Muse

Ĕratosthĕn·ēs -is *m* famous Alexandrine geographer, poet, and philosopher (276-196 B.C.)

erc- see **herc-**

Ĕrĕb·us -ī *m* god of darkness, son of Chaos and brother of Night; lower world

Ĕrechth·eus -ĕī *m* mythical king of Athens, son of Hephaestus

ērect·us -a -um *pp* of **erigo**; *adj* erect, upright; noble, elevated, lofty; haughty; attentive, alert, tense; resolute, courageous

ē·rēpō -rēpĕre -repsī *vt* to crawl through (*field*); to crawl up (*mountain*); *vi* to crawl out

ēreptī·ō -ōnis *f* robbery

ērept·or -ōris *m* robber

ēreptus *pp* of **eripio**

ergā *prep* (with *acc*) to, towards; against

ergastŭl·um -ī *n* prison; *n pl* inmates

ergō *adv* therefore, consequently; (resumptive) well then, I say, as I was saying; (with *imperatives*) then, now; **quid ergo?** why then?; *prep* (with preceding *genit*) for the sake of; **illius ergo** for his sake

Ĕrichthŏn·ius -īī or **-ī** *m* mythical king of Athens; son of Dardanus, father of Tros, and king of Troy

ēric·ius -īī or **-ī** *m* hedgehog; (mil) beam with iron spikes

Ĕrĭdăn·us -ī *m* Po river (*so called by the Greeks*)

erĭfŭg·a -ae *m* runaway slave

ē·rĭgō -rigĕre -rexī -rectum *vt* to set up straight, straighten out (*e.g., tree*); to set up, erect; to cheer up, encourage; to arouse, excite; (mil) to deploy troops on a slope; **erigi** or **se erigere** to raise oneself, arise

Ĕrigŏn·ē -ēs *f* Virgo (*constellation*)

erīl·is -e *adj* master's, mistress's

Ĕrīn·ys -ўos *f* Fury; (fig) frenzy

Ĕriphŷl·a -ae or **Ĕriphŷl·ē -ēs** *f* wife of the seer Amphiaraus and the mother of Alcmaeon, who killed her for betraying Amphiaraus

ē·rĭpĭō -rĭpĕre -rĭpŭī -reptum *vt* to snatch away, pull out, tear out; to deliver, rescue; to rob; (with *dat* or with **ab** or **ex** + *abl*) to take away from, wrest from, rescue from; **se eripere** to escape

ērogātī·ō -ōnis *f* paying out, payment

ērogĭt·ō -āre *vt* to try to find out

ērŏg·ō -āre *vt* to allocate, expend; to bequeath; (with **in** + *acc*) to allocate to, expend on; **b** to bequeath to

Ĕr·ōs -ōtis *m* Cupid

errābund·us -a -um *adj* wandering, straggling

errātĭc·us -a -um *adj* erratic, roving, wandering

errātĭ·ō -ōnis *f* wandering

errāt·um -ī *n* error, mistake

errāt·us -ūs *m* roving, wandering about

err·ō -āre *vi* to wander, lose one's way, stray, roam; to waver; to err, make a mistake, be mistaken; (with **in** + *abl*) to be mistaken about

err·ō -ōnis *m* vagrant, vagabond

err·or -ōris *m* wandering, wavering, uncertainty; error; cause of error, deception; maze, winding, intricacy

ērub·escō -escĕre -ŭī *vt* to blush at; to be ashamed of; to respect; *vi* to grow red, redden; to blush

ērūc·a -ae *f* colewort

ēruct·ō -āre *vt* to belch, vomit, throw up; (fig) to belch

ērud·ĭō -īre -īī -ītum *vt* to educate, teach, instruct

ērudītē *adv* learnedly

ērudītĭ·ō -ōnis *f* instructing, instruction; erudition

ērudītŭl·us -a -um *adj* somewhat experienced, somewhat skilled

ērudīt·us -a -um *adj* educated, learned, accomplished

ē·rumpō -rumpĕre -rūpī -ruptum *vt* to cause to break out; to give vent to; **iram in hostes erumpere** to vent one's wrath on the enemy; *vi* to burst out, break out

ē·ruō -ruĕre -rŭī -rŭtum *vt* to root up, uproot, dig out; to undermine, demolish, destroy; to draw out, elicit; to rescue; to plow up

ēruptĭ·ō -ōnis *f* eruption; (mil) sortie, sally

ēruptus *pp* of **erumpo**

er·us -ī *m* master of the house, head of the family; lord, owner, proprietor

ērūtus *pp* of **eruo**

erv·um -ī *n* pulse, vetch

Ĕrycīn·us -a -um *adj* of Mt. Eryx (*in Sicily*); of Venus; Sicilian; *f* Venus

Ĕrymanth·is -ĭdis *f* Callisto (*changed into a bear and made a constellation*)

Ĕrymanth·us -ī *m* mountain range in Arcadia, where Hercules killed a boar

Ĕrysichth·ōn -ōnis *m* son of Thessalian king Triopas, punished with insatiable hunger for having cut down a grove sacred to Ceres

erythīn·us -ī *m* red mullet

Er·yx -ўcis or **Ĕrўc·us -ī** *m* mountain on W. coast of Sicily, famous for its temple to Venus

esc·a -ae *f* dish; food; bait

escāri·us -a -um *adj* of food; of bait; *n pl* dishes, courses

e·scendō -scendĕre -scendī -scensum *vt* & *vi* to climb, climb up

escensi·ō or **exscensī·ō -ōnis** *f* climb, climbing

esculent·us -a -um *adj* edible; *n pl* edibles

esculētum see **aesculetum**

escŭlus see **aesculus**

ēsĭt·ō -āre *vt* to be accustomed to eating

Esquili·ae -ārum *f pl* Esquiline Hill in Rome

Esquilīn·us -a -um *adj* Esquiline; *f* Esquiline gate

essedār·ius -iī or **-ī** *m* soldier fighting from a chariot

esse *inf* of **sum**; *inf* of **edo**

essĕd·um -ī *n* combat chariot (*used by Gauls and Britons*)

essenti·a -ae *f* essence

estr·ix -īcis *f* glutton (*female*)

essit·ō -āre *vt* to be accustomed to eating

ēsuriāl·is -e *adj* of hunger

ēsur·iō -īre — -ītum *vt* to be hungry; *vi* to be hungry

ēsurītī·ō -ōnis *f* hunger

ēsus *pp* of **edo**

et *adv* besides, also; even, I mean

et *conj* and; (for emphasis) and even, yes and; (antithetical) however, but; **et . . . et** both . . . and, not only . . . but also

etĕnim *conj* for, and as a matter of fact

etēsi·ae -ārum *m pl* periodic winds (*on the Aegean Sea*)

ēthĭc·ē -ēs *f* ethics

ēthologī·a -ae *f* portrayal of character

ētholŏg·us -ī *m* impersonator

etiam *conj* also, and also, besides, likewise; (of time) yet, as yet, still, even now; (in affirmation) yes, yes indeed, certainly, by all means; (emphatic) even, rather; (with emphatic imperatives) but just; **etiam atque etiam** again and again, repeatedly

etiamnunc or **etiamnum** *adv* even now, even at the present time, still

etiamsī *conj* even if, although

etiamtum or **etiamnunc** *adv* even then, till then, still

Etrūri·a -ae *f* district N. of Rome

Etrusc·us -a -um *adj* & *mf* Etruscan

etsī *conj* even if, although

etymologi·a -ae *f* etymology

eu *interj* well done!, bravo!

Euan or **Euhan** *m* Bacchus

Euand·er or **Euandr·us -rī** *m* Evander (*Arcadian who founded Pallanteum at the foot of the Palatine hill*)

eu·ans or **euh·ans -antis** *adj* crying Euan or Euhan (*Bacchic cry*)

euax *interj* hurray!

Euboe·a -ae *f* island off the E. coast of Attica and Boeotia

Euēn·us -ī *m* river in Aetolia

euge or **eugĕpae** *interj* well done!, terrific!

euh·ans -antis *adj* shouting Euan (*Bacchic cry*)

Euhēmĕr·us -ī *m* Greek writer who attempted to prove that all the ancient myths were actually historical events (*fl* 316 B.C.)

Euh·ius -iī or **-ī** *m* Bacchus

Euhoe or **Euoe** *interj* ecstatic cry of revelers at festival of Bacchus

Eu·ius -iī or **-ī** *m* Bacchus

Eumenĭd·es -um *f pl* Erinyes or Furies (*goddesses of vengeance*)

eunūch·us -ī *m* eunuch

Euoe see **Euhoe**

Euphorb·us -ī *m* brave Trojan warrior whose soul Pythagoras asserted had transmigrated to himself

Euphrāt·ēs -is *m* Euphrates River

Eupōl·is -ĭdis *m* famous Athenian comic poet (4467-411 B.C.)

Euripīd·ēs -is *m* Athenian tragic poet (485-405 B.C.)

Eurīp·us -ī *m* strait between Boeotia and Euboea; channel, canal

Eurōp·a -ae or **Eurōp·ē -ēs** *f* daughter of Agenor and mother of Sarpedon and Minos by Jupiter; he, in the shape of a bull, carried her off to Crete

Eurōt·as -ae *m* chief river in Laconia

Eur·us -ī *m* S.E. wind; east wind; wind

Eurydĭc·ē -ēs *f* wife of Orpheus

Eurypŷl·us -ī *m* Greek warrior who fought at Troy

Eurysth·eus -eī *m* son of Sthenelus, grandson of Perseus, and king of Nycenae, who imposed the twelve labors of Hercules

Eurŷt·is -ĭdis *f* Iole (*with whom Hercules fell in love*)

Eurŷt·us -ī *m* king of Oechalia and father of Iole

euschēmē *adv* gracefully

Euterp·ē -ēs *f* Muse of lyric poetry

Euxīn·us Pont·us or **Euxīn·us -ī** *m* or **Pont·us -ī** *m* Black Sea

ē·vādō -vādĕre -vāsī -vāsum *vt* to pass, pass by; to pass through, escape; *vi* to go out; to turn out, become, prove to be, turn out to be; to get away, escape; to leap, climb

ēvăg·or -ārī -ātus sum *vt* to stray beyond, transgress; *vi* (mil) to maneuver; (fig) to spread

ēval·escō -escĕre -uī *vi* to grow strong; to increase; (of a word or expression) to gain currency; (with *inf*) to be able to; (with **in** + *acc*) to develop into

ēvān·escō -escĕre -uī *vi* to vanish, pass away, die away; (of wine) to become vapid; to be forgotten, perish

ēvānĭd·us -a -um *adj* vanishing

ēvast·ō -āre *vt* to devastate, wreck completely

evasus *pp* of **evado**

ē·věhō -vehěre -vexī -vectum vt
to carry out, convey out; to carry
abroad, spread abroad; to lift up,
raise; evehi to ride, sail, drift

ē·vellō -vellěre -vellī or -vulsī
-vulsum vt to tear or pluck out;
to eradicate

ē·veniō -venīre -vēnī -ventum vi
to come out, come forth; to come
to pass, happen; to follow, result,
turn out, end; v impers it happens

ēvent·um -ī n event, occurrence; result, effect, consequence; fortune,
experience

ēvent·us -ūs m event, accident, fortune, lot, fate; good fortune, success; issue, consequence, result

ēverběr·ō -āre vt to strike hard; to
beat violently

ēverricŭl·um -ī n broom; dragnet

ē·verrō -verrěre -verrī -versum
vt to sweep out; (fig) to clean out,
strip

ēversĭ·ō -ōnis f overthrow, subversion, destruction

ēvers·or -ōris m subverter, destroyer

ēversus pp of everro; pp of everto

ē·vertō or ē·vortō -vertěre -vertī
-versum vt to overturn, turn upside down; to overthrow, upset; to
turn out, expel, eject; to subvert,
destroy, ruin

ēvestīgāt·us -a -um adj tracked
down

ēvictus pp of evinco

ēvĭd·ens -entis adj evident, visible,
plain

ēvidenter adv evidently, plainly,
clearly

ēvidentĭ·a -ae f distinctness, clearness (in speech)

ēvigĭl·ō -āre vt to watch through
(the night); to work through the
night writing (e.g., books); vi to be
wide-awake; (fig) to be on one's
toes

ēvil·escō -escěre -ŭī vi to depreciate, become worthless

ē·vinciō -vincīre -vinxī -vinctum
vt to tie up; to crown, wreathe

e·vincō -vincěre -vīcī -victum vt
to conquer completely, trounce; to
prevail over

ēvinctus pp of evincio

ēvīr·ō -āre vt to unman, castrate

ēviscěr·ō -āre vt to disembowel; to
mangle

ēvitābĭl·is -e adj avoidable

ēvitātĭ·ō -ōnis f avoidance

ēvĭt·ō -āre vt to avoid, escape

ēvocāt·ī -ōrum m pl veterans called
up again; reenlisted veterans

ēvocāt·or -ōris m recruiter

ēvŏc·ō -āre vt to call out, summon;
to challenge; (mil) to call up (for
service); to evoke, excite, stir

ēvolgō see evulgo

ēvŏl·ō -āre vi to fly out, fly away; to
rush out, dash out; (fig) to soar

ēvolūtĭ·ō -ōnis f unrolling a book;
(fig) reading

ē·volvō -volvěre -volvī -volūtum
vt to roll out, unroll, unfold; to
spread; to unroll, read, study; to
unfold, disclose; to free, extricate;
to repel; to evolve, develop

ē·vōmō -voměre -vomŭī -vomī-
tum vt to vomit, spew out, disgorge

ēvulg·ō or ēvolg·ō -āre vt to divulge, make public

ēvulsĭ·ō -ōnis f pulling out, extraction (of a tooth)

ēvulsus pp of evello

ex or ē prep (with abl) (of space) out
of, from; down from; up from,
above; (of time) from, from . . . onward, immediately after, following,
since; (cause or origin) from,
through, by, on account of, by reason of; (transition) from, out of;
from being; (conformity) after, according to, in conformity with;
(means) with, by means of; (parti-
tive) out of, from among, among;
made of, out of

exacerb·ō -āre vt to exasperate,
provoke

exactĭ·ō -ōnis f driving out, expulsion; supervision; exaction, collection; tax, tribute

exact·or -ōris m expeller; supervisor; tax collector

exact·us -a -um pp of exigo; adj
exact, precise

exac·ŭō -ŭěre -ŭī -ūtum vt to
sharpen; to sharpen, stimulate, excite, inflame

exadversum or exadvorsum or
exadversus adv on the opposite
side; prep (with dat or acc) across
from, right opposite

exaedificātĭ·ō -ōnis f construction

exaedifĭc·ō -āre vt to finish building, build, construct; (fig) to complete

exaequātĭ·ō -ōnis f leveling; uniformity

exaequ·ō -āre vt to level, make level; (fig) to equal, regard as equal;
exaequari (with dat) to be put on
the same level with

exaestŭ·ō -āre vi to seethe, boil; to
ferment

exaggerātĭ·ō -ōnis f (fig) elevation,
enlargement; animi exaggeratio
broadening of the mind

exaggěr·ō -āre vt to pile up; to enlarge; to enhance

exagitāt·or -ōris m critic

exagĭt·ō -āre vt to stir up, keep on
the move; to scare away; to criticize, satirize; to irritate; to excite,
stir up (feelings)

exagŏg·a -ae f exportation

exalb·escō -escěre -ŭī vi to turn
pale

exām·en -ĭnis n swarm; crowd;
tongue of scale; weighing, consideration; examination

exāmĭn·ō -āre vt to weigh; to consider; to try, test, examine

examussim adv exactly

exancl·ō -āre vt to draw off, drain; to drain to the dregs

exanimāl·is -ē adj dead, lifeless; deadly

exanimātĭ·ō -ōnis f breathlessness; terror, panic

exanim·is -e or **exanim·us -a -um** adj breathless, terrified; dead, lifeless; fainting (e.g., from fear)

exanim·ō -āre vt to knock the breath out of; to wind, tire, weaken; to deprive of life, kill; to scare out of one's wits; to dishearten; to agitate

exanimus see **exanimis**

ex·ardēscĕre -ardēscĕre -arsī -arsum vi to catch fire; to flare up; (fig) to flare up, be provoked, be exasperated

exār·escō -escĕre -ŭī vi to become quite dry, dry up

exarm·ō -āre vt to disarm

exăr·ō -āre vt to plow up; to raise, produce; to write (on wax with a stylus), write down, note; to furrow, wrinkle; **frontem rugis exarare** to knit one's brow

exasciāt·us -a -um adj hewn out; properly planned, properly worked out

exaspĕr·ō -āre vt to make rough, roughen; to exasperate

exauctōr·ō -āre vt (mil) to discharge, cashier

exaud·ĭō -īre -īvī -ītum vt to hear clearly; to discern; to perceive, understand; to listen to; to grant

exaug·ĕō -ēre vt to increase; to confirm

exaugurātĭ·ō -ōnis f desecration, profaning

exaugŭr·ō -āre vt to desecrate, profane

exauspĭc·ō -āre vi to find the omens good

exballist·ō -āre vt to put an end to, finish off

exbĭbō see **ebibo**

excaec·ō -āre vt to blind; to stop up (a river, pipe, etc.); to darken

excandescentĭ·a -ae f mounting anger, outburst of anger

excand·escō -escĕre -ŭī vi to grow white hot; to reach a pitch (of emotion)

excant·ō -āre vt to charm away

excarnĭfĭc·ō -āre vt to tear to pieces, torture to death

excăv·ō -āre vt to hollow out

ex·cēdō -cēdĕre -cessī -cessum vt to exceed, pass, surpass; vi to go out, go away, withdraw, depart, disappear; to die; **e medio excedere** or **e vita excedere** to depart from life, die

excell·ens -entis adj excellent, outstanding, distinguished; superior

excellenter adv excellently

excellentĭ·a -ae f excellence, superiority

ex·cellō -cellĕre vi to excel, be superior

excelsē adv high, loftily

excelsĭt·ās -ātis f loftiness

excels·us -a -um adj high, lofty; eminent; n height; high social status; **in excelso aetatem** or **vitam agere** to be in the limelight

exceptĭ·ō -ōnis f exception, restriction, limitation; (law) objection raised by a defendant against an accuser's statement

except·ō -āre vt to catch, catch up to

exceptus pp of **excipio**

ex·cernō -cernĕre -crēvī -crētum vt to sift out, separate

ex·cerpō -cerpĕre -cerpsī -cerptum vt to pick out, extract; to pick out, choose, gather; to leave out, omit, except

excerpt·um -ī n excerpt

excess·us -ūs m departure; death; digression

excētr·a -ae f snake

excidĭ·ō -ōnis f destruction

excid·ĭum -ĭī or **-ī** n overthrow, destruction; cause of destruction

ex·cĭdō -cidĕre -cĭdī vi to fall out; (of an utterance) to slip out, escape; to pass away, perish; to degenerate; to disappear; to be forgotten; (with **in** + acc) to degenerate into; (with abl or **ex** + abl) **a** to be deprived of, lose; **b** to forget, miss; (with dat or **de** + abl) **a** to fall from; **b** to escape from (lips); **e memoria excidere** to slip the memory

ex·cīdō -cīdĕre -cīdī -cīsum vt to cut out, cut off, cut down; to raze, demolish; (fig) to banish, eliminate

excĭĕō see **excio**

exc·ĭō -īre -īvī or **-ĭī -ītum** or **exci·ĕō -ēre** vt to call (someone) out, summon; to awaken (from sleep); to disturb; to frighten; to stir up, excite; to produce, occasion

ex·cipĭō -cipĕre -cēpī -ceptum vt to take out, remove; to rescue; to exempt; to take, receive, catch, capture; to follow, succeed; to catch, intercept; to be exposed to; to incur; to receive, welcome; to take up eagerly; to listen to, overhear; to except, make an exception of; to reach (a place); to mention in particular; to take on, withstand

excīsĭ·ō -ōnis f destruction

excīsus pp of **excido**

excitāt·us -a -um adj excited, lively, vigorous; loud

excĭt·ō -āre vt to wake, rouse; to raise, stir up; to erect, construct, produce; to cause, occasion; (fig) to arouse, awaken, incite, inspire, stimulate, enliven, encourage; to startle

excītus pp of **excio**

exclāmātĭ·ō -ōnis f exclamation

exclām·ō -āre vt to exclaim; vi to shout, yell

ex·clūdō -clūdĕre -clūsī -clūsum vt to exclude, shut out, shut off; to remove, separate; to hatch; (coll) to knock out (an eye); to prevent

exclūsi·ō -ōnis f exclusion

exclūsus pp of excludo

excoctus pp of excoquo

excōgitāti·ō -ōnis f thinking out, inventing, contriving

excōgitāt·us -a -um adj choice

excōgit·ō -āre vt to think out, devise, contrive

ex·cōlō -colēre -coluī -cultum vt to tend, cultivate, work carefully; to refine, ennoble, perfect, improve; to worship

ex·cōquō -coquēre -coxī -coctum vt to cook out, boil away; to dry up, bake thoroughly; to harden, temper (steel)

excor·s -dis adj senseless, silly, stupid

excrēment·um -ī n excretion

excrēō see exscreo

ex·crescō -crescēre -crēvī -crētum vi to grow out; to grow up, rise up

exoruciābil·is -e adj deserving torture

excrucī·ō -āre vt to torture, torment; to trouble, harass, distress

excubi·ae -ārum f pl standing guard; sentry; watchfire

excubīt·or -ōris m sentry

excūb·ō -āre -uī -itum vi to sleep out of doors; to stand guard; to be attentive, be on the alert

ex·cūdō -cūdēre -cūdī -cūsum vt to beat or strike out; to hammer out; to forge; (fig) to hatch (eggs); (fig) to hammer out, write up, hammer into shape

exculc·ō -āre vt to kick out; to tread down on; to stomp

exoultus pp of excolo

excūrāt·us -a -um adj carefully attended to

ex·currō -currēre -cucurrī or **-currī -cursum** vi to run or dash out; (mil) to sally forth, make an incursion; to project, extend; (fig) to fan out, expand

excursi·ō -ōnis f sally, sortie; inroad, invasion; outset, opening (of a speech)

excurs·or -ōris m skirmisher, scout

excurs·us -ūs m reconnoitering, running out ahead; raid, charge, attack, invasion; digression

excūsābil·is -e adj excusable

excūsātē adv excusably, without blame

excūsāti·ō -ōnis f excuse

excūsāt·us -a -um adj free from blame, exempt

excūs·ō -āre vt to free from blame; excuse; to exempt; to make excuses for, apologize for; to allege in excuse, plead as an excuse

excussus pp of excutio

excūsus pp of excudo

ex·cutiō -cutēre -cussī -cussum vt to shake out, shake off, shake loose; to knock out (e.g., teeth); (of

horse) to throw, throw off; to shake out (garment); to jilt, give a cold shoulder to; to toss, throw; to shake out, search; to examine, investigate; (fig) to shake off, discard, banish

exdorsū·ō -āre vt to fillet

exec- see exsec-

ex·ēdō -esse -ēdī -ēsum vt to eat up, consume; to destroy; to prey on; to hollow; to wear away, corrode

exēdr·a -ae f sitting room; lecture room; hall

exedr·ium -iī or **-ī** n sitting room, parlor, living room

exempl·ar or **exempl·āre -āris** n copy; likeness; pattern, model, ideal

exemplār·is -e adj following a model

exempl·um -ī n sample, example, typical instance; precedent; pattern, make, character; model, pattern (of conduct); object lesson; warning; copy, transcript; portrait

exemptus pp of eximo

exentēr·ō -āre vt to disembowel; to empty, exhaust; to torture, torment

ex·eō -īre -iī -itum vt to pass beyond, cross; to parry, ward off, avoid; (fig) to exceed; vi to go out, go forth; to go away, withdraw, depart, retire; to march out; to disembark; to pour out, gush out, flow out; to escape, be freed; to pass away, perish; (of time) to run out, expire; to get out, become public; to burgeon forth; (of hills) to rise; **ex urna exire** to come out of, fall out of the urn (said of lots)

exeq- = exseq-

exerc·eō -ēre -uī -itum vt to exercise, train; (mil) to drill, exercise, train; to keep (someone) busy, keep (someone) going; to supervise; to cultivate, work (the soil); to engage, occupy (the mind); to practice, follow (a trade, occupation); to carry into effect; to disturb, worry

exercitāti·ō -ōnis f exercise, practice, experience, training; (with genit) practice in

exercitāt·us -a -um adj experienced, trained, disciplined; troubled, worried, disturbed

exercit·ium -iī or **-ī** exercise, training

exercit·ō -āre vt to keep in training, exercise

exercit·or -ōris m trainer

exercit·us -a -um pp of excerceo; adj disciplined; experienced; trying, tough, harassing; harassed, vexed

exercit·us -ūs m army; infantry; (pol) assembly of the people; army of followers; swarm, flock, multitude

exērō see exsero

exēs·or -ōris m corrosive factor, underminer

exēsus pp of exedo

exhālāti·ō -ōnis f exhalation, vapor

exhāl·ō -āre vt to exhale, breathe out; vi to steam; to breathe one's last, expire

ex·haurĭō -haurīre -hausī -haus-tum *vt* to draw out, empty, exhaust; to take away, remove; to drain dry; to bring to an end; to undergo, endure (*troubles*); to discuss fully

exhērēd·ō -āre *vt* to disinherit

exhēr·ēs -ēdis *adj* disinherited

exhĭb·ĕō -ēre -ŭī -ĭtum *vt* to hold out; to present, produce; to display, exhibit; to cause, occasion; to render, make

exhĭlăr·ō -āre *vt* to cheer up

exhorr·escō -escĕre -ŭī *vt* to shudder at; *vi* to be terrified

exhortātĭ·ō -ōnis *f* encouragement; *f pl* words of encouragement

exhort·or -ārī -ātus sum *vt* to encourage

ex·ĭgō -igĕre -ēgī -actum *vt* to drive out, push out, thrust out, expel; to demand, exact, collect, require; to pass, spend, complete, close (*life, time*); to finish, complete, conclude; to ascertain, determine; to weigh, consider, estimate, examine, try, test; to dispose of

exĭgŭē *adv* briefly, slightly, sparingly, barely

exiguĭt·ās -ātis *f* shortness, smallness, meagerness, scantiness, scarcity

exigŭ·us -a -um *adj* short, small, meager, scanty, poor, paltry, inadequate; a little, a bit of

exilĭō see **exsilio**

exĭl·is -e *adj* thin, small, meager, feeble, poor; cheerless, dreary; depleted (*ranks*); worthless, insincere; dry, flat (*style*)

exīlĭt·ās -ātis *f* thinness; meagerness, dreariness

exīlĭter *adv* drily, drearily, jejunely

exilĭum see **exsilium**

exim see **exinde**

eximĭē *adv* exceptionally

eximĭ·us -a -um *adj* taken out, exempted; exempt; select, special, exceptional

ex·ĭmō -imĕre -ēmī -emptum *vt* to take out, take away, remove; to exempt; to free, release, let off; to make an exception of; to waste, lose (*time*); to banish (*e.g., worries*)

exin see **exinde**

exĭnān·ĭō -īre -ĭī -ītum *vt* to empty completely; to plunder; (fig) to clean out, fleece

exinde or **exim** or **exin** *adv* from that place, from that point; (in enumerating) after that, next, then; (of time) from that point, after that, then, furthermore, next; accordingly

existĭmātĭ·ō -ōnis *f* appraisal, judgment, estimate, opinion, decision, verdict; reputation, good name, character; (com) credit; **vulgi existimatio** public opinion

existĭmāt·or -ōris *m* critic, judge

existĭm·ō or **existŭm·ō -āre** *vt* to appraise, evaluate, value, estimate;

to think, judge, consider, regard; **in hostium numero existimare** to regard as an enemy

existō see **exsisto**

exitĭābĭl·is -e *adj* deadly, fatal, destructive; (with *dat*) fatal to

exitĭāl·is -e *adj* deadly, fatal

exitĭ·ō -ōnis *f* going out, exit

exitĭōs·us -a -um *adj* deadly, destructive

exit·ĭum -ĭī or **-ī** *n* destruction, ruin; cause of destruction

exit·us -ūs *m* going out, exit, departure; way out, outlet, exit; end, close, conclusion; **ad exitum adducere** to bring to a close

execĕbra see **elecebra**

ex·lex -lēgis *adj* without law, bound by no law; lawless, heedless of laws

exobsēcr·ō or **exopsēcr·ō -āre** *vi* to make an earnest entreaty

exocŭl·ō -āre *vt* to knock the eyes out of

exod·ĭum -ĭī or **-ī** *n* farce (*presented after the main feature*)

exol·escō -escĕre -ēvī -ētum *vi* to decay, fade; to become obsolete

exolēt·us -a -um *adj* full-grown; *m* (fig) old rake

exonĕr·ō -āre *vt* to unload; (fig) to relieve, free, exonerate

exoptābĭl·is -e *adj* highly desirable, long-awaited

exoptāt·us -a -um *adj* longed-for, welcome, desired

exopt·ō -āre *vt* to long for, wish earnestly, desire greatly

exōrābĭl·is -e *adj* accessible, sympathetic, placable

exōrābŭl·a -ōrum *n pl* enticements, bait, arguments

exōrāt·or -ōris *m* lucky petitioner

ex·ordĭor -ordīrī -orsus sum *vt* & *vi* to begin, start, commence

exord·ĭum -ĭī or **-ī** *n* beginning, start, commencement, origin; introduction

ex·orĭor -orīrī -ortus sum *vi* to come out, come forth, rise, appear; to begin, arise, be caused, be produced

exornātĭ·ō -ōnis *f* embellishment

exorn·ō -āre *vt* to fit out, furnish, equip, provide, supply; to adorn, embellish, decorate, set off, give luster to

exōr·ō -āre *vt* to prevail upon, win over; to gain or obtain by entreaty; to appease

exorsus *pp* of **exordior;** *n pl* beginning, commencement; introduction, preamble

exors·us -ūs *m* beginning, commencement; introduction

exortus *pp* of **exorior**

exort·us -ūs *m* rising; the East, the Orient

ex·os -ossis *adj* boneless

exoscŭl·or -ārī -ātus sum *vt* to kiss lovingly, kiss tenderly

exoss·ō -āre *vt* to bone, take the bones out of

exostr·a -ae *f* movable stage; **in exostra** in public

exōs·us -a -um *adj* hating, detesting; hated, detested

exōtic·us -a -um *adj* foreign, exotic

expall·escō -escĕre -ŭī *vt* to turn pale at, dread; *vi* to turn pale

expalliāt·us -a -um *adj* robbed of one's cloak

expalp·ō -āre *vt* to coax out

ex·pandō -pandĕre -pandī -pansum *vt* to spread out, unfold, expand

expātr·ō -āre *vt* to waste, squander

expav·escō -escĕre -ŭī *vt* to panic at; *vi* to panic

expect- = exspect-

expecūliāt·us -a -um *adj* stripped of property

exped·īō -īre -īī or -īvī -ītum *vt* to unfetter, extricate, disentangle; to get out, get ready; to clear for action; to clear (*roads of obstacles*); to free, extricate (*from troubles*); to put in order, arrange, settle, adjust, set right; to explain, unfold, clear up, disclose, recount, relate; **expedit** *v impers* it is expedient, useful, advantageous

expedītē *adv* without obstacles, without difficulty, quickly, promptly

expedītī·ō -ōnis *f* expedition, campaign, special mission

expedīt·us -a -um *adj* unencumbered, unhampered, unobstructed; (mil) lightly equipped; ready, prompt; ready at hand, convenient; **in expedito habere** to have at hand

ex·pellō -pellĕre -pŭlī -pulsum *vt* to drive out, eject, expel; to disown

ex·pendō -pendĕre -pendī -pensum *vt* to weigh out; to pay out, pay down, lay out, expend; to rate, estimate; to ponder, consider; to pay (*penalty*)

expens·us -a -um *adj* paid out, spent; *n* payment, expenditure

expergē·faciō -facĕre -fēcī -factum *vt* to awaken, wake up; to arouse, excite

exper·giscor -gisci -rectus sum *vi* to wake up; to be alert

expergō -ĕre -ī -ītum *vt* to awaken, wake up

experi·ens -entis *adj* enterprising, active; (with *genit*) ready to undergo

experienti·a -ae *f* test, trial, experiment; experience, practice; effort

experiment·um -ī *n* test, experiment, proof; experience

exper·ior -īrī -tus sum *vt* to test, try, prove; to experience, endure, find out; to try to do, attempt; to measure strength with; *vi* to go to court

experrectus *pp* of **expergiscor**

exper·s -tis *adj* (with *genit*) having no share in, devoid of, free from, without

expert·us -a -um *pp* of **experior**;

adj tried, proved, tested; (with *genit*) experienced in

expetess·ō -ĕre *vt* to desire, long for

expet·ō -ĕre -īvī or -īī -ītum *vt* to ask for, demand; to aim at, head for; to desire, long for, wish; *vi* (with **in** + *acc*) to befall; to fall upon, assail

expiātī·ō -ōnis *f* expiation, atonement; satisfaction

expictus *pp* of **expingo**

expīlātī·ō -ōnis *f* pillaging, plundering, ransacking

expīlāt·or -ōris *m* plunderer, robber

expīl·ō -āre *vt* to pillage, plunder, rob, ransack; to plagiarize

ex·pingō -pingĕre -pinxī -pictum *vt* to paint up; to depict; to paint true to life

expī·ō -āre *vt* to purify, cleanse ritually; to atone for, expiate; to avert (*curse, bad omen*)

expīrō see **exspiro**

expisc·or -ārī -ātus sum *vt* to fish for (*information*), ferret out, try to find out

explānātē *adv* plainly, clearly, distinctly

explānātī·ō -ōnis *f* explanation; clear pronunciation

explānāt·or -ōris *m* explainer; interpreter

explānāt·us -a -um *adj* plain, distinct

explān·ō -āre *vt* to explain, make clear; to pronounce clearly

ex·plaudō -plaudĕre -plausī -plausum *vt* to boo at, hiss at; to reject

explēment·um -ī *n* filling, stuffing

ex·plēō -ēre -ēvī -ētum *vt* to fill out, fill up; to complete; to satisfy (*desires*); to make good, repair (*losses*); to fulfill, perform, accomplish, discharge

explētī·ō -ōnis *f* satisfying

explēt·us -a -um *adj* full, complete, perfect

explicātē *adv* clearly, plainly

explicātī·ō -ōnis *f* unfolding, uncoiling; analysis; interpretation

explicāt·or -ōris *m* or explicātr·īx -īcis *f* explainer

explicāt·us -a -um *adj* plain, clear-cut

explicāt·us -ūs *m* unfolding; explanation, interpretation

explicit·us -a -um *adj* disentangled; simple, easy

explic·ō -āre -āvī or -ŭī -ātum or -ītum *vt* to unfold, unroll; to spread out; to loosen, undo; (mil) to exceed, deploy; to set free, release; to set in order, arrange, adjust, settle; to set forth, exhibit, explain

ex·plōdō or ex·plaudō -plōdĕre -lōsī -plōsum *vt* to drive off by clapping; to boo (*off the stage*); to disapprove, discredit

explōrātē *adv* after careful examination; for sure, for certain

explōrātĭ·ō -ōnis f exploration, examination

explōrāt·or -ōris m scout, spy

explōrāt·us -a -um adj sure, certain

explōr·ō -āre vt to explore, investigate; (mil) to reconnoiter; to probe, search; to test, try, try out

explōsĭ·ō -ōnis f booing (of an actor)

expolĭō -īre -īvī or **-ĭī -ītum** vt to polish; (fig) to polish, refine, adorn

expolītĭ·ō -ōnis f polishing, finishing off, embellishing

expolīt·us -a -um adj polished, lustrous; refined

ex·pōnō -pōnĕre -posŭī -positum or **-postum** vt to put out; to expose, abandon; to expose, lay open; to reveal, publish; to exhibit, relate, explain; to offer, tender; to set on shore, disembark, land

expor·rĭgō -rĭgĕre -rexī -rectum vt to stretch out, spread, spread out; **exporge frontem** (coll) smooth out your brow, quit frowning

exportātĭ·ō -ōnis f exportation

export·ō -āre vt to carry out; to export

ex·poscō -poscĕre -poposcī vt to demand, beg, insist upon; to demand the surrender of

expositīcĭ·us -a -um adj foundling

expositĭ·ō -ōnis f exposing; (rhet) narration, explanation (of details of a case)

exposĭt·us -a -um pp of **expono**; adj accessible; accessible, affable

expostulātĭ·ō -ōnis f insistent demand; complaint

expostŭl·ō -āre vt to demand, insist on; to complain of; (with cum + abl of person) to complain of (something) to (someone); vi to lodge a complaint; (with cum + abl) to lodge a complaint with

expostus pp of **expono**

expōtus see **epotus**

express·us -a -um adj distinct, clear, express; distinct, real

ex·prĭmō -prĭmĕre -pressī -pressum vt to press out, squeeze out; (fig) to squeeze out, wring, extort; to model, form, portray; to represent, imitate, copy, describe, express; to translate; to pronounce, articulate

exprobrātĭ·ō -ōnis f reproach

exprŏbr·ō -āre vt to reproach, find fault with; (with dat) to cast (something) up to, put the blame for (something) on; vi (with dat) to complain to

ex·prōmō -prōmĕre -prompsī -promptum vt to bring out, fetch out; to give vent to; to disclose, display, exhibit; to give utterance to, utter, express, state

expugnābĭl·is -e adj vulnerable to attack, pregnable

expugnācĭ·or -us adj more potent

expugnātĭ·ō -ōnis f assault; (with genit) assault on

expugnāt·or -ōris m attacker; **expugnator pudicitiae** assailant

expugn·ō -āre vt to assault, storm; to conquer (persons) in war; (fig) to conquer, overcome; (fig) to achieve, accomplish; (fig) to wrest, extort

expulsĭ·ō -ōnis f expulsion

expuls·ō -āre vt to drive out, expel

expuls·or -ōris m expeller

expulsus pp of **expello**

expultr·ix -īcis f expeller (female)

ex·pungō -pungĕre -punxī -punctum vt to expunge; to cancel; to remove

expurgātĭ·ō -ōnis f justification, excuse

expurg·ō -āre vt to cleanse, purify; to cure; to vindicate, excuse, justify

expūtescō -ĕre vi to rot away

expūt·ō -āre vt to prune, lop off; to consider; to comprehend

ex·quīrō -quīrĕre -quīsīvī -quīsītum vt to investigate, scrutinize; to search for, look for; to ransack; to devise

exquīsītē adv carefully, accurately; exquisitely

exquīsīt·us -a -um pp of **exquiro**; adj carefully considered, choice, exquisite

exrādīcĭtus adv from the very roots

exsaev·ĭō -īre vi to cease raging, calm down

exsangu·is -e adj bloodless; pale; feeble; causing paleness

ex·sarcĭō or **ex·sercĭō -sarcīre — -sartum** vt to patch up; (fig) to repair

exsatĭ·ō -āre vt to satiate, satisfy fully, glut

exsaturābĭl·is -e adj appeasable

exsatŭr·ō -āre vt to satiate, satisfy completely

exscē- = **esce**

ex·scindō -scindĕre -scĭdī -scissum vt to annihilate, destroy

exscrĕ·ō -āre vt to cough up, spit out

ex·scrībō -scrībĕre -scripsī -scriptum vt to write down; to write out in full; to copy; (fig) to copy, take after, resemble

exsculp·ō -ĕre -sī -tum vt to carve out; to scratch out, erase; (fig) to extort

exsĕc·ō or **exsĭc·ō -āre -ŭī -tum** vt to cut out, cut away, cut off; to castrate; to deduct

exsecrābĭl·is -e adj accursed; bitter, merciless, deadly; execrating, cursing

exsecrātĭ·ō -ōnis f curse, execration; solemn oath

exsecrāt·us -a -um adj accursed, detestable

exsĕcr·or -ārī -ātus sum vt to curse, execrate; vi to take a solemn oath

exsectĭ·ō -ōnis f cutting out

exsecūtĭ·ō -ōnis f execution, performance; discussion

exsecūtus pp of exsequor

exsequi·ae -ārum f pl funeral procession, funeral rites

exsequiāl·is -e adj funeral; **carmina exsequialia** dirges

ex·sĕquor -sĕquī -secūtus sum vt to follow out; to accompany to the grave; to perform, execute, accomplish, carry out; to follow up, investigate: to pursue, go after; to avenge, punish; to say, tell, describe, relate

exsĕr·ō -ĕre -ŭī -tum vt to untie, disconnect; to stretch out (one's arms); to stick out (the tongue in disdain); to bare, uncover

exsert·ō -āre vt to keep on stretching or sticking out

exsertus pp of exsero; adj uncovered, bare; protruding

exsībĭl·ō -āre vt to hiss off the stage

exsiccāt·us -a -um adj dry, uninteresting

exsicc·ō -āre vt to dry up; to drain dry

exsicō see exseco

exsign·ō -āre vt to mark down exactly, write down in detail

ex·silĭō -silīre -silŭī vi to jump out, leap up; to start; **exsilīre gaudio** to jump for joy

exsil·ĭum -ĭī or **-ī** n exile, banishment (voluntary or involuntary); place of exile

ex·sistō -sistĕre -stĭtī -stĭtum vi to come out, come forth; to appear, emerge; to exist, be; to arise, proceed; to turn into, become; to be visible

ex·solvō -solvĕre -solvī -solūtum vt to loosen, untie; to release, free, set free; to discharge, pay; to keep, fulfill; to satisfy (hunger); to break open, wound; to solve, explain; to throw off, get rid of; to repay, requite; to give out (awards, punishment)

exsomn·is -e adj sleepless

exsorb·ĕō -ēre -ŭī vt to suck up, drain; to drain, exhaust; to grasp at eagerly, welcome

exsor·s -tis adj without lots; chosen specially; (with genit) having no share in, free from

exspatĭ·or -ārī -ātus sum vi to go off course; to digress

exspectābĭl·is -e adj expected, anticipated

exspectātĭ·ō -ōnis f expectation, suspense; **exspectationem facere** to cause suspense

exspectāt·us -a -um adj expected, awaited, desired

exspect·ō -āre vt to await, wait for, look out for; to hope for, long for, anticipate

ex·spergō -spergĕre — -spersum vt to sprinkle, scatter

exspēs adj hopeless, forlorn; (with genit) without hope of

exspīrātĭ·ō -ōnis f breathing out, exhalation

exspīr·ō -āre or **expīr·ō -āre** vt to breathe out, exhale, emit; vi to expire, breathe one's last; (fig) to come to an end, cease

exsplend·escō -escĕre -ŭī vi to glitter, shine

exspolĭ·ō -āre vt to strip; to pillage

es·spŭō -spuĕre -spŭī -spūtum vt to spit out; (fig) to banish (e.g., worries)

extern·ō -āre vt to startle, scare; to terrify; to stampede (horses)

exstill·ō -āre vi to drop, trickle out; to melt

exstimulāt·or -ōris m instigator

exstimŭl·ō -āre vt to instigate, goad on

exstinctĭ·ō -ōnis f extinction

exstinct·or -ōris m extinguisher; suppressor; destroyer

ex·stinguō -stinguĕre -stinxī -stinctum vt to extinguish, put out; to destroy, kill; to abolish, annul; **extingui** to die, die out; to be forgotten

exstirp·ō -āre vt to extirpate, root out, eradicate

exst·ō -āre vi to stand out, protrude, project; to stand out, be prominent, be conspicuous; to be visible; to appear; to exist, be extant

exstructĭ·ō -ōnis f erection

ex·strŭō -struĕre -struxī -structum vt to pile up, heap up; to build, erect

exsuct·us -a -um pp of exsugo; adj dried up

exsūd·ō -āre vt to sweat; (fig) to sweat out, sweat over; vi to pour out

ex·sūgō -sūgĕre -suxī -suctum vt to suck out

exs·ul or **ex·ul -ŭlis** m or f exile, refugee

exsŭl·ō -āre vi to be an exile, be a refugee

exsultātĭ·ō -ōnis f exultation, jumping for joy

exsultim adv friskily

exsult·ō or **exult·ō -āre** vi to jump up; to frisk about; (of horses) to rear, prance; to exult, rejoice, jump for joy; to revel, run riot; to boast; (of speech) to range freely

exsuperābĭl·is -e adj climbable; superable

exsuperantĭ·a -ae f superiority

exsupĕr·ō -āre vt to surmount; to exceed, surpass; to overpower; vi to rise; (of flames) to shoot up; to be superior, excel, be conspicuous, prevail

exsurd·ō -āre vt to deafen; (fig) to dull

ex·surgō -surgĕre -surrexī vi to get up, rise, stand up; (fig) to rise, recover strength; **foras exsurgĕre** to get up and go out

exsuscĭt·ō -āre vt to rouse from sleep; to fan (fire); to excite, stir up

ext·a -ōrum *n pl* vital organs (*of sacrificial animals*)

extāb·escō -escĕre -ŭī *vi* to waste away, pine away; to disappear

extār·is -e *adj* used for cooking the sacrificial victim; sacrificial

extemplō or **extempŭlō** *adv* immediately, right away; on the spur of the moment

ex·tendō -tendĕre -tendī -tentum or **-tensum** *vt* to stretch out, spread out, extend; to enlarge, increase; to widen, broaden; to prolong, continue; to pass, spend; to exert, strain; **extendi** to stretch out, extend; **labellum extendere** to pout

extent·ō -āre *vt* to exert, strain

extent·us -a -um *pp* of **extendo**; *adj* extensive, wide; **extentis itineribus** by forced marches

extenuātī·ō -ōnis *f* extenuation; thinning out

extenuāt·us -a -um *adj* thinned, reduced; trifling; weak, faint

extenŭ·ō -āre *vt* to thin out; to lessen, diminish, extenuate, detract from

exter or **extĕr·us -a -um** *adj* external, outward; foreign, strange

exterĕbr·ō -āre *vt* to bore out; to extort

ex·tergĕō -tergēre -tersī -tersum *vt* to wipe out, wipe clean; (fig) to wipe out, plunder

exterī·or -us *adj* outer, exterior

exterīus *adv* on the outside

extermin·ō -āre *vt* to drive out, banish; to put aside, put away, remove

extern·us -a -um *adj* external, outward; foreign, strange; *m* foreigner, stranger, foreign enemy; *n pl* foreign goods

ex·tĕrō -terĕre -trīvī -trītum *vt* to rub out, wear away; (fig) to crush

exterr·ĕō -ēre -ŭī -ĭtum *vt* to frighten, terrify

extersus *pp* of **extergeo**

extĕrus see **exter**

extex·ō -ĕre *vt* to unweave; (fig) to cheat

extim·escō -escĕre -ŭī *vt* to become terribly afraid of, dread; *vi* to become afraid

extīm·us -a -um *adj* outermost, farthest, most remote

extisp·ex -ĭcis *m* soothsayer, diviner (*who makes predictions by inspecting the entrails of animals*)

extoll·ō -ĕre *vt* to lift up; to erect; to postpone; to extol, praise; to raise, exalt; to beautify; **animos extollere** to raise the morale

ex·torquĕō -torquēre -torsī -tortum *vt* to wrench, wrest; to dislocate; to extort

extorr·is -e *adj* driven out of one's country, banished, exiled

extort·or -ōris *m* extorter

extortus *pp* of **extorqueo**; *adj* deformed

extrā *adv* outside, on the outside; **extra quam** except in the case that; **extra quam sī** unless; *prep* (*with acc*) outside, outside of, beyond; apart from, aside from; contrary to; except, besides; without; **extra jocum** all joking aside

ex·trăhō -trahĕre -traxī -tractum *vt* to pull out, drag out; to drag out, prolong; to waste (*time*); to extricate, release, rescue; to remove

extrānĕ·us -a -um *adj* extraneous, external, irrevelant, strange; *m* stranger

extrāordinārī·us -a -um *adj* extraordinary

extrārī·us -a -um *adj* outward, external; unrelated (*by family ties*)

extrēm·a -ōrum *n pl* end (*e.g.*, *of a marching column, of strip of land, of life*)

extrēmit·ās -ātis *f* extremity, end

extrēmō *adv* finally, at last

extrēmum *adv* finally, at last; for the last time

extrēm·us -a -um *adj* extreme, outermost, on the end; latest, last; (of degree) utmost, extreme; lowest, meanest; **extrema aetas** advanced old age; **extrema cauda** tip of the tail; **extremā lineā amare** to love at a distance; **extrema manus** final touches; **extremis digitis attingere** to touch lightly; to touch lightly on; to hold tenderly; **extremus ignis** flickering flame; **in extremo libro secundo** at the end of the second book; *n* end; extremity; **ad extremum** at last; at the end; utterly; **in extremo** in mortal danger, in a crisis

extrīc·ō -āre or **extrīc·or -ārī -ātus sum** *vt* to extricate; to clear up; to obtain with difficulty

extrinsĕcus *adv* from outside, from abroad; on the outside, outside

extrītus *pp* of **extero**

ex·trūdō -trūdĕre -trūsī -trūsum *vt* to thrust out, drive out; to get rid of

extum·ĕō -ēre *vi* to swell up

ex·tundō -tundĕre -tūdī -tūsum *vt* to beat out, hammer out; to fashion; to devise; to extort

exturb·ō -āre *vt* to drive out, chase out, drive away; to divorce; to knock out

exūbĕr·ō -āre *vi* to grow luxuriantly; to abound

exulcĕr·ō -āre *vt* to make sore, aggravate; to exasperate

exulŭl·ō -āre *vt* to invoke with cries; *vi* to howl

exunctus *pp* of **exungo**

exund·ō -āre *vi* to overflow; **in lītora exundare** to wash up on the shores

ex·ungō -ungĕre — -unctum *vt* to oil down, rub with oil

ex·ŭō **-uĕre** **-ŭī** **-ūtum** *vt* to take off, pull off; to shake off; to unclothe; to strip, deprive; to cast aside, cast off; to bare

exurge·ĕō **-ēre** *vt* to squeeze out

ex·ūrō **-ūrĕre** **-ussī** **-ustum** *vt* to burn out, burn up; to dry up; to consume, destroy; (fig) to inflame

exustī·ō **-ōnis** *f* conflagration

exustus *pp* of **exuro**

exūtus *pp* of **exuo**

exuvĭ·ae **-ārum** *f pl* clothing; equipment; arms; hide; slough; booty, spoils

F

fab·a **-ae** *f* bean

fabāl·is **-e** *adj* bean; **stipulae fabales** bean stalks

fābell·a **-ae** *f* short story; fable, tale; short play

fab·er **-ra** **-rum** *adj* skilled; *m* craftsman; smith; carpenter; (mil) engineer; **faber ferrarius** blacksmith; **faber tignarius** carpenter

Fab·ĭus **-ĭī** or **-ī** *m* Quintus Fabius Maximus Cunctator, elected consul five times and appointed dictator in 217 B.C. to conduct the war against Hannibal (d. 203 B.C.); Quintus Fabius Pictor, first Roman historian to use prose (*fl* 225 B.C.)

fabrē *adv* skillfully

fabrē·facĭō **-facĕre** **-fēcī** **-factum** *vt* to build, make; to forge

fabric·a **-ae** *f* trade, industry; workshop, factory; piece of work, structure, production; **fabricam fingere** (with **ad** + *acc*) (coll) to pull a trick on

fabricātĭ·ō **-ōnis** *f* structure, construction

fabricāt·or **-ōris** *m* builder, architect, producer, creator

fabric·or **-ārī** **-ātus sum** or **fabrĭc·ō** **-āre** *vt* to build, construct, produce, forge; to prepare, form; to coin (*words*)

fabrīl·is **-e** *adj* craftman's, carpenter's, sculptor's; *n pl* tools

fābŭl·a **-ae** *f* story, tale; talk, conversation, conversation piece; small talk; affair, matter, concern; myth, legend; drama, play; dramatic poem; **fabulae!** (coll) baloney!; **lupus in fabula!** (coll) speak of the devil!

fābulār·is **-e** *adj* legendary

fābŭl·or **-ārī** **-ātus sum** *vt* to say, invent; *vi* to talk, chat, gossip

fābulōs·us **-a** **-um** *adj* legendary

fabŭl·us **-ī** *m* small bean

facess·ō **-ĕre** **-īvī** **-ĭtum** *vt* to do eagerly, perform, accomplish; to bring on, cause, create; **negotium alicui facessere** to cause someone trouble; *vi* to go away, depart

facētē *adv* facetiously, humorously, wittily, brilliantly

facētĭ·ae **-ārum** *f pl* clever thing, clever talk, witticism, humor

facēt·us **-a** **-um** *adj* witty, humorous; fine, polite; elegant; brilliant

facĭ·ēs **-ēī** *f* make, form, shape; face, look; look, appearance; nature, character; external appearance, pretense, pretext

facĭl·is **-e** *adj* easy; nimble; suitable, convenient; ready, quick; easy, easygoing, good-natured; favorable, prosperous; gentle (*breeze*); easily-borne, slight (*loss*); **ex** or **e facili** easily; **in facili esse** to be easy; **facilis victu** prosperous, well-off, well-to-do

facĭle *adv* easily, without trouble; unquestionably, by far, far; quite, fully; promptly, readily, willingly; pleasantly, well; **non facile** hardly

facilit·ās **-ātis** *f* facility, easiness, ease; readiness; fluency; suitability; good nature, affability, courteousness; levity

facinorōs·us or **facinerōs·us** **-a** **-um** *adj & m* criminal

facĭn·us **-ŏris** *n* deed, action; crime, villany

facĭō facĕre fēcī factum (**faxim** = **fēcĕrim**; **faxō** = **fēcĕrō**) *vt* to make, fashion, frame, create, build, erect; to do, perform; to make, produce, compose; to bring about, cause, occasion; to acquire, gain, get, accumulate; to incur, suffer; to render, grant, give, confer; to grant, admit; to assume, suppose; to assert, say, represent, depict; to choose, appoint; to follow, practice; to regard, prize, value; **certiorem facere** to inform; **copiam facere** to afford the opportunity; **fac ita esse** suppose it were so, granted that it is so; **fidem facere** to give one's word; **pecuniam facere** or **stipendium facere** to make money, earn money; **promissum facere** to fulfill a promise; **sacra facere** to sacrifice; **verbum facere** to speak; **viam facere** (with *dat*) to make way for; *vi* to do, act; to take part, take sides; (with *dat* or with **ad** + *acc*) to be satisfactory for, be fit for, do for

factĕon = **faciendum**

factĭ·ō **-ōnis** *f* doing; making; party, faction; partisanship; company, social set, association, class; oligarchy; (with *genit*) right to make (*e.g., a will*)

factiōs·us **-a** **-um** *adj* busy; partisan; oligarchical; factious, revolutionary, seditious

factĭt·ō -āre *vt* to keep doing or making; to practice (*e.g.*, *trade*); (with double *acc*) to declare (*someone*) to be (*e.g.*, *heir*)

fact·or -ōris *m* (in playing ball) batter

fact·us -a -um *pp* of **facio;** *n* deed, act; accomplishment, exploit

facŭl·a -ae *f* little torch

facult·ās -ātis *f* opportunity, means; feasibility; ability, capacity, mental resources; material resources, means, supplies, abundance

fācundē *adv* eloquently

fācundi·a -ae *f* eloquence

fācundĭt·ās -ātis *f* eloquence

fācund·us -a -um *adj* eloquent, fluent

faecē·us -a -um *adj* morally impure, morally rotten

faecŭl·a -ae *f* wine lees

faenĕbr·is -e *adj* of interest, regarding interest; **res faenebris** indebtedness

faenerāti·ō -ōnis *f* lending at interest, investment

faenerātō *adv* with interest

faenerāt·or -ōris *m* money lender, investor, capitalist

faenĕr·or -ārī -ātus sum or **faenĕr·ō -āre** *vt* to lend at interest; to invest; to ruin through high interest rates; *vi* to bring interest, bring profit; **faeneratum beneficium** (fig) a favor richly repaid

faenē·us -a -um *adj* made of hay

faenīl·ĭa -ĭum *n pl* hayloft

faenisĕc·a -ae *m* peasant

faen·um or **fēn·um -ī** *n* hay; **faenum habet in cornu** (fig) he's crazy

faen·us or **fēn·us -ōris** *n* interest; debt (*as result of heavy interest*); capital; (fig) profit, gain, advantage

faenuscŭl·um or **fēnuscŭl·um -ī** *n* a little interest

fae·x -cis *f* dregs, sediments, grounds, lees; (fig) dregs

fāginē·us or **fāgĭn·us** or **fāgĕ·us -a -um** *adj* beech

fāg·us -ī *f* beech tree

fal·a or **phal·a -ae** *f* movable wooden siege tower; scaffold

falārĭc·a or **phalārĭc·a -ae** *f* incendiary missile

falcār·ĭus -ĭī or **-ī** *m* sickle maker

falcāt·us -a -um *adj* fitted with scythes, scythed; sickle-shaped, curved

falcĭf·er -ĕra -ĕrum *adj* scythe-bearing

Falern·us -a -um *adj* Falernian; **ager Falernus** district in N. Campania, famous for its wine; *n* Falernian wine

Falisc·ī -ōrum *m pl* a people of S.E. Etruria

fallācĭ·a -ae *f* deception, deceit, trick

fallācĭter *adv* deceptively, deceitfully, fallaciously

fall·ax -ācis *adj* deceptive, deceitful, fallacious

fallō fallĕre fefellī falsum *vt* to cause to fall, trip; to lead into error; to deceive, trick, dupe, cheat; to fail to live up to, disappoint; to wile away; to escape the notice of, slip by; **fĭdem fallere** to break one's word; **me fallit** I do not know; **nisi** or **ni fallor** unless I'm mistaken; **opinionem fallere** (with *genit*) to fail to live up to the expectations of

falsē *adv* falsely

falsidĭc·us -a -um *adj* speaking falsely, lying

falsific·us -a -um *adj* acting dishonestly

falsijūri·us -a -um *adj* swearing falsely

falsilŏqu·us -a -um *adj* lying

falsimōni·a -ae *f* trick

falsipār·ens -entis *adj* bastard

falsō *adv* mistakenly, wrongly, erroneously; falsely, deceitfully, untruly

fals·us -a -um *pp* of **fallo;** *adj* mistaken, wrong, erroneous; false, untrue; lying, deceitful; vain, groundless, empty; spurious, sham, fictitious; *n* error; lying, perjury; lie, untruth, falsehood

fal·x -cis *f* sickle; pruning hook, pruning knife; (mil) hook for pulling down walls

fām·a -ae *f* talk, rumor, report; saying, tradition; reputation; fame, renown, glory, name; infamy, notoriety; public opinion

famēlĭc·us -a -um *adj* famished, starved

fam·ēs -is *f* hunger, starvation; poverty; famine; greed; (rhet) bald style, poverty of expression

fāmigerāti·ō -ōnis *f* rumor

fāmigerāt·or -ōris *m* gossip, rumormonger

famĭlĭ·a -ae or **-ās** *f* household slaves, domestics; household; house, family; family estate; fraternity; sect, school; **familiam ducere** to be the head of a sect; **pater familĭas** head of the household

familĭār·is -e *adj* domestic, family, household; familiar, intimate; (in augury) one's own (*part of the sacrificial animal*); *m* servant, slave; acquaintance, friend, companion

familĭārĭt·ās -ātis *f* familiarity, intimacy; association, friendship

familĭārĭter *adv* on friendly terms

fāmōs·us -a -um *adj* much talked of; famous, renowned; infamous, notorious; slanderous, libelous; **carmen famosum** lampoon

famŭl·a -ae *f* slave, maid, maidservant

famulār·is -e *adj* of slaves, of servants

famulāt·us -ūs *m* servitude, slavery

famŭl·or -ārī -ātus sum *vi* to be a slave; (with *dat*) to serve

famŭl·us -a -um *adj* serviceable; *m* servant, attendant

fānātic·us -a -um *adj* fanatic, enthusiastic, inspired; wild, frantic

fān·um -ī *n* shrine, sanctuary, temple

fār farris *n* spelt; coarse meal, grits; sacrificial meal; bread; dog biscuit; *n pl* grain

far·ciō -cīre -sī -tum *vt* to stuff, cram

farfăr·us or **farfĕr·us -ī** *m* coltsfoot (*plant*)

farīn·a -ae *f* flour; powder; character, quality

farrāg·ō -inis *f* mash (*for cattle*); medley, hodgepodge

farrāt·us -a -um *adj* filled with grain; made with grain

fart·is -is *f* stuffing, filling, mincemeat; **fartim facere ex hostibus** to make mincemeat of the enemy

fart·or -ōris *m* fattener of fowls

fartus *pp* of **farcio**

fās (indecl) *n* divine law; sacred duty; divine will, fate; right; **fas est** it is right, it is lawful, it is permitted

fasci·a -ae *f* bandage, swathe; girth; fillet; wisp of cloud

fasciātim *adv* in bundles

fascicŭl·us -ī *m* small bundle

fascin·ō -āre *vt* to cast an evil eye on, bewitch; jinx; to envy

fascin·um -ī *n* or **fascin·us -ī** *m* evil eye; jinx; witchcraft; charm, amulet; penis

fasciŏl·a -ae *f* small bandage

fasc·is -is *m* bundle, pack, parcel, fagot; load, burden; baggage; *m pl* fasces (*bundle of rods and ax, carried before high magistrates by lictors as symbols of authority*); high office, supreme power, consulship

fassus *pp* of **fateor**

fast·ī -ōrum *m pl* calendar, almanac; annals; register of higher magistrates

fastīd·iō -īre -īvī or **-iī -ītum** *vt* to disdain, despise, snub, turn up the nose at; *vi* to feel disgust, feel squeamish; to be snobbish, be haughty

fastīdiōsē *adv* fastidiously, squeamishly; disdainfully, snobbishly

fastīdiōs·us -a -um *adj* fastidious, squeamish; disdainful, snobbish; refined, delicate

fastīd·ium -iī or **-ī** *n* fastidiousness, squeamishness, distaste, disgust, loathing; snobbishness, haughtiness, contempt

fastīgātē *adv* sloped (*like a gable*), sloping up, sloping down

fastīgāt·us -a -um *adj* rising to a point; sloping down

fastīg·ium -iī or **-ī** *n* gable; pediment; roof, ceiling; slope; height, elevation, top, edge; depth, depression; finish, completion; rank, dig-

nity; main point, heading, highlight (*of story, etc.*)

fast·us -a -um *adj* legal (*day*); **dies fastus** court day

fast·us -ūs *m* disdain, contempt, arrogance; *m pl* brash deeds; calendar

fātāl·is -e *adj* fateful, destined, preordained; fatal, deadly; **deae fatales** the Fates

fātāliter *adv* according to fate, by fate

fatĕor fatērī fassus sum *vt* to admit, acknowledge; to disclose, reveal

fāticăn·us or **fāticin·us -a -um** *adj* prophetic

fātidic·us -a -um *adj* prophetic

fātif·er -ĕra -ĕrum *adj* fatal, deadly

fatigāti·ō -ōnis *f* fatigue, weariness

fatig·ō -āre *vt* to fatigue, weary, tire; to worry, torment, harass, wear down; to importune, pray to constantly

fātilŏqu·a -ae *f* prophetess

fatisc·ō -ĕre or **fatisc·or -ī** *vi* to split, crack, give way; (fig) to crack, break down, collapse from exhaustion

fatuīt·ās -ātis *f* silliness

fāt·um -ī *n* divine utterance, oracle; fate, destiny, doom; calamity, mishap, ruin; death; **ad fata novissima** to the last; **fato obire** to meet death, die; **fatum proferre** to prolong life

fātus *pp* of **for**

fatŭ·us -a -um *adj* silly, foolish; clumsy; *m* fool

fauc·ēs -ium *f pl* upper part of the throat, throat, gullet; strait, channel; pass, defile, gorge; (fig) jaws; **fauces premere** (with *genit*) to choke, throttle

Faun·us -ī *m* mythical king of Latium, father of Latinus, and worshiped as the Italian Pan; *m pl* Fauns, woodland spirits

faustē *adv* favorably, auspiciously

faustit·ās -ātis *f* fertility; good fortune, happiness

Faustŭl·us -ī *m* shepherd who raised Romulus and Remus

faust·us -a -um *adj* auspicious, favorable, fortunate, lucky

faut·or or **favit·or -ōris** *m* promoter, patron, supporter, fan

fautr·ix -īcis *f* patroness, protectress

favĕ·a -ae *f* favorite girl, pet slave girl

favĕō favēre fāvī fautum *vi* (with *dat*) to be favorable to, favor, support, side with; (with *inf*) to be eager to; **favere linguis** or **favere ore** to observe a reverent silence

favill·a -ae *f* ashes, embers; (fig) spark, beginning

favitor see **fautor**

Favŏn·ius -iī or **-ī** *m* west wind (*also called Zephyrus*)

fav·or -ōris *m* favor, support; applause; appreciation (*shown by applause*)

favōrābil·is -e *adj* popular

fav·us -ī *m* honeycomb

fa·x -cis *f* torch; wedding torch; wedding; funeral torch; funeral; meteor, shooting star, comet; firebrand; fire, flame; guiding light; instigator; flame of love; stimulus, incitement; cause of ruin, destruction; **dicendi faces** fiery eloquence; **dolorum faces** pangs of grief

faxim see **facio**

febrīcul·a -ae *f* slight fever

febr·is -is *f* fever

Febru·a -ōrum *n pl* Roman festival of purification and expiation, celebrated on February 15th

Februāri·us -a -um *adj* & *m* February

febru·um -ī *n* purgation, purification

fēcundĭt·ās -ātis *f* fertility, fruitfulness; (rhet) overstatement

fēcund·ō -āre *vt* to fertilize

fēcund·us -a -um *adj* fertile, fruitful; abundant, rich; fertilizing; (with *genit* or *abl*) rich in, abounding in

fe·l -llis *n* gallbladder; gall, bile; bitterness, animosity; poison

fēl·ēs -is *f* cat

fēlicĭt·ās -ātis *f* fertility; luck, good fortune, piece of luck; felicity, happiness

fēlicĭter *adv* fruitfully, abundantly; favorably, auspiciously; luckily; happily; successful

fēl·ix -īcis *adj* fruit-bearing; fruitful, fertile; favorable, auspicious; lucky; happy; successful

fēmell·a -ae *f* girl

fēmin·a -ae *f* female; woman

fēmināt·us -a -um *adj* effeminate

fēminĕ·us -a -um *adj* woman's; effeminate, unmanly

fēminīn·us -a -um *adj* (gram) feminine

fem·ur -ŏris or **-ĭnis** *n* thigh

fēn- = faen-

fenestr·a -ae *f* window; hole (*for earrings*); (fig) opening, opportunity; (mil) breach (*in a wall*)

fer·a -ae *f* wild beast, wild animal

ferācĭus *adv* more fruitfully

Fērāl·ia -ĭum *n pl* festival of the dead, celebrated on February 17th or 21st

fērāl·is -e *adj* funeral; deadly, fatal; gloomy, dismal

fer·ax -ācis *adj* fertile, fruitful; (with *genit*) productive of

fercŭl·um -ī *n* food tray; dish, course; litter for carrying spoils in a victory parade or cult images in religious processions

fercŭl·us -ī *m* litter bearer

ferē or **fermē** *adv* approximately, nearly, almost, about, just about; generally, as a rule, usually; (with

negatives) practically; **nemo fere** practically no one

ferentār·ius -iī or **-ī** *m* light-armed soldier; eager helper

Feretr·ius -iī or **-ī** *m* epithet of Jupiter

ferētr·um -ī *n* litter, bier

fēri·ae -ārum *f pl* holidays, vacation; (fig) leisure

fēriāt·us -a -um *adj* vacationing, taking it easy, relaxing, taking time off

ferīn·us -a -um *adj* of wild animals; **caro ferina** venison; *f* game, venison

fer·iō -īre *vt* to strike, hit, shoot, knock; to kill; to slaughter, sacrifice (*an animal*); to coin; (fig) to strike, reach, affect; (fig) to cheat, trick; **cornu ferire** to butt; **foedus ferire** to make a treaty; **securi ferire** to behead; **verba ferire** to coin words

ferĭt·ās -ātis *f* wildness, fierceness

fermē see **fere**

ferment·um -ī *n* yeast; beer; (fig) ferment, provocation, vexation, anger, passion

ferō ferre tulī or **tetŭlī lātum** *vt* to bear, carry; to bear, produce, bring forth; to bear, endure; to lead, drive, conduct, direct; to bring, offer; to receive, acquire, obtain, win; to take by force, carry off, plunder, ravage; to manifest, display, make known, report, relate, say, tell; to propose, bring forward; to allow, permit; to cause, create; to set in motion; to call, name; (in accounting) to enter; **aegre ferre** to be annoyed at; **caelo supinas manus ferre** to raise the hands heavenward in prayer; **ferri** to move, rush; to sail; to fly; to flow along; (fig) to be carried away (*e.g., with ambition, greed*); **ferri** or **se ferre** to rush, flee; **iter ferre** to pursue a course; **laudibus ferre** to extol; **legem ferre** to propose a bill; **moleste ferre** to be annoyed at; **pedem ferre** to come, go, move, get going; **prae se ferre** to display, manifest; **se ferre obviam** (with *dat*) to rush to meet; **repulsam ferre** to experience defeat (*at the polls*); **sententiam ferre** to pass judgment; to cast a vote; **signa ferre** (mil) to begin marching; **ventrem ferre** to be pregnant; *vi* to say, e.g., **ut ferunt** as people say, as they say; to allow, permit, e.g., **si oocasio tulerit** if occasion permit; to lead, e.g., **iter ad oppidum ferebat** the road led to the town

ferōci·a -ae *f* courage, bravery, spirit; ferocity, barbarity; presumption

ferōcĭt·ās -ātis *f* courage, spirit, fierceness, aggressiveness; ferocity, barbarity; pride, presumption

ferōcĭter *adv* bravely, courageously, aggressively; defiantly; haughtily

Fērōnĭ·a -ae *f* early Italic goddess of groves and fountains, and patroness of ex-slaves

fer·ox -ōcis *adj* brave, intrepid, warlike; defiant; overbearing, haughty, insolent

ferrāment·um -ī *n* tool, implement

ferrārĭ·us -a -um *adj* iron; **faber ferrarius** blacksmith; *m* blacksmith; *f pl* iron mines, iron works

ferrātĭl·is -e *adj* fit to be chained

ferrāt·us -a -um *adj* iron-plated; iron-tipped; in chains; in armor; **calx ferrata** spur; *m pl* soldiers in armor

ferrĕ·us -a -um *adj* iron, made of iron; hardhearted, cruel; firm, unyielding

ferricrepīn·us -a -um *adj* (coll) clanking chains

ferritĕr·ĭum -iī or **-ī** *n* (coll) brig, jug

ferritĕr·us -ī *m* (coll) glutton for punishment

ferritrīb·ax -ācis *adj* (coll) chainsore (*sore from dragging chains*)

ferrūgĭnĕ·us or **ferrūgĭn·us -a -um** *adj* rust-colored, dark, dusky

ferrūg·ō -ĭnis *f* rust; verdigris; dark red; dark color; gloom

ferr·um -ī *n* iron; tool, implement; iron object: sword, dart, arrowhead, ax, plowshare, crowbar, spade, scissors, curling iron; **ferro atque igni** with fire and sword; **ferro decernere** to decide by force of arms

fertĭl·is -e *adj* fertile, fruitful, productive; fertilizing; (with *genit*) productive of

fertĭlĭt·ās -ātis *f* fertility, fruitfulness

ferŭl·a -ae *f* reed, stalk; rod, whip

fer·us -a -um *adj* wild; uncultivated, untamed; savage, uncivilized; rude, cruel, fierce; wild, desert (*place*); *m* wild beast, wild horse, lion, stag; *f* wild beast

fervĕ·facĭō -facĕre -fēcī -factum *vt* to heat, boil

ferv·ens -entis *adj* seething, burning, hot; (fig) hot, heated, violent, impetuous

ferventer *adv* (fig) heatedly, impetuously

ferv·ĕō -ēre or **ferv·ō -ĕre -ī** *vi* to boil, seethe, steam; to foam; to swarm; to be busy, bustle about; (fig) to burn, glow, rage, rave

fervesc·ō -ĕre *vi* to become boiling hot, begin to boil, grow hot

fervĭd·us -a -um *adj* boiling, seething, hot; fermenting (*grapes*); hot, highly spiced; (fig) hot, fiery, violent, impetuous, hot-blooded

fervō see **ferveo**

ferv·or -ōris *m* heat, boiling heat; boiling; fermenting; fever; raging (*of the sea*); (fig) heat, vehemence, ardor, passion

Fescennĭ·a -ae *f* town in Etruria

Fescennīn·us -a -um *adj* Fescennine, of Fescennia; *m pl* Fescennine verses (*rude form of dramatic dialogue*)

fess·us -a -um *adj* tired, exhausted, worn out

festīnanter *adv* quickly

festīnātĭ·ō -ōnis *f* hurrying, haste, hurry

festīnātō *adv* hurriedly

festīn·ō -āre *vt & vi* to rush, hurry, accelerate; **jussa festīnare** to carry out orders promptly

festīn·us -a -um *adj* hasty, quick, speedy

festīvē *adv* gaily; humorously

festīvĭt·ās -ātis *f* gaiety, fun; humor

festīv·us -a -um *adj* holiday, festal; gay, merry; agreeable, pleasing, pretty; humorous

festūc·a -ae *f* stalk; rod with which slaves were tapped when freed

fest·us -a -um *adj* joyous, festive, in holiday mood; *n* holiday; feast; **festum agere** to observe a holiday

fētĭāl·is -is *m* member of a college of priests who performed the ritual in connection with declaring war and making peace

fētĭāl·is -e *adj* negotiating, diplomatic; fetial, of the fetial priests

fetĭd·us -a -um *adj* fetid, stinking

fētūr·a -ae *f* breeding, bearing; offspring, young

fēt·us -a -um *adj* pregnant, breeding; fruitful, teeming, productive

fēt·us -ūs *m* breeding; (of plants) producing; bearing; offspring, young, brood; fruit, produce; (fig) growth, production

fī *interj* (expressing disgust at a bad smell) phew!

fīb·er -rī *m* beaver

fibr·a -ae *f* fiber, filament; *f pl* entrails

fībŭl·a -ae *f* clasp, pin, brooch, buckle; brace, clamp

fīcedŭl·a or **fīcēdŭl·a -ae** *f* beccafico (*small bird*)

fictē *adv* falsely, fictitiously

fictĭl·is -e *adj* clay, earthen; *n* jar; clay statue; *n pl* earthenware

fictĭ·ō -ōnis *f* forming, formation; disguising; supposition; fiction

fict·or -ōris *m* sculptor, molder, shaper

fictr·ix -īcis *f* maker, creator (*female*)

fict·um -ī *n* falsehood, fiction, pretense

fictūr·a -ae *f* shaping, fashioning

fict·us -a -um *pp* of **fingo**; *adj* false, fictitious; **vox ficta** falsehood

fīcŭl·us -ī *m* little fig

fīculn·us or **fīculnĕ·us -a -um** *adj* of a fig tree

fīc·us -ī or **-ūs** *f* fig; fig tree

fīdēcommiss·um or **fīdeīcommiss·um -ī** *n* trust fund

fīdēlĭ·a -ae *f* earthen pot, pail,

bucket; **duo parietes de eadem fidelia dealbare** to whitewash two walls with one pail, to kill two birds with one stone

fidēl·is -e *adj* faithful, loyal; trusty, trustworthy, true, sure, safe (*ship, port, advice, etc.*); (with *dat* or **in** + *acc*) faithful to; *m* confidant

fidelit·ās -ātis *f* faithfulness, loyalty, fidelity

fidēliter *adv* faithfully, loyally; securely, certainly

Fidēn·ae -ārum *f pl* ancient town in Latium

fīd·ens -entis *adj* confident; resolute; bold

fīdenter *adv* confidently; resolutely; boldly

fīdentī·a -ae *f* self-confidence, boldness

fīd·ēs -ēī *f* trust, faith, reliance, confidence; credence, belief; trustworthiness, conscientiousness, honesty; promise, assurance, word, word of honor; protection, guarantee; promise of protection, safe conduct; (com) credit; confirmation, proof, fulfilment; **de fide mala** in bad faith, dishonestly; **Di vostram fidem!** for heaven's sake!; **ex fide bona** in good faith, honestly; **fidem dare** to give one's word, offer a guarantee; **fidem facere** to inspire confidence; **fidem fallere** to break one's word; **fidem habere** (with *dat*) to have confidence in; to convince; **fidem servare** to keep one's word; **pro fidem deum!** for heaven's sake!; **res fidesque** capital and credit

fīd·ēs -is *f* string (*of a musical instrument*); *f pl* stringed instrument: lyre, lute, zither

fidic·en -inis *m* lutist, lyre player; lyric poet

fidicīn·us -a -um *adj* stringed-instrument; *f* lutist, lyre player (*female*)

fidicul·a -ae *f* or **fidicul·ae -ārum** *f pl* small lute

fīdissimē *adv* most faithfully

Fīd·ius -iī or **-ī** *m* epithet of Jupiter; **medius fidius!** honest to goodness!

fīdō fīdĕre fīsus sum *vi* (with *dat* or *abl*) to trust, put confidence in

fīdūcī·a -ae *f* trust, confidence, reliance; self-confidence; trustworthiness; (law) deposit, pledge, security, mortgage

fīdūcīārī·us -a -um *adj* held in trust

fīd·us -a -um *adj* trusty, dependable; certain, sure, safe

figlīn·us or **figulīn·us -a -um** *adj* potter's

fīgō fīgĕre fixī fixum *vt* to fix, fasten, affix, attach, nail; to drive in; to pierce; to erect, set up; to build; to post up, hang up

figulār·is -e *adj* potter's

figŭl·us -ī *m* potter; bricklayer

figūr·a -ae *f* figure, shape, form;

phantom, ghost; nature, kind; figure of speech

figūrāt·us -a -um *adj* figurative

figūr·ō -āre *vt* to shape, form, mold, fashion; to train, educate

fīlātim *adv* thread by thread

fīli·a -ae *f* daughter

filicāt·us -a -um *adj* engraved with fern patterns

fīliŏl·a -ae *f* little daughter

fīliŏl·us -ī *m* little son

fīl·ius -iī or **-ī** *m* son; **terrae filius** a nobody

fīl·ix -īcis *f* fern

fīl·um -ī *n* thread; fillet; string, cord; wick; figure, shape (*of a woman*); texture, quality, style (*of speech*)

fimbrī·ae -ārum *f pl* fringe, border, end

fim·us -ī *m* dung, manure; mire

findō findĕre fidī fissum *vt* to split, split in half

fingō fingĕre finxī fictum *vt* to shape, form; to mold, model (*in clay, stone, etc.*); to arrange, dress, trim; to imagine, suppose, think, conceive; to contrive, invent, pretend, feign; to compose (*poetry*); to disguise (*looks*); to trump up (*charges*); (with double *acc*) to represent as, depict as; **ars fingendi** sculpture; **linguā fingere** to lick; **se fingere** (with **ad** + *acc*) to adapt oneself to; to be subservient to

finient·ēs -ium *m pl* horizon

fīn·iō -īre -īvī or **-iī -ītum** *vt* to limit; (fig) to set bounds to, limit, restrain; to mark out, fix, determine; to put an end to, finish complete; **finiri** to come to an end, end; *vi* to come to an end; to die

fīn·is -is *m* or *f* boundary, border, limit; end; purpose, aim; extreme limit, summit, highest degree; starting point; goal; death; **fine** (with *genit*) up to, as far as; **finem facere** (with *genit* or *dat*) to put an end to; **quem ad finem** how long, to what extent; *m pl* boundaries, country, territory, land

finītē *adv* to a limited degree

fīnitim·us or **fīnitŭm·us -a -um** *adj* neighboring, bordering; (with *dat*) a bordering upon; **b** (fig) bordering upon, akin to; *m pl* neighbors

fīnīt·or -ōris *m* surveyor

fīnīt·us -a -um *adj* limited; (rhet) rhythmical

fīō fiĕrī factus sum *vi* to come into being, arise; to be made, become, get; to happen; **fieri non potest quin** it is inevitable that; **fieri potest ut** it is possible that; **ita fīt ut** or **quo fīt ut** thus it happens that

firmām·en -inis *n* prop, support

firmāment·um -ī *n* prop, support; support, mainstay; main point

firmāt·or -ōris *m* establisher, promoter

firmē adv firmly, steadily

firmĭt·ās -ātis f firmness, strength; steadfastness, stamina, endurance

firmĭter adv firmly, steadily

firmĭtūd·ō -ĭnis f firmness, strength, durability; (fig) stability, constancy

firm·ō -āre vt to strengthen, fortify, support; to encourage, strengthen, fortify, assure, reinforce; to establish, prove, confirm; to declare, aver

firm·us -a -um adj firm, strong, hardy, stable; (fig) firm, steadfast, trusty, true, faithful, lasting; **firmus ad bellum** toughened for combat

fiscāl·is -e adj fiscal

fiscell·a -ae f small basket

fiscĭn·a -ae f small basket

fisc·us -ī m basket; money box; state treasury; imperial treasury, emperor's privy purse, imperial revenues

fissĭl·is -e adj easy to split; split

fissĭ·ō -ōnis f dividing, splitting

fiss·us -a -um pp of **findo**; adj cloven; n slit, fissure

fistūc·a -ae f mallet

fistūl·a -ae f pipe, tube; water pipe; hollow stalk or reed; flute; fistula, ulcer

fīsus pp of **fido**

fix·us -a -um pp of **figo**; adj fixed, immovable; permanent

flābellĭfĕr·a -ae f female slave who waved a fan

flābell·um -ī n fan

flābĭl·is -e adj of air

flābr·a -ōrum n pl gusts of wind; breezes, winds

flacc·ĕō -ēre vi to be flabby; to lose heart; (of a speech) to get dull

flacc·escō -escēre -ŭī vi to become flabby; to wither, droop

flaccĭd·us -a -um adj flabby; languid, feeble

flacc·us -a -um adj flabby

flagell·ō -āre vt to whip

flagell·um -ī n whip; scourge; riding crop; young shoot, sucker; arm (of a polypus); sting (e.g., of conscience)

flāgĭtātĭ·ō -ōnis f demand

flāgĭtāt·or -ōris m persistent demander

flāgĭtĭōsē adv shamefully, disgracefully

flāgĭtĭōs·us -a -um adj shameful, disgraceful, profligate

flāgĭt·ĭum -ĭī or **-ī** n shame, disgrace, scandalous conduct, scandal; rascal, good-for-nothing

flāgĭt·ō -āre vt to demand; (with double acc or with acc of thing or **ab + abl** of person) to demand (something) from (someone)

flagr·ans -antis adj blazing, flaming, hot; shining, glowing, glittering; ardent, hot, vehement, eager

flagranter adv vehemently, ardently

flagrantĭ·a -ae f blazing, glow; **flagiti flagrantia** utter disgrace

flagrĭtrīb·a -ae m (coll) (said of a slave) victim of constant whipping

flagr·ō -āre vi to blaze, be on fire; (with abl) **a** to glow with, flare up in; **b** to be the victim of (e.g., envy)

flagr·um -ī n whip

flām·en -ĭnis m flamen (priest of a specific deity); **flamen Dialis** priest of Jupiter

flām·en -ĭnis n gust, gale; breeze

flāminĭc·a -ae f wife of a flamen

Flāminīn·us -ī m T. Quintus Flamininus (consul of 198 B.C., and conqueror of Philip of Macedon at Cynoscephalae, in Thessaly, in 197 B.C.)

flāmin·ĭum -ĭī or **-ī** n office of flamen, priesthood

Flāminĭ·us -a -um adj Flaminian; **via Flaminia** road leading from Rome to Ariminum; m Gaius Flaminius (conqueror of Insubrian Gauls in 223 B.C., builder of the Circus Flaminius and the Flaminian highway in 220 B.C., and casualty in the battle at Lake Trasimenus in 217 B.C.)

flamm·a -ae f flame, fire, blaze; star; torch; flame of passion, fire of love, glow, passion; sweetheart; danger, destruction; **flamma fumo est proxima** where there's smoke there's fire; **flammam concipere** to catch fire

flammār·ĭus -ĭī or **-ī** m maker of bridal veils

flammĕŏl·um -ī n bridal veil

flammesc·ō -ĕre vi to become inflamed, become fiery

flammĕ·us -a -um adj flaming, fiery; flashing (eyes); flame-covered; n bridal veil

flammĭf·er -ĕra -ĕrum adj fiery

flamm·ō -āre vt to set on fire; (fig) to inflame, incense; vi to burn, glow, blaze

flammŭl·a -ae f little flame

flāt·us -ūs m blowing, breathing, breath; breeze, wind; snorting; arrogance

flāv·ens -entis adj yellow, golden

flāvesc·ō -ĕre vi to become yellow, become golden-yellow

Flāvĭ·us -a -um adj Flavian; **gens Flavia** Flavian clan (to which the emperors Vespasian, Titus, and Domitian belonged)

flāv·us -a -um adj yellow, blond, reddish-yellow, golden

flēbĭl·is -e adj pitiful, pathetic, deplorable; crying, tearful

flēbĭlĭter adv tearfully, mournfully

flectō flectĕre flexī flexum vt to bend, curve; to turn, wheel about, turn around; to wind, twist, curl; to direct, avert, turn away (eyes, mind, etc.); to double, sail around (a cape); to modulate (voice); to change (the mind); to persuade, move, appease; **viam** or **iter flectere** (with **ad + acc**) to make one's way toward, head toward; vi to turn, go, march

fēmĭn·a -um *n* *pl* swollen, bloody ankles

fl·ĕō -ēre -ēvī -ētum *vt* to cry for, mourn for; *vi* to cry

flēt·us -ūs *m* crying; *m* *pl* tears

flexanĭm·us -a -um *adj* moving, touching

flexibĭl·is -e *adj* flexible; shifty, fickle

flexĭl·is -e *adj* flexible, pliant

flexĭlŏqu·us -a -um *adj* ambiguous

flexĭ·ō -ōnis *f* bending, turning; modulation (*of the voice*)

flexĭp·ēs -ĕdis *adj* creeping (*ivy*)

flexuŏs·us -a -um *adj* winding (*road*)

flexūr·a -ae *f* bending, winding

flexus *pp* of **flecto**

flex·us -ūs *m* bending, turning, winding; shift, change, transition, crisis

flict·us -ūs *m* clashing, banging together

fl·ō -āre *vt* to blow, breathe; to coin (*money*); *vi* to blow

flocc·us -ī *m* lock (*of hair, wool*); down; **flocci facere** to think little of, disregard, not give a hoot about

Flōr·a -ae *f* goddess of flowers, whose festival was celebrated on April 28th

flōr·ens -entis *adj* blooming; prosperous; flourishing, in the prime; (with *abl*) in the prime of, at the height of

flōr·ĕō -ēre -ŭī *vi* to bloom, blossom; to be in one's prime; (*of wine*) to foam, ferment; to be prosperous, be eminent; (with *abl*) **a** to abound in; **b** to swarm with, be filled with

flōr·escō -escĕre -ŭī *vi* to begin to bloom, begin to blossom

flōrĕ·us -a -um *adj* flowery; made of flowers

flōrĭd·us -a -um *adj* flowery; fresh, pretty; florid (*style*)

flōrĭf·er -ĕra -ĕrum *adj* flowery

flōrĭlĕg·us -a -um *adj* (of bees) going from flower to flower

flōr·us -a -um *adj* luxuriant

fl·ōs -ōris *m* flower; bud, blossom; best (*of anything*); prime (*of life*); youthful beauty, innocence; crown, glory; nectar; literary ornament

floscŭl·us -ī *m* little flower, floweret; flower, pride, glory

fluctĭfrăg·us -a -um *adj* wave-breaking (*shore*), surging

fluctŭātĭ·ō -ōnis *f* wavering, vacillating

fluctŭ·ō -āre or **fluctŭ·or -ārī -ātus sum** *vi* to fluctuate, undulate, wave; to be restless; to waver, vacillate, fluctuate

fluctŭŏs·us -a -um *adj* running (*sea*)

fluct·us -ūs *m* wave, billow; flowing, undulating; turbulence, commotion; disorder, unrest; **fluctus in simpulo** tempest in a tea cup

flu·ens -entis *adj* loose, flowing; (morally) loose; effeminate; fluent

fluent·a -ōrum *n* *pl* flow, stream, river

fluenter *adv* like a wave

fluĭd·us or **flūvĭd·us -a -um** *adj* flowing, fluid; soft; relaxing

fluĭt·ō or **flūt·ō -āre** *vi* to float, swim; to sail; to toss about; to hang loose, flap; to be uncertain, waver; to stagger

flūm·en -ĭnis *n* flowing, stream, river, flood; fluency; (fig) flood (*e.g.*, *of tears, words, etc.*); **flumine adverso** upstream; **secundo flumine** downstream

flūmĭnĕ·us -a -um *adj* river

flu·ō -ĕre -xī -xum *vi* to flow; to run down, drip; to overflow; (of branches) to spread; to sink, drop, droop; to pass away, vanish, perish; to be fluent; to be monotonous; to spring, arise, proceed

flūtō see **fluito**

fluvĭāl·is -e *adj* river, of a river

fluvĭātĭl·is -e *adj* river, of a river

flūvĭdus see **fluidus**

fluv·ĭus -ĭī or **-ī** *m* river; running water, stream

flux·us -a -um *adj* flowing, loose; careless; loose, dissolute; frail, weak; transient, perishable

fōcāl·e -is *n* scarf

fōcĭll·ō -āre *vt* to warm, revive

focŭl·um -ī *n* stove

focŭl·us -ī *m* brazier; (fig) fire

foc·us -ī *m* hearth, fireplace; brazier; funeral pile; altar; home, family

fodĭc·ō -āre *vt* to poke, nudge

fodĭō fodĕre fōdī fossum *vt* to dig, dig out; (fig) to prod, goad, prick

foecund- = fecund-

foedē *adv* foully, cruelly, shamefully

foederāt·us -a -um *adj* confederated, allied

foedĭfrăg·us -a -um *adj* treacherous, perfidious

foedĭt·ās -ātis *f* foulness, hideousness

foed·ō -āre *vt* to make hideous, disfigure; to pollute, defile, disgrace

foed·us -a -um *adj* foul, filthy, horrible, ugly, disgusting, repulsive; disgraceful, vile

foed·us -ĕris *n* treaty, charter, league; compact, agreement; law; **aequo foedere** on equal terms, mutually; **foedere certo** by fixed law; **foedere pacto** by fixed agreement

foen- = faen-

foet·ĕō -ēre *vi* to stink

foetĭd·us -a -um *adj* stinking

foet·or -ōris *m* stink, stench

foetu- = fētu-

folĭāt·us -a -um *adj* leafy; *n* nard oil

fol·ĭum -ĭī or **-ī** *n* leaf; **folium recĭtare Sibyllae** to tell the gospel truth

follĭcŭl·us -ī *m* small bag, sack; shell, skin; eggshell

foll·is -is *m* bag; punching bag; bellows; money bag; puffed-out cheeks

fōment·um -ī n bandage; mitigation, alleviation

fōm·es -ĭtis m tinder

fon·s -tis m spring, fountain; spring water, water; stream; lake; source, origin, fountainhead

fontān·us -a -um adj spring

fonticŭl·us -ī m little spring, little fountain

for fārī fātus sum vt & vi to say, speak, utter

forābĭl·is -e adj vulnerable

forām·en -ĭnis n hole, opening

forās adv out, outside; **foras dare** to publish (writings)

forc·eps -ĭpis m or f forceps, tongs

ford·a -ae f pregnant cow

fore = futūr·us -a -um esse to be about to be

forem = essem

forens·is -e adj of the forum, in the forum; public, forensic

forf·ex -ĭcis f scissors

for·is -is f door, gate; f pl double doors; opening, entrance; (fig) door

forīs adv outside, out of doors; abroad, in foreign countries; from outside, from abroad

form·a -ae f form, shape, figure; beauty; shape, image; mold, stamp; shoemaker's last; vision, apparition, phantom; species, form, nature, sort, kind; outline, design, sketch, plan

formāment·um -ī n shape

formāt·or -ōris m fashioner

formātūr·a -ae f fashioning, shaping

Formĭ·ae -ārum f pl town in S. Latium

formīc·a -ae f ant

formīcīn·us -a -um adj ant-like

formīdābĭl·is -e adj terrifying

formīd·ō -āre vt to fear, dread; vi to be frightened

formīd·ō -ĭnis f fear, dread, awe, terror; scarecrow; threats

formīdolōsē adv dreadfully, terribly

formīdolōs·us -a -um adj dreadful, terrifying, terrible; afraid, terrified

form·ō -āre vt to form, shape, mold, build; to make, produce, invent; to imagine; to regulate, direct

formōsē adv beautifully, gracefully

formōsit·ās -ātis f beauty

formōs·us -a -um adj shapely, beautiful, handsome

formŭl·a -ae f nice shape, beauty; form, formula, draft; contract, agreement; rule, regulation; (law) regular method, formula, rule; (phil) principle

fornācāl·is -e adj of an oven

fornācŭl·a -ae f small oven

forn·ax -ācis f oven, furnace, kiln; forge

fornicāt·us -a -um adj arched

forn·ix -ĭcis m arch, vault; arcade; brothel

fornus see furnus

for·ō -āre vt to bore, pierce

fors adv perhaps, chances are, there is a chance, possibly

for·s -tis f chance, luck, fortune, accident; **forte** by chance, accidentally, by accident; as it happens, as it happened; perhaps

forsan, forsit, or **forsĭtan** adv perhaps

fortasse or **fortassis** adv perhaps

forte see fors

fortĭcŭl·us -a -um adj quite bold, rather brave

fort·is -e adj strong, mighty, powerful; brave, courageous, valiant, resolute, steadfast, firm

fortĭter adv strongly, vigorously, firmly, bravely, boldly

fortitūd·ō -ĭnis f strength; bravery, courage, resolution

fortuītō adv by chance, accidentally, casually

fortuīt·us -a -um adj accidental, fortuitous, casual

fortūn·a -ae f chance, luck, fate, fortune; good luck, prosperity; bad luck, misfortune; lot, circumstances, state, rank, position; property, goods, fortune

fortūnātē adv fortunately, prosperously

fortūnāt·us -a -um adj fortunate, lucky, prosperous, happy; rich, well-off

fortūn·ō -āre vt to make happy, make prosperous, bless

forŭl·ī -ōrum m pl bookcase

for·um -ī n shopping center, market, marketplace; market town; trade, commerce; forum, civic center; court; public life, public affairs; jurisdiction; **cedere foro** to go bankrupt; **extra suum forum** beyond his jurisdiction; **forum agere** to hold court; **forum attingere** to enter public life; **in foro versari** to be engaged in commerce

For·um Appĭī (genit: **For·ī Appĭī**) n town in Latium on the Via Appia

For·um Aurēlĭī (genit: **For·ī Aurēlĭī**) n town N. of Rome on the Via Aurelia

For·um Jūlĭī (genit: **For·ī Jūlĭī**) n town in S. Gaul, colony of the eighth legion

for·us -ī m gangway; tier of seats; tier of a beehive

foss·a -ae f ditch, trench; **fossam deprimere** to dig a deep trench

fossĭl·ō -ōnis f digging

foss·or -ōris m digger; lout, clown

fossŭr·a -ae f digging

fossus pp of **fodio**

fōtus pp of **foveo**

fov·ē·a -ae f small pit; (fig) pitfall

fovĕō fovēre fōvī fōtum vt to warm, keep warm; to fondle, caress; to love, cherish; to support, encourage; to pamper

fract·us -a -um pp of **frango**; adj interrupted, irregular; weak, feeble

frāg·a -ōrum n pl strawberries

fragĭl·is -e adj fragile, brittle;

crackling; weak, frail; unstable, fickle

fragilit·ās -ātis *f* weakness, frailty

fragilō see **fragro**

fragm·en -inis *n* fragment; *n pl* debris, ruins, wreckage

fragment·um -ī *n* fragment, remnant

frag·or -ōris *m* crash, noise, uproar, din; applause; clap of thunder

fragōs·us -a -um *adj* broken, uneven, rough; crashing, roaring

fragr·ō or **fragl·ō -āre** *vi* to smell sweet, be fragrant; to reek

framē·a -ae *f* German spear

frangō frangĕre frēgī fractum *vt* to break in pieces, smash to pieces, shatter; to grind, crush; (fig) to break down, overcome, crush, dishearten, humble, weaken, soften, move, touch; **diem mero frangere** to break up the day with wine

frāt·er -ris *m* brother; cousin; friend, comrade

frātercŭl·us -ī *m* little brother

frāternē *adv* like a brother

frāternit·ās -ātis *f* brotherhood

frātern·us -a -um *adj* brotherly; brother's; fraternal

frātricīd·a -ae *m* murderer of a brother, a fratricide

fraudātī·ō -ōnis *f* swindling

fraudāt·or -ōris *m* swindler

fraud·ō -āre *vt* to swindle, cheat, defraud; to embezzle; (with *abl*) to defraud (*someone*) of, cheat (*someone*) of

fraudulentī·a -ae *f* tendency to swindle, deceitfulness

fraudulent·us -a -um *adj* fraudulent; deceitful, treacherous

frau·s -dis *f* fraud, deception, trickery; error, delusion; crime, offense; harm, damage; deceiver, fraud, cheat; **sine fraude** without harm

fraxinĕ·us or **fraxin·us -a -um** *adj* of ash wood, ashen

fraxin·us -ī *f* ash tree; spear (*made of ash wood*)

Fregell·ae -ārum *f pl* ancient Volscan city on the Liris River, in Latium, made a Roman colony in 328 B.C.

fremebund·us -a -um *adj* roaring

fremit·us -ūs *m* roaring, growling, snorting; din, noise

frem·ō -ĕre -ŭī -itum *vt* to grumble at, complain loudly of; to demand angrily; *vi* to roar, growl, snort, howl, grumble, murmur; to resound

frem·or -ōris *m* roaring, grumbling, murmuring

frend·ō -ĕre -ŭī *vi* to gnash the teeth; **dentibus frendere** to gnash the teeth

frēnī see **frenum**

frēn·ō -āre *vt* to bridle, curb; (fig) to curb, control

frēn·um -ī *n* or **frēn·a -ōrum** *n pl* or **frēn·ī -ōrum** *m pl* bridle, bit; (fig) curb, control, restraint

frequ·ens -entis *adj* crowded, in crowds, numerous, filled; frequent, repeated, usual, common; (may be rendered adverbially) often, repeatedly

frequentātī·ō -ōnis *f* piling up

frequenter *adv* frequently, often; in great numbers

frequentī·a -ae *f* crowd, throng; crowded assembly, large attendance

frequent·ō -āre *vt* to visit often, frequent, resort to; to do often, repeat; to crowd, people, stock; to attend (*e.g., games*) in large numbers

fretens·is -e *adj* **fretensæ mare** Strait of Messina

fret·um -ī *n* strait, channel; sea, waters; (fig) seething flood

frēt·us -a -um *adj* confident; (with *dat* or *abl*) supported by, relying on, depending on

fret·us -ūs *m* strait

fric·ō -āre -ŭī -tum *vt* to rub, rub down

frictus *pp* of **frigo**

frigefact·ō -āre *vt* to make cold or cool

frig·ĕō -ēre *vi* to be cold, be chilly; to freeze; (fig) to be numbed, be lifeless, be dull; (fig) to get a cool reception, be snubbed, get a cold shoulder; (fig) to fall flat

frigesc·ō -ĕre *vi* to become cold, become chilled; to become lifeless

frigidārī·us -a -um *adj* cooling

frigidē *adv* feebly

frigidŭl·us -a -um *adj* rather cold; rather faint

frigid·us -a -um *adj* cold, cool; numbed, dull, lifeless, indifferent, unimpassioned, feeble; flat, insipid, trivial; *f* cold water

frigō frigĕre frixī frictum *vt* to fry, roast

frīg·us -ōris *n* cold, coldness, chill, coolness; frost; cold of winter, winter; coldness of death, death; chill, fever; cold shudder, chill; cold region; cold reception; coolness, indifference; slowness, inactivity; *n pl* cold spell, cold season

frigutt·iō -īre *vi* to stutter

fri·ō -āre *vt* to crumble

fritill·us -ī *m* dice box

frivŏl·us -a -um *adj* frivolous, trifling, worthless, sorry, pitiful; *n pl* trifles

frondāt·or -ōris *m* pruner

frond·ĕō -ēre *vi* to have leaves; to become green

frondesc·ō -ĕre *vi* to get leaves

frond·us -a -um *adj* leafy, covered with leaves

frondif·er -ĕra -ĕrum *adj* leafy

frondōs·us -a -um *adj* full of leaves, leafy

fron·s -dis *f* foliage; leafy bough, green bough; chaplet, garland

fron·s -tis *f* forehead, brow; front end, front; countenance, face, look; face, façade; van, vanguard; exterior, appearance; outer end of a scroll; sense of shame; **a fronte** in front; **frontem contrahere** to knit the brow, frown; **frontem fe-rire** to hit oneself on the head (*in self-annoyance*); **frontem remit-tere** to smooth the brow, to cheer up; **in fronte** (in measuring land) in breadth, frontage; **salvā fronte** without shame; **tenuis frons** low forehead

frontāl·ia -ium *n pl* frontlet (*orna-ment for forehead of a horse*)

front·ō -ōnis *m* one with a large forehead

frūctuāri·us -a -um *adj* produc-tive; subject to land tax

frūctuōs·us -a -um *adj* fruitful, productive

frūctus *pp of* fruor

frūct·us -ūs *m* produce, fruit; pro-ceeds, profit, income, return, reve-nue; enjoyment, satisfaction; bene-fit, reward, results, consequence

frūgāl·is -e *adj* frugal; honest; worthy

frūgālit·ās -ātis *f* frugality, econ-omy; temperance; honesty; worth

frūgāliter *adv* frugally, economical-ly; temperately

frūgēs see frux

frūgī (indecl) *adj* frugal; temperate; honest, worthy; useful, proper

frūgif·er -ĕra -ĕrum *adj* fruitful, productive, fertile; profitable

frūgifer·ens -entis *adj* fruitful

frūgilĕg·us -a -um *adj* (of ants) food-gathering

frūgipăr·us -a -um *adj* fruitful

frūitus *pp of* fruor

frūmentāri·us -a -um *adj* of grain, grain; grain-producing; of provi-sions; **res frumentaria** (mil) sup-plies, quartermaster corps; *m* grain dealer

frūmentātĭ·ō -ōnis *f* (mil) foraging

frūmentāt·or -ōris *m* grain mer-chant; (mil) forager

frūment·or -ārī -ātus sum *vi* (mil) to forage

frūment·um -ī *n* grain; wheat; *n pl* grain fields, crops

frūn·iscor -iscī -ītus sum *vt* to enjoy

fruor fruī fructus sum or **frui-tus sum** *vt* to enjoy; *vi* (with *abl*) **a** to enjoy, delight in; **b** to enjoy the company of; **c** (law) to have the use and enjoyment of

frūstillātim *adv* in bits

frūstrā *adv* in vain, uselessly, for nothing; without reason, ground-lessly; **frustra discedere** to go away disappointed; **frustra esse** to be mistaken; **frustra habere** to have (*someone*) confused or baffled

frūstrām·en -inis *n* deception

frūstrātĭ·ō -ōnis *f* deception; frus-tration

frūstrāt·us -ūs *m* deception; **frus-tratui habere** (coll) to take for a sucker

frūstr·or -ārī -ātus sum or **frus-tr·ō -āre** *vt* to deceive, trick; to

disappoint; to frustrate

frūstulent·us -a -um *adj* crumby, full of crumbs

frūst·um -ī *n* crumb, bit, scrap; **frustum pueri** (coll) whipper-snapper

frut·ex -icis *m* shrub, bush; (coll) blockhead

fruticēt·um -ī *n* thicket, shrubbery

frutic·ō -āre or **frutic·or -ārī -ātus sum** *vi* to sprout; (of the hair) to become bushy; (fig) (of the hair) to become bushy

fruticōs·us -a -um *adj* bushy, over-grown with bushes

frux frūgis *f* or **frūg·ēs -um** *f pl* fruit, produce, grain, vegetables; barley meal (*for sacrifice*); fruits, benefit, result; **se ad frugem bo-nam recipere** to turn over a new leaf; **expers frugis** worthless

fūcāt·us -a -um *adj* dyed, colored, painted; artificial, spurious

fūc·ō -āre *vt* to dye red, redden, paint red; to disguise, falsify

fūcōs·us -a -um *adj* painted, col-ored; spurious, phoney

fūc·us -ī *m* red paint; rouge; drone; bee glue; disguise, pretense, deceit

fue or **fu** *interj* phui!

fug·a -ae *f* flight, escape; avoidance; exile; speed, swift passage; disap-pearance; (with *genit*) avoidance of, escape from; **fugae sese man-dare, fugam capere, fugam ca-pessere, fugam facere, se in fugam conferre, se in fugam conjicere,** or **sese in fugam dare** to flee, take flight; **in fugam conferre, in fugam conjicere, in fugam dare,** or **in fugam im-pellere** to put to flight

fugācius *adv* more cautiously, with one eye on flight

fug·ax -ācis *adj* apt to flee, fleeing; shy, timid; swift; passing, transi-tory; (with *genit*) shy of, shunning, avoiding, steering clear of, averse to

fugĭ·ens -entis *adj* fleeing, retreat-ing; (with *genit*) avoiding, averse to

fugĭō fugĕre fūgī fugitum *vt* to escape, escape from, run away from, shun, avoid; to leave (*esp. one's country*); to be averse to, dis-like; to escape the notice of, escape, be unknown to; **fuge** (with *inf*) do not; **fugit me scribere** I forgot to write; *vi* to flee, escape, run away; to go into exile; to speed, hasten; to vanish, disappear; to pass away, perish

fugĭt·ans -antis *adj* fleeing; (with *genit*) averse to

fugitīv·us -a -um *adj & m* runaway, fugitive

fugĭt·ō -āre *vt* to run away from

fugĭt·or -ōris *m* deserter

fug·ō -āre *vt* to put to flight, drive away, chase away; to exile, banish; to avert

fulcīm·en -inis *n* support, prop, pillar

fulciō fulcīre fulsī fultum *vt* to prop up, support; to secure, sustain

fulcr·um -ī *n* bed post; couch, bed

fulgĕō fulgēre fulsī or **fulg·ō -ĕre** *vi* to gleam, flash, blaze, shine, glare; to shine, be conspicuous, be illustrious

fulgid·us -a -um *adj* flashing, shining

fulgō see **fulgeo**

fulg·or -ōris *m* flash of lightning, lightning; brightness; thing struck by lightning

fulgurāl·is -e *adj* of lightning; **libri fulgurales** books on lightning

fulgurāt·or -ōris *m* interpreter of lightning

fulgurīt·us -a -um *adj* struck by lightning

fulgur·ō -āre *vi* to lighten, send lightning; *v impers* it is lightning

fulic·a -ae or **ful·ix -icis** *f* coot (*waterfowl*)

fūlīg·ō -inis *f* soot; black paint

fulix see **fulica**

full·ō -ōnis *m* fuller

fullōnic·a -ae *f* fuller's craft, fulling

fullōni·us -a -um *adj* fuller's

fulm·en -inis *n* thunderbolt, lightning bolt; (*fig*) bolt, bolt out of the blue

fulminĕ·us -a -um *adj* of lightning, lightning; shine, sparkling, flashing

fulmin·ō -āre *vi* to lighten; (*fig*) to flash

fultūr·a -ae *f* support, prop

fultus *pp* of **fulcio**

fulv·us -a -um *adj* yellow, yellowish brown, reddish yellow, tawny; blond

fūmĕ·us -a -um *adj* smoky

fūmid·us -a -um *adj* smoking, smoky

fūmif·er -ĕra -ĕrum *adj* smoking

fūmific·ō -āre *vi* to smoke; to burn incense

fūmific·us -a -um *adj* smoking, steaming

fūm·ō -āre *vi* to smoke, fume, steam, reek

fūmōs·us -a -um *adj* smoked, smoky

fūm·us -ī *m* smoke, steam, fume

fūnāl·e -is *n* rope; torch; chandelier, candelabrum

fūnambul·us -ī *m* tightrope walker

functi·ō -ōnis *f* performance

functus *pp* of **fungor**

fund·a -ae *f* sling; sling stone; dragnet

fundām·en -inis *n* foundation

fundāment·um -ī *n* foundation; (*fig*) basis, ground, beginning; **a fundamentis** utterly, completely; **fundamenta agere, jacere,** or **locare** to lay the foundations

fundāt·or -ōris *m* founder

fundāt·us -a -um *adj* well-founded, established

fundit·ō -āre *vt* to sling, shoot with a sling; (*fig*) to sling (*e.g., words*) around

fundit·or -ōris *m* slinger

funditus *adv* from the bottom, utterly, entirely

fund·ō -āre *vt* to found, build, establish; to secure to the ground, make fast

fundō fundĕre fūdī fūsum *vt* to pour, pour out; to melt (*metals*); to cast (*in metal*); to pour in streams, shower, hurl; (*mil*) to pour in (*troops*); (*mil*) to rout; to pour out, empty; to spread, extend, diffuse; to bring forth, bear, yield in abundance; to throw to the ground, bring down; to give up, lose, waste; to utter, pour out (*words*)

fund·us -ī *m* bottom; farm, estate; (*law*) sanctioner, authority

fūnĕbr·is -e *adj* funeral; deadly, murderous

fūnerāt·us -a -um *adj* done in, killed

fūnerĕ·us -a -um *adj* funeral; deadly, fatal

fūner·ō -āre *vt* to bury; **prope funeratus** almost sent to my (*his, etc.*) grave

fūnest·ō -āre *vt* to defile with murder, desecrate

fūnest·us -a -um *adj* deadly, fatal, calamitous; sad, dismal, mournful; **annales funesti** obituary column

fungīn·us -a -um *adj* of a mushroom

fungor fungī functus sum *vi* (with *abl*) **a** to perform, execute, discharge, do; **b** to busy oneself with, be engaged in; **c** to finish, complete; **morte fungi** to suffer death, die

fung·us -ī *m* mushroom, fungus; candle snuff; (*fig*) clown

fūnicul·us -ī *m* cord

fūn·is -is *m* rope, cable, cord; rigging; **funem ducere** (*fig*) to command; **funem reducere** (*fig*) to change one's mind; **funem sequi** (*fig*) to serve, follow

fūn·us -ĕris *n* funeral rites, funeral, burial; corpse; death, murder; havoc; ruin, destruction; **sub funus** on the brink of the grave; *n pl* shades of the dead

fūr fūris *m* or *f* thief; (*fig*) rogue, rascal

fūrācissimē *adv* quite like a thief

fūr·ax -ācis *adj* thievish

furc·a -ae *f* fork; fork-shaped prop (*for supporting vines, bleachers, etc.*); wooden yoke (*put around slave's neck as punishment*)

furcif·er -ĕrī *m* rogue, rascal

furcill·a -ae *f* little fork

furcill·ō -āre *vt* to support, prop up

furcŭl·a -ae *f* fork-shaped prop; *f pl* narrow pass, defile

Furcŭl·ae Caudīn·ae (*genit:* **Furcŭl·ārum Caudīn·ārum**) *f pl* Caudine Forks (*mountain pass near Caudium, in Samnium, where the Roman army was trapped in 321 B.C. by the Samnites and made to pass under the yoke*)

furenter adv furiously

furf·ur -ŭris m chaff; bran

Furi·a -ae f Fury (one of the three goddesses of frenzy and vengeance, who were named Megaera, Tisiphone, and Alecto)

furi·a -ae f frenzy, madness, rage; remorse; madman

furiâl·is -e adj of the Furies; frenzied, frantic, furious; infuriated

furiâliter adv frantically

furibund·us -a -um adj frenzied, frantic, mad; inspired

fûrin·us -a -um adj of thieves

furi·ô -âre vt to drive mad, infuriate

furiôsê adv in a rage, in a frenzy

furiôs·us -a -um adj frenzied, frantic, mad, furious; maddening

furn·us or **forn·us -î** m oven; bakery

fur·ô -ĕre vi to be crazy, be out of one's mind, rage, rave

fûr·or -ârî -âtus sum vt to steal, pilfer; to pillage; to plagiarize; to obtain by fraud; to withdraw in secret; to impersonate

fur·or -ôris m madness, rage, fury, passion, furor, excitement; prophetic frenzy, inspiration; passionate love

furtific·us -a -um adj thievish

furtim adv secretly, by stealth, clandestinely

furtîvê adv secretly, stealthily

furtîv·us -a -um adj stolen; secret, hidden, furtive

furt·um -î n theft, robbery; trick, stratagem; secret action, intrigue; secret love; n pl intrigues; secret love affair; stolen goods

fûruncŭl·us -î m petty thief

furv·us -a -um adj black, dark, gloomy, eerie

fuscĭn·a -ae f trident

fusc·ô -âre vt to blacken

fusc·us -a -um adj dark, swarthy; low, muffled, indistinct (sound)

fûsê adv widely; in great detail

fûsĭl·is -e adj molten, liquid

fûsĭ·ô -ônis f outpouring, effusion

fust·is -is m club, stick, cudgel; beating to death (as a military punishment)

fustitudĭn·us -a -um adj (coll) whip-happy (jail)

fustuâr·ium -iî or **-î** n beating to death (as a military punishment)

fûs·us -a -um pp of **fundo**; adj spread out; broad, wide; diffuse (style)

fûs·us -î m spindle

futtĭl·is or **fûtĭl·is -e** adj brittle; futile, worthless, untrustworthy

fnttilit·âs or **fûtilit·âs -âtis** f futility, worthlessness

fut·ŭ -ŭĕre -ŭî -ûtum vt to have sexual intercourse with (a woman)

futûr·us -a -um fut p of **sum**; adj & n future

G

Gabĭ·î -ôrum m pl ancient town in Latium

Gad·ês -ĭum f pl Cadiz (town in S. Spain)

gaes·um -î n Gallic spear

Gaetûl·î -ôrum m pl a people in N.W. Africa along the Sahara Desert

Gâ·ius -î m Roman praenomen (the names of Gaius and Gaia were formally given to the bridegroom and bride at the wedding ceremony)

Galăt·ae -ârum m pl Galatians (a people of central Asia Minor)

Galati·a -ae f Galatia (country in central Asia Minor)

Galb·a -ae m Servius Sulpicius Galba, the Roman emperor from June, 68 A.D., to January, 69 A.D. (5 B.C.-69 A.D.)

galbanè·us -a -um adj of galbanum

galban·um -î n galbanum (resinous sap of a Syrian plant)

galbĭn·us -a -um adj chartreuse; (fig) effeminate; n pl pale green clothes

galè·a -ae f helmet

galeăt·us -a -um adj helmeted

galêricŭl·um -î n cap

galêrît·us -a -um adj wearing a farmer's cap, countryish

galêr·um -î n or **galêr·us -î** m cap; (fig) wig

gall·a -ae f gallnut

Gall·î -ôrum m pl Gauls (inhabitants of modern France and N. Italy)

Galli·a -ae f Gaul

Gallic·us -a -um adj Gallic

gallîn·a -ae f chicken, hen; (as term of endearment) chick

gallînâcĕ·us or **gallînâcĭ·us -a -um** adj poultry

gallînâr·ius -iî or **-î** m poultry farmer

Gallograec·î -ôrum m pl Galatians (Celts who migrated from Gaul to Asia Minor in the 3rd cent. B.C.)

Gall·us -a -um adj Gallic; m Gaul; priest of Cybele; C. Cornelius Gallus, lyric poet and friend of Virgil (69-27 B.C.)

gall·us -î m rooster, cock

gănĕ·a -ae f or **gănĕ·um -î** n brothel, dive; cheap restaurant

gănĕ·ô -ônis m glutton

gănĕum see **ganea**

Gangarîd·ae -ârum m pl an Indian people on the Ganges

Gang·es -is m Ganges River

gann·ĭō -īre *vi* to snarl, growl

gannīt·us -ūs *m* snarling, growling

Ganymēd·ēs -is *m* Ganymede (*handsome youth carried off to Olympus by the eagle of Jupiter to become the cupbearer of the gods*)

Garamant·es -um *m pl* tribe in N. Africa

Gargaphĭ·ē -ēs *f* valley in Boeotia sacred to Diana

Gargān·us -ī *m* mountain in S.E. Italy

garr·ĭō -īre *vt* to chatter, prattle, talk; nugas garrire to talk nonsense; *vi* to chatter, chat; (of frogs) to croak

garrŭlĭt·ās -ātis *f* talkativeness; chattering

garrŭl·us -a -um *adj* talkative, babbling, garrulous

gar·um -ī *n* fish sauce

gaud·ens -entis *adj* cheerful

gaudĕō gaudēre gāvīsus sum *vt* to rejoice at; gaudium gaudere to feel joy; *vi* to rejoice, be glad, feel pleased; (with *abl*) to delight in; in se gaudere or in sinu gaudere to be secretly glad

gaud·ĭum -iī or -ī *n* joy, gladness, delight; sensual pleasure, enjoyment; joy, cause of joy; mala mentis gaudia gloating

gaul·us -ī *m* bucket

gausăp·e -is or gausăp·um -ī *n* felt; (fig) shaggy beard

gāvīsus *pp* of gaudeo

gaz·a -ae *f* royal treasure; treasure, riches

gelĭdē *adv* coldly, indifferently

gelĭd·us -a -um *adj* cold, icy, frosty; icy cold, stiff, numbed; *f* cold water

gel·ō -āre *vt* & *vi* to freeze

Gelōn·ī -ōrum *m pl* Scythian tribe

gel·u -ūs *n* or gel·um -ī *n* or gel·us -ūs *m* coldness, cold, frost, ice; chill, coldness (*of death, old age, fear*)

gemebund·us -a -um *adj* sighing, groaning

gemellĭpăr·a -ae *f* mother of twins

gemell·us -a -um *adj* & *m* twin

gemĭnātĭ·ō -ōnis *f* doubling; compounding

gemĭn·ō -āre *vt* to double; to join, unite, pair; to repeat, reproduce

gemĭn·us -a -um *adj* twin; double, twofold, two, both; similar; *m pl* twins

gemĭt·us -ūs *m* sigh, groan

gemm·a -ae *f* bud; gem, jewel; jeweled goblet; signet ring, signet; eye of a peacock's tail; literary gem

gemmāt·us -a -um *adj* set with jewels, jeweled

gemmĕ·us -a -um *adj* set with jewels, jeweled; brilliant, glittering, sparkling

gemmĭf·er -ĕra -ĕrum *adj* gemproducing

gemm·ō -āre *vi* to sprout, bud; to sparkle

gem·ō -ĕre -ŭī -ĭtum *vt* to sigh

over, lament; *vi* to sigh, groan, moan; to creak

Gemōni·ae -ārum *f pl* steps on the Capitoline slope from which criminals were thrown

gen·a -ae *f* or gen·ae -ārum *f pl* cheek; cheekbone; eye socket; eye

geneālŏg·us -ī *m* genealogist

gen·er -ĕrī *m* son-in-law; daughter's boyfriend or fiancé

generāl·is -e *adj* of a species, generic; general, universal

generālĭter *adv* in general, generally

generasc·ō -ĕre *vi* to be generated

generātim *adv* by species, by classes; in general, generally

generāt·or -ōris *m* producer, breeder

genĕr·ō -āre *vt* to beget, procreate, produce, engender

generōsĭus *adv* more nobly

generōs·us -a -um *adj* of good stock, highborn, noble; noble, nobleminded

genĕs·is -is *f* birth, creation; horoscope

genesta see genista ..

genetīv·us -a -um *adj* inborn, innate; (gram) genitive; *m* genitive case

genĕtr·ix -īcis *f* mother, ancestress

geniāl·is -e *adj* nuptial, bridal; genial; joyous, festive, merry

geniālĭter *adv* merrily

genĭculāt·us -a -um *adj* knotted, having knots, jointed

genist·a or genest·a -ae *f* broom plant; broom

genĭtābĭl·is -e *adj* productive

genĭtāl·is -e *adj* generative, productive; of birth; dies genitalis birthday

genĭtālĭter *adv* fruitfully

genĭtīvus see genetivus

genĭt·or -ōris *m* father, creator

genĭtrix see genetrix

genĭtus *pp* of gigno

gen·ĭus -iī or -ī *m* guardian spirit; taste, appetite, natural inclination; talent, genius

gen·s -tis *f* clan; stock; tribe; folk, nation, people; species; breed; descendant, offspring; *f pl* foreign nations; longe gentium abire to be far, far away; minime gentium by no means; ubi gentium where in the world, where on earth

gentĭc·us -a -um *adj* tribal; national

gentīlicĭ·us -a -um *adj* family

gentīl·is -e *adj* family, hereditary; tribal; national; *m* clansman, kinsman

gentīlĭt·ās -ātis *f* clan relationship

gen·ū -ūs *n* knee; genibus minor kneeling; genibus nixus on one's knees; genuum junctura knee joint

genuāl·ia -ĭum *n pl* garters

genuīn·us -a -um *adj* innate, natural; of the cheek; jaw, of the jaw; *m pl* back teeth

gen·us -ĕris n race, descent, lineage, breed, stock, family; noble birth; tribe; nation, people; descendant, offspring, posterity; kind, sort, species, class; rank, order, division; fashion, way, style; matter, respect; genus; sex; gender; **aliquid id genus** (acc of description instead of genit of quality) something of that sort; **in omni genere** in every respect

geographi·a -ae f geography

geōmĕtr·ēs -ae m geometer, mathematician

geōmetri·a -ae f geometry

geōmetric·us -a -um adj geometrical; n pl geometry

georgic·us -a -um adj agricultural; n pl Georgics (poems on farming by Virgil)

ger·ens -entis adj (with genit) managing (e.g., a business)

germān·a -ae f full sister, real sister

germānē adv sincerely

Germān·ī -ōrum m pl Germans

Germānī·a -ae f Germany

Germānic·us -a -um adj Germanic; m cognomen of Tiberius' nephew and adoptive son (15 B.C.-19 A.D.)

germānit·ās -ātis f brotherhood, sisterhood (relationship between brothers and sisters of the same parents); relationship between colonies of the same mother-city

germān·us -a -um adj having the same parents; brotherly; sisterly; genuine, real, true; m full brother, own brother; f see **germana**

germ·en -ĭnis n sprout, bud, shoot, offspring; embryo

germĭn·ō -āre vt to put forth, grow (hair, wings, etc.); vi to sprout

gerō gerĕre gessī gestum vt to bear, carry, wear, have, hold; to bring; to display; exhibit, assume; to bear, produce; to carry on, manage, govern, regulate, administer; to carry out, transact, do, accomplish; **bellum gerere** to fight, carry on war; **dum ea geruntur** while that was going on; **gerere morem** (with dat) to gratify, please, humor; **personam gerere** (with genit) to play the part of; **rem gerere** to run a business, conduct an affair; **se gerere** to behave; **se gerere** (with pro + abl) to claim to be for; **se medium gerere** to remain neutral

ger·ō -ōnis m porter

gerr·ae -ārum f pl trifles, nonsense

gerr·ō -ōnis m (coll) loafer

gerulifigŭl·us -ī m accomplice; (with genit) accomplice in

gerŭl·us -ī m porter

Gēry·ōn -ŏnis or **Gēryŏn·ēs -ae** m mythical three-headed king of Spain who was slain by Hercules

gestām·en -ĭnis n that which is worn or carried, load; vehicle, litter; n pl ornaments; accouterments; arms

gestāti·ō -ōnis f drive (place where one drives)

gestāt·or -ōris m bearer, carrier

gestī·ō -ōnis f performance

gest·ĭō -īre -īvī or **-iī -ītum** vi to be delighted, be thrilled, be excited; to be eager; (with inf) to be itching to, long to

gestĭt·ō -āre vt to be in the habit of carrying or wearing

gest·ō -āre vt to bear, wear, carry; to carry about, blab, tell; to cherish; **gestari** to ride, drive, sail (esp. for pleasure)

gest·or -ōris m tattler

gestus pp of gero; adj **res gestae** accomplishments, exploits

gest·us -ūs m gesture; gesticulation; posture, bearing, attitude

Get·ae -ārum m pl Thracian tribe of the lower Danube

gibb·us -ī m hump

Gigant·es -um m pl Giants (race of gigantic size, sprung from Earth as the blood of Uranus fell upon her. They tried to storm heaven but were repelled by the gods with the aid of Hercules and placed under various volcanoes)

gignō gignĕre genŭī genĭtum vt to beget, bear, produce; to cause, occasion, create, begin

gilv·us -a -um adj pale-yellow; **equus gilvus** palomino

gingīv·a -ae f gum (of the mouth)

glab·er -ra -rum adj hairless, bald, smooth; m young slave, favorite slave

glaciāl·is -e adj icy, frozen

glaci·ēs -ēī f ice; f pl ice fields

glaci·ō -āre vt to turn into ice, freeze

gladiāt·or -ōris m gladiator; m pl gladiatorial combat, gladiatorial show; **gladiatores dare** or **gladiatores edere** to stage a gladiatorial show

gladiātōrĭ·us -a -um adj gladiatorial; n gladiator's pay

gladiātūr·a -ae f gladiatorial profession

gladĭ·us -iī or **-ī** m sword; murder, death; **gladium educere** or **gladium stringere** to draw the sword; **gladium recondere** to sheathe the sword

glaeb·a -ae f lump of earth, clod; soil, land; lump, piece

glaebŭl·a -ae f small lump; bit of land, small farm

glaesum see **glesum**

glandĭf·er -ĕra -ĕrum adj acorn-producing

glandiōnĭd·a -ae f choice morsel

gland·ĭum -iī or **-ī** n choice cut (of meat)

glan·s -dis f mast; nut; acorn; chestnut; bullet

glārĕ·a -ae f gravel

glāreōs·us -a -um adj full of gravel, gravelly

glaucōm·a -ătis n cataract; **glaucomam ob oculos objicere** (with dat) to throw dust into the eyes of

glauc·us -a -um adj grey-green, greyish; bright, sparkling

Glauc·us -ī m leader of the Lycians in the Trojan War; fisherman of Anthedon, in Euboea, who was changed into a sea deity

glēba see **glaeba**

glēs·um or **glaes·um -ī** n amber

glī·s -ris m dormouse

glīsc·ō -ĕre vi to grow, swell up, spread, blaze up; to grow, increase

globōs·us -a -um adj spherical

glob·us -ī m ball, sphere, globe; crowd, throng, gathering; clique

glomerām·en -inis n ball, globe

glomĕr·ō -āre vt to form into a ball, gather up, roll up; to collect, gather together, assemble

glom·us -ĕris n ball of yarn

glōri·a -ae f glory, fame; glorious deed; thirst for glory, ambition; pride, boasting, bragging

glōriāti·ō -ōnis f boasting, bragging

glōriŏl·a -ae f bit of glory

glōri·or -ārī -ātus sum vt (only with neut pron as object) to boast about, e.g., **haec gloriari** to boast about this; **idem gloriari** to make the same boast; vi to boast, brag; (with abl or with de or in + abl) to take pride in, boast about; (with **adversus** + acc) to boast or brag to (someone)

glōriōsē adv gloriously; boastfully, pompously

glōriōs·us -a -um adj glorious, famous; boastful

glossēm·a -ătis n word to be glossed

glūt·en -inis n glue

glūtināt·or -ōris m bookbinder

glūtin·ō -āre vt to glue together

glutt·iō or **glūt·iō -īre** vt to gulp down

glutt·ō -ōnis m glutton

Gnae·us or **Gnē·us -ī** m Roman praenomen

gnār·us -a -um or **gnārūr·is -e** adj skillful, expert; known; (with genit) familiar with, versed in, expert in

gnātus see **natus**

gnāv· = **nav-**

gnōbilis see **nobilis**

Gnōsi·a -ae or **Gnōsi·as -ădis** or **Gnōs·is -ĭdis** f Ariadne (daughter of King Minos)

gnoscō see **nosco**

Gnoss·us or **Gnōs·us -ī** f Cnossos (ancient capital of Crete and residence of Minos)

gnōtus see **nosco**

gōb·ius or **cōb·ius -iī** or **-ī** or **gōbi·ō -ōnis** m goby (small fish)

Gorgi·as -ae m famous orator and sophist of Leontini, in Sicily (c. 480-390 B.C.)

Gorg·ō -ōnis f Gorgon (a daughter of Phorcys and Ceto); f pl Gorgons (Stheno, Medusa, and Euryale)

Gorgŏnē·us -a -um adj Gorgonian; **Gorgoneus equus** Pegasus; **Gorgoneus lacus** fountain Hippocrene on Mount Helicon

grabāt·us -ī m cot

Gracch·us -ī m Tiberius Sempronius Gracchus (social reformer and tribune in 133 B.C.); Gaius Sempronius Gracchus (younger brother of Tiberius and tribune in 123 B.C.)

gracil·is -e or **gracil·us -a -um** adj slim, slender; thin, skinny; poor; slight, insignificant; plain, simple (style)

gracilit·ās -ātis f slenderness; thinness, leanness, meagerness

grācŭl·us or **graccŭl·us -ī** m jackdaw

gradātim adv step by step, gradually, little by little

gradāti·ō -ōnis f climax

gradior gradī gressus sum vi to go, walk, step

Grādīv·us or **Grādĭv·us -ī** m epithet of Mars

grad·us -ūs m step, pace, walk, gait; step, degree, grade, stage; approach, advance, progress; status, rank; station, position; step, rung, stair; footing; **concito gradu** on the double; **de gradu dejicere** (fig) to throw off balance; **gradum celerare** or **gradum corripere** to pick up the pace, speed up the pace; **gradum conferre** (mil) to come to close quarters; **gradūs ferre** (mil) to charge; **pleno gradu** on the double; **suspenso gradu** on tiptoe

Graecē adv Greek, in Greek; **Graece loqui** to speak Greek; **Graece scire** to know Greek

Graeci·a -ae f Greece; **Magna Graecia** southern Italy

graeciss·ō -āre vi to ape the Greeks

graec·or -ārī -ātus sum vi to go Greek, act like a Greek

Graecŭl·us -a -um adj (in contemptuous sense) Greek through and through, hundred-percent Greek; mf Greekling, dirty little Greek

Graec·us -a -um adj & mf Greek; n Greek, Greek language

Grā·iī or **Grā·ī -ōrum** m pl Greeks

Grāiŭgĕn·a -ae m Greek, Greek by birth

grall·ae -ārum f pl stilts

grallāt·or -ōris m stilt walker

grām·en -inis n grass; meadow, pasture; plant, herb

grāminĕ·us -a -um adj grassy, of grass; of bamboo

grammatĭc·us -a -um adj grammatical, of grammar; m teacher of literature and language; philologist; f & n pl grammar; philology

grānāri·a -ōrum n pl granary

grandaev·us -a -um adj old, aged

grandesc·ō -ĕre vi to grow, grow big

grandicŭl·us -a -um *adj* rather large; pretty tall

grandĭf·er -ĕra -ĕrum *adj* productive

grandĭlŏqu·us -ī *m* braggart

grandĭn·at -āre *v impers* it is hailing

grand·ĭō -īre *vt* to enlarge, increase

grand·is -e *adj* full-grown, grown up, tall; large, great; aged; important, powerful, strong; grand, lofty, dignified (*style*); loud, strong (*voice*); heavy (*debt*); dignified (*speaker*)

grandĭt·ās -ātis *f* grandeur

grand·ō -ĭnis *f* hail

grānĭf·er -ĕra -ĕrum *adj* (of ants) grain-carrying

grān·um -ī *n* grain, seed

graphĭcē *adv* masterfully

graphĭc·us -a -um *adj* masterful

graph·ĭum -ĭī or **-ī** *n* stilus

grassāt·or -ōris *m* vagabond, tramp; bully; prowler

grass·or -ārī -ātus sum *vi* to walk about, prowl around; to hang around, loiter; to go, move, proceed; (with **adversus** or **in** + *acc*) to attack, waylay

grātē *adv* willingly, with pleasure; gratefully

grātēs (*genit* not in use) *f pl* thanks, gratitude; **grates agere** (with *dat*) to thank, give thanks to; **grates habere** (with *dat*) to feel grateful to

grātĭ·a -ae *f* grace, charm, pleasantness, loveliness; influence, prestige; love, friendship; service, favor, kindness; thanks, gratitude, acknowledgment; cause, reason, motive; **cum gratia** (with *genit*) to the satisfaction of; with the approval of; **eā gratiā ut** for the reason that; **exempli gratiā** for example; **gratiā** (with *genit*) for the sake of, on account of; **gratiam facere** (with *dat* of person and *genit* of thing) to pardon (*someone*) for (*a fault*); **gratias agere** (with *dat*) to thank, give thanks to; **gratias habere** (with *dat*) to feel grateful to; **in gratiam** (with *genit*) in order to win the favor of, in order to please; **in gratiam habere** to regard (*something*) as a favor; **meā gratiā** for my sake; **quā gratiā** why

Grātĭ·ae -ārum *f pl* Graces (*Aglaia, Euphrosyne, and Thalia, daughters of Jupiter by Eurynome*)

grātĭfĭcātĭ·ō -ōnis *f* kindness

grātĭfĭc·or -ārī -ātus sum *vt* to give up, surrender, sacrifice; *vi* (with *dat*) **a** to do (*someone*) a favor; **b** to gratify, please

grātĭis *adv* gratis, free, for nothing, gratuitously

grātĭōs·us -a -um *adj* popular, influential; obliging

grātĭs *adv* gratis, free, for nothing, gratuitously

grāt·or -ārī -ātus sum *vi* to rejoice; to express gratitude; (with

dat) to congratulate; **invicem inter se gratari** to congratulate one another

grātuītō *adv* gratuitously, gratis, for nothing; for no particular reason

grātuīt·us -a -um *adj* gratuitous, free, spontaneous; voluntary; unprovoked

grātŭlābund·us -a -um *adj* congratulating

grātŭlātĭ·ō -ōnis *f* congratulation; rejoicing, joy; public thanksgiving

grātŭlāt·or -ōris *m* congratulator, well-wisher

grātŭl·or -ārī -ātus sum *vi* to be glad, rejoice, manifest joy; (with *dat*) **a** to congratulate; **b** to render thanks to

grāt·us -a -um *adj* pleasing, pleasant, agreeable, welcome; thankful, grateful; deserving thanks, earning gratitude; *n* favor; **gratum facere** (with *dat*) to do (*someone*) a favor

gravanter *adv* reluctantly

gravātē *adv* with difficulty; unwillingly, grudgingly

gravātim *adv* with difficulty; unwillingly

gravēdĭnōs·us -a -um *adj* prone to catch colds

gravēd·ō -ĭnis *f* cold, head cold

gravesc·ō -ĕre *vi* to grow heavy; (fig) to become worse

gravĭdĭt·ās -ātis *f* pregnancy

gravĭd·ō -āre *vt* to impregnate

gravĭd·us -a -um *adj* loaded, filled, full; pregnant; (with *abl*) teeming with

grav·is -e *adj* heavy, weighty; burdensome; troublesome, oppressive, painful, harsh, hard, severe, unpleasant; unwholesome, indigestible; important, influential, venerable, grave, serious; pregnant; hostile; low, deep, bass; flat (*note*); harsh, bitter, offensive (*smell or taste*); impressive (*speech*); stormy (*weather*); oppressive (*heat*)

gravĭt·ās -ātis *f* weight; severity, harshness, seriousness; importance; dignity, influence; pregnancy; violence, vehemence

gravĭter *adv* heavily, ponderously; hard, violently, vehemently; severely, harshly, unpleasantly, disagreeably; sadly, sorrowfully; with dignity, with propriety, with authority; (to feel) deeply; (to smell) offensive, strong; (to speak) impressively; **graviter ferre** to take (*something*) hard

grav·ō -āre *vt* to weigh down, load, load down; to burden, be oppressive to; to aggravate; to increase

grav·or -ārī -ātus sum *vt* to feel annoyed at, object to, refuse, decline; to bear with reluctance, regard as a burden; *vi* to feel annoyed, be vexed

gregāl·is -e *adj* of the herd or flock; common; **sagulum gregale** uniform of a private; *m pl* comrades, companions

gregāri·us -a -um *adj* common; (mil) of the same rank; **miles gregārius** private

gregātim *adv* in flocks, in herds, in crowds

grem·ium -iī or **-ī** *n* lap, bosom; womb

gressus *pp* of **gradior**

gress·us -ūs *m* step; course, way

gre·x -gis *m* flock, herd; swarm; company, group, crowd, troop, set, clique, gang; theatrical cast

gruis see **grus**

grunn·iō or **grund·iō -īre -īvī** or **-iī -ītum** *vi* to grunt

grunnīt·us -ūs *m* grunt, grunting

grū·s or **gru·is -is** *m* or *f* crane

grȳ (indecl) *n* scrap, crumb

gryps grȳpis *m* griffin

gubernācul·um or **gubernācl·um -ī** *n* rudder, tiller, helm; *n pl* (fig) helm

gubernātǐ·ō -ōnis *f* navigation

gubernāt·or -ōris *m* navigator, pilot; governor

gubernāt·rix -īcis *f* directress

gubern·ō -āre *vt* to navigate, pilot; to direct, govern

gul·a -ae *f* gullet, throat; palate, appetite, gluttony

gulōs·us -a -um *adj* appetizing, dainty

gurg·es -itis *m* abyss, gulf, whirl-

pool; waters, flood, depths, sea; spendthrift

gurguli·ō -ōnis *m* gullet, windpipe

gurgust·ium -iī or **-ī** *n* dark hovel; (fig) hole in the wall

gustātōr·ium -iī or **-ī** *n* appetizer

gustāt·us -ūs *m* sense of taste; flavor, taste

gust·ō -āre *vt* to taste; (fig) to enjoy; to overhear; *vi* to have a snack

gust·us -ūs *m* tasting; appetizer

gutt·a -ae *f* drop; spot, speck

guttātim *adv* drop by drop

guttul·a -ae *f* tiny drop

gutt·ur -ŭris *n* gullet, throat, neck; *n pl* throat, neck

gūt·us or **gutt·us -ī** *m* cruet, flask

Gy·ās -ae *m* hundred-armed giant

Gȳg·ēs -is or **-ae** *m* king of Lydia (716–678 B.C.)

gymnasiarch·us -ī *m* manager of a gymnasium

gymnas·ium -iī or **-ī** *n* gymnasium

gymnastic·us -a -um *adj* gymnastic

gymnǐc·us -a -um *adj* gymnastic

gymnosophist·ae -ārum *m pl* Hindu Stoics

gynaecē·um or **gynaecī·um -ī** *n* women's apartments

gypsāt·us -a -um *adj* covered with plaster

gyps·um -ī *n* gypsum, plaster

gȳr·us -ī *m* circle, cycle, ring, orbit, course

H

ha, hahae, hahahae *interj* expression of joy, satisfaction, or laughter

habēn·a -ae *f* strap; *f pl* reins; (fig) reins, control; **habenae rerum** reins of the state; **habenas adducere, dare, effundere,** or **immittere** (with *dat*) to give free rein to

hab·eō -ēre -uī -itum *vt* to have, hold, keep; to retain, detain; to contain; to possess, own; to wear; to treat, handle, use; to hold, conduct (*meeting*); to deliver (*speech*); to occupy, inhabit; to pronounce, utter (*words*); to hold, manage, govern, wield; to hold, think, consider, believe; to occupy, engage, busy; to occasion, produce, render; to know, be informed of, be acquainted with; to take, accept, endure, bear; **in animo habere** to have on one's mind; **in animo habere** (with *inf*) to intend to; **pro certo habere** to regard as certain; **secum** or **sibi habere** to keep (*something*) to oneself, keep secret; **se habere** (with *adv*) to be,feel (*well, etc.*); *vi* **bene habet** it is well, all is well; **sic habet** that's how it is

habil·is -e *adj* handy; suitable, con-

venient; active, nimble; skillful

habilit·ās -ātis *f* aptitude

habitābil·is -e *adj* habitable, fit to live in

habitātǐ·ō -ōnis *f* dwelling, house

habitāt·or -ōris *m* inhabitant, tenant

habit·ō -āre *vt* to inhabit; *vi* to dwell, live, stay, reside; (with **in** + *abl*) **a** to live in, reside at; **b** to be always in (*a certain place*); **c** (fig) to dwell upon

habitūd·ō -inis *f* condition, appearance

habit·us -a -um *adj* well-kept, fat, stout

habit·us -ūs *m* condition (*of the body*); character, quality; style, style of dress, attire; disposition, state of feeling; habit

hāc *adv* this way, in this way

hactēnus *adv* to this place, thus far; up till now, hitherto, so far; to this extent, so far, so much

Hadrǐ·a -ae *f* city in Picenum, the birthplace of Hadrian; city in the country of the Veneti, on the coast of the sea named after it; *m* Adriatic Sea

Hadriān·us -ī *m* Hadrian (*Roman emperor*, 117-138 A.D.)

haec hōrum (*neut pl* of **hoc**) *adj* & *pron* these

haec hūjus (older form; **haece**; *gen-it:* **hujusce**) (*fem* of **hic**) *adj* this; the present, the actual; the latter; (occasionally) the former; **haec . . . haec** one . . . another; *pron* this one, she; the latter; (occasionally) the former; **haec . . . haec** one . . . another one; **haecine** (**haec** with *interrog* enclitic **-ne**) is this . . .?

haece see **haec**

haecine see **haec**

Haed·ī -ōrum *m pl* pair of stars in the constellation Auriga

haedīli·a -ae *f* little kid

haedill·us -ī *m* (term of endear-ment) little kid or goat

haedīn·us -a -um *adj* kid's, goat's

haedǔl·us -ī *m* little kid, little goat

haed·us -ī *m* young goat, kid

Haemoni·a -ae *f* Thessaly

Haem·us or **Haem·os -ī** *m* moun-tain range in Thrace

haerĕō haerēre haesī haesum *vi* to cling, stick; to hang around, lin-ger, stay, remain fixed, remain in place; to be rooted to the spot, come to a standstill, stop; to be embar-rassed, be at a loss, hesitate, be in doubt; with *dat* or *abl* or with *in* + *abl*) **a** to cling to, stick to, ad-here to, be attached to; **b** to loiter in, hang around in, waste time in (*a place*) or at (*an activity*); **c** to adhere to, stick by (*an opinion, purpose*); **d** to gaze upon; **e** to keep close to; **in terga, in tergis,** or **tergis hostium haerere** to pur-sue the enemy closely

haeresc·ō -ĕre *vi* to adhere

haerĕs·is -is *f* sect, school of thought

haesitābund·us -a -um *adj* hesi-tating, faltering

haesitanti·a -ae *f* stammering

haesitātǐ·ō -ōnis *f* hesitation, inde-cision; stammering

haesitāt·or -ōris *m* hesitator

haesīt·ō -āre *vi* to get stuck; to stammer; to hesitate, be undecided, be at a loss

hahae hahahae *interj* expression of joy, satisfaction, or laughter

halagŏra -ae *f* salt market

hāl·ans -antis *adj* fragrant

hāl·ĕc -ēcis *n* fish sauce

haliaeĕt·os -ī *m* sea eagle, osprey

hālǐt·us -ūs *m* breath; steam, vapor

hall·ex -ĭcis *m* big toe

hallūcīn·or or **hālūcǐn·or -ārī -ātus sum** *vi* to daydream, have hallucinations, talk wildly

hāl·ō -āre *vt* to exhale; *vi* to exhale; to be fragrant

halophant·a -ae *m* scoundrel

hālūcinor see **hallucinor**

ham·a or **am·a -ae** *f* bucket, pail

Hamādry·as -ādis *f* wood nymph

hāmātǐl·is -e *adj* with hooks

hāmāt·us -a -um *adj* hooked, hook-shaped

Hamilc·ar -āris *m* famous Cartha-ginian general in the First Punic War, surnamed Barca, and father of Hannibal (*d.* 228 B.C.)

hāmǐōt·a -ae *m* angler

hāmǔl·us -ī *m* small hook

hām·us -ī *m* hook, fishhook

Hannǐb·al -ālis *m* son of Hamilcar Barca and famous general in the Second Punic War (246-172 B.C.)

har·a -ae *f* pen, coop, stye

harēn·a -ae *f* sand; seashore, beach; arena; *f pl* desert

harēnōs·us -a -um *adj* sandy

hariŏl·or -ārī -ātus sum *vi* to fore-tell the future; to talk gibberish

hariŏl·us -ī *m* or **hariŏl·a -ae** *f* soothsayer

harmoni·a -ae *f* harmony

harpăg·ō -āre *vt* to steal

harpăg·ō -ōnis *m* hook, harpoon, grappling hook; greedy person

Harpalўc·ē -ēs *f* daughter of a Thracian king, brought up as a warrior

harp·ē -ēs *f* scimitar

Harpўǐ·ae -ārum *f pl* Harpies (*mythical monsters, half woman, half bird*)

harundǐf·er -ĕra -ĕrum *adj* reed-bearing

harundǐnĕ·us -a -um *adj* made of reed

harundǐnōs·us -a -um *adj* over-grown with reeds

harund·ō -ǐnis *f* reed, cane; fishing rod; pen; shepherd's pipe; arrow shaft, arrow; fowler's rod; weaver's comb; hobbyhorse (*toy*)

harusp·ex -ǐcis *m* soothsayer who foretold the future from the inspec-tion of the vital organs of animals; prophet

haruspǐc·a -ae *f* soothsayer (*female*)

haruspǐcǐn·us -a -um *adj* of divin-ation; *f* art of divination

haruspǐc·ǐum -ǐī or **-ī** *n* divination

Hasdrǔb·al or **Asdrǔb·al -ālis** *m* brother of Hannibal (*d.* 207 B.C.); son-in-law of Hamilcar Barca (*d.* 221 B.C.)

hast·a -ae *f* spear; **sub hasta ven-dere** to sell at auction, auction off

hastāt·us -a -um *adj* armed with a spear; *m pl* soldiers in first line of a Roman battle formation

hastīl·e -is *n* shaft; spear, javelin

hau or **au** *interj* cry of pain or grief

haud or **haut** or **hau** *adv* not, hard-ly, not at all, by no means

hauddum *adv* not yet

haudquāquam *adv* not at all, by no means

haurǐō haurīre hausī haustum *vt* to draw, draw up, draw out; to drain, drink up; to spill, shed; to swallow, devour, consume, exhaust; to derive; (fig) to drink in, seize upon, imbibe

haustr·um -ī *n* scoop, bucket

haustus *pp* of **haurio**

haust·us -ūs *m* drawing (*of water*); drinking, swallowing; drink, draught; handful; stream (*of blood*)

haut see **haud**

havēō see **aveo**

hebdŏm·as -ădis *f* week

Hēb·ē -ēs *f* goddess of youth, daughter of Juno, and cupbearer of the gods

hebĕn·us -ī *f* ebony

heb·ĕō -ēre *vi* to be blunt, be dull; (fig) to be inactive, be sluggish

heb·es -ĕtis *adj* blunt, dull; faint, dim; dull, obtuse, stupid

hebesc·ō -ĕre *vi* to grow blunt, grow dull; to become faint or dim; to lose vigor

hebĕt·ō -āre *vt* to blunt, dull, dim

Hebr·us -ī *m* principal river in Thrace

Hecăt·ē -ēs *f* goddess of magic and witchcraft and often identified with Diana

hecatomb·ē -ēs *f* hecatomb

Hect·or -ŏris *m* son of Priam and Hecuba, husband of Andromache, and bravest Trojan warrior in fighting the Greeks

Hecŭb·a -ae *or* **Hecŭb·ē** -ēs *f* wife of Priam who, after the destruction of Troy, became a captive of the Greeks and was eventually changed into a dog

hedĕr·a -ae *f* ivy

hederĭg·er -ĕra -ĕrum *adj* wearing ivy

hederŏs·us -a -um *adj* overgrown with ivy

hēdўchr·um -ī *n* perfume

hei hēia see **ei, ēia**

Helĕn·a -ae *or* **Helĕn·ē** -ēs *f* Helen (*wife of Menelaus, sister of Clytemnestra, Castor, and Pollux, who was abducted by Paris*)

Helĕn·us -ī *m* prophetic son of Priam and Hecuba

Hēliăd·es -um *f pl* daughters of Helios and sisters of Phaëthon, who were changed into poplars and whose tears were changed to amber

Helic·ē -ēs *f* Big Bear (*constellation*)

Helic·ōn -ōnis *m* mountain in Boeotia sacred to the Muses and to Apollo

Helicōniăd·es *or* **Helicōnid·es** -um *f pl* Muses

Hell·as -ădis *f* Greece

Hell·ē -ēs *f* daughter of Athamas and Nephele who, while riding the golden-fleeced ram, fell into the Hellespont and drowned

hellĕbor· = **ellebor-**

Hellespont·us -ī *m* Dardanelles

hellŭ·ō -ōnis *m* glutton, squanderer

hellŭ·or -ārī -ātus sum *vi* to be a glutton

hel·ops *or* **el·ops** *or* **ell·ops** -ōpis *m* highly-prized fish (*perhaps the sturgeon*)

helvell·a -ae *f* delicious herb

Helvĕtĭ·ī -ōrum *m pl* people of Gallia Lugdunensis (*modern Switzerland*)

helv·us -a -um *adj* light-bay

hem *interj* (expression of surprise) well!

hēmerodrŏm·us -ī *m* courier

hēmicill·us -ī *m* mule

hēmicycl·ium -iī *or* -ī *n* semicircle of seats

hēmin·a -ae *f* half of a sextarius (*half a pint*)

hendecasyllăb·ī -ōrum *m pl* hendecasyllabics (*verses with eleven syllables*)

hēpatārĭ·us -a -um *adj* of the liver

hептĕr·is -is *f* galley with seven banks of oars

hera see **era**

Hēr·a -ae *f* Greek goddess identified with Juno

Hēraclīt·us -ī *m* early Greek philosopher of Ephesus who believed that fire was the primary element of all matter (*fl* 513 B.C.)

herb·a -ae *f* blade, stalk; herb, plant; grass, lawn; weed

herbesc·ō -ĕre *vi* to sprout

herbĕ·us -a -um *adj* grass-green

herbĭd·us -a -um *adj* grassy

herbĭf·er -ĕra -ĕrum *adj* grassy, grass-producing; made of herbs

herbōs·us -a -um *adj* grassy; made with herbs

herbŭl·a -ae *f* little herb

hercisc·ō -ĕre *vi* to divide an inheritance

herct·um *or* **erct·um** -ī *n* inheritance

Herculănĕ·um -ī *n* town on the seacoast of Campania which was destroyed with Pompeii in an eruption of Vesuvius in 79 A.D.

Hercŭl·ēs -is *or* -ī *m* son of Jupiter and Alcmena, husband of Deianira, and after his death and deification, husband of Hebe

hercŭlēs *or* **hercŭle** *or* **hercle** *interj* by Hercules!

here *adv* yesterday

hērēditārĭ·us -a -um *adj* of or about an inheritance; inherited, hereditary

hērēdĭt·ās -ātis *f* inheritance

hērēd·ium -iī *or* -ī *n* inherited estate

hēr·ēs -ēdis *m* heir; (fig) heir, successor; *f* heiress

herī *or* **here** *adv* yesterday

herif· **herīl·** = **erif· eril-**

Hermāphrodīt·us -ī *m* son of Hermes and Aphrodite who combined with the nymph Salmacis to become one person

Herm·ēs *or* **Herm·a** -ae *m* Greek god identified with Mercury

Hermiŏn·ē -ēs *or* **Hermiŏn·a** -ae *f* daughter of Helen and Menelaus and wife of Orestes

Hērodŏt·us -ī *m* father of Greek history, born at Halicarnassus on coast of Asia Minor (484-425 B.C.)

hērŏĭc·us -a -um adj heroic, epic

hērŏīn·a -ae f demigoddess

hērŏ·is -ĭdis f demigoddess

hēr·ōs -ōĭs m demigod, hero (rarely used of men born of human parents)

hērō·us -a -um adj heroic, epic

herus see **erus**

Hēsiŏd·us -ī m Hesiod (early Greek poet, born in Boeotia, 8th cent. B.C.)

Hēsiŏn·ē -ēs or **Hēsiŏn·a -ae** f daughter of Laomedon, king of Troy, whom Hercules rescued from a sea monster

Hespĕr·us or **Hespĕr·os -ī** m evening star

hestern·us -a -um adj yesterday's

hetairī·a -ae f secret society

hetairĭc·ē -ēs f Macedonian mounted guard

heu! interj (expression of pain or dismay) oh!, ah!

heus! interj (to draw attention) say there!, hey!

hexamĕt·er -rī m hexameter verse

hexēr·is -is f ship with six banks of oars

hĭāt·us -ūs m opening; open or gaping mouth; mouthing, bluster; basin (of fountain); chasm; (gram) hiatus

Hibēr·es -um m pl Spaniards

hibern·a -ōrum n pl winter quarters

hībernācŭl·a -ōrum n pl winter bivouac; winter residence

hibern·ō -āre vi to spend the winter; to stay in winter quarters; (fig) to hibernate

hibern·us -a -um adj winter, in winter, wintry

hibisc·um -ī n hibiscus

hibrĭd·a or **hybrĭd·a -ae** m or f hybrid, mongrel, half-breed

hīc (or **hio**) **hūjus** (older form: **hīce hūjusce**) adj this; the present, the actual; the latter; (occasionally) the former; **hic . . . hic** one . . . another; **pron** this one, he; this man, myself, your's truly (i.e., the speaker or writer); the latter; (occasionally) the former; (in court) the defendant, my defendant; **hic . . . hic** one . . . another; **hicine** (**hic** with interrog enclitic **-ne**) is this . . . ?

hīc adv here, in this place; at this point; in this affair, in this particular, herein

hīce see **hic**

hicine see **hic**

hiemāl·is -e adj winter, wintry; stormy

hiĕm·ō -āre vi to spend the winter, pass the winter; to be wintry, be cold, be stormy

hiem·s or **hiem·ps -is** f winter; cold; storm

Hiĕr·ō -ōnis m ruler of Syracuse and patron of philosophers and poets (?-466 B.C.); friend of the Romans in the First Punic War (306?-215 B.C.)

Hierosolȳm·a ōrum m pl Jerusalem

hiĕt·ō -āre vi to keep yawing

hilāre adv cheerfully, merrily, gaily

hilār·is -e or **hilār·us -a -um** adj cheerful, merry, gay

hilarĭt·ās -ātis f cheerfulness, gaiety

hilaritūd·ō -ĭnis f cheerfulness

hilār·ō -āre vt to cheer up

hilarŭl·us -a -um adj merry little

hilārus see **hilaris**

hill·ae -ārum f pl smoked sausage

Hĭlōt·ae or **Ilōt·ae -ārum** m pl Helots (slaves of the Spartans)

hĭl·um -ī n something, trifle

hinc adv from here, from this place; on this side, here; for this reason; from this source; after this, henceforth, from now on

hinn·iō -īre vi to whinny, neigh

hinnīt·us -ūs m neighing

hinnŭl·us -ī m fawn

hĭ·ō -āre vt to sing; vi to open, be open; to gape; to yawn; to make eyes (in surprise or greedy longing)

hippagōg·ī -ōrum f pl ships for transporting horses and cavalry

Hipparch·us -ī m son of Pisistratus, the tyrant of Athens, who was slain by Harmodius and Aristogiton in 514 B.C.

Hippi·ās -ae m son of Pisistratus, the tyrant of Athens, and tyrant of Athens himself, 527-510 B.C.

hippocentaur·us -ī m centaur

Hippocrăt·ēs -is m famous physician, founder of scientific medicine (c. 460-380 B.C.)

Hippocrēn·ē -ēs f spring on Mt. Helicon, sacred to the Muses and produced when the hoof of Pegasus hit the spot

Hippodăm·ē -ēs or **Hippodamē·a** or **Hippodami·a -ae** f daughter of Oenomaus, the king of Elis, and wife of Pelops; daughter of Adrastus and wife of Pirithous

hippodrŏm·os -ī m racetrack

Hippolȳt·ē -ēs or **Hippolȳt·a -ae** f Amazonian wife of Theseus; wife of Acastus, king of Magnesia

Hippolȳt·us -ī m son of Theseus and Hippolyte

hippomăn·es -is n membrane of the head of a new-born foal; discharge of a mare in heat

Hippomĕn·ēs -ae m son of Megareus who competed with Atalanta in a race and won her as his bride

Hippōn·ax -actis m Greek satirist (fl 540 B.C.)

hippotoxŏt·ae -ārum m pl mounted archers

hippūr·us -ī m goldfish

hir·a -ae f empty gut

hircīn·us or **hirquīn·us -a -um** adj goat, of a goat

hircōs·us -a -um adj smelling like a goat

hirc·us -ī m goat

hirně·a -ae f jug

hirsūt·us -a -um adj hairy, shaggy, bristly; prickly; rude

Hirt·ius -iī or -ī m Aulus Hirtius (consul in 43 B.C. and author of the eighth book of Caesar's Memoirs on the Gallic War)

hirt·us -a -um adj hairy, shaggy; uncouth

hirūd·ō -inis f bloodsucker, leech

hirundinīn·us -a -um adj swallow's

hirund·ō -inis f swallow

hisc·ō -ĕre vt to murmur, utter; vi to open, gape, yawn; to open the mouth

Hispān·ī -ōrum m pl Spaniards

Hispāni·a -ae f Spain

Hispāniens·is -e adj Spanish

hispĭd·us -a -um adj hairy, shaggy, rough

Hist·er or Ist·er -rī m lower Danube

historĭ·a -ae f history; account, story; theme (of a story)

historĭo·us -a -um adj historical; m historian

histric·us -a -um adj theatrical

histri·ō -ōnis m actor

histriōnāl·is -e adj theatrical; histrionic

histriōnĭ·a -ae f dramatics, art of acting

hiulcē adv with frequent hiatus

hiulc·ō -āre vt to split open

hiulc·us -a -um adj split, split open; open, gaping; with hiatus

hōc hūjus (older form: hōce; genit: hūjusce) (neut of hic) adj this; the present, the actual; the latter; (occasionally) the former; pron this one, it; the latter; (occasionally) the former; (with genit) this amount of, this degree of, so much; hoc erat quod this was the reason why; hoc est that is, I mean, namely; hocine (hoc with interrog enclitic -ne) is this . . . ?; hoc facilius all the more easily

hōce see hoc

hōcine see hoc

hodiē adv today; now, nowadays; still, to the present; at once, immediately; hodiē mane this morning; numquam hodiē (coll) never at all, never in the world

hodiern·us -a -um adj today's; hodiernus diēs this day, today

holĭt·or -ōris m grocer

holitōri·us -a -um adj vegetable

hol·us -ĕris n vegetables

Homēr·us -ī m Homer

homicĭd·a -ae m or f murderer, killer

homicīd·ĭum -iī or -ī n murder, manslaughter

hom·ō -inis m or f human being, man, person, mortal; mankind, human race; fellow; fellow creature; (coll) this one; m pl persons, people; infantry; bodies, corpses; members (of the senate); inter homi-

nes esse to be alive; to see the world

homull·us -ī or homucĭ·ō -ōnis or homuncŭl·us -ī m poor man, poor creature

honest·a -ae f lady

honestāment·um -ī n ornament

honest·ās -ātis f good reputation, respectability; sense of honor, respect; beauty, grace; honesty, integrity, uprightness; decency; f pl respectable persons, decent people

honestē adv honorably, respectably, decently, virtuously

honest·ō -āre vt to honor, dignify, embellish, grace

honest·us -a -um adj honored, respected; honorable, decent, respectable, virtuous; handsome; m gentleman; n virtue, good

hon·or or hon·ōs -ōris m honor, esteem; position, office, post; mark of honor, reward, acknowledgment; offering, rites (to the gods or the dead); beauty, grace, charm; glory, fame, reputation; honoris causā out of respect, with all respect

honōrābĭl·is -e adj honorable

honōrārĭ·us -a -um adj honored, respected, highly esteemed; honorary, conferring honor

honōrātē adv with honor, honorably

honōrāt·us -a -um adj honored, respected; in high office; honorable, respectable; honoratum habere to hold in honor

honōrificē adv honorably, respectfully

honōrific·us -a -um adj honorable, complimentary

honōr·ō -āre vt to honor, respect; to embellish, decorate

honōr·us -a -um adj honorable, complimentary

honōs see honor

hoplomăch·us -ī m gladiator

hōr·a -ae f hour; time; season; in diem et horam continually; in horam vivere to live from hand to mouth; quota hora est? what time is it?; f pl clock; in horas from hour to hour, every hour

Hor·a -ae f wife of Quirinus (i.e., of deified Romulus), called Hersilia before her death

Hōr·ae -ārum f pl Hours (daughters of Jupiter and Themis and goddesses who kept watch at the gates of heaven)

hōrae·us -a -um adj pickled

Horāt·ius -iī or -ī m Quintus Horatius Flaccus (65-8 B.C.); Horatius Cocles (defender of the bridge across the Tiber in the war with Porsenna)

hordĕ·um -ī n barley

horĭ·a -ae f fishing boat

horĭŏl·a -ae f small fishing boat

hornō adv this year, during this year

hornōtĭn·us -a -um adj this year's

horn·us -a -um adj this year's

hōrolog·ium -iī or **-ī** n clock; water clock; sundial

horrend·us -a -um adj horrendous, horrible, terrible; awesome

horr·ens -entis adj bristling, bristly, shaggy

horr·eō -ēre -uī vt to dread; to shudder at, shrink from; to be amazed at; vi to stand on end, stand up straight; to get gooseflesh; to shiver, tremble, quake, shake; to look frightful, be rough

horr·escō -escĕre -uī vt to dread, become terrified at; vi to stand on end; (of the sea) to become rough; to begin to shake or shiver; to start (in fear)

horr·eum -ī n barn, shed; silo, granary; wine cellar; beehive

horribil·is -e adj horrible, terrifying; amazing

horridē adv roughly, rudely, sternly

horridŭl·us -a -um adj rather shaggy; somewhat shabby; somewhat unsophisticated (style)

horrid·us -a -um adj bristling, bristly, shaggy, prickly; rude, uncouth, rough, rugged, wild; disheveled; blunt, unpolished, coarse (manner); frightful, frightened, awful

horrif·er -ĕra -ĕrum adj causing shudders; freezing, chilling; terrifying

horrificē adv awfully

horrific·ō -āre vt to make rough, ruffle; to terrify, appall

horrific·us -a -um adj frightful, terrifying

horrisŏn·us -a -um adj frightening (sound), frightening to hear

horr·or -ōris m bristling; shivering, shuddering, quaking; dread, horror; awe, reverence; chill; thrill

horsum adv this way, here

hortām·en -ĭnis n injunction; encouragement

hortāment·um -ī n encouragement

hortātĭ·ō -ōnis f exhortation, encouragement

hortāt·or -ōris m backer, supporter, rooter, instigator

hortāt·us -ūs m encouragement, cheering, cheer

Hortens·ius -iī or **-ī** m Quintus Hortensius (famous orator and friendly competitor of Cicero, 114-50 B.C.)

hort·or -ārī -ātus sum vt to encourage, cheer, incite, instigate; to give a pep talk to (soldiers)

hortŭl·us -ī m little garden, garden plot

hort·us -ī m garden; m pl park

hosp·es -ĭtis m host, entertainer; guest, visitor; friend; stranger, foreigner

hospĭt·a -ae f hostess; guest, visitor; friend; stranger, foreigner

hospĭtāl·is -e adj host's; guest's; hospitable

hospĭtālĭt·ās -ātis f hospitality

hospĭtālĭter adv hospitably, as a guest

hospĭt·ium -iī or **-ī** n hospitality, friendship; welcome; guest room; lodging; inn

hostĭ·a -ae f victim, sacrifice

hostiāt·us -a -um adj bringing offerings

hostĭc·us -a -um adj hostile; foreign, strange; n enemy territory

hostĭl·is -e adj enemy's, enemy, hostile

hostīlĭter adv hostilely, like an enemy

Hostīl·ius -iī or **-ī** m Tullus Hostilius (third king of Rome)

hostĭment·um -ī n compensation, recompense

host·iō -īre vi to return like for like

host·is -is m or f enemy

hūc adv here, to this place; to this, to this point, so far; to such a pitch; for this purpose; **hūc atque illūc** here and there, in different directions; **hucine?** (**hūc** + interrog enclitic) so far?

huī interj (expressing surprise or admiration) wow!

hūjusmŏdī or **hūjuscemŏdī** adj of this sort, such

humānē or **hūmānĭter** adv like a man; politely, gently, with compassion

hūmānĭt·ās -ātis f human nature; mankind; kindness, compassion; courtesy; culture, refinement, civilization

hūmānĭtus adv humanly; humanely, kindly, compassionately

hūmān·us -a -um adj of man, human; humane, kind, compassionate; courteous; cultured, refined, civilized, well educated

humātĭ·ō -ōnis f burial

hūme- = ume-

humī adv on or in the ground

hūmid- = umid-

humĭl·is -e adj low, low-lying, lowgrowing; shallow; stunted; low, common, colloquial; lowly, humble, poor, obscure, insignificant; base, mean, small-minded, cheap

humilĭt·ās -ātis f lowness; lowliness, insignificance; smallness of mind, meanness, cheapness

humilĭter adv low, deeply; meanly, abjectly

hum·ō -āre vt to bury

hum·us -ī f ground, earth; land, region, country

hyacinthĭn·us -a -um adj of the hyacinth; crimson

hyacinth·us or **hyacinth·os -ī** m hyacinth

Hyacinth·us or **Hyacinth·os -ī** m Spartan youth, who was accidently killed by his friend Apollo and from whose blood flowers of the same name sprang

Hyăd·es -um f Hyads (group of sev-

en stars in the head of the constellation Taurus whose rising with the sun was accompanied by rainy weather)

hyaen·a -ae *f* hyena

hyăl·us -ī *m* glass

Hybl·a -ae or **Hybl·ē -ēs** *f* Sicilian mountain, famous for its honey

hybrĭd·a -ae *m* or *f* hybrid, mongrel, half-breed

Hydasp·ēs -is *m* tributary of the Indus River

Hȳdr·a -ae *f* Hydra (*seven-headed dragon killed by Hercules*); Hydra or Anguis (*constellation*); fifty-headed monster at the gates of the lower world

hydraulic·us -a -um *adj* hydraulic

hydraul·us -ī water organ

hydrĭ·a -ae *f* jug, urn

Hydrochŏ·us -ī *m* Aquarius (*constellation*)

hydrŏpic·us -a -um *adj* dropsical

hydr·ops -ōpis *m* dropsy

hydr·us or **hydr·os -ī** *m* serpent

Hyl·ās -ae *m* youthful companion of Hercules who was carried off by the nymphs as he was drawing water

Hyll·us or **Hŭl·us -ī** *m* son of Hercules and husband of Iole

Hym·ēn -ēnis or **Hymenae·us** or

Hymenae·os -ī *m* Hymen (*god of marriage*); wedding ceremony; wedding; wedding song

Hymett·us or **Hymett·os -ī** *m* mountain in E. Attica, famous for its honey

Hypăn·is -is *m* river in Sarmatia (*modern Bug*)

hyperbăt·on -ī *n* (rhet) transposition of words

hyperbŏl·ē -ēs *f* hyperbole

Hyperbŏrĕ·ī -ōrum *m pl* legendary people in the land of the midnight sun

Hyperī·ōn -ŏnis *m* son of Titan and Earth, father of the Sun

Hypermestr·a -ae or **Hypermestr·ē -ēs** *f* the only one of the fifty daughters of Danaus who did not kill her husband on her wedding night

hypocaust·um or **hypocaust·on -ī** *n* sweat bath

hypodidascăl·us -ī *m* instructor

hypomnēm·a -ătis *n* memorandum, note

Hypsipȳl·ē -ēs *f* queen of Lemnos at the time of the Argonauts

Hyrcăn·ī -ōrum *m pl* a people on the Caspian Sea

I

ia- = ja-

Iacch·us -ī *m* Bacchus; wine

iambĕ·us -a -um *adj* iambic

iamb·us -ī *m* iamb; iambic poem, iambic poetry

ianthĭn·a -ōrum *n pl* violet-colored garments

Iapĕt·us -ī *m* Titan, father of Prometheus, Epimetheus, and Atlas

Iăpȳd·es -um *m pl* Illyrian tribe

Iăp·yx -ȳgis *m* son of Daedalus who ruled in S. Italy; wind that blew from Apulia to Greece

Iăs·ius -iī or **-ī** *m* son of Jupiter and Electra and brother of Dardanus

Iăs·ōn -ŏnis *m* Jason (*son of Aeson, leader of the Argonauts, and husband of Medea and afterwards of Creusa*)

iasp·is -ĭdis *f* jasper

Ibēr- = Hiber-

ibi or **ibī** *adv* there, in that place; then, on that occasion; therein

ibīdem *adv* in the same place, just there; at that very moment; at the same time; in the same matter

īb·is -is or **-ĭdis** *f* ibis (*bird sacred to the Egyptians*)

Icăr·us -ī *m* son of Daedalus, who, on his flight from Crete with his father, fell into the sea; father of Penelope

ichneum·ōn -ŏnis *m* ichneumon

(*Egyptian rat that eats crocodile eggs*)

īcō īcĕre īcī ictum *vt* to hit, strike, shoot

īc·ōn -ŏnis *f* image

icterĭc·us -a -um *adj* jaundiced

ict·is -ĭdis *f* weasel

ictus *pp* of **īcō**

ict·us -ūs *m* stroke, blow, hit; cut, sting, bite, wound; range; stress, beat; **sub ictum** within range

id *adv* for that reason, therefore

id ejus (*neut* of **is**) *adj* this, that, the said, the aforesaid; *pron* it; a thing, the thing; **ad id** for that purpose; **aliquid id genus** something of that sort, something like that; **cum eo . . . ut** on condition that, with the stipulation that; **eo plus** the more; **ex eo** from that time on; as a result of that, consequently; **id consili** some sort of plan, some plan; **id quod** a thing which, the thing which; **id temporis** at that time; of that age; **in id** to that end; **in eo esse** to depend on it; **in eo esse . . . ut** to be so far gone that, to get to the point where

Īd·a -ae or **Id·ē -ēs** *f* mountain near Troy; mountain in Crete where Jupiter was brought up

Īdăl·ium -iī or **-ī** *n* city in Cyprus dear to Venus

idcircō adv on that account, for that reason, therefore

idem eădem idem adj the same, the very same, exactly this; (often equivalent to a mere connective) also, likewise; pron the same one

identidem adv again and again, continually, habitually; now and then, at intervals

ideō adv therefore

idiōt·a -ae m uneducated person, ignorant person, layman

īdōl·on -ī n apparition, ghost

idōněē adv suitably

idōně·us -a -um adj suitable, fit, proper; (with dat or with ad or in + acc) fit for, capable of, suited for, convenient for, sufficient for

Īd·ūs -ŭum f pl Ides (fifteenth day of March, May, July, and October, and thirteenth of the other months; interest, debts, and tuition were often paid on the Ides)

ie- = je-

iens euntis pres p of eo

igitur adv then, therefore, accordingly; (resumptive after parenthetical matter) as I was saying; (in summing up) so then, in short

ignār·us -a -um adj ignorant, unaware, inexperienced; unsuspecting; senseless; unknown, strange, unfamiliar; (with genit) unaware of, unfamiliar with

ignāvē adv listlessly, lazily

ignāvi·a -ae f listlessness, laziness; cowardice

ignāviter adv listlessly

ignāv·us -a -um adj listless, lazy, idle, inactive; relaxing; cowardly, bastardly; unproductive (field, etc.)

ignesc·ō -ĕre vi to catch fire, become inflamed, burn; (fig) to flare up

igně·us -a -um adj of fire, on fire, fiery; red-hot, fiery

igniciŭl·us -ī m small fire, little flame, spark

ignif·er -ĕra -ĕrum adj fiery

ignigĕn·a -ae m son of fire (epithet of Bacchus)

ignip·ēs -ēdis adj fiery-footed

ignipŏt·ens -entis adj lord of fire (epithet of Vulcan)

ign·is -is m fire; conflagration; watch fire, signal fire; torch; lightning, bolt of lightning; funeral pyre; star; brightness, glow, brilliancy, splendor; (fig) fire, rage, fury, love, passion; flame, sweetheart; agent of destruction, fanatic; m pl love poems

ignōbĭl·is -e adj insignificant, obscure, unknown, undistinguished; low-born, ignoble

ignōbilĭt·ās -ātis f obscurity; humble birth

ignōmini·a -ea f ignominy, dishonor, disgrace; **ignominiā afficere** to dishonor, disgrace; **ignominia senatūs** public censure imposed by the senate

ignōminiōs·us -a -um adj disgraced, degraded; disgraceful, shameful, ignominious; m infamous person

ignōrābĭl·is -e adj unknown

ignōranti·a -ae f ignorance

ignōrātĭ·ō -ōnis f ignorance

ignōr·ō -āre vt to not know, be ignorant of, be unfamiliar with; to mistake, misunderstand; to ignore, disregard, take no notice of

ignosc·ens -entis adj forgiving

ig·noscō -noscĕre -nōvī -nōtum vt (with dat of person and acc of the offense) to pardon, forgive, excuse (someone a fault); vi (with dat) to pardon, forgive, excuse

ignōt·us -a -um adj unknown, unfamiliar, strange; inglorious; unnoticed; low-born, ignoble; vulgar; ignorant

īl·ex -ĭcis f holm oak

Īlĭ·a -ae f Rhea Silvia (mother of Romulus and Remus)

īl·ia -ĭum n pl guts, intestines; groin, belly

Īlĭăc·us -a -um adj Trojan

Īlĭ·as -ădis f Iliad; Trojan woman

īlicet adv (ancient form for adjourning an assembly) let us go; all is lost, kaput; at once, immediately, instantly

īlicō adv on the spot, right then and there; immediately

īlign·us or **īligně·us -a -um** adj of holm oak, oak

Īl·ios -ī or **-ī** f Troy

Īlithyi·a -ae f goddess who aided women in childbirth

Īl·ium -ī or **-ĭ** or **Īlĭ·on -ī** n Troy

Īlĭ·us -a -um adj Trojan

illa adv that way

ill·a -īus adj fem that; that famous; pron that one; she

illabefact·us -a -um adj unbroken, uninterrupted

il·lābor -lābī -lapsus sum vi to flow; to sink, fall in, cave in; to slip; (with dat or with ad or in + acc) to flow into, enter into, penetrate

illabōr·ō -āre vi (with dat) to work at, work on

illāc adv that way

illacessīt·us -a -um adj unprovoked

illacrimābĭl·is -e adj unlamented; unwept; inexorable

illacrĭm·ō -āre or **illacrĭm·or -ārī -ātus sum** vi (with dat) to cry over

ill·aec (acc: -anc; abl: -āc) adj fem that; pron she

illaes·us -a -um adj unhurt, unharmed

illaetābĭl·is -e adj sad, melancholy

illapsus pp of illabor

illaquě·ō -āre vt to trap

illātus pp of infero

illaudāt·us -a -um adj without fame, obscure; detestable

ill·e -īus adj masc that; that famous; the former; **ille aut ille** this or that, such and such; *pron* that one; he; the former one

illecebr·a -ae *f* attraction, allurement

illecebrōs·us -a -um *adj* alluring, seductive

illect·us -a -um *adj* unread

illect·us -ūs *m* allurement

illepidē *adv* inelegantly, rudely, impolitely

illepid·us -a -um *adj* inelegant, impolite, churlish

ill·ex -icis *m* or *f* lure, decoy

ill·ex -ēgis *adj* lawless

illibāt·us -a -um *adj* undiminished, unimpaired

illiberāl·is -e *adj* ungenerous, stingy

illiberālit·ās -ātis *f* stinginess

ill·ic (*acc:* -unc; *abl:* -ōō) *adj masc* that; *pron* he

illic *adv* there, yonder, in that place; in that matter, therein

il·liciō -licēre -lexī -lectum *vt* to allure, attract, seduce, mislead, lead astray

illicitāt·or -ōris *m* fake bidder (*one who bids at an auction to make others bid higher*)

illicit·us -a -um *adj* unlawful

il·līdō -līdēre -līsī -līsum *vt* to smash to pieces, crush; (with *dat* or with **ad** or **in** + *acc*) to smash (*something*) against

illig·ō -āre *vt* to attach, connect; to tie, bind; to oblige; to impede, hamper

illim *adv* from there

illīm·is -e *adj* unmuddied, clear

illinc *adv* from there; on that side; **hinc illinc** from one side to another

il·linō -linēre -lēvī -litum *vt* to cover; to smear; (with *dat*) to smear or spread (*something*) on

illiquefact·us -a -um *adj* melted

illīsus *pp* of **illīdō**

illiterāt·us -a -um *adj* uneducated, illiterate

illitus *pp* of **illinō**

illō or **illōc** *adv* there, to that place; to that point

illōt·us -a -um *adj* unwashed, dirty

illūc *adv* to that place, in that direction; to that person, to him, to her; to that matter; to that point

ill·ūc (*acc:* -ūc; *abl:* -ōō) *adj neut* that; *pron* it

illuc·eō -ēre *vt* to shine on; *vi* to blaze

il·lucescō -lucescēre -luxī *vi* to grow light, dawn, to begin to shine

ill·ud -īus *adj neut* that; the former; *pron* it

il·lūdō -lūdere -lūsī -lūsum *vt* to make fun of, ridicule; to waste, abuse; *vi* (with *dat*) to play around with, do mischief to

illūmināte *adv* clearly

illūmin·ō -āre *vt* to light up, make bright, illuminate; to illustrate

illūsi·ō -ōnis *f* irony

illustr·is -e *adj* bright, clear, bril-

liant; plain, distinct, evident; distinguished, famous, illustrious, noble

illustr·ō -āre *vt* to light up, illuminate; to make clear, clear up, explain, illustrate; to adorn, embellish; to make famous

illūsus *pp* of **illūdo**

illuvi·ēs -ēī *f* inundation; offscouring, filth, dirt

Illyric·us -a -um *adj* Illyrian; *n* Illyria

Illyri·us -a -um *adj & m* Illyrian; *f* Illyria (*country on the E. coast of the Adriatic Sea*)

Īl·us -ī *m* son of Tros, father of Laomedon, and founder of Ilium; Ascanius

imāgināri·us -a -um *adj* imaginary

imāginātiōn·ēs -um *f pl* imaginings

imāgin·or -ārī -ātus sum *vt* to imagine

imāg·ō -inis *f* image, likeness, picture, bust; bust of ancestor; ghost, vision; echo; appearance, semblance, shadow; mental picture, image, conception, thought, idea; figure of speech, simile, metaphor

imbēcillit·ās -ātis *f* weakness, feebleness; helplessness

imbēcillius *adv* more weakly, more faintly

imbēcill·us -a -um *adj* weak, feeble; helpless

imbell·is -e *adj* anti-war, pacifistic; peaceful; unfit for war, soft, cowardly; peaceful, quiet

imb·er -ris *m* rain, shower, rain storm; rain cloud; water; stream of tears; shower (*of gold, spears, etc.*)

imberb·is -e or **imberb·us -a -um** *adj* beardless

im·bibō -bibere -bibī *vt* to imbibe, drink in; to resolve on; **animo imbibere** to conceive, form (*e.g., an opinion*)

imbr·ex -icis *f* tile

imbric·us -a -um *adj* rainy

imbrif·er -ēra -ērum *adj* rainy

im·buō -buere -buī -būtum *vt* to wet, soak, saturate; to stain, taint, infect, imbue, fill, steep; to instruct, train, educate

imitābil·is -e *adj* imitable

imitām·en -inis *n* imitation; *n pl* likeness, image

imitāment·a -ōrum *n pl* pretense

imitāti·ō -ōnis *f* imitation; pretense

imitāt·or -ōris *m* or **imitātr·ix -īcis** *f* imitator

imitāt·us -a -um *adj* fictitious, copied

imit·or -ārī -ātus sum *vt* to imitate, copy, portray; to ape

immad·escō -escere -uī *vi* to become wet

immāne *adv* savagely

immān·is -e *adj* huge, enormous, monstrous; inhuman, savage, monstrous

immānit·ās -ātis *f* vastness, enor-

mity; savageness, cruelty, mon-
strousness, barbarity

immansuēt·us -a -um *adj* wild,
savage

immātūrit·ās -ātis *f* overanxious-
ness

immātūr·us -a -um *adj* immature,
unripe, premature

immedicābil·is -e *adj* incurable

immĕm·or -ŏris *adj* forgetful, forgetting; negligent

immemorābil·is -e *adj* not worth
mentioning; untold

immemorāt·a -ōrum *n pl* novelties

immensit·ās -ātis *f* immensity; *f pl*
immense stretches

immens·us -a -um *adj* immense,
unending; *n* infinite space, infinity

immĕr·ens -entis *adj* undeserving,
innocent

im·mergō -mergĕre -mersī -mer-
sum *vt* to immerse, dip, plunge;
(with **in** + *acc*) to dip (*something*)
into; **se immergere** (with **in** +
acc) a to plunge into; **b** to insinuate
oneself into

immeritō *adv* undeservedly, innocently

immerit·us -a -um *adj* undeserving, innocent; undeserved, unmer-
ited; **immerito meo** through no
fault of mine

immersābil·is -e *adj* unsinkable

immersus *pp* of **immergo**

immētāt·us -a -um *adj* unmeasured

immigr·ō -āre *vi* to immigrate;
(with **in** + *acc*) a to move into;
b (fig) to invade

immin·ĕō -ēre *vi* to project, stick
out; to be near, be imminent, be
near at hand; to threaten, menace;
(with *dat*) a to jut out over; **b** to
look out over, overlook (*a view*); **c**
to hover over, loom over, threaten;
(with *dat* or **in** + *acc*) to be intent
on, be eager for

immin·ŭō -ŭĕre -ŭī -ūtum *vt* to
lessen, curtail; to weaken, impair;
to infringe upon, encroach upon,
violate, subvert, destroy

imminūtī·ō -ōnis *f* lessening; mutilation; understatement

im·miscĕō -miscēre -miscŭī
-mixtum *vt* to mix in, intermix,
blend; (fig) to mix up, confound;
immisceri or **se immiscere** (with
dat) a to join, join in with, mingle
with, get lost in (*e.g., a crowd*); **b**
to blend with, disappear in (*e.g.,
night, cloud, etc.*); **manūs manibus immiscere** (of boxers) to mix
it up

immiserābil·is -e *adj* unpitied

immisericordĭter *adv* unmercifully

immisericor·s -dis *adj* merciless,
pitiless

immissi·ō -ōnis *f* letting grow, letting alone

immissus *pp* of **immitto**

immīt·is -e *adj* unripe, sour, green;
rude, harsh, stern, severe; pitiless,
inexorable

im·mittō -mittĕre -mīsī -missum
vt to insert; to let in, let go in, admit; let go of, let drop; to let go,
let fly, launch; to set on, incite,
egg on; **immitti** or **se immittere**
(with *dat* or **in** + *acc*) a to plunge
or dive into; **b** to rush against, attack; **in terram immittere** to
ground

immixtus *pp* of **immisceo**

immo or **immō** *adv* (in contradiction or correction of preceding
words) no, on the contrary, or
rather; (in confirmation of preceding words) quite so, yes indeed;
immo vero yes and in fact

immōbil·is -e *adj* motionless, unshaken; immovable; clumsy

immoderātē *adv* without limit; immoderately, extravagantly

immoderātī·ō -ōnis *f* lack of moderation, excess

immoderāt·us -a -um *adj* unmeasured, limitless; immoderate, uncontrolled, excessive

immodestē *adv* immoderately,
shamelessly

immodestĭ·a -ae *f* excesses; insubordination

immodest·us -a -um *adj* immoderate, uncontrolled

immodicē *adv* excessively

immodic·us -a -um *adj* huge, enormous; immoderate, excessive; (with
genit or *abl*) given to, excessive in

immodulāt·us -a -um *adj* unrhythmical

immolātĭ·ō -ōnis *f* sacrifice

immolāt·or -ōris *m* sacrificer

immōlīt·us -a -um *adj* constructed,
erected; *n pl* buildings

immōl·ō or **inmōl·ō** -āre *vt* to immolate, sacrifice, offer

im·morior -mŏrī -mortŭus sum
vi (with *dat*) to die in, die upon;
(fig) to get sick over

immŏr·or -ārī -ātus sum *vi* (with
dat) to dwell upon

immors·us -a -um *adj* bitten into;
excited

immortāl·is -e *adj* immortal

immortālit·ās -ātis *f* immortality

immortālĭter *adv* infinitely

immortŭus *pp* of **immorior**

immōt·us -a -um *adj* unmoved, immovable; unshaken, undisturbed,
steadfast

immūg·ĭō -īre -īvī or -ĭī -ītum *vi*
to bellow, roar

immulg·ĕō -ēre *vt* to milk

immundit·a -ae *f* dirtiness, filth

immund·us -a -um *adj* dirty, filthy,
foul

immūn·ĭō -īre -īvī *vt* to reinforce,
fortify

immūn·is -e *adj* without duty or office; tax-exempt, free, exempt;
pure, innocent; (with *abl* or **ab** +
abl) free from, exempt from; (with
genit) free of, free from, devoid of,
without

immūnit·ās -ātis *f* immunity, exemption, exemption from taxes

immūnit·us -a -um *adj* unfortified, undefended; unpaved (*street*)

immurmur·ō -āre *vi* to grumble; (with *dat*) (of the wind) to whisper among

immūtābil·is -e *adj* immutable, unchangeable

immūtābilit·ās -ātis *f* immutability

immūtātī·ō -ōnis *f* exchange, substitution; metonymy

immūtāt·us -a -um *adj* unchanged

immūt·ō -āre *vt* to change, alter; to substitute

impācāt·us -a -um *adj* restless; aggressive

impactus *pp* of **impingo**

impall·escō -escēre -uī *vi* (with *abl*) to turn pale at

im·pār -āris *adj* uneven, odd (*numbers*); uneven (*in size or length*); not matching, unlike (*in color or appearance*); unequal; unfair; ill-matched; uneven, crooked; (with *dat*) not a match for, inferior to, unable to cope with

imparāt·us -a -um *adj* unprepared

impariter *adv* unequally

impast·us -a -um *adj* unfed, hungry

impati·ens -entis *adj* impatient; (with *genit*) unable to stand, endure, tolerate

impatienter *adv* impatiently; intolerably

impatienti·a -ae *f* impatience; (with *genit*) inability to stand or endure

impavidē *adv* fearlessly

impavid·us -a -um *adj* fearless, dauntless

impedīment·um -ī *n* impediment, hindrance; difficulty; *n pl* baggage, luggage; mule train

imped·iō -īre -īvī or **-iī -ītum** *vt* to entangle; to hamper, hinder; to entwine, encircle; to clasp, embrace; to block up (*road*); to hinder, prevent; to embarrass; **impedīre** (with **ne, quin,** or **quominus**) to prevent (*someone*) from

impedītī·ō -ōnis *f* obstacle, obstruction

impedīt·us -a -um *adj* hampered; obstructed, blocked; difficult, intricate; impassable; busy, occupied

im·pellō -pellěre -pŭlī -pulsum *vt* to strike against, strike, reach; to push, drive, drive forward, impel, propel; to urge, persuade, stimulate, induce; to force, compel; to put to rout; to swell (*sails*)

impend·eō -ēre *vi* to be near, be at hand, be imminent, threaten; (with *dat*) to hang over; (with *dat* or **in** + *acc*) to hover or loom over, threaten

impendiōs·us -a -um *adj* extravagant

impend·ium -iī or **-ī** *n* expense, cost, outlay; interest (*paid out*); loss

im·pendō -penděre -pendī -pen- **sum** *vt* to weigh out, pay out; to expend, devote, apply, employ; (with **in** + *acc*) a to spend (*money*) on; **b** to expend (*effort*) on, pay (*attention*)

impenetrābil·is -e *adj* impenetrable

impens·a -ae *f* expense, cost, outlay; waste; contribution; **meis impensis** at my expense

impensē *adv* at a high cost, expensively; with great effort

impens·us -a -um *pp* of **impendo**; *adj* high, costly, expensive; strong, vehement, earnest; *n* high price

impěr·ans -antis *m* master, ruler, conqueror

imperāt·or -ōris *m* commander, general; commander in chief; emperor; director, master, ruler, leader

imperātōri·us -a -um *adj* of a general, general's; imperial

imperātr·ix -īcis *f* controller, mistress

imperāt·um -ī *n* command, order

impercept·us -a -um *adj* unperceived, unknown

impercuss·us -a -um *adj* noiseless

imperdīt·us -a -um *adj* unscathed

imperfect·us -a -um *adj* unfinished, imperfect

imperfoss·us -a -um *adj* unpierced, not stabbed

imperiōs·us -a -um *adj* imperial; magisterial; tyrannical, overbearing, domineering, imperious

imperītē *adv* unskillfully, clumsily, ignorantly

imperīti·a -ae *f* inexperience, awkwardness, ignorance

imperīt·ō -āre *vt & vi* to command, rule, govern

imperīt·us -a -um *adj* inexperienced, unfamiliar, ignorant, unskilled; (with *genit*) inexperienced in, unacquainted with, ignorant of

imper·ium -iī or **-ī** *n* command, order; right to command; exercise of authority; military commission, supreme command; mastery, sovereignty; realm, empire, dominion, supremacy, authority; public office, magistracy; term of office

imperjūrāt·us -a -um *adj* sacrosanct, inviolable

impermiss·us -a -um *adj* forbidden, unlawful

impěr·ō -āre *vt* to requisition, give orders for, order, demand; (with *acc* of thing demanded and *dat* of source demanded from) to demand (*e.g., hostages*) from; *vi* to be in command, rule, be master; (with *dat*) to give orders to, order, command, govern, master

imperterrit·us -a -um *adj* undaunted, unterrified

impert·iō -īre *vt* (with *dat*) to impart, communicate, bestow, assign, direct (*something*) to, share (*something*) with; (with *acc* of person and *abl* of thing) to present (*someone*) with

imperturbāt·us -a -um *adj* unperturbed, unruffled

impervi·us -a -um *adj* impassable; (with *dat*) impervious to

impetibil·is -e *adj* intolerable

impět·ō -ěre *vt* to make for; to attack

impetrābil·is -e *adj* obtainable; successful

impetrātī·ō -ōnis *f* obtaining, procurement

impetr·ĭō -īre *vt* to try to obtain through favorable omens

impětr·ō -āre *vt* to obtain, procure (*by asking*); to achieve, accomplish, bring to pass

impět·us -ūs *m* attack, assault; rush; impetus, impetuosity, vehemence, vigor, violence, fury, force; impulse, passion

impex·us -a -um *adj* uncombed; unpolished

impiē *adv* wickedly

impiět·ās -ātis *f* impiety, irreverence; disloyalty; treason

impǐg·er -ra -rum *adj* diligent, active, energetic

impigrē *adv* energetically, actively, quickly

impigrǐt·ās -ātis *f* energy, activity

im·pingō -pingěre -pēgī -pactum *vt* (with *dat* or in + *acc*) **a** to fasten to; **b** to pin against, force against, dash against; **c** to press or force (*something*) on; **d** to fling at

impǐ·ō -āre *vt* to make irreverent

impǐ·us -a -um *adj* impious, irreverent; disobedient, undutiful; disloyal, unpatriotic; wicked, unscrupulous, shameless

implācābil·is -e *adj* implacable, unappeasable

implācāt·us -a -um *adj* unappeased, unsatisfied

implācĭd·us -a -um *adj* fierce, savage

impl·ěō -ēre -ēvī -ētum *vt* to fill up; to satisfy; to fatten; to impregnate, make pregnant; to enrich; to cover with writing, fill up (*a book*); to discharge, fulfill, execute, implement; to complete, finish, end; to spend (*time*)

implex·us -a -um *adj* enfolded, entwined; involved

implicātī·ō -ōnis *f* entanglement; incorporation; embarrassment

implicāt·us -a -um *adj* entangled, involved, complicated, confused

implicīsc·or -ī *vi* to become confused

implicǐtē *adv* intricately

implicǐtus *pp* of **implico**; *adj* confused, confounded; **implicitus morbo** disabled by sickness, sick

implǐc·ō -āre -āvī -ātum or **-āre -ŭī -ĭtum** *vt* to entangle, involve, enfold, envelop; to embrace, clasp, grasp; to connect, unite, join; to involve, implicate, engage; to embarrass; **se dextrae implicare** to embrace, shake hands

implōrātī·ō -ōnis *f* begging, imploring

implōr·ō -āre *vt* to implore, appeal to, call upon for aid; (with double *acc*) to beg (*someone*) for; (with **ab** + *abl*) to ask for (*something*) from

implūm·is -e *adj* without feathers, unfledged

impl·ŭō -ŭěre -ŭī -ūtum *vi* (with *dat*) to rain on

impluviāt·us -a -um *adj* shaped like an impluvium, square

impluv·ium -ī or **-ī** *n* skylight, impluvium (*opening in the roof of the atrium of the Roman house to get rid of smoke and let in light*); built-in basin in the atrium to catch the rain water; uncovered space in the atrium

impolītē *adv* simply, without fancy words

impolīt·us -a -um *adj* unpolished, rough; unrefined, inelegant; unfinished

impollūt·us -a -um *adj* unsullied

im·pōnō -pōněre -posŭī -positum or **-postum** *vt* to impose; to establish, introduce; to place, set; to inflict, impose, dictate; to assign; to apply, give; to impose, assess, exact; to put (*someone*) in charge; (with *dat*, with in + *acc*, in + *abl*, or **supra** + *acc*) to place, put, set, lay (*someone or something*) on or in; (with *dat*) **a** to impose (*taxes, etc.*) upon; **b** to put (*someone*) in charge of; *vi* (with *dat*) to impose upon, trick, cheat

import·ō -āre *vt* to bring in, import; to introduce

importūnǐt·ās -ātis *f* importunity, rudeness, insolence; unfitness

importūn·us -a -um *adj* inconvenient, unsuitable; troublesome, annoying; lacking consideration for others, rude, ruthless, churlish; stormy; ill-omened

importuōs·us -a -um *adj* without a harbor

imp·os -ōtis *adj* without control; (with *genit*) without control of

imposǐtus *pp* of **impono**

impossibǐl·is -e *adj* impossible

impostus *pp* of **impono**

impŏt·ens -entis *adj* impotent, powerless; having no control of oneself, wild, uncontrollable, impetuous, violent

impotenter *adv* impotently, weakly

impotentǐ·a -ae *f* weakness, helplessness; lack of self-control, violence, fury, passion

impraesentiārum *adv* for the present, under present circumstances

imprans·us -a -um *adj* without breakfast, fasting

imprecātī·ō -ōnis *f* imprecation, curse

imprěc·or -ārī -ātus sum *vt* to call down (*a curse*); to invoke

impressǐ·ō -ōnis *f* pressure; assault, attack, charge; rhythmical beat;

emphasis; impression (*on the mind*)

impressus *pp of* **imprimo**

imprimis or **in primis** *adv* in the first place, chiefly, especially

im·primō -primĕre -pressī -pressum *vt* to press down; to impress, imprint, stamp; (*fig*) to impress, engrave, mark

improbātī·ō -ōnis *f* disapprobation, blame

improbē *adv* badly, wickedly, wrongfully; recklessly; persistently

improbĭt·ās -ātis *f* wickedness, depravity; roguishness

improb·ō -āre *vt* disapprove, condemn, blame, reject

improbŭl·us -a -um *adj* naughty

improb·us -a -um *adj* below standard, poor, inferior, bad, shameless; rebellious, unruly; restless, indomitable, self-willed; cruel, merciless; persistent

imprōcēr·us -a -um *adj* undersized

imprōdict·us -a -um *adj* not postponed

imprompt·us -a -um *adj* slow

improperāt·us -a -um *adj* slow, deliberate

impropri·us -a -um *adj* unsuitable

imprōsp·er -ĕra -ĕrum *adj* unfortunate

imprōspĕrē *adv* unfortunately

imprōvīdē *adv* without foresight, thoughtlessly

imprōvĭd·us -a -um *adj* not foreseeing, not anticipating; (*with genit*) indifferent to

imprōvīs·us -a -um *adj* unexpected; **de imprōvīso, ex imprōvīso** or **imprōviso** unexpectedly; *n pl* emergencies

imprūd·ens -entis *adj* not foreseeing, not anticipating, unsuspecting, off one's guard; inconsiderate; (*with genit*) unaware of, ignorant of, heedless of, not experienced in

imprūdenter *adv* without foresight, thoughtlessly, inconsiderately, imprudently

imprūdenti·a -ae *f* thoughtlessness; ignorance, imprudence

impūb·ēs -ĕris or **-is** *adj* youthful, young; innocent, chaste, celibate, virgin

impūd·ens -entis *adj* shameless

impūdenter *adv* shamelessly

impūdenti·a -ae *f* shamelessness

impūdĭciti·a -ae *f* immodesty, lewdness, shamelessness

impūdīc·us -a -um *adj* immodest, lewd, shameless

impugnātĭ·ō -ōnis *f* assault, attack

impugn·ō -āre *vt* to assault, attack; (*fig*) to impugn

impulsĭ·ō -ōnis *f* pressure; impulse

impuls·or -ōris *m* instigator

impulsus *pp of* **impello**

impuls·us -ūs *m* push, pressure, impulse, shock; instigation, incitement

impūne or **inpūne** *adv* with impunity, unpunished, scot-free; safely,

unscathed

impūnĭt·ās -ātis *f* impunity

impūnītē *adv* with impunity

impūnīt·us -a -um *adj* unpunished; unrestrained

impūrē *adv* impurely

impūrĭt·ās -ātis *f* impurity

impūr·us -a -um *adj* impure, unclean, filthy; (morally) impure, filthy, vile

imputāt·us -a -um *adj* unpruned, untrimmed

imput·ō -āre *vt* to charge to someone's account, enter in an account; (with *dat*) to charge to, ascribe to, give credit for (*something*) to, put the blame for (*something*) on

imŭl·us -a -um *adj* cute little

īm·us -a -um *adj* deepest, lowest; last; the bottom of, the foot of, the tip of; *n* bottom, depth; **ab imo** utterly; **ab imo ad summum** from top to bottom; **ex imo** utterly, completely; *n pl* lower world

in *prep* (with *abl*) in, on, upon, among, at; before; under; during, within, in, at, in the course of, on the point of, in case of, in relation to; subject to, affected by, engaged in, involved in; (with *acc*) into, up to, towards; till, to, for; in relation to, about, respecting, against; for, with a view to, according to, after

inaccess·us -a -um *adj* inaccessible

inac·escō -escĕre -ŭī *vi* to turn sour

Inachĭd·ēs -ae *m* descendant of Inachus; Perseus; Epaphus

Inăch·is -ĭdis *f* female descendant of Inachus (*esp.* Io)

Inăch·us or **Inăch·os -ī** *m* first king or Argos and father of Io

inadsc- = **inasc-**

inadt- = **inatt-**

inadust·us -a -um *adj* unburned

inaedĭfĭc·ō -āre *vt* to build on, build as an addition, erect, construct; to wall up, barricade; (with *in + abl*) to build (*something*) on top of

inaequābĭl·is -e *adj* uneven

inaequābĭlĭter *adv* unevenly, unequally

inaequāl·is -e *adj* uneven, unequal; unlike, changeable, inconstant

inaequālĭt·ās -ātis *f* unevenness

inaequālĭter *adv* unevenly

inaequāt·us -a -um *adj* unequal

inaequ·ō -āre *vt* to level off

inaestĭmābĭl·is -e *adj* inestimable; invaluable; valueless

inaestŭ·ō -āre *vi* **bilis inaestuat** anger flares up

inaffectāt·us -a -um *adj* unaffected, natural

inamābĭl·is -e *adj* hateful, revolting

inamārescō -ĕre *vi* to become bitter

inambĭtiōs·us -um *adj* unambitious

inambulātĭ·ō -ōnis *f* walking about, strutting about

inambŭl·ō -āre vi to walk up and down

inamoen·us -a -um adj unpleasant

ināni·ae -ārum f pl emptiness

inānilogist·a -ae m chatterbox

inānīment·um -ī n empty space

inānim·us -a -um adj inanimate

inān·e -is n empty space, vacuum; emptiness; worthlessness

inān·is -e adj empty, void; deserted, abandoned, unoccupied; hollow; worthless, idle; lifeless, unsubstantial; penniless, poor; unprofitable; groundless, unfounded

inānǐt·ās -ātis f empty space, emptiness; uselessness, worthlessness

inānǐter adv uselessly, vainly

inarāt·us -a -um adj untilled, fallow

in·ardescō -ardescĕre -arsī vi to catch fire, burn, glow

ināresc·ō -ĕre vi to become dry, dry up

inascens·us -a -um adj not climbed

inassuēt·us -a -um adj unaccustomed

inattenuāt·us -a -um adj undiminished; unappeased

inaud·ax -ācis adj timid, cowed

inaud·ǐō -īre -īvī or -ǐī -ǐtum vt to hear, learn

inaudīt·us -a -um adj unheard-of, unusual; without a hearing in court

inaugurātō adv after taking the auspices

inaugŭr·ō -āre vt to inaugurate, consecrate, install; vi to take the auspices

inaurāt·us -a -um adj gilded, gilt

inaur·ēs -ǐum f pl earrings

inaur·ō -āre vt to goldplate, gild; to line the pockets of (someone) with gold, to make rich

inauspicātō adv without consulting the auspices

inauspicāt·us -a -um adj undertaken without auspices; unlucky

inaus·us -a -um adj unattempted

inb- = imb-

inbīt·ō -ĕre vt enter

incaedŭ·us -a -um adj uncut

incal·escō -escĕre -ŭī vi to grow warm or hot; to get excited

incalfac·ǐō -ĕre vt to warm, heat

incallǐdē adv unskillfully

incallǐd·us -a -um adj unskillful; stupid, simple, clumsy

incand·escō -escĕre -ŭī vi to become white; to get white-hot

incān·escō -escĕre -ŭī vi to get grey

incantāt·us -a -um adj enchanted

incān·us -a -um adj grown grey

incassum adv in vain

incastīgāt·us -a -um adj unscolded, unpunished

incautē adv incautiously, recklessly

incaut·us -a -um adj incautious, inconsiderate, thoughtless, reckless; unforeseen, unexpected; unguarded

in·cēdō -cēdĕre -cessī -cessum vi to go, step, move, walk, stalk; to

proceed, go forward; to come along, happen, occur, appear, arrive; to advance, go on

incelebrāt·us -a -um adj unheralded

incēnāt·us -a -um adj supperless

incendiār·ius -ǐī or -ī m agitator

incend·ium -ǐī or -ī fire; heat

in·cendō -cendĕre -cendī -censum vt to light, set on fire, burn; to light up, make bright; (fig) to inflame, fire, excite, enrage

incēn·is -e adj dinnerless, without dinner

incensǐ·ō -ōnis f burning

incensus pp of incendo

incens·us -a -um adj not registered (with the censor)

inceptǐ·ō -ōnis f beginning; undertaking

incept·ō -āre vt to begin; to undertake

incept·or -ōris m beginner, originator

incept·us -a -um pp of incipio; n beginning; undertaking, attempt, enterprise; subject, theme

in·cernō -cernĕre -crēvī -crētum vt to sift

incēr·ō -āre vt to wax, cover with wax

incertō adv not for certain

incert·ō -āre vt to render doubtful, make uncertain

incert·us -a -um adj uncertain, vague, obscure; doubtful, dubious; unsure, hesitant; n uncertainty, insecurity; contingency; in incertum for an indefinite time

incess·ō -ĕre -īvī vt to fall upon, assault, reproach, accuse, attack; (fig) to attack

incess·us -ūs m walk, gait, pace; tread, trampling; invasion, attack

incestē adv impurely, sinfully; indecently

incest·ō -āre vt to pollute, defile; to violate (a girl)

incest·us -a -um adj polluted, defiled, unclean, impure, sinful; lewd, unchaste, incestuous

incest·us -ūs m indecency, incest

in·cǐdō -cǐdĕre -cǐdī -cāsum vi to happen, occur; (with in or ad + acc) to fall into, fall upon; (with in + acc) a to come upon unexpectedly, fall in with; b to attack; (with dat or in + acc) a to occur to (mentally); b to fall on (a certain day); c to befall; d to agree with

in·cǐdō -cǐdĕre -cǐdī -cīsum vt to carve, engrave, inscribe; to cut, sever; (fig) to cut into, cut short, put an end to, break off, interrupt

incīl·e -is n ditch, trench

in·cingō -cingĕre -cinxī -cinctum vt to drape; to wreathe; to invest, surround

incǐn·ō -ĕre vt to sing; to play

incipessō see incipisso

in·cipǐō -cipĕre -cēpī -ceptum vt & vi to begin, start

incipiss·ō -ĕre *vt* to begin

incīsē or incīsim *adv* in short phrases

incisi·ō -ōnis *f* or incīs·um -ī *n* clause

incīsus *pp* of incido

incitāment·um -ī *n* incitement, incentive

incitātī·ō -ōnis *f* inciting, rousing; speed

incitātius *adv* rather impetuously

incitāt·us -a -um *adj* rapid, speedy; equo incitato at full gallop

incit·ō -āre *vt* to incite, urge on, spur on, drive on; to stimulate; to inspire; to stir up, arouse; to increase, augment; currentem incitare (fig) to spur a willing horse; se incitare to rush

incit·us -a -um *adj* rapid, swift; immovable; ad incita redigere to bring to a standstill

inclāmit·ō -āre *vt* to cry out against, abuse

inclām·ō -āre *vt* to shout at, scold, chide; *vi* to yell

inclār·escō -escĕre -ŭī *vi* to become famous

inclēm·ens -entis *adj* inclement, harsh, unmerciful

inclēmenter *adv* harshly, severely

inclēmentĭ·a -ae *f* harshness, severity, rigor

inclīnātĭ·ō -ōnis *f* leaning; inclination, tendency, bias; change; inflection

inclīnāt·us -a -um *adj* inclined, prone; sinking; low, deep

inclīn·ō -āre *vt* to bend, turn, to turn back, drive back, repulse; (fig) to divert, shift (*e.g., blame*); to change, alter; inclinari (mil) to fall back, give way; inclinari or se inclinare to lean, bend, turn; to change (*esp. for the worse*); *vi* to bend, turn, lean, dip, sink, (mil) to fall back, give way; (fig) to change, deteriorate; (fig) to change for the better

inclit·us -a -um *adj* famous

in·clūdō -clūdĕre -clūsī -clūsum *vt* to shut in, confine, lock up; to include, insert; to block, obstruct, shut off, stop up; (fig) to include, embrace, comprehend; to restrain, control; to close, end (*e.g., day*)

inclūsĭ·ō -ōnis *f* locking up, confinement

inclŭt·us or inclĭt·us -a -um *adj* famous

incoct·us -a -um *pp* of incoquo; *adj* uncooked, raw

incōgitābil·is -e *adj* thoughtless, inconsiderate

incōgit·ans -antis *adj* unthinking, thoughtless

incōgitantĭ·a -ae *f* thoughtlessness

incōgitāt·us -a -um *adj* thoughtless, inconsiderate

incōgit·ō -āre *vt* to think up

incognit·us -a -um *adj* not investigated; unknown, unrecognized,

unidentified; unparalleled

incohāt·us -a -um *adj* unfinished

incŏh·ō -āre *vt* to begin, start

incŏl·a -ae *m & f* inhabitant, resident

incŏl·ō -ĕre -ŭī *vt* to live in, inhabit, occupy; *vi* to live, reside

incolŭm·is -e *adj* unharmed, safe and sound, unscathed, alive; (with *abl*) safe from

incolumit·ās -ātis *f* safety

incomitāt·us -a -um *adj* unaccompanied

incommendāt·us -a -um *adj* unprotected

incommŏdē *adv* at the wrong time; inconveniently; unfortunately

incommodestic·us -a -um *adj* (coll) ill-timed, inconvenient

incommŏdĭt·ās -ātis *f* inconvenience; unsuitableness; disadvantage

incommŏd·ō -āre *vi* (with *dat*) to be inconvenient to, to be annoying to, to inconvenience

incommŏd·us -a -um *adj* inconvenient, annoying; *n* inconvenience; trouble, setback, disaster

incommūtābil·is -e *adj* unchangeable

incomparābil·is -e *adj* unequaled, incomparable

incompert·us -a -um *adj* unknown, forgotten

incompositē *adv* in disorder

incomposĭt·us -a -um *adj* disordered, confused, unstudied, uncouth; irregular

incomprehensĭbil·is -e *adj* incomprehensible

incompt·us -a -um *adj* unkempt, messy; primitive, rude (*discourse*)

inconcess·us -a -um *adj* forbidden, unlawful

inconcĭlĭ·ō -āre *vt* to deceive, trick, to rob, fleece

inconcinn·us -a -um *adj* clumsy, awkward; absurd

inconcuss·us -a -um *adj* unshaken

incondītē *adv* confusedly

incondĭt·us -a -um *adj* unorganized, disorderly, confused, irregular; rough, undeveloped (*style*); raw (*jokes*)

inconsīderātē *adv* thoughtlessly

inconsīderāt·us -a -um *adj* thoughtless

inconsōlābĭl·is -e *adj* incurable

inconst·ans -antis *adj* inconsistent, fickle, shifty

inconstanter *adv* inconsistently

inconstantĭ·a -ae *f* inconsistency, fickleness

inconsultē *adv* indiscreetly

inconsult·us -a -um *adj* indiscreet, ill-advised, imprudent; not consulted

inconsult·us -ūs *m* inconsultu meo without consulting me

inconsumpt·us -a -um *adj* unconsumed

incontāmĭnāt·us -a -um *adj* untainted

incontent·us -a -um *adj* loose, untuned (*string*)

incontin·ens -entis *adj* incontinent

incontinenter *adv* without self-control, incontinently

incontinentï·a -ae *f* lack of self-control

inconveni·ens -entis *adj* unsuitable, dissimilar

in·cóquõ -coquère -coxï -coctum *vt* to boil, cook; to dye

incorrect·us -a -um *adj* uncorrected, unrevised

incorruptê *adv* justly, fairly

incorrupt·us -a -um *adj* untainted; uncorrupted, unspoiled; genuine, pure

increbr·escô or **increb·escô -escère -ûï** *vi* to grow, rise, increase, spread

incrêdibil·is -e *adj* incredible

incredibiliter *adv* incredibly

incrêdûl·us -a -um *adj* incredulous

increment·um -ï *n* growth, increase; increment, addition; addition to the family, offspring

increpitô -āre *vt* to scold, rebuke

incrêp·ô -āre -ûï (or **-āvï**) **-ïtum** (or **-ātum**) *vt* to cause to make noise; to rattle; (*of Jupiter*) to thunder at; to scold, rebuke; *vi* to make a noise, to rustle, rattle, clatter, clash; to speak angrily

incr·escô -escère -êvï *vi* to grow, increase; (with *dat* or *abl*) to grow in or upon

incrētus *pp* of **incerno**

incruentāt·us -a -um *adj* unbloodied

incruent·us -a -um *adj* bloodless, without bloodshed

incrustô -āre *vt* to cover with a coat, encrust

incûb·ô -āre -ûï -ïtum *vi* (with *dat*) a to lie in or upon; b to lean on; c to brood over; d to watch jealously over

inculcô -āre *vt* to impress, inculcate; (with *dat*) to force (*something*) upon

inculpāt·us -a -um *adj* blameless

incultê *adv* uncouthly, roughly

incult·us -a -um *adj* untilled, uncultivated; neglected, slovenly; rough, uneducated, uncivilized; *n pl* desert, wilderness

incult·us -ûs *m* neglect; dirt, squalor

in·cumbô -cumbère -cubûï -cubïtum *vi* (with *dat* or **in** + *acc*) a to lean on or against; b to lie down on (*a couch, bed*); c to bend to (*the oars*); d to light on, fall on; e (*fig*) to press upon, burden, oppress, weigh down; f to apply onself to, take pains with, pay attention to; (with **ad** or **in** + *acc*) to be inclined towards, lean towards

incûnābûl·a -ôrum *n pl* baby clothes, swaddling clothes; (*fig*) cra-dle, infancy, birthplace, source, origin

incûrāt·us -a -um *adj* neglected; uncured

incûri·a -ae *f* carelessness, negligence

incûriôsê *adv* carelessly

incûriôs·us -a -um *adj* careless, unconcerned, indifferent; neglected

in·currô -currère -currï or -cucurrï -cursum *vt* to attack; *vi* (with *dat* or **in** + *acc*) a to run into, rush at, charge, attack, invade; b to extend to; c to meet, run into; d to fall on, coincide with

incursï·ô -ônis *f* incursion, invasion, raid; assault, attack, collision

incurs·ô -āre *vt* to assault, attack; to invade; *vi* (with *dat* or **in** + *acc*) a to assault, attack; b to run into, bump against; c to strike, meet (*e.g., the eyes*); d to affect, touch, move

incurs·us -ûs *m* assault, attack; invasion; impulse

incurv·ô -āre *vt* to bend, curve

incurv·us -a -um *adj* bent, crooked

inc·ûs -ûdis *f* anvil

incûsātï·ô -ônis *f* accusation

incûs·ô -āre *vt* to blame, find fault with, accuse

incuss·us -ûs *m* shock

incussus *pp* of **incutio**

incustôdīt·us -a -um *adj* unguarded; unconcealed; imprudent

incûs·us -a -um *adj* forged; **lapis incusus** indented millstone

in·cutiô -cutère -cussï -cussum *vt* to throw; to produce; (with *dat* or **in** + *acc*) to strike (*something*) on or against; (with *dat*) a to strike into, instill in; b to throw at, to fling upon; **metum incutere** (with *dat*) to inspire fear in, strike fear in; **scipionem in caput alicujus incutere** to beat someone over the head with a stick

indāgātï·ô -ônis *f* investigation, search

indāgāt·or -ôris *m* or **indāgātr·ix -ïcis** *f* investigator

indāg·ô -āre *vt* to track down, hunt; (*fig*) to track down, investigate, explore

indāg·ô -ïnis *f* dragnet; **indagine agere** to ferret out

indaudiô see **inaudio**

inde *adv* from there; from that source, therefrom; from that time on, after that, thereafter; then; from that cause

indêbit·us -a -um *adj* not owed, not due

indêc·ens -entis *adj* unbecoming, improper, indecent

indecenter *adv* improperly, indecently

indec·eô -êre *vt* to be improper for

indeclïnāt·us -a -um *adj* unchanged, constant

indêc·or -ôris or **indecōr·is -e** *adj* disgraceful, dishonorable, cowardly

indecōrē *adv* indecently, improperly

indecŏr·ō -āre *vt* to disgrace

indecōr·us -a -um *adj* unsightly, improper, disgraceful

indēfens·us -a -um *adj* undefended

indēfess·us -a -um *adj* tireless; not tired

indēflēt·us -a -um *adj* unwept

indēject·us -a -um *adj* undemolished

indēlēbĭl·is -e *adj* indestructible, indelible

indēlībāt·us -a -um *adj* undiminished

indemnāt·us -a -um *adj* unconvicted

indeplōrāt·us -a -um *adj* unwept

indeprens·us -a -um *adj* undetected

indeptus *pp of* **indipiscor**

indēsert·us -a -um *adj* unforsaken

indespect·us -a -um *adj* unfathomable

indestrict·us -a -um *adj* unscathed

indētons·us -a -um *adj* unshorn

indēvītāt·us -a -um *adj* unerring (*e.g., arrow*)

ind·ex -ĭcis *m* index, sign, mark, indication, proof; title (*of book*); informer, spy; index finger

Indĭ·a -ae *f* India

indicātĭ·ō -ōnis *f* value; price

indīc·ens -entis *adj* not speaking; **me indicente** without a word from me

indĭc·ĭum -ĭī or **-ī** *n* information, disclosure, evidence; indication, proof, permission to give evidence; reward for giving evidence

indĭc·ō -āre *vt* to point out; to reveal, disclose, make known; to betray, inform against, accuse; to put a price on; *vi* to give evidence

in·dīcō -dīcĕre -dīxī -dictum *vt* to proclaim, announce, publish; to summon, convoke; to impose (*a fine*); **bellum indīcere** to declare war; **diem indīcere** to set a date

indict·us -a -um *adj* unsaid; **causā indictā** without a hearing

Indĭc·us -a -um *adj* Indian; *m* Indian; *n* indigo

indĭdem *adv* from the same place; from the same source, from the same thing

indiffĕr·ens -entis *adj* (morally) indifferent, unconcerned, indifferent

indĭgĕn·a -ae *adj masc & fem* native

indĭg·ens -entis *adj* indigent; (with *genit*) in need of

indĭgentĭ·a -ae *f* indigence, want, need; craving

indĭg·ĕō -ēre -ŭī *vi* (with *genit* or *abl*) to need, be in need of, require; (with *genit*) to crave, desire

indĭg·es -ĕtis *adj* indigenous, native; *m* native god; national hero

indĭgest·us -a -um *adj* unarranged, confused

indignābund·us -a -um *adj* indignant, highly indignant

indign·ans -antis *adj* indignant; impatient, reluctant

indignātĭ·ō -ōnis *f* indignation, displeasure; provocation, occasion for indignation; *f pl* expressions of indignation

indignē *adv* unworthily, undeservedly; indignantly

indignĭt·ās -ātis *f* unworthiness; indignation; indignity, shameful treatment; enormity, shamefulness

indign·or -ārī -ātus sum *vt* to be indignant at, displeased at, angry at, offended at

indign·us -a -um *adj* unworthy, undeserving; undeserved; (with *abl*) a unworthy of; b not deserving; c not worth; (with *genit*) unworthy of, undeserving of; **indignum!** shame!

indĭg·us -a -um *adj* (with *genit* or *abl*) in need of, needing

indīlĭg·ens -entis *adj* careless

indīligenter *adv* carelessly

indīligentĭ·a -ae *f* carelessness

ind·ipiscor -ipiscī -eptus sum or **indipisc·ō -ĕre** *vt* to obtain, get; to attain, reach

indirept·us -a -um *adj* unplundered

indiscrēt·us -a -um *adj* closely connected; indiscriminate, undistinguishable; confused

indisertē *adv* without eloquence

indisert·us -a -um *adj* not eloquent; at a loss for words

indisposĭt·us -a -um *adj* confused, disorderly

indissolŭbĭl·is -e *adj* imperishable, indestructible

indistinct·us -a -um *adj* indistinct, obscure; confused

indĭtus *pp of* **indo**

indivĭdŭ·us -a -um *adj* indivisible; inseparable; *n* atom, indivisible particle

in·dō -dĕre -dĭdī -dĭtum *vt* to put, place; to introduce; to impart, give; (with **in** + *acc*) to put or place (*something*) into or on, insert in

indocĭl·is -e *adj* difficult to teach, slow to learn; hard to learn; untaught

indoctē *adv* unskillfully

indoct·us -a -um *adj* untaught, untrained, unschooled; illiterate, ignorant

indolentĭ·a -ae *f* freedom from pain, insensibility

indŏl·ēs -is *f* inborn quality, natural quality; nature, character, disposition; natural ability, talent, genius

indol·escō -escĕre -ŭī *vi* to feel sorry; to feel resentment

indomābĭl·is -e *adj* untameable

indomĭt·us -a -um *adj* untamed, wild; (fig) wild, unmanageable

indorm·ĭō -īre -īvī or **-ĭī -ītum** *vi* to fall asleep; to grow careless; (with *dat* or *abl* or with **in** + *abl*) a to fall asleep at or on; b to fall asleep over; c to become careless about

indōtāt·us -a -um *adj* without dowry; poor; without funeral rites or funeral honors; **ars indotata** unadorned style; **corpora indotata** bodies that have not been accorded the usual honors paid to the dead

indubitābil·is -e *adj* indubitable

indubitāt·us -a -um *adj* undoubted

indubit·ō -āre *vi* (with *dat*) to begin to distrust, begin to doubt

indubi·us -a -um *adj* undoubted, certain

indūci·ae -ārum *f pl* armistice, truce

in·dūcō -dūcere -duxī -ductum *vt* to lead or bring in; to bring in, introduce; to induce, persuade, seduce, move; to overlay, drape, wrap, cover, put on, clothe; to strike out, erase; to repeal, cancel; to present, exhibit; to mislead, delude; (with in + *acc*) **a** to lead to, lead into, lead against; **b** to bring into, introduce into; **c** (fig) to introduce (*e.g., a new custom*) into; **d** to enter into (*account books*), charge to (*someone's account*); (with *dat* or **super** + *acc*) to put (*item of apparel*) on, spread over, wrap around, draw over; **animum inducere** or **in animum inducere** to make up one's mind, convince oneself, be convinced, conclude, suppose, imagine

inducti·ō -ōnis *f* bringing in, introduction, admission; resolution, determination; intention; induction, generalization; **animi inductio** inclination; **erroris inductio** deception

induct·or -ōris *m* (referring to a whip) persuader

induct·us -ūs *m* persuasion, inducement

indūcŭl·a -ae *f* skirt, petticoat

indulg·ens -entis *adj* indulgent, lenient; (with *dat* or **in** + *acc*) lenient toward, kind toward

indulgenter *adv* indulgently, leniently, kindly

indulgenti·a -ae *f* indulgence, leniency, kindness

in·dulgeō -dulgēre -dulsī *vt* (with *dat*) to grant, concede (*something*) to; **veniam indulgere** (with *dat*) to make allowances for; *vi* (with *dat*) **a** to be lenient toward, be kind to, be tender to; **b** to yield to, give way to; **c** to indulge in, be addicted to; **sibi indulgere** to be self-indulgent, take liberties

ind·uō -ŭĕre -ŭī -ūtum *vt* to put on (*e.g., a tunic*); to cover, wrap, clothe, array, envelop; to engage in; to assume, put on; to assume the part of; to involve, entangle; (with *dat*) to put (*e.g., a tunic*) on (*someone*)

indup- = **imp-**

indūr·escō -escĕre -ŭī *vi* to become hard, harden

indūr·ō -āre *vt* to harden

Ind·us -a -um *adj* Indian; *m* Indian; Ethiopian; mahout

industri·a -ae *f* industry, diligence;

industriā or **de** or **ex industriā** or **ob industriam** on purpose

industriē *adv* industriously, diligently

industri·us -a -um *adj* industrious, diligent, painstaking

indūti·ae or **indūci·ae** -ārum *f pl* armistice, truce

indūtus *pp* of **induo**; *adj* (with *acc* or *abl*) dressed in, wearing

indūt·us -ūs *m* wearing; clothing

induvi·ae -ārum *f pl* clothes

inebri·ō -āre *vt* to make drunk; (fig) to fill (*e.g., ear with gossip*)

inedi·a -ae *f* fasting; starvation

inēdit·us -a -um *adj* not made known, unknown, unpublished

inēlĕg·ans -antis *adj* inelegant, undistinguished

inēleganter *adv* without distinction

inēluctābil·is -e *adj* inescapable

inēmor·ior -ī *vi* (with *dat*) to die in or at

inempt·us -a -um *adj* unpurchased; without ransom

inēnarrābil·is -e *adj* indescribable

inēnarrābiliter *adv* indescribably

inēnōdābil·is -e *adj* inexplicable

in·ĕō -īre -iī -ĭtum *vt* to enter; to enter upon, undertake, form; to begin, engage in; **consilium inire** to form a plan; **consilium inire ut, qua,** or **quemadmodum** to plan how to (*do something*); **inire numerum** (with *genit*) to go into an enumeration of, enumerate; **inire rationem** (with *genit*) to form an estimate of; **inire rationem ut, qua,** or **quemadmodum** to consider, find out, or figure out how to (*do something*); **viam inire** to begin a trip; to find a way, devise a means

inepte *adv* foolishly, absurdly, inappropriately, pointlessly

inepti·a -ae *f* foolishness; *f pl* nonsense; trifles

ineptiō -īre *vi* to be absurd, make a fool of oneself

inept·us -a -um *adj* foolish, silly; inept, awkward, absurd; unsuitable, out of place; tactless, tasteless

inerm·is -e or **inerm·us** -a -um *adj* unarmed, defenseless; undefended; toothless (*gums*); harmless

inerr·ans -antis *adj* not wandering, fixed

inerr·ō -āre *vi* to wander about

iner·s -tis *adj* unskillful, incompetent; inactive, sluggish; weak, soft, helpless; stagnant, motionless; ineffective, dull, insipid; numbing (*cold*); expressionless (*eyes*); uneventful, leisurely (*time*)

inerti·a -ae *f* lack of skill, ignorance, rudeness; inactivity, laziness

inērūdīt·us -a -um *adj* uneducated; crude, inconsiderate

inesc·ō -āre *vt* to bait; (fig) to bait, trap, deceive

inēvect·us -a -um *adj* mounted

inēvītābĭl·is -e adj inevitable, inescapable

inexcĭt·us -a -um adj unexcited, calm

inexcūsābĭl·is -e adj without excuse; admitting no excuse

inexercĭtāt·us -a -um adj untrained

inexhaust·us -a -um adj unexhausted, not wasted; inexhaustible

inexōrābĭl·is -e adj inexorable, relentless; unswerving, strict

inexperrect·us -a -um adj unawakened

inexpert·us -a -um adj untried, untested; novel (with abl, or with in or adversus + acc) inexperienced in, unaccustomed to

inexpĭābĭl·is -e adj inexpiable, not to be atoned for; irreconcilable, implacable

inexplēbĭl·is -e adj insatiable

inexplēt·us -a -um adj unsatisfied, unfilled

inexplĭcābĭl·is -e adj inextricable; inexplicable; impassable (road); involved, unending (war)

inexplōrātō adv without reconnoitering

inexplōrāt·us -a -um adj unexplored; unfamiliar

inexpugnābĭl·is -e adj impregnable, unassailable; invincible

inexspectāt·us -a -um adj unexpected

inexstinct·us -a -um adj unextinguished; insatiable

inexsuperābĭl·is -e adj insuperable, insurmountable

inextrĭcābĭl·is -e adj inextricable

infābrē adv unskillfully

infabrĭcāt·us -a -um adj unshaped, untrimmed

infacētē adv witlessly

infacētĭ·ae -ārum f pl coarse jokes

infacēt·us -a -um adj not witty, not funny, dull, stupid

infācund·us -a -um adj ineloquent

infāmĭ·a -ae f bad reputation, bad name; disrepute, disgrace, scandal; embarrassment

infām·is -e adj infamous, notorious, disreputable, disgraceful

infām·ō -āre vt to defame, dishonor, disgrace

infand·us -a -um adj unspeakable, shocking

inf·ans -antis adj speechless, unable to speak; baby, infant, young; childish, silly; (fig) incapable of speaking, tongue-tied; m or f infant

infantĭ·a -ae f infancy; childishness; inability to speak; lack of eloquence

infar- = infer-

infatŭ·ō -āre vt to make a fool of

infaust·us -a -um adj ill-omened, unpropitious; unfortunate

infect·or -ōris m dyer

infect·us -a -um pp of inficio; adj not made, not done, undone, unfinished, unachieved; unfeasible; impossible

infēcundĭt·ās -ātis f unfruitfulness

infēcund·us -a -um adj unfruitful

infēlĭcĭt·ās -ātis f bad luck, misfortune

infēlĭcĭter adv unhappily; unluckily, unsuccessfully

infēlĭc·ō -āre vt to make unhappy

infēl·ix -īcis adj unfruitful; unhappy, unfortunate; causing misfortune, ruinous; ill-omened; pessimistic

infensē adv hostilely, aggressively

infens·ō -āre vt to antagonize; to make dangerous; vi to be hostile

infens·us -a -um adj hostile, antagonistic; dangerous; (with dat or in + acc) a hostile to, antagonistic toward; b dangerous to

in-fercĭō or infarcĭō -fercīre -fersī -fersum or -fertum vt to stuff, cram

infĕr·a -ōrum n pl lower world

infĕr·ī -ōrum m pl the dead; the world below

inferĭ·ae -ārum f pl rites and offerings to the dead

inferĭ·or -us adj lower, farther down; (fig) inferior, lower; subsequent, later

inferĭus adv lower, too low

infernē adv below, beneath

infern·us -a -um adj lower; infernal, of the lower world

inferō inferre intŭlī illātum vt to bring in, introduce, carry in; to import; to bring forward, adduce, produce, make, occasion, incite, cause; to offer, render, sacrifice; to bury, inter; arma, bellum, gradum, pedem, or signa inferre to make an attack, make an advance, begin hostilities; arma, bellum, pedem or signa inferre (with dat or with in or contra + acc) to attack, advance against, invade; conversa signa inferre (with dat) to turn around and attack; ignem inferre (with dat) to set fire to; se inferre to go, march, rush, charge, plunge; se in periculum inferre to expose oneself to danger; vi to infer, conclude

infĕr·us -a -um adj lower; southern

in-fervescō -fervescĕre -ferbŭī vi to simmer, boil

infestē adv hostilely, violently, outrageously

infest·ō -āre vt to annoy; to infest; to attack

infest·us -a -um adj infested, molested, disturbed, unsafe; hostile, aggressive; dangerous; threatening

inficēt- = infacēt-

in-ficĭō -ficĕre -fēcī -fectum vt to dip, dye, tint; to infect; to stain; to corrupt, spoil; to imbue, instruct; (fig) to poison, infect

infidēl·is -e adj unfaithful, untrue, disloyal

infidēlĭt·ās -ātis f infidelity, unfaithfulness, disloyalty

infidēlĭter adv disloyally

infĭd·us -a -um *adj* untrustworthy, treacherous

in·fĭgō -fĭgĕre -fĭxī -fĭxum *vt* to drive in, nail, thrust; to imprint, fix, impress; (with *dat*) **a** to drive into, thrust into; **b** to impale on; **c** to imprint on or in

infĭmātis see **infumatis**

infĭm·us or **infŭm·us -a -um** (*superl* of **inferus**) *adj* lowest, last; lowest, worst, humblest; **ab infimo colle** at the foot of the hill; **infĭmum mare** the bottom of the sea; *n* bottom

in·fĭndō -fĭndĕre -fĭdī -fissum *vt* (with *dat*) to cut (*e.g.*, *furrows*) into

infĭnĭt·ās -ātis *f* endlessness, infinity

infĭnĭtē *adv* without bounds, without end, infinitely; without exception

infĭnĭtĭ·ō -ōnis *f* boundlessness, infinity

infĭnĭt·us -a -um *adj* unlimited, boundless; without end, endless, infinite; countless; indefinite

infirmātĭ·ō -ōnis *f* invalidation; refutation

infirmē *adv* weakly, faintly, feebly

infirmĭt·ās -ātis *f* weakness, feebleness; infirmity, sickness; inconstancy

infirm·ō -āre *vt* to weaken, enfeeble; to refute, disprove; to annul

infirm·us -a -um *adj* weak, faint, feeble; infirm, sick; trivial; inconstant

infissus *pp* of **infindo**

infĭt *v defect* he, she, it begins

infĭtĭ·ae -ārum *f pl* denial; **infĭtĭas ire** (with *acc*) to deny

infĭtĭāl·is -e *adj* negative

infĭtĭātĭ·ō -ōnis *f* denial

infĭtĭāt·or -ōris *m* repudiator

infĭtĭ·or -ārī -ātus sum *vt* to deny, repudiate, contradict, disown

infixus *pp* of **infigo**

inflammātĭ·ō -ōnis *f* setting on fire; **inflammationem inferre** (with *dat*) to set on fire

inflamm·ō -āre *vt* to set on fire, kindle, light up; (fig) to inflame, excite

inflatĭ·ō -ōnis *f* swelling up; **habet inflationem faba** beans cause gas

inflātĭus *adv* too pompously

inflāt·us -a -um *adj* blown up, swollen, inflated; haughty; turgid (*style*)

inflāt·us -ūs *m* puff, blast; inspiration

in·flectō -flectĕre -flexī -flexum *vt* to bend, curve, bow, turn aside; to change; to influence; to inflect

inflēt·us -a -um *adj* unwept

inflexibĭl·is -e *adj* inflexible

inflexĭ·ō -ōnis *f* bending

inflexus *pp* of **inflecto**

inflex·us -ūs *m* curve

in·flīgō -flīgĕre -flīxī -flīctum *vt* to strike, smash, dash, swing; to inflict (*wound*); to bring (*e.g.*, *disgrace*)

inflō -āre *vt* to blow (*horn*), play (*flute*); to inspire; to inflate, puff up, fill

in·fluō -fluĕre -fluxī *vi* (with **in** + *acc*) **a** to flow into; **b** (fig) to flow over into, stream into, pour into

in·fodĭō -fodĕre -fōdī -fossum *vt* to dig; to bury

informātĭ·ō -ōnis *f* sketch; idea

inform·is -e *adj* unformed, shapeless; ugly, hideous

inform·ō -āre *vt* to form, shape

infŏr·ō -āre *vt* to bring into court

infortūnāt·us -a -um *adj* unfortunate

infortū·ĭum -ĭī or **-ī** *n* misfortune, calamity; punishment

infossus *pp* of **infodio**

infrā *adv* below, underneath; down south, down the coast; *prep* (with *acc*) below, beneath, under; later than

infractĭ·ō -ōnis *f* weakening; **animi infractio** discouragement

infract·us -a -um *pp* of **infringo**; *adj* broken, weakened, exhausted; **infractos animos gerere** to feel down and out

infragĭl·is -e *adj* unbreakable, strong

infrĕm·ō -ĕre -ŭī *vi* to growl, bellow, roar; to rage

infrēnāt·us -a -um *adj* unbridled

infrend·ĕō -ēre or **infrend·ō -ĕre** *vi* **dentibus infrendere** to gnash the teeth

infrēn·is -e or **infrēn·us -a -um** *adj* unbridled

infrēn·ō -āre *vt* to put a bridle on; to harness; (fig) to curb

infrēnus see **infrenis**

infrĕqu·ens -entis *adj* uncrowded, not numerous; poorly attended; thinly populated; inconstant, irregular

infrequentĭ·a -ae *f* small number, scantiness; poor attendance; emptiness

in·fringō -fringĕre -frēgī -fractum *vt* to break, break in; to impair, affect, subdue, weaken, break down

infr·ons -ondis *adj* leafless

infructuōs·us -a -um *adj* unfruitful; pointless

infŭcāt·us -a -um *adj* painted over, varnished; hidden

infŭl·a -ae *f* bandage; fillet; mark of distinction, badge of honor

infŭmāt·is or **infĭmāt·is -is** *m* one of the lowest (*in rank*)

infŭmus see **infimus**

in·fundō -fundĕre -fūdī -fūsum *vt* to pour in, pour on, pour out; (with *dat* or **in** + *acc*) **a** to pour into, pour upon; **b** to administer to; **infundi** or **se infundere** (with *dat*) to lay on, spread out on

infusc·ō -āre *vt* to darken, obscure; to stain, corrupt, sully

infūsus *pp* of **infundo**; *adj* diffused, permeating; fallen (*snow*); crowded

ingemin‧ō -āre *vt* to redouble; to repeat, reiterate; *vi* to redouble

ingem‧iscō or **ingem‧escō -iscĕre -ŭī** *vi* to groan, heave a sigh; (with *dat* or **in** + *abl*) to groan over, sigh over

ingĕm‧ō -ĕre -ŭī *vt* to groan over, sigh over; *vi* (with *dat*) to sigh over

ingenĕr‧ō -āre *vt* to engender, generate, produce, create

ingeniāt‧us -a -um *adj* naturally endowed, talented

ingeniōsē *adv* ingeniously

ingeniōs‧us -a -um *adj* ingenious, clever, talented; (with *dat* or **ad** + *acc*) naturally suited to

ingenĭt‧us -a -um *adj* inborn, natural

ingen‧ium -iī or **-ī** *n* innate or natural quality; nature, temperament, character, bent, inclination; natural ability, talent, genius; clever person, genius

ing‧ens -entis *adj* huge, vast; great, mighty, powerful

ingenŭē *adv* liberally; frankly

ingenuĭt‧ās -ātis *f* noble birth; noble character; frankness

ingenŭ‧us -a -um *adj* native, indigenous; natural; free-born; like a freeman, noble; frank

in‧gĕrō -gerĕre -gessī -gestum *vt* to carry in, throw in, heap; to hurl, shoot (*weapon*); to pour out (*angry words*), heap (*abuse*)

inglōri‧us -a -um *adj* inglorious, without glory, inconspicuous

ingluvi‧ēs -ēī *f* crop, maw; gluttony

ingrātē *adv* unpleasantly; unwillingly; ungratefully

ingrātīfic‧us -a -um *adj* ungrateful

ingrātīis or **ingrātīs** *adv* without thanks; unwillingly

ingrāt‧us -a -um *adj* unpleasant, unwelcome; ungrateful; receiving no thanks, unappreciated; thankless

ingravesc‧ō -ĕre *vi* to grow heavier; to become pregnant; to grow worse; to become more serious; to become weary; to become dearer (*in price*); to become more important

in‧gredior -grĕdī -gressus sum *vt* to enter; to undertake; to begin; to walk in, follow (*footsteps*); *vi* to go in, enter; to go, walk, walk along; to begin, commence; to begin to speak; (with **in** + *acc*) **a** to go in, enter; **b** to enter upon, begin, take up, undertake; **in rem publicam ingredi** to enter politics, enter public life

ingressi‧ō -ōnis *f* entering; walking; gait, pace; beginning

ingress‧us -ūs *m* entering; (*mil*) inroad; walking; gait; beginning

ingru‧ō -ĕre -ī *vi* to come, come on, rush on; (*of war*) to break out; (*of rain*) to pour down; (with *dat* or **in** + *acc*) to fall upon, attack

ingu‧en -ĭnis *n* groin; swelling, tumor; *n pl* private parts

ingurgĭt‧ō -āre *vt* to gorge, stuff; **se ingurgitare** to stuff oneself; **se ingurgitare** (with **in** + *acc*) to steep oneself in, devote oneself to

ingustāt‧us -a -um *adj* untasted

inhabĭl‧is -e *adj* clumsy, unhandy; (with *dat* or **ad** + *acc*) unfit for

inhabitābĭl‧is -e *adj* uninhabitable

inhabĭt‧ō -āre *vt* inhabit

in‧haerĕō -haerēre -haesī -haesum *vi* to stick, cling; (*fig*) to cling, adhere; to be inherent; (with *dat*, with **ad** + *acc*, or with **in** + *abl*) **a** to cling to; **b** to be closely connected with; **c** to gaze upon

in‧haerescō -haerescĕre -haesī *vi* to stick fast, take hold

inhăl‧ō -āre *vt* (with *dat*) to breathe (*e.g., bad breath*) on (*someone*)

inhib‧ĕō -ēre -ŭī -ĭtum *vt* to hold back, curb, check, control; to use, practice, perform; to apply, inflict; **retro navem inhibere** to back up the ship; *vi* to row backwards, backwater

inhibĭti‧ō -ōnis *f* backing up

inhĭ‧ō -āre *vt* to gape at; to covet; *vi* to stand open-mouthed, be amazed

inhonestē *adv* dishonorably, disgracefully; dishonestly

inhonest‧ō -āre *vt* to dishonor, disgrace

inhonest‧us -a -um *adj* dishonorable, disgraceful, shameful, inglorious; indecent; ugly, degrading

inhonōrāt‧us -a -um *adj* unhonored, disregarded, unrewarded

inhonōr‧us -a -um *adj* defaced

inhorr‧ĕō -ēre -ŭī *vi* to stand on end, bristle

inhorr‧escō -escĕre -ŭī *vi* to stand on end, bristle; to vibrate; to shiver, tremble, shudder

inhospitāl‧is -e *adj* inhospitable, unfriendly

inhospitālĭt‧ās -ātis *f* inhospitality

inhospĭt‧us -a -um *adj* inhospitable

inhūmānē *adv* inhumanly, savagely

inhūmānĭt‧ās -ātis *f* inhumanity, barbarity; churlishness; extreme stinginess

inhūmānĭter *adv* impolitely

inhūmān‧us -a -um *adj* inhuman, savage; brutal; crude, impolite

inhumāt‧us -a -um *adj* unburied

inĭbi or **inĭbī** *adv* there, in that place; near at hand

inimĭc‧a -ae *f* (personal) enemy (*female*)

inimĭcē *adv* hostilely, in an unfriendly way

inimīcĭtĭ‧a -ae *f* unfriendliness, enmity; *f pl* feuds

inimĭc‧ō -āre *vt* to make into enemies, set at odds

inimīc‧us -a -um *adj* unfriendly, hostile; harmful; *m* (personal) enemy; **inimicissimus suus** his bitterest enemy

inīquē *adv* unequally, unevenly; unfairly

inīquĭt‧ās -ātis *f* unevenness; inequality; disadvantage; unfairness

iniqu·us -a -um *adj* uneven, unequal; not level, sloping; unfair; adverse, harmful; dangerous, unfavorable; prejudiced; excessive; impatient, discontented; **iniquo animo** impatiently, unwillingly; *m* enemy, foe

initi·ō -īī or **-ī** *vt* to initiate, begin; to initiate (*into mysteries*)

init·ium -ī or **-ī** *n* entrance; beginning; *n pl* elements; first principles; sacred rites, sacred mysteries

initus *pp* of **ineo**

init·us -ūs *m* entrance; beginning

in·jiciō -jicēre -jēcī -jectum *vt* to throw, inject; to impose, apply; to inspire, infuse; to cause, occasion; to furnish (*a cause*); to bring up, mention (*a name*); (with *dat* or **in** + *acc*) to throw or fling into, on or over; (with *dat* or **in** + *acc*) **a** to throw oneself into, rush into, expose oneself to; **b** to fling oneself down on; **c** (of the mind) to turn itself to, concentrate on, reflect on; **manum injicere** (with *dat*) to lay hands on, take possession of

injūcundit·ās -ātis *f* unpleasantness

injūcundius *adv* rather unpleasantly

injūcund·us -a -um *adj* unpleasant

injūdicāt·us -a -um *adj* undecided

in·jungō -jungere -junxī -junctum *vt* to join, attach, fasten; to inflict, impose; (with *dat*) **a** to join, attach, fasten to; **b** to inflict on, impose (*e.g., taxes, obligations*) on

injūrāt·us -a -um *adj* not under oath

injūri·a -ae *f* injury, wrong, outrage, injustice; insult, affront; harshness, severity; revenge; damage, harm; ill-gotten goods; **injuriā** unjustly, undeservedly, innocently; **per injuriam** unjustly, outrageously

injūriōsē *adv* unjustly, wrongfully

injūriōs·us -a -um *adj* unjust, wrongful; harmful

injūri·us -a -um *adj* unjust, wrong

injūr·us -a -um *adj* wrongful

injussū (*abl* only) *m* without orders; **injussu meo** without my orders

injuss·us -a -um *adj* unasked, unbidden, voluntary

injustē *adv* unjustly

injustiti·a -ae *f* injustice

injust·us -a -um *adj* unjust

inl- = **ill-**

inm- = **imm-**

innābil·is -e *adj* unswimmable

in·nascor -nascī -nātus sum *vi* (with *dat*) to be born in, grow in or on; (with **in** + *abl*) (fig) to originate in

innāt·ō -āre *vt* to swim; *vi* (with *dat*) to swim around in, float on; (with **in** + *acc*) to swim into

innāt·us -a -um *pp* of **innascor**; *adj* inborn, natural

innāvigābil·is -e *adj* unnavigable

in·nectō -nectēre -nexuī -nexum *vt* to entwine; to tie, fasten together; to join, attach, connect; (fig) to devise, invent, plan

in·nītor -nītī -nixus sum or **-nīsus sum** *vi* (with *abl*) to lean on, rest on, be supported by

inn·ō -āre *vt* to swim; to sail, sail over; *vi* (with *abl*) **a** to swim in, float on; **b** to sail on; **c** (of the sea) to wash against (*a shore*)

innŏc·ens -entis *adj* harmless; guiltless, innocent; upright; unselfish; (with *genit*) innocent of

innocenter *adv* blamelessly

innocenti·a -ae *f* innocence; integrity; unselfishness

innocuē *adv* harmlessly; innocently

innocŭ·us -a -um *adj* harmless, innocuous; innocent; unharmed

innōt·escō -escĕre -ŭī *vi* to become known; to become notorious

innŏv·ō -āre *vt* to renew, restore; **se innovare** (with **ad** + *acc*) to return to

innoxi·us -a -um *adj* harmless; safe; innocent; unhurt; (with *genit*) innocent of

innūbil·us -a -um *adj* cloudless

innūb·a -ae (*fem* only) *adj* unmarried

in·nūbō -nūbĕre -nupsī *vi* (with *dat*) to marry into

innumerābil·is -e *adj* innumerable

innumerābilit·ās -ātis *f* countless number

innumerābiliter *adv* innumerably

innumerāl·is -e *adj* innumerable

innumĕr·us -a -um *adj* countless

in·nŭō -nuĕre -nŭī -nŭtum *vi* to give a nod; (with *dat*) to nod to

innupt·a -ae (*fem* only) *adj* unmarried; *f* unmarried girl, maiden

innutr·iō -īre -īvī or **-iī -ītum** *vt* (with *dat*) to bring up in

In·ō -ūs *f* daughter of Cadmus and Harmonia, wife of Athamas, mother of Learchus and Melicerta, and stepmother of Phrixus and Helle; pursued by mad Athamas, she and Melicerta hurled themselves into the sea, whereupon they were changed into sea deities

inoblīt·us -a -um *adj* unforgetful

inobrŭt·us -a -um *adj* not overwhelmed

inobservābil·is -e *adj* unnoticed

inobservanti·a -ae *f* inattention

inobservāt·us -a -um *adj* unobserved

inoccidŭ·us -a -um *adj* never setting

inodōr·us -a -um *adj* odorless

inoffens·us -a -um *adj* unobstructed, uninterrupted, unhindered

inofficiōs·us -a -um *adj* irresponsible; not obliging

inŏl·ens -entis *adj* odorless

inol·escō -escĕre -ēvī *vi* to become inveterate; (with *dat*) to grow on or in

inōmināt·us -a -um *adj* ill-omened, inauspicious

inopi·a -ae *f* lack, want, need, poverty; scarcity; barrenness (*of style*); helplessness

inopīn·ans -antis *adj* unsuspecting, taken by surprise

inopīnanter *adv* unexpectedly

inopīnātō *adv* unexpectedly, by surprise

inopīnāt·us -a -um *adj* not expected, unexpected, unsuspected, surprising; *n* surprise; **ex inopīnato** by surprise

inopīn·us -a -um *adj* unexpected

inopiōs·us -a -um *adj* (with *genit*) in need of

in·ops -ōpis *adj* without means or resources; poor, needy, destitute; helpless, weak, forlorn; bald (*style*); poor (*expression*); pitiful, wretched, contemptible; (with *genit*) destitute of, stripped of, without; (with *abl*) lacking in, deficient in, poor in

inōrāt·us -a -um *adj* not presented; **re inorata** without presenting one's case

inordināt·us -a -um *adj* disordered

inornāt·us -a -um *adj* unadorned; plain (*style*); unheralded

inp- = imp-

inpendiōs·us -a -um *adj* extravagant

inperc·ō -ĕre *vi* (with *dat*) to spare

inpluviāt·us -a -um *adj* square, shaped like an impluvium

inpūrāt·us -a -um *adj* (morally) defiled

inpūritī·ae -ārum *f pl* (moral) impurity

inquam *v defect* say; after one or more words of direct quotation, e.g., **Desilite, inquit, milites et . . .** "Jump down, fellow soldiers", he says, "and . . ."; in emphatic repetition, e.g., **tuas, tuas inquam suspiciones . . .** your suspicions, yes I say yours . . . ; **inquit** it is said, one says

inquī·ēs -ētis *adj* restless

inquiēt·ō -āre *vt* to disquiet, disturb

inquiēt·us -a -um *adj* restless, unsettled

inquilīn·us -ī *m* tenant, inhabitant

inquinātē *adv* filthily

inquināt·us -a -um *adj* filthy, foul

inquīn·ō -āre *vt* to mess up, defile, contaminate

in·quīrō -quīrĕre quīsīvī -quīsitum *vt* to search for, inquire into, examine, pry into; *vi* to hold an investigation; to hold a preliminary hearing

inquīsītī·ō -ōnis *f* search, inquiry, investigation; preliminary hearing; (with *genit*) search for, inquiry into, investigation of

inquīsīt·or -ōris *m* inspector, examiner; spy; (law) investigator

inquīsīt·us -a -um *pp* of **inquiro**; *adj* not investigated

inquit see **inquam**

inr- = irr-

insalūbr·is -e *adj* unhealthy

insalūtāt·us -a -um *adj* ungreeted

insānābil·is -e *adj* incurable

insānē *adv* crazily, madly

insāni·a -ae *f* insanity, madness, frenzy; rapture; mania; excess; inspiration

insān·iō -īre -īvī or **-iī -ītum** *vi* to be crazy, be mad, be insane; to be absurd, be wild

insānit·ās -ātis *f* unsoundness, disease

insān·us -a -um *adj* insane, mad, crazy; absurd, foolish; excessive, extravagant; monstrous, outrageous; inspired; maddening

insatiābil·is -e *adj* insatiable; that cannot cloy, uncloying

insatiābiliter *adv* insatiably

insatiēt·ās -ātis *f* insatiety

insaturābil·is -e *adj* insatiable

insaturābiliter *adv* insatiably

in·scendō -scendĕre -scendī -scensum *vt* & *vi* to climb up, mount

inscensi·ō -ōnis *f* mounting; **in navem inscensio** boarding a ship

inscensus *pp* of **inscendo**

insci·ens -entis *adj* unaware; silly, stupid

inscienter *adv* ignorantly, inadvertently

inscientī·a -ae *f* ignorance; inexperience; foolishness; awkwardness

inscīt·us -a -um *adj* ignorant, clumsy, stupid

inscī·us -a -um *adj* ignorant, unaware

in·scrībō -scrībĕre -scripsī -scriptum *vt* to inscribe; to ascribe; to title (*a book*); to assign, attribute, appropriate; to advertise; to address (*a letter*); (with *dat* or **in** + *abl*) to write (*something*) on or in

inscriptī·ō -ōnis *f* inscribing

inscript·us -a -um *pp* of **inscribo**; *adj* unwritten

in·sculpō -sculpĕre -sculpsī -sculptum *vt* to cut, carve, engrave; (with *abl* or **in** + *abl*) to cut, carve, or engrave upon

insectātī·ō -ōnis *f* hot pursuit

insectāt·or -ōris *m* persecutor

insect·ō -āre *vt* to pursue, attack; to attack with words, criticize

insect·us -a -um *adj* indented, notched

insecūtus *pp* of **insequor**

insēdābiliter *adv* incessantly

insen·escō -escĕre -uī *vi* (with *dat*) to grow old amidst, grow old over

insensil·is -e *adj* imperceptible

insepult·us -a -um *adj* unburied

insequ·ens -entis *adj* next, following, succeeding

in·sequor -sĕquī -secūtus sum *vt* to follow, follow after; to succeed, to follow up; to attack; to prosecute; to pass, overtake; to reproach;

to strive after; vi to follow, come next

in·sĕrō -serĕre -sēvī -sĭtum vt to graft; (fig) to implant

in·sĕrō -serĕre -serŭī -sertum vt to insert; to introduce; to involve; to join, enroll, associate; to mingle, blend; to let in

insert·ō -āre vt to insert

inserv·ĭō -īre -īvī or **-ĭī -ītum** vt to serve, obey; vi to be a slave, be a subject; (with dat) to serve, be subservient to, be devoted to

insessus pp of insido

insĭbĭl·ō -āre vi (of the wind) to whistle, hiss

in·sĭdĕō -sĭdĕre -sēdī -sessum vt to hold, occupy; vi to sit down; to settle down; to be deep-seated; (with abl or in + abl) **a** to sit on; **b** to settle down on or in; **c** (fig) to be fixed in, stamped in

insĭdĭ·ae -ārum f pl ambush; plot, trap; insidias dare, comparare, collocare, parare, or struere (with dat) to lay a trap for

insĭdĭāt·or -ōris m soldier in ambush; (fig) plotter, subversive

insĭdĭ·or -ārī -ātus sum vi to lie in wait; (with dat) **a** to lie in wait for; **b** (fig) to plot against; **c** (fig) to watch for (an opportunity)

insĭdĭōsē adv insidiously, by underhand means

insĭdĭōs·us -a -um adj insidious, treacherous, tricky

in·sĭdō -sĭdĕre -sēdī -sessum vt to occupy, keep possession of, possess; vi (with dat) to settle in or on; (with in + abl) (fig) to become fixed in

insign·e -is n insignia, mark, token; (mil) decoration, medal; standard; coat of arms; signal; honor, distinction; brilliant passage, gem; n pl insignia, regalia, uniform, attire, accouterments

insign·ĭō -īre -īvī or **-ĭī -ītum** vt to make conspicuous, distinguish

insign·is -e adj conspicuous, distinguished; prominent, eminent, extraordinary, singular

insignĭtē adv extraordinarily, notably

insignĭter adv remarkably

insignĭt·us -a -um adj marked, conspicuous, clear, glaring; distinguished, striking, notable

insĭl·a -ĭum n pl treadle (of a loom)

insĭl·ĭō -īre -ŭī or **-īvī** vt to jump up on, mount; vi (with dat) to jump on; (with in + acc) **a** to jump into or on; **b** to jump on, mount, climb aboard

insĭmŭlātĭ·ō -ōnis f charge, accusation

insĭmŭl·ō -āre vt to accuse, accuse falsely, allege

insincēr·us -a -um adj mixed, spoiled, not pure

insĭnŭātĭ·ō -ōnis f winning sympathy

insĭnŭ·ō -āre vt to bring in secretly, sneak in; **se insĭnuare** (with inter + acc) to wriggle in between, work one's way between or among; **se insinuare in familiaritatem** (with genit) to ingratiate oneself with

insĭpĭ·ens -entis adj foolish

insĭpĭenter adv foolishly

insĭpĭentĭ·a -ae f foolishness

in·sĭstō -sĭstĕre -stĭtī vt to stand on, trample on; to set about, keep at (a task, etc.); to follow, chase after, pursue; **iter insistere** or **viam insistere** to enter upon a course, pursue a course; vi to stand, stop, come to a standstill; to pause; (with dat) **a** to tread on the heels of, pursue closely; **b** to press on with; **c** (fig) to dwell upon; (with dat or in + acc) to set foot on or in, step on, tread on, stand on; (with dat or in + abl) to persist in; (with ad or in + acc) to keep at, keep after, keep the pressure on, pursue vigorously

insĭtĭ·ō -ōnis f grafting; grafting time

insĭtīv·us -a -um adj grafted; (fig) spurious

insĭt·or -ōris m grafter

insĭt·us -a -um pp of insero; adj inborn, innate; incorporated

insŏcĭābĭl·is -e adj incompatible

insōlābĭlĭter adv unconsolably

insŏl·ens -entis adj unaccustomed, unusual; immoderate, excessive; extravagant, insolent; (with genit or in + abl) unaccustomed to, inexperienced in; **in aliena re insolens** free with someone else's money

insŏlenter adv unusually; excessively; insolently

insŏlentĭ·a -ae f unusualness, strangeness, novelty; inexperience; affectation; insolence, arrogance

insŏlesc·ō -ĕre vi to become strange; to become insolent; to become elated

insŏlĭd·us -a -um adj soft

insŏlĭt·us -a -um adj unaccustomed, inexperienced; unusual, strange, uncommon; n the unusual

insomnĭ·a -ae f insomnia, sleeplessness

insomn·is -e adj sleepless

insomn·ĭum -ĭī or **-ī** n nightmare; dream

insŏn·ō -āre -ŭī vi to make noise; to sound, resound, roar; **calamis insonare** to make music with a reed pipe; **flagello insonare** to crack the whip; **pennis insonare** to flap the wings

ins·ons -ontis adj innocent; harmless

insŏpīt·us -a -um adj sleepless

insŏp·or -ōris adj sleepless

inspect·ō -āre vt to look at, view, observe

inspectus pp of inspicio

inspēr·ans -antis adj not expecting

insperāt·us -a -um *adj* unhoped for, unexpected, unforeseen; unwelcome; **ex insperato** unexpectedly

in·spergō -spergĕre -spersī -spersum *vt* to sprinkle

in·spiciō -spicĕre -spexī -spectum *vt* to inspect, look into, examine, consider; to inspect, review; to look at, consult (*books*)

inspīc·ō -āre *vt* to make pointed; to sharpen

inspīr·ō -āre *vt* to inspire, infuse, enkindle; *vi* (with *dat*) to blow on, breathe on

inspoliāt·us -a -um *adj* undespoiled

insput·ō -āre *vt* to spit on

instābil·is -e *adj* unstable, unsteady; (fig) unsteady, changeable

inst·ans -antis *adj* present; immediate, threatening, urgent

instanter *adv* vehemently

instanti·a -ae *f* presence; vehemence

instar (indecl) *n* image, likeness, appearance, resemblance; (with *genit*) like, equal to, as large as, worth, as good as

instaurātī·ō -ōnis *f* renewal, repetition

instaurātīv·us -a -um *adj* begun anew, repeated

instaur·ō -āre *vt* to set up; to renew, repeat, start all over again (*esp. games and celebrations*); to repay, requite

in·sternō -sternĕre -strāvī -strātum *vt* to cover

instigāt·or -ōris *m* or **instigātr·ix -īcis** *f* instigator, ringleader

instig·ō -āre *vt* to instigate, goad on, stimulate, incite

instill·ō -āre *vt* (with *dat*) to pour (*something*) on, instill (*something*) in

instimulāt·or -ōris *m* instigator

instimul·ō -āre *vt* to stimulate, urge on

instinct·or -ōris *m* instigator

instinct·us -a -um *adj* incited, inspired

instinct·us -ūs *m* inspiration, impulse

instipul·or -ārī -ātus sum *vi* to bargain

instit·a -ae *f* border, flounce; (fig) lady

institī·ō -ōnis *f* standing still

instit·or -ōris *m* salesman, huckster, hawker

instit·uō -uĕre -uī -ūtum *vt* to set, fix, plant; to set up, erect, establish; to arrange; to build, make, construct; to prepare, make ready; to provide, furnish; to institute, organize, set up; to appoint, designate; to undertake, begin; to decide, determine; to control, direct, govern; to teach, train, instruct, educate

institūtī·ō -ōnis *f* arrangement; custom; instruction, education; *f pl* principles of education

institūt·um -ī *n* practice, custom,

usage; precedent; principle; decree, regulation, stipulation, terms; purpose, intention; **ex instituto** according to custom

in·stō -stāre -stitī *vt* to follow, pursue; to work hard at; to menace, threaten; *vi* to be at hand, approach, be impending; to insist; (with *dat* or **in** + *abl*) to stand on or in; (with *dat*) **a** to be close to; **b** to be on the heels of, pursue closely; **c** to harass

instrātus *pp* of **insterno**

instrēnŭ·us -a -um *adj* lethargic

instrĕp·ō -āre -uī -itum *vi* to creak, rattle

instructī·ō -ōnis *f* construction; array

instructius *adv* with better preparation

instruct·or -ōris *m* supervisor

instruct·us -a -um *pp* of **instruo**; *adj* provided, equipped, furnished; prepared, arranged; instructed, versed

instruct·us -ūs *m* equipment; stock-in-trade (*of an orator*)

instrūment·um -ī *n* instrument, tool, utensil; equipment; dress, outfit; repertory, stock-in-trade; means, supply, provisions; document

in·struō -struĕre -struxī -structum *vt* to build up, construct; to furnish, prepare, provide, fit out; to instruct; (mil) to deploy

insuās·um -ī *n* dark-orange color

insuāv·is -e *adj* unpleasant, disagreeable

insūd·ō -āre *vi* (with *dat*) to sweat on, drip sweat on

insuēfact·us -a -um *adj* accustomed

in·suescō -suescĕre -suēvī -suētum *vt* to accustom, familiarize; *vi* (with *dat*, with **ad** + *acc*, or with *inf*) to get used to

insuēt·us -a -um *adj* unusual; (with *genit* or *dat*, with **ad** + *acc*, or with *inf*) unused to

insŭl·a -ae *f* island; apartment building

insulān·us -ī *m* islander

insulsē *adv* in poor taste; insipidly, absurdly

insulsit·ās -ātis *f* lack of taste; silliness, absurdity

insuls·us -a -um *adj* unsalted, without taste; coarse, tasteless, insipid; silly, absurd; bungling; *f pl* silly creatures (*i.e., women*)

insult·ō -āre *vt* to insult, scoff at, taunt; (of votaries) to dance about in; *vi* to jump, gambol, prance; to gloat; (with *abl*) **a** to jump in, cavort in, gambol on, jump upon; **b** to gloat over; (with *dat* or **in** + *acc*) to scoff at, gloat over

insultūr·a -ae *f* jumping in

insum inesse infuī *vi* to be there; (with *dat* or **in** + *abl*) **a** to be in, be on; **b** to be implied in, be contained in, be in, belong to

in·sūmō -sūmĕre -sumpsī -sump-
tum vt to spend, devote, waste;
(with dat or in + acc) to devote to,
apply to; (with abl or in + abl)
to expend on; operam insumere
(with dat) to devote effort to, waste
effort on

in·sŭō -suĕre -sŭī -sūtum vt to
sew up; (with dat) a to sew up in;
b to embroider (something) on

insŭper adv above, overhead, on the
top; from above; moreover, besides,
in addition; prep (with acc) above,
over, over and above; (with abl) in
addition to, besides

insŭperābĭl·is -e adj insurmountable; unconquerable

in·surgō -surgĕre -surrexī -sur-
rectum vi to rise, stand up; to rise,
stand high, tower; to rise, increase,
grow, grow intense; to rise to power; (with dat) a to rise up against;
b to strain at (e.g., oars)

insusurr·ō -āre vt (with dat) to
whisper (something) to; insusurrare in aurem (with genit) to
whisper into the ear of; sibi cantilenam insusurrare to hum a
tune to oneself; vi to whisper; (of
wind) to blow gently

intāb·escō -escĕre -ŭī vi to melt
away gradually, dissolve gradually;
(fig) to waste away, pine away

intactĭl·is -e adj intangible

intact·us -a -um adj untouched; uninjured, intact; unpolluted; untried; unmarried; virgin, chaste

intact·us -ūs m intangibility

intāmĭnāt·us -a -um adj unsullied

intect·us -a -um pp of intego; adj
uncovered; naked; open, frank

integell·us -a -um adj fairly pure
or chaste; in fair condition

intĕg·er -ra -rum adj whole, complete, intact, unimpaired; unhurt,
unwounded; healthy, sound, fresh;
new, fresh; pure, chaste; untouched,
unaffected; unbiased, unprejudiced;
unattempted; unsubdued, unconquered; unbroken (horse); not worn,
unused; inexperienced, ignorant;
virtuous, honest, blameless, irreproachable; healthy, sane; ab integro or de integro anew, all over
again; in integrum restituere to
restore to a former condition; to
pardon; integrum alicui esse
(with inf) to be in someone's power to

in·tĕgō -tegĕre -texī -tectum vt
to cover up; to protect

integrasc·ō -ĕre vi to break out
fresh, start all over again

integrātĭ·ō -ōnis f renewal, new beginning

intĕgrē adv wholly, entirely; honestly; correctly

integrĭt·ās -ātis f soundness; integrity; innocence; purity, chastity;
correctness

intĕgr·ō -āre vt to make whole; to
heal, repair; to renew, begin again;

to refresh

integumtn·um -ī n covering; lid;
protection

intellectus pp of intellego

intellect·us -ūs m perception; comprehension, understanding; intellect

intellĕg·ens -entis adj intelligent;
(with genit) appreciative of; (with
in + abl) versed in

intellegenter adv intelligently

intellegentĭ·a -ae f intelligence; understanding, knowledge; perception,
judgment, discrimination, taste,
skill; concept, notion; (with genit)
knowledge or understanding of;
(with in + abl) judgment in

intel·lĕgō -legĕre -lexī -lectum
vt to understand, perceive, discern,
comprehend, gather; to realize, recognize; to have an accurate knowledge of, be an expert in; vi intellego (in answers) I understand, I
get it

intemerāt·us -a -um adj undefiled,
pure; pure, undiluted

intempĕr·ans -antis adj intemperate, without restraint; profligate;
excessive

intemperanter adv intemperately

intemperantĭ·a -ae f intemperance,
lack of self-control; extravagance,
excess

intemperātē adv intemperately

intemperāt·us -a -um adj excessive

intemperārĭ·ae -ārum f pl wild
outbursts, wildness

intemperĭ·ēs -ēī f wildness, excess;
outrageous conduct, excesses; intemperies aquarum heavy rain;
intemperies caeli stormy weather

intempestīvē adv at a bad time, in-
opportunely

intempestīv·us -a -um adj untimely, unseasonable; poorly timed

intempest·us -a -um adj unseasonable; dark, dismal; unhealthy; nox
intempesta dead of night

intemptāt·us or intentāt·us -a
-um adj unattempted

in·tendō -tendĕre -tendī -tentum
or -tensum vt to stretch, stretch
out, extend, spread out; to stretch,
bend (e.g., bow); to aim, direct, shoot
(weapon); to increase, magnify, intensify; to intend; to urge, incite;
to aim at, intend; to assert, maintain; to aim, turn, direct; to raise
(voice); to stretch (truth); to direct,
turn, focus (mind, attention); to
pitch (tent)

intentātus see intemptatus

intentē adv intently, attentively

intentĭ·ō -ōnis f stretching, straining, tension; attention; effort, exertion; accusation

intent·ō -āre vt to stretch out; to
aim, direct; to threaten

intent·us -a -um pp of intendo;
adj taut, tense; intent, attentive;
eager, waiting, tense; strict (discipline); vigorous, tense, nervous
(speech)

intent·us -ūs *m* stretching out, extending (*of the palms*)

intep·ēŏ -ēre -ŭī *vi* to be lukewarm

intep·escō -pescĕre -ŭī *vi* to grow warm, be warmed

inter *prep* (with *acc*) between, among, amidst; during, within, in the course of; in spite of; (in classifying) among, in, with; **inter se** each other, one another, mutual, mutually

interaestŭ·ō -āre *vi* to retch

interāment·a -ōrum *n pl* framework of a ship

Interamn·a -ae *f* town in Latium, on the Liris; town in Umbria, birthplace of Tacitus

interapt·us -a -um *adj* joined together

interāresc·ō -ĕre *vi* to dry up

interātim *adv* meanwhile

interbib·ō -ĕre *vt* to drink up

interbĭt·ō -ĕre *vi* to come to nothing

intercalār·is -e *adj* intercalary, inserted

intercalāri·us -a -um *adj* intercalary, inserted

intercăl·ō -āre *vt* to intercalate, insert

intercapēd·ō -ĭnis *f* interruption, break, pause

inter·cēdō -cēdĕre -cessī -cessum *vi* to come or go in between; (of time) to intervene, pass, occur; to act as an intermediary; to intercede; (of tribunes) to exercise the veto; (with *dat*) a to veto, protest against; **b** to interfere with, obstruct, hinder

intercepti·ō -ōnis *f* interception

intercept·or -ōris *m* embezzler

interceptus *pp* of **intercipio**

intercessi·ō -ōnis *f* intercession, mediation; (tribune's) veto

intercess·or -ōris *m* intercessor, mediator; interferer, obstructor; tribune exercising the veto

inter·cĭdō -cĭdĕre -cĭdī *vi* to fall short, miss the mark; to happen in the meantime; to drop out, be lost

inter·cĭdō -cĭdĕre -cĭdī -cīsum *vt* to cut through, sever, cut down

intercĭn·ō -ĕre *vt* to interrupt with song or music

inter·cĭpĭō -cĭpĕre -cēpī -ceptum *vt* to intercept; to cut off (*the enemy*); to interrupt, cut off, preclude; to appropriate; to misappropriate; to receive by mistake (*e.g.*, poison)

intercīsē *adv* piecemeal

intercīsus *pp* of **intercido**

inter·clūdō -clūdĕre -clūsī -clūsum *vt* to shut off, shut out, cut off; to stop, block up; to hinder, prevent; to blockade, shut in; to cut off, intercept, separate, divide

interclūsi·ō -ōnis *f* stopping; parenthesis; **animae interclusio** shortwindedness

interclūsus *pp* of **intercludo**

intercolumn·ium -iī or **-ī** *n* space between columns, intercolumniation

inter·currō -currĕre -cucurrī -cursum *vi* to intervene, mediate; to mingle; to rush in

intercurs·ō -āre *vi* to crisscross; to infiltrate; **inter se intercursare** to crisscross each other

intercurs·us -ūs *m* intervention

interc·us -ūtis *adj* between the skin and flesh; **aqua intercus** dropsy

inter·dīcō -dīcĕre -dīxī -dictum *vt* to forbid, prohibit; *vi* to make a provisional decree; **aquā et igni interdicere** (with *dat*) to outlaw, banish

interdictĭ·ō -ōnis *f* prohibiting; **aquae et igni interdictio** banishment

interdict·um -ī *n* prohibition; contraband; provisional decree (*of a praetor*)

interdictus *pp* of **interdico**

interdĭū or **interdĭūs** *adv* by day, in the daytime

interd·ō -āre *vt* to give intermittently; to distribute

interduct·us -ūs *m* punctuation

interdum *adv* sometimes, now and then, occasionally; meanwhile

interdŭ·ō -āre *vt* **floccum interduo** or **nihil interduo** I don't give a hoot

intereā *adv* meanwhile, in the interim; meanwhile, anyhow, nevertheless

interemptus *pp* of **interimo**

inter·eō -īre -iī -itum *vi* to be done for, be finished, perish, be lost; to become extinct

ride in between

interequit·ō -āre *vt* to ride between (*e.g.*, the ranks or columns); *vi* to ride

interfāti·ō -ōnis *f* interruption

interfecti·ō -ōnis *f* killing

interfect·or -ōris *m* or **interfectrīx -īcis** *f* killer

inter·ficĭō -ficĕre -fēcī -fectum *vt* to destroy; to kill

inter·flĭō -flĭĕrī *vi* to pass away, be destroyed

inter·fluō -fluĕre -fluxī *vt* to flow between; *vi* to flow in between

inter·fodĭō -fodĕre -fōdī -fossum *vi* to pierce

interf·or -ārī -ātus sum *vt & vi* to interrupt

interfug·ĭō -ĕre *vi* to scatter

interfulg·ĕō -ēre *vi* (with *abl*) to shine amidst or among

interfūs·us -a -um *adj* spread here and there; (with *acc*) flowing between

interĭbī *adv* in the meantime

interim *adv* meanwhile; for the moment; sometimes; however, anyhow

inter·ĭmō -ĭmĕre -ēmī -emptum *vt* to do away with, abolish; to kill

inter·ĭor -ĭus *adj* inner, interior; inner side of; secret, private; deeper, more profound; more intimate, more personal, more confidential

interitĭ·ō -ōnis *f* ruin, destruction

interĭt·us -ūs *m* ruin; death

interius *adv* on the inside, in the middle; too short; (to listen) closely

interjac·ĕō -ēre *vi* (with *dat*) to lie between

interjaciō see **interjicio**

interjectī·ō -ōnis *f* interjection; parenthesis

interject·us -a -um *pp* of **interjicio**; *adj* (with *dat* or **inter** + *acc*) set or lying between

interject·us -ūs *m* interposition; interval

inter·jiciō -jicĕre -jēcī -jectum *vt* to interpose; (with *dat* or **inter** + *acc*) **a** to throw or set (*something*) between; **b** to intermingle (*something*) with, intermix (*something*) with

inter·jungō -jungĕre -junxī -junctum *vt* to join together; to clasp

inter·lābor -lābī -lapsus *vi* to glide or flow in between

inter·lĕgō -legĕre -lēgī -lectum *vt* to pick or pluck here and there

inter·linō -linĕre -lēvī -litum *vt* to smear; to alter by erasing

inter·lŏquor -lŏquī -locūtus sum *vi* to interrupt; (with *dat*) to interrupt (*someone*)

inter·lūcĕō -lūcĕre -luxī *vi* to shine through; to lighten now and then; to be transparent; to be plainly visible

interlūnĭ·a -ōrum *n pl* new moon

interlŭ·ō -ĕre *vt* to flow between, wash

intermenstrŭ·us -a -um *adj* of the new moon; *n* new moon

intermināt·us -a -um *adj* endless

intermĭn·or -ārī -ātus sum *vt* (with *dat*) to threaten (*someone*) with (*something*); *vi* to threaten

inter·miscĕō -miscēre -miscŭī -mixtum *vt* to intermingle

intermissĭ·ō -ōnis *f* interruption

inter·mittō -mittĕre -mīsī -missum *vt* to interrupt, break off, suspend, omit, neglect; to leave gaps in, leave unoccupied, leave undefended; to allow (*time*) to pass; *vi* to pause, stop

intermixtus *pp* of **intermisceo**

inter·morior -mŏrī -mortŭus sum *vi* to die suddenly; to faint

intermortŭ·us -a -um *adj* dead; unconscious; (fig) half-dead, moribund

intermundĭ·a -ōrum *n pl* outer space

intermūrāl·is -e *adj* intermural, between two walls

internāt·us -a -um *adj* (with *dat*) growing among or between

internecīn·us -a -um *adj* internecine, exterminating, of extermination

internecĭ·ō -ōnis *f* massacre, extermination

internecīv·us -a -um *adj* exterminating; **bellum internecivum** war of extermination

internĕc·ō -āre *vt* to kill off, exterminate

internect·ō -ĕre *vt* to intertwine

internit·ĕō -ēre *vi* to shine out

internōd·ĭum -iī or ·-ī *n* space between two joints

inter·noscō -noscĕre -nōvī -nōtum *vt* to distinguish, recognize; (with *ab* + *abl*) to distinguish (*one thing*) from (*another*)

internuntĭ·ō -āre *vi* to exchange messages

internunt·ĭus -iī or ·-ī *m* or **internuntĭ·a -ae** *f* messenger, courier, mediator, go-between

intern·us -a -um *adj* internal; civil, domestic

in·tĕrō -terĕre -trivī -trītum *vt* to rub in, mash together

interpellātĭ·ō -ōnis *f* interruption

interpellāt·or -ōris *m* interrupter, disturber

interpell·ō -āre *vt* to interrupt, break in on; to disturb, obstruct, hinder; to raise as an objection

interpŏl·is -e *adj* patched up

interpŏl·ō -āre *vt* to polish, dress up; to interpolate, falsify

inter·pōnō -pōnĕre -posŭī -posĭtum *vt* to insert, interpose, insert sperse; to introduce, insert; to introduce, admit (*a person*); to let (*time*) pass or elapse; to alter, falsify (*writings*); to allege, use as pretext; **operam** or **studium interponere** to apply effort; **se interponere** (with *dat* or **in** + *acc*) to interfere with, meddle with, get mixed up with

interposĭtĭ·ō -ōnis *f* insertion; introduction; parenthesis

interposĭtus *pp* of **interpono**

interposĭt·us -ūs *m* interposition

interpr·es -ĕtis *m & f* mediator, negotiator; middleman, broker; interpreter; expounder; translator

interpretātĭ·ō -ōnis *f* interpretation, explanation; meaning; translation

interprĕt·or -ārī -ātus sum *vt* to interpret, put a construction on, construe; to understand, infer, conclude; to decide, determine; to translate

inter·prīmō -prīmĕre -pressī -pressum *vt* to squeeze

interpunct·a -ōrum *n pl* pauses, punctuation

interpunctĭ·ō -ōnis *f* punctuation

interpunct·us -a -um *adj* well-divided

inter·quiescō -quiescĕre -quiēvī *vi* to rest awhile; to pause awhile

interregn·um -ī *n* interregnum (*time between death of one king and election of another or similar interval between consuls*)

inter·rex -rēgis *m* interrex, regent

interrĭt·us -a -um *adj* undaunted

interrogātĭ·ō -ōnis *f* question; interrogation, cross-examination; syllogism

interrogāt·um -ī *n* question.

interrŏg·ō -āre *vt* to ask, question; to interrogate, cross-examine; to indict, sue

inter·rumpō -rumpĕre -rūpī -ruptum *vt* to break apart, break in half, break up, smash; to divide, scatter; to interrupt, break off

interruptē *adv* with interruptions

interruptus *pp* of **interrumpo**

inter·saepiō -saepīre -saepsī -saeptum *vt* to fence off, enclose; to stop up, close, cut off

inter·scindō -scindĕre -scīdī -scissum *vt* to tear apart, tear down; to cut off, separate

inter·scrībō -scrībĕre -scrīpsī -scrīptum *vt* to write (*something*) in between

inter·sĕrō -gerĕre -seruī *vt* to interpose; to allege as an excuse

interspīrātī·ō -ōnis *f* breathing pause, correct breathing (*in delivering a speech*)

interstinct·us -a -um *adj* blotchy

inter·stinguō -stinguĕre — -stinctum *vt* to spot, blotch; to extinguish

interstring·ō -ĕre *vt* to strangle

inter·sum -esse -fuī *vi* to be present, assist, take part; to differ; to be of interest; (with *dat*) to be present at, attend, take part in; (with **in** + *abl*) to be present at; *v impers* there is a difference; it makes a difference; it is of importance; it is of interest; (with **inter** + *acc*) there is a difference between; (with **in** + *abl*) there is a difference among; (with *genit* or with *fem* of possessive pronouns **meā, tuā, nostrā,** *etc.*) it make a difference to, it is of importance to, it concerns (*me, you, us, etc.*); (with *genit* of value, e.g., **magni, permagni, tanti,** or with *adv* **multum, plurimum, maxime**) it makes a (*great, very great, such a great*) difference, it is of (*great, very great, such great*) importance, it is of (*great, very great, such great*) concern; **ne minimum quidem interest** there is not the slightest difference; **nihil omnino interest** there is no difference whatever

intertext·us -a -um *adj* interwoven

inter·trāhō -trahĕre -traxī *vt* (with *dat*) to take (*something*) away from

intertrīment·um -ī *n* wear and tear; loss, wastage

interturbātī·ō -ōnis *f* confusion, turmoil

interturb·ō -āre *vt* to confuse

intervall·um -ī *n* interval, space, distance; interval of time, spell, pause, intermission; contrast, difference

inter·vellō -vellĕre -vulsī -vulsum *vt* to pluck here and there

inter·veniō -venīre -vēnī -ventum *vt* to interfere with; *vi* to happen along; to intervene, intrude; to happen, occur; (with *dat*) to interfere with, interrupt, put a stop to, come in the way of, oppose, prevent

intervent·or -ōris *m* intruder, untimely visitor.

intervent·us -ūs *m* intervention, intrusion; mediation

inter·vertō or **inter·vortō -ver-tĕre -vertī -versum** *vt* to divert, embezzle; (with *acc* of person and *abl* of thing) to rob or cheat (*someone*) of

inter·vīsō -vīsĕre -vīsī -vīsum *vt* to visit from time to time; to look after

intervŏlĭt·ō -āre *vi* to flit about

intervŏm·ō -ĕre -uī -ĭtum *vt* (with **inter** + *acc*) to throw up amongst

intervulsus *pp* of **intervello**

intestābĭl·is -e *adj* infamous, notorious; wicked

intestātō *adv* intestate

intestāt·us -a -um *adj* intestate; unconvicted by witnesses.

intestāt·us -a -um *adj* castrated

intestīn·us -a -um *adj* internal; *n & n pl* intestines

in·texō -texĕre -texuī -textum *vt* to interweave, interlace; to weave; to embroider; to surround, envelop

intĭb·um -ī *n* endive

intĭmē *adv* intimately, cordially

intĭm·us or **intŭm·us -a -um** *adj* innermost; deepest, most profound; most secret, most intimate; *m* intimate friend

in·tingō or **in·tinguō -tingĕre -tinxī -tinctum** *vt* to dip, soak

intolerābĭl·is -e *adj* intolerable; irresistible

intolerand·us -a -um *adj* intolerable

intolĕr·ans -antis *adj* intolerable, insufferable; (with *genit*) unable to stand, unable to put up with

intoleranter *adv* intolerably, immoderately, excessively

intolerantĭ·a -ae *f* unbearableness, insolence

intŏn·ō -āre -uī -ātus *vt* to thunder out; *vi* to thunder

intons·us -a -um *adj* unshorn, untrimmed; long-haired; rude

in·torquĕō -torquēre -torsī -tortum *vt* to twist, turn, roll; (with **circum** + *acc*) to wrap (*something*) around; (with *dat* or **in** + *acc*) to aim, cast, throw (*a weapon*) at

intort·us -a -um *adj* twisted; tangled; (fig) crooked

intrā *adv* on the inside, inside, within; inward; *prep* (with *acc*) inside, within; during, within, in the course of, in less than; less than, fewer than, within the limits of

intrābĭl·is -e *adj* inaccessible

intractābĭl·is -e *adj* intractable, unmanageable; formidable, dangerous

intractāt·us -a -um *adj* untamed, wild; unbroken (*horse*); unattempted intrem·iscō -iscĕre -ŭī *vi* to begin to shake or tremble

intrĕm·ō -ĕre -ŭī *vi* to shake, tremble, shiver

intrepidē *adv* calmly, intrepidly

intrepid·us -a -um *adj* calm, intrepid, not nervous

intrīc·ō -āre *vt* to entangle, involve

intrinsĕcus *adv* on the inside

intrīt·us -a -um *adj* not worn away; (fig) not worn out

intrō *adv* inwards, inside, in

intr·ō -āre *vt* & *vi* to enter; to penetrate

intrō·dūcō -dūcĕre -duxī -ductum *vt* to introduce

introductĭ·ō -ōnis *f* introduction

intro·ĕō -īre -ĭī -ĭtum *vt* & *vi* to enter

intrō·fĕrō -ferre -tŭlī -lātum *vt* to carry in

intrō·gredĭor -gredī -gressus sum *vi* to step inside

introīt·us -ūs *m* entrance; beginning, prelude

intrōlātus *pp* of introfero

intrō·mittō -mittĕre -mīsī -missum *vt* to let in, admit

introrsum or introrsus *adv* inwards, towards the inside; (fig) inwardly, inside

intrō·rumpō -rumpĕre -rūpī -ruptum *vi* to break in, enter by force

introspect·ō -āre *vt* to look in on

intrō·spicĭō -spicĕre -spexī -spectum *vt* to look into, look at; (fig) to inspect, examine, observe; *vi* (with in + *acc*) to look into; (fig) to look into, inspect, examine

intŭb·um -ī *n* endive

in·tŭeor -tŭērī -tŭĭtus sum *vt* to look at, gaze upon; to contemplate, consider; to look up to, have regard for, admire; to keep an eye on

intum·escō -escĕre -ŭī *vi* to swell up, rise; (of voice) to grow louder; (of river) to rise; to become angry; to get a big head, swell with pride

intumulāt·us -a -um *adj* unburied

in·tŭor -tŭī *vt* to look at, gaze at; to consider

inturbĭd·us -a -um *adj* undisturbed, quiet

intus *adv* inside, within; at home, in; to the inside; from within

intūt·us -a -um *adj* unguarded; unsafe

inūl·a -ae *f* elecampane (*plant*)

inult·us -a -um *adj* unavenged; unpunished, without being punished

inumbr·ō -āre *vt* to shade; to cover

inundātĭ·ō -ōnis *f* inundation

inund·ō -āre *vt* to flood, inundate; *vi* to overflow; sanguine inundare to run red with blood

in·ungō -ungĕre -unxī -unctum *vt* to anoint

inurbānē *adv* impolitely, rudely; without wit

inurbān·us -a -um *adj* impolite, rude, rustic

in·urgĕō -urgēre -ursī *vi* to butt

in·ūrō -ūrĕre -ussī -ustum *vt* to burn in, brand, imprint; (with *dat*) a to brand upon, imprint upon, affix to; b to inflict upon

inūsĭtātē *adv* unusually, strangely

inūsĭtāt·us .-a -um *adj* unusual, strange, uncommon, extraordinary

inustus *pp* of inuro

inūtĭl·is -e *adj* useless, unprofitable; impractical; injurious, harmful

inūtĭlĭt·ās -ātis *f* uselessness; harmfulness

inūtĭliter *adv* uselessly, unprofitably

in·vādō -vādĕre -vāsī -vāsum *vt* to come or go into, enter; to enter upon, undertake, attempt; to invade, attack, assault, rush upon; (fig) to seize, take possession of; *vi* to come or go in; to invade; (with in + *acc*) a to assail, attack, invade; b to seize, get possession of, usurp

inval·escō -escĕre -ŭī *vi* to grow stronger

invalĭd·us -a -um *adj* weak, feeble, impotent; inadequate, unsuitable

invāsus *pp* of invado

invectĭ·ō -ōnis *f* importing, importation; arrival by boat

in·vĕhō -vehĕre -vexī -vectum *vt* to carry in, bring in (*by cart, horse, boat, etc.*); (with *dat*) to bring (*e.g., evils*) upon; invehi (with *acc* or in + *acc*) a to ride into, sail into; b to attack; c to inveigh against, attack (*with words*); inveheq equo to ride a horse; invehi nave to sail; se invehere (with *acc* or in + *acc*) to rush against, attack

invendĭbĭl·is -e *adj* unsalable

in·venĭō -venīre -vēnī -ventum *vt* to come upon, find, come across, discover; to find out, invent, devise; to learn, ascertain; to acquire, get, reach, earn

inventĭ·ō -ōnis *f* inventiveness; inventing, invention

invent·or -ōris *m* or inventr·īx -īcis *f* inventor, author, discoverer

invent·us -a -um *pp* of invenio; *n* invention, discovery

invenust·us -a -um *adj* having no sex appeal; homely, unattractive; unlucky in love

inverēcund·us -a -um *adj* disrespectful, immodest, shameless

inverg·ō -ĕre *vt* to pour upon

inversĭ·ō -ōnis *f* inversion (*of words*); irony; allegory

invers·us -a -um *adj* turned upside down; turned inside out

in·vertō -vertĕre -vertī -versum *vt* to invert, turn upside down, upset, reverse, turn inside out; to transpose, reverse; to pervert, abuse, misrepresent; to use ironically

invesperasc·it -ĕre *v impers* evening is approaching, twilight is falling

investĭgātĭ·ō -ōnis *f* investigation

investigāt·or -ōris *m* investigator, researcher

investīg·ō -āre *vt* to track, trace, search after; to investigate, search into, search after

inveter·ascō -ascěre -āvī *vi* to begin to grow old, grow old; to become fixed, become established; to become rooted, grow inveterate; to become obsolete

inveterāti·ō -ōnis *f* chronic illness

inveterāt·us -a -um *adj* inveterate, long-standing

invicem or **in vicem** *adv* in turn, taking turns, one after another, alternately; mutually, each other

invict·us -a -um *adj* unconquered; invincible

invid·ens -entis *adj* envious, jealous

invidenti·a -ae *f* enviousness, jealousy

in·vidĕō -vidēre -vīdī -vīsum *vt* to cast an evil eye on; to envy, begrudge; *vi* (with *dat*) to envy, begrudge; (with *dat* of person and *abl* of cause or **in** + *abl*) to begrudge (*someone something*), envy (*someone because of something*)

invidi·a -ae *f* envy, jealousy; unpopularity; **invidiae esse** (with *dat*) to be a cause of envy to; **invidiam habere** to be unpopular, be hated

invidiōsē *adv* spitefully

invidiōs·us -a -um *adj* envious, spiteful; envied; causing envy

invid·us -a -um *adj* envious, jealous; (with *dat*) hostile to, unfavorable to

invigil·ō -āre *vi* to be alert, be on one's toes; (with *dat*) to be on the lookout for, keep an eye on, pay attention to, watch over; (with **pro** + *abl*) to watch over

inviolābil·is -e *adj* inviolable; invulnerable, indestructible

inviolātē *adv* inviolately

inviolāt·us -a -um *adj* inviolate, unhurt; inviolable

invisitāt·us -a -um *adj* rarely seen; not seen before, unknown, strange

in·vīsō -vīsěre -vīsī -vīsum *vt* to visit, get to see; to look into, inspect; to look after; to get sight of

invīs·us -a -um *pp* of **invideo**; *adj* unseen; hateful, detested; hostile

invītāment·um -ī *n* attraction, allurement, inducement

invītāti·ō -ōnis *f* invitation; challenge

invītāt·us -ūs *m* invitation

invītē *adv* unwillingly, against one's wish

invīt·ō -āre *vt* to invite; to entertain; to summon, challenge; to ask, request; to allure, attract; to encourage, court

invīt·us -a -um *adj* reluctant, unwilling, against one's will; **invītā Minervā** against one's better judgment, against the grain

invi·us -a -um *adj* without a road, trackless, impassable; *n pl* rough terrain

invocāti·ō -ōnis *f* invocation

invocāt·us -a -um *adj* unbidden

invŏc·ō -āre *vt* to invoke, call upon, appeal to

involāt·us -ūs *m* flight

involgō see **invulgo**

involit·ō -āre *vi* (with *dat*) (of long hair) to float over, trail over

invol·ō -āre *vt* to swoop down upon, pounce upon; *vi* to swoop down; (with **in** + *acc*) to swoop down upon, pounce upon

involūcr·e -is *n* smock

involūcr·um -ī *n* wrapper, cover, case, envelope; (fig) cover-up, front

involūt·us -a -um *adj* complicated

in·volvō -volvěre -volvī -volūtum *vt* to wrap up, involve, envelop; to cover completely, overwhelm; (with *dat* or **in** + *acc*) to pile (*something*) on; **se involvere** (with *dat*) (fig) to get all wrapped up in

involvŏl·us -ī *m* caterpillar

invulg·ō -āre *vi* to give evidence

invulnerāt·us -a -um *adj* unwounded

iō *interj* ho!

io- = jo-

Ī·ō -ūs or **Ī·ōn -ōnis** *f* Io (*daughter of Argive King Inachus, changed by Jupiter into a heifer, and driven by Juno in this form over the world under the surveillance of hundred-eyed Argus*)

Īocast·a -ae or **Īocast·ē -ēs** *f* wife of Laius and mother as well as wife of Oedipus

Īol·a -ī *m* son of Iphicles and companion of Hercules

Īol·ē -ēs *f* daughter of Eurytus, the king of Oechalia, who fell in love with Hercules

Īōn see **Io**

Īōn·es -um *m pl* Ionians (*Greek inhabitants of the W. coast of Asia Minor*)

Īōnǐc·us -a -um *adj* Ionic; *m* Ionic dancer; *n pl* Ionic dance

Īōnǐ·us -a -um *adj* Ionian; *f* Ionia (*coastal district of Asia Minor*); *n* Ionian Sea (*off the W. Coast of Greece*)

īōta (*indecl*) *n* iota (*ninth letter of the Greek alphabet*)

Īphianass·a -ae *f* Iphigenia

Īphigenī·a -ae *f* daughter of Agamemnon and Clytemnestra, who was to have been sacrificed at Aulis but was saved by Diana and conveyed to the Tauric Chersonese, where she became priestess of Diana

Īphǐt·us -ī *m* Argonaut, son of Eurytus and Antiope

ips·a -īus or **-īus** *adj* self, very, just, mere, precisely; in person; by herself, alone; of herself, of her own accord; *pron* she herself; mistress of the house

ips·e (or **ips·us**) **-īus** (or **-īus**) *adj* self, very, just, mere, precisely; in person; by himself, alone; of himself, of his own accord; *pron* he himself; master; host

ips·um -īus or **-īus** *adj* self, very, just, mere, precisely; by itself, alone; of itself, spontaneously; **nunc ipsum** just now; **tunc ipsum** just then; *pron* it itself, that itself; **ipsum quod . . .** the very fact that . . .

ipsus see **ipse**

īr·a -ae *f* ire, wrath, resentment

īrācundē *adv* angrily; passionately

īrācundi·a -ae *f* quick temper; anger, wrath, violence, passion; resentment

īrācund·us -a -um *adj* hot-tempered, quick-tempered, irritable; angry; resentful

īrasc·or -ī *vi* to get angry, fly into a rage; (with *dat*) to get angry at

īrātē *adv* angrily

īrāt·us -a -um *adj* angry, irate, enraged; (with *dat*) angry at

Īr·is -idis *f* goddess of the rainbow and messenger of the gods

īrōni·a -ae *f* irony

irrās·us -a -um *adj* unshaven

irrationāl·is -e *adj* irrational

ir·rauescō -raucescĕre -rausī *vi* to become hoarse

irredivīv·us -a -um *adj* irreparable

irrĕd·ux -ŭcis *adj* one-way (*road*)

irreligāt·us -a -um *adj* not tied

irreligiōsē *adv* impiously

irreligiōs·us -a -um *adj* impious, irreligious

irremeābil·is -e *adj* not to be traversed; one-way

irreparābil·is -e *adj* irretrievable

irrepert·us -a -um *adj* undiscovered, not found

ir·rēpō -rēpĕre -repsī -reptum *vi* to creep in; (fig) to sneak in; (with **ad** or **in** + *acc*) to creep toward or into; (fig) to sneak up on

irreprehens·us -a -um *adj* blameless

irrequiēt·us -a -um *adj* restless

irresect·us -a -um *adj* untrimmed

irresolūt·us -a -um *adj* not loosened, still tied

irrēt·iō -īre -īvī or **-iī -ītum** *vt* to trap

irretort·us -a -um *adj* not turned back

irrevĕr·ens -entis *adj* irreverent, disrespectful

irreverenter *adv* irreverently, disrespectfully

irreverenti·a -ae *f* irreverence, disrespect

irrevocābil·is -e *adj* irrevocable; implacable, relentless

irrevocāt·us -a -um *adj* not called back, not asked back

ir·rīdĕō -rīdēre -rīsī -rīsum *vt* to

ridicule, laugh at, mock; *vi* to laugh, joke; (with *dat*) to laugh at

irrīdiculē *adv* with no sense of humor

irrigāti·ō -ōnis *f* irrigation

irrig·ō -āre *vt* to irrigate, water; to inundate; (fig) to diffuse; (fig) to flood, steep, soak

irrigu·us -a -um *adj* wet, soaked, well-watered; refreshing

irrīsi·ō -ōnis *f* ridicule, mockery

irrīs·or -ōris *m* reviler, mocker

irrīsus *pp* of **irrideo**

irrīs·us -ūs *m* mockery, derision; laughing stock, object of derision

irrītābil·is -e *adj* easily excited, easily enraged, irritable, sensitive

irrītām·en -inis *n* incentive; provocation

irrītāment·um -ī *n* incentive; provocation

irrītāti·ō -ōnis *f* incitement; irritation, provocation; stimulant

irrīt·ō -āre *vt* to incite, excite, provoke, enrage

irrīt·us -a -um *adj* invalid, null and void; futile, pointless, useless; unsuccessful (*person*)

irrogāti·ō -ōnis *f* imposing (*e.g.*, of a *fine*)

irrŏg·ō -āre *vt* to impose, inflict; to object to (*proposals*)

irrŏr·ō -āre *vt* to wet, moisten, sprinkle

irruct·ō -āre *vi* to belch

ir·rumpō -rumpĕre -rūpī -ruptum *vt* to rush into, break down; *vi* to rush in; (with *dat* or **in** + *acc*) **a** to rush into, rush through; **b** (fig) to intrude upon

ir·ruō -ruĕre -ruī *vi* to rush in, force one's way in; to make a slip (*in speaking*); (with **in** + *acc*) to rush into, rush on, invade, attack; **inruere in odium** (with *genit*) to incur the anger of

irrupti·ō -ōnis *f* invasion

irrupt·us -a -um *pp* of **irrumpo;** *adj* unbroken

Īr·us -ī *m* beggar in the palace of Ulysses in Ithaca

is ejus *adj* this, that, the said, the aforesaid; *pron* he; **is qui** he who, the person who, the one who

Īs·is -is or **-īdis** *f* Egyptian goddess

Ismar·us -a -um *adj* of Mt. Ismarus in Thrace; Thracian

Īsocrāt·ēs -is *m* famous orator and teacher of rhetoric at Athens (436-338 B.C.)

ista see **iste**

istāc *adv* that way

istactĕnus *adv* thus far

istaec see **istic**

ist·e -a -ud *adj* that of yours; this, that, the, the very, that particular; such, of such a kind; that terrible, that despicable; *pron* that one; (in court) your client

Isthm·us or **Isthm·os -ī** *m* Isthmus of Corinth

ist·ic -aec -oc or **-uc** *adj* that, that of yours; *pron* the one, that one

istic *adv* there, in that place; here-in; on this occasion

istinc *adv* from there, from where you are

istīusmŏdī or **istīmŏdī** or **istīus modī** or **istī modī** *adj* that kind of, such

istō *adv* where you are; therefore; in that matter

istōc *adv* there, to where you are, yonder

istorsum *adv* in that direction

istūc *adv* there, to that place, to where you are, that way; **istuc ve-niam** I'll come to that matter

istūcĭne see **istic**

istud see **iste**

ita *adv* thus, so, in this manner, in this way; (of natural consequence) thus, accordingly, therefore, under these circumstances; (in affirma-tion) yes, true, exactly; (in ques-tions) really?, truly?; **ita . . . ut** (in comparisons) just as, although . . . nevertheless; (as correlatives) both . . . and, both . . . as well as; (in restriction) on condition that, in sofar as, on the assumption that; (of degree) to such a degree . . . that, so much . . . that, so . . . that; **non ita** not very, not especially; **quid ita?** how so?, what do you mean?

Itali·a -ae *f* Italy

Italic·us -a -um *adj* Italian

Ĭtăl·is -ĭdis *adj* Italian; *f pl* Italian women

Ĭtali·us -a -um *adj* Italian; *f* see **Italia**

Ĭtăl·us -a -um *adj* Italian

ităque *conj* and so, and thus, accord-ingly, therefore, consequently

item *adv* likewise, besides, moreover, also

it·er -inĕris *n·* journey, trip, march, walk; day's march, day's journey; route; right of way; passage (*of voice, etc.*); method, course, way, road; **ex itinere** or **in itinere** en route; **iter flectere** to change course; **iter terrestre** overland route; **maximis itineribus** by marching at top speed

iterāti·ō -ōnis *f* repetition

itĕr·ō -āre *vt·* to repeat, renew; to plow again

itĕrum *adv* again, a second time; **iterum atque iterum** repeatedly, again and again

Ithăc·a -ae or **Ithăc·ē -ēs** *f* island off the W. coast of Greece in the Ionian Sea and home of Odysseus

itĭdem *adv* in the same way

itĭ·ō -ōnis *f* going, walking

it·ō -āre *vi* to go

it·us -ūs *m* going; going away, de-parture

Ĭt·ys -ўos *m* son of Tereus and Procne, who was killed by Procne and served up as food to Tereus

iu- = ju-

Ixī·ōn -ōnis *m* son of Antion, or of Jupiter, king of the Laipthae in Thessaly, and father of Pirithous; he was allowed into heaven by Jūpi-ter after killing his father-in-law, but for trying to seduce Juno, was tied to a wheel and sent flying into Tartarus

J

jac·ĕŏ -ēre -ŭi *vi* to lie, lie down; to lie ill, be sick; to lie dead, to have fallen; to lie in ruins; to hang loose; to lie idle, rest; to lie, be situated; to lie flat, lie low; to feel low, be despondent; to lie prostrate, be powerless; to fall, fail, be refuted; to be low in someone's opinion; to linger, stay

jaciō jacĕre jēcī jactum *vt* to lay, build, establish, set, found, con-struct; to throw, cast, fling; to emit, produce; to sow, scatter; to throw away; to mention, utter, declare, intimate

jact·ans -antis *adj* boasting, brag-ging, showing off

jactanter *adv* boastfully

jactanti·a -ae *f* boasting, showing off

jactāti·ō -ōnis *f* tossing to and fro; swaying; shaking; writhing; boast-ing, bragging, showing off; gesticu-lation; **jactatio animi** agitation; **jactatio maritima** seasickness

jactāt·us -ūs *m* tossing, waving

jactĭt·ō -āre *vt* to display, show off

jact·ō -āre *vt* to throw, hurl; to toss about, shake; to throw away, throw out, throw overboard; to disturb, disquiet, stir up; to consider, dis-cuss; to throw out, mention; to brag about, show off; **jactari** to toss, rock; (of money) to fluctuate in value; **se jactare** to boast, show off, throw one's weight around

jactūr·a -ae *f* throwing away, throw-ing overboard; loss, sacrifice

jactus *pp* of **jacio**

jact·us -ūs *m* toss, throw, cast

jaculābĭl·is -e *adj* missile

jaculāt·or -ōris *m* thrower, shooter; light-armed soldier; spearman

jaculātr·ix -īcis *f* huntress

jacŭl·or -ārī -ātus sum *vt* to throw; to shoot at; (fig) to aim at, strive after

jacŭl·us -a -um *adj* throwing, cast-ing; *n* dart, javelin; casting net

jājūn- = jejun-

jam adv (present) now, already; (past) already, by then; (future) very soon, right away; (in transition) now, next, moreover; (for emphasis) actually, precisely, quite; (in a conclusion) then surely; **jam dudum** long ago, long since; **jam inde** immediately; **jam jam** even now, at every moment; **jam . . . jam** at one time . . . at another; **jam nunc** even now; **jam pridem** long since; **jam tum** even then, even at that time

Jānicŭl·um -ī n Roman hill on the right bank of the Tiber

jānĭt·or -ōris m doorman

jānĭtr·ix -īcis f portress

jānŭ·a -ae f door, house door; entrance; (fig) entrance, approach

Jānuārĭ·us -a -um adj & m January

jān·us -ī m covered passage, arcade

Jān·us -ī m Janus (old Italian deity, represented as having two faces); temple of Janus (at the bottom of the Argiletum in the Forum)

jec·ur -ŏris n liver; (as the seat of emotions) anger, lust

jecuscŭl·um -ī n little liver

jējūnē adv (fig) drily

jējūniōs·ior or **jājūniōs·ior -ius** adj fasting, hungry

jējūnĭt·ās or **jājūnĭt·ās -ātis** f fasting; dryness (of style)

jējūn·ium -ĭī or **-ī** n fasting, fast; hunger; leanness

jējūn·us or **jājūn·us -a -um** adj fasting; hungry; poor (land); thin; insignificant, paltry, contemptible; low; dry (style)

jentācŭl·um -ī n breakfast

joc·or -ārī -ātus sum or **joc·ō -āre** vt to say in jest; vi to joke, crack a joke, be joking

jocōsē adv humorously, as a joke, jokingly

jocōs·us -a -um adj humorous, funny, clowning

joculār·is -e adj humorous, funny

joculārĭ·us -a -um adj ludicrous

joculāt·or -ōris m joker

jocul·or -ārī -ātus sum vi to joke

jocŭl·us -ī m joke

joc·us -ī (pl: **joc·ī -ōrum** m or **joc·a -ōrum** n) m joke; laughingstock; child's play; **joco remoto** all joking aside; **per jocum** as a joke, jokingly

jub·a -ae f mane; crest

jub·ar -ăris n radiance, brightness; sunshine

jubāt·us -a -um adj crested

jubĕō jubēre jussī jussum vt to order; (pol) to order, decree, enact, ratify; to designate, appoint, assign; (med) to prescribe; **jube fratrem tuum salvere** (in letters) best regards to your brother

jūcundē adv pleasantly, delightfully, agreeably

jūcundĭt·ās -ātis f pleasantness, delight, enjoyment, agreeableness; f pl favors

jūcund·us -a -um adj pleasant, delightful, agreeable

Jūdae·us -a -um adj Jewish; m Jew; f Jewess; Judaea, Palestine

jūd·ex -ĭcis m judge; juror; arbitrator; umpire; critic, scholar; **judex morum** censor; **me judice** in my judgment

jūdĭcātĭ·ō -ōnis f judicial investigation; (fig) judgment, opinion

jūdĭcāt·us -a -um adj decided, determined; m condemned person; n decision, precedent; fine; **judicatum facere** to carry out a decision; **judicatum solvere** to pay a fine

jūdĭcāt·us -ūs m judgeship

jūdĭcĭāl·is -e adj judicial, forensic

jūdĭcĭārĭ·us -a -um adj judiciary

jūdĭc·ium -ĭī or **-ī** n trial, court, court of justice; sentence; jurisdiction; opinion, decision; faculty of judging, judgment, good judgment, taste, tact, discretion

jūdĭc·ō -āre vt to judge; to examine; to sentence, condemn; to form an opinion of; to conclude; to declare, proclaim; (with dat of person and acc of the offense) to convict (someone) of; (with genit) to find (someone) guilty of; (with dat of person and genit of the offense) to convict (someone) of

jugāl·is -e adj yoked together; nuptial

jugātĭ·ō -ōnis f tying up

jūgĕr·um -ī n jugerum (land measure: about two thirds of an acre)

jūg·is -e adj continual, perennial, inexhaustible

jugl·ans -andis f walnut tree

jugōs·us -a -um adj hilly

Jugŭl·ae -ārum f pl Orion's belt (three stars in the constellation Orion)

jugŭl·ō -āre vt to cut the throat of, kill, murder; to destroy; to silence

jugŭl·um -ī n or **jugŭl·us -ī** m throat

jug·um -ī n yoke, collar; pair, team; (mil) yoke (consisting of a spear laid crosswise on two upright spears, under which the conquered had to pass); crossbar (of a loom); thwart (of a boat); common bond, union; wedlock; pair, couple; mountain ridge; n pl heights

Jugurth·a -ae m king of Numidia (160–104 B.C.)

Jūlĭ·a -ae f aunt of Julius Caesar and wife of Marius; daughter of Julius Caesar and wife of Pompey (d. 54 B.C.); daughter of Augustus by Scribonia (39 B.C.–14 A.D.)

Jūlĭ·us -a -um adj Julian; of July; m Roman praenomen; July

jūment·um -ī n beast of burden, horse, mule

junce·us -a -um adj of reeds; slim, slender

juncōs·us -a -um adj overgrown with reeds

junctĭ·ō -ōnis f joining

junctūr·a -ae f joining, uniting, joint, juncture; connection, relationship; combination

junct·us -a -um pp of jungo; adj connected, associated, united, attached

junc·us -ī m reed

jungō jungĕre junxī junctum vt to join, join together, unite, connect; to yoke, harness; to couple, pair, mate; to bridge (a river); to bring together, unite, associate, ally; to add; to compose (poems); to combine (words)

jūnĭ·or -ōris adj younger

jūnĭpĕr·us -ī f juniper

Jūnĭ·us -a -um adj June, of June; m Roman praenomen; June

jūn·ix -īcis f heifer

Jūn·ō -ōnis f daughter of Saturn and wife and sister of Jupiter

Juppĭter (or **Jupĭter** or **Diespĭter**) **Jovis** m son of Saturn, brother and husband of Juno, and chief god of the Romans

jūrāt·or -ōris m judge; assistant censor

jūreconsult·us -ī m legal expert, lawyer

jūrejūr·ō -āre vi to swear

jūreperītus see jurisperitus

jurg·ĭum -ī or **-ī** n quarrel; n pl reproaches

jurg·ō -āre vi to quarrel

jūridĭcĭāl·is -e adj juridical

jūrisconsult·us or **jūreconsult·us -ī** m legal expert, lawyer

jūrisdictĭ·ō -ōnis f administration of justice; jurisdiction

jūrisperīt·us or **jūreperīt·us -ī** m legal expert, lawyer

jūr·ō -āre vt to swear; to swear by, attest, call to witness; to swear to, attest; vi to swear, take an oath; to conspire; (with **in** + acc) to swear allegiance to, swear to observe, vow obedience to; **in haec verba jurare** to swear according to the prescribed form; to conspire against; **jurare calumniam** to swear that the accusation is not false

jū·s -ris n juice, broth, gravy, soup; law (as established by society and custom rather than statute law); right, justice; law court, court of justice; legal right, authority, permission, prerogative; jurisdiction; **in jus ire** to go to court; **jure** by right, rightfully, in justice; **jus dicere** to sit as judge, hold court; **jus**

gentium international law; **jus publicum** common right; **summum jus** strict letter of the law

jūs jūrand·um (genit: **jūr·is jūrand·ī**) n oath

jussū (abl only) m by order; **meo jussu** by my order

juss·us -a -um pp of jubeo; n order, command, bidding

justē adv justly, rightly

justĭfĭc·us -a -um adj just-dealing

justĭtĭ·a -ae f justice, fairness

justĭt·ĭum -ĭī or **-ī** n suspension of legal business; (fig) standstill

just·us -a -um adj just, fair; justified, well-founded; formal; in due order, according to protocol, regular; n justice; due measure; **plus quam justo** more than due measure, too much; n pl rights; formalities; ceremonies, due ceremony; funeral rites, obsequies

Jūturn·a -ae f nymph, sister of Turnus, the king of the Rutuli

jūtus pp of juvo

juvenāl·is -e adj youthful; juvenile

Juvenāl·is -is m Juvenal (D. Junius Juvenalis, Roman satirist in the time of Domitian and Trajan, c. 62-142 A.D.)

juvenc·us -a -um adj young; m bullock; young man; f heifer; girl

juven·escō -escĕre -uī vi to grow up; to get young again

juvenīl·is -e adj youthful; juvenile; cheerful

juvenīlĭter adv youthfully, boyishly

juvĕn·is -e adj young; m young man (between the ages of twenty and forty-five); warrior; f young lady

juvĕn·or -ārī -ātus sum vi to act like a kid

juvent·a -ae f youth

juvent·ās -ātis f youth, prime of life, manhood; (collectively) young people, youth

juvent·ūs -ūtis f youth, prime of life, manhood; (collectively) young people, youth

juvō juvāre jūvī jūtum vt to help; to please, delight; **juvat** (with inf) it helps to; **juvat me** it delights me, I am glad

juxtā adv nearby, in close proximity; alike, in like manner, equally; (with **ac, atque, et, quam**, or **cum**) as well as, just the same as; prep (with acc) close to, near to, next to; next to, immediately after; near, bordering upon; next door to

juxtim adv near; equally

K

Kalend·ae or **Calend·ae -ārum** f pl Kalends (first day of the Roman month); **tristes Kalendae** gloomy Kalends (because interest was due on the Kalends)

Kalendār·ĭum -ĭī or **-ī** n account book

Karthāginiens·is -e adj Carthaginian

Karthāg·ō -ĭnis f Carthage (city of N. Africa)

L

labasc·ō -ĕre *vi* to waver; to give in, yield

lābēcŭl·a -ae *f* blemish, spot, stain (*e.g., on someone's reputation*)

labe·faciō -facĕre -fēcī -factum *vt* to cause to totter, to shake, to weaken; (fig) to weaken, ruin, destroy

labefact·ō -āre *vt* to shake; (fig) to weaken, ruin, destroy

labell·um -ī *n* lip

lābell·um -ī *n* small basin

lāb·ēs -is *f* fall, falling down; stroke, blow, ruin, destruction; blemish, spot, defect; disgrace, discredit

labi·a -ae *f* lip

Labiēn·us -ī *m* Caesar's officer who defected to Pompey

labiōs·us -a -um *adj* thick-lipped

lab·ium -iī or **-ī** *n* lip

lab·ō -āre *vi* to totter, wobble; to waver, hesitate, be undecided; to fall to pieces, go to ruin

lābor lābī lapsus sum *vi* to glide, slide, slip; to slip, fall, sink; to slip away, disappear, escape; (of time) to slip by, pass, elapse; (fig) to fade

lab·or or **lab·ōs -ōris** *m* effort; trouble, distress, suffering; work, task

labōrif·er -ĕra -ĕrum *adj* struggling

labōriōs·us -a -um *adj* full of troubles, troublesome; energetic, industrious

labōr·ō -āre *vt* to work out, make, produce; *vi* to work; to suffer, be troubled; to be in danger; (with *inf*) to try to

labōs see **labor**

labr·um -ī *n* lip, edge

lābr·um -ī *n* basin, tub, bathtub

labrusc·a -ae *f* wild vine

labrusc·um -ī *n* wild grape

labyrinthē·us -a -um *adj* labyrinthine

labyrinth·us -ī *m* labyrinth

lac lactis *n* milk; milk of plants

Lacaen·a -ae *f* Spartan woman

Lacedaem·ōn -ŏnis *f* Sparta

Lacedaemŏni·a -a -um *adj* Spartan

lac·er -ĕra -ĕrum *adj* mangled, torn, lacerated, mutilated; lacerating, tearing

lacerāti·ō -ōnis *f* tearing, laceration, mangling

lacern·a -ae *f* coat, topcoat, overcoat

lacernāt·us -a -um *adj* wearing an overcoat

lacĕr·ō -āre *vt* to lacerate, tear, mangle; to slander, abuse; to waste, squander, destroy; to wreck (*ship*)

lacert·us -a -um *adj* muscular, brawny; *m* lizard; upper arm, muscle; *m pl* muscles, strength, brawn; *f* lizard

lacess·ō -ĕre -īvī or **-iī -ītum** *vt* to provoke, exasperate; to challenge; to move, arouse

Lachĕs·is -is *f* one of the three Fates

lacini·a -ae *f* flap (*of a garment*)

Lacīn·ium -iī or **-ī** *n* promontory in Bruttium with a temple to Juno

Lac·ō or **Lac·ōn -ōnis** *m* Spartan; Spartan dog

Lacōni·a -ae *f* district of the Peloponnesus of which Sparta was the chief city

Lacōnic·us -a -um *adj* Spartan; *n* sweat bath

lacrim·a or **lacrŭm·a -ae** *f* tear; gumdrop (*plant*)

lacrimābil·is -e *adj* worthy of tears, deplorable

lacrimābund·us -a -um *adj* tearful, about to break into tears

lacrim·ō or **lacrŭm·ō -āre** *vt* to cry for, shed tears over; (of trees) to drip; *vi* to cry, shed tears

lacrimōs·us -a -um *adj* crying, tearful; causing tears, bringing tears to the eyes

lacrimŭl·a -ae *f* teardrop, little tear; (fig) crocodile tear

lacrum· = lacrim·

lact·ans -antis *adj* milk-giving

lactāri·us -a -um *adj* milky

lactāti·ō -ōnis *f* allurement

lact·ens -entis *adj* suckling; milky, juicy, tender; full of milk; *m* suckling

lacteŏl·us -a -um *adj* milk-white

lact·ēs -ium *f pl* intestines; **laxae lactes** empty stomach

lactesc·ō -ĕre *vi* to turn to milk

lactē·us -a -um *adj* milky, full of milk, milk-colored, milk-white

lact·ō -āre *vt* to cajole, wheedle

lactūc·a -ae *f* lettuce

lacūn·a -ae *f* ditch, hole, pit; pond, pool; (fig) hole, gap

lacūn·ar -āris *n* paneled ceiling

lacūn·ō -āre *vt* to panel

lacūnōs·us -a -um *adj* sunken

lac·us -ūs *m* vat; tank, pool, reservoir, cistern; lake

laedō laedĕre laesī laesum *vt* to knock, strike; to hurt, rub open; to wound; to break (*promise, pledge*); to offend, outrage, violate; (with **ad + acc**) to smash (*something*) against

laen·a -ae *f* lined coat

Lāërt·ēs -ae *m* father of Ulysses

Lāërtiăd·ēs -ae *m* Ulysses

laesi·ō -ōnis *f* attack, provocation

Laestrȳg·ōn -ōnis *m* Laestrygonian (one of the mythical race of cannibals in Italy, founders of Formiae)

laes·us *pp* of **laedō**

laetābil·is -e *adj* cheerful, glad

laet·ans -antis *adj* joyful, glad

laetāti·ō -ōnis *f* rejoicing, joy

laetē *adv* joyfully, gladly

laetific·ans -antis *adj* joyous

laetific·ō -āre *vt* to gladden, cheer up; **laetificari** to rejoice

laetific·us -a -um *adj* joyful, cheerful

laetiti·a -ae *f* joyfulness, gladness, exuberance

laet·or -ārī -ātus sum *vi* to rejoice, be glad

laet·us -a -um *adj* rejoicing, glad, cheerful; happy, fortunate, auspicious; fertile, rich, smiling (*grain*); sleek, fat (*cattle*); bright, cheerful (*appearance*); cheering, welcome (*news*)

laevē *adv* awkwardly

laev·us -a -um *adj* left, on the left side; awkward, stupid; ill-omened; lucky, propitious; *f* left hand, left side; *n* the left; *n pl* the area on the left

lagăn·um -ī *n* pancake

lagē·os -ī *f* Greek vine

lagoen·a or **lagŏn·a -ae** *f* jug

lagō·is -ĭdis *f* grouse

laguncŭl·a -ae *f* flask

Lāĭăd·ēs -ae *m* son of Laius (*Oedipus*)

Lāi·us -ī *m* Laius (*father of Oedipus*)

lall·ō -āre *vi* to sing a lullaby

lām·a -ae *f* swamp, bog

lambĕr·ō -āre *vt* to tear to pieces

lamb·ō -ĕre -ī *vt* to lick, lap; (of a river) to wash, flow by; (of ivy) to cling to

lāment·a -ōrum *n pl* wailing, moaning, lamentation

lāmentābil·is -e *adj* pitiable; doleful; mournful, sorrowful

lāmentārĭ·us -a -um *adj* sorrowful, pitiful

lāmentātĭ·ō -ōnis *f* lamentation

lāment·or -ārī -ātus sum *vt* to cry over, lament; *vi* to wail, cry

lami·a -ae *f* witch, sorceress

lāmin·a or **lammĭn·a** or **lamn·a -ae** *f* plate, leaf (*of metal or wood*); blade; coin; peel, shell

lamp·as -ădis *f* torch; brightness; day; meteor; lamp

Lam·us -ī *m* mythical king of the Laestrygonians; son of Hercules and Omphale

lān·a -ae *f* wool; working in wool, spinning, **lana aurea** golden fleece; **lanam trahere** to card wool; **lanas ducere** to spin wool; **rixari de lana caprina** to argue over nothing

lānăr·ĭus -ĭī or **-ī** *m* wool worker

lānāt·us -a -um *adj* woolly; *f pl* sheep

lancĕ·a -ae *f* lance, spear

lancĭn·ō -āre *vt* to squander, waste

lānĕ·us -a -um *adj* woolen; soft

langue·facĭō -facĕre -fēcī -factum *vt* to make tired

langu·ens -entis *adj* languid, drooping, listless

langu·ĕō -ēre *vi* to be tired, be weary; to be weak, feeble (*from disease*); (fig) to be dull, languid, listless; to be without energy

langu·escō -escĕre -ŭī *vi* to become weak, grow faint; (fig) to become listless; to decline, decrease; to relax

languĭdē *adj* weakly, faintly, without energy

languĭdŭl·us -a -um *adj* languid; withered, faded

languĭd·us -a -um *adj* weak, faint, languid, sluggish; listless; enervating

langu·or -ōris *m* weakness, faintness, languor; dullness, listlessness, sluggishness

lanĭāt·us -ūs *m* mangling; *f pl* mental anguish

laniēn·a -ae *f* butcher shop

lānific·ĭum -ĭī or **-ī** *n* weaving

lānifĭc·us -a -um *adj* spinning, weaving, of spinning, of weaving

lānĭg·er -ĕra -ĕrum *adj* fleecy; *m* sheep (*ram*); *f* sheep (*ewe*)

lanĭ·ō -āre *vt* to tear to pieces, mangle

lanist·a -ae *m* gladiator trainer, fencing master; (*in derision*) ringleader

lānĭt·ĭum -ĭī or **-ī** *n* wool

lan·ĭus -ĭī or **-ī** *m* butcher; (*in derision*) executioner, butcher

lantern·a -ae *f* lantern

lanternār·ĭus -ĭī or **-ī** *m* guide

lānūg·ō -ĭnis *f* down (*of plants, cheeks, etc.*)

Lānuv·ĭum -ĭī or **-ī** *n* town in Latium on the Appian Way

lan·x -cis *f* dish, platter; scale

Lāocŏ·ŏn -ontis *m* son of Priam and priest of Apollo, who, with his two sons, was killed by two serpents from the sea

Lāomĕd·ōn -ontis *m* king of Troy and father of Priam and Ganymede

Lāomedontē·us or **Lāomedontĭ·us -a -um** *adj* Trojan

Lāomedontĭăd·ēs -ae *m* son of Laomedon; Priam; *m pl* Trojans

lapăth·um -ī *n* or **lapăth·us -ī** *f* sorrel (*plant*)

lapicīd·a -ae *m* stonecutter, quarry worker

lapicīdīn·ae -ārum *f pl* stone quarry

lapidārĭ·us -a -um *adj* stone; **latomiae lapidariae** stone quarries

lapidātĭ·ō -ōnis *f* throwing stones

lapidāt·or -ōris *m* stone thrower

lapidĕ·us -a -um *adj* of stones, stone, stony; **lapideus sum** (fig) I am petrified

lapid·ō -āre *vt* to throw stones at; *v impers* it is raining stones, it is hailing stones

lapidōs·us -a -um *adj* full of stones, stony; hard as stone; gritty (*bread*)

lapill·us -ī *m* pebble; precious stone, gem, jewel; *m pl* small stones (*esp. for mosaics*)

lap·is -ĭdis *m* stone; milestone; platform; boundary stone, landmark; tombstone; precious stone, gem, pearl, jewel, stone statue; marble table; **lapides loqui** to speak harsh words

Lapith·ae -ārum *m pl* mountain tribe in Thessaly that fought the centaurs at the marriage of their king Pirithous

lapp·a -ae *f* burr

lapsi·ō -ōnis *f* sliding, slipping; (fig) tendency

laps·ō -āre *vi* to keep slipping, stumble

laps·us -a -um *pp of* **labor;** *adj* fallen

laps·us -ūs *m* falling, fall, sliding, slipping, gliding, flow, flight; blunder, error, fault, slip

laqueăr·ia -ĭum *n pl* paneled ceiling

laqueăt·us -a -um *adj* paneled, having a paneled ceiling

laquě·us -ī *m* noose; snare; (fig) snare, trap; *m pl* (fig) subtleties

Lăr Laris *m* tutelary deity, household god; hearth, home; *m pl* hearth, home, house, household, family

lard·um -ī *n* lard, fat

Larenti·a -ae *f* wife of Faustulus who reared Romulus and Remus

largē *adv* liberally, generously

largific·us -a -um *adj* bountiful

largiflŭ·us -a -um *adj* gushing

largilŏqu·us -a -um *adj* talkative

larg·ior -īrī -ītus sum *vt* to give generously, bestow freely; to lavish; to bestow, confer; to grant, concede; *vi* to give bribes, bribe

largĭt·ās -ātis *f* generosity, bounty

largītĭ·ō -ōnis *f* generosity; bribery

largīt·or -ōris *m* generous donor; spendthrift; briber

larg·us -a -um *adj* abundant, plentiful, large, much; generous, liberal, bountiful, profuse

lārĭd·um -ī *n* lard, bacon fat

Lāriss·a -ae *f* town in Thessaly on the Peneus River

Lār·ius -ii *or* **-ī** *m* Lake Como

lar·ix -ĭcis *f* larch tree

larv·a -ae *f* mask; ghost

larvāt·us -a -um *adj* bewitched

lasăn·um -ī *n* chamber pot

lasarpīcĭ·er -ěra -ěrum *adj* producing asafetida (*used as an antispasmodic*)

lascīvĭ·a -ae *f* playfulness; petulence; lewdness

lascīvĭbund·us -a -um *adj* petulant, roguish

lascīv·ĭō -īre -ĭī -ītum *vi* to frolic, be frisky; to run riot, run wild

lascīv·us -a -um *adj* playful, frisky; brash, impudent, petulant; licentious, lustful; luxuriant (*growth*)

lāserpīcĭ·um -ĭī *or* **-ī** *n* silphium (*plant which yielded asafetida*)

lassĭtūd·ō -ĭnis *f* physical weariness, lassitude

lass·ō -āre *vt* to fatigue, exhaust

lassŭl·us -a -um *adj* somewhat tired

lass·us -a -um *adj* tired, weary, fatigued, exhausted

lātē *adv* widely, extensively; pro-

fusely; **late longeque** far and wide

latĕbr·a -ae *f* hiding place, hideaway, hideout; (fig) loophole

latebricŏl·a -ae *m or f* person who hangs around dives or brothels

latebrōsē *adv* secretly

latebrōs·us -a -um *adj* full of holes; hidden, secret; porous

lat·ens -entis *adj* hidden, secret

latenter *adv* in secret

lat·ĕō -ēre -ŭī *vi* to lie hidden, lie concealed, lurk; to keep out of sight, sulk; to live a retired life, remain in obscurity, remain unknown, escape notice; to be in safety; to avoid a summons, lie low; to be obscure

later·ĕris *m* brick, tile; **laterem lavare** to waste effort

laterām·en -ĭnis *n* earthenware

latercŭl·us -ī *m* small brick; tile; biscuit

latericĭ·us -a -um *adj* brick, made of brick; *n* brickwork

lātern·a -ae *f* lantern

latesc·ō -ěre *vi* to hide

lat·ex -ĭcis *m* liquid, fluid; water; spring; wine; oil

latibŭl·um -ī *n* hiding place, hideout, lair, den; (fig) refuge

lāticlāvĭ·us -a -um *adj* having a broad crimson stripe (*distinctive mark of senators, military tribunes of the equestrian order, and of sons of distinguished families*)

Latīnē *adv* Latin, in Latin; in proper Latin; in plain Latin; **Latīne loqui** to speak Latin; to speak correct Latin; **Latīne reddere** to translate into Latin; **Latīne scire** to understand Latin

Latīnĭt·ās -ātis *f* pure Latin, Latinity; Latin rights and privileges

Latīn·us -a -um *adj* Latin; possessing Latin rights and privileges; *m* Latinus (*king of the Laurentians, who gave his daughter Lavinia in marriage to Aeneas*); *n* Latin language; **in Latinum convertere** to translate into Latin

lātĭ·ō -ōnis *f* bringing, rendering; proposing

latĭt·ō -āre *vi* to keep hiding oneself; to be concealed, hide, lurk; to lie low (*in order to avoid a summons*)

lātĭtūd·ō -ĭnis *f* breadth, width; size, extent; broad pronunciation; richness of expression

lātĭus *adv of* late

Latĭ·us -a -um *adj* of Latium, Latin, Roman; *n* Latium (*district in W. central Italy, in which Rome was situated*); **jus Latĭ** *or* **Latĭum** Latin political rights and privileges

Latŏ·is -ĭdis *f* Diana

lātom· = lautom·

Lātōn·a -ae *f* daughter of the Titan Coeus and Phoebe, and mother of Apollo and Diana

Lātōnigĕn·a -ae *m or f* child of Latona; *m pl* children of Latona, i.e., Apollo and Diana

Lătōnĭ·us -a -um *adj* of Latona; *f* Diana

lāt·or -ōris *m* bringer, bearer; proposer (*of a law*)

Lātō·us -ī *m* Apollo

lātrāt·or -ōris *m* barker; dog

lātrāt·us -ūs *m* barking

lātrīn·a -ae *f* wash room, toilet

lātr·ō -āre *vt* to bark at, snarl at; to clamor for; *vi* to bark; (fig) to rant

latr·ō -ōnis *m* mercenary; freebooter; brigand, bandit; (in chess) pawn

latrōcĭn·ium -iī or **-ī** *n* military service (*as a mercenary*); freebooting; brigandage, banditry, vandalism, piracy, robbery, highway robbery; villany, outrage; band of robbers

latrōcĭn·or -ārī -ātus sum *vi* to serve as a mercenary, be a mercenary soldier; to be a bandit, be a highwayman, be a pirate

latruncŭl·us -ī *m* small-time bandit

lātumĭ·ae -ārum *f pl* stone quarry; prison

lātus *pp* of **fero**

lāt·us -a -um *adj* wide, broad; extensive; widespread; broad (*pronunciation*); diffuse (*style*)

lat·us -ĕris *n* side, flank; body, person; lungs; lateral surface; coast; (mil) flank, wing; **a latere** (mil) on the flank; **a latere** (with *genit*) **a** at the side of, in the company of; **b** from among the friends of; **aperto latere** (mil) on the exposed flank; **latere tecto** scot free; **latus dare** to expose oneself; **latus tegere** (with *genit*) to walk by the side of, to escort (*someone*)

latuscŭl·um -ī *n* small side

laudābĭl·is -e *adj* laudable, praiseworthy

laudābĭlĭter *adv* laudably

laudātĭ·ō -ōnis *f* commendation; eulogy, panegyric, funeral oration; (in court) testimony by a character witness

laudāt·or -ōris *m* praiser; eulogist, panegyrist; (law) character witness

laudāt·us -a -um *adj* praiseworthy, commendable, excellent

laud·ō -āre *vt* to praise, commend; to name, quote, cite; to pronounce a funeral oration over

laurĕ·a -ae *f* laurel tree; laurel, laurel branch, laurel crown, bay wreath; triumph

laureāt·us -a -um *adj* laureate, laureled, crowned with laurel; **litterae laureatae** communiqué announcing victory

Laurent·ēs -um *m pl* Laurentians (*people of Lanuvium*)

Laurentīn·us or **Laurentĭ·us -a -um** *adj* Laurentian

laureŏl·a -ae *f* little laurel crown; triumph

laurĕ·us -a -um *adj* laurel, of laurel; *f see* **laurea**

lauricŏm·us -a -um *adj* laurel-covered (*mountain*)

laurĭf·er -ĕra -ĕrum *adj* crowned with laurel

laurĭg·er -ĕra -ĕrum *adj* wearing laurel

laur·us -ī *f* laurel tree, bay tree; triumph, victory

laus laudis *f* praise, commendation; fame, glory; approval, praiseworthy deed; merit, worth

Laus·us -ī *m* son of Numitor and brother of Rhea Silvia; son of Mezentius, killed by Aeneas

lautē *adv* sumptuously, splendidly; excellently

lautĭ·a -ōrum *n pl* state banquet (*given to foreign ambassadors and official guests*)

lautĭtĭ·a -ae *f* luxury, high living

lautumĭ·ae or **lātomĭ·ae** or **lātumĭ·ae -ārum** *f pl* stone quarry; prison

laut·us -a -um *adj* expensive, elegant, fine; well-heeled; refined, fashionable

lavābr·um -ī *n* bath

lavātĭ·o -ōnis *f* washing, bathing, bath; bathing kit

Lāvīnĭ·us -a -um *adj* Lavinian, of Lavinium; *n* town in Latium founded by Aeneas; *f* wife of Aeneas

lavō lavāre (or **lavĕre**) **lāvī lautum** (or **lavātum** or **lōtum**) *vt* to wash, bathe; to wet, drench; to wash away; **lavi** to wash, wash oneself, bathe; *vi* to wash, wash oneself, bathe

laxāment·um -ī *n* relaxation, respite, letup, mitigation

laxāt·us -a -um *adj* loose, extended (*e.g., ranks*)

laxē *adv* loosely, widely; freely

laxĭt·ās -ātis *f* roominess, extent

lax·ō -āre *vt* to extend, widen, expand, open; to open, undo, release; to relax, slacken; to mitigate; (fig) to release, relieve; *vi* (of price) to go down

lax·us -a -um *adj* roomy, wide; loose, slack; prolonged, extended (*time*); (fig) relaxed, easygoing, free; low (*price*)

le·a -ae *f* lioness

leaen·a -ae *f* lioness

Lēand·er -rī *m* youth of Abydos who swam across the Hellespont every night to his lover Hero of Sestos

Learch·us -ī *m* son of Athamas and Ino, killed by his mad father

leb·ēs -ētis *m* pan, cauldron, basin

lectĭc·a -ae *f* litter; sofa, couch

lectĭcār·ius -iī or **-ī** *m* litter bearer

lectĭcŭl·a -ae *f* small litter; small bier

lectĭ·ō -ōnis *f* selection; reading, reading aloud; perusal; **lectio senatūs** revision of the senate roll (*by the censor*)

lectisterniāt·or -ōris *m* slave who arranged the seating at table

lestistern·ium -iī or **-ī** *n* ritual feast (*at which images of the gods were placed on couches at the table*)

lectĭt·ō -āre vt to read and reread; to like to read

lectiuncŭl·a -ae f light reading

lect·or -ōris m reader (esp. slave who read aloud to his master)

lectŭl·us -ī m cot; small couch, settee; humble bier

lect·us -ī or **-ūs** m bed, couch; bier

lect·us -a -um pp of **lego**; adj select, choice, special, elite

Lēd·a -ae or **Lēd·ē -ēs** f Tyndarus's wife, whom Jupiter visited in the form of a swan and who bore Helen, Clytemnestra, Castor, and Pollux

lēgātĭ·ō -ōnis f embassy, mission, legation; members of an embassy; work or report of a work of a mission; nominal staff appointment; command of a legion; **legatio libera** junket (all-expenses-paid trip, a privilege granted to senators, nominally in an official capacity, to visit the provinces to transact private business)

lēgāt·um -ī n bequest, legacy

lēgāt·us -ī m deputy, representative; ambassador, envoy; adjutant (of a consul, proconsul, or praetor); commander of a legion

lēgĭf·er -ĕra -ĕrum adj law-giving

legĭ·ō -ōnis f legion (divided into 10 cohorts and numbering between 4,200 and 6,000 men); army

legiōnārĭ·us -a -um adj legionary

lēgirŭp·a -ae or **lēgirup·ĭō -ōnis** m lawbreaker

lēgitĭmē adv legitimately, lawfully; properly

lēgitĭm·us -a -um adj legitimate, lawful; regular, right, just, proper; n pl legal formalities

legiuncŭl·a -ae f under-manned legion

lēg·ō -āre vt to commission; to send on a public mission, despatch; to delegate, deputize; to bequeath, will; (fig) to entrust

legō legĕre lēgī lectum vt to gather, collect, pick; to pick out, choose; to pick one's way through, cross; to sail by, coast along; to read, peruse; to recite, read out loud; to pick up, steal; to pick up (news, rumor); **fila legere** to wind up the thread of life; **senatum legere** to read off the senate roll

lēgŭlē·ĭus -ĭī or **-ī** pettifogger

legŭm·en -ĭnis n leguminous plant; vegetable; pulse; bean

lemb·us -ī m cutter, yacht (built for speed), speedboat

lemm·a -ătis n theme, subject matter; epigram

Lemnicŏl·a -ae m inhabitant of Lemnos, i.e., Vulcan

lemniscāt·us -a -um adj heavily decorated (with combat ribbons)

lemnisc·us -ī m ribbon which hung down from a victor's wreath

Lemnĭ·us -a -um adj Lemnian; m Lemnian; Vulcan

Lemn·os or **Lemn·us -ī** f large island in the Aegean

Lemŭr·ēs -um m pl ghosts

Lemŭrĭ·a -ōrum n pl night festival to drive ghosts from the house

lēn·a -ae f procuress, madame; seductress

Lēnae·us -a -um adj Lenaean, Bacchic; m Bacchus

lēnē adv gently

lēnīm·en -ĭnis n consolation, comfort, compensation, reward

lēnīment·um -ī n alleviation

lēnĭ·ō -īre -īvī or **-ĭī -ītum** vt to soften, alleviate, soothe, calm; vi to calm down

lēn·is -e adj soft, gentle, mild, smooth, calm; gradual (slope); (fig) gentle, mild, kind

lēnĭt·ās -ātis f softness, gentleness, mildness, smoothness; (fig) gentleness, mildness, tenderness, clemency

lēnĭter adv softly, gently, mildly; (fig) mildly, quietly, calmly; (of style) smoothly; halfheartedly

lēnĭtūd·ō -ĭnis f softness, mildness, gentleness, smoothness

lēn·ō -ōnis m pander, procurer, pimp; seducer

lēnōcin·ĭum -ĭī or **-ī** n pandering, pimping; allurement, attraction; bawdy or gaudy clothes; flattery

lēnōcĭn·or -ārī -ātus sum vi to be a pimp; (with dat) to play up to, humor, pander to; **b** to stimulate, promote

lēnōnĭ·us -a -um adj pimp's

len·s -tis f lentil

lentē adv slowly; indifferently, halfheartedly; calmly, leisurely, deliberately

lent·escō·ō -ĕre vi to get sticky, soften; (fig) to soften, weaken; (with ad + acc) to stick to

lentiscĭf·er -ĕra -ĕrum adj (of a region) producing mastic trees

lentisc·us -ī f mastic tree; toothpick (made of mastic wood)

lentitūd·ō -ĭnis f slowness; insensibility, apathy, dullness

lent·ō -āre vt to bend

lentŭl·us -a -um adj somewhat slow

lent·us -a -um adj sticky, clinging; pliant, limber; slow, sluggish; lingering; irresponsive, reluctant, indifferent, backward; slow-moving; tedious; drawling; at rest, at leisure, lazy; calm, unconcerned

lēnŭl·us -ī m little pimp

lēnuncŭl·us -ī m little pimp; small sailboat, skiff

le·ō -ōnis m lion

Le·ō -ōnis m Lion (constellation)

Leōnĭd·ās -ae m king of Sparta (487–480 B.C.), who fell at Thermopylae in 480 B.C. after a gallant stand

leōnīn·us -a -um adj lion's, of a lion

Leontīn·ī -ōrum m pl town in E. Sicily

lep·as -ădis f limpet

lepĭdē adv pleasantly, charmingly,

neatly; (as affirmative answer) yes, indeed; (of approval) bravo!

lepid·us -a -um *adj* pleasant, charming, neat; effeminate

lep·ōs or **lep·or -ōris** *m* pleasantness, charm, attractiveness

lep·us -ŏris *m* hare

Lep·us -ŏris *m* Hare (*constellation*)

lepuscŭl·us -ī *m* little hare

Lern·a -ae or **Lern·ē -ēs** *f* marsh near Argos, where Hercules slew the Hydra

Lernae·us -a -um *adj* Lernaean

Lesbĭ·us -a -um *adj* Lesbian; *f* pseudonym for the girl friend of the poet Catullus; *n* Lesbian wine

Lesb·os or **Lesb·us -ī** *f* large island in the N. Aegean, the birthplace of the lyric poets Alcaeus and Sappho

less·us (only *acc*: **lessum** in use) *m* wailing

lētāl·is -e *adj* lethal, fatal, mortal

Lēthae·us -a -um *adj* of Lethe; infernal; causing drowsiness

lēthargĭc·us -ī *m* lazy fellow

lētharg·us -ī *m* lethargy

Lēth·ē -ēs *f* Lethe (*river of oblivion in the lower world*); forgetfulness

lētĭf·er -ěra -ěrum *adj* deadly, fatal; **locus letifer** mortal spot

lēt·ō -āre *vt* to kill

lēt·um -ī *n* death; ruin, destruction; **leto dare** to put to death

Leuc·as -ădis *f* island off W. Greece

leucasp·is -ĭdis *adj* armed with a white shield

Leucipp·us -ī *m* philosopher, teacher of Democritus, and one of the founders of Atomism (5th *cent.* B.C.)

Leucothĕ·a -ae or **Leucothĕ·ē -ēs** *f* name of Ino, daughter of Cadmus, after she was changed into a sea deity

Leuctr·a -ōrum *n pl* small town in Boeotia where Epaminondas defeated the Spartans in 371 B.C.

levām·en -ĭnis *n* alleviation, comfort, consolation

levāment·um -ī *n* alleviation, comfort, consolation

levātĭ·ō -ōnis *f* lightening; relief; comfort; lessening

levicŭl·us -a -um *adj* somewhat vain

levidens·is -e *adj* poor, inferior

levifīd·us -a -um *adj* untrustworthy

lēv·is -e *adj* light, not heavy; lightarmed; lightly dressed; light, easily digested; thin, poor (*soil*); light, nimble; flitting; slight, small; unimportant, trivial; unfounded (*rumor*); easy, simple; mild; gentle, easygoing; capricious, unreliable, fickle

lēv·is -e *adj* smooth; slippery; smooth, hairless, beardless; delicate, tender; effeminate; smooth (*style*)

levisomn·us -a -um *adj* light-sleeping

levĭt·ās -ātis *f* lightness; mobility, nimbleness; levity, frivolity; (fig) shallowness

lēvĭt·ās -ātis *f* smoothness; (fig) smoothness, fluency

levĭter *adv* lightly; slightly, a little, somewhat; easily, without difficulty; nimbly

lēv·ō -āre *vt* to lift up, raise; to lighten, relieve, ease; to console, comfort; to lessen, weaken; to release, free; to take away; to avert

lēv·ō -āre *vt* to make smooth, polish; to soothe

lēv·or -ōris *m* smoothness

lex lēgis *f* motion, bill; law, statute; rule, regulation, principle, precept; condition, stipulation; **eā lege ut** with the stipulation that, on condition that; **lege** or **legibus** legally; **lege agere** to proceed legally; **legem abrogare** to repeal a law; **legem ferre** to propose a bill; **legem derogare** to amend a bill or law; **legem jubere** to sanction a law; **legem perferre** to pass a law; **sine legibus** without restraint, without control

lībām·en -ĭnis *n* libation; firstfruits

lībāment·um -ī *n* libation; firstfruits

lībātĭ·ō -ōnis *f* libation

libell·a -ae *f* small silver coin, ace; small sum; level (*instrument*); **ad libellam** to a tee, exactly; **heres ex libella** sole heir

libell·us -ī *m* small book, pamphlet; notebook; journal, diary; program; handbill, advertisement; petition; answer to a petition; letter; written accusation, indictment, libel; satirical verse

lib·ens or **lub·ens -entis** *adj* willing, ready, glad; merry, cheerful

libenter or **lubenter** *adv* willingly, gladly, with pleasure

lib·er -rī *m* bark of a tree; book; work, treatise; catalog, list, register; letter, rescript

lib·er -ěra -ěrum *adj* free; open, unoccupied; unrestricted; unprejudiced; outspoken, frank; uncontrolled, unrestricted; (not slave) free; (of states or municipalities) independent, autonomous; exempt; free of charge; (with *abl* or *ab* + *abl*) free from, exempt from; (with *genit*) free of; *m pl* see **liberi**

Līb·er -ěrī *m* Italian fertility god, later identified with Bacchus; wine

Lībĕr·a -ae *f* Proserpina; Ariadne, the wife of Bacchus

Lībĕrāl·ia -ĭum *n pl* festival of Liber, held on March 17th, at which young men received the toga virilis

lībĕrāl·is -e *adj* relating to freedom, relating to civil status, of free citizens; worthy of a freeman, honorable, gentleman's; courteous; liberal, generous; handsome

lībĕrālĭt·ās -ātis *f* courtesy, politeness; liberality, generosity; grant, gift

lībĕrālĭter *adv* like a freeman, nobly; liberally (*e.g.*, *educated*); courteously; liberally, generously

līberātĭ·ō -ōnis f liberation, delivery, freeing, release; acquittal

līberāt·or -ōris m liberator

lībĕrē adv freely; frankly, outspokenly; ungrudgingly; like a freeman, liberally

lībĕr·ī -ōrum m pl children

lībĕr·ō -āre vt to set free, free, release; to acquit, discharge; to cancel, get rid of (e.g., debts); to exempt; to manumit, set free; (with abl or with ab or ex + abl) to free or release from, acquit of; fidem liberare to keep one's promise; nomina liberare to cancel debts; se aere alieno liberare to pay up a debt

lībert·a -ae f freedwoman, ex-slave

lībert·ās -ātis f liberty, freedom; status of a freeman; political freedom; freedom of speech, freedom of thought; frankness

lībertīn·us -a -um adj & mf ex-slave; m freedman; f freedwoman

lībert·us -ī m freedman, ex-slave

lib·et (or lub·et) -ēre -ŭit (or lĭbĭtum est) v impers (with dat) it pleases, is pleasant, is agreeable to, is nice for (someone); (with inf) it is nice, pleasant to (do something); si lubet if you please; ut lubet as you please

lĭbīdĭn·or -ārī -ātus sum vi to gratify lust

lĭbīdĭnōsē adv willfully; arbitrarily

lĭbīdĭnōs·us -a -um adj willful; arbitrary; lustful, sensual

lĭbīd·ō or lŭbīd·ō -ĭnis f desire, longing, inclination, pleasure; will, willfulness, arbitrariness, caprice; fancy; lust; rut, heat; ex libidine arbitrarily

lĭbĭt·a -ōrum n pl will, pleasure, liking

Lĭbītīn·a -ae f burial goddess; implements for burial; grave, death

līb·ō -āre vt to taste, sip; to pour as a libation, offer, consecrate; to touch lightly, barely touch, graze; to spill, waste; to extract, collect, compile

lībr·a -ae f balance, scales; plummet, level; pound (of twelve ounces)

lībrāment·um -ī n weight; balance, ballast; plane surface; gravity

lībrārĭ·a -ae f forelady (who weighed out wool for slaves to spin)

lībrārĭŏl·us -ī m copyist, scribe

lībrārĭ·us -a -um adj book, of books; taberna libraria bookstore; m copyist, scribe; n bookcase

lībrāt·us -a -um adj poised; hurled; powerful

lībrīl·is -e adj one-pound, weighing a pound

lībrīt·or -ōris m artilleryman

lībr·ō -āre vt to balance; to poise, level, hurl, launch; to sway

līb·um -ī n cake; birthday cake

Lĭburnĭ·a -ae f district of Illyria between Istria and Dalmatia

Lĭburn·us -a -um adj & mf Liburnian; f Liburnian galley

Lĭbў·a -ae or Lĭbў·ē -ēs f Libya (Africa)

Lĭbў·es -um m pl Libyans

Lĭbўc·us or Lĭbyss·us or Lĭbystīn·us or Lĭbў·us -a -um or Lĭbyst·is -ĭdis adj Libyan; (in general) African

lic·ens -entis adj free, bold

licenter adv freely, boldly, without restraint, licentiously

licentĭ·a -ae f license, liberty, freedom; lawlessness, licentiousness

lic·ĕō -ēre vi to cost; to be for sale

lic·ĕor -ērī -ĭtus sum vt to bid on, bid for, make an offer for; vi to bid, make a bid

lic·et -ēre -ŭit or -ĭtum est v impers it is permitted or lawful; (with dat & inf) it is all right for (someone) to; licet (to express assent) yes, all right

licet conj granted that, even if, although

Līch·ās -ae m companion of Hercules

līch·ēn -ēnis m ringworm

lĭcĭtātĭ·ō -ōnis f bidding (at auction); haggling

lĭcĭt·or -ārī -ātus sum vt to bid for

lĭcĭt·us -a -um adj permissible, lawful

līc·ium -ĭī or -ī n thread

līct·or -ōris m lictor (attendant and bodyguard of a magistrate, of whom twenty-four attended a dictator, twelve a consul, and six a praetor)

lĭ·ēn -ēnis m spleen

liēnōs·us -a -um adj splenetic

lĭgām·en -ĭnis n bandage

lĭgāment·um -ī n bandage

lĭgnār·ĭus -ĭī or -ī m carpenter

lĭgnātĭ·ō -ōnis f gathering of lumber

lĭgnāt·or -ōris m woodcutter, lumberjack

lĭgnĕŏl·us -a -um adj wooden

lĭgnĕ·us -a -um adj wooden

lĭgn·or -ārī -ātus sum vi to gather wood

lĭgn·um -ī n wood; timber, firewood, log, plank; writing tablet; tree; in silvam ligna ferre to carry coals to Newcastle

lĭg·ō -āre vt to tie, tie up, bandage; to close (a deal)

lĭg·ō -ōnis m mattock, hoe; farming

lĭgŭl·a -ae f shoe strap

Lĭg·ur or Lĭg·us -ŭris m or f Ligurian

Lĭgŭrĭ·a -ae f Liguria (district along the N.W. coast of Italy)

lĭgŭrĭ·ō or lĭgurr·ĭō -īre -īvī or -ĭī -ītum vt to lick, pick at; to eat daintily; (fig) to prey on; (fig) to be dying for

lĭgŭrītĭ·ō -ōnis f daintiness

Lĭgus see Lĭgur

Lĭgusc·us or Lĭgustĭc·us or Lĭgustīn·us -a -um adj Ligurian

lĭgustr·um -ī n privet

līl·ĭum -ĭī or **-ī** *n* lily; (mil) trench lined with sharp stakes

līm·a -ae *f* file; (fig) polishing, revision

līmātĭus *adv* in a more polished manner

līmātŭl·us -a -um *adj* (fig) rather sharp (*judgment*)

līmāt·us -a -um *adj* (fig) polished, refined

līm·ax -ācis *m* or *f* snail

līmbŏlārĭ·us -a -um *adj* **textores līmbolarii** tassel makers, hemmers

līmb·us -ī *m* fringe, hem, tassel

līm·en -ĭnis *n* lintel, threshold; doorway, entrance; threshold, outset, beginning; starting gate (*at racetrack*); house, home

līm·es -ĭtis *m* country trail; path; road along a boundary; boundary, frontier; channel, course, way; zodiac

līm·ō -āre *vt* to file; (fig) to polish, refine; to file down, take away from, lessen; to get down to (*the truth*)

līmōs·us -a -um *adj* muddy; mud, growing in mud

līmpĭd·us -a -um *adj* limpid, clear

līmŭl·us -a -um *adj* squinting

līm·us -a -um *adj* squinting; sidelong, askance; *m* mud; dirt; grime; ceremonial apron (*worn by priests at sacrifice*)

līnĕ·a -ae *f* line, string, thread; fishing line; plumb line; outline; boundary line, limit; **ad līneam** or **rectā līneā** in a straight line, vertically; horizontally; **extrēmā līneā amare** to love at a distance; **līneas transire** to go out of bounds

līneāment·um -ī *n* line; characteristic, feature; outline

līnĕ·ō -āre *vt* to make straight, make perpendicular

līnĕ·us -a -um *adj* flaxen, linen

līngō līngĕre līnxī līnctum *vt* to lick up, lap up

līngu·a -ae *f* tongue; speech, language, dialect; (of animals) note, song, bark; tongue of land; eloquence; **līnguā promptus** insolent; **utraque līngua** Greek and Latin

līngŭl·a -ae *f* tongue of land

līngulāc·a -ae *m* or *f* gossip, chatterbox

līnĭg·er -ĕra -ĕrum *adj* wearing linen

līnō līnĕre lēvī or **līvī lītum** *vt* to smear; to erase; to cover, overlay; (fig) to mess up

līnquō līnquĕre līquī *vt* to leave, forsake, depart from; to leave or let alone; to leave in a pinch; **līnqui animo** or **līnqui** to faint; **līnquitur** (with **ut**) it remains to (*do something*)

līntĕāt·us -a -um *adj* canvas

līntĕ·ō -ōnis *m* linen weaver

līntĕŏl·um -ī *n* small linen cloth

līnt·er -ris *f* skiff; tub, vat

līntĕ·us -a -um *adj* linen; *n* linen,

linen cloth; canvas, sail; kerchief

līntrĭcŭl·us -ī *m* small boat

līn·um -ī *n* flax; linen; thread, rope, line; fishing line; net

Līn·us -ī *m* son of Apollo and instructor of Orpheus and Hercules

Lĭpăr·a -ae or **Lĭpăr·ē -ēs** *f* island off the N. coast of Sicily; *f pl* the Aeolian islands

Lĭparaē·us -a -um or **Lĭparens·is -e** *adj* of Lipara

līpp·ĭō -īre -īvī or **-ĭī -ītum** *vi* to have sore eyes; (of eyes) to burn, ache

līppĭtūd·ō -ĭnis *f* running eyes, inflammation of the eyes

līpp·us -a -um *adj* with sore eyes, sore-eyed; burning (*eyes*); (fig) blind

lĭque·făcĭō -facĕre -fēcī -factum (*passive*: **lĭque·fĭō -fĭerī -factus sum**) *vt* to melt, dissolve; to decompose; to waste, weaken

lĭqu·ens -entis *adj* clear, limpid; flowing, gliding; liquid, fluid

lĭquĕō lĭquēre lĭcŭī *vi* to be liquid; *v impers* it is clear, is apparent, is evident; **lĭquet mĭhī** (with *inf*) I am free to; **non lĭquet** (law) it is not clear (*legal formula used by a hung jury*)

lĭquescō lĭquescĕre lĭcŭī *vi* to melt; to decompose; to grow soft, grow effeminate; (fig) to melt away; to become clear

lĭquĭdē *adv* clearly; (fig) clearly, plainly

lĭquĭdĭuscŭl·us -a -um *adj* somewhat softer

lĭquĭdō *adv* clearly, plainly, certainly

lĭquĭd·us -a -um *adj* liquid, fluid, flowing; clear, transparent; pure (*pleasure*); clear (*voice*); calm (*mind*); clear, evident, certain; *n* liquid, water; clearness, certainty

lĭqu·ō -āre *vt* to melt, dissolve; to strain, filter

lĭqu·or -ī *vi* to flow; to melt, dissolve; (fig) to melt away, waste away

lĭqu·or -ōris *m* fluidity; liquid, fluid; sea

Līr·is -is *m* river between Campania and Latium

līs lītis *f* lawsuit, litigation; matter of dispute; quarrel, wrangling; charge, accusation; **lītem intendere** or **lītem inferre** (with *dat*) to sue (*someone*); **lītem aestimare** to assess damages; **līs capitis** criminal charge

lītātĭ·ō -ōnis *f* success in sacrificing, efficacious sacrifice

lītātō *adv* with favorable omens

lītĕra see **littĕra**

lītĭc·en -ĭnis *m* clarion player

lītĭgāt·or -ōris *m* litigant

lītĭgĭōs·us -a -um *adj* quarrelsome, litigious; contested, disputed

lītĭg·ĭum -ĭī or **-ī** *n* quarrel, dispute

lītĭg·ō -āre *vi* to quarrel, squabble; to go to court

lĭt·ō -āre *vt* to offer duly or acceptably; *vi* to offer acceptable sacrifice; to receive a good omen; (with *dat*) to propitiate, satisfy, appease

litorāl·is *-e adj* shore, of the shore

litorĕ·us *-a -um adj* seashore, at or along the seashore

littĕr·a or **lītĕr·a** *-ae f* letter (*of the alphabet*); handwriting; *f pl* epistle, letter, dispatch; edict, ordinance; literature, books, literary works; learning, liberal education, scholarship; records, accounts; **littera salutaris** (*i.e.,* **A** = **absolvo**) vote of acquittal; **littera tristis** (*i.e.,* **C** = **condemno**) vote of guilty; **litteras discere** to learn to read and write; **litteras scire** to know how to read and write

litterāri·us *-a -um adj* of reading and writing; **ludus litterarius** elementary school

litterātē *adv* legibly, in a clear handwriting; literally; learnedly

litterāt·or *-ōris m* elementary-school teacher; grammarian, philologist

litterātūr·a *-ae f* alphabet

litterāt·us *-a -um adj* marked with letters, engraved; learned, scholarly; liberally educated; devoted to literature

litterŭl·a *-ae f* small letter; *f pl* short letter, note; slight literary endeavors

litūr·a *-ae f* erasure; erased passage; correction, emendation; blot, smear; wrinkle

litus *pp* of **lino**

lit·us *-ōris n* seashore, beach, coast; river bank; **in litus harenas fundere** to carry coals to Newcastle; **litus arare** to waste effort

litŭ·us *-ī m* cavalry trumpet, clarion; (fig) signal; augur's wand (*crooked staff carried by an augur*); **lituus meae profectionis** signal for my departure

līv·ens *-entis adj* black-and-blue, livid

līv·ĕō *-ēre vi* to be black and blue, be livid; to be envious; (with *dat*) to be jealous of

līvesc·ō *-ĕre vi* to turn black and blue

Līvi·a *-ae f* second wife of Augustus (58 B.C.-29 A.D.)

līvidŭl·us *-a -um adj* inclined to be jealous, somewhat envious

līvĭd·us *-a -um adj* leaden (*in color*); blue; black and blue; jealous, envious, spiteful

Līv·ius *-iī* or *-ī m* T. Livius Patavinus or Livy (*famous historian*, 59 B.C.-17 A.D.)

līv·or *-ōris m* leaden color; bluish color; black-and-blue mark; jealousy, envy, spite

lix·a *-ae m* camp follower

locāti·ō *-ōnis f* arrangement, placement; renting out, contract, lease

locāt·um *-ī n* lease, contract

locit·ō *-āre vt* to lease out

loc·ō *-āre vt* to place, put, set, lay; to establish, constitute, lay, set; to give in marriage, marry off; to let, rent out; to contract for; to invest

locŭl·us *-ī m* little place, spot; pocket

locŭplēt·ēs *-ētis adj* rich; reliable, responsible

locuplēt·ō *-āre vt* to make rich, enrich

loc·us *-ī* (*pl*: **loc·ī** *-ōrum m*; **loc·a** *-ōrum n*) *m* place, site, spot, locality, district; place, seat; period, period of time; opportunity, room, occasion; situation, position, category; rank, degree, birth; passage in a book; topic, subject, point, division; (mil) position, post, station; **adhuc locorum** till now; **ad id locorum** till then; **ex aequo loco dicere** to speak in the senate; to hold a conversation; **ex** or **de loco superiore dicere** to speak from the rostrum; **ex loco inferiore dicere** to speak before a judge, speak in court; **inde loci** since then; **in eo loci** in such a condition; **interea loci** meanwhile; **loci communes** general topics; public places, parks; **loco** (with *genit*) instead of; **loco** or **in loco** at the right time; **loco cedere** to give way, yield; **postea loci** afterwards; **post id locorum** afterwards; **ubicumque loci** whenever

lōcust·a *-ae f* locust

Lōcust·a *-ae f* woman notorious as poisoner in the time of Claudius and Nero

locūti·ō *-ōnis f* speech; way of speaking, pronunciation

locūtus *pp* of **loquor**

lōd·ix *-īcis f* blanket

logic·us *-a -um adj* logical; *n pl* logic

log·os or **log·us** *-ī m* word; witticism; *m pl* mere words, empty talk

lōligō see **lolligo**

lol·ium *-iī* or *-ī n* darnel

lollīg·o or **lōlīg·ō** *-ĭnis f* cuttlefish

lolliguncŭl·a *-ae f* small cuttlefish

lōment·um *-ī n* face cream

Londīn·ium *-iī* or *-ī n* London

longaev·us *-a -um adj* aged

longē *adv* far, far off, long way off; away, distant; out of reach, of no avail; long, for a long period; (to speak) at greater length; (with comparatives) far, by far, much; **longe lateque** far and wide, everywhere

longinquit·ās *-ātis f* length, extent; remoteness, distance; length, duration

longinqu·us *-a -um adj* long, extensive; far off, distant, remote; from afar, foreign; long, prolonged, continued, tedious; **ex** or **e longinquo** from far away

longĭter *adv* far

longitūd·ō *-ĭnis f* length; **in longitudinem** lengthwise

longiuscŭl·us -a -um *adj* pretty long

longur·ius -iī or **-ī** *m* long pole

long·us -a -um *adj* long; spacious; long, protracted, drawn-out; tedious; **longa navis** battleship; **longum esse** (with *inf*) to be tedious to; *n* length; **in longum** for a long while; **ne longum faciam** in short

loquācĭt·ās -ātis *f* talkativeness

loquācĭter *adv* long-windedly; at length, in detail

loquācŭl·us -a -um *adj* rather talkative

loqu·ax -ācis *adj* talkative, loquacious

loquell·a -ae *f* speech, language

loquĭt·or -ārī -ātus *vi* to chatter away

loquor loquī locūtus sum *vt* to say; to talk of, speak about; to tell, tell of, mention; (fig) to declare, show, indicate; *vi* to speak; to rustle, murmur

lōrār·ius -iī or **-ī** *m* flogger, slave driver

lōrāt·us -a -um *adj* tied with thongs

lōrĕ·us -a -um *adj* striped

lōrīc·a -ae *f* breastplate; parapet; **libros mūtare loricis** to exchange books for arms

lōrīcāt·us -a -um *adj* wearing a breastplate

lōrĭp·ēs -ēdis *adj* bowlegged

lōr·um -ī *n* strip of leather, thong, strap; whip, scourge; leather badge; *n pl* reins

lōt·os or **lōt·us -ī** *f* lotus; flute (*of lotus wood*)

lōtus *pp* of **lavo**

lub- = lĭb-

lubentĭ·a -ae *f* pleasure

lubrĭc·ō -āre *vt* to oil, grease, make smooth

lubrĭc·us -a -um *adj* slippery; smooth; slimy; gliding; deceitful, tricky; precarious; *n* precarious situation, critical period

Lūc·a bōs (*genit*: **Lūc·ae bovis**) *f* elephant

Lūcānĭ·a -ae *f* district in S.W. Italy

Lūcānĭc·us -a -um *adj* Lucanian; *f* Lucanian sausage

Lūcān·us -a -um *adj* Lucanian; *m* Lucanian; Lucan (*M. Annaeus Lucanus, epic poet, 39-65 A.D.*)

lūc·ar -āris *n* forest tax

lucell·um -ī *n* slight profit

lūcĕō lūcēre luxī *vi* to shine, be light, glow, glitter, be clear; (fig) to be clear, be apparent, be conspicuous; *v impers* it is light, day is dawning

Lūcĕr·ēs -um *m pl* one of the three original Roman tribes

lucern·ae -ae *f* lamp; (fig) midnight oil

lūcescō or **lūciscō lūcescĕre luxī** *vi* to begin to shine; *v impers* it is getting light

lūcĭdē *adv* clearly, distinctly

lūcĭd·us -a -um *adj* shining, bright, clear; lucid, clear

lūcĭf·er -ĕra -ĕrum *adj* shiny

Lūcĭf·er -ĕrī *m* morning star; planet Venus; son of Aurora and Cephalus; day

lūcĭfŭg·us -a -um *adj* light-shunning

Lūcīl·ĭus -iī or **-ī** *m* C. Lucilius (*first Roman satiric poet, c. 180-102 B.C.*)

Lūcīn·a -ae *f* goddess of childbirth; childbirth

lūciscō see **lucesco**

Lucrētĭ·a -ae *f* daughter of Spurius Lucretius and wife of Collatinus, who, having been raped by Sextus Tarquinius, committed suicide in 509 B.C.

Lūcrēt·ĭus -iī or **-ī** *m* Spurius Lucretius (*father of Lucretia and consul in 509 B.C.*); Titus Lucretius Carus (*philosophical poet, 94?-55? B.C.*)

lucrĭfĭcābĭl·is -e or **lucrĭfĭc·us -a -um** *adj* profitable

lucrĭfŭg·a -ae *m* or *f* person not out for gain, disinterested person

Lucrīn·us -a -um *adj* Lucrine; *m* Lake Lucrine (*small lake near Baiae, famous for its oysters*)

lucrĭpĕt·a -ae *m* profiteer

lucr·or -ārī -ātus sum *vt* to gain, win, get

lucrōs·us -a -um *adj* profitable

lucr·um -ī *n* profit, gain; wealth; greed, love of gain; **lucrī facĕre** to gain; **lucrī fĭerī** to be gained; **lucro esse** (with *dat*) to be advantageous for (*someone*); **ponere in lucro** or **in lucris** to regard as gain

luctām·en -ĭnis *n* wrestling; struggle, effort

luct·ans -antis *adj* reluctant

luctātĭ·ō -ōnis *f* wrestling; struggle, contest

luctāt·or -ōris *m* wrestler

luctĭfĭc·us -a -um *adj* causing sorrow, doleful, woeful

luctĭsŏn·us -a -um *adj* sad-sounding

luct·or -ārī -ātus sum or **luct·ō -āre** *vi* to wrestle; (with *inf*) to struggle to

luctuōsĭus *adv* more pitifully

luctuōs·us -a -um *adj* causing sorrow, sorrowful; sad, feeling sad

luct·us -ūs *m* sorrow, mourning, grief, distress; signs of sorrow, mourning clothes; source of grief, affliction

lūcŭbrātĭ·ō -ōnis *f* moonlighting, working by lamp light; evening gossip; nighttime writing

lūcŭbr·ō -āre *vt* to compose at night; *vi* to moonlight, burn the midnight oil

lūcŭlentē *adv* splendidly, well; (to beat) soundly

lūcŭlenter *adv* brilliantly, smartly, very well

lūculent·us -a -um *adj* bright, brilliant; (fig) brilliant, smart, excellent; considerable (*wealth*); sound (*beating*); trustworthy (*sources*)

Lūcull·us -ī *m* Lucius Licinius Lucullus (*Roman general and politician,* 117-56 B.C.)

Lucūm·ō or **Lucm·ō -ōnis** *m* Etruscan prince, Etruscan priest

lūc·us -ī *m* sacred grove; woods

lūdi·a -ae *f* actress; gladiator (*female*)

lūdibr·ium -iī or **-ī** *n* derision; subject of derision, butt of ridicule; (fig) plaything, sucker; **ludibrio esse** (with *dat*) to be made a fool of by (*someone*), be taken in by (*someone*); **ludibrio habere** to take for a sucker, make fun of

lūdibund·us -a -um *adj* playful, playing around; without effort, without danger

lūdic·er -ra -rum *adj* for sport, in sport; **ludicra exercitatio** sports; athletics; **ludicrum praemium** sports award; **ludicra res** drama; *n* sport, game; toy; show, public game; stage play

lūdificābil·is -e *adj* used in mockery

lūdificāti·ō -ōnis *f* ridiculing, mocking; fooling, tricking

lūdificāt·or -ōris *m* mocker

lūdificāt·us -ūs *m* mockery

lūdific·ō -āre or **lūdific·or -ārī -ātus sum** *vt* to make a fool of, fool, take for a sucker; to fool, trick, baffle

lūdi·ō -ōnis or **lūd·ius -iī** or **-ī** *m* actor

lūdō lūdēre lūsī lūsum *vt* to play; to spend in play; to amuse oneself with, do for amusement, practice as a pastime; to imitate, mimic, mock, do a takeoff on, ridicule; to deceive, delude; *vi* to play; to frisk, frolic; to play around, make love; **aleā ludere** to shoot craps; **pilā ludere** to play ball, play tennis

lūd·us -ī *m* play, game, sport, pastime, diversion; school; mere child's play; joke, fun; playing around, fooling around, lovemaking; public show, public game; **amoto ludo** all joking aside; **in ludum ire** to go to school; **per ludum** as a joke, for fun; *m pl* public games, public exhibition; games, tricks; **ludos facere** or **ludos reddere** (with *dat*) to play tricks on, make fun of

luell·a -ae *f* expiation, atonement

lu·ēs -is *f* infection, contagion, plague, pestilence; calamity

Lugdūnens·is -e *adj* of Lyons

Lugdūn·um -ī *n* Lyons (*town in E. Gaul*)

lūgēō lugēre luxī *vt* to mourn, lament, deplore; *vi* to mourn, be in mourning; to be in mourning clothes

lūgubr·ia -ium *n pl* mourning clothes

lūgubr·is -e *adj* mourning; doleful; disastrous

lumbifrag·ium -iī or **-ī** *n* physical wreck

lumbric·us -ī *m* worm; (as term of reproach) worm

lumb·us -ī *m* loin; *m pl* loins; genital organs

lūm·en -inis *n* light; lamp, torch; brightness, sheen, gleam; daylight; light of the eye, eye; light of life, life; window, window light; distinguished person, luminary, celebrity; glory, pride

lūminār·e -is *n* window

lūminōs·us -a -um *adj* luminous; (fig) bright, conspicuous

lūn·a -ae *f* moon; month; night; crescent (*worn as ornament by senators on their shoes*); **luna laborans** moon in eclipse, eclipse of the moon; **luna minor** waning moon

lūnār·is -e *adj* lunar, of the moon

lūnāt·us -a -um *adj* crescent-shaped

lūn·ō -āre *vt* to make crescent-shaped, to shape like a crescent

lūnŭl·a -ae *f* little crescent (*ornament worn by women*)

lu·ō -ĕre -ī *vt* to wash; to cleanse, purge; to set free, let go; to pay (*debt of penalty*); to suffer, undergo; to atone for, expiate; to satisfy, appease; to avert by expiation or punishment

lup·a -ae *f* she-wolf; flirt, prostitute

lupān·ar -āris *n* brothel

lupāt·us -a -um *adj* jagged (*like wolf's teeth*); *m pl* or *n pl* jagged bit

Luperc·al -ālis *n* shrine on the Palatine hill sacred to Pan

Lupercāl·ia -ium *n pl* festival of Lycaean Pan, celebrated in February

Luperc·us -ī *m* Pan

lupill·us -ī *m* small lupine (*plant*)

lupīn·us -a -um *adj* lupine, wolf's; *m & n* lupine, wolf's-bane (*plant*); stage money

lup·us -ī *m* wolf; (fish) pike; jagged bit; grapnel

lurc·ō -ōnis *m* glutton

lūrĭd·us -a -um *adj* pale-yellow, wan, ghastly, lurid; making pale

lūr·or -ōris *m* sallowness

luscini·a -ae *f* nightingale

lusciniŏl·a -ae *f* little nightingale

luscin·ius -iī or **-ī** *m* nightingale

lusciōs·us or **luscitiōs·us -a -um** *adj* purblind, partly blind

lusc·us -a -um *adj* one-eyed

lūsi·ō -ōnis *f* play, game

Lūsitān·ī -ōrum *m pl* Lusitanians

Lūsitāni·a -ae *f* Lusitania (*modern Portugal and W. part of Spain*)

lūsit·ō -āre *vi* to like to play

lūs·or -ōris *m* player, gambler; humorous writer; joker

lustrāl·is -e *adj* lustral, propitiatory; quinquennial

lustrāti·ō -ōnis *f* purification, lustration; wandering

lustr·ō -āre *vt* to purify; to travel

over, traverse; to check, examine; to go around, encircle; to survey; (mil) to review (*troops*); to light up, make bright, illuminate; to scan (*with the eyes*); to consider, review

lustr·or -ārī -ātus sum *vi* to frequent brothels

lustr·um -ī *n* haunt, den, lair; wilderness; brothel; sensuality; purificatory sacrifice, lustration; lustrum, period of five years; period of years; **ingens lustrum** one hundred years, century

lūsus *pp* of **ludo**

lūs·us -ūs *m* play, game, sport, amusement; playing around (*amorously*)

lūteŏl·us -a -um *adj* yellowish

lūtĕ·us -a -um *adj* of mud, of clay; muddy; dirty, grimy; (fig) dirty; mud-colored; golden-yellow, yellow, orange

lutit·ō -āre *vt* to splatter with mud; (fig) to throw mud at

lut·ō -āre *vt* to make dirty

lutulent·us -a -um *adj* muddy, filthy; (fig) filthy; turbid (*style*)

lut·um -ī *n* mud, mire; clay; yellow

lux lūcis *f* light; light of day, daylight; light of day, life; public view, publicity; the public, the world; light of hope, encouragement; glory; elucidation; **luce** or **luci** by daylight, in the daytime; **lux aestiva** summer; **lux brumalis** winter

lux·ō -āre *vt* to put out of joint, dislocate

lux·or -ārī -ātus sum *vi* to live riotously, have a ball

luxurĭ·a -ae or **luxurĭ·ēs -ēī** *f* luxurience; luxury, extravagance, excess

luxurĭ·ō -āre or **luxurĭ·or -ārī -ātus sum** *vi* to grow luxuriantly; to luxuriate; (of the body) to swell up; (of animals) to be frisky; to run riot, lead a wild life

luxurĭōs·us -a -um *adj* luxuriant; exuberant; extravagant, voluptuous

lux·us -ūs *m* extravagance, excess, luxury; splendor, pomp, magnificence

Lyae·us -a -um *adj* Bacchic; *m* Bac-

chus; wine

Lycae·us -a -um *adj* Lycaean (*esp. applied to Pan*); *m* mountain in Arcadia where Jupiter and Pan were worshiped

Lycā·ōn -ŏnis *m* king of Arcadia, the father of Callisto, who was changed into a wolf

Lycāŏn·is -ĭdis *f* Callisto, who was changed into the Great Bear

Lycē·um or **Lycī·um -ī** *n* Aristotle's school at Athens

Lycĭ·us -a -um *adj* & *m* Lycian; *f* country in S.W. Asia Minor

lychnūch·us -ī *m* lamp stand; chandelier

lychn·us -ī *m* lamp

Lyctĭ·us -a -um *adj* Cretan

Lycurg·us -ī *m* Thracian king who prohibited the worship of Bacchus and was punished with madness and death; Spartan lawgiver (*date unknown*); Athenian orator and friend of Demosthenes (390-324 B.C.)

Lyc·us or **Lyc·os -ī** *m* husband of Antiope, who divorced her to marry Dirce

Lўdĭ·us -a -um *adj* & *m* Lydian; Etruscan; *f* country of Asia Minor, whose capital was Sardis

Lўd·us -a -um *adj* & *m* Lydian; Etruscan

lymph·a -ae *f* water, spring water; water nymph

lymphātĭc·us -a -um *adj* crazy, frantic; *n* craziness

lymphāt·us -a -um *adj* crazy, mad

Lyncĕ·us -a -um *adj* sharp-eyed; *m* Argonaut, famous for keen vision; son of Egyptus and Hyperaestra

lyn·x -cis *m* or *f* lynx

lyr·a -ae *f* lyre; lyric poetry, lyric

Lyr·a -ae *f* Lyra (*constellation*)

lyrĭc·us -a -um *adj* lyric; of the lyre; *m pl* lyric poets; *n pl* lyric poems

lyrist·ēs -ae *m* lyrist

Lyrnēs·is or **Lyrness·is -ĭdis** *f* Briseis

Lyrnēs·us -ī *f* town in the Troad, the birthplace of Briseis

Lysĭ·ās -ae *m* Athenian orator in the time of Socrates (*c.* 450-370 B.C.)

M

Macăr·eus -ĕī or **-ĕos** *m* son of Aeolus, who lived in incest with his sister Canace

Macĕd·ō -ŏnis *m* Macedonian

Macedonĭc·us -a -um *adj* Macedonian

Macedonĭ·us -a -um *adj* Macedonian; *f* Macedonia (*country lying between Thessaly and Thrace*)

macell·um -ī *n* butcher shop, meat market

mac·ĕō -ēre *vi* to be lean, be skinny

mac·er -ĕra -ĕrum *adj* lean; skinny; thin, poor (*soil*)

Mac·er -rī *m* C. Licinius Macer (*Roman historian and orator who was impeached by Cicero and committed suicide in 66 B.C.*); C. Licinius Macer Calvus (*son of the former, and distinguished orator and poet,* 82–46 B.C.)

mācerī·a -ae *f* brick or stone wall; garden wall

mācĕr·ō -āre *vt* to knead, soften, make tender; to weaken, waste; to distress, vex, torment

macesc·ō -ĕre *vi* to grow thin

machaer·a -ae *f* sword

machaerophŏr·us -ī *m* soldier armed with sword

Machā·ōn -ŏnis *m* famous physician of the Greeks in the Trojan War and son of Aesculapius

Machāonī·us -a -um *adj* surgical

māchin·a -ae *f* machine; engine; crane; pulley, windlass, winch; (fig) scheme, stratagem

māchināment·um -ī *n* machine, engine, contrivance

māchinātī·ō -ōnis *f* mechanism; machine; trick

māchināt·or -ōris *m* engineer, machinist; (fig) contriver

māchin·or -ārī -ātus sum *vt* to engineer, design, contrive; to scheme, plot

macĭ·ēs -ēī *f* leanness, thinness; barrenness; poverty (*of style*)

macilent·us -a -um *adj* skinny

macresc·ō -ĕre *vi* to grow thin, get skinny

macritūd·ō -ĭnis *f* leanness, skinniness

macrocoll·um -ī *n* large-size sheet of paper

mactābil·is -e *adj* deadly

mactāt·us -ūs *m* sacrifice

mactē *interj* well done! good luck!

mact·ō -āre *vt* to magnify, glorify, honor; to sacrifice; to slaughter, put to death; to destroy, ruin, overthrow; to trouble, afflict

mact·us -a -um *adj* glorified, honored, adored; **macte virtute (esto)** (congratulatory exclamation) good luck!; well done!

macŭl·a -ae *f* spot, stain, blemish; mesh (*of a net*); (fig) stigma, blemish, disgrace, defect

macŭl·ō -āre *vt* to spot; to stain; to defile, pollute; to dishonor

maculōs·us -a -um *adj* spotted; stained

made·faciō -facĕre -fēcī -factus (*passive:* **made·fīō -fĭerī -factus sum**) *vt* to wet, moisten, drench, soak, steep

mad·ens -entis *adj* wet, moist; flowing (*hair*); melting (*snow*); reeking (*with blood*)

mad·ĕō -ēre -uī *vi* to be wet, be moist, be soaked, be drenched; to drip; to flow; to be soused; to be full, overflow

mad·escō -escĕre -uī *vi* to become wet, become moist

madĭdē *adv* drunkenly

madĭd·us -a -um *adj* wet, moist, drenched; dyed, steeped; drunk

mad·or -ōris *m* moisture

maduls·a -ae *m* souse, drunkard

Maeand·er or **Maeandr·os** or **Maeandr·us -ī** *m* river in Asia Minor, famous for its winding course; winding; winding border; devious course

Maecēn·ās -ātis *m* C. Cilnius Maecenas (*adviser to Augustus and friend of Virgil and Horace,* d. 8 B.C.)

maen·a -ae *f* sprat (*fish*)

Maenăl·is -ĭdis *adj* **Maenalis ursa** Callisto (*who was changed into the Great Bear*)

Maenăl·us or **Maenăl·os -ī** *m* or **Maenăl·a -ōrum** *n pl* Mt. Maenalus (*mountain range in Arcadia, sacred to Pan*)

Maen·as -ădis *f* Bacchante

Maenĭ·us -a -um *adj* Maenian; **Maenia Columna** pillar in the forum at which thieves, slaves, and debtors were tried and flogged

Maeŏn·es -um *m pl* Maeonians (*ancient name of the Lydians*)

Maeonĭd·ēs -ae *m* native of Maeonia; Homer; Etrurian

Maeŏn·is -ĭdis *f* Maeonian woman (*esp. Arachne or Omphale*)

Maeonĭ·us -a -um *adj* Lydians; Homeric; Etruscan; *f* Maeonia, Lydia; Etruria

Maeōt·ae -ārum *m pl* Scythian tribe on Lake Maeotis on the N.E. coast of the Black Sea

Maeōt·is -ĭdis *adj* Maetoic; Scythian; **Maeotis lacus** Sea of Azov

maer·ĕō -ēre *vi* to mourn

maer·or -ōris *m* mourning, sadness

maestĭter *adv* like a mourner

maestitĭ·a -ae *f* sadness, gloom, melancholy

maestitūd·ō -ĭnis *f* sadness

maest·us -a -um *adj* mourning, sad, gloomy

Maev·ius -iī or **-ī** *m* poetaster often ridiculed by Virgil and Horace

māgāl·ia -ĭum *n pl* huts

mage see **magis**

magĭc·us -a -um *adj* magic; **artes magicae** magic

magis or **mage** *adv* more, in a higher degree, rather; **eo magis** all the more, the more; **magis magisque** more and more; **magis ... quam** or **magis ... atque** rather **... than**; **non magis ... quam** not so much **... as**

magist·er -rī *m* chief, master, director; teacher; adviser, guardian; ringleader, author; captain, pilot; (in apposition with another noun) expert; **magister morum** censor; **magister sacrorum** chief priest

magister·ium -iī or **-ī** *n* directorship, presidency; **magisterium morum** censorship

magistr·a -ae *f* directress, mistress, instructress

magistrāt·us -ūs *m* magisterial office, magistracy; magistrate, offi-

cial; body of magistrates; military
command

magnanimit·ās -ātis _f_ magnanimity; bravery

magnanim·us -a -um _adj_ magnanimous; brave

Magn·ēs -ētis _adj_ & _m_ Magnesian;
_f_ city in Caria, near the Meander;
city in Lydia near Mt. Sipylus; district in Thessaly on the Aegean Sea

magnidic·us -a -um _adj_ talking big

magnificē _adv_ magnificently, splendidly; pompously

magnificenti·a -ae _f_ magnificence,
grandeur, splendor; pompousness

magnific·ō -āre _vt_ to think much of

magnific·us -a -um _adj_ grand,
great, splendid, august; rich, costly, magnificent; pompous

magniloquenti·a -ae _f_ lofty style;
pompous language

magnilŏqu·us -a -um _adj_ sublime;
bragging

magnitūd·ō -ĭnis _f_ greatness, magnitude, size; large quantity, large
number; vastness, extent

magnopĕre or **magnō opĕre** _adv_
greatly, very much, particularly;
strongly, earnestly, heartily, ur-
gently

magn·us -a -um (_comp:_ **major;**
superl: **maximus**) _adj_ big, large,
great; long (_time_); high (_price_); important, momentous; significant;
impressive; high, powerful (_in
rank_); loud (_voice_); heavy (_rain_); advanced (_age_); noble (_character_);
proud, boastful; _n_ great thing;
great value; **magni (pretii) aestimare** or **magni habere** to value
highly, have a high regard for;
magno emere to buy at a high
price; **magno vendere** to sell at
a high price; **vir magno jam natu** aged man, man advanced in
years

mag·us -a -um _adj_ magic; **artes
magae** magic; _m_ learned man
(_among the Persians_); magician

Māi·us -a -um _adj_ & _m_ May; _f_
daughter of Atlas and Pleione, and
mother of Mercury by Jupiter

mājāl·is -is _m_ castrated hog; (as
term of abuse) swine

mājest·ās -ātis _f_ majesty, dignity,
grandeur; high treason; sovereign
power, sovereignty; authority

māj·or (_comp_ of **magnus**) _adj_
bigger, larger, greater; **annos natu major quadraginta** forty
years older; **in majus ferre** to exaggerate; **majoris (pretii)** at a
higher price; more highly; **major
natu** elder, older

mājōr·ēs -um _m pl_ ancestors, forefathers

mājuscŭl·us -a -um _adj_ somewhat
greater; a little older

māl·a -ae _f_ cheekbone, upper jaw;
_f pl_ cheek; (fig) jaws (_e.g._, of death)

malacĭ·a -ae _f_ calm at sea, dead calm

malaciss·ō -āre _vt_ to soften, soft-

en up

malăc·us -a -um _adj_ soft; luxurious

male _adv_ badly, wrongly; wickedly,
cruelly, maliciously; unfortunately,
unsuccessfully, awkwardly; excessively, extremely, very much; (with
adjectives having a good sense) not,
scarcely, not at all; (with adjectives
having a bad sense) very much; terribly; **male audire** to be ill spoken
of; **male dicere** (with _dat_) to say
nasty things to, abuse; **male emere** to buy at a high price; **male
facere** (with _dat_) to treat badly or
cruelly; **male habere** to harass;
male metuere to be terribly
afraid of; **male vendere** to sell at
a loss; **male vivere** to be a failure
in life

maledĭc·ax -ācis _adj_ abusive, foul-
mouthed

maledĭcē _adv_ abusively, slanderously

maledĭc·ens -entis _adj_ abusive,
foul-mouthed

male·dīcō -dīcĕre -dixī -dictum _vi_
(with _dat_) **a** to speak ill of, abuse,
slander; **b** to say nasty things to

maledictĭ·ō -ōnis _f_ abusive language, abuse

maledictĭt·ō -āre _vi_ (with _dat_) to
keep saying nasty things to

maledict·um -ī _n_ curse; abuse

maledĭc·us -a -um _adj_ abusive,
scurrilous, foul-mouthed

malefact·or -ōris _m_ malefactor

malefact·um or **malfact·um -ī** _n_
wrong, injury

maleficē _adv_ mischievously

maleficenti·a -ae _f_ harm, wrong,
mischief

malefic·ium -iī or **-ī** _n_ evil deed,
crime, offense; harm, injury, wrong,
mischief; **maleficium admittere**
or **committere** to commit an offense or crime

malefic·us -a -um _adj_ wicked, vicious, criminal; _m_ mischief-maker

malesuād·us -a -um _adj_ seductive,
tempting

malevŏl·ens -entis _adj_ spiteful

malevolenti·a -ae _f_ spitefulness,
malice, meanness

malevŏl·us -a -um _adj_ spiteful,
malicious, mean; _mf_ enemy; jealous
person

malif·er -ĕra -ĕrum _adj_ apple-
growing

malignē _adv_ spitefully, jealously,
meanly; stingily, grudgingly

malignit·ās -ātis _f_ spite, malice,
jealousy, meanness; stinginess

malign·us -a -um _adj_ spiteful, malicious, jealous, mean; stingy; (fig)
stingy, unproductive (_soil_); scanty
(_light_)

malitĭ·a -ae _f_ malice, ill-will, bad
behavior; _f pl_ devilish tricks

malitiōsē _adv_ craftily, wickedly

malitiōs·us -a -um _adj_ crafty,
wicked, malicious, devilish

malleŏl·us -ī _m_ small hammer, small
mallet; fiery arrow

mallĕ·us -ī m hammer, mallet; pole-ax (for slaughtering animals)

mālō or **māvŏlō malle mālŭī** vt to prefer; vi (with dat) to incline toward, be more favorably disposed to

malobăthr·um -ī n malobathrum oil, betel juice

māl·um -ī n apple; **aureum malum** quince; **felix malum** lemon; **malum Punicum** or **malum granatum** pomegranate

mal·um -ī n evil, ill; harm; punishment; disaster; hardship

māl·us -ī m mast (of ship); pole; f apple tree

mal·us -a -um adj bad; ill, evil; ugly; unpatriotic; adverse, unsuccessful; unlucky; **i in malam rem** go to hell!; n see **malum**

malv·a -ae f mallow

Mām·ers -ertis m Mars

Māmertin·ī -ōrum m pl (mercenaries of Agathocles who after his death seized Messana, c. 282 B.C., and precipitated the First Punic War)

mamill·a -ae f breast, teat

mamm·a -ae f breast (of a woman); dug

mammeāt·us -a -um adj largebreasted, full-bosomed

mānābil·is -e adj penetrating (cold)

manc·eps -ĭpis m purchaser; contractor

mancip·ium or **mancup·ium -iī** or **-ī** n formal purchase; possession, right of ownership; slave; **mancipio accipere** to take possession of; **mancipio dare** to turn over possession of; **res mancipi** possessions basic to running a farm (e.g., land, slaves, livestock, farm implements); **res nec mancipi** possessions other than those needed to run a farm

mancip·ō or **mancup·ō -āre** vt to sell, transfer

manc·us -a -um adj crippled, maimed; (fig) defective, imperfect

mandāt·um -ī n command, order, commission; n pl instructions

mandāt·us -ūs m command, order

mand·ō -āre vt to commit, entrust; to command, order, enjoin, commission

mandō mandĕre mandī mansum vt to chew; to champ; to eat, devour; **humum mandere** to bite the dust (said of those who fall in battle)

mandr·a -ae f stable, stall; drove of cattle; checkerboard

manduc·us -ī m mask representing a glutton

māne (indecl) n morning; adv early in the morning; **bene mane** very early; **cras mane** tomorrow morning; **heri mane** yesterday morning; **hodie mane** this morning; **postridie ejus diei mane** the following morning

manĕō manēre mansī mansum vt

to wait for, await; vi to stay, remain; to stop off, pass the night; to last, endure, continue, persist; **in condicione manere** to stick by an agreement; **in sententia manere** to stick to an opinion

mān·ēs -ium m pl souls of the dead; ghosts; lower world; last remains (of the body), ashes

mang·ō -ōnis m pushy salesman; slave dealer

manic·ae -ārum f pl handcuffs; grappling hook; long sleeves; gloves

manicāt·us -a -um adj long-sleeved

manicŭl·a -ae f little hand

manifestē adv plainly, distinctly

manifestō adv manifestly, evidently, plainly

manifest·ō -āre vt to reveal, betray

manifest·us -a -um adj manifest, plain, clear, distinct; exposed, brought to light, detected, caught; (with genit) convicted of, caught in; (with inf) known to

manipl- = manipul-

manipulār·is -e adj of a maniple or company; **miles manipularis** private

manipulār·is -is m private; soldier of the same company; comrade

manipulātim adv by companies

manipŭl·us or **manipl·us -ī** m handful (esp. of hay); (coll) gang; (mil) maniple, company (three of which constituted a cohort)

Manl·ius -iī or **-ī** m M. Manlius Capitolinus (consul in 392 B.C., who, in 389 B.C., saved the Capitoline from the invading Gauls); T. Manlius Torquatus (consul in 340 B.C., famous for his military discipline)

mannŭl·us -ī m pony

mann·us -ī m small Gallic horse

mān·ō -āre vi to drip, trickle, flow; to stream; (fig) to spread, emanate

mansi·ō -ōnis f stopover

mansit·ō -āre vi to stay on

mansuē·faciō -facĕre -fēcī -factum (passive: **mansuē·fiō -fiĕrī -factus sum**) vt to tame; (fig) to tame, pacify, civilize

mansu·ēs -is or **-ētis** adj tame, mild

mansu·escō -escĕre -ēvī -ētum vt to tame; vi to grow tame, become tame; (fig) to grow gentle, grow mild

mansuētē adv gently, mildly

mansuētūd·ō -ĭnis f mildness, gentleness

mansuēt·us -a -um adj tame; mild, gentle

mansus pp of **mando** and **maneo**

mantēl·e -is n napkin, towel

mantell·um or **mantēl·um -ī** n mantle

mantic·a -ae f knapsack

manticĭn·or -ārī -ātus sum vi to predict, prophesy

mant·ō -āre vt to wait for; vi to stay, remain, wait

Mant·ō -ūs f prophetic daughter of Tiresias

Mantŭ·a -ae f birthplace of Virgil, in N. Italy

manuāl·is -e adj that can be held in hand, hand-sized (e.g., rocks)

manubĭ·ae -ārum f pl money derived from the sale of booty

manubĭārĭ·us -a -um adj (coll) bringing in the loot

manūbrĭ·um -ĭī or **-ī** n handle; hilt

manufestārĭ·us -a -um adj plain, obvious

manŭlĕ·a -ae f long sleeve

manŭlĕăr·ĭus -ĭī or **-ī** m sleeve maker

manŭlĕăt·us -a -um adj longsleeved

manūmissĭ·ō -ōnis f manumission, freeing of a slave

manŭ·mittō or **manŭ·mittō -mittĕre -mīsī -missum** vt to manumit, emancipate, set free (a slave)

manupretĭ·um -ĭī or **-ī** n workman's pay, wages; (fig) pay, reward

man·us -ūs f hand; band, company; gang; force, violence, close combat; finishing touch; handwriting; work; workmanship; elephant's trunk; grappling irons; power; (law) power of the husband over his wife; **ad manum habere** to have at hand, have in readiness; **ad manum venire** to come within reach; **e manu** at a distance, from a distance; **in manibus esse** to be in everyone's hands, be well known; to be near, be at hand; to be present; **in manu esse** (with genit) to be in the power of, be under the jurisdiction of; **in manu esse** (with dat) to be obvious to; **inter manus** under one's hands, with one's care; in one's hands, in one's arms; **manibus pedibusque** (fig) with might and main; **manu** by hand, artificially; (mil) by force of arms; **manu tenere** to know for sure; **manum committere, conserere,** or **conferre** to begin to fight; **manum dare** to lend a hand; **manum injicere** (with dat) to lay hands on, arrest; **manus dare** or **manus dedere** to give oneself up, surrender; **per manus** by hand; by force, by main force; from hand to hand, from mouth to mouth, from father to son; **plēnā manu** generously; **prae manibus** or **prae manu** at hand, in readiness; **sub manu** or **sub manum** at hand, near; immediately

mapāl·ĭa -ĭum n pl African huts; African village, kraal

mapp·a -ae f napkin; flag (used in starting races at the racetrack)

Marăth·ōn -ōnis f site, in E. Attica, of victory by Miltiades over the Persians (490 B.C.)

Marcell·us -ī m Roman cognomen in the gens Claudia; M. Claudius Marcellus (nephew of Augustus, whose premature death is referred to in the Aeneid, 43-23 B.C.)

marc·ĕō -ēre vi to wither, droop, shrivel; to be weak, be feeble, be decrepit, be run-down; to slack off

marcesc·ō -ēre vi to begin to wither, begin to droop; to become weak, become run-down; to become lazy

marcĭd·us -a -um adj withered, drooping; groggy

Marc·ĭus -ĭī or **-ī** m Ancus Marcius (fourth king of Rome)

marcŭl·us -ī m small hammer

mar·e -is n sea; seawater, saltwater; **mare inferum** Tyrrhenian Sea; **mare nostrum** Mediterranean Sea; **mare superum** Adriatic Sea

Marĕŏt·a -ae f town and lake near Alexandria in Egypt

Marĕōtĭc·us -a -um adj Mareotic; Egyptian

margarīt·a -ae f or **margarīt·um -ī** n pearl

margĭn·ō -āre vt to furnish with a border; to curb (a street)

marg·ō -ĭnis f margin, edge, border; frontier

Marĭān·ī -ōrum m pl partisans of Marius

Marĭc·a -ae f nymph of Minturnae, mother of Latinus

marīn·us -a -um adj sea, of the sea, marine

marisc·a -ae f fig; tumidae mariscae the piles

marīt·a -ae f wife, married woman

marītāl·is -e adj marital, nuptial, matrimonial

marītĭmus or **marītŭm·us -a -um** adj sea, of the sea; seafaring, maritime; (fig) changeable (like the sea); **ora maritima** seacoast; n pl seacoast

marīt·ō -āre vt to marry; to train (a vine to a tree)

marīt·us -a -um adj matrimonial nuptial; m husband, married man; lover; f see **marita**

Mar·ĭus -ĭī or **-ī** m C. Marius (conqueror of Jugurtha and of the Cimbri and Teutons, and seven times consul, 157-86 B.C.)

marm·or -ŏris n marble; marble statue, marble monument; smooth surface of the sea

marmŏrĕ·us -a -um adj marble, made of marble; marble-like

Mar·ō -ōnis m cognomen of Virgil

marr·a -ae f hoe, weeding hook

Mar·s -tis m god of war and father of Romulus and Remus; battle, war; engagement; planet; **aequo Marte** on an equal footing; **suo Marte** by one's own exertions, independently

Mars·ī -ōrum m pl Marsians (a people of S. central Italy, regarded as tough warriors)

marsupp·ĭum -ĭī or **-ī** n pouch, purse

Marsy̆·ās or **Marsy̆·a -ae** m satyr who challenged Apollo with the flute and was flayed alive upon his defeat; statue in the Roman forum of Marsyas

Martiāl·is -is *m* M. Valerius Martialis (*commonly called Martial and famous for his epigrams, c.* 40-120 A.D.)

Marticŏl·a -ae *m* worshiper of Mars

Marti·us -a -um *adj* Martian, of Mars; sacred to Mars; descended from Mars; March; *m* March, month of March

mās maris *adj* male, masculine; manly, masculine, brave; *m* male

masculīn·us -a -um *adj* male, masculine

mascŭl·us -a -um *adj* male, masculine; manly, vigorous; *m* male

mass·a -ae *f* mass, lump; (coll) chunk of money

Massic·us -a -um *adj* Massic; *m* Mt. Massicus (*between Latium and Campania, famous for its wine*); *n* Massic (*wine*)

Massilī·a -ae *f* Greek colony on S. coast of Gaul (*modern Marseilles*)

Massȳl·ī -ōrum *m pl* tribe of E. Numidia

mastīgī·a ae *m* rascal

mastrūc·a -ae *f* sheepskin; (as term of abuse) ninny

mastrūcāt·us -a -um *adj* clothed in sheepskin

matăr·a -ae or **matăr·is -is** *f* Celtic javelin

matell·a -ae *f* chamber pot

matell·ō -ōnis *m* pot

māt·er -ris *f* mother; matron; **mater familias** lady of the house; (of animals) dam; cause, origin, source

mātercŭl·a -ae *f* a little mother, poor mother

māt·erfamiliās -risfamiliās *f* lady of the house, mistress of the household

māterī·a -ae or **māterī·ēs -ēī** *f* matter, stuff, material; lumber, wood, timber; fuel; subject, subject matter, theme, topic; cause, source, occasion, opportunity; capacity, natural ability, disposition

māteriār·ius -iī or **-ī** *m* timber merchant

māteriāt·us -a -um *adj* built with lumber; **male materiatus** built with poor lumber

māteriēs see **materia**

māterī·or -ārī -ātus sum *vi* to fetch or gather wood

mātern·us -a -um *adj* maternal, mother's, of a mother

mātertĕr·a -ae *f* aunt, mother's sister

mathēmatic·us -ī *m* mathematician; astrologer

Matīn·us -ī *m* mountain in Apulia, near Horace's birthplace

mātricīd·a -ae *m* matricide, mother's murderer

mātricīd·ium -iī or **-ī** *n* matricide, murder of one's mother

mātrimōn·ium -iī or **-ī** *n* matrimony, marriage; **in matrimonium ire** to enter matrimony, get mar-

ried; **in matrimonium aliquam ducere** to marry some girl

mātrīm·us -a -um *adj* having a mother still living

mātrōn·a -ae *f* married woman, matron, wife; woman of quality, lady

Mātrōnāl·ia -ium *n pl* festival celebrated by matrons on March 1 in honor of Mars

mātrōnāl·is -e *adj* matronly, womanly, wifely

matt·a -ae *f* straw mat

matŭl·a -ae *f* pot; chamber pot

mātūrātē *adv* in good time

mātūrē *adv* at the right time; in time; betimes, in good time, promptly, quickly; prematurely

mātūr·escō -escĕre -ŭī *vi* to get ripe, ripen, mature

mātūrit·ās -ātis *f* ripeness, maturity; (fig) maturity, height, perfection

mātūr·ō -āre *vt* to ripen, bring to maturity; to accelerate, speed up; (with *inf*) to be too quick in doing; *vi* to hasten

mātūr·us -a -um *adj* ripe, mature, full-grown; opportune, at the right time; early, coming early (*e.g., winter*); advanced in years; marriageable; mellow (*with age*)

Mātūt·a -ae *f* goddess of the dawn

mātūtīn·us -a -um *adj* morning, early; **tempora matutina** morning hours

Mauritānī·a -ae *f* country of N.W. Africa

Maur·us -a -um *adj* Moorish; African

Maurūsī·us -a -um *adj* Moorish, Mauretanian

Māvor·s -tis *m* Mars

Māvortī·us -a -um *adj* Martian, of Mars

maxill·a -ae *f* jaw

maximē or **maxŭmē** *adv* very, most, especially, particularly; just, precisely, exactly; (in sequences) in the first place, first of all; (in affirmations) by all means, certainly, yes; **immo maxime** certainly not; **nuper maxime** just recently; **quam maxime** as much as possible; **tum cum maxime** at the precise moment when; **tum maxime** just then, precisely at that time; **ut maxime . . . ita maxime** the more . . . so much the more

maximit·ās -ātis *f* magnitude

maximus or **maxŭmus** (*superl* of **magnus**) see **magnus**

mazonŏm·us -ī *m* large dish

meāmet = meā, *abl fem sing* of **meus**, strengthened by **-met**

meapte = mea, *nom fem sing* of **meus**, strengthened by **-pte**

meāt·us -ūs *m* motion, movement; course, channel

mecastor *interj* by Castor!

mēd = me

mēcum = cum me

medd·ix or **med·ix -īcis** *m* magistrate (*among the Oscans*); **meddix tuticus** senior magistrate (*among the Oscans*)

Mēdē·a -ae *f* daughter of Aeetes, the king of Colchis, and wife of Jason, famous for her magic

Mēdē·is -ĭdis *adj* magic

med·ens -entis *m* physician

med·ĕor -ērī *vt* to heal; *vi* (with *dat*) to heal, cure, be good for, remedy

Mēd·ī -ōrum *m pl* Medes; Persians; Parthians

Mēdĭ·a -ae *f* Asian country between Armenia, Parthia, Hyrcania, and Assyria

mediastīn·us -ī *m* servant, drudge

mēdĭc·a -ae *f* alfalfa

medicābĭl·is -e *adj* curable

medicām·en -ĭnis *n* medicine, remedy, drug, antidote; tincture; cosmetic; (fig) cure, remedy

medicāment·um -ī *n* medication, medicine; potion; (fig) relief, antidote; (rhet) embellishment

medicāt·us -ūs *m* magic charm

medicīn·a -ae *f* medicine, medical science; medicine, remedy; doctor's office; (with *genit*) (fig) cure for, remedy for

medic·ō -āre *vt* to medicate, cure; to dye

medic·or -ārī -ātus sum *vt* to cure; *vi* (with *dat*) to heal, cure

medic·us -a -um *adj* medical; healing; *m* doctor, surgeon

Mēdic·us -a -um *adj* Median, of the Medes

mediē *adv* moderately

mediēt·ās -ātis *f* mean

medimn·um -ī *n* or **medimn·us -ī** *m* bushel, medimnus (*containing six modii*)

mediŏcr·is -e *adj* medium, average, ordinary; mediocre; narrow, small

mediocrĭt·ās -ātis *f* mean; moderation; mediocrity; *f pl* moderate passions

mediocriter *adv* moderately, fairly; not particularly, not very, not much; calmly

Mediolān·um -ī *n* Milan

mediŏxĭm·us -a -um *adj* (coll) in the middle

meditāment·um -ī *n* practice, drill

meditātē *adv* purposely

meditātĭ·ō -ōnis *f* reflection, contemplation; practice; rehearsal; (with *genit*) reflection on, contemplation of

meditāt·us -a -um *adj* premeditated

mediterrānĕ·us -a -um *adj* inland

medĭt·or -ārī -ātus sum *vt* to think over, reflect on; to practice; to plan, design

medĭ·us -a -um *adj* middle, central, the middle of, in the middle; intervening (*time*); middling, ordinary, common; undecided, neutral, ambiguous; meddling; **in mediā insulā** in the middle of the island; **media pars** half, one half; *m* mediator; *n* middle, center; commu-

nity, common good; public, publicity; **e medio abīre** to disappear; **in medio relinquere** to leave undecided, leave hanging in the air; **in medium** into the center; on behalf of the public; for the common good; **in medium proferre** to publish

medĭus fīdĭus *interj* by Heaven!

med·ix -ĭcis *m* magistrate (*among the Oscans*); **medix tuticus** senior magistrate

medull·a -ae *f* marrow; middle, center

medullĭtus *adv* (fig) with all one's heart

Medūs·a -ae *f* one of the three Gorgons, the daughter of Phorcys, whose eyes turned everything they looked upon into stone

Medūsae·us -a -um *adj* Medusan; **equus Medusaeus** Pegasus

Megaer·a -ae *f* one of the three Furies

Megalens·ĭa or **Megalēs·ĭa -ĭum** *n pl* festival of Cybele, celebrated on the 4th of April

Megăr·a -ae *f* or **Megăr·a -ōrum** *n pl* town near Athens

Megarē·us or **Megarĭc·us -a -um** *adj* Megarean

megistān·es -um *m pl* grandees

mehercle or **mehercūle** or **mehercūles** *interj* by Hercules!

mēī·ō -ĕre *vi* to urinate

mel mellis *n* honey; **meum mel** (as term of endearment) my honey!; *n pl* drops of honey

melanchŏlĭc·us -a -um *adj* melancholy

melandry·um -ī *n* piece of salted tuna

Melanth·ĭus -ĭī or **-ī** *m* goatherd of Ulysses

melcŭl·um -ī *n* (*term of endearment*) little honey

Meleăg·er or **Meleăg·ros -rī** *m* son of King Oeneus of Calydon and participant in the famous Calydonian boar hunt

Meleagrĭd·es -um *f pl* sisters of Meleager, who were changed into birds

Melicert·a or **Melicert·ēs -ae** *m* son of Ino and Athamas, who was changed into a sea god, called by the Greeks Palaemon and by the Romans Portunus

melic·us -a -um *adj* musical; lyric

melilōt·os -ī *m* clover

melimēl·a -ōrum *n pl* honey apples

melīn·a -ae *f* mead

melīn·a -ae *f* leather wallet

Melīn·um -ī *n* pigment; Melian white

melĭ·or -us (*comp of* **bonus**) *adj* better

melisphyll·um -ī *n* balm

Melĭt·a or **Melĭt·ē -ēs** *f* Malta

Melitens·is -e *adj* Maltese

melĭus (*comp of* **bene**) *adv* better

meliuscūlē *adv* pretty well

meliuscŭl·us -a -um *adj* a little better

mell·a -ae *f* mead

mellicŭl·us -a -um *adj* sweet as honey

mellif·er -ĕra -ĕrum *adj* honey-producing

mellific·ō -āre *vi* to make honey

mellill·a -ae *f* (term of endearment) little honey

mellīn·a -ae *f* sweetness, delight

mellīn·a -ae *f* leather wallet

mellīt·a -a -um *adj* honeyed, sweetened with honey; sweet as honey

mel·os -ī (Greek *pl*: **mel·e**) *n* tune, melody, song

Melpomĕn·ē -ēs *f* Muse of tragic poetry

membrān·a -ae *f* membrane, skin; slough; parchment; film

membrānŭl·a -ae *f* small piece of parchment

membrātim *adv* limb by limb; piecemeal, singly; in short sentences

membr·um -ī *n* limb, member; part, division; clause

mēmet *pron* (emphatic form of me) me

memĭn·ī -isse *vt* to remember; *vi* (with *genit*) to be mindful of, remember

Memn·ōn -ŏnis *m* son of Tithonus and Aurora, king of the Ethiopians, and ally of the Trojans, who was killed by Achilles

Memnŏnĭd·es -um *f pl* birds that rose from the pyre of Memnon

Memnŏnĭ·us -a -um *adj* Memnonian; Oriental, Moorish, black

mem·or -ŏris *adj* mindful, remembering; having a good memory; reminding; (with *genit*) mindful of, remembering

memorābĭl·is -e *adj* memorable, remarkable

memorand·us -a -um *adj* worth mentioning, notable

memorāt·us -ūs *m* mention

memorĭ·a -ae *f* memory; remembrance; period of recollection, recollection, time, lifetime; a memory, past event, history; historical account; **memoriae prodere** to hand down to posterity; **paulo supra hanc memoriam** not long ago; **post hominum memoriam** within the memory of man; **superiore memoriā** in earlier times

memoriŏl·a -ae *f* weak memory

memorĭter *adv* from memory, by heart; accurately, correctly

memŏr·ō -āre *vt* to mention, bring up, relate; to name, call; *vi* (with **de** + *abl*) to speak of

Memph·is or -ĭdos *f* city in central Egypt

Memphītĭc·us -a -um *adj* Egyptian

Menand·er or Menand·ros -rī *m* Greek comic playwright, the most important representative of the Attic New Comedy (342-291 B.C.)

Menandrē·us -a -um *adj* of Menander

mend·a -ae *f* fault, blemish

mendācĭloquī·or -us *adj* more false, more mendacious

mendāc·ĭnm -ĭī or -ĭ *n* lie

mendācĭuncŭl·um *n* white lie, fib

mend·ax -ācis *adj* mendacious, given to lying, false; *m* liar

mendicābŭl·um -ī *n* beggar

mendicĭt·ās -ātis *f* beggary

mendic·ō -āre or mendic·or -ārī -ātus sum *vt* to beg, beg for; *vi* to beg, go begging

mendicŭl·us -a -um *adj* beggarly

mendīc·us -a -um *adj* needy, poor, poverty-stricken; (fig) poor, sorry, paltry; *m* beggar

mendōsē *adv* faultily, carelessly

mendōs·us -a -um *adj* full of physical defects; full of faults, faulty, incorrect, erroneous; blundering

mend·um -ī *n* defect, fault; blunder

Menelā·us -ī *m* son of Atreus, brother of Agamemnon, and husband of Helen

Menen·ĭus -ī or -ĭ *m* Menenius Agrippa (*patriotic Roman who told the plebs the fable of the belly and the limbs during the secession of the plebs in 494 B.C.*)

Menoec·eus -ĕī or -ĕos *m* son of Theban king Creon, who hurled himself off the city walls to save the city

Menoetĭăd·es -ae *m* Patroclus

Menoet·ĭus -ĭī or -ĭ *m* father of Patroclus

men·s -tis *f* mind, intellect; understanding, reason; thought, opinion, intention, plan; courage, boldness; passion, impulse; idea; feeling, heart, soul; purpose, **addere mentem** to give courage; **captus mente** crazy; **demittere mentem** to lose heart; **in mentem venire** to come to mind; **mentis suae esse** to be in one's right mind

mens·a -ae *f* table; meal, course, dinner; guests at table; counter; bank; sacrificial table, altar; **mensa secunda** dessert

mensār·ĭus -ĭī or -ĭ *m* banker; treasurer, treasury-board member

mensĭ·ō -ōnis *f* measure, measuring; quantity (*of a syllable*)

mens·is -is *m* month; **primo mense** at the beginning of the month

mens·or -ōris *m* surveyor

menstruāl·is -e *adj* for a month

menstru·us -a -um *adj* monthly; lasting for a month; *n* rations for a month; month's term of office

mensŭl·a -ae *f* little table

mensūr·a -ae *f* measuring, measurement; standard of measure; amount, size, proportion, capacity, extent, limit, degree

mensus *pp* of **metior**

ment·a or menth·a -ae *f* mint

menti·ens -entis *m* sophism, fallacy

mentĭ·ō -ōnis *f* mention; **mentĭo-**

nem facere (with *genit* or *de* + *abl*) to make mention of; **mentiones serere** (with *ad* + *acc*) to throw hints to

ment·ior -īrī -ītus sum *vt* to invent, fabricate; to feign, imitate, fake; *vi* to lie; to act deceitfully

Ment·or -ōris *m* friend of Ulysses; famous artist in metalwork; ornamental cup

ment·um -ī *n* chin

mē·ō -āre *vi* to go, pass

mephīt·is -is *f* malaria

mepte *pron* (emphatic form of **mē**) me, me myself

merācŭl·us or **merācl·us -a -um** *adj* pretty pure, rather pure

merāc·us -a -um *adj* pure, unmixed, undiluted, straight

mercābĭl·is -e *adj* buyable

mercāt·or -ōris *m* merchant, trader, dealer, wholesale dealer

mercātōrĭ·us -a -um *adj* merchant, trading; **navis mercatoria** merchant ship

mercātūr·a -ae *f* trading, trade, commerce; purchase; *f pl* goods

mercāt·us -ūs *m* trade, traffic; market, marketplace; fair

mercēdŭl·a -ae *f* poor pay; low rent, low income

mercēnārĭ·us -a -um *adj* hired, paid, mercenary; *m common* laborer, servant

merc·ēs -ēdis *f* pay, wages, salary; bribe; reward, recompense; cost; injury, detriment; stipulation, condition, retribution, punishment; rent, income, interest

mercimōn·ĭum -ĭī or **-ī** *n* merchandise

mer·cor -ārī -ātus sum *vt* to deal in, trade in, purchase

Mercŭriāl·is -e *adj* of Mercury; *m pl* corporation of merchants in Rome

Mercŭr·ĭus -ĭī or **-ī** *m* Mercury (*son of Jupiter and Maia, messenger of the gods, patron of commerce, diplomacy, lying, gambling, and conductor of departed souls to the world below*); Mercury (*planet*)

merd·a -ae *f* droppings, excrement

merend·a -ae *f* lunch, snack

mer·ĕo -ēre -ŭī -ĭtum or **mer·ĕor -ērī -ĭtus sum** *vt* to deserve, merit, be entitled to; to win, earn, acquire, merit; *vi* to serve; to serve in the army; (with **de** + *abl*) to serve, render service to, do a favor for: **bene de re publica merere** or **mereri** to serve one's country well; **de te merui** I have done you a favor, I have treated you well; **equo merere** to serve in the cavalry

meretrīcĭ·us -a -um *adj* prostitute's

meretrīcŭl·a -ae *f* cute little wench

merētr·ix -īcis *f* prostitute, harlot, wench, strumpet

merg·ae -ārum *f pl* pitchfork

merg·es -ĭtis *f* sheaf

mergō mergĕre mersī mersum *vt* to dip, plunge, sink; to engulf, swallow up; to swamp, overwhelm, bury, drown; **mergi** to sink, drown; to go bankrupt

merg·us -ī *m* diver (*bird*)

merīdĭān·us -a -um *adj* midday, noon; southern, southerly

merīdĭātĭ·ō -ōnis *f* siesta

merīdĭ·ēs -ēī *m* midday, noon; south; **spectare ad meridiem** to face south

merīdĭ·ō -āre *vi* to take a siesta

Mērĭŏn·ēs -ae *m* charioteer of Idomeneus

merītō *adv* deservedly, rightly

merīt·ō -āre *vt* to earn regularly

merītōr·ĭus -a -um *adj* rented, hired; *n pl* rented apartment

merīt·us -a -um *adj* deserved, just, right, proper, deserving; guilty; *n* service, favor, kindness; blame, fault, offense; merit, worth

merobĭb·us -a -um *adj* drinking unmixed wine

Merŏp·ē -ēs *f* one of the Pleiades, the daughter of Atlas and Pleione

Mer·ops -ŏpis *m* king of Ethiopia, husband of Clymene, and reputed father of Phaethon

mer·ops -ŏpis *f* bee eater (*bird*)

mers·ō -āre *vt* to keep dipping or plunging, to immerse; (fig) to engulf; **mersari** (with *dat*) to plunge into

mersus *pp* of **mergo**

merŭl·a -ae *f* blackbird

mer·us -a -um *adj* pure, unmixed, undiluted, unadulterated; (fig) undiluted; (fig) nothing but, mere; *n* wine

mer·x -cis *f* merchandise, wares; **mala merx** (fig) bad lot

Messallīn·a -ae *f* wife of the Emperor Claudius; wife of Nero

Messān·a -ae *f* town in N.E. Sicily

Messāpĭ·us -a -um *adj* Apulian; *f* town and district in S.E. Italy, named after the mythical founder Messapus

mess·is -is *f* harvest; harvest time; **adhuc tua messis in herba est** (fig) don't count your chickens before they are hatched

mess·or -ōris *m* reaper, mower

messōr·ĭus -a -um *adj* reaper's

messus *pp* of **meto**

mēt·a -ae *f* marker for measuring the distance at a racetrack; (fig) goal, end; (fig) turning point, critical moment

metall·um -ī *n* metal; *n pl* mine

metamorphōs·is -is *f* transformation

metaphŏr·a -ae *f* metaphor

mētāt·or -ōris *m* planner; **metator urbis** city planner

Metaur·us -ī *m* small river in Umbria, at the banks of which Hasdrubal was defeated in 207 B.C.

Metell·us -ī *m* Roman surname; Q. Caecilius Metellus Numidicus (*commander of the Roman forces against Jugurtha from 109 B.C. until replaced by Marius in 107 B.C.*)

Methymn·a -ae *f* town on the island of Lesbos

mētior mētīrī mensus sum *vt* to measure; to traverse, travel; to judge, estimate; (with *dat*) to measure (*something*) out to, distribute (*something*) among; (with *abl*) to judge (*someone*) by the standard of

metō metĕre messuī messum *vt* to reap, mow, gather, collect, harvest; (fig) to mow down (*e.g., with the sword*)

mēt·or -ārī -ātus sum *vt* to measure off; to lay out (*e.g., a camp*)

metrēt·a -ae *f* liquid measure (*about nine gallons*)

metuculōs·us -a -um *adj* fearful; scary

metŭ·ens -entis *adj* afraid, apprehensive, anxious

metŭ·ō -ĕre -ī *vt* to fear, be afraid of; *vi* to be afraid, be apprehensive

met·us -ūs *m* fear, anxiety, apprehension

me·us -a -um *adj* my; *pron* mine; **meā interest** it is of importance to me; **meum est** (with *inf*) it is my duty to; **meus est** (coll) I've got him

Mezent·ĭus -ĭī or **-ī** *m* Etruscan tyrant of Caere, slain by Aeneas

mī = mihi

mīc·a -ae *f* crumb, morsel

Micips·a -ae *m* son of Masinissa and king of Numidia (148-118 B.C.); *m pl* (fig) Numidians, Africans

mic·ō -āre *vi* to vibrate, quiver, twinkle, sparkle, flash

micturĭō -īre *vi* to have to urinate

Mid·ās -ae *m* king of Phrygia, at whose touch everything turned to gold (*8th cent. B.C.*)

migrātĭ·ō -ōnis *f* moving, changing residence; metaphorical use

migrāt·us -ūs *m* transporting

migr·ō -āre *vt* to transport; (fig) to transgress, violate; *vi* to move, change residence, depart, migrate; (fig) to go away, change, turn

mīl·es -ĭtis *m* soldier; infantryman; private; army

Mīlēsĭ·us -a -um *adj* Milesian, of Miletus

Mīlēt·us -ī *f* Miletus (*town on the W. coast of Asia Minor*)

mil·ĭa -ĭum *n pl* thousands; see **mille**

mīlĭār·ĭum -ĭī or **-ī** *n* milestone

mīlitār·is -e *adj* military

mīlitārĭter *adv* in a military manner, like a soldier

mīlitār·ĭus -a -um *adj* soldierly, military

mīlitĭ·a -ae *f* army; war; the military; military discipline; **militiae** in war, on the battlefield, in the army; **militiae domique** abroad

and at home, on the war front and on the home front

milit·ō -āre *vt* to carry on (*war*); *vi* to serve as a soldier, be in the service

mil·ĭum -ĭī or **-ī** *n* millet

mille (indecl) *adj* thousand; *n* thousand; **mille homines** a thousand men; **milia** *n pl* thousands; **duo milia passuum** two miles

millēsĭm·us or **millensĭm·us -a -um** *adj* thousandth

milliār·ĭum -ĭī or **-ī** *n* milestone

milliens or **milliēs** *adv* a thousand times; innumerable times

Mil·ō -ōnis *m* T. Annius Milo (*friend of Cicero and enemy of Clodius, defended by Cicero on a charge of having murdered Clodius in 52 B.C.*)

Miltĭăd·ēs -is *m* Athenian general victorious at Marathon (490 B.C.)

mīlnīn·us -a -um *adj* rapacious

mīlŭ·us or **mīlŭ·os -ī** *m* kite (*bird of prey*); gurnard (*fish*)

Mīlŭ·us -ī *m* Kite (*constellation*)

mīm·a -ae *f* actress

Mimallŏn·is -ĭdis *f* Bacchante

Mīm·ās -antis *m* one of the giants

mīmicē *adv* like a mime actor

mīmĭc·us -a -um *adj* suitable for the mime, farcical

Mimnerm·us -ī *m* Greek elegiac poet of Colophon (*fl. 560 B.C.*)

mīmŭl·a -ae *f* miserable little actress

mīm·us -ī *m* mime, farce; actor of a mime; (fig) farce

min·a -ae *f* Greek coin (*about 100 denarii*)

minācĭ·ae -ārum *f pl* menaces, threats

minācĭter *adv* threateningly

min·ae -ārum *f pl* menaces, threats; projecting points of a wall

minanter *adv* threateningly

minātĭ·ō -ōnis *f* threatening

min·ax -ācis *adj* threatening, menacing; projecting, jutting out

min·eō -ēre *vi* to project, jut out

Minerv·a -ae *f* goddess of wisdom and of the arts and sciences, identified with Pallas Athene; (fig) skill, genius; spinning and weaving; **invitā Minervā** against one's better judgment

mingō mingĕre minxī mictum *vi* to urinate

minĭān·us -a -um *adj* vermilion

miniātŭl·us -a -um *adj* reddish

minimē or **minŭmē** *adv* least of all, least, very little; by no means, certainly not, not in the least; **minume gentium** (coll) by no means

minĭm·us or **minŭm·us -a -um** (*superl of* **parvus**) *adj* smallest, least, very small; slightest, very insignificant; youngest; shortest (*time*); **minimus natū** youngest; *n* the least, minimum; lowest price; **minimo emere** to buy at a very low price; **minimo provocare** to provoke for the least thing or on the flimsiest pretext

mini·ō -āre vt to color red, paint red

minist·er -rī m servant, attendant, helper; agent, tool, instrument

minister·ium -iī or **-ī** n office, ministry, service, occupation, work, employment; retinue

ministr·a -ae f servant, attendant, helper; waitress; handmaid

ministrāt·or -ōris m or **ministrātr·ix -īcis** f assistant, helper

ministr·ō -āre vt to serve, wait on; to tend; to execute, carry out (orders); (with dat) to hand out (something) to; (with abl) to supply (someone or something) with

minitābund·us -a -um adj threatening

minit·ō -āre or **minit·or -ārī -ātus sum** vt to make threats of (e.g., war); (with acc of thing and dat of person) to threaten to bring (e.g., evil, death) upon, hold (something) threateningly over (someone); vi to make threats; (with dat of person threatened and abl of means) to threaten (someone) with

min·ium -iī or **-ī** n vermilion; red lead

Mīnō·is -idis f Ariadne

Mīnō·us or **Mīnō·us -a -um** adj of Minos, Cretan

min·or -ārī -ātus sum vt to threaten; to promise boastfully; (with dat of person and acc of thing) to threaten (someone) with (something), to hold (something) over (someone) as a threat; vi to jut out, project; to be menacing, make threats; (with dat) to threaten, make threats to

min·or -us (comp of **parvus**) adj smaller, less; less, shorter (time); younger; inferior, less important; (with abl) a (of time) too short for; b inferior to; c unworthy of; **dimidio minor quam** half as small as; **minores facere filios quam** to think less of the sons than of; **minor natu** younger; m pl descendants, posterity; n less, smaller amount; **minoris emere** to buy at a lower price; **minus praedae** less booty

Mīn·ōs -ōis or **-ōnis** m son of Zeus and Europa, king of Crete, and, after his death, judge in the lower world; grandson of the former, likewise king of Crete, husband of Pasiphaë, and father of Ariadne and Phaedra

Mīnōtaur·us -ī m monstrous offspring of Pasiphaë, half man and half bull, and kept in the labyrinth

minūme see **minime**

minūmus see **minimus**

min·uō -uĕre -uī -ūtum vt to diminish, lessen, reduce; to weaken, lower; to modify (plans); to settle (controversies); to limit, restrict (authority); to offend against, try to cheapen (e.g., the majesty of the Roman people); vi to diminish, abate, ebb; **minuente aestū** at ebbtide

minus adv less; not; by no means, not at all

minuscul·us -a -um adj rather small, smallish

minūt·al -ālis n hamburger, hash

minūtātim adv piecemeal; bit by bit

minūtē adv in a small-minded way

minūtul·us -a -um adj tiny

minūt·us -a -um adj small, minute; petty, narrow-minded

Minў·ae -ārum m pl Argonauts, the companions of Jason

Minў·ās -ae m mythical king of Thessaly

mīrābil·is -e adj wonderful, marvelous, amazing, extraordinary

mīrābiliter adv wonderfully, amazingly

mīrābund·us -a -um adj full of amazement, astonished

mīrācul·um -ī n wonder, marvel; surprise, amazement

mīrand·us -a -um adj fantastic

mīrāti·ō -ōnis f admiration, wonder

mīrāt·or -ōris m admirer

mīrātr·ix -īcis adj fem admiring

mīrē adv wonderfully, uncommonly, strangely; **mīre quam** it is strange how, strangely

mīrificē adv wonderfully

mīrific·us -a -um adj causing wonder, wonderful

mīrimŏdīs adv in a strange way

mirmill·ō -ōnis m gladiator (who fought with Gallic arms)

mīr·or -ārī -ātus sum vt to be amazed at, be surprised at; to look at with wonder, admire

mīr·us -a -um adj amazing, surprising, astonishing; wonderful; **mīrum est** (with acc & inf) it is surprising that; **mīrum quam** or **mīrum quantum** it is amazing how, it is amazing to what extent

miscellāně·a -ōrum n pl hash

miscĕō miscēre miscŭī mixtum vt to mix, blend, mingle; to combine, associate, share; to mix up, confuse, turn upside down; to mix, prepare, brew

misell·us -a -um adj poor little

Mīsēn·um -ī n promontory and town near the bay of Naples

mis·er -ĕra -ĕrum adj poor; wretched, miserable, unhappy; sorry, worthless

miserābil·is -e adj miserable, pitiable; piteous

miserābiliter adv pitiably; piteously

miserand·us -a -um adj pitiful, deplorable

miserāti·ō -ōnis f pity, compassion, sympathy; appeal for sympathy

miserē adv wretchedly, miserably, unhappily; pitifully; desperately

miser·ĕō -ēre -uī -itum or **miser·ĕor -ērī -itus sum** vi (with genit) to pity, feel sorry for, sympathize with; v impers (with acc of person who feels pity and *genit* of object of pity), e.g., **miseret** or **miseretur me aliorum** I feel sorry for the others

miseresc·ō -ĕre *vi* to feel pity, feel sympathetic; (with *genit*) to pity, feel sorry for; *v impers* (with *acc* of person who feels pity and *genit* of object of pity), e.g., **me miserescit tuī** I feel sorry for you, I pity you

miserĭ·a -ae *f* poverty; misery, unhappiness, distress, trouble

misericordĭ·a -ae *f* pity, sympathy, compassion; mercy

misericor·s -dis *adj* sympathetic, merciful

miserĭter *adv* sadly

misĕr·or -ārī -ātus sum *vt* to deplore; to pity; *vi* to feel pity

missicŭl·ō -āre *vt* to keep sending

missĭl·is -e *adj* missile, flying; *n pl* missiles

missĭ·ō -ōnis *f* release, liberation; sending off, despatching; military discharge; dismissal from office; cessation, end; **sine missione** without letup, to the death

missĭt·ō -āre *vt* to keep sending

missus *pp* of **mitto**

miss·us -ūs *m* letting go, throwing, hurling; sending

mītesc·ō -ĕre *vi* to grow mild, grow mellow, become ripe; (fig) to get soft; (fig) to become gentle, become tame

Mithr·ās -ae *m* Mithra (*sun-god of the Persians*)

Mithridāt·ēs -is *m* Mithridates the Great (*king of Pontus from 120 B.C. to 63 B.C.*)

Mithridātē·us or **Mithridātĭc·us -a -um** *adj* Mithridatic

mītigātĭ·ō -ōnis *f* mitigation, soothing

mītig·ō -āre *vt* to mellow, ripen; to soften; to calm down, appease, pacify

mīt·is -e *adj* mellow, ripe, soft; calm, placid; mild, gentle

mitr·a -ae *f* miter, turban

mittō mittĕre mīsī missum *vt* to send; let fly, throw, fling, launch; to emit, shed; to let out, utter; to let go of, drop; to free, release, discharge, dismiss; to pass over in silence, omit; to send for, invite; to pass up, forego; to dedicate (*a book*); to yield, produce, export; to dismiss, forget; **sanguinem mittere** to bleed; **sanguinem provinciae mittere** (fig) to bleed a province dry

mītŭl·us -ī *m* limpet

mixtim *adv* promiscuously

mixtūr·a -ae *f* mixing, blending

Mnēmosўn·ē -ēs *f* mother of the Muses

mnēmosўn·on -ī *n* souvenir

mōbĭl·is -e *adj* mobile, moveable, portable; nimble, active; shifty, changing; impressionable, excitable

mōbilĭt·ās -ātis *f* mobility; agility, quickness; shiftiness

mōbilĭter *adv* quickly, rapidly

mōbilĭt·ō -āre *vt* to impart motion to, endow with motion

moderābĭl·is -e *adj* moderate

moderām·en -ĭnis *n* control

moderanter *adv* under control

moderātē *adv* with moderation

moderātim *adv* gradually

moderātĭ·ō -ōnis *f* controlling, control, regulation, guidance; moderation, self-control; rules, regulation

moderāt·or -ōris *m* or **moderātr·ix -īcis** *f* controller, director, guide

moderāt·us -a -um *adj* controlled, well regulated, orderly, restrained

modĕr·ō -āre or **modĕr·or -ārī -ātus sum** *vt* to control, direct, guide; *vi* (with *dat*) **a** to moderate, restrain, put restraint upon; **b** to allay, mitigate

modestē *adv* with moderation, discreetly; modestly

modestĭ·a -ae *f* moderation, restraint; discretion; modesty, sense of shame, sense of honor, dignity; propriety; mildness (*of weather*)

modest·us -a -um *adj* moderate, restrained; modest, discreet; orderly, obedient

modiāl·is -e *adj* containing a modius or peck

modĭcē *adv* moderately, with restraint; in an orderly manner; only slightly

modĭc·us -a -um *adj* moderate; small; modest, unassuming; ordinary, puny, trifling

modificāt·us -a -um *adj* regulated (*in length*)

mod·ĭus -ĭī or **-ī** *m* modius, peck (*one sixth of a medimnus*); measure; **plēno modĭo** in full measure

modo *adv* only, merely, simply, solely; (of time) just now, just recently, lately; presently, in a moment; **modo ... deinde** (or **tum** or **postea** or **interdum**) first ... then, at one time ... next time; **modo ... modo** now ... now, sometimes ... sometimes, at one moment ... at another; **non modo ... sed etiam** or **verum etiam** not only ... but also; *conj* if only, provided that

modulātē *adv* according to measure, in time; melodiously

modulāt·or -ōris *m* director, musician

modŭl·or -ārī -ātus sum *vt* to regulate the time of, measure rhythmically; to modulate; to sing; to play

modŭl·us -ī *m* small measure, small stature

mod·us -ī *m* standard of measurement, measure; time, rhythm; size; limit, boundary; rule, regulation; way, manner, mode; **ad modum** (with *genit*) or **in modum** (with *genit*) or **modo** (with *genit*) in the manner of, according to the style of, like; **ejus modi homo** that kind of man; **hujus modi homo** this kind of man

moech·a **-ae** f adultress

moechiss·ō **-āre** vt to ravish, rape

moech·or **-ārī** **-ātus sum** vi to have an affair, commit adultery

moech·us **-ī** m adulterer

moen·ia **-ium** n pl town walls, ramparts, fortifications; fortified town; castle, stronghold; defenses

moeniō see **munio**

moerus see **murus**

Moes·ī **-ōrum** m pl a people on the lower Danube

mol·a **-ae** f millstone; mill; flour; f pl mill

molār·is **-is** m millstone; molar (tooth)

mōl·ēs **-is** f mass, bulk, pile; massive structure, dam, mole, pier; mass (of people, etc.); burden, effort, trouble; calamity; might, greatness

molestē adv with annoyance; with difficulty, with trouble; **molestē ferre** to be annoyed at, be disgruntled at, just about stand

molesti·a **-ae** f annoyance, trouble; worry; affectation (in style)

molest·us **-a** **-um** adj annoying, troublesome, distressing; labored, affected (style)

mōlīm·en **-inis** n great exertion, great effort; attempt, undertaking

mōlīment·um **-ī** n great exertion, great effort

mōl·ior **-īrī** **-ītus sum** vt to do with great effort, strain at, exert oneself over; to wield, heave, hurl; to work hard at; to build, erect; to rouse; to displace; to undertake, attempt; to perform; to cause, occasion; vi to exert oneself, struggle, take great pains

mōlīti·ō **-ōnis** f building, erection; demolition

mōlīt·or **-ōris** m builder

molītus pp of **molo**

mōlītus pp of **mōlior**

mollesc·ō **-ēre** vi to become soft; to become gentle; to become effeminate

mollicul·us **-a** **-um** adj tender, dainty

moll·iō **-īre** **-īvī** or **-iī** **-ītum** vt to make soft, soften; (fig) to soften, mitigate; to demoralize

mollip·ēs **-ēdis** adj soft-footed

moll·is **-e** adj soft; springy; flexible; flabby; mild, calm; easy; gentle (slope); sensitive, impressionable; tender, touching; weak, effeminate; amatory (verses); complaint; changeable, untrustworthy

molliter adv softly; gently, smoothly; effeminately; voluptuously; patiently, with fortitude

mollīti·a **-ae** or **mollīti·ēs** **-ēī** f softness; flexibility; tenderness; sensitivity; weakness, irresolution; effeminacy, voluptuousness

mollītūd·ō **-inis** f softness; flexibility; susceptibility

mol·ō **-ēre** **-uī** **-itum** vt to grind

Moloss·us **-a** **-um** adj Molossian; m Molossian hound; m pl Molassians (a people of Epirus)

mōl·y **-ўos** n magic herb

mōm·en **-inis** n movement, motion; momentum

mōment·um **-ī** n movement, motion; alteration; turn, critical time; moment; impulse; momentum; influence, importance; motive

Mon·a **-ae** f Isle of Man

monēdūl·a **-ae** f jackdaw

mon·eō **-ēre** **-uī** **-itum** vt to call to mind, remind, advise, point out; to warn; to foretell; to teach, instruct, inform

monēr·is **-is** f galley

Monēt·a **-ae** f Juno Moneta, in whose temple on the Capitoline Hill money was kept; coin, money; stamp or die (for money)

monētāl·is **-e** adj of the mint; m (coll) money man

monil·e **-is** n necklace

monim- = **monum-**

monit·a **-ōrum** n pl warnings; prophecies

moniti·ō **-ōnis** f reminder

monit·or **-ōris** m reminder, counselor; teacher

monit·us **-ūs** m reminder, warning

monogramm·us **-a** **-um** adj sketchy, shadowy

monopod·ium **-iī** or **-ī** n table with a single central leg

monotrop·us **-a** **-um** adj single, alone

mon·s **-tis** m mountain, mountain range; mass, heap; hill; **montis aurī polliceri** to make wild promises; **summus mons** mountain top

monstrāti·ō **-ōnis** f pointing out

monstrāt·or **-ōris** m displayer; inventor

monstr·ō **-āre** vt to show, to point out, exhibit, make known, advise, teach; to appoint, institute, ordain; to advise, urge

monstr·um **-ī** n sign, portent, wonder; warning; monster, monstrosity; miracle, marvel

monstruōsē adv unnaturally

monstruōs·us **-a** **-um** adj unnatural, strange, monstrous

montān·us **-a** **-um** adj mountain, of a mountain; mountainous; m pl mountaineers; n pl mountainous regions

monticol·a **-ae** m mountaineer, highlander

montivǎg·us **-a** **-um** adj wandering over the mountains

montōs·us or **montuōs·us** **-a** **-um** adj mountainous

monument·um **-ī** n reminder; monument, memorial; record (written or oral); token of identification

Mopsopi·us **-a** **-um** adj Athenian; f Attica, Athens

mor·a -ae f delay; pause; spell, period of time; stop-off; division of the Spartan army consisting of from three to seven hundred men

morāl·is -e adj moral

morāt·or -ōris m obstructionist; (in court) lawyer who spoke only to gain time

morāt·us -a -um adj -mannered; -natured; in character; **bene morātus** well-mannered; **male morātus** ill-mannered, rude

morbĭd·us -a -um adj sickly; causing sickness, unwholesome

morbōs·us -a -um adj debauched

morb·us -ī m sickness, disease; fault, vice; distress; **in morbum cadere** or **in morbum incidere** to fall sick

mordācĭus adv more bitingly; (fig) more radically

mord·ax -ācis adj biting, snapping; (fig) sharp, stinging, caustic, snarling; pungent (taste)

mordĕō mordēre momordī morsum vt to bite; to eat, devour; to bite, grip, (of cold) to nip; (of words) to cut, hurt; (of a river) to bite its way through

mordīc·ēs -um m pl bites

mordĭcus adv by biting, with the teeth; (fig) tightly, doggedly

mōrē adv foolishly

morēt·um -ī n salad

moribund·us -a -um adj dying, at the point of death; mortal; deadly

mōrigĕr·ō -āre or **mōrigĕr·or -ārī -ātus sum** vi (with dat) to humor, pamper, yield to, comply with

mōrigĕr·us -a -um adj obedient, obsequious

morĭor morī mortŭus sum vi to die; (fig) to die out, wither, decay, pass away

morm·yr -ȳris f Pontic fish

mōrolŏg·us -a -um adj speaking nonsense, foolish

mor·or -ārī -ātus sum vt to delay, detain; to entertain, hold the attention of; to hinder, prevent; **nihil morari** (with acc) **a** to disregard, care nothing for, not value; **b** to have nothing against, have nothing to say against; vi to delay, linger, tarry, loiter; to stay, remain, wait; **quid moror?** or **quid multis morer?** why should I drag out the point?, to make a long story short

mōrōsē adv morosely, crabbily

mōrōsĭt·ās -ātis f moroseness, peevishness, crabbiness

mōrōs·us -a -um adj morose, peevish, crabby; fastidious, particular; (fig) stubborn (disease)

Morph·eus -ĕos m god of dreams

mors mortis f death; destruction; corpse; **mortem obīre** to meet death; **mortis poena** death penalty; **sibi mortem consciscere** to commit suicide

mors·a -ōrum n pl bits, little pieces

morsiuncŭl·a -ae f peck, kiss

morsus pp of **mordeo**

mors·us -ūs m bite; pungency; grip; corrosion; gnawing pain; sting, vicious attack

mortāl·is -e adj mortal, subject to death; human, mortal; transient; man-made; m mortal, human being

mortālĭt·ās -ātis f mortality; mortals, mankind

mortĭcīn·us -a -um adj dead; corpse-like, rotting

mortĭf·er or **mortĭf·ĕrus -ĕra -ĕrum** adj lethal, deadly

mortĭfĕrē adv mortally

mortuāl·ia -ium n pl dirges

mortŭ·us -a -um pp of **morior**; adj dead, deceased; withered, decayed; scared to death; m corpse

mōrŭl·us -a -um adj dark, black

mōr·um -ī n blackberry, mulberry

mōr·us -ī f mulberry tree

mōr·us -a -um adj foolish; mf fool

mōs mōris m caprice, mood; nature, manner; custom, usage, practice; fashion, style; rule, regulation, law; **de more** or **ex more** according to custom; **morem gerere** (with dat) to humor (someone); m pl morals, character, behavior; customs; laws

Mōs·ēs or **Moys·ēs -is** m Moses

mōtĭ·ō -ōnis f motion

mōt·ō -āre vt to keep moving, keep shifting

mōtus pp of **moveo**

mōt·us -ūs m motion, movement; gesture; dancing; change (e.g., of fortune); impulse, inspiration; emotion, passion; rebellion, riot; **motus animi** emotion; **motus terrae** earthquake

mov·ens -entis adj movable; **res moventes** personal property; n pl motives

movĕō movēre mōvī mōtum vt to move; to stir, shake, disturb; to dislodge (the enemy); to eject, expel; to degrade; to remove, take away; to plow; to cause, occasion, promote; to begin; to undertake; to trouble, torment; to move, influence, affect; to dissuade; to exert, exercise; to turn over in the mind, ponder; **se ex loco movere** to budge from the spot; **se movere** to dance; vi to move

mox adv soon, presently; hereafter; next, then, later on

Moys·ēs -is m Moses

mūcĭd·us -a -um adj sniveling, driveling; moldy, musty

Mūc·ĭus -ĭī or **-ī** m Roman family name

mūcr·ō -ōnis m sharp point, sharp edge; sword; edge, boundary; keenness

mūc·us -ī m nasal mucus

mūgient·ēs -ĭum m pl oxen

mūgil or **mūgĭl·is -is** m mullet

mugin·or -ārī -ātus sum vi to dillydally

mŭg·ĭō -īre -īvī or -ĭī -ītum *vi* to bellow, low; to rumble, roar

mŭgīt·us -ūs *m* bellowing, lowing; rumbling, roaring

mūl·a -ae *f* mule

mulcĕō mulcēre mulsī mulsum *vt* to stroke, pet; to stir gently; to soothe, alleviate; to appease; to flatter, delight

Mulcīb·er -ērī or -ēris *m* Vulcan; fire

mulc·ō -āre *vt* to beat, cudgel; to mistreat, injure

mulctr·a -ae *f* milk pail

muctrār·ĭum -ĭī or -ī or **muctr·um** -ī *n* milk pail

mulgĕō mulgēre mulsī mulsum or **mulctum** *vt* to milk

muliēbr·is -e *adj* woman's, womanly, feminine; womanish, effeminate

muliēbrĭter *adv* like a woman; effeminately

muli·er -ĕris *f* woman; wife

mulierārĭ·us -a -um *adj* woman's; *m* woman chaser, wolf

muliercŭl·a -ae *f* little woman; little hussy

mulierōsĭt·ās -ātis *f* weakness for women

mulierōs·us -a -um *adj* woman-crazy

mūlīn·us -a -um *adj* mulish

mūl·ō -ōnis *m* mule driver

mūlōnĭ·us -a -um *adj* mule driver's

mullŭl·us -ī *m* little mullet

mull·us -ī *m* mullet

muls·us -a -um *pp* of **mulceo**; *adj* honeyed, sweet as honey; *f* (term of endearment) honey; *n* mead (*wine mixed with honey*)

mult·a -ae *f* fine; penalty; loss of money; **multam certare** to contest a fine; **multam committere** to incur a fine; **multam dicere** (with *dat* of person and *acc* of the fine) to fine (*someone a certain amount*); **multam subire** to incur a fine, be fined

multa *adv* much, very, greatly, earnestly

mult·a -ōrum *n pl* many things; much; **ne multa** in short, to be brief

multangŭl·us -a -um *adj* many-angled

multātīcĭ·us -a -um *adj* fine, of a fine; **multaticia pecunia** fine

multātĭ·ō -ōnis *f* fine, penalty

multēsĭm·us -a -um *adj* trifling, negligible

mult·ī -ōrum *m pl* many men, many; multitude, mass, common people

multibĭb·us -a -um *adj* heavy-drinking

multicăv·us -a -um *adj* porous

multicĭ·a -ōrum *n pl* diaphanous garments

multifārĭam *adv* in many places

multifĭd·us -a -um *adj* divided into many parts; (of a river) having many tributaries; **dens multifida** comb

multiform·is -e *adj* multiform, manifold

multifōr·us -a -um *adj* many-holed; (flute) having many stops

multigenĕr·is -e or **multigĕn·us** -a -um *adj* of many kinds, various, complex

multijŭg·is -e or **multijŭg·us** -a -um *adj* yoked together; (fig) various, complex

multilŏqu·ax -ācis *adj* talkative

multiloqu·ĭum -ĭī or -ī *n* talkativeness

multilŏqu·us -a -um *adj* talkative

multimŏdīs *adv* in many ways

multipl·ex -ĭcis *adj* with many folds; winding, labyrinthine, serpentine; manifold; many; (in implied comparisons) many times as great, far greater; varied, complicated; changeable, versatile, many-sided; sly, cunning; *n* manifold return

multiplicăbĭl·is -e *adj* manifold, many

multiplicĭter *adv* in various ways

multiplic·ō -āre *vt* to multiply, increase, enlarge

multipŏt·ens -entis *adj* mighty, powerful

multitūd·ō -ĭnis *f* great number, multitude, crowd, throng; rabble, common people

multivŏl·us -a -um *adj* passionate

multō *adv* (with comparatives) much, far, by far, a great deal; **multo aliter ac** far otherwise than, much different from; **multo ante** long before; **multo post** long after; **non multo secus fieri** to turn out just about the same

mult·ō -āre *vt* to punish, fine

mult·us -a -um (*comp*: **plures**; *superl*: **plurimus**) *adj* many a, much, great; abundant, considerable, extensive; tedious, long-winded; full, numerous, thick, loud, heavy, constant; **ad multum diem** till late in the day; **multā nocte** late at night; **multo die** late in the day; (with plural nouns) many; *m pl* see **multi**; *n* much; **multi** of great value, highly; **multi facere** to think highly of, make much of, think much of; **multum est** it is of great importance; **multum temporis** a great deal of time, much time; *n pl* see **multa**

multum *adv* much, greatly, very, often, frequently, far; (with comparatives) much, far; **multum valere** to have considerable influence

mūl·us -ī *m* mule

Mulvĭ·us -a -um *adj* Mulvian; **Mulvius pons** Mulvian bridge (*across the Tiber, above Rome, on the Via Flaminia*)

Mumm·ĭus -ĭī or -ī *m* L. Mummius Achaicus (*conqueror of Corinth*, 146 B.C.)

mundān·us -ī *m* world citizen

mundē or **mundĭter** adv neatly, cleanly

munditĭ·a -ae or **munditĭ·ēs -ēī** f neatness, cleanness; elegance; politeness

mundŭl·us -a -um adj trim, neat, sharp

mund·us -a -um adj neat, clean, nice; fine, smart, sharp, elegant; choice (words); m neat person; world, universe, heavens; earth, mankind; beauty aids

mūnerigerŭl·us -ī m bearer of presents

mūnĕr·ō -āre or **mūnĕr·or -ārī -ātus sum** vt to reward, honor, present; (with acc of thing and dat of person) to present to

mūni·a -ōrum n pl official duties or functions

mūnĭc·eps -ĭpis m or f citizen of a municipality; fellow citizen, fellow countryman

mūnicipāl·is -e adj municipal; (as term of contempt) provincial, country

mūnicip·ĭum -ĭī or **-ī** n municipality, town (whose people were Roman citizens, but otherwise autonomous)

mūnificē adv generously

mūnificentĭ·a -ae f generosity

mūnific·ō -āre vt to treat generously

mūnific·us -a -um adj generous; splendid

mūnīm·en -ĭnis f defense

mūnīment·um -ī n defense, protection, fortification, rampart; (fig) shelter, defense

mūn·ĭō or **moen·ĭō -īre -īvī** or **-ī -ītum** vt to wall, defend with a wall, fortify, strengthen, defend, protect, guard, secure; to build (road); (fig) to guard, shelter, protect, support

mūn·is -e adj obliging

mūnītĭ·ō -ōnis f building, fortifying, defending; fortification, rampart, trenches, lines; **munitio fluminum** bridging of rivers; **munitio viae** road construction

mūnīt·ō -āre vt to open up (a road)

mūnīt·or -ōris m builder, engineer

mūnīt·us -a -um adj fortified; (fig) protected, safe

mūn·us or **moen·us -ĕris** n service, function, duty; gift; service, favor, kindness; duty, tribute; public entertainment, gladiatorial show, extravaganza; tribute (to the dead), rite, sacrifice; public office

mūnuscŭl·um -ī n small present

mūraen·a -ae f moray (eel-like fish)

mūrāl·is -e adj wall; wall-destroying; wall-defending; **corona mūralis** mural crown (award for being the first to scale the enemy walls)

mūr·ex -ĭcis m murex, mollusk (yielding purple dye); purple dye, purple; jagged rock; spiked trap (as defense against cavalry attack)

murĭ·a -ae f brine

muriātĭc·um -ī n pickled fish

mūricīd·us -ī m mouse killer; (fig) coward

murmill·ō -ōnis m gladiator with Gallic arms, who fought against a retarius

murm·ur -ŭris n murmur, murmuring; buzz, hum; roar, crash; growling, grumbling; rumbling; hubbub

murmurill·um -ī n low murmur

murmŭr·ō -āre vi to murmur; to mutter, grumble; to rumble, roar

murr·a or **murrh·a** or **myrrh·a -ae** f myrrh tree; myrrh

murrĕ·us or **myrrhĕ·us -a -um** adj made of myrrh; perfumed with myrrh; myrrh-colored, yellowish

murrĭn·us or **myrrhĭn·us -a -um** adj of myrrh; f drink flavored with myrrh; n pl vases

murt- = myrt-

mūr·us -ī m wall, city wall; dam, dike; rim (of dish or pot); (fig) wall, protection

mūs mūris m or f mouse, rat

Mūs·a -ae f Muse (patron goddess of poetry, song, dance, literature, astronomy, etc.); poem, song; talent, genius, taste; f pl studies

Mūsae·us -ī m mythical pre-Homeric bard and musician in the time of Orpheus

musc·a -ae f fly

muscār·ĭum -ĭī or **-ī** n fly swatter

muscĭpŭl·a -ae f or **muscipŭl·um -ī** n mousetrap

muscōs·us -a -um adj mossy

muscŭl·us -ī m little mouse; muscle; (mil) mantelet

musc·us -ī m moss

Mūse·us or **Mūsae·us -a -um** adj of the Muses, musical, poetic

mūsic·a -ae or **mūsic·ē -ēs** f or **mūsic·ă -ōrum** n pl music, art of music (including poetry)

mūsicē adv pleasantly

mūsic·us -a -um adj musical; poetic; cultural; m musician

mussit·ō -āre vt to bear in silence; vi to be silent; to mutter, grumble

muss·ō -āre vt to bear in silence, bear silently; to brood over; vi to mutter, murmur; (of bees) to hum; to hesitate

mustācĕ·us -ī m or **mustācĕ·um -ī** n cake, wedding cake

mustell·a or **mustēl·a -ae** f weasel

mustellīn·us or **mustēlīn·us -a -um** adj of a weasel

must·um -ī n fresh grape juice, unfermented wine, must; vintage

mūtābĭl·is -e adj changeable; fickle

mūtābĭlĭt·ās -ātis f mutability; fickleness

mūtātĭ·ō -ōnis f mutation, change, alteration; exchange, interchange

mutĭl·ō -āre vt to cut off, lop off, crop; to mutilate; to reduce, shorten, lessen; to rob

mutĭl·us -a -um adj maimed, mutilated; defective

Mutīn·a -ae *f* town of N. central Italy, S. of the Po, which played a role in the civil war after the death of Julius Caesar

mūtiō see **muttio**

mūtītiō see **muttitio**

mūt·ō -āre *vt* to move, shift, change, alter; to exchange, interchange, barter, sell; to modify, transform, vary; to change for the better; to change for the worse; (with *abl* or **pro** + *abl*) to exchange or substitute (*something or someone*) for; *vi* to change

mūt·ō -ōnis *m* penis

mutt·iō or **mūt·iō -īre -īvī -ītum** *vi* to mutter, mumble

muttīti·ō or **mūtīti·ō -ōnis** *f* muttering, mumbling

mūtuāti·ō -ōnis *f* borrowing

mūtuē *adv* mutually; in return

mūtuit·ō -āre *vt* to wish to borrow

mūtuō *adv* mutually, in return

mūtu·or -ārī -ātus sum *vt* to borrow; to derive, obtain, get

mūt·us -a -um *adj* mute, speechless; silent, still; *n pl* brutes

mūtu·us -a -um *adj* mutual, reciprocal, interchangeable; borrowed, lent; *n* reciprocity; loan; **mutuum dare** (with **cum** + *abl*) to lend to (*someone*); **mutuas pecunias sumere** (with **ab** + *abl*) to borrow money from (*someone*); **mutuum argentum rogare** to ask for a loan of cash

Mycēn·ae -ārum *f pl* or **Mycēn·ē -ēs** *f* Mycene (*city of Agamemnon in Argolis*)

Mycēnae·us -a -um or **Mycēnens·is -e** *adj* Mycenaean

Mycēn·is -idis *f* Mycenaean girl (*Iphigenia*)

Mygdŏn·es -um *m pl* a people of Thrace, some of whom later migrated to Phrygia

Mygdoni·a -a -um *adj* Phrygian

myopār·ō -ōnis *m* pirate ship

myric·a -ae or **myric·ē -ēs** *f* tamarisk

Myrmidŏn·es -um *m pl* Myrmidons (*people of Thessaly whom Achilles led in battle*)

Myr·ōn -ōnis *m* famous Greek sculptor, whose most famous work is the Discus Thrower, 5th cent. B.C.

myropōl·a -ae *m* perfumer

myropōl·ium -iī or **-ī** *n* perfume shop

myrrh- = **murr-**

myrtēt·um or **murtēt·um -ī** *n* myrtle grove

myrtĕ·us or **murtĕ·us -a -um** *adj* myrtle; crowned with myrtle

Myrtō·um mar·e (*genit:* **Myrtō·ī mar·is**) *n* sea between the Peloponnesus and the Cyclades

myrt·um -ī *n* myrtle berry

myrt·us -ūs or **-ī** *f* myrtle

Mȳsi·us -a -um *adj* Mysian; *f* Mysia (*country in N.W. Asia Minor*)

myst·a or **myst·ēs -ae** *m* priest of the mysteries of Ceres; an initiate

mystagōg·us -ī *m* initiator

mystēr·ium -iī or **-ī** *n* secret religion, secret service, secret rite or worship, divine mystery; secret; **mysteria facere** to hold service; **mysteria Romana** festival of Bona Dea

myst·ēs -ae *m* priest of the mysteries of Ceres

mystic·us -a -um *adj* mystic

Mytilēn·ae -ārum *f pl* or **Mytilēn·ē -ēs** *f* capital of the island of Lesbos

N

Nabatae·us -a -um *adj* Nabataean; Arabian, Eastern, Oriental; *m pl* Nabataeans; *f* Nabataea (*ancient Arab kingdom S.E. of Palestine*)

nabl·ium -iī or **-ī** *n* Phoenician harp (*an instrument of ten or twelve strings, played with both hands*)

nactus *pp* of **nanciscor**

Naeviān·us -a -um *adj* of Naevius

Naev·ius -iī or **-ī** *m* Cn. Naevius (*early Roman dramatic and epic poet, c. 270-200 B.C.*)

naev·us -ī *m* body mole

Nāi·as -ādis or **Nā·is -idis** or **-idos** *f* Naiad, water nymph

nam *conj* for; for instance; (transitional) now, but now, on the other hand

namque *conj* for, for in fact, for no doubt, for surely

nanciscor nanciscī nanctus sum or **nactus sum** *vt* to get by accident (*esp. by good luck*), obtain, chance upon, find

nān·us -ī *m* dwarf, midget

Napae·ae -ārum *f pl* dell nymphs

nāp·us -ī *m* turnip

Narb·ō -ōnis *m* town in S. Gaul, from which the province of Narbonese Gaul took its name

Narbōnens·is -e *adj* Narbonese

narciss·us -ī *m* narcissus

Narciss·us -ī *m* son of Cephisus and the nymph Liriope, who was changed into a flower of the same name; powerful freedman of Claudius

nard·um -ī *n* or **nard·us -ī** *f* nard, spikenard (*fragrant ointment*)

nār·is -is *f* nostril; *f pl* nostrils; nose; **acutae nares** keen perception; **homo naris obesae** dimwit;

naribus ducere to smell; **naribus uti** (with **ad** + *acc*) to turn up the nose at

narrābil·is -e *adj* to be told

narrāti·ō -ōnis *f* narration, narrative

narrātiuncul·a -ae *f* short story

narrāt·or -ōris *m* narrator, historian

narrāt·um -ī *n* account, statement, narrative

narrāt·us -ūs *m* narration, narrative

narr·ō -āre *vt* to tell, relate, narrate, recount; to describe; *vi* to speak, tell; **bene narrare** (with **de** + *abl*) to tell good news about (*someone*); **male narrare** (with **de** + *abl*) to tell bad news about (*someone*); **tibi narro** I'm telling you, I assure you

narthēc·ium -iī or **-ī** *n* medicine chest

narus see **gnarus**

Nāryci·us -a -um *adj* of Naryx (*city of the Opuntian Locrians and birthplace of Ajax Oileus*)

nascor nascī nātus sum or **gnātus sum** *vi* to be born; to rise, begin, originate, be produced, spring forth, proceed, grow, be found; **post homines natos** since the beginning of the world

Nās·ō -ōnis *m* Publius Ovidius Naso (*Roman poet, born in Sulmo, in central Italy,* 43 B.C.-c. 17 A.D.)

nass·a -ae *f* wicker trap (*for catching fish*); (fig) trap

nassitern·a -ae *f* large water jug

nasturc·ium -iī or **-ī** *n* garden cress

nās·us -ī *m* or **nās·um -ī** *n* nose; sense of smell; sagacity; anger; scorn; nozzle, spout

nāsūtē *adv* sarcastically

nāsūt·us -a -um *adj* big-nosed; satirical, sarcastic

nāt·a or **gnāt·a -ae** *f* daughter

nātālici·us -a -um *adj* birthday, natal; *n pl* birthday party

nātāl·is -e *adj* of birth, natal; *m* birthday; *m pl* birth, origin, lineage

nat·ans -antis *m* or *f* fish

natāti·ō -ōnis *f* swimming

natāt·or -ōris *m* swimmer

nat·ēs -ium *f pl* buttocks, rear, rear end

nāti·ō -ōnis *f* race, stock; tribe, nation, people; (in contemptuous sense) breed, set

nat·is -is *f* buttock, rump; *f pl* see **nates**

nātīv·us -a -um *adj* born; inborn, innate, original; produced by nature, natural; primitive (*words*)

nat·ō -āre *vi* to swim, float; to flow; to swim, overflow, be flooded; (of the eyes) to be glassy; (of birds) to fly, glide; to waver, fluctuate, be uncertain; to hover, move to and fro

nātr·ix -īcis *f* water snake

nātūr·a -ae *f* blood relationship,

natural affinity, birth; nature, natural constitution, quality, property; nature, natural disposition, character; physical nature, world, universe; order of the world, course of things; element, substance; reproductive organs

nātūrāl·is -e *adj* natural; by birth, one's own (*e.g., father, son*); produced by nature; according to nature

nātūrāliter *adv* naturally, by nature

nāt·us or **gnāt·us -a -um** *pp* of **nascor**; *adj* born, made, destined, fit; (with *dat* or with **ad** or **in** or **propter** + *acc*) born for, made for, naturally suited to; (with **annos**) at the age of . . . . years old, *e.g.*, **annos viginti natus** at the age of twenty, twenty years old; **non amplius novem annos natus** no more than nine years old; **pro** or **e re nata** under the existing circumstances, as matters stand; *m* son; *m pl* children; *f* see **nata**

nauarch·us -ī *m* captain of a ship, skipper

nauclēric·us -a -um *adj* ship owner's, skipper's

nauclēr·us -ī *m* ship owner, skipper

nauc·um -ī *n* trifle; (mostly in genitive of value with a negative) **non nauci esse** to be of no value, be good for nothing; **non nauci facere** or **non nauci habere** to regard as worthless, regard as good for nothing

naufrag·ium -iī or **-ī** *n* shipwreck; wreck, ruin, destruction; wreckage; **naufragium facere** to be shipwrecked

naufrāg·us -a -um *adj* shipwrecked, wrecked, of the shipwrecked; causing shipwreck, dangerous to shipping; (fig) ruined; *m* shipwrecked person

naul·um -ī *n* fare

naumachi·a -ae *f* simulated sea engagement (*staged as an exercise or for amusement*)

nausē·a -ae *f* seasickness; vomiting, nausea

nauseō -āre *vt* to make (*someone*) throw up; (fig) to belch forth, throw up, utter; *vi* to be seasick; to vomit; to feel squeamish, feel disgust; to cause disgust

nauseol·a -ae *f* slight squeamishness

Nausicǎ·a -ae *f* daughter of Alcinous, king of the Phaeacians

naut·a or **nāvit·a -ae** *m* sailor, seaman, mariner; captain

nautē·a -ae *f* nausea; stinking liquid

nautic·us -a -um *adj* nautical, sailors'; *m pl* sailors, seamen

nāvāl·is -e *adj* naval, of ships, of a ship; **castra navalia** camp for the protection of ships; **forma navalis** shape of a ship; *n* tackle, rigging; *n pl* dock, dockyard, shipyard; rigging

nāvicŭl·a -ae *f* small ship

nāviculārī·us -a -um *adj* of a small ship; *m* skipper; ship owner; *f* shipping business

nāvifrāg·us -a -um *adj* dangerous, treacherous, causing shipwreck

nāvigābil·is -e *adj* navigable

nāvigātī·ō -ōnis *f* sailing, navigation, voyage

nāvig·er -ĕra -ĕrum *adj* navigable

nāvig·ium -iī or -ī *n* ship

nāvig·ō -āre *vt* to sail across, navigate; *vi* to sail, put to sea; (fig) to swim

nāv·is -is *f* ship; **navem appellere** or **navem terrae applicare** to land a ship; **navem deducere** to launch a ship; **navem solvere** to set sail; **navem subducere** to beach a ship; **navis aperta** ship without a deck; **navis longa** battleship; **navis mercatoria** merchant vessel; **navis oneraria** transport, cargo ship; **navis praetoria** flagship; **navis tecta** ship with a deck

nāvĭt·a -ae *m* sailor, seaman; captain

nāvĭt·ās -ātis *f* energy, zeal

nāviter *adv* energetically, zealously, actively, busily; utterly, completely

nāv·ō -āre *vt* to do or perform energetically, conduct or prosecute with vigor; **operam navare** to act energetically; **operam navare** (with *dat*) to render assistance to

nāv·us or gnāv·us -a -um *adj* energetic, busy

Nax·os -ī *f* largest island of the Cyclades, famous for its wine and as the place where Theseus abandoned Ariadne

nē *interj* (always with a personal or demonstrative pronoun) indeed, certainly, surely; *adv* not; **ne ... quidem** (to negate emphatically the words placed between) not even; (in negative commands) not; **ne time-te** do not fear; *conj* that not, lest; (after verbs and nouns denoting fear) lest, that

-ne *enclitic* (introducing a question and added to the first important word of a clause)

nebŭl·a -ae *f* mist, fog, vapor; cloud; smoke; darkness, obscurity

nebŭl·ō -ōnis *m* loafer, good-for-nothing

nebulōs·us -a -um *adj* foggy

nec or **neque** *adv* not; *conj* nor, and not; **nec ... et** not only not ... but also; **nec ... nec** or **neque ... neque** neither ... nor; **nec non** (introducing an emphatic affirmative) and certainly, and besides

necdum or **neque dum** *conj* and not yet, nor yet

necessāriē or **necessāriō** *adv* necessarily, of necessity

necessāri·us -a -um *adj* necessary, indispensable, needful, requisite; necessary, inevitable; pressing, urgent; connected by blood or friend-

ship, related, closely connected; *mf* relative, kinsman; friend; *n pl* necessities

necesse (indecl) *adj* necessary; unavoidable, inevitable; requisite; **ne-cesse esse** to be necessary; **ne-cesse habere** to regard as necessary, regard as inevitable

necessĭt·ās -ātis *f* necessity, inevitableness, compulsion, urgency; requirement; privation, want; relationship, friendship, connection

necessitūd·ō -ĭnis *f* necessity, need, want, distress; relationship, bond, connection, relationship, friendship; *f pl* ties of friendship; relatives, friends, personal connections

necessum (indecl) *adj* necessary, requisite; inevitable

necne *adv* or not

necnōn *adv* also, besides, moreover

nec·ō -āre *vt* to kill, murder, slay, destroy

necopīn·ans -antis *adj* unaware

necopīnātō *adv* unexpectedly, by surprise

necopīnāt·us -a -um *adj* unexpected

necopīn·us -a -um *adj* unexpected; unsuspecting, careless, off guard

nect·ar -ăris *n* nectar (*drink of the gods*); nectar (*as term for honey, milk, wine, poetry, sweetness, etc.*)

nectarĕ·us -a -um *adj* of nectar, sweet or delicious as nectar

nectō **nectĕre nexŭī** or **nexī nexum** *vt* to tie, connect, fasten together, join; to weave; to clasp; to imprison, fetter; to devise, contrive; (fig) to attach, affix

nēcŭbi *conj* lest anywhere, so that nowhere

nēcunde *conj* lest from anywhere

nēdum *adv* (after an expressed or implied negative) much less, still less; (after an affirmative) not to say, much more

nefand·us -a -um *adj* unspeakable, impious, abominable

nefāriē *adv* impiously, abominably

nefāri·us -a -um *adj* impious, abominable, criminal; *n* crime, criminal act

nefās (indecl) *n* crime, wrong, wickedness, act contrary to divine law, sin; criminal, monster; **per omne fas ac nefas** by hook or by crook

nefast·us -a -um *adj* forbidden, unlawful; impious, irreligious; criminal; unlucky, inauspicious; *n* crime, outrage

negātī·ō -ōnis *f* denial

negĭt·ō -āre *vt* to deny, refuse, turn down

neglecti·ō -ōnis *f* neglect

neglectus *pp* of neglego

neglect·us -ūs *m* neglect

neglĕg·ens -entis *adj* negligent, careless, indifferent

neglegenter *adv* carelessly

neglegenti·a -ae *f* negligence, carelessness, neglect

neg·lĕgō -legĕre -lexī -lectum *vt*

to be unconcerned about; to neglect, disregard, overlook; to slight, despise

neg·ō -āre vt to deny, refuse, decline; vi to say no; to refuse

negōtiāl·is -e adj business

negōti·ans -antis m business man

negōtiātī·ō -ōnis f banking, banking business

negōtiāt·or -ōris m business man; banker; salesman, dealer

negōtiōl·um -ī n minor matter

negōti·or -ārī -ātus sum vi to do business, do banking; to trade

negōtiōs·us -a -um adj business; busy

negōt·ium -iī or **-ī** n business, occupation, employment; matter, thing, affair; situation; trouble; banking, money lending; trade, commerce; **negotium suum** private affairs; **quid negoti est?** what's the matter?; **quid negoti tibi est?** what business is it of yours?

Nēl·eus -ĕī or **-ĕos** m son of Neptune and the nymph Tyro, king of Pylos, and father of Nestor

Nemae·us -a -um adj Nemean

Nemĕ·a -ae or **Nemĕ·ē -ēs** f town in Argolis, where Hercules slew the Nemean lion and founded the Nemean games

Nemĕ·a -ōrum n pl Nemean games (held every two years at Nemea)

Nemĕs·is -is or **-ios** f goddess of vengeance

nēm·ō -inis m or f no one, nobody; **nemo quisquam** nobody at all; **nemo unus** no single person, no one by himself; **non nemo** someone, many a one

nemorāl·is -e adj sylvan

nemorens·is -e adj of a grove; of Diana's grove

nemoricultr·ix -īcis f denizen of the forest

nemorivāg·us -a -um adj roaming the woods

nemorōs·us -a -um adj wooded; covered with foliage

nempe adv (in confirmation or in sarcasm) certainly, to be sure, of course, naturally; (in questions) do you mean?

nem·us -ŏris n grove; sacred grove; plantation

nēni·a or **naeni·a -ae** f funeral dirge; doleful song; incantation; ditty

neō nēre nēvī nētum vt to spin; to weave

Neoptolĕm·us -ī m Pyrrhus, the son of Achilles

nep·a -ae f scorpion; crab

Nephelē·is -idos f Helle (daughter of Nephele and Athamas)

nep·ōs -ōtis m grandson; nephew; descendant; spendthrift

Nep·ōs -ōtis m Cornelius Nepos (Roman biographer and friend of Cicero, c. 100- c. 25 B.C.)

nepōtul·us -ī m little grandson

nept·is -is f granddaughter

Neptūnī·us -a -um adj of Neptune

Neptūn·us -ī m Neptune (god of the sea and brother of Jupiter)

nēquam (indecl) adj worthless, bad, good for nothing

nēquāquam adv by no means, not at all

neque see **nec**

nequedum see **necdum**

nequ·eō -īre -īvī or **-iī -ītum** vi to be unable; (with inf) to be unable to, not to be able to, be incapable of; **nequit** (with quin) it is impossible to

nēqui·or -us adj (comp of **nequam**) worse, more worthless

nēquiquam or **nēquicquam** adv pointlessly, for nothing, to no purpose; without good reason; with impunity

nēquissim·us -a -um adj (superl of **nequam**) worst, most worthless

nēquiter adv worthlessly, wretchedly, miserably, vilely, wrongly

nēquiti·a -ae or **nēquiti·ēs -ēī** f worthlessness, vileness, wickedness

Nērē·is -idis f sea nymph, Nereid (daughter of Nereus, of whom there were 50)

Nēr·eus -ĕī or **-ĕos** m son of Oceanus and Tethys, husband of Doris and father of the Nereids; sea

Nērīn·ē -ēs f daughter of Nereus

Nēritī·us -a -um adj of Neritos; **Neritius dux** Ulysses

Nērit·os or **Nērit·us -ī** m island near Ithaca

Nēr·ō -ōnis m Nero Claudius Caesar (Roman emperor 38-68 A.D.; reigned 54-68 A.D.)

Nērōniān·us -a -um adj Nero's, Neronian

Nerv·a -ae m M. Cocceius Nerva (Roman emperor 30-98 A.D., reigned 96-98 A.D.)

nervōsē adv strongly, vigorously

nervōs·us -a -um adj sinewy, brawny, strong

nervŭl·us -ī m a little vigor

nerv·us -ī m sinew, tendon, muscle; string, wire; bowstring; thong, strap; penis; leather covering of a shield; prison; power, vigor, strength, nerve, force, energy

nesc·iō -īre -īvī or **-iī -ītum** vt not to know, be ignorant of, be unacquainted with; (with inf) a not to know how to; b to be unable to; **nescio modo** somehow or other; **nescio quando** sometime or other; **nescio quid** something or other; **nescio quis** someone or other

nesci·us -a -um adj unaware, not knowing, ignorant; unknown; (with genit or de + abl) ignorant of, unaware of; (with inf) not knowing how to, unable to, incapable of; (with acc & inf) unaware that, not knowing that

Ness·us -ī m centaur who was slain by Hercules with a poisoned arrow for trying to molest his wife

Nest·or -ōris m son of Neleus, king

of Pylos, and wise counselor of the Greeks at Troy

neu see **neve**

neut·er -ra -rum *adj* neither (*of two*); neuter; of neither sex; *pron* neither one (*of two*)

neutiquam or **ne utiquam** *adv* on no account, in no way

neutrō *adv* to neither side

neutrŭbi *adv* in neither the one place nor the other

nēve or **neu** *conj* or not, and not; **neve . . . neve** or **neu . . . neu** neither . . . nor

nex necis *f* death, murder, slaughter

nexĭl·is -e *adj* tied up, bound together

nex·um -ī *n* slavery for debt; voluntary servitude for debt

nex·us -a -um *pp* of **necto**; *m* free person who has pledged his person as security for a debt

nex·us -ūs *m* grip; bond; enslavement for debt

nī *adv* not; **quid nī?** why not?; *conj* (in prohibition or negative purpose) that not; (in negative condition) if not, unless

nīcētēr·ium -īī or **-ī** *n* prize

nic·ō -ĕre -ī *vi* to beckon

nict·ō -āre *vi* to wink; (with *dat*) to wink at

nīdāment·um -ī *n* material for a nest

nīd·or -ōris *m* steam, vapor, smell

nīdŭl·us -ī *m* little nest

nīd·us -ī *m* nest; (fig) home; *m pl* nestlings, brood

nig·er -ra -rum *adj* black; swarthy, dark; dismal; unlucky, ill-omened; black, bad (*character*); malicious

nigr·ans -antis *adj* black, dusky

nigr·escō -escĕre -ŭī *vi* to grow black, grow dark

nigr·ō -āre *vi* to be black

nigr·or -ōris *m* blackness, darkness

nihil or **nīl** (indecl) *n* nothing; (with *genit*) no, not a bit of; **nihil boni** no good, not a bit of good; **nil est** it is pointless, it's no good

nihil or **nīl** *adv* not, not at all, in no respect

nihilōminus *adv* nonetheless, nevertheless, just the same; no less

nihil·um or **nīl·um -ī** *n* nothing; **de nihilo** for nothing, for no reason; **nihil est quod, cur,** or **quam ob rem** there is no reason why; **nihili esse** to be worthless, be of no value; **nihili facere** or **nihili pandere** to consider as worthless; **nihil quicquam** nothing whatever, nothing at all; **pro nihilo putare** to regard as worthless

nīl see **nihil**

Nīliăc·us -a -um *adj* Nile, of the Nile, Egyptian

Nīligĕn·a -ae *masc & fem adj* born on the Nile, Egyptian

nīlum see **nihilum**

Nīl·us -ī *m* Nile River; god of the Nile

nimbāt·us -a -um *adj* light, frivolous

nimbif·er -ĕra -ĕrum *adj* stormy

nimbōs·us -a -um *adj* stormy, rainy

nimb·us -ī *m* cloud; storm cloud, black rain cloud; rainstorm, heavy shower, pouring rain; (fig) storm

nimiō *adv* far, much; **nimio plus** far more, much more

nimīrum *adv* no doubt, certainly, surely; (ironically) doubtless, of course

nimis *adv* very, very much, too much; **non nimis** not particularly

nimium *adv* too, too much; very, very much; **nimium quam** or **nimium quantum** very much indeed, ever so much, very; **nimium quam es barbarus** you are as barbarous as can be; **non nimium** not particularly, not very much

nimi·us -a -um *adj* very much, very great; too great, excessive; *n* excess, abundance

ningit (or **ninguit**) **ningĕre ninguit** (or **ninxit**) *v impers* it is snowing

ningu·ēs -ium *f pl* snowflakes, snow

Nin·us -ī *m* son of Belus, the first king of Assyria, husband of Semiramis, and builder of Nineveh; Nineveh

Nĭŏb·a -ae or **Nĭŏb·ē -ēs** *f* daughter of Tantalus and wife of Amphion, who was turned into a weeping mountain after Apollo and Diana had slain her seven sons and seven daughters

Nīr·eus -ĕī or **-ĕos** *m* handsomest Greek at Troy

Nīsē·is -ĭdis *f* Scylla (*daughter of Nisus*)

nisi *conj* unless, if not; except, but

nīsus *pp* of **nitor**

nis·us or **nix·us -ūs** *m* pressure, effort; labor pain (*of childbirth*); soaring, flight; posture; **nisu immotus eodem** immobile in the same posture

Nis·us -ī *m* king of Megara, father of Scylla, who betrayed her country by cutting off his purple lock of hair; friend of Euryalus in the Aeneid

nītēdŭl·a -ae *f* dormouse

nit·ens -entis *adj* shining, bright; brilliant; beautiful, glowing with beauty, glamorous; sleek (*cattle*); greasy

nit·ĕō -ēre -ŭī *vi* to shine, gleam, glisten; to be glamorous; to glow with health; (of animals) to be sleek; to be greasy; to be flashy

nit·escō -escĕre -ŭī *vi* to become shiny, become bright; to begin to glow (*with health or beauty*); to grow sleek

nitidē *adv* brightly

nitidiuscŭlē *adv* somewhat more sprucely

nitidiuscŭl·us -a -um *adj* a little more shiny

nitid·us -a -um adj shining, bright; glowing (with health or beauty); shiny, greasy; glamorous, flashy; smart, spruce, handsome; cultivated, refined; sleek (cattle)

nit·or -ōris m brightness, sheen; luster; glamour, beauty, healthy glow; elegance (of style); dignity (of character)

nītor nītī nixus sum (usually in the literal sense) or **nīsus sum** (usually in the figurative sense) vi to make an effort, struggle, strain, strive; to be in labor; to push forward, advance, climb, fly; to contend, insist; (with abl or in + acc) to lean on, support oneself on; (with abl or in + abl) (fig) to depend on, rely on, trust to; (with ad + acc) to aspire to; (with inf) to try to, endeavor to, struggle to

nitr·um -ī n soda; soap, cleanser

nivāl·is -e adj snowy; covered with snow; cold, wintry; (fig) cold, chilly

nivĕ·us -a -um adj of snow, snowy, snow; covered with snow; snow-white

nivōs·us -a -um adj snowy

nix nivis f snow; f pl (fig) grey hair

nix·or -ārī -ātus sum vi to struggle hard; (with abl) to lean upon, rest on

nixus pp of **nitor**

nix·us -ūs see **nisus**

nō nāre vi to swim, float; to sail; to fly; (of eyes) to be glazed

nōbil·is -e adj known; noted; notable, famous; notorious; noble; thorough-bred (horse); fine, excellent; m pl notables, nobles

nōbilit·ās -ātis f fame, renown; noble birth; the nobility; excellence

nōbilit·ō -āre vt to make famous; to make notorious

noc·ens -entis adj harmful; guilty criminal

noc·ĕō -ēre -ŭī -ĭtum vi (with dat) to harm, injure

nocīv·us -a -um adj harmful, injurious

noctif·er -ĕrī m evening star

noctilūc·a -ae f moon

noctivăg·us -a -um adj night-wandering

noctū adv by night, at night

noctŭ·a -ae f owl

noctuābund·us -a -um adj traveling by night

noctuīn·us -a -um adj of owls

nocturn·us -a -um adj nocturnal, of night, at night, by night, night

noctuvigil·us -a -um adj awake at night

nocŭ·us -a -um adj harmful, injurious

nōd·ō -āre vt to tie in a knot, knot, tie

nōdōs·us -a -um adj knotty

nōd·us -ī m knot; knob, knot (in wood); girdle; bond, tie; obligation; knotty point, difficulty; crisis

nōlō nolle nōlŭī vt (with inf) to be unwilling to, wish not to, refuse to; vi to be unwilling

nom·as -ădis m or f nomad; Numidian

nōm·en -inis n name; gentile name (e.g., Julius, as distinct from the praenomen); race, stock; title; noun; bond, claim, debt; debtor; name, fame, reputation; title, pretext, pretense, excuse, account, reason, responsibility, authority, sake, behalf; mere name (as opposed to reality); **aetatis nomine** on the pretext of age, on account of age; **eo nomine** on that account; **nomen dare** or **nomen profiteri** to enlist (in the army); **nomen deferre** (with genit) to bring an accusation against, accuse (someone); **nomen dissolvere** or **nomen expedire** or **nomen solvere** to liquidate an account, pay a debt; **nomina sua exigere** to collect one's debt

nōmenclāt·or -ōris m name caller (slave who accompanied his master and identified those whom they met, esp. during a political campaign)

nōminātim adv by name, expressly

nōminātĭ·ō -ōnis f nomination for office

nōminātīv·us -a -um adj & m nominative

nōmināt·us -a -um adj renowned

nōminĭt·ō -āre vt to usually call

nōmin·ō -āre vt to name, call by name; to mention by name; to make famous; to nominate for an office; to denounce, arraign

nomism·a -ătis n coin

nōn adv not; no; by no means

Nōn·ae -ārum f pl Nones (fifth day in all months, except March, May, July, and October, in which they occurred on the seventh)

nōnāgensĭm·us or **nōnāgēsĭm·us -a -um** adj ninetieth

nōnāgĭens or **nōnāgĭēs** adv ninety times

nōnāgintā (indecl) adj ninety

nōnān·us -a -um adj of the ninth legion; m soldier of the ninth legion

nōnārĭ·a -ae f prostitute

nondum adv not yet

nongent·ī -ae -a adj nine hundred

nonne adv is it not?; (in indirect questions) whether not; **nonne vides?** don't you see?, you see, don't you?; **quaeritur nonne ire statim velis** the question is whether you do not wish to go at once

nonnull·us -a -um adj some, many a; **nonnulli** some, some people

nonnunquam adv sometimes

nonnusquam adv in some places

nōn·us -a -um adj ninth; f ninth hour

nōn·us decĭm·us -a -um adj nineteenth

Nōric·us -a -um adj of Noricum; n region between the Danube and the Alps

norm·a -ae f square (carpenter's tool); (fig) rule, standard

nōs pron we; us

noscīt·ō -āre vt to examine closely, observe; to recognize, know

nōscō nōscĕre nōvī nōtum or **gnōscō — gnōvī gnōtum** vt to get to know, become acquainted with, recognize, learn; to examine, inquire into; to approve of; **no-vīsse** to have become acquainted with, (and therefore) to know

nōsmet pron (emphatic form of **nōs**) we ourselves; us

noster·ra -rum adj our, our own; pron ours; **noster** our friend; **nostrī** our men, our soldiers, our side

nostr·ās -ātis adj native, of our country

not·a -ae f note, mark, sign; letter, character; note, short letter; punctuation mark; brand (of wine); marginal note, critical mark; tattoo marks, brand; distinctive mark, distinctive quality; stamp (on coin); brand, stigma; nickname; black mark (against one's name); reproach, disgrace; nod, sign, beck; f pl letters of the alphabet; shorthand notes; memoranda

notābil·is -e adj notable, noteworthy, memorable; notorious

notābilĭter adv notably, remarkably; perceptibly

notār·ius -iī or **-ī** m stenographer; secretary

notātĭ·ō -ōnis f notation, mark; black mark (of a censor); choice; observation; etymology

notāt·us -a -um adj noted, distinguished

nōt·escō -escĕre -uī vi to become known

noth·us -a -um adj bastard, illegitimate; mongrel; not genuine, phoney

nōtĭ·ō -ōnis f acquaintance; (law) investigation; (fig) notion, idea

nōtĭtĭ·a -ae or **nōtĭtĭ·ēs -ēī** f acquaintance; fame; notion, conception

not·ō -āre vt to mark; to mark out; to note, mark, observe; to write down; to record; to take down in shorthand; to mark critically; to brand; to indicate, denote; to brand, reproach

not·us or **not·os -ī** m south wind; wind

nōt·us -a -um pp of **nosco**; adj known, well known; notorious; familiar, customary; m pl acquaintances

novācŭl·a -ae f razor

novāl·is -is f or **novāl·e -is** n field plowed for the first time, reclaimed land; cultivated field; fallow land; crops

novātr·ix -īcis f renovator, renewer (female)

novē adv newly, in an unusual manner

novell·us -a -um adj new, fresh, young, newly acquired

novem (indecl) adj nine

Novemb·er or **Novemb·ris -re** adj & m November

novendĕcim or **novemdĕcim** (indecl) adj nineteen

novendĭāl·is or **novemdĭāl·is -e** adj nine-day; occurring on the ninth day

novensil·ēs -ium m pl new gods (introduced from abroad)

novēn·ī -ae -a adj in groups of nine, nine each, nine

noverc·a -ae f stepmother

novercāl·is -e adj stepmother's, of a stepmother, like a stepmother

novīcĭ·us -a -um adj new, brand new

noviens or **noviēs** adv nine times

novissĭmē adv very recently, of late

novissĭm·us -a -um adj latest, last, most recent; **novissimum agmen** (mil) the rear; **novissima verba** parting words; m pl (mil) rear guard

novĭt·ās -ātis f newness, novelty; rareness, strangeness, unusualness; novelty of high rank, recently acquired rank

nov·ō -āre vt to make new, renovate, renew; to repair, fix; to refresh; to change, alter; to invent, coin (words); **res novare** to bring about a revolution

nov·us -a -um adj new, young, fresh, novel; strange, unusual, unheard-of; recent, modern; new, unused; inexperienced; renewed, revived; **homo novus** self-made man (first man of a family to reach a curule office); **res novae** political innovations, revolution; n news

nox noctis f night; night activity; sleep; death; darkness, blindness; mental darkness, ignorance; gloom; **ad multam noctem** till late at night; **nocte** or **de nocte** at night, by night; **noctem et dies** night and day; **sub noctem** at nightfall

nox·a -ae f harm, injury; offense, fault, guilt, responsibility; punishment

noxĭ·us -a -um adj harmful, noxious; guilty; (with genit or abl) guilty of; f harm, damage, injury; blame, guilt; fault, offense; **in noxia esse** to be at fault

nūbēcŭl·a -ae f little cloud; gloomy expression

nūb·ēs -is f or **nūb·is -is** m cloud; gloom; veil

nūbĭf·er -ĕra -ĕrum adj cloudy; cloud-capped (mountain); cloud-bringing (wind)

nūbĭgĕn·a -ae adj masc or fem born of clouds

nūbĭl·is -e adj marriageable

nūbĭl·us -a -um adj cloudy; cloud-bringing (wind); troubled; dark, gloomy, melancholy

nūbō nūbĕre nupsī nuptum vi (of women) to marry; (with dat) to marry (a man), be married to (a man)

nucifrangibŭl·um -ī n (colloquially of teeth) nutcracker

nuclĕ·us -ī m nut; kernel, stone (of fruit)

nudius adv it is now the . . . day since, e.g., **nudius tertius dedi ad te epistolam** it is now the third day since I mailed you a letter; ago, e.g., **nudius tertius decimus** twelve days ago

nūd·ō -āre vt to strip, bare; to lay bare, uncover; (mil) to leave undefended; (with abl) to divest of

nūd·us -a -um adj nude, naked; lightly clothed; bare, empty; defenseless; poor, needy; bare, mere, simple, sole, only; (with genit or abl or with **ab +** abl) bare of, without, stripped of, destitute of, deprived of

nūg·ae -ārum f pl trifles, nonsense; good-for-nothing, a nobody

nūgāt·or -ōris m joker; fibber, babbler, braggart

nūgātōri·us -a -um adj worthless, useless, nonsensical

nūg·ax -ācis adj nonsensical

nūgivend·us -ī m dealer in women's apparel

nūg·or -ārī -ātus sum vi to talk nonsense; (with dat) to trick, cheat

null·us -a -um adj no; (coll) not, not at all; non-existent, of no account; pron none

num adv (of time, used only with **etiam**) now, e.g., **etiam num** now, even now, still; interrog particle (expecting negative answer) surely not, really, actually, e.g., **num ista est nostra culpa?** is that really our fault?, that isn't our fault, is it?; conj (in indirect questions) whether

Num·a -ae m Numa Pompilius (second king of Rome)

numcŭbi adv ever?, at any time?

numell·a -ae f shackle

nūm·en -inis n nod; will, consent; divine will; divine power, divinity; deity, godhead

numerābil·is -e adj easily counted, few in number

numerāt·um -ī n ready cash

numĕrō adv at the right time, just now; too soon

numĕr·ō -āre vt to number, count; to pay out (money); to consider; to enumerate, mention; to relate, recount; to reckon as one's own, possess, own

numerōsē adv rhythmically

numerōs·us -a -um adj numerous; rhythmical

numĕr·us -ī m member; (mil) division, troop; mere cipher; class, category; rank, position; estimation, regard; rhythm, meter, verse; quantity, measure; portion (of work), part, function; **aliquo numero esse** to be of some account; **in numero haberi** (with genit) to be regarded as, be ranked among; **nul-**

lo numero esse to be of no account; m pl mathematics, astronomy

Numĭd·a -ae m Numidian

Numĭdi·a -ae f Numidia (a country of N. Africa)

Numĭdic·us -a -um adj Numidian

Numĭt·or -ōris m king of Alba, brother of Amulius, father of Ilia, and grandfather of Romulus and Remus

nummārĭ·us -a -um adj financial; mercenary

nummāt·us -a -um adj rich; **bene nummatus** well-off, well-to-do

nummulār·ĭus -ĭī or **-ī** m banker

nummŭl·ī -ōrum m pl petty cash

numm·us -ī m coin, cash, money; sesterce (small silver coin, worth about a nickel); small sum, trifle, mere nothing; **in nummis habere** to have in ready cash

numquam or **nunquam** adv never; **non numquam** sometimes

numquid adv (to introduce direct question): **numquid meministi?** do you remember?; (to introduce indirect question): whether

nunc adv now; nowadays, today; now, in view of this, but as matters now stand; **nunc . . . nunc** at one time . . . at another, once . . . once

nuncupātĭ·ō -ōnis f name, appellation; public pronouncing (of vows)

nuncŭp·ō -āre vt to name, call; to take or make (a vow) publicly; to proclaim publicly

nundĭn·ae -ārum f pl market day; marketplace, market town; trade, sale

nundĭnāl·is -e adj market

nundĭnātĭ·ō -ōnis f trading, bargaining, buying and selling

nundĭn·or -ārī -ātus sum vt to buy; vi to hold a market, attend a market; to trade; to gather in large numbers

nundĭn·um -ī n market time; **trinum nundinum** period of three market times, i.e., seventeen days

nunq- = numq-

nuntiātĭ·ō -ōnis f announcement (by an augur)

nuntĭ·ō -āre vt to announce, declare, report, relate

nuntĭ·us -a -um adj bringing news; m messenger, courier; news, message; order, injunction; **nuntium remittere** (with dat) to send a letter of divorce to, to divorce (a wife); n pl message, news

nūper adv recently

nūpĕr·us -a -um adj recent

nupt·a -ae f bride, wife

nuptĭ·ae -ārum f pl marriage, wedding

nuptĭāl·is -e adj nuptial, wedding

nur·us -ūs f daughter-in-law; young lady, young married woman

nusquam adv nowhere; on no occasion; for nothing, to nothing; **nus-**

quam alibi nowhere else; **nusquam esse** to not exist; **nusquam gentium** nowhere in the world

nūt·ō -āre *vi* to keep nodding; to sway to and fro, totter; to hesitate, waver

nūtrīcāt·us -ūs *m* nursing (*of babies*)

nūtrīc·ius -iī or **-ī** *m* tutor

nūtrīc·ō -āre or **nūtrīc·or -ārī -ātus sum** *vt* to nurse, suckle; to rear, bring up

nūtrīcŭl·a -ae *f* nurse

nūtrīm·en -inis *n* nourishment

nūtrīment·um -ī *n* nutriment, nourishment, support; fuel (*for fire*)

nūtr·iō -īre -īvī or **-iī -ītum** *vt* to nurse, suckle, nourish, feed; to rear, bring up, support, maintain, foster; to take care of, attend to; to cherish, cultivate

nūtr·ix -īcis *f* nurse; *f pl* breasts

nūt·us -ūs *m* nod; hint, intimation; will, pleasure, command; gravity

nux nucis *f* nut; nut tree, almond tree; **nuces relinquere** (fig) to put away childish things

Nyctē·is -idis *f* Antiope (*wife of Lycus, the king of Thebes, and mother of Amphion and Zethus*)

Nyct·eus -ěī or **-ěos** *m* father of Antiope

nymph·a -ae or **nymph·ē -ēs** *f* bride; nymph (*demi-goddesses who inhabit fountains, rivers, sea, woods, and mountains*); water

Nȳs·a -ae *f* mythical birthplace of Bacchus

Nȳsae·us or **Nȳsī·us -a -um** *adj* of Nysa, Nysaean

Nȳs·eus -ěī or **-ěos** *m* Bacchus

Nȳsigĕn·a -ae *m* native of Nysa

O

ō *interj* oh!

Oax·ēs or **Oax·is -is** *m* river in Crete

ob *prep* (with *acc*) before, in front of; on account of, because of; for the sake of, in the interest of; in return for, instead of; in proportion to, balanced against; **ob rem** to the purpose, usefully, profitably; **quam ob rem** wherefore, accordingly

obaerāt·us -a -um *adj* deeply in debt; *m* debtor

obambŭl·ō -āre *vt* to prowl all over, prowl about (*e.g., the city*); *vi* to walk about, wander, prowl about; (with *dat*) to prowl about near; (with **ante** + *acc*) to wander around in front of

obarm·ō -āre *vt* to arm

obăr·ō -āre *vt* to plow up, plow over

obbrūtēsc·ō -ĕre *vi* to grow dull

obc- = occ-

ob·dō -děre -dīdī -ditum *vt* to close, lock; to expose

obdorm·iō -īre -īvī or **-iī -ītum** *vi* to fall asleep

**obdorm·iscō -iscĕre -īvī — ** *vi* to fall asleep

ob·dūcō -dūcĕre -duxī -ductum *vt* to put on (*clothes*); to cover, veil, surround, envelop; to hide; to swallow; to pass (*time*); to bring forward as a candidate; to run or dig (*ditch*); (with *dat* of thing protected) to draw or place (*something*) over; (with *dat* or **ad** + *acc*) to pit (*someone or something*) against

obductī·ō -ōnis *f* veiling

obduct·ō -āre *vt* to introduce as a rival

obdūr·escō -escĕre -ŭī *vi* to grow hard, harden; to become insensitive

obdūr·ō -āre *vi* to persist, stick it out

ob·eō -īre -īvī or **-iī -ītum** *vt* to go to meet; to travel, travel to, travel over, wander through, traverse, encircle, visit; to run over, review, enumerate (*in a speech*); to undertake, engage in; **diem edicti obire** to meet one's death; *vi* to go; to pass away, die; to fade, disappear; (of heavenly bodies) to go down, set

obequit·ō -āre *vi* to ride up; (with *dat*) to ride up to

oberr·ō -āre *vi* to ramble about, wander around; (with *abl*) **a** to wander about, wander among; **b** to make a mistake on or at

obēs·us -a -um *adj* fat, plump; swollen; crude, coarse

ōb·ex -icis *m* or *f* bar, bolt; barrier; obstacle, hindrance

obf- = off-

obg- = ogg-

ob·haerescō -haerescĕre -haesī *vi* to get stuck

obīr·ascor -ascī -ātus sum *vi* (with *dat*) to get angry at

obīter *adv* on the way, as one goes along; (fig) in passing, incidentally

obītus *pp* of **obeo**

obīt·us -ūs *m* approach, visit; death, passing, ruin, downfall; setting (*of heavenly bodies*)

objac·ĕō -ēre -ŭī *vi* (with *dat*) to lie before, lie at

objectāti·ō -ōnis *f* reproach

object·ō -āre *vt* to oppose; to expose, endanger; to throw in the way; to cause (*delay*); (with *dat*) **a** to expose, abandon to; **b** to impute to, throw up (*faults*) to, bring a charge of (*e.g., madness*) against, fling (*charges, abuse*) at; (with *dat & acc & inf*) to throw a hint to (*someone*) that

object·us -a -um *adj* lying in the

way, lying in front; (with *dat*) a opposite; **b** exposed to; *n pl* charges, accusations

object·us -ūs *m* interposition; obstacle, hindrance; protection; (with *genit*) protection afforded by

ob·jiciō -jicĕre -jēcī -jectum *vt* to cast, hurl; to present, offer, expose; to hold up as an example; to set up as a defense, use as a defense; (with *dat*) a to cast before, throw to, offer to, expose to, set up as a defense against; **b** to throw up (*faults, weaknesses, etc.*) to; **c** to bring upon, inflict on, inspire in; **objici** (with *dat*) to happen to, befall, occur to; **se objicere** (with *dat*) to expose oneself to

objurgāti·ō -ōnis *f* scolding, rebuke

objurgāt·or -ōris *m* critic

objurgātōrǐ·us -a -um *adj* scolding, reproachful

objurgǐt·ō -āre *vt* to keep on scolding

objurg·ō -āre *vt* to scold, rebuke, blame, reprimand; to chastise, correct; to deter

oblangu·escō -escĕre -ŭī *vi* to taper off

oblātrātr·ix -īcis *f* nagging woman, nag

oblātus *pp of* **offero**

oblectām·en -inis *n* delight

oblectāment·um -ī *n* delight, amusement, pastime

oblectātǐ·ō -ōnis *f* delight, amusement; attraction; (with *genit*) diversion from

oblect·ō -āre *vt* to attract, delight, amuse, divert; to spend (*time*) pleasantly; **se oblectare** to amuse oneself, enjoy oneself

ob·līdō -līdĕre -līsī -līsum *vt* to crush; to squeeze together, strangle

obligāti·ō -ōnis *f* binding, pledging, obligation

obligāt·us -a -um *adj* obliged, under obligation; (with *dat*) (vow) made to

oblīg·ō -āre *vt* to tie up, bandage; to bind, oblige, put under obligation, make liable; to hamper, tie down; to embarrass; to mortgage; **fidem obligare** to pledge one's word; **obligari** (with *abl*) a to be guilty of; **b** to be obliged to, compelled to

oblīm·ō -āre *vt* to cover with mud; to dissipate, squander

ob·linō -linĕre -lēvī -litum *vt* to smear; (fig) to smear, defile; (fig) to overload

oblīquē *adv* sideways; (fig) indirectly

oblīqu·ō -āre *vt* to turn aside, twist, shift, slant

oblīqu·us -a -um *adj* slanting, crosswise; from the side; indirect; sly; envious; downhill (*road*); **oblīquus oculus** disapproving look, envious look; *n* side; **ab obliquo** from the side; **per obliquum** across

oblīsus *pp of* **oblīdo**

oblit·escō -escĕre -ŭī *vi* to hide

oblittĕr·ō -āre *vt* to erase; to cancel; (fig) to blot out; **nomina oblitterare** to cancel debts

oblītus *pp of* **oblino**

oblītus *pp of* **obliviscor**

oblivī·ō -ōnis *f* oblivion; forgetting; forgetfulness

obliviōs·us -a -um *adj* forgetful, oblivious; (wine) causing forgetfulness

ob·līviscor -līvisci -lītus sum *vt* to forget; *vi* to forget; (with *genit*) to forget, neglect, disregard, be indifferent to

oblīv·ium -iī or **-ī** *n* forgetfulness, oblivion

oblocūt·or -ōris *m* contradictor

oblong·us -a -um *adj* oblong

ob·lǒquor -lǒquī -locūtus sum *vt* (with *dat*) a to interrupt; **b** to answer (*in argument*), contradict; **c** to speak against, abuse, rail at; **d** to accompany (*in music*), sing to

obluct·or -ārī -ātus sum *vi* (with *dat*) to struggle with, fight against, struggle against

oblūd·ō -ĕre *vi* to play jokes on

obmōl·ior -īrī -ītus sum *vt* to make a barricade of

obmurmǔr·ō -āre *vi* (with *dat*) to roar in answer to

obmūt·escō -escĕre '-ŭī *vi* to become silent, hush up; to cease

obnāt·us -a -um *adj* growing on (*e.g., the bank of a river*)

ob·nītor -nītī -nixus sum *vi* to strain, struggle, put on the pressure; (with *dat*) a to press against, lean against; **b** to resist, oppose

obnixē *adv* with all one's might, obstinately

obnix·us -a -um *pp of* **obnitor;** *adj* steadfast, firm, resolute

obnoxiē *adv* guiltily; timidly

obnoxiōsǐus *adv* more slavishly

obnoxiōs·us -a -um *adj* submissive

obnoxǐ·us -a -um *adj* liable, addicted, guilty; submissive, servile, obedient; weak, timid; obliged, under obligation, indebted; answerable, responsible; liable, subject, exposed; **obnoxium est** (with *inf*) it is dangerous to

ob·nūbō -nūbĕre -nupsī -nuptum *vt* to veil, cover

obnuntiātǐ·ō -ōnis *f* announcement (of omens)

obnuntǐ·ō -āre *vi* to make an announcement; to make an announcement that the omens are adverse; to announce bad news

oboedǐ·ens -entis *adj* obedient; (with *dat* or **ad** + *acc*) obedient to

oboedienter *adv* obediently

oboedientǐ·a -ae *f* obedience

oboed·ǐō -īre -īvī or **-iī -ītum** *vi* (with *dat*) to give ear to, listen to, obey

obol·ĕō -ēre -ŭī *vt* to smell of; *vi* to smell

ob·orior -orīrī -ortus sum vi to rise, appear

obp- = opp-

ob·rēpō -rēpēre -repsī -reptum vt to creep up on, sneak up on; vi to creep up; (with dat) **a** to creep up on, sneak up on, take by surprise; **b** to trick, cheat; (with in + acc) to steal over; **obrepere ad honores** to worm one's way into high positions

obrept·ō -āre vi to sneak up

obrēt·iō -īre -īvī or **-iī -ītum** vt to entangle

obrig·escō -escēre -uī vi to stiffen; to freeze

obrōd·ō -ēre vt to gnaw at

obrōg·ō -āre vi (with dat) to supersede (a law)

ob·ruō -ruēre -ruī -rutum vt to cover up, cover, hide, bury; to overwhelm, overthrow; to sink, cover with water, swamp, overflow; to overpower, surpass, obscure, eclipse; vi to fall to ruin

obruss·a -ae f test, proof

obsaep·iō -īre -sī -tum vt to fence in; to block (road); (fig) to close, block

obsatūr·ō -āre vt to sate, cloy; **istius obsaturari** to have enough of him

obscaen- = obscen-

obscaev·ō -āre vi to give a bad omen

obscēnē adv obscenely

obscēnit·ās -ātis f obscenity

obscēn·us -a -um adj dirty, filthy; indecent, obscene; ominous

obscūrāti·ō -ōnis f obscuring, darkening; disappearance

obscūrē adv indistinctly; secretly, imperceptibly

obscūrit·ās -ātis f obscurity

obscūr·ō -āre vt to obscure, darken; to cover, hide; to veil (words); (of love) to blind; to hide, suppress

obscūr·us -a -um adj obscure, dark, shady; obscure, lowly, mean; dim, indistinct, unintelligible; secret; reserved; vague, uncertain; gloomy; n the dark, darkness; obscurity

obsecrāti·ō -ōnis f entreaty; public appeal to the gods

obsecr·ō -āre vt to entreat, appeal to, implore

obsecund·ō -āre vi (with dat) to comply with, humor

obsecūtus pp of **obsequor**

obsēp- = obsaep-

obsēqu·ens -entis adj compliant, obedient; indulgent, gracious (gods); (with dat) obedient to

obsequenter adv compliantly, obsequiously

obsequenti·a -ae f obsequiousness

obsequiōs·us -a -um adj obsequious

obsequ·ium -iī or **-ī** n compliance, indulgence; obedience, allegiance

ob·sĕquor -sĕquī -secūtus sum vi (with dat) to comply with, yield to, give into, gratify, humor

obser·ō -āre vt to bolt, bar, lock up

ob·sĕrō -serēre -sēvī -situm vt to sow or plant thickly; to fill, cover

observ·ans -antis adj attentive, respectful; (with genit) respectful of, attentive to, careful about

observanti·a -ae f regard, respect; (with genit or in + acc) regard for, respect for

observāti·ō -ōnis f observation; caution, care

observāt·or -ōris m observer

observit·ō -āre vt to watch carefully, note carefully

observ·ō -āre vt to watch, watch out for, take careful note of; to guard; to observe, keep, obey, comply with; to pay attention to, pay respect to

obs·es -idis m or f hostage; guarantee

obsessi·ō -ōnis f blockade

obsess·or -ōris m frequenter, regular visitor; blockader

ob·sidĕō -sidēre -sēdī -sessum vt to sit near or at, remain by or near; to frequent; (mil) to besiege, invest, blockade; to block, choke; to occupy, fill; to look out for, watch closely; to keep guard over

obsidiāl·is -e adj for breaking a blockade; **corona obsidialis** decoration for breaking a blockade

obsidi·ō -ōnis f blockade, siege; imminent danger

obsid·ium -iī or **-ī** n blockade, siege; imminent danger, great peril; status of hostage

ob·sidō -sidĕre -sēdī -sessum vt to besiege, invest, beset, blockade; to take possession of, occupy

obsignāt·or -ōris m sealer; witness; **obsignator testamenti** witness to a will

obsign·ō -āre vt to seal, seal up; to sign and seal; (fig) to stamp, impress

ob·sistō -sistĕre -stĭtī -stĭtum vi (with dat) to stand in the way of, block, resist, oppose, disapprove of, forbid

obsitus pp of **obsero** (to sow)

obsole·fīō -fĭerī -factus sum vi to wear out, become spoiled; to become worthless

obsol·escō -escĕre -ēvī -ētum vi to wear out, go out of style, become obsolete, get shabby, lose value

obsolētius adv rather shabbily

obsolēt·us -a -um adj out of date, old, obsolete, worn out; shabby, threadbare; low, mean, poor

obsōnāt·or -ōris m shopper

obsōnāt·us -ūs m shopping

obsōn·ium -iī or **-ī** n shopping items, food

obsōn·ō -āre or **obsōn·or -ārī -ātus sum** vt to shop for; **famem obsonare** to work up an appetite; vi to go shopping; to provide food; (with de + abl) to provide a feast for

obsŏn·ō -āre vi (with dat) to drown out

obsorb·ĕō -ēre -uī vt to gulp down

obstant·ia -ium n pl obstacles, obstructions

obstĕtr·īx -īcis f midwife

obstinātē adv resolutely, with determination; obstinately, stubbornly

obstināti·ō -ōnis f resolution, determination; obstinacy, stubbornness

obstināt·us -a -um adj resolute, determined, fixed; obstinate, stubborn

obstin·ō -āre vt to be resolved on, resolve, determine; (with inf) to resolve to, determine to; vi to be determined, be resolved; (with **ad +** acc) to be set on

obstipescō see **obstupesco**

obstip·us -a -um adj bent, bent to one side; bent forwards, bowed; **capite obstipo stare** to stand with head bowed

ob·stō -stāre -stĕtī vi to stand in the way, be in the way, raise opposition; (with dat) to stand in the way of, oppose, object to, resist, hinder, obstruct; (with **ne**, **quin**, **quominus**, or **cur non**) to prevent (someone) from

obstrĕp·ō -ĕre -ŭī -ĭtum vt to fill with noise, drown out; vi to make a racket, make noise; a (with dat) to shout at, drown out with shouts, interrupt with shouts; b (of the sea) to resound against

ob·stringō -stringĕre -strinxī -strictum vt to shut in, confine, tie up; (fig) to tie up, involve, put under obligation, oblige; **fidem obstringere** (with dat) to pledge one's word to; **obstringi** or **se obstringere** (with abl) to get involved in, be guilty of

obstructi·ō -ōnis f obstruction

obstructus pp of **obstruo**

obs·trūdō or **ob·trūdō -trūdĕre -trūsī -trūsum** vt to gulp down; (with dat) to force (something) upon, thrust (something) upon

ob·strūō -struĕre -struxī -structum vt to pile up, block up, stop up; (with dat) to block or close (e.g., the road) against

obstrūsus pp of **obstrudo**

obstupe·faciō -facĕre -fēcī -factum vt to astound, astonish, paralyze, stupefy

obstup·escō or **obstip·escō -escĕre -ŭī** vi to be astounded, be struck dumb, be paralyzed

obstupĭd·us -a -um adj stupefied

ob·sum -esse -fŭī vi (with dat) to be opposed to, be against; to be prejudicial to, harm; **nihil obest dicere** there is no harm in saying

ob·suō -suĕre -sŭī -sūtum vt to sew on; to sew up

obsurd·escō -escĕre -ŭī vi to become deaf; (fig) to turn a deaf ear

ob·tĕgō -tegĕre -texī -tectum vt to cover up; to protect; (fig) to conceal, keep secret; **animus sui obtegens** secretive mind

obtemperāti·ō -ōnis f compliance, obedience

obtempĕr·ō -āre vi (with dat) to comply with, submit to, obey

ob·tendō -tendĕre -tendī -tentum vt to spread, stretch out; to offer as an excuse; to envelop, conceal; **obtendī** (with dat) to lie opposite; **obtentā nocte** under cover of darkness

obtentus pp of **obtineo**

obtent·us -ūs m screen, cover; pretext, pretense

ob·tĕrō -terĕre -trīvī -trītum vt to trample on, trample down, crush; (fig) to trample on, crush, degrade, destroy

obtestāti·ō -ōnis f adjuring, adjuration; solemn entreaty, supplication

obtest·or -ārī -ātum sum vt to call as witness; to make an appeal to, implore, entreat

obtex·ō -ĕre -ŭī vt to cover, veil

obtic·ĕō -ēre vi to be silent

obtic·escō -escĕre -ŭī vi to fall silent, be dumbstruck

ob·tinĕō -tinēre -tinŭī -tentum vt to get hold of; to hold on to, keep, maintain, preserve, uphold; to assert, maintain; to obtain, gain, acquire; vi to continue

ob·tingō -tingĕre -tigī vi to happen, occur; (with dat) to happen to, befall, occur to

obtorp·escō -escĕre -ŭī vi to become numb, become stiff, become insensible

ob·torquĕō -torquēre -torsī -tortum vt to twist

obtrectāti·ō -ōnis f detraction, disparagement

obtrectāt·or -ōris m detractor, disparager

obtrect·ō -āre vt to treat spitefully, mistreat, disparage; to carp at; vi (with dat) to detract from, disparage, belittle

obtrītus pp of **obtero**

obtrūdō see **obstrudo**

obtrunc·ō -āre vt to cut off, cut down; (in battle) to cut down, kill

ob·tuĕor -tuērī -tuītus sum vt to gaze at, gaze upon; to see clearly

ob·tundō -tundĕre -tŭdī -tūsum or **-tunsum** vt to beat, beat on, thump on; to blunt; (fig) to pound away at, stun, deafen, annoy, molest, importune

obturb·ō -āre vt to throw into disorder; (fig) to disturb, confuse, distract

obturgesc·ō -ĕre vi to begin to swell up

obtūr·ō -āre vt to block up, stop up, plug up; **aures obturare** to refuse to listen

obtūsus or **obtunsus** pp of **obtundō**; adj blunt, dull; (fig) dulled, blurred

obtūt·us -ūs m stare, gaze

obumbr·ō -āre vt to overshadow, shade; to darken, obscure; to cover, screen

obunc·us -a -um adj hooked

obust·us -a -um *adj* singed; hardened in the fire; nipped (*by cold*)

obvāg·ĭō -īre *vi* to whimper

obvall·ō -āre *vt* to fortify

ob·venĭō -venīre -vēnī -ventum *vi* to come up, happen, occur; (with *dat*) to fall to the lot of, be alloted to

obvers·or -ārī -ātus sum *vi* to make an appearance, show oneself; (fig) hover

obvers·us -a -um *adj* (with **ad** + *acc*) a turned toward, facing; **b** inclined to; (with *dat*) engaged in; *m pl* opponents

ob·vertō or **ob·vortō -vertěre -vertī -versum** *vt* (with *dat* or **ad** + *acc*) to turn (*something*) towards or in the direction of; (with **in** + *acc*) to turn (*e.g., the soldiers*) to face (*e.g., the enemy*); **obvertī** (with **ad** + *acc*) to turn toward

obviam or **ob viam** *adv* (with *dat*) a to meet, in order to meet, in the way of; **b** (fig) opposed to; **effundi obviam** (with *dat*) to pour out to meet, go out in great numbers to meet; **obviam esse** (with *dat*) a to meet; **b** to oppose, resist; **obviam ire** (with *dat*) or **obviam procedere** (with *dat*) to go to meet; **obviam obsistere** (with *dat*) to stand in the way of (*someone*); **obviam prodire** or **obviam proficisci** or **obviam progredi** (with *dat*) to go out to meet; **obviam venire** (with *dat*) to go to meet, come to meet

obvigilāt·um -ī *n* vigilance

obvi·us -a -um *adj* in the way; exposed, open; accessible (*person*); ready, at hand; (with *dat*) a to meet, so as to meet; **b** opposed to; **c** exposed or open to; **obvius esse** (with *dat*) to meet, encounter; **obvius venire** (with *dat*) to come to meet

ob·volvō -volvěre -volvī -volūtum *vt* to wrap up, cover up

occaec·ō -āre *vt* to blind, make blind; to darken, obscure; to hide; to numb

occall·escō -escěre -ŭī *vi* to become thick-skinned; (fig) to become callous

occăn·ō -ěre -ŭī *vi* to sound the charge

occāsĭ·ō -ōnis *f* occasion, opportunity, good time, chance; pretext; (mil) surprise, raid; **occasionem amittere** to lose the opportunity; **occasionem arripere** to seize the opportunity; **per occasionem** at the right time

occāsiuncŭl·a -ae *f* nice little opportunity

occās·us -ūs *m* setting; sunset; west; (fig) downfall, ruin, death

occātĭ·ō -ōnis *f* harrowing

occāt·or -ōris *m* harrower

oc·cēdō -cēděre -cessī -cessum *vi* to go up; **obviam occedere** (with *dat*) to go to meet

occent·ō -āre *vt* to serenade; to satirize in verse

occept·ō -āre *vt* to begin

occid·ens -entis *m* the setting sun; west

occīdĭ·ō -ōnis *f* massacre, annihilation; **occidione occidere** to massacre, annihilate, wipe out

oc·cīdō -cīděre -cīdī -cīsum *vt* to knock down; to cut down, slay, kill; to murder; to ruin; to pester to death; **se occidere** to commit suicide

oc·cĭdō -cĭděre -cĭdī -cāsum *vi* to fall, fall down; (of the sun) to go down, set; to fall, be slain, perish; (of hope, etc.) to fade, die; (fig) to be ruined, be lost; **occidī!** I'm finished!

occidŭ·us -a -um *adj* setting; western; (fig) sinking, fading, dying

occill·ō -āre *vt* to smash

oc·cĭnō -cĭněre -cecĭnī or **-cĭnŭī** *vi* to sound ominous

oc·cipĭō -cipěre -cēpī -ceptum *vt & vi* to begin

occipit·ĭum -ĭī or **-ī** or **occĭp·ut -ĭtis** *n* back of the head

occīsĭ·ō -ōnis *f* massacre; **occisionem facere** to cause a massacre

occīs·or -ōris *m* killer, murderer

occīsus *pp* of **occīdo**

occlāmĭt·ō -āre *vt* to shout at; *vi* to cry out, bawl

oc·clūdō -clūděre -clūsī -clūsum *vt* to close up, shut up, lock up; to check, control

occ·ō -āre *vt* to harrow

occŭb·ō -āre *vi* to lie; to rest

occulc·ō -āre *vt* to trample down

occŭl·ō -ěre -ŭī -tum *vt* to cover; to cover up, hide

occultātĭ·ō -ōnis *f* concealment, hiding

occultāt·or -ōris *m* hideout

occultē *adv* secretly, in concealment

occult·ō -āre *vt* to hide

occult·us -a -um *adj* hidden, secret; reserved (*person*); *n* concealment; secret; **ex occulto** from a place of concealment; secretly

oc·cumbō -cumběre -cubŭī -cubĭtum *vt* to fall to, meet; **mortem occumbere** to meet death; *vi* to sink down in death, fall dying; **certae morti occumbere** to meet certain death; **morti occumbere** to fall prey to death; **occumbere** (with **per** + *acc*) to die at the hands of

occupātĭ·ō -ōnis *f* occupation (*e.g., of a town*); occupation, employment, business; business engagement, task; job; involvement, concern

occupāt·us -a -um *adj* occupied, busied, engaged, involved

occŭp·ō -āre *vt* to occupy, seize; to win, gain; to attack, strike down; to outstrip, overtake; to fill, take up; to invest, loan, lend; (with *inf*) to be the first to

oc·currō -currěre -currī or **-cu-**

currī -cursum *vi* to run up: (with *dat*) **a** to run up to, run to meet, meet; **b** to rush against, attack; **c** to resist, oppose, counteract; **d** to meet, answer, reply to, object to; **e** to relieve, remedy; **f** to occur to, suggest itself to, present itself to; **g** (fig) to run into, run up against, get involved in

occursātĭ·ō -ōnis *f* hustle and bustle; excited welcome; officiousness

occurs·ō -āre *vt* to run to meet; *vi* (with *dat*) **a** to run to meet, go or come to meet, meet; **b** to go to meet (*the enemy*), attack, charge, oppose; **c** (of thoughts) to occur to

occurs·us -ūs *m* meeting; (with *genit*) running into (*someone or something*)

ōceanīt·is -ĭdis *f* ocean nymph

ōcean·us -ī *m* ocean; Oceanus (*son of Caelus and Terra, husband of Tethys, and father of rivers and of ocean nymphs*)

ocell·us -ī *m* eye; gem; darling

ōcĭm·um -ī *n* basil

ōcĭ·or -us *adj* swifter, quicker

ōcĭus *adv* more swiftly, more quickly; sooner; more easily; immediately, on the spot; (with *abl*) rather than; **ocius serius** sooner or later; **quam ocissime** as quickly as possible

ocrĕ·a -ae *f* greave, shin guard

ocreāt·us -a -um *adj* wearing shin guards

Octāvĭ·a -ae *f* sister of Augustus, wife of C. Marcellus, and later of M. Antony (64-11 B.C.); daughter of Claudius and wife of Nero (*murdered in 62 A.D.*)

Octāv·ĭus -ĭī or **-ī** *m* C. Octavius (*Emperor Augustus, who, upon adoption by Julius Caesar, became C. Julius Caesar Octavianus, 63 B.C.-14 A.D.*)

octāvum *adv* for the eighth time

octāv·us -a -um *adj* eighth; **octava pars** one eighth; *f* eighth hour of the day (*i.e.*, 2 p.m.); *n* **cum octavo efficere** to produce eightfold

octāv·us decĭm·us -a -um *adj* eighteenth

octĭens or **octĭēs** *adv* eight times

octingentēsĭm·us or **octingentensĭm·us -a -um** *adj* eight hundredth

octingent·ī -ae -a *adj* eight hundred

octĭp·ēs -ĕdis *adj* eight-footed

octō (*indecl*) *adj* eight

Octōb·er -ris *adj & m* October

octōdĕcim (*indecl*) *adj* eighteen

octōgēnārĭ·us -a -um *adj & m* octogenarian

octōgēn·ī -ae -a *adj* eighty each

octōgēsĭm·us or **octōgensĭm·us -a -um** *adj* eightieth

octōgĭēs or **octōgĭens** *adv* eighty times

octōgintā (*indecl*) *adj* eighty

octōjŭg·is -e *adj* eight-team

octōn·ī -ae -a *adj* eight at a time, eight each

octōphŏr·os -on *adj* carried by eight carriers; *n* eight-man litter

octuplicāt·us -a -um *adj* eightfold

octŭpl·us -a -um *adj* eightfold; *n* eightfold fine

octuss·is *m* sum of eight aces

ocŭlāt·us -a -um *adj* having eyes; exposed to view, conspicuous; **oculatus testis** eyewitness

ocŭlĕ·us -a -um *adj* many-eyed

oculissĭm·us -a -um *adj* dearest

ocŭlĭtus *adv* like one's own eyes, dearly

ocŭl·us -ī *m* eye; eye, bud (*in plants*); sight, vision; mind's eye; apple of the eye; **aequis oculis** contentedly; **altero oculo captus** blind in one eye; **ante oculos** in full view; (fig) obvious; **ante oculos ponere** to imagine; **ex oculis abire** to go out of sight, disappear; **in oculis** in view, in public, in the limelight; **in oculis ferre** or **gestare** to hold dear, value; **oculos adjicere** (with **ad** + *acc*) to eye; to covet; **oculos dejicere** (with **ab** + *abl*) to take one's eyes off; (fig) to lose sight of; **oculos pascere** (with *abl*) to feast one's eyes on; **sub oculis** (with *genit*) in the presence of, under the very nose of

ōd·ī -isse *vt* to have taken a dislike to, dislike, hate, be disgusted at

ōdĭōsē *adv* hatefully; unpleasantly

ōdĭōsĭc·us -a -um *adj* odious, unpleasant, annoying

ōdĭōs·us -a -um *adj* odious, unpleasant, annoying

ōd·ĭum -ĭī or **-ī** *n* dislike, hatred, aversion; object of hatred, nuisance; dissatisfaction, disgust; offensive conduct, insolence; **odio esse** (with *dat*) to be hateful to, be disliked by, be hated by; *n pl* feelings of hatred

od·or or **od·ōs -ōris** *m* odor, smell, scent; stench, stink; pleasant smell, fragrance, perfume; inkling, suggestion, hint; *m pl* perfume

odōrātĭ·ō -ōnis *f* smell, smelling

odōrāt·us -a -um *adj* fragrant, scented

odōrāt·us -ūs *m* smell, smelling; sense of smell

odōrĭf·er -ĕra -ĕrum *adj* fragrant

odōr·ō -āre *vt* to make fragrant

odōr·or -ārī -ātus sum *vt* to sniff at, scent; to aspire to, aim at; to be sniffing after, search for, investigate; to get a smattering of

odōr·us -a -um *adj* smelly, fragrant; keen-scented

odōs see **odor**

Odrysĭ·us -a -um *adj & m* Thracian

Odyssē·a or **Odyssī·a -ae** *f* the Odyssey

Oeăg·er -rī *m* king of Thrace and father of Orpheus

Oeagrĭ·us -a -um *adj* Thracian

Oebalĭd·ēs -ae *m* male descendant of Oebalus; *m pl* Castor and Pollux

Oebalⁱ·us -a -um *adj* Spartan; Tarentine; Sabine; *f* Tarentum (*Spartan colony in S. Italy*)

Oebăl·us -ī *m* king of Sparta, father of Tyndareus, and grandfather of Helen and Clytemnestra

Oedĭp·us -ŏdis *or* -ī *m* Oedipus

Oen·eus -ĕī *or* -ĕos *m* king of Calydon, husband of Althaea, and father of Meleager and Deianira

Oenĭd·ēs -ae *m* descendant of Oeneus; Meleager; Diomedes (*son of Tydeus*)

Oenomă·us -ī *m* king of Pisa in the Peloponnesus and father of Hippodamia

oenophŏr·um -ī *n* wine-bottle basket

Oenopⁱ·a -ae *f* ancient name of Aegina (*island between Attica and Argolis*)

oenopōl·ium -iī *or* -ī *n* wine shop, tavern

Oenōtrⁱ·us -a -um *adj* Oenotrian, Italian; *f* ancient name of S.E. Italy; Italy

oestr·us -ī *m* horsefly, gadfly; fancy, inspiration

oesȳp·um -ī *n* lanolin

Oet·a -ae *or* Oet·ē -ēs *f* Mt. Oete (*mountain in S. Thessaly, on which Hercules died*)

Oetae·us -a -um *adj* Oetean; *m* Hercules

ofell·a -ae *f* bit, morsel

off·a -ae *f* pellet, lump, dumpling; swelling; shapeless mass

offātim *adv* in bits, in little lumps

offectus *pp* of officio

of·fendō -fendĕre -fendī -fensum *vt* to bump, bump against, stub, strike, hit; to hit upon, come upon, meet with, bump into, stumble upon, find; to offend, shock, vex, disgust; to hurt (*feelings*); to injure (*reputation*); nihil offendere to suffer no damage, receive no injury; *vi* to make a blunder, make a mistake, blunder; to give offense, be offensive; to fail, take a loss, be defeated, come to grief; to run aground; (with *dat* or in + *abl*) to hit against, bump against; (with *dat*) to give offense to; (with in + *acc*) to take offense at; terrae offendere to run aground

offens·a -ae *f* offense, affront, injury; displeasure, resentment, hatred; crime; offensā (with *genit*) out of hatred for

offensⁱ·ō -ōnis *f* stubbing; tripping, stumbling; dislike, displeasure, hatred, disgust, aversion; discredit, bad reputation, mishap, failure, disaster, accident, defeat; *f pl* offensive acts; feelings of displeasure

offensiuncŭl·a -ae *f* slight displeasure; minor setback; disappointment

offens·ō -āre *vt & vi* to bump

offens·us -a -um *pp* of offendo; *adj* offensive, odious; offended, displeased, annoyed

offens·us -ūs *m* bump; shock; offense

offĕrō offerre obtŭlī oblātum *vt* to offer, bring forward, present, show; to cause, occasion; to confer, bestow, inflict; se offerre (with *dat*) a to meet, encounter; b to expose oneself to

offerūment·a -ae *f* (*said humorously of a blow or welt*) present

officīn·a *or* opificīn·a -ae *f* shop, workshop, factory, office

of·ficiō -ficĕre -fēcī -fectum *vi* (with *dat*) to get in the way of, interfere with, oppose, obstruct, be detrimental to, hinder

officiōsē *adv* obligingly, courteously

officiōs·us -a -um *adj* ready to serve, obliging; dutiful, obligatory

officⁱ·um -iī *or* -ī *n* service, favor, kindness, courtesy; obligation, duty, function, office, part; social obligation, social call, social visit; ceremony, ceremonial observance, attendance; official duty; employment, business, job; sense of duty, conscience; allegiance

of·fīgō -fīgĕre -fīxī -fīxum *vt* to fasten down, nail down, drive in

offirmāt·us -a -um *adj* determined, resolute

offirm·ō -āre *vt* se offirmare to steel oneself, be determined; *vi* to be determined

offlect·ō -ĕre *vt* to turn (*something*) around

offrēnāt·us -a -um *adj* curbed

offūcⁱ·a -ae *f* cosmetic; (fig) trick

of·fulgĕō -fulgēre -fulsī -fulsum *vi* (with *dat*) to shine on

of·fundō -fundĕre -fūdī -fūsum *vt* to pour out; to cover, fill; to eclipse; offundī (with *dat*) to pour out over, spread over

oggan·iō -īre -īvī *or* -iī -ītum *vt & vi* to growl

og·gerō -gerĕre *vt* to bring, offer, give

Ōgȳg·ēs -is *or* Ōgȳg·us -ī *m* mythical king of Thebes, in whose reign the Deluge occurred

Ōgȳgⁱ·us -a -um *adj* Theban

oh *interj* oh!

ōhē *or* ōhē *interj* whoa!

oi *interj* (*express complaint*) oh no!

Oīl·eus -ĕī *or* -ĕos *m* king of Locris and father of Ajax the archer

olĕ·a -ae *f* olive; olive tree

oleāgĭn·us -a -um *adj* olive, of an olive tree

oleārⁱ·us -a -um *adj* oil, of oil; *m* oil merchant

oleast·er -rī *m* oleaster, wild olive tree

ōlenⁱ·us -a -um *adj* of Olenus (*town in Achaia and Aetolia*); Achaian, Aetolian

ol·ens -entis *adj* smelling; fragrant; smelly, stinking; musty

ol·ĕō -ēre -uī *vt* to smell of, smell like; (fig) to betray; *vi* to smell; (with *abl*) to smell of

olĕ·um -ī *n* olive oil, oil; (fig) palaestra; oleum addere camino (fig) to pour oil on the fire; oleum et operam perdere to waste time and effort

ol·faciō -facère -fēcī -factum vt to smell

olfact·ō -āre vt to sniff at

olid·us -a -um adj smelly

ōlim adv once, once upon a time; at the time; for a good while; someday, in the future, hereafter; now and then, at times; ever, at any time

olit- = holit-

olīv·a -ae f olive; olive tree; olive wreath; olive branch; olive staff

olivēt·um -ī n olive grove

olivif·er -èra -èrum adj olive-producing, olive-growing

olīv·um -ī n oil; ointment; (fig) palaestra

oll·a -ae f pot, jar

olle or ollus = ille

ol·or -ōris m swan

olōrīn·us -a -um adj swan, of a swan

olus see holus

Olympi·a -ae f Olympia (region in Elis, in the Peloponnesus, where the Olympian games were held)

Olympi·a -ōrum n pl Olympian games

Olympiăc·us -a -um adj Olympian

Olympi·as -ădis f Olympiad (period of four years between Olympian games, starting in the year 776 B.C., according to which the Greeks reckoned time); wife of Philip V of Macedon and mother of Alexander the Great

Olympic·us or Olympi·us -a -um adj Olympian

Olympionic·ēs -ae m Olympic victor

Olymp·us -ī m Mt. Olympus (mountain on the boundary of Macedonia and Thessaly, regarded as the home of the gods or heaven)

omās·um -ī n tripe; (fig) paunch, belly

ōm·en -inis n omen, sign, token, foreboding; solemn assurance

ōment·um -ī n fat; bowels

ōmināt·or -ōris m diviner

ōmin·or -ārī -ātus sum vt to forebode, predict, prophesy

ōminōs·us -a -um adj ominous

omiss·us -a -um adj remiss, negligent

omitto omittère omīsī omissum vt to let go, let fall, let go of; to give up, abandon; to omit, pass over, say nothing of; to overlook, disregard

omnif·er -èra -èrum adj all-sustaining

omnigĕn·us -a -um adj of every kind

omnimŏdīs or omnimŏdo adv by all means, wholly

omnīnō adv altogether, entirely, wholly; (with numerals) in all; (in generalizations) in general; (in concessions) no doubt, to be sure; yes, by all means, certainly; haud om-

nino or non omnino not quite, not entirely; absolutely not, not at all; not expressly; omnino nemo no one at all

omnipăr·ens -entis adj all-producing (earth)

omnipŏt·ens -entis adj almighty

omn·is -e adj all, every; every kind of, every sort of; the whole; m pl all, all men, everybody; n the universe; n pl all things, everything, all nature, all the world

omnitŭ·ens -entis adj all-seeing

omnivăg·us -a -um adj roving everywhere

omnivŏl·us -a -um adj all-craving

Omphăl·ō -ēs f Lydian queen whom Hercules had to serve

onăg·er or onagr·us -ī m wild ass

onăg·os -ī m ass driver

Onchesmit·ēs -ae m wind blowing from Onchesmus (harbor in Epirus)

onerāri·us -a -um adj carrying freight; jumenta oneraria beasts of burden; oneraria or navis oneraria freighter, transport

onĕr·ō -āre vt to load, load down, burden; (fig) to overload, oppress; (fig) to pile on, aggravate

onerōs·us -a -um adj onerous, burdensome, oppressive, heavy

on·us -ĕris n load, burden; freight, cargo; burden, difficulty; trouble; tax expense; foetus, embryo; oneri esse (with dat) to be a burden to

onust·us -a -um adj loaded, burdened; filled, full

on·yx -ȳchis m or f onyx; onyx box

opăcĭt·ās -ātis f shade, darkness

opăc·ō -āre vt to shade

opăc·us -a -um adj shady; dark, obscure; n pl per opaca locorum through shady places

opell·a -ae f light work

opĕr·a -ae f effort, pains, exertion, work, labor; care, attention; service, assistance; leisure, spare time; laborer, workman, artisan; operae esse or operae pretium esse to be worthwhile; operam dare to take pains, exert oneself, be busied, pay attention, give attention; operam funeri dare to attend a funeral; operam sermoni dare to listen to a conversation; operam tonsori dare to see a barber, get a haircut; operā meā (tuā, etc.) through my (your, etc.) agency, thanks to me (you, etc.)

operāri·us -a -um adj working; m working man, workman, laborer; f working woman

opercŭl·um -ī n lid, cover

operiment·um -ī n lid, cover

oper·iō -īre -ŭī -tum vt to cover, cover up; to shut, close; to hide; to overwhelm

opĕr·or -ārī -ātus sum vi to work, work hard, take pains; (with dat) a to work hard at, be busied with, be engaged in; b to perform (religious services); c to attend; d to worship

operōsē *adv* with great effort, at great pains

operōs·us -a -um *adj* active, busy, painstaking; troublesome, difficult, elaborate; efficacious, powerful (*drugs*)

opert·us -a -um *pp* of **operio**; *adj* closed; hidden; secret; *n* secret; secret place; **in operto** inside, in secret; *n pl* depths; veiled oracles

opēs see **ops**

ophit·ēs -ae *m* serpentine (*type of marble*)

Ophiūsi·us -a -um *adj* Cyprian; *f* old name of Cyprus

ophthalmi·ās -ae *m* a fish

opic·us -a -um *adj* boorish

opif·er -ěra -ěrum *adj* helpful

opif·ex -ĭcis *m* maker, framer, creator; craftsman, mechanic

opificīn·a -ae *f* workshop

ōpili·ō -ōnis *m* shepherd

opīmē *adv* richly, splendidly

opīmit·ās -ātis *f* abundance

opīm·us -a -um *adj* fat, plump; fertile, fruitful; rich, enriched; abundant, copious, plentiful; sumptuous, splendid; lucrative; noble; **spolia opima** armor stripped from one general by another on the field of battle

opīnābil·is -e *adj* conjectural, imaginary

opīnātĭ·ō -ōnis *f* mere opinion, conjecture, supposition, hunch

opīnāt·or -ōris *m* guesser

opīnāt·us -a -um *adj* supposed, imagined

opīnāt·us -ūs *m* supposition

opīnĭ·ō -ōnis *f* opinion, conjecture, supposition, guess, belief, expectation; general impression, estimation; rumor; reputation, bad reputation; **amplius opinione** beyond expectation, beyond all hopes; **celerius opinione** sooner than expected; **hac opinione ut** under the impression that; **in opinione esse** (with *acc & inf*) to be of the opinion that; **praebere opinionem timoris** to convey the impression of fear; **praeter opinionem** contrary to expectation, sooner than expected; **ut opinio mea est** as I suppose

opīniōs·us -a -um *adj* opinionated

opīn·ō -āre or **opīn·or -ārī -ātus sum** *vt* to suppose, imagine, conjecture; *vi* (parenthetical) to suppose, imagine

opipārē *adv* splendidly, sumptuously

opipăr·us -a -um *adj* splendid, sumptuous, ritzy

opisthogrăph·us -a -um *adj* written on the back

opitŭl·or -ārī -ātus sum *vi* (with *dat*) to bring help to, assist

oport·et -ēre -ŭit *v impers* it is right, it is proper; **me ire oportet** I ought to go, should go

op·pangō -pangěre -pēgī -pactum *vt* to affix, imprint

oppect·ō -ěre *vt* to comb off; (coll) to pluck, pick, eat

oppēd·ō -ěre *vi* (with *dat*) **a** to break wind at; **b** (fig) to deride, mock

opper·ior -īrī -tus sum *vt* to wait for, await; (with **num**) to wait and see whether; *vi* to wait

oppět·ō -ěre -īvī or **-ĭī -ītum** *vt* to go to meet; **mortem oppetere** to go to meet death, perish, die; *vi* to perish, die

oppidān·us -a -um *adj* of a town, in a town; (disparagingly) provincial; *m pl* townsfolk, townspeople

oppĭdō *adv* absolutely, quite, completely; (as affirmative answer) exactly

oppidŭl·um -ī *n* small town

oppĭd·um -ī *n* town

oppignĕr·ō -āre *vt* to pledge

oppĭl·ō -āre *vt* to stop up, shut off

op·plĕō -plēre -plēvī -plētum *vt* to fill up, choke up

op·pōnō -pōněre -posŭī -posĭtum *vt* to put, place, station; to oppose; to expose, lay bare, open; to wager, mortgage; to bring forward, present, adduce, allege; to reply, respond, object; to compare

opportūnē *adv* opportunely, at the right time

opportūnit·ās -ātis *f* suitableness, fitness, convenience; opportunity, right time; advantage

opportūn·us -a -um *adj* suitable, fit, convenient; advantageous, useful; exposed; **tempore opportunissimo** in the nick of time; *n pl* exposed parts

oppositĭ·ō -ōnis *f* opposition

opposĭt·us -a -um *pp* of **oppono**; *adj* opposite; (with *dat*) opposite, across from

opposĭt·us -ūs *m* opposing, opposition

oppressĭ·ō -ōnis *f* force, violence; violent seizure; suppression, overthrow

oppressiuncŭl·a -ae *f* slight pressure

oppressus *pp* of **opprimo**

oppress·us -ūs *m* pressure

op·primō -priměre -pressī -pressum *vt* to press down, weigh down; to pressure, put pressure on; to close, shut; to overwhelm; to put down, suppress, quell; to sink (*a ship*); to subvert, overthrow, crush, subdue, overpower; to conceal, suppress; to seize, catch, surprise

opprobrāment·um -ī *n* disgrace, scandal

opprobr·ĭum -ĭī or **-ī** *n* disgrace, scandal, reproach; cause of disgrace; taunt, abuse, abusive word

opprŏbr·ō -āre *vt* to taunt

oppugnātĭ·ō -ōnis *f* assault; (fig) attack, assault, accusation

oppugnāt·or -ōris *m* assailant, attacker

oppugn·ō -āre *vt* to assault, assail, attack, storm; (fig) to attack, assail

ops opis *f* power, might; help, aid; influence, weight; **opem ferre** (with *dat*) to bring help to, help; *f pl* wealth, resources, means; military or political resources

Ops Opis *f* goddess of abundance, sister and wife of Saturn, and identified with Earth

ops- = **obs-**

optābil·is -e *adj* desirable

optātī·ō -ōnis *f* wishing, wish

optātō *adv* according to one's wish

optāt·us -a -um *adj* longed-for, desired, welcome; *n* wish, desire

optigō see **obtego**

optim·ās -ātis *m* aristocrat; *m pl* aristocracy, aristocratic party

optimē or **optumē** (*superl* of **bene**) *adv* very well, thoroughly, best; most opportunely, just in time

optim·us or **optum·us -a -um** (*superl* of **bonus**) *adj* very good, best; excellent

optī·ō -ōnis *m* helper, assistant; (mil) adjutant

optiv·us -a -um *adj* chosen

opt·ō -āre *vt* to choose, select; to wish for, desire

optum- = **optim-**

opulēns -entis *adj* opulent, rich

opulentē or **opulenter** *adv* richly, splendidly

opulenti·a -ae *f* opulence, wealth; resources; power

opulentit·ās -ātis *f* opulence; power

opulent·ō -āre *vt* to make rich, enrich

opulent·us -a -um *adj* opulent, rich, wealthy; powerful; sumptuous

op·us -ōris *n* work; product of work, structure, building; literary work, composition, book; work of art, workmanship; deed, achievement; (mil) offensive works, siege works; (mil) defensive works, fortifications; **magno opere** greatly; **quanto opere** how much, how greatly; **tanto opere** so much, so greatly; **opus est** (with *inf*) it is useful or beneficial to; **opus est** (with *dat* of person in need and *abl* of person or thing needed) to need, e.g., **vo-bis duce opus est** you need a leader

opuscŭl·um -ī *n* little work, minor work

ōr·a -ae *f* boundary, border, edge; coastline, coast; region, district; cable, hawser; (fig) people of the coast, people of the region; **ora maritima** seacoast

ōracŭl·um or **ōracl·um -ī** *n* oracle; prophesy

ōrāri·us -a -um *adj* coasting; **navis oraria** coaster, coasting vessel

ōrāt·a -ōrum *n pl* prayers, requests

ōrātī·ō -ōnis *f* faculty of speech; speech, language; style of speech, manner of speaking, style, expression; oration, speech; theme, subject; prose; eloquence; imperial rescript; **orationem habere** to give a speech

ōrātiuncŭl·a -ae *f* short speech, insignificant speech

ōrāt·or -ōris *m* orator, speaker; spokesman; suppliant

ōrātōriē *adv* oratorically

ōrātōri·us -a -um *adj* orator's, oratorical

ōrātr·ix -īcis *f* suppliant (*female*)

ōrāt·us -ūs *m* request

orb·a -ae *f* orphan; widow

orbāt·or -ōris *m* murderer (*of someone's children or parents*)

Orbil·ĭus -ī or **-ĭ** *m* Horace's teacher in Venusia

orb·is -is *m* circle; disk, ring, orbit; quoit; hoop; wheel; round shield; eye socket, eye; globe, earth, world, universe; region, territory, country; circuit, round; rotation; cycle, period; (rhet) balance; zodiac; **orbis lacteus** Milky Way; **orbis terrae** or **terrarum** earth, world, universe

orbit·a -ae *f* rut, wheel track; (fig) rut, routine

orbit·ās -ātis *f* childlessness, widowhood, orphanhood

orbitōs·us -a -um *adj* full of ruts

orb·ō -āre *vt* to bereave of parents, father, mother, children, husband, or wife; to strip, rob, deprive, make destitute

orb·us -a -um *adj* bereaved, bereft; destitute; orphaned, fatherless; childless; widowed; (with *genit* or *abl* or with **ab + abl**) bereft of, deprived of, without; *m* orphan; *f* see **orba**

orc·a -ae *f* vat, barrel

Orcăd·es -um *f pl* islands N. of Scotland (*modern Orkneys*)

orch·as -ădis *f* olive

orchestr·a -ae *f* senatorial seats (*in the theater*); (fig) senate

Orc·us -ī *m* lower world; Pluto (*king of the lower world*); death

orde- = **horde-**

ordināri·us -a -um *adj* ordinary, usual, regular

ordinātim *adv* in order, in good order, in succession; regularly, properly

ordinātī·ō -ōnis *f* orderly arrangement; orderly government

ordināt·us -a -um *adj* regular; appointed

ordin·ō -āre *vt* to set in order, arrange, regulate; to govern, rule; to record chronologically

ordior ordīrī orsus sum *vt* to begin, undertake; to describe; *vi* to begin, begin to speak

ord·ō -inis *m* line, row, series; row of seats (*in a theater*); order, methodical arrangement; (pol) rank, order, class; (mil) line, file (*of soldiers*), company, century, command of a company or century; *m pl* officers of a company; promotions; **amplissimus ordo** senatorial order; **ex ordine** in succession, without a break; **extra ordinem** extraordinarily, especially, uncommonly; **ordine, in ordine,** or **per ordinem** in order, in sequence, in detail, with regularity, regularly

Orē·as -ǎdis f Oread, mountain nymph

Orest·ēs -is or **-ae** m son of Agamemnon and Clytemnestra who avenged his father's death by killing his mother

orex·is -is f longing, appetite

organic·us -ī m organist

orgăn·um -ī n instrument, implement; musical instrument, organ

orgi·a -ōrum n pl Bacchic revels; orgies

orichalc·um -ī n copper ore; brass

ōricill·a -ae f lobe

ori·ens -entis m rising sun, morning sun; morning; day; land of the rising sun, Orient, the East

orig·ō -inis f origin, source, beginning, start; birth, lineage, descent; race, stock, family; founder, progenitor

Ōri·ōn or **Orī·ōn -ōnis** or **-ōnis** m mythical hunter, turned into a constellation

orior orīrī ortus sum vi to rise, get up; to become visible, appear; to be born, originate, be descended; to proceed, begin, start

ōrithyi·a -ae f daughter of Erechtheus and mother of Calais and Zetes by Boreas

oriund·us -a -um adj descended, sprung, born

ornāment·um -ī n equipment, trappings, apparatus; ornament, adornment, decoration; trinket, jewel; (fig) distinction; rhetorical ornament; pride and joy

ornātē adv ornately, elegantly

ornātr·ix -īcis f hairdresser (female)

ornātŭl·us -a -um adj fancy

ornāt·us -a -um adj equipped, fitted out, furnished, dressed, harnessed; adorned, decorated, embellished; handsome; illustrious, excellent

ornāt·us -ūs m equipment; attire, apparel, outfit; furniture; decoration, ornament; world, universe

orn·ō -āre vt to equip, fit out, furnish, dress; to set off, decorate, adorn; to honor, praise, commend

orn·us -ī f mountain ash

ōr·ō -āre vt to beg, entreat, implore, plead with; to ask for; to plead (a case); (with double acc) to ask (someone) for; vi to plead, beg, pray; (with **cum** + abl) to plead or argue with

Oront·ēs -is or **-ae** m chief river of Syria; companion of Aeneas

Orontē·us -a -um adj Syrian

Orph·eus -ĕī or **-ĕos** m son of Oeagrus and Calliope, husband of Eurydice, and famous musician and poet

Orphē·us or **Orphic·us -a -um** adj Orphic

ors·us -a -um pp of **ordior**; n pl beginnings; utterance, words; attempt

ors·us -ūs m beginning; attempt, undertaking

ortus pp of **orior**

ort·us -ūs m rising; the East; birth, origin; source

Ortygi·a -ae or **Ortygi·ē -ēs** f Delos; island in the port of Syracuse

or·yx -ȳgis m gazelle

oryz·a -ae f rice

os ossis n bone; marrow, innermost parts; n pl skeleton

ōs ōris n mouth; beak; voice, speech, expression; lip, face, countenance, look; sight, presence (of a person); impudence; mask, mouth, opening, orifice, front; **habere aliquid in ore** to be talking about something continually; **in ore omnium esse** to be on the lips of everyone, be talked about

osc·en -inis m bird of augury (e.g., crow, raven, owl)

oscill·um -ī n small mask

oscit·ans -antis adj yawning; (fig) indifferent, bored

oscit·ō -āre or **oscit·or -ārī -ātus sum** vi to gape; to yawn

osculāti·ō -ōnis f kissing

oscŭl·or -ārī -ātus sum vt to kiss; (fig) to make a fuss over

oscŭl·um -ī n little mouth; kiss; **breve osculum** peck

Osc·us -a -um adj Oscan; m pl Oscans (ancient people of Campania and Samnium)

Osīr·is -is or **-idis** m Egyptian god, the husband of Isis

ōs·or -ōris m hater

Oss·a -ae f mountain in N.E. Thessaly

ossĕ·us -a -um adj bony

ossifrăg·a -ae f osprey

ostendō ostendĕre ostendī ostentum vt to stretch out, stretch forth; to expose; to show, exhibit, display, present; to reveal, disclose; to declare, make known

ostentāti·ō -ōnis f display; ostentation, showing off; mere show, pretense

ostentāt·or -ōris m show-off

ostent·ō -āre vt to show, exhibit; to show off, display, parade, boast of; to declare, point out, set forth

ostent·um -ī n portent, prodigy

ostent·us -ūs m display, show; **ostentui** for appearances, in pretense

Osti·a -ae f or **Osti·a -ōrum** n pl Ostia (port and town at the mouth of the Tiber)

ostiār·ium -iī or **-ī** n tax on doors

ostiātim adv from door to door

ost·ium -iī or **-ī** n door; entrance, mouth

ostrĕ·a -ae f or **ostrĕ·um -ī** n oyster

ostreāt·us -a -um adj covered with oyster shells; (fig) black and blue ostreōs·us -a -um adj abounding in oysters

ostrif·er -ĕra -ĕrum adj oyster-growing

ostrīn·us -a -um adj purple

ostr·um -ī n purple; purple dress, purple covering

ōsus pp of odi

Oth·ō -ōnis m L. Roscius Otho (author of the law in 67 B.C. reserving fourteen rows in the theaters for the equestrian order); M. Salvius Otho (Roman emperor in 69 A.D.)

Othr·ys -ўos m mountain in S. Thessaly

ōtĭŏl·um -ī n bit of leisure

ōtĭ·or -ārī -ātus sum vi to take it easy

ōtĭōsē adv at leisure; leisurely; without haste; calmly, fearlessly

ōtĭōs·us -a -um adj at leisure, relaxing; free from official obligations; quiet, calm; unconcerned, in-different, neutral; passionless; m private person (not holding public office); m pl civilians, non-combatants

ōt·ĭum -ĭī or -ī n leisure, free time, relaxation; freedom from public affairs, retirement; peace, quiet; ease, idleness, inactivity

Ovid·ĭus -ĭī or -ī m P. Ovidius Naso or Ovid (Latin poet, born at Sulmo, 43 B.C.-17 A.D.)

ovīl·e -is n sheepfold; voting enclosures in the Campus Martius

ovīl·is -e adj sheep, of sheep

ovīl·us -a -um adj sheep, of sheep

ov·is -is f sheep; wool; simpleton

ov·ō -āre vi to rejoice; to hold a celebration; to celebrate a minor triumph

ōv·um -ī n egg; n pl wooden balls used to mark the laps at the race-track

P

pābulātĭ·ō -ōnis f foraging

pābulāt·or -ōris m forager

pābul·or -ārī -ātus sum vi to forage; (coll) to make a living

pābul·um -ī n food, fodder; pasturage, grass; (fig) nourishment

pācāl·is -e adj of peace

pācāt·us -a -um adj peaceful, quiet, calm; n friendly country

Pachўn·um -ī n S.E. point of Sicily

pācif·er -ĕra -ĕrum adj peace-bringing, peaceful

pācĭficātĭ·ō -ōnis f pacification

pācĭficāt·or -ōris m peacemaker

pācĭficātōri·us -a -um adj peace-making

pācĭfic·ō -āre vt to pacify, appease; vi to make peace, conclude peace

pācĭfic·us -a -um adj peace-making; peaceable

paciscor pasciscī pactus sum vt to bargain for, agree upon; to stipulate; to barter; to betroth; vi to come to an agreement, agree, make a bargain, make a contract; (with inf) to agree to, pledge oneself to

pac·ō -āre vt to pacify, soothe, subdue

pact·a -ae f fiancee; bride

pactĭ·ō -ōnis f pact, contract, agreement, treaty; condition, stipulation; collusion

Pactŏl·us -ī m river in Lydia famous for its gold

pact·or -ōris m contractor, negotiator, party (in a contract)

pact·us -a -um pp of paciscor and of pango; n pact, contract, agreement; way, manner; aliquo pacto somehow; hoc pacto in this way; in pacto manere to stick to the agreement; quo pacto how, in what way

Pācuv·ĭus -ĭī or -ī m Roman tragic poet, native of Brundisium, and nephew of Ennius (c. 220-130 B.C.)

Pad·us -ī m Po River (in N. Italy)

pae·ān -ānis m epithet of Apollo as the god of healing; paean, hymn of praise, victory song

paedagōg·ĭum -ĭī or -ī n training school for pages

paedagōg·us -ī m slave in charge of school children; (fig) guide, leader

paedĭc·ō -āre vt to have abnormal relations with (young boys)

paed·or -ōris m filth

pael·ex -ĭcis f concubine, mistress

paelicāt·us -ūs m concubinage

Paelign·ī -ōrum m pl a people of central Italy

paenē adv almost, nearly

paeninsŭl·a -ae f peninsula

paenĭtend·us -a -um adj regrettable

paenĭtentĭ·a -ae f repentance, regret

paenit·ĕō -ēre -ŭī vt to cause to regret; to displease; vi (with genit) to regret; v impers (with acc of person), e.g., me paenitet I am sorry; (with acc of person and genit of thing), e.g., me paenitet consilī I regret the plan, I am dissatisfied with the plan; (with acc of person and inf or quod), e.g., eos paenitet animum tuum offendisse or eos paenitet quod animum tuum offenderint they regret having offended your feelings

paenŭl·a -ae f traveling coat; raincoat

paenŭlāt·us -a -um adj wearing a traveling coat

pae·ōn -ōnis m metrical foot containing one long and three short syllables

paeŏni·us -a -um *adj* healing, medicinal

Paest·um -ī *n* town in Lucania in S. Italy

paetŭl·us -a -um *adj* slightly squint-eyed

paet·us -a -um *adj* squinting, squint-eyed; leering

pāgān·us -a -um *adj* of a village, rustic; ignorant, untaught; *m* villager, peasant; (as term of contempt) yokel

Pagăs·a -ae *f* or **Pagăs·ae -ārum** *f pl* town on the coast of Thessaly, from which the Argonauts sailed

Pagasae·us -a -um *adj* Pagasaean; *m* Jason

pāgātim *adv* by villages, in every village

pāgell·a -ae *f* small page

pāgin·a -ae *f* page (*of book*)

pāginŭl·a -ae *f* small page

pāg·us -ī *m* village; canton, province; country people, villagers

pāl·a -ae *f* spade

palaestr·a -ae *f* palaestra, wrestling school, gymnasium; school of rhetoric; rhetorical training; school; wrestling; exercise; brothel

palaestricē *adv* as at the palaestra

palaestric·us -a -um *adj* of the palaestra, gymnastic; *f* gymnastics

palaestrīt·a -ae *m* professional wrestler; director of a palaestra

palam *adv* openly, publicly, plainly; **palam esse** to be public, be well known; **palam facere** to make public, disclose; *prep* (with *abl*) before, in the presence of, face to face with

Palātīn·us -a -um *adj* Palatine; imperial

Palāt·ium -iī or **-ī** *n* Palatine Hill (*residential area of distinguished Romans and several Roman emperors*); palace

palāt·um -ī *n* or **palāt·us -ī** *m* palate; taste; literary taste

palĕ·a -ae *f* chaff

paleār·ia -ium *n pl* dewlap

Pal·ēs -is *f* Italic goddess of shepherds and flocks

Palīc·ī -ōrum *m pl* twin sons of Jupiter and the nymph Thalia

Palīl·is -e *adj* of Pales; *n pl* festival of Pales celebrated on April 21st

palimpsest·us -ī *m* palimpsest

Palinūr·us -ī *m* pilot of Aeneas who fell overboard and drowned; promontory named after him

palіūr·us -ī *m* Christ's thorn (*plant*)

pall·a -ae *f* ladies' long robe; outer garment, mantle; tragic actor's costume

Palladĭ·us -a -um *adj* of Pallas; *n* statue of Pallas, Palladium

Pall·as -ădis or **-ădos** *f* Athene; olive oil, oil; olive tree; Palladium (*Trojan statue of Pallas*)

pall·ens -entis *adj* pale, sallow;

grey-green, yellow-green, chartreuse, yellowish, sickly-looking

pall·ĕō -ēre -ŭī *vi* to be pale, look pale; to be yellow, look yellow; to change color, fade; (with *dat*) to grow pale over, worry about

pall·escō -escĕre -ŭī *vt* to turn pale at; *vi* to turn pale; to turn yellow; to fade

palliāt·us -a -um *adj* wearing a Greek cloak; **fabula palliata** Latin play with Greek setting and characters

pallidŭl·us -a -um *adj* somewhat pale

pallĭd·us -a -um *adj* pale, sallow; grey-green, yellow-green, chartreuse

palliolātim *adv* in a mantle

palliolāt·us -a -um *adj* wearing a short mantle, wearing a hood

palliŏl·um -ī *n* short cloak; cape, hood

pall·ium -iī or **-ī** *n* coverlet, cover; Greek cloak

pall·or -ōris *m* paleness, pallor; **pallorem dūcere** to turn pale

pallŭl·a -ae *f* short cloak

palm·a -ae *f* palm of the hand, hand; palm tree, date; palm branch, palm wreath; palm of victory, prize, victory, honor, distinction; blade of an oar

palmār·is -e *adj* excellent, deserving the palm or prize

palmārī·us -a -um *adj* prize-winning, excellent; *n* masterpiece

palmāt·us -a -um *adj* embroidered with palm branches; **tunica palmata** palm-embroidered tunic (*worn by a general*)

palm·es -ĭtis *m* vine sprout, vine branch; branch, bough

palmēt·um -ī *n* palm grove

palmif·er -ĕra -ĕrum *adj* palm-growing, full of palm trees

palmōs·us -a -um *adj* full of palm trees

palmŭl·a -ae *f* oar blade

pāl·or -ārī -ātus sum *vi* to roam about, wander aimlessly

palpāti·ō -ōnis *f* stroking; *f pl* flattering

palpāt·or -ōris *m* flatterer

palpĕbr·a -ae *f* eyelid

palpit·ō -āre *vi* to throb, palpitate, quiver

palp·ō -āre or **palp·or -ārī -ātus sum** *vt* to stroke, pat; to wheedle, coax; to flatter; *vi* (with *dat*) **a** to coax; **b** to flatter

palp·us -ī *m* palm of the hand; coaxing

palūdāment·um -ī *n* military coat; general's coat

palūdāt·us -a -um *adj* wearing a general's coat

palūdōs·us -a -um *adj* swampy, marshy

palumb·ēs -is *m* or *f* pigeon, dove

pāl·us -ī *m* stake, post; wooden post used in sword practice pal·us ·ūdis f swamp, marsh; sedge

palust·er ·ris ·re adj swampy, marshy, in the swamps

pampine·us ·a ·um adj of vine tendrils, made of vine leaves; **odor pampineus** bouquet of wines

pampīn·us ·ī m vine shoot, tendril; vine leaf; tendril (of any plant)

Pān Pānos m Pan (Greek god of flocks, shepherds, and woods, often identified with Faunus)

panacē·a ·ae f or panăc·es ·is n panacea

Panaetōlic·us ·a ·um adj Pan-Aetolian

pānār·ium ·iī or ·ī n bread basket

Panchāĭ·a ·ae f region in Arabia famous for its frankincense

panchrest·us or panchrist·us ·a ·um adj good for everything, universally useful

pancratice adv (coll) fine, splendidly; **pancratice valere** to get along splendidly

pancrat·ium or pancrat·ĭon ·iī or ·ī n contest which included both boxing and wrestling

Pandăr·us ·ī m famous Lycian archer in the Trojan army; companion of Aeneas, killed by Turnus

pandicŭl·or ·ārī ·ātus sum vi to stretch oneself

Pandī·ōn ·ōnis m king of Athens and father of Procne and Philomela

Pandīoni·us ·a ·um adj of Pandion

pandō pandĕre pandī pansum or **passum** vt to spread out, extend, expand, unfold; to open, lay open, throw open; to reveal, make known, publish

pand·us ·a ·um adj crooked, bent, curved

pangō pangĕre panxī or pepēgī ·pactum vt to fasten, fix, drive in; to fix, settle, agree upon, determine; to write, compose, celebrate, record; to promise in marriage; **indutias pangere** (with cum + abl) to conclude an armistice with

pānĭce·us ·a ·um adj made of bread; **milites panicei** (coll) Breadville brigade

pānicŭl·a ·ae f tuft

pānĭc·um ·ī n millet

pān·is ·is m bread, loaf; **panis cibarius** coarse bread; **panis secundus** stale bread

Pānisc·us ·ī m little Pan

pannicŭl·us ·ī m rag

Pannoni·us ·a ·um adj Pannonian; f Pannonia (country on the Danube)

pannōs·us ·a ·um adj tattered, ragged; shriveled, wrinkled, sad-looking

pannŭcē·us or pannŭci·us ·a ·um adj ragged; shriveled, wrinkled

pann·us ·ī m patch; rag

Panŏp·ē ·ēs or Panopē·a ·ae f a sea nymph

pans·a ·ae masc & fem adj flat-footed, splayfooted

pansus pp of pando

panthēr·a ·ae f panther

Panthoïd·ēs ·ae m Euphorbus (Trojan warrior)

Panth·us ·ī m priest of Apollo at Troy and father of Euphorbus

pantĭc·ēs ·um m pl bowels; sausages

papae interj great!, wonderful!

pāp·as ·ae or ·ătis m tutor

papăv·er ·ĕris n poppy

papāverĕ·us ·a ·um adj of poppies

Paphĭ·ē ·ēs f Venus

Paphĭ·us ·a ·um adj Paphian, of Paphos

Paph·os ·ī f town in Cyprus sacred to Venus

pāpĭli·ō ·ōnis m butterfly

papill·a ·ae f nipple, teat; breast

papp·ō ·āre vi to eat baby food, eat pap

papp·us ·ī m hairy seed (of certain plants)

papŭl·a ·ae f pimple

papȳrif·er ·ĕra ·ĕrum adj papyrus-producing

papȳr·us ·ī m & f or papȳr·um ·ī n papyrus; paper; garment (made of papyrus)

pār paris adj equal, like, on a par, equally matched, well matched; suitable, adequate; of equal size; (with dat or cum + abl) equal to, comparable to, similar to, as large as; (with limiting abl, ad + acc, or in + abl) equal, similar, alike in; **par est** it is right, it is proper; **par proelium** indecisive battle; **ut par est** (used parenthetically) as is only right; m companion, comrade; equal; mate, spouse; **pares cum paribus facillime congregantur** birds of a feather flock together; n pair, couple; the like; **par pari** like for like, tit for tat

parābĭl·is ·e adj available

parasīt·a ·ae f parasite (female)

parasītast·er ·rī m poor parasite

parasītāti·ō ·ōnis f sponging

parasītĭc·us ·a ·um adj parasitical

parasīt·or ·ārī ·ātus sum vi to sponge, freeload, be a parasite

parasīt·us ·ī m parasite, sponger, freeloader

parātē adv with preparation; carefully; readily, promptly

parātĭ·ō ·ōnis f preparing, procuring, acquisition

paratragoed·ō ·āre vi to talk in a tragic style, be melodramatic

parāt·us ·a ·um adj prepared, ready; well prepared, furnished, equipped; learned, well versed, skilled; (with dat or ad + acc) a ready for; b equipped to; (with inf) prepared to, ready to; (with abl or in + abl) versed in, experienced in

parāt·us ·ūs m preparation, provision, equipment, outfit; clothing, apparel

Parc·a ·ae f goddess of Fate, Fate

parcē adv sparingly, thriftily; moderately, with restraint; stingily; rarely, seldom

parceprōm·us -ī *m* stingy person

parcō parcēre pepercī parsum *vt* to spare, use sparingly; *vi* to be sparing, economize; (with *dat*) **a** to spare, use carefully; **b** to show mercy to; **c** to abstain from, refrain from; **d** to refuse (*help*); (with *inf*) to cease, stop (*e.g., doing, talking*)

parc·us -a -um *adj* thrifty, economical, frugal; niggardly, stingy; moderate, conservative; slight, little, scanty, paltry (*thing given*)

pard·us -ī *m* panther

par·ens -entis *adj* obedient; *m* parent, father; ancestor, grandparent; founder, inventor; *m pl* subjects; ancestors; *f* parent, mother

parentāl·is -e *adj* parental; **dies parentalis** memorial day; *n pl* festival in honor of dead ancestors and relatives

parent·ō -āre *vi* to hold memorial service in honor of dead parents or relatives; (with *dat*) **a** to offer sacrifice to (*the dead*); **b** to avenge (*a dead person*) with the death of another person; **c** to appease, satisfy

pār·eō -ēre -uī *vi* to appear, be visible, be evident, be at hand; (with *dat*) **a** to obey, be obedient to, comply with, be subject to, be subservient to; **b** to yield to, gratify, satisfy (*pleasures, etc.*); **c** to fulfill (*promises*)

pari·ēs -ētis *m* wall (*esp. partition in a house or building*)

parietin·ae -ārum *f pl* tumbled-down walls; ruins; (fig) ruins

Parīl·ia -ium *n pl* festival of Pales (*celebrated on April 21st*)

parīl·is -e *adj* equal, like; **aetas parilis** same age, like age

pariō parĕre pepĕrī partum *vt* to bear, bring forth, give birth to; (of animals) to lay, spawn, produce; (fig) to produce, create, devise, cause, effect, accomplish, acquire, obtain

Par·is -ĭdis *m* son of Priam and Hecuba, also called Alexandros; famous pantomime actor in the reign of Nero; famous pantomime actor in the reign of Domitian, the freedman of Domitia

pariter *adv* equally, in like manner, as well, alike; at the same time, simultaneously, together, at once; **pariter ac** (or **atque**), **pariter ut** as well as; **pariter ac si** just as if; **pariter** (with *cum* + *abl*) together with, at the same time as

parit·ō -āre *vt* (with *inf*) to get ready to

Parī·us -a -um *adj & mf* Parian

parm·a -ae *f* small round shield; shield

parmāt·us -a -um *adj* armed with a shield, light-armed

parmŭl·a -ae *f* small shield

Parnās·is -ĭdis or **Parnāsi·us -a -um** *adj* of Parnassus, Parnassian

Parnās·us or **Parnās·os -ī** *m* mountain in Phocis, in central Greece, sacred to Apollo and the Muses, on whose slopes Delphi was located

par·ō -āre *vt* to prepare, make ready, provide, furnish; to get, procure, acquire, gather, purchase; **se parare** to prepare oneself, get ready; *vi* to get ready, make preparations, make arrangements; (with *dat* or *ad* + *acc*) to get ready for

parŏch·a -ae *f* room and board (*required of provincials for traveling Roman officials*)

parŏch·us -ī *m* official host (*local official who provided accommodations for traveling Roman dignitaries*); host

parops·is -ĭdis *f* dish, dessert dish

Par·os or **Par·us -ī** *f* island of the Cyclades, famous for its white marble

parr·a -ae *f* owl

Parrhās·is -ĭdis *f* Arcadian woman; Callisto

Parrhasi·us -a -um *adj* Arcadian; **Parrhasia virgo** Callisto; *f* district in Arcadia

parricīd·a -ae *m* or *f* parricide (*murder of a parent or close relative*); assassin of a high magistrate; murderer, assassin; traitor, outlaw, criminal

parricīd·ium -iī or **-ī** *n* parricide (*murderer of a parent or close relative*); murder, assassination; treason, high treason

par·s -tis *f* part, portion, share, section, fraction; side, direction, region; part, function, duty; part of body, member (*esp. genital organs*); *f pl* part, role, character; political party; **ab omni parte** in all respects; **ex altera parte** on the other hand; **ex magna parte** to a great extent; **ex parte** partly; **in eam partem** in that direction; in that sense; in such a manner; **in perjorem partem rapere** to put a worse construction on; **in utramque partem** in both directions; **major pars populi** the majority; **maximam partem** for the most part; **minor pars populi** the minority; **omnibus partibus** in all respects; **pars ... pars, pars ... alii** some . . . others; **parte** in part, partly; **pro mea parte** to the best of my abilities; **tres partes** three fourths

parsimōni·a -ae *f* parsimony

parsus *pp* of **parco**

parthenic·ē -ēs *f* parthenium (*plant*)

Parthenopae·us -ī *m* son of Meleager and Atalanta and one of the Seven who fought against Thebes

Parthenŏp·ē -ēs *f* one of the Sirens, after whom Naples was originally named

Parthi·a -ae *f* Parthia (*country located S.E. of the Caspian*)

Parthĭc·us -a -um *adj* Parthian

Parth·us -a -um *adj & m* Parthian

partĭc·eps -ĭpis *adj* (with *genit*)
sharing in, taking part in; *m* partner, confederate

particĭp·ō -āre *vt* to make (*someone*)
a partner; to share (*something*)

particŭl·a -ae *f* bit, particle, grain

partim *adv* partly, in part, to some
extent; for the most part, mostly;
(with *genit* or **ex** + *abl*) some of;
partim . . . partim some . . .
others

partĭ·ō -ōnis *f* bringing forth, producing

part·ĭō -īre -īvī or **-ĭī -ītum** or
part·ĭor -īrī -ītus sum *vt* to
share, distribute, apportion, divide

partītē *adv* with proper divisions,
methodically

partītĭ·ō -ōnis *f* division, distribution, sharing; division of a speech

partĭtūd·ō -ĭnis *f* bearing (*of young*)

partŭr·ĭō -īre -īvī or **-ĭī** *vt* to teem
with; to be ready to produce; to
bring forth, yield; (fig) to brood
over; *vi* to be in labor

partus *pp* of **parĭō**; *adj* acquired; *n*
acquisition, gain, store

part·us -ūs *m* birth; young, offspring; (fig) beginnings

parum *adv* a little, too little, insuffi-
ciently; **parum est** it is not
enough, it does not suffice; **parum**
habere to regard as unsatisfactory;
satis eloquentiae sapientiae
parum enough eloquence but too
little wisdom

parumper *adv* for a little while, a
moment; **operire parumper** wait
a moment

parvĭt·ās -ātis *f* smallness

parvŭl·us or **parvŏl·us -a -um** *adj*
tiny; slight, petty; young; *n* childhood, infancy; **ab parvulis** from
childhood, from infancy

parv·us -a -um (*comp* **minor**; *su-*
perl **minimus**) *adj* small, little,
puny; short; young; brief, short
(*time*); small, insignificant, unimportant; low, cheap (*price*); *n* a little, trifle; childhood, infancy; **a**
parvis or **a parvo** from childhood,
from infancy; **parvi esse** to be of
little importance; **parvi facere**,
aestimare, **habere**, or **ducere** to
think little of, care little for; **parvi**
refert it makes little difference, it
matters little

pascĕŏl·us -ī *m* money bag

pascō pascĕre pāvī pastum *vt* to
feed, pasture, keep, raise (*animals*);
to cultivate, cherish; to feed (*flames*,
passions); to pile up (*debts*); to grow
(*beard*); to lay waste, ravage (*fields*);
to feast, gratify (*the eyes*); to cherish (*hope*)

pascor pascī pastus sum *vi* to
graze, browse, be fed; (with *abl*) **a**
to graze on; **b** (fig) to feed on, feast
on, thrive on

pascŭ·us -a -um *adj* grazing, pasture; *n* pasture

Pāsĭphǎ·ē -ēs or **Pāsĭphǎ·a -ae** *f*
daughter of Helios, sister of Circe,
husband of Minos, and mother of
Androgeos, Ariadne, Phaedra, and
the Minotaur

pass·er -ĕris *m* sparrow; plaice,
flounder; **passer marinus** ostrich

passercŭl·us -ī *m* little sparrow

passim *adv* here and there, all over,
at random; without order, indiscriminately, promiscuously

passus *pp* of **pando** and of **patior**;
adj spread out, extended, open; disheveled; dried, dry; *n* wine made
from dried grapes, raisin wine

pass·us -ūs *m* step, pace; footstep,
track; **mille passūs** mile; **tria**
milia passuum three miles

pastill·us -ī *m* lozenge

pastĭ·ō -ōnis *f* pasture, grazing

past·or -ōris *m* shepherd

pastorāl·is -e *adj* shepherd's, pastoral

pastorĭcĭ·us or **pastorĭ·us -a -um**
adj shepherd's, pastoral

pastus *pp* of **pasco**

past·us -ūs *m* pasture, fodder, food;
(fig) food

patagĭār·ĭus -ĭī or **-ī** *m* fringe
maker

patagĭāt·us -a -um *adj* (tunic) with
fringes

Patăr·a -ae *f* town in Lycia with an
oracle of Apollo

Patăr·eus -ěī or **-ĕos** *m* Apollo

Patavīn·us -a -um *adj* of Patavium

Patav·ĭum -ĭī or **-ī** *n* city in N.
Italy, the birthplace of Livy (*mod-*
ern Padua)

pate·facĭō -facĕre -fēcī -factus
(passive: **pate·fĭō -fĭěrī**) *vt* to
throw open; to open up, make accessible; to bring to light

patefactĭ·ō -ōnis *f* disclosure

patell·a -ae *f* pan, dish, plate

pat·ens -entis *adj* open, accessible;
extensive; exposed; evident

patentĭus *adv* more openly, more
clearly

pat·ĕō -ēre -ŭī *vi* to stand open, be
open; to be accessible; to be exposed; to open, stretch out, extend;
to be clear, be plain, be well known;
to be accessible, be attainable, be
free; (of the mind) to be open, be
receptive

pat·er -ris *m* father; **pater cenae**
host; **pater familias** head of the
household, head of the family; *m pl*
forefathers; senators

patěr·a -ae *f* flat dish (*used esp. in*
making libations)

pat·erfamilĭās -risfamilĭās *m*
head of the household, head of the
family

patern·us -a -um *adj* father's, paternal; ancestral; of a native country, native

pat·escō -escĕre -ŭī *vi* to be opened,
be open; to stretch out, extend; to
be disclosed, be divulged, become
evident

pathĭc·us -a -um *adj* lustful

patĭbĭl·is -e *adj* tolerable, endurable;
sensitive

patibulāt·us -a -um adj gibbeted; wearing a yoke

patibŭl·um -ī m fork-shaped yoke (tied around the neck of a criminal); fork-shaped gibbet

patĭ·ens -entis adj hardy, tough; hard; stubborn, unyielding, patient, tolerant; (with genit or ad + acc) able to endure, inured to, able to take; **amnis patiens navium** navigable river

patienter adv patiently

patientĭ·a -ae f patience, endurance; resignation, forbearance; submissiveness; sexual submission

patĭn·a -ae f dish, pan

patinārĭ·us -a -um adj of pans; in a pan; **strues patinaria** pile of dishes

patĭor pātī passus sum vt to experience, undergo, suffer; to put up with, allow; to submit to sexually; **aequo animo pati** to suffer patiently; **aegre pati** to resent, be displeased with

patrāt·or -ōris m perpetrator

patrāt·us -ī masc **pater patratus** plenipotentiary

patrĭ·a -ae f native land, native city, home

patricē adv paternally

patricĭ·us -a -um adj of patrician status, patrician; m pl patricians, patrician class

patrimōnĭ·um -ĭī or **-ī** n patrimony, inheritance

patrĭm·us -a -um adj having a father living

patriss·ō -āre vi to take after one's father

patrīt·us -a -um adj father's, inherited from one's father

patrĭ·us -a -um adj father's, of a father, fatherly, paternal; ancestral, traditional, heriditary; native; f see **patria**

patr·ō -āre vt to bring about, effect, achieve, accomplish, perform, finish, conclude; **bellum patrare** to bring the war to an end; **jus jurandum patrare** to take an oath (confirming a treaty); **pacem patrare** to conclude a peace

patrōcĭnĭ·um -ĭī or **-ī** n patronage, protection, legal defense, legal representation

patrōcĭn·or -ārī -ātus sum vi to be a patron, afford protection; (with dat) to serve (someone) as patron, protect, defend

Patrōcl·us -ī m son of Menoetius and friend of Achilles, who wearing the armor of Achilles, was killed by Hector

patrōn·a -ae f legal protectress, patroness; advocate; defender, safeguard

patrōn·us -ī m legal protector, patron; advocate (in court); defender

patruēl·is -e adj of or descended from a father's brother, cousin's; m cousin

patrŭ·us -a -um adj uncle's; m (paternal) uncle

patŭl·us -a -um adj open, standing open; spreading, spread out, broad

pauciloqu·ĭum -ĭī or **-ī** n reticence

paucĭt·ās -ātis f paucity, scarcity, small number

paucŭl·ī -ae -a adj just a few, very few; n pl few words

pauc·us -a -um adj few, little; pron masc pl few, a few; the select few, elite; **inter paucos (paucas)** or **in paucis** especially; pron neut pl a few things, a few words; **paucis** in a few words, briefly

paulātim adv little by little, gradually, by degrees; a few at a time

paulisper adv for a little while

paulō adv (as abl of degree of difference in expressions of comparison) by a little, a little, somewhat; **paulo antea** a little before; **paulo post** a little later

paulŭlō adv somewhat, a little; cheaply, at a low price

paulŭlum adv somewhat, a little

paulŭl·us -a -um adj very little; n a bit; **paululum pecuniae** a bit of money

paulum adv a little, to some extent, to some degree

paul·us -a -um adj small, little; n bit, trifle; **post paulum** after a bit, after a while

Paul·us -ī m L. Aemilius Paulus (conqueror of Macedonia through the victory at Pydna in 168 B.C.)

paup·er -ĕris adj poor; scanty, meager; (with genit) poor in; m poor man, pauper

paupercŭl·us -a -um adj poor

pauperĭ·ēs -ēī f poverty

pauper·ō -āre vt to impoverish; (with abl) to rob (someone) of

paupert·ās -ātis f poverty

paus·a -ae f pause, stop, end

pausĭ·a -ae f plump olive

pauxillātim adv bit by bit, little by little

pauxillisper adv by degrees

pauxillŭlum adv a little, a bit

pauxillŭl·us -a -um adj very little, tiny; n bit

pauxillum adv a little, a bit

pauxill·us -a -um adj very little, tiny; n small amount

pavefact·us -a -um adj frightened, scared

pavĕō pavēre pāvī vt to be scared of; vi to be terrified, tremble, or shiver with fear

pavesc·ō -ĕre vt to get scared of; vi to begin to be alarmed

pavĭdē adv in panic

pavĭd·us -a -um adj panicky, alarmed, shivering or trembling with fear, startled; with beating heart, nervous; causing alarm

pavīment·ō -āre vt to pave

pavīment·um -ī n pavement; floor

pav·ĭō -īre -īvī or **-ĭī -ītum** vt to strike, beat

pavīt·ō -āre *vt* to be panicky over; *vi* to quake with fear, be scared to death; to shiver (*with fever*)

pāv·ō -ōnis *m* peacock

pav·or -ōris *m* panic, terror, dismay, quaking, shivering; **pavorem injicere** (with *dat*) to throw the fear of the Lord into, to terrify

pax pācis *f* peace; peace treaty, reconciliation, compact, agreement; harmony, tranquility; favor, pardon (*from the gods*); **pace tuā** with your permission, with your leave

peccāns -antis *m* offender, sinner

peccāt·um -ī *n* fault, mistake, slip, transgression, sin

pecc·ō -āre *vi* to make a mistake, commit a fault, sin

pecorōs·us -a -um *adj* rich in cattle

pect·en -ĭnis *m* comb; plectrum (*for strumming a lyre*); scallop (*sea food*)

pectō pectĕre pexī pexum *vt* to comb; to card (*wool*); (coll) to clobber (*with stick or fist*)

pect·us -ŏris *n* breast; heart, feeling; soul, conscience, mind, understanding; character, person

pecŭ (*genit not in use*) *n* flock; *n pl* cattle; pastures

pecuārĭ·us -a -um *adj* of sheep, of cattle; **res pecuāria** livestock; *m* cattle man, cattle breeder, rancher; *f* livestock; *n pl* herds of cattle, herds of sheep

pecŭlāt·or -ōris *m* embezzler

pecŭlāt·us -ūs *m* embezzlement

pecŭlĭār·is -e *adj* one's own, as one's own private property; special

pecŭlĭāt·us -a -um *adj* rich, well off

pecŭlĭ·ō -āre *vt* to give away for good

pecŭlĭōs·us -a -um *adj* owning private property

pecŭl·ĭum -iī *or* **-ī** *n* small savings (*esp. accumulated by slaves*); private property

pecūnĭ·a -ae *f* money; **pecunia praesēns** ready cash

pecūnĭārĭ·us -a -um *adj* pecuniary, financial, money

pecūnĭōs·us -a -um *adj* rich, wealthy, loaded with money; profitable, bringing in money

pec·us -ŏris *n* cattle, herd, flock; sheep; head of cattle; **pecus equīnum** stud; (as term of scorn) cattle

pec·us -ŭdis *f* head of cattle; beast; sheep; domestic animal; beast, animal (*as opposed to birds*); (as term of abuse) brute, beast, swine

pedāl·is -e *adj* one-foot-long

pedārĭ·ius -iī *or* **-ī** *m* inferior senator (*who let others step all over him*)

ped·es -ĭtis *m* infantryman; pedestrian; infantry

pedest·er -ris -re *adj* infantry; pedestrian; on land, by land; written in prose; prosaic, plain

pedetemptim *adv* by feeling one's

way, step by step, slowly, cautiously

pedĭc·a -ae *f* foot chain; trap, snare

pedĭculōs·us -a -um *adj* lousy

ped·is -is *m or f* louse

pedĭsĕqu·a -ae *f* attendant, handmaid

pedĭsĕqu·us -ī *m* footman, page, lackey

pedĭtastell·us -ī *m* poor infantryman

pedĭtāt·us -ūs *m* infantry

pēdĭt·um -ī *n* wind, gas

pēdō pēdĕre pepēdī *vi* to break wind

ped·um -ī *n* shepherd's hook

Pēgasē·us *or* **Pēgasēi·us -a -um** *adj* of Pegasus, Pegasean

Pēgasĭd·es -um *f pl* Muses

Pēgăs·us -ī *m* winged horse which sprang from the blood of Medusa and whose hoof, as it hit Mt. Helicon, caused Hippocrene, a fountain dear to the Muses, to flow

pegm·a -ătis *n* bookcase; scaffolding

pējĕrātiunŭl·a -ae *f* petty oath

pējĕrāt·us *or* **pējŭrāt·us -a -um** *adj* offended by false oaths; **jus pejeratum** false oath

pējĕr·ō *or* **perjūr·ō -āre** *vt* to swear falsely by; *vi* to swear a false oath; (coll) to lie

pējĕrōs·us -a -um *adj* perjured

pēj·or -us (*comp of* **malus**) *adj* worse

pējus (*comp of* **male**) *adv* worse

pelagĭ·us -a -um *adj* of the sea

pelăg·us -ī *n* sea, open sea

pēlăm·is -ĭdis *or* **pēlăm·ys -ўdis** *f* young tuna fish

Pelasg·ī -ōrum *m pl* aborigines of Greece

Pēl·eus -ĕī *or* **-ĕos** *m* king of Thessaly, son of Aeacus, husband of Thetis, and father of Achilles

Pelĭ·ās -ae *m* king of Iolcos in Thessaly and uncle of Jason

Pēlĭd·ēs -ae *m* descendant of Peleus; Achilles; Neoptolemus

Pēlĭ·on -ī *n* mountain in E. Thessaly

Pēlĭ·us *or* **Pēlĭăc·us -a -um** *adj* of Mt. Pelion

Pell·a -ae *or* **Pell·ē -ēs** *f* city of Macedonia and birthplace of Alexander the Great

pellācĭ·a -ae *f* charm, allurement

Pellae·us -a -um *adj* of or from Apella; **Pellaeus juvenis** Alexander

pell·ax -ācis *adj* seductive, alluring

pellectĭ·ō -ōnis *f* perusal

pel·lĭciō -lĭcĕre -lexī -lectum *vt* to allure, entice, coax, wheedle

pellĭcŭl·a -ae *f* small hide, skin, fleece

pellĭ·ō -ōnis *m* furrier

pell·is -is *f* skin, hide; leather; felt; tent; shield cover; **detrahere pellem** to expose one's true character

pellīt·us -a -um *adj* clothed in skins, wearing leather coat

pellō pellĕre pepŭlī pulsum *vt* to push, beat, strike, knock, hurl; to drive out or away, expel, banish; to repel, drive back, rout; to play or strum (*lyre, etc.*); to affect, impress, move, strike; to stamp (*the earth*)

pelluc- = **perl-**

Pelopēi·as -ădis or **Pelopē·is -ĭdis** *adj* Peloponnesian

Pelopēi·us or **Pelopē·us -a -um** *adj* Pelopian; Mycenaean; Phrygian

Pelopĭd·ae -ārum *m pl* descendants of Pelops

Peloponnēns·is -e *adj* Peloponnesian

Peloponnēsiăc·us or **Peloponnēsi·us -a -um** *adj* Peloponnesian

Peloponnēs·us -ī *f* the Peloponnesus (*modern Morea*)

Pel·ops -ŏpis *m* son of Tantalus, father of Atreus and Thyestes, and grandfather of Agamemnon and Menelaus

pelōr·is -ĭdis *f* large shellfish

Pelōr·us or **Pelŏr·os -ī** *m* N.E. promontory of Sicily

pelt·a -ae *f* small leather shield

peltast·ēs or **peltast·a -ae** *m* soldier armed with a small leather shield

peltāt·us -a -um *adj* armed with a small leather shield

Pēlūs·ĭum -ĭī or **-ī** *n* city on the E. mouth of the Nile

pelv·is -is *f* bucket, basin

penāri·us -a -um *adj* food, supply, storage

Penāt·ēs -ĭum *m pl* Penates, household gods; hearth, home, house; cells (*of bees*)

penātig·er -ĕra -ĕrum *adj* carrying the household gods

pendĕō pendēre pependī *vi* to hang, hang down, be suspended; to hang loose; to hang down, be flabby, be weak; to depend, be dependent; to be in suspense, be uncertain, hesitate; to hang around, loiter; to hang in the air, be suspended, hover, float, overhang; (*with abl or with* **ab, dē** *or* **ex** + *abl*) a to hang down from, hang by; **b** to depend on, be dependent upon; **c** to hang on to, be devoted to; (*with* **in** + *abl*) to be poised on, hover in, hover over

pendō pendĕre pependī pensum *vt* to weigh, weigh out; to pay, pay out; to weigh, ponder, consider, value, esteem; to pay (*penalty*); **floccī pendere** to think little of; **magnī pendere** to think much of, value highly; *vi* to weigh, have weight

pendŭl·us -a -um *adj* hanging, hanging down; doubtful, uncertain

Pēnē·is -ĭdis or **Pēnēi·us -a -um** *adj* of Peneus

Pēnelŏp·a -ae or **Pēnelŏp·ē -ēs** *f* daughter of Icarius and Periboea and wife of Ulysses

penes *prep* (*with acc of person only*) in the possession of, in the power of, belonging to, resting with; at the house of, with; **penes sē esse** to be in one's senses

penetrābĭl·is -e *adj* penetrating, piercing; penetrable

penetrāl·is -e *adj* penetrating, piercing; inner, internal, interior; *n pl* the interior, center; inner chambers; sanctuary; the interior, hinterlands

penētr·ō -āre *vt & vi* to penetrate, enter

Pēnē·us -a -um *adj* of Peneus, of the Peneus River; *m* Peneus River (*largest river in Thessaly*); river god, the father of Cyrene and Daphne

pēnicill·us -ī *m* paint brush, pencil

pēnicŭl·us -ī *m* brush; sponge

pēn·is -is *m* tail; penis; lechery

penitē *adv* inwardly

penĭtus *adv* internally, inside, deep within, deeply; from within; thoroughly, completely, through and through; heartily

penĭt·us -a -um *adj* inner, inward

penn·a -ae *f* feather; wing; flight

pennāt·us -a -um *adj* feathered

pennĭg·er -ĕra -ĕrum *adj* winged, feathered

pennipŏt·ens -entis *adj* winged, able to fly

pennŭl·a -ae *f* little wing

pensĭl·is -e *adj* hanging; **ūva pensilis** grape hung out to dry

pensĭ·ō -ōnis *f* payment, instalment

pensĭt·ō -āre *vt* to pay; to weigh, ponder, consider; *vi* to be taxable

pens·ō -āre *vt* to weigh out; to weigh, ponder, consider, examine; to compare, contrast; to pay, atone for; to repay, compensate, requite

pens·um -ī *n* work quota; duty, task; consideration, scruple; **pensī esse** to be of value, be of importance; **pensī habēre** to value, consider of importance

pensus *pp* of **pendo**

pentēr·is -is *f* galley, quinquereme

Penthesilē·a -ae *f* Amazon, warrior queen who was killed by Achilles at Troy

Penth·eus -ĕī *or* **-ĕos** *m* king of Thebes, son of Echion and Agave, grandson of Cadmus, and opponent of the Bacchic cult

pen·um -ī *n* supplies, provisions, food

pēnūri·a -ae *f* want, need, dearth

pen·us -ūs *or* **-ī** *m* or **pen·us -ŏris** *n* supplies, provisions, food

pepl·um -ī *n* or **pepl·us -ī** *m* robe for the statue of Athena

per *prep* (*with acc*) (*of space*) through, throughout, all over, along; (*of time*) through, during, for, in the course of, at, at the time of; (*of agency*) through, by, by means of, at the hands of; (*of means or manner*) through, by, under pretense of; for the sake of, with a view to; (*in oath*) by

pēr·a -ae *f* wallet

perabsurd·us -a -um *adj* completely absurd

peraccommodāt·us -a -um *adj* very convenient

perāc·er -ris -re *adj* very sharp

peracerb·us -a -um *adj* very harsh, very sour

perac·escō -escĕre -ŭī *vi* to become completely sour

practī·ō -ōnis *f* conclusion, last act (of a play)

peractus *pp* of **perago**

peracūtē *adv* very acutely

peracūt·us -a -um *adj* very sharp; very clear (voice, intellect)

peradulesc·ens -entis *adj* very young

peradulescentŭl·us -ī *m* very young man

peraequē *adv* quite evenly, uniformly

peragĭt·ō -āre *vt* to harass

per·agō -agĕre -ēgī -actum *vt* to carry through to the end, complete, accomplish; to pierce; to travel through; to harass, disturb, trouble; to describe, relate, go over; to work over, till, cultivate; to deliver (speech); (law) to prosecute to a conviction

peragrātī·ō -ōnis *f* traveling

perāgr·ō -āre *vt* to travel through, travel, traverse; *vi* (fig) to spread, penetrate

peralt·us -a -um *adj* very high

perăm·ans -antis *adj* (with genit) very fond of

peramanter *adv* very lovingly

perambŭl·ō -āre *vt* to travel, traverse, walk through

peramoen·us -a -um *adj* very pleasant, very charming

perampl·us -a -um *adj* very large, very spacious

perangustē *adv* very narrowly

perangust·us -a -um *adj* very narrow

perantīqu·us -a -um *adj* very ancient, very old

perapposĭt·us -a -um *adj* very suitable

perardŭ·us -a -um *adj* very difficult

perargūt·us -a -um *adj* very clear; very sharp, very witty

perarmāt·us -a -um *adj* heavily armed

per·arō -āre *vt* to plow through; to furrow; to write on (a wax tablet); to write

pērātim *adv* bag by bag

perattentē *adv* very attentively

perattent·us -a -um *adj* very attentive

peraudiend·us -a -um *adj* that must be heard to the end

perbacch·or -ārī -ātus sum *vt* to carouse through (e.g., many days)

perbeāt·us -a -um *adj* very happy

perbellē *adv* very prettily

perbĕne *adv* very well

perbenevŏl·us -a -um *adj* very friendly

perbenignē *adv* very kindly

perbĭb·ō -ĕre -ī *vt* to drink up, drink in, imbibe

perbit·ō -ĕre *vi* to go to ruin

perbland·us -a -um *adj* very attractive, very charming

perbŏn·us -a -um *adj* very good, excellent

perbrĕv·is -e *adj* very short, very brief; **perbrevi** or **perbrevi tempore** in a very short time

perbrevĭter *adv* very briefly

perc·a -ae *f* perch

percalefact·us -a -um *adj* warmed through and through

percal·escō -escĕre -ŭī *vi* to become quite hot

percall·escō -escĕre -ŭī *vt* to become thoroughly versed in; *vi* to become very hardened

percār·us -a -um *adj* very dear, very costly; very dear, much loved

percaut·us -a -um *adj* very cautious

percelĕbr·or -ārī -ātus sum *vi* to be quite famous

percĕl·er -ĕris *adj* very quick

perceleriter *adv* very quickly

per·cellō -cellĕre -cŭlī -culsum *vt* to knock down, beat down, overthrow; to scare to death; to overthrow, ruin; to send scurrying; to hit hard

percens·ĕō -ēre -ŭī *vt* to count up; to review, survey; to travel through, traverse

perceptĭ·ō -ōnis *f* harvesting; comprehension; *f pl* concepts

percept·us -a -um *pp* of **percipio**; *n* precept, rule, doctrine

per·cīdō -cīdĕre -cīdī -cīsum *vt* to smash to pieces

perci·ĕō -ēre or **perc·īō -īre -īvī** or **-iī -itum** *vt* to stir up, excite

per·cipiō -cipĕre -cēpī -ceptum *vt* to get a good hold of; to catch; to occupy, seize; to gather in, harvest, reap; (of the senses) to take in, perceive, feel; (of feelings) to get hold of, get the better of; to learn, know, comprehend, understand, perceive

percĭt·us -a -um *pp* of **percieo**; *adj* aroused, provoked; impetuous, excitable

percoctus *pp* of **percoquo**

percŏl·ō -āre *vt* to strain, filter

per·cōlō -colĕre -colŭī -cultum *vt* to reverence, revere, worship; to beautify; to crown, complete

percōm·is -e *adj* very courteous

percommŏdē *adv* very conveniently, very well, very suitably

percommŏd·us -a -um *adj* very convenient, very suitable

percontātĭ·ō -ōnis *f* thorough investigation

percontāt·or -ōris *m* inquisitive fellow

percont·or -ārī -ātus sum *vt* to question, investigate, interrogate; (with double acc) to ask (someone something)

percontŭm·ax -ācis *adj* very stubborn

per·cŏquŏ -coquĕre -coxī -coctum *vt* to cook through and through, cook thoroughly; to heat thoroughly; to ripen; to scorch, blacken

percrēb·escŏ or **percrēbr·escŏ -escĕre -uī** *vi* to become prevalent, be spread abroad

percrēp·ŏ -āre -uī -ĭtum *vi* to resound, ring

perorucī·or -ārī -ātus sum *vi* to torment oneself

perculsus *pp* of **percello**

percult·us -a -um *pp* of **percolo**; *adj* decked out; (coll) dolled up (*woman*)

percupĭd·us -a -um *adj* (with *genit*) very fond of

percup·ĭŏ -ĕre *vt* (with *inf*) to be eager to, desire very much to, be dying to

percūrĭŏs·us -a -um *adj* very curious

percūr·ŏ -āre *vt* to heal completely

per·currŏ -currĕre -cucurrī or **currī -cursum** *vt* to run through, run along, run over, pass over, speed over; (fig) to scan briefly, look over; (in a speech) to treat in succession, go over, run over; (of feelings) to run through, penetrate, pierce; *vi* to run fast, hurry along; (with **ad** + *acc*) to dash to (*e.g.*, *the Forum*); (with **per** + *acc*) **a** to run through or across, travel through; **b** (fig) to run through, mention quickly, treat in succession

percursātĭ·ŏ -ōnis *f* traveling; **percursātio Italiae** traveling through Italy

percursĭ·ŏ -ōnis *f* quick survey

percurs·ŏ -āre *vi* to roam about, range about

percussĭ·ŏ -ōnis *f* hitting, striking; snapping (*of fingers*); (mus) beat, time

percuss·or -ōris *m* assailant; assassin

percussus *pp* of **percutio**

percuss·us -ūs *m* beating, striking

per·cutĭŏ -cutĕre -cussī -cussum *vt* to beat or hit hard; to pierce, transfix, run through; to shoot, kill; to shock, impress, move, astound; to cut through; to dig (*ditch*); to coin, stamp (*money*); to cheat, trick

perdecōr·us -a -um *adj* very pretty

perdēlīr·us -a -um *adj* very silly, quite mad

perdeps·ŏ -ĕre -uī *vt* to knead thoroughly; (fig) to seduce

perdiffĭcĭl·is -e *adj* very difficult

perdiffĭcĭlĭter *adv* with great difficulty

perdign·us -a -um *adj* (with *abl*) quite worthy of

perdīlĭg·ens -entis *adj* very diligent, very conscientious

perdīlĭgenter *adv* diligently, very conscientiously

per·discŏ -discĕre -dĭdĭcī *vt* to learn thoroughly, learn by heart

perdīsertē *adv* very eloquently

perdĭtē *adv* recklessly, desperately

perdĭt·or -ōris *m* destroyer

perdĭt·us -a -um *adj* ruined, lost; profligate, degenerate, infamous, reckless, incorrigible, hopeless

perdiū *adv* for a very long time

perdiūturn·us -a -um *adj* longlasting, protracted

perdīv·es -ĭtis *adj* very rich

perd·ix -īcis *m* partridge

per·dŏ -dĕre -dĭdī -dĭtum *vt* to wreck, ruin, destroy; to waste, squander; to lose

perdoc·ĕŏ -ēre -uī -tum *vt* to teach thoroughly

perdoctē *adv* very skillfully

perdoct·us -a -um *pp* of **perdoceo**; *adj* very learned, very skillful

perdol·escŏ -escĕre -uī *vi* to become resentful

perdŏm·ŏ -āre -uī -ĭtum *vt* to tame completely, subdue, subjugate

perdormiscŏ·ŏ -ĕre *vi* to sleep on, keep on sleeping

per·dūcŏ -dūcĕre -duxī -ductum *vt* to lead, guide; to cover, spread; to prolong, drag out; to induce; to seduce; (with **ad** + *acc*) **a** to lead, bring, guide, escort to; **b** to build, run (*wall, ditch, road, etc.*) to; **c** to prolong, protract, drag out, continue (*something*) to or till; **d** to win over to, convince of

perduct·ŏ -āre *vt* to lead, conduct

perduct·or -ōris *m* guide; pimp

perdūdum *adv* long long ago

perduellĭ·ŏ -ōnis *f* treason, high treason

perduell·is -is *m* enemy

perdūr·ŏ -āre *vi* to hold out, last, endure

per·ĕdŏ -esse -ēdī -ēsum *vt* to eat up, devour

perĕgrē *adv* abroad, away from home; from abroad; **peregre abire** or **peregre exire** to go abroad

perĕgrīnābund·us -a -um *adj* traveling around

perĕgrīnātĭ·ŏ -ōnis *f* living abroad, travel, touring; roaming, ranging (*said of animals*)

perĕgrīnāt·or -ōris *m* traveler, wanderer

perĕgrīnĭt·ās -ātis *f* foreign manners, strange ways

perĕgrīn·or -ārī -ātus sum *vi* to live abroad, travel abroad, travel around; (fig) to be a stranger

perĕgrīn·us -a -um *adj* foreign, strange, alien, exotic; (fig) strange, inexperienced; **amores peregrini** love affairs with foreign women; **praetor peregrinus** praetor who tried cases involving foreigners and Roman citizens; **terror peregrinus** fear of a foreign enemy; *mf* foreigner, alien

perēlĕg·ans -antis *adj* very elegant

perēlĕganter *adv* very elegantly

perēlŏqu·ens -entis *adv* very eloquent

peremn·ia -ium n pl auspices taken before crossing a river

peremptus pp of **perimo**

perendiē adv the day after tomorrow

perendĭn·us -a -um adj **dies perendĭnus** the day after tomorrow; m the day after tomorrow

perenn·is -e adj perennial, continual, everlasting

perenniserv·os -ī m slave for life

perennĭt·ās -ātis f continuance, perpetuity

perenn·ō -āre vi to last

pĕrenticīd·a -ae m (coll) crook

per·ĕō -īre -iī -ĭtum vi to pass away, pass on, die; to go to waste, perish, be destroyed; to be lost, be ruined, be undone; to be desperately in love, pine away; (of snow) to melt away; (of iron) to rust away; **periī!** I'm ruined!, I'm finished!, I'm washed up!

perequit·ō -āre vt to ride up through; vi to ride around

pererr·ō -āre vt to roam around, wander through; to survey, look (someone) over

perērudīt·us -a -um adj very learned

perēsus pp of **peredo**

perexcels·us -a -um adj very high, exalted

perexiguē adv very sparingly

perexigu·us -a -um adj tiny; insignificant; very short (day)

perfacētē adv very wittily

perfacēt·us -a -um adj very witty, very sharp

perfacile adv very easily, very readily

perfacĭl·is -ē adj very easy; very courteous

perfamiliār·is -e adj very close, intimate; m very close friend

perfectē adv completely, perfectly

perfecti·ō -ōnis f completion; perfection

perfect·or -ōris m perfecter; **dicendi perfector** stylist

perfect·us -a -um pp of **perficio**; adj complete, finished, perfect, excellent

per·ferō -ferre -tŭlī -lātum vt to carry through; to endure to the end, bear with patience, put up with; to pass (a law); to bring, announce, report (news)

per·ficĭō -ficĕre -fēcī -fectum vt to complete, finish, accomplish, carry out, perform, execute, bring to an end; to bring to completion, finish, perfect; to bring about, cause

perfic·us -a -um adj perfecting; **natura perfica** nature which perfects

perfidēl·is -e adj very faithful, very trusty

perfidĭ·a -ae f perfidy, treachery

perfidiōsē adv treacherously

perfidiōs·us -a -um adj treacherous, faithless

perfīd·us -a -um adj treacherous, untrustworthy, dishonest, sneaky; m sneak

per·figō -figĕre -fixī -fixum vt to pierce

perflābĭl·is -e adj airy; invisible (gods)

perflāgitiōs·us -a -um adj utterly disgraceful

perfl·ō -āre vt to blow through, blow across

perfluctŭ·ō -āre vt to surge through

per·fodĭō -fodĕre -fōdī -fossum vt to dig through; to pierce

perfŏr·ō -āre vt to bore through, pierce; to make by boring

perfortĭter adv very bravely

perfoss·or -ōris m **perfossor parietum** burglar

perfossus pp of **perfodio**

perfractus pp of **perfringo**

perfrĕm·ō -ĕre -ŭī vi to snort loud

perfrĕqu·ens -entis adj very crowded, over-crowded

perfric·ō -āre -ŭī -ātum or **-tum** vt to rub well, rub all over; **os perfricare** to rub away blushes, put on a bold front

perfrīgefac·ĭō -ĕre vt (fig) to send a chill over, make shudder

per·frīgescō -frīgescĕre -frixī vi to catch a bad cold

perfrīgĭd·us -a -um adj very cold, ice-cold

per·fringō -fringĕre -frēgī -fractum vt to break through; to break to pieces, batter in, smash; (fig) to break (laws, etc.), break up (conspiracy)

per·fruor -frŭī -fructus sum vi (with abl) to experience to the full, fully enjoy, be delighted by, perform gladly

perfŭg·a -ae m military deserter; political turncoat

per·fugĭō -fugĕre -fūgī vi (with **ad** or **in** + acc) a to flee to for refuge; **b** to desert to; **c** (fig) to have recourse to, find comfort in

perfuncti·ō -ōnis f performance, performing, discharge

perfunctus pp of **perfungor**

per·fundō -fundĕre -fūdī -fūsum vt to drench, bathe; to sprinkle; to dye; (fig) to fill, flood, steep, inspire

per·fungor -fungī -functus sum vt to enjoy; vi (with abl) a to perform, discharge, fulfill; **b** to go through, endure, undergo; **c** to get rid of; **d** to be finished with, be done with; **e** to enjoy

perfŭr·ō -ĕre vi to rage wildly, rage on

perfūsus pp of **perfundo**

Pergăm·a -ōrum n pl or **Pergăm·us -ī** f citadel of Troy, Troy

Pergamē·us -a -um adj Trojan; m pl Trojans

Pergăm·um -ī n Troy; Pergamum (city in Mysia, the capital of the Attalid kingdom, famous for its library)

pergaud·ĕō -ēre *vi* to be very glad

per·gō -gĕre -rexī -rectum *vt* to go on uninterruptedly with, continue; (with *inf*) to continue to; *vi* to go straight on, continue, proceed; (with ad + *acc*) to pass on to, proceed to (*esp. in speaking*)

pergraec·or -ārī -ātus sum *vi* to go completely Greek, have a ball

pergrand·is -e *adj* very large, huge; **pergrandis natu** very old

pergraphic·us -a -um *adj* very cunning

pergrāt·us -a -um *adj* very pleasant; *n* distinct pleasure

pergrav·is -e *adj* very heavy; very important; very impressive

pergravĭter *adv* very seriously

pergŭl·a -ae *f* veranda, balcony; school; brothel

Perg·us -ī *m* lake in Sicily, near Henna, where Pluto carried off Proserpina

perhĭb·ĕō -ēre -ŭī -ĭtum *vt* to hold, assert, maintain; to call, name; to adduce, cite

perhīlum *adv* very little

perhonōrĭfĭcē *adv* very respectfully, with all due respect

perhonōrĭfĭc·us -a -um *adj* very honorable, very complimentary; very respectful

perhorr·escō -escĕre -ŭī *vt* to begin to shudder at; to develop a terror of; *vi* to begin to quake, begin to tremble violently

perhorrĭd·us -a -um *adj* horrible, dreadful

perhūmanĭter *adv* very kindly

perhūmān·us -a -um *adj* very courteous

Pericl·ēs -is or -ī *m* Athenian statesman, son of Xanthippus and political leader of Athens during the city's most flourishing period (c. 495-429 B.C.)

perīclĭtātĭ·ō -ōnis *f* test, experiment

perīclĭt·or -ārī -ātus sum *vt* to test, put to the test, try; to jeopardize; to risk; *vi* to be in danger, be in jeopardy; to run a risk; (with *abl*) to be in danger of losing (*e.g.*, *life*, *reputation*); **capite perīclĭtari** to be in danger of losing one's life, risk one's life

perīculōsē *adv* dangerously

perīculōs·us -a -um *adj* dangerous, perilous, risky

perīcŭl·um or **perīcl·um** -ī *n* danger, peril, risk; trial, attempt, experiment, test; literary venture; (law) trial, case, lawsuit, legal record, writ, sentence

perĭdōnĕ·us -a -um *adj* very suitable; (with *dat* or ad + *acc*) well adapted to, well suited to

perillustr·is -e *adj* very clear; very illustrious, very distinguished

perimbēcill·us -a -um *adj* very weak, very feeble

per·ĭmō -ĭmĕre -ēmī -emptum *vt* to take away completely; to destroy; to slay, kill

perimpedīt·us -a -um *adj* rough (*terrain*), full of obstacles

perincommŏdē *adv* very inconveniently

perincommŏd·us -a -um *adj* very inconvenient

perinde *adv* in the same manner, equally, just as, quite as; (with **at-que**, **ac**, **ut**, or **quam**) just as, exactly as; (with **ac si, quasi, tamquam**, or **quam si**) just as if

perindulg·ēns -entis *adj* very tender; (with ad + *acc*) very tender toward

perinfirm·us -a -um *adj* very weak

peringenĭōs·us -a -um *adj* very clever

perinīqu·us -a -um *adj* very unfair; very upset, very annoyed, very impatient, very reluctant; **perinīquo animo patī** or **ferre** to be quite upset at, be quite annoyed at, be very reluctant about

perinsign·is -e *adj* very remarkable

perinvīt·us -a -um *adj* very unwilling

perĭŏd·us -ī *f* sentence, rhetorical period

peripatētĭc·us -a -um *adj* peripatetic, Aristotelian; *m pl* peripatetics, Aristotelians

peripetasmăt·a -um *n pl* curtains, drapes

perīrāt·us -a -um *adj* very angry; (with *dat*) very angry with

periscĕl·is -ĭdis *f* anklet

peristrōm·a -ătis *n* carpet

peristȳl·ĭum -iī or -ī *n* peristyle (*open court surrounded by a colonnade*)

peristȳl·um -ī *n* colonnade around a building, peristyle

perītē *adv* skillfully, expertly

perītĭ·a -ae *f* experience, practical knowledge, skill; (with *genit*) experience in, familiarity with, knowledge of

perīt·us -a -um *adj* experienced, skillful, expert, familiar; (with *genit* or *abl*, with **in** + *abl*, or with ad + *acc*) experienced in, skillful in, expert in or at, familiar with; (with *inf*) skilled in, expert at, e.g., **perĭtus cantare** skilled in singing, expert at singing

perjūcundē *adv* very pleasantly

perjūcund·us -a -um *adj* very pleasant

perjūr·ĭum -iī or -ī *n* perjury, false oath

perjūrō see **pejero**

perjūr·us or **pejĕr·us** -a -um *adj* perjured, oath-breaking; lying, dishonest

per·lābor -lābī -lapsus sum *vi* to glide along, skim across or over; (with **per** + *acc*) to slip through; (with ad + *acc*) to come, move, glide, or slip toward; (with **in** + *acc*) to glide into, slip into

perlaet·us -a -um *adv* very glad, most joyful

perlapsus *pp* of **perlabor**

perlātē *adv* very extensively

perlat·ěō -ēre -ŭī *vi* to be completely hidden

perlātus *pp* of **perfero**

perlecti·ō -ōnis *f* thorough perusal

per·lěgō -legěre -lēgī -lectum *vt* to scan, survey thoroughly; to read through

perlepidē *adv* very nicely

perlěv·is -e *adj* very light, very slight

perleviter *adv* very lightly, very slightly

perlib·ens or **perlūb·ens -entis** *adj* very willing

perlibenter or **perlubenter** *adv* very gladly

perlīberāl·is -e *adj* very genteel

perlib·et or **perlūb·et -ēre** *v impers* (with *inf*) I should very much like to

perliciō see **pellicio**

perlīt·ō -āre *vi* to sacrifice with favorable omens

perlongē *adv* a long way off, very far

perlonginqu·us -a -um *adj* very long; very tedious

perlub- = **perlib-**

per·lūcěō or **pel·lūcěō -lūcěre -luxī** *vi* to shine clearly, be bright; to be clearly visible; to be transparent; to be clear, be intelligible

perlūcidŭl·us -a -um *adj* somewhat transparent

perlūcid·us or **pellūcid·us -a -um** *adj* very bright; transparent

perluctuōs·us -a -um *adj* very sad

per·lŭō -luěre -lŭī -lūtum *vt* to wash thoroughly, wash off, bathe

perlustr·ō -āre *vt* to traverse; to scan, survey, review

permadefac·iō -ěre *vt* to soak through and through, drench

permagn·us -a -um *adj* very great; very important; *n* great thing; **permagno** at a very high price, very dearly; **permagnum aestimare** (with *inf*) to think it quite something to

permānanter *adv* by flowing through

permānasc·ō -ěre *vi* (*of a report*) to begin to spread

per·maněō -manēre -mansī -mansum *vi* to last, continue, hold out, remain, persist, endure

permān·ō -āre *vt* to seep through, penetrate; *vi* to penetrate; (with **ad** or **in** + *acc*) **a** to seep through to, seep into, penetrate; **b** (fig) to reach, extend to, penetrate

permansi·ō -ōnis *f* persistence, continuance

permarīn·us -a -um *adj* sea-going

permātūr·escō -escěre -ŭī *vi* to become fully ripe

permediōcr·is -e *adj* completely normal

permeditāt·us -a -um *adj* well rehearsed, well trained

permensus *pp* of **permetior**

permě·ō -āre *vt* to go through, cross over, cross; *vi* (with **in** + *acc*) to penetrate; (with **per** + *acc*) to penetrate, permeate

Permess·us -ī *m* river in Boeotia sacred to Apollo and the Muses

per·mētior -mētīrī -mensus sum *vt* to measure out, measure; to traverse, travel, travel over

per·mingō -mingěre -minxī *vt* to soak with urine; to pollute

permīr·us -a -um *adj* very surprising, truly amazing

per·miscěō -miscēre -miscŭī -mixtum *vt* to mix together, intermingle; (fig) to mix together, mix up, confuse

permissi·ō -ōnis *f* unconditional surrender; permission

permiss·us -a -um *pp* of **permitto**; *n* permission

permiss·us -ūs *m* permission, leave

permitiāl·is -e *adj* destructive, deadly

permiti·ēs -ēī *f* wasting away; ruin, decay

per·mittō -mittěre -mīsī -missum *vt* to let through, let go through; to throw, hurl; to give up, surrender; to concede, relinquish; to let loose, let go; to let, permit, allow, grant; (with *dat*) to give up to, surrender (*something*) to, entrust (*something*) to, grant (*something*) to; (with **in** + *acc*) to send flying at, hurl or throw at

permixtē or **permixtim** *adv* confusedly, promiscuously

permixti·ō -ōnis *f* mixture; confusion, bedlam

permixt·us -a -um *pp* of **permisceo**; *adj* confused, promiscuous

permodest·us -a -um *adj* very modest, very moderate

permolestē *adv* with much trouble; **permoleste ferre** to be quite annoyed at

permolest·us -a -um *adj* very troublesome, very annoying

permŏl·ō -ěre *vt* to grind up; **aliēnas uxores permolere** (fig) to seduce other men's wives

permōti·ō -ōnis *f* excitement; **animi permotio** or **mentis permotio** excitement, deep emotion

per·mověō -movēre -mōvī -mōtum *vt* to stir up, churn up (*the sea*); to move deeply, make a deep impression upon; to excite, agitate, rouse; to influence, induce, prevail on

per·mulcěō -mulcēre -mulsī -mulsum *vt* to stroke, pet, caress; to soothe, charm; to delight, flatter; to appease, tame, mitigate, allay

permultō *adv* (with comparatives) by far, far, much

permultum *adv* very much; **permultum ante** very often before; **permultum interest** it makes a world of difference

permult·us -a -um *adj* very much, very many; *n* a lot, much

permūn·iō -īre -īvī or **-iī -ītum** *vt* to fortify thoroughly; to finish fortifying

permūtāti·ō -ōnis *f* permutation, complete change; change, alteration; crisis, revolution; exchange, barter; substitution

permūt·ō -āre *vt* to change completely, alter completely; to exchange, interchange

pern·a -ae *f* ham

pernecessāri·us -a -um *adj* very necessary; very closely related; *m* close friend; close relative

pernecesse (indecl) *adj* very necessary, indispensable

pernēg·ō -āre *vt* to deny flatly; to turn down flat

per·neō -nēre -nēvī -nētum *vt* (of the Fates) to spin out

perniciābil·is -e *adj* ruinous

pernici·ēs -ēī *f* ruin, destruction, disaster, calamity; pest, curse

perniciōsē *adv* perniciously, ruinously

perniciōs·us -a -um *adj* pernicious, ruinous

pernicit·ās -ātis *f* agility, nimbleness, swiftness

perniciter *adv* nimbly, swiftly

pernig·er -ra -rum *adj* jet black

pernimi·us -a -um *adj* much too much

pern·ix -īcis *adj* agile, nimble, active, swift

pernōbil·is -e *adj* famous, illustrious

pernoct·ō -āre *vi* to spend the night

per·nōscō -nōscere -nōvī -nōtum *vt* to examine thoroughly; to become fully acquainted with, get an accurate knowledge of

pernōt·escō -escere -ŭī *vi* to become generally known

pern·ox -octis *adj* all-night; **luna pernox** full moon

pernumer·ō -āre *vt* to count up

pēr·ō -ōnis *m* clodhopper, brogue (*worn by peasants and soldiers*)

perobscūr·us -a -um *adj* very obscure

perodiōs·us -a -um *adj* very annoying

perofficiōsē *adv* with devotion, with attention

perol·eō -ēre *vi* to have a strong odor

pērōnāt·us -a -um *adj* wearing clodhoppers

peropportūnē *adv* very opportunely, very conveniently

peropportūn·us -a -um *adj* very opportune, very convenient, well timed

peroptātō *adv* very much to one's wish

perōpus (indecl) *n* great need; **peropus est** it is absolutely essential

perōrāti·ō -ōnis *f* peroration, conclusion of a speech

perōrnāt·us -a -um *adj* very flowery (*style*)

perorn·ō -āre *vt* to enhance the prestige of (*e.g., the senate*)

perōr·ō -āre *vt* to plead (*a case*) all by oneself; to wind up, conclude (*a speech, case*), rest (*a case*); *vi* to give the summation

perōs·us -a -um *adj* hating, detesting

perpāc·ō -āre *vt* to silence completely; to pacify thoroughly

perparcē *adv* very stingily

perparvŭl·us -a -um *adj* tiny

perparv·us -a -um *adj* very small

perpast·us -a -um *adj* well fed

perpauc·ī -ae -a *adj* very few; *n pl* very few words; **perpauca dicere** to speak very briefly

perpaucŭl·ī -ae -a *adj* very few

perpaulum *adv* somewhat, slightly

perpaul·um -ī *n* small bit

perpaup·er -eris *adj* very poor

perpauxill·um -ī *n* little bit

perpavefac·iō -ere *vt* to frighten the daylight out of

per·pellō -pellĕre -pulsī -pulsum *vt* to push hard; to urge strongly, force

perpendicŭl·um -ī *n* plumb line, plummet; **ad perpendiculum** perpendicularly

per·pendō -pendĕre -pendī -pensum *vt* to weigh carefully, consider; to value, judge

perpĕram *adv* incorrectly, falsely

perp·es -ĕtis *adj* continuous, uninterrupted

perpessi·ō -ōnis *f* suffering, endurance

per·petior -pĕtī -pessus sum *vt* to endure, put up with, stand; to allow, permit

perpĕtr·ō -āre *vt* to accomplish, go through with, carry out, achieve, perform; to perpetrate, commit

perpetuĭt·ās -ātis *f* perpetuity

perpetuō *adv* constantly, without interruption, forever

perpetu·ō -āre *vt* to perpetuate

perpetu·us -a -um *adj* perpetual, continuous, uninterrupted; general, universal; whole, entire; **quaestiones perpetuae** standing courts; permanent committee; *n* **in perpetuum** without a break, continuously; for all time, forever

perplac·eō -ēre -ŭī *vi* (with *dat*) to please immensely

perplexābil·is -e *adj* obscure, perplexing

perplexābiliter *adv* perplexingly

perplexē or **perplexim** *adv* confusedly, unintelligibly

perplex·or -ārī -ātus sum *vi* to cause confusion

perplex·us -a -um *adj* intricate, confused; ambiguous, obscure; *n* ambiguity, confusion

perplicāt·us -a -um *adj* entangled

perplŭ·ō -ĕre *vt* (fig) to rain, pour; *vi* (of roof, etc.) to leak, let the rain in

perpŏl·ĭō -īre -īvī or **-ĭī -ītum** *vt* to polish well, bring to a high polish; (fig) to polish up, perfect

perpŏlīt·us -a -um *adj* polished, refined

perpŏpŭl·or -ārī -ātus sum *vt* to ravage, devastate

perpŏtātĭ·ō -ōnis *f* heavy drinking; drinking party

perpŏt·ō -āre *vt* to drink off; *vi* to drink heavily, drink constantly

per·prĭmō -prĭmĕre -pressī *vt* to press hard, squeeze hard; to lie on near

perpropinqu·us -a -um *adj* very near

perprūrisc·ō -ĕre *vi* to begin to itch all over

perpugn·ax -ācis *adj* very belligerent

perpulch·er -ra -rum *adj* very beautiful, very handsome

perpulsus *pp* of perpello

perpurg·ō -āre *vt* to cleanse thoroughly, clean up; (fig) to clear up, explain

perpusill·us -a -um *adj* puny

perpŭt·ō -āre *vt* to prune back hard; to clear up, explain in detail

perquam *adv* very, extremely

per·quīrō -quīrĕre -quīsīvī -quīsītum *vt* to search carefully for; to examine carefully

perquīsītīus *adv* more accurately, more critically

perquīsīt·or -ōris *m* enthusiast; **auctiōnum perquīsītor** auction enthusiast

perrārō *adv* very rarely, very seldom

perrār·us -a -um *adj* very rare, quite uncommon

perrecondĭt·us -a -um *adj* recondite, abstruse

perrectus *pp* of pergo

per·rēpō -rēpĕre -repsī -reptum *vt* to crawl over, crawl along

perrept·ō -āre *vt* to creep through, sneak through; *vi* to creep around

perrīdĭcŭlē *adv* most absurdly

perrīdĭcŭl·us -a -um *adj* utterly absurd

perrŏgātĭ·ō -ōnis *f* passage (*of a law*)

perrŏg·ō -āre *vt* to ask in succession; to poll (*opinions*); **sententĭas perrŏgāre** to have roll call (*in the senate*)

per·rumpō -rumpĕre -rūpī -ruptum *vt* to break through, force one's way through; to break in two, shatter, smash; to offend against, violate; *vi* to break through, make a breakthrough

Pers·a or **Pers·ēs -ae** *m* Persian

persaepe *adv* very often

persalsē *adv* very wittily

persals·us -a -um *adj* very witty

persalūtātĭ·ō -ōnis *f* round of greetings, greeting all in turn

persalūt·ō -āre *vt* to salute one after another

persanctē *adv* very solemnly

persapĭ·ens -entis *adj* very wise

persapĭenter *adv* very wisely

perscĭenter *adv* very wisely, very discreetly

per·scindō -scindĕre -scĭdī -scissum *vt* to tear to pieces; to scatter (*e.g., clouds*)

perscīt·us -a -um *adj* very clever, very smart

per·scrībō -scrībĕre -scrīpsī -scrīptum *vt* to write out; to describe fully, give in detail; to record, register; to enter (*into an account book*); to make over by writing; to pay by check

perscrīptĭ·ō -ōnis *f* entry, official record; check, payment by check

perscrīpt·or -ōris *m* bookkeeper, accountant

perscrīptus *pp* of perscribo

perscrūt·ō -āre or **perscrūt·or -ārī -ātus sum** *vt* to search or examine thoroughly, scrutinize

per·sĕcō -secāre -secŭī -sectum *vt* to dissect, cut into pieces; (fig) to cut through, cut out, eliminate

persect·or -ārī -ātus sum *vt* to follow eagerly, investigate

persecūtĭ·ō -ōnis *f* prosecution, suing, lawsuit

persecūtus *pp* of persequor

per·sedĕō or **per·sĭdĕō -sedēre -sēdī -sessum** *vi* to remain seated

persegn·is -e *adj* very slow-moving, dull, tedious

per·sentĭō -sentīre -sensī -sensum *vt* to perceive clearly; to feel deeply

persentisc·ō -ĕre *vt* to detect; to feel deeply

Persephŏn·ē -ēs *f* daughter of Demeter and queen of the lower world, called Proserpina by the Romans

persĕqu·ens -entis *adj* pursuing; (with *genit*) given to the practice of

per·sĕquor -sĕquī -secūtus sum *vt* to follow persistently, follow up; to be in hot pursuit of, be on the heels of; to chase after, catch up to; to follow verbatim; to imitate, copy; to prosecute; to take vengeance on; to follow out, execute, perform; to describe, explain

Pers·ēs -ae or **Pers·eus -ĕī** *m* last king of Macedonia, conquered by Aemilius Paulus at Pydna (169 B.C.)

Pers·eus -ĕī or **-ĕos** *m* son of Jupiter and Danae, who killed Medusa and slew the sea monster who was about to devour Andromeda

Pers·eus or **Persĕ·us -a -um** *adj* of Perseus

persevēr·ans -antis *adj* persevering, persistent, relentless

persevēranter *adv* persistently, relentlessly

persevērantĭ·a -ae *f* perseverance, persistence

persevēr·ō -āre *vt* to persist in; *vi* to persist

persevēr·us -a -um *adj* very strict

Persi·a -ae or **Pers·is -ĭdis** f Persia

Persĭc·us -a -um adj Persian; (fig) luxurious, soft; of Perses (king of Macedonia); m pl Persians; f peach tree; n peach; n pl Persian history

per·sīdō -sīdĕre -sēdī -sessum vi to sink down, penetrate

persign·ō -āre vt to record in detail

persimil·is -e adj very similar; (with genit or dat) very similar to, very much like

persimpl·ex -ĭcis adj very plain, very simple

Pers·is -ĭdis adj Persian; f Persia; Persian woman

Pers·ius -iī or **-ī** m A. Persius Flaccus (famous satirist in the reign of Nero, 34-62 A.D.)

persoll·a -ae f little mask; (as term of abuse) you ugly little thing!

persōl·us -a -um adj completely alone

per·solvō -solvĕre -solvī -solūtum vt to solve, explain; to pay up; to pay (a penalty); to fulfill (a vow); to render (thanks); to offer (sacrifice); **poenas persolvere** (with dat) to suffer at the hands of

persōn·a -ae f mask; part, character; mask, pretense; personality, person, character

personāt·us -a -um adj wearing a mask, masked; under false pretenses; **pater personatus** father on the stage

persŏn·ō -āre vt to make resound, make ring; to shout; **aurem personare** to make the ear ring; vi to resound, reecho; **citharā personare** to play the zither loudly

perspectē adv intelligently

perspect·ō -āre vt to look all around

perspect·us -a -um pp of **perspicio**; adj well known, clear, evident

perspecŭl·or -ārī -ātus sum vt to examine thoroughly, explore thoroughly

persperg·ō -ĕre vt to sprinkle

perspĭc·ax -ācis adj sharp-sighted; keen, penetrating, perspicacious

perspicientĭ·a -ae f clear perception

per·spiciō -spicĕre -spexī -spectum vt to see through; to look closely at, examine, inspect, observe

perspicŭē adv clearly

perspicuit·ās -ātis f clarity

perspicŭ·us -a -um adj clear, transparent; clear, evident, perspicuous

per·sternō -sternĕre -strāvī -strātum vt to pave

perstimŭl·ō -āre vt to stimulate violently

per·stō -stāre -stĭtī -stātum vi to stand firm, hold one's ground; to keep standing; to remain unchanged, last; to be firm, persevere, persist, hold out

perstrātus pp of **persterno**

perstrĕp·ō -ĕre -ŭī -ĭtum vi to make a loud noise, make a lot of noise

per·stringō -stringĕre -strinxī -strictum vt to tie, tie up; to blunt, deaden (the senses), dazzle (the eyes), deafen (the ears); to touch lightly, graze, graze against; to glance over, touch lightly on; to belittle, slight

perstudiōsē adv enthusiastically

perstudiōs·us -a -um adj very eager, enthusiastic; (with genit) very fond of, enthusiastic about

per·suādĕō -suādēre -suāsī -suāsum vi (with dat) to persuade, convince; **sibi persuasum habere** to convince oneself, be convinced

persuāsĭ·ō -ōnis f convincing

persuastr·ix -īcis f seductress

persuāsus pp of **persuadeo**

persuās·us -ūs m persuasion

persubtīl·is -e adj very subtle, very ingenious

persult·ō -āre vt to gambol about, prance about; to scour (woods); vi to gambol, prance, run around

per·taedet -taedēre -taesum est v impers (with acc of person = subject in English and genit of thing = object in English) to be weary of, be sick and tired of, be bored with, e.g., **me negotii pertaedet** I am sick and tired of this business

per·tĕgō -tegĕre -texī -tectum vt to cover, cover up

pertempt·ō -āre vt to test thoroughly; to sound (someone) out; to consider well; (fig) to pervade, fill, overwhelm; **gaudia pertemptant pectus** joy fills (their) hearts

per·tendō -tendĕre -tendī -tensum or **-tentum** vt to press on with, continue, carry out; vi to press on, continue, persevere, persist, keep going

pertenŭ·is -e adj very thin, very slight, very small, very fine

perterebr·ō -āre vt to bore through

per·tergĕō -tergēre -tersī -tersum vt to wipe off; (of air) to brush lightly against

perterre·faciō -facĕre -fēcī -factum vt to scare the life out of

perterr·ĕō -ēre -ŭī -itum vt to frighten, terrify; (with **ab + abl**) to frighten (someone) away from

perterricrĕp·us -a -um adj terrible-sounding, rattling frightfully

per·texō -texĕre -texŭī -textum vt to bring to an end, go through with, accomplish

pertĭc·a -ae f pole, rod, staff; measuring pole; (fig) measure

pertim·escō -escĕre -ŭī vt to be alarmed at, become afraid of; vi to become very frightened, become alarmed

pertināci·ā -ae f stubbornness; perseverance, determination

pertināciter adv stubbornly, tenaciously; perseveringly, constantly

pertin·ax -ācis adj very tenacious; persevering, steadfast; unyielding, stubborn, obstinate

pertin·ĕō -ēre -uī *vi* to reach, extend; (with per + *acc*) to pervade, reach; (with ad + *acc*) a to extend to, reach; **b** to pertain to, relate to, concern; **c** to apply to, be applicable to, suit, be suitable to; **d** to tend toward, be conducive to; **e** to belong to; **quod pertinet** (with ad + *acc*) as regards, as far as concerns

perting·ō -ĕre *vi* to extend

pertolĕr·ō -āre *vt* to put up with, endure to the end

pertorqu·ĕō -ēre *vt* to twist, distort

pertractātē *adv* systematically

pertractāti·ō -ōnis *f* handling, treatment

pertract·ō -āre *vt* to handle, fondle; (fig) to handle carefully, treat systematically; to influence

per·trăhō -trahĕre -traxī -tractum *vt* to drag; to allure, lead on, decoy

pertrect- = pertract-

pertrist·is -e *adj* very sad, very gloomy

pertumultuōsē *adv* very excitedly, hysterically

per·tundō -tundĕre -tŭdī -tūsum *vt* to punch a hole through, perforate

perturbātē *adv* confusedly, in confusion

perturbāti·ō -ōnis *f* confusion, disorder; political disturbance, revolution; mental disturbance; disturbing emotion

perturbātr·ix -īcis *f* disturbing element

perturbāt·us -a -um *adj* disturbed, troubled; excited, alarmed; embarrassed

perturb·is -e *adj* downright shameful

perturb·ō -āre *vt* to throw into confusion, confuse, disturb; to embarrass; to upset, alarm

pertūs·us -a -um *pp* of **pertundō**; *adj* perforated; tattered (*clothes*)

per·ungō -ungĕre -unxī -unctum *vt* to oil well, anoint thoroughly

perurbān·us -a -um *adj* very urbane, very sophisticated; *m* sophisticate

per·ūrō -ūrĕre -ussī -ustum *vt* to burn up; to consume; to inflame, rub sore; to scorch; (of cold) to nip, bite; (fig) to fire, inflame

Perusi·a -ae *f* town in Etruria

perustus *pp* of **peruro**

perūtil·is -e *adj* very useful, very practical

per·vādō -vādĕre -vāsī -vāsum *vt* to pass through, go through; to spread throughout, pervade; to penetrate, reach; *vi* to spread, penetrate; (with ad or in + *acc*) to go as far as, spread to, reach, arrive at, penetrate; (with per + *acc*) to spread through or over

pervagāt·us -a -um *adj* widespread,

prevalent, well known; general, common

pervăg·or -ārī -ātus sum *vt* to spread through or over, pervade; *vi* to wander all over, range about; (with ad + *acc*) to spread to, extend to, be known as far as

pervăg·us -a -um *adj* wandering about

pervariē *adv* in various versions

pervast·ō -āre *vt* to devastate

pervāsus *pp* of **pervado**

per·vĕhō -vehĕre -vexī -vectum *vt* to bring, carry, convey; to bring (*e.g., supplies*) through; **pervehī** to ride, drive, sail; to reach; **in portum pervehī** to sail into port, reach port

per·vellō -vellĕre -vellī *vt* to pull hard; to pinch hard; to excite, arouse; (fig) to tear apart (*with words*), disparage

per·veniō -venīre -vēnī -ventum *vt* to come to, reach; *vi* to come up, arrive; (with ad or in + *acc*) a to arrive at, reach; **b** (fig) to attain to

pervĕn·or -ārī -ātus sum *vt* to search through (*e.g., all the city*)

perversē or **pervorsē** *adv* wrongly, perversely

perversit·ās -ātis *f* perversity, distortion

pervers·us or **pervors·us -a -um** *adj* turned the wrong way, awry, crooked; cross-eyed; (fig) crooked, wrong, perverse; spiteful, malicious

per·vertō or **per·vortō -vertĕre -vertī -versum** *vt* to overturn, upset, knock down; (fig) to abuse, misuse, undo, destroy, pervert

pervespĕrī *adv* late in the evening

pervestīgāti·ō -ōnis *f* thorough search, examining, investigation

pervestīg·ō -āre *vt* to track down, hunt down; (fig) to trace, detect

pervĕt·us -ĕris *adj* very old, ancient

pervetust·us -a -um *adj* outdated, antiquated

perviam *adv* **perviam facere** to make accessible

pervicāci·a -ae *f* persistence; stubbornness

pervicācius *adv* more obstinately, more stubbornly

pervic·ax -ācis *adj* persistent, determined; headstrong, stubborn, obstinate

pervictus *pp* of **pervinco**

per·vidĕō -vidēre -vīdī -vīsum *vt* to look over, overlook, survey; to see through; to examine, investigate; to realize

pervig·ĕō -ēre -uī *vi* to continue to thrive

pervig·il (*genit:* **-īlis**) *adj* wide awake, ever watchful

pervigilāti·ō -ōnis *f* religious vigil

pervigil·ium -iī or **-ī** *n* all-night vigil

pervigil·ō -āre *vt* to spend or pass (*nights, days*) without sleep; *vi* to stay awake all night, keep an all-night vigil

pervíl·is -e *adj* very cheap

per·vincō -vincĕre -vīcī -victum *vt* to defeat completely, completely overcome, completely get the better of; to outdo, surpass, exceed; to outbid; to convince; to prove; *vi* to win, succeed; to carry a point; (with *ut*) to succeed in, bring it about that; **non pervicit ut referrent consules** he did not succeed in having the consuls make a formal proposal

pervīsus *pp* of **pervideo**

pervi·us -a -um *adj* crossable, passable, accessible; *n* passage, thoroughfare

per·vīvō -vīvĕre -vixī *vi* to live on; **pervivere usque ad summam aetatem** to live on to a ripe old age

pervolgō see **pervulgo**

pervolit·ō -āre *vt & vi* to fly about, flit about

pervol·ō -āre *vt* to fly through or about, flit about; to dart through, pass quickly over; *vi* to fly about, flit about; (with **in** + *acc*) to fly through to, arrive at, reach

per·volō -velle -voluī *vt* to want badly, wish very much; (with *inf*) to wish very much to; (with *acc & inf*) to eagerly wish (*someone*)

pervolūt·ō -āre *vt* to turn over often, read through (*books*)

per·volvō -volvĕre -volvī -volū-tum *vt* to roll (*someone*) over; to keep reading, read through (*books*); **pervolvi** to be busy, be engaged

pervor- see **perver-**

pervulgāt·us or **pervolgāt·us -a -um** *adj* widely known, very common

pervulg·ō or **pervolg·ō -āre** *vt* to make known, make public, publicize; to frequent; **se pervulgare** to prostitute oneself, become a prostitute

pēs pedis *m* foot; foot (*measure*); foot, meter (*in verse*); leg (*of table, couch, etc.*); sail rope, sheet; **ad pedes descendere** to dismount (*in order to fight on foot*); **aequis pedibus labi** to sail on an even keel; **ante pedes** in plain view; **pede dextro, felice**, or **secundo** auspiciously; **pedem conferre** to come to close quarters; **pedem ferre** to come; to go; **pedem ponere** (with **in** + *abl*) to set foot on; **pedem referre** to go back, retreat; **pedibus** on foot; **pedibus claudere** to set to verse, put in meter; **pedibus ire in sententiam** (with *genit*) to vote in favor of the proposal of; **pedibus itur in sententiam** the proposal is put to a vote, a vote is taken on the proposal; **pedibus merere** or **pedibus mereri** to serve in the infantry; **pedibus vincere** to win a footrace; **pugna ad pedes** infantry battle; **se in pedes conjicere** to take to one's heels; **servus a pedibus** footman; **sub pedibus** under one's sway

pessímē (*superl* of **male**) *adv* very badly, most wretchedly

pessim·us -a -um (*superl* of **malus**) *adj* worst; *m* scoundrel

pessŭl·us -ī *m* bolt (*of a door*)

pessum *adv* down, to the ground, to the bottom; **pessum dare** to send to the bottom, sink, drown, ruin, destroy; **pessum ire** to go down, sink, go to ruin

pestif·er -ĕra -ĕrum *adj* pestilential; destructive, pernicious; *m* troublemaker

pestifĕrē *adv* balefully

pestíl·ens -entis *adj* pestilential, unhealthful; (*fig*) destructive, pernicious

pestilenti·a -ae *f* unhealthful atmosphere, unhealthful climate; pestilence, plague; destruction; death

pestilit·ās -ātis *f* pestilence, plague

pest·is -is *f* contagious disease, plague; destruction; death; trouble-maker, anarchist, subversive

petasāt·us -a -um *adj* wearing a hat; (*fig*) ready to travel

petasi·ō or **petās·ō -ōnis** *m* ham

petasuncŭl·us -ī *m* little ham

petās·us -ī *m* hat

petaur·um -ī *n* springboard

petess·ō or **petiss·ō -ĕre** *vt* to be eager for, pursue; **pugnam petessere** to be spoiling for a fight

petíti·ō -ōnis *f* attack, blow, thrust, aim; petition, request, application; candidacy, political campaign; claim, suit, suing; right to sue; **petitioni se dare** to become a candidate

petīt·or -ōris *m* applicant; political candidate; plaintiff

petitur·iō -ire *vi* to be eager for office

petīt·us -a -um *pp* of **peto**; *n* request, desire

petīt·us -ūs *m* (with *genit*) heading for

pet·ō -ĕre -īvī or **-iī -ītum** *vt* to make for, head for; to attack; to strive for, aim at; to demand, require, exact; to claim, sue for; to beg, desire, entreat; to look for, go in search of, search for; to run after, chase, court (*girls*); to fetch, bring, obtain, draw; to run for (*office*); to refer to, relate to

petorrīt·um -ī *n* open four-wheeled carriage

petr·a -ae *f* rock, crag

petr·ō -ōnis *m* yokel

Petrōn·ius -iī or **-ī** *m* Petronius Arbiter (*author and master of ceremonies at the court of Nero*)

petŭl·ans -antis *adj* pert, impudent, smart-alecky, petulant, forward

petulanter *adv* pertly, impudently, petulantly

petulantī·a -ae *f* pertness, impudence, forwardness; carelessness

petulc·us -a -um *adj* butting, apt to butt

pex·us -a -um *pp* of **pecto**; *adj* combed; new, still having the nap on

Phaeāc·es -um *m pl* Phaeacians (*people described in the Odyssey as living on a utopian island*)

Phaeācī·us -a -um *adj* Phaeacian; *f* Phaeacia

Phaeāc·us -a -um *adj* Phaeacian

Phaedr·a -ae *f* daughter of Minos and Pasiphae and wife of Theseus

Phaedr·us -ī *m* pupil of Socrates; freedman of Augustus and famous writer of Latin fables

Phaest·um -ī *n* town in Crete

Phaëth·ōn -ontis *m* son of Helios and Clymene who was killed trying to drive his father's chariot

Phaëthontē·us -a -um *adj* of Phaethon

Phaëthontiăd·es -um *f pl* sisters of Phaethon

phalang·ae -ārum *f pl* wooden rollers

phalangīt·ae -ārum *m pl* soldiers belonging to a Macedonian phalanx

phal·anx -angis *f* phalanx, battalion (*compact body of heavy-armed men in battle array first developed by the Macedonians*)

phalāric·a or **falāric·a -ae** *f* firebrand, fiery missile (*shot by a catapult or thrown by hand*)

phalēr·ae -ārum *f pl* military medals; medallions (*worn by horses on forehead and chest*)

phalerāt·us -a -um *adj* wearing medals, decorated; ornamental

Phalērīc·us -a -um *adj* of Phaleron

Phalēr·um -ī *n* Athenian harbor

pharĕtr·a -ae *f* quiver

pharetrāt·us -a -um *adj* wearing a quiver

pharmaceutrī·a -ae *f* witch, sorceress

pharmacopōl·a -ae *m* druggist; quack

Pharsālic·us -a -um *adj* of Pharsalus

Pharsāli·us -a -um *adj* Pharsalian; *f* district of Pharsalia

Pharsāl·os or **Pharsāl·us -ī** *f* town in Thessaly near which Caesar defeated Pompey (48 B.C.)

Phar·os or **Phar·us -ī** *m* or *f* island in the harbor at Alexandria famous for its lighthouse; lighthouse

phasel·us -ī *m* or *f* kidney bean; pinnace (*light boat*); yacht

Phāsiāc·us -a -um *adj* Colchian

Phāsiān·a -ae *f* pheasant (*female*)

Phāsiān·us -ī *m* pheasant

Phāsi·as -ădis *adj* Colchian

Phās·is -ĭdis or **-ĭdos** *m* river in Colchis

phasm·a -ătis *n* ghost

Pher·ae -ārum *f pl* city in Thessaly, the home of Admetus

Pherae·us -a -um *adj* of Pherae

phiăl·a -ae *f* saucer

Phīdĭ·ās -ae *m* famous Greek sculptor and friend of Pericles (*fl* 440 B.C.)

philēm·a -ătis *n* kiss

Philēm·ōn -ŏnis *m* pious rustic who was changed into an oak tree while his wife Baucis was changed into a linden tree

Philipp·ī -ōrum *m pl* city in Macedonia where Octavian and Antony defeated Brutus and Cassius (42 B.C.)

Philippĭc·ae -ārum *f pl* series of vitriolic speeches directed at Antony by Cicero

Philipp·us -ī *m* name of several kings of Macedon (*esp. Philip II, son of Amyntas, and father of Alexander the Great, c. 382-336 B.C.*)

philitĭ·a or **phiditĭ·a -ōrum** *n pl* communal meals at Sparta

Phil·ō or **Phil·ōn -ōnis** *m* Academic philosopher and teacher of Cicero

Philoctēt·ēs -ae *m* Greek warrior and famous archer who was abandoned by the Greek army on the island of Lemnos

philologī·a -ae *f* love of study, study of literature

philolŏg·us -a -um *adj* learned, scholarly

Philomēl·a -ae *f* daughter of Pandion and sister of Procne, who was changed into a nightingale

philosŏphē *adv* philosophically

philosŏphi·a -ae *f* philosophy

philosŏph·or -ārī *vi* to pursue philosophy

philosŏph·us -a -um *adj* philosophical; *mf* philosopher

phitr·um -ī *n* love potion

philўr·a -ae *f* inner bark of the lime tree; linden tree

phīm·us -ī *m* dice box

Phīn·eus -ěī or **-ěos** *m* king of Salmydessus in Thrace, whom the Argonauts rescued from the torments which the Harpies visited upon him

Phlegěth·ōn -ontis *m* river of fire in the lower world

Phlegethont·is -ĭdis *adj* of Phlegethon

Phlegў·ās -ae *m* king of the Lapiths and father of Ixion

Phlī·ūs -untis *f* city in N.E. Peloponnesus

phōc·a -ae or **phōc·ē -ēs** *f* seal

Phōcaĭc·us or **Phōcē·us** or **Phōci·us -a -um** *adj* & *mf* Phocian

Phōc·is -ĭdis *f* a country of Greece W. of Boeotia

Phoeb·as -ădis *f* prophetess, priestess of Apollo

Phoeb·ē -ēs *f* moon goddess, the sister of Phoebus; night

Phoebigěn·a -ae *m* son of Phoebus (*i.e., Asculapius*)

Phoeb·us -ī *m* Apollo as sun god; sun

Phoenīc·ē -ēs *f* Phoenicia

Phoenic·es -um *m pl* Phoenicians

phoenicoptĕr·us -ī *m* flamingo

Phoeniss·a -ae *f* Phoenician woman (*esp. Dido*)

phoen·ix -īcis *m* phoenix (*famous Arabian bird which was said to live 500 years and from whose ashes a young phoenix would be born*)

Phoen·ix -īcis *m* son of Amyntor and companion of Achilles

Phorc·is -īdos *f* female descendant of Phorcus; Medusa

Phorc·us -ī *m* son of Neptune and father of Medusa and the other Gorgons

Phorcȳn·is -īdis or **-īdos** *f* Medusa

Phraāt·ēs or **Phrahāt·ēs -ae** *m* king of Parthia

phrenēs·is -is *f* frenzy, delirium

phrenētic·us -a -um *adj* frenetic, frantic, delirious

Phrix·us -ī *m* son of Athamas and Nephele and brother of Helle, with whom he fled to Colchis mounted on the ram with the golden fleece

Phryg·es -um *m pl* Phrygians (*a people of Asia Minor*)

phrygi·ō -ōnis *m* embroiderer

Phrygi·us -a -um *adj* & *mf* Phrygian; Trojan; *f* Phrygia (*a country of Asia Minor*)

Phthi·a -ae *f* home of Achilles in Thessaly

Phthiōt·a or **Phthiōt·ēs -ae** *m* native of Phthia

phthis·is -is *f* consumption, tuberculosis

phy *interj* bah!

phylāc·a -ae *f* jail

phylacist·a -ae *m* jailer; overanxious creditor

phylarch·us -ī *m* tribal chief

physic·a -ae or **physic·ē -ēs** *f* physics

physic·us -a -um *adj* natural, physical, belonging to natural philosophy or physics; *m* natural philosopher, physicist, scientist; *n pl* physics

physiognōm·ōn -ŏnis *m* physiognomist

physiologi·a -ae *f* natural philosophy, natural science

piābil·is -e *adj* expiable

piăculār·is -e *adj* expiatory, atoning; *n pl* expiatory sacrifices

piăcŭl·um -ī *n* propitiatory sacrifice; victim; atonement, expiation; remedy; crime, sacrilege; punishment

piām·en -inis *n* atonement

pīc·a -ae *f* magpie

picāri·a -ae *f* place where pitch is made

picĕ·a -ae *f* pine tree

Pīc·ens -entis *adj* Picene, of Picenum

Pīcēn·us -a -um *adj* & *m* Picene; *n* district of Central Italy on the Adriatic coast

picĕ·us -a -um *adj* made of pitch; pitch-black

pict·or -ōris *m* painter

Pict·or -ōris *m* Q. Fabius Pictor (*earliest Roman historian, who wrote a history of Rome in Greek, fl 225 B.C.*)

pictūr·a -ae *f* painting, art of painting; a painting, picture; embroidery

pictūrāt·us -a -um *adj* painted; embroidered

pict·us -a -um *pp* of **pingo**; *adj* decorated, colored; tattooed; ornate (*style*); false, unreal

pīc·us -ī *m* woodpecker; griffin (*fabulous bird*)

Pīc·us -ī *m* son of Saturn and grandfather of Latinus, who was changed by Circe into a woodpecker

piē *adv* dutifully, affectionately

Pieri·a -ae *f* district in Macedonia

Piĕr·is -īdis or **-īdos** *f* daughter of Pieros; Muse; *f pl* the nine Muses

Pieri·us -a -um *adj* Pierian; poetic; musical; *f* see **Pieria**; *f pl* Muses

Piĕr·os or **Piĕr·us -ī** *m* father of the nine Muses

piĕt·ās -ātis *f* responsibility, sense of responsibility, sense of duty; devotion, piety; kindness, tenderness; loyalty, patriotism

pig·er -ra -rum *adj* reluctant, unwilling; apathetic, slow, lazy; numbing (*cold*); slow-moving, tedious, dull (*war, etc.*); backward, slow, dull (*person*)

pig·et -ēre -ŭit or **-itum est** *v impers* it irks, pains, annoys, makes regretful; (*with genit* of cause of feeling), e.g., **piget stultitiae meae** I am irked by my foolishness; (*with inf*), e.g., **illa me composuisse piget** I repent having written those verses

pigmentār·ius -iī or **-ī** *m* paint dealer

pigment·um -ī *n* pigment, paint, color; coloring, color (*of style*)

pignerāt·or -ōris *m* mortgagee

pignĕr·ō -āre *vt* to pledge, mortgage, pawn; (fig) to pledge

pignĕr·or -ārī -ātus sum *vt* to take as pledge, accept in good faith; to claim to

pign·us -ĕris or **-ŏris** *n* pledge, security, guarantee; hostage; mortgage; income from mortgages; wager, stake; (fig) pledge, assurance, proof; *n pl* children

pigrē *adv* slowly, sluggishly

pigriti·a -ae or **pigriti·ēs -ēī** *f* sluggishness, laziness

pigr·ō -āre or **pigr·or -ārī -ātus sum** *vi* to be slow, be sluggish, be lazy

pīl·a -ae *f* a mortar; pillar; pier

pīl·a -ae *f* ball; ball game; ballot (*used by jury*); **mea pila est** the ball is mine, I've won; **pilā ludere** to play ball

pīlān·us -ī *m* soldier in the third rank in battle

pīlāt·us -a -um *adj* armed with javelin

pīlent·um -ī *n* ladies' carriage

pilleāt·us -a -um *adj* wearing a felt skullcap (*as a symbol of free status*)

pilleŏl·us -ī *m* skullcap

pillĕ·um -ī *n* or **pille·us -ī** *m* felt cap or hat (*worn by Romans at festivals, esp. at the Saturnalia, and given to a slave when freed as a symbol of his freedom*); freedom, liberty

pilōs·us -a -um *adj* hairy

pīl·um -ī *n* javelin

pīl·us -ī *m* maniple or company of the triarii, company of veteran reserves; **primī pilī centuriō** chief centurion of a legion (*centurion of the first century of the triarii*); **primus pilus** chief centurion of the triarii and therefore of the legion

pīl·us -ī *m* hair; (fig) whit; **non pilī facere** to care not a whit for

Pimpl·a -ae *f* town in Pieria sacred to the Muses

Pimplē·a -ae or **Pimplē·is -ĭdis** *f* Muse

Pindaric·us -a -um *adj* Pindaric

Pindăr·us -ī *m* Pindar (*famous lyric poet from Thebes in Boeotia, 518-438 B.C.*)

Pind·us -ī *m* mountain range separating Thessaly from Epirus

pīnēt·um -ī *n* pine forest

pīnē·us -a -um *adj* pine, of pine

pingō pingĕre pinxī pictum *vt* to draw, paint; to embroider; to depict, represent, portray; to stain, color; to decorate; to color, embellish (*style*)

pingu·e -is *n* fat, grease

pinguescō -ĕre *vi* to get fat; to become fertile

pingu·is -e *adj* fat; oily, greasy; juicy; rich, fertile; thick, dense; stupid, dull; quiet, comfortable

pīnif·er -ĕra -ĕrum *adj* pine-producing, pine-covered

pīnig·er -ĕra -ĕrum *adj* pine-producing, pine-covered

pinn·a -ae *f* feather; wing; flight; fin; feathered arrow; pinnacle, battlement

pinnāt·us -a -um *adj* feathered, winged

pinnig·er -ĕra -ĕrum *adj* winged; having fins, finny

pinnip·ēs -ēdis *adj* wing-footed

pinnirăp·us -ī *m* crest-snatcher (*gladiator who tried to get his opponent's helmet crest*)

pinnŭl·a -ae *f* little wing

pīnotēr·ēs -ae *m* hermit crab

pins·ō -ĕre -ī (or **-ŭī**) **-um** (or **-ĭtum**) *vt* to pound

pīn·us -ūs or **-ī** *f* pine tree, fir tree; pine forest; ship; torch; wreath of pine

pi·ō -āre *vt* to appease by sacrifice, propitiate; to honor with religious rites, worship; to purify with religious rites; to atone for, expiate; to avert

pip·er -ĕris *n* pepper

pīpil·ō -āre *vi* to chirp

pīpŭl·um -ī *n* or **pīpŭl·us -ī** *m* shrieking, yelling

Pīrae·eus or **Pīrae·us -ī** *m* or **Pīrae·a -ōrum** *n pl* principal harbor of Athens

pīrāt·a -ae *m* pirate

pīrātic·us -a -um *adj* pirate; *f* piracy; **pirāticam facere** to practice piracy

Pīrēn·ē -ēs *f* fountain on the citadel of Corinth near which Bellerophon caught Pegasus

Pīrithŏ·us -ī *m* son of Ixion and king of the Lapiths

pir·um -ī *n* pear

pir·us -ī *f* pear tree

Pīs·a -ae *f* of **Pīs·ae -ārum** *f pl* Pisa (*city in Elis on the Alpheus River near which the Olympic games were held*)

Pīs·ae -ārum *f pl* Pisa (*ancient city of N. Etruria*)

Pīsae·us -a -um *adj* of Pisa; *f* Hippodamia

piscārĭ·us -a -um *adj* fish, of fishing or fish; **forum piscārium** fish market

piscāt·or -ōris *m* fisherman; fishmonger

piscātōrĭ·us -a -um *adj* fishing; fish

piscāt·us -ūs *m* fishing; fish; (fig) good haul

piscicŭl·us -ī *m* little fish

piscīn·a -ae *f* fish pond; swimming pool

piscīnār·ĭus -ĭī or **-ī** *m* person fond of swimming pools or fish ponds

pisc·is -is *m* fish

Pisc·is -is *m* Pisces (*constellation*)

pisc·or -ārī -ātus sum *vi* to fish

piscōs·us -a -um *adj* full of fish

pisculent·us -a -um *adj* well stocked with fish

Pīsistratĭd·ae -ārum *m pl* sons of Pisistratus (*i.e., Hippias and Hipparchus*)

Pīsistrăt·us -ī *m* enlightened tyrant of Athens (560-527 B.C.)

pistill·um -ī *n* pestle

pist·or -ōris *m* miller; baker

pistrill·a -ae *f* little mill

pistrīn·um -ī *n* flour mill; bakery; drudgery

pistr·is -is or **pistr·ix -īcis** *f* sea monster (*of any kind*); whale, shark; swift ship

pithēc·ium -ĭī or **-ī** *n* little ape

Pitth·eus -ĕī or **-ĕos** *m* king of Troezen and father of Aethra, the mother of Theseus

pītuīt·a -ae *f* phlegm; rheum; head cold

pītuītōs·us -a -um *adj* full of phlegm, phlegmatic

pi·us -a -um *adj* conscientious; god-fearing, godly, holy; fatherly, motherly, brotherly, sisterly; affectionate; patriotic; good; sacred, holy (*objects connected with religion*)

pix picis *f* pitch; *f pl* chunks of pitch

plăcābĭl·is -e *adj* easily appeased; pacifying, appeasing

plăcābĭlit·ās -ātis *f* readiness to forgive, conciliatory disposition plācām·en -ĭnis n means of appeasing, peace offering

plācāment·um -ī n means of appeasing, peace offering

plācātē adv calmly, quietly

plācātĭ·ō -ōnis f pacifying, propitiating

plācāt·us -a -um adj calm, quiet; appeased, reconciled

plac·ens -entis adj pleasing

placent·a -ae f cake

plac·ĕō -ēre -ŭī -ĭtum vi (with dat) to please, satisfy, give pleasure to, be acceptable to; **sibi placere** to be satisfied with oneself, pride oneself; v impers it seems right, seems proper; it is settled, is agreed; it is resolved, is decided; **eis placitum est ut considerent** they decided to consider; **senatui placuit** the senate decreed

placĭdē adv calmly, placidly, gently, quietly

placĭd·us -a -um adj calm, placid, gentle, quiet

placĭt·ō -āre vi to be very pleasing

placĭt·us -a -um adj pleasing, acceptable; agreed upon; n principle, belief, tenet; **ultra placitum laudare** to praise excessively

plāc·ō -āre vt to calm, quiet; to appease; to reconcile

plāg·a -ae f blow; wound; (fig) blow

plāg·a -ae f region, tract, zone; hunting net; mesh of a net; curtain; (fig) trap

plagiār·ĭus -ĭī or -ī n plunderer; kidnapper; plagiarist

plāgĭg·er -ĕra -ĕrum adj covered with welts

plāgigerŭl·us -a -um adj covered with welts

plāgipatĭd·a -ae m whipping boy

plāgōs·us -a -um adj quick to use the rod

plagŭl·a -ae f curtain

plagūsĭ·a -ae f a fish

planctus pp of plango

planct·us -ūs m beating

plānē adv clearly, distinctly; legibly; completely, entirely, quite; certainly, to be sure

plangō plangĕre planxī planctum vt to strike, beat; to beat (breast, head as sigh of grief); to lament, bewail; vi to wail, lament, (fig) to wring the hands

plang·or -ōris m striking, beating; beating of the breast; wailing

plānilŏqu·os -a -om adj speaking clearly

plānĭp·ēs -ĕdis m ballet dancer

plānĭt·ās -ātis f distinctness

plānĭtĭ·ēs -ēī or plānĭtĭ·a -ae f flat surface, level ground, plain

plant·a -ae f sprout, shoot; young plant, slip; sole (of the foot)

plantār·ĭa -ĭum n pl slips; young trees; hair

plān·us -a -um adj flat, level, even; plai., clear; n level ground, plain

plan·us -ī m tramp; imposter, cheat

plasm·a -ătis n phoney accent

Platae·ae -ārum f pl Plataea (town in Boeotia near which the Greeks defeated the Persians in 479 B.C.)

platalĕ·a -ae f waterfowl, spoonbill

platăn·us -ī or -ūs f plane tree

platē·a or platĕ·a -ae f street

Plat·ō or Plat·ōn -ōnis m Plato (famous Greek philosopher, 429-348 B.C.)

Platōnĭc·us -a -um adj Platonic; m pl Platonists

plaudō plaudĕre plausī plausum vt to slap, clap, beat; vi to flap, beat, clap; (with dat) to applaud, approve of; **alis plaudere** to flap the wings; **manibus plaudere** to clap the hands

plausibĭl·is -e adj deserving applause

plaus·or -ōris m applauder

plaustr·um -ī n wagon, cart

Plaustr·um -ī n the Great Bear (constellation)

plausus pp of plaudo

plaus·us -ūs m clapping, flapping; clapping of the hands; applause

Plaut·us -ī m T. Maccius Plautus (famous Roman writer of comedies, born at Sarsina in Umbria, c. 254-184 B.C.)

plēbēcŭl·a -ae f rabble

plēbēĭ·us or plēbēj·us -a -um adj plebeian, of the common people; common, low, vulgar

plēbĭcŏl·a -ae m democrat; demagogue

plēbiscīt·um -ī n decree of the commons

pleb·s -is or plēb·ēs -ēī or -ī f plebeians, common people; the masses, proletariat

plectĭl·is -e adj plaited

plectō plectĕre plexī or plexŭī plexum vt to plait, braid

plect·ō -ĕre vt to punish

Plēĭ·as -ădis f Pleiad; f pl Pleiades (seven daughters of Atlas and Pleione, who were placed among the stars)

Plēĭŏn·ē -ēs f daughter of Oceanus and Tethys, wife of Atlas, and mother of the Pleiades

plēnē adv fully, completely

plēn·us -a -um adj full; stout, plump; pregnant; filled, satisfied; full, packed; full, strong, loud (voice); full-length, unabridged, uncontracted; abundant, plentiful; advanced, mature (years); complete, finished

plērumque adv generally, mostly; often, frequently

plēr·usque -ăque -umque adj a very great part of, the greater part of, most; very many, a good many; n the greatest part

plex·us -a -um pp of plecto; adj plaited

plicātr·ix -īcis f woman who folds clothes, folder

plic·ō -āre -āvī or -ŭī -ātum or -ĭtum *vt* to fold, wind, coil up

Plīn·ius -iī or -ī *m* C. Plinius Secundus (*author of a work on natural history, who perished in the eruption of Vesuvius in 79 A.D.*); C. Plinius Caecilius (*his nephew, author of Letters and a Panegyric to Trajan, 62 A.D.-c. 114 A.D.*)

plōrābil·is -e *adj* deplorable

plōrāt·or -ōris *m* mourner

plōrāt·us -ūs *m* wailing, wail

plōr·ō -āre *vt* to cry over; *vi* to cry aloud, wail

plostell·um -ī *n* cart

ploxĕm·um -ī *n* wagon frame

pluit pluĕre pluit *vt* it is raining (*stones, blood, etc.*); *vi* it is raining; (*with abl*) it is raining (*stones, etc.*)

plūm·a -ae *f* down, soft feather; (*collectively*) feathers, down

plūmātil·e -is *n* dress embroidered with feathers

plūmāt·us -a -um *adj* covered with feathers

plumbĕ·us -a -um *adj* lead, of lead; leaden, oppressive (*weather*); dull, stupid

plumb·um -ī *n* lead; bullet; pipe; ruler (*for drawing lines*); **plumbum album** tin

plūmĕ·us -a -um *adj* downy, filled with down; like feathers

plūmip·ēs -ĕdis *adj* with feathered feet

plūmōs·us -a -um *adj* downy, feathered

plūrimum *adv* very much, especially, commonly, generally, most

plūrim·us -a -um (*superl of multus*) *adj* many a; most; very much; very many; very great, very intense; **plurimam salutem dare** to send warmest greetings; *n* a great deal; **plurimi facere** to think very highly of, think a great deal of; **quam plurimum** as much as possible

plūs *adv* more; **multo plus** much more; **paulo plus** a little more

plūs plūris (*comp of multus*) *adj* more; *n* more; too much; **et, quod plus est, Romani estis** and what is more, you are Romans; **plus animi** more courage; **plus nimio** much too much; **plus plusque** more and more; **uno viro plus habere** to have one man too much; **pluris esse** (*genit* of value) to be of more value, of a higher price, worth more, be higher, be dearer; *n pl* more words; **quid plura?** why should I say more?, in short

pluscŭl·us -a -um *adj* a little more, somewhat more; *n* a little more; **plusculum negoti** a little more business

plutĕ·us -ī *m* or **plutĕ·um** -ī *n* (*mil*) movable mantlet or shed used to protect soldiers in siege work; parapet; couch, dining couch; book shelf; book case; board, slab

Plūt·ō or **Plūt·ōn** -ōnis *m* king of the lower world, husband of Proserpina, and brother of Jupiter and Neptune

pluvi·a -ae *f* rain

pluviāl·is -e *adj* rain, of rain, rainy; **fungi pluviales** mushrooms brought out by the rain

pluvi·us -a -um *adj* rain, of rain, rainy; **pluvia aqua** rain water; **pluvius arcus** rainbow; *f* see **pluvia**

pōcill·um -ī *n* small drinking cup

pōcŭl·um -ī *n* drinking cup; drink, draught; **poculum ducere** or **exhaurire** to drain a cup

podăgr·a -ae *f* arthritis

podagrōs·us -a -um *adj* arthritic

pōd·ex -icis *m* anus, rectum

pod·ium -iī or -ī *n* balcony; box seat (*for the emperor*)

Poeantiăd·ēs -ae *m* Philoctetes

Poe·ās -antis *m* father of Philoctetes

poēm·a -ătis *n* poem

poēmat·ium -iī or -ī *n* short poem

poen·a -ae *f* compensation, recompense, retribution, satisfaction, penalty, fine, punishment; hardship, loss, pain; (*in games*) penalty; **poenam** or **poenas dare, dependere, pendere, persolvere, reddere, solvere, suscipere,** or **sufferre** to pay the penalty, make restitution, give satisfaction; **poenam** or **poenas capere, persequi, petere, repetere,** or **reposcere** to exact a penalty, demand satisfaction; **poena mortis** capital punishment, death penalty

poeniō see **punio**

Poen·us -a -um *adj & m* Carthaginian

poēs·is -is *f* art of poetry; poetry, poems

poēt·a -ae *m* maker, contriver; poet

poētic·a -ae or **poētic·ē** -ēs *f* art of poetry; poetics

poēticē *adv* poetically

poētic·us -a -um *adj* poetic, poetical; *f* see **poetica**

poētri·a -ae *f* poetess

poētr·is -īdis or -īdos *f* poetess

pol *interj* by Pollux!; Lord!

polent·a -ae *f* pearl barley

polentārī·us -a -um *adj* caused by eating barley

pol·iō -īre -īvī or -iī -ītum *vt* to polish, smooth; (*fig*) to polish, improve, perfect

politē *adv* in a polished manner, with taste, smoothly, elegantly

polītic·us -a -um *adj* political

polīt·us -a -um *adj* polished, smooth; (*fig*) polished, smooth, smooth-spoken, smooth-mannered, refined, cultivated

poll·en -inis *n* or **poll·is** -inis *m* or *f* flour

poll·ens -entis *adj* strong, powerful, thriving, able

pollentī·a -ae *f* might, power

poll·ĕŏ -ēre *vi* to be strong, be powerful; to be capable, be able; (of medicines) to be powerful, be efficacious; to have influence; **in re publica plurimum pollere** to have tremendous influence in politics

poll·ex -ĭcis *m* thumb; big toe

pollic·ĕor -ērī -ĭtus sum *vt* to promise

pollicitātĭ·ō -ōnis *f* promise

pollicĭt·or -ārī -ātus sum *vt* to keep promising

pollicĭt·us -a -um *pp* of **polliceor;** *n* promise

pollinārĭ·us -a -um *adj* flour, for flour

pollinct·or -ōris *m* embalmer

pol·lingō -lingĕre -linxī -linctum *vt* to lay out, embalm

Pollĭ·ō -ōnis *m* C. Asinius Pollio (*distinguished orator, poet, historian, patron of literature, and statesman,* 76 B.C.-4 A.D.)

poll·is -ĭnis *m* or *f* flour

pol·lŭcĕŏ -lŭcēre -luxī -luctum *vt* to offer, offer up as sacrifice; to serve (*meal*); to entertain

pollūcibilĭter *adv* sumptuously, in grand style

polluctūr·a -ae *f* sumptuous dinner

polluct·us -a -um *pp* of **polluceo;** *n* offering, sacrificial meal

pol·lŭŏ -lŭĕre -luī -lūtum *vt* to pollute, defile, soil, mess up; to defile, violate

Poll·ux or **Poll·ūcēs -ūcis** *m* son of Tyndareus and Leda, twin brother of Castor, and famous boxer

pol·us -ī *m* end of an axis, pole; North Pole; **polus australis** South Pole

Polyb·ĭus -ĭī or **-ī** *m* Greek historian and friend of Scipio Aemilianus (*c.* 203-120 B.C.)

Polydăm·ās -antis *m* son of Panthus and friend of Hector

Polydōr·us -ī *m* son of Priam and Hecuba, murdered by Polymestor the king of Thrace

Polyhymnĭ·a -ae *f* one of the nine Muses

Polymest·ōr -ōris *m* king of the Thracian Chersonese, husband of Ilione the daughter of Priam

Polynīc·ēs -is *m* son of Oedipus and Jocasta and brother of Eteocles

Polyphēm·us -ī *m* son of Neptune and one of the Cyclops of Sicily

pōlyp·us -ī *m* polyp (*sea animal; tumor*)

Polyxĕn·a -ae *f* daughter of Priam whom Pyrrhus, the son of Achilles, sacrificed at his father's tomb

pōmārĭ·us -a -um *adj* fruit, of fruit trees; *m* fruit vendor; *n* orchard

pōmerīdĭān·us -a -um *adj* afternoon

pōmer·ĭum or **pōmoer·ĭum -ĭī** or **-ī** *n* space kept free of buildings inside and outside a city wall

pōmif·er -ĕra -ĕrum *adj* fruit-bearing

pōmōs·us -a -um *adj* loaded with fruit

pomp·a -ae *f* solemn or religious procession; retinue; pomp, ostentation

Pompēĭ·us or **Pompēj·us -ī** *m* Pompey the Great (*Roman general and statesman,* 106-48 B.C.)

Pompējān·us -a -um *adj* Pompeian; *m pl* inhabitants of Pompeii; soldiers or followers of Pompey

Pompēj·ī -ōrum *m pl* city south of Naples, destroyed by the eruption of Vesuvius in 79 A.D.

Pompil·ĭus -ĭī or **-ī** *m* Numa Pompilius (*second king of Rome and traditional founder of Roman state religion*)

Pomptīn·us -a -um *adj* Pomptine; **Pomptinae paludes** Pomptine Marshes in Latium

pōm·um -ī *n* fruit; fruit tree

pōm·us -ī *f* fruit tree

pondĕr·ō -āre *vt* to weigh; to consider, ponder

ponderōs·us -a -um *adj* weighty, heavy; full of meaning

pondō *adv* in weight

pondō (*indecl*) *n* pound, pounds; **auri quinque pondo** five pounds of gold

pond·us -ĕris *n* weight; mass; burden; importance; stability of character; *n pl* balance, equilibrium

pōne *adv* behind, after, back; *prep* (with *acc*) behind

pōnō pōnĕre posŭī posĭtum or **postum** *vt* to put, place, put down, set down, set, fix, deposit; to lay aside, lay down; to lay out, spend; to stake; to place, station, post; to set up, erect, build, found; to regard, consider; to cite, assert; to suppose, assume; to lay out for burial; to smooth, calm; to arrange, smooth (*hair*); *vi* to abate, calm down

pons pontis *m* bridge; gangway; drawbridge; deck

pontĭcŭl·us -ī *m* small bridge

pontĭf·ex -ĭcis *m* pontiff, pontifex, priest (*one of a board of fifteen*); **pontifex maximus** chief pontiff

pontĭfĭcāl·is -e *adj* pontifical

pontĭfĭcāt·us -ūs *m* pontificate

pontĭfĭc·us -a -um *adj* pontifical

pont·ō -ōnis *m* ferry

pont·us -ī *m* sea; sea water

Pont·us -ī *m* Euxine or Black Sea; region around the Black Sea; kingdom of Mithridates between Bithynia and Armenia, subsequently a Roman province

pop·a -ae *m* priest's assistant (*attendant who slew the victim*)

popān·um -ī *n* sacrificial cake

popell·us -ī *m* rabble, mob

popīn·a -ae *f* restaurant; food sold at a restaurant

popīn·ō -ōnis *m* diner at a restaurant

popl·es -ĭtis *m* hollow of the knee;

knee; **duplicato poplite** on bended knee; **contento poplite** with a stiff knee

Pōplicŏla see **Publicola**

poppysm·a -ătis n clicking with the tongue (as sign of approval)

populābĭl·is -e adj destructible

populābund·us -a -um adj ravaging, laying waste

populār·ēs -ĭum m pl people's party, democrats

populār·ĭa -ĭum n pl general-admission seats

populār·is -e adj of the people, by the people, for the people, people's, popular; approved by the people, popular; favoring the people, democratic; demagogic; of the same country, native; common, coarse

populār·is -is m or f fellow countryman; party member; fellow member, associate; (with genit) partner or associate in

populārĭt·ās -ātis f fellow citizenship; popularity

populārĭter adv like the people; like a demagogue; **populariter loqui** to use slang

populātĭ·ō -ōnis f ravaging, devastation

populāt·or -ōris m ravager, destroyer

populāt·us -ūs m devastation

pōpulĕ·us -a -um adj of poplars, poplar

pōpulĭf·er -ĕra -ĕrum adj filled with poplar trees

pōpuln·us -a -um adj of poplars, poplar

popŭl·ō -āre or **popŭl·or -ārī -ātus sum** vt to ravage, devastate, lay waste; (fig) to pillage, ruin, destroy, spoil

popŭl·us -ī m people (as a political community), nation; people, crowd, public; citizens (as opposed to soldiers), civilians; region, district

pōpul·us -ī f poplar tree

porc·a -ae f sow

porcell·a -ae f little sow

porcell·us -ī m little hog

porcīnār·ius -ĭī or **-ī** m pork seller

porcīn·us -a -um adj hog's, pig's; f pork

Porc·ius -ĭī or **-ī** m M. Porcius Cato the Censor (235-149 B.C.); M. Porcius Cato Uticensis (95-46 B.C.)

porcŭl·a or **porculēn·a -ae** f little sow

porcŭl·us -ī m little pig

porc·us -ī m pig, hog

porgō see **porrigo**

Porphyr·iōn -ōnis m a Giant

porrect·a -ōrum n pl offering; **inter caesa et porrecta** (fig) at the eleventh hour

porrectĭ·ō -ōnis f extending, stretching out

porrect·us -a -um pp of **porrigo**; adj stretched out, extended, extensive, long; protracted (delay); laid out, dead; (fig) wide-spread

porric·ĭō -ĕre vt to offer up, make an offering of

por·rĭgō or **porg·ō -rigĕre -rexī -rectum** vt to reach out, stretch out, extend; to offer, present, hand; to lengthen (a syllable); **se porrigere** to extend

porrig·ō -ĭnis f dandruff

porrō adv forwards, farther on, on; far off, at a distance; long ago; in the future, hereafter; again, in turn; next, furthermore, moreover, on the other hand

porr·um -ī n leek; chive

Porsenn·a or **Porsēn·a** or **Porsinn·a -ae** m king of Clusium in Etruria who sided with Tarquin in a war against Rome

port·a -ae f city gate; gate; entrance; outlet; camp gate (of which there were always four)

portātĭ·ō -ōnis f carrying, conveyance

por·tendō -tendĕre -tendī -tentum vt to indicate, foretell, portend, predict

portentĭfĭc·us -a -um adj monstrous, abnormal

portentōs·us -a -um adj monstrous, abnormal, unnatural, portentous

portent·um -ī n portent, omen, sign; monstrosity, monster; fantasy, far-fetched fiction; (as term of contempt) monster, demon

portentus pp of **portendo**

porthm·eus -ĕī or **-ĕos** m ferryman (i.e., Charon, who piloted the ferry across the Styx)

portĭcŭl·a -ae f small portico

portĭc·us -ūs f colonnade, portico; (mil) gallery (formed by placing vineae end to end); Stoicism

portĭ·ō -ōnis f portion, share; ratio, portion; instalment, payment; **pro portione** proportionally, relatively

portiscŭl·us -ī m gavel

portĭt·or -ōris m customs officer; ferryman, boatman

port·ō -āre vt to carry; to bring

portōr·ium -ĭī or **-ī** n port duty, customs duty; tax (on peddlers)

portŭl·a -ae f small gate

Portūn·us -ī m tutelary deity of harbors

portuōs·us -a -um adj having good harbors

port·us -ūs m port, harbor; haven, refuge; mouth of a river

pōsc·a -ae f sour drink

poscō poscĕre poposcī vt to ask, request, beg, demand; (of things) to require, demand, need, call for, make necessary; (with **ab** + abl) to ask for (something) from, demand (something) of; (with double acc) to demand (something) of, ask (someone) for

Posīdōn·ius -ĭī or **-ī** m Stoic philosopher at Rhodes, teacher of Cicero

positĭ·ō -ōnis f putting, placing, setting; position, posture; situation

posit·or -ōris m builder

positūr·a -ae f posture; formation

posit·us -a -um pp of **pono**; adj situated, located

posit·us -ūs m position; arrangement

possessi·ō -ōnis f possession; getting possession, occupation; possession, estate

possessiuncŭl·a -ae f small estate

possess·or -ōris m possessor, occupant; (law) defendant

possibil·is -e adj possible

pos·sīdĕō -sīdēre -sēdī -sessum vt to possess, occupy; to have, own; to dwell in, live in; (fig) to take hold of

pos·sīdo -sīdĕre -sēdī -sessum vt to take possession of, occupy, seize

possum posse potŭī vi to be able; **multum (plus, plurimum) posse** to have much (more, very great) influence; **non possum quin exclamem** I can't help exclaiming; **quantum** or **ut fieri potest** as far as is possible

post adv (of place) behind, back, backwards; (of time) later, afterwards; (of order) next; **aliquanto post** somewhat later; **multis post annis** many years later; prep (with acc) (of place) behind; (of time) after, since

posteā adv afterwards, after this, after that, hereafter, thereafter

posteāquam conj after

posterī·or -us adj later, next, following; latter, posterior; inferior, worse; hind

posterit·ās -ātis f the future, afterages, posterity, later generations; offspring (of animals); **in posteritatem** in the future

posterĭus adv later, at a later date

poster·us -a -um adj following, ensuing, next, subsequent, future; m pl future generations, posterity, descendants; n future time; next day; consequence; **in posterum** till the next day; for the future

post·fĕrō -ferre vt to put after; to esteem less; to sacrifice

postgenit·us -a -um adj born later; m pl later generations

posthab·ĕō -ēre -ŭī -ĭtum vt to consider of secondary importance; to slight, neglect; (with dat) to think (something) less important than

posthāc adv hereafter, in the future

posthinc or **post hinc** adv from here, from this place, next

posthōc or **post hōc** adv after this, afterwards

postĭbī adv afterwards, then

postĭcŭl·um -ī n small building in the rear

postĭc·us -a -um adj hind, back, rear; n back door

postĭdeā adv afterwards, after that

postilēn·a -ae f crupper; buttocks

postillā adv afterwards

post·is -is m door post; door; m pl double doors

postlīmin·ium -iī or **-ī** n right to return home and resume one's former rank and privileges, right of recovery; **postliminio** by the right of recovery

postmerīdiān·us -a -um adj afternoon

postmŏdo or **postmŏdum** adv after a bit, a little later, afterwards

postpart·or -ōris m successor, heir

post·pōnō -pōnĕre -posŭī -positum or **-postum** vt to consider of secondary importance; to neglect, disregard; (with dat) to consider (something) of less importance than, set (something) aside in favor of

postprincipĭ·a -ōrum n pl sequel

postpŭt·ō -āre vt to consider of secondary importance; (with **prae +** abl) to consider (something) less important than

postquam conj after, when

postrēmō adv at last, finally; **primo ... deinde ... postremo** first ... then ... finally

postrēmum adv for the last time, last of all

postrēm·us -a -um (superl of **posterus**) adj last, last in line, rear; lowest, worst

postrīdiē adv on the day after, on the following day; **postridie mane** the next morning; prep (with genit), e.g., **postridie ejus diei** on the day after that; (with acc), e.g., **postridie ludos** on the day after the games

postrīdŭō adv on the day after

postscaen·ium -iī or **-ī** n backstage

post·scrībō -scrībĕre -scripsī scriptum vt (with dat) to add (e.g., a name) to; **Tiberi nomen suo postscribere** to add the name of Tiberius to his own name

postulāt·a -ōrum n pl demands, claims, requests

postulātĭ·ō -ōnis f demand, request, desire; complaint; (law) application for permission to present a claim

postulāt·us -ūs m claim, suit

postŭl·ō -āre vt to demand, claim; to arraign, prosecute; to apply for (a writ from the praetor to prosecute)

postŭm·us -a -um adj last, latest-born

postus pp of **pono**

pōtātĭ·ō -ōnis f drinking, drinking party

pōtāt·or -ōris m drinker

pot·ens -entis adj capable; mighty, powerful, strong; efficacious, potent; fit, capable, equal; influential; (with genit) a capable of, equal to, fit for; **b** having power over; **c** presiding over; **d** having obtained (one's wish); **e** having carried out (an order)

potentāt·us **-ūs** *m* political power, rule, dominion

potenter *adv* powerfully, mightily, effectually, vigorously; according to one's ability

potenti·a **-ae** *f* force, power; political power (*esp. unconstitutional power*)

poter·ium **-iī** or **-ī** *n* goblet

potest·ās **-ātis** *f* power, ability, capacity; efficacy, force; public authority, rule, power, sway, dominion, sovereignty, empire; rule; magisterial power, magistracy, office; possibility, opportunity, permission; person in office, magistrate, ruler; property, quality

potin or **potin'** = **potisne** can you?, are you able?

pōti·ō **-ōnis** *f* drinking; drink, draught; magic potion

pot·ior **-īrī** **-ītus sum** *vt* to acquire, get possession of; *vi* (with *genit* or *abl*) to acquire, get possession of, become master of, get hold of, get

poti·or **-us** (*comp of* **potis**) *adj* better, preferable, superior; more important

potis or **pote** (*indecl*) *adj* able, capable; possible

potissimum *adv* chiefly, especially, eminently

potissim·us **-a** **-um** *adj* chief, principal, most important

potius *adv* rather, more, by preference; **potius quam** more than, rather than

pōt·ō **-āre** *vt* to drink; to absorb

pōt·or **-ōris** *m* drinker

pōtr·ix **-īcis** *f* drinker (*female*)

pōtulent·us **-a** **-um** *adj* drinkable; *n pl* drinks

pōt·us **-a** **-um** *adj* drunk

pōt·us **-ūs** *m* drink

prae *adv* before, in front; in preference; *prep* (with *abl*) before, in front of; compared with, in comparison with; in view of; because of; by reason of, on account of, through; **prae manu** at hand; **prae se** publicly, openly, plainly; **prae se ferre** to display, manifest, exhibit, profess

praeacū·ō **-ěre** *vt* to sharpen to a point

praeacūt·us **-a** **-um** *adj* pointed

praealt·us **-a** **-um** *adj* very high; very deep

praeb·ěō **-ēre** **-uī** **-ĭtum** *vt* to hold out, offer, present; to supply, give; to exhibit, represent, show; to give up, yield, surrender; to cause, occasion; to permit, allow; **se praebere** to show oneself, behave

praebĭb·ō **-ěre** **-ī** *vt* (with *dat*) to drink (*e.g., a toast*) to

praebĭt·or **-ōris** *m* supplier

praecalĭd·us **-a** **-um** *adj* very warm, hot

praecantr·ix **-īcis** *f* witch, enchantress

praecān·us **-a** **-um** *adj* prematurely grey

prae·cavěō **-cavēre** **-cāvī** **-cautum** *vt* to guard against, try to avoid; *vi* to take precautions, be on one's guard; (with *dat*) to look out for, look after; (with *abl*) to guard against, be on one's guard against

prae·cēdō **-cēděre** **-cessī** **-cessum** *vt* to precede, go out before, lead; to surpass, excel; *vi* to excel, be superior; (with *dat*) to excel, be superior to

praecell·ens **-entis** *adj* superior, excellent, preeminent

praecell·ō **-ěre** *vt* to surpass, outdo; *vi* to distinguish oneself, excel; (with *dat*) to rule over

praecels·us **-a** **-um** *adj* towering

praecentī·ō **-ōnis** *f* musical prelude (*before a sacrifice*)

praecent·ō **-āre** *vi* (with *dat*) to sing to

praecentus *pp of* **praecino**

praec·eps **-ipĭtis** *adj* headfirst; downhill, steep, precipitous; sinking (*sun*); swift, rushing, violent; hasty, rash, inconsiderate; dangerous; *n* edge of a cliff, cliff, precipice; danger, critical situation

praeceps *adv* headfirst

praeceptī·ō **-ōnis** *f* preconception; precept, rule; priority

praecept·or **-ōris** *m* or **praeceptr·ix** **-īcis** *f* teacher, preceptor

praecept·um **-ī** *n* rule, maxim; order, command, direction

prae·cerpō **-cerpěre** **-cerpsī** **-cerptum** *vt* to pick or gather before time; (with *dat*) (fig) to snatch away from

prae·cīdō **-cīděre** **-cīdī** **-cīsum** *vt* to lop off, cut short; to cut, cut through; to damage, mutilate; to break off, finish abruptly, end suddenly (*a speech, etc.*); to end, destroy (*hopes, etc.*); to refuse, decline

prae·cingō **-cingěre** **-cinxī** **-cinctum** *vt* to gird; to surround, ring; to dress; **ense cingi** to wear a sword; **male cinctus** improperly dressed; **recte cinctus** properly dressed

prae·cĭnō **-ciněre** **-cinuī** **-centum** *vt* to predict; (with *dat*) to predict (*something*) to; *vi* to make predictions; (with *dat*) to sing or play before or at (*e.g., dinner, sacrifice*)

prae·cipĭō **-cipěre** **-cēpī** **-ceptum** *vt* to take or receive in advance; to grasp beforehand, anticipate; to teach, instruct, direct, warn; to prescribe; **animo praecipere** or **cogitatione praecipere** to imagine beforehand, reckon on, anticipate, expect; **oculis praecipere** to see beforehand, get a preview of; **opinione praecipere** to suspect in advance; **pecuniam mutuam praecipere** to get an advance loan

praecipitanter *adv* at a high speed

praecipĭt·ō **-āre** *vt* to throw down

head first; to hasten, hurry, precipitate; **se praecipitare** to throw oneself down, throw oneself down headfirst, jump down, dive; to sink; *vi* to rush headfirst, rush at top speed, rush thoughtlessly; to fall, sink; to be ruined

praecipŭē *adv* especially, chiefly

praecipŭ·us -a -um *adj* special, peculiar, particular; chief, principal; distinguished, excellent, extraordinary; *n* excellence, superiority; *n pl* outstanding or important elements; **praecipua rerum** highlights

praecīsē *adv* briefly, concisely; absolutely

praecīs·us -a -um *pp* of **praecido**; *adj* abrupt, precipitous; rugged, rough; brief, abrupt (*speech*)

praeclārē *adv* very clearly; excellently; (to express agreement) very good, splendid

praeclār·us -a -um *adj* very clear; very nice; splendid, noble, distinguished, excellent; famous, distinguished; notorious

prae-clūdŏ -clūdĕre -clūsī -clūsum *vt* to shut, shut off, obstruct; to hinder, stop, impede; **portas consuli praecludere** to shut the gates on the consul, shut the gates in the consul's face; **vocem praecludere alicui** to shut someone up, to hush someone up

praec·ō -ōnis *m* crier, herald; auctioneer; (fig) panygyrist

precōgit·ō -āre *vt* to premeditate

praecognĭt·us -a -um *adj* known beforehand, foreseen

prae-cōlō -colĕre — -cultum *vt* to cultivate prematurely; (fig) to embrace prematurely

praecomposĭt·us -a -um *adj* arranged beforehand; studied, self-conscious

praecōnĭ·us -a -um *adj* of a public crier, of an auctioneer; *n* crier's office; proclamation, announcement; praising, praise

praecon·sūmō -sūmĕre -sumpsī -sumptum *vt* to spend or use up beforehand

praecontract·ō -āre *vt* to consider in advance

praecordĭ·a -ōrum *n pl* diaphragm, midriff; insides, stomach; breast, heart

praecor·rumpō -rumpĕre -rūpī -ruptum *vt* to bribe in advance

praec·ox -ōcis *adj* premature, hasty, rash

praecurrent·ĭa -ĭum *n pl* antecedents

prae-currō -currĕre -cucurrī or **-currī -cursum** *vt* to precede, anticipate; to outdo, surpass; *vi* to run out ahead, take the lead; (with **ante** + *acc*) to run out ahead of; (with *dat*) to outdo

praecursĭ·ō -ōnis *f* previous occurrence; (mil) skirmish; (rhet) warm-up (*of the audience*)

praecurs·or -ōris *m* forerunner; spy; (mil) scout; advance guard

praecursōrĭ·us -a -um *adj* sent in advance

prae-cutĭō -cutĕre -cussī -cussum *vt* to wave, brandish in front

praed·a -ae *f* booty, spoils, plunder; prey; **praedae esse** (with *dat*) to fall prey to

praedābund·us -a -um *adj* pillaging, plundering

praedamn·ō -āre *vt* to condemn beforehand; **spem praedamnare** to give up hope too soon

praedātĭ·ō -ōnis *f* pillaging, plunder

praedāt·or -ōris *m* marauder, looter, vandal; hunter; greedy man

praedātōrĭ·us -a -um *adj* marauding, looting; graspy, greedy

praedēlass·ō -āre *vt* to tire out, weaken beforehand

praedestĭn·ō -āre *vt* to predetermine

praedĭāt·or -ōris *m* real-estate agent

praedĭātōrĭ·us -a -um *adj* real-estate; **jus praediatorium** mortgage law

praedicābĭl·is -e *adj* praiseworthy, laudable

praedicātĭ·ō -ōnis *f* announcement, publication; praising

praedicāt·or -ōris *m* appreciator; eulogist

praedĭc·ō -āre *vt* to announce, proclaim; to report; to assert; to praise

prae-dīcō -dīcĕre -dixī -dictum *vt* to mention beforehand or earlier; to prearrange; to predict; to order, command beforehand

praedictĭ·ō -ōnis *f* prediction

praedict·um -ī *n* prediction, prophecy; command, order; **velut ex praedicto** as if by prearrangement

praedĭŏl·um -ī *n* small estate, small farm

praedisc·ō -ĕre *vt* to learn beforehand, find out in advance

praedisposĭt·us -a -um *adj* previously arranged

praedĭt·us -a -um *adj* endowed, gifted, provided, furnished; (with *abl*) endowed with, provided with, furnished with

praed·ĭum -ĭī or **-ĭ** *n* estate, farm; **praedia urbana** city lots

praedīv·es -ĭtis *adj* very rich

praedīvĭn·ō -āre *vt* to know in advance, have a presentiment of

praed·ō -ōnis *m* marauder, looter, robber, pirate

praedoct·us -a -um *adj* instructed beforehand

praed·or -ārī -ātus sum *vt* to raid, plunder, loot, rob; (fig) to rob, ravish; **amores alicujus praedari** to steal away someone's sweetheart; *vi* to plunder, loot, make a raid; (with **ex** + *abl*) to prey on, profit by, take advantage of, e.g., **ex al-**

terius inscientiā praedari to prey on someone else's ignorance

prae·dūcō -dūcĕre -duxī -ductum *vt* to run or construct (*trench, wall*) out in front (*for defensive purposes*)

praedulc·is -e *adj* very sweet; (fig) very satisfying (*honor, reward*)

praedūr·us -a -um *adj* very tough (*skin*); tough, brawny

praeēmin·ĕō -ēre *vt* to surpass, excel; *vi* to project forward, stick out

prae·ĕō -īre -īvī or **-iī -ĭtum** *vt* to lead, precede; to read out, dictate, lead (*prayers*); *vi* to go out ahead, take the lead; (with *dat*) to walk in front of

praefāti·ō -ōnis *f* preface, introduction; formula

praefātus *pp* of **praefor**

praefectūr·a -ae *f* supervision, superintendence; prefectship, office of prefect, superintendency; government of a district; prefecture (*Italian city governed by a Roman prefect*); territory of a prefecture, district

praefect·us -ī *m* prefect, supervisor, superintendent; commander; governor; (with *genit* or *dat*) supervisor of, commander of, prefect or governor of

prae·fĕrō -ferre -tŭlī -lātum *vt* to hold out, carry in front; to prefer; to anticipate; to display, reveal, betray; to offer, present; to offer as a model; **praeferri** to ride past, ride by, march past, outflank; **praeferri** or **se praeferri** (with *dat*) to surpass

praefĕr·ox -ōcis *adj* very belligerent, very defiant

praeferrāt·us -a -um *adj* iron-tipped; (coll) chained (*slave*)

praefervĭd·us -a -um *adj* boiling; (fig) boiling; **ira praefervĭda** boiling anger

praefestīn·ō -āre *vt* to hurry past; (with *inf*) to be in a hurry to

praefĭc·a -ae *f* hired mourner (*female*)

prae·ficiō -ficĕre -fēcī -fectum *vt* to put (*someone*) in charge; (with double *acc*) to appoint (*someone*) as; (with *dat*) to put (*someone*) in charge of, set (*someone*) over, appoint (*someone*) to command

praefīd·ens -entis *adj* too trustful, overconfident; (with *dat*) too trustful of; **homines sibi praefīdentes** overconfident men

prae·fīgō -fīgĕre -fixī -fixum *vt* to fix, fasten, set up in front, fasten on the end; to tip, point; to transfix; **capistris praefīgere** to muzzle; **cuspidibus praefixus** pointed; **ferro praefixus** iron-tipped

praefīn·iō -īre -īvī or **-iī -ĭtum** *vt* to determine in advance; to prescribe, appoint; to limit

praefīnītō *adv* in the prescribed manner

praefiscinē or **praefiscinī** *adv* meaning no offense

praefiōr·ō -āre *vt* to deflower, deprive of its bloom; (fig) to tarnish, spoil

praefiŭ·ō -ĕre *vt & vi* to flow by

praefōc·ō -āre *vt* to choke, choke up, strangle

prae·fodiō -fodĕre -fōdī *vt* to bury beforehand; to dig in front of; **portas praefodire** to dig trenches in front of the gates

prae·for -fārī -fātus sum *vt* to say beforehand, utter in advance, preface; to address in prayer beforehand; to foretell; to invoke; *vi* to pray beforehand; (with *dat*) to pray before

praefractē *adv* obstinately

praefract·us -a -um *pp* of **praefringo**; resolute, determined; abrupt

praefrĭgĭd·us -a -um *adj* very cold, freezing

prae·fringō -fringĕre -frēgī -fractum *vt* to break off at the tip or end, break to pieces, smash

prae·fulciō -fulcĭre -fulsī -fultum *vt* to prop up, support in front; (with *dat*) to use (*someone*) as a prop or support for; **illud praefulci ut** make sure that

prae·fulgĕō -fulgēre -fulsī *vi* to shine forth, glitter, sparkle

praegelĭd·us -a -um *adj* very cold

praegest·ĭō -īre *vi* to be very eager

praegn·ans -antis or **praegn·ās -ātis** *adj* pregnant; (with *abl*) full of, swollen with

praegracĭl·is -e *adj* very lean or slender

praegrand·is -e *adj* huge, very great; very powerful

praegrăv·is -e *adj* very heavy; very fat; oppressive; very tiresome

praegrăv·ō -āre *vt* to weigh down; to outweigh; (fig) to burden

prae·gredior -grĕdī -gressus sum *vt* to go in advance of, go ahead of; to go by, go past; *vi* to walk out in front; (with *dat*) to precede, lead

praegressi·ō -ōnis *f* procession; (fig) precedence

praegustāt·or -ōris *m* taster, sampler

praegust·ō -āre *vt* to taste beforehand, get a sample of

praehib·ĕō -ēre *vt* to offer, furnish, supply; to utter, speak (*words*); **praehibere operam** (with *dat*) to offer to help

praejac·ĕō -ēre *vt* to lie before, be located in front of; *vi* (with *dat*) to lie before

praejūdicāt·us -a -um *adj* decided beforehand; prejudiced; *n* prejudged matter; prejudice; **id pro praejudicato ferre** to take it as a foregone conclusion

praejūdic·ĭum -ĭī or **-ī** *n* preliminary hearing; prejudgment; precedent, example

praejūdic·ō -āre vt to decide beforehand, prejudge

prae·jŭvō -jŭvāre -jŭvī vt to help in advance

prae·lābor -lābī -lapsus sum vt & vi to glide along, glide by, float by

praelamb·ō -ĕre vt to pretaste

praelarg·us -a -um adj very ample

praelātus pp of **praefero**

prae·lēgō -legĕre -lēgī -lectum vt to sail past

praelĭg·ō -āre vt to tie up; (with dat) to tie (something) to

praelong·us -a -um adj very long

prae·lŏquor -lŏquī -locūtus sum vt to make (a speech) before someone else; to present (a case) first; to say by way of preface; vi to speak first

prae·lūcĕō -lūcĕre -luxī vi (with dat) a to throw light on; b to outshine, outdo, surpass

praelūsī·ō -ōnis f prelude

praelustr·is -e adj magnificent

praemandāt·a -ōrum n pl warrant for arrest

praemand·ō -āre vt to order in advance

praemātūrē adv too soon, prematurely

praemātūr·us -a -um adj premature

praemedicāt·us -a -um adj protected by charms

praemeditātī·ō -ōnis f premeditation, prior consideration

praemedĭt·or -ārī -ātus sum vt to think over beforehand; to practice, practice on (a musical instrument)

praemerc·or -ārī -ātus sum vt to buy in advance

praemetŭ·ens -entis adj apprehensive

praemetŭenter adv anxiously

praemetŭ·ō -ĕre vt to fear beforehand; vi (with dat) to be apprehensive about

prae·mittō -mittĕre -mīsī -missum vt to send out ahead, send in advance; vi to send word

praem·ium -iī or **-ī** n prize, reward, recompense; exploit (worthy of reward); gift, bribe

praemolesti·a -ae f apprehension, presentiment of trouble

praemŏl·ior -īrī vt to prepare beforehand

praemon·ĕō -ēre -ŭī -ĭtum vt to forewarn; to warn of; to foreshadow, presage, predict

praemonĭt·us -ūs m forewarning, premonition

praemonstrāt·or -ōris m director, guide

praemonstr·ō -āre vt to point out the way to, guide, direct; to predict

prae·mordĕō -mordēre -mordī or **morsī -morsum** vt to bite the tip off of; (fig) to crib, pilfer

prae·morior -mŏrī -mortŭus sum vi to die too soon, die prematurely

praemūn·iō -īre -īvī -ītum vt to fortify, protect, secure

praemūnītī·ō -ōnis f (rhet) preparation, conditioning (of the minds of the hearers)

praenarr·ō -āre vt to relate beforehand

praenăt·ō -āre vt to float past, flow by

Praenest·e -is n or f ancient town in Latium (modern Palestrina)

Praenestīn·us -a -um adj & m Praenestine

praenit·ĕō -ēre -ŭī vi (with dat) a to outshine; b to appear more attractive to

praenōm·en -ĭnis n first name

praenosc·ō -ĕre vt to find out beforehand, foreknow

praenŏtī·ō -ōnis f innate idea, preconception

praenūbil·us -a -um adj heavily clouded; dark, gloomy

praenunti·a -ae f harbinger, foreteller, omen

praenunti·ō -āre vt to foretell

praenunti·us -a -um adj foreboding; m forecaster, harbinger, omen

praeoccupātī·ō -ōnis f seizing beforehand, advance occupation

praeoccŭp·ō -āre vt to occupy before another; to preoccupy; to anticipate, prevent

praeŏl·it -ĕre v impers a smell is emitted, there is a strong smell; **praeolit mihi quod tu velis** I scent your wishes before you express them

praeopt·ō -āre vt to prefer

praepand·ō -ĕre vt to spread, extend

praeparātī·ō -ōnis f preparation

praeparāt·us -a -um adj prepared, supplied, furnished, ready; n stores; **ex ante preparato** from the stores; (fig) by previous arrangement

praepăr·ō -āre vt to get ready, prepare, prepare for; to gather together

praepedīment·um -ī n impediment, hindrance

praeped·iō -īre -īvī -ī̆ī -ītum vt to shackle, chain; to hinder, obstruct, hamper; to embarrass

praepend·ĕō -ēre vi to hang down in front

praep·es -ĕtis adj nimble, fast; winged; of good omen, favorable; m or f bird of good omen; bird, large bird

praepilāt·us -a -um adj tipped with a ball; **missile prapilatum** blunted missile

praepingu·is -e adj very fat; very fertile

praepoll·ĕō -ēre vi to be powerful; to be superior; (with dat) to surpass in power

praepondĕr·ō -āre vt to outweigh; to regard as superior

prae·pōnō -pōnĕre -posŭī -posĭ-

tum *vt* (with *dat*) **a** to place, set, put (*something*) in front of or before; **b** to entrust (*someone*) with, put (*someone*) in command of, in charge of; **c** to prefer (*someone or something*) to

praeport·ō -āre *vt* to carry before oneself

praepositi·ō -ōnis *f* preference; prefixing

praeposit·us -a -um *pp* of **praepono**; *adj* preferred, preferable; *m* prefect, commander; *n* that which is desirable, a desirable good

prae·possum -posse -potuī *vi* to get the upper hand, have the better of it

praepostērē *adv* in reversed order, out of order

praepostēr·us -a -um *adj* inverted, in reverse order; absurd, preposterous

praepot·ens -entis *adj* very powerful; (with *genit*) in full control of, fully controlling

praeproperanter or **praepropērē** *adv* very quickly

praepropēr·us -a -um *adj* very quick; overhasty, sudden

praepūt·ium -iī or **-ī** *n* foreskin

praequam *conj* in comparison to; **nihil hoc est, praequam alios sumptus facit** this is nothing in comparison to the other expenses that he runs up

praequest·us -a -um *adj* complaining beforehand; **multa praequestus** having first raised many complaints

praeradi·ō -āre *vt* to outshine

praerapid·us -a -um *adj* very swift

praereptus *pp* of **praeripio**

praerig·escō -escēre -uī *vi* to become very stiff

prae·ripiō -ripēre -ripuī -reptum *vt* to snatch away, carry off; to anticipate, forestall; to count on too soon, presume upon; (with *dat*) to snatch from, steal from

prae·rōdō -rōdēre -rōsī -rōsum *vt* to bite the ends of, nibble at; **digitos praerodere** to bite the fingernails

praerogātīv·us -a -um *adj* asked before others; voting first, privileged; *f* first tribe or century to vote; vote of the first tribe or century; previous election; sure sign, omen

praerōsus *pp* of **praerodo**

prae·rumpō -rumpēre -rūpī -ruptum *vt* to break off, tear away (*something*) in front

praerupt·us -a -um *adj* broken off, broken up; broken up, rough (*terrain*); steep; hasty, impetuous

praes praedis *m* bondsman, surety; collateral

praesaep- = praesep-

praesāg·iō -īre -īvī or **praesāg·ior -īrī** *vt* to have forebodings of, feel beforehand; to cause

praesāgīti·ō -ōnis *f* presentiment, strange feeling, foreboding, prophetic power

praesāg·ium -iī or **-ī** *n* presentiment, presage, prediction

praesāg·us -a -um *adj* divining, prophetic

praesc·iō -īre -īvī *vt* to know beforehand

praescisc·ō -ēre *vt* to find out or learn beforehand

praesci·us -a -um *adj* prescient; (with *genit*) foreseeing; **praescius venturi** foreseeing the future

prae·scrībō -scrībēre -scripsī -scriptum *vt* to prefix in writing; to describe beforehand; to determine in advance, prescribe, ordain; to dictate; to outline, map out; to put forward as an excuse

praescripti·ō -ōnis *f* heading, title; preface; pretext; rule, law; limit, restriction

praescript·um -ī *n* regulation, rule, proviso

praesēc·ō -āre -uī -tum *vt* to cut off, cut out, cut short

praesegmin·a -um *n pl* clippings

praes·ens -entis *adj* present, in person, at hand; existing, contemporary; prompt, immediate, impending; efficacious, powerful, effective; influential; resolute; propitious; **sermo praesens** a face-to-face talk; *n* present time; **ad praesens** or **in praesens** for the present

praesensi·ō -ōnis *f* presentiment; preconception

praesensus *pp* of **praesentio**

praesentāri·us -a -um *adj* ready, at hand

praesenti·a -ae *f* presence; efficacy, effect; **animi praesentia** presence of mind; **in praesentia** at the present time, just now, for the present

praesent·ia -ium *n pl* present circumstances, present state of affairs

prae·sentiō -sentīre -sensī -sensum *vt* to feel beforehand, to realize in advance, have strange feelings about, divine

praesēp·e or **praesaep·e -is** *n* or **praesēp·is** or **praesēp·es -is** *f* stall, stable; crib, manger; room, lodgings; tavern; hovel; beehive

praesēp·iō or **praesaep·iō -īre -sī -tum** *vt* to fence in, barricade

praesertim *adv* especially, particularly, principally; **praesertim cum** especially because

praeserv·iō -īre *vi* (with *dat*) to serve as a slave to

praes·es -idis *m* guard, guardian, protector, defender; president, superintendent; captain, pilot; *f* guardian, protectress

praesīd·ens -entis *m* president, ruler

prae·sīdeō -sidēre -sēdī *vt* to guard, protect, defend; to command, be in comand of; *vi* to be in charge, be in command; (with *dat*) **a** to watch over, guard, protect; **b** to preside over, direct, manage, command

praesidiāri·us -a -um *adj* on garrison duty

praesid·ium -iī or **-ī** *n* protection, defense; help, assistance; guard, garrison; convoy, escort; garrison post, defensive position

praesignific·ō -āre *vt* to indicate in advance, foretoken

praesign·is -e *adj* outstanding

praesŏn·ō -āre -ŭī *vi* to sound beforehand

praesparg·ō -ĕre *vt* to strew, scatter

praestābil·is -e *adj* excellent, outstanding

praest·ans -antis *adj* outstanding, eminent, exceptional

praestanti·a -ae *f* excellence, superiority, preeminence

praestern·ō -ĕre *vt* to strew

praest·es -ĭtis *adj* guardian, protecting, presiding

praestigi·ae -ārum *f pl* sleight of hand, juggling, tricks, illusion, deception

praestigiāt·or -ōris *m* or **praestigiātr·ix -īcis** *f* juggler, magician; imposter

praestin·ō -āre *vt* to buy, shop for

prae·stĭtŭō -stituĕre -stĭtŭī -stĭtūtum *vt* to fix or set up beforehand, prescribe

praestĭtus *pp* of **praesto**

praestō *adv* at hand, ready, present; **praesto esse** (with *dat*) **a** to be on hand for, attend, serve, be helpful to, aid; **b** to be in the way of, resist, oppose

prae·stō -stāre -stĭtī -stĭtum *vt* to excel, be superior to; to show, exhibit, give evidence of, display; to answer for, be responsible for, take upon oneself; to perform, discharge, fulfill; to keep, maintain, retain; **fidem praestare** to keep one's word; **impetūs populi praestare** to be responsible for popular outbreaks; **nihil praestare** to be answerable for nothing; **officia praestare** to perform duties; **se praestare** to show oneself, behave; **socios salvos praestare** to keep the allies safe; **terga hosti praestare** to show one's back to the enemy, retreat; **virtutem praestare** to display courage; *vi* to stand out, be outstanding, be preeminent, be superior; *v impers* it is preferable, it is better

praestōl·or -ārī -ātus sum *vt* to wait for, expect; *vi* (with *dat*) to wait for

prae·stringō -stringĕre -strinxī -strictum *vt* to draw together, squeeze; to blunt (*an edge*); to blind, dazzle (*the eyes*); to dazzle, baffle, confuse

prae·strŭō -struĕre -struxī -structum *vt* to build up, block up,

block, stop up; to build up (*e.g., confidence*) beforehand

praes·ul -ŭlis *m* or *f* public dancer

praesult·ō -āre *vi* (with *dat*) to jump around in front of

prae·sum -esse -fŭī *vi* to preside, be in charge, be in command; (with *dat*) **a** to preside over, be in charge of, be in command of; **b** to protect; (with **in** + *abl*) to be governor in

prae·sūmō -sūmĕre -sumpsī -sumptum *vt* to take in advance; to anticipate, take for granted, presume

praesumptī·ō -ōnis *f* anticipation

praesūt·us -a -um *adj* sewed up; covered

praetĕg·ō -ĕre *vt* to protect

praetempt·ō -āre *vt* to try out in advance, test in advance; to grope for

prae·tendō -tendĕre -tendī -tentum *vt* to hold or stretch in front of oneself; to present; to offer as an excuse, give as pretext, allege, pretend; (with *dat*) to hold or draw (*e.g., a toga*) in front of (*e.g., the eyes*); **praetendi** (of places) to lie to the front or opposite; **praetendi** (with *dat*) to lie or be situated opposite or over against

praetentō see **praetempto**

praetentus *pp* of **praetendo**

praetep·escō -escĕre -ŭī *vi* (of love) to glow

praeter *conj* besides, other than; *prep* (with *acc*) (of place) past, by, along, before, in front of; (in comparison) above, beyond, more than; against, contrary to, aside from; besides, apart from, except; besides, in addition to

praeterăg·ō -ĕre *vt* (with double *acc*) to drive (*e.g., a horse*) past (*a place*)

praeterbĭt·ō -ĕre *vt & vi* to go by or past

praeterĕā *adv* besides, moreover; hereafter, thereafter

praeter·ĕō -īre -īvī or **-iī -ĭtum** *vt* to go past, pass by; to skip, pass over in silence, neglect; to escape the notice of; to go beyond; to surpass

praeterequĭt·ans -antis *adj* riding by

praeter·fĕrō -ferre -tŭlī -lātum *vt* (with double *acc*) to carry or take (*someone*) past (*something*); **praeterferri** to move or sweep by (*a place*)

praeterflŭ·ō -ĕre *vt & vi* to flow by

praeter·grĕdĭor -grĕdī -gressus sum *vt* to march by, go past; to surpass

praeterhāc *adv* in addition

praeterĭt·us -a -um *pp* of **praetereo**; *adj* past, past and gone, bygone; *n pl* bygone events, the past

praeter·lābor -lābī -lapsus sum *vt* to glide by; *vi* to glide by, slip away

praeterlātus *pp* of **praeterfero**

praetermĕ·ō -āre *vt & vi* to go past or by

praetermissī·ō -ōnis *f* leaving out, omission; passing over, neglecting; (with *genit*) omission of, neglecting of

praeter·mittō -mittĕre -mīsī -missum *vt* to let pass, let go by; to leave undone; to pass over, omit, disregard, overlook, neglect

praetĕr·ō -ĕre *vt* to wear down in front

praeterquam *adv* besides, other than; **praeterquam quod** apart from the fact that

praetervectī·ō -ōnis *f* passing by

praeter·vĕhor -vĕhī -vectus sum *vt & vi* to ride by; to sail by; to march or go by

praetervŏl·ō -āre *vt & vi* to fly by; (of opportunity) to slip by; to escape

praetex·ō -ĕre -uī -tum *vt* to border, edge, fringe; to adorn in front; (fig) to cloak, conceal, disguise; to allege as a pretext

praetextāt·us -a -um wearing the toga praetexta (*crimson-bordered toga*); underage, juvenile, **mores praetextati** loose morals

praetext·us -a -um *pp* of **praetexo**; *adj* bordered; wearing the crimson-bordered toga; **fabula praetexta** Roman tragic drama; *f* toga praetexta (*crimson-bordered toga which was worn by higher magistrates and by freeborn boys*); *tragedy*; **praetextas docere** to put on tragedies; *n* pretext, pretense, excuse

praetext·us -ūs *m* outward show, splendor; pretense, pretext

praetim·ĕō -ēre *vi* to be apprehensive

praetinct·us -a -um *adj* previously dipped

praet·or -ōris *m* praetor (*judicial magistrate, accompanied by six lictors*); commander; (during the early years of the republic) chief magistrate, chief executive; (in Italian municipalities) chief magistrate; **praetor peregrinus** praetor who had jurisdiction over cases involving foreigners; **praetor urbanus** or **praetor urbis** praetor who had jurisdiction over cases involving Roman citizens

praetōriān·us -a -um *adj* praetorian, belonging to the emperor's bodyguard; *m pl* praetorian guard, soldiers of the praetorian guard

praetōricĭ·us -a -um *adj* received from the praetor (*at public games*)

praetōrĭ·us -a -um *adj* of the commander in chief, of the commander or general; praetor's, of the praetor; propraetor's; **cohors praetoria** general's bodyguard; **comitia praetoria** praetorian elections; **navis praetoria** flagship; **porta praetoria** camp gate nearest the general's tent; **turba praetoria**

crowd around the praetor; *n* general's quarters, headquarters; official residence of the governor in a province; council of war; emperor's bodyguard; palace, mansion

praetorqu·ĕō -ēre *vt* to twist beforehand; to strangle first

praetrepĭd·ans -antis *adj* very nervous

praetrepĭd·us -a -um *adj* very nervous, trembling

praetrunc·ō -āre *vt* to cut off, cut short

praetūr·a -ae *f* praetorship; **praeturā se abdicare** to resign the praetorship

praeumbr·ans -antis *adj* casting a shadow; (fig) overshadowing

praeust·us -a -um *adj* burnt at the tip; hardened by fire at the point; frost-bitten

praeut *conj* as compared with, when compared with

praeval·ĕō -ēre -uī *vi* to be stronger, have more power; to have greater influence; to have the upper hand

praevalĭd·us -a -um *adj* of superior strength, unusually strong, unusually powerful, imposing; too strong

praevāricātĭ·ō -ōnis *f* collusion

praevāricāt·or -ōris *m* phoney accuser, prosecutor in collusion, prevaricator

praevāric·or -ārī -ātus sum *vi* to make a sham defense or prosecution; (with *dat*) to favor because of collusion

prae·vĕhor -vĕhī -vectus sum *vt* (of a river) to flow past; *vi* to ride in front, ride by; to sail by

prae·venio -venīre -vēnī -ventum *vt* to come before, precede, get the jump on, anticipate; to prevent; *vi* to come before, precede

praeverr·ō -ĕre *vt* to sweep before

praevert·ō -ĕre -ī or **prae·vertor -vertī** *vt* to go before, precede, outrun, outstrip; to turn to first, attend to first; to prefer; to come before, anticipate, prevent; to preoccupy; (with *dat* or **prae** + *abl*) to prefer (*someone or something*) to; *vi* (with *dat* or **ad** + *acc*) to go to first, turn to first, attend to first

prae·vidĕō -vidēre -vīdī -vīsum *vt* to foresee

praevitĭ·ō -āre *vt* to taint or pollute beforehand

praevĭ·us -a -um *adj* going before, leading the way

praevŏl·ō -āre *vi* to fly out in front

pragmatĭc·us -a -um *adj* experienced; *m* lawyer, attorney

prandĕō prandēre prandī pransum *vt* to eat for breakfast, eat for lunch; *vi* to have breakfast, have lunch

prand·ium -iī or **-ī** *n* breakfast, lunch

pransĭt·ō -āre *vt* to usually eat for lunch

prans·or -ōris *m* guest at lunch

prans·us -a -um *pp of* **prandeo**; *adj* having had breakfast, after eating; well fed; **pransus potus** having been wined and dined

prasín·us -a -um *adj* green; **factio prasina** the Greens (*one of the stables of horses at the racetrack in Rome*)

prātens·is -e *adj* meadow, growing in the meadow

prātŭl·um -ī *n* small meadow

prāt·um -ī *n* meadow; (fig) plain (*of the sea*); *n pl* meadow grass

prāvē *adv* crookedly; improperly, wrongly, badly, poorly; **prave facti versūs** poorly written verses

prāvit·ās -ātis *f* crookedness, distortion; impropriety, irregularity; perverseness, depravity

prāv·us -a -um *adj* crooked, distorted, deformed; irregular, improper, wrong, bad; perverse, vicious

Praxitěl·ēs -is *m* famous Greek Athenian sculptor (*4th cent. B.C.*)

precāriō *adv* upon request

precāri·us -a -um *adj* obtained by prayer; dependent on another's will, uncertain, precarious

precātí·ō -ōnis *f* prayer; **precationes facere** to say prayers

precāt·or -ōris *m* intercessor, suppliant

precēs = *pl of* **prex**

preci·ae -ārum *f pl* grapevine

prec·or -ārī -ātus sum *vt* to entreat; supplicate, pray to; to pray for; to wish for; (with double *acc*) to pray to (*someone*) for; (with *acc* of thing and *abl* of person) to request (*something*) from; (with **pro** + *abl*) to entreat (*e.g., the gods*) on behalf of; (with **ut** or **ne**) to pray that; pray that not; **longum Augusto diem precari** to wish Augustus long life; *vi* to pray; (with **ad** + *acc*) to pray to, e.g., **di ad quos precantur** the gods to whom they pray; **male precari** to curse, utter curses

pre·hendō -hendĕre -hendī -hensum *or* **prendō prendĕre prendī prensum** *vt* to take hold of, grasp, seize; to detain; to arrest; to occupy; to catch, surprise; to reach, arrive at; to grasp, understand

prēl·um -ī *n* wine press, oil press; clothes press

premō premĕre pressī pressum *vt* to press, squeeze; to lie down on; to hug (*shore*); to suppress, hide; to cover, crown; to press hard, bear down on; to chase, attack; to weigh down, load; to press together, close; to curb, stop; to depress, lower; to mark, impress; to prune; to pressure, urge, importune; to degrade, humble, disparage; to abridge; to subjugate

prensāti·ō -ōnis *f* campaigning (*for office*)

prens·ō *or* **prehens·ō -āre** *vt* to take hold of, clutch at, grab; to stop, detain; *vi* to campaign, be a candidate

prensus *pp of* **prendo**

pressē *adv* distinctly, with articulation; concisely; accurately; simply

pressí·ō -ōnis *f* fulcrum; leverage

press·ō -āre *vt* to press

press·us -a -um *pp of* **premo**; *adj* closed, shut tight; suppressed; slow; lowered, low, subdued; concise, precise, accurate; articulate

press·us -ūs *m* pressing, pressure; expression (*of the face*)

prest·ēr -ēris *m* waterspout

pretiōsē *adv* at great cost, expensively

pretiōs·us -a -um *adj* previous, valuable; expensive; extravagant

pret·ium -iī *or* **-ī** *n* price; value, worth; reward, return, recompense; bribe; pay, wages; **in pretio esse** to be prized; to be held in high esteem; **in pretio habere** to prize, hold in high esteem; **pretium curae esse** to be worth the trouble; **pretium habere** to have value, be worth something; **pretium facere** to set a price; **pretium operae esse** to be worth the effort, be worthwhile

prex precis *f* prayer, request; curse, imprecation; intercession

Priamē·is -ĭdis *f* daughter of Priam

Priamēi·us -a -um *adj* Priam's, of Priam

Priamĭd·ēs -ae *m* son of Priam

Priăm·us -ī *m* Priam (*son of Laomedon, husband of Hecuba, father of Hector, Paris, etc., king of Troy at the time of its fall*)

prīdem *adv* long ago, long, since; **haud ita pridem** not so long ago; not long before; **quam pridem** how long ago

prīdiē *adv* the day before, the previous day

prīm·a -ōrum *n pl* first part, beginning; first principles or elements; **cum primus** among the first, especially; **in primis** above all, chiefly, particularly, especially, principally

prīm·ae -ārum *f pl* lead, first rank, highest place, highest importance; **primas dare** (with *dat*) to attach supreme importance to

prīmaev·us -a -um *adj* young, youthful

prīmān·ī -ōrum *m pl* soldiers of the first legion

prīmāri·us -a -um *adj* first in rank; first-rate

prīmigĕn·us -a -um *adj* original

prīmipīl·us -ī *m* first-ranking centurion of a legion

prīmitĭ·ae -ārum *f pl* firstfruits

prīmĭtus *adv* originally, at first; for the first time

prīmō *adv* first, in the first place; at first, at the beginning

prīmord·ium -iī *or* **-ī** *n* origin, beginning; commencement; beginning of a new reign

prīmōr·ēs -um *m pl* chiefs, nobles, leaders; (mil) front line

prīmōr·is -e *adj* first, foremost, extreme, tip of; first, principal; **digitulī prīmōres** fingertips; **prīmōrī in acie** all the way up front

prīmŭlum *adv* first of all, at first

prīmŭl·us -a -um *adj* very first

prīmum *adv* first, in the first place, before all else; at first; for the first time; **cum prīmum, ubī prīmum, ut prīmum** as soon as; **prīmum dum** in the first place; **quam prīmum** as soon as possible

prīm·us -a -um *adj* first, foremost; principal; eminent, distinguished; earliest; **prīmas partes agere** to play the lead role; **prīmīs digitis** with or at the fingertips; **prīmo annō** at the beginning of the year or season; **prīmus in prōvinciam introiit** he was the first to enter the province; **prīmus quisque** the very first, the first possible; *f pl* see **prīmae;** *n* beginning, front; **a prīmo** from the first, from the beginning; **in prīmo** in the beginning; (mil) at the head of the column; *n pl* see **prīma**

prīnc·eps -ipis *adj* first, in front; foremost, chief; *m* leader, chief; emperor; (mil) maniple, company; captain, company commander, centurion; captaincy, centurionship; *m pl* soldiers of the second line (*between the hastati and triarii*), second line

prīncipāl·is -e *adj* first, foremost; original, primitive; chief, principal; of the emperor; **via prīncipālis** (mil) main street of a camp; **porta prīncipālis** (mil) main gate of a camp

prīncipāt·us -ūs *m* first place; post of commander in chief; principate, rule, sovereignty; origin, beginning

prīncip·a -ōrum *n pl* first principles; foundations; front line, front-line troops; headquarters

prīncipiāl·is -e *adj* initial

prīncip·ium -iī or **-ī** *n* start, commencement, origin; beginner, originator; first to vote; right to vote first; **a prīncipiō** or **prīncipiō** at the beginning, at first

pri·or -us *adj* previous, preceding, prior, former; first; better, superior, preferable

priōr·ēs -um *m pl* forefathers, ancestors, ancients; *f pl* (only *acc*) lead, preference

priscē *adv* in the old-fashioned style

prisc·us -a -um *adj* old, ancient; old-time, old-fashioned; former, previous

pristīn·us -a -um *adj* former, earlier; pristine, primitive, original; preceding, previous, yesterday's; *n* former condition; **in pristīnum restituere** to restore to its former condition

pristis see **pistrix**

prius *adv* earlier, before, previously,

sooner, first; sooner, rather

priusquam *conj* before

prīvātim *adv* privately, in private, in a private capacity, as a private citizen; at home

prīvāti·ō -ōnis *f* removal

prīvātō *adv* at home

prīvāt·us -a -um *adj* private; personal, individual, peculiar; isolated, withdrawn; ordinary (*language*); *m* private citizen, civilian; *n* privacy, retirement; private property, private land; **ex prīvātō** out of one's own pocket; **in prīvātō** in private; **in prīvātum** for private use

prīvign·a -ae *f* stepdaughter

prīvign·us -ī *m* stepson; *m pl* stepchildren

prīvilēg·ium -iī or **-ī** *n* special bill directed against an individual; special bill in favor of an individual

prīv·ō -āre *vt* to deprive, rob, strip; to free, release

prīv·us -a -um *adj* every, each single; own, private; (with *genit*) deprived of

prō *adv* (with **quam** or **ut**) just as, according as; *prep* (with *abl*) before, in front of, in, on, in the presence of; for, in behalf of, in favor of, in the service of, on the side of; instead of, in place of, for; in return for, in exchange for, for; just as, as, the same as, for; in proportion to, according to, in comparison with, by virtue of; **prō eō** just the same; **prō eō atque** or **ac** just as, the same as; **prō eō quod** in view of the fact that; **prō sē quisque** each one for himself, individually; **prō ut** or **prō eō quantum** as, in proportion as; *interj* oh!; **prō dī immortālēs!** Oh, heavens above!

proāgŏr·us -ī *m* chief magistrate in some provincial towns

proāvi·a -ae *f* great-grandmother

proāvīt·us -a -um *adj* great-grandfather's, ancestral

proāv·us -ī *m* great-grandfather; ancestor, forefather

probābil·is -e *adj* worthy of approval, commendable, acceptable, pleasing, agreeable; probable, plausible, credible, likely

probābilit·ās -ātis *f* probability, plausibility

probābiliter *adv* probably

probāti·ō -ōnis *f* approval, approbation, assent; test, trial; proof

probāt·or -ōris *m* approver, supporter, backer

probāt·us -a -um *adj* approved, acceptable; tried, tested, good; esteemed

probē *adv* well, properly, correctly; well, thoroughly, very, very much

probit·ās -ātis *f* probity, honesty, worth, goodness

prob·ō -āre *vt* to approve, commend, esteem; to make good, represent as good, make acceptable; to pronounce judgment on; to pronounce approval of; to make credible, prove, show, demonstrate; to test, try, inspect; **probare pro** (with *abl*) to pass (*someone*) off for; **probari pro** (with *abl*) to pass for, be taken for

probriperlecĕbr·ae -ārum *f pl* temptations

probrōs·us -a -um *adj* scandalous, shameful, abusive

probr·um -ī *n* abuse, invective, reproach; shameful act, vile deed; lewdness, indecency; shame, disgrace; charge of disgraceful conduct

prob·us -a -um *adj* good, honest, upright, virtuous, decent; (coll) real, proper, downright

Proc·a or **Proc·ās -ae** *m* king of Alba and father of Numitor and Amulius

procācit·ās -ātis *f* brashness

procāciter *adv* brashly

proc·ax -ācis *adj* brash

prō·cēdō -cēdĕre -cessī -cessum *vi* to proceed, go forward, advance; to make progress, advance; to come out (*in public*), show oneself, appear; to come forth, arise; (of time) to pass, elapse; to turn out, result, succeed; to continue

procell·a -ae *f* violent wind, squall, hurricane, storm; (fig) violence, commotion, storm; (mil) charge, sudden attack

procell·ō -ĕre *vt* to throw down; **se procellere in mensam** to lie down at the table

procellōs·us -a -um *adj* gusty

proc·er -ĕris *m* chief, noble, prince, leader

prōcērit·ās -ātis *f* height, tallness; length; *f pl* the different heights

prōcērius *adv* farther, to a greater extent, more

prōcēr·us -a -um *adj* tall; long; **palmae procerae** upraised palms

prōcessi·ō -ōnis *f* advance

prōcessus *pp* of **procedo**

prōcess·us -ūs *m* advance, progress

Prochўt·a -ae or **Prochўt·ē -ēs** *f* small island off the Campanian coast

prō·cĭdō -cĭdĕre -cĭdī *vi* to fall forwards, fall over, fall down, fall prostrate

prōcinctū (*abl* only) *m* **in procinctu** under arms, ready for combat

prōclāmāt·or -ōris *m* loudmouth

prōclām·ō -āre *vi* to yell

prōclīn·ō -āre *vt* to bend forward, bend; **res proclinata** critical situation, crisis

prōclīv·e -is *n* slope, descent; **in proclivi esse** to be easy

prōclīve *adv* downward, downhill; rapidly

prōclīv·is -e or **prōclīv·us -a -um** *adj* sloping forward; downhill; easy; inclined, disposed, subject, ready, willing

prōclīvĭt·ās -ātis *f* proclivity, tendency, predisposition

prōclīvus see **proclivis**

Procn·ē or **Progn·ē -ēs** *f* daughter of Pandion, sister of Philomela, wife of Tereus, and mother of Itys, who was changed into a swallow; swallow

proc·ō -āre *vt* to require, demand

prōcons·ul -ŭlis *m* vice-consul, proconsul; governor of a province; military commander

prōconsulār·is -e *adj* proconsular

prōconsulāt·us -ūs *m* proconsulship, proconsulate

prōcrastināti·ō -ōnis *f* procrastination

prōcrastin·ō -āre *vt* to postpone, put off from day to day

prōcreāti·ō -ōnis *f* procreation, breeding

prōcreāt·or -ōris *m* procreator, sire, parent, father

prōcreātr·ix -īcis *f* mother

prōcrĕ·ō -āre *vt* to procreate, beget, produce

prōcresc·ō -ĕre *vi* to spring forth, be produced; to continue to grow, grow up

Procr·is -is or **-ĭdis** *f* wife of Cephalus who mistook her for a wild beast and shot her

Procrust·ēs -ae *m* notorious robber in Attica who stretched his victims to the length of his bed or mutilated them if they were too tall

prōcŭb·ō -āre *vi* to lie stretched out

prō·cūdō -cūdĕre -cūdī -cūsum *vt* to forge, fashion; to bring forth, produce

procul *adv* at a distance, in the distance, far; from a distance, from far; **haud procul afuit quin legatos violarent** they came close to outraging the ambassadors

prōculc·ō -āre *vt* to trample upon, trample down

prō·cumbō -cumbĕre -cubŭī -cubĭtum *vi* to fall down, sink down; to lean forward, bend over, be broken down; to extend, spread; (fig) to go to ruin

prōcūrāti·ō -ōnis *f* management, administration, superintendence; expiation, expiatory sacrifice

prōcūrāt·or -ōris *m* procurator, manager, administrator, superintendent, agent, deputy; governor of a province

prōcūrātr·ix -īcis *f* governess, protectress

prōcūr·ō -āre *vt* to manage, administer; to take care of, attend to; to avert by sacrifice; to expiate; *vi* to serve as procurator

prō·currō -currĕre -cucurrī or **-currī -cursum** *vi* to run out ahead, dash forward; to jut out, project

prōcursāti·ō -ōnis *f* sally, charge

prōcursātōr·ēs -um *m pl* skirmishers

prōcurs·ō -āre *vi* to keep charging out, continue to skirmish

prōcurs·us -ūs *m* sally, charge, onset

prōcurv·us -a -um *adj* curving forwards; curving, winding (*shore*)

proc·us -ī *m* noble; gigolo; **impudentes proci** shameless candidates

Procy·ōn -ōnis *m* Lesser Dog Star, Sirius

prōdactus *pp* of **prodigo**

prōdeambul·ō -āre *vi* to go out for a walk

prōd·eō -īre -iī -itum *vi* to go out, come out, go forth, come forth; (of a cliff) to project; (of plants) to come out, appear; to appear in public; to go ahead, advance, proceed

prō·dīcō -dīcere -dīxī -dictum *vt* to put off, defer, postpone; **diem prodicere** to adjourn a case to a later date

prōdictāt·or -ōris *m* vice-dictator

prōdigē *adv* lavishly

prōdigenti·a -ae *f* profusion, extravagance; openhandedness

prōdigiāliter *adv* to a fantastic degree

prōdigiōs·us -a -um *adj* prodigious; freakish

prōdig·ium -iī or **-ī** *n* portent; unnatural crime, monstrous crime; monster, freak

prōd·īgō -igēre -ēgī -actum *vt* to squander, waste

prōdig·us -a -um *adj* wasteful; lavish, openhanded; (with *genit*) free with; **animae prodigus** free with or careless with one's life; **herbae prodigus locus** spot with luxuriant growth of grass

prōditi·ō -ōnis *f* betrayal, treason; **proditionem agere** (with *dat*) to commit treason against, betray

prōdit·or -ōris *m* betrayer, traitor

prō·dō -dere -didī -ditum *vt* to bring out, bring forth, produce; to reveal, disclose; to record, relate, report, hand down, transmit; to proclaim, appoint, elect; to give up, surrender; to forsake, betray; to prolong, protract; (fig) to display, exhibit

prōdoc·eō -ēre *vt* to preach publicly

prōdrōm·us -ī *m* forerunner, advance messenger

prō·dūcō -dūcere -duxī -ductum *vt* to bring out, bring forth; to produce; to promote, advance; to bring to light, reveal; to bring into the world, produce, raise, bring up; to educate; to drag out, protract, stretch out, lengthen; to lead on, induce; to put off, adjourn; to put (a *slave*) up for sale; to produce (*on the stage*), perform; to bring to court

prōductē *adv* long; **producte litteram dicere** to lengthen the letter or vowel

prōducti·ō -ōnis *f* lengthening

prōduct·ō -āre *vt* to drag out, delay

prōduct·us -a -um *pp* of **produco**; *adj* lengthened, prolonged, long

proēgmén·on -ī *n* preference

proeliār·is -e *adj* battle, of battle

proeliāt·or -ōris *m* combatant

proel·ior -ārī -ātus sum *vi* to battle, fight

proel·ium -iī or **-ī** *n* battle, combat, fight; *n pl* fighting men, warriors

Proet·us -ī *m* king of Tiryns

prōfān·ō -āre *vt* to profane, desecrate

prōfān·us -a -um *adj* unconsecrated, ordinary, common; impious, wicked; ill-omened

prōfātus *pp* of **profor**

prōfecti·ō -ōnis *f* setting out, departure; source (*of money*)

prōfectō *adv* really, actually

prōfectus *pp* of **proficiscor**

prōfectus *pp* of **proficio**

prōfect·us -ūs *m* progress, advance, success; increase, profit

prō·ferō -ferre -tulī -lātum *vt* to bring forward, advance, bring out; to extend, enlarge; to put off, postpone, defer; to produce, discover, invent; to make known, reveal, publish; to mention, cite, quote; **pedem proferre** to advance; **signa proferre** to march forward

profess·ae -ārum *f pl* professional prostitutes, professionals

professi·ō -ōnis *f* public acknowledgment, profession, declaration; registration (*at which property, etc., was declared*); profession, business

profess·or -ōris *m* professor, teacher

professōri·us -a -um *adj* professorial; professional, expert

professus *pp* of **profiteor**

profest·us -a -um *adj* non-holiday, ordinary; **dies profestus** working day

prō·ficiō -ficere -fēcī -fectum *vi* to make progress, make headway, advance, have success, succeed; to be useful, do good, help, be conducive; **nihil proficere** to do no good

prō·ficiscor -ficiscī -fectus sum *vi* to set out, start, go, depart; to originate, proceed, arise

prō·fiteor -fitērī -fessus sum *vt* to declare publicly, acknowledge, confess, profess; to offer freely, promise, volunteer; to follow as a profession, practice (*e.g., law*); to make a declaration of, register (*property, etc.*) before a public official; **indicium profiteri** to volunteer evidence, testify freely; **nomen profiteri** to put one's name in as a candidate, announce oneself a candidate; **se adjutorem profiteri** (with **ad + acc**) to volunteer to help (*someone*); **se amicum profiteri** to avow oneself a friend, profess to be a friend; *vi* to make a confession, make an admission; to be a professor, be a teacher

prōflīgāt·or -ōris m big spender

prōflīgāt·us -a -um adj profligate, dissolute

prōflīg·ō -āre vt to knock to the ground, knock down; to defeat, conquer; to bring to an end, do away with, finish off; to ruin, crush; to debase, degrade

prōfl·ō -āre vt to breathe out

prōflū·ens -entis adj flowing along; fluent (speech); f running water

prōfluenter adv easily, effortlessly

prōfluenti·a -ae f fluency

prō·fluō -fluēre -flūxi vi to flow out; to flow along; (fig) to proceed

prōfluv·ium -iī or **-ī** n flow

prof·or -ārī -ātus sum vt to say, declare; vi to speak out

prō·fugiō -fugēre -fūgī vt to run away from, escape from; vi to run away, escape; (with ad + acc) to take refuge with, take refuge at the house of

profug·us -a -um adj fugitive; banished, exile; nomadic; m fugitive, refugee

prō·fundō -fundēre -fūdī -fūsum vt to pour, pour out; to shed; to utter; to give vent to; to spend freely, waste, squander; **se profundere** (of things) to come pouring out; (of persons) to come pouring out, come charging out, break out

profund·us -a -um adj deep; boundless, vast; dense (forest, cloud); high (heaven); infernal; (fig) bottomless, boundless; n depth; the deep, deep sea; (fig) abyss

profūsē adv in disorder, helter-skelter, haphazardly; extravagantly

profūsi·ō -ōnis f profusion

profūs·us -a -um pp of **profundo**; adj extravagant, lavish, profuse; excessive, expensive

prōgen·er -erī m granddaughter's husband

prōgener·ō -āre vt to beget, produce

prōgeni·ēs -ēī f line, lineage; progeny, descendants, offspring, posterity

prōgenit·or -ōris m progenitor, founder, ancestor

prō·gignō -gignēre -genuī -genitum vt to beget, produce

prōgnāriter adv precisely, exactly

prōgnāt·us -a -um adj born, descended; (with abl or with ab or ex + abl) born of, descended from; m child; grandson

Prognē see **Procne**

prognōstic·on or **prognōstic·um -ī** n sign of the future, prognostic

prō·gredior -gredī -gressus sum vi to go forward, march forward, proceed, advance; to go on, make headway, make progress; to go forth, go out

prōgressi·ō -ōnis f progress, advancement; increase, growth; (rhet) climax

prōgressus pp of **progredior**

prōgress·us -ūs m progress, advance; march (of time or events)

prōh interj oh!, O!

prohib·eō -ēre -uī -itum vt to hold back, check, hinder, prevent, avert, keep off; to prohibit, forbid; to keep away; to defend, protect

prohibiti·ō -ōnis f prohibition

proinde or **proīn** adv consequently, accordingly; **proinde atque** (or **ac**), **proinde ut**, or **proinde quam** just as, exactly as; **proinde atque si** (or **ac si**), **proinde quasi** just as if

prōjectīcī·us -a -um adj exposed (child)

prōjectī·ō -ōnis f stretching out; **projectio bracchii** stretching out of the arm

prōject·ō -āre vt to accuse, blame

prōject·us -a -um pp of **projicio**; adj jutting out, projecting; prostrate, stretched out; inclined; prone; abject, contemptible; downcast

prōject·us -ūs m projection, extension

prō·jiciō -jicēre -jēcī -jectum vt to throw down, throw out, throw; to throw away, abandon, forsake; to hold out, extend; to throw out, banish, exile; to neglect, desert; to blurt out; to throw away, give up, sacrifice; to put off, delay; to throw overboard; **se projicere ad pedes** (with genit) to throw oneself at the feet of, fall prostrate before; **se projicere ex nave** to jump overboard; **se projicere in forum** to rush into the forum

prō·lābor -lābī -lapsus sum vi to glide forward, slip or move forward; to fall forwards, fall on one's face; to slip out; (of words) to slip out, escape; to be led on, led astray (by greed, fear, etc.); (fig) to fail, go to ruin, collapse

prōlapsi·ō -ōnis f falling, collapse

prōlapsus pp of **prolabor**

prōlāti·ō -ōnis f expansion, extension (of territory); adducing, mentioning (of precedents); delay, postponement

prōlāt·ō -āre vt to extend; to put off, delay

prōlātus pp of **profero**

prōl·ēs -is f offspring, progeny, children, descendants; race, stock; child; young man

prōlētār·ius -iī or **-ī** m proletarian; m pl proletariat

prō·liciō -licere -lixī vt to entice, bring out, incite

prōlixē adv freely, wildly; readily, cheerfully, freely

prōlix·us -a -um adj long, freely growing, wild (beard, hair, etc.); obliging, ready and unwilling; favorable (circumstances)

prōlocūtus pp of **proloquor**

prōlŏg·us -ī m prologue (of a play); actor who gives the prologue prō·lŏquor -lŏquī -locūtus sum vt & vi to speak out

prōlub·ium -iī or -ī n desire, inclination, yen

prō·lūdō -lūdĕre -lūsī -lūsum vi to practice; (of boxers) to spar, shadowbox

prō·lŭō -luĕre -lŭī -lūtum vt to wash out, flush, wash off, wash away; to wet, drench

prōlūsi·ō -ōnis f sparring, shadowboxing

prōlūtus pp of proluo

prōluvi·ēs -ēī f flood; refuse, sewage

prōmer·ĕō -ēre -ŭī -ĭtum or prōmer·ĕor -ērī -ĭtus sum vt to deserve, merit, earn; vi to be deserving; (with de + abl) to deserve the gratitude of; bene de multis promerere or promereri to deserve the full gratitude of many people

prōmerit·um -ī n reward, due; merit; guilt

Promēth·eus -ĕī or -ĕos m son of Iapetus and Clymene, brother of Epimetheus, and father of Deucalion, who by teaching men the use of fire, incurred the wrath of Jupiter

Promēthē·us -a -um adj Promethean, of Prometheus

Promēthīd·ēs -ae m son of Prometheus, Deucalion (who, with his wife Pyrrha, was the sole survivor of the Deluge)

prōmin·ēns -entis adj projecting, prominent; n headland

prōmin·ĕō -ēre -ŭī vi to jut out, hang forward, bend forward, extend; (with in + acc) to reach down to

prōmiscam or prōmiscē adv in common, without distinction, indiscriminately

prōmiscuē adv indiscriminately, promiscuously

prōmiscu·us or prōmisc·us -a -um adj promiscuous, haphazard, indiscriminate, in common, open to all; common, ordinary

prōmissi·ō -ōnis f promise

prōmiss·or -ōris m promiser, fourflusher

prōmiss·us -a -um adj allowed to grow, long, hanging down; n promise

prō·mittō -mittĕre -mīsī -missum vt to let (e.g., the hair) grow; to promise; to give promise of, give hope of; vi to promise to go; ad cenam promittere to promise to go to dinner, make a dinner engagement

prōmō prōmĕre prompsī promptum vt to bring out, draw out; to produce (arguments); to bring to light, reveal; to bring out, express (feelings, ideas, emotions)

prōmontōr·ium -iī or -ī n promontory

prōmōt·a -ōrum n pl second choice

(things preferred next after absolute good)

prō·movĕō -movēre -mōvī -mōtum vt to move (something) forward, cause to advance; to enlarge, extend; to effect, accomplish; to promote (to higher office); to bring to light, reveal; to put off, postpone; nihil promovere to accomplish nothing, do no good, make no progress

promptē adv readily, quickly; easily; frankly

prompt·ō -āre vt to give out, distribute

promptū (only abl) m in promptu in readiness, ready, at hand; public, visible, manifest; in promptu gerere, habere, or ponere to display

promptuāri·us -a -um adj of a storehouse, storage; cella promptuaria (coll) jail

prompt·us -a -um pp of promo; adj prompt, ready; easy; brought to light, evident; bold, enterprising; (with dat or with ad or in + acc) a ready or prepared for, set for; b inclined to, disposed to; (with in + abl) quick at, prompt at; (with adversus + acc) ready for, prepared against; (with inf) ready to, quick to

prōmulgāti·ō -ōnis f promulgation, publication

prōmulg·ō -āre vt to promulgate, publish

prōmuls·is -ĭdis f hors d'oeuvres

prōmuntŭr·ium -iī or -ī n promontory

prōm·us -ī m butler

prōmūtŭ·us -a -um adj on credit, advanced, given in advance

prōnē adv downwards

prōnĕp·ōs -ōtis m great-grandson

prōnept·is -is f great-granddaughter

prōnoe·a -ae f providence

prōnŭb·a -ae f patroness of marriage

prōnuntiāti·ō -ōnis f proclamation, declaration; announcement (of the jury's verdict); delivery (of a speech); proposition (in logic)

prōnuntiāt·or -ōris m narrator

prōnuntiāt·um -ī n proposition (in logic)

prōnunti·ō -āre vt to proclaim, announce; to utter, pronounce, express (opinion, judgment); to hold out, promise, offer; to recite, deliver, narrate, relate; (in the senate) to formulate, announce, put to a vote

prōnŭr·us -ūs f grandson's wife

prōn·us -a -um adj leaning, inclined, bending, stooping, bent over, bent forwards; swift, rushing, dashing, moving swiftly along; sloping, steep (hill, road); sinking, setting (sun, etc.); downhill; easy; inclined, disposed, prone; n downward tendency, gravity; n pl slopes

prooemĭ·or -ārī *vi* to make an introduction or preface

prooem·ĭum -ĭī or **-ī** *n* preface; prelude; (fig) prelude (*e.g., to a fight*)

propāgātĭ·ō -ōnis *f* propagation; extension, prolongation; **nominis propagatio** perpetuation of the name

propāg·ō -āre *vt* to propagate (*race*); to extend (*territory*); to prolong (*life*)

prōpalam *adv* openly, publicly

prōpatŭl·us -a -um *adj* open; *n* open space; **in propatulo habere** to display

prope *adv* near, nearby; (of time) near, at hand; (of degree) nearly, almost, practically, just about; (with **ab** + *abl*) close by, near to; **prope est cum** the time has come when; *prep* (with *acc*) near, near to; **prope diem** very soon, presently

prō·pellō -pellĕre -pŭlī -pulsum *vt* to drive forward, push forward; to drive away, drive out

propemŏdo or **propemŏdum** *adv* nearly, practically, almost

prō·pendĕō -pendĕre -pendī -pensum *vi* to hang down; to preponderate; (with **in** + *acc*) to be inclined to, be favorably disposed to

propensē *adv* readily, willingly

prōpensĭ·ō -ōnis *f* propensity, inclination, tendency

prōpens·us -a -um *pp* of **propendeo**; *adj* important; coming near, approaching; inclined, disposed, ready, willing; **propenso animo** with a ready mind, willingly; **propensus in alteram partem** inclined toward the other point of view

properanter *adv* quickly, hastily

properantĭ·a -ae *f* haste

properātĭ·ō -ōnis *f* haste

properātō *adv* quickly, speedily

properāt·us -a -um *adj* hurried, quick, speedy; *n* haste, speed; **properato opus est** speed is required

properē *adv* quickly, in haste, hastily

properĭp·ēs -ēdis *adj* quick-moving

properŏ·ō -āre *vt* to speed up, accelerate; to prepare hastily, do in haste; *vi* to be quick; to go or move quickly

Propert·ĭus -ĭī or **-ī** *m* Sextus Propertius (*Latin elegiac poet, c. 50-15 B.C.*)

proper·us -a -um *adj* quick, speedy

prōpex·us -a -um *adj* combed forward

prōpīnātĭ·ō -ōnis *f* toast

propīn·ō or **prōpīn·ō -āre** *vt* to drink (*e.g., a cup of wine*) as a toast; to drink a toast to, toast; (with *dat*) **a** to drink (*e.g., a cup of wine*) as a toast to; **b** to pass on (*a cup*) to

propinqu·a -ae *f* relative (*female*)

propinquē *adv* near at hand

propinquĭt·ās -ātis *f* proximity, nearness, vicinity; (fig) relationship; affinity; friendship

propinqu·ō -āre *vt* to bring on; to accelerate, hasten; *vi* to draw near, approach; (with *dat*) to draw near to, approach

propinqu·us -a -um *adj* near, neighboring; (of time) near, at hand; related; *m* relative; *f* see **propinqua**; *n* neighborhood, vicinity

propĭ·or -us *adj* nearer, closer; later, more recent; more closely related, more like, more nearly resembling; more intimate, closer; of more concern, of greater import; (with *dat*) **a** nearer to, closer to; **b** closer to in resemblance, more like; (with *acc* or with **ab** + *abl*) closer to

propĭŏr·a -um *n pl* closer side (*e.g., of a river*); more recent events

propitĭ·ō -āre *vt* to propitiate, appease

propitĭ·us -a -um *adj* propitious, well-disposed, favorable

propnigē·um -ī *n* room where the bath was heated

prōpōl·a -ae *m* retailer

prōpollŭ·ō -ĕre *vt* to pollute further

prō·pōnō -pōnĕre -posŭī -positum *vt* to put or place forward, expose to view, display; to propose; to imagine; to offer, propose; to say, report, relate, publish; to threaten; to denounce; to design, determine, intend

Propont·is -ĭdis or **-ĭdos** *f* Sea of Marmora

prōporrō *adv* furthermore; wholly, completely

prōportĭ·ō -ōnis *f* proportion, symmetry; analogy

prōpositĭ·ō -ōnis *f* proposition; intention, purpose; theme; basic assumption (*in logic*)

prōposit·us -a -um *pp* of **propono**; *adj* exposed, open; accessible; impending, at hand; *n* intention, design, purpose, resolution; main point, theme; first premise (*in logic*)

prōpraet·or -ōris *m* propraetor (*ex-praetor who was made governor of a province*)

propriē *adv* in the strict sense; strictly for oneself, personally; peculiarly, especially

propriĕt·ās -ātis *f* property, peculiarity, quality

proprītim *adv* specifically, properly

propri·us -a -um *adj* own; very own; special, peculiar, individual, particular, personal; lasting, permanent

propter *adv* near, near at hand

propter *prep* (with *acc*) near, close to, next to; on account of, because of, for the sake of; through, by means of

propterĕā *adv* for that reason, therefore, on that account; **propterea quod** for the very reason that

prōpudĭōs·us -a -um *adj* shameful, disgraceful

prōpud·ium -iī or **-ī** *n* shameful act; (said of a person) disgrace

prōpugnācŭl·um -ī *n* rampart, battlement; defense; (fig) safeguard

prōpugnāti·ō -ōnis *f* defense, vindication

prōpugnāt·or -ōris *m* defender, champion

prōpugn·ō -āre *vt* to defend; *vi* to come out and fight; to fight a defensive action, repel an assault; (fig) to put up a defense

prōpulsāti·ō -ōnis *f* repulse

prōpuls·ō -āre *vt* to drive back, repel, repulse; (fig) to ward off, repel

prōpulsus *pp* of **propello**

Propylae·a -ōrum *n pl* entrance to the Athenian Acropolis

prōquam *conj* according as

prōr·a -ae *f* prow; (fig) ship; **mihi prora et puppis est** my intention from first to last is

prō·rēpō -rēpĕre -repsī *vi* to creep ahead, crawl out

prōrēt·a -ae *m* look-out at the prow

prōrē·us -ī *m* look-out at the prow

prō·ripiō -ripĕre -ripŭī -reptum *vt* to drag forth, drag out; to rush; **se proripere** to rush, dash

prōrogāti·ō -ōnis *f* extension, prolongation (*of a term of office*); postponement

prōrŏg·ō -āre *vt* to prolong, extend; to put off, postpone

prorsum *adv* forwards; (with a negative) absolutely, at all, e.g., **prorsum nihil** absolutely nothing, nothing at all

prorsus *adv* forward; by all means, certainly; in short, in a word; (with a negative) absolutely, at all, e.g., **nullo prorsus modo assentior** I don't agree in any way at all

prō·rumpō -rumpĕre -rūpī -ruptum *vt* to make (*something*) break forth, fling forth; **prorumpi** to burst forth; *vi* to break out, rush out, make an attack

prō·ruō -ruĕre -ruī -rŭtum *vt* to overthrow, demolish; *vi* to rush forth; to tumble

prōrupt·us -a -um *pp* of **prorumpo**; *adj* unrestrained

prōsāpi·a -ae *f* stock, race, line

proscaen·ium -iī or **-ī** *n* front part of a stage; *n pl* stage; theater

pro·scindō -scindĕre -scīdī -scissum *vt* to plow up, break up; (fig) to criticize harshly, satirize, cut to pieces

pro·scrībō -scrībĕre -scripsī -scriptum *vt* to publish in writing; to proclaim, announce; to advertise (*for sale, etc.*); to confiscate (*property*); to punish with confiscation of property, deprive of property; to proscribe, outlaw

proscripti·ō -ōnis *f* advertisement; proscription, notice of confiscation, notice of outlawry

proscriptur·iō -īre *vi* to be anxious to hold a proscription

proscript·us -a -um *pp* of **proscrībo**; *m* proscribed person, outlaw

prōsĕc·ō -āre -ŭī -tum *vt* to cut off (*esp. parts of a sacrificial victim*)

prōsecūtus *pp* of **prosequor**

prōsĕd·a -ae *f* prostitute

prōsēmin·ō -āre *vt* to sow, scatter about, plant; to propagate, raise (*family*)

prō·sentiō -sentīre -sensī *vt* to sense or realize beforehand

prō·sĕquor -sĕquī -secūtus sum *vt* to escort, attend; to pursue (*enemy*); to chase, follow; to pursue, go on with, continue (*a topic*); to describe in detail; to follow, imitate; to attend, honor

Proserpĭn·a -ae *f* daughter of Ceres and wife of Pluto

prōserp·ō -ĕre *vi* to creep or crawl forwards, creep along

proseuch·a -ae *f* synagogue

prōsil·iō -īre -ŭī *vi* to jump forward, jump up; to jump to one's feet; (of blood) to spurt; (of sparks) to shoot out; to rush, dash

prōsŏc·er -ĕrī *m* wife's grandfather

prospect·ō -āre *vt* to view, look out at, gaze upon; (of places) to look towards, command a view of; to look for, hope for, expect, await

prospectus *pp* of **prospicio**

prospect·us -ūs *m* distant view; sight, view; faculty of sight; sight (*thing seen*)

prospecŭl·or -ārī -ātus sum *vt* to look out for, watch for; *vi* to look around, reconnoiter

prosp·er see **prosperus**

prospĕrē *adv* favorably, luckily, as desired, successfully

prosperĭt·ās -ātis *f* success, good fortune, prosperity; **prosperitas valetudinis** good health

prospĕr·ō -āre *vt* to cause to succeed, make happy, make fortunate

prosp·ĕrus or **prosp·er -ĕra -ĕrum** *adj* successful, fortunate, lucky, favorable, prosperous

prospicientĭ·a -ae *f* foresight, precaution

pro·spiciō -spicĕre -spexī -spectum *vt* to see far off, see in the distance; to spot; to command a view of; to watch for; to look out for, provide for; to foresee; *vi* to look forward; to look into the distance, have a distant view, have a view; to be on the lookout, exercise foresight; (with **in** + *acc*) to command a view of, overlook; **ex superioribus in urbem prospicere** to have a view of the city from a vantage point; **parum prospiciunt oculi** the eyes are nearsighted

pro·sternō -sternĕre -strāvī -strātum *vt* to throw to the ground, throw down, knock down; to wreck, ruin, overthrow, subvert; to debase; **se prosternere** to debase oneself; **se prosternere ad**

pedes (with *genit*) to throw oneself at the feet of, fall down before

prostibil·is -is *f* prostitute

prostibŭl·um -ī *n* prostitute

prostit·ŭō -ŭēre -ŭī -ūtum *vt* to expose for sale; to prostitute

pro·stō -stāre -stĭtī *vi* to project; (of wares) to be set out for sale; to prostitute oneself, be a prostitute

prostrātus *pp* of **prosterno**

prōsubĭg·ō -ĕre *vt* to dig up, root up

prō·sum -desse -fŭī *vi* to be useful, be of use, do good, be profitable; **multum prodesse** to do a lot of good

Prōtagŏr·ās -ae *m* Greek sophist, contemporary of Socrates, born at Abdera (*c.* 485-415 B.C.)

prō·tĕgō -tegĕre -texī -tectum *vt* to cover in front, cover, cover up; to cover with a roof; to shelter, protect; (fig) to cover, defend, protect

prōtĕl·ō -āre *vt* to chase away, drive off

prōtĕl·um -ī *n* team of oxen; (fig) row, series

prō·tendō -tendĕre -tendī -tentum *vt* to stretch forth, stretch out, extend

prōtent·us -a -um *adj* extended

prōtĕnus see **protinus**

prō·tĕrō -terĕre -trīvī -trītum *vt* to wear down, rub out; to trample down, trample under foot; (fig) to trample upon, rub out, crush

prōterr·ĕō -ēre -ŭī -ĭtum *vt* to scare away

protervē *adv* boldly, brashly, impudently, brazenly

protervĭt·ās -ātis *f* brashness, brazenness

proterv·us -a -um *adj* bold, brash, brazen, impudent

Prōtesĭlā·us -ī *m* first Greek casualty in the Trojan War

Prōt·eus -ĕī or **-ĕos** *m* god of the sea with power to assume various forms

prothȳmē *adv* willingly, readily

prothymĭ·a -ae *f* willingness, readiness

prōtĭnam *adv* immediately

prōtĭnus or **prōtĕnus** *adv* straight on, forward, farther on; continuously, right on, without pause; immediately, at once, on the spot

prōtoll·ō -ĕre *vt* to stretch out (*hand*); to put off, postpone

prōtopraxĭ·a -ae *f* priority (*among creditors in receiving payment*)

prō·trăhō -trahĕre -traxī -tractum *vt* to drag forward, drag out; to produce; to reveal, expose, disclose, bring to light

prōtrītus *pp* of **protero**

prō·trūdō -trūdĕre -trūsī -trūsum *vt* to push forwards, push out; to push off, postpone

prōtŭrb·ō -āre *vt* to drive ahead, drive on, drive away, repel; to knock down

proüt *conj* as, just as

prōvect·us -a -um *adj* advanced; **aetate provectus** advanced in years; **nox provecta erat** the night had been far advanced

prō·vĕhō -vehĕre -vexī -vectum *vt* to carry forwards; to transport, convey; to lead, lead on; to promote, advance, raise; **provehi** to ride, drive, move, or sail ahead

prō·venĭō -venīre -vēnī -ventum *vi* to go on, proceed; to succeed; to come out, appear; to come out, grow, be produced; to come about, happen

prōvent·us -ūs *m* result, outcome; success; yield, produce; harvest

prōverb·ĭum -ĭī or **-ī** *n* proverb

prōvĭd·ens -entis *adj* prudent

prōvĭdenter *adv* prudently, with foresight

prōvĭdentĭ·a -ae *f* foresight, foreknowledge; precaution; **providentia deorum** providence

prō·vĭdĕō -vidēre -vīdī -vīsum *vt* to see in the distance; to see coming; to foresee; to provide for; to provide against, guard against, avert, avoid; to look after, look out for, care for; to prepare, make ready

prōvĭd·us -a -um *adj* foreseeing; prudent, cautious; provident; (with *genit*) providing

prōvincĭ·a -ae *f* sphere of administration; sphere of jurisdiction: office, duty, charge; public office, commission, command, administration; sphere of action; province

prōvincĭāl·is -e *adj* provincial, of a province, in a province; **bellum provinciale** war in a province; **molestia provincialis** annoyance of administering a province; *m* provincial

prōvisĭ·ō -ōnis *f* foresight; precaution; (with *genit*) precaution against

prōvisō *adv* with forethought

prōvis·ō -ĕre *vt* to go out to see; to be on the lookout for

prōvis·or -ōris *m* lookout (*person*); provider

prōvisū (only *abl*) *m* by looking forward; (with objective *genit*) **a** by foreseeing (*e.g., danger*); **b** by providing, providing for

prōvisus *pp* of **provideo**

prō·vīvō -vivĕre -vixī *vi* to live on

prōvocātĭ·ō -ōnis *f* appeal (*to a higher court*); challenge

prōvocāt·or -ōris *m* challenger; type of gladiator

prōvŏc·ō -āre *vt* to challenge; to provoke; to exasperate; to stir, stimulate; **bellum provocare** to provoke a war; **beneficio provocatus** touched or stirred by an act of kindness; **in aleam provocare** to challenge to a game of dice; **provocare maledictis** to provoke or exasperate with nasty remarks

prōvŏl·ō -āre *vi* to fly out, rush out, dash out

prō·volvō -volvĕre -volvī -volū-
tum *vt* to roll forward, roll along;
to roll over, overturn; to humble,
ruin; **se provolvere** to prostrate
oneself, fall down, grovel, humble
oneself

prōvŏm·ō -ĕre *vt* to vomit, throw
up

proximē or proxŭmē *adv* (of place)
nearest, next; (of time) most recently, just recently; (with *acc*)
close to, next to, at the side of, very
much like, closely resembling; (with
dat) (of place) next to; **proxime
atque** almost as much as, nearly
the same as; **proxime Pompeium
sedebam** I was sitting next to
Pompey; **quam proxime** (with
dat or *acc*) as close as possible to

proxĭmĭt·ās -ātis *f* proximity, vicinity; resemblance, similarity; close
relationship

proximō *adv* very recently, just recently

proxĭm·us or proxŭm·us -a -um
adj nearest, next; next, following,
ensuing; previous, most recent, latest, last; closely related; adjoining;
most direct (*route*); *m* close relative,
next of kin; *n* neighborhood; next
door, next-door neighbor

prūd·ens -entis *adj* foreseeing, fore-
knowing; conscious, aware; skilled,
skillful, experienced, versed; prudent, discreet, sensible, intelligent;
(with *genit* or *abl* or with **in** + *abl*)
aware of, conscious of, familiar
with, skilled in, experienced in

prūdenter *adv* prudently, cautiously;
skillfully

prūdentĭ·a -ae *f* foreseeing; prudence, discretion, good sense; **prudentia juris publici** knowledge of
or experience in public law

pruīn·a -ae *f* frost; winter

pruīnōs·us -a -um *adj* frosty

prūn·a -ae *f* live coal

prūnĭtĭ·us -a -um *adj* of plum-tree
wood

prūn·um -ī *n* plum

prūn·us -ī *f* plum tree

prūrīg·ō -ĭnis *f* itching, itch; yen

prūrĭō -īre *vi* to itch; to have an
itch; (with **in** + *acc*) to be itching
for

prytanē·um -ī *n* state dining hall
(*where the Prytanes dined*)

prytăn·is -is *m* prytane (*member of
the executive body in some Greek
states*)

psall·ō -ĕre -ī *vi* to play the lyre or
lute

psaltēr·ĭum -ĭī or -ī *n* stringed instrument, lute

psaltrĭ·a -ae *f* lutist, musician (*female*)

psec·as -ădis *f* female slave who
perfumed her lady's hair

psēphism·a -ătis *n* plebiscite of the
Greek assembly

pseudocăt·ō -ōnis *m* a make-believe
Cato

pseudomĕn·os or pseudomĕn·us -ī
m fallacious syllogism

pseudothȳr·um -ī *n* back door

psittăc·us -ī *m* parrot

Psych·ē -ēs *f* maiden loved by Cupid
and made immortal by Jupiter

psychomantī·um or psychoman-
tē·um -ī *n* place where people attempted to communicate with the
dead

-pte *enclitic* (added to pronouns) self,
own

ptisanār·ĭum -ĭī or -ī *n* gruel

Ptolemae·us -ī *m* Ptolemy (*name
of a series of Egyptian kings descended from Lagus, a general of
Alexander the Great*)

pūb·ens -entis *adj* mature; juicy
(*plant*)

pūber see pubes

pūbert·ās -ātis *f* puberty; manhood,
virility; sign of maturity, beard

pūb·ēs or pūb·er -ĕris *adj* grown
up, adult; downy, covered with
down; *m pl* grown-ups, adults, men;

pūb·ēs -is *f* pubic hair; groin;
youth, young men, grown-up males;
throng, people; bullocks

pūb·escō -escĕre -ŭī *vi* to reach the
age of puberty, arrive at maturity;
(of plants) to grow up, ripen; (of
meadows, etc.) to be clothed, covered (*e.g., with flowers*)

pūblĭcān·us -a -um *adj* of public
revenues; *m* revenue agent

pūblĭcātĭ·ō -ōnis *f* confiscation

pūblĭcē *adv* publicly, officially, in behalf of the state, for the state;
at public expense; generally, universally; **publice dicere** to speak
officially

pūblĭcĭtus *adv* at public expense, at
the expense of the state; publicly

pūblĭc·ō -āre *vt* to confiscate; to
throw open to the general public;
to prostitute

Pūblĭcŏl·a or Pōplĭcŏl·a -ae *m* Publius Valerius Publicola (*fl 509 B.C.*)

pūblĭc·us -a -um *adj* of the people,
public, common; of the state, state,
federal, national; common, ordinary, vulgar; common, general,
public; **causa publica** affair of national importance; (law) federal
case (*i.e., criminal case*); **res publica** state, government, politics,
public life, country; *m* public official; *n* public, publicity; public
property, national treasury, federal
revenue; **de publico** at public expense; **in publico** in public, publicly; **in publicum prodire** to go
out in public; **in publicum redigere** to hand over to the national
treasury

pudend·us -a -um *adj* shameful,
scandalous

pud·ens -entis *adj* modest, bashful

pudenter *adv* modestly, bashfully

pud·ĕō -ēre -ŭī or **puditum est** *vt*
to make ashamed; *v impers* (with
acc of person and *genit* or *abl* of

cause of feeling), e.g., **me tui pu-det** I am ashamed of you

pudibund·us -a -um adj modest, bashful

pudīcē adv chastely, modestly, virtuously

pudiciti·a -ae f chastity, modesty, purity

pudīc·us -a -um adj chaste, modest, virtuous, pure

pud·or -ōris m shame, decency, modesty, sense of shame; sense of honor, propriety; cause for shame, shame, disgrace; blush

puell·a -ae f girl; girl friend, sweetheart; young wife

puellār·is -e adj young girl's, girlish, youthful

puellāriter adv girlishly

puellŭl·a -ae f little girl; little sweetheart

puell·us -ī m little boy, lad

pu·er -ērī m boy, lad, young man; servant, slave, page; bachelor; **a pueris** or **a puero** from boyhood, from childhood; **ex pueris excedere** to outgrow childhood

puerīl·is -e adj boyish, childish, youthful, puerile

puerīliter adv like a child, childishly

pueriti·a or **puertĭ·a -ae** f childhood, boyhood

puerper·ium -iī or **-ī** n childbirth, lying-in, giving birth

puerpĕr·us -a -um adj helping childbirth, easing labor pains; f woman in labor

puertĭa see **pueritia**

puerŭl·us -ī m little boy, little slave

pūg·a or **pȳg·a -ae** f rump, rear, buttocks

pug·il -ilis m boxer

pugilātĭ·ō -ōnis f boxing

pugilāt·us -ūs m boxing

pugilicē adv like a boxer

pugillār·is -e adj hand-size; m pl & n pl notebook

pugillātōrĭ·us -a -um adj boxing, punching; **follis pugillatorius** punching bag

pugi·ō -ōnis m dagger

pugiuncŭl·us -ī m small dagger

pugn·a -ae f fist fight, brawl; fight, combat, battle

pugnācĭt·ās -ātis f pugnacity, aggressiveness

pugnācĭter adv pugnaciously, doggedly

pugnācŭl·um -ī n fortress

pugnant·ēs -ium m pl fighters, warriors

pugnant·ĭa -ium n pl contradictions, inconsistencies

pugnāt·or -ōris m fighter, combatant

pugn·ax -ācis adj pugnacious, scrappy, aggressive; quarrelsome; dogged, obstinate

pugnĕ·us -a -um adj of the fist; **mergae pugneae** punches

pugn·ō -āre vt to fight; vi to fight; to contend, dispute; (with dat or

cum + abl) **a** to fight, fight against, struggle with, oppose; **b** to contradict

pugn·us -ī m fist

pulchell·us -a -um adj cute little

pulch·er -ra -rum adj beautiful, fair, handsome

pulchrē adv beautifully; (as exclamation of applause) fine!; **pulchre mihi est** I am fine

pulchritūd·ō -ĭnis f beauty; excellence, attractiveness

pūlē·ĭum or **pūleg·ĭum -iī** or **-ī** n pennyroyal, mint; (fig) fragrance, pleasantness

pūl·ex -ĭcis m flea

pullār·ĭus -ĭī or **-ī** m keeper of the sacred chickens

pullāt·us -a -um adj wearing black, in black, in mourning

pullŭl·ō -āre vi to sprout; (of animals) to produce young

pull·us -a -um adj dark-grey, dark, blackish; mourning; **toga pulla** mourning toga; n dark-grey garment

pull·us -ī m young (of animals), foal, offspring, chick, chicken

pulmentār·ĭum -iī or **-ī** n relish, appetizer

pulment·um -ī n relish; food, rations

pulm·ō -ōnis f lung

pulmōnĕ·us -a -um adj of the lungs, pulmonary

pulp·a -ae f meat, flesh

pulpāment·um -ī n meat; game

pulpĭt·um -ī n platform; stage

puls pultis f pulse, porridge, mush

pulsātĭ·ō -ōnis f knock

puls·ō -āre vt to batter, keep hitting; to knock at; to strum (lyre); to beat on, strike against; (fig) to jolt, disquiet; vi to throb

pulsus pp of **pello**

puls·us -ūs m push, pushing; beat, beating, striking, stamping, blow, stroke; trample; (fig) impression, influence

pultātĭ·ō -ōnis f knocking (at the door)

pultiphagōnĭd·ēs -ae m porridge eater

pultiphăg·us -ī m porridge eater

pult·ō -āre vt to knock at

pulverĕ·us -a -um adj dust, of dust; dusty; fine as dust; raising dust

pulverulent·us -a -um adj dusty; raising dust; covered with dust

pulvill·us -ī m small cushion

pulvīn·ar -āris n cushioned couch, couch; sacred couch for the images of the gods; seat of honor; shrine, temple

pulvīnār·ĭum -iī or **-ī** n cushioned seat of a god; dry dock

pulvīn·us -ī m pillow, cushion; seat of honor

pulv·is -ĕris m dust, powder; scene of action, arena, field; effort, work

pulviscŭl·us -ī m fine dust, fine powder

pūm·ex -ĭcis *m* pumice stone; porous stone, lava

pūmĭcě·us -a -um *adj* pumice, lava

pūmĭc·ō -āre *vt* to smooth or polish with pumice stone

pūmĭl·ĭ·ō -ōnis *m* or *f* midget, dwarf, pygmy

punctim *adv* with the point, with the pointed end

punct·um -ī *n* prick, puncture; point, mathematical point; point, spot; vote, ballot; clause, phrase; moment; **puncto temporis eodem** at the same instant; **punctum temporis** moment, instant, point of time

pungō pungěre pupŭgī punctum *vt* to prick, puncture, dent; to sting, bite; to cause (*a wound*); to stab; (fig) to sting, annoy, trouble, disturb

Pūnĭcān·us -a -um *adj* Punic, Carthaginian, in the Carthaginian style

Pūnĭcē *adv* Punic, in the Punic language

pūnĭcě·us -a -um *adj* reddish, red, crimson, pink

Pūnĭc·us -a -um *adj* Punic, Carthaginian; red, crimson, reddish, pink; *n* pomegranate

pūn·ĭo -īre -īvī or **-iī -ītum** or **pūn·ĭor -īrī -ītus sum** *vt* to punish, chastise; to avenge, revenge

pūnīt·or -ōris *m* avenger

pūp·a -ae *f* doll, puppet; girl, lass

pūpĭll·a -ae *f* orphan girl, ward; minor; pupil (*of the eye*)

pūpillār·is -e *adj* of an orphan, belonging to an orphan

pūpĭll·us -ī *m* orphan boy, orphan, ward

pupp·is -is *f* stern; ship; (coll) back; **a puppī astern**

pūpŭl·a -ae *f* pupil; eye

pūpŭl·us -ī *m* little boy

pūrē *adv* clearly, brightly; plainly, simply; purely, chastely

purgām·en -ĭnis *n* dirt, filth; means of expiation, purification

purgāment·a -ōrum *n pl* offscourings, refuse, dirt, filth, garbage; (term of abuse) trash, dregs, garbage

purgātĭ·ō -ōnis *f* cleansing, cleaning, cleanup; apology, justification

purgāt·us -a -um *adj* cleansed, clean, pure

purg·ō -āre *vt* to clean, cleanse, clear, clear away, remove; to clear of a charge, exculpate, excuse, justify; to refute; to cleanse, purify ritually; to purge (*the body*)

pūrĭfic·ō -āre *vt* to purify

pūriter *adv* purely, cleanly; **vitam puriter agere** to lead a clean life

purpŭr·a -ae *f* purple, deep-red, dark-red; purple or deep-red cloth or garment; royal-purple robe; royalty; consular dignity, imperial dignity

purpūrāt·us -a -um *adj* wearing royal purple; *m* courtier

purpŭrě·us -a -um *adj* deep-red, crimson, pink, violet, royal-purple (*and various shades, as applied to roses, poppies, lips, flesh, blood, wine, dawn, hair*)

purpūrissāt·us -a -um *adj* rouged

purpūriss·um -ī *m* rouge; red dye

pūr·us -a -um *adj* pure, clear, clean; cleared, cleansed; cleansing, purifying; pure, chaste; plain, naked, unadorned, natural; plain (*toga*), without crimson border; pure, accurate, faultless (*style*); (law) unconditional, absolute; subject to no religious claims; *n* clear sky

pūs pūris *n* pus; (fig) venom, malice

pusill·us -a -um *adj* petty, puny; *n* bit, trifle

pūsĭ·ō -ōnis *m* little boy

pustŭl·a -ae *f* pimple; blister

pustŭlāt·us or **pusŭlāt·us -a -um** *adj* refined, purified

putām·en -ĭnis *n* clipping, peeling, shell, husk

putātĭ·ō -ōnis *f* pruning

putāt·or -ōris *m* pruner

putě·al -ālis *n* low wall (*around a well or sacred spot*), stone enclosure; **puteal Libonis** stone enclosure in the Roman Forum near which much business was transacted

puteāl·is -e *adj* well, of a well

pūt·ěō -ēre *vi* to stink; to be rotten, be putrid

Puteolān·us -a -um *adj* of Puteoli

Puteŏl·ī -ōrum *m pl* commercial city on the coast of Campania (*modern Pozzuolo*)

put·er or **put·ris -e** *adj* putrid, rotting; crumbling; flabby

pūt·escō -escěre -ŭī *vi* to become rotten

pŭtě·us -ī *m* well; pit; dungeon

pūtĭdē *adv* disgustingly, disagreeably

pūtĭdiuscŭl·us -a -um *adj* rather tedious

pūtĭd·us -a -um *adj* stinking, rotten; affected, unnatural (*style*)

putill·us -a -um *adj* tiny

put·ō -āre *vt* to trim, prune; to think, ponder, consider, judge, suppose, imagine; to reckon, estimate, value; to believe in, recognize (*gods*); to clear up, settle (*accounts*); **magnī putare** to think highly of; **pro certo putare** to regard as certain; *vi* to think, imagine, suppose

pūt·or -ōris *m* stench

putre·facĭō -facěre -fēcī -factum *vt* to make rotten, rot; to cause to crumble, soften

putresc·ō -ěre *vi* to become rotten, get moldy

putrĭd·us -a -um *adj* rotten; flabby

putris see **puter**

pūt·us -a -um *adj* pure, bright, perfectly pure; splendid; unmixed; unmitigated; *m* boy

pyct·a or **pyct·ēs -ae** *m* boxer

Pydn·a -ae *f* city in Macedonia near which Aemilius Paulus defeated

Perseus, the Macedonian king (169 B.C.)

pȳg·a -ae f rump, rear, buttocks

Pygmalǐ·ōn -ōnis m son of Belus the king of Cyprus and brother of Dido; king of Cyprus who fell in love with a statue

Pylǎd·ēs -ae m son of Strophius and friend of Orestes

Pyl·ae -ārum f pl Thermopylae (narrow pass in E. Thessaly)

Pylǐ·us -a -um adj of Pylos

Pyl·os -ī f Pylos (home of Nestor in S.E. Peloponnesus)

pyr·a -ae f pyre

pȳrăm·is -ǐdis f pyramid; cone

Pȳrăm·us -ī m neighbor and boy friend of Thisbe

Pȳrēnae·us -a -um adj of the Pyrenees

Pȳrēn·ē -ēs f the Pyrenees Mountains

pyrĕthr·on or pyrĕthr·um -ī n Spanish camomile (plant)

pyrōp·us -ī m bronze

Pyrrh·a -ae or Pyrrh·ē -ēs f daughter of Epimetheus, wife of Deucalion, and survivor of the Deluge

Pyrrh·ō -ōnis m philosopher of Elis, contemporary of Aristotle, and founder of the philosophical school of Skepticism (c. 360-270 B.C.)

Pyrrh·us -ī m son of Achilles and founder of Epirus (also called Neoptolemus); king of Epirus who invaded Italy to assist the Tarentines against the Romans in 280 B.C. (319-272 B.C.)

Pȳthagŏr·ās -ae m Greek philosopher and mathematician (6th cent. B.C.)

Pȳthagŏrē·us or Pythagorǐc·us -a -um adj Pythagorean

Pȳthǐ·us -a -um adj Pythian, Delphic; m Apollo; f Pythia (priestess of Apollo at Delphi); n pl Pythian games (held in honor of Apollo every four years)

Pȳth·ō -ūs f Delphi

Pȳth·ōn -ōnis m dragon slain by Apollo near Delphi

pȳtism·a -ătis n spit, squirt of wine

pȳtiss·ō -āre vt to spit, spit out (wine)

pyx·is -ǐdis f powder box, cosmetic box

Q

quā adv where, in what direction, by what way; to what extent, as far as; whereby, how, by what means; in any way, to any degree; quā . . . quā partly . . . partly, both . . . and

quācumque adv wherever, by whatever way, in whatever way; by whatever means, howsoever

quādam tenus adv to a certain point, only so far and no farther

quadr·a -ae f square table, dining table; square crust; square morsel, square bit (of cheese, etc.)

quadrāgēni -ae -a adj forty each

quadrāgēsǐm·us or quadrāgensǐm·us -a -um adj fortieth; f one fortieth; 2½ percent tax

quadrāgǐēs or quadrāgǐens adv forty times

quadrāgintā (indecl) adj forty

quadr·ans -antis m fourth part, a fourth, a quarter; cent (smallest coin, worth one sixth of an ace); quarter of a pound; quarter pint (quarter of a sextarius); quadrante lavatum ire take a bath for one cent (usual price of a bath)

quadrant·al -ālis n five-gallon jar

quadrantārǐ·us -a -um adj quarter; mulier quadrantaria two-bit wench (woman who sold herself for a pittance); tabulae quadrantariae record of debts reduced to a fourth

quadrāt·us -a -um adj squared, square; n square

quadrīdǔ·um -ī n four-day period, four days

quadrǐenn·ǐum -ǐī or -ī n four-year period, four years

quadrǐfārǐam adv in four parts

quadrǐfǐd·us -a -um adj split into four parts

quadrīg·ae -ārum f pl four-horse team; four-horse chariot

quadrīgār·ǐus -ǐī or -ī m chariot racer

quadrīgāt·us -a -um adj stamped with a four-horse chariot

quadrīgǔl·ae -ārum f pl little four-horse team

quadrijǔg·is -e adj four-horse-team

quadrijǔg·us -a -um adj four-horse-team; m pl four-horse team

quadrǐlibr·is -e adj four-pound

quadrǐmǔl·us -a -um adj only four years old

quadrīm·us -a -um adj four-year-old

quadringēnārǐ·us -a -um adj consisting of four hundred men each

quadringēn·ī -ae -a adj four hundred each

quadringentēsǐm·us -a -um adj four-hundredth

quadringentǐēs adv four hundred times

quadrǐpertīt·us -a -um adj four-fold

quadrǐrēm·is -e adj having four banks of oars; f quadrireme

quadrǐv·ǐum -ǐī or -ī n crossroads

quadr·ō -āre *vt* to make square; to complete; to round out, give rhythmic finish to (*a speech*); *vi* to make a square; to be exact; (of accounts) to agree, come out right, tally; (with *dat* or in + *acc*) to suit, fit, seem proper to

quadr·um -ī *n* square; **in quadrum redigere sententias** to balance sentences

quadrupĕd·ans -antis *adj* galloping; *m pl* horses

quadrŭp·ēs -ĕdis *adj* four-footed; on all fours; *mf* quadruped

quadruplāt·or -ōris *m* informer (*who received one fourth of the forfeiture*); corrupt judge

quadrŭpl·ex -ĭcis *adj* quadruple, fourfold

quadruplĭc·ō -āre *vt* to quadruple, increase fourfold

quadrŭpl·or -ārī -ātus sum *vi* to be an informer

quadrŭpl·us -a -um *adj* quadruple, fourfold; *n* four times the amount

quaerĭt·ō -āre *vt* to keep looking for; to keep asking

quaerō quaerĕre quaesīvī quaesītum *vt* to look for, search for; to try to get; to get, obtain; to try to gain, earn, acquire; to miss, lack; to require, demand, call for; to ask, interrogate; to examine, investigate; to plan, devise, aim at; (with *inf*) ▸to try to, wish to; (with ab or de or ex + *abl*) to ask (*something*) of or from (*someone*); *vi* to hold an examination; (with de + *abl*) to ask about, inquire about; si quaeris or si quaerimus (coll) to tell the truth

quaesītĭ·ō -ōnis *f* questioning under torture

quaesīt·or -ōris *m* judge (*praetor or other official who presided over a criminal trial*)

quaesīt·us -a -um *pp* of quaero; *adj* select, special; far-fetched, artificial, affected; *n* question; *n pl* gains, earnings, acquisitions, store

quaes·ō -ĕre *vt* to beg, ask; **quaeso** (usually parenthetical) please

quaestĭcŭl·us -ī *m* slight profit

quaestĭ·ō -ōnis *f* inquiry, investigation, questioning, examination; judicial investigation, criminal trial; court of inquiry, court; questioning under torture, third degree; question, subject of investigation, case; court record; (with de + *abl* of the nature of the charge) court investigating a charge of (*e.g., forgery, etc.*); **in quaestione versare** to be under investigation; **quaestio extraordinaria** investigation by a special board; **quaestio inter sicarios** murder trial, court investigating a murder; **quaestio perpetua** standing court; **quaestioni praeesse** to preside over a case, be judge at a trial; **servos in quaestionem dare** or **ferre** to hand over

slaves for questioning under torture

quaestiuncŭl·a -ae *f* minor or trifling question

quaest·or -ōris *m* quaestor; financial officer; treasury official; public prosecutor of criminal offenses

quaestōrĭ·us -a -um *adj* quaestor's, of a quaestor; *m* ex-quaestor; *n* quaestor's tent in a camp; quaestor's residence in a province

quaestuōs·us -a -um *adj* profitable, lucrative, productive; acquiring wealth; eager to make a profit, acquisitive; enriched, wealthy

quaestūr·a -ae *f* quaestorship; quaestor's safe, public funds

quaest·us -ūs *m* gain, profit; acquisition; way of making money, job, occupation, business, trade; (fig) profit, gain, benefit, advantage; ad **quaestum** for profit, to make a profit; **quaestui rem publicam habere** to use public office for personal profit; **quaestum facere** to make money

quālĭbet or **quālŭbet** *adv* anywhere, everywhere; in any way, as you please

quāl·is -e *adj* what sort of, what kind of; of such a kind, such as, as; (with quotations and citations) as, as for example; **in hoc bello, quale** in this war, the likes of which; **qualis erat!** what a man he was!

quāl·iscumque -ecumque *adj* of whatever kind; of any kind whatever, any at all; **homines, qualescumque sunt** men, no matter what kind they are

quāl·islibet -elibet *adj* of whatever kind, of whatever sort

quālit·ās -ātis *f* quality, nature, property

quālĭter *adv* as, just as

quāl·us -ī *m* wicker basket, straw basket

quam *adv* (in questions and exclamations) to what extent, how, how much; (in comparisons) as, than; (with superlatives) as . . . as possible, e.g., **quam celerrime** as fast as possible; **quam plurimo vendere** to sell at the highest price possible; **quam primum** as soon as possible; (*after verbs implying preference*) rather than

quamdĭū or **quam dĭū** *adv* how long; *conj* as long as, until

quamlĭbet or **quamlŭbet** *adv* as much as you please

quamŏbrem or **quam ob rem** *adv* for what reason, why; for which reason, wherefore, why

quamquam *conj* though, although

quamvīs *adv* (with *adj* or *adv*) however; ever so; *conj* although

quānam *adv* by what route, by what way

quandō *adv* (in questions) when, at what time; (indefinite, after si, ne,

num) ever, at any time; *conj* when; because, since

quandōcumque or **quandōcunque** *adv* at some time or other, some day; *conj* whenever; as often as, no matter when

quandōque *adv* at some time, at one time or other, some day; *conj* whenever; as often as; since

quandōquidem *conj* in as much as, whereas, seeing that

quantill·us -a -um *adj* how much, how little

quantit·ās -ātis *f* quantity

quantō *adv* by how much, how much; **quanto ante** how much earlier; **quanto . . . tanto** the . . . the

quantopēre *adv* how much, how greatly; with how great effort, how carefully

quantŭlum *adv* how little; **quantulum interest utrum** how little difference it makes whether

quantŭl·us -a -um *adj* how great, how much, how little, how small, how insignificant

quantul·uscumque -acumque -umcumque *adj* however small, however unimportant

quantum *adv* as much as, so much as, as great an extent; how much, how far, to what extent; (with comparatives) the more, the greater; **quantum in me fuit** as much as I could, to the best of my ability; **quantum maximā voce potuit** at the the top of his voice; **quantum potest** as much (or *fast, quickly, soon, long, etc.*) as possible

quantumcumque *adv* as much as

quantumlibet *adv* however much

quantumvis *adv* however; **quantumvis rusticus** however unsophisticated, although unsophisticated

quant·us -a -um *adj* how great, how much; **quantus quantus** however great, however much; *pron neut* what amount; (with *genit*) how much; **in quantum** to whatever extent, as far as; **quanti** (*genit* of price) at what price, how much, how dearly, how high; **quanto** (*abl* of price) at what price, for how much; **quantum frumenti** how much grain

quant·uscumque -acumque -umcumque *adj* however great; of whatever size; however small, however trifling, however unimportant

quant·uslibet -alibet -umlibet *adj* however great; ever so great

quant·usvis -āvis -umvis *adj* however great

quāpropter *adv* wherefore, why

quāquā *adv* by whatever route, whatever way

quāquam *adv* by any way

quārē or **quā rē** *adv* by what means, how; from what cause, why; whereby; wherefore

quartadecumān·ī -ōrum *m pl* sol-

diers of the fourteenth legion

quartān·us -a -um *adj* occurring every fourth day; *f* quartan fever; *m pl* soldiers of the fourteenth legion

quartār·ius -iī or **-ī** *m* quarter pint

quartō *adv* for the fourth time

quartum *adv* for the fourth time

quart·us -a -um *adj* fourth

quart·us decim·us -a -um *adj* fourteenth

quasi *conj* as if, just as if, as though

quasi *adv* as it were, so to speak; about, nearly, almost

quasill·um -ī *n* or **quasill·us -ī** *m* small basket

quassāti·ō -ōnis *f* shaking

quass·ō -āre *vt* to keep shaking, keep tossing, keep waving; to batter, shatter, smash to pieces; (fig) to shake, weaken

quass·us -a -um *pp* of **quatio**; *adj* shattered, broken; **vox quassa** weak voice

quate·faciō -facĕre -fēcī -factum *vt* to shake; (fig) to weaken

quatēnus *adv* how far, to what point; as far as; till when, how long; to what extent; **est quatenus** there is an extent to which; *conj* as far as; insofar as, inasmuch as, seeing that, since, as

quater *adv* four times

quater deciens or **quater deciēs** *adv* fourteen times

quatern·ī -ae -a *adj* four together, four in a group, four each

quatiō quatĕre — -quassum *vt* to shake, cause to tremble, cause to vibrate; to brandish, wave about; to beat, strike, drive; to batter, crush; (fig) to touch, move, affect; (fig) to plague, harass

quattuor (indecl) *adj* four

quattuordĕcim (indecl) *adj* fourteen

quattuorvirāt·us -ūs *m* membership on the board of four

quattuorvir·ī -ōrum *m pl* board of four officials (*executive board of municipalities and colonies*)

-que *conj* and

quemadmŏdum or **quem ad mŏdum** *adv* in what way, how; *conj* just as, as

qu·eō -īre -īvī or **-iī -ītum** *vi* to be able; (with *inf*) to be able to

quercēt·um -ī *n* oak forest

quercĕ·us -a -um *adj* oak, of oak

querc·us -ūs *f* oak tree; oak-leaf crown (*awarded to a soldier who saved citizen in battle*); acorns

querell·a or **querēl·a -ae** *f* complaint

queribund·us -a -um *adj* complaining; **vox queribunda** whining voice

querimōni·a -ae *f* complaint, grievance; elegy

querit·or -ārī -ātus sum *vi* to keep complaining

quern·us -a -um *adj* oak, of oak

queror querī questus sum *vt* to

complain of, complain about; to lament; *vi* to complain; (of birds) to sing, warble, sing sadly, coo mournfully

querquētulān·us -a -um *adj* oak, covered with oak trees

querūl·us -a -um *adj* complaining, full of complaints, querulous; plaintive; warbling, cooing

questus *pp of* **queror**

quest·us -ūs *m* complaint; plaintive note (*of the nightingale*)

quī quae quod *adj* (interrog) which, what, what kind of; (indefinite) any; *pron* (rel) who, that; (indef, after **sī, nisi, num, nē**) anyone

quī *adv* how; why; at what price; whereby; in some way, somehow

quia *conj* because

quiănam *adv* why

quicquam cūjusquam *pron* anything

quicque cūjusque *pron* each, each one

quidquid (*genit* not in use) *pron* whatever

quīcum (old *abl* + **cum**) *pron* with whom, with which

quīcumque quaecumque quodcumque or **quīcunque quaecunque quodcunque** *pron* (rel) whoever, whosoever, everyone who, whatever, whatsoever, everything that, all that; (indef) any whatsoever, any possible, every possible

quid *adv* why

quid cūjus *pron* (interrog) what; (indef, after **sī, nisi, num,** or **nē**) anything

quīdam quaedam quiddam *pron* a certain one, a certain person, a certain thing

quīdam quaedam quoddam *adj* a certain; (to soften an expression) a kind of, what one might call

quidem *adv* (emphasizing the word that is placed before it) indeed, in fact; (qualifying or limiting) at least, at any rate; (concessive) it is true; of course; all right; (exemplifying) for example; **ne . . . quidem** (emphasizing the intervening word) not even, e.g., **ne tu quidem** not even you

quidnam cūjusnam *pron* (interrog) what

quidnam *adv* why, why in the world

quidnī *adv* why not

quidpiam cūjuspiam *pron* anything, something

quidquid (*genit* not in use; *abl:* **quōquo**) *pron* whatever, whatsoever, everything which; **per quidquid deorum** by all the gods

quidquid *adv* to whatever extent, the further

quĭ·ēs -ētis *f* quiet, peace, rest; calm, lull; neutrality; sleep; dream; sleep of death, death

quiēscō -ēscere -ēvī -ētum *vt* to stand by and watch, quietly allow; *vi* to rest, keep quiet, be inactive;

to rest, sleep, be asleep; to lie still, be still, be undisturbed; to pause, make a pause; to be calm, be unruffled; to be neutral, keep neutral; (with *inf*) to cease to, stop; (with **ab** + *abl*) to be free from

quiētē *adv* quietly, calmly

quiēt·us -a -um *adj* at rest, resting, free from exertion, inactive; quiet, peaceful, undisturbed; neutral; calm, quiet; still, silent; idle; *n pl* period of peace

quīlibet quaelibet quidlibet *pron* anyone, any you wish, no matter who, anything, anything you wish, not matter what, everything

quīlibet quaelibet quodlibet *adj* any, any at all, any you wish

quīn *adv* (interrog) why not; (corroborative) in fact, as a matter of fact; *conj* so that not, without; **facere non possum, quīn ad tē mittam librum** I can't help sending you the book; **nullō modō introīre possem, quīn vīderent mē** I just couldn't walk in without their seeing me; (after verbs of preventing, opposing) from: **mīlitēs aegrē sunt retentī quīn oppidum oppugnārent** the soldiers could barely be kept from assaulting the town; (after verbs of hesitation, doubt, suspicion): **nōn dubitō quīn** I do not doubt that; (esp. representing a nominative of a relative pronoun with a negative) that . . . not, without: **nēmo aspicere potest quīn dīcat** no one can look on without saying; **nēmo est quīn velit** there is no one who does not prefer

quīnam quaenam quodnam *adj* which, what, just which, just what

Quīnct- = Quīnt-

quīnc·unx -uncis *m* five twelfths; five percent (*interest*); the figure five (*as arranged on dice or cards*)

quīndeciēns or **quīndeciēs** *adv* fifteen times

quīndĕcim (indecl) *adj* fifteen

quīndecimprīm·ī -ōrum *m pl* executive board of fifteen (*magistrates of a municipality*)

quīndecimvīrāl·is -e *adj* of the board of fifteen

quīndecimvir·ī -ōrum *m pl* board of fifteen; **quīndecimvirī Sibyllīnī** board of fifteen in charge of the Sibylline Books

quīngēnāri·us -a -um *adj* of five hundred each, consisting of five hundred men

quīngēn·ī -ae -a *adj* five hundred each

quīngentēsim·us -a -um *adj* five-hundredth

quīngent·ī -ae -a *adj* five hundred

quīngentiēns or **quīngentiēs** *adv* five hundred times

quīn·ī -ae -a *adj* five each; **quīnī dēnī** fifteen each; **quīnī vīcēnī** twenty-five each

quīnquāgēn·ī -ae -a *adj* fifty each

quinquāgēsĭm·us -a -um *adj* fiftieth; *f* two-percent tax

quinquāginta (indecl) *adj* fifty

Quinquātr·ūs -ŭum *f pl* or **Quinquātr·ĭa -ĭum** *n pl* festival in honor of Minerva (*celebrated from March 19th to 23rd*)

quinque (indecl) *adj* five

quinquennāl·is -e *adj* quinquennial, occurring every five years; five-year, lasting five years

quinquenn·is -e *adj* five years old, of five years

quinquenn·ĭum -ĭī or **-ĭ** *n* five-year period, five years

quinquepartīt·us -a -um *adj* fivefold, divided into five parts

quinqueprīm·ī -ōrum *m pl* fiveman board of magistrates

quinquerēm·is -e *adj* having five banks of oars; *f* quinquereme

quinquĕ·vir -vĭrī *m* member of a five-man board

quinquevirāt·us -ūs *m* membership on a board of five

quinquevĭr·ī -ōrum *m pl* five-man board (*created at various times to serve various purposes*)

quinquĭens or **quinquĭēs** *adv* five times

quinquĭplĭc·ō -āre *vt* to multiply by five

quintadecĭmān·ī -ōrum *m pl* soldiers of the fifteenth legion

quintān·us -a -um *adj* of the fifth; *m pl* members of the fifth legion; *f* camp street running between the fifth and sixth maniple (*used as the market street of the camp*)

Quintĭliān·us or **Quinctiliān·us -ī** *m* M. Fabius Quintilianus (*Quintilian, famous orator and rhetoric teacher, c. 35-c. 95 A.D.*)

Quintĭl·is or **Quinctīl·is -e** *adj & m* July

quintō or **quintum** *adv* for the fifth time

quint·us -a -um *adj* fifth

Quint·us -ī *m* Roman first name

quint·us decĭm·us -a -um *adj* fifteenth

quippe *adv* of course, naturally, obviously, by all means; *conj* since, for; **quippe qui** since he (*is, was, will be one who*), inasmuch as he; **multa Caesar questus est quippe qui vidisset** Caesar complained a lot since he had seen

quippĭam = quidpiam

quippĭnī *adv* why not?; of course, to be sure

Quirīnāl·ĭa -ĭum *n pl* festival in honor of Romulus (*celebrated on the 17th of February*)

Quirīnāl·is -e *adj* of Quirinus; **collis Quirinālis** Quirinal Hill (*one of the seven hills of Rome*)

Quirīn·us -a -um *adj* of Quirinus; *m* Quirinus (*epithet applied to Romulus after his deification, to Janus, to Augustus, and to Antony*)

Quir·is -ītis *m* Roman citizen; inhabitant of Cures (*Sabine town*)

quirĭtātĭ·ō -ōnis *f* shrieking, shriek

quirĭtāt·us -ūs *m* scream, shriek

Quirītēs = pl of Quiris

quirĭt·ō -āre *vi* to scream, shriek

quis cūjus *pron* (interrog) who, which one; (indef) anyone

quīs = quibus

quisnam quaenam (see **quidnam**) *pron* (interrog) who

quispĭam cūjuspĭam *pron* someone

quispĭam quaepĭam quodpĭam *adj* any

quisquam cūjusquam *pron* anyone, anybody, any person

quisque cūjusque *pron* each, each one, everybody, every one; **doctissimus quisque** every one of great learning, all the most learned; **optĭmus quisque** all the best ones

quisque quaeque quodque *adj* each

quisquĭlĭ·ae -ārum *f pl* refuse, trash, junk, rubbish, odds and ends

quisquis (*genit* not in use; *abl:* **quoquo**) *pron* whoever, whosoever, every one who; every one, each

quīvīs quaevīs quidvīs *pron* anyone, anyone you please, anyone at all; **quivis unus** any one person

quīvīs quaevīs quodvīs *adj* any, any you please, any at all

quō *adv* (interrog) where, to what place; what for, to what purpose; (after **si, nisi,** or **ne**) to any place, anywhere; **quo . . . eo . . . the; quo magis . . . eo magis the more** . . . the more; *conj* where, to which place; whereby, wherefore; (replacing **ut** when the clause contains a comparative) in order that, so that

quoad *adv* how far; how long; *conj* as long as; as far as; until

quōcircā *adv* for which reason, wherefore, therefore, that's the reason why

quōcumque *adv* to whatever place, wherever

quod *conj* because; as for the fact that; for the fact that; insofar as; as far as; **quod sī** or **quodsī** but if

quōdammŏdo or **quōdam modo** *adv* in a way

quoi = cui

quōjus = cujus

quōlĭbet *adv* anywhere you please

quom see **cum**

quōmĭnus *conj* that not; (after verbs of hindering) from, e.g., **deterrere aliquem quominus habeat** to keep someone from having

quōmŏdo *adv* (interrog) in what way, how; (rel) just as, as

quōmŏdocumque *adv* in whatever way, however

quōmŏdŏnam *adv* in just what way, how then

quōnam *adv* where, where to; to what purpose, to what end

quondam *adv* once, at one time, formerly; at times, sometimes, once in a while; some day, one day (*in the future*)

quŏnĭam *conj* because, seeing that, now that

quŏpĭam *adv* to any place, anywhere

quŏque *adv* too, also

quŏquŏ *adv* to whatever place, wherever

quŏquŏmŏdŏ *adv* in whatever way, however

quŏquŏversum or **quŏquŏversus** *adv* in every direction, every way

quorsum or **quorsus** *adv* in what direction, where to; to what end, why

quot (indecl) *adj* (interrog) how many; (correlative) as many; **quot Kalendis** every first of the month; **quot mensibus** every month

quŏtannis *adv* every year

quŏtcumque (indecl) *adj* however many

quŏtēn·ī -ae -a *adj* how many each

quŏtīdĭē *adv* daily

quŏtĭens or **quŏtĭēs** *adv* (interrog) how many times; (correlative) as often as

quŏtĭenscumque or **quŏtĭenscunque** *adv* however often, as often as

quotquot (indecl) *adj* however many, no matter how many

quŏtŭm·us -a -um *adj* which in number, which in order

quot·us -a -um *adj* which, what; what a small, what a trifling; **quota hora est?** what time is it?; **quota pars** what part; **quot erit iste liber qui . . .** which will be the book which . . .; **quotus quisque philosophorum invenitur** how rarely is one of the philosophers found, how few philosophers are found

quot·uscumque -acumque -umcumque *adj* just what, just which; **quotacumque pars** just what part

quŏusque *adv* how far, how long

quŏvīs *adv* to any place whatsoever, anywhere; **quovis gentium** anywhere in the world

quum see **cum** *conj*

R

răbĭdē *adv* rabidly, madly, furiously

răbĭd·us -a -um *adj* rabid, mad, furious, raving, uncontrolled

răbĭ·ēs (*genit* not in use) *f* rage, madness; (fig) rage, anger, fury, wild passion, eagerness

răbĭōsē *adv* furiously, ravingly

răbĭōsŭl·us -a -um *adj* half-crazy

răbĭōs·us -a -um *adj* rabid, mad, raving, crazy

răbŭl·a -ae *m* ranting lawyer

răcēmĭf·er -ĕra -ĕrum *adj* clustered; covered with grape clusters

răcēm·us -ī *m* cluster, bunch (*esp. of grapes*); (fig) wine

rădĭ·ans -antis *adj* shining, beaming, radiant

rădĭāt·us -a -um *adj* spoked; having rays, radiant

rādīcĭtus *adv* by the roots, root and all; completely

rādīcŭl·a -ae *f* small root

rădĭ·ō -āre or **rădĭ·or -ārī -ātus sum** *vt* to radiate; *vi* to radiate, shine, gleam

rădĭōs·us -a -um *adj* radiant

rad·ĭus -ĭī or **-ī** *m* stake, stick; spoke; ray, beam; shuttle; radius; measuring rod; elongated olive

rād·ix -īcis *f* root; radish; foot (*of hill or mountain*); base, foundation; basis, origin

rādō rādĕre rāsī rāsum *vt* to scrape, scratch; to shave; to scratch out, erase; to graze, touch in passing; to strip off; (of the wind) to lash

raed·a -ae *f* four-wheeled carriage, coach

raedār·ĭus -ĭī or **-ī** *m* coach driver

Raetĭ·us -a -um *adj* Raetian; *f* Raetia (*Alpine country between Germany and Italy*)

Raet·us -a -um *adj* & *m* Raetian

rall·us -a -um *adj* thin, threadbare

rāmāl·ĭa -ĭum *n pl* brushwood, undergrowth

rāment·um -ī *n* or **rament·a -ae** *f* chip, shaving

rāmĕ·us -a -um *adj* of branches, of boughs

rām·ex -ĭcis *m* hernia, rupture; blood vessel of the lung

Ramn·ēs or **Ramnens·ēs -ĭum** *m pl* one of the three original Roman tribes; (fig) blue bloods

rāmōs·us -a -um *adj* branchy, branching; branch-like

rāmŭl·us -ī *m* twig

rām·us -ī *m* branch, bough; branch (*of an antler*); stick, club

rān·a -ae *f* frog; **rana marina** frog fish

ranc·ens -entis *adj* putrid, stinking

rancĭdŭl·us -a -um *adj* rank, stinking; disgusting

rancĭd·us -a -um *adj* rancid, rank, stinking; disgusting

rānuncŭl·us -ī *m* little frog, tadpole

răpācĭd·a -ae *m* son of a thief

răpācĭt·ās -ātis *f* rapacity, greediness

răp·ax -ācis *adj* rapacious, grasping, grabby, greedy for plunder; insatiable

răphăn·us -ī *m* radish

răpĭdē *adv* rapidly; (to burn) fiercely

răpĭdĭt·ās -ātis *f* rapidity, velocity, swiftness, rush

răpĭd·us -a -um *adj* tearing away,

seizing; fierce, consuming, white-hot (*fire*); rapid, swift, rushing, hurrying, impetuous

rapīn·a -ae *f* rapine, pillage; prey, booty

rapiō rapĕre rapŭī raptum *vt* to seize and carry off, to snatch, tear, pluck; to drag off; to hurry, drive, cause to rush; to carry off by force, rob, ravish, ravage, lay waste; to lead on hurriedly; **flammam rapere** to catch fire; **in jus rapere** to drag off to court, hale before a court; **se rapere** to hurry, dash, take off

raptim *adv* hurriedly, speedily, suddenly

raptī·ō -ōnis *f* abduction, ravishing, rape

rapt·ō -āre *vt* to seize and carry off, drag away; to drag along; to plunder; to hale, arraign

rapt·or -ōris *m* plunderer, robber; rapist

rapt·or -a -um *pp* of **rapio**; *n* plunder, loot

rapt·us -ūs *m* snatching away; looting, robbery; rape, abduction

rāpŭl·um -ī *n* little turnip

rāp·um -ī *n* turnip

rārē *adv* rarely, seldom

rārē·faciō -facĕre -fēcī -factum *vt* to rarefy, thin out

rāresc·ō -ĕre *vi* to grow thin, lose density, become rarefied; to grow wider, widen out, open up; to become fewer; to disappear, die away

rārĭt·ās -ātis *f* looseness of texture; thinness; small number

rārō *adv* rarely, seldom

rār·us -a -um *adj* wide apart, of loose texture, thin; far apart, scattered far apart; scarce, sparse; few; (mil) in open rank; uncommon, rare, unusual

rāsĭl·is -e *adj* shaved smooth, scraped, polished

rastr·um -ī *n* rake; mattock

rāsus *pp* of **rado**

ratĭ·ō -ōnis *f* calculation, computation, reckoning, account; matter, affair, business, transaction; consideration, respect, regard; grounds; scheme, system, method, procedure; theory, doctrine; science; relation, connection, reference; fashion, way, style; reasoning, reason, judgment, understanding; reasonableness, order, law, rule; view, opinion; **propter rationem** (with *genit*) out of regard for; **ratio aeraria** rate of exchange; **ratio atque usus** theory and practice; **ratio constat** the accounts tally; **rationem conferre, referre,** or **deferre** (with *genit*) to render or give an account of, account for; **rationem ducere** to make a calculation, reckon; **rationem habere** (with **cum +** *abl*) to have to do with; **rationem inire** to calculate, make a calculation

ratĭōcĭnātĭ·ō -ōnis *f* (rhet) exercise

of the reasoning powers, reasoning; syllogism

ratĭōcĭnātīv·us -a -um *adj* syllogistic

ratĭōcĭnāt·or -ōris *m* accountant

ratĭōcĭn·or -ārī -ātus sum *vt & vi* to calculate, reckon; to reason, argue, conclude, infer

rat·is -is *f* raft; boat; *f pl* pontoons

ratiuncŭl·a -ae *f* small account; trifling reason; petty syllogism

rat·us -a -um *pp* of **reor**; *adj* reckoned, calculated; fixed, established, settled, certain, sure, approved; **pro rata parte** or **pro rata** in proportion, proportionately; **ratum facere** or **ratum efficere** to confirm, ratify, approve; **ratum habere** or **ducere** to consider valid, regard as certain or sure

raucĭsŏn·us -a -um *adj* hoarse

rauc·us -a -um *adj* raucous, hoarse; screaming, strident; scraping; deep, deep-voiced

raud·us or **rūd·us -ĕris** *n* copper coin

rauduscŭl·um or **rūduscŭl·um -ī** *n* bit of money

rāv·iō -īre *vi* to talk oneself hoarse

rāv·is -is *f* hoarseness

rāv·us -a -um *adj* greyish

re·a -ae *f* defendant, guilty woman

reapse *adv* in fact, actually, really

Reāt·e -is *n* Sabine town

Reātīn·us -a -um *adj & m* Reatine

rebellātĭ·ō -ōnis *f* rebellion

rebellātr·ix -īcis *f* rebel; **Germania rebellatrix** rebel Germany

rebellĭ·ō -ōnis *f* rebellion

rebell·is -e *adj* rebellious; *m pl* rebels

rebellĭum -ĭī or **-ī** *n* rebellion

rebell·ō -āre *vi* to rebel

rebĭt·ō -ĕre *vi* to go back

rebŏ·ō -āre *vt* to make reecho; *vi* to reecho, bellow back

recalcĭtr·ō -āre *vi* to kick back

recal·ĕō -ēre *vi* to be warmed; (of a river) to run warm (*e.g., with blood*)

recal·escō -escĕre -ŭī *vi* to grow warm again

recal·faciō -facĕre -fēcī *vt* to make warm again, warm up again

recalv·us -a -um *adj* bald in front, with receding hairline

recand·escō -escĕre -ŭī *vi* to grow white; to grow hot, glow; (with *dat*) to grow white, grow hot, glow in response to

recant·ō -āre *vt* to recant; to charm back, charm away; *vi* to reecho

re·cēdō -cēdĕre -cessī -cessum *vi* to go back, go away, withdraw, recede, give ground, fall back; to depart; to vanish, disappear; to stand back, be distant

recell·ō -ĕre *vi* to spring back, recoil

rec·ens -entis *adj* recent, fresh, young; newly arrived, just arrived; modern; fresh, rested; *n pl* recent events

recens *adv* just, recently, lately, newly

recens-ĕō -ēre -ŭī -um *vt* to count, enumerate, number, survey; to review, hold a review of (*the army*); (*of a censor*) to revise the roll of, review, enroll; to recount, go over again, retell

recensĭ-ō -ōnis *f* revision

recensus *pp* of **recenseo**

recens-us -ūs *m* review

receptācŭl-um -ī *n* receptacle, container; reservoir; place of refuge, shelter; hiding place

receptĭ-ō -ōnis *f* reception

recept-ō -āre *vt* to take back; to welcome frequently into the home, entertain; to tug at; **se receptare** to beat a hasty retreat

recept-or -ōris *m* or **receptr-ix -īcis** *f* shelterer; concealer

recept-us -a -um *pp* of **recipio**; *n* obligation

recept-us -ūs *m* taking back, recantation; (mil) retreat; way of escape; refuge, place of retreat; return; (**signum**) **receptui canere** to sound retreat

recessim *adv* backwards

recess-us -ūs *m* retreat, withdrawal; departure; secluded spot, retreat; inner room, central chamber; recess; background

recharmīd-ō -āre *vi* to stop being a Charmides (*character in Roman comedy*)

recidīv-us -a -um *adj* recurring, returning; rebuilt

re-cĭdo -cĭdĕre -cĭdī -cīsum *vt* to cut back, cut away, cut off, cut down; to abridge, cut short

re-cĭdō -cĭdĕre -cĭdī -cāsum or **rec-cĭdō -cĭdĕre** *vi* to fall back; to jump back, recoil; to suffer a relapse; (fig) to fall back, fall, sink, relapse; to turn out, result; (with **ad** or **in** + *acc*) to pass to, be handed over to

re-cingō -cingĕre — -cinctum *vt* to loosen, undo, take off

recĭn-ō -ĕre *vi* to repeat, reecho; *vi* to sound a warning

reciper- = recuper-

re-cĭpĭō -cĭpĕre -cēpī -ceptum *vt* to keep back, keep in reserve; to take back, withdraw, bring back, carry back, retake, recover, regain; to take in, accept, receive, welcome; to gain, collect, take in, make (*money*); to take up, assume, undertake; to guarantee, pledge; (mil) to retake, reoccupy, recapture, seize, take, occupy; **ad se** or **in se recipere** to take upon oneself, take responsibility for, promise, guarantee; **se recipere** to get hold of oneself again, regain self-composure, recover, come to again; to retreat, escape; **se recipere** (with **ad** or **in** + *acc*) to retreat to, escape to, find refuge in

reciprŏc-ō -āre *vt* to move back and forth; to turn back; to back (*e.g., a ship*) about, reverse the direction of; to reverse, convert (*a proposition*); *vi* (of the tide) to ebb and flow, rise and fall

reciprŏc-us -a -um *adj* ebbing and flowing, going backwards and forwards

recisus *pp* of **recido**

recitātĭ-ō -ōnis *f* reading aloud, recitation

recitāt-or -ōris *m* reader, reciter

recit-ō -āre *vt* to read out, read aloud, recite; to name in writing, appoint, constitute; **senatum recitare** to have roll call in the senate

reclāmātĭ-ō -ōnis *f* cry of disapproval

reclāmĭt-ō -āre *vi* to voice disapproval

reclām-ō -āre *vt* to protest; *vi* to raise a protest, voice disapproval, shout objections; to reverberate; (with *dat*) to express disapproval to, contradict

reclīn-is -e *adj* reclining, leaning back

reclīn-ō -āre *vt* to bend back, lean back, rest; (with **ab** + *abl*) to distract (*someone*) from; **se reclinare** to lean

re-clūdō -clūdĕre -clūsī -clūsum *vt* to open; to lay open, disclose; to draw (*sword*); to break up (*the soil*)

recoctus *pp* of **recoquo**

recōgĭt-ō -āre *vi* (with **de** + *abl*) to think again about, reconsider, reflect on

recognitĭ-ō -ōnis *f* reinvestigation

reco-gnoscō -gnoscĕre -gnōvī -gnitum *vt* to call to mind again, review; to recognize; to look over, examine, inspect, investigate; to certify, authorize

recol-lĭgō -lĭgĕre -lēgī -lectum *vt* to gather again, gather up, collect; **te recollige** get hold of yourself, pluck up your courage

re-cŏlō -cŏlĕre -cŏlŭī -cultum *vt* to till again; to honor again; to recall to mind, think over, consider; to cultivate once more, practice again, resume

recommĭnisc-or -ī *vt* to call to mind again, recall

recomposĭt-us -a -um *adj* rearranged

reconciliātĭ-ō -ōnis *f* winning back again, reestablishment, restoration; reconciling, reconciliation

reconcili-ō -āre *vt* to bring back, regain, recover; to restore, reestablish; to win over again, conciliate; to bring together again, reconcile

reconcinn-ō -āre *vt* to set right again, repair

recondĭt-us -a -um *adj* hidden, concealed; recondite, abstruse, profound; reserved (*person*)

recon-dō -dĕre -dĭdī -dĭtum *vt* to put back again, put away, hoard; to hide, conceal; to plunge (*sword*); to close (*eyes*) again; to store up (*in the mind*)

reconfl·ō -āre *vt* to blow up again, rekindle

re·cŏquō -coquĕre -coxī -coctum *vt* to cook, boil, or bake again; to recast, remold

recordātĭ·ō -ōnis *f* recollection, remembrance

record·or -ārī -ātus sum *vt* to recall, recollect, remember

recrĕ·ō -āre *vt* to recreate, restore, renew; (fig) to revive, refresh

recrĕp·ō -āre *vt & vi* to reecho

re·crescō -crescĕre -crēvī *vi* to grow again; to be renewed

recrūd·escō -escĕre -ŭī *vi* to become raw again; (of a wound) to open up again; (of a revolt) to break out again

rectā *adv* by a direct route, right on, directly

rectē *adv* in a straight line; rightly, correctly, suitably, properly, well; quite; (in answers) well, right, quite well, fine

rectĭ·ō -ōnis *f* direction, controlling

rect·or -ōris *m* guide, controller, leader, ruler, master, pilot

rect·us -a -um *pp of* **rego**; *adj* in a straight line, straight, direct; correct, right, proper, appropriate; just, upright, conscientious, virtuous; *n* right; uprightness, rectitude, virtue

recŭb·ō -āre *vi* to lie on one's back, lie down, rest

rēcŭl·a -ae *f* little thing

recultus *pp of* **recolo**

re·cumbō -cumbĕre -cubŭī *vi* to lie down again, lie down; to recline (*esp. at table*); to sink down (*e.g., in a swamp*); to fall; (of fog) to settle down

recuperātĭ·ō -ōnis *f* recovery

recuperāt·or or **reciperāt·or -ōris** *m* recoverer, regainer; (law) arbiter (*member of a bench of from three to five men who expedited cases needing speedy decisions*)

recuperātōrĭ·us or **reciperātōrĭ·us -a -um** *adj* of the special court for summary civil suits

recupĕr·ō or **recipĕr·ō -āre** *vt* to regain, recover, get back; to win over again

recŭr·ō -āre *vt* to restore, refresh, restore to health

re·currō -currĕre -currī *vi* to run back, hurry back; to return, recur, come back

recurs·ō -āre *vi* to keep running back; to keep recurring

recurs·us -ūs *m* return; retreat

recurv·ō -āre *vt* to curve, bend back

recurv·us -a -um *adj* curving, curved, bent, crooked

recusātĭ·ō -ōnis *f* refusal; (law) objection, protest; counterplea

recūs·ō -āre *vt* to raise objections to, reject, refuse; (with *inf*) to be

reluctant to, refuse to; *vi* to raise an objection, object; to make a rebuttal

recuss·us -a -um *adj* reverberating

recutīt·us -a -um *adj* with the foreskin cut back, circumcised; Jewish

redactus *pp of* **redigo**

redambŭl·ō -āre *vi* to walk back

redăm·ō -āre *vt* to love in return

redargu·ō -ĕre -ī *vt* to disprove, contradict, refute

redauspĭc·ō -āre *vi* to take the return auspices; (coll) to return

red·dō -dĕre -dĭdī -dĭtum *vt* to give back, return, restore, replace; to repay; to repeat, recite (*words*); to translate; to render, make; to give as due, pay, deliver; to reflect, produce, imitate; **se reddere** to return, come back

redemptĭ·ō -ōnis *f* ransoming; bribing; revenue collection

redempt·ō -āre *vt* to ransom, repeatedly

redempt·or -ōris *m* contractor; revenue agent

redemptūr·a -ae *f* revenue collection

redemptus *pp of* **redimo**

red·ĕō -īre -ĭī -ĭtum *vi* to go or come back, return; (of a speaker) to return (*to the main theme*); (with **ad** + *acc*) **a** to return to, revert to; **b** to fall back on, have recourse to, be reduced to; **c** (of power, inheritances, etc.) to revert to, devolve upon; **ad se redire** to come to again, regain consciousness; to control oneself

redhāl·ō -āre *vt* to exhale

redhĭb·ĕō -ēre — -ĭtum *vt* to take back

red·igō -igĕre -ēgī -actum *vt* to drive back, lead back, bring back; to call in, collect, raise (*money, revenues*); to reduce, diminish (*numbers*); to force, compel, subdue, reduce; (with double *acc*) to render, make; (with **in** or **sub** + *acc*) to bring under the power of; **ad vanum et irritum redigere** to make meaningless; **in memoriam redigere** to remember, recall; **in provinciam redigere** to reduce to the rank of a province

redimīcŭl·um -ī *n* band, chaplet, fillet; chain, fetter

redim·ĭō -īre -ĭī -ĭtum *vt* to crown, wreathe

red·imō -imĕre -ēmī -emptum *vt* to buy back; to ransom, redeem; to buy off, rescue by payment, rescue, release, set free; to buy up; to buy off, ward off, avert; to pay for, compensate for, atone for; to get by contract, collect under contract

redintĕgr·ō -āre *vt* to make whole again, restore, refresh; (mil) to bring to full strength

redipisc·or -ī *vt* to get back

reditĭ·ō -ōnis *f* return

redĭt·us -ūs *m* return; revenue, proceeds, returns; (of heavenly bodies) revolution, orbit; (fig) restoration

redivia see **reduvia**

redivīv·us -a -um *adj* second-hand (*building materials*)

redol·ĕō -ēre -ŭī *vt* to smell of; *vi* to smell, be redolent

redomĭt·us -a -um *adj* retamed, broken in again

redōn·ō -āre *vt* to restore, give back again; to give up, abandon

redorm·ĭō -īre *vi* to go to sleep again

re·dūcō -dūcĕre -dūxī -ductum *vt* to draw back; to lead back, bring back; to escort (*official as mark of honor to his home*); to remarry (*after a separation*); to restore to normal; to withdraw (*troops*); **in gratiam reducere** to restore to favor

reductĭ·ō -ōnis *f* restoration

reduct·or -ōris *m* restorer

reduct·us -a -um *pp* of **reduco**; remote, secluded, aloof, removed

redunc·us -a -um *adj* bent backwards, curved backwards

redundantĭ·a -ae *f* excess; redundancy

redund·ō -āre *vi* to overflow; to be too numerous, be too large; to be soaked (*e.g., with blood*); (with *abl*) to abound in; (with **de** or **ex** + *abl*) to stream from, overflow with

reduvĭ·a or **redivĭ·a -ae** *f* hangnail, loose fingernail

red·ux -ūcis *adj* guiding back, rescuing; brought back, restored

refectus *pp* of **reficio**

refell·ō -ĕre -ī *vt* to refute, disprove

re·fercĭō -fercīre -fersī -fertum *vt* to stuff, cram, choke, crowd

refer·ĭō -īre *vt* to strike back, hit back

refĕrō referre rettŭlī relātum *vt* to bring back, carry back; to give back, return, restore, pay back, repay; to bring back, return, echo (*a sound*); to renew, revive, repeat; to bring back, direct, focus, turn (*mind, attention*); to present again, represent; to say in turn, answer, reply; to announce, report, relate, tell; to note down, enter, register, record; to reckon, consider, regard; to refer, attribute, ascribe; to bring up, spit out, vomit; **gradum referre** to go back, retreat; **gratiam** or **gratias referre** to return thanks, show gratitude; **in rationibus referendis** in accounting; **pedem referre** to go back, retreat, withdraw, retire; **pedes fertque refertque** he walks up and down; **rationes referre ad aerarium** to make an accounting to the treasury; **se referre** to go back, return; **vestigia referre** to retrace footsteps, return; *vi* to make a motion, make a proposal; **ad senatum referre** (with **de** + *abl*) to bring before the senate the matter of, make a proposal to the senate about; *v impers* it is of importance, it is of consequence; **meā (tuā, nostrā) refert** it is of importance, of consequence, of advantage to me (*you, us*); **non refert utrum** it makes no difference whether; **parvi refert** (with *inf*) it is of little importance, of little advantage to; **quid refert?** what's the difference?

refert·us -a -um *pp* of **refercio**; *adj* stuffed, packed, crammed; crowded

referv·ĕō -ēre *vi* to boil over, bubble over

refervesc·ō -ĕre *vi* to begin to boil or bubble

re·ficĭō -ficĕre -fēcī -fectum *vt* to rebuild, repair, restore; to revive (*hope, etc.*); to refresh, invigorate; to get (*e.g., money*) back again; to reappoint, reelect

re·fīgō -fīgĕre -fīxī -fīxum *vt* to unfasten, undo; to take down (*pictures, posters, etc.*); to annul (*laws*)

refingō -ĕre *vt* to refashion

refixus *pp* of **refigo**

reflāgĭt·ō -āre *vt* to demand again, ask back

reflāt·us -ūs *m* head wind

re·flectō -flectĕre -flexī -flexum *vt* to bend back or backwards, turn around, turn away; (fig) to turn back, bring back, change

refl·ō -āre *vt* to breathe out again; *vi* to blow in the wrong direction

reflŭ·ō -ĕre *vi* to flow back, run back; to overflow

reflŭ·us -a -um *adj* ebbing, receding

refocill·ō -āre *vt* to rewarm; to revive

reformāt·or -ōris *m* reformer

reformĭdātĭ·ō -ōnis *f* dread

reformĭd·ō -āre *vt* to dread, stand in awe of; to shrink from, shun

reform·ō -āre *vt* to reshape, remold, transform

re·fovĕō -fovēre -fōvī -fōtum *vt* to warm again; to restore, revive, refresh

refractārĭŏl·us -a -um *adj* a bit refractory, somewhat stubborn

refractus *pp* of **refringo**

refrāg·or -ārī -ātus sum *vi* (with *dat*) to oppose, resist, thwart

refrēn·ō -āre *vt* to curb, restrain, keep down, control

refric·ō -āre -ŭī -ātum *vt* to rub open, scratch open; to irritate, reopen, inflame (*a wound*); (fig) to irritate, exasperate; (fig) to renew; *vi* to break out again

refrīgerātĭ·ō -ōnis *f* coolness

refrīgĕr·ō -āre *vt* to cool off, cool, chill; to refresh; to weary, exhaust; **refrigerari** to grow cool, grow weary

re·frīgescō -frīgescĕre -frīxī *vi* to grow cool, become cool; (fig) to lose

force, flag, abate, fail, grow dull,
grow stale, fall flat

re·fringō -fringĕre -frēgī -frac·
tum *vt* to break open, break down;
to tear off (*clothes*); (fig) to break,
check, destroy, put an end to

re·fugiō -fugĕre -fūgī *vt* to run
away from; to avoid; *vi* to run away,
escape; to disappear

refug·ium -iī or -ī *n* place of refuge;
recourse

refūg·us -a -um *adj* receding, van·
ishing; *m* fugitive

re·fulgĕō -fulgēre -fulsī *vi* to
gleam, reflect, reflect light, glitter

re·fundō -fundĕre -fūdī -fūsum
vt to pour back, pour out; refundī
to flow back, overflow

refūtātī·ō -ōnis *f* refutation

refūtāt·us -ūs *m* refutation

refūt·ō -āre *vt* to repress, suppress;
to refute, disprove

rēgāl·is -e *adj* kingly, regal; king's,
of a king, royal

rēgāliter *adv* royally, in royal style,
splendidly; despotically

regel·ō -āre *vt* to cool off; to thaw

re·gĕrō -gerĕre -gessī -gestum *vt*
to carry back, throw back; (fig) to
throw back (*remarks*)

rēgi·a -ae *f* palace, castle, court;
fortress, residence; (in camp) king's
tent; royal family, king and cour·
tiers, court; regia (*originally the
palace of King Numa on the Sacred
Way in the Roman Forum and la·
ter the residence of the Pontifex
Maximus*)

rēgiē *adv* royally; despotically

Rēgiens·is -e or Rēgīn·us -a -um
adj of Regium; *m pl* inhabitants of
Regium

rēgific·us -a -um *adj* royal, king·
ly, magnificent

regign·ō -ēre *vt* to reproduce

Rēgillān·us -a -um or Rēgil·
lens·is -e *adj* of or at Lake Regil·
lus

rēgill·us -a -um *adj* royal, magnifi·
cent

Rēgill·us -ī *m* lake in Latium fa·
mous for the victory over the Latins
won by the Romans under the dic·
tator Postumius (496 B.C.)

regim·en -inis *n* steering, control·
ling; rudder; government, rule,
command, guidance; director, ruler,
governor

rēgīn·a -ae *f* queen; princess; noble
woman, lady

regi·ō -ōnis *f* straight line, line, di·
rection; boundary, boundary line;
region, area, quarter, neighborhood;
ward (*of Rome*); district, province
(*of a country*); department, sphere;
ab recta regione in a straight
line; de recta regione deflectere
to veer off from a straight path; e
regione in a straight line, direct·
ly; e regione (with *genit*) in the
opposite direction to, exactly oppo·
site; rectā regione by a direct
route

regiōnātim *adv* by wards, by dis·
tricts

Rēg·ium or Rhēg·ium -iī or -ī *n*
city on the toe of Italy; town in
Cisalpine Gaul

rēgi·us -a -um *adj* king's, kingly,
royal, regal; like a king, worthy of
a king, magnificent; *m pl* the king's
troops; *f* see regia

reglūtin·ō -āre *vt* to unglue

regnāt·or -ōris *m* ruler, sovereign

regnātr·ix -īcis *adj fem* imperial

regn·ō -āre *vi* to be king, reign; to
be supreme, hold sway; to domi·
neer; (with *genit*) to be king of;
(with in + *acc*) to rule over; reg·
nārī to be ruled by a king, be un·
der a king

regn·um -ī *n* monarchy, royal pow·
er, kingship; absolute power, des·
potism, power; supremacy, control,
direction, sovereignty; realm, king·
dom; domain, estate

regō regĕre rexī rectum *vt* to keep
in a straight line; keep in a proper
course; to guide, conduct; to gov·
ern, rule, command; to manage, di·
rect; regere fīnīs (law) to mark
out the limits

re·gredior -grēdī -gressus sum
vi to step or go back; to come back,
return; to march back, retreat

regress·us -ūs *m* return; retreat

rēgul·a -ae *f* ruler (*for measuring*);
straight stick; straight board; rule,
standard, example, model, principle

rēgul·us -ī *m* petty king, prince,
chieftain; prince

Rēgul·us -ī *m* M. Atilius Regulus
(*Roman general who was taken
prisoner by the Carthaginians in
the First Punic War, refused to let
himself be ransomed, and was killed
in 250 B.C.*)

regust·ō -āre *vt* to taste again; (fig)
to delve again into (*e.g., literature*)

rē·iciō -icĕre -jēcī -jectum *vt* to
throw back, fling back; to throw
over one's shoulders or behind one;
to beat back, repel, repulse; to re·
ject, refuse, disdain, scorn; (of
judges) to challenge, overrule; to
refer, direct, assign; to postpone;
rem reicere (with ad + *acc*) to
turn over or refer the matter to
(*someone for consideration or de·
cision*); potestas reiciendi (law)
right to challenge

rējectānĕ·us -a -um *adj* to be re·
jected

rējectī·ō -ōnis *f* rejection; (law)
challenging; rejectio judicum
challenging of the members of the
jury

rēject·ō -āre *vt* to throw back

rējectus *pp* of reicio

re·lābor -lābī -lapsus sum *vi* to
slide or glide back; to sink down
(*upon a couch*); (of rivers) to flow
back; to sail back; (fig) to relapse

relangu·escō -escĕre -ī *vi* to faint;
to be relaxed, relax; to weaken

relātī·ō -ōnis *f* report (*made by a*

magistrate to the senate or emperor); repetition, reiteration; **relatio criminis** (law) answering to a charge

relāt·or -ōris *m* proposer of a motion

relātus *pp of* **refero**

relāt·us -ūs *m* official report; narration, recital, listing; **relatus carminum** recital of poems

relaxātī·ō -ōnis *f* relaxation, easing; mitigation

relax·ō -āre *vt* to stretch out, widen, open; to loosen, open; to release, set free; to ease, ease the tensions of, relieve, cheer up; to alleviate, mitigate

relectus *pp of* **relego**

relēgātī·ō -ōnis *f* banishment, sending into retirement

relēg·ō -āre *vt* to send away, remove, send into retirement, retire; to banish; to put aside, reject; to refer

re·lēgō -legĕre -lēgī -lectum *vt* to collect again, gather up, gather together, to travel over, sail over again; to go over, review (*in thought, in a speech*); to reread

relentesc·ō -ĕre *vi* to slack off, cool off

relĕv·ō -āre *vt* to lighten; to lift up or raise again; (fig) to relieve, free, lighten, soothe, alleviate

relictī·ō -ōnis *f* abandonment

relictus *pp of* **relinquo**

relicŭus *see* **reliquus**

religātī·ō -ōnis *f* tying back, tying up

religi·ō -ōnis *f* religious scruple, conscientiousness, sense of right; misgivings; reverence, awe; religion; superstition; sanctity, holiness; religion, sect, cult, mode of worship; object of veneration, sacred object, sacred place; divine service, worship, religious observation

religiōsē *adv* scrupulously, conscientiously, carefully, exactly; reverently, piously, religiously

religiōs·us -a -um *adj* scrupulous, conscientious, exact, precise, accurate; religious, reverent, pious, devout; superstitious; sacred, holy, consecrated; subject to religious claims, under religious liability

relig·ō -āre *vt* to bind back, tie up; to moor (*a ship*); to unbind, untie, loosen; (fig) to bind

re·linō -linĕre -lēvī — *vt* to unseal, open

re·linquō -linquĕre -līquī -lictum *vt* to leave behind, not take along; to leave behind, bequeath; to permit to remain, let remain; to leave alive; to forsake, abandon, desert, leave in a lurch; to give up, abandon, relinquish, resign; to leave unmentioned; **locum integrum relinquere** to leave the place untouched

reliqui·ae -ārum *f pl* remains, remnants

relĭqu·us or **relicŭ·us -a -um** *adj* remaining, left over, left; remaining, subsequent, future (*time*); outstanding (*debt*); *m pl* the others; *n* remainder, rest, residue; **in reliquum** in the future, for the future; **nihil reliqui facere** to leave nothing undone, omit nothing, leave no stone unturned; **reliqui omnes** all the rest; **reliquum est** (with *inf* or **ut**) it only remains to; **reliquum aliquem facere** to leave someone behind; to spare someone; **reliquum aliquid facere** or **aliquid reliqui facere** to leave something remaining, leave something behind, neglect something

rellig- = relig-

relliq- = reliq-

re·lūceō -lūcēre -luxī *vi* to reflect light, gleam, shine out, blaze

re·lūcescō -lūcescĕre -luxī *vi* to grow bright again, clear

reluct·or -ārī -ātus sum *vi* to fight back, put up a struggle, resist; to be reluctant

re·maneō -manēre -mansī *vi* to stay behind; to remain, continue (*in a certain state*)

remān·ō -āre *vi* to flow back

remansī·ō -ōnis *f* staying behind, stay

remed·ĭum -ĭī or **-ĭ** *n* remedy, cure, antidote, medicine

remensus *pp of* **remetior**

remĕ·ō -āre *vt* to retrace, relive; *vi* to go or come back, return

re·mētĭor -mētīrī -mensus sum *vt* to remeasure; to retrace, go back over

rēm·ex -ĭgis *m* rower, crew member, oarsman

Rēm·ī -ōrum *m pl* a people of Gaul (*near modern Rheims*)

rēmigātī·ō -ōnis *f* rowing

rēmig·ĭum -ĭī or **-ĭ** *n* rowing; oars; oarsmen, rowers

rēmig·ō -āre *vi* to row

remigr·ō -āre *vi* to move back, go back, return

reminisc·or -ī *vt* to call to mind, remember; *vi* to remember; (with *genit*) to be mindful of, conscious of, remember

re·misceō -miscēre — -mixtum *vt* to mix up, intermingle; **veris falsa remiscere** to intermingle lies with truth

remissē *adv* mildly, gently

remissi·ō -ōnis *f* release; easing, letting down, lowering; relaxing (*of muscles*); relaxation, recreation; mildness, gentleness; submissiveness; abatement, diminishing; remission (*of debts*)

remiss·us -a -um *adj* relaxed, loose, slack; mild, gentle; negligent, remiss; easy-going, indulgent, yielding; gay, merry, light; low, cheap (*price*)

re·mittō -mittĕre -mīsī -missum *vt* to send back; to release; to slacken, loosen; to emit, produce, let out, yield, send forth, give off; to send back, return, restore; to give up, reject, resign, concede; to relax, relieve (*the mind*); to pardon; to remit, remove (*penalty*); (with *inf*) to stop (*doing something*); *vi* (of wind, rain, etc.) to slack off, abate

remixtus *pp* of **remisceo**

remōl·ior -īrī -ītus sum *vt* to push or move back or away, heave back

remollēsc·ō -ĕre *vi* to get soft again, soften; to weaken

remŏr·a -ae *f* hindrance, delay

remorāmin·a -um *n pl* hindrances, delays

re·mordĕō -mordēre — -morsum *vt* to bite back; to attack in return; to disturb, annoy, worry, torture

remŏr·or -ārī -ātus sum *vt* to delay, hinder, hold back, detain; *vi* to loiter, delay, linger, stay behind

remōtē *adv* at a distance, far away

remōti·ō -ōnis *f* removal

remōt·us -a -um *adj* removed, out of the way, far off, remote, distant; (fig) remote, apart, separate, clear, free; dead; (with **ab** + *abl*) removed from, separate from, apart from, clear of, free from

re·movĕō -movēre -mōvī -mōtum *vt* to move back, withdraw, put away, remove; to shroud, veil; (fig) put out of sight, set aside, abolish; to subtract

remūg·iō -īre *vi* to bellow back; to resound, reecho

re·mulcĕō -mulcēre -mulsī *vt* to stroke, smooth back; **caudam remulcēre** to put the tail between the legs (*in fear*)

remulc·um -ī *n* tow rope, tow line

remūnerāti·ō -ōnis *f* remuneration, reward, recompense, repayment

remūnĕr·or -ārī -ātus sum *vt* to repay, reward

remurmŭr·ō -āre *vi* to murmur back in reply

rēm·us -ī *m* oar; (fig) wing; **remi corporis** hands and feet (*of a swimmer*)

Rem·us -ī *m* brother of Romulus

renarr·ō -āre *vt* to tell over again, recount

re·nascor -nascī -nātus sum *vi* to be born again; to rise again, spring up again, to be restored; to reappear; to recur

renāvig·ō -āre *vi* to sail back

ren·eō -ēre *vt* to unravel, undo

rēn·ēs -um *m pl* kidneys

renīd·ens -entis *adj* beaming, glad

renīd·ĕō -ēre *vi* to reflect, reflect light, glitter, shine; to smile, grin all over; to beam with joy

renīdesc·ō -ĕre *vi* to begin to reflect light, begin to glitter

renīt·or -ī *vi* to put up a struggle, fight back, resist

ren·ō -āre *vi* to swim back, float back

rēn·ō or **rhēn·ō -ōnis** *m* fur

renōd·ō -āre *vt* to tie back in a knot; to untie

renovām·en -ĭnis *n* renewal, new condition

renovāti·ō -ōnis *f* renovation, renewal; revision; compound interest

renŏv·ō -āre *vt* to make new again; to renovate, repair, restore; to plow up (*a fallow field*); to reopen (*wounds*); to revive (*old customs, etc.*); to start (*battles*) all over again; to refresh (*the memory*); to repeat, keep repeating, reaffirm; **faenus renovare in singulos annos** to compound the interest on a yearly basis

renumĕr·ō -āre *vt* to count over again, recount; to pay back, repay

renuntiāti·ō -ōnis *f* formal or official report, announcement

renunti·ō -āre *vt* to report; to announce; to retract (*promise, etc.*); to renounce, call off, reject; (with double *acc*) to announce or declare elected as; (with *acc & inf*) to bring back word that

renunt·ius -ii or **-ī** *m* bringer of news, reporter

re·nuō -nuĕre -nuī *vt* to nod refusal to, deny, refuse, turn down, decline, say not to, reject; *vi* to shake the head in refusal, refuse, say no; (with *dat*) to say no to, deny (*a charge*)

renūt·ō -āre *vt* to refuse emphatically

reor rērī ratus sum *vt* to think, deem; (with *acc & inf*) to think that; (with *acc & adj* as objective complement) to regard (*something*) as; *vi* to think, suppose

repāgŭl·a -ōrum *n pl* bolts, bars; (fig) restraints, regulations, rules, limits

repand·us -a -um *adj* curved backwards, concave; (*shoes*) with turned-up toes

reparābĭl·is -e *adj* capable of being repaired, reparable, retrievable

repar·ō -ĕre *vi* (with *dat*) to be sparing with, take it easy with

repăr·ō -āre *vt* to get again, acquire again; to recover, retrieve, make good; to restore, renew, repair; to recruit (*a new army*); **vīna merce reparare** to get wine in exchange for wares, barter for wine

repastināti·ō -ōnis *f* digging up again

re·pectō -pectĕre — -pexum *vt* to comb back; to comb again, recomb

repellō repellĕre reppŭlī repulsum *vt* to drive back, push back, repel, repulse; to reject; to remove; to refute

re·pendō -pendĕre -pendī -pensum *vt* to repay, pay back; to ransom, redeem; (fig) to repay in kind, requite, recompense, reward; to compensate for; to balance, balance out; **magna rependere** to pay back in full

rep·ens -entis *adj* sudden, unexpected, unlooked-for, hasty

repensus *pp* of **rependo**

repentē adv suddenly, unexpectedly, all of a sudden

repentīnō adv suddenly, unexpectedly

repentīn·us -a -um adj sudden, unpected, unlooked-for; hasty, impetuous

reperc·ō -ēre vi (with dat) **a** to be sparing with; **b** to refrain from

repercussus pp of **repercutio**; adj rebounding; reflected, reflecting; echoed, echoing

repercuss·us -ūs m rebounding, reverberation, echo, repercussion

reper·cutiō -cutĕre -cussī -cussum vt to make (something) rebound, reverberate, or reflect

reperiō reperīre reppĕrī repertum vt to find, find again, discover; to get, procure, obtain, win; to find out, ascertain, learn, realize; to invent, devise

repert·or -ōris m discoverer, inventor, author

repert·us -a -um pp of **reperio**; n pl discoveries, inventions

repetītĭ·ō -ōnis f repetition; (rhet) anaphora, repetition

repetīt·or -ōris m claimant

repĕt·ō -ĕre -īvī or **-ĭī -ītum** vt to head back to, try to reach again, return to; to aim at again; to fetch back; to attack again; to prosecute again; to demand anew; to demand back, claim, demand in compensation, retake; to trace back, retrace; to trace in thought, think over, recall, recollect; to trace back (in speech); to repeat, undertake again, resume, renew; **lex de pecuniis** (or **rebus**) **repetundis** law on extortion, extortion law; **pecuniam repetere** to sue for the recovery of money; **res repetere** to sue for the recovery of property; **reus pecuniarum repetundarum** guilty of extortion

repetund·ae -ārum f pl extortion; money extorted; **repetundarum argui** to be charged with extortion; **repetundarum teneri** to be held on an extortion charge

repexus pp of **repecto**

replĕō -plēre -plēvī -plētum vt to refill, fill up, replenish; to fill to overflowing; to make up for, replace, compensate for; to recruit, bring (an army) to full strength

replēt·us -a -um adj filled, full; well provided

replicātĭ·ō -ōnis f folding back, rolling back, rolling up; reflex action

replic·ō -āre vt to fold back, unfold, turn back

rēp·ō -ĕre -sī vi to creep, crawl

re·pōnō -pōnĕre -posŭī -positum or **repostum** vt to put back, set back, lay (e.g., the head) back; to replace; to restore; to substitute; to lay out, stretch out (the body); to lay aside, store, keep, preserve; to lay aside, put away; to renew, repeat; to place, class; to replay, requite;

in sceptra reponere to reinstate in power; **membra reponere** (with abl or in + abl) to stretch out on (e.g., a bed); **se in cubitum reponere** to rest on one's elbow, prop oneself up on one's elbow; **spem reponere** (with in + abl) to put one's hope in or on, count on

report·ō -āre vt to bring back; to report; to carry off, gain, obtain; **victoriam reportare** to win a victory

reposc·ō -ĕre vt to demand back; to ask for, claim, require, demand

reposĭt·us -a -um pp of **repono**; adj distant, remote

repost·or -ōris m restorer

repostus pp of **repono**

repōtĭ·a -ōrum n pl second round of drinks

repraesentātĭ·ō -ōnis f vivid presentation; cash payment

repraesent·ō -āre vt to present again, show, exhibit, display, depict; to pay in cash; to do immediately, accomplish instantly, do on the spot; to rush, speed up (e.g., plans); to anticipate; to apply (medicines) immediately

repreh·endō or **repr·endō -endĕre -endī -ensum** vt to hold back; to restrain, check; to blame, find fault with, rebuke, criticize; (law) to prosecute, convict, condemn; to refute

reprehensĭ·ō -ōnis f checking, check; interruption (of a speech); blame, rebuke, criticism; refutation

reprehens·ō -āre vt to hold back continually; to detain from time to time

reprehens·or -ōris m critic

repress·or -ōris m restrainer

re·prīmō -prīmĕre -pressī -pressum vt to hold back, keep back; to restrain, limit, confine, curb, repress, suppress; **se reprimere** to control oneself; **se reprimere** (with ab + abl) to refrain from

reprōmissĭ·ō -ōnis f return promise

reprō·mittō -mittĕre -misī -missum vt to promise in return

repudiātĭ·ō -ōnis f repudiation; refusal, rejection

repudĭ·ō -āre vt to repudiate, scorn; to refuse, reject; to jilt; to divorce

repudiōs·us -a -um adj objectionable, offensive

repudĭ·um -lī or **-ī** n repudiation, separation, divorce; **repudium renuntiare** or **repudium remittere** (with dat) to send a letter of divorce to, divorce

repuerasc·ō -ĕre vi to become a child again; to behave childishly

repugn·ans -antis n contradiction

repugnanter adv reluctantly

repugnantĭ·a -ae f incompatibility

repugn·ō -āre vi to fight back; (with dat) **a** to oppose, offer opposition to, fight against, be against; **b** to disagree with, be inconsistent with, be incompatible with; (with **contra** + *acc*) to fight against

repuls·a -ae *f* defeat at the polls; rebuff, cold shoulder; **repulsa consulatūs** defeat in running for the consulship; **repulsam ferre** to lose an election

repuls·ans -antis *adj* throbbing; re-echoing

repulsus *pp* of **repello**

repuls·us -ūs *m* reverberation, echo

repung·ō -ĕre *vt* to goad again

repurg·ō -āre *vt* to clean or clear again; to purge away, remove

reputātī·ō -ōnis *f* reconsideration, review

reput·ō -āre *vt* to count back, calculate; to think over, reflect upon, reconsider

requi·ēs -ētis *f* rest, relief; relaxation, recreation

requi·escō -escĕre -ēvī -ētum *vt* to put to rest, quiet down, calm down; *vi* to rest, take a rest, come to rest, stop, end; to rest, relax; to find rest, be consoled, find relief; to rest, lie quietly, sleep; (of the dead) to rest, sleep

requiēt·us -a -um *adj* rested up, refreshed

requirit·ō -āre *vt* to keep asking for, be on a constant lookout for

re·quirō -quirĕre -quisīvī or -quisīi -quisītum *vt* to look for, search for, hunt for; to look around for, miss; to ask; to ask for, demand, require; (with **ab** or **de** + *abl*) to ask or demand (*something*) from or of

rēs reī or **rēī** *f* thing, matter, affair, object, business, circumstance, event, occurrence, deed, condition, case; reality, truth, fact; property, possessions, estate, effects; benefit, advantage, interest, profit; business affair, transaction; cause, reason, motive, ground; (law) case, suit; (mil) operation, campaign, battle; state, government, politics; historical event; theme, topic, subject matter; **ab re** contrary to interests, disadvantageous, useless; **contra rem publicam** unconstitutional(ly), contrary to public interests; **eā re** therefore, for that reason; **ex re** according to the circumstances, according to the situation; **ex re istius** for his good; **ex re publica** constitutionally, for the common good, in the public interest; **ex tuā re** to your advantage; **in re** in fact, in reality; **in rem** for the good; useful, advantageous; **ob eam rem** for that reason; **ob rem** to the purpose; **pro re** according to circumstances; **re** in fact, in practice, in reality, in truth, actually, really; **rem gerere** to conduct a military operation; **rerum potiri** to get control of the government; **rerum scriptor** historian, annalist; **res est mihi tecum** I have some busi-

ness with you; **res sit mihi cum his** let me handle them; **res frumentaria** foraging; grain situation, grain supply; **res gestae** exploits, achievements, military achievements; **res judiciaria** administration of justice, department of justice; **res novae** revolution; **res pecuaria et rustica** livestock; **res Persicae** Persian history, Parthian history; **res rustica** agriculture; **res publica** state, government, politics, public life, commonwealth, country; **res secundae** prosperous times, prosperity; **res uxoria** marriage; dowry; **summa rerum** world, universe

resacr·ō -āre *vt* to ask again for; to free from a curse

resaev·iō -īre *vi* to go wild again

resalūt·ō -āre *vt* to greet in return

resān·escō -escĕre -ŭī *vi* to heal up again

re·sarciō -sarcīre — -sartum *vt* to patch up, repair; to make good (*a loss*)

re·scindō -scindĕre -scīdī -scissum *vt* to tear off; to cut down; to tear open; to rescind, repeal, abrogate; (fig) to tear open, expose

re·sciscō -sciscĕre -scīvī or -sciī -scītum *vt* to find out, learn, ascertain

re·scrībō -scrībĕre -scripsī -scriptum *vt* to write back in reply; to rewrite, revise; to enlist, enroll; to repay, pay back; *vi* to write a reply

rescript·um -ī *n* imperial rescript

resĕc·ō -āre -ŭī -tum *vt* to cut back, cut short; to reap; (fig) to trim, curtail; **ad vivum resecare** to cut to the quick

resăcr·ō or **resăcr·ō -āre** *vt* to ask again for; to free from a curse

resectus *pp* of **reseco**

resecūtus *pp* of **resequor**

resēmin·ō -āre *vt* to reproduce

re·sēquor -sĕquī -secūtus sum *vt* to reply to, answer

resĕr·ō -āre *vt* to unlock, unbar, open; to disclose; to open, begin (*a year*)

reserv·ō -āre *vt* to reserve, hold back; to spare; to hold on to

res·es -idis *adj* remaining, left; lazy, idle, inactive; slow, sluggish; calm

re·sidĕō -sidēre -sēdī *vi* to remain seated; to stay behind, be left, remain; to tarry, linger; to stay, reside

re·sīdō -sīdĕre -sēdī *vi* to sit down, settle back; to sink down, sink, settle, subside; to calm down

residŭ·us -a -um *adj* remaining, left; in arrears, outstanding (*money*); *n* the remainder, rest

resign·ō -āre *vt* to unseal, open; to disclose, reveal; to give up, resign; to annul, cancel; to destroy (*confidence*)

resil·iō -īre -ŭī *vi* to spring back,

jump back; to recoil; to contract; to shrink back

resīm·us -a -um *adj* turned up, snub

rēsin·a -ae *f* resin

resīnāt·us -a -um *adj* resined, rubbed with resin

resip·iō -ĕre *vt* to taste of, have the flavor of

resip·iscō -iscĕre -īvī or -iī or -ŭī *vi* to come to one's senses

resist·ens -entis *adj* firm, tough

re·sistō -sistĕre -stitī *vi* to stand still, stop, pause; to stay, stay behind, remain, continue; to resist, put up resistance; to rise again; (with *dat*) **a** to be opposed to, resist; **b** to reply to

re·solvō -solvĕre -solvī -solūtum *vt* to untie, unfasten, undo; to open; to dissolve, melt, thaw; to relax (*the body*); stretch out (*the limbs*); to unravel; to cancel; to dispel; to unnerve, enervate; to release, set free

resonābil·is -e *adj* resounding, answering (*echo*)

resŏn·ō -āre *vt* to repeat, reecho, resound with, make ring; *vi* to resound, ring, reecho; (with *dat* or **ad** + *acc*) to resound in answer to

resŏn·us -a -um *adj* resounding, reechoing

resorb·ĕō -ēre *vt* to suck in, swallow again

respect·ō -āre *vt* to look back on; to keep an eye on, care for; to have regard for; to gaze at, look at; *vi* to look back; to look around

respectus *pp of* **respicio**

respect·us -ūs *m* backward glance, looking back; looking around; refuge, asylum; regard, respect, consideration; **respectum habere** (with *dat* or **ad** + *acc*) to have respect for

re·spergō -spergĕre -spersī spersum *vt* to sprinkle, splash, spray; to defile

respersi·ō -ōnis *f* sprinkling, splashing

respersus *pp of* **respergo**

re·spiciō -spicĕre -spexī -spectum *vt* to look back at, see behind oneself; to look back for, look around for; to look back upon (*the past, etc.*); to look at, gaze at, look upon, regard, contemplate, consider; to notice; to look after, take care of, see to; to respect; *vi* to look back; to look around; (with **ad** + *acc*) to look at, gaze at

respīrām·en -inis *n* windpipe

respīrāti·ō -ōnis *f* respiration, breathing; exhalation; letup, rest, pause (*to catch one's breath*), breathing space

respīrāt·us -ūs *m* respiration

respīr·ō -āre *vt* to breathe, breathe out, exhale; *vi* to breathe, take a breath; to catch one's breath, breathe again, recover (*from fright, etc.*); (of combat, passions, etc.) to slack off, die down, subside; **a con-**tinuis cladibus respirare to catch one's breathe again after continuous fighting; **ab metu respirare** to breathe again after a shock

resplend·ĕō -ēre *vi* to glitter

re·spondĕō -spondēre -spondī -sponsum *vt* to answer; to say in reply; **ficta respondere** to make up answers; **multa respondere** to give a lengthy reply; **par pari respondere** to answer tit for tat; **verbum verbo respondere** to answer word for word; *vi* to answer, respond, reply; to echo; (law) to answer (*to bail*), appeal (*in court*); (of lawyers) to give an opinion, give legal advice; (of priests, oracles) to give a response; (with *dat*) **a** to answer, reply to; **b** to match, balance, correspond to, be equal to, resemble, measure up to; **amori amore respondere** to return love for love

responsi·ō -ōnis *f* response, answer, reply; refutation; **sibi ipsi responsio** a reply to one's own arguments

responsit·ō -āre *vi* to give professional advice

respons·ō -āre *vi* to answer, reply; to reecho; (with *dat*) **a** to answer to, agree with; **b** to resist, defy; **c** to answer back to (*in disobedience or defiance*)

respons·or -ōris *m* answerer

respons·us -a -um *pp of* **respondeo**; *n* answer, response, reply; professional advice, oracular response; **responsum auferre** or **ferre** (with **ab** + *abl*) to receive an answer from; **responsum referre** to deliver an answer

rēspūblica reīpūblicae *f* state, government, politics, public life, commonwealth, country

respŭ·ō -ĕre -ī *vt* to spit out, cast out, eject, expel; to reject, refuse, dislike, spurn

restagn·ō -āre *vi* to form pools; to run over, overflow; to be inundated

restaur·ō -āre *vt* to restore, rebuild

resticŭl·a -ae *f* thin rope, cord

restincti·ō -ōnis *f* quenching

re·stinguō -stinguĕre -stinxī -stinctum *vt* to quench, extinguish, put out; to snuff out, extinguish, exterminate, destroy

resti·ō -ōnis *m* rope maker; (coll) roper (*person who whipped with ropes*)

restipulāti·ō -ōnis *f* counterclaim

restipŭl·or -ārī -ātus sum *vt* to stipulate in return

rest·is -is *f* rope

restit·ō -āre *vi* to stay behind, lag behind, hold back, hang back

restitr·ix -īcis *f* stay-behind (*female*)

re·stituō -stituĕre -stituī -stitūtum *vt* to set up again; to restore, rebuild, reconstruct; to renew, reestablish, revive; to bring back, restore, reinstate; to give back, return, replace; to restore, repair, remedy; to reenact (*a law*); to reverse, revoke, make void, undo, cancel; to make good, compensate for, repair

restitūti·ō **-ōnis** *f* restoration; reinstatement, pardon; recall (*from exile*)

restitūt·or **-ōris** *m* restorer, rebuilder

restitūtus *pp* of **restituo**

re·stō **-stāre** **-stĭtī** *vi* to stand firm, stand one's ground, resist; to stay behind, stay in reserve; to be left, be left over; *v impers* (*with inf* or *ut*) it remains to (*do something*)

restrictē *adv* sparingly; exactly, precisely

restrict·us **-a** **-um** *adj* tied back, tight; stingy; moderate; strict, stern

re·stringō **-stringĕre** **-strinxī** **-strictum** *vt* to draw back tightly, tie back, tighten; (of dogs) to show (*the teeth*); (fig) to restrain

resūd·ō **-āre** *vt & vi* to sweat

result·ō **-āre** *vi* to rebound; to reverberate, resound

re·sūmō **-sūmĕre** **-sumpsī** **-sumptum** *vt* to take up again, resume; to recover (*strength*)

resupīn·ō **-āre** *vt* to throw (*someone*) on his back, throw over, throw down; (coll) to knock for a loop; to break down (*doors*)

resupīn·us **-a** **-um** *adj* bent back, thrown back; supine, lying on the back; leaning backward; proud, haughty (*gait*)

re·surgō **-surgĕre** **-surrexī** **-surrectum** *vi* to rise again, appear again

resuscit·ō **-āre** *vt* to resuscitate, revive, renew

retardāti·ō **-ōnis** *f* retarding, delaying

retard·ō **-āre** *vt* to slow down, retard, hold back, delay, keep back, check, hinder

rēt·e **-is** *n* net; (fig) trap

re·tēgō **-tegĕre** **-texī** **-tectum** *vt* to uncover; to open

retempt·ō **-āre** *vt* to attempt again, try again, test again

re·tendō **-tendĕre** **-tendī** **-tentum** or **-tensum** *vt* to release from tension, unbend, relax

retenti·ō **-ōnis** *f* holding back, slowing down; withholding (*of assent*)

retent·ō **-āre** *vt* to hold back, hold tight; to attempt again, try again, test again

retentus *pp* of **retendo** and **retineo**

re·texō **-texĕre** **-texŭī** **-textum** *vt.* to unravel; to cancel, annul, reverse, undo; to weave anew; to renew, repeat; to correct, revise; to take back, retract (*words*)

rētiār·ius **-iī** or **-ī** *m* gladiator who tried to entangle his opponent in a net

reticenti·a **-ae** *f* reticence, silence; (rhet) abrupt pause; **poena reticentiae** punishment for suppressing the truth

retic·ĕō **-ēre** *vt* to be silent about, suppress, keep secret; *vi* to be silent, keep silence; (with *dat*) to make no answer to

rētĭcŭl·um **-ī** *n* small net; hair net; network bag, reticule (*for protecting bottles*); racket (*for playing ball*)

retināĕŭl·a **-ōrum** *n pl* cable, rope, hawser, tether

retĭn·ens **-entis** *adj* (with *genit*) clinging to

retinenti·a **-ae** *f* recollection, retention

re·tinĕō **-tinēre** **-tinŭī** **-tentum** *vt* to hold back, keep back; to restrain; to keep, retain; to hold in reserve; to keep, preserve, maintain, uphold; to hold, engross (*attention*); to detain, delay

retinn·iō **-īre** *vi* to ring again, ring out

retŏn·ō **-āre** *vi* to resound

re·torquĕō **-torquēre** **-torsī** **-tortum** *vt* to twist or bend back; to hurl back (*weapons*); **mentem retorquere** to change the mind; **oculos retorquere** (with **ad +** *acc*) to look back wistfully at

retorrĭd·us **-a** **-um** *adj* parched, dried out, withered; wily, old, shrewd

retortus *pp* of **retorqueo**

retractāti·ō **-ōnis** *f* rehandling, retreatment; hesitation

retract·ō or **retrect·ō** **-āre** *vt* to rehandle, take in hand again, undertake once more, take up once more; to reexamine, review; to revise; *vi* to refuse, decline; to be reluctant

retract·us **-a** **-um** *adj* withdrawn, distant, remote

re·trăhō **-trahĕre** **-traxī** **-tractum** *vt* to draw back, withdraw, drag back; to bring to light again, make known again; (fig) to drag away, divert, remove, turn

retrectō see **retracto**

retrĭb·ŭō **-ŭĕre** **-ŭī** **-ūtum** *vt* to give back, restore, repay

retrō *adv* backwards, back, to the rear; behind, on the rear; in the past, formerly, back, past; in return, on the contrary, on the other hand

retrorsum or **retrorsus** *adv* back, backwards, behind; in reversed order

re·trūdō **-trūdĕre** — **-trūsum** *vt* to push back; to hide, conceal

retundō **retundĕre** **retŭdī** (or **rettŭdī**) **retunsum** (or **retūsum**) *vt* to pound back; to dull, blunt; (fig) to deaden, weaken, repress, restrain

retuns·us or **retūs·us** **-a** **-um** *adj* blunt, dull; (fig) dull

re·us **-ī** *m* defendant, plaintiff, the accused; convict, criminal, culprit

reval·escō -escĕre -ŭī *vi* to regain one's strength, recover; to become valid again

re·vĕhō -vehĕre -vexī -vectum *vt* to carry back, bring back; **revehi** to ride or drive back, sail back; (fig) to go back (*e.g., to an earlier period*)

re·vellō -vellĕre -vellī -vulsum *vt* to pull out, pull back, tear off, tear out; to tear up (*the ground*), dig up; (fig) to abolish, remove

revēl·ō -āre *vt* to unveil, uncover

re·veniō -venīre -vēnī -ventum *vi* to come again, come back, return

rēvērā *adv* in fact, actually

rēverbĕr·ō -āre *vt* to beat back, repel

reverend·us -a -um *adj* venerable, awe-inspiring

revĕr·ens -entis *adj* reverent, respectful

reverenter *adv* respectfully

reverenti·a -ae *f* awe, respect, reverence

rever·ĕor -ērī -ĭtus sum *vt* to revere, respect, stand in awe of

reversi·ō or **revorsi·ō -ōnis** *f* turning back (*before reaching one's destination*); recurrence (*of fever, etc.*)

revert·ō -ĕre -ī or **re·vertor** (or **re·vortor**) **-vertī -versus sum** *vi* to turn back, turn around, come back, return; (in speaking) to return, revert, recur

revictus *pp* of **revinco**

revid·ĕō -ēre *vt* to go back to see, revisit

re·vinciō -vincīre -vinxī -vinctum *vt* to tie back, tie behind, tie up

re·vincō -vincĕre -vīcī -victum *vt* to conquer, crush, repress; to refute, disprove, convict

revinctus *pp* of **revincio**

revir·escō -escĕre -ŭī *vi* to grow green again, become green again; to grow young again; to grow again, grow strong again, revive

revīs·ō -ĕre *vt* to go to see again, revisit; to look back to see; *vi* to come or go back; (with **ad** + *acc*) a to look at again, look back at; b to return to, revisit

re·vīvīscō or **re·vīvescō -vīvescĕre -vixī** *vi* to come back to life, be restored to life, revive; (fig) to revive, recover, gain strength

revocābil·is -e *adj* revocable, capable of being recalled

revocām·en -ĭnis *n* recall

revocāti·ō -ōnis *f* calling back, calling away, recall; revoking, retracting (*of a word*)

revŏc·ō -āre *vt* to call back, recall; to recall, call off, withdraw (*troops*); to call back (*an actor, singer*) for an encore; to bring back to life, revive; (law) to arraign again; to recover, regain (*strength, etc.*); to resume (*career, studies*); to revoke, retract;

to check, control; to cancel; (with **ad** + *acc*) to refer, apply, subject, submit (*someone or something*) to

revŏl·ō -āre *vi* to fly back

revolsus see **revulsus**

revolūbil·is -e *adj* able to be rolled back; **non revolubilis** irrevocable (*fate*)

re·volvō -volvĕre -volvī -volūtum *vt* to roll back, unroll, unwind; to retravel (*a road*); to unroll, read over, read again (*a book*); to reexperience; to go over, think over; **revolvi** to revolve, come around again, recur, return

revŏm·ō -ĕre -ŭī *vt* to vomit forth again, disgorge

revor- = rever-

revorr·ō -ĕre *vt* to sweep back, scatter again

revulsus *pp* of **revello**

rex rēgis *m* king; (with bad connotations during the republican period) tyrant, dictator; patron; rich man; leader, king (*in children's game*); queen bee

Rhadamanth·us -ī *m* son of Jupiter, brother of Minos, and one of the three judges in the lower world

Rhaet·ī -ōrum *m pl* people of Raetia

Rhaeti·a -ae *f* Alpine country between Germany and Italy

rhapsōdi·a -ae *f* Homeric lay, selection from Homer

Rhe·a -ae *f* Cybele

Rhe·a Silvi·a -ae *f* daughter of Numitor and mother of Romulus and Remus

rhēd- = raed-

Rhēgĭum -ĭī or **-ī** *n* town on the toe of Italy

rhēn·ō -ōnis *m* fur

Rhēnān·us -a -um *adj* Rhenish

Rhēn·us -ī *m* Rhine

Rhēs·us -ī *m* Thracian king who fought as an ally of Troy

rhēt·or -ŏris *m* rhetorician, teacher of rhetoric; orator

rhētoric·a -ae or **rhētoric·ē -ēs** *f* rhetoric

rhētoric·a -ōrum *n pl* treatise on rhetoric

rhētoricē *adv* rhetorically, in an oratorical manner

rhētoric·us -a -um *adj* rhetorician's, rhetorical; **doctores rhetorici** rhetoric professors; **libri rhetorici** rhetoric textbooks

rhīnocĕr·ōs -ōtis *m* rhinoceros; vessel made of a rhinoceros's tusk

rhō (indecl) *n* seventeenth letter of the Greek alphabet

Rhodān·us -ī *m* Rhone

Rhodiens·is -e or **Rhodĭ·us -a -um** *adj* Rhodian, of Rhodes; *m pl* Rhodians

Rhodŏp·ē -ēs *f* mountain range in Thrace

Rhodopēĭ·us -a -um *adj* Thracian

Rhod·os or **Rhod·us -ī** *f* Rhodes (*island off the coast of Asia Minor*)

Rhoetē·us -a -um *adj* Trojan;

Rhoeteus ductor Aeneas; *m* promontory on the Dardanelles near Troy; sea near the promontory of Rhoeteum

rhomb·us -ī *m* magic wheel; turbot (*fish*)

rhomphae·a -ae *f* long javelin

rhythmic·us -a -um *adj* rhythmical; *m* teacher of prose rhythm

rhythm·os or **rhythm·us -ī** *m* rhythm, symmetry

ric·a -ae *f* veil (*worn by Roman women at sacrifices*)

rīcīn·ium -iī or **-ī** *n* short mantle with a cowl

rict·um -ī *n* snout; wide-open mouth

rict·us -ūs *m* snout; wide-open mouth; **rīsū rictum dīducere** to break into a grin; *m pl* jaws, gaping jaws

rīdĕō rīdēre rīsī rīsum *vt* to laugh at, ridicule; to smile upon; *vi* to smile, laugh; (*with dat or* **ad** + *acc*) to smile to

rīdibund·us -a -um *adj* laughing

rīdiculārī·us -a -um *adj* laughable, funny; *n pl* jokes

rīdiculē *adv* jokingly, humorously; ridiculously, absurdly

rīdiculōs·us -a -um *adj* funny, amusing; ridiculous

rīdicul·us -a -um *adj* funny, amusing, laughable; ridiculous, silly; *m* joker, clown; *n* joke

rig·ens -entis *adj* stiff, rigid, unbending

rig·ĕō -ēre *vi* to be still, be numb, stiffen; to be rigid, stand on end, stand erect; to stand stiff, rise

rig·escō -escĕre -uī *vi* to grow stiff, become numbed, stiffen, harden; to stand on end

rigidē *adv* rigorously, severely

rigid·us -a -um *adj* rigid, stiff, hard, inflexible; stern, rigid, severe; rough, rude

rig·ō -āre *vt* to wet, moisten, water; to conduct, convey (*water*)

rig·or -ōris *m* stiffness; numbness, cold; hardness; sternness, severity

rigu·us -a -um *adj* irrigating, watering; irrigated, watered

rīm·a -ae *f* crack; **rimas agere** to be cracked

rīm·or -ārī -ātus sum *vt* to lay open, tear open; to pry into, search, tear at, examine; to ransack; **naribus rimari** to sniff at

rīmōs·us -a -um *adj* full of cracks, leaky

ringor ringī rictus sum *vi* to open the mouth wide, to show the teeth; to snarl; (fig) to be snappy, snarl

rīp·a -ae *f* bank, shore

rīpul·a -ae *f* river bank

risc·us -ī *m* chest, trunk

rīsiōn·ēs -um *f pl* laughs

rīs·or -ōris *m* scoffer, teaser

rīs·us -ūs *m* laugh, smile, laughter; laughingstock; **risum continere** to keep back a laugh, keep from laughing; **risum movere** (*with dat*

of person) to make (*someone*) laugh; **rīsūs captāre** to try to make people laugh, try to get laughs

rīte *adv* according to religious usage; duly, justly, rightly, fitly; in the usual way, customarily

rīt·us -ūs *m* ceremony, rite; custom, habit, way, manner, style; **ritū** (*with genit*) in the manner of, like; **pecudum ritū** like cattle

rīvāl·is -is *m* one who uses the same stream, neighbor; one who uses the same mistress, rival

rīvālit·ās -ātis *f* rivalry in love

rīvul·us or **rīvōl·us -ī** *m* brook, rivulet

rīv·us -ī *m* brook, stream

rix·a -ae *f* brawl, fight; quarrel, squabble

rix·or -ārī -ātus sum *vi* to brawl, come to blows, fight; to quarrel, squabble

rōbiginōs·us or **rūbiginōs·us -a -um** *adj* rusty; envious

rōbīg·ō -inis *f* rust; blight, mildew; film (*on teeth*), tartar

rōborĕ·us -a -um *adj* oak, of oak

rōbŏr·ō -āre *vt* to make strong, strengthen

rōb·ur or **rōb·us -ŏris** *n* hard wood; oak; prison (*at Rome, also called Tullianum*); objects made of hard wood: lance, club, bench; physical strength, power, vigor, toughness; vigor, strength, power, quality (*of mind*); best part, flower, choice, cream, élite; stronghold

rōbust·us -a -um *adj* hardwood; oak; robust, strong, firm, tough (*body*); firm, vigorous, solid (*character*)

rōdō rōdĕre rōsī rōsum *vt* to gnaw, gnaw at; to rust, corrode; to say nasty things about, slander, run down

rogāl·is -e *adj* of a pyre

rogātī·ō -ōnis *f* proposal, referendum, bill, resolution; request; (rhet) question; **rogationem ferre** to introduce a bill; **rogationem perferre** to pass a bill; **rogationem suadere** to back, push, speak in favor of a bill; **rogationi intercedere** to veto a bill

rogātiuncul·a -ae *f* inconsequential bill; little question

rogāt·or -ōris *m* proposer (*of a bill to the people*); poll clerk (*who collected and counted votes*); beggar

rogāt·us -ūs *m* request

rogitātī·ō -ōnis *f* proposal

rogit·ō -āre *vt* to keep asking, keep asking for

rog·ō -āre *vt* to ask, ask for, beg, request, solicit, question; to invite; to nominate for election; to bring forward for approval, introduce, propose (*bill or resolution*); (with double *acc*) to ask (*someone for something*), ask (*someone something*); **legem rogare** to introduce a bill; **milites sacramento rogare** to swear in soldiers; **senatorem sententiam rogāre** to ask a senator for his opinion, ask a senator how he votes; **sententias rogāre** to call the roll (in the senate); **populum rogāre** to ask the people about a bill, to propose or introduce a bill; **primus sententiam rogāri** to have the honor of being the first (senator) to be asked his view, be the first to vote

rog·us -ī m funeral pile, pyre; (fig) grave, destruction

Rōm·a -ae f Rome

Rōmān·us -a -um adj Roman; m pl Romans

Rōmulē·us -a -um adj of Romulus

Rōmulid·ae -ārum m pl descendants of Romulus, Romans

Rōmul·us -a -um adj of Romulus; m Romulus (son of Rhea Silvia and Mars, twin brother of Remus, and founder as well as first king of Rome)

rōrāri·ī -ōrum m pl skirmishers (light-armed Roman troops who usually initiated an attack and then withdrew)

rōrid·us -a -um adj dewy

rōrif·er -ēra -ērum adj dew-bringing, dewy

rōr·ō -āre vt to drip, trickle, pour drop by drop; to moisten; vi to drop dew, scatter dew

rōs rōris m dew; moisture; water; teardrop; **ros Arabus** perfume; **ros marinus** or **ros maris** rosemary; **rores pluvii** rain drops; **rores sanguinei** drops of blood

ros·a -ae f rose; rose bush; rose bed; wreath of roses

rosār·ium -iī or **-ī** n rose garden

roscid·us -a -um adj dewy; moistened, sprayed

Rosc·ius -iī or **-ī** m L. Roscius Otho (friend of Cicero, whose law in 67 B.C. reserved fourteen rows of seats in the theater for members of equestrian order); Q. Roscius (famous Roman actor and friend of Cicero, d. 62 B.C.); Sextus Roscius (of Ameria, defended by Cicero in a patricide trial in 80 B.C.)

rosēt·um -ī n rose bed, rose garden

rosē·us -a -um adj rosy, rose-colored; of roses

rosmarīn·um -ī n rosemary (spice)

rostrāt·us -a -um adj beaked; (ship) having a pointed bow; **columna rostrata** column adorned with the beaks of conquered vessels to commemorate a naval victory; **corona rostrata** navy medal (awarded to the first man to board the enemy's ship)

rostr·um -ī n bill, beak; snout, muzzle; curved bow (of a ship); n pl speaker's stand in the Roman Forum (so called because it was adorned with the beaks of ships taken from the battle of Antium, 338 B.C.)

rōsus pp of rodo

rot·a -ae f wheel; potter's wheel; torture wheel; disk; chariot, car

rot·ō -āre vt to turn, whirl about; **rotari** to roll around; to revolve

rotūl·a -ae f little wheel

rotundē adv smoothly, elegantly

rotund·ō -āre vt to make round, round off; to round out, complete

rotund·us -a -um adj rolling, revolving; round, circular, spherical; rounded, perfect; well-turned, smooth, polished, balanced (style)

rube·faciō -facĕre -fēcī -factum vt to make red, redden

rubell·us -a -um adj reddish

rub·ens -entis adj red; blushing

rub·eō -ēre vi to be red, be ruddy; to be bloody; to blush

rub·er -ra -rum adj red; ruddy

rub·escō -escĕre -uī vi to grow red, redden; to blush

rubēt·a -ae f toad

rubēt·a -ōrum n pl bramble bush

rubē·us -a -um adj bramble, of brambles

Rubic·ō -ōnis m small stream marking the boundary between Italy and Cisalpine Gaul

rubicundul·us -a -um adj reddish

rubicund·us -a -um adj red; ruddy

rubid·us -a -um adj reddish, red

rubīg- = robig-

rub·or -ōris m redness; blush; bashfulness, sense of shame; shame, disgrace

rubrīc·a -ae f red clay; red ochre; red chalk; rubric, law

rub·us -ī m bramble bush; blackberry bush; blackberry

ruct·ō -āre or **ruct·or -ārī -ātus sum** vt & vi to belch

ruct·us -ūs m belch, belching

rud·ens -entis m rope; m pl rigging

Rudi·ae -ārum f pl town in Calabria in S. Italy (birthplace of Ennius)

rudiār·ius -iī or **-ī** m retired gladiator

rudiment·um -ī n first attempt, beginning, commencement; **rudimentum adulescentiae ponere** to pass the novitiate; **rudimentum militare** basic training

Rudīn·us -a -um adj of Rudiae

rud·is -e adj in the natural state; raw, undeveloped, rough, wild, unformed; inexperienced, unskilled, ignorant, awkward, uncultured, uncivilized; (with genit or abl, with ad + acc, or with in + abl) inexperienced in, ignorant of, awkward at

rud·is -is f stick, rod; practice sword

rud·ō -ĕre -īvī -ītum vi to roar, bellow, bray; to creak

rūd·us -ĕris n crushed stone; rubble; rubbish; piece of brass or copper

rūfŭl·us -a -um adj reddish

Rūfŭl·ī -ōrum m pl military tribunes appointed by a general (as opposed to military tribunes elected by the people)

rūf·us -a -um *adj* red, reddish

rūg·a -ae *f* wrinkle

rūg·ō -āre *vi* to become wrinkled, become creased

rūgōs·us -a -um *adj* wrinkled, shriveled; corrugated

ruīn·a -ae *f* tumbling down, falling down, fall; collapse; debris, ruins; crash; catastrophe, disaster, destruction, defeat; wrecker, destroyer; **ruīnam dare** or **trahere** to fall with a crash

ruīnōs·us -a -um *adj* going to ruin, ruinous, ruined, tumbling, fallen

rum·ex -icis *f* sorrel

rūmific·ō -āre *vt* to report

Rūmin·a -ae *f* Roman goddess who was worshiped near the fig tree under which the she-wolf had suckled Romulus and Remus

Rūmināl·is -e *adj* ficus **Ruminalis** fig tree of Romulus and Remus

rūminātī·ō -ōnis *f* chewing of the cud; (fig) rumination

rūmin·ō -āre *vt* to chew again; *vi* to chew the cud

rūm·or -ōris *m* shouting, cheering, noise; rumor, hearsay; popular opinion, current opinion; reputation, fame; notoriety; calumny; **adverso rumore esse** to be in bad repute, be unpopular

rumpi·a -ae *f* long javelin

rump·ō rumpĕre rūpī ruptum *vt* to break, break down, break open; to burst, burst through; to tear, split; to force, make (*e.g., a path*) by force; to break in on, interrupt, cut short; to break (*a law, treaty*); to break out in, utter (*complaints, etc.*)

rāmuscŭl·ī -ōrum *m pl* gossip

rūn·a -ae *f* dart

runc·ō -āre *vt* to weed, weed out

ru·ō -ĕre -ī -tum *vt* to throw down, hurl to the ground; to level (*e.g., sand dunes*); to destroy, overthrow, lay waste; to throw up, upturn, churn up; *vi* to fall hard, fall in ruins, totter; to run, dash, rush on, hurry; (of rain) to come pouring down; (of the sun) to set rapidly

rūp·ēs -is *f* cliff

rupt·or -ōris *m* breaker, violator

ruptus *pp* of **rumpo**

rūricŏl·a -ae *m* or *f* rustic, peasant, farmer; *m* ox

rūrigĕn·a -ae *m* rustic, peasant, farmer

rūr·ō -āre *vi* to live in the country

rursus or **rursum** or **rūsum** *adv* back, backwards; on the contrary, on the other hand, in turn; again, back again, once more; **rursus rursusque** again and again

rūs rūris *n* the country, countryside, lands, fields; farm, estate; **rure redire** to return from the country; **rurī** or **rure vitam agere** to live in the country; **rus īre** to go into the country; *n pl* countryside

rusc·um -ī *n* or **rusc·us** -ī *f* broom (*of twigs*)

russ·us -a -um *adj* red, russet

rusticān·us -a -um *adj* rustic, country, rural

rusticātī·ō -ōnis *f* country life

rusticē *adv* like a farmer; plainly, simply; unsophisticatedly, boorishly

rusticīt·ās -ātis *f* simple country ways, rusticity; boorishness, coarseness

rustic·or -ārī -ātus sum *vi* to live in the country

rusticŭl·us -a -um *adj* somewhat coarse; *m* peasant

rustic·us -a -um *adj* of or in the country, country, rural; plain, simple, unspoiled, unsophisticated; coarse, boorish, rude; *m* farmer, peasant; *f* country girl

rūsum see **rursus**

rūt·a -ae *f* rue (*bitter herb*); bitterness, unpleasantness

rūt·a -ōrum *n pl* minerals; **ruta caesa** or **ruta et caesa** (law) everything mined or cut down on an estate, timber and minerals

rutil·ō -āre *vt* to make red, color red, dye red; *vi* to glow red

rutīl·us -a -um *adj* red, reddish yellow; strawberry-blond

rutr·um -ī *n* spade

rūtŭl·a -ae *f* a bit of rue

Rūtŭl·ī -ōrum *m pl* ancient people of Latium whose capital was Ardea

rutus *pp* of **ruo**

S

Sab·a -ae *f* town in Arabia Felix, famous for its incense

Sabae·us -a -um *adj* Sabaean

Sabāz·ius -iī or -ī *m* Bacchus; *n pl* festival in honor of Bacchus

sabbāt·a -ōrum *n pl* Sabbath

sabbatāri·ī -ōrum *m pl* Sabbathkeepers, Jews

Sabell·us -a -um *adj* Sabellian, Sabine; *m* Sabine (*i.e., Horace*)

Sabīn·us -a -um *adj & mf* Sabine; *n* Sabine wine; Horace's Sabine estate

Sabrīn·a -ae *f* Severn River

saburr·a -ae *f* sand, ballast

saburr·ō -āre *vt* to ballast; (coll) to gorge with food

Sac·ae -ārum *m pl* Scythian tribe

saccipēr·ium -iī or -ī *n* purse pocket

sacc·ō -āre *vt* to filter, strain

saccŭl·us -ī m little bag; purse

sacc·us -ī m sack, bag; wallet; filter, strainer

sacell·um -ī n chapel

sac·er -ra -rum adj sacred, holy, consecrated; devoted to a deity for destruction, accursed; detestable; criminal, infamous; n see sacrum

sacerd·ōs -ōtis m priest; f priestess

sacerdōtāl·is -e adj sacerdotal

sacerdōt·ium -iī or -ī n priesthood

sacrāment·um -ī n guarantee, deposit (sum of money which each of the parties to a law suit deposited and which was forfeited by the loser); civil law suit; dispute; oath; voluntary oath of recruits; military oath; eum obligare militiae sacramento to swear him in; justis sacramentis contendere to argue on equal terms; omnes sacramento adigere or rogare to swear in everyone; sacramentum dicere to sign up, swear in; sacramentum dicere (with dat) to swear allegiance to (a general or emperor)

sacrār·ium -iī or -ī n sacristy; shrine, chapel

sacrāt·us -a -um adj hallowed, consecrated, holy, sacred

sacrif·er -ĕra -ĕrum adj carrying sacred objects

sacrificāl·is -e adj sacrificial

sacrificāti·ō -ōnis f sacrifice, sacrificing

sacrific·ium -iī or -ī n sacrifice

sacrific·ō or sacrufic·ō -āre vt & vi to sacrifice

sacrificŭl·us -ī m sacrificing priest

sacrific·us -a -um adj sacrificial

sacrileg·ium -iī or -ī n sacrilege; temple robbing

sacrileg·us -a -um adj sacrilegious; profane, impious, wicked; m temple robber; wicked person; f impious woman

sacr·ō -āre vt to consecrate; to dedicate; to set apart, devote, give; to doom, curse; to hallow, declare inviolable; to hold sacred, worship; to immortalize

sacrōsanct·us -a -um adj sacred, inviolable, sacrosanct

sacrufic·ō see sacrifico

sacr·um -ī n holy object, sacred vessel; holy place, temple, sanctuary; religious rite, act of worship, religious service, sacrifice; victim; n pl worship, religion; secret, mystery; sacra facere to sacrifice

saeclum see saeculum

saeculār·is or sēculār·is -e adj centennial

saecul·um or sēcul·um or saecl·um -ī n generation, lifetime; century; spirit of the age, fashion

saepe adv often

saepenumĕrō or saepe numĕrō adv very often, again and again, oftentimes

saep·ēs or sēp·ēs -is f hedge, fence, enclosure

saepiment·um or sēpiment·um -ī n hedge, fence, enclosure

saep·iō or sēp·iō -īre -sī -tum vt to fence in, hedge in, enclose; to surround, encircle; to guard, fortify, protect, strengthen

saept·um or sept·um -ī n fence, wall, enclosure; stake; sheepfold; voting booth; n pl enclosure; voting booths, polls

saet·a -ae or sēt·a -ae f stiff hair, bristle

saetig·er -ĕra -ĕrum adj bristly; m boar

saetōs·us -a -um adj bristly, hairy

saevē adv fiercely, savagely

saevidic·us -a -um adj spoken in anger, savage

saev·iō -īre -iī -ītum vi to be fierce, be savage, be furious; (of persons) to be brutal, be violent

saeviter adv savagely, ferociously, cruelly

saeviti·a -ae f rage, fierceness; brutality, savageness, barbarity (of persons)

saev·us -a -um adj raging, fierce, furious, cruel; brutal, savage, barbarous (persons)

sāg·a -ae f fortune-teller (female)

sagācit·ās -ātis f keenness; sagacity, keenness of perception, shrewdness

sagāciter adv keenly; shrewdly, accurately, acutely, sagaciously

sagāt·us -a -um adj wearing a military coat

sag·ax -ācis adj keen, sharp, acute; intellectually quick, sharp, shrewd; prophetic

sagīn·a -ae f stuffing, cramming, fattening up; food, rations; rich food; fattened animal; fatness (from overeating)

sagīn·ō -āre vt to fatten

sāg·iō -īre vi to perceive quickly, catch on quickly

sagitt·a -ae f arrow

Sagitt·a -ae f Sagitta (constellation)

sagittāri·us -a -um adj of or for an arrow; m archer, bowman

Sagittār·ius -iī or -ī m Sagittarius (constellation)

sagittif·er -ĕra -ĕrum adj arrow-bearing

Sagittipŏt·ens -entis m Sagittarius (constellation)

sagitt·ō -āre vt to shoot (arrows); vi to shoot arrows

sagm·en -inis n tuft of sacred herbs (plucked in the Capitol by the consul or praetor and worn by the fetiales as a sign of inviolability)

sagŭl·um -ī n short military coat (esp. that of general officers)

sag·um -ī n coarse mantle; military uniform; ad sagum ire or sagum sumere to get into uniform; in sagis esse to be in uniform, be in the armed forces

Saguntīn·us -a -um *adj & m* Saguntine

Sagunt·um -ī *m* Saguntum (*city on the E. coast of Spain which Hannibal attacked and which thereby brought on the First Punic War*)

sāl salis *m* salt; salt water, sea water, sea; seasoning, flavor; good taste, elegance; pungency (*of words*), wit, humor; sarcasm; *m pl* witticisms, jokes, sarcastic remarks

salāc·ō -ōnis *m* braggart, show-off

salamandr·a -ae *f* salamander

Salamīni·us -a -um *adj* of Salamis; *m pl* people of Salamis

Salām·īs -īnis *f* island in the Saronic gulf near Athens; city in Cyprus founded by Teucer

salaput·ium -iī or **-ī** *n* midget

Salāri·a -ae *f* Via Salaria (*from the Porta Collina to the Sabine district*)

salāri·us -a -um *adj* salt, of salt; **annona salaria** revenue from salt mines; *m* salt-fish dealer; *n* salary; allowance; a meal

sal·ax -ācis *adj* lustful; salacious, provocative

salēbr·a -ae *f* jolting; rut; harshness, roughness (*of speech*)

Saliār·is -e *adj* Salian, of the Salii; sumptuous

Saliāt·us -ūs *m* office of Salius, Salian priesthood

salict·um -ī *n* willow grove

salient·ēs -ium *f pl* springs, fountains

salign·us -a -um *adj* willow, of willow

Sali·ī -ōrum *m pl* college of twelve priests dedicated to Mars who went in solemn procession through Rome on the Kalends of March

salill·um -ī *n* small salt cellar

salīn·ae -ārum *f pl* salt pits, salt works; **salinae Romanae** salt works at Ostia (*a state monopoly*)

salīn·um -ī *n* salt cellar

sal·iō -īre -uī or **-iī -tum** *vi* to jump, leap, bound, hop

Salisubsŭl·ī -ōrum *m pl* dancing priests of Mars

saliunc·a -ae *f* wild nard (*aromatic plant*)

salīv·a -ae *f* saliva; taste, flavor

sal·ix -īcis *f* willow tree

Sallust·ius -iī or **-ī** *m* Sallust (*C. Sallustius Crispus, a Roman historian, 86-35 B.C.*)

Salmāc·is -īdis *f* fountain in Caria which made all who drank from it soft and effeminate

Salmōn·eus -ĕos *m* son of Aeolus and brother of Sisyphus who imitated lightning and was thrown by Jupiter into Tartarus

Salmōn·is -īdis *f* Tyro (*daughter of Salmoneus*)

salsāment·um -ī *n* salted or pickled fish; brine

salsē *adv* facetiously, humorously

Salsipŏt·ens -entis *adj* ruling the sea

sals·us -a -um *adj* salted; briny, salty; facetious, humorous, sharp, witty; *n pl* salty food; witty remarks, satirical writings

saltāti·ō -ōnis *f* dancing, dance

saltāt·or -ōris *m* dancer

saltātōri·us -a -um *adj* dance, for dancing

saltātr·ix -īcis *f* dancing girl, dancer

saltāt·us -ūs *m* dance, religious dance

saltem *adv* at least, in any event, anyhow; **non saltem** not even

salt·ō -āre *vt & vi* to dance

saltuōs·us -a -um *adj* wooded, covered with forest

salt·us -ūs *m* wooded pasture, forest; upland; jungle; ravine; valley, glen; (*coll*) female organ; leap, leaping; **saltum dare** to leap

salūb·er (or **salūb·ris**) **-re** *adj* healthful, healthy, wholesome; (with *dat* or with ad + *acc*) healthful for, good for, beneficial to

salūbrit·ās -ātis *f* healthiness, wholesomeness; health, soundness

salūbriter *adv* healthfully; healthily; beneficially

sal·um -ī *n* seas, high seas

sal·ūs -ūtis *f* health; welfare; prosperity, safety; greeting, good wish, best regards; **salutem dicere** (abbreviated **s. d.**) to say hello, send greetings; (at the end of a letter) to say good-bye; **salutem magnam dicere** to send warm greetings; (at the end of a letter) to say good-bye; **salutem plurimam dicere** (abbreviated **s.p.d.**) to send warmest greetings; (at the end of a letter) to give best regards

salūtār·is -e *adj* salutary, healthful, wholesome; beneficial, advantageous, useful; **ars salutaris** art of healing; **salutaris littera** vote of acquittal

salūtāriter *adv* beneficially, profitably, advantageously

salūtāti·ō -ōnis *f* greeting, salutation; formal morning reception or morning call at the house of an important person; callers; **ubi salutatio defluxit** when the morning callers have dispersed

salūtāt·or -ōris *m* or **salūtātr·ix -īcis** *f* morning caller

salūtif·er -ĕra -ĕrum *adj* healthgiving

salūtiger·ŭl·us -a -um *adj* bringing greetings

salūt·ō -āre *vt* to greet, wish well, salute; to send greetings to; to visit, pay respects to, pay a morning call on; to pay reverence to (*gods*); to greet, welcome; (with double *acc*) to salute as, hail as, e.g., **aliquem imperatorem salutare** to hail someone as a victorious general

salvē *adv* well; in good health; **satine salve?** (*coll*) everything O.K.?

salv·ĕō -ēre *vi* to be well, be in good

health; to be getting along well; **salve, salvete,** or **salveto!** hello!, good morning!, good day!; goodbye!; **te salvere jubeo** I bid you good day

salv·us or **salv·os -a -um** or **-om** *adj* well, sound, safe, unharmed, unscathed; living, alive; (with substantive in an *abl* absolute) without violation of, without breaking, e.g., **salvā lege** without breaking the law; **salvos sum** (coll) I'm all right, I'm O.K.

sambūc·a -ae *f* triangular stringed instrument, harp

sambūcin·a -ae *f* harpist (*female*)

sambūcistri·a -ae *f* harpist (*female*)

Sam·ē -ēs *f* ancient name of the island of Cephallenia

Sami·us -a -um *adj* of Samos; **Juno Samia** Juno worshiped at Samos; **vir Samius** Pythagoras

Samn·īs -ītis *adj* Samnite; *m* Samnite gladiator; *m pl* Samnites

Samn·ium -iī or **-ī** *n* district of central Italy

Sam·os or **Sam·us -ī** *f* island off the W. coast of Asia Minor, famous for temple to Juno and as the birthplace of Pythagoras

Samothrāc·ēs -um *m pl* Samothracians

Samothrāci·us -a -um *adj* Samothracian; *f* Samothrace (*island in the N. Aegean*)

sānābil·is -e *adj* curable

sānāti·ō -ōnis *f* healing, curing

sanciō sancīre sanxī sanctum *vt* to consecrate, hallow, make inviolable; to ratify; to condemn; (with *abl*) to forbid under penalty of

sanctē *adv* solemnly, reverently, religiously, conscientiously, purely

sanctimōni·a -ae *f* sanctity, sacredness; chastity

sancti·ō -ōnis *f* consecration, confirmation, sanctioning; penalty clause (*that part of the law that provided for penalties against those breaking that law*), sanction

sanctit·ās -ātis *f* sanctity, sacredness, inviolability; integrity, purity, chastity, holiness

sanctitūd·ō -inis *f* sanctity, sacredness

sanct·or -ōris *m* enactor (*of laws*)

sanct·us -a -um *adj* consecrated, hallowed, sacred, inviolable, venerable, august, divine; pure, holy, chaste, virtuous

sandaligerūl·ae -ārum *f pl* maids who brought their mistress's slippers

sandal·ium -iī or **-ī** *n* slipper, sandal

sandapil·a -ae *f* cheap coffin (*for people of the lower classes*)

sand·yx -ȳcis *f* vermilion

sānē *adv* reasonably, sanely, sensibly; certainly, doubtless, truly, very; (ironically) of course, naturally;

(with negatives) really, at all; (in concessions) to be sure, however; (in answers) yes, of course, to be sure; (with imperatives) then; (with **quam**) how very

sanguen see **sanguis**

sanguin·ans -antis *adj* bleeding; (fig) bloodthirsty, savage

sanguināri·us -a -um *adj* bloodthirsty, savage

sanguin·eus -a -um *adj* bloody, bloodstained; bloodred

sanguinolent·us -a -um *adj* bloody, bloodstained; bloodred; sanguinary

sangu·is or **sangu·īs -inis** *m* or **sangu·en -inis** *n* blood; blood, consanguinity, descent, family; descendant, offspring; slaughter, murder, bloodshed; forcefulness, life, vigor (*of a speech*); life, strength; **pugnatum plurimo sanguine** fought out in a real massacre; **sanguinem dare** to bleed; **sanguinem effundere** or **profundere** to bleed heavily; **sanguinem haurire** to shed (*someone else's*) blood; **sanguinem mittere** (of a physician) to let blood, bleed

saniēs (*genit* not found) *f* blood (*from a wound*); gore; foam, froth, slaver; venom

sānit·ās -ātis *f* health; sanity; common sense, discretion; solidity, healthy foundation (*for victory, etc.*); soundness, propriety (*of style*)

sann·a -ae *f* mocking grimace, face

sanni·ō -ōnis *m* one who makes faces, clown

sān·ō -āre *vt* to cure, heal; to correct, repair; to allay, quiet, relieve

Sanquāl·is -e *adj* of Sangus (*Sabine deity*); **Sanqualis avis** osprey (*bird*)

sān·us -a -um *adj* sound, hale, healthy; sane, rational, sensible; sober; (with **ab** + *abl*) free from (*faults, vices*)

sap·a -ae *f* new wine

sāperd·a -ae *m* a fish (*from the Black Sea*)

sapi·ens -entis *adj* wise, sensible, judicious, discreet; *m* sensible person; sage, philosopher; man of discriminating taste, connoisseur

sapienter *adv* wisely, sensibly, prudently

sapienti·a -ae *f* good taste, common sense, prudence, wisdom; science; philosophy

sapi·ō -ĕre -īvī or **-iī** *vt* to have the flavor of, taste of; to have the smell of, smell like; to have knowledge of, understand; *vi* to have a sense of taste; to have sense, be sensible, be discreet, be wise; **sero sapiunt** they are wise too late

sāp·ō -ōnis *m* soap

sap·or -ōris *m* taste, flavor; delicacy, dainty; elegance, refinement, sense of taste

Sapph·ō -ūs *f* celebrated Greek lyric poetess of Lesbos

sarcĭn·a -ae *f* package, bundle, pack; burden (*of the womb*); sorrow, trouble; *f pl* luggage, gear

sarcĭnārĭ·us -a -um *adj* pack, of luggage; **jumenta sarcinaria** pack animals

sarcĭnāt·or -ōris *m* patcher, botcher

sarcĭnāt·us -a -um *adj* loaded down, burdened

sarcĭnŭl·ae -ārum *f pl* small bundles, little trousseau

sarcĭō sarcīre sarsī sartum *vt* to patch, fix, repair

sarcŏphăg·us -ī *m* sarcophagus, tomb

sarcŭl·um -ī *n* light hoe, garden hoe

Sard·ēs or **Sard·is -ĭum** *f pl* Sardis (*capital of Lydia*)

Sardiān·us -a -um *adj* Sardian

Sardinĭ·a -ae *f* Sardinia

Sardĭnĭens·is -e *adj* Sardinian

Sardīs see **Sardes**

sardŏn·yx -ȳchis *m* sardonyx (*precious stone*)

Sardŏ·us or **Sard·us -a -um** *adj* & *m* Sardianian

sarg·us -ī *m* bream (*fish*)

sar·ĭō or **sarr·ĭō -īre -īvī** or **-ŭī** *vt* to hoe, weed

sarīs·a -ae *f* long Macedonian lance

sarīsophŏr·os -ī *m* Macedonian lancer

sarīt·or or **sart·or -ōris** *m* hoer, weeder

Sarmăt·ae -ārum *m pl* Sarmatians (*barbarous people of S.E. Russia*)

Sarmatĭ·a -ae *f* Sarmatia

Sarmatĭc·us -a -um *adj* Sarmatian

sarm·en -ĭnis or **sarment·um -ī** *n* brushwood; *n pl* twigs, fagots

Sarpēd·ōn -ŏnis *m* king of Lycia who was killed by Patroclus at Troy

Sarr·a -ae *f* Tyre

sarrāc·um or **serrāc·um -ī** *n* cart

Sarrān·us -a -um *adj* Tyrian

sarrĭō see **sario**

sartāg·ō -ĭnis *f* frying pan

sartor see **saritor**

sart·us -a -um *pp* of **sarcio**; *adj* (occurring only with **tectus**) in good repair; **aedem Castoris sartam tectam tradere** to hand over the temple of Castor in good repair; *n pl* repairs; **sarta tecta exigere** to complete the repairs

sat (indecl) *adj* enough, sufficient, adequate; *n* enough; **sat agere** (with *genit*) to have enough of, have the hands full with

sat *adv* sufficiently, quite; **sat scio** I am quite sure

sat·a -ae *f* daughter

sat·a -ōrum *n pl* crops

satăg·ō -ĕre *vi* to have trouble enough, have one's hands full

satell·es -ĭtis *m* or *f* attendant, follower; partisan; accomplice

satĭ·ās -ātis *f* sufficiency; overabundance, satiety, satisfied desire

satĭĕt·ās -ātis *f* sufficiency, adequacy; satiety, weariness, disgust

satin' or **satine** *adv* quite, really

satĭ·ō -āre *vt* to satisfy, appease; to fill, glut; to saturate; to cloy

satĭ·ō -ōnis *f* sowing, planting; *f pl* sown fields

satis (indecl) *adj* enough, sufficient, adequate; *n* enough; (law) satisfaction, security, guarantee; **satis accipere** to accept a guarantee; **satis dare** (with *dat*) to give a guarantee to; **satis facere** (with *dat*) to satisfy; to pay (*a creditor*); to make amends to (*by word or deed*), apologize to; **satis facere** (with *dat* of person and *acc & inf*) to satisfy (*someone*) with proof that, demonstrate sufficiently to (*someone*) that; **satis superque dictum est** more than enough has been said

satis *adv* enough, sufficiently, adequately, fully; **satis bene** pretty well

satisdatĭ·ō -ōnis *f* putting up bail, giving a guarantee

satisfactĭ·ō -ōnis *f* amends, satisfaction, apology

satĭus (*comp* of **satis**) *adj* **satius est** (with *inf*) it is better or preferable to

sat·or -ōris *m* sower, planter; father; promoter, author

satrapē·a or **satrapī·a -ae** *f* satrapy (*office or province of a satrap*)

satrăp·ēs -is *m* satrap (*governor of a province of the Persian empire*)

sat·ur -ŭra -ŭrum *adj* full, well fed, stuffed; plump; rich, fertile; rich, deep (*colors*); *f* mixture, hotchpotch; medley; satire, satirical poem; **per saturam** at random, pell-mell

saturei·a -ōrum *n pl* savory (*aromatic herb used as seasoning*)

saturĭt·ās -ātis *f* satiety; plenty, overabundance

Sāturnālĭ·a -ōrum *n pl* festival in honor of Saturn, beginning on the 17th of December and lasting several days

Sāturnĭ·a -ae *f* Juno (*daughter of Saturn*)

Sāturnīn·us -ī *m* L. Appuleius Saturninus (*demagogic tribune in 103 B.C. and 100 B.C.*)

Sāturnĭ·us -a -um *adj* Saturnian; **Saturnius numerus** Saturnian meter (*archaic Latin meter based on stress accent*); *m* Jupiter; Pluto

Sātur·nus -ī *m* Saturn (*Italic god of agriculture, equated with the Greek god Cronos, ruler of the Golden Age, and father of Jupiter, Neptune, Juno, and Pluto*)

satŭr·ō -āre *vt* to fill, satisfy, glut, cloy, saturate; to satisfy, content

sat·us -a -um *pp* of **sero**; *m* son; *f* see **sata**; *n pl* see **sata**

sat·us -ūs *m* sowing, planting; begetting; race, stock; seed (*of knowledge*)

satyrĭsc·us -ī *m* little satyr

satȳr·us -ī *m* satyr; satyr play (*Greek drama in which satyrs often formed the chorus*)

sanciāti·ō -ōnis *f* wounding

sancī·ō -āre *vt* to wound

sauci·us -a -um *adj* wounded; (fig) smitten, offended, hurt; melted (*snow*)

Sauromăt·ae -ārum *m pl* Sarmatians (*barbaric tribe of S. Russia*)

sāviāti·ō or **suāviāti·ō -ōnis** *f* kissing

sāviŏl·um or **suāviŏl·um -ī** *n* little kiss

sāvī·or -ārī -ātus sum *vt* to kiss

sāv·ium or **suāv·ium -iī** or **-ī** *n* puckered lips; kiss

saxātĭl·is -e *adj* rock, living among rocks; *m* saxatile (*fish*)

saxēt·um -ī *n* rocky place

saxĕ·us -a -um *adj* rocky, stony; **umbra saxea** shade of the rocks

saxific·us -a -um *adj* petrifying, changing objects into stone

saxōs·us -a -um *adj* rocky, stony

saxŭl·um -ī *n* small rock, little crag

sax·um -ī *n* bolder, rock; Tarpeian Cliff (*W. side of the Capitoline Hill*)

scabellum see **scabillum**

scab·er -ra -rum *adj* itchy; rough, scurfy

scab·ĭēs (*genit* not found) *f* itch; roughness, scurf; (fig) itch

scabill·um or **scabell·um -ī** *n* stool, footstool; castanet tied to the foot

scabiōs·us -a -um *adj* itchy, mangy; moldy

scab·ō -ĕre -ī *vt* to scratch

Scae·a port·a -ae *f* Scaean gate (*W. gate of Troy*)

scaen·a or **scēn·a -ae** *f* stage setting, stage; scene; (fig) public view, publicity; pretense, pretext; **tibi scenae serviendum est** you must keep yourself in the limelight

scaenāl·is or **scēnāl·is -e** *adj* theatrical, scenic

scaenĭc·us or **scēnĭc·us -a -um** *adj* of the stage, theatrical, scenic; *m* actor

Scaevŏl·a -ae *m* C. Mucius Scaevola (*Roman hero who infiltrated into Porsenna's camp to kill Porsenna, and, on being discovered, burned off his own right hand*)

scaev·us -a -um *adj* left, on the left; perverse; *f* sign or omen appearing on the left

scāl·ae -ārum *f pl* ladder, flight of steps, stairs

scalm·us -ī *m* oarlock; oar; boat

scalpell·um -ī *n* scalpel

scalp·ō -ĕre -sī -tum *vt* to carve; to scratch; to tickle

scalpr·um -ī *n* chisel; knife; penknife

scalpurr·iō -īre *vi* to scratch

Scamand·er -rī *m* river at Troy, also called Xanthus

scammōnĕ·a -ae *f* scammony (*plant*)

scamn·um -ī *n* bench, stool; throne

scandō scandĕre scandī scansum *vt & vi* to climb, mount, ascend

scandŭl·a -ae *f* shingle (*for roof*)

scaph·a -ae *f* light boat, skiff

scaph·ium -iī or **-ī** *n* boat-shaped drinking cup; chamber pot

scapŭl·ae -ārum *f pl* shoulder blades; shoulders, back

scāp·us -ī *m* shaft; yarn beam (*of a loom*)

scarif·ō -āre *vt* to scratch open

scar·us -ī *m* scar (*fish*)

scatēbr·a -ae *f* bubbling, gushing, jet

scat·ĕō -ēre or **scat·ō -ĕre** *vi* to bubble up, gush out, jet; to teem

scatūrīgin·ēs or **scaturrīgin·ēs -um** *f pl* springs

scaturr·iō -īre *vi* to bubble, gush; to bubble over with enthusiasm

scaur·us -a -um *adj* clubfooted

scaz·ōn -ōntis *m* scazon (*iambic trimeter with a spondee or trochee in the last foot*)

scelerātē *adv* criminally, wickedly

scelerāt·us -a -um *adj* profaned, desecrated; outlawed; criminal, wicked, infamous; *m* villain, criminal

scelĕr·ō -āre *vt* to pollute, desecrate

scelerōs·us -a -um *adj* full of wickedness, vicious

scel·us -ĕris *n* wicked deed, crime, wickedness; calamity; scoundrel, criminal

scēn- = scaen-

sceptrĭf·er -ĕra -ĕrum *adj* sceptered

sceptr·um -ī *n* scepter; kingship; dominion, authority; kingdom

sceptŭch·us -ī *m* scepter-bearer (*high officer of state in the East*)

sched·a or **scid·a -ae** *f* sheet, page

schēm·a -ae *f* figure, form, style; figure of speech

Schoenē·is -ĭdis *f* Atalanta

Schoenei·us -a -um *adj* of Schoeneus; *f* Atalanta

Schoen·eus -ĕī *m* king of Boeotia and father of Atalanta

schoenobăt·ēs -ae *m* ropewalker

schol·a -ae *f* learned debate, dissertation, lecture; school; sect, followers

scholastĭc·us -a -um *adj* school, scholastic; *m* rhetoric teacher, rhetorician

scida see **scheda**

sci·ens -entis *adj* having knowledge; having full knowledge, with one's eyes open; (with *genit*) having knowledge of, familiar or acquainted with, expert in; (with *inf*) knowing how to

scienter *adv* wisely, expertly

scientĭ·a -ae *f* knowledge, skill

scīlicet *adv* of course, evidently, certainly; (ironically) naturally, of course, to be sure; (as an explanatory particle) namely, that is to say, in other words

scill·a or **squill·a -ae** f shrimp

scīn = **scisne**, i.e., **scis** + **ne**

scindō scindĕre scidī scissum vt to cut, split, tear apart or open; to divide, separate; to interrupt

scindŭla see **scandula**

scintill·a -ae f spark

scintill·ō -āre vi to sparkle, flash

scintillŭl·a -ae f little spark

sciō scīre scīvī or **sciī scītum** vt to know; to realize, understand; to have skill in; (with inf) to know how to

Scīpiăd·ēs -ae m a Scipio, one of the Scipio family

Scīpi·ō -ōnis m famous family in the gens Cornelia; P. Cornelius Scipio Africanus Major (conqueror of the Carthaginians in the Second Punic War, 236-184 B.C.); P. Cornelius Scipio Aemilianus Africanus Minor (conqueror of the Carthaginians in the Third Punic War, c. 185-132 B.C.)

scirpĕ·us or **sirpĕ·us -a -um** adj wicker, of wicker; f wickerwork

scirpicŭl·a -ae f wicker basket

scirpicŭl·us -ī m wicker basket

scirp·us or **sirp·us -ī** m bulrush

sciscĭt·ō -āre or **sciscĭt·or -ārī -ātus sum** vt to ask, question, interrogate; to consult; (with acc of thing asked about and ex or ab + abl of person) to ask (something) of (someone), check on (something) with (someone); vi (with de + abl) to ask about

sciscō sciscĕre scīvī scītum vt (pol) to approve, adopt, enact, decree; to learn, ascertain

sciss·us -a -um pp of **scindo**; adj split, rent; furrowed (cheeks); shrill, harsh (voice)

scītāment·a -ōrum n pl dainties, delicacies

scītē adv expertly

scīt·or -ārī -ātus sum vt to ask; to consult (oracle); (with acc of thing and ab or ex + abl) to ask (something) of (someone); vi (with de + abl) to ask or inquire about

scītŭl·us -a -um adj neat, trim, smart

scīt·um -ī n statute, decree

scīt·us -a -um adj experienced, skillful; suitable, proper; judicious, sensible, witty (words); smart, sharp (appearance); (with genit) skilled in, expert at

scīt·us -ūs m decree, enactment

scīūr·us -ī m squirrel

scob·is -is f sawdust, scrapings, filings

scomb·er -rī m mackerel

scōp·ae -ārum f pl twigs, shoots; broom

Scop·ās -ae m famous Greek sculptor of Paros (4th cent. B.C.)

scopulōs·us -a -um adj rocky, craggy

scopŭl·us -ī m rock, cliff, crag; promontory

scorpi·ō -ōnis or **scorp·īus** or **scorp·ios -īī** or **-ī** m scorpion; (mil) artillery piece, catapult

Scorpi·ō -ōnis m Scorpion (sign of the zodiac)

scortāt·or -ōris m fornicator, lecher

scortĕ·us -a -um adj leather, of leather

scort·or -ārī -ātus sum vi to associate with prostitutes

scort·um -ī n prostitute; sex fiend

screāt·or -ōris m one who clears his throat noisily, hawker

screāt·us -ūs m clearing the throat, hawking

scre·ō -āre vi to clear the throat, hawk, hem

scrīb·a -ae m clerk, secretary

scrīblīt·a -ae f tart

scrībō scrībĕre scrīpsī scrīptum vt to write, draw; to write down; to write out, compose, produce; to enlist (soldiers); (with double acc) to appoint (someone) as

scrīn·ium -iī or **-ī** n bookcase, letter case, portfolio

scrīpti·ō -ōnis f writing, composition, authorship; wording, text

scrīptĭt·ō -āre vt to keep writing, write regularly

scrīpt·or -ōris m writer; scribe, secretary; composer, author; **rerum scrīptor** historian

scrīptŭl·a -ōrum n pl lines on a game board

scrīptūr·a -ae f writing; composing; a writing, written work; tax paid on public pastures; testamentary provision

scrīpt·us -a -um pp of **scribo**; n written composition, treatise, work, book; literal meaning, letter; **orationem de scripto dicere** to read off a speech; **scriptum legis** or **scriptum** written ordinance, law

scrīpŭl·um or **scrūpŭl·um -ī** n small weight, smallest measure of weight, scruple (one twenty fourth of an uncia)

scrob·is -is m ditch, trench; grave

scrōf·a -ae f breeding sow

scrōfipasc·us -ī m swine keeper, pig breeder

scrūpĕ·us -a -um adj stony, rugged, jagged, rough

scrūpōs·us -a -um adj full of sharp stones, rugged, jagged, rough

scrūpŭlōsē adv precisely, carefully

scrūpŭlōs·us -a -um adj rough, rugged, jagged; precise, careful

scrūpŭlum see **scripulum**

scrūpŭl·us -ī m small sharp pebble; uneasy feeling, scruple

scrūp·us -ī m rough or sharp stone; uneasiness

scrūt·a -ōrum n pl trash, junk

scrūtāt·or -ōris m examiner

scrūt·or -ārī -ātus sum vt to scrutinize, examine

sculp·ō -ĕre -sī -tum vt to carve, chisel, engrave

sculpōnĕ·ae -ārum f pl clogs

sculptĭl·is -e adj carved, engraved

sculpt·or -ōris m sculptor

sculptūr·a -ae f carving; sculpture

sculptus pp of **sculpo**

scurr·a -ae m jester, comedian; man-about-town

scurrīl·is -e adj scurrilous

scurrīlĭt·ās -ātis f scurrility

scurrīlĭter adv jeeringly

scurr·or -ārī -ātus sum vi to clown around

scŭtāl·e -is n thong of a sling

scŭtār·ĭus -iī or **-ī** m shield maker

scŭtāt·us -a -um adj carrying a shield; m pl troops armed with shields

scutell·a -ae f saucer, shallow bowl

scutĭc·a -ae f whip

scūtigerŭl·us -ī m shield bearer

scutr·a -ae f pan, flat dish

scutŭl·a or **scytăl·a** or **scytăl·ē -ae** f platter; eye patch; wooden cylinder; secret letter

scutŭlāt·us -a -um adj diamond-shaped; n pl checkered clothing

scŭtŭl·um -ī n small shield

scūt·um -ī n oblong shield; (fig) shield, defense, protection

Scyll·a -ae f dangerous rock on the Italian side of Straits of Messina, said to have been the daughter of Phorcus and transformed by Circe into a sea monster with howling dogs about her midriff; daughter of Nisus who betrayed her father by cutting off his purple lock of hair

Scyllae·us -a -um adj Scyllan

scymn·us -ī m cub, whelp

scyph·us -ī m goblet, cup

Scyr·os or **Scyr·us -ī** f island off Euboea

scytăla see **scutula**

scytălē see **scutula**

Scyth·a or **Scyth·ēs -ae** m Scythian; m pl Scythians (general name for the nomadic tribes of the section of Europe and Asia beyond the Black Sea)

Scythĭ·a -ae f Scythia

Scythĭc·us -a -um adj Scythian

Scyth·is -ĭdis f Scythian woman

sē or **sēsē** (genit: **suī;** dat: **sibī** or **sibī;** abl **sē** or **sēsē**) pron acc (reflex) himself, herself, itself, themselves; one another; **ad sē** or **apud sē** at home; **apud se** in one's senses; **inter se** one another, mutually

sēb·um -ī n tallow, grease

sē·cēdō -cēdĕre -cessī -cessum vi to go apart, go aside, withdraw; to rebel

sē·cernō -cernĕre -crēvī -crētum vt to separate; to dissociate; to distinguish; to reject, set aside

sēcessĭ·ō -ōnis f withdrawal; secession

sēcess·us -ūs m retirement, retreat; isolated spot

sē·clūdō -clūdĕre -clūsī -clūsum vt to shut off, shut up; to seclude, bar; to hide

sec·ō -āre -ŭī -tum vt to cut, cut off, reap, carve; (in surgery) to cut out, excise, cut off, amputate; to scratch, tear, wound, injure; to cut through, traverse; to cut short, settle, decide; to follow, chase

sēcordĭa see **socordia**

sēcrētĭ·ō -ōnis f dividing, separating

sēcrētō adv separately, apart; secretly; in private

sēcrēt·us -a -um pp of **secerno;** separate; isolated, solitary; secret; (with genit or abl) deprived of, in need of; n secret, mystery; private conversation or interview; isolated place, solitude

sect·a -ae f path; way, method, course; school of thought; political party

sectārĭ·us -a -um adj gelded; leading

sectāt·or -ōris m follower, adherent

sectĭl·is -e adj cut, divided

sectĭ·ō -ōnis f cutting; auctioning off of confiscated property; right to confiscated property; confiscated property

sect·or -ōris m cutter; buyer at a sale of confiscated property, speculator in confiscated estates

sect·or -ārī -ātus sum vt to keep following, follow eagerly, run after, keep trailing after; to chase, hunt

sectūr·a -ae f digging, excavation; f pl diggings, mines

sectus pp of **seco**

sēcubĭt·us -ūs m sleeping alone

sēcŭb·ō -āre -ŭī vi to lie alone, sleep by oneself; to live alone

sēcul- = **saecul-**

secund·a -ōrum n pl success, good fortune

secund·ae -ārum f pl secondary role (in a play); second fiddle

secundān·ī -ōrum m pl soldiers of the second legion

secundārĭ·us -a -um adj secondary, second-rate, inferior

secundō adv secondly

secund·ō -āre vt to favor, further, back, support

secundum adv after, behind; prep (with acc) (of space) beside, by, along; (of time) immediately after, after; (in rank) next to, after; (of agreement) according to, in compliance with; in favor of, to the advantage of

secund·us -a -um adj following; next, second (in time); backing, favorable, supporting; next, second (in rank); secondary, subordinate, inferior, second-string; **anno secundo** the next year; **a mensis fine secunda dies** the second-last day of the month; **in secundam aquam** with the current; **secunda mensa** dessert; **secundo flumine** downstream, with the current; **se-**

cundo lumine on the following day; **secundo mari** with the tide; **secundo populo** with the backing of the people; **secundus panis** inferior bread, stale bread; **secundus ventus** tail wind, fair wind; *f pl* see **secundae**; *n pl* see **secunda**

sēcūrē *adv* securely, safely

secūricŭl·a -ae *f* hatchet

secūrif·er -ĕra -ĕrum *adj* carrying an ax, ax-carrying

secūrig·er -ĕra -ĕrum *adj* ax-carrying

secūr·is -is *f* ax, hatchet; blow, mortal blow; power of life and death; supreme authority, sovereignty

sēcūrit·ās -ātis *f* freedom from care, unconcern, composure; freedom from danger, security, safety; false sense of security; carelessness

sēcūr·us -a -um *adj* carefree; secure, safe; cheerful; careless; offhand

secus (indecl) *n* sex; **secus muliebre** females; **secus viriles** males

secus *adv* otherwise, differently; **non secus ac** or **non secus quam** not otherwise than, just as, exactly as; **si secus accidet** if it turns out otherwise (*than expected*), if it turns out badly

secut·or -ōris *m* gladiator (*who fought against an opponent who had a net*)

secūtus *pp* of **sequor**

sed or **set** *conj* but; but also; but in fact

sēdātē *adv* sedately, calmly

sēdāti·ō -ōnis *f* calming

sēdāt·us -a -um *adj* calm, composed

sēdĕcim (indecl) *adj* sixteen

sēdēcŭl·a -ae *f* little seat, low stool

sedentāri·us -a -um *adj* sedentary

sedĕō sedēre sēdī sessum *vi* to sit, remain sitting; (of magistrates, esp. judges) to sit, preside, hold court, be a judge; (of an army) to remain encamped; to keep the field; to settle down in blockade; to be idle, be inactive; (of clothes) to fit; (of places) to be low-lying; to sink, settle; to be firm, be fixed, be established; to stick fast, be stuck; to be determined, be firmly resolved

sēd·ēs -is *f* seat, chair, throne; residence, home; last home, burial place; base, foundation, bottom

sedīl·e -is *n* seat, chair, bench, stool; *n pl* seats in the theater; rowers' benches

sēditi·ō -ōnis *f* sedition, insurrection, mutiny; dissension, quarrel, disagreement; warring (*of elements, etc.*)

sēditiōsē *adv* seditiously

sēditiōs·us -a -um *adj* seditious, mutinous; quarrelsome; troubled, disturbed

sēd·ō -āre *vt* to calm, settle, still, allay

sē·dūcō -dūcĕre -duxī -ductum *vt* to lead aside, draw aside, lead

away, carry off; to put aside; to separate, divide

sēductī·ō -ōnis *f* taking sides, siding

sēduct·us -a -um *pp* of **sēduco**; distant, remote

sēdŭlit·ās -ātis *f* application, earnestness; officiousness

sēdŭlō *adv* diligently; intentionally, on purpose

sēdŭl·us -a -um *adj* diligent, busy; officious

seg·es -ĕtis *f* grain field; crop

Segest·a -ae *f* town in N.W. Sicily

Segestān·us -a -um *adj* of Segesta; *m pl* people of Segesta; *n* territory of Segesta

segmentāt·us -a -um *adj* trimmed with a flounce

segment·um -ī *n* trimming, flounce; brocade

segnip·ēs -ĕdis *adj* slow-footed

segn·is -e *adj* slow, inactive; sluggish, lazy

segniter *adv* slowly, lazily

segniti·a -ae or **segniti·ēs** (*genit* not found) *f* slowness, inactivity, laziness

sēgrĕg·ō -āre *vt* to segregate, separate

sējugāt·us -a -um *adj* separated

sējŭg·is -is *m* six-horse chariot

sējunctim *adv* separately

sējunctī·ō -ōnis *f* separation, division

sē·jungō -jungĕre -junxī -junctum *vt* to separate, disunite, part, sever; (fig) to sever, part, disconnect; to distinguish

sēlectī·ō -ōnis *f* selection

sēlectus *pp* of **seligo**

Seleuc·us -ī *m* name of a line of kings of Syria

sēlibr·a -ae *f* half pound

sē·ligō -ligĕre -lēgī -lectum *vt* to pick out, select, choose

sell·a -ae *f* chair, stool; sedan; magistrate's chair

sellāriōl·us -a -um *adj* (place) for sitting or lounging

sellār·ius -iī or **-ī** *m* lecherer

sellisterni·a -ōrum *n pl* sacred banquets in honor of goddesses

selltŭl·a -ae *f* stool; sedan

sellulār·ius -iī or **-ī** *m* mechanic

sēmanimis see **semianimis**

semel *adv* once, one time; but once, once for all; first, the first time; once, ever, at some time, at any time

Semĕl·ē -ēs or **Semĕl·a -ae** *f* daughter of Cadmus and mother of Bacchus by Jupiter

Semelei·us -a -um *adj* of Semele

sēm·en -inis *n* seed, germ; seedling, young plant, shoot; offspring; race, stock; (in physics) particle; instigator, cause

sēmenstris see **semestris**

sēmentif·er -ĕra -ĕrum *adj* seed-bearing, fruitful

sēmentīn·us -a -um *adj* of the sowing season

sément·is -is *f* sowing, planting; young crops

sementiv·us -a -um *adj* at seed time, of the sowing season

sēmerm·is -e *adj* half-armed

sēmestr·is or **sēmenstr·is -e** *adj* for six months, half-yearly, semi-annual

sēmēs·us -a -um *adj* half-eaten

sēmet = emphatic form of **se**

sēmiadapert·us -a -um *adj* half-open

sēmianim·is -e or **sēmianim·us** or **sēmanim·us -a -um** *adj* half-dead

sēmiapert·us -a -um *adj* half-open

sēmīb·ōs -ōvis *adj masc* half-ox; **semibos vir** Minotaur

sēmicáp·er -rī *adj masc* half-goat

sēmicremāt·us or **sēmicrēm·us -a -um** *adj* half-burned

sēmicubitāl·is -e *adj* half-cubit long

sēmidé·us -a -um *adj* semidivine; *m* demigod

sēmidoct·us -a -um *adj* half-educated

sēmierm·is -e or **sēmierm·us -a -um** *adj* half-armed

sēmiēs·us -a -um *adj* half-eaten

sēmifact·us -a -um *adj* half-finished

sēmif·er -ēra -ērum *adj* half-beast; half-savage; *m* centaur

sēmifult·us -a -um *adj* half-propped

sēmigermān·us -a -um *adj* half-German

sēmigráv·is -e *adj* half-drunk

sēmigr·ō -āre *vi* to go away, depart

sēmihi·ans -antis *adj* half-open

sēmihōm·ō -īnis *m* half man, half beast; subhuman

sēmihōr·a -ae *f* half hour

sēmilác·er -ēra -ērum *adj* half-mangled

sēmilaut·us -a -um *adj* half-washed

sēmilīb·er -ēra -ērum *adj* half-free

sēmilix -a -ae *m* (term of reproach) sad sack

sēmimarin·us -a -um *adj* semisubmerged (*in the sea*)

sēmim·ās -āris *adj* gelded, castrated; *m* hermaphrodite

sēmimortu·us -a -um *adj* half-dead

sēminār·ium -iī or **-ī** *n* nursery garden; (fig) breeding ground

sēminat·or -ōris *m* originator, cause, source

sēminéc·is (*genit*; *nom* does not occur) *adj* half-killed, half-dead

sēmin·ium -iī or **-ī** *n* breeding; stock

sēmin·ō -āre *vt* to sow; to beget, procreate; to produce

sēminūd·us -a -um *adj* half-stripped; half-unarmed

sēmipāgān·us -ī *m* little clown

sēmiplēn·us -a -um *adj* (garrison) at half strength

sēmiputāt·us -a -um *adj* half-pruned

Semīrām·is -is or **-ĭdis** *f* famous queen of Assyria, the consort and successor of Ninus

Semiramī·us -a -um *adj* of Semiramis

sēmirās·us -a -um *adj* half-shaven

sēmireduct·us -a -um *adj* bent back halfway

sēmirefect·us -a -um *adj* half-repaired

sēmirūt·us -a -um *adj* half-ruined, half-demolished

sēm·is -issis *m* half; half an ace (*coin*); one half percent a month or six-percent per annum; **non semissis homo** man not worth a penny, worthless fellow

sēmisēn·ex -is *m* elderly gent

sēmisepult·us -a -um *adj* half-buried

sēmisomn·is -e or **sēmisomn·us -a -um** *adj* half-asleep

sēmisupīn·us -a -um *adj* half-prone

sēmit·a -ae *f* path, lane

sēmitāl·is -a -um *adj* of byways

sēmitāri·us -a -um *adj* back-alley

sēmiustilāt·us or **sēmiustulāt·us -a -um** *adj* half-burned

sēmiv·ir -īrī *adj* half-man, half-beast; unmanned; unmanly, effeminate; *m* half-man; eunuch

sēmivīv·us -a -um *adj* half-alive, half-dead

sēmod·ius -iī or **-ī** *m* half a peck

sēmōt·us -a -um *adj* remote, distant; *n pl* faraway places

sē-moveō -movēre -mōvī -mōtum *vt* to move apart, separate, remove, put aside

semper *adv* always, ever; regularly, on each occasion

sempitern·us -a -um *adj* everlasting

Semprōnĭus see **Gracchus**

sēmunci·a -ae *f* half ounce (*one twenty-fourth of a Roman pound*); trifle

sēmunciāri·us -a -um *adj* half-ounce; **faenus semunciarium** interest at the rate of one twenty-fourth of the capital (*i.e., about five percent per annum*)

sēmust·us -a -um *adj* half-burned

senācŭl·um -ī *n* open-air meeting place of the senate in the Forum

sēnāriŏl·us -ī *m* trifling trimeter

sēnāri·us -a -um *adj* six-foot (*verse*); *m* iambic trimeter

senāt·or -ōris *m* senator

senātōri·us -a -um *adj* senatorial; in the senate; of a senator

senāt·us -ūs *m* senate; senate session; **senatūs consultum** decree of the senate

Senéc·a -ae *m* L. Annaeus Seneca (*Stoic philosopher and instructor of Nero, 4 B.C.-65 A.D.*)

senect·us -a -um *adj* aged, old; *f* old age, senility

senect·ūs -ūtis *f* old age; old people

sen·ĕŏ -ēre *vi* to be old

sen·escō -escĕre -ŭī *vi* to grow old; to decline, become feeble, lose strength; to wane, draw to a close

sen·ex -is *adj* aged, old; *m* old man; *f* old woman

sēn·ī -ae -a *adj* six each, six in a group, six at a time; **seni deni** sixteen each

senīl·is -e *adj* of old people, of an old man; aged; senile

sēnī·ō -ōnis *m* a six (*on dice*)

seni·or -us (*comp of* **senex**) *adj* older, elder; more mature (*years*); *m* elderly person, an elder (*over forty-five years of age*)

sen·ium -iī *or* **-ī** *n* feebleness of age, decline, senility; decay; grief, trouble; gloom; crabbiness; old man

sens·a -ōrum *n pl* thoughts, sentiments, ideas

sensicŭl·us -ī *m* short sentence

sensif·er -ĕra -ĕrum *adj* producing sensation

sensil·is -e *adj* capable of sensation, sentient

sensim *adv* gropingly; tentatively; carefully, gradually, gently

sens·us -a -um *pp of* **sentio**; *n pl* see **sensa**

sens·us -ūs *m* sense faculty, capacity for feeling, sensation; feeling, emotion, sentiment; attitude, frame of mind, view; understanding, judgment, intelligence; meaning, intent, sense; sentence; **communes sensūs** commonplaces; universal human feelings

sententi·a -ae *f* opinion, view, judgment; purpose, intention; (*law*) sentence, verdict; (in the senate) motion, proposal, view; meaning, sense; sentence; maxim; **de sententia** (with *genit*) in accordance with the wishes of; **ex animi (mei) sententia** (in an oath) to the best of (*my*) knowledge and belief; **ex mea sententia** in my opinion, to my liking; **in sententiam alicujus pedibus ire** to vote in favor of someone's proposal; **sententia est** (with *inf*) I intend to; **sententiam dicere** (in the senate) to express a view; **sententiam pronuntiare** *or* **dicere** to pronounce or give the verdict

sententiŏl·a -ae *f* phrase; maxim

sententiōsē *adv* sententiously

sententiōs·us -a -um sententious, full of meaning

senticēt·um -ī *n* thorny bush

sentin·a -ae *f* bilge water; cesspool; bilge; (fig) dregs, scum, rabble

sentiō sentīre sensī sensum *vt* to perceive with the senses, feel, hear, see, smell; to realize; to feel, observe, notice; to experience; to think, judge; *vi* (law) to vote, decide

sent·is -is *m* thorny bush, bramble, brier

sentisc·ō -ĕre *vt* to begin to realize;

to begin to observe, perceive

sent·us -a -um *adj* thorny; untidy (*person*)

seorsum *or* **seorsus** *adv* apart, separately; (with *abl* or **ab** + *abl*) apart from

sēparābil·is -e *adj* separable

sēparātim *adv* apart, separately

sēparāti·ō -ōnis *f* severing, separation

sēparātius *adv* less closely, more widely

sēparāt·us -a -um *adj* separate, distinct, different

sēpăr·ō -āre *vt* to separate, divide, part; to distinguish

sepelībil·is -e *adj* that may be buried

sepeliō sepelīre sepelīvī *or* **sepeliī sepultum** *vt* to bury; (fig) to bury, overwhelm, ruin, destroy, suppress

sēpēs see **saepes**

sēpi·a -ae *f* cuttlefish

sēpīmentum see **saepimentum**

sēpiō see **saepio**

sēpiŏl·a -ae *f* little cuttlefish

sē·pōnō -pōnĕre -posuī -positum *vt* to put aside; to separate, pick out, select; to assign, reserve; to remove, take away, exclude; to distinguish

sēposit·us -a -um *adj* remote, distant; select; distinct, private

seps sēpis *m* or *f* snake

sēpse = emphatic **sē**

septem (indecl) *adj* seven

September -ris *adj & m* September

septemdĕcim (indecl) *adj* seventeen

septemflu·us -a -um *adj* seven-mouthed (*Nile*)

septemgemīn·us -a -um *adj* sevenfold

septempedāl·is -e *adj* seven-foot, seven-feet-high

septempl·ex -ĭcis *adj* sevenfold

septemtriōnāl·ia -ium *n pl* northern regions, northern part

septemtriōnāl·is -e *adj* northern

septemtriōn·ēs *or* **septentriōn·ēs -um** *m pl* seven stars near the North Pole belonging to the Great Bear; the seven stars of the Little Bear; northern regions, the North; north wind

septemvirāl·is -e *adj* of the septemvirs, septemviral; *m pl* septemvirs

septemvirāt·us -ūs *m* septemvirate, office of the septemvirs

septemvir·ī -ōrum *m pl* septemvirs (*board of seven officials*)

septēnār·ius -iī *or* **-ī** *m* heptameter (*verse of seven feet*)

septendĕcim *or* **septemdĕcim** (indecl) *adj* seventeen

septēn·ī -ae -a *adj* seven each, seven in a group; **septeni deni** seventeen each, seventeen in a group

septentr- = **septemtr-**

septiens *or* **septiēs** *adv* seven times

septimān·us -a -um *adj* of or on the seventh; *n pl* soldiers of the seventh legion

septimum *adv* for the seventh time

septim·us or **septŭm·us -a -um** *adj* seventh

septim·us decim·us -a -um *adj* seventeenth

septingentēsim·us -a -um *adj* seven hundredth

septingent·ī -ae -a *adj* seven hundred

septuāgēsim·us -a -um *adj* seventieth

septuāgintā (indecl) *adj* seventy

septuenn·is -e *adj* seven-year-old

septum see **saeptum**

septun·x -cis *m* seven ounces; seven twelfths

septus *pp* of **saepio**

sepulcrāl·is -e *adj* of a tomb, sepulchral, funeral

sepulcrēt·um -ī *n* grave, tomb

sepulcr·um -ī *n* grave, tomb

sepultūr·a -ae *f* burial

sepultus *pp* of **sepelio**

Sēquān·a -ae *m* Seine

sequ·ax -ācis *adj* following, pursuing; penetrating (*fumes*); eager

sequ·ens -entis *adj* next, following

sequest·er -ris (or **-ra**) **-re** *adj* intermediate; negotiating, mediating; **pace sequestrā** under the protection of a truce; *m* trustee; agent, mediator, go-between

sequius or **sētius** (*comp* of **secus**) *adv* less; worse, more unfavorably; **nihilo setius** or **nilo setius** nevertheless

sequor sequī secūtus sum *vt* to follow, escort, accompany, go with; to chase, pursue; to come after (*in time*); to go after, aim at; to head for (*a place*); *vi* to go after, follow, come next; (of words) to come naturally

ser·a -ae *f* bolt, bar (*of door*)

Serāp·is -is or **-idis** *m* Egyptian god of healing

serēnit·ās -ātis *f* fair weather; serenity; favorableness

serēn·ō -āre *vt* to make fair, clear up, brighten

serēn·us -a -um *adj* clear, bright, fair, cloudless; cheerful, serene; *n* clear sky, fair weather

Sēr·es -um *m pl* Chinese

seresc·ō -ĕre *vi* to dry off

sēri·a -ae *f* large jar

sēri·a -ōrum *n pl* serious matters, serious business

Sēric·us -a -um *adj* Chinese; *n pl* silks

seri·ēs (*genit* not found) series, row, succession; train, sequence, order, connection; lineage

sēriō *adv* seriously, in all sincerity

sēri·us -a -um *adj* serious, earnest; *n* serious matter; seriousness, earnestness; *n pl* see **seria**

serm·ō -ōnis *m* conversation, talk; discussion, discourse; common talk,

rumor, gossip; language, diction; prose, everyday language

sermōcin·or -ārī -ātus sum *vi* to talk, converse

sermuncŭl·us -ī *m* small talk, chit-chat

serō serĕre serŭī sertum *vt* to join, connect; to entwine, wreathe; to compose, combine, contrive

serō serĕre -sēvī satum *vt* to sow, plant; (fig) to sow the seeds of

sērō *adv* late

serp·ens -entis *m* or *f* creeping thing, snake, serpent, dragon

Serp·ens -entis *m* Serpent, Draco (*constellation*)

serpentigĕn·a -ae *m* dragon offspring

serpentĭp·ēs -ĕdis *adj* dragon-footed

serperastr·a -ōrum *n pl* splints (*for straightening the crooked legs of children*); officer who keeps his soldiers in check

serpillum see **serpyllum**

serpō serpĕre serpsī serptum *vi* to creep, crawl; to move along slowly, spread slowly

serpyll·um or **serpill·um** or **serpull·um -ī** *n* wild thyme

serr·a -ae *f* saw

serrāt·us -a -um *adj* serrated, notched

serrŭl·a -ae *f* small saw

sert·a -ae *f* wreath

sert·a -ōrum *n pl* wreaths, festoons

Sertōr·ius -iī or **-ī** *m* general of Marius who held out in Spain against the partisans of Sulla until he was assassinated by Perperna (*c.* 122-72 B.C.)

sert·us -a -um *pp* of **sero** (to join); *f* see **serta**; *n pl* see **serta**

ser·um -ī *n* whey; serum

sēr·us -a -um *adj* late; too late; **anni seri** ripe years; **ulmus sera** slow-growing elm; *n* late hour; in **serum rem trahere** to drag out the matter until late

serv·a -ae *f* slave (*female*)

servābil·is -e *adj* retrievable

serv·ans -antis *adj* keeping; (with *genit*) observant of

servāt·or -ōris *m* or **servātr·ix -īcis** *f* savior, preserver, deliverer

servīl·is -e *adj* slave, servile

servīliter *adv* slavishly

serv·iō -īre -īvī or **-iī -ītum** *vi* to be a servant or slave; to be obedient; (of buildings, land) to be mortgaged; (with *dat*) **a** to be a slave to, be subservient to; **b** to serve; **c** to comply with, conform to, humor; **d** to be devoted to, work at; **e** to serve, be of use to

servit·ium -iī or **-ī** *n* slavery, servitude; slaves

servitūd·ō -inis *f* servitude, slavery

servit·ūs -ūtis *f* slavery; serfdom; slaves; property liability, easement

Serv·ius Tull·ius -iī or **-ī** *m* sixth king of Rome

serv·ō -āre vt to watch over, preserve, protect; to store, reserve; to keep, retain; to observe; to keep to, continue to dwell in

servŏl·a -ae f young slave girl

servolicŏl·a -ae f slave of a slave (female)

servŏl·us -ī m young slave

serv·us or **serv·os -a -um** adj slave, servant; mf slave, servant

sescēnār·is -e adj a year and a half old

sescēnāri·us -a -um adj six-hundred-man (cohort)

sescēn·ī -ae -a adj six hundred each, six hundred in a group

sescentēsim·us -a -um adj six hundredth

sescent·ī -ae -a adj six hundred

sescentiēns or **sescentiēs** adv six hundred times

sēsē see se

sescunci·us -a -um adj inch and a half thick

sesēl·is -is f seseli (plant)

sesqui adv more by a half, one and a half times

sesquialt·er -ĕra -ĕrum adj one and a half

sesquihōr·a -ae f an hour and a half

sesquimod·ius -iī or **-ī** m peck and a half

sesquioctāv·us -a -um adj having a ratio of nine to eight

sesquiŏp·us -ĕris n day and a half's work

sesquipedāl·is -e adj foot and a half long or wide

sesquiplāg·a -ae f blow and a half

sesquipl·ex -icis adj one and a half times as much

sesquiterti·us -a -um adj containing one and a third; having a ratio of four to three

sessibŭl·um -ī n chair, seat, easy chair

sessil·is -e adj for sitting on; (plants) growing close to the ground, low-growing

sessi·ō -ōnis f sitting; session; loafing

sessit·ō -āre vi to sit much, keep sitting, rest

sessiuncŭl·a -ae f small group, small circle

sess·or -ōris m spectator; resident

sestert·ium -iī or **-ī** n sesterce

sestert·ius -iī or **-ī** (genit pl: **sestertium**) (abbreviated HS) m sesterce (small silver coin, equal to one fourth of a denarius, i.e., about 8¢, and used as the ordinary Roman unit in accounting); **centena milia sestertium** 100,000 sesterces; **deciens** (i.e., **deciens centena milia**) **sestertium** 1,000,000 sesterces

Sest·os or **Sest·us -ī** f city on the Hellespont

sēt- = **saet-**

Sēti·a -ae f town in Latium famous for its wine

Sētīn·us -a -um adj Setine; n Setine wine

sētius see sequius

seu conj or if; or; **seu . . . seu** whether . . . or

sevērē adv seriously; severely, austerely

sevērit·ās -ātis f severity, sternness, strictness

sevēritūd·ō -inis f austerity

sevēr·us -a -um adj serious, grave; severe, strict, austere; ruthless, grim

sēvŏc·ō -āre vt to call aside, call away; to remove, withdraw, separate

sēv·um -ī n tallow, grease

sex (indecl) adj six

sexāgēnāri·us -a -um adj sixty-year-old

sexāgēn·ī -ae -a adj sixty each, sixty in a group

sexāgēsim·us -a -um adj sixtieth

sexāgiens or **sexāgiēs** adv sixty times

sexāgintā (indecl) adj sixty

sexangŭl·us -a -um adj hexagonal

sexcen- = **sescen-**

sexcēnāri·us -a -um adj six-hundred-man (cohort)

sexenn·is -e adj six-year-old, of six years; **sexenni die** in a six-year period

sexenn·ium -iī or **-ī** n six-year period, six years

sexiens or **sexiēs** adv six times

sexprim·ī or **sex prim·ī -ōrum** m pl six-member council (in provincial towns)

sextadecimān·ī -ōrum m pl soldiers of the sixteenth legion

sext·ans -antis m one sixth; small coin (one sixth of an ace); one sixth of a pint

sextār·ius -iī or **-ī** m pint

Sextīl·is -e adj of or belonging to the sixth month of the old Roman year which was afterwards called August in honor of Augustus

sextŭl·a -ae f sixth of an ounce

sextum adv for the sixth time

sext·us -a -um adj sixth

sext·us decim·us -a -um adj sixteenth

sexungŭl·a -ae f six-clawed woman, rapacious woman

sex·us -ūs m sex

sī conj if, if only; **quod sī** but if; **sī forte** if perchance, in the hope that; **sī minus** if not

sibī see se

sībil·a -ōrum n pl hisses, hissing

sībil·ō -āre vt to hiss at; vi to hiss

sībil·us -a -um adj & m hissing

Sibyll·a or **Sibull·a -ae** f sibyl, prophetess

Sibyllīn·us -a -um adj sibylline

sīc adv thus, so, in this way; thus, as follows; in these circumstances; in such a way, to such a degree; (in assent) yes

Sicān·ī -ōrum *m pl* ancient people of Italy who migrated to Sicily

Sicānі·a -ae *f* Sicily

Sicān·is -idis *adj* Sicilian

Sicān·is -a -um *adj* Sicilian; *f* see **Sicania**

Sicān·us -a -um *adj* Sicilian; *m pl* see **Sicani**

sicār·ius -ī or **-ī** *m* murderer, assassin; **inter sicarios accusare (defendere)** to prosecute (defend) on a murder charge

sicce *adv* firmly, solidly

siccit·ās -ātis *f* dryness; drought; firmness, solidity; dullness (*of style*)

sicc·ō -āre *vt* to dry, dry up, drain; to stanch, heal

siccocŭl·us -a -um *adj* dry-eyed

sicc·us -a -um *adj* dry; thirsty; sober; firm, solid (*body*); solid (*argument*); dry, insipid (*style*)

Sicilі·a -ae *f* Sicily

sicilicissit·ō -āre *vi* to act like a Sicilian

sicilicŭl·a -ae *f* sickle

Siciliens·is -e *adj* Sicilian

sicine *adv* is this how . . . ?

sicŭbi *adv* if anywhere, wheresoever

sicŭl·a -ae *f* little dagger

Sicŭl·ī -ōrum *m pl* ancient Italian people who migrated to Sicily

sicunde *conj* if from some place, if from anywhere

sicut or **sicŭti** *conj* as, just as; (in elliptical clauses) just as, like; (introducing a comparison) as it were, so to speak; (introducing an example) as, as for instance; (of condition) as, in the same condition as; as if, just as if; **sicut . . . ita** although . . . yet

Sicy·ōn -ōnis *f* town in the N. Peloponnesus

Sicyōnі·us -a -um *adj* of Sicyon; *m pl* inhabitants of Sicyon

siderĕ·us -a -um *adj* starry; star-spangled; heavenly, divine

sidō sidĕre sidī or **sēdī sessum** *vi* to sit down; to settle; (of birds) to alight, land; to sink; to settle down, subside; (of ships) to be grounded

Sīd·ōn -ōnis *f* city of Phoenicia

Sīdōn·is -idis *adj* Phoenician; *f* Dido; Europa

Sīdōnі·us -a -um *adj* Sidonian, Phoenician; Theban; *m pl* Sidonians

sīd·us -ĕris *n* constellation; star, heavenly body; sky, heaven; light, glory, beauty, pride; season; climate, weather; (in astrology) star, destiny

Sigambr·ī -ōrum *m pl* powerful German tribe

Sīgē·um -ī *n* promontory near Troy where Achilles was said to have been buried

Sīgē·us -a -um *adj* Sigean

sigill·a -ōrum *n pl* figurines; seal (*on a seal ring*)

sigillāt·us -a -um *adj* adorned with little figures

signāt·or -ōris *m* sealer, signer; witness

signāt·us -a -um *adj* sealed, secured

signif·er -ĕra -ĕrum *adj* bearing the constellations, starry; *m* standard-bearer; chief, leader

signific·ans -antis *adj* clear, distinct, expressive

significanter *adv* clearly, graphically

significāti·ō -ōnis *f* signal, indication, sign, mark; expression of approval, applause; meaning, sense, signification; emphasis

signific·ō -āre *vt* to show, indicate, point out, express; to intimate; to notify, publish, make known; to portend; to mean, signify

sign·ō -āre *vt* to mark, stamp, impress, imprint; to seal, seal up; to coin; to point out, signify, indicate, express; to adorn, decorate; to distinguish, mark, note

sign·um -ī *n* sign, indication, proof; military standard, banner; password; cohort, maniple; omen, symptom; statue, picture; device on a seal, seal, signet; heavenly sign, constellation; **ab signis discedere** to break ranks, disband; **signa conferre** to engage in close combat; to concentrate troops; **signa constituere** to halt; **signa conversa ferre** to wheel around and attack; **signa ferre** to break camp; **signa movere** to advance; **signa movere in hostem** to advance against the enemy, attack the enemy; **signa proferre** to march forward, advance; **signa servare** to keep the order of battle; **signa sequi** to march in rank; **signa subsequi** to keep the order of battle; **signa transferre** to desert, join the other side; **signis collatis** in regular battle

silān·us -ī *m* jet of water

Silăr·us -ī *m* river forming the boundary between Lucania and Campania

sil·ens -entis *adj* silent, calm, quiet; *m f pl* the dead

silent·ium -ī or **-ī** *n* silence; inactivity; **silentium facere** to obtain silence; to keep silence; **silentium significare** to call for silence

Sīlēn·us -ī *m* teacher and constant companion of Bacchus, usually drunk

sil·ĕō -ēre -ŭī *vt* to leave unmentioned, say nothing about; *vi* to be silent, be still; to keep silence; to be hushed; to rest, cease

sil·er -ĕris *n* willow

silesc·ō -ĕre *vi* to become silent, fall silent, become hushed

sil·ex -icis *m* flint, flint stone; cliff, crag; hardheartedness

silicern·ium -ī or **-ī** *n* funeral feast; (coll) old fossil

silīg·ō -inis *f* winter wheat; wheat flour

siliqu·a -ae f pod, husk; f pl pulse

sillyb·us -ī m label giving book's title

sīl·ō -ōnis m (man) button nose, snub nose

silūr·us -ī m sheatfish

sīl·us -a -um adj having a turned-up nose, snub-nosed

silv·a or **silŭ·a -ae** f woods, forest; shrubbery, bush, foliage, crop, growth; mass, abundance, quantity, material, supply

Silvān·us -ī m god of woods; m pl woodland gods

silvesc·ō -ĕre vi (of a vine) to run wild

silvestr·is -e adj wooded, overgrown with woods; woodland, living in woods; wild, growing wild; rural, pastoral; n pl woodlands

silvicŏl·a -ae m or f denizen of the forest

silvicultr·ix -īcis adj fem living in the woods

silvifrăg·us -a -um adj forest-smashing (wind)

silvōs·us -a -um adj wooded, woody

sīmĭ·a -ae f ape

simil·is -e adj similar; (with genit or dat) resembling, like, similar to; **homines inter se similes** men resembling one another; **veri similis** probable; realistic; n comparison, parallel

similĭter adv similarly; **similiter atque** or **ac** just as; **similiter ut si** just as if

similitūd·ō -ĭnis f likeness, resemblance; imitation; analogy; comparison, simile; monotony; (with genit) similarity to; **est homini cum deo similitudo** there is a resemblance between a god and man

sīmiŏl·us -ī m monkey

simĭtū adv at the same time; (with **cum + abl**) together with

sīm·ius -ī or **-ĭ** m ape

Simō·is -entis m river at Troy

Simōnĭd·ēs -is m famous lyric poet of Ceos (fl 500 B.C.); celebrated iambic poet of Amorgos (7th cent. B.C.)

simpl·ex -ĭcis adj single, simple, unmixed; plain, natural; frank; naive; in single file

simplicĭt·ās -ātis f simplicity; candor, frankness

simplicĭter adv simply, plainly; candidly, frankly

simpl·us -a -um adj simple; n simple sum

simpŭl·um -ī n small ladle

simpuv·ium -ĭī or **-ĭ** n libation bowl

simul adv together, at the same time; likewise, also; (with **abl** or **cum + abl**) with, together with; **simul atque** or **ac** or **et** as soon as; **simul . . . simul** both . . . and; conj as soon as

simulăcr·um -ī n image, likeness, representation; form, shape, phantom, ghost; conception; sign, emblem; mere shadow; portraiture, characterization

simulām·en -ĭnis n imitation, copy

simŭl·ans -antis adj imitating; (with genit) imitative of

simulātē adv insincerely, deceitfully

simulātĭ·ō -ōnis f faking, bluffing, bluff, pretense; **simulatione** (with genit) under the pretense of, under the guise of

simulāt·or -ōris m imitator; pretender, phoney

simŭl·ō -āre vt to imitate, copy, represent; to put on the appearance of, simulate

simult·ās -ātis f enmity, rivalry, feud, jealousy, grudge

sīmŭl·us -a -um adj rather snub-nosed

sīm·us -a -um adj snub-nosed, pug-nosed

sīn conj if however, if on the other hand, but if

sināp·i -is n or **sināp·is -is** f mustard

sincērē adv sincerely, honestly, frankly

sincērĭt·ās -ātis f soundness, integrity

sincĕr·us -a -um adj sound, whole, clean, untainted; real, genuine

sincĭp·ut -ĭtis or **sincipitāment·um -ī** n half a head; cheek, jowl (of a hog); brain

sind·ōn -ōnis f fine cotton or linen fabric, muslin

sine prep (with abl) without; **flammā sine** flameless

singillātim adv one by one, singly

singlārĭter see **singulariter**

singulār·is -e adj single, alone, one at a time; unique, unparalleled; m pl crack troops

singulārĭter or **singlārĭter** adv singly; particularly

singulārĭ·us -a -um adj single, separate

singulātim adv singly, individually

singŭl·ī -ae -a adj single, one at a time, individual; one each, one apiece; **in singulos dies** on each successive day; every day, daily; m pl individuals

singultim adv sobbingly, gaspingly; falteringly

singult·ĭō -īre vi to hiccup; to throb

singult·ō -āre vt to gasp out, spurt out; vi to sob, gasp; to gurgle

singult·us -ūs m sob, gasp; squirt (of water, etc.); death rattle

singŭl·us -a -um adj one by one, single; each one, one apiece

sinist·er -ra -rum adj left, on the left; (because in Roman augury the augur faced south, having the East on the left) favorable, auspicious, lucky; (because in Greek augury the augur faced north, having the East on his right) unfavorable, inauspicious, unlucky; wrong, perverse, improper; m pl soldiers on the left flank; *f* left, left hand; left side; *n* left side; **a sinistra** on the left

sinisterit·ās -ātis *f* awkwardness

sinistrē *adv* badly, wrongly, perversely

sinistrorsum or **sinistrorsus** *adv* to the left

sinō sinĕre sīvī or **siī situm** *vt* to allow; **sine modo** only let, if only

Sin·ōn -ōnis *m* Greek soldier through whose treachery the Greeks were able to get the horse into Troy

Sinōp·a -ae or **Sinōp·ē -ēs** *f* Greek colony on the S. coast of the Euxine Sea

Sinuess·a -ae *f* city on the border between Latium and Campania

sīn·um -ī *n* large drinking cup

sinŭ·ō -āre *vt* to wind, curve, arch

sinuōs·us -a -um *adj* winding, sinuous, serpentine

sin·us -ūs *m* curved or bent surface, indentation, curve, fold, hollow; fold of the toga about the breast; pocket, purse; breast, bosom, lap; bay, gulf, lagoon; winding coast; valley, hollow; heart (*e.g., of a city*), interior; intimacy; **in sinu meo est** he is dear to me

sīn·us -ī *m* large drinking cup

sīpar·ium -iī or **-ī** *n* theater curtain; **post siparium** behind the scenes

sīph·ō -ōnis *m* siphon; fire engine

sīphuncŭl·us -ī *m* small pipe

Sipўl·us -ī *m* mountain in Lydia

siquandō or **sī quandō** *conj* if ever

siquīdem *conj* if in fact

siremps or **sirempse** = **sī rem ipsam** *adj* the same, e.g., **sirempse legem** the same law

Sīr·ēn -ēnis *f* Siren (*sea nymph who had the power of charming with her song*)

Sīri·us -a -um *adj* of Sirius, of the Dog Star; *m* Sirius, Dog Star

sirp·e -is *n* silphium (*plant*)

sīr·us -ī *m* underground granary

sīs = **sī vīs** please, if you please

sistō sistĕre stiti statum *vt* to cause to stand, make stand, put, place, set; to set up (*monument*); to establish; to stop, check, arrest; to put an end to; to produce in court; **pedem sistere** or **gradum sistere** to halt, stop; **se sistere** to present oneself, appear, come; **sisti non potest** the crisis cannot be met, the case is hopeless; **vadimonium sistere** to answer bail, show up in court; *vi* to stand, rest; to stop, stay; to stand firm, last, endure; to show up in court; (with *dat* or **contra** + *acc*) to stand firm against

sistrāt·us -a -um *adj* with a tambourine

sistr·um -ī *n* rattle, tambourine

Sīsyphĭd·ēs -ae *m* descendant of Sisyphus, i.e., Ulysses

Sīsyph·us -ī *m* son of Aeolus, king of Corinth, whose punishment in

Hades was to roll a rock repeatedly up a hill

sitell·a -ae *f* lottery urn

Sīth·ōn -ōnis *adj* Thracian

Sīthōn·is -idis or **Sīthonī·us -a -um** *adj* Thracian; *m pl* Thracians

siticulōs·us -a -um *adj* thirsty, dry

siti·ens -entis *adj* thirsting, thirsty; arid, parched; parching; (with *genit*) eager for

sitienter *adv* thirstily, eagerly

sit·iō -īre -īvī -ī *vt* to thirst for; *vi* to be thirsty

sit·is -is *f* thirst; (with *genit*) thirst for

sitit·or -ōris *m* thirsty person; **sititor aquae** thirster for water

sittўbus see **sillybus**

sitŭl·a -ae *f* bucket

sit·us -a -um *pp* of **sino**; *adj* lying, situated; founded; (with **in** + *abl*) resting on, dependent on

sit·us -ūs *m* position, situation, site; structure; neglect; mustiness; dust, dirt; idleness, inactivity, lack of use

sīve *conj* or if; or; **sīve . . . sīve** whether . . . or

smaragd·us -ī *m* or *f* emerald

smar·is -idis *f* a small sea fish

smīl·ax -ăcis *f* smilax, bindweed (*plant*)

Sminth·eus -ĕī *m* epithet of Apollo

Smyrn·a -ae *f* town in Asia Minor

sobol· = **subol-**

sōbriē *adv* soberly, moderately; sensibly

sōbriet·ās -ātis *f* temperance (*in drinking*)

sōbrīn·a -ae *f* cousin (*female, on the mother's side*)

sōbrīn·us -ī *m* cousin (*on the mother's side*)

sōbri·us -a -um *adj* sober; temperate, continent; sensible, reasonable

soccŭl·us -ī *m* small or short sock

socc·us -ī *m* sock; slipper; low shoe worn by actors in comedies; comedy

soc·er or **soc·ĕrus -ĕrī** *m* father-in-law

soci·a -ae *f* associate, companion, ally, partner (*female*)

sociābil·is -e *adj* compatible, intimate

sociāl·is -e *adj* allied, confederate; nuptial, conjugal; companionable, sociable

sociāliter *adv* sociably, in comradeship

socienn·us -ī *m* comrade

sociĕt·ās -ātis *f* companionship, fellowship; association, society, partnership, alliance, confederacy

soci·ō -āre *vt* to unite, associate; to share

sociofraud·us -ī *m* heel, double crosser

soci·us -a -um *adj* joint, allied, confederate; held in common, common; *m* associate, companion, ally, partner; *f* see **socia**

sōcordi·a or **sēcordi·a -ae** *f* silliness, stupidity; apathy, laziness

sŏcordĭus *adv* too apathetically

sŏc·ors -ordis *adj* silly, stupid; apathetic, lazy, inactive

Sŏcrăt·ēs -is *m* famous Athenian philosopher (469-399 B.C.)

Sŏcratĭc·ī -ōrum *m pl* Socratics, disciples of Socrates

socr·us -ūs *f* mother-in-law

sodālĭcĭ·us -a -um *adj* of companionship; *n* companionship, intimacy; society, secret society

sodāl·is -is *m or f* comrade, companion, fellow; member (*of a society, priestly college, etc.*); accomplice, conspirator; gallant

sodālĭt·ās -ātis *f* companionship, fellowship; society, club, association; secret society

sodālĭt- = sodalĭc-

sōdēs = si audes if you will, please

sōl sōlis *m* sun; sunlight, sunshine; day

sōlācĭŏl·um -ī *n* bit of comfort

sōlāc·ĭum -ĭī or -ī *n* comfort, relief

sōlām·en -ĭnis *n* comfort

sōlār·is -e *adj* sun; **lumen solare** sunlight, sunshine

sōlār·ĭum -ĭī or -ī *n* sundial; clock; sunny spot, balcony

sōlāt- = solac-

sōlāt·or -ōris *m* comforter

soldūrĭ·ī -ōrum *m pl* retainers (*of a chieftain*)

soldus see **solidus**

solĕ·a -ae *f* sole; sandal; fetter; sole (*flat fish*)

soleār·ĭus -ĭī or -ī *m* sandal maker

soleāt·us -a -um *adj* wearing sandals

solĕō solēre solĭtus sum *vi* (with *inf*) to be in the habit of, usually, e.g., **solet cenare sero** he usually eats late; (with **cum + abl**) to have intercourse with

solĭdē *adv* for certain; fully, wholly

solidĭt·ās -ātis *f* solidity

solĭd·ō -āre *vt* to make firm, make dense; to strengthen

solĭd·us or sold·us -a -um *adj* solid, firm, dense; whole, entire; genuine, real; trustworthy; firm, resolute; *n* entire sum, total; solid, solid body, mass, substance; solid earth

sōliferrĕ·um -ī *n* all-iron spear

sōlistĭm·us -a -um *adj* perfect; **tripudium solistimum** perfectly auspicious omen

sōlĭtārĭ·us -a -um *adj* solitary, lonely

sōlĭtūd·ō -ĭnis *f* loneliness; deprivation; wilderness

solĭt·us -a -um *adj* usual, customary, characteristic; *n* the usual, the customary; **formosior solito** more handsome than usual, unusually handsome; **magis solito or plus solito** more than usual

sol·ĭum -ĭī or -ī *n* seat, chair; throne; dominion, sway; bathtub; stone coffin, sarcophagus

sōlivăg·us -a -um *adj* roaming

alone; single, solitary

sollemn·is -e *adj* annual, periodic; religious, solemn; usual; *n* usage, practice; solemn rite, solemnity, ceremony, feast, sacrifice; festival, games (*in observance of Roman holy days*)

sollemnĭter *adv* solemnly, religiously

soll·ers -ertis *adj* skilled, skillful, expert, clever

sollerter *adv* skillfully, expertly, cleverly

sollertĭ·a -ae *f* skill, ingenuity, shrewdness; clever plan; (with *genit*) skill in

sollicĭtātĭ·ō -ōnis *f* vexation, anxiety; incitement, instigation

sollicĭtē *adv* anxiously, with solicitude; diligently

sollicĭt·ō -āre *vt* to shake, disturb; to disquiet, annoy, molest; to worry, make anxious; to provoke, tempt; to stir up, incite, incite to revolt

sollicĭtūd·ō -ĭnis *f* anxiety, uneasiness

sollicĭt·us -a -um *adj* stirred up, stormy (*sea*); tossed (*by the waves*); troubled, disturbed, disquieted, restless; anxious, solicitous, apprehensive, worried

sollif- = solif-

sollist- = solist-

soloecism·us -ī *m* grammatical mistake, solecism

Sol·ōn -ōnis *m* famous Athenian legislator (c. 640-c. 560 B.C.)

sōl·or -ārī -ātus sum *vt* to console, comfort; to relieve, mitigate (*fear, worry*)

sōlstĭtĭāl·is -e *adj* of the summer solstice; midsummer's; solar

sōlstĭt·ĭum -ĭī or -ī *n* summer solstice; midsummer, summer heat

sol·um -ī *n* bottom, ground, floor; soil, land, country; sole (*of foot or shoe*)

sōlum *adv* only, merely, barely; **non solum ... sed etiam** not only ... but also

sōl·us -a -um *adj* only, single, sole, alone; lonely, solitary

sŏlūtē *adv* loosely, freely, without hindrance; negligently; without vigor

sŏlūt·us -a -um *adj* loose, untied, unbandaged; negligent; free; fluent; unrhythmical; uncontrolled; exempt, free; unbiased; unbridled, loose

sŏlūtĭ·ō -ōnis *f* loosening; payment

solvō solvĕre solvī or solŭī solūtum *vt* to loosen, untie; to free, release; to dissolve, break up; detach, disengage; to unlock, open; to melt, turn, change; to relax, smooth, soothe; to impair, weaken, destroy; to acquit, absolve; to accomplish, fulfill; to pay, pay off; to solve, explain; to suffer, undergo (*punishment*); to remove, get rid of (*feelings*); *vi* to weigh anchor, set sail

Solym·a -ōrum *n pl* Jerusalem

somniculōsē *adv* sleepily, drowsily

somniculōs·us -a -um *adj* sleepy, drowsy

somnif·er -ĕra -ĕrum *adj* sleep-inducing, soporific; deadly (*poison*)

somni·ō -āre *vt* to dream of; to daydream about, imagine; **somnium somniare** to have a dream

somn·ium -iī or **-ī** *n* dream; daydreaming; nightmare

somn·us -ī *m* sleep; night; sleep of death; indolence

sonābil·is -e *adj* noisy

sonĭp·ēs -ēdis *adj* loud-hoofed; *m* steed

sonĭt·us -ūs *m* sound, noise

sonĭvĭ·us -a -um *adj* noisy

son·ō -āre -uī -ĭtum *vt* to speak, sound, express; to mean; to sound like; *vi* to sound, ring, resound, make a noise

son·or -ōris *m* sound, noise, clang

sonōr·us -a -um *adj* sonorous, loud, noisy, clanging

sons sontis *adj* guilty, criminal

sontĭc·us -a -um *adj* important

son·us -ī *m* sound, noise; tone (*of style*)

sophī·a -ae *f* wisdom

sophist·ēs -ae *m* sophist

Sophŏcl·ēs -is *m* famous Greek writer of tragedies (*c.* 495-406 B.C.)

Sophoclē·us -a -um *adj* Sophoclean, of Sophocles

soph·us -a -um *adj* wise; *m* wise man, sage

sōp·ĭō -īre -īvī or **-ĭī -ītum** *vt* to put to sleep; to stun, knock unconscious; (*fig*) to calm, still, settle, lull

sop·or -ōris *m* deep sleep; stupor; apathy, indifference; sleeping potion

sopōrāt·us -a -um *adj* stupefied; unconscious; buried in sleep; allayed (*grief*); soporific

sopōrĭf·er -ĕra -ĕrum *adj* sleep-inducing

sopōr·us -a -um *adj* drowsy

Sōract·e -is *n* mountain in Etruria about twenty-six miles from Rome

sōrăc·um -ī *n* hamper

sorb·ĕō -ēre -uī *vt* to suck in, gulp down; to absorb; (*fig*) to swallow (*e.g., hatred*)

sorbill·ō -āre *vt* to sip

sorbĭlō *adv* drop by drop, bit by bit

sorbĭtĭ·ō -ōnis *f* drink, pleasant drink

sorb·um -ī *n* Juneberry, service-berry

sorb·us -ī *f* Juneberry tree, service-berry tree

sord·ĕō -ēre *vi* to be dirty, be shabby; to appear worthless

sord·ēs -is *f* dirt, filth; shabbiness, squalor; (*often worn as a sign of mourning*) mourning; meanness (*of behavior*); low rank, low condition, vileness; dregs, rabble; vulgarity

sord·escō -escĕre -uī *vi* to become dirty, become soiled

sordidāt·us -a -um *adj* in dirty or shabby clothes (*esp. as a sign of mourning*)

sordĭdē *adv* vilely, meanly, vulgarly

sordĭdŭl·us -a -um *adj* rather soiled, rather shabby; (*fig*) low, mean

sordĭd·us -a -um *adj* dirty, filthy, shabby; soiled, stained; dressed in mourning clothes; low (*rank*); vile, vulgar (*behavior*)

sordĭtūd·ō -ĭnis *f* dirt, filth

sōr·ex -ĭcis *m* shrewmouse

sōrĭcĭn·us -a -um *adj* squealing like mice

sōrīt·ēs -ae *m* sorites (*logical conclusion drawn from cumulative arguments*)

sor·or -ōris *f* sister; cousin; companion, playmate; **sorores doctae** Muses; **sorores tres** three Fates; **sorores tristes** gloomy Fates

sorōrĭcĭd·a -ae *f* murderer of a sister

sorōrĭ·us -a -um *adj* sister's, of a sister; sisterly; **stuprum sororium** incest with a sister

sors sortis *f* lot; casting of lots, decision by lot; prophecy; fate, destiny, lot in life; portion, share; sort, kind, class

sorsum see **seorsum**

sortĭlĕg·us -a -um *adj* prophetic; *m* soothsayer, fortune-teller

sortĭ·ō -īre or **sort·ĭor -īrī -ītus sum** *vt* to cast or draw lots for; to allot, assign by lot, appoint by lot; to obtain by lot; to choose, select; to share, divide; to receive, get by chance; *vi* to cast or draw lots

sortītĭ·ō -ōnis *f* drawing lots, determining by lots

sortītō *adv* by lot; by fate

sortīt·us -ūs *m* lottery

Sosĭ·ī -ōrum *m pl* the Sosii (*two brothers famous as booksellers in Rome at the time of Horace*)

sosp·es -ĭtis *adj* safe and sound; auspicious, lucky

sospĭt·a -ae *f* preserver (*epithet of Juno*)

sospĭtāl·is -e *adj* beneficial

sospĭt·ō -āre *vt* to preserve, protect

sōt·ēr -ēris *m* savior, deliverer, protector

sōtērĭ·a -ōrum *n pl* party thrown for a person recovering from an illness

spād·ix -īcis *adj* chestnut-brown

spad·ō -ōnis *m* eunuch

spargō spargĕre sparsī sparsum *vt* to scatter, sprinkle, strew; to scatter, disperse; to disseminate, broadcast; to spot, dapple

sparsĭ·ō -ōnis *f* sprinkling

spars·us -a -um *pp* of **spargo;** *adj* freckled, spotty

Spart·a -ae or **Spart·ē -ēs** *f* Sparta (*capital of Laconia, also called Lacedaemon*)

Spartăc·us -ī *m* Thracian gladiator who led a revolt of gladiators against Rome in 73-71 B.C.

Spartān·us -a -um adj Spartan

Spartiāt·ēs -ae m Spartan

Spartiātic·us or **Spartic·us -a -um** adj Spartan

spart·um -ī n Spanish broom (plant, used in making ropes, nets, etc.)

sparŭl·us -ī m bream (fish)

spar·us -ī m hunting spear

spath·a -ae f broad two-edged sword

spati·or -ārī -ātus sum vi to walk, stroll, take a walk; to walk solemnly; to spread out

spatiōsē adv extensively; long, for a long time

spatiōs·us -a -um adj spacious; broad, large; prolonged

spat·ium -iī or **-ī** n room, space, extent; open space, public square; distance (between two points); walk, promenade (place); interval, period; time, opportunity; measure, quantity (in metrics); lap; race track

speci·ēs -ēī f sight, view; outward appearance, outline, shape; fine appearance, beauty; deceptive appearance, show, semblance, pretense, pretext; resemblance, likeness; display, splendor; vision, apparition; image, statue; idea, notion; reputation; species, sort; **in speciem** or **per speciem** as a pretext, for the sake of appearances

specill·um -ī n probe (surgical instrument)

specīm·en -Inis n mark, sign, proof, example; model, ideal

speciō specēre spexī vt to look at, behold

speciōsē adv splendidly

speciōs·us -a -um adj handsome, good-looking, beautiful; plausible; specious

spectābil·is -e adj visible; remarkable

spectācŭl·um or **spectācl·um -ī** n sight, spectacle; public performance; stage play; theater

spectām·en -Inis n sign, proof

spectāti·ō -ōnis f observation, view; examining, testing

spectāt·or -ōris m observer; spectator; critic, judge

spectātr·ix -īcis f on-looker, observer; spectator

spectāt·us -a -um adj tried, tested, proved; esteemed

specti·ō -ōnis f observing the auspices; right to take the auspices

spect·ō -āre vt to observe, watch; to face in the direction of; to consider; to bear in mind; to aim at, tend towards; to examine, test

spectr·um -ī n specter, apparition

specŭl·a -ae f look-out, watch tower; summit

spēcŭl·a -ae f bit of hope

speculābund·us -a -um adj on the look-out

speculār·is -e adj transparent; n pl windowpane, window

speculāt·or -ōris m spy; explorer

speculātōri·us -a -um adj for spying, for reconnaissance; f reconnaissance ship

speculātr·ix -īcis f spy (female)

specŭl·or -ārī -ātus sum vt to reconnoiter, observe, watch for

specŭl·um -ī n mirror (made of polished metal)

spec·us -ūs m or n cave, cavern; artificial excavation, ditch, canal, channel, pit; hole, cavity (of a wound, etc.)

spēlae·um -ī n den, cave

spēlunc·a -ae f cave

spērābil·is -e adj possible (able to be hoped for)

spērāt·us -a -um adj hoped for, longed for, desired; f fiancée, bride-to-be

Sperchē·is -Idis adj of the Spercheos

Sperchē·os or **Sperchi·us -ī** m large river in S. Thessaly

spernō spernēre sprēvī sprētum vt to remove; to scorn, reject

spēr·ō -āre vt to hope for, expect, look forward to; to trust, trust in; to anticipate, await with fear

spēs speī f hope, expectation; anticipation, apprehension (of evil); **praeter spem** beyond all expectation; unexpectedly

Speusipp·us -ī m nephew of Plato and his successor as head of the Academy (347-339 B.C.)

sphaer·a -ae f sphere, globe, ball

sphaeristēr·ium -iī or **-ī** n tennis court

Sphin·x -gis f sphinx

spīc·a -ae f point; ear (of grain); tuft, top, head (of plants)

spīcě·us -a -um adj made of ears of grain

spīcŭl·um -ī n point; sting; dart, arrow

spīc·um -ī n ear (of grain)

spīn·a -ae f thorn; thorn bush; prickle (of animals); backbone, spine; back; f pl subtleties

spīnēt·um -ī n thorn hedge, thorny thicket

spīně·us -a -um adj made of thorns, thorn

spīnif·er -ěra -ěrum adj prickly

spīnōs·us -a -um adj thorny, prickly; (fig) stinging, irritating (worries); confused, obscure (style)

spint·ēr -ēris m elastic bracelet

spintri·a -ae m male prostitute

spinturnic·ium -iī or **-ī** n bird of ill omen

spīn·us -ī f blackthorn, sloe tree

spīr·a -ae f coil (of a serpent); chin strap

spīrābil·is -e adj good to breathe, life-giving (air)

spīrācŭl·um -ī n pore, vent; breathing space

spīrāment·um -ī n pore, vent; breathing space, pause, instant

spīrit·us -ūs m breathing, breath; breeze; air; breath of life; life; inspiration; spirit, character, courage; pride, arrogance; morale; **spiritum ducere** to take a breath, breathe

spīr·ō -āre vt to exhale, breathe out; to aspire to, aim at; vi to breathe; to be alive; to be favorable; to have poetic inspiration

spissāt·us -a -um adj condensed, concentrated

spissē adv thickly, closely, tightly; slowly

spissesc·ō -ĕre vi to condense, become thick

spissigrăd·us -a -um adj slow-paced

spiss·ō -āre vt to condense, concentrate

spiss·us -a -um adj thick, tight, dense; slow; late; difficult

splēn splēnis m spleen

splend·ĕō -ēre vi to be clear and bright, shine, gleam; to be illustrious, be glorious

splendesc·ō -ĕre vi to become clear and bright

splendid·us -a -um adj clear and bright, gleaming, glistening, sparkling; spotless, noble (character); splendid, magnificent; sumptuous; showy; illustrious

splend·or -ōris m brightness, brilliance; clearness; splendor, magnificence; noble

splēniăt·us -a -um adj wearing a patch

splēn·ium -iī or **-ī** n patch (for the face)

spoliātǐ·ō -ōnis f stripping, plundering; unjust deprivation (of honor or dignity); ousting (from public office)

spoliāt·or -ōris m or **spoliātr·ix -ǐcis** f despoiler, robber

spoliāt·us -a -um adj stripped, robbed

spolǐ·ō -āre vt to strip of clothes; to pillage, plunder, rob

spol·ium -iī or **-ī** n hide, skin; spoils, booty, loot

spond·a -ae f bed frame, sofa frame; bed, sofa

spondāl·ium or **spondaul·ium -iī** or **-ī** n ritual hymn accompanied by a flute

spondĕō spondēre spopondī sponsum vt to promise solemnly, pledge, vow; to promise in marriage; vi (law) to give a guarantee, put up bail; (with **pro** + abl) to vouch for

spondē·us -ī m spondee

spondŷl·us -ī m mussel

spongǐ·a -ae f sponge; coat of mail

spons·a -ae f fiancée

sponsāl·ia -ium n pl engagement; engagement party

sponsǐ·ō -ōnis f solemn promise, guarantee; bet; (law) agreement between two parties that the loser pay a certain sum to the other

spons·or -ōris m guarantor, surety

spons·us -a -um pp of **spondeo**; m fiancé, bridegroom; f see **sponsa**; n agreement, engagement

spons·us -ūs m contract

sponte (only abl) f (of persons, mostly with possessive adj) of one's own accord, voluntarily; by oneself, unaided; (of things) of itself, spontaneously; on its own account, for its own sake

sport·a -ae f plaited basket; sieve

sportell·a -ae f little basket, lunch basket

sportūl·a -ae f little basket (in which gifts of food were given by the patron to his clients); dole, present (of food or money); gift

sprētǐ·ō -ōnis f scorn, contempt

sprēt·or -ōris m despiser

sprētus pp of **sperno**

spūm·a -ae f foam, froth; lather; scum

spūmāt·us -a -um adj covered with foam

spūmesc·ō -ĕre vi to grow foamy

spūmě·us -a -um adj foaming, frothing

spūmif·er -ěra -ěrum adj foaming

spūmig·er -ěra -ěrum adj foaming

spūm·ō -āre vi to foam, froth

spūmōs·us -a -um adj full of foam, foaming; bombastic (poem)

spuō spuěre spuī spūtum vt to spit, spit out; vi to spit

spurcāt·us -a -um adj foul, filthy

spurcē adv filthily; in filthy language

spurcidǐc·us -a -um adj foul-mouthed, filthy, smutty, obscene

spurcǐfic·us -a -um adj smutty, obscene

spurc·ō -āre vt to make filthy, foul up; to defile

spurc·us -a -um adj (morally) filthy, dirty

spūtātilǐc·us -a -um adj deserving to be spit at, contemptible, disgusting

spūtāt·or -ōris m spitter

spūt·ō -āre vt to spit, spit out; to avert by spitting

spūt·um -ī n spit

squāl·ĕō -ēre -ǔī vi to be rough, be scaly, be parched, be wrankled; to be coated, be clotted, be stiff; to be covered with filth; to be covered with weeds, be overgrown; to wear mourning clothes, go in mourning

squālǐdē adv coarsely

squālǐd·us -a -um adj rough, scaly; stiff, coated with dirt, squalid; in mourning; rough, coarse (speech); cracked, parched (land)

squāl·or -ōris m squalor, dirtiness; desolation; filthy garments (neglected as a sign of mourning)

squal·us -ī m shark

squām·a -ae f scale; scale armor; fish

squāmě·us -a -um adj scaly

squāmif·er -ěra -ěrum adj scaly

squāmig·er -ĕra -ĕrum *adj* scaly; *m pl* fish

squāmōs·us -a -um *adj* covered with scales, scaly

squill·a or scill·a -ae *f* shrimp

st *interj* sh!

stabiliment·um -ī *n* support

stabil·iō -īre -īvī -ītum *vt* to stabilize; to establish

stabil·is -ē *adj* stable, firm, steady; steadfast, unwavering, immutable

stabilit·ās -ātis *f* stability, firmness, steadiness, durability

stabiliter *adv* firmly

stabŭl·ō -āre *vt* to stable or house (*animals*); *vi* to have a stall

stabŭl·um -ī *n* stable, stall; lair; hut; brothel

stact·a -ae or stact·ē -ēs *f* myrrh oil

stad·ium -iī or -ī *n* furlong; race track

Stagīr·a -ōrum *n pl* town in Macedonia, the birthplace of Aristotle

Stagīrīt·es -ae *m* Aristotle

stagn·ō -āre *vt* to overflow, inundate; *vi* to form a pool; to be inundated

stagn·um -ī *n* pool, swamp, lake, lagoon; straits; waters

stalagm·ium -iī or -ī *n* eardrop, earring (*with pendant*)

stām·en -inis *n* warp (*of a loom*); thread; string (*of an instrument*); fillet (*worn by priests*)

stāminĕ·us -a -um *adj* full of threads, consisting of threads, wrapped in threads

Stat·a -ae *f* surname of Vesta

statāri·us -a -um *adj* standing, stationary; steady, calm; *m pl* actors in a type of comedy; *f* quiet or refined comedy

statēr·a -ae *f* scales; statera aurificis goldsmith's scales

staticŭl·us -ī *m* a dance

statim *adv* at once, immediately, on the spot

stati·ō -ōnis *f* standing still; station, post; position; residence; anchorage; *f pl* sentries

Stāt·ius -iī or -ī *m* P. Papinius Statius (*poet of the Silver Age of Latin literature, c.* 40-96 A.D.)

statīv·us -a -um *adj* stationary; *n pl* bivouac

stat·or -ōris *m* magistrate's attendant

Stat·or -ōris *m* Stayer (*epithet of Jupiter, who kept the Roman soldiers from retreating*)

statŭ·a -ae *f* statue

statūm·en -inis *n* rib (*of a hull*)

stat·ŭō -ŭĕre -ŭī -ūtum *vt* to cause to stand, bring to a stop; to set up, erect; to establish (*precedent, etc.*); to set, fix, determine; to decide, settle; to decree; to strengthen, support; to appoint, create; to inflict, pass (*sentence, punishment*); to hold, think, consider; to fix (*a price*); to draw up, arrange (*a battle line*)

stat·us -a -um *pp* of sisto; *adj* fixed, set, appointed

stat·us -ūs *m* position, posture; position, situation, condition; social status, rank; form of government; (*mil*) position; status rei publicae type of government

statūt·us -a -um *adj* tall

steg·a -ae *f* deck

stell·a -ae *f* star; constellation; stella comans comet; stella diurna Lucifer; stella errans planet

stell·ans -antis *adj* starry

stellāt·us -a -um *adj* set with stars, starry; made into a star

stellif·er -ĕra -ĕrum *adj* star-bearing, starry

stellig·er -ĕra -ĕrum *adj* star-bearing, starry

stelli·ō -ōnis *m* newt, lizard with spotted back

stemm·a -ătis *n* genealogical tree, pedigree; *n pl* antiquity, history

stercorĕ·us -a -um *adj* full of dung

stercŏr·ō -āre *vt* to manure, fertilize

sterc·us -ŏris *n* manure, dung

steril·is -e *adj* sterile, barren; causing barrenness, blighting; empty, bare; unprofitable; unrequited (*love*): wild (*trees*)

sterilit·ās -ātis *f* sterility, barrenness

stern·ax -ācis *adj* bucking (*horse*)

sternō sternĕre strāvī strātum *vt* to strew, spread; to pave (*roads, etc.*); to knock down, bring low, slay; to raze, level; to flatten, smooth; to calm, calm down; sterni to stretch out (*on the ground*)

sternūment·um -ī *n* sneezing, sneeze

sternŭ·ō -ĕre -ī *vt* to give (*e.g., an omen*) by sneezing; *vi* to sneeze; to sputter

Sterŏp·ē -ēs *f* one of the Pleiades

sterquilīni·um -iī or -ī or sterquilīn·um -ī *n* dung heap; (term of abuse) heap of dung

stert·ō -ĕre *vi* to snore

Stēsichŏr·us -ī *m* Greek lyric poet of Himera in Sicily (*c.* 640-*c.* 555 B.C.)

Sthenĕl·us -ī *m* king of Mycenae, son of Perseus, and father of Eurystheus; king of the Ligurians and father of Cycnus who was changed into a swan

stibad·ium -iī or -ī *n* semicircular seat

stigm·a -ătis *n* mark, brand; stigma (*of disgrace*)

stigmati·ās -ae *m* branded slave

stigmōs·us -a -um *adj* branded

still·a -ae *f* drop; mere drop

still·ō -āre *vt & vi* to drip

stil·us -ī *m* stylus (*pointed instrument for writing*); writing, composition; style (*of writing or speaking*)

stimulāti·ō -ōnis *f* stimulation, incitement

stimulātr·ix -īcis f inciter (female)

stimulē·us -a -um adj of goads

stimulō -āre vt to goad, torment; to spur on, incite, excite

stimŭl·us -ī m or **stimŭl·um -ī** n goad, prick; (mil) pointed stake concealed below the ground; (fig) stimulus, incentive, spur

stingu·ō -ĕre vt to quench, extinguish

stīpātī·ō -ōnis f crowd, throng

stīpāt·or -ōris m attendant; m pl retinue

stīpendāri·us -a -um adj liable to tax, tributary; m pl tributary peoples; mercenary troops

stīpend·ium -iī or **-ī** n tax, tribute, tariff; (mil) pay; military service; year's service, campaign; **emereri stipendia** to have served out one's term; **emeritis stipendiis** at the end of one's military service, at discharge; **merere stipendia** or **mereri stipendia** to serve, serve in the army

stīp·es -itis m log, trunk; branch, tree; blockhead

stīp·ō -āre vt to crowd, cram, pack; to crowd around, accompany in a group

stips stipis f gift, donation, alms

stipŭl·a -ae f stalk, blade; stubble; reed pipe

stipulāti·ō -ōnis f agreement, bargain; (law) formal promise

stipulātiuncŭl·a -ae f insignificant promise, slight stipulation

stipulāt·us -a -um adj promised

stipŭl·or -ārī -ātus sum vt to stipulate; vi to bargain; (law) to make a formal promise

stīrĭ·a -ae f icicle

stirpĭtus adv by the roots

stirp·s or **stirp·ēs** or **stirp·is -is** f stock, stem, stalk, root; plant, shrub; race, lineage; offspring, descendant; character, nature; root, source, foundation, beginning, origin

stīv·a -ae f plow handle

stlattāri·us or **stlātāri·us -a -um** adj imported, costly

stlopp·us -ī m slap (sound produced by slapping an inflated cheek)

stō stāre stetī statum vi to stand, stand still, remain standing; to stand firm, hold one's ground; to stand upright; (of hair) to stand up straight, stand on end; (of eyes) to remain fixed; (of battle) to continue; (of a ship) to be moored, ride at anchor; to be motionless; to be stuck; to depend, rest; to take sides, take part; (with abl of price) to come to, cost; (with abl or **in** + abl) to depend on, rest with; (with **per** + acc of person) to depend on, be due to, be the fault of, thanks to

Stōĭc·a -ōrum n pl Stoic philosophy

Stōĭcē adv like a Stoic

Stōĭc·us -a -um adj Stoic; m Stoic, Stoic philosopher; n pl see **Stoica**

stol·a -ae f dress (long outer gar-

ment worn by Roman women and reaching from the neck to the ankles); ceremonial gown (worn by musicians)

stolāt·us -a -um adj wearing a stola; (fig) proper for a lady, lady-like

stolĭdē adv stupidly

stolĭd·us -a -um adj dull, stupid, solid, slow

stomāch·or -ārī -ātus sum vi to be annoyed, fret, fume, glower

stomachōsius adv rather angrily

stomachōs·us -a -um adj irritable, resentful

stomāch·us -ī m stomach; taste, appetite; irritation, anger, resentment; **stomachus bonus** good appetite; good humor, patience

storē·a or **storĭ·a -ae** f straw mat, rope mat

strab·ō -ōnis m squinter

strāg·ēs -is f heap, confused mass, pile of debris; havoc, massacre

strāgŭl·us -a -um adj covering, serving as a covering; n rug, carpet; bedspread; horse blanket

strām·en -inis n straw

strāment·um -ī n straw; covering, saddle cloth; **stramentum agreste** straw bed

strāminĕ·us -a -um adj straw, made of straw

strangŭl·ō -āre vt to choke, stifle

strangūri·a -ae f strangury

stratēgēm·a -ătis n stratagem; trick

stratēg·us -ī m commander, general; master of ceremonies

stratiōtic·us -a -um adj soldier-like, soldierly, military

strāt·us -a -um pp of **sterno**; n quilt, blanket; bed, couch; horse blanket, pack saddle; pavement

strēn·a -ae f good-luck omen

strēnuē adv briskly, quickly, actively, strenuously

strēnuĭt·ās -ātis f briskness, vigor, liveliness

strēnŭ·ō -āre vi to be brisk

strēnŭ·us -a -um adj brisk, vigorous, active; fast (ship); restless

strepĭt·ō -āre vi to be noisy, clatter, rustle

strepĭt·us -ūs m noise, din, racket; crash, bang, clank, rumble, rustle, creak, squeak; sound (of musical instruments)

strep·ō -ĕre -ŭī -ĭtum vt to shout; vi to make a noise (of any kind); to rattle, clatter, clang, rumble, rustle, creak, squeak; to roar; to hum, murmur; (of musical instruments) to sound, blare; (of places) to ring, resound, be filled

striāt·a -ae f scallop

strictim adv superficially, cursorily

strictūr·a -ae f mass of molten iron

strict·us -a -um pp of **stringo**; adj close, tight, narrow

strīd·ĕō -ēre -ī or **strīd·ō -ĕre -ī** vi to make a high-pitched noise; to hiss, whistle, whizz, shriek, scream; to grate, buzz, rattle

strīd·or -ōris *m* shrill sound, hiss, shriek, scream, whine; harsh noise, grating, rattle, buzz

strīdŭl·us -a -um *adj* shrill, strident, hissing, whistling, creaking

strigil·is -is *f* scraper

strig·ō -āre *vi* to stop, halt; to lose strength, give out

strigōs·us -a -um *adj* lean, thin; bald (*style*)

string·ō stringĕre strinxī strictum *vt* to strip, clip; to draw (*sword*); to draw tight, tie tight; to press together, compress; to touch lightly, graze; to border on, touch (*places*); to affect, touch, move, pain, wound (*mind, good name, etc.*); to waste, consume

string·or -ōris *m* twinge, shock

strix strigis *f* owl, screech owl

stroph·a -ae *f* trick

Strophăd·es -um *f pl* island home of the Harpies

strophiăr·ius -iī or -ī *m* brassiere maker

stroph·ĭum -iī or -ī *n* brassiere; head band, chaplet

Stroph·ĭus -iī or -ī *m* king of Phocis and father of Pylades

structĭl·is -e *adj* building, for building

struct·or -ōris *m* builder, mason, carpenter; carver (*at table*)

structūr·a -ae *f* construction; structure

structus *pp* of struo

stru·ēs -is *f* pile, heap

stru·ix -īcis *f* pile, heap

strūm·a -ae *f* tumor, swollen gland

strūmōs·us -a -um *adj* scrofulous

struō struĕre struxī structum *vt* to build, build up, erect; to arrange, deploy (*troops*); to arrange, regulate; to occasion, contrive, plot

strūthĕ·us -a -um *adj* sparrow's

strūthiocamēl·us -ī *m* ostrich

Strȳm·ōn -ŏnis *m* river forming the border between Macedonia and Thrace

Strȳmonĭ·us -a -um *adj* Strymonian, Thracian

stud·ĕō -ēre -ŭī *vt* to desire, be eager for; *vi* to be eager; (with *dat*) **a** to be eager for, be keen on, be enthusiastic about, take pains with, busy oneself with, apply oneself to; **b** to study; **c** to be a partisan of

studĭōsē *adv* eagerly, enthusiastically, diligently

studĭōs·us -a -um *adj* eager, keen, enthusiastic; studious; (with *genit*) partial to (*a person or cause*); (with *genit* or *dat*) eager for, keen on, enthusiastic about, devoted to, fond of, desirous of; **litterarum studiosus** studious

stud·ĭum -iī or -ī *n* eagerness, keenness, enthusiasm; devotion (*to a person*); party spirit; study; (with *genit*) eagerness for, enthusiasm for

stultē *adv* foolishly

stutiloquentĭ·a -ae *f* or **stultiloqu·ĭum -iī or -ī** *n* silly talk

stultĭlŏqu·us -a -um *adj* talking foolishly

stultiti·a -ae *f* foolishness, silliness

stultivĭd·us -a -um *adj* foolish-looking

stult·us -a -um *adj* foolish, silly, stupid

stūp·a -ae *f* tow, coarse flax, hemp

stupe·faciō -facĕre -fēcī -factum (passive: **stupe·fīō -fĭerī -factus sum**) *vt* to stupefy, stun, astonish, knock senseless

stup·ĕō -ēre -ŭī *vt* to be amazed at; *vi* to be knocked senseless, be stunned, be stupefied, be astounded, be amazed; to be stopped in one's tracks

stup·escō -escĕre -ŭī *vi* to become amazed, become bewildered

stūpĕ·us -a -um *adj* of tow, hempen

stupidit·ās -ātis *f* stupidity

stupĭd·us -a -um *adj* amazed, astounded; dull, stupid

stup·or -ōris *m* numbness, bewilderment, confusion; dullness, stupidity

stupp·a -ae *f* tow, coarse flax, hemp

stuppĕ·us -a -um *adj* of tow, hempen

stupr·ō -āre *vt* to ravish, rape; to defile

stupr·um -ī *n* immorality; rape; disgrace (*esp. from a sex crime*)

sturn·us -ī *m* starling

Stygĭăl·is -e *adj* Stygian

Stygĭ·us -a -um *adj* Stygian, infernal; deadly

Stymphālĭc·us or **Stymphālĭ·us -a -um** *adj* Stymphalian

Stymphāl·um -ī *n* or **Stymphăl·us -ī** *m* district in Arcadia famous for its vicious birds of prey which were killed by Hercules in one of his twelve labors

Stȳ·x -gis or **-gos** *f* chief river in the lower world; river in Arcadia

suādēl·a -ae *f* persuasion

suādĕō suādēre suāsī suāsum *vt* to recommend, propose, suggest; to urge, impel, induce; *vi* (with *dat*) to advise, urge, suggest to, propose to; **sibi suadere** (with *acc & inf*) to satisfy oneself that

suās·ĭō -ōnis *f* recommendation; support, backing (*a proposal*); persuasive eloquence

suās·or -ōris *m* adviser; advocate, supporter

suās·um -ī *n* dye

suāsus *pp* of suadeo

suās·us -ūs *m* advice

snāvĕŏl·ens -entis *adj* fragrant

suāvĭātĭō see saviatio

suāvĭdĭc·us -a -um *adj* charming

suāvĭlŏqu·ens -entis *adj* charming

suāvĭloquentĭ·a -ae *f* charming manner of speech

suāvĭŏlum see saviolum

suāvĭor see savior

suāv·is -e *adj* charming, pleasant, agreeable, attractive

suāvĭt·ās -ātis *f* charm, pleasantness, sweetness, attractiveness

suāvĭter *adv* pleasantly, sweetly, charmingly, attractively

suāvĭtūd·ō -ĭnis *f* (term of endearment) honey

suāvĭum see **savium**

sub *prep* (with *abl*) under, beneath, underneath, behind; at the foot of, close to, near (*mountain, wall*); during, in, within, at, by, in the time of, just before; during the reign of; (with *acc*) under, along under; up to (*walls*); approaching, about, just before, just after

subabsurdē *adv* a bit absurdly

subabsurd·us -a -um *adj* rather absurd

subaccūs·ō -āre *vt* to blame, find fault with

subactĭ·ō -ōnis *f* working (*of the soil*); development (*of the mind*)

subactus *pp* of **subigo**

subaerāt·us -a -um *adj* (gold) having an inner layer of bronze

subagrest·is -e *adj* rather uncouth

subālār·is -e *adj* carried under the arms

subalb·us -a -um *adj* whitish

subamār·us -a -um *adj* somewhat bitter

subaquĭl·us -a -um *adj* somewhat dark, brownish

subarroganter *adv* rather arrogantly

subauscult·ō -āre *vt* to eavesdrop on; *vi* to eavesdrop

subbasilicān·us -ī *m* loafer (*person who hangs around the basilicas*)

subbĭb·ō -ere -ī *vt* to drink a little

subbland·ior -īrī -ītus sum *vi* (with *dat*) to flirt with

subc- = succ-

subdifficĭl·is -e *adj* rather difficult

subdiffīd·ō -ĕre *vi* to be a little distrustful

subditicĭ·us -a -um *adj* substituted, phoney

subditīv·us -a -um *adj* substituted, phoney

subditus *pp* of **subdo**

subdĭū *adv* by day

sub·dō -dĕre -dĭdī -dĭtum *vt* to put under; to subdue; to substitute; to forge, make up; to spread (*a rumor*) falsely; (with *dat*) a to put or apply (*something*) to, add (*something*) to; b to subject (*someone*) to; **se aquis subdere** to plunge into the water

subdoc·ĕō -ēre *vt* to instruct (*as an assistant teacher*)

subdŏlē *adv* rather cunningly

subdŏl·us -a -um *adj* underhand, sly, cunning

subdŏm·ō -āre *vt* to tame somewhat

subdŭbĭt·ō -āre *vi* to be rather undecided

sub·dūcō -dūcĕre -duxī -ductum *vt* to draw up from below; to pull up, raise, to remove, take away, steal; to haul up, beach (*a ship*); to

withdraw (*troops*); to balance (*accounts*)

subductĭ·ō -ōnis *f* drydocking, beaching; calculation, computation

sub·ĕdō -esse -ēdī *vt* to eat away or wear away at the bottom; **scopulum unda subedit** water wears away the bottom of the cliff

sub·ĕō -īre -īvī or **-īi -ĭtum** *vt* to enter (*a place*), enter (*the mind*); to approach, attack; to undergo (*dangers, punishment, etc.*); to help, support; to climb; to slip under; to dodge (*a blow*); *vi* to come or go up, climb; to follow; to advance, press forward; (with **ad** or **in** + *acc*) a to come up against, attack; b to climb (*a mountain*); c to approach, enter

sūb·er -ĕris *n* cork tree; cork

subf- = suff-

subg- = sugg-

subhorrĭd·us -a -um *adj* rather coarse, rather uncouth

sub·iciō -icĕre -jēcī -jectum *vt* to throw up, fling up; to bring up; to bring up close, expose; to suggest; to add, append; to suborn; to substitute; to forge; (with *dat* or **sub** + *acc*) a to put, place (*something*) under; b to subject (*someone*) to (*authority, danger, risk*); c to classify (*something*) under; d to submit (*something*) to (*one's judgment*)

subigĭtātĭ·ō -ōnis *f* lewdness; intercourse

subigĭtātr·ix -īcis *f* loose woman

subigĭt·ō -āre *vt* to lie with

sub·igō -igĕre -ēgī -actum *vt* to turn up, till, plow; to knead; to whet, sharpen; to rub down; to tame; to train, discipline (*the mind*); to conquer, subdue, subjugate, reduce; to force, impel, constrain; to incite; to row, propel (*a boat*)

subimpŭd·ens -entis *adj* rather shameless

subinān·is -e *adj* rather empty, rather pointless

subinde *adv* immediately afterwards; from time to time

subinsuls·us -a -um *adj* rather insipid

subinvĭd·ĕō -ēre *vi* (with *dat*) to envy (*someone*) a little

subinvīs·us -a -um *adj* rather disliked, rather unpopular

subinvīt·ō -āre *vt* to invite unenthusiastically

subīr·ascor -ascī -ātus sum *vi* to be annoyed; (with *dat*) to be peeved at

subitārĭ·us -a -um *adj* (mil) suddenly called up (*to meet an emergency*); built in a hurry

subĭtō *adv* suddenly, unexpectedly, at once; **subito dicere** to speak ex-tempore

subĭt·us -a -um *adj* coming on suddenly, sudden, unexpected; rash (*man*); emergency (*troops*); *n* emergency

subjac·ĕō -ēre -ŭī *vi* to lie nearby; (with *dat*) to lie under or close to; **monti subjacere** to lie at the foot of the mountain

subjecti·ō -ōnis *f* subjection; substitution; forgery

subjectissimē *adv* most humbly

subject·ō -āre *vt* to toss up

subject·or -ōris *m* forger

subject·us -a -um *pp* of **subicio**; *adj* (with *dat*) a located near, bordering on; b subject to; *m* subject (*conquered person*)

sub·jungō -jungĕre -junxī -junctum *vt* (with *dat*) a to yoke or harness to; b to join to, connect with, add to; c to make subject to

sub·lābor -lābī -lapsus sum *vi* to sink, fall down, collapse; to glide imperceptibly; to fall back, fail

sublātē *adv* loftily, in lofty tones

sublāti·ō -ōnis *f* elevation, raising

sublāt·us -a -um *pp* of **suffero** and of **tollo**; *adj* elated

sublect·ō -āre *vt* to coax, cajole

sub·lĕgō -legĕre -lēgī -lectum *vt* to gather up, pick up; to pick up stealthily, steal, kidnap; to substitute; to overhear, pick up

sublest·us -a -um *adj* weak, trifling

sublevāti·ō -ōnis *f* alleviation, lightening

sublĕv·ō -āre *vt* to lift up, raise, support

sublīc·a -ae *f* stake, pile (*esp. for a bridge*)

sublici·us -a -um *adj* resting upon piles; **pons sublicius** wooden bridge across the Tiber, built by Ancus Marcius

subligācŭl·um -ī *n* short apron

sublig·ar -āris *n* apron

sublig·ō -āre *vt* (with *dat*) to tie or fasten (*e.g., a sword*) to or below

sublīmē *adv* aloft, on high

sublimen *adv* upwards, on high

sublim·is -e *adj* high, raised up, lifted high; lofty, elevated, exalted; raised high, borne aloft, through the sky; aspiring; eminent, distinguished

sublim·us -a -um *adj* high, lofty

sublimit·ās -ātis *f* loftiness, sublimity

subling1·ō -ōnis *m* scullion

sub·linō -linĕre -lēvī -litum *vt* to smear secretly; **os sublinere** (with *dat*) to cheat (*someone*)

sublūc·ĕō -ēre *vi* to shine faintly, glimmer

sub·luō -luĕre — -lūtum *vt* to wash underneath; to flow at the foot of (*a mountain*)

sublustr·is -e *adj* dimly lighted, throwing some light, glimmering, flickering

subm- = summ-

sub·nascor -nascī -nātus sum *vi* (with *dat*) to grow up underneath

sub·nectō -nectĕre -nexŭī -nex-

---

um *vt* to fasten, tie (*something*) underneath; to confine; (with *dat*) to fasten or tie (*something*) below (*something else*)

subnĕg·ō -āre *vt* to halfway refuse; (with *dat*) to halfway refuse (*something*) to (*someone*)

subnig·er -ra -rum *adj* blackish

subnimi·a -ae *f* robe

subnīs·us or **subnix·us -a -um** *adj* propped up, resting, leaning; (with *dat*) a propped up on, resting on, leaning on; b relying on, depending on, confiding in

subnŏt·ō -āre *vt* to note down, record, register; to observe secretly

subnūb·a -ae *f* rival (*female*)

subnūbil·us -a -um *adj* somewhat cloudy, overcast

sub·ō -āre *vi* to be in heat

subobscēn·us -a -um *adj* somewhat obscene, shady

subobscūr·us -a -um *adj* rather obscure

subodiōs·us -a -um *adj* annoying

suboffend·ō -ĕre *vi* to give some offense

subŏl·et -ēre *v impers* there is a faint smell; **mihi subolet** I have an inkling, I have a sneaking suspicion, I have a faint idea

subŏl·ēs -is *f* offspring

subolesc·ō -ĕre *vi* to grow up instead

subor·ior -īrī *vi* to rise up in succession, arise, proceed

suborn·ō -āre *vt* to equip, supply, provide; to employ as a secret agent, incite secretly, suborn

subp- = supp-

subr- = surr-

sub·scrībō -scrībĕre -scripsī -scriptum *vt* to write underneath; to sign; to write down, record, register; *vi* to sign an accusation, act as prosecutor; (with *dat*) a to add (*something*) to, attach (*something*) in writing to; b to assent to, agree to; (with **in** + *acc*) to sign an accusation against, indict, accuse, prosecute

subscripti·ō -ōnis *f* inscription underneath; signature; (law) subscription; recording (*of an offense by the censor*); record, register

subscript·or -ōris *m* signer or joint-signer (*of an accusation*)

subscriptus *pp* of **subscribo**

subsc·us -ūdis *f* tenon of a dovetail

subsecīvus see **subsicivus**

subsĕc·ō -āre -ŭī -tum *vt* to clip, trim, cut off

subsecūtus *pp* of **subsĕquor**

subsell·ĭum -ĭī or **-ī** *n* low seat or bench; seat or bench on a lower level; judge's seat, the bench; tribunal, court; seat in the senate, senator's seat; bleachers (*where the poor people sat*); **versatus in utrisque subsellis** experienced as judge and lawyer

sub·sentiō -sentīre -sensī *vt* to have some inkling of

sub·sequor -sequī -secūtus sum *vt* to follow close after, chase, pursue; to back up, support; to imitate; to adhere to, conform to; to come after, succeed (*in time or order*); *vi* to ensue

subserv·iō -īre *vi* (with *dat*) **a** to be subject to; **b** to accommodate oneself to, humor; **c** to support, aid

subsiciv·us -a -um *adj* left over; extra, spare (*time*); extra, overtime (*work*)

subsidiārī·us -a -um *adj* (mil) reserve; *m pl* reserves

subsid·ium -ī or **-ī** *n* aid, support; place of refuge, asylum; protection; (mil) reserves, triarii; military support, relief, aid; **subsidiō esse** (with *dat*) to act as support to; **subsidiō mittere** to send in support

sub·sīdō -sīdĕre -sēdī -sessum *vt* to lie in wait for; *vi* to sit down, crouch down, settle down; to sink, subside, settle; to establish oneself, settle down, establish residence, stay

subsignān·us -a -um *adj* special reserve (*troops*)

subsign·ō -āre *vt* to endorse, subscribe to (*an opinion*); to register, enter, record; to guarantee

subsil·iō -īre -īī *vi* to jump up

sub·sistō -sistĕre -stitī *vt* to hold out against; *vi* to stand up; to make a stand, take a firm stand; to come to a standstill, stop; to stay behind; (with *dat*) **a** to take a stand against, oppose, fight; **b** to meet (*an expense*)

subsort·ior -īrī -ītus sum *vt* to choose as a substitute by lot; *vi* to choose a substitute by lot; (in a passive sense) to be chosen as a substitute

subsortīti·ō -ōnis *f* substitution by lot

substanti·a -ae *f* substance, essence; means, wealth, property

sub·sternō -sternĕre -strāvī -strātum *vt* to spread underneath; to cover; (with *dat*) to put at the disposal of, make subservient to; **rem publicam libīdini suae substernere** to misuse high office to serve one's lust

substit·uō -uĕre -uī -ūtum *vt* to submit, present; to substitute; (with *dat* or **in locum** with *genit*) to substitute for or in place of; **animo** or **oculis substituere** to imagine

subst·ō -āre *vi* to stand firm, hold out; (with *dat*) to stand up to

substrātus *pp* of **substerno**

substrict·us -a -um *adj* tight, narrow, small

sub·stringō -stringĕre -strinxī -strictum *vt* to tie up, draw up; to restrain, control; (with *dat*) to press (*something*) close to

substructi·ō -ōnis *f* substructure, foundation

sub·struō -struĕre -struxī -structum *vt* to lay (*foundation*); **vias glareā substruere** to lay a foundation of gravel on the roads

subsult·ō -āre *vi* to jump up, jump up and down

sub·sum -esse *vi* to be near, be at hand; (with *dat*) **a** to be below or beneath, be under; **b** to be concealed in; **c** to be subject to, subservient to

subsūt·us -a -um *adj* trimmed at the bottom

subtēm·en -inis *n* woof; thread, yarn

subter *adv* below, underneath; *prep* (with *abl*) beneath, below, underneath, under; (with *acc*) underneath, beneath; up to, close to, close beneath

subter·dūcō -dūcĕre -duxī -ductum *vt* to withdraw secretly, lead away secretly

subter·fugiō -fugĕre -fūgī *vt* to evade, avoid; *vi* to run away secretly, get off

subter·lābor -lābī *vt* to glide or flow under; *vi* to slip away, escape

sub·tĕrō -terĕre -trivī -trītum *vt* to wear away underneath

subterrānē·us -a -um *adj* subterranean, underground

subtex·ō -ĕre -uī -tum *vt* to sew on; to veil, cover; (fig) to work up, compose; (with *dat*) **a** to sew onto; **b** to throw (*a covering*) over; **c** to work (*something*) into (*a story or plot*)

subtīl·is -e *adj* woven fine, of fine texture; delicate; subtle; discriminating, precise; plain, direct (*style*)

subtīlit·ās -ātis *f* fineness, minuteness; slenderness; exactness, precision; simplicity (of *style*)

subtīliter *adv* finely, delicately; accurately; plainly, simply

subtim·ĕō -ēre *vt* to be a bit afraid of

sub·trahō -trahĕre -traxī -tractum *vt* to drag up from beneath, drag out, draw off, withdraw, remove; to avert (*the eyes*); (with *dat*) to drag or draw (*something*) away from

subtrist·is -e *adj* rather sad

subtrītus *pp* of **subtero**

subturpicul·us -a -um *adj* somewhat disgraceful

subturp·is -e *adj* rather disgraceful

subtus *adv* below, underneath

subtūs·us -a -um *adj* somewhat bruised

subūcul·a -ae *f* man's undershirt

sūbūl·a -ae *f* awl

subulc·us -ī *m* swineherd

Subūr·a -ae *f* rough, noisy district in Rome, N.E. of the Forum between the Esquiline and Quirinal

Subūrān·us -a -um *adj* of the Subura

suburbānit·ās -ātis *f* nearness to Rome

suburbān·us -a -um adj suburban, near Rome; m suburbanite; n suburban home

suburb·ium -iī or **-ī** n suburb

suburg·ĕō -ēre vt (with ad + acc) to keep or turn (a ship) close to

subvecti·ō -ōnis f transportation

subvect·ō -āre vt to bring up regularly

subvectus pp of **suveho**

subvect·us -ūs m bringing up, transportation

sub·vĕhō -vehĕre -vexī -vectum vt to carry or bring up, transport

sub·vĕniō -venīre -vēnī -ventum vi (with dat) to come up to aid, reinforce, relieve

subvent·ō -āre vi (with dat) to rush to the aid of

subver·eor -ērī vi to be a bit apprehensive

subvers·ō or **subvors·ō -āre** vt to ruin completely

subvers·or -ōris m subverter, repealer

sub·vertō or **sub·vortō -vertĕre -vertī -versum** vt to turn upside down, upset, overthrow, throw over, subvert

subvex·us -a -um adj sloping upward

subvŏl·ō -āre vi to fly up

subvolv·ō -ĕre vt to roll up

subvor- = **subver-**

subvulturi·us -a -um adj vulture-like

succăv·us -a -um adj hollow underneath

succēdānĕ·us or **succīdānĕ·us -a -um** adj substitute

suc·cēdō -cēdĕre -cessī -cessum vt to climb; to march on or against, advance to or as far as; vi to come up, climb; to come next, follow in succession; to turn out (successfully); (with ad, in, or sub + acc) to climb, climb up; (with dat) a to come next to, follow; b to succeed in (an undertaking); c to yield to, submit to; d to relieve, take the place of (e.g., tired troops); e to enter, go below to (e.g., a shelter; grave); (with in or ad + acc) (fig) to reach, attain (e.g., high honors), receive by succession, enter upon (an inheritance)

suc·cendō -cendĕre -cendī -censum vt to set on fire, set fire to; to light (a fire); (fig) to inflame

succens·ĕō or **suscens·ĕō -ēre -ī** vi to be angry, be enraged; (with dat) to be enraged at

succensus pp of **succendo**

succenturiāt·us -a -um adj in reserve

succenturi·ō -āre vt to receive (someone) as a substitute into a century or company

succenturi·ō -ōnis m assistant centurion, substitute for a centurion

successi·ō -ōnis f succession

success·or -ōris m successor

success·us -ūs m approach, advance uphill; outcome, success

succīdānĕus see **succedaneus**

succīdi·a -ae f leg or side of meat; (fig) extra income

suc·cīdō -cīdĕre -cīdī -cīsum vt to cut down, cut off, mow down

suc·cīdō -cīdĕre -cīdī vi to sink, give way; to collapse, fail

succīd·us or **sūcīd·us -a -um** adj juicy; (coll) fresh, plump (girl)

succĭdŭ·us -a -um adj sinking, falling

suc·cingō -cingĕre -cinxī -cinctum vt to tuck up; to put on (e.g., a sword); to equip, arm, fit out

succingŭl·um -ī n belt

succĭn·ō -ĕre vi to chime in (in conversation)

succīsus pp of **succīdo**

succlāmāti·ō -ōnis f shouting in reply

succlām·ō -āre vt to shout out after, interrupt with shouts; (with dat) to shout out (words) at

succontumēliōsē adv rather insolently

suc·crescō -crescĕre -crēvī vi to grow up; to be replenished; (with dat) to attain to

succrisp·us -a -um adj rather curled

suc·cumbō -cumbĕre -cubŭī -cubĭtum vi to fall or sink back; to yield, succumb, submit

suc·currō -currĕre -currī -cursum vi (with dat) a to run up to; b to run to help; c to occur to, enter the mind of

succ·us or **sūc·us -ī** m sap, juice; taste, flavor

succuss·us -ūs m shaking, jolt

succust·ōs -ōdis m assistant guard

suc·cutiō -cutĕre -cussī -cussum vt to toss up

sūcĭdus see **succidus**

sūcĭn·us -a -um adj & n amber

suctus pp of **sūgō**

sūcŭl·a -ae f little pig; winch, windlass

sūcus see **succus**

sūdār·ium -iī or **-ī** n handkerchief, towel

sūdātōri·us -a -um adj sweat, for sweating; n sweat room

sūdātr·ix -īcis adj causing sweat

sud·is -is f stake, pile; pike (weapon); dorsal fin

sūd·ō -āre vt to sweat, exude; to soak with sweat; (fig) to sweat over; vi to sweat; to drip

sūd·or -ōris m sweat; moisture; hard work

sūducŭl·um -ī n sweat-maker (i.e., whip)

sūd·us -a -um adj dry; clear, cloudless (weather); n clear weather, bright sky

su·ĕō -ēre vi to be accustomed; (with inf) be accustomed or used to

su·escō -escĕre -ēvī -ētum vt to

accustom, familiarize; *vi* to become used; (with *dat*) to get used to

Suess·a -ae *f* town in Latium

suet·us *pp* of **suesco**; *adj* usual, familiar

Suēv·ī -ōrum *m pl* a people of N.E. Germany

sūf·es -ĕtis *m* chief magistrate at Carthage

suffarcināt·us -a -um *adj* stuffed full

suffarcīn·ō -āre *vt* to stuff full, cram

suffectus *pp* of **sufficio**

suffĕrō sufferre sustŭlī sublātum *vt* to suffer, bear, endure

suf·ficiō -ficĕre -fēcī -fectum *vt* to lay the foundation for; to dip, tinge, dye; to appoint to a vacancy; to yield, supply, afford; **consul suffectus** substitute cousul (*consul appointed to complete an unexpired term of another consul*); *vi* to suffice, be sufficient; (with *dat* or with **ad** or **in** + *acc*) to suffice for, be adequate to

suf·fīgō -fīgĕre -fīxī -fixum *vt* to nail up, fasten

suffīm·en -ĭnis *n* incense

suffīment·um -ī *n* incense

suffixus *pp* of **suffigo**

sufflām·en -ĭnis *n* brake (*on a vehicle*)

sufflāt·us -a -um *adj* puffed up, bloated; (fig) fuming (*with anger*)

suffl·ō -āre *vt* to blow up, inflate; *vi* to blow, puff

suffōc·ō -āre *vt* to choke, strangle

suf·fodiō -fodĕre -fōdī -fossum *vt* to stab, pierce; to dig under (*walls*)

suffrāgātĭ·ō -ōnis *f* voting (*in someone's favor*), support

suffrāgāt·or -ōris *m* supporter (*at the polls*), partisan

suffrāgātōri·us -a -um *adj* partisan

suffrāg·ium -iī or **-ī** *n* ballot, vote; right to vote, franchise; decision, judgment; applause, approbation; **suffragium ferre** to cast a ballot; **suffragium ferre** (with **de** or **in** + *abl*) to vote on

suffrāg·or -ārī -ātus sum *vi* to cast a favorable vote; (with *dat*) to vote in favor of, support, vote for; **fortunā suffragante** with luck on our side

suffring·ō -ĕre *vt* to break, smash

suf·fugiō -fugĕre -fūgī *vt* to escape, avoid; *vi* (with **in** + *acc*) to run to for cover

suffug·ium -iī or **-ī** *n* shelter, cover

suf·fulciō -fulcīre -fulsī -fultum *vt* to prop up, underpin, support

suf·fundō -fundĕre -fūdī -fūsum *vt* to pour in, fill; to suffuse, spread; to tinge, color; to infuse; **virgineum ore ruborem suffundere** (with *dat*) to cause (*someone*) to blush

suffūr·or -ārī *vt* to filch

suffusc·us -a -um *adj* darkish, brownish

suffūsus *pp* of **suffundo**

sug·gĕrō -gerĕre -gessī -gestum *vt* to supply, add; to prompt, suggest

suggest·um -ī *m* platform; stage

suggestus *pp* of **suggero**

suggest·us -ūs *m* platform; stage

suggrand·is -e *adj* rather huge

sug·gredior -grēdī -gressus sum *vt & vi* to approach

sūgillātĭ·ō -ōnis *f* bruise; affront

sūgill·ō -āre *vt* to beat black and blue; to affront, insult

sūgō sūgĕre suxī suctum *vt* to suck

suī see **se**

suill·us -a -um *adj* of swine; **grex suillus** herd of swine

sulc·ō -āre *vt* to furrow, plow; to make a line in (*sand*)

sulc·us -ī *m* furrow; ditch, trench (*for plants*); track (*of a wheel or meteor*); wrinkle; plowing; wake (*of ship*)

sulf·ur -ŭris *m* sulfur

Sull·a -ae *m* Sulla (*Cornelius Sulla Felix, Roman general, dictator, champion of the aristocratic party, and political reformer, 138–78 B.C.*)

Sullān·ī -ōrum *m pl* partisans of Sulla

sullātur·iō -īre *vi* to wish to be a Sulla

Sulm·ō -ōnis *m* town about ninety miles east of Rome and birthplace of Ovid

Sulmōnens·is -e *adj* of Sulmo

sulp·ur or **sulf·ur -ŭris** *m* sulfur

sulpurāt·us -a -um *adj* saturated with sulfur; *n pl* matches

sulpurĕ·us -a -um *adj* sulfurous

sultis = si vultis if you please, please

sum esse fuī *vi* to be, exist; (with *genit* of possession) to belong to, pertain to, be characteristic of, be the duty of; (with *genit* or *abl* of quality) to be of, be possessed of, have; (with *genit* or *abl* of value) to be valued at, cost; (with *dat*) to belong to; (with **ab** + *abl*) to belong to; (with **ad** + *acc*) to be designed for; (with **ex** + *abl*) to consist of; **est** (with *inf*) it is possible to, it is permissible to; **est** (with **ut**) it is possible that; **sunt qui** there are those who, there are people who, they are of the type that

sūm·en -ĭnis *n* breast, teat, udder; breeding sow

summ·a -ae *f* main thing; chief point, gist, summary; sum, amount, contents, substance; sum of money; **ad summam** generally, on the whole; in short; **summa rerum** the world; supreme power; **summa summarum** the whole universe

summān·ō -āre *vi* to drip a bit

Summān·us -ī *m* Roman god of night lightning

summ·ās -ātis adj high-born, aristocratic, noble

summātim adv on the surface; generally, summarily

summāt·us -ūs m supremacy, supreme power

summē adv very, extremely

sum·mergō -mergĕre -mersī -mersum vt to sink, submerge, drown

summĕr·us -a -um adj pure, straight (wine)

sumministr·ō -āre vt to supply, furnish

summissē or **summissim** adv in a low voice, softly; modestly, humbly

summissi·ō -ōnis f lowering, dropping

summiss·us -a -um adj lowered, stooping; lowered, soft (voice); humble, unassuming; submissive; too submissive, abject

sum·mittō -mittĕre -mīsī -missum vt to let down, lower, sink, drop; to let (hair) grow long; to lower, reduce, moderate, relax, lessen; to bring down, humble; to rear, put forth, produce; to send secretly; to send as a reinforcement; to send as a substitute; **animum summittere** (with dat) to yield to; **se summittere** to bend down, stoop over; to condescend; **se summittere** (with dat) to yield to, give in to

summolestē adv with some annoyance

summolest·us -a -um adj rather annoying

summon·ĕō -ēre -uī vt to give (someone) a gentle reminder, remind privately

summopere adv with the greatest diligence, completely

summōrōs·us -a -um adj rather crabby

sum·movĕō -movēre -mōvī -mōtum vt to move up, advance; to clear (e.g., the court); to remove; to expel, banish; (mil) to dislodge; (fig) to drive away, forget about (e.g., worries)

summ·us -a -um adj uppermost, highest; the top of, the surface of; last, latest, the end of; greatest, best, top, consummate; most distinguished; most important; m head of the table; f see **summa**; n top, surface, highest place, head of the table

summum adv at most; at latest; **uno aut summum altero proelio** in one or at most in two battles

sūmō sūmĕre sumpsī sumptum vt to take up; to put on, dress oneself in, wear; to exact, inflict (penalty); to take up, begin, enter upon; to eat, consume; to assume, suppose, take for granted; to cite, adduce, mention; to assume, appropriate; to select; to purchase, buy

sumptī·ō -ōnis f assumption

sumptuāri·us -a -um adj expense, relating to expenses, sumptuary, against extravagance

sumptuōsē adv sumptuously, expensively

sumptuōs·us -a -um adj costly, expensive; lavish, wasteful

sumptus pp of **sumo**

sumpt·us -ūs m cost, expense, charge; **sumptui esse** (with dat) to be costly to, be expensive to; **sumptum suum exercere** to earn one's keep; **sumptu tuo** at your expense, out of your pocket

Sūn·ium -iī or **-ī** n S.E. promontory of Attica

suō suĕre suī sūtum vt to sew, stitch, tack together

suōmet = emphatic form of **suo**

suopte = emphatic form of **suo**

suovetauril·ia -ium n pl sacrifice of a pig, sheep, and bull

supell·ex -ectilis f furniture, household utensils; (fig) outfit, qualification

super adv on the top, above; besides; moreover; **super esse** to be left over; prep (with abl) above, over, upon, on; concerning, about; besides, in addition to; at, on (time); (with acc) over, above, upon; (with numbers) over, more than; besides, over and above

supĕr·a -ōrum n pl upper world, sky, Heaven; heavenly bodies

supĕrā adv above

superābil·is -e adj surmountable, climbable; conquerable

super·addō -addĕre — -addītum vt to add besides, add to boot

supĕr·ans -antis adj predominant

superast·ō -āre vi (with dat) to stand on

superāt·or -ōris m conqueror

superbē adv arrogantly, haughtily, snobbishly

superbi·a -ae f arrogance, haughtiness, snobbishness; (justifiable) pride

superbiloquenti·a -ae f haughty tone, arrogant speech

superb·iō -īre vi to be haughty; to be superb, be magnificent; (with abl) to take pride in

superb·us -a -um adj arrogant, haughty, snobbish; overbearing, tyrannical, despotic; fastidious, disdainful; superb, magnificent

supercil·ium -iī or **-ī** n eyebrow; frown, will (of Jupiter); summit, brow (of a hill, etc.); arrogance, superciliousness

superēmin·ĕō -ēre -uī vt to tower over, top

superfici·ēs -ēī f top, surface; (law) fixtures, improvements, buildings (i.e., anything upon the property, but not the land itself)

super·fiō -fiĕrī vi to be over and above; to be left over

superfix·us -a -um *adj* attached above

superflu·ens -entis *adj* superabundant, running over; (with *abl*) abounding in

superflu·ō -ĕre *vi* to overflow

super·fundō -fundĕre -fūdī -fūsum *vt* (with *abl*) to shower (*something*) with; (with *dat*) to pour (*something*) upon; **superfundi** *or* **sē superfundere** to spread, spread out, extend; **fama superfudit sē in Asiam** the report spread to Asia

super·gredior -grĕdī -gressus sum *vt* to walk or step over; to surpass

supĕr·ī -ōrum *m pl* the gods above; men on earth; mortals; upper world

superimmin·ĕō -ēre *vt* to tower above

superimpend·ens -entis *adj* overhanging, towering overhead

superim·pōnō -pōnĕre -posŭī -positum *vt* to place on top, place overhead

superposit·us -a -um *adj* superimposed

superincĭd·ens -entis *adj* falling from above

superincŭb·ans -antis *adj* lying above or on top

superin·cumbō -cumbĕre -cubŭī *vi* (with *dat*) to lay oneself down upon

superingĕr·ō -ĕre *vt* to pour down

superin·iciō -icĕre — -jectum *vt* to throw on top

superin·sternō -sternĕre -strāvī *vt* to cover

superi·or -us (*comp of* **supĕrus**) *adj* higher, upper; the upper part of; past, previous, preceding; older, elder, more advanced; victorious, conquering; superior, stronger; superior, greater; **dē locō superiōre dicere** to speak from the tribunal, handle a case in court; to speak from the rostra, deliver a formal address; **ex locō superiōre pugnāre** to fight from a vantage point

superin·jaciō -jacĕre -jēcī -jectum *or* **-jactum** *vt* to overspread, overwhelm; to overdo, exaggerate

superinjectus *pp of* **superinicio**

superlātĭ·ō -ōnis *f* exaggeration

superlāt·us -a -um *adj* exaggerated

supernē *adv* above, from above

supern·us -a -um *adj* upper; situated high up; supernal, celestial

supĕr·ō -āre *vt* to go over, pass over, rise above; to pass or go past, go beyond; to sail past, double; to outdo, surpass; to overcome, vanquish; *vi* to mount, ascend; to be superior, have the advantage; to be left over, survive; to be superfluous; to be abundant; (with *dat*) to pass over, pass above

superobru·ō -ĕre *vt* to cover completely, smother

superpend·ens -entis *adj* towering overhead

super·pōnō -pōnĕre -posŭī -positum *vt* (with *dat*) to put or place (*something*) upon; (with **in** + *acc*) to put (*someone*) in charge of

superscand·ō -ĕre *vt* to step over, climb over

super·sedĕō -sedēre -sēdī -sessum *vi* (with *abl*) to refrain from, give up

superstagn·ō -āre *vi* (of a river) to overflow and form swamps

superst·es -ĭtis *adj* standing by as a witness; surviving; posthumous; (with *genit* or *dat*) outliving, surviving; **superstes esse** to live on; **superstes esse** (with *genit* or *dat*) to outlive (*someone or something*)

superstitĭ·ō -ōnis *f* excessive fear; superstition

superstitiōsē *adv* superstitiously

superstitiōs·us -a -um *adj* superstitious; having magical powers

superstĭt·ō -āre *vi* to be remaining, be left

superst·ō -āre *vt* to stand over; *vi* (with *dat*) to stand on, stand over

superstrāt·us -a -um *adj* spread over (*as a covering*)

super·struō -struĕre -struxī -structum *vt* to build on top

super·sum -esse -fŭī *vi* to be left over, still exist, survive; to abound; to be in excess, be superfluous; to be adequate, suffice; (with *dat*) to outlive, survive (*someone*)

supertĕg·ō -ĕre *vt* to cover, cover over

superurg·ens -entis *adj* putting on pressure, adding pressure

supĕr·us -a -um *adj* upper; of this world, of this life; northern; **ad auras superas redire** to return to the upper air, come back to life; **mare superum** Adriatic Sea; *m pl* see **superi**; *n pl* see **supera**

supervacānĕ·us -a -um *adj* superfluous

supervacu·us -a -um *adj* superfluous, needless

supervād·ō -ĕre *vt* to go over, climb over

super·vĕhor -vĕhī -vectus sum *vt* to sail, ride, or drive by or past

super·veniō -venīre -vēnī -ventum *vt* to come upon, come on top of; to overtake; to come over, close over, cover; to surprise; *vi* to arrive suddenly; (with *dat*) to come upon by surprise

supervent·us -ūs *m* sudden arrival, unexpected arrival

supervolĭt·ō -āre *vt* to hover over

supervŏl·ō -āre *vt* to fly over; *vi* to fly across

supīn·ō -āre *vt* to turn up, lay on its back; to turn over (*by plowing*)

supīn·us -a -um *adj* face-up; lying

upwards, turned upwards; sloping, sloping upwards; (streams) flowing upwards (to their source); on one's back; lazy, careless, indifferent

suppactus pp of **suppingo**

suppaenīt·et -ēre v impers (with acc of person and genit of thing regretted), e.g., **illum furoris suppaenitet** he somewhat regrets the outburst

suppalp·or -ārī vi (with dat) to coax (someone) a little

supp·ār -āris adj nearly equal

supparasīt·or -ārī -ātus sum vi (with dat) to flatter (someone) a little like a parasite

suppăr·um -ī n or **suppăr·us -ī** m linen dress; small sail

suppeditātĭ·ō -ōnis f good supply, abundance

suppedĭt·ō -āre vt to supply, furnish; vi to stand by; to be at hand, be in stock, be available; (with dat) to be at hand for; (with **ad** or **in** + acc) to be adequate for, suffice for

suppēd·ō -ēre vi to break wind quietly

suppetĭ·ae -ārum f pl help, assistance

suppetĭ·or -ārī -ātus sum vi (with dat) to help, assist

suppĕt·ō -ĕre -īvī or **-ĭī -ītum** vi to be at hand, be in stock, be available; (with dat) a to be at hand for, be available to; **b** to be equal to, suffice for, be sufficient for; **c** to correspond to

suppīl·ō -āre vt to filch

sup·pingō -pingĕre — -pactum vt to fasten underneath

supplant·ō -āre vt to trip up

supplēment·um -ī n full complement; reinforcements

suppl·ĕō -ēre -ēvī -ētum vt to fill up; to make good (losses, damage, etc.); (mil) to bring to full strength

suppl·ex -ĭcis adj kneeling, on one's knees, in entreaty; humble, submissive; m suppliant

supplicātĭ·ō -ōnis f public thanksgiving, day of prayer; thanksgiving for victory; day of humiliation

suppliciter adv suppliantly, humbly, submissively

supplic·ĭum -ĭī or **-ī** n kneeling down, bowing down, humble entreaty; public prayer, supplication; (because criminals were beheaded kneeling) execution, death penalty; punishment, torture; suffering, distress, pain

supplĭc·ō -āre vi (with dat) to go on one's knees to, entreat, beg

sup·plōdō -plōdĕre -plōsī vt to stamp (the foot)

supplōsĭ·ō -ōnis f stamping; **supplosio pedis** stamping of the foot

sup·pōnō -pōnĕre -posŭī -positum vt (with dat) a to put, place, set (something) under; **b** to put (something) next to, add (something) to; **c** to substitute (some-

thing) for; **potentiam in gratiae locum supponere** to put power in place of influence, substitute power for influence

support·ō -āre vt to bring or carry up, transport

supposīticĭ·us -a -um adj spurious

suppositĭ·ō -ōnis f substitution

suppositus pp of **suppono**

suppostr·ix -īcis f unfair substituter (female)

suppressĭ·ō -ōnis f holding back (of money), embezzlement

sup·primō -primĕre -pressī -ressum vt to press down or under; to sink; to repress, stop; to suppress, keep secret

supprōm·us -ī m assistant butler

suppŭd·et -ēre v impers to cause (someone) a slight feeling of shame; (with acc of person and genit of cause), e.g., **eorum me suppudet** I am a bit ashamed of them

suppūr·ō -āre vi to fester

supp·us -a -um adj (animals) facing the ground

supput·ō -āre vt to trim up; to count, compute

suprā adv on top, above; up above; earlier; beyond; more; **supra quam** more than; prep (with acc) over, above; beyond; (of time) before; (of amount) over, beyond; in charge of

suprascand·ō -ĕre vt to climb over

suprēmum adv for the last time

suprēm·us -a -um (superl of **superus**) adj highest, topmost; the top of; last, latest, final; greatest, supreme, extreme; closing, dying, final; **suprema manus** the finishing touches; **supremus mons** summit of the mountain, mountain top; n last moment; n pl moment of death; funeral rites, obsequies; testament

sūr·a -ae f calf of the leg

surcŭl·us -ī m shoot, sprout, twig; slip, graft

surdast·er -ra -rum adj somewhat deaf

surdĭt·ās -ātis f deafness

surd·us -a -um adj deaf; silent, noiseless; unheeding; dull, faint, indistinct

surēn·a -ae f grand vizier (in the Parthian empire)

surgō surgĕre surrexī surrectum vi to get up, rise, stand up; to get up (from sleep); to grow up, spring up

surp·ō -ĕre -ŭī vt to snatch, wrest; to pilfer

surrancĭd·us or **subrancĭd·us -a -um** adj somewhat rancid

surrauc·us or **subrauc·us -a -um** adj somewhat hoarse

surrectus pp of **surgo**

surrēmīg·ō or **subrēmīg·ō -āre** vi to row along

sur·rēpō or **sub·rēpō -rēpĕre -repsī -reptum** vt to creep under, crawl under; vi to creep up; (with dat) to creep up on, steal upon

surreptĭcĭ·us or **subreptĭcĭ·us -a -um** *adj* surreptitious; stolen

surreptus *pp* of **surrepo** and of **surripio**

sur·rīdĕŏ or **sub·rīdĕŏ -rīdēre -rīsī** *vi* to smile

surrīdĭcŭlē or **subrīdĭcŭlē** *adv* rather humorously

sur·rĭgŏ or **sub·rĭgŏ -rĭgĕre -rexī -rectum** *vt* to raise, lift up, erect

surring·or or **subring·or -ī** *vi* to grimace, make a face; to be somewhat annoyed

sur·rĭpĭŏ or **sub·rĭpĭŏ -rĭpĕre -rĭpŭī -reptum** *vt* to snatch secretly, pilfer; (with *dat*) to pilfer (*something*) from

surrŏg·ŏ -āre *vt* to propose as a substitute

surrostrān·ī or **subrostrān·ī -ōrum** *m pl* loafers around the rostra

surrub·ĕŏ or **subrub·ĕŏ -ēre** *vi* to blush slightly

surrūf·us or **subrūf·us -a -um** *adj* reddish

sur·rŭŏ or **sub·rŭŏ -ruĕre -rŭī -rŭtum** *vt* to undermine, dig under; to tear down, demolish; (fig) to wreck, stamp out, destroy

surrustĭc·us or **subrustĭc·us -a -um** *adj* rather unsophisticated

surrŭtus *pp* of **surruo**

sursum or **sursus** *adv* upwards, high up; **sursum deorsum** up and down, to and fro

sūs suis *m* pig, hog, boar; *f* sow

Sūs·a -ōrum *n pl* capital of Persia

suscensĕŏ see **succenseo**

susceptĭ·ŏ -ōnis *f* undertaking

sus·cĭpĭŏ -cĭpĕre -cēpī -ceptum *vt* to catch (*something before it falls*); to support; to pick up, resume (*conversation*); to bear (*children*); to accept, receive (*under one's protection*); to take up, undertake; to acknowledge, recognize (a *child*) as one's own

suscĭt·ŏ -āre *vt* to stir up; to erect, build; to awaken; to encourage; (fig) to stir up (*rebellion, love, etc.*)

suspect·ŏ -āre *vt* to gaze up at; to distrust, suspect

suspect·us -a -um *pp* of **suspicio**; *adj* suspected, mistrusted

suspect·us -ūs *m* respect, esteem

suspend·ĭum -ĭī or **-ī** *n* hanging; hanging oneself

sus·pendŏ -pendĕre -pendī -pensum *vt* to hang up, hang; to prop up, support; to keep in suspense; to check (*temporarily*); to interrupt; **suspendi** (with **ex** + *abl*) to depend on

suspens·us -a -um *adj* hanging, balanced; raised, poised; in suspense, uncertain, hesitant; (with **ex** + *abl*) dependent upon

suspĭc·ax -ācis *adj* suspicious; mistrusted, causing mistrust, suspicious

su·spĭcĭŏ -spĭcĕre -spexī -spec-

tum *vt* to look up at; to look up to, admire; to mistrust, suspect; *vi* to look up; (with **in** + *acc*) to look up at or into

suspĭcĭōsē *adv* suspiciously

suspĭcĭōs·us -a -um *adj* mistrustful, suspicious; suspicious-looking, suspicious; (with **in** + *acc*) suspicious of

suspĭc·ŏ -āre or **suspĭc·or -ārī -ātus sum** *vt* to mistrust, suspect; to suppose, believe, surmise

suspīrāt·us -ūs *m* deep breath, sigh

suspīr·ĭum -ĭī or **-ī** *n* deep breath, sigh; **suspirium ducere, repetere,** or **trahere** to draw a deep breath, sigh

suspīr·ŏ -āre *vt* to sigh for; *vi* to sigh, heave a sigh

susque deque *adv* up and down; **de Octavio susque deque est** it's all one (i.e., *of no consequence*) as far as Octavian is concerned

sustentācŭl·um -ī *n* prop, support

sustentātĭ·ŏ -ōnis *f* forbearance, patience

sustent·ŏ -āre *vt* to hold up, hold upright, support; to sustain (*with food*); to hold (*enemy*); to uphold (*law*); to delay; to postpone

sus·tinĕŏ -tinēre -tinŭī -tentum *vt* to hold up, support; to hold back, hold in, check; to uphold (*law*); to sustain, support (*with food*); to bear (*trouble*); to hold up, delay, put off

sustoll·ŏ -ĕre *vt* to lift up, raise; to destroy

susurrāt·or -ōris *m* mutterer, whisperer

susurr·ŏ -āre *vt & vi* to mutter, murmur, whisper

susurr·us -ī *m* low, gentle noise; murmur, whisper, buzz, hum

sūtēl·ae -ārum *f pl* patches; tricks

sūtĭl·is -e *adj* sewn together, fastened together

sūt·or -ōris *m* shoemaker

sūtōrĭ·us -a -um *adj* shoemaker's; *m* ex-shoemaker

sūtrīn·us -a -um *adj* shoemaker's; *f* shoemaker's shop; shoemaker's trade

sūtūr·a -ae *f* seam; suture

sūt·us -a -um *pp* of **suo**; *n pl* joints

su·us -a -um *adj* his, her, its, their, one's own; due, proper, peculiar; *pron masc pl* one's own people, one's own friends, one's own family; *pron neut pl* one's own property

Sybăr·is -is *f* town in S. Italy noted for its luxurious living

Sybarīt·a -ae *m* Sybarite

Sychae·us -ī *m* husband of Dido

sycophant·a -ae *m* sycophant; blackmailer; cheat; slanderer

sycophantĭ·a -ae *f* cunning, deceit

sycophantĭōsē *adv* deceitfully

sycophant·or -ārī -ātus sum *vi* to cheat; (with *dat*) to play a trick on

Syēn·ē -ēs *f* town in S. Egypt

syllăb·a -ae *f* syllable

syllabātim *adv* syllable by syllable

symbŏl·a -ae *f* contribution *(of money to a feast)*; (coll) blows
symbŏl·us -ī *m* symbol, mark, token
symphōnǐ·a -ae *f* agreement of sound, symphony, harmony
symphōnǐăc·us -a -um *adj* concert, musical; **puerī symphoniaci** choristers; *m pl* musicians
Symplēgăd·es -um *f pl* two islands in the Euxine which floated about and dashed against each other until they were fixed in place as the Argo sailed by them
symplegm·a -ătis *m* group *(of persons embracing or wrestling)*
synĕdr·us -ī *m* senator *(in Macedonia)*
syngrăph·a -ae *f* promissory note
syngrăph·us -ī *m* written contract; pass, passport
synŏd·us -ontis *m* bream *(fish)*
synthĕs·is -is *f* dinner service; suit of clothes; dinner clothes
Syph·ax -ăcis *m* king of Numidia

at the time of the Second Punic War, siding with Carthage *(d.* 203 B.C.)
Syrācosǐ·us -a -um *adj* Syracusan; *m pl* Syracusans
Syrācūs·ae -ārum *f pl* Syracuse *(chief city in Sicily)*
Syrācūsān·us or **Syrācūsǐ·us -a -um** *adj* Syracusan
Syrǐ·us -a -um *adj* Syrian; *m pl* Syrians; *f* Syria
Syr·us -a -um *adj* Syrian; *m pl* Syrians
Syr·inx -ingis *f* nymph who was pursued by Pan and changed into a reed
syrm·a -ae *f* robe with a train *(worn esp. by actors in tragedies)*; tragedy
syrt·is -is *f* sand dune; quicksand
Syrt·is -is *f* Gulf of Sidra in N. Africa; Gulf of Cabes; *f pl* the Syrtes *(lakes and sand dunes of that area as representative of a wild, forbidding place)*

T

tabell·a -ae *f* small board; door sill; game board; writing tablet; ballot; picture, painting; votive tablet
tabellārǐ·us -a -um *adj* (law) regulating voting; *m* mailman; courier
tāb·ĕō -ēre *vi* to waste away; to melt away; to stream, run
tabern·a -ae *f* hut, hovel, cottage; booth, stall, shop; inn
tabernācŭl·um -ī *n* tent; **tabernaculum capere** to choose a place for a tent outside the city in which to take the auspices
tabernārǐ·ī -ōrum *m pl* shopkeepers
tāb·ēs -is *f* melting, wasting, decay, dwindling, shrinking; decaying matter, rot; disease, pestilence
tāb·escō -escĕre -ŭī to begin to decay, begin to melt, melt gradually
tābidŭl·us -a -um *adj* wasting, consuming
tābǐd·us -a -um *adj* wasting, decaying, melting; corrupting, infectious
tābǐfic·us -a -um *adj* melting, wasting; (fig) gnawing
tabŭl·a -ae *f* plank, board; writing tablet; advertisement; auction; picture, painting; map; votive tablet; *f pl* account books, records, register, lists
tabulār·ǐum -ǐī or **-ǐ** *n* archives, archives building
tabulātǐ·ō -ōnis *f* flooring, floor, story
tabulāt·us -a -um *adj* boarded; *n* floor, story; layer; row *(of trees)*
tāb·um -ī *n* putrid matter, decay, rot; disease, plague, pestilence
tac·ĕō -ēre -ŭī -ǐtum *vt* to be silent

about, pass over in silence; *vi* to be silent, hold one's tongue; to be still, be noiseless
tacitē *adv* silently, secretly
taciturnǐt·ās -ātis *f* silence, taciturnity
taciturn·us -a -um *adj* silent, taciturn; noiseless, hushed, quiet
tacǐt·us -a -um *adj* silent, mute; unmentioned, secret; (law) assumed, implied, tacit; **per tacitum** in silence
Tacǐt·us -ī *m* C. Cornelius Tacitus *(Roman historian, c.* 55-*c.* 115 A.D.)
tactǐl·is -e *adj* tangible
tactǐ·ō -ōnis *f* touch, touching; feeling, sense of touch
tactus *pp* of **tango**
tact·us -ūs *m* touch; handling; influence, effect
taed·a -ae *f* pine wood, pitch pine; torch; wedding torch; wedding; pine board
taedet taedēre taedŭit or **taesum est** *v impers* it irks; (with *acc of* person and *genit* of the cause), e.g., **mē taedet stultitiae meae** my foolishness irks me, I am annoyed at my foolishness
taedǐf·er -ĕra -ĕrum *adj* torch-bearing
taed·ǐum -ǐī or **-ǐ** *n* irksomeness, tediousness, weariness, boredom
taenǐ·a -ae *f* band, ribbon
Taenarǐd·ēs -ae *m* Spartan *(esp. Hyacinthus)*
Taenăr·is -ǐdis *adj* Spartan
Taenăr·um or **Taenăr·on -ī** *n* or **Taenăr·us** or **Taenăr·os -ī** *m* or *f* most southerly point of the Pelo-

ponnesus (*thought to be the entrance to the lower world*); lower world, Hades

taet·er -ra -rum *adj* foul, revolting, offensive, shocking, loathsome; ugly, hideous; disgraceful; *n* offensiveness, repulsiveness

taetrē *adv* foully, hideously, shockingly

taetricus see tetricus

tag·ax -ācis *adj* light-fingered

tālār·is -e *adj* ankle-length; *n pl* angle-length clothes; sandals

tālār·ius -a -um *adj* of dice; ludus talarius game of dice

talāsiō or talassiō *interj* wedding cry

tālĕ·a -ae *f* rod, bar, stake

talent·um -ī *n* talent (*Greek weight, varying from state to state, but equal to about fifty pounds*); sum of money (*consisting of sixty minae*)

tāli·ō -ōnis *f* (law) punishment in kind

tāl·is -e *adj* such, of such kind, of that kind; so great, so excellent, so distinguished

talp·a -ae *m* or *f* mole (*animal*)

Talthyb·ius -iī or -ī *m* herald of Agamemnon

tāl·us -ī *m* ankle, anklebone; heel, foot; die (*used in playing dice*)

tam *adv* to such an extent, to such a degree, so, so much; tam . . . quam the . . . the; tam magis . . . quam magis the more . . . the more

tamār·ix -īcis *f* tamarisk

tamdiū *adv* so long, how long; tuamdiu quam or tuamdiu dum as long as

tamen *adv* yet, nevertheless, still, all the same; in the same way

Tāmĕs·is -is or Tāmĕs·a -ae *m* Thames

tametsī *conj* even if, although

tamquam or tanquam *conj* as, just as, as much as; just as if; tamquam sī just as if

Tanăgr·a -ae *f* town in Boeotia

Tană·is -is *m* river of Sarmatia (*modern Don*)

Tanăqu·il -īlis *f* wife of the elder Tarquin

tandem *adv* at last, in the end, finally; (*expressing urgency or impatience*) now, tell me, please

tangō tangĕre tetigī tactum *vt* to touch; to handle, meddle with; to taste; to come to, reach; to border on; to hit, beat; to wash, anoint; to affect, gall, move to pity; to dupe; to touch upon, mention; to touch, be related to; to undertake

Tantălĕ·us -a -um *adj* of Tantalus

Tantalĭd·ēs -ae *m* descendant of Tantalus

Tantăl·is -ĭdis *f* descendant of Tantalus (*female*)

Tantăl·us -ī *m* son of Jupiter and father of Pelops who was punished in the lower world with constant hunger and thirst

tantill·us -a -um *adj* so small, so little; *n* a bit

tantisper *adv* just so long (*and no longer*); just for the moment

tantopĕre or tantō opĕre *adv* so much, so greatly, to such a degree, so earnestly, so hard

tantŭlum *adv* so little, in the least

tantŭl·us -a -um *adj* so little, so small; *n* so little, such a trifle; tantulo vendere to sell for such a trifling amount

tantum *adv* so much, so greatly, to such a degree, so far, so long, so; only, just, but just, hardly, scarcely; tantum modo only

tantummŏdo *adv* only

tantundem *adv* just so much, just as far, to the same extent

tant·us -a -um *adj* of such size, so great; so much; so little; so important; *pron neut* so much; so little; so small an amount, so small a number; tanti of such value, worth so much, at so high a price; of little account, of such small importance; tanto (*with comparatives*) by so much, so much the; tanto melior! so much the better!, bravo!, excellent!; tanto nequior! so much the worse!

tant·usdem -ădem -undem *adj* so great, just as great, just as large

tapēt·a -ae *m* or tapēt·a -ōrum or tapēt·ia -ium *n pl* carpet; tapestry; coverlet

tardē *adv* slowly

tardesc·ō -ĕre *vi* to become slow; to falter

tardip·ēs -ĕdis *adj* limping

tardit·ās -ātis *f* tardiness, slowness; dullness, stupidity

tarditūd·ō -īnis *f* tardiness, slowness

tardiuscŭl·us -a -um *adj* rather slow, slowish, dragging

tard·ō -āre *vt* to slow down, delay, hinder; *vi* to go slow, take it easy

tard·us -a -um *adj* tardy, slow; lingering; mentally slow, mentally retarded; deliberate; crippling

Tarentīn·us -a -um *adj* Tarentine; *m pl* Tarentines

Tarent·um -ī *n* town on S. coast of Italy, founded by the Spartans around 700 B.C.

tarm·es -ĭtis *m* wood worm, borer

Tarpēi·us -a -um *adj* Tarpeian; mons Tarpeius Tarpeian cliff on the Capitoline Hill from which criminals were thrown; *f* Roman girl who treacherously opened the citadel to the Sabine attackers

tarpezīt·a or trapezīt·a -ae *m* banker

Tarquiniens·is -e *adj* of the town of Tarquinii

Tarquini·us -a -um *adj* Tarquinian; *m* Tarquinius Priscus (*fifth king of Rome and husband of Tanaquil*); Tarquinius Superbus (*seventh and last king of Rome*); *m pl* important Etrurian town

Tarracīn·a -ae *f* or **Terracīn·ae -ārum** *f pl* town in Latium

Tartăr·a -ōrum *n pl* or **Tartăr·us** or **Tartăr·os -ī** *m* Tartarus (*lower level of Hades reserved for criminals*)

Tartărĕ·us -a -um *adj* of Tartarus, infernal

tat or **tatae** *interj* exclamation of surprise

tat·a -ae *m* (coll) daddy

Tat·ius -iī or **-ī** *m* Titus Tatius (*king of the Sabines who later ruled jointly with Romulus until the latter had him killed*)

taurĕ·us -a -um *adj* bull's, of a bull; **terga taurea** bulls' hides; drums; *f* rawhide, whip

Taur·ī -ōrum *m pl* barbarous people living in the peninsula now called the Crimea

Tauric·us -a -um *adj* Tauric

taurĭf·er -ĕra -ĕrum *adj* bull-producing (*regions*)

tauriform·is -e *adj* bull-shaped

taurīn·us -a -um *adj* bull's; made of bull's hide; bull-like

taur·us -ī *m* bull

Taur·us -ī *m* Taurus (*constellation*)

taxāti·ō -ōnis *f* rating, appraisal

taxill·us -ī *m* small die (*for playing dice*)

tax·ō -āre *vt* to appraise

tax·us -ī *f* yew, yew tree

Tāygĕt·ē -ēs *f* one of the Pleiades, the daughter of Atlas and Pleione

Tāygĕt·us -ī *m* mountain range in Laconia

tē *acc & abl* of **tu**

-te = suffix for **tu** and **te**

Teān·um -ī *n* town in Campania; town in Apulia

techn·a or **techĭn·a -ae** *f* trick

Tecmess·a -ae *f* wife of Ajax the son of Telamon

tectē *adv* cautiously, guardedly

tect·or -ōris *m* plasterer

tectōriŏl·um -ī *n* bit of plaster work

tectōri·us -a -um *adj* roofing; plasterer's; painter's; *n* plaster, stucco; fresco painting; beauty preparation

tect·us -a -um *pp* of **tego;** *adj* concealed; secret; guarded (*words*); reserved, secretive (*person*); *n* roof; ceiling; canopy; cover, shelter; house

tēcum = **cum te**

Tegĕ·a -ae *f* town in Arcadia

Tegeae·us -a -um *adj* Tegean, Arcadian; *m* Pan; *f* Arcadian maiden (*i.e., Atalanta*)

Tegeāt·ae -ārum *m pl* Tegeans

teg·es -ĕtis *f* mat

tegill·um -ī *n* hood, cowl

tegĭm·en or **tegm·en** or **tegŭm·en -ĭnis** *n* cover, covering; vault (*of heaven*)

tegiment·um or **tegment·um** or **tegument·um -ī** *n* cover, covering

teg·ō tegĕre texī tectum *vt* to cover; to protect, shelter, defend; to hide; to bury; **tegĕre latus** (with *genit*) to escort (*someone*)

tēgŭl·a -ae *f* tile; *f pl* roof tiles, tiled roof

tegŭmen see **tegimen**

tegumentum see **tegimentum**

tēl·a -ae *f* web; warp (*threads that run lengthwise in the loom*); yarn beam; loom; design, plan

Telăm·ōn -ōnis *m* son of Aeacus, brother of Peleus, king of Salamis, and father of Ajax and Teucer

Telamōniăd·ēs -ae *m* son of Telamon (*i.e., Ajax*)

Telamōn·ius -iī or **-ī** *m* Ajax

Tēlĕgŏn·us -ī *m* son of Ulysses and Circe

Tēlĕmăch·us -ī *m* son of Ulysses and Penelope

Tēlĕph·us -ī *m* king of Mysia, wounded by the spear of Achilles and later cured by its rust

tell·ūs -ūris *f* the earth; ground, earth; land, country

tēl·um -ī *n* missile, weapon; spear, javelin, dart; sword, dagger, ax; shaft

temerāri·us -a -um *adj* casual, accidental; rash, thoughtless

temĕre *adv* by chance, without cause; at random; rashly, thoughtlessly; **non temere** not lightly; not easily; hardly ever; **nullus dies temere intercessit quo non scriberet** hardly a day ever passed without his writing

temerit·ās -ātis *f* chance, accident; rashness, thoughtlessness; *f pl* foolhardy acts

temĕr·ō -āre *vt* to darken, blacken; to violate, disgrace, defile

tēmēt·um -ī *n* alcohol, wine

temnō temnĕre tempsī temptum *vt* to slight, offend

tēm·ō -ōnis *m* pole, tongue (*of a carriage or plow*); wagon

Tempē (indecl) *n pl* scenic valley between Olympus and Ossa in Thessaly

temperāment·um -ī *n* moderation

tempĕr·ans -antis *adj* moderate, temperate

temperanter *adv* moderately

temperanti·a -ae *f* self-control, moderation

temperātē *adv* moderately, with due moderation

temperāti·ō -ōnis *f* blending, proportion, symmetry; temperament; organization, constitution; control

temperāt·or -ōris *m* controller

temperāt·us -a -um *adj* tempered; self-controlled, temperate

tempĕrī *adv* in time, on time; in due time, at the right time

temperi·ēs -ēī *f* blending, tempering; temperature, mild temperature

tempĕr·ō -āre *vt* to compound, combine, blend, temper; to regulate, moderate; to tune; to govern, control, rule; *vi* to be moderate, exercise restraint; (with *abl* or *ab* + *abl*) to abstain from

tempest·ās -ātis *f* time, period, season; stormy weather, storm, tempest

tempestīvē *adv* at the right time, seasonably

tempestīvit·ās -ātis *f* right time, timeliness

tempestīv·us -a -um *adv* timely, seasonable, fit; ripe, mature; in good time, early

templ·um -ī *n* space marked off in the sky or on the earth for observation of omens; open space, quarter; temple, shrine, sanctuary

temporāl·is -e *adj* temporary, transitory

temporāri·us -a -um *adj* temporary; changeable (*character*)

tempŏre or **tempŏrī** *adv* in time, on time; in due time, at the right time

temptābund·us -a -um *adj* making constant attempts, trying

temptāment·um -ī *n* attempt, effort; temptation, trial

temptāmin·a -um *n pl* attempts, trials

temptātĭ·ō -ōnis *f* trial; attack (*of sickness*)

temptāt·or -ōris *m* assailant

tempt·ō or **tent·ō -āre** *vt* to test, feel, probe; to try, attempt; to attack; to try to influence, tamper with, tempt, try to induce; to urge, incite, sound out; to worry, distress, disquiet

temptus *pp* of temno

temp·us -ŏris *n* temple (*of the head*); time, period, season; occasion, opportunity; right time, good time, proper period; times, condition, state, position; need, emergency; measure, quantity, cadence (*in metrics*); **ad tempus** punctually; at the right time, at the appointed time; for the time being, for the moment; for the occasion; **ante tempus** before time, too soon, prematurely; **ex tempore** on the spur of the moment; **id temporis** at that time; **in ipso tempore** in the nick of time; **in tempore** at the right moment, just in time; **in tempus** temporarily, for a time; **per tempus** just in time; **pro tempore** as time permits, according to circumstances; **tempori cedere** to yield to circumstances; **tempus in ultimum** to the last extremity

tēmulent·us -a -um *adj* intoxicated

tenācĭt·ās -ātis *f* tenacity; miserliness

tenācĭter *adv* tightly, firmly

ten·ax -ācis *adj* holding tight, gripping, clinging; sticky; firm; obstinate; stingy; (with *genit*) clinging to, holding on to

tendĭcŭl·ae -ārum *f pl* little snare, little noose, little trap

tendō tendĕre tetendī tentum or **tensum** *vt* to stretch, stretch out, hold out, spread, strain; to head for (*a place*); to aim, shoot (*an arrow*); to bend (*a bow*); to tune (*an instrument*); to pitch (*a tent*); *vi* to pitch tents, be encamped; to travel, sail, move, march; to endeavor; to contend, fight; to exert oneself; (with *inf*) to try to, endeavor to; (with **ad** + *acc*) a to tend toward, be inclined toward; **b** to move toward, travel to, aim for; (with **contra** + *acc*) to fight against

tenĕbr·ae -ārum *f pl* darkness; night; blindness; dark place, haunts; lower world; unconsciousness; death; obscurity, low station; ignorance

tenĕbricōs·us -a -um *adj* gloomy; darkened (*senses*); blind (*lust*)

tenĕbric·us -a -um *adj* dark, gloomy

tenĕbrōs·us -a -um *adj* dark, gloomy

Tenĕd·os or **Tenĕd·us -ī** *f* Island off the coast of Troy

tenellŭl·us -a -um *adj* tender little, dainty little

tenell·us -a -um *adj* dainty

ten·ĕō -ēre -ŭī -tum *vt* to hold, hold tight, keep; to grasp, comprehend; to comprise; to possess, occupy, be master of; to hold back, restrain, repress; to hold, charm, amuse; to have control of, get the better of; to keep, detain; *vi* to hold out, last, keep on

ten·er -ĕra -ĕrum *adj* tender, soft, delicate; young, youthful; impressionable; weak; effeminate; voluptuous

tenerasc·ō -ĕre *vi* to grow weak

tenĕrē *adv* softly

tenerĭt·ās -ātis *f* weakness

tēnesm·os -ī *m* straining at stool

ten·or -ōris *m* uninterrupted course; **uno tenore** uninterruptedly

tens·a -ae *f* car carrying images of the gods in procession

tens·us -a -um *pp* of tendo; *adj* stretched, drawn tight, stretched out

tentīg·ō -ĭnis *f* lust

tentō see tempto

tentōr·ium -iī or **-ī** *n* tent

tent·us -a -um *pp* of tendo and of teneo; *adj* stretched, drawn tight, stretched out

tenuicŭl·us -a -um *adj* poor, paltry

tenŭ·is -e *adj* thin, fine; delicate; precise; shallow (*groove, etc.*); slight, puny, poor, insignificant; plain, simple; small, narrow

tenŭĭt·ās -ātis *f* thinness, fineness; leanness; simplicity; precision; poverty

tenŭĭter *adv* thinly; slightly; poorly, indifferently; exactly, minutely; superficially

tenŭ·ō -āre *vt* to make thin; to contract; to dissolve; to lessen, diminish, weaken

ten·us -ōris *n* trap, snare

tenus *prep* (with *abl*, always placed after the noun) as far as, up to, down to; **nomine tenus** or **verbo tenus** as far as the name goes, nominally, in name

Te·os or **Te·us -ī** *f* town on the coast of Asia Minor, the birthplace of Anacreon

tepe·faciō -facĕre -fēcī -factum *vt* to make warm, warm up

tep·ĕō -ēre -uī *vi* to be warm, be lukewarm; to glow with love; to be lukewarm, indifferent

tep·escō -escĕre -uī *vi* to grow warm; to grow lukewarm, grow indifferent

tepidius *adv* rather tepidly

tepĭd·us -a -um *adj* warm, lukewarm, tepid

tep·or -ōris *m* warmth; coolness; lack of heat (*in the bath*); lack of fire (*in a speech*)

ter *adv* three times, thrice

terdecĭens or **terdecĭēs** *adv* thirteen times

terebinth·us -ī *f* terebinth, turpentine tree

terĕbr·a -ae *f* borer, drill

terĕbr·ō -āre *vt* to bore, drill, bore out

terēd·ō -ĭnis *f* grub worm

Tēreĭd·ēs -ae *m* Itys (*son of Tereus*)

Terent·ius -iī or **-ī** *m* Terence (*M. Terentius Afer, Roman comic poet, c. 190-159 B.C.*)

ter·es -ĕtis *adj* smooth, well-rounded; smooth and round, polished, shapely; round, cylindrical; (*fig*) smooth, elegant, fine

Tēr·eus -ĕī or **-ĕos** *m* king of Thrace, husband of Procne, and father of Itys

tergemĭn·us -a -um *adj* triple, threefold

tergĕō tergēre tersī tersum or **terg·ō -ēre** *vt* to scour, wipe off, wipe dry, clean, cleanse

tergĭn·um -ī *n* rawhide; scourge

tergiversātĭ·ō -ōnis *f* refusal; evasion, subterfuge

tergivers·or -ārī -ātus sum *vi* to keep turning one's back; to be shifty, be evasive

tergō see **tergeo**

terg·um -ī or **terg·us -ŏris** *n* back; ridge; hide, leather; leather objects: bag, shield, drum; (*mil*) rear; **a tergo** in the rear, from behind; **in tergum** backward

term·es -ĭtis *m* branch

Termināl·ia -ĭum or **-iōrum** *n pl* festival of Terminus (*the god of boundaries, celebrated on the 23rd of February*)

terminātĭ·ō -ōnis *f* decision, determining; arrangement, ending (*of a sentence*)

termĭn·ō -āre *vt* to mark off with boundaries, bound, limit; to fix, de-

termine, define; (rhet) to end, round out (*a sentence*)

termĭn·us -ī *m* boundary, limit

Termĭn·us -ī *m* god of boundaries

tern·ī -ae -a *adj* three in a group, three apiece, three each

terō terĕre trīvī trītum *vt* to wear, rub, wear out, crush; to spend, waste; to smooth, grind, sharpen

Terpsichŏr·ē -ēs *f* Muse of dancing; poetry

terr·a -ae *f* the earth; land; earth, ground, soil; country, region, territory

terrāneŏl·a -ae *f* crested lark

terrēn·us -a -um *adj* earthly, terrestrial; earthen, made of earth; *n* land, ground

terr·ĕō -ēre -uī -ĭtum *vt* to frighten, scare, terrify; to deter

terrestr·is -e *adj* of the earth, on the earth; land, earth; **proelium terrestre** land battle

terrĕ·us -a -um *adj* sprung from the earth, earth-born

terrĭbĭl·is -e *adj* terrible, frightful

terrĭcŭl·a -ōrum *n pl* scarecrow

terrĭfĭc·ō -āre *vt* to terrify

terrĭfĭc·us -a -um *adj* terrifying, awe-inspiring, alarming

terrĭgĕn·a -ae *m* or *f* earth-born creature

terrĭlŏqu·us -a -um *adj* ominous, alarming

territ·ō -āre *vt* to keep frightening; to intimidate

territōr·ium -iī or **-ī** *n* land around a town, territory, suburbs

terr·or -ōris *m* terror, alarm, dread, fright

ters·us -a -um *pp* of **tergeo;** *adj* clean, neat; neat, terse

tertiadecĭmān·ī -ōrum *m pl* soldiers of the thirteenth legion

tertiān·us -a -um *adj* recurring every second day, tertian; *m pl* soldiers of the third legion; *f* tertian fever

tertĭō *adv* in the third place, thirdly; the third time

tertĭum *adv* for the third time

tertĭ·us -a -um *adj* third

tertĭ·us decĭm·us -a -um *adj* thirteenth

terunc·ius -iī or **-ī** *m* three twelfths of an ace, quarter ace; **heres ex teruncio** heir to one fourth of the estate

tervenēfĭc·us -ī *m* (term of abuse) three-time killer

tesqu·a -ōrum *n pl* wilderness, wilds

tessell·a -ae *f* cubed mosaic stone

tessellāt·us -a -um *adj* tesselated

tessĕr·a -ae *f* cube; die; watchword, countersign; tally, token; ticket

tesserār·ius -iī or **-ī** *m* officer of the day

tesserŭl·a -ae *f* small cube; ticket

test·a -ae *f* brick, tile; jug, crock; potsherd; shell fish; shell

testāmentārĭ·us -a -um *adj* pertaining to a will or testament; *m* forger of a will

testāment·um -ī *n* will, testament

testātī·ō -ōnis *f* invoking as witness

testāt·us -a -um *adj* attested, public

testicŭl·us -ī *m* testicle

testificātī·ō -ōnis *f* giving evidence, testifying; proof, evidence

testífíc·or -ārī -ātus sum *vt* to give as evidence, attest; to vouch for; to bring to light; to call to witness

testimōn·ĭum -ĭī or **-ī** *n* testimony, deposition

test·is -is *m* or *f* witness; *m* testicle

test·or -ārī -ātus sum *vt* to give as evidence; to show, prove, vouch for; to call to witness, appeal to; *vi* to be a witness, testify; to make a will

testūdĭnĕ·us -a -um *adj* of a tortoise; made of tortoise shell

testūd·ō -ĭnis *f* tortoise; tortoise shell; lyre, lute; arch, vault; (mil) protective shed (*for besiegers*)

test·um -ī *n* earthenware lid; pot with a lid

tēte = emphatic form of **te**

Tēth·ys -ўos *f* wife of Oceanus and mother of the sea nymphs; sea

tetradrachm·um or **tetrachm·um -ī** *n* Greek silver coin (*worth four drachmas*)

tetrarch·ēs -ae *m* tetrarch (*ruler of one fourth of a country*); petty prince

tetrarchĭ·a -ae *f* tetrarchy

tetrĭc·us -a -um *adj* gloomy, sour, crabby

Teuc·er or **Teuc·rus -rī** *m* son of Telamon and brother of Ajax; son of Scamander of Crete, son-in-law of Dardanus, and later king of Troy

Teucr·ĭa -ae *f* Troy

Teucr·us -a -um *adj* Teucrian, Trojan; *m pl* Trojans

Teutōn·ēs -um or **Teutōn·ī -ōrum** *m pl* Teutons

texō texĕre texŭī textum *vt* to weave; to plait; to build; to compose

textĭl·is -e *adj* woven; brocaded; *n* fabric

text·or -ōris *m* weaver

textrīn·um -ī *n* weaving

textr·ix -īcis *f* weaver (*female*)

textūr·a -ae *f* texture; web; fabric

text·us -a -um *pp* of **texo**; *n* woven cloth, fabric; web

text·us -ūs *m* texture

Thā·is -ĭdis *f* Athenian courtesan

thalăm·us -ī *m* woman's room; bedroom; marriage bed; marriage

thalassĭc·us -a -um *adj* sea-green

thalassĭn·us -a -um *adj* sea-green

Thal·ēs -is or **-ētis** *m* early Ionian philosopher of Miletus, regarded as one of the Seven Sages (*fl 575 B.C.*)

Thalī·a -ae *f* Muse of comedy; sea nymph

thall·us -ī *m* green bough, green stalk

Thaps·os or **Thaps·us -ī** *f* city in Africa where Caesar defeated the Pompeians (46 B.C.)

Thas·os or **Thas·us -ī** *f* island in the Aegean Sea, off the coast of Thrace

Thaumantĭ·as -ădis or **Thaumant·is -ĭdis** *f* Iris (*daughter of Thaumas*)

theātrāl·is -e *adj* theatrical

theātr·um -ī *n* theater

Thēb·ae -ārum *f pl* Thebes (*capital of Boeotia, founded by Cadmus*); Thebes (*city of Upper Egypt*)

Thēbae·us -a -um *adj* & *mf* Theban (*of Egypt*)

Thēbān·us -a -um *adj* & *mf* Theban (*of Boeotia*)

thēc·a -ae *f* case; envelope

Them·is -ĭdis *f* goddess of justice and of prophecy

Themistŏcl·ēs -is or **-ī** *m* Themistocles (*Athenian general and statesman, c. 528-459 B.C.*)

thensaurārĭ·us -a -um *adj* treasure, of treasure

thensaurus see **thesaurus**

Theocrĭt·us -ī *m* founder of Greek pastoral poetry, born at Syracuse (*3rd cent. B.C.*)

theolŏg·us -ī *m* theologian

therm·ae -ārum *f pl* hot springs, hot baths

thermopōl·ĭum -ĭī or **-ī** *n* hot-drink shop

thermopŏt·ō -āre *vt* to warm with a drink

Thermopўl·ae -ārum *f pl* famous pass in Thessaly between Mt. Oeta and the sea, defended by Leonidas and his four hundred Spartans (490 B.C.)

thermŭl·ae -ārum *f pl* little hot bath

Thersīt·ēs -ae *m* Greek soldier at Troy notorious for his ugliness

thēsaur·us or **thensaur·us -ī** *m* storehouse; store, treasure, hoard

Thēs·eus -ĕī or **-ĕos** *m* king of Athens, son of Aegeus and Aethra, and husband first of Ariadne and later of Phaedra

Thēsē·us -a -um *adj* of Theseus

Thēsīd·ae -ārum *m pl* Athenians

Thēsīd·ēs -ae *m* Hippolytus (*son of Theseus*)

Thespĭăd·ēs -um *f pl* Muses

Thesp·is -is *m* traditional founder of Greek tragedy

Thespĭ·us -a -um *adj* Thespian; *f pl* town in Boeotia near Mt. Helicon

Thessalĭ·a -ae *f* Thessaly (*most northerly district of Greece*)

Thessalĭc·us -a -um *adj* Thessalian

Thessăl·us -a -um *adj* Thessalian; *m pl* people of Thessaly, Thessalians

Thestorĭd·ēs -ae *m* Calchas (*famous Greek seer who joined the expedition to Troy*)

Thet·is -ĭdis or **-ĭdos** *f* sea nymph, daughter of Nereus and Doris, wife of Peleus, and mother of Achilles

thiás·us -ī *m* Bacchic dance; Bacchic troop of dancers

Thisb·ē -ēs *f* girl in Babylon, loved by Pyramus

Tho·ás -antis *m* king of Tauris, slain by Orestes; king of Lemnos and father of Hypsipyle

thol·us -ī *m* rotunda

thōr·ax -ācis *m* breastplate

Thrác·a -ae or **Thrác·ē -ēs** *f* Thrace (*wild country to the N. of the Aegean*)

Thrácì·us -a -um *adj* Thracian; *f* Thrace

Thress·a or **Threiss·a -ae** *f* Thracian woman

Thr·ex -ēcis or **Thr·ax -ācis** *m* Thracian gladiator

thron·us -ī *m* throne

Thúcýdíd·ēs -is *m* Thucydides (*famous Greek historian of the Peloponnesian War, c. 456-c. 400 B.C.*)

thunn·us -ī *m* tuna fish

thūr· = tur·

Thūrí·ī -ōrum *m pl* city on the Tarentine Gulf in S. Italy

Thūrín·us -a -um *adj & m* Thurian

thūs thúris *n* incense, frankincense

Thybris see **Tiberis**

Thyén·ē -ēs *f* nymph who nursed Bacchus

Thyest·ēs -ae *m* son of Pelops, brother of Atreus, and father of Aegisthus

thymbr·a -ae *f* savory (*plant*)

thym·um -ī *n* thyme

Thyní·a -ae *f* Bithynia (*country in Asia Minor*)

Thyníác·us -a -um *adj* Bithynian

Thýn·us -a -um *adj & m* Bithynian

thynn·us -ī *m* tuna fish

Thyōn·eus -ěī *m* Bacchus

thyrs·us -ī *m* Bacchic wand twined with vine tendrils and ivy, and crowned with a fir cone

tiár·a -ae *f* or **tiár·ās -ae** *m* tiara

Tiberín·is -ídis *adj* of the Tiber

Tiberín·us -a -um *adj* of the Tiber; *m* river god of the Tiber

Tibér·is or **Tibr·is** or **Thybr·is -is** *m* Tiber River

Tiber·ius -iī or **-ī** *m* Tiberius (*Tiberius Claudius Nero Caesar, successor of Augustus, 42 B.C.-37 A.D., ruling from 14 A.D. to 37 A.D.*)

tíbí·a -ae *f* shinbone, tibia; flute

tíbíc·en -inis *m* flutist; prop; pillar

tíbícín·a -ae *f* flutist (*female*)

Tibull·us -ī *m* Albius Tibullus (*Roman elegiac poet, c. 54-c. 19 B.C.*)

Tib·ur -úris *n* town of Latium on the Anio (*modern Tivoli*)

Tiburt·ēs -um *m pl* Tiburtines

Tiburtín·us or **Tiburn·us -a -um** *adj* Tiburtine

Ticín·us -ī *m* tributary of the Po

Tigellín·us -ī *m* notorious favorite of the emperor Nero

tigill·um -ī *n* beam, log

tignári·us -a -um *adj* **faber tignarius** carpenter

tign·um -ī *n* trunk, log, beam, board

tigr·is -is or **-ídis** *f* tigress

Tigr·is -is or **-ídis** *m* large river of W. Asia which joins with the Euphrates

tíli·a -ae *f* lime tree

Tímae·us -ī *m* Greek historian of Sicily (*c. 346-c. 250 B.C.*); Pythagorean philosopher of Locri in S. Italy after whom Plato named one of his dialogues (*5th cent. B.C.*)

Tímágěn·ēs -is *m* brilliant rhetorician in the time of Augustus

timefact·us -a -um *adj* alarmed, frightened

timídē *adv* timidly, fearfully

timídít·ās -ātis *f* timidity, fearfulness, cowardice

timíd·us -a -um *adj* timid, fearful, cowardly; (*with genit*) fearful of, afraid of

tim·or -ōris *m* fear, alarm; dread; a terror

tinctíl·is -e *adj* used for dipping

tinct·us -a -um *pp* of **tingo**

tiné·a -ae *f* moth; bookworm

tingō tíngěre tinxī tinctum *vt* to dip, soak; to dye, color; to tinge, imbue

tinniment·um -ī *n* ringing

tinn·iō -īre -īvī -īī -ītum *vt & vi* to ring

tinnit·us -ūs *m* ring, ringing, tinkling, jingling

tinnúl·us -a -um *adj* ringing, tinkling; shrill

tintinnábul·um -ī *n* bell, door bell, cattle bell

tintinnácul·us -a -um *adj* jingling; *m pl* chain gang

tintin·ō -āre *vi* to ring

tín·us -ī *m* laurustinus (*shrub*)

Típh·ys -yos *m* pilot of the Argo

tippúl·a -ae *f* water spider

Tiresí·ās -ae *m* famous seer at Thebes at the time of Oedipus

Tíridát·ēs -ae *m* king of Armenia

tír·ō -ōnis *m* recruit; beginner

tírócín·ium -iī or **-ī** *n* first campaign; inexperience in military life; body of raw recruits; beginning, first try

tíruncúl·us -ī *m* young beginner

Tíryn·s -this or **-thos** *f* town in Argolis where Hercules was raised

Tírynthí·us -a -um *adj* Tirynthian

Tísamén·us -ī *m* son of Orestes and king of Argos

Tísiphŏn·ē -ēs *f* one of the three Furies who haunted murderers

Tísiphoné·us -a -um *adj* guilty

Tít·ān -ānis or **Títān·us -ī** *m* Titan; sun; *m pl* giant sons of Uranus and Ge who rebelled against Uranus and put Cronus on the throne

Títāni·us -a -um *adj* of the Titans, Titanic; *f* Latona (*the mother of Apollo and Diana*); Pyrrha (*as descendant of Prometheus*); Circe (*as daughter of Sol*)

Tīthōni·us -a -um adj Tithonian; f Aurora

Tīthōn·us -ī m son of Laomedon and husband of Aurora from whom he received the gift of immortality without eternal youth

Tit·iēs -ium m pl one of the three original tribes of Rome

tītīllātī·ō -ōnis f tickling

tītīll·ō -āre vt to tickle

titivillīt·ium -iī or **-ī** n trifle

titubanter adv falteringly

titubātī·ō -ōnis f staggering

titūb·ō -āre vi to stagger, reel, totter; to falter, waver (in speech)

titūl·us -ī m inscription; label; notice, advertisement; title of honor; renown; pretext

Tity·os -ī m giant slain by Apollo for insulting Latona and thrown into Tartarus

Tītyr·us -ī m shepherd in Vergil's pastorals, sometimes identified with Vergil himself

Tlēpolēm·us -ī m son of Hercules

Tmōl·us or **Timōl·us -ī** m mountain in Lydia famous for its wines

tocull·ō-ōnis m banker

tōf·us or **tōph·us -ī** m tufa (volcanic rock)

tog·a -ae f outer garment of a Roman citizen; **toga candida** white toga (worn by candidates for office); **toga picta** brocaded toga (worn by triumphant generals); **toga praetexta** crimson-bordered toga (worn by magistrates and freeborn children); **toga pulla** dark-grey toga (worn by mourners); **toga pura** or **virilis** or **libera** toga of manhood (worn by young men from about the age of sixteen)

togāt·us -a -um adj wearing a toga; m Roman citizen; civilian; humble client; f Roman drama (treating of Roman themes); prostitute

togul·a -ae f little toga

tolerābil·is -e adj tolerable; patient

tolerābilius adv more patiently, fairly patiently

toler·ans -antis adj tolerant; (with genit) tolerant of, enduring

toleranter adv patiently

tolerantí·a -ae f toleration, endurance

tolerātī·ō -ōnis f toleration, endurance

tolerāt·us -a -um adj tolerable, endurable

tolēr·ō -āre vt to tolerate, bear, endure; to support, maintain, sustain

tollēn·ō -ōnis m crane, lift, derrick

tollō tollēre sustūlī sublātum vt to lift, raise; to have (a child); to acknowledge (a child); to raise, educate; to weigh (anchor); to take on, take on board; to remove; to do away with, destroy; to cancel, abolish, abrogate; to lift, steal; to uplift, cheer up, excite; to erect, build up; to waste (time); **amicum tollere** to cheer up a friend; **animos**

tollere to boost the morale; **deos tollere** to deny the existence of the gods; **hominem de medio tollere** to make away with or kill a man; **pecunias ex fano tollere** to steal money from a shrine; **signa tollere** to break camp

tolūtim adv at a trot

tomācul·um or **tomācl·um -ī** n sausage

tōment·um -ī n stuffing (for pillows)

Tom·ī -ōrum m pl or **Tom·is -is** f town in Moesia on the Black Sea to which Ovid was exiled

Tomīt·ae -ārum m pl people of Tomi

Tomītān·us -a -um adj of Tomi

Ton·ans -antis m Thunderer (epithet of several gods, esp. Jupiter)

tondeō tondēre totondī tonsum vt to clip, shear, shave; to prune; to reap, mow; to crop, browse on; (fig) to fleece, rob; **usque ad cutem tondere** to swindle, fleece

tonitrāl·is -e adj thunderous

tonitr·us -ūs m or **tonitrū·um -ī** n thunder; m pl or n pl claps of thunder

ton·ō -āre -uī -itum vt to thunder out (words); vi to thunder

tons·a -ae f oar blade

tonsil·is -e adj clipped

tonsill·ae -ārum f pl tonsils

tonsīt·ō -āre vt to shear regularly

tons·or -ōris m shearer, barber

tonsōrí·us -a -um adj shaving; barber's

tonstrīcul·a -ae f little hairdresser, little barber (female)

tonstrīn·a -ae f barber shop

tonstr·ix -īcis f hairdresser, barber (female)

tonsūr·a -ae f clipping, shearing; **capillorum tonsura** haircut

tons·us -a -um pp of **tondeo**; f see **tonsa**

tons·us -ūs m haircut; hairdo

tōph·us -ī m tufa (volcanic rock)

topiāri·us -a -um adj garden, landscape; m gardener, landscaper; f landscaping

topíc·e -ēs f resourcefulness in finding topics for speeches

tor·al -ālis n valance

torcul·ar -āris or **torcūl·um -ī** n wine press, oil press

toreum·a -ātis n embossing, relief

torment·um -ī n windlass; catapult, artillery piece; shot; torture rack, torture; (fig) torture; n pl artillery

tormīn·a -um n pl colic

torminōs·us -a -um adj prone to colic

torn·ō -āre vt to form with a lathe, turn on a lathe

torn·us -ī m lathe; burin

torōs·us -a -um adj brawny, muscular

torpēd·ō -īnis f numbness, lethargy, listnessness; crampfish, torpedo (fish)

torp·ĕō -ēre -ŭī vi to be numb; to be stiff; to be stupefied; to be groggy

torp·escō -escĕre -ŭī vi to grow numb, grow listless

torpĭd·us -a -um adj groggy

torp·or -ōris m torpor, numbness; grogginess

torquāt·us -a -um adj wearing a necklace

Torquāt·us -ī m T. Manlius Torquatus (*legendary Roman hero who is said to have slain a gigantic Gaul in single combat and to have worn the Gaul's necklace*)

torquĕō torquēre torsī tortum vt to twist, turn, wind, wrench; to whirl, hurl, wind up and hurl; to rack; (fig) to torment

torqu·ēs or **torqu·is -is** m or f necklace; collar; festoon

torr·ens -entis adj burning, seething; rushing, roaring (*stream*); fiery (*speech*); m roaring stream, torrent

torrĕō torrēre torrŭī tostum vt to roast, bake, burn, scorch; to parch, dry up

torr·escō -escĕre -ŭī vi to become burned or parched

torrĭd·us -a -um adj baked, parched, dried up; frostbitten

torr·is -is m firebrand

tortē adv crookedly

tortĭl·is -e adj twisted, winding, spiral

tort·ō -āre vt to twist; **tortāri** to writhe

tort·or -ōris m torturer, executioner

tortŭōs·us -a -um adj full of turns, winding; (fig) tortuous, complicated

tort·us -a -um pp of **torqueo**; adj twisted, crooked; gnarled (*oak*); complicated

tort·us -ūs m twisting, twist, spiral; **tortūs dare** (of a serpent) to form loops

torŭl·us -ī m tuft (*of hair*)

tor·us -ī m knot; bulge; muscle; brawn; bed, couch; mattress; mound; boss; flowery expression

torvĭt·ās -ātis f grimness, wildness

torv·us -a -um adj grim, fierce, stern, savage

tostus pp of **torreo**

tot (indecl) adj so many, as many

totĭdem (indecl) adj just so many, just as many

totiens or **totiēs** adv so often, so many times

tōt·us -a -um adj the whole, all, entire; **totus in illis** wholly absorbed in those matters; n the whole matter, all; **ex toto** wholly, totally; **in toto** on the whole, in general; **in totum** wholly, totally

toxic·um -ī n poison

trabāl·is -e adj of or for beams; **clavus trabalis** spike; **telum trabale** beam-like shaft

trabĕ·a -ae f ceremonial robe (*woven in stripes and worn by magistrates, augurs, etc.*)

trabeāt·us -a -um adj wearing a ceremonial robe

trab·s -is f beam, plank; timber; tree; object made of beams: roof, shaft, table, battering ram

tractābĭl·is -e adj manageable; (weather) fit for navigation

tractātĭ·ō -ōnis f handling, management, treatment; discussion, treatment (*of a subject*)

tractāt·us -ūs m touching, handling, management

tractim adv little by little, slowly; at length, in a drawn-out manner

tract·ō -āre vt to drag around, haul, pull; to touch, handle; to manage, control, wield; to conduct, carry on, transact, practice; to discuss; **se tractare** to behave oneself, conduct oneself

tract·us -a -um pp of **traho**; adj flowing, fluent, continuous (*discourse*)

tract·us -ūs m dragging; drawing out, dragging out, extension (*e.g., of a war*); track, trail; tract, extent, distance; region, district

trādĭtĭ·ō -ōnis f handing over, surrender; transmission

trādĭt·or -ōris m betrayer, traitor

trādō trādĕre trādĭdī trādĭtum vt to hand over, surrender, deliver; to betray; to hand down, bequeath, transmit, pass on; to relate, recount; to teach; **se tradere** (with dat) a to surrender to; b to devote oneself to

trā·dūcō -dūcĕre -duxī -ductum vt to lead across, bring over, transfer, to lead in parade, make a show of; to disgrace, degrade; to broadcast, proclaim; to pass, spend

trāductĭ·ō -ōnis f transfer, transference; course, passage (*of time*); metonymy

trāduct·or -ōris m conveyor

trāductus pp of **traduco**

trād·ux -ŭcis m vine branch

tragicē adv as in tragedy

tragicōcŏmoedĭ·a -ae f melodrama

tragic·us -a -um adj of tragedy, tragic; in the tragic style, grand, solemn; of a tragic nature, tragic, moving, terrible; **actor tragicus** tragedian; m tragic playwright

tragoedĭ·a -ae f tragedy

tragoed·us -ī m tragic actor, tragedian

trāgŭl·a -ae f javelin

trag·us -ī m body odor of the armpits; a fish (*of unknown type*)

trah·ax -ācis adj greedy

trahĕ·a -ae f sledge, drag

trahō trahĕre traxī tractum vt to draw, drag, trail; to draw out, pull out, extract; to lead, take along, be followed by; to contract, wrinkle; to inhale; to quaff; to take on, assume, acquire, get; to squander, dissipate; to spin, manufacture; to attract, allure, influence; to win over (*to the other side*); to refer, ascribe; to distract; to consider, ponder; to spin out, prolong, protract

Trājān·us -ī m Trajan (*M. Ulpius Trajanus, Roman emperor,* 97-117 A.D.)

trājectī·ō -ōnis f crossing, passage; transposition (*of words*); shift of meaning; exaggeration

trājectus pp of **trajicio**

trāject·us -ūs m crossing over, passage

trā·jiciō or **trans·iciō** or **trans·jiciō -jicĕre -jēcī -jectum** vt to have go across, cause to go across, transfer; to ship across, transport; to pass through, break through; to stab through, pierce; (with double *acc*) to bring (*e.g., troops*) across (*river, mountain*); (with **trans** + *acc*) to lead across; (with **in** + *acc*) to lead over into

trālāt- = **translat-**

Trall·ēs -ĭum f pl town in Lydia

trālŏqu·or -ī vt to talk over, enumerate, recount

trālūcĕō see **transluceo**

trām·a -ae f woof, web

trāmĕō = **transmeo**

trām·es -ĭtis m path, track, trail

trāmi- = **transmi-**

trānātō = **transnato**

trān·ō or **transn·ō -āre** vt to swim across; to pass through, permeate; vi to swim across; to pass through

tranquillē adv quietly, calmly

tranquillĭt·ās -ātis f tranquillity, stillness, calmness

tranquill·ō -āre vt to calm, quiet, tranquillize

tranquill·us -a -um adj calm, quiet, tranquil; n calm, calmness, peace, quiet, tranquillity; quiet sea

trans prep (with *acc*) across, over, beyond

transab·ĕō -īre -ĭī vt to go through, pierce

transact·or -ōris m manager

transactus pp of **transigo**

transad·igō -igĕre -ēgī -actum vt to pierce; to run (*someone*) through; (with double *acc*) to run (*e.g., a sword*) through (*someone*)

Transalpīn·us -a -um adj Transalpine, lying beyond the Alps

tran·scendō or **trans·scendō -scendĕre -scendī -scensum** vt to climb or step over, surmount; to overstep, transgress; vi to climb or step across

trans·cīdō -cīdĕre -cīdī vt to flog soundly

tran·scrībō or **trans·scrībō -scrībĕre -scripsī -scriptum** vt to transcribe, copy off; (law) to transfer, convey; to transfer, remove

trans·currō -currĕre -currī or **-cucurrī -cursum** vt & vi to run or dash over; to run or dash through; to run or dash by or past

transcurs·us -ūs m running through, passage; cursory mention

transd- = **trad-**

transenn·a -ae f grating; lattice work, trellis work; lattice window; fowler's net

trans·ĕō -īre -ĭī -ĭtum vt to pass over, cross; to desert; to pass (*in a race*); to pass over, make no mention of; to treat cursorily; to overstep, pass beyond; to surpass; vi to go over, go across, pass over; to pass by, go by; to shift (*to another opinion, topic, etc.*); (of time) to pass, go by; to pass away; (with **ad** + *acc*) to a cross over to (*a place*); **b** to cross over to, desert to; (with **in** + *acc*) to change into, be transformed into; (with **per** + *acc*) to penetrate, permeate, pervade

trans·fĕrō -ferre -tŭlī -lātum (or **trālātum**) vt to carry or bring across; to transfer by writing, to copy; to shift, transfer; to transform; to postpone; to translate; to use (*words*) figuratively

trans·fīgō -fīgĕre -fixī -fixum vt to pierce, transfix; to run (*someone*) through

transfigūr·ō -āre vt to transform

transfixus pp of **transfigo**

trans·fodiō -fodĕre -fōdī -fossum vt to run through, stab, pierce

transform·is -e adj transformed, changed in shape

transform·ō -āre vt to change in shape, transform

transfossus pp of **transfodio**

transfŭg·a -ae m or f deserter, turncoat

trans·fugiō -fugĕre -fūgī vi to desert

transfŭg·ĭum -ĭī or **-ī** n desertion

trans·fundō -fundĕre -fūdī -fūsum vt to transfuse; to pour; (with **in** + *acc*) to pour (*a liquid*) into; (with **ad** + *acc*) (fig) to shift (*affection, allegiance*) to (*another person*)

transfūsi·ō -ōnis f transmigration

transfūsus pp of **transfundo**

trans·gredĭor -grĕdī -gressus sum vt to cross, pass over; to exceed; vi to go across; to cross over (*to another party*)

transgressi·ō -ōnis f crossing, passage; transposition (*of words*)

transgressus pp of **transgredior**

transgress·us -ūs m crossing

transiciō see **trajicio**

transiect- = **traject-**

trans·igō -igĕre -ēgī -actum vt to pierce, run through; to finish, settle, transact, accomplish, perform, conclude; to pass, spend (*time*); vi to come to an agreement, reach an understanding

transil·iō or **transsil·iō -īre -ŭī** vt to jump over, jump across; to overstep; exceed; to skip, omit; vi to jump across

transit·ans -antis adj passing through

transiti·ō -ōnis f crossing, passage;

switching (*to another party*); contagion, infection; passageway

transitus *pp of* **transeo**

transit·us -ūs *m* crossing; passage; passing; traffic; crossing over, desertion; change, period of change, transition; fading (*of colors*); **in transitu** in passing

translāticī·us or **trālātīcī·us -a -um** *adj* transmitted, traditional, customary; usual, common

translātī·ō or **trālātī·ō -ōnis** *f* transfer, shift; transporting; translation; metaphor, figure

translātīv·us -a -um *adj* transferable

translāt·or -ōris *m* middleman (*in a transfer*)

translātus *pp of* **transfero**

translĕg·ō -ĕre *vt* to read through

translūc·ĕō or **trālūc·ĕō -ēre** *vi* to be reflected; to shine through

transmarīn·us -a -um *adj* from beyond the seas, foreign, overseas

transmĕ·ō or **trāmĕ·ō -āre** *vi* to cross, pass

transmigr·ō -āre *vi* to move, migrate, emigrate

transmissi·ō -ōnis *f* crossing, passage

transmissus *pp of* **transmitto**

transmiss·us -ūs *m* passing over, crossing, passage

trans·mittō or **trā·mittō -mittĕre -mīsī -missum** *vt* to send across; to transmit; to let pass; to hand over, entrust, commit; to pass over, leave unmentioned; to pass through, endure; (with **in** + *acc*) to send (*someone*) across to or into; (with **per** + *acc*) to let (*someone*) pass through; *vi* to cross over, cross, pass (*from one place to another*)

transmontān·ī -ōrum *m pl* people across the mountains

trans·movĕō -movēre -mōvī -mōtum *vt* to move, transfer

transmūt·ō -āre *vt* to change, shift

transnat·ō or **trānat·ō -āre** *vt* to swim; *vi* to swim across

transnō see **trano**

Transpadān·us -a -um *adj* Transpadane, beyond or N. of the Po River

transpect·us -ūs *m* view, prospect

transpic·iō or **transspic·iō -ĕre** *vt* to look through

trans·pōnō -pōnĕre -posŭī -posĭtum *vt* to transfer

transport·ō -āre *vt* to transport

transposĭtus *pp of* **transpono**

Transrhēnān·us -a -um *adj* beyond the Rhine, E. of the Rhine

transs- = **trans-**

Transtĭberīn·us -a -um *adj* across the Tiber

transtin·ĕō -ēre *vi* to pass through

transtr·um -ī *n* thwart

transult·ō -āre *vi* to jump across

transult·us -a -um *adj* pierced through

transvectĭ·ō or **trāvectĭ·ō -ōnis** *f*

transportation, crossing

trans·vĕhō or **trā·vĕhō -vehĕre vexī -vectum** *vt* to transport; to carry, lead (*in a parade*); **transvehī** to ride by (*in a parade*); (of time) to elapse

transverbĕr·ō -āre *vt* to pierce through and through, transfix

transversa *adv* sideways; across one's course

transversārĭ·us -a -um *adj* transverse, lying crosswise

transvers·us or **trāvers·us** or **transvors·us -a -um** *adj* lying across, lying crosswise; inopportune; astray; in the wrong direction; *n* wrong direction, opposite direction; **de transverso** unexpectedly; **ex transverso** unexpectedly; sideways

transvolit·ō -āre *vt* to flit through, fly through

transvŏl·ō or **trāvŏl·ō -āre** *vt & vi* to fly over, fly across, fly by, zip by

transvorsus see **transversus**

trapēt·us -ī *m* oil press

trapezīt·a -ae *m* banker

Trapēz·ūs -untis *f* city in Pontus on the Black Sea

Trasimenn·us or **Trasumenn·us -ī** *m* lake in Etruria where Hannibal defeated the Romans (217 B.C.)

trāv- = **transv-**

trecēn·ī -ae -a *adj* three hundred each

trecentēsĭm·us -a -um *adj* three hundredth

trecentĭēs *adv* three hundred times

trechedipn·um -ī *n* light garment worn to dinner

tredĕcim (*indecl*) *adj* thirteen

tremebund·us -a -um *adj* trembling, shivering

treme·facĭō -facĕre -fēcī -factum *vt* to shake, cause to shake

tremend·us -a -um *adj* terrible, frightful

trem·escō or **trem·iscō -escĕre -ŭī** *vt* to tremble at; *vi* to tremble

trem·ō -ĕre -ŭī *vt* to tremble at; *vi* to tremble, shiver, quake

trem·or -ōris *adj* trembling, shaking, shivering; dread

tremŭl·us -a -um *adj* trembling, quivering, tremulous, shivering

trepidanter *adv* tremblingly, nervously

trepidātĭ·ō -ōnis *f* nervousness, alarm

trepĭdē *adv* nervously, in alarm

trepĭd·ō -āre *vt* to start at, be jumpy or nervous at; *vi* to be nervous, be jumpy, be alarmed; (of a flame) to flicker; (of streams) to rush along

trepĭd·us -a -um *adj* nervous, jumpy, agitated, hurried, restless; bubbling; perilous, critical, alarming; **in re trepida** in a ticklish situation

trēs (or **trīs**) **tria** *adj* three; (denoting a small number) a couple of

tress·is -is *m* small coin: mere trifle

tresvīrī (*genit:* **triumvirōrum**) *m pl* three-man board, triumvirs

Trēvĕr·ī -ōrum *m pl* people of E. Gaul

triangŭl·us -a -um *adj* triangular; *n* triangle

triārī·ī -ōrum *m pl* soldiers of the third rank in a battle line, reserves

tribuārī·us -a -um *adj* tribal

tribŭl·is -is *m* fellow tribesman

tribŭl·um -ī *n* threshing sledge (*wooden platform with iron teeth underneath*)

tribŭl·us -ī *m* caltrop (*thistle*)

tribūn·al -ālis *n* raised platform; tribunal, judgment seat; (in camp) general's platform; cenotaph

tribūnāt·us -ūs *m* tribuneship, rank of tribune

tribūnici·us -a -um *adj* tribunician, tribune's; *m* ex-tribune

tribūn·us -ī *m* tribune; **tribunus aerarius** paymaster; **tribunus militaris** or **tribunus militum** military tribune (*six in each legion, serving under the legatus, and elected by the people or at times appointed by a commander*); **tribunus plebis** tribune of the people (*ten in number, serving the interests of the plebeians*)

trib·ŭō -ŭĕre -ŭī -ūtum *vt* to divide; to distribute, bestow, confer, assign; to give, present; to concede, grant, allow; to ascribe, impute; to devote, spend

trib·us -ūs *m* tribe (*originally three in number and eventually increased to thirty-five*)

tribŭtārī·us -a -um *adj* subject to tribute; **tributariae tabellae** letters of credit

tribūtim *adv* by tribes

tribūtī·ō -ōnis *f* distribution

tribūt·us -a -um *pp* of **tribuo**; *adj* arranged by tribes; *n* tribute, tax, contribution

trīc·ae -ārum *f pl* tricks; nonsense

trīcēn·ī -ae -a *adj* thirty each

tric·eps -ipĭtis *adj* three-headed

trīcēsim·us -a -um *adj* thirtieth

trichil·a -ae *f* bower, arbor; summer home

trīciens or **trīciēs** *adv* thirty times

trīclīn·ium -iī or -ī *n* dining couch (*running around three sides of a table*); dining room

trīc·ō -ōnis *m* practical joker, trickster

trīc·or -ārī -ātus sum *vi* to cause trouble; to pull tricks

tricorp·or -ŏris *adj* three-bodied

tricusp·is -ĭdis *adj* three-pronged

trid·ens -entis *adj* three-pronged; *m* trident

Tridentif·er or **Tridentĭg·er** -ĕrī *m* Trident Bearer (*epithet of Neptune*)

tridŭ·um -ī *n* three-day period, three days

trienn·ia -ium *n pl* triennial festi-

val, festival celebrated every three years

trienn·ium -iī or -ī *n* three-year period, three years

tri·ens -entis *m* one third; coin (*one third of an ace*); third of a pint

trientābŭl·um -ī *n* land given by the state as an equivalent for one third of the sum which the state owed

trienti·us -a -um *adj* sold for a third

triērarch·us -ī *m* captain of a trireme

triēr·is -is *f* trireme

trietēric·us -a -um *adj* triennial, recurring every three years; *n pl* festival of Bacchus

trietēr·is -ĭdis *f* three-year period; triennial festival

trifāriam *adv* in three places, on three sides

trifau·x -cis *adj* triple-throated

trifĭd·us -a -um *adj* three-forked; split into three parts

triform·is -e *adj* triple

trifĭl·is -e *adj* having three threads or hairs

tri·fūr -fūris *m* archthief

trifurcif·er -ĕrī *m* archvillain, hardened criminal

trigemĭn·us or **tergemĭn·us** -a -um *adj* threefold, triple; *m pl* triplets

trigintā (indecl) *adj* thirty

trig·ōn -ōnis *m* ball game

trilībr·is -e *adj* three-pound

trilingu·is -e *adj* triple-tongued

tril·ix -īcis *adj* three-ply, triple-stranded

trimestr·is -e *adj* of three months

trimĕtr·us -ī *m* trimeter

trīm·us -a -um *adj* three-year-old

Trīnăcr·is -ĭdis *adj* Sicilian

Trīnacrī·us -a -um *adj* Sicilian; *f* Sicily

trīn·ī -ae -a *adj* threefold, triple; three each

trinōd·is -e *adj* having three knots, triple-knotted

triōbōl·us -ī *m* three-obol coin, half-drachma piece

Trīŏn·es -um *m pl* Great Bear and Little Bear (*constellation*)

tripartītō *adv* in three parts, into three parts

tripartīt·us or **tripertīt·us** -a -um *adj* divided into three parts, threefold

tripectŏr·us -a -um *adj* triple-bodied, triple-breasted

tripedāl·is -e *adj* three-foot

tripertītus see **tripartitus**

trip·ēs -ĕdis *adj* three-legged

tripl·ex -īcis *adj* threefold, triple; *n* three times as much, threefold portion

tripl·us -a -um *adj* triple, threefold

Triptolĕm·us -a -um *m* son of Celeus the king of Eleusis, favorite of Ceres, inventor of agriculture, and one of the judges in the lower world

tripudi·ō -āre vi to dance (as a religious act); to do a war dance; to leap, dance, hop about

tripudium -iī or **-ī** n solemn religious dance; war dance; dance (in general); favorable omen (when the sacred chickens ate hungrily)

trip·us -ŏdis f tripod (three-footed vessel); oracle, Delphic oracle

triquĕtr·us -a -um adj triangular; Sicilian

trirēm·is -e adj having three banks of oars; f trireme

trīs see **trēs**

triscurri·a -ōrum n pl broad humor, fantastic nonsense

tristicŭl·us -a -um adj somewhat sad

tristific·us -a -um adj ominous; saddening

tristimōni·a -ae f sadness

trist·is -e adj sad, sorrowful, melancholy, glum, dispirited; bringing sorrow, saddening; dismal; gloomy, sullen; stern, harsh; disagreeable, offensive (odor); bitter (taste)

tristiti·a -ae f sadness, gloom, gloominess, melancholy; severity, sternness

tristiti·ēs -ēī f sadness, sorrow, melancholy

trisulc·us -a -um adj three-forked

tritāv·us -ī m great-great-great-grandfather

triticē·us -a -um adj wheat, of wheat

tritic·um -ī n wheat

Trīt·ōn -ōnis m son of Neptune who blows through a shell to calm the seas; lake in Africa where Minerva was said to be born

Trītōniāc·us -a -um adj Tritonian

Trītōn·is -idis or **-idos** f Minerva

Trītōni·us -a -um adj Tritonian; f Minerva

trīt·or -ōris m grinder

trītūr·a -ae f threshing

trīt·us -a -um pp of **tero**; adj worn, well-worn; beaten (path); experienced, expert; common, trite (language)

trīt·us -ūs m rubbing, friction

triumphāl·is -e adj triumphal; having had a triumph; n pl triumphal insignia (without the actual triumph)

triumph·ō -āre vt to triumph over, conquer completely, vanquish; vi to make a triumphal procession, celebrate a triumph, triumph

triumph·us or **triump·us -ī** m victory parade, triumph; victory, triumph; **triumphum agere** (with **dē** or **ex** + abl) to celebrate a triumph over

triumvir -īrī m triumvir, commissioner; mayor (of a provincial town)

triumvirāl·is -e adj triumviral, of the triumvirs

triumvirāt·us -ūs m triumvirate, office of triumvir

triumvir·ī -ōrum m pl triumvirs, three commissioners, three-man commission (appointed at various times to serve various purposes); **triumviri capitales** police commissioners, superintendents of prisons and executions

trivenēfic·a -ae f nasty old witch

Trivi·a -ae f Diana

triviāl·is adj of the crossroads; found everywhere, common, ordinary

triv·ium -iī or **-ī** n crossroads, intersection; public street, highway

trivi·us -a -um adj of or at the crossroads

Trō·as -ădis adj Trojan; f Troad, district of Troy; Trojan woman

trochae·us -ī m trochee; tribrach (metrical foot of three short syllables)

trochlē·a -ae f block and tackle

troch·us -ī m hoop

Trōi·a or **Trōj·a -ae** f Troy

Trōiăd·es -um f pl Trojan women

Trōic·us -a -um adj Trojan

Trōīl·us -ī m son of Priam, killed by Achilles

Trōi·us -a -um adj Trojan; f see **Troia**

Trōjān·us -a -um adj Trojan; m pl Trojans

Trōjugĕn·a masc & fem adj Trojan-born, born at Troy, of Trojan descent, Trojan; m Trojan

tropae·um -ī n trophy, victory memorial; victory; mark, token, memorial, monument

Trōs Trōis m Tros (king of Phrygia after whom Troy was named)

trucīdāti·ō -ōnis f slaughter, massacre, butchery

trucīd·ō -āre vt to slaughter, massacre, cut down

truculentē or **truculenter** adv grimly, fiercely

truculenti·a -ae f savagery, ferocity; harshness; inclemency

truculent·us -a -um adj savage, grim, fierce, cruel

trud·is -is f pointed pole, pike

trūdō trūdĕre trūsī trūsum vt to push, thrust, drive, shove; to put forth (buds)

trull·a -ae f dipper, ladle, scoop; brazier; wash basin

trunc·ō -āre vt to lop off, mutilate, maim

trunc·us -a -um adj lopped; stripped (of branches and leaves), trimmed; maimed, mutilated; imperfect, undeveloped; m trunk, tree trunk; trunk, body (of human being); chunk of meat; blockhead

trūsit·ō -āre vt to keep pushing, keep shoving

trūsus pp of **trudo**

trutin·a -ae f balance, pair of scales; criterion

trutin·or -ārī -ātus sum vt to weigh, balance

trux trucis *adj* savage, grim, fierce, wild

trȳgŏn·us -ī *m* stingray

tu *pron* you (*singular*)

tuātim *adv* in your manner, as is typical of you

tub·a -ae *f* bugle, war trumpet

tūb·er -ĕris *n* lump, bump, swelling; truffle (*food*)

tub·er -ĕris *f* apple tree; *m* apple

tubīc·en -ĭnis *m* bugler, trumpeter

tubilustr·ium -iī or **-ī** *n* festival of bugles or trumpets (*celebrated on March 23rd and May 23rd and including a ritual cleaning of the bugles or trumpets*)

tuburcin·or -ārī -ātus sum *vt* to devour, gobble up

tub·us -ī *m* tube, pipe

tuccēt·um or **tūcēt·um -ī** *n* sausage

tudĭt·ō -āre *vt* to keep hitting, keep beating

tuĕor or **tu·or tuērī tuĭtus sum** or **tūtus sum** *vt* to see, look at, gaze at, watch, observe; to look after, take care of, guard, defend, protect

tugur·ium -iī or **-ī** *n* hut, hovel, cottage

tuĭti·ō -ōnis *f* guarding, defense; **tuĭtio sui** self-defense

Tulliān·um -ī *n* state prison in Rome, reputedly built by Servius Tullius

Tulliŏl·a -ae *f* little Tullia (*Cicero's daughter*)

Tull·ius -iī or **-ī** *m* Servius Tullius (*sixth king of Rome*)

tum *adv* then, at that time; next; moreover, besides; **cum . . . tum** both . . . and especially, not only . . . but also, if . . . then surely; **tum cum** at the point when, at the time when, just then when; **tum . . . tum** first . . . then, at one time . . . at another, now . . . now, both . . . and, partly . . . partly

tume·faciō -facĕre -fēcī -factum *vt* to make swell; (fig) to inflate

tum·ĕō -ēre -uī *vi* to be swollen, swell up, be inflated; (of business) to be in ferment, be cooking; (of language) to be bombastic; (of a person) to be excited, be in a dither, be in a rage; to be proud

tum·escō -escĕre -uī *vi* to begin to swell, begin to swell up; (of wars) to brew; to grow excited, become enraged, become inflated

tumĭd·us -a -um *adj* swollen, swelling; bloated; rising high; proud, inflated, puffed up; arrogant; incensed, enraged, exasperated; bombastic

tum·or -ōris *m* tumor, swelling; protuberance, bulging; elevation (*of the ground*); commotion, excitement, anger, rage; vanity, pride, arrogance

tumŭl·ō -āre *vt* to bury

tumulōs·us -a -um *adj* full of hills, hilly, rolling

tumultuārĭ·us -a -um *adj* hurried, confused, disorderly; (mil) emergency, drafted hurriedly to meet an emergency; **exercĭtus tumultuārius** emergency army; **pugna tumultuāria** irregular fight or battle (*i.e., not fought in regular battle formation*)

tumultuātĭ·ō -ōnis *f* confusion, hustle and bustle, panic

tumultŭ·ō -āre or **tumultŭ·or -ārī -ātus sum** *vi* to make a disturbance; to be in uproar, be topsyturvy

tumultuōsē *adv* disorderly, in confusion

tumultuōs·us -a -um *adj* boisterous, uproarious, turbulent, panicky

tumŭlt·us -ūs *m* commotion, uproar; insurrection, rebellion, civil war; confusion, agitation (*of the mind*); outbreak (*of crime*)

tumŭl·us -ī *m* mound; rising; ground swell; burial mound; **tumulus inanis** cenotaph

tūn = tūne (**tū & ne**)

tunc *adv* (of time past) then, at that time, on that occasion, just then; (of future time) then, at that time, in that event; (of succession in time) thereupon; (in conclusion) accordingly, consequently, in that case; **tunc . . . cum** then . . . when, just when, just at the time when; only when, whenever; **tunc dēmum** not until, then only, not till then; **tunc prīmum** then for the first time; **tunc quandō** whenever; **tunc quoque** then too; **tunc vērō** then to be sure, exactly then

tundō tundĕre tutŭdī tunsum or **tūsum** *vt* to beat, pound, hammer, thump; to buffet; to thresh; (fig) to harp on, keep at, importune

tunic·a -ae *f* tunic (*ordinary sleeved garment worn by both sexes*); skin, peel, husk, coating

tunicāt·us -a -um *adj* wearing a tunic; in shirt sleeves; coated, covered with skin

tunicŭl·a -ae *f* short tunic; thin skin or coating

tunsus *pp* of **tundo**

tuor see **tueor**

turb·a -ae *f* turmoil, disorder, uproar, commotion; brawl; crowd, disorderly crowd, mob, gang; multitude; common crowd, the masses; a large number

turbāment·a -ōrum *n pl* means of disturbance

turbātē *adv* in confusion, confusedly

turbātĭ·ō -ōnis *f* confusion, disorder

turbāt·or -ōris *m* ringleader, troublemaker, disturber

turbāt·us -a -um *adj* confused, disorderly; disturbed, annoyed

turbell·ae -ārum *f pl* stir, row; **turbellas facere** to cause a row

turben see **turbo** *m*

turbĭdē *adv* confusedly, in disorder

turbĭd·us -a -um *adj* wild, confused, boisterous; muddy, turbid;

troubled, perplexed; vehement; disheveled (*hair*); stormy (*sky, weather*)

turbĭnĕ·us -a -um *adj* cone-shaped

turb·ŏ -ĭnis *m* or **turb·en -ĭnis** *n* whirl, twirl, eddy; spinning, revolution; coil; spinning top; reel; spindle; wheel; tornado, whirlwind; wheel of fortune; (fig) whirlwind, storm

turb·ŏ -āre *vt* to throw into confusion, disturb, agitate; to break, disorganize (*in battle*), cause to break ranks; to confuse, confound; to muddy

turbulentē or **turbulenter** *adv* boisterously, tumultuously, confusedly

turbulent·us -a -um *adj* turbulent, wild, stormy; disturbed, confused; seditious, trouble-making

turd·a -ae *f* or **turd·us -ī** *m* thrush

tūrĕ·us -a -um *adj* of frankincense

turgĕŏ turgēre tursī *vi* to be swollen, be puffed up; to be bombastic

turgesc·ŏ -ĕre *vi* to begin to swell, begin to swell up; to begin to blow up (*in anger*)

turgĭdŭl·us -a -um *adj* poor swollen, swollen little (*eyes*)

turgĭd·us -a -um *adj* swollen, puffed up, inflated; turgid, bombastic

tūrĭbŭl·um -ī *n* censer

tūricrĕm·us -a -um *adj* incense-burning

tūrĭf·er -ĕra -ĕrum *adj* incense-producing

tūrĭlĕg·us -a -um *adj* incense-gathering

turm·a -ae *f* troop, squadron (*of cavalry*); crowd, group

turmāl·is -e *adj* of a squadron; equestrian; *m pl* troopers

turmātim *adv* by troops, by squadrons, squadron by squadron

Turn·us -ī *m* king of the Rutuli, killed by Aeneas

turpĭcŭl·us -a -um *adj* ugly little; somewhat indecent

turpĭfĭcāt·us -a -um *adj* corrupted, debased, degenerate

turpĭlucrĭcupĭd·us -a -um *adj* (coll) eager to make a fast buck

turp·is -e *adj* ugly, deformed; foul, filthy, nasty; disgraceful, shameless; dirty, obscene, indecent

turpĭter *adv* repulsively; disgracefully, scandalously, shamelessly

turpĭtūd·ŏ -ĭnis *f* ugliness, deformity; foulness; disgrace; moral turpitude

turp·ŏ -āre *vt* to make ugly, disfigure; to soil, dirty, defile, pollute

turrĭg·er -ĕra -ĕrum *adj* turreted; (Cybele) wearing a turreted crown (*representing the earth with its cities*)

turr·is -is *f* turret, tower; howdah (*on an elephant*); (fig) castle, mansion

turrīt·us -a -um *adj* turreted; for-

tified with turrets; crowned with turrets, adorned with a turret crown

turt·ur -ŭris *m* turtledove

tūs tūris *m* incense, frankincense

Tusculān·us -a -um or **Tusculens·is -e** *adj* Tusculan, of Tusculum; *m pl* Tusculans

Tuscŭl·us -a -um *adj* Tusculan; *n* Tusculum (*town in Latium near Alba Longa, about twelve miles from Rome*)

Tusc·us -a -um *adj* Etruscan

tussĭcŭl·a -ae *f* slight cough

tuss·iŏ -īre *vi* to cough, have a cough

tuss·is -is *f* cough

tūsus *pp* of **tundo**

tūtām·en -ĭnis or **tūtāment·um -ī** *n* means of defense, defense, protection

tūte = **tū** & **te** emphatic form of **tū**

tūtē *adv* safely

tūtēl·a or **tūtell·a -ae** *f* care, charge, patronage, protection, defense; guardianship; charge, thing protected; guardian, keeper, watcher

tūtĕmet = **tū** & **te** & **met** emphatic form of **tū**

tūt·ŏ -āre or **tūt·or -ārī -ātus sum** *vt* to guard, protect, defend; to keep safe, watch, preserve; to ward off, avert; (with **ab** + *abl* or with **ad** or **adversus** + *acc*) to protect (*someone*) from, guard (*someone*) against

tūt·or -ōris *m* protector; guardian (*of minors, women, etc.*)

tūt·us -a -um *pp* of **tueor**; *adj* safe, secure; cautious, prudent; *n* safe place, safety, shelter, security; **ex tuto** from a safe place, in safety, safely

tūtŏ *adv* safely, in safety

tu·us -a -um *adj* your; right for you, proper for you; *pron* yours; **tuā interest** it is of importance to you; **tui** your friends, your people, your family; **tuum est** (with *inf*) it is your duty to, it is up to you to

tuxtax *adv* (word meant to imitate the sound of blows) whack, wham; **tuxtax meo tergo erit** (coll) it's going to go whack, wham, bang over my back

Tȳd·eus -ĕī or **-ĕos** *m* Tydeus (*son of Oeneus, one of the Seven against Thebes, and father of Diomedes*)

Tȳdĭd·ēs -ae *m* Diomedes (*son of Tydeus*)

tympanotrīb·a -ae *m* timbrel player, drummer

tympăn·um or **typăn·um -ī** *n* timbrel, drum

Tyndăr·eus -ĕī or **Tyndăr·us -ī** *m* king of Sparta, husband of Leda, father of Castor and Clytemnestra, and reputed father of Pollux and Helen

Tyndarid·ēs -ae *m* descendant of Tyndareus

Tyndăr·is -ĭdis *f* descendant of Tyndareus (*female*)

Typhō·ēus -ĕi or **ĕos** or **Typh·ōn -ōnis** *m* giant who was struck with lightning by Jupiter and buried under Mount Etna

typ·us -ī *m* figure, image (*on the wall*)

tyrannactŏn·us -ī *m* tyrannicide, assassin of a tyrant

tyrannĭcē *adv* tyrannically; arbitrarily, cruelly

tyrannĭcīd·a -ae *m* tyrannicide, assassin of a tyrant

tyrannĭc·us -a -um *adj* tyrannical; arbitrary, cruel

tyrann·is -ĭdis *f* tyranny, despotism

tyrianthin·a -ōrum *n pl* violet-colored clothes

Tyri·us -a -um *adj* Tyrian, Phoeni-

cian; Carthaginian; Theban; crimson (*because of the famous dye produced at Tyre*); *m pl* Tyrians, Carthaginians

Tyr·ō -ūs *f* daughter of Salmoneus and mother of Pelias and Neleus by Poseidon

Tyr·os or **Tyr·us -ī** *f* Tyre (*famous commercial city of Phoenicia*)

tyrotarich·os -ī *m* dish of salted fish and cheese

Tyrrhēni·a -ae *f* Etruria

Tyrrhēnĭc·us -a -um *adj* Etrurian, Etruscan

Tyrrhēn·us -a -um *adj* Etrurian, Etruscan; *m pl* Etruscans (*Pelasgian people who migrated to Italy perhaps from Lydia in Asia Minor and settled to the N. of the Tiber*)

Tyrtae·us -ī *m* Spartan poet (7th cent. B.C.)

U

ŭb·er -ĕris *adj* rich, fruitful, fertile, plentiful, productive; rich, imaginative (*style*); (fig) fruitful, productive; *n* richness, fruitfulness, fertility; fertile soil, fruitful field; breast, teat; udder, dug

ŭberius *adv* more fully, more copiously, more fruitfully

ŭbert·ās -ātis *f* richness, fertility, productiveness

ŭbertim *adv* abundantly, copiously

ubī *adv* (interrog) where; **ubi gentium** (coll) where in the world; *conj* where, in which, whereby, with whom, by whom; when, whenever

ubĭcumque *adv* wherever, wheresoever; anywhere, everywhere

Ubĭ·ī -ōrum *m pl* German tribe on the lower Rhine

ubĭnam *adv* where; **ubĭnam gentium** (coll) where in the world

ubĭquāque *adv* everywhere

ubĭque *adv* anywhere, everywhere

ubĭŭbī *adv* wherever

ubīvīs *adv* anywhere, everywhere, wherever you please; **ubīvis gentium** (coll) anywhere in the world

ūd·us -a -um *adj* wet, moist, damp, humid

ulcĕr·ō -āre *vt* to make sore; (fig) to wound

ulcerōs·us -a -um *adj* full of sores, ulcerous

ulciscor ulciscī ultus sum *vt* to avenge oneself on, take vengeance on, punish; to avenge, requite, repay

ulc·us -ĕris *n* sore, ulcer

ūlīg·ō -ĭnis *f* moisture, dampness

Ulix·ēs -is or **-ēī** or **-ei** *m* Ulysses (*king of Ithaca, son of Laertes, hus-*

band of Penelope, and father of Telemachus and Telegonus)

ull·us -a -um *adj* any

ulmĕ·us -a -um *adj* elm, made of elm

ulmitrĭb·a -ae *m* (coll) slaphappy (*from being flogged with elm whips*)

ulm·us -ī *f* elm tree; *f pl* elm rods

uln·a -ae *f* elbow; arm; (as measure of length) ell

ulpĭc·um -ī *n* leek

ulteri·or -ūs *adj* farther, on the farther side, more remote; further, more, longer, in a higher degree; worse; *m pl* more remote people, those beyond; *n pl* things beyond

ultĭmum *adv* finally, for the last time

ultĭm·us -a -um *adj* farthest, most distant, extreme; earliest; latest; final, last; greatest; lowest; meanest; *n* last thing; end; **ad ultĭmum** to the end, to the extreme, in the highest degree, to the last degree, utterly; *n pl* extremes; the worst

ultĭ·ō -ōnis *f* vengeance, revenge

ult·or -ōris *m* avenger, punisher, revenger

ultrā *adv* beyond, farther, besides; *prep* (with *acc*) beyond, past; (of number, measure, degree) over, beyond, more than, over and above

ultr·ix īcis *adj* avenging

ultrō *adv* to the farther side, beyond; on the other side; besides, moreover, too; of one's own accord, without being asked; without being spoken to; **ultrō tribūta** expenditure incurred by the government for public works

ultus *pp* of **ulciscor**

ulŭl·a -ae f screech owl

ululāt·us -ūs m crying, wailing (esp. of mourners); war cry

ulŭl·ō -āre vt to cry out to; vi to shriek, yell; (of places) to ring, resound

ulv·a -ae f sedge

umbell·a -ae f umbrella, parasol

umbilīc·us -ī m navel, belly button; midriff; middle, center; projecting end of dowels on which books were rolled; cockle, sea snail

umb·ō -ōnis m boss (of a shield); shield; elbow

umbr·a -ae f shade, shadow; phantom, shade, ghost; mere shadow (of one's former self, etc.); shelter, cover; constant companion; grayling, umber (fish); rhetorica umbra rhetorician's school

umbrācŭl·um -ī n bower, arbor; school; umbrella, parasol

umbrātĭcŏl·a -ae m lounger, loafer (in the shade)

umbrātĭc·us -a -um adj too fond of the shade, lazy

umbrātĭl·is -e adj remaining in the shade, private, retired; academic

Umbrĭ·a -ae f Umbria (district in central Italy)

umbrĭf·er -ĕra -ĕrum adj shady

umbr·ō -āre vt to shade, cover

umbrōs·us -a -um adj shady

ūmect·ō -āre vt to wet, moisten

ūmect·us -a -um adj moist, damp

ūm·ĕō -ēre vi to be moist, be damp, be wet

umĕr·us -ī m shoulder

ūmesc·ō -ēre vi to become moist or wet

ūmidŭl·us -a -um adj dampish

ūmĭd·us -a -um adj moist, damp, wet; green (lumber); n wet place

ūm·or -ōris m moisture; liquid, fluid

umquam or unquam adv ever, at any time

ūnā adv together; ūnā venīre to come along

ūnanĭm·ans -antis adj of one mind, of one accord

ūnanĭmĭt·ās -ātis f unanimity

ūnanĭm·us -a -um adj unanimous; of one mind, of one heart, harmonious

ūncĭ·a -ae f a twelfth; ounce (one twelfth of a pound or libra)

ūnciārĭ·us -a -um adj containing a twelfth; faenus unciarium eight and one third percent interest per annum

ūnciātim adv little by little

uncĭnāt·us -a -um adj hooked, barbed

ūnciŏl·a -ae f a mere twelfth

unctĭ·ō -ōnis f rubdown; (fig) wrestling

unctĭt·ō -āre vt to keep rubbing with oil, keep oiling

unctiuscŭl·us -a -um adj somewhat too unctuous

·unct·or -ōris m anointer, rubdown man

unct·um -ī n sumptuous dinner; ointment

unctūr·a -ae f anointing

unct·us -a -um pp of ungo; adj greasy; resinous; sumptuous; n sumptuous dinner; ointment

unc·us -a -um adj hooked, crooked, barbed; m hook, clamp; grappling iron

und·a -ae f water; liquid; wave, billow; (fig) stream, tide, agitated mass

unde adv from where, whence; from whom; unde unde or undeunde from some place or other, somehow or other, by hook or by crook

undecĭens or undecĭēs adv eleven times

undĕcim (indecl) adj eleven

undecĭm·us -a -um adj eleventh

undecumque or undecunque adv from whatever place, from whatever source

undēn·ō -ae '-a adj eleven in a group, eleven each, eleven

undēnōnāgintā (indecl) adj eightynine

undeoctōgintā (indecl) adj seventynine

undēquadrāgintā (indecl) adj thirty-nine

undēquinquāgensĭm·us or undēquinquāgēsĭm·us -a -um adj forty-ninth

undēquinquāgintā (indecl) adj forty-nine

undēsexāgintā (indecl) adj fifty-nine

undētrīcensĭm·us or undētrīcēsĭm·us -a -um adj twenty-ninth

undēvīcēsĭmān·ī -ōrum m pl soldiers of the nineteenth legion

undēvīcēsĭm·us -a -um adj nineteenth

undēvīgintī (indecl) adj nineteen

undĭque adv from all directions, on all sides, everywhere; in all respects, completely

undisŏn·us -a -um adj sea-roaring; undisoni dei gods of the roaring waves

und·ō -āre vi to move in waves, undulate; to billow; to overflow

undōs·us -a -um adj full of waves, billowy

ūnetvīcensĭm·us or ūnetvīcēsĭm·us -a -um adj twenty-first

ūnetvīcēsĭmān·ī -ōrum m pl soldiers of the twenty-first legion

ungō or unguō ungĕre unxī unctum vt to oil, grease, anoint

ungu·en -ĭnis n fat, grease, ointment

unguentār·ius -ĭī or -ī m perfumer

unguentāt·us -a -um adj anointed; perfumed, wearing perfume

unguent·um -ī n ointment; perfume

unguicŭl·us -ī m fingernail; toenail; a teneris unguiculis from earliest childhood

ungu·is -ī m fingernail; toenail; claw, talon, hoof; ad unguen to a tee, complete, perfect; **de tenero ungui** from earliest childhood; **transversum unguem** a hair's breadth

ungŭl·a -ae f hoof, claw, talon; (fig) horse

unguō see **ungo**

ūnicē adv singularly, solely

ūnicŏl·or -ōris adj of one and the same color

ūnicorn·is -e adj one-horned

ūni·ous -a -um adj sole, only, single, singular, unique; uncommon, unparalleled, outstanding, unique

ūniform·is -e adj uniform

ūnigĕn·a -ae masc & fem adj only-begotten, only; of the same parentage

ūnimăn·us -a -um adj with one hand, one-handed

ūni·ō -ōnis m single large pearl

ūniter adv jointly, conjointly

ūniversāl·is -e adj universal

ūniversē adv generally, in general

ūniversit·ās -ātis f aggregate, entirety, whole; whole world, universe

ūnivers·us -a -um adj all together, all taken collectively, whole, entire; n the whole; whole world, universe; **in universum** on the whole, in general

ūnocŭl·us -ī m one-eyed person

ūnomammĭ·a -ae f (coll) single-breasted land (country of the Amazons)

unquam or **umquam** adv ever, at any time

ūn·us -a -um adj one; single, only, sole; one and the same; (indef) **a**, an, one, some; pron some one, a mere individual; **ad ūnum** to a man; **ūnus et alter** one or two; **ūnus quisque** every one individually, every single one

ūpĭli·ō or **ōpĭli·ō -ōnis** m shepherd

ūpŭp·a -ae f hoopoe; hoe, mattock

Ūrani·a -ae or **Ūrani·ē -ēs** f Muse of astronomy

urbānē adv politely, courteously; with sophistication; wittily, elegantly

urbānĭt·ās -ātis f living in the city, city life; refinement, politeness; sophistication; wit; raillery

urbān·us -a -um adj of the city, of the town, city, town; courteous; sophisticated; witty, facetious, humorous; forward, brash; m city man; city slicker

urbicăp·us -ī m conqueror of cities

urbs urbis f city; the city of Rome, the capital

urceŏl·us -ī m little pitcher, little pot

urcĕ·us -ī m pitcher, water pot

ūrēd·ō -ĭnis f blight (of plants)

urgeō urgēre ursī vt to prod on, urge, urge forward; to pressure, put pressure on (someone); to crowd, hem in; to follow up, keep at, stick by; vi to be pressing, be urgent; to be insistent

ūrīn·a -ae f urine

ūrīnāt·or -ōris m diver

ūrīn·ō -āre or **ūrīn·or -ārī -ātus sum** vi to dive

urn·a -ae f pot, jar; water pot; voting urn; urn of fate; cinerary urn; money jar

ūrō ūrĕre ussī ustum vt to burn; to burn up, reduce to ashes, consume; to scorch, parch, dry up; to sting, pain; to nip, frostbite; to rub sore; to corrode; to annoy, gall, burn up, make angry; to inflame (with love); kindle, set on fire

urnŭl·a -ae f small urn

urs·a -ae f she-bear

Urs·a Major (genit: **Urs·ae Major·is**) f Great Bear (constellation)

Urs·a Minor (genit: **Urs·ae Minor·is**) f Little Bear (constellation)

ursīn·us -a -um adj bear, bear's

urs·us -ī m bear

urtīc·a -ae f nettle; desire, itch

ūr·us -ī m wild ox

Usipĕt·ēs -um m pl German tribe on the Rhine

ūsitātē adv in the usual way, as usual

ūsitāt·us -a -um adj usual, customary, familiar; **usitatum est** (with inf) it is customary to

uspiam adv anywhere, somewhere; in any matter

usquam adv anywhere, in any place; anywhere, to any place

usque adv all the way, right on, straight on; all the time, continuously; even, as much as; **usque** (with **ab** + abl) all the way from; **usque** (with **ad** + acc) all the way to; **usque quaque** every moment, continually; on all occasions, in everything

ust·or -ōris m cremator

ustŭl·ō -āre vt to burn a little, scorch, singe; to burn up

ustus pp of **uro**

ūsū·capiō -capĕre -cēpī -captum vt (law) to acquire possession of, acquire ownership of (by long use, by prescription)

ūsūcapĭ·ō -ōnis f (law) acquisition of ownership through long use or long possession

ūsūr·a -ae f use, enjoyment; interest (on capital)

ūsūrārĭ·us -a -um adj for use and enjoyment; paying interest

ūsūrpātĭ·ō -ōnis f use; (with genit) making use of, use of

ūsūrp·ō -āre vt to make use of, use, employ, adopt, practice, exercise; (law) to take possession of, acquire; to seize wrongfully, usurp; to name, call, speak of; to adopt, assume; to perceive (with the senses), observe, experience

ūsus pp of **utor**

ūs·us -ūs m use, enjoyment; practice, employment; experience, skill; usage, custom; familiarity; usefulness, advantage, benefit; occasion, need, necessity; **ex usu esse** or **usui esse** (with *dat*) to be useful to, be beneficial to, be a good thing for; **si usus veniat** if the need should arise, if the opportunity should present itself; **usus adest** a good opportunity comes along; **usus est** (with *abl*) there is need of; **usus et fructus** use and enjoyment; **usu venit** it happens, it occurs

ūsusfructus (*genit*: **ūsūsfructūs**) *m* use and enjoyment

ut or **utī** *adv* how, in what way; *conj* (comparative) as; (adversative) although; (temporal) when, while; (purpose) in order that; (result) that; (concessive) granted that; (introducing examples) as, as for example; (after verbs of fearing) lest, that not; (introducing an explanation or reason) as, as being, inasmuch as; (introducing indirect commands) that

utcumque or **utcunque** *adv* however; whenever; one way or another

ūtensīl·is -e *adj* useful; *n pl* utensils, materials

ūt·er -ris *m* bag, skin, bottle

ut·er -ra -rum *adj* which (*of the two*); *pron* which one (*of the two*); one or the other

ut·ercumque -racumque -rumcumque *adj* whichever (*of the two*); *pron* whichever one (*of the two*)

ut·erlibet -ralibet -rumlibet *adj* whichever (*of the two*) you please; *pron* whichever one (*of the two*) you please, either one (*of the two*)

ut·erque -răque -rumque *adj* each (*of the two*), both; **sermones utriusque linguae** conversations in both languages; *pron* each one (*of the two*), both; **uterque insaniunt** both are insane

utĕr·us -ī *m* or **utĕr·um -ī** *n* womb; belly, paunch (*of a man*)

ut·ŏrvis -răvis -rumvis *adj* whichever (*of the two*) you please; either; *pron* whichever one (*of the two*) you please, either one

utī see ut

ūtibĭl·is -e *adj* useful, practical

Utic·a -ae *f* city in Africa, N.W. of Carthage, where the younger Cato committed suicide

Uticens·is -is *adj* of Utica, Utican

ūtĭl·is -e *adj* useful, profitable, expedient, practical; (with *dat* or **ad** + *acc*) fit for, useful for, practical in

ūtĭlĭt·ās -ātis *f* usefulness, advantage

ūtĭlĭter *adv* usefully, profitably

utĭnam *conj* (introducing a wish) if only ,would that

utĭque *adv* anyhow, at least, at any rate

ūtor ūtī ūsus sum *vi* (with *abl*) **a** to use, make use of; **b** to enjoy; **c** to practice, experience; **d** to enjoy the friendship or companionship of

utpŏte *conj* as, inasmuch as; **utpote qui** inasmuch as (*he is one*) who, inasmuch as he, because he

ūtrār·ĭus -ī or **-ī** *m* water carrier, water boy

utrimque or **utrinque** *adv* from or on both sides, on either side; **utrimque constitit fides** on both sides the word of honor held good, both parties kept their word

utrō *adv* to which of the two sides, in which direction

utrobĭque *adv* on both sides, on either hand

utrōlĭbet *adv* to either side

utrŏque *adv* to both places, in both directions

utrŭbi or **utrŭbī** *adv* at or on which of two sides

utrubĭque *adv* on both sides, on either hand

utrum *conj* either; whether

utut or **ut ut** *adv* however, in whatever way

ūv·a -ae *f* grape; bunch or cluster of grapes; vine; cluster of bees

ūvesc·ō -ĕre *vi* to become moist; (fig) to get drunk

ūvĭdŭl·us -a -um *adj* moist

ūvĭd·us -a -um *adj* wet, moist, damp, humid; drunken

ux·or -ōris *f* wife; mate (*of animals*)

uxorcŭl·a -ae *f* dear little wife

uxōri·us -a -um *adj* of a wife, wifely; very fond of a wife; henpecked

V

vac·ans -antis *adj* vacant, unoccupied; at leisure, unemployed; unengaged, single; (with *abl*) lacking, without; *n pl* unoccupied estates

vacātĭ·ō -ōnis *f* freedom, exemption (*from duty, service, etc.*); exemption from military service; payment for exemption from military service

vacc·a -ae *f* cow

vaccīn·ĭum -ī ī or **-ī** *n* hyacinth

vaccŭl·a -ae *f* heifer

vacē·fīō -fiĕrī -factus sum *vi* to become empty, be emptied

vacill·ō -āre *vi* to stagger, reel; to vacillate, waver; to be untrustworthy

vacīvē *adv* at leisure

vacīvĭt·ās -ātis *f* want, lack

vacīv·us or **vocīv·us -a -um** *adj* empty; free; (with *genit*) free of, void of, free from

vac·ō -āre *vi* to be empty, be vacant,

be unoccupied; to be free, be care-free; to be at leisure, have free time; (with *abl* or **ab** + *abl*) to be free from; (with *dat* or with **ad** or **in** + *acc*) to be free for, have time for; *v impers* there is time, room, leisure; (with *inf*) there is time to or for

vacuāt·us -a -um *adj* empty

vacuē·faciō -facere -fēcī -factum *vt* to empty, clear, free

vacuit·ās -ātis *f* freedom, exemption; vacancy (*in an office*)

vacu·ō -āre *vt* to empty, clear, free

vacu·us -a -um *adj* empty, clear, free; vacant; worthless, useless; single, unmarried; widowed; at leisure; carefree; (with *genit* or *abl* or with **ab** + *abl*) free from, devoid of, without; (with *dat*) free for

vadimōn·ium -iī or **-ī** *n* (law) promise (*to appear in court*), bail (*given as a guarantee of one's appearance in court*); **vadimonium deserere** to default, fail to show up in court; **vadimonium differre** to postpone appearance in court, grant a continuance; **vadimonium facere** to put up bail; **vadimonium sistere** to appear in court

vād·ō -ere *vi* to go, make one's way, advance

vad·or -ārī -ātus sum *vt* to put (*someone*) under bail

vadōs·us -a -um *adj* shallow

vad·um -ī *n* shallow place, shallow, shoal, ford; body of water, stream, sea; bottom, depths

vae *interj* woe! (with *acc* or *dat*) woe to

vaf·er -ra -rum *adj* sly, cunning; subtle

vafrē *adv* slyly, cunningly

vagē *adv* far and wide

vāgin·a -ae *f* sheath, scabbard; sheath (*of ear of grain*), hull, husk; vagina

vāg·iō -īre -īvī -ī *vi* (esp. of an infant) to cry; (of swine) to squeal

vāgīt·us -ūs *m* cry; bleating

vāg·or -ōris *m* cry, wail (*of an infant*)

vag·or -ārī -ātus sum or **vag·ō -āre** *vi* to wander, range, roam

vag·us -a -um *adj* wandering, ranging, roaming; unsteady, inconstant; vague, uncertain

vah *interj* ah!, oh!

valdē *adv* greatly, intensely; (with *adj* or *adv*) very; (as affirmative reply) yes, certainly; to be sure

valē *interj* good-bye

val·ens -entis *adj* strong, powerful; healthy, hale, well

valenter *adv* strongly; energetically

valentul·us -a -um *adj* a strong little

val·eō -ēre -uī *vi* to be strong, be vigorous; to be powerful, be effective; to avail, prevail, succeed; to be influential; to be valid; to be strong enough, be adequate, be ca-

pable, be able; to be of value, be of worth; to mean, signify; **te valere jubeo** I bid you farewell, good-by to you; **vale!** or **valete!** good-bye! **vale dicere** to say good-bye, take leave

valesc·ō -ere *vi* to grow strong, acquire strength, thrive

valētūdinār·ium -iī or **-ī** *n* hospital

valētūd·ō -inis *f* state of health; good health; ill health, illness

valg·us -a -um *adj* bowlegged

validē *adv* strongly, vehemently; (in replies) of course, certainly, definitely

valid·us -a -um *adj* strong, powerful, able; healthy, robust; fortified; influential; efficacious

vallār·is -e *adj* (decoration) awarded for scaling a rampart

vall·ēs or **vall·is -is** *f* valley

vall·ō -āre *vt* to fortify with a rampart, wall in; to protect, defend

vall·um -ī *n* rampart, palisade, entrenchment; protection

val·us -ī *m* stake, pale; rampart with palisades, stockade; tooth (*of a comb*)

valv·ae -ārum *f pl* folding doors, double doors

vanesc·ō -ere *vi* to vanish, fade, disappear

vānidīc·us -a -um *adj* lying, boasting; *m* liar, boaster

vāniloquenti·a -ae *f* empty talk

vāniloquidōr·us -ī *m* liar

vāniloqu·us -a -um *adj* talking nonsense; lying, boasting, bragging

vānit·ās -ātis *f* falsity, unreality, deception, untruth; boasting, lying; vanity, conceit; worthlessness, frivolity, fickleness

vānitūd·ō -inis *f* falsehood

vann·us -ī *f* fan, winnowing fan

vān·us -a -um *adj* empty, vacant; groundless, pointless; hollow, unreal; lying, false; boastful, conceited, vain; *n* emptiness, uselessness, deceptive appearance

vapidē *adv* poorly, badly

vapid·us -a -um *adj* flat, vapid, spoiled, bad; morally corrupt

vap·or -ōris *m* vapor, steam, smoke; exhalation, warmth, heat

vapōrār·ium -iī or **-ī** *n* steam pipe

vapōr·ō -āre *vt* to steam, steam up; to warm, heat; *vi* to steam, smoke

vapp·a -ae *f* sour wine; spoiled lad, good-for-nothing

vāpulār·is -e *adj* in for a flogging

vāpul·ō -āre *vi* to get a beating; (of savings, etc.) (fig) to take a beating

varianti·a -ae *f* diversity, variations

variāti·ō -ōnis *f* variation, difference

vāric·ō -āre *vt* to straddle

varicōs·us -a -um *adj* varicose

vāric·us -a -um *adj* with legs wide apart

variē *adv* variously, in various ways, differently

variět·ās -ātis f variety, difference, diversity; vicissitudes; inconstancy

vari·ō -āre vt to diversify, vary, change, make different; to variegate; vi to change color; to vary, differ, change; to differ in opinion; to waver

vari·us -a -um adj colored, variegated, spotted, striped; different, varying, various, changeable; versatile; inconstant, unsteady, untrustworthy

Var·ius -iī or **-ī** m epic and tragic poet and friend of Virgil and Horace (d. c. 12 B.C.)

var·ix -icis f varicose vein

Varr·ō -ōnis m M. Terentius Varro (*Roman antiquarian and philologist whose wide erudition earned him the title of the most learned of the Romans,* 116-27 B.C.)

văr·us -a -um adj knock-kneed; bent, crooked; opposed, contrary

vas vadis m bail, surety

vās vāsis or **vās·um -ī** (*pl:* **vās·a -ōrum**) n vessel, dish; utensil, implement; n pl equipment, gear; **va-sa conclamare** (mil) to give the signal to pack the gear

vāsār·ium -iī or **-ī** n allowance for furnishings (*given to a provincial governor*)

vasculār·ius -iī or **-ī** m metal worker; goldsmith

vascul·um -ī n small vessel

vastāti·ō -ōnis f devastation, ravaging

vastāt·or -ōris m devastator, ravager

vastē adv vastly, widely; coarsely, harshly; violently

vastific·us -a -um adj devastating

vastit·ās -ātis f wasteland, desert; state of desolation, emptiness; devastation, destruction; vastness, immensity; (fig) destroyer

vastiti·ēs -ēī f ruin, destruction

vast·ō -āre vt to make empty, make desolate, vacate, empty; (mil) to lay waste, ravage, devastate, destroy

vast·us -a -um adj empty, deserted, desolate; ravaged, devastated; vast, enormous; uncouth, rude, uncultivated, clumsy

vāt·ēs -is m soothsayer, prophet; bard, poet; f prophetess; poetess

Vătīcăn·us -a -um adj Vatican; **mons** or **collis Vaticanus** hill in Rome on the right bank of the Tiber

văticināti·ō -ōnis f prophesying, prediction, soothsaying

văticināt·or -ōris m prophet, soothsayer

văticīn·ium -iī or **-ī** n prediction, prophecy

văticīn·us -a -um adj prophetic

văticīn·or -ārī -ātus sum vt to foretell, prophesy; to keep harping on; vi to prophesy; to rant and rave, talk wildly

vatill·um -ī n brazier

-ve conj (enclitic) or; **-ve ... -ve** either ... or

vēcordī·a -ae f senselessness; insanity, madness

vēc·ors -ordis adj senseless; foolish; mad

vectīg·al -ālis n tax, toll, tariff; revenue, income (*of an individual*); honorarium (*given to a magistrate*)

vectīgāl·is -e adj tax, toll, tariff; paying tribute, subject to taxes, taxable, taxed; **pecunia vectigalis** tax money, tribute

vecti·ō -ōnis f conveyance, transporting

vect·is -is m crowbar, lever; bar, bolt (*on a door or gate*)

vect·ō -āre vt to carry around; **vectari** to keep riding around

vect·or -ōris m bearer, carrier; rider, passenger

vectōri·us -a -um adj transportation, of transportation; **navigia vectoria** transport ships, transports

vectūr·a -ae f transport, transportation, conveyance; freight costs; fare

vectus pp of **veho**

Vēdiŏv·is or **Vējŏv·is -is** m Anti-Jove (*Etruscan divinity of the lower world, identified with Apollo and with the Jupiter of the lower world*); Little Jove (*identified with the infant Jupiter*)

vegět·us -a -um adj lively, vigorous, vivacious

vēgrand·is -e adj not huge, small

vehěm·ens -entis adj vehement, violent, impetuous, ardent; great, tremendous; vigorous, active

vehementer or **vēmenter** adv vehemently, impetuously, violently, eagerly

vehementī·a -ae f vehemence

vehicŭl·um -ī n vehicle, carriage, cart; vessel, ship

vehō vehěre vexī vectum vt to carry, convey, transport; **vehi** to ride, sail, be borne along

Vei·ens -entis or **Veientān·us -a -um** adj of Veii

Vei·ī -ōrum m pl old Etrurian city about twelve miles from Rome, captured by Camillus (396 B.C.)

vel adv even, actually; perhaps; for instance; conj or, or perhaps; or rather; **vel ... vel** either ... or

Vēlābr·um -ī n low ground between the Capitoline and Palatine

vēlām·en -inis n drape, covering, veil; clothing, robe

vēlāment·um -ī n curtain, veil; n pl olive branches draped with woolen fillets

vēlār·ium -iī or **-ī** n awning (*over the open-air theater*)

vēlăt·ī -ōrum m pl (mil) reserves

vēl·es -itis m light-armed soldier; skirmisher

vēlif·er -ěra -ěrum adj sail, sailing;

carīna velifera sail boat, sailing ship

vēlificātī·ō -ōnis f sailing

vēlific·ō -āre or **vēlific·or -ārī -ātus sum** vt to sail through; vi to sail; (with dat) (fig) to be under full sail toward, be hell-bent for (e.g., high office)

Velīn·us -ī m river and lake in the Sabine territory

vēlitār·is -e adj of the light-armed troops

vēlitātī·ō -ōnis f skirmishing

vēlitēs = pl of **veles**

vēlīt·or -ōris m skirmisher

vēlivŏl·us -a -um adj sail-flying (ship); sail-covered (sea)

vellĭc·ō -āre vt to pluck, pinch, nip; to carp at, rail at

vellō vellĕre vellī (or **vulsī**) **vulsum** (or **volsum**) vt to pluck, pull, tear at, tear away, tear out; to tear up, tear down, destroy

vell·us -ĕris n fleece; skin, pelt; wool; m pl fleecy clouds

vēl·ō -āre vt to veil, wrap, envelop, cover, cover up; to encircle, crown; to cover up, hide, conceal

vēlōcĭt·ās -ātis f speed, velocity

vēlōcĭter adv speedily, swiftly

vēl·ox -ōcis adj speedy, swift

vēl·um -ī n sail; veil, curtain, awning, covering; **vela dare** or **vela facere** to set sail; **remis velisque** with might and main

velut or **velutī** conj as, just as, even as; as for example; (to introduce a simile) as, as it were; (in elliptical clauses) like; **velut** or **velut sī** just as if, just as though, as if, as though

vēmens see **vehemens**

vēn·a -ae f vein, artery; vein of metal; water course; vein (in wood, stone, etc.); natural bent or disposition, genius; penis; strength; f pl (fig) heart, core

vēnābŭl·um -ī n hunting spear

Venāfrān·us -a -um adj of Venafrum

Venāfr·um -ī n town in S. central Italy

vēnālici·us -a -um adj for sale; m slave dealer; n pl merchandise, imports and exports

vēnāl·is -e adj for sale; open to bribes; mf slave offered for sale

vēnātĭc·us -a -um adj hunting

vēnātĭ·ō -ōnis f hunt, hunting; wild-beast show; game

vēnāt·or -ōris m hunter

vēnātōri·us -a -um adj hunter's

vēnātr·ix -īcis f huntress

vēnātūr·a -ae f hunting

vēnāt·us -ūs m hunting

vendibĭl·is -e adj salable; attractive, popular, acceptable, on sale

venditātĭ·ō -ōnis f boasting, showing off

venditĭ·ō -ōnis f sale

venditō -āre vt to try to sell; to advertise; to give as a bribe; **se**

venditāre (with dat) to ingratiate oneself with

vendĭt·or -ōris m vendor, seller; recipient of a bribe

vend·ō -ĕre -ĭdī -ĭtum vt to put up for sale; to sell, vend; to sell (someone) out, betray; to advertise; to praise, recommend

venēfĭc·a -ae f poisoner; sorceress, witch; (term of abuse) hag, witch

venēfĭc·ium -ĭī or **-ī** n poisoning, witchcraft, magic

venēfĭc·us -a -um adj poisoning, poisonous; magic; m poisoner; sorcerer, magician

venēnāt·us -a -um adj poisonous, venomous; filled with poison; magic; bewitched, enchanted; (fig) venomous, bitter

venēnĭf·er -ĕra -ĕrum adj poisonous, venemous

venēn·ō -āre vt to poison; (fig) to poison, injure by slander

venēn·um -ī n poison; drug, potion; magic charm; sorcery; ruin, destruction

vēn·ĕō -īre -ĭī -ĭtum vi to go up for sale, be sold

venerābĭl·is -e adj venerable

venerābund·us -a -um adj reverent, reverential

venerand·us -a -um adj venerable

venerātĭ·ō -ōnis f veneration, reverence, great respect

venerāt·or -ōris m respecter, adorer; admirer

Venĕr·us or **Veneri·us -a -um** adj of Venus; of sexual love, venereal; m Venus-throw (best throw in playing dice); m pl attendants in Venus's temple

venĕr·or -ārī -ātus sum vt to venerate, revere, worship, pray to; to implore, beg; to pray for

Venĕt·ī -ōrum m pl a people in N.E. Italy in the region around modern Venice

Venetĭ·a -ae f district of the Veneti

Venetĭc·us -a -um adj Venetian

Venĕt·us -a -um adj Venetian; bluish; m Venetian; a Blue (i.e., a member of one of the racing factions in Rome which were called Blues, Greens, etc.)

veni·a -ae f kindness, favor, goodwill; permission; pardon, forgiveness; **veniam dare** (with dat) to grant forgiveness to, to do a favor to, grant permission to; **veniam petere** to ask for permission; **veniā vestrā** with your leave

venĭō venīre vēnī ventum vi to come; (with in + acc) a to come into, enter into (e.g., agreement, friendship); b to fall into (e.g., trouble, disgrace)

vēn·or -ārī -ātus sum vt & vi to hunt

vent·er -ris m stomach, belly; womb; embryo, unborn child; belly, protuberance; appetite; gluttony

ventĭl·ō -āre vt to fan, wave; to display, show off

ventĭ·ō -ōnis f coming

ventĭt·ō -āre vi to keep coming, come regularly

ventōs·us -a -um adj windy, full of wind; of the wind; wind-like, swift as the wind; conceited; fickle

ventrĭcŭl·us -ī m belly; ventricle (of the heart)

ventriōs·us -a -um adj pot-bellied

ventŭl·us -ī m breeze

vent·us -ī m wind

vēnŭcŭl·a -ae f grape (of the type well suited for preserving)

vēnum (genit not in use; dat: **vēnō**) n sale, that which is for sale; **venum** or **veno dare** to sell, sell as a slave; **venum** or **veno dari** to be sold; **venum** or **veno ire** to go up for sale, be sold

vēnum·dō or **vēnun·dō -dare -dō̆dī -dātum** vt to put up for sale, sell

ven·us -ĕris f beauty, charm; pleasure of love, sexual indulgence, mating; beloved, love

Vĕn·us -ĕris f Venus (goddess of love and beauty; planet); Venus-throw (highest throw of the dice)

Venŭsĭ·a -ae f town in Apulia, the birthplace of Horace

Venŭsīn·us -a -um adj of Venusia

venust·ās -ātis f beauty, charm, attraction

venustē adv prettily, charmingly

venustŭl·us -a -um adj cute, pretty, charming little

venust·us -a -um adj beautiful, charming, attractive

vēpallĭd·us -a -um adj very pale

veprēcŭl·a -ae f little brier bush

vepr·ēs -is m thorn bush, bramble bush

vēr vēris n spring, springtime; youth

vērātr·um -ī n hellebore

vēr·ax -ācis adj truthful

verbēn·a -ae f vervain; f pl sacred branches worn by heralds and priests

verb·er -ĕris n scourge, rod, whip; flogging, scourging; thong (of a sling and similar weapons); n pl strokes, flogging

verberābilissŭm·us -a -um adj altogether deserving of a flogging

verberātĭ·ō -ōnis f flogging

verberĕ·us -a -um adj deserving of a flogging

verber̆·ō -āre vt to scourge, flog, whip; to batter, beat

verber̆·ō -ōnis m rascal

verbōsē adv verbosely

verbōs·us -a -um adj verbose, wordy

verb·um -ī n word; saying, expression; verb; proverb; mere words; formula; **ad verbum** word for word, verbatim; **verba dare** (with dat) to cheat (someone); **verba facere** to speak, make a

---

speech; **verbi causā** or **verbi gratiā** for instance; **verbo** orally; in a word, briefly; nominally, in name only; in theory; **verbum de verbo**, **verbum pro verbo**, **verbum verbo** word for word

Vercingetŏr·ix -ĭgis m famous leader of the Arverni in the Gallic War

vercŭl·um -ī n (term of endearment) sweet springtime

vērē adv really, truly

verēcundē adv bashfully, shyly, modestly

verēcundĭ·a -ae f bashfulness, shyness, modesty; respect, awe, reverence; sense of shame, feeling of disgrace, disgrace, shame

verēcund·or -ārī vi to be bashful, be shy, feel ashamed

verēcund·us -a -um adj bashful, shy, modest, reserved

verēd·us -ī m fast hunting horse

verend·us -a -um adj venerable; n pl the private parts

ver·eor -ērī -ĭtus sum vt to revere, have respect for, respect; to fear; vi to feel uneasy, be apprehensive, be afraid, be anxious; (with genit) to stand in awe of, be afraid of; (with dat) to be afraid for; (with **dē + abl**) to be apprehensive about; (with **ut**) to be afraid that not; (with **ne**) to be afraid that

verētr·um -ī n the private parts

Vergilĭ·ae -ārum f pl Pleiads

Vergil·ĭus or **Virgil·ĭus -ĭī** or **-ī** m Virgil (P. Vergilius Maro, famous epic poet of the Augustan Age, 70-19 B.C.)

verg·ō -ĕre vt to turn, incline; vi to turn, incline; to decline; to lie, be situated; (with **ad + acc**) a to verge toward; **b** to face, face toward

vērĭdĭc·us -a -um adj truthful, speaking the truth; truly spoken

vērīsimĭl·is -e adj probable, likely; realistic

vērīsimĭlitūd·ō -ĭnis f probability, likelihood

vērĭt·ās -ātis f truth, truthfulness; the truth, the real facts; real life, reality; honesty, integrity; correctness (in etymology or grammar); **ex veritate** in accordance with the truth

vēriverb·ĭum -ĭī or **-ī** n truthfulness

vermĭcŭlāt·us -a -um adj inlaid with wavy lines, vermiculated

vermĭcŭl·us -ī m grub worm

vermĭn·a -um n pl stomach pains

verm·is -is m worm

vern·a -ae m or f slave (born in the master's house), home-born slave; native

vernācŭl·us -a -um adj of home-born slaves; native, domestic; m pl jesters

vernīl·is -e adj slavish, servile; pert, smart

vernīlĭt·ās -ātis f slavishness, subservience; pertness

verniliter adv slavishly

vern·ō -āre vi to show signs of spring; to burgeon, break into bloom; to be young

vernŭl·a -ae m or f little home-born slave, young home-born slave; native

vern·us -a -um adj spring; **tempus vernum** springtime

vērō adv in truth, in fact; certainly, to be sure; even; however

Verōn·a -ae f city in N. Italy, the birthplace of Catullus and of Pliny the Elder

Vērōnens·is -e adj Veronese

verp·a -ae f penis

verp·us -ī m circumcised man

verr·ēs -is m boar, pig

Verr·ēs -is m C. Cornelius Verres (notorious for outrageous conduct in governing Sicily in 73-70 B.C.)

verrīn·us -a -um adj of a boar, boar, hog, pork

verrō verrēre verrī versum vt to pull, drag, drag away, carry off; to sweep, scour, brush; (of the wind) to whip across, sweep (the land)

verrūc·a -ae f wart (on the body); small failing, minor blemish

verrūcōs·us -a -um adj full of warts; (fig) faulty, full of blemishes

verrunc·ō -āre vi to turn out well

versābil·is -e adj shifting, movable

versābund·us -a -um adj revolving

versātil·is -e adj capable of turning, revolving, movable; versatile

versicŏl·or -ōris adj changing color, of various colors

versicŭl·us -ī m short line, single line (of verse or prose), versicle; m pl poor little verses

versificāt·or -ōris m versifier

versipell·is -e adj changing appearance, of changed appearance; sly; m werwolf

vers·ō or **vors·ō -āre** vt to keep turning, twist, wind; to roll; to bend, shift; to move about, agitate; to disturb, harass; to handle; to consider

vers·or or **vors·or -ārī -ātus sum** vi to live, stay; (with **in** + abl) to be involved in, be engaged in, be busy with

versum or **vorsum** adv (usually after another adv of direction) back; **rusum vorsum** backward; **sursum versum** up and down

versūr·a or **vorsūr·a -ae** f rotation; loan (of money to pay another debt); **versuram facere** (with **ab** + abl) to get a loan from (someone to pay another); **versurā solvere** to pay off (another debt) with borrowed money

versus pp of **verro** and of **verto**

vers·us or **vors·us -ūs** m turning; furrow; line, row; line, verse; line (in writing); turn, step (in a dance)

versus or **vorsus** adv (with **ad** + acc) towards, in the direction of; (with **in** + acc) into, in towards;

si in urbem versus venturi erunt if they intend to come into the city; **sursum versus** upwards

versūtē adv cunningly

versūti·ae -ārum f pl cunning

versūtilŏqu·us -a -um adj smooth-speaking, sly

versūt·us or **vorsūt·us -a -um** adj clever, shrewd, ingenious; sly, crafty, cunning, deceitful

vert·ex or **vort·ex -ĭcis** m whirlpool, eddy, strong current; whirlwind, tornado; crown or top of the head; head; top, summit (of mountain); pole (of the heavens); **ex vertice** from above

verticōs·us or **vorticōs·us -a -um** adj swirling, full of whirlpools

vertīg·ō -ĭnis f turning, whirling; dizziness

vert·ō or **vort·ō vertĕre vertī versum** vt to turn, turn around; to invert, tilt; to change, alter, transform; to overturn, overthrow, destroy; to ascribe, impute; to translate; **se vertere** or **verti** (with **in** + acc) to change into, change oneself into; **verti** (with **in** + abl) a to be in (a place or condition); **b** to be engaged in, be involved in; vi to turn; to change; to turn out; (with **in** + abl) to center upon, depend upon

Vertumn·us -ī m god of the changing seasons

ver·ū -ūs n spit (for roasting); javelin, dart

verŭīn·a -ae f small javelin

vērum adv truly, yes; true but; but in fact; but yet, but even; yet, still; **verum tamen** or **verumtamen** nevertheless, but yet

vēr·us -a -um adj true, actual, genuine, real; fair, reasonable; n truth, the truth, reality; honor, duty, right; **veri similis** probable; realistic; **veri similitūdo** probability

verūt·um -ī n dart, javelin

verūt·us -a -um adj armed with a dart or a javelin

verv·ex -ēcis m wether, castrated hog; (term of abuse) muttonhead

vēsāni·a -ae f insanity, madness

vēsāni·ens -entis adj furious

vēsān·us -a -um adj insane, mad; furious, savage, raging

vesc·or -ī vi (with abl) to feed on, eat, feast on, enjoy

vesc·us -a -um adj nibbled off; little, feeble; corroding, consuming

vēsīc·a or **vensīc·a -ae** f bladder; bombast; objects made of bladder; purse, cap, football, lantern

vēsīcŭl·a -ae f little bladder; little bag

vesp·a -ae f wasp

Vespasiān·us -ī m Vespasian (T. Flavius Vespasianus Sabinus, Roman emperor, 70-79 A.D., and father of Domitian and Titus)

vesp·er -ĕris or **-ĕrī** m evening; supper; the West; **ad vesperum**

towards evening; **primo vespere** early in the evening; **sub vesperum** towards evening; **tam vesperi** so late in the evening; **vespere** or **vesperi** in the evening

vesper·a -ae f evening

vesperasco·ō -āre vi to become evening, grow towards evening; to get late

vespertīlī·ō -ōnis m bat

vespertīn·us -a -um adj evening, in the evening; eastern

vesperūg·ō -inis f evening star

vespill·ō -ōnis m undertaker

Vest·a -ae f Roman goddess of the hearth

Vestāl·is -e adj Vestal, of Vesta, Vesta's; f Vestal, Vestal virgin

vest·er or **vost·er -ra -rum** adj (in addressing more than one person) your; pron yours; **voster** your master; your own stock or lineage

vestibūl·um -ī n entrance, forecourt; beginning

vestīg·ium -ī or **-ī** n footstep, step; footprint, track; trace, vestige; moment, instant

vestīg·ō -āre vt to track, trace; to check, find out

vestiment·um -ī n garment, clothes

vest·iō -īre -īvī or **-ī -ītum** vt to dress, clothe; to adorn, deck, array, attire; (fig) to dress, clothe

vestiplic·a -ae f laundress

vest·is -is f garment, clothing; coverlet, tapestry; blanket; slough, skin (of a snake); **mutare vestem** to change one's clothes; to put on mourning clothes

vestispic·a -ae f wardrobe woman

vestīt·us -ūs m clothes, clothing, dress, apparel, attire; ornament (of speech); **mutare vestitum** to put on mourning clothes; **redire ad suum vestitum** to end the mourning period

veter·a -um n pl tradition, antiquity

veterān·us -a -um adj & m veteran

veter·ascō -āscere -āvī vi to grow old

veterāt·or -ōris m old hand, expert; sly old fox

veterātōriē adv cunningly, slyly

veterātōri·us -a -um adj cunning, sly

veter·ēs -um m pl the ancients; ancient authors

veterīn·us -a -um adj of burden; f pl & n pl beasts of burden

veternōs·us -a -um adj lethargic, sleepy, drowsy

vetern·us -ī m lethargy; old age; drowsiness; listlessness

vetit·um -ī n prohibition

vet·ō or **vot·ō -āre -uī** or **-āvī -itum** vt to forbid, prohibit, oppose

vetūl·us -a -um adj poor old

vet·us -ĕris adj old, aged; longstanding; m pl see **veteres**; n pl see **vetera**

vetust·ās -ātis f age; ancient times, antiquity; long duration, great age

vetust·us -a -um adj old, ancient; old-time, old-fashioned, good old (days, etc.); antiquated

vexām·en -inis n shaking, quaking

vexātī·ō -ōnis f shaking, jolting, tossing; distress

vexāt·or -ōris m jostler; harasser; troublemaker

vexillār·ius -ī or **-ī** m standard-bearer, ensign; m pl special reserves

vexill·um -ī n standard, ensign, flag (esp. the red flag hoisted above the general's tent as a signal for battle); troops; **vexillum praeponere** to hoist the red flag (as a signal for battle)

vex·ō -āre vt to shake, toss; to vex, annoy; to harass (troops), attack

vi·a -ae f way, road, street, highway; march, journey; method; right way, right method; **inter vias** on the road

viāl·is -e adj highway

viāri·us -a -um adj for highway maintenance

viāticāt·us -a -um adj provided with traveling money

viātic·us -a -um adj for a trip, for traveling, travel; n travel allowance, provisions for the journey; (mil) soldiers' saving fund

viāt·or -ōris m traveler; passenger; (law) summoner

vīb·ix -icis f weal, welt (from a blow)

vibr·ō -āre vt to brandish, shake, wave around; to hurl, fling; vi to vibrate, quiver; (of the tongue) to flick

viburn·um -ī n wayfaring tree, guelder rose

vīcān·us -a -um adj village; m pl villagers

Vic·a Pot·a (genit: **Vic·ae Pot·ae**) f goddess of victory

vicāri·us -a -um adj substituted; m substitute, deputy, proxy; underslave (kept by another slave)

vīcātim adv from street to street; from village to village; in hamlets

vice prep (with genit) on account of; like, after the manner of

vicem adv in turn; prep (with genit) instead of, in place of; on account of; like, after the manner of

vīcēnāri·us -a -um adj of the number twenty

vīcēn·ī -ae -a adj twenty each, twenty in a group

vīcēsimān·ī -ōrum m pl soldiers of the twentieth legion

vīcēsimāri·us -a -um adj derived from the five-percent tax

vīcēsim·us -a -um adj twentieth; f five-percent tax

vici·a -ae f vetch

viciens or **viciēs** adv twenty times

vīcīnāl·is -e adj neighboring, nearby

vīcīni·a -ae f neighborhood, nearness, proximity

vīcīnit·ās -ātis f neighborhood, proximity; the neighborhood (i.e., the neighbors) vīcīn·us -a -um *adj* neighboring, nearby, near; *mf* neighbor; *n* neighborhood

vicis (*genit;* the *nom* does not occur; *acc:* vicem; *abl:* vice) *f* change, interchange, alteration, succession; return, recompense, retaliation; fortune, misfortune, condition, fate, changes of fate; duty, office, position; function, office; **in vicem** or **invicem** by turns, alternately, mutually; **in vicem** or **invicem** (with *genit*) instead of, in place of; **in vicis** by turns, alternately, mutually

vicissim or vicissātim *adv* in turn, again

vicissitūd·ō -inis *f* change, interchange, alternation

victim·a -ae *f* victim; sacrifice

victimār·ius -iī or -ī *m* assistant at sacrifices

victit·ō -āre *vi* to live, subsist; (with *abl*) to live on, subsist on

vict·or -ōris *m* conqueror; (in apposition) victor exercitus victorious army

victōriāt·us -ī *m* silver coin stamped with the image of victory

Victōriŏl·a -ae *f* small statue of Victory

victr·ix -īcis *f* or *n* conqueror, victor

victus *pp* of vinco

vict·us -ūs *m* living, means of livelihood; way of life

vīcŭl·us -ī *m* hamlet

vīc·us -ī *m* village, hamlet; ward, quarter (*in a town or city*); street, alley (*running through the quarter*)

vidēlicet *adv* clearly, evidently; (in irony) of course, naturally; (in explanations) namely

viden = vidēsne? do you see?, do you get it?

vidĕō vidēre vīdī vīsum *vt* to see, look at; to know; to consider; to understand, realize; (with ut) to see to it that, take care that; vidĕrī to seem, appear, seem right, seem good

vidŭ·a -ae *f* widow; spinster

vidŭit·ās -ātis *f* bereavement; want, lack; widowhood

vīdŭl·us -ī *m* leather travel bag, suitcase, knapsack

vidŭ·ō -āre *vt* to deprive, bereave; (with *genit* or *abl*) to deprive of, bereave of; viduata left a widow

vidŭ·us -a -um *adj* bereft, destitute; unmarried; (with *abl* or **ab** + *abl*) bereft of, destitute of, without; *f* see vidua

viĕt·or -ōris *m* cooper

viĕt·us -a -um *adj* shriveled

vig·ĕō -ēre -uī *vi* to thrive, be vigorous, flourish

vig·escō -escĕre -uī *vi* to become vigorous, gain strength, become lively

vīgēsim·us -a -um *adj* twentieth

vig·il -ilis *adj* awake, wakeful; alert, on one's toes; *m* watchman,

guard, sentinel

vigil·ans -antis *adj* watchful, alert; disquieting (*worries*)

vigilanter *adv* vigilantly, alertly

vigilanti·a -ae *f* wakefulness; alertness

vigil·ax -ācis *adj* alert; sleep-disturbing, disquieting (*worries*)

vigili·a -ae *f* wakefulness, sleeplessness, insomnia; standing guard; guards, sentinels; vigil; vigilance, alertness

vigil·ō -āre *vt* to spend (*the night*) awake; to make, do, perform, write (*something*) while awake at night; *vi* to remain awake, stay awake; to be alert; (with *dat*) to be attentive to

vīgintī (indecl) *adj* twenty

vīgintivirāt·us -ūs *m* membership on a board of twenty

vīgintivir·ī -ōrum *m pl* twenty-man board or commission

vig·or -ōris *m* vigor, liveliness, energy

vīlic·a -ae *f* foreman's wife, manager's wife

vīlic·ō -āre *vi* to be a foreman, be a manager

vīlic·us -ī *m* foreman, manager (*of an estate*)

vīl·is -e *adj* cheap, inexpensive; cheap, mean, common, worthless

vīlit·ās -ātis *f* lowness of price, cheapness, low price; worthlessness

vīliter *adv* cheaply

vīll·a -ae *f* villa, country home, farm

vīllic- = vīlic-

vīllōs·us -a -um *adj* hairy, shaggy

vīllŭl·a -ae *f* small villa

vīll·um -ī *n* drop of wine

vīll·us -ī *m* hair, fleece; nap (*of cloth*)

vīm·en -inis *n* osier; basket

vīment·um -ī *n* osier

Vīmināl·is coll·is (*genit:* Vīmināl·is coll·is) *m* one of the seven hills of Rome

vīminĕ·us -a -um *adj* made of osiers

vīn or vīn' = vīsne? do you wish

vīnācĕ·us -a -um *adj* grape, of a grape; *m* a grape seed

Vīnāl·ia -ium *n pl* wine festival (*celebrated on the 23rd of April and on the 19th of August*)

vīnāri·us -a -um *adj* wine; *m* wine dealer, vintner; *n pl* wine flasks

vincibil·is -e *adj* easily won

vinciō vincīre vinxī vinctum *vt* to bind; to encircle, surround; to restrain; (rhet) to bind together, link together, arrange rhythmically

vincō vincĕre vīcī victum *vt* to conquer, vanquish; to get the better of, beat, defeat, outdo; to surpass, excel; to convince, refute, persuade; to prove, demonstrate; to outlast, outlive; *vi* to be victorious; to prevail, succeed

vinctus *pp* of vincio

vincŭl·um or vincl·um -ī *n* chain, fetter, cord, band; *n pl* prison

vindēmi·a -ae *f* vintage

vindēmiāt·or -ōris *m* vintager, grape gatherer

vindēmiŏl·a -ae *f* small vintage; minor sources of income

vind·ex -ĭcis *adj* avenging; *m* (law) claimant; defender, protector, champion; deliverer, liberator, avenger, punisher

vindicāti·ō -ōnis *f* (law) claim; avenging, punishment

vindici·ae -ārum *f pl* legal claim; things or persons claimed; championship, protection; **vindicias dare, dicere,** or **decernere** to hand over the things or persons claimed

vindic·ō -āre *vt* to lay a legal claim to; to protect, defend; to appropriate; to demand; to demand unfairly; to claim as one's own; to avenge, punish; **in libertatem vindicare** to claim for freedom, set free, free, liberate, emancipate

vindict·a -ae *f* rod used in the ceremony of setting slaves free; defense, protection; vengeance, revenge, satisfaction

vīnē·a -ae *f* vineyard; vine; (mil) shed (*used to defend besiegers against the missiles of the enemy*)

vīnēt·um -ī *n* vineyard

vīnit·or -ōris *m* vinedresser

vinnŭl·us -a -um *adj* charming, pleasant

vīnolenti·a -ae *f* wine drinking, intoxication

vīnolent·us -a -um *adj* intoxicated, drunk

vīnōs·us -a -um *adj* fond of wine

vīn·um -ī *n* wine

viŏl·a -ae *f* violet; violet color

violābĭl·is -e *adj* vulnerable

violār·ium -ĭī or **-ī** *n* bed of violets

violār·ĭus -ĭī or **-ī** *m* dyer of violet color

violāti·ō -ōnis *f* violation, profanation

violāt·or -ōris *m* violator, profaner, desecrator

viŏl·ens -entis *adj* violent, raging, impetuous

violenter *adv* violently, vehemently, impetuously

violenti·a -ae *f* violence, vehemence, impetuosity

violent·us -a -um *adj* violent, vehement, impetuous, boisterous

viŏl·ō -āre *vt* to do violence to, outrage, harm or injure by violence; to violate, break

vīpĕr·a -ae *f* viper; adder, snake

vīperĕ·us -a -um *adj* viper's, adder's, snake's

vīperīn·us -a -um *adj* of a viper or snake

vir virī *m* male person, man; real man; hero; husband; manhood, virility; (mil) infantryman

virāg·ō -ĭnis *f* female warrior; heroine

virect·a -ōrum *n pl* green places; lawn

vir·ĕŏ -ēre -ŭī *vi* to be green; to be fresh, be vigorous, flourish

vīrēs = *pl* of **vīs**

vir·escō -escĕre -ŭī *vt* to grow green

virg·a -ae *f* twig, sprout; graft; rod, switch (*for flogging*); walking stick, cane, staff; magic wand; wand; colored stripe in a garment; branch of a family tree

virgāt·or -ōris *m* flogger

virgāt·us -a -um *adj* made of twigs or osiers; striped

virgēt·um -ī *n* osier thicket

virgĕ·us -a -um *adj* of twigs, of kindling wood

virgidēmi·a -ae *f* (coll) harvest of birch rods (*i.e., sound flogging*)

virgināl·is -e *adj* maiden's, girl's, girlish; *n* female organ

virginārī·us -a -um *adj* maiden's, girl's

virginĕ·us -a -um *adj* maidenly, virgin, of virgins

virginĭt·ās -ātis *f* virginity, girlhood

virg·ō -ĭnis *f* virgin, maiden, girl, young woman; young married woman

Virg·ō -ĭnis *f* Virgo (*constellation; aqueduct constructed by M. Vipsanius Agrippa*)

virgŭl·a -ae *f* little twig; wand; **virgula divina** divining rod

virgult·a -ōrum *n pl* thickets, brushwood; slips (*of trees*)

virguncŭl·a -ae *f* lass, young girl

virid·ans -antis *adj* growing green, green

viridār·ĭum -ĭī or **-ī** *n* garden; plantation

virĭd·is -e *adj* green; fresh, young; *n pl* greenery

viridĭt·ās -ātis *f* greenness; freshness

virĭd·or -ārī *vi* to become green

virīl·is -e *adj* male, masculine; adult; manly; **pro virili parte** or **partione** to the best of one's ability; *n pl* manly or heroic deeds

virīlĭt·ās -ātis *f* manhood, virility

virīliter *adv* manfully

vīripŏt·ens -entis *adj* almighty

virītim *adv* individually, separately

vīrōs·us -a -um *adj* slimy; strong-smelling, fetid, stinking

virt·ūs -ūtis *f* manliness, manhood, virility; strength; valor, bravery, gallantry; gallant deeds; excellence, worth; virtue, moral perfection, good quality; *f pl* achievements

vīr·us -ī *n* slime; poison; pungency; saltiness

vīs (*genit* not in use) *f* power, strength, force; energy; hostile force, violence, attack, assault; amount, quantity; meaning (*of words*); **vīres** *f pl* strength, resources; (mil) troops; **per vim** forcibly, violently; **pro viribus** with all one's might

viscāt·us -a -um *adj* limed

viscěr·a ‑um n pl viscera, internal organs; womb; heart, vitals, bowels; (fig) innermost part, bowels, heart, center; bosom friend, favorite

visceratǐ·ō ‑ōnis f public distribution of meat

visc·ō ‑āre vt to make sticky

visc·um ‑ī n mistletoe; birdlime

visc·us ‑ěris n organ (of the body); entrails

vīsǐ·ō ‑ōnis f appearance, apparition; notion, idea

vīsǐt·ō ‑āre vt to keep seeing; to visit, go to visit

vīs·ō ‑ěre ‑ī ‑um vt to look at with attention, view; to come or go to look at; to find out; to visit

vīs·um ‑ī n sight, appearance

vīs·us ‑ūs m faculty of sight, sight; thing seen, sight, vision

vīt·a ‑ae f life, way of life; livelihood; course of life, career; biography

vītābǐl·is ‑e adj undesirable, deserving to be shunned

vītābund·us ‑a ‑um adj avoiding, evading

vītāl·is ‑e adj of life, vital; likely to live, staying alive; n means of life; n pl vital parts

vītālǐter adv vitally

vītātǐ·ō ‑ōnis f avoidance

Vitell·ǐus ‑ǐī or ‑ī m A. Vitellius (Roman emperor, 69 A.D.)

vitell·us ‑ī m little calf; yolk (of egg)

vīt·us ‑a ‑um adj of the vine

vītǐcǔl·a ‑ae f little vine

vītǐf·er ‑ěra ‑ěrum adj vine-producing

vītǐgěn·us ‑a ‑um adj produced from the vine

vitǐlēn·a ‑ae f procuress

vitǐ·ō ‑āre vt to corrupt, spoil, violate, mar; to falsify

vitǐōsē adv faultily, badly, corruptly

vitǐōsǐt·ās ‑ātis f corrupt or bad condition

vitǐōs·us ‑a ‑um adj faulty, defective, corrupt, bad; vicious

vīt·is ‑is f vine; vine branch; centurion's staff; centurionship

vītǐsāt·or ‑ōris m vine planter

vit·ǐum ‑ǐī or ‑ī n fault, defect, flaw; sin, offense, vice; flaw in the auspices

vīt·ō ‑āre vt to avoid, evade

vīt·or ‑ōris m basket maker

vitrě·us ‑a ‑um adj glass, of glass; glassy; n pl glassware

vītrǐc·us ‑ī m stepfather

vitr·um ‑ī n glass

vitt·a ‑ae f headband, fillet

vittāt·us ‑a ‑um adj wearing a fillet

vitǔl·a ‑ae f heifer

vitulīn·us ‑a ‑um adj & f veal

vitǔl·or ‑ārī vi to celebrate, hold a celebration

vitǔl·us ‑ī m calf, young bull; foal; seal

vituperābǐl·is ‑e adj blameworthy

vituperātǐ·ō ‑ōnis f blaming, censuring; blame; scandalous conduct, blameworthiness

vituperāt·or ‑ōris m censurer

vitupěr·ō ‑āre vt to spoil (omen), render void; to blame

vīvācǐt·ās ‑ātis f will to live

vīvār·ǐum ‑ǐī or ‑ī n game preserve; fish pond

vīvāt·us ‑a ‑um adj animated, lively

vīv·ax ‑ācis adj long-lived; long-lasting, enduring; quick to learn

vīvescō or vīvǐscō vīvescěre vixī vi to become alive, come to life; to grow lively, get full of life

vīvǐd·us ‑a ‑um adj teeming with life, full of life; true to life, vivid, realistic; quick, lively (mind)

vīvīrād·ix ‑īcis f development of roots

vīvīscō see vivesco

vīvō vīvěre vixī victum vi to be alive, live; to be still alive, survive; to reside; (with abl or de + abl) to live on, subsist on

vīv·us ‑a ‑um adj alive, living; lively; fresh; natural (rock); speaking (voice); n (com) capital; ad vivum resecare to cut to the quick

vix adv with difficulty, hardly; scarcely

vixdum adv hardly then, scarcely yet

vocābǔl·um ‑ī n designation, name; noun

vōcāl·is ‑e adj having a voice, gifted with speech or song, singing, speaking; tuneful; f vowel

vocām·en ‑ǐnis f designation, name

vocātǐ·ō ‑ōnis f summons (to court); invitation (to dinner)

vocāt·or ‑ōris m inviter, host

vocāt·us ‑ūs m summons, call

vōcǐferātǐ·ō ‑ōnis f loud cry, yell

vōcǐfěr·ō ‑āre or vōcǐfěr·or ‑ārī ‑ātus sum vt & vi to shout, yell

vocǐt·ō ‑āre vt to usually call, name; to shout out again and again

voc·ō ‑āre vt to summon; to call, name; to call upon (the gods); to invite; (mil) to challenge; in dubium vocare to call in question; in odium vocare to bring into disfavor; in periculum vocare to lead into danger

vōcǔl·a ‑ae f small or weak voice; soft note, soft tone; whisper, gossip

volaem·um ‑ī n large pear

Volaterr·ae ‑ārum f pl old Etruscan town

Volaterrān·us ‑a ‑um adj of Volaterrae

volātǐc·us ‑a ‑um adj flying, winged; transitory, passing; inconstant

volātǐl·is ‑e adj flying, winged; rapid, swift; fleeting, transitory

volāt·us ‑ūs m flight

Volcānāl·ǐa ‑ǐum n pl festival of Vulcan (celebrated on the 23rd of August)

Volcān·us or Vulcān·us ‑ī m Vulcan (god of fire and son of Juno and Jupiter)

vol·ens -entis *adj* willing, permitting; willing, ready; favorable; *m* well-wisher

volg- = vulg-

volĭt·ans -antis *m* winged insect

volĭt·ō -āre *vi* to flit about, fly about, flutter; to move quickly; to hover, soar

volō velle voluī *vt* to wish, want; to propose, determine; to hold, maintain; to mean; to prefer; *vi* to be willing

volōn·ēs -um *m pl* volunteers (*slaves who enlisted after the battle of Cannae*, 216 B.C.)

volpēs see **vulpes**

Volsc·us -a -um *adj* Vulscan; *m pl* an ancient people in S. Latium

volsell·a -ae *f* tweezers

volsus *pp* of **vello**

volt = older form of **vult** he, she, it wishes

voltis = older form of **vultis** you wish

Voltumn·a -ae *f* Etruscan goddess in whose temple the Etruscan states met

voltus see **vultus**

volūbĭl·is -e *adj* turning, spinning, revolving, swirling; voluble, rapid, fluent; changeable

volūbĭlĭt·ās -ātis *f* whirling motion; roundness; volubility, fluency; mutability

volūbĭlĭter *adv* volubly, rapidly, fluently

volūc·er -ris -re *adj* flying, winged; rapid, speedy; *mf* bird; *f* insect

volūm·en -ĭnis *n* roll, book; chapter, book; whirl, eddy; coil; fold

voluntārĭ·us -a -um *adj* voluntary; *m pl* volunteers

volunt·ās -ātis *f* will, wish, desire, purpose, aim; goodwill; last will, testament; attitude (*good or bad*); **ad voluntatem** (with *genit*) according to the wishes of; **de** or **ex voluntate** (with *genit*) at the desire of

volup *adv* to one's satisfaction, agreeably

voluptābĭl·is -e *adj* agreeable, pleasant

voluptārĭ·us -a -um *adj* pleasant, agreeable; voluptuous; *m* voluptary

volupt·ās -ātis *f* pleasure, enjoyment, delight; *f pl* sensual pleasures; games, sports, public performances

voluptuōs·us -a -um *adj* pleasant, agreeable

volūtābr·um -ī *n* wallow (*for swine*)

volūtābund·us -a -um *adj* wallowing about

volūtātĭ·ō -ōnis *f* rolling about, tossing about; wallowing; restlessness

volūt·ō -āre *vt* to roll about, turn over; to engross; to think over; **volutari** to wallow, luxuriate

volūtus *pp* of **volvo**

volv·a or **vulv·a -ae** *f* wrapper, cover; womb; sow's womb (*as a favorite dish*)

volvō volvēre volvī volūtum *vt* to roll, turn about, wind; (e.g., of a river) to roll (*rocks, etc.*) along; to breathe; to unroll, read (*books*); to pour out, utter fluently; to consider, weigh; (of time) to bring on, bring around; to form (*a circle*); to undergo (*troubles*); **volvī** to roll, tumble, revolve; *vi* to revolve; to roll on, elapse

vōm·er or **vōm·is -ĕris** *m* plowshare; penis

vomĭc·a -ae *f* sore, boil, abscess, ulcer; annoyance

vōmis see **vomer**

vomĭtĭ·ō -ōnis *f* vomiting

vom·ō -ĕre -ŭī -ĭtum *vt & vi* to vomit, throw up

vorāg·ō -ĭnis *f* deep hole, abyss, chasm, depth

vor·ax -ācis *adj* swallowing, devouring; greedy, ravenous

vor·ō -āre *vt* to swallow, devour; (fig) to devour (*by reading*)

vors- = vers-

vort- = vert-

vōs *pron* you; (reflex) yourselves

vosmet *pron* (emphatic form of **vōs**) you yourselves

voster see **vester**

vōtīv·us -a -um *adj* votive, promised in a vow

votō see **veto**

vōt·um -ī *n* solemn vow (*made to a deity*), vow; votive offering; wish, prayer

vovĕō vovēre vōvī vōtum *vt* to vow, promise solemnly, pledge, devote (*to a deity*); to wish, wish for, desire

vox vōcis *f* voice; sound, tone, cry, call; word, utterance, saying, expression; proverb; language; accent

Vulcānus see **Volcanus**

vulgār·is or **volgār·is -e** *adj* common, general, usual

vulgārĭter or **volgārĭter** *adv* in the common or usual way

vulgāt·or or **volgāt·or -ōris** *m* divulger

vulgāt·us or **volgāt·us -a -um** *adj* common, general; well known; notorious

vulgĭvāg·us or **volgĭvāg·us -a -um** *adj* roving; inconstant

vulg·ō or **volg·ō -āre** *vt* to spread, publish, broadcast; to divulge; to prostitute; to level, make common

vulgō or **volgō** *adv* generally, publicly, everywhere

vulg·us or **volg·us -ī** *n* masses, people, public; crowd, herd; rabble, populace

vulnerātĭ·ō or **volnerātĭ·ō -ōnis** *f* wounding, wound

vulnĕr·ō or **volnĕr·ō -āre** *vt* to wound; to damage

vulnĭfĭc·us -a -um *adj* inflicting wounds

vuln·us or **voln·us -ĕris** *n* wound; blow, stroke; blow, disaster

vulpēcŭl·a or **volpēcŭl·a -ae** *f* little fox, sly little fox

vulp·ēs or **volp·ēs -is** *f* fox; craftiness, cunning

vuls·us or **vols·us -a -um** *pp* of **vello**; *adj* plucked, beardless, effeminate

vulticŭl·us or **volticŭl·us -ī** *m* mere look

vult·um -ī *n* face; looks, expression, features; look, appearance

vultuōs·us or **voltuōs·us -a -um** *adj* full of airs, affected

vult·ur or **volt·ur -ŭris** *m* vulture

Vult·ur or **Volt·ur -ŭris** *m* mountain in Apulia near Venusia

vulturīn·us or **volturīn·us -a -um** *adj* of a vulture, vulture-like

vultur·ĭus or **voltur·ĭus -iī** or **-ī** *m* vulture

Vulturn·us or **Volturn·us -ī** *m* principal river of Campania (*modern Volturno*)

vult·us or **volt·us -ūs** *m* face; looks, expression, features; look, appearance

vulv·a or **volv·a -ae** *f* wrapper, cover; womb; sow's womb (*as a delicacy*)

X

Xanthipp·ē -ēs *f* wife of Socrates

Xanth·us -ī *m* river at Troy, identified with Scamander River

xen·ĭum -iī or **-ī** *n* gift, present

Xenophăn·ēs -is *m* early Greek philosopher (*c.* 565-470 B.C.)

Xenŏph·ōn -ontis *m* Greek historian and pupil of Socrates (*c.* 430-*c.* 354

B.C.)

xērampelĭn·ae -ārum *f pl* dark-colored clothes

Xerx·ēs -is *m* Persian king, defeated at Salamis (*c.* 519-465 B.C.)

xiphĭ·ās -ae *m* swordfish

xyst·us -ī *m* or **xyst·um -ī** *n* open colonnade or portico, walk, avenue

Z

Zacynth·us or **Zacynth·os -ī** *f* island off W. Greece

Zam·a -ae *f* town in Numidia where Scipio defeated Hannibal and brought the Second Punic War to an end

zāmĭ·a -ae *f* harm, damage, loss

Zancl·ē -ēs *f* old name of Messana in Sicily

Zēn·ō or **Zēn·ōn -ōnis** *m* founder of Stoic philosophy and a native of Citium in Cyprus (335-263 B.C.); Epicurean philosopher, the teacher of Cicero and Atticus

Zephўr·us -ī *m* zephyr; west wind; wind

Zēth·us -ī *m* son of Jupiter and Antiope and brother of Amphion

zmaragd·us -ī *f* emerald

zōdĭăc·us -ī *m* zodiac

Zōĭl·us -ī *m* proverbially stern Alexandrine critic of Homer

zōn·a -ae *f* belt, sash, girdle (*worn by women*); money belt; zone

zōnārĭ·us -a -um *adj* of a belt or girdle; *m* belt maker, girdle maker

zōnŭl·a -ae *f* little girdle

zōthēc·a -ae *f* small room

zōthēcŭl·a -ae *f* small bedroom

A

a *indefinite article, unexpressed in Latin;* **twice — year** bis in anno

aback *adv* **taken** — stupefactus, attonitus, consternatus

abandon *vt* (to) (de)relinquĕre, destituĕre, deserĕre, abjicĕre, omittĕre

abandoned *adj* derelictus, desertus; (*fig*) nefarius, perditus, flagitiosus

abandonment *s* derelictio, destitutio *f*

abase *vt* deprimĕre, comprimĕre, frangĕre, (de)minuĕre

abash *vt* perturbare, confundĕre, pudefacĕre, percellĕre

abashed *adj* pudendus, erubescens

abate *vt* (to lower) imminuĕre; (to slacken) laxare; (the price) remittĕre, detrahĕre; *vi* (to lessen) imminuĕre, decrescĕre; (to decline) cadĕre, decedĕre; (of passion) defervescĕre

abbess *s* abbatissa *f*

abbey *s* abbatia *f*

abbot *s* abbas *m*

abbreviate *vt* abbreviare, contrahĕre, imminuĕre

abbreviation *s* abbreviatio, contractio *f*, compendium *n*

abdicate *vt* abdicare; *vi* se abdicare

abdication *s* abdicatio *f*

abdomen *s* abdomen *n*

abduct *vt* abducĕre, rapĕre

abduction *s* raptio *f*, rapt·us -ūs *m*

aberration *s* error *m*; declinatio *f*

abet *vt* adjuvare, instigare; favēre (with dat)

abeyance *s* **to be in** — jacēre, intermitti

abhor *vt* abhorrēre ab (with abl), detestari, odio habēre

abhorrence *s* detestatio *f*, odium *n*

abhorrent *adj* perosus; alienus, repugnans, abhorrens

abide *vt* tolerare, subire; *vi* (to dwell) habitare, manēre; **to — by** stare in (with abl)

abiding *adj* diuturnus, mansurus; constans, fidus

ability *s* facultas, potestas *f*; ingenium *n*; **to the best of one's** — summa ope; pro sua parte

abject *adj* abjectus, vilis; humilis; **—ly** abjecte; humiliter

abjure *vt* abjurare, ejurare

ablative *s* ablativus *m*

able *adj* potens; valens, capax, peritus; ingeniosus; **to be** — **to** posse, valēre, quire, sufficĕre

ablution *s* ablutio, lavatio *f*

ably *adv* experte; ingeniose

aboard *adv* in *or* super nave; **to go — a ship** navem conscendĕre

abode *s* domicilium *n*; sedes *f*; commoratio, mansio *f*

abolish *vt* abolēre; exstinguĕre, tollĕre, rescindĕre

abolition *s* abolitio, dissolutio *f*

abominable *adj* detestabilis, infandus, execrabilis; odiosus

abominably *adv* execrabiliter; odiose

abominate *vt* abominari, detestari

abomination *s* destestatio *f*

aborigines *s* aborigines, indigenae *m pl*

abortion *s* abortio *f*; abort·us -ūs *m*

abortive *adj* abortivus; (*fig*) irritus, frustratus

abound *vi* abundare, redundare, superesse; **to — in** abundare (with abl)

abounding *adj* abundans; copiosus, largus; creber

about *adv* circa, circiter; fere, ferme

about *prep* (of place) circa, circum (with acc); (of number) circa, ad (with acc); (of time) circa, sub (with acc); (of respect) de (with abl)

above *adv* supra; insuper; **from** — desuper, superne

above *prep* supra, super (with acc)

abrasion *s* attrit·us -ūs *m*

abreast *adv* pariter; ex adverso

abridge *vt* contrahĕre; abbreviare; (*fig*) privare

abridgment *s* compendium *n*, epitome *f*

abroad *adv* (in a foreign land) peregre; (of motion, out of doors) foras; (of rest, out of doors) foris; **from** — extrinsecus; peregre; **to be** *or* **live abroad** peregrinari; patriā carēre; **to get** — (*fig*) divulgari

abrogate *vt* rescindĕre, abrogare, dissolvĕre

abrupt *adj* praeruptus; (*fig*) subitus, repentinus; (of style) abruptus; **—ly** abrupte; raptim

abruptness *s* declivitas, rapiditas, festinatio *f*

abscess *s* abscess·us -ūs *m*; suppuratio *f*; vomica *f*

absence *s* absentia *f*; **in my** — me absente

absent *adj* absens; **to be** — abesse

absent *vt* **to** — **oneself** se removēre, non comparēre

absentee *s* qui abest *m*; peregrinator *m*

absolute *adj* absolutus, summus, perfectus; (unlimited) infinitus; **—ly** absolute; prorsus; penitus, omnino

absolution *s* absolutio *f*; venia, indulgentia *f*

absolve *vt* veniam dare (with dat); absolvĕre; dimittĕre; (from punishment) condonare

absorb vt absorbēre, combibēre; (*fig*) distringēre, tenēre

absorbent adj bibulus; absorbens

abstain vi abstinēre, se abstinēre

abstinence s abstinentia f; continentia f; jejunium n

abstract vt abstrahēre; separare, sejungēre, excludēre

abstract adj abstractus; mente perceptus

abstract s compendium n; epitome f; **in the** — in abstracto

abstracted adj abstractus; separatus; contractus; (*in mind*) parum attentus; **—ly** separatim; in abstracto

abstraction s separatio f; (*idea*) notio f

abstruse adj abstrusus; reconditus; obscurus, occultus; **—ly** abdite, occulte

absurd adj absurdus, insulsus; ridiculus; **—ly** inepte, absurde

absurdity s ineptia, insulsitas f

abundance s abundantia, copia f

abundant adj abundans; amplus; copiosus, plenus; uber; **to be** — abundare; **—ly** abundanter, copiose; cumulate; (*fruitfully*) feliciter

abuse s (*wrong use*) abus·us -ūs m; (*insult*) injuria f, convicium n; contumelia f; probra n pl, maledicta n pl

abuse vt (*misuse*) abuti (*with abl*); (*a woman*) stuprare; (*with words*) maledicēre (*with dat*); lacerare

abusive adj contumeliosus; dicax, maledicus; injuriosus; **—ly** contumeliose; maledice, injuriose

abyss s profundum n, vorago f, gurges m; (*fig*) barathrum n

academic adj scholasticus; academicus

academy s Academia f; schola f, collegium n; societas f

accede vi accedēre, assentire or assentiri

accelerate vt accelerare, festinare, maturare

acceleration s acceleratio f

accent s accent·us -ūs m; sonus m; vox f; (*mark*) apex m

accent vt (*in speaking*) acuēre; (*in writing*) fastigare

accentuation s accent·us -ūs m

accept vt accipēre; recipēre

acceptable adj acceptus, aptus, gratus; probabilis; **to be** — placēre

acceptably adv apte; grate

acceptance s acceptio f; approbatio f

access s adit·us -ūs, access·us -ūs m; **to have** — admitti

accessible adj (*of places*) patens; (*fig*) facilis, affabilis

accession s (*addition*) accessio f, cumulus m; (*to the throne*) regni principium n

accessory adj adjunctus; (*of crimes*) conscius

accessory s affinis, conscius m, par-

ticeps m & f

accident s cas·us -ūs m; calamitas f

accidental adj fortuitus; adventicius; **—ly** casu, forte, fortuito

acclaim s acclamatio f; clamor m

acclaim vt acclamare

acclamation s acclamatio f, clamor, consens·us -ūs, plaus·us -ūs m

accommodate vt accommodare, aptare; (*with lodgings*) hospitium parare (*with dat*)

accommodation s accommodatio f; (*convenience*) commoditas f; (*lodgings*) hospitium, deversorium f

accompaniment s concinentia f

accompany vt comitari; deducēre; (*mus*) concinēre (*with dat*)

accomplice s particeps, socius, conscius m; satelles m

accomplish vt efficēre, perficēre; peragēre, implēre

accomplished adj completus; (*fig*) doctus, eruditus; (*eloquent*) disertus

accomplishment s exsecutio, peractio f; eruditio f

accord s consens·us, -ūs m, concordia f; **of one's own** — sua sponte; ultro; **with one** — unanimiter

accord vt concedēre, dare, praebēre, praestare; vi convenire; inter se congruēre; inter se consentire

accordance s **in** — **with** ex, de (*with abl*); secundum (*with acc*); pro (*with abl*)

accordingly adv itaque; ita; pariter; sic

according to prep de, ex, pro (*with abl*); secundum (*with acc*)

accost vt appellare; compellare; alloqui, affari

account s (*financial*) ratio f; (*statement*) memoria f; (*esteem*) reputatio f; (*story*) narratio f; **of little** — parvi pretii; vilis; **of no** — nullius pretii; on — of, propter (*with acc*); causā (*with genit*); **on that** — propterea; ideo; **to call to** — rationem poscēre; **to give an** — rationem reddēre; **to take** — of rationem habēre (*with genit*)

account vt numerare; (*esteem*) aestimare, habēre, pendēre; **to** — **for** rationem reddēre (*with genit*)

accountable adj reus

accountant s calculator m; a rationibus (procurator) m

accredited adj aestimatus, honoratus

accretion s accessio f

accrue vi accrescēre; advenire; cedēre; (*advantage*) redundare

accumulate vt accumulare, coacervare; vi crescēre, augēri

accumulation s cumulus, acervus, congest·us -ūs m; collectio f

accuracy s cura f; subtilitas f

accurate adj exactus; subtilis; diligens; **—ly** accurate, exacte; subtiliter; diligenter

accursed adj exsecratus; scelestus

accusation s accusatio f; (*charge*) crimen n; **to bring an** — **against** accusare

accusative *s* accusativus *m*

accuse *vt* accusare; criminari; *(to blame)* reprehendĕre; **to — falsely** calumniari, insimulare

accuser *s* accusator, delator *m*; *(in civil suit)* petitor *m*

accustom *vt* assuefacĕre; **to — one-self** assuefieri, consuescĕre; **to be accustomed to** solēre *(with inf)*

acerbity *s* acerbitas *f*; *(fig)* severitas *f*; rigor *m*

ache *s* dolor *m*

ache *vi* dolēre; **my head —s** caput mihi dolet

achieve *vt* patrare, conficĕre, perficĕre; *(to win)* consequi

achievement *s* res gesta *f*; facinus *n*

acid *adj* acidus; vinosus

acid *s* acidum *n*

acknowledge *vt* agnoscĕre, recognoscĕre; confitēri; *(a child)* tollĕre

acknowledgment *s* recognito *f*, confessio *f*; *(receipt for money)* apocha *f*

acme *s* fastigium *n*

acorn *s* glans *f*; balanus *f*

acoustics *s* acustica *n pl*; res auditoria *f*

acquaint *vt* certiorem facĕre; **to — oneself with** noscĕre, cognoscĕre

acquaintance *s* familiaritas, notitia *f*; *(person)* familiaris *m & f*

acquainted *adj* notus; **— with** gnarus *(with genit)*; peritus *(with genit or abl)*; **to become — with** noscĕre, cognoscĕre, pernoscĕre

acquiesce *vi* acquiescĕre, assentire

acquiescence *s* assensˑus -ūs *m*

acquire *vt* acquirĕre; adipisci, nancisci

acquisition *s* *(act of acquiring)* conciliatio *f*; quaestˑus -ūs *m*; *(thing acquired)* quaesitum *n*

acquisitive *adj* quaestuosus

acquit *vt* absolvĕre, liberare; **to — oneself** se gerere

acquittal *s* absolutio *f*

acre *s* jugerum *n*; **— by —** jugeratim

acrid *adj* acer, asper

acrimonious *adj* acerbus; asper, truculentus

acrimony *s* acrimonia *f*; acerbitas, amaritudo *f*; acor *m*

acrobat *s* funambulus *m*

across *adv* transversus

across *prep* trans *(with acc)*

act *s* *(deed, action)* factum, gestum *n*; *(decree)* decretum *n*; *(in a play)* actˑus -ūs *m*; **caught in the —** deprehensus; **in the very —** in flagranti

act *vt* *(role, part)* agĕre; *vi* agĕre, facĕre, gerĕre

acting *s* actio, gesticulatio *f*

action *s* actio *f*, actˑus -ūs *m*; *(deed)* factum, facinus *n*; *(law)* actio *f*; *(mil)* pugna *f*, proelium *n*; *(of speaker)* gestˑus -ūs *m*; **to bring an — against** actionem intendĕre *(with dat)*

active *adj* actuosus; activus; agilis; impiger, vegetus, strenuus, sedulus,

navus; **—ly** impigre; strenue; *(gram)* active

activity *s* agilitas, mobilitas *f*; *(motion)* motˑus -ūs *m*; *(energy)* industria, sedulitas, gnavitas *f*

actor *s* histrio *m*; mimus *m*; *(in comedy)* comoedus *m*; *(in tragedy)* tragoedus *m*

actress *s* mima, scenica *f*

actual *adj* verus, ipse; **—ly** re vera

actuality *s* veritas *f*

acumen *s* acumen *n*; sagacitas *f*; ingenii acies *f*

acute *adj* acutus; acer; *(fig)* sagax, subtilis; **—ly** acute, acriter

acuteness *s* acies *f*; *(of the mind)* acumen *n*, subtilitas *f*

adage *s* proverbium *n*

adamant *adj* obstinatus

adamant *s* adamas *m*

adapt *vt* accommodare, aptare

adaptation *s* accommodatio *f*

adapted *adj* aptus

add *vt* addĕre, apponĕre, adjungĕre; *(in speaking)* superdicĕre; *(in writing)* subjungĕre; *(to reckon)* adscribĕre; **to — up** computare, supputare; **to be added** accedĕre

adder *s* coluber *m*, vipera *f*

addict *vt* **to be addicted** se addicĕre, se tradĕre, se dare

addition *s* additamentum *n*; adjectio, accessio *f*; appendix *f*; incrementum *n*; **in —** praeterea, insuper; **in —** to praeter *(with acc)*

additional *adj* novus, addititius, adjunctus

address *s* alloquium *n*; allocutio, compellatio *f*; *(on letter)* forma directionis, inscriptio *f*; *(speech)* contio, oratio *f*; *(adroitness)* dexteritas, comitas *f*

address *vt* *(to speak to)* alloqui, aggredi, compellare; *(letter)* inscribĕre

adduce *vt* *(witnesses)* producĕre; *(arguments)* afferre

adept *adj* peritus

adequacy *s* sufficientia *f*

adequate *adj* adaequatus, sufficiens, par; **to be — sufficĕre; —ly** satis, apte

adhere *vi* adhaerēre, cohaerēre; **to — to** inhaerēre *(with dat)*; *(fig)* stare in *(with abl)*

adherence *s* adhaesio *f*

adherent *s* assectator, fautor, cliens *m*

adhesion *s* adhaesio *f*

adhesive *adj* tenax

adieu *interj* vale, valete; **to bid —** valedicĕre; valēre jubēre

adjacent *adj* confinis, conterminus; vicinus

adjective *s* adjectivum (nomen) *n*

adjectively *adv* adjective; ut apposito; pro apposito

adjoin *vt* adjungĕre, adjacĕre *(with dat)*; *vi* adjacēre

adjoining *adj* adjacens, confinis

adjourn *vt* comperendinare, differre, prorogare; *vi* deferri

adjournment *s* dilatio *f*

adjudge vt addicĕre, adjudicare

adjudicate vt addicĕre, decernĕre

adjudication s addictio, adjudicatio f; sententia f; arbitrium n

adjunct s adjunctum n, accessio, appendix f

adjuration s obtestatio f; obsecratio f

adjure vt adjurare; obtestari

adjust vt aptare, accommodare; (put in order) componĕre

adjustment s accommodatio, compositio f; (of a robe) structura f

adjutant s optio m

administer vt (to manage) administrare; (medicine, etc.) adhibēre; (oath) adigĕre; (justice) dispensare, reddĕre

administration s administratio, cura, procuratio f; jurisdictio f; magistrat·us -ūs m

administrative adj ad administrationem pertinens

administrator s administrator, procurator m

admirable adj admirabilis, mirabilis, admirandus; insignis, egregius

admiral s classis praefectus m

admiration s admiratio f

admire vt admirari; amare

admirer s admirator, mirator, laudator m; amator m

admiringly adv admirans

admissible adj accipiendus, aptus, aequus

admission s admissio, confessio f; adit·us -ūs, access·us -ūs m

admit vt admittĕre; recipĕre; (to recognize) asciscĕre; noscĕre; **it is admitted** constat

admittedly adv sane

admonish vt monēre, admonēre, commonēre; hortari

admonition s monitio, admonitio f; monitum n

adolescence s prima adulescentia f

adolescent adj adolescens, adulescens

adolescent s adulescentulus, adulescens m

adopt vt (a minor) adoptare; (an adult) arrogare; (a custom) asciscĕre; (a plan) capĕre, inire

adoption s adoptio, adoptatio f; (of an adult) arrogatio f; (of a custom) assumptio f; **by —** adoptivus

adoptive adj adoptivus

adorable adj adorandus, venerandus

adoration s adoratio f; cult·us -ūs m; (of kings) veneratio f

adore vt adorare, venerari; (fig) admirari, amare

adorn vt ornare, decorare, distinguĕre, illustrare; excolĕre, comare

adornment s exornatio f; ornat·us -ūs m; ornamentum n

Adriatic Sea s Hadria m or Adria m

adrift adv fluctuans; **to be —** fluctuare

adroit adj callidus, dexter, sollers, peritus; **—ly** callide, scite

adroitness s dexteritas, sollertia,

calliditas f

adulation s adulatio, assentatio f

adult adj adultus

adult s adultus homo, puber m

adulterate vt adulterare, vitiare, commiscēre

adulteration s adulteratio, commixtio f

adulterer s adulter m; moechus m

adulteress s adultera f; moecha f

adulterous adj stuprosus, adulterinus, incestus

adultery s adulterium, stuprum n; **to commit —** moechari; adulterare

advance vt promovēre; admovēre; (money) praerogare; (a cause) fovēre; (an opinion) exhibēre, praeferre; (to honors) provehēre; vi procedĕre, progredi, incedĕre; (mil) gradum or pedem inferre; signa proferre; (to progress) proficĕre

advance s progress·us -ūs m; (step) pass·us -ūs m; (attack) incursio f; impet·us -ūs m; (money) mutuae pecuniae f pl; **in —** maturius

advanced adj provectus; (of age) grandis

advance guard s primum agmen n

advancement s dignitatis accessio, promotio f; honos m

advantage s (benefit) commodum n, us·us -ūs m, bonum n; (profit) lucrum, emolumentum n; utilitas f, fruct·us -ūs m; **to be of —** prodesse; **to have an — over** praestare (with dat); superior esse (with dat); **to take —** of uti (with abl); (to deceive) decipĕre, fallĕre; **with —** faenerato

advantageous adj fructuosus, utilis; **—ly** utiliter; bene

advent s advent·us -ūs m

adventure s cas·us -ūs m; fors f; facinus n

adventurer s periclitator m; latro m; pirata m

adventurous adj audax

adverb s adverbium n

adverbial adj adverbialis; **—ly** adverbialiter

adversary s adversarius m, hostis m; adversatrix f

adverse adj adversus, infestus; asper; **—ly** male, contrarie, infeliciter

adversity s res adversae f pl; calamitas f

advertise vt communefacĕre; proscribĕre

advertisement s proscriptio f; libellus m; indicium n

advice s consilium n; **to ask — of** consulĕre; **to give —** suadēre (with dat)

advisable adj commodus, utilis

advise vt suadēre (with dat), censēre (with dat), monēre; **to — to the contrary** dissuadēre (with dat)

adviser s consultor m

advocate s (law) actor, causidicus m; (fig) patronus m; suasor m; auctor m

aedile s aedilis m

aegis *s* aegis *f*

aerial *adj* aërius, aethereus

affability *s* comitas, affabilitas, facilitas *f*

affable *adj* affabilis, comis, facilis

affably *adv* comiter

affair *s* negotium *n*; res *f*; *(love)* amores *m pl*

affect *vt* afficĕre; commovēre; jactare; ostentare; attingĕre

affectation *s* simulatio, affectatio *f*

affected *adj* simulatus, fictus; *(in style)* putidus; —ly putide

affection *s* amor *m*; benevolentia *f*; studium *n*

affectionate *adj* amans, benevolus; —ly amanter

affidavit *s* testimonium *n*

affiliate *vt* adoptare; attribuĕre

affinity *s* affinitas *f*; cognatio *f*

affirm *vt* affirmare, asseverare, testificari

affirmation *s* affirmatio *f*

affirmative *adj* affirmans; I reply in the — aio; —ly affirmative

affix *vt* affigĕre, annectĕre

afflict *vt* affligĕre, afflictare

affliction *s* afflictio, miseria *f*; res adversae *f pl*

affluence *s* abundantia, copia *f*; divitiae *f pl*

affluent *adj* affluens, abundans; divites; —ly abundanter

afford *vt* praebēre; *(to yield)* reddĕre, ferre; I cannot — res mihi non suppetit ad *(with acc)*

affront *vt* irritare; contumeliā afficĕre; offendĕre

affront *s* contumelia, injuria *f*

afield *adv* foris

afloat *adj* natans; fluctuans; to be — natare, fluctuare

afoot *adv* pedestris, pedibus; to be — geri

afraid *adj* timidus, pavidus; to be — timēre; to make — terrefacĕre

afresh *adv* de integro, iterum, de novo

after *prep* post *(with acc)*; a, de, e, ex *(with abl)*; *(following immediately upon)* sub *(with acc)*; *(in rank or degree)* secundum *(with acc)*; *(in imitation of)* ad *(with acc)*; — all tamen; saltem; a little — paulo post; the day — postridie

after *conj* postquam

afternoon *adj* postmeridianus, pomeridianus

afternoon *s* pomeridianum *n*; in the — post meridiem

afterthought *s* posterior cogitatio *f*

afterwards *adv* post, postea; deinde, deinceps, dehinc

again *adv* iterum, rursus, denuo, rursum; deinde; *(hereafter)* posthac; *(likewise, in turn)* invicem, mutuo, vicissim; contra; — and — etiam atque etiam; identidem; once — de novo; over — de novo

against *prep* contra *(with acc)*; adversus *(with acc)*; *(in a hostile manner)* in *(with acc)*; — the current adverso flumine; to be — adversari

age *s* *(life)* aetas *f*; *(era)* saeculum *n*, aetas *f*; of the same — aequaevus, aequalis; old — senectus *f*; to be of — sui juris esse; twelve years of — duodecim annos natus; under — impubis

age *vi* senescĕre; maturescĕre

aged *adj* aetate provectus; senilis; *(things)* antiquus

agency *s* actio *f*; *(medium)* opera *f*; *(office)* procuratio *f*; through the — of per *(with acc)*

agent *s* actor, auctor *m*; *(in crime)* minister *m*

aggravate *vt* aggravare; *(pain)* augēre; provocare; *(a wound)* ulcerare; to become aggravated ingravescĕre

aggravating *adj* molestus

aggravation *s* exaggeratio *f*

aggregate *adj* aggregatus, totus

aggregate *s* summa *f*

aggregation *s* collatio *f*; aggregatum *n*

aggression *s* incursio *f*

aggressive *adj* hostilis, infensus; ferox

aggressor *s* qui bellum infert *m*; qui alterum prior lacessit *m*

aggrieve *vt* dolore afficĕre

aggrieved *adj* iratus

aghast *adj* attonitus, consternatus, stupefactus; to stand — obstupescĕre

agile *adj* agilis; pernix

agility *s* agilitas *f*; pernicitas *f*

agitate *vt* agitare; commovēre; perturbare

agitated *adj* tumultuosus; turbulentus; *(fig)* sollicitus

agitation *s* agitatio, commotio *f*; *(of the sea)* jactatio *f*; trepidatio *f*

agitator *s* concitator, turbator *m*

ago *adv* abhinc; a short time — haud ita pridem; dudum; long — iamdudum, iampridem, antiquitus; some time — pridem

agonize *vt* crueiare, excruciare; *vi* discruciari

agonizing *adj* crucians; horribilis

agony *s* dolor *m*; agonia *f*; cruciat·us -ūs *m*

agrarian *adj* agrarius

agree *vi* assentire, assentiri; convenire; *(to make a bargain)* pacisci; *(of facts)* constare, convenire; to — with assentiri *(with dat)*, sentire cum *(with abl)*

agreeable *adj* gratus, acceptus; amabilis; congruens, conveniens; very — pergratus

agreeably *adv* grate, jucunde; suaviter

agreement *s* consens·us -ūs *m*; concordia *f*; *(pact)* pactio *f*, pactum *n*; *(bargain)* conditio *f*; *(proportion)* symmetria *f*; reconciliatio *f*

agricultural *adj* rusticus, agrestis

agriculture *s* agricultura *f*; res rustica *f*

agriculturist *s* agricola *m*

ah *interj* ah!, eja!, vah!, vae!

ahead *adv use verb with prefix prae-* or *pro-*

aid *s* auxilium, subsidium *n*

aid *vt* succurrĕre (*with dat*), subvenire (*with dat*), adjuvare

aide-de-camp *s* optio *m*

ail *vt* dolēre; *vi* aegrotare

ailing *adj* aegrotus, aeger

ailment *s* aegrotatio *f*; malum *n*; morbus *m*

aim *s* (*mark*) scopus *m*; (*fig*) finis *m*, propositum *n*

aim *vt* intendĕre, tendĕre; *vi* to — **at** affectare, spectare, petĕre, quaerĕre

aimless *adj* vanus, inanis; —**ly** sine ratione

air *s* aër *m*; caelum *n*; (*breeze*) aura *f*; (*attitude*) habit·us ·ūs *m*, gest·us ·ūs *m*; (*tune*) modus *m*; **in the open** — sub divo *or* sub caelo; **to take the** — deambulare

air *vt* ventilare

airily *adv* hilare

airy *adj* aërius; apertus, patens; ventosus; (*fig*) hilaris

aisle *s* ala *f*

ajar *adj* semiapertus

akin *adj* cognatus, agnatus, consanguineus, propinquus

alabaster *s* alabaster *m*

alacrity *s* alacritas *f*

alarm *s* (*signal*) classicum *n*; (*sudden fright*) trepidatio *f*, pavor *m*; tumult·us ·ūs *m*; **to give the** — increpare

alarm *vt* perterrefacĕre, consternĕre, perturbare

alarming *adj* formidolosus

alas *interj* eheu!, heu!

alchemist *s* alchemista *m*

alchemy *s* alchemistica *f*

alcohol *s* spirit·us ·ūs vini *m*

alcoholic *adj* alcoolicus

alcove *s* zotheca *f*, cubiculum *n*

ale *s* cerevisia *f*

alert *adj* alacer, promptus, vegetus

alertness *s* alacritas *f*

alias *adv* aliter

alias *s* falsum nomen *n*

alibi *s* (*law*) absentia rei *f*; (*excuse*) species *f*

alien *adj* peregrinus

alien *s* peregrinus *m*; alienigena, advena *m*

alienate *vt* alienare, abalienare, avertĕre, avocare

alienation *s* abalienatio, alienatio *f*

alight *vi* descendĕre; (*from a horse*) desilire; (*of birds*) subsidĕre

alike *adj* aequus, par, similis

alike *adv* pariter, similiter, aeque

alimony *s* alimentum, alimonium *n*

alive *adj* vivus; (*fig*) alacer; **to be** — vivĕre; superesse

all *adj* omnis, cunctus, totus; integer; universus; — **over** undique, passim; — **the better** tanto melius; — **the more** eo plus

all *s* omnia *n pl*; **at** — omnino; **in** — in summa; **not at** — haudquaquam; **one's all** proprium *n*

allay *vt* sedare, lenire, mitigare; **to**

be allayed defervescĕre, temperari

allegation *s* affirmatio *f*; insimulatio *f*

allege *vt* affirmare, arguĕre; citare, allegare

allegiance *s* fides, fidelitas *f*; **to swear** — sacramentum dicĕre

allegorical *adj* allegoricus; —**ly** allegorice

allegorize *vi* allegorice scribĕre; allegorice explicare

allegory *s* allegoria *f*

alleviate *vt* levare, allevare, sublevare

alleviation *s* allevamentum *n*, levatio *f*

alley *s* angiport·us ·ūs *m*

alliance *s* (*by blood*) consanguinitas *f*; (*by marriage*) affinitas *f*; (*of states*) foedus *n*; societas *f*

allied *adj* foederatus, socius; junctus, propinquus

alligator *s* crocodilus *m*

alliteration *s* alliteratio *f*

allocate *vt* impertire, assignare

allot *vt* distribuĕre, assignare

allotment *s* assignatio, portio *f*; assignatum *n*

allow *vt* concedĕre (*with dat*), permittĕre (*with dat*), sinĕre, pati; **it is allowed** licet; **to** — **for** indulgēre (*with dat*); **to** — **of** admittĕre

allowable *adj* licitus

allowance *s* (*permission*) licentia, permissio *f*; (*concession*) venia, indulgentia *f*; (*portion*) portio *f*; salarium *n*; diaria *n pl*; cibaria *n pl*; demensum *n*; **to make** — **for** ignoscĕre (*with dat*), condonare

alloy *s* mixtura *f*

alloy *vt* miscēre, adulterare, diluĕre

allude *vi* **to** — **to** attingĕre, designare, denotare, spectare

allure *vt* allicĕre, allectare, pellicĕre

allurement *s* illecebra, blanditia *f*; blandimentum *n*

alluring *adj* blandus; —**ly** blande

allusion *s* parodia *f*; indicium *n*, mentio *f*

allusive *adj* obliquus; —**ly** oblique

alluvial *adj* alluvius

ally *s* socius *m*, socia *f*

ally *vt* sociare

almanac *s* fasti *m pl*

almighty *adj* omnipotens

almond *s* amygdala *f*

almond tree *s* amygdalus *f*

almost *adv* fere, paene, prope, ferme

alms *s* stips *f*

aloft *adv* sublime

alone *adj* solus, unus, solitarius, unicus; **all** — persolus; **to leave** — deserĕre; **to let** — omittĕre, mittĕre

alone *adv* solum

along *adv* porro, protinus; **all** — jamdudum; — **with** una cum (*with abl*)

along *prep* per (*with acc*), praeter (*with acc*), secundum (*with acc*)

aloof *adv* procul; **to stand** — discedĕre, abstare

aloud *adv* magna voce; clare

alphabet s alphabetum n; prima elementa n pl
alphabetical adj litterarum ordine
Alpine adj alpinus
already adv jam
also adv etiam, quoque, et, idem, necnon
altar s ara f; altaria n pl
alter vt mutare, commutare; variare; vertĕre
alterable adj mutabilis
alteration s mutatio, commutatio f
altercation s altercatio f, jurgium n
alternate adj alternus; —ly invicem, per vices; alternis
alternate vt & vi alternare, variare
alternation s vicissitudo f
alternative adj alter
alternative s discrimen n, optio f; alternata conditio f
although conj etsi, etiamsi, tametsi, quamquam, licet, cum
altitude s altitudo f
altogether adv omnino; prorsus, plane
altruism s beneficentia f
always adv semper
amalgamate vt miscēre, conjungĕre
amalgamation s mixtio f
amass vt coacervare, cumulare
amateur s artium amator m; tiro m
amaze vt obstupefacĕre
amazed adj attonitus, stupefactus; to be — stupēre; obstupescĕre
amazement s stupor m; in — attonitus, stupefactus
amazing adj mirus, mirandus, mirabilis; —ly mirabiliter
Amazon s Amazon f
Amazonian adj amazonius, amazonicus
ambassador s legatus m
amber s sucinum n; electrum n
ambiguity s ambiguitas f, ambages f pl
ambiguous adj ambiguus, dubius, anceps; —ly ambigue
ambition s ambitio f; studium n
ambitious adj laudis or gloriae cupidus; studiosus; ambitiosus
amble vi ambulare
ambrosia s ambrosia f
ambush s insidiae f pl
ambush vt insidiari (with dat)
ameliorate vt meliorem or melius facĕre, corrigĕre
amenable adj docilis, obediens
amend vt emendare, corrigĕre; vi proficĕre
amendment s emendatio, correctio f
amends s compensatio, satisfactio f; to make — expiare, satisfacĕre, compensare
amenity s amoenitas f; (comfort) commodum n
amethyst s amethystus f
amiable adj amabilis, suavis
amiably adv amabiliter, suaviter
amicable adj amicus; pacatus; benevolus
amicably adv amice; pacate; benevole
amid prep inter (with acc)

amity s amicitia f
ammonia s ammoniaca f
ammunition s belli apparat-us -ūs m; missilium copia f
amnesty s venia, abolitio f
among prep inter (with acc); apud (with acc); ad (with acc); from — e, ex (with abl)
amorous adj amatorius; libidinosus, mulierosus; —ly amatorie; cum amore
amount s summa f, totum n
amount vi to — to crescĕre, exsurgĕre; (fig) esse
amour s amores m pl
amphitheater s amphitheatrum n
ample adj amplus; copiosus; satis
amplification s amplificatio, auctio, dilatatio f
amplify vt amplificare, dilatare
amply adv ample, abunde
amputate vt amputare, secare
amputation s amputatio, sectio f
amuck adv furiose; to run — delirare
amulet s amuletum n
amuse vt oblectare, delectare; to — oneself ludĕre
amusement s delectatio, oblectatio f; delectamentum n; ludibrium n
amusing adj ridiculus; festivus; facetus
an indefinite article, unexpressed in Latin
anachronism s temporum inversio f
analogous adj analogus
analogy s analogia, comparatio f
analysis s analysis f; explicatio f; separatio f
analytical adj analyticus; —ly per analysin
analyze vt in principia resolvĕre; (words) subtiliter enodare
anapest s anapaestus m
anapestic adj anapaesticus
anarchist s civis seditiosus m
anarchy s anarchia f; rei publicae perturbatio f; licentia f
anathema s anathema n; exsecratio f
anatomical adj anatomicus
anatomy s anatomia, dissectio f
ancestor s proavus m; auctor m; —s majores, priores m pl
ancestral adj avitus; proavitus; patrius
ancestry s genus n; stirps f; origo f
anchor s ancora f; to lie at — in ancoris stare; to weigh — ancoram tollĕre or solvĕre
anchor vt in ancoris tenēre; vi ancoram jacĕre
anchorage s statio f
ancient adj antiquus, vetustus; priscus; pristinus; in — times antiquitus; the —s veteres m pl; barbati m pl
and conj et, ac, atque, -que
anecdote s fabella f
anemic adj exsanguis
anew adv denuo; ab integro
angel s angelus m

angelic *adj* angelicus; (*fig*) egregius, excellens
anger *s* ira *f*; bilis *f*
anger *vt* irritare, exacerbare
angle *s* angulus *m*
angle *vi* hamo piscari
angler *s* piscator *m*
angrily *adv* irate, iracunde
angry *adj* iratus, iracundus, indignans; **to be** — irasci, succensēre, stomachari; **to make** — irritare, exacerbare
anguish *s* angor *m*; dolor *m*; cruciat·us -ūs *m*
anguished *adj* animo fractus
angular *adj* angularis; angulosus
animal *s* animal *n*; (*wild beast*) bestia, fera *f*; (*domestic*) pecus *n*
animal *adj* animalis
animate *vt* animare; (*fig*) excitare
animated *adj* excitatus, vegetus
animation *s* animatio *f*; vigor, ardor, spirit·us -ūs *m*
animosity *s* acerbitas *f*; invidia *f*; odium *n*; inimicitia *f*
ankle *s* talus *m*
annalist *s* annalium scriptor *m*
annals *s* annales, fasti *m pl*
annex *s* appendix *f*
annex *vt* annectĕre, adjungĕre, addĕre, supponĕre
annexation *s* adjectio *f*
annihilate *vt* delēre, exstinguĕre
annihilation *s* exstinctio *f*; internecio *f*
anniversary *adj* anniversarius; annuus
anniversary *s* festus dies anniversarius *m*
annotate *vt* annotare, commentari
annotation *s* annotatio, nota *f*
announce *vt* nuntiare; (*to report*) renuntiare; (*officially*) denuntiare, pronuntiare; (*laws, etc.*) proscribĕre
announcement *s* denuntiatio, pronuntiatio *f*; (*news*) nuntius *m*
announcer *s* nuntius *m*
annoy *vt* incommodare, vexare, male habēre; **to be annoyed** stomachari, offensus esse
annoyance *s* vexatio, molestia *f*; dolor *m*
annoying *adj* molestus, odiosus
annual *adj* anniversarius, annuus; **—ly** quotannis
annuity *s* annua pecunia *f*; annuus redit·us -ūs *m*; (*law*) annuum *n*
annul *vt* rescindĕre, tollĕre, dissolvĕre, abrogare
annulment *s* abolitio *f*; abrogatio *f*
anoint *vt* ung(u)ĕre
anointing *s* unctio *f*
anomalous *adj* anomalus; enormis
anomaly *s* anomalia *f*; enormitas *f*
anonymous *adj* sine nomine; **—ly** sine nomine
another *adj* alius; **—'s** alienus; **one after** — alius ex alio; **one** — **inter** se; alius alium; **to** — **place** alio
answer *vt* respondēre (*with dat*); (*by letter*) rescribĕre (*with dat*); (*to correspond to*) congruĕre cum (*with abl*); *vi* **to** — **for** rationem reddēre

(*with genit*); **to** — **to the name of** vocari
answer *s* responsio *f*, responsum *n*; (*solution*) explicatio *f*
answerable *adj* reus; **to be** — **for** praestare
ant *s* formica *f*
antagonism *s* adversitas, inimicitia *f*
antagonist *s* adversarius *m*; adversatrix *f*; hostis *m*
antarctic *adj* antarcticus
antecedent *adj* antecedens; prior
antecedent *s* antecedens *n*
antechamber *s* atriolum *n*; antithalamus *m*
antedate *vt* diem vero antiquiorem ascribĕre (*with dat*)
antelope *s* antilope *f*; dorcas *f*
antepenult *s* syllaba antepenultima *f*
anterior *adj* anterior, prior
anteroom *s* antithalamus *m*; vestibulum *n*
anthem *s* canticum sacrum *n*; hymnus elatior *m*
anthology *s* anthologia *f*; excerpta *n pl*
anticipate *vt* anticipare; (*to expect*) spectare; (*to forestall*) praevenire, praeoccupare; (*mentally*) praesumĕre
anticipation *s* anticipatio, praesumptio, anteoccupatio *f*
anticlimax *s* climax inversa *f*
antics *s* joca *n pl*; ineptiae *f pl*
antidote *s* antidotum *n*
antipathy *s* repugnantia, antipathia *f*; fastidium, odium *n*
antiquarian *adj* historicus
antiquarian *s* antiquitatis peritus *m*; antiquarius *m*
antiquated *adj* antiquatus, obsoletus
antique *adj* antiquus, vetus, priscus
antique *s* antiqui artificis opus *n*
antiquity *s* antiquitas, vetustas *f*
antithesis *s* contrarium *n*, contentio *f*
antler *s* cornu *n*
anvil *s* incus *f*
anxiety *s* anxietas, sollicitudo *f*
anxious *adj* anxius, sollicitus; trepidus; avidus; **—ly** anxie, sollicite; trepide; avide
any *adj* ullus; quivis, quilibet; aliquis; **— longer** diutius; **— more** amplius
anybody *pron* aliquis; quivis; quilibet; (*after si, nisi, num, ne*) quis; (*interrog*) ecquis, numquis; (*after negative*) quisquam
anyhow *adv* quoquomodo
anyone *see* **anybody**
anything *pron* aliquid, quicquam, quidpiam, quodvis; (*after si, nisi, num, ne*) quid; (*interrog*) ecquid, numquid; (*after negative*) quicquam; **hardly** — nihil fere
anywhere *adv* ubilibet, alicubi, ubivis
apart *adv* seorsum, separatim; **to be** — distare; **to set** — seponĕre; **to stand** — distare
apart from *prep* praeter (*with acc*)
apartment *s* conclave *n*; insula *f*

apathetic *adj* lentus, languidus

apathy *s* apathia, lentitudo *f*, languor *m*

ape *s* simius *m*, simia *f*

ape *vt* imitari

aperture *s* apertura *f*; foramen *n*

apex *s* cacumen *n*; fastigium *n*

aphorism *s* sententia *f*

apiary *s* alvearium *n*

apiece *adv* singuli

aplomb *s* confidentia *f*

apocalypse *s* apocalypsis *f*

apocryphal *adj* apocryphus, commenticius

apogee *s* apogaeum *n*

apologetic *adj* apologeticus; confitens

apologist *s* defensor *m*

apologize *vi* se excusare; veniam petēre

apology *s* excusatio, defensio *f*; (*written treatise*) apologia *f*, liber apologeticus *m*; **to make an —** for excusare

apoplectic *adj* apoplecticus

apoplexy *s* apoplexia *f*; apoplexis *f*

apostasy *s* apostasia *f*

apostate *s* apostata *m*

apostle *s* apostolus *m*

apostolic *adj* apostolicus

apostrophe *s* apostrophe *f*; (*gram*) apostrophus *f*

apostrophize *vt* abrupte compellare

apothecary *s* (*druggist*) medicamentarius *m*; (*drugstore*) medicina taberna *f*, pharmacopolium *n*

apotheosis *s* apotheosis *f*

appall *vt* exterrēre, percellēre

apparatus *s* apparat·us -ūs *m*

apparel *s* vestis *f*, vestit·us -ūs *m*; vestimenta *n pl*

apparel *vt* vestire; adornare

apparent *adj* manifestus, apertus, conspicuus; **to be — apparēre; —ly** manifeste, aperte, specie, per speciem

apparition *s* spectrum *n*; visum *n*; species *f*

appeal *vi* appellare; provocare; **to — to** (*a magistrate*) appellare; (*the people*) provocare ad (*with acc*); (*the gods*) obsecrare, invocare, testari

appeal *s* (*law*) appellatio *f*; (*entreaty*) obsecratio, testatio *f*; (*to the people*) provocatio *f*

appear *vi* apparēre, comparēre; se ostendēre; (*to seem*) vidēri; (*to arise*) exoriri, surgēre; **to begin to — patescēre**

appearance *s* (*becoming visible*) aspect·us -ūs *m*; (*outward show*) species *f*; (*likelihood*) similitudo *f*; (*vision*) visum *n*; **first —** exort·us -ūs *m*; **to all —s** probabilissime; **to make an —** prodire

appease *vt* placare, sedare; mitigare; (*fig*) expiare

appeasement *s* placatio *f*; (*of an enemy*) pacificatio *f*

appellation *s* nomen *n*

appendage *s* appendix, accessio, appendicula *f*

appendix *s* appendix *f*

appetite *s* appetit·us -ūs *m*, cupiditas *f*; **to have an —** esurire

applaud *vt* applaudēre; laudare

applause *s* plaus·us -ūs, applaus·us ūs *m*; laus f

apple *s* malum, pomum *n*; **— of my eye** ocellus meus *m*

apple tree *s* malus *f*

appliance *s* instrumentum *n*, apparat·us -ūs *m*

applicable *adj* commodus, conveniens

applicant *s* petitor *m*

application *s* petito *f*; adhibitio, appositio *f*; studium *n*, sedulitas, industria, diligentia *f*; (*med*) fomentum *n*

apply *vt* adhibēre, admovēre, apponēre; aptare, accommodare; (*fig*) applicare; *vi* **to — to** pertinēre ad (*with acc*); **to — for** petēre

appoint *vt* creare; facēre; designare; destinare; constituēre

appointment *s* creatio *f*; (*rendezvous*) constitutum *n*; (*order*) mandatum *n*; (*office*) magistrat·us -ūs *m*

apportion *vt* dividēre, distribuēre

apportionment *s* divisio, distributio *f*

apposition *s* appositio *f*

appraisal *s* aestimatio *f*

appraise *vt* aestimare

appraiser *s* aestimator *m*

appreciable *adj* aestimabilis, haud exiguus

appreciate *vt* aestimare

appreciation *s* aestimatio *f*

apprehend *vt* apprehendēre, comprehendēre, percipēre; (*to seize*) capēre; (*to take by surprise*) intercipēre; (*to fear*) timēre, metuēre

apprehension *s* comprehensio *f*; facultas, intelligentia *f*; suspicio *f*; (*seizing*) captura *f*; (*fear*) timor, met·us -ūs *m*

apprehensive *adj* timidus, sollicitus

apprentice *s* discipulus *m*; tiro *m*

apprenticeship *s* identura *f*; tirocinium *n*

apprize *vt* docēre

approach *vt* appropinquare (*with dat*), accedēre ad (*with acc*), adire; *vi* appropinquare, appetēre

approach *s* access·us -ūs, adit·us -ūs *m*; appropinquatio *f*; (*by sea*) appuls·us -ūs *m*

approachable *adj* (*person*) facilis, affabilis; (*place*) patens

approbation *s* approbatio, laus *f*

appropriate *adj* proprius, aptus, idoneus; **—ly** apte, congruenter

appropriate *vt* asciscēre, asserēre, vindicare; assumēre

appropriation *s* vindicatio *f*

approval *s* approbatio *f*

approve *vt* approbare, probare; (*law*) sciscēre; *vi* **to — of** probare

approved *adj* probatus, spectatus

approximate *adj* propinquus, proximus; **—ly** prope, propemodum; (*with numbers*) ad (*with acc*)

approximate *vt* appropinquare (*with dat*); accedēre ad (*with acc*)

approximation *s* appropinquatio *f*

apricot *s* malum armeniacum *n*

April *s* (mensis) Aprilis *m*

apron *s* praecinctorium *n*; operimentum *n*

apt *adj* aptus, idoneus; *(inclined, prone)* pronus, propensus; **—ly** apte

aptitude *s* habilitas *f*, ingenium *n*

aptness *s* convenientia, congruentia *f*; *(tendency)* proclivitas *f*

aquatic *adj* aquatilis, aquaticus

aqueduct *s* aquaeduct·us -ūs *m*, aquarum duct·us -ūs *m*

aquiline *adj* (of the nose) aduncus

arable *adj* arabilis, culturae idoneus; **— land** arvum *n*

arbiter *s* arbiter *m*

arbitrament *s* arbitrat·us -ūs *m*, arbitrium *n*

arbitrarily *adv* ad arbitrium; ad libidinem; libidinoso

arbitrary *adj* libidinosus; imperiosus, superbus

arbitrate *vt & vi* disceptare

arbitration *s* arbitrium *n*, dijudicatio *f*

arbitrator *s* arbiter *m*; disceptator *m*

arbor *s* umbraculum *n*, pergula *f*

arc *s* arc·us -ūs *m*

arcade *s* portic·us -ūs *f*

arch *s* arc·us -ūs, fornix *m*

arch *adj* astutus, callidus, vafer; nimius

arch *vt* arcuare, fornicare

archaeological *adj* archaeologiae *(genit)*

archaeologist *s* antiquitatis investigator *m*

archaeology *s* rerum antiquarum scientia *f*

archaism *s* locutio obsoleta *f*

archbishop *s* archiepiscopus *m*

archer *s* sagittarius *m*; *(constellation)* Arcitenens *m*

archery *s* ars sagittandi *f*

archetype *s* archetypum *n*

archipelago *s* insulis crebrum mare *n*

architect *s* architectus *m*

architectural *adj* architectonicus

architecture *s* architectura *f*

archives *s* tabulae *f pl*; tabularium *n*

arctic *adj* arcticus

ardent *adj* ardens, fervidus; **—ly** ardenter

ardor *s* ardor, fervor *m*

arduous *adj* arduus

area *s* regio *f*; area *f*; superficies *f*

arena *s* (h)arena *f*

argonaut *s* argonauta *m*

argue *vt* arguěre, probare; *vi* argumentari, disputare, disserěre

argument *s* *(discussion)* disputatio *f*; controversia *f*; *(theme)* argumentum, thema *n*, ratio *f*

argumentation *s* argumentatio *f*

argumentative *adj* ratiocinativus, litigiosus

aria *s* canticum *n*

arid *adj* aridus, siccus

aright *adv* recte

arise *vi* surgěre, exoriri, exsistěre;

to — from nasci ex *(with abl)*

aristocracy *s* *(class)* optimates, nobiles *m pl*; *(government)* optimatum dominat·us -ūs *m*

aristocrat *s* optimas *m*

aristocratic *adj* patricius, generosus

arithmetic *s* arithmetica *n pl*

ark *s* arca *f*

arm *s* bracchium *n*; *(of the sea)* sin·us -ūs *m*; fretum *n*; **—s** arma *n pl*; **by force of —s** vi et armis; **to be under —s** in armis esse; **to lay down —s** ab armis disceděre; arma deděre; **to take up —s** armare; arma suměre

arm *vt* armare; *vi* armari; bellum parare

armada *s* classis magna *f*

armament *s* belli apparat·us -ūs *m*; copiae *f pl*

armchair *s* anconibus fabrefacta sella *f*

armistice *s* indutiae *f pl*

armlet *s* bracchiolum *n*; *(bracelet)* bracchiale *n*

armor *s* armatura *f*, armat·us -ūs *m*; arma *n pl*

armorbearer *s* armiger *m*

armory *s* armamentarium *n*

armpit *s* ala *f*

army *s* exercit·us -ūs *m*; *(in battle)* acies *f*; *(on the march)* agmen *n*

aroma *s* aroma *n*; *(of wine)* flos *m*

aromatic *adj* armomaticus

around *adv* circum, circa; **all — undique**, passim

around *prep* circum *(with acc)*

arouse *vt* suscitare; *(fig)* erigěre; **to — oneself** expergisci

arraign *vt* accusare

arraignment *s* accusatio, actio *f*

arrange *vt* instruěre, struěre, ordinare, disponěre, componěre; *(to agree)* pacisci

arrangement *s* ordo *m*, collocatio *f*; dispositio *f*; pactum n

array *s* vestis f, vestit·us -ūs *m*; habit·us -ūs *m*; *(mil)* acies *f*

array *vt* vestire; adornare; instruěre

arrears *s* reliqua *n pl*; residuum *n*, residuae pecuniae *f pl*; **to be in — relinqui**

arrest *s* prehensio *f*

arrest *vt* *(to seize)* prehenděre, deprehenděre, arripěre; *(movement)* tardare, morari; *(attention)* in se convertěre

arrival *s* advent·us -ūs *m*; *(by sea)* appuls·us -ūs *m*

arrive *vi* pervenire, advenire; *(of a ship)* advehi, appelli

arrogance *s* arrogantia, superbia *f*

arrogant *adj* arrogans, superbus; **—ly** arroganter, insolenter, superbe

arrogate *vt* arrogare, assuměre

arrow *s* sagitta, arundo *f*

arsenal *s* armamentarium *n*; navalia *n pl*

arsenic *s* arsenicum *n*

arson *s* incendium dolo malo *n*

art *s* ars *f*; artificium *n*

artery *s* arteria *f*

artful *adj* artificialis; callidus, subtilis; **—ly** callide, eleganter

article *s* (*object*) res *f*; (*ware*) merx *f*; (*term*) condicio *f*; (*clause*) caput *n*; (*gram*) articulus *m*

articulate *adj* distinctus, dilucidus; **—ly** articulatim, distincte

articulate *vt* explanare, exprimĕre; articulatim dicĕre

articulation *s* commissura *f*; (*fig*) explanatio *f*

artifice *s* artificium *n*; ars *f*; dolum *n*

artificial *adj* artificiosus; factitius; **—ly** arte

artillery *s* tormenta *n pl*

artisan *s* faber *m*; artifex, opifex *m*

artist *s* artifex *m*

artistic *adj* artificiosus, elegans; **—ally** artificiose; affabre

as *conj & adv* ut; quam; (*of time*) dum, cum; ita ut; sicut, velut; **— far —** quoad, usque ad, quantum; **— if** quasi, perinde ac si; ita ut si; **— it were** seu, tamquam; **— long — tamdiu, tantisper dum; — many — tot, totidem; quotquot, quodcumque; — much** tantum; **— often — toties quoties; — soon — cum** primum, simul, simul ac, simul atque; **— well —** ut, tamquam; **— yet** adhuc; **not — yet** nondum, necdum

ascend *vt & vi* ascendĕre

ascendency *s* auctoritas *f*

ascent *s* ascensio *f*; ascens·us -ūs *m*; acclivitas *f*

ascertain *vt* confirmare, comperire

ascetic *adj* asceticus

ascetic *s* asceta *m*

asceticism *s* duritia *f*

ascribe *vt* imputare, tribuĕre, ascribĕre

ash *s* cinis *m*; (*tree*) fraxinus *f*

ashamed *adj* pudibundus; **I am — of** pudet me (*with genit*)

ashen *adj* pallidus

ashore *adv* (*motion*) in litus; (*rest*) in litore

Asiatic *adj* Asiaticus

aside *adv* seorsum, oblique; **to call — sevocare; to lay** *or* **set — ponĕre, seponĕre**

aside from *prep* praeter (*with acc*)

asinine *adj* asininus

ask *vt* rogare, poscĕre; interrogare; requirĕre; *vi* **to — for** petĕre

askance *adv* oblique

askew *adv* traverse

asleep *adj* dormiens; **to be —** dormire; **to fall —** obdormire, obdormiscĕre

asp *s* aspis *f*

asparagus *s* asparagus *m*

aspect *s* aspect·us -ūs, prospect·us -ūs *m*; facies *f*

aspen *s* populus tremula *f*

asperity *s* acerbitas *f*

aspersion *s* opprobrium *n*, calumniatio *f*

asphalt *s* bitumen *n*

asphyxia *s* asphyxia *f*

aspirant *s* petitor *m*

aspiration *s* affectatio, spes *f*; (*pol*) ambitio *f*

aspire *vi* **to — to** affectare, spectare, petĕre, anniti

aspiring *adj* appetens; **aspiring to** appetens (*with genit*)

ass *s* asinus *m*; asina *f*; onager *m*; (*fig*) stultus *m*

assail *vt* appetĕre; oppugnare, invehi

assailable *adj* expugnabilis

assailant *s* oppugnator *m*

assassin *s* sicarius *m*; percussor *m*

assassinate *vt* insidiis interficĕre, occidĕre

assassination *s* caedes *f*

assault *s* impet·us -ūs *m*; oppugnatio, vis *f*; **aggravated — (**law*) vis *f*; **sexual — stupratio *f*; **to take by — expugnare

assault *vt* adoriri, oppugnare; manus inferre (*with dat*); aggredi; (*in speech*) invehi in (*with acc*)

assay *vt* (*metals*) spectare; tentare, conari

assay *s* (*of metals*) obrussa *f*; spectatio *f*

assemblage *s* congregatio *f*; coacervatio *f*

assemble *vt* congregare, convocare; contrahĕre; *vi* convenire

assembly *s* coet·us -ūs *m*; convent·us -ūs *m*; (*pol*) comitia *n pl*; concilium *n*; (*of troops*) contio *f*; synodus *f*

assent *s* assens·us -ūs *m*

assent *vi* assentiri, adnuĕre

assert *vt* asserĕre, affirmare, asseverare; (*to vindicate*) defendĕre

assertion *s* affirmatio, asseveratio *f*; postulatio *f*

assess *vt* (*to tax*) censĕre; (*to value*) aestimare

assessment *s* cens·us -ūs *m*; aestimatio *f*; vectigal, tributum *n*

assessor *s* (*judge*) consessor *m*; (*of taxes*) censor *m*

assets *s* bona *n pl*

assiduous *adj* assiduus; **—ly** assidue

assign *vt* attribuĕre, tribuĕre; (*land*) assignare; (*place*) indicare; (*time*) praestituĕre; (*task*) delegare; (*to allege*) suggerĕre, afferre

assignment *s* assignatio, attributio *f*; delegatio *f*

assimilate *vt* assimulare; (*food*) concoquĕre; (*knowledge*) concipĕre

assimilation *s* assimilatio, appropriatio *f*

assist *vt* adesse (*with dat*), succurrĕre (*with dat*), juvare, adjuvare

assistance *s* auxilium *n*; opem (*no nominative*) *f*; **to be of — to** auxilio esse (*with dat*)

assistant *s* adjutor *m*, adjutrix *f*, administer *m*

associate *adj* socius; collegialis

associate *s* socius, sodalis, consors *m*

associate *vt* consociare, adsciscĕre, conjungĕre; *vi* **to — with** familiariter uti (*with abl*); se adjungĕre (*with dat*)

association s societas f; communi-
tas f; consociatio f; congregatio f

assort vt digerĕre, disponĕre; vi
congruĕre

assortment s digestio, dispositio f;
variae res f pl

assuage vt allevare, placare, lenire,
mitigare

assume vt assumĕre, arrogare; induĕre; (office) inire

assuming adj arrogans

assumption s assumptio f; arrogan-
tio f; (hypothesis) sumptio f

assurance s fiducia f; (guarantee) fides f; (boldness) confidentia, audacia f

assure vt confirmare, affirmare; promittĕre (with dat); adhortari; **to be
assured** confidĕre

assuredly adv certo, profecto

asterisk s asteriscus m

asthmatic adj asthmaticus; **to be
— suspirio laborare**

astonish vt obstupefacĕre; **to be
astonished at** mirari

astonishingly adv admirabiliter

astonishment s admiratio f; stupor
m

astound vt (ob)stupefacĕre

astray adj vagus; **to go — errare;
to lead —** seducĕre

astride adj varicus

astrologer s astrologus m; Chal-
daeus m; mathematicus m

astrological adj astrologicus

astrology s astrologia f; Chaldaeo-
rum divinatio f

astronomer s astrologus m; astrono-
mus m

astronomical adj astronomicus

astronomy s astrologia, astronomia
f

astute adj callidus

asunder adv seorsum, separatim;
use verb with prefix dis- or se-

asylum s asylum, perfugium n

at prep (of place) ad (with acc), apud
(with acc), in (with abl), or loca-
tive case; (of time) in (with abl),
ad (with acc), or abl case

atheism s deos esse negare (used as
neuter noun)

atheist s atheos m

athlete s athleta m

athletic adj athleticus; lacertosus

atlas s orbis terrarum descriptio f

atmosphere s aër m; caelum n;
inane n

atmospheric adj aërius (genit)

atom s atomus f; corpus individuum
n; (fig) mica, particula f

atomic adj atomicus; **— theory**
atomorum doctrina f

atone vi **to — for** piare, expiare

atonement s piaculum n; expiatio,
compensatio f

atrocious adj atrox, dirus; nefarius,
nefandus; immanis; **—ly** nefarie

atrocity s atrocitas f; atrox facinus n

atrophy s tabes, atrophia f

atrophy vi tabescĕre, macrescĕre

attach vt annectĕre, adjungĕre; ap-

plicare; affigĕre; **to be attached
to** adhaerēre (with dat)

attachment s adhaesio f; (emotional) amor m; vinculum n; studium n

attack s impet·us -ūs m; oppugnatio
f; (of cavalry) incurs·us -ūs m; (of
disease, etc.) tentatio f

attack vt adoriri, aggredi, oppugnare; (with words) invehi in (with
acc), insequi; (of diseases) corripĕre, invadĕre, tentare

attacker s oppugnator, provocator m

attain vt adipisci, consequi; **to — to**
pervenire ad (with acc)

attainable adj impetrabilis, obti-
nendus

attempt s conat·us -ūs m, inceptum
n; (risk) ausum, periculum n; **first
—** tirocinium n

attempt vt conari, niti, temptare,
moliri

attend vt (to accompany) comitari;
(to escort) deducĕre; (to be present
at) adesse (with dat), interesse
(with dat); vi **to — on** apparēre
(with dat); frequentare, assectari;
adesse (with dat); **to — to** animadvertĕre, procurare; (to comply with)
obtemperare (with dat); invigilare

attendance s frequentia f; expecta-
tio, adsectatio, cura, diligentia f;
obsequium n; (retinue) comitat·us
-ūs m

attendant adj adjunctus

attendant s comes m; assecla, apparitor m; famulus m, famula f

attention s animadversio f; animi
attentio f; (to duty) cura, diligentia f; **to call —** to indicare; **to
pay —** to operam dare (with dat),
studēre (with dat)

attentive adj attentus; sedulus; officiosus; **—ly** attente, intento animo;
sedulo; officiose

attenuate vt attenuare, extenuare

attenuation s extenuatio f

attest vt testari, testificari

attestation s testificatio f

attic s cenaculum n

Attic adj Atticus; (fig) subtilis, elegans

attire s ornat·us -ūs m; vestis f; ha-
bit·us -ūs m; vestit·us -ūs m

attire vt vestire; adornare

attitude s habit·us -ūs, stat·us -ūs
m; (mental) ratio f

attorney s cognitor, procurator, advocatus, actor m

attorney general s advocatus fisci,
procurator publicus m

attract vt trahĕre, attrahĕre; (fig)
allicĕre

attraction s vis attractionis f; (fig)
illecebra f, invitamentum n

attractive adj blandus, suavis, lepidus, venustus; **—ly** blande, suaviter, venuste, lepide

attractiveness s lepos m, venustas f

attribute s proprium, attributum n

attribute vt tribuĕre, attribuĕre; assignare, delegare

attrition s attrit·us -ūs m

attune *vt* modulari
auburn *adj* fulvus; aureus
auction *s* auctio *f*; *(public)* hasta *f*; **to hold an —** auctionem facĕre; **to sell by —** sub hasta vendĕre
auctioneer *s* praeco *m*
audacious *adj* audax; **—ly** audacter
audacity *s* audacia *f*
audible *adj* quod audiri potest
audibly *adv* clara voce
audience *s* auditores *m pl*; *(bystanders)* corona *f*
audit *s* rationum inspectio *f*
audit *vt* inspicĕre
auditory *adj* auditorius
Augean *adj* Augiae *(genit)*
auger *s* terebra *f*
augment *vt* augēre, ampliare; *vi* augēri, accrescĕre
augur *s* augur *m*
augur *vi* augurari
augury *s* augurium, auspicium *n*; auguratio *f*
august *adj* augustus; magnificus
August *s* (mensis) Sextilis, (mensis) Augustus *m*
Augustan *adj* Augustalis
aunt *s* *(on father's side)* amita *f*; *(on mother's side)* matertera *f*
auspices *s* auspicium *n*; **to take —** auspicari; **without taking —** inauspicato
auspicious *adj* auspicatus; faustus, felix; **—ly** auspicato; feliciter
austere *adj* austerus, severus; **—ly** austere, severe
austerity *s* austeritas, severitas *f*
authentic *adj* certus; verus; ratus; *(law)* authenticus; fide dignus; genuinus
authenticate *vt* recognoscĕre
authentication *s* auctoritas *f*; legibus confirmatio *f*
authenticity *s* auctoritas, fides *f*
author *s* auctor, scriptor *m*; *(inventor)* conditor *m*; *(of a crime)* caput *n*
authoress *s* auctor *f*
authoritative *adj* imperiosus; fidus; **—ly** praecise
authority *s* auctoritas, potestas *f*; *(leave)* licentia *f*; jus *n*; imperium *n*; magistrat·us -ūs *m*; **to have it on good —** bono auctore habēre
authorization *s* auctoritate confirmatio *f*; licentia *f*
authorize *vt* potestatem *or* auctoritatem dare *(with dat)*, mandare; *(law)* sancire
authorship *s* scriptoris munus *n*; auctoritas *f*
autobiography *s* de vita sua scriptus liber *m*
autocrat *s* dominus *m*
autograph *s* chirographum *n*
autograph *vt* manu propria scribĕre
automatic *adj* necessarius
automaton *s* automaton *n*
autumn *s* autumnus *m*
autumnal *adj* autumnalis
auxiliaries *s* *(mil)* auxilia *n pl*; auxiliarii *m pl*

auxiliary *adj* auxiliaris, auxiliarius
auxiliary *s* adjutor *m*
avail *vt* prodesse *(with dat)*; **to — oneself of** uti *(with abl)*; *vi* valēre
avail *s* **to be of no —** usui non esse
availability *s* utilitas *f*
available *adj* in promptu; utilis
avalanche *s* montis ruina *f*
avarice *s* avaritia *f*; sordes *f*
avaricious *adj* avarus, avidus; **—ly** avare
avenge *vt* vindicare, ulcisci
avenger *s* ultor *m*, vindex *m* & *f*
avenging *adj* ultrix, vindex
avenue *s* xystus *m*, xystum *n*
average *s* medium *n*; **on the — fere**
average *vi* fere esse
averse *adj* aversus; **to be — to** abhorrēre ab *(with abl)*; **—ly** averse
aversion *s* odium, fastidium *n*; **to have an — for** fastidire
avert *vt* avertĕre, amovēre, abducĕre
aviary *s* aviarium *n*
avid *adj* avidus
avocation *s* officium *n*, negotia *n pl*
avoid *vt* vitare, fugĕre; *(a blow)* declinare
avoidable *adj* evitabilis
avoidance *s* vitatio *f*; declinatio *f*
avow *vt* asserĕre, profitēri
avowal *s* confessio *f*
avowedly *adv* palam, aperte, ex confesso
await *vt* exspectare
awake *adj* vigil, vigilans; **to be — vigilare**
awaken *vt* excitare, suscitare, expergefacĕre; *vi* expergisci
award *s* praemium *n*; *(decision)* arbitrium, judicium *n*
award *vt* tribuĕre; *(law)* adjudicare, addicĕre
aware *adj* gnarus, sciens; **to be — of** scire
away *adv* use verbs with prefix a- *or* ab-; **far —** procul, longe; **to be — abesse**; **to go — abire**
awe *s* reverentia *f*; formido *f*, met·us -ūs, terror *m*; **to stand in — of** verēri; venerari
awful *adj* formidulosus, dirus, terribilis; **—ly** terribiliter, formidulose
awhile *adv* paulisper, aliquamdiu, parumper
awkward *adj* ineptus; rusticus, rudis; inhabilis; *(fig)* molestus; **—ly** inepte; rustice; dure; inscite
awkwardness *s* ineptia *f*; imperitia, rusticitas *f*
awl *s* subula *f*
awning *s* velarium *n*; inductio *f*
awry *adj* obliquus; pravus
awry *adv* oblique; prave
ax *s* securis *f*
axiom *s* axioma, pronuntiatum *n*, sententia *f*
axis *s* axis *m*
axle *s* axis *m*
azure *adj* caeruleus

B

baa *s* balat·us -ūs *m*
baa *vi* balare
babble *s* garrulitas *f*
babble *vi* blaterare, garrire
babbler *s* blatero, garrulus *m*
babbling *adj* garrulus, loquax
babe *s* infans *m* & *f*
baboon *s* cynocephalus *m*
baby *s* infans *m* & *f*
babyish *adj* infantilis
bacchanal *s* bacchans *m*, baccha *f*
bacchanalian *adj* bacchanalis
Bacchic *adj* bacchicus
bachelor *s* caelebs *m*; (*degree*) baccalaureus *m*
back *s* tergum, dorsum *n*; aversum *n*; at one's — a tergo
back *adv* retro, retrorsum; *or use verbs with prefix* re- *or* retro-
back *vt* adjuvare; favēre (*with dat*), obsecundare (*with dat*), adesse (*with dat*); *vi* to — away from defugēre; to — up retrogradi
backboard *s* pluteus *m*
backbone *s* spina *f*
backdoor *s* posticum *n*
backer *s* adjutor, fautor *m*
background *s* recess·us -ūs *m*
backstairs *s* scalae posticae *f pl*
backward *adv* retro; retrorsum; rursus
backward *adj* (*reversed*) supinus; (*slow*) piger, tardus; (*late*) serus; to be — cunctari
backwardness *s* tarditas *f*; pigritia *f*
bacon *s* lardum *n*
bad *adj* malus, parvus, nequam; improbus; aegrotus; (*of weather*) adversus; to go — corrumpi; —ly male, prave; improbe
badge *s* insigne, signum *n*
badger *s* meles *f*
badger *vt* vexare, inquietare, sollicitare
badness *s* malitia, pravitas, nequitia, improbitas *f*
baffle *vt* decipēre, fallēre, eludēre
bag *s* saccus *m*; (*of leather*) uter *m*; (*of network*) reticulum *n*
baggage *s* sarcinae *f pl*; impedimenta *n pl*; scruta *n pl*
bail *s* vadimonium *n*; vas *m*; (*for debt*) praes *m*; to accept — for vadari; to put up — for spondēre pro (*with abl*), fidepromittēre
bailiff *s* (*sergeant of court of justice*) apparitor *m*; (*manager of estate*) villicus *m*
bailiwick *s* jurisdictio *f*
bait *s* esca *f*; (*fig*) incitamentum *n*, illecebra *f*
bait *vt* inescare; (*to tease*) lacessēre
bake *vt* torrēre, coquēre
baker *s* pistor *m*
bakery *s* pistrina *f*, pistrinum *n*
balance *s* libra, trutina, statera *f*; (*equipoise*) aequipondium *n*; (*in bookkeeping*) reliquum *n*; (*fig*) compensatio *f*

balance *vt* librare; compensare; (*accounts*) consolidare, dispungēre; *vi* constare; the account balances ratio constat
balance sheet *s* ratio accepti et expensi *f*
balcony *s* maenianum *n*; podium *n*
bald *adj* calvus, glaber; (*fig*) aridus; —ly (*in style*) jejune
baldness *s* calvitium *n*; (*of style*) ariditas, jejunitas *f*
bale *s* sarcina *f*, fascis *m*
bale *vt* (*e.g., hay*) involvēre; to — out exhaurire
baleful *adj* funestus; perniciosus, noxius
balk *s* (*of wood*) tignum *n*; (*fig*) frustratio *f*
balk *vt* frustrari, eludēre, decipēre
ball *s* globulus *m*; (*for playing*) pila *f*; to play — pilā ludēre
ballad *s* carmen *n*
ballast *s* saburra *f*
ballast *vt* saburrare
ballet *s* pantomimus *m*
ballet dancer *s* pantomimus *m*, pantomima *f*
ballot *s* tabella *f*; suffragium *n*
ballot box *s* cista, cistula *f*
balm *s* balsamum *n*; unguentum *n*; (*fig*) solatium *n*
balmy *adj* balsaminus; suavis, lenis
balsam *s* balsamum *n*
bamboo *s* arundo indica *f*
ban *s* edictum *n*; proscriptio *f*; interdictum *n*
ban *vt* interdicēre (*with dat*), vetare
banana *s* ariena *f*
band *s* vinculum, ligamentum *n*; (*for the head*) redimiculum *n*, infula *f*; (*troop*) caterva *f*, chorus *m*; grex *f*; man·us -ūs *f*; in —s turmatim
band *vi* to — together conjungi, consociari
bandage *s* fascia, ligatura *f*
bandage *vt* ligare, obligare
bandit *s* latro *m*
banditry *s* latrocinium *n*
bandy *vt* jactare; to — words altercari
bane *s* venenum *n*; virus *n*; (*fig*) pestis, pernicies *f*
baneful *adj* pestiferus, perniciosus, exitiosus
bang *s* crepit·us -ūs, sonit·us -ūs *m*
bang *vt* verberare; *vi* sonare, crepare
banish *vt* expellēre, pellēre, relegare, deportare; aquā et igni interdicēre (*with dat*)
banishment *s* (*act*) ejectio, relegatio *f*; interdictio aquae et ignis *f*; (*state*) exilium *n*
banister *s* epimedion *n*
bank *s* (*of a river*) ripa *f*; (*of earth*) agger *m*; (*com*) argentaria *f*, mensa publica *f*

banker s argentarius, mensarius m
banking s argentaria negotiatio f
bank note s tessera mensae publicae f
bankrupt s conturbator, decoctor m; **to be** or **become** — rationes conturbare; decoquěre; **to go** — foro cedēre
bankruptcy s rationum conturbatio f; (*fig*) naufragium patrimonii n
banner s vexillum n
banquet s convivium n, epulae f pl
banter s cavillatio f; jocus m
banter vi cavillari
bantering s cavillatio f
baptism s baptisma n, baptismus m
baptize vt baptizare
bar s vectis f; (*of door*) obex m; repagulum n; (*fig*) impedimentum n; (*ingot*) later m; (*in court of justice*) cancelli m pl, claustra n pl; (*legal profession*) forum n; (*counter*) abacus m; **of the** — forensis; **to practice at the** — causas agěre
bar vt (*door*) obserare; (*to keep away*) obstare (*with dat*), prohibēre, includěre
barb s hamus m; aculeus m
barbarian adj barbarus
barbarian s barbarus m
barbaric adj barbaricus
barbarism s barbaria, barbaries f; feritas f; (*of language*) barbarismus m
barbarity s ferocia, saevitia, immanitas f
barbarous adj barbarus; ferus, immanis; —**ly** barbare; saeve
barbed adj hamatus
barber s tonsor m, tonstrix f
bard s vates m
bare adj nudus; merus; (*of style*) pressus; **to lay** — nudare, detegěre
bare vt nudare, denudare; detegěre, aperire
barefaced adj impudens; —**ly** impudenter
barefoot adj nudis pedibus; discalceatus
bareheaded adj nudo capite
barely adv vix, aegre
bargain s pactio f, pactum n; **to strike a** — pacisci
bargain vi pacisci
barge s linter f
bark s (*of tree*) cortex m & f, liber m; (*of dog*) latrat·us -ūs m; (*ship*) navis, ratis f
bark vi latrare; **to** — **at** allatrare
barley s hordeum n
barley adj hordeacus
barmaid s ministra cauponae f
barn s granarium, horreum n
barometer s barometrum n
barometric adj barometricus
baron s baro m
barracks s castra (stativa) n pl
barrel s cadus m, dolium n, cupa f
barren adj sterilis; macer; jejunus; (*fig*) angustus
barrenness s sterilitas f

barricade s munimentum n; claustrum n
barricade vt obsaepire, obstruěre, oppilare
barrier s limes m; cancelli m pl; (*fig*) claustra n pl
barrister s advocatus m
barter s permutatio f; merx f
barter vt mutare, commutare; vi merces mutare, merces pacisci
base adj humilis, ignobilis, obscurus; inferior; servilis; infamis, vilis, turpis; —**ly** abjecte; turpiter
base s basis f; (*mus*) sonus gravis m; (*fig*) fundamentum n; (*mil*) castra n pl
baseless adj inanis, vanus, falsus
basement s fundamentum n, basis f; imum tabulatum n
baseness s humilitas f; turpitudo f
bashful adj erubescens; pudens; modestus; verecundus; —**ly** timide, verecunde; modeste
bashfulness s pudor m; rubor m; verecundia f
basic adj primus, principalis
basilica s basilica f
basin s (*for washing*) trulleum n, trulla f; (*reservoir*) labrum n
basis s fundamentum n
bask vi apricari
basket s corbis f, canistrum n; (*for wool*) quasillum n; cophinus m
bas-relief s caelamen n; toreuma n
bass s sonus gravissimus m
bast s tilia f
bastard adj spurius
bastard s nothus, spurius m
baste vt lardo perfunděre
bastion s propugnaculum, castellum n
bat s (*bird*) vespertilio m; (*club*) clava f
batch s massa n; numerus m
bath s balneum n; (*public*) balnea n pl; (*tub*) alveus m, labrum n; lavatio f; **cold** — frigidarium n; **hot** — cal(i)darium n
bathe vt lavare; vi balneo uti, lavari, perlui
bathing s lavatio f; natatio f
bathtub s alveus m
batman s calo m
baton s virga f
battalion s cohors f
batter vt percutěre, obtunděre, diruěre, verberare, quassare
battering ram s aries m
battle s proelium n, pugna f; acies f
battle vi pugnare, proeliari
battle array s acies f
battle-ax s bipennis f
battlement s pinna f
bauble s tricae f pl
bawd s lena f
bawdry s lenocinium n
bawl vi vociferari, clamitare
bawling s vociferatio f; indecorus clamor m
bay s (*sea*) sin·us -ūs m; (*tree*) laurea, laurus f; **at** — interclusus
bay adj (*light-colored*) helvus; (*dark-colored*) spadix; (*of bay*) laureus

bay *vi* latrare
bayonet *s* pugio *f*
bayonet *vt* pugione fodĕre
bazaar *s* forum rerum venalium *n*
be *vi* esse; exsistĕre; (*condition*) se habēre; **to — absent** abesse; **to — against** adversari; **to — amongst** interesse (*with dat*); **to — for** (*to side with*) favēre (*with dat*), stare cum (*with abl*); **to — present** adesse
beach *s* litus *n*, acta *f*
beach *vt* subducĕre; *vi* vadis impingĕre
beacon *s* ignis in specula *m*; (*lighthouse*) pharus *m*
bead *s* pilula, sphaerula *f*
beagle *s* parvus canis venaticus *m*
beak *s* rostrum *n*
beaked *adj* rostratus
beaker *s* poculum *n*, cantharus *m*
beam *s* (*of wood*) tignum *n*, trabs *f*; (*of light*) radius *m*, jubar *n*; nitor *m*
beam *vi* radiare, refulgēre; (*of a person*) arridēre
beaming *adj* nitens, lucidus
bean *s* faba *f*; phaselus *m & f*
bear *vt* (*to carry*) portare, ferre; (*to endure*) ferre, pati, tolerare; (*to produce*) ferre; (*to beget*) parĕre; **to — away** auferre; **to — out** (*to confirm*) arguĕre; **to — witness to** testari; *vi* **to — down on** appropinquare; **to — upon** (*to refer to*) pertinēre ad (*with acc*); **to — up under** obsistĕre (*with dat*), sustinēre; **to — with** indulgēre (*with dat*)
bear *s* ursus *m*, ursa *f*
bearable *adj* tolerandus, tolerabilis
beard *s* barba *f*; (*of grain*) arista *f*
bearded *adj* barbatus; intonsus
beardless *adj* inberbis
bearer *s* (*porter*) bajulus *m*; (*of litter*) lecticarius *m*; (*of letter*) tabellarius *m*; (*of news*) nuntius *m*
bearing *s* (*posture*) gest·us -ūs, vult·us -ūs *m*; (*direction*) regio *f*; **to have a — on** pertinēre ad (*with acc*)
beast *s* belua *f*; bestia *f*; (*wild*) fera *f*; (*domestic*) pecus *f*
beast of burden *s* jumentum *n*
beastly *adj* obscenus, foedus, spurcus
beat *vt* (*to punish*) verberare; (*to knock*) pulsare; (*to conquer*) superare, vincĕre; (*the body in grief*) plangĕre; **to — back** repellĕre; **to — down** demoliri; **to — in** perfringĕre; *vi* palpitare; **to — upon** (*of rain*) impluĕre; (*of waves*) illidĕre
beat *s* (*blow*) plaga *f*, ict·us -ūs *m*; (*of the heart*) palpitatio *f*; (*mus*) percussio *f*; (*patrol*) vigiles nocte ambulantes *m pl*
beaten *adj* victus; (*worn*) tritus
beating *s* verberatio *f*; ict·us -ūs *m*; verbera *n pl*; (*defeat*) repulsa *f*; clades *f*; (*of the heart*) palpitatio *f*
beautiful *adj* pulcher; (*shapely*) formosus; **—ly** pulchre, belle
beautify *vt* ornare, decorare

beauty *s* pulchritudo *f*; forma *f*; (*of places*) amoenitas *f*
beaver *s* castor, fiber *m*; (*of helmet*) buccula *f*
because *conj* quod, quia, quoniam; quippe qui
because of *prep* ob (*with acc*), propter (*with acc*), gratiā (*with genit*)
beck *s* nut·us -ūs *m*; **at the — and call** ad arbitrium
beckon *vt* nutare, annuĕre
become *vt* decēre; *vi* fieri
becoming *adj* decens; decorus; conveniens; **—ly** decenter; digne; honeste
bed *s* lectus *m*, cubile *n*; (*in a garden*) areola *f*; (*of a river*) alveus *m*; **to go to —** cubitum ire; **to make the — lectum sternĕre**
bedding *s* stragulum *n*
bedeck *vt* decorare, ornare
bedevil *vt* (*to enchant*) fascinare
bedfellow *s* tori socius *m*, tori socia *f*
bedlam *s* tumult·us -ūs *m*
bedpost *s* fulcrum *n*
bedraggled *adj* sordidus
bedridden *adj* **to be — lecto tenēri**
bedroom *s* cubiculum *n*
bedtime *s* hora somni *f*
bee *s* apis *f*
beef *s* bubula caro *f*
beehive *s* alveus *m*; alvearium *n*
beekeeper *s* apiarius *m*
beer *s* cerevisia *f*
beet *s* beta *f*
beetle *s* scarabaeus *m*
befall *vt* accidĕre (*with dat*); contingĕre (*with dat*); *vi* accidĕre, contingĕre, evenire
befit *vt* decēre, convenire in (*with acc*)
befitting *adj* decens; conveniens, idoneus; **it is — decet**
before *prep* ante (*with acc*); prae (*with abl*); pro (*with abl*); coram (*with abl*); apud (*with acc*); **— all things** imprimis; **— long** jamdudum; **— now** antehac
before *conj* antequam, priusquam
beforehand *adv* antea
befriend *vt* favēre (*with dat*), sublevare, adjuvare
beg *vt* petĕre, poscĕre, orare, obsecrare; *vi* mendicare
beget *vt* gignĕre, procreare, generare
beggar *s* mendicus *m*
begging *s* mendicitas *f*; **to go — mendicare**
begin *vt & vi* incipĕre, incohare, exordiri; **to — with** incipĕre ab (*with abl*)
beginner *s* auctor *m*; inceptor *m*; tiro *m*
beginning *s* inceptio *f*; initium *n*; exordium *n*; origo *f*; principium *n*; **at the — of winter** ineunte hieme
begone *interj* apage!
beguile *vt* fallĕre, fraudare
behalf *s* **on — of** pro (*with abl*)
behave *vi* se gerĕre; **to — towards**

uti (with abl); **well behaved** bene moratus

behavior s mores m pl

behead vt detruncare, obtruncare

beheading s decollatio f

behest s jussum n

behind adv pone, a tergo, post; **to be left** — relinqui

behind prep pone (with acc); post (with acc)

behold vt conspicěre; obtuěri

behold interj ecce!, en!

being s ens n; natura f; essentia f; homo m

bejewelled adj gemmatus, gemmeus

belabor vt mulcare, verberare

belch s ruct·us -ūs m

belch vi ructare, eructare

belfry s campanile n

belie vt repugnare; (to refute) refutare, refellěre

belief s fides f; opinio, persuasio f

believe vt (thing) creděre; (person) creděre (with dat); (to suppose) existimare, opinari, putare, creděre, arbitrari; **to make** — simulare

believer s credens m & f; Christianus m

bell s (large) campana f; (small) tintinnabulum n

belle s formosa puella f

belles lettres s litterae f pl

belligerent adj belliger, belligerans, bellans

bellow vi rugire, mugire

bellowing s mugit·us -ūs m

bellows s follis m

belly s venter m; abdomen n

bellyache s tormina n pl

belong vi to — to esse (with genit); inesse (with dat); pertinēre ad (with acc)

beloved adj dilectus, carus; **dearly** — carissimus

below adj inferus

below adv infra; subter

below prep infra (with acc); sub (with abl or acc)

belt s cingulum n; (swordbelt) balteus m; zona f

bemoan vt deplorare, lamentari

bemused adj attonitus

bench s scamnum, sedile, subsellium n; (for rowers) transtrum n

bend vt flectěre, curvare; inclinare; (bow) intenděre; (to persuade) intenděre; vi se inflectěre; **to** — **back** reflectěre; **to** — **down** or **over** se demittěre

bend s plica f; flex·us -ūs m; curvamen n; (fig) inclinatio f

bending s flexura, curvatura, inclinatio f

bending adj flexus; inclinans; acclivis; declivis; (concave) concavus

beneath adv subter

beneath prep sub (with acc or abl)

benediction s benedictio f

benefaction s beneficium n

benefactor s largitor m; patronus m

benefactress s patrona f

beneficence s beneficentia f

beneficent adj beneficus, benignus, liberalis; —**ly** benefice

beneficial adj utilis, commodus; salutaris; —**ly** utiliter

benefit s beneficium n, gratia f; fruct·us -ūs m; **to have the** — **of** frui (with abl)

benefit vt juvare; prodesse (with dat); vi proficěre; lucrari

benevolence s benevolentia f

benevolent s benevolus, beneficus; benignus, liberalis; —**ly** benevole

benign adj benignus; —**ly** benigne

bent adj curvus, flexus; (of the mind) attentus; — **backwards** recurvus; — **forwards** pronus; — **inwards** camur; sinuosus

bent s flex·us -ūs m, plica f; curvatura f; (inclination) ingenium n, inclinatio f

benumb vt torpore afficěre

bequeath vt legare

bequest s legatum n

bereave vt orbare; privare; spoliare

bereavement s orbitas f; damnum n

bereft adj orbus, orbatus, privatus

berry s bacca f; acinus m

berth s statio f; (cabin) diaeta f; **to give wide** — **to** devitare

beseech vt obsecrare, implorare, supplicare

beset vt circumdare, obsiděre, circumsedēre; urgēre

beside prep ad (with acc), apud (with acc), juxta (with acc); — **the point** nihil ad rem; **to be** — **oneself** delirare

besides adv praeterea, ultro, insuper

besides prep praeter (with acc)

besiege vt circumsedēre, obsiděre

besieging s obsessio, circumsessio f

besmirch vt maculare

best adj optimus, praestantissimus; **the** — **part** major pars f

best s flos m; **to do one's** — **pro** virili parte agěre; **to have the** — **of it** praevalēre, valēre; **to make the** — **of** aequo animo ferre; **to the** — **of one's ability** pro viribus

bestial adj bestialis; immanis

bestir vt **to** — **oneself** expergisci

bestow vt tribuěre, conferre; donare, largiri

bestower s largitor, dator m

bet s pignus, depositum n

bet vt deponěre; vi pignore contendēre

betide vi evenire, acciděre

betoken vt indicare, portenděre

betray vt traděre, proděre; (feelings) arguěre

betrayer s proditor, traditor m

betroth vt spondēre, despondēre

betrothal s sponsalia n pl; pactio nuptialis f

betrothed adj sponsus, pactus

better adj melior; potior, praestantior; superior; **it is** — praestat; **to get** — convalescěre; **to get the** — **of** superare, vincěre

better adv melius, potius; praestantius; rectius; satius

better *vt* meliorem facĕre; corrigĕre; to — **oneself** proficĕre

betters *s* superiores *m pl*

between *prep* inter (*with acc*); — **whiles** interim

betwixt *prep* inter (*with acc*)

bevel *vt* obliquare

beverage *s* potio *f*, pot·us -ūs *m*

bevy *s* grex *f*

bewail *vt* deplorare, ingemĕre, queri, lamentari

beware *vi* cavēre; to — **of** cavēre

bewilder *vt* perturbare, confundĕre

bewilderment *s* perturbatio *f*

bewitch *vt* fascinare; (*to charm*) demulcēre

beyond *adv* supra, ultra; ulterius

beyond *prep* ultra (*with acc*); (*motion*) trans (*with acc*); supra (*with acc*), extra (*with acc*); **to go —** excedĕre

bias *s* inclinatio *f*; praeponderatio *f*

bias *vt* inclinare

Bible *s* divina scriptura *f*, biblia *n pl*

Biblical *adj* biblicus

bibliography *s* bibliographia *f*

bicker *vi* jurgare, altercari

bickering *s* altercatio *f*

bid *vt* jubēre, mandare, rogare; (*to invite*) invitare; (*at auction*) licitari, licēri; to — **farewell** valedicĕre

bid *s* licitatio *f*; **to make a —** licēri

bidder *s* licitator *m*

bidding *s* jussum *n*; (*auction*) licitatio *f*

bide *vt* exspectare, manēre

biennial *adj* biennalis, bimus

bier *s* feretrum *n*, sandapila *f*

big *adj* ingens, vastus; grandis, amplus; — **with child** gravida; — **with young** praegnans; **very —** permagnus

bigamist *s* bimaritus *m*

bigamy *s* bigamia *f*

bigot *s* nimis obstinatus fautor *m*

bigoted *adj* nimis obstinatus

bigotry *s* contumacia *f*; nimia obstinatio *f*

bile *s* bilis *f*

bilge water *s* sentina *f*

bilious *adj* biliosus

bilk *vt* fraudare; frustrari

bill *s* (*of a bird*) rostrum *n*; (*proposed law*) rogatio *f*; lex *f*; plebiscitum *n*; (*com*) ratio debiti *f*; syngrapha *f*; (*notice*) libellus *m*; **to introduce a —** ferre, legem ferre; populum rogare; **to pass a —** legem perferre; **to turn down a —** antiquare

billet *s* hospitium *n*

billet *vt* per hospitia dispargĕre

billion *s* billio *m*

billow *s* fluct·us -ūs *m*

billowy *adj* fluctuosus, undabundus

bin *s* (*in wine cellar*) loculus *m*; (*for grain*) cista *f*, panarium *n*

bind *vt* ligare, nectĕre, stringĕre, vincire; (*by obligation*) obligare; (*books*) conglutinare; (*wounds*) obligare; **to — fast** devincire; **to — together** colligare; **to — up** alligare; (*med*) astringĕre

binding *adj* obligatorius; (*law*) ratus

binding *s* religatio *f*; compages *f*

biographer *s* vitae scriptor *m*

biography *s* vita *f*

biped *s* bipes *m*

birch *adj* betulinus

birch tree *s* betula *f*

bird *s* avis, volucris *f*

birdcage *s* cavea *f*

birdcall *s* fistula aucupatoria *f*

birdlime *s* viscum *n*

bird's nest *s* nidus *m*

birth *s* part·us -ūs *m*; ort·us -ūs *m*; (*race*) genus *n*

birthday *s* dies natalis *m*

birthday cake *s* libum *n*

birthplace *s* patria *f*

birthright *s* patrimonium *n*

biscuit *s* crustulum *n*

bisect *vt* dividĕre

bishop *s* episcopus *m*

bison *s* bison *m*; urus *m*

bit *s* (*for a horse*) frenum *n*; (*small amount*) pars *f*, fragmentum *n*; (*of food*) frustum *n*; — **by** — minutatim

bitch *s* canis *f*

bite *s* mors·us -ūs *m*; (*fig*) sarcasmus *m*

bite *vt* mordēre; (*as pepper, frost, etc.*) urĕre

biting *adj* mordax; (*fig*) asper; mordens

bitter *adj* amarus; (*fig*) acerbus; asper; gravis; —**ly** acerbe; aspere

bitterness *s* amaritas *f*; (*fig*) acerbitas *f*; asperitas *f*

bitters *s* absinthium *n*

bivouac *s* excubiae *f pl*

blab *s* garrulus *m*

blab *vi* garrire, deblaterare

black *adj* niger; ater; (*in looks*) trux; (*of character*) scelestus

black *s* nigrum *n*; (*negro*) Aethiops *m*; **in — pullatus

black-and-blue *adj* lividus

blackberry *s* morum *n*

blackbird *s* merula *f*

black death *s* pestis *f*

blacken *vt* nigrare; denigrare

blackguard *s* nebulo *m*

blacklist *s* proscriptio *f*

black magic *s* magicae artes *f pl*

blackness *s* nigritia, nigrities *f*

blacksmith *s* ferrarius faber *m*

bladder *s* vesica *f*

blade *s* (*edge*) lamina *f*; (*of grass*) caulis *m*, herba *f*; (*of oar*) palma *f*

blamable *adj* culpabilis; reus

blame *vt* reprehendĕre, culpare, vituperare

blame *s* culpa *f*; reprehensio *f*

blameless *adj* integer, innoxius; irreprehensus; —**ly** integre, innocenter

blanch *vt* candefacĕre; *vi* exalbescĕre, pallescĕre

bland *adj* blandus

blandishment *s* blanditia *f*, blandimentum *n*; (*charm*) lenocinium *n*

blank *adj* vacuus, albus, purus; (*expression*) stolidus

blanket *s* lodix *f*; stragulum *n*
blare *s* strepit·us –ūs, clangor, stridor *m*
blare *vi* stridēre, canēre
blaspheme *vi* maledicēre, execrari; blasphemare
blasphemous *adj* maledicus, impius; blasphemus
blasphemy *s* maledicta *n pl*, impietas *f*; blasphemia, blasphematio *f*
blast *s* flat·us –ūs *m*, flamen *n*
blast *vt* discutēre, disjicēre; (*crops*) urēre, robigine afficēre
blaze *s* flamma *f*; fulgor *m*
blaze *vi* flagrare, ardēre; **to — up** exardescēre
bleach *vt* dealbare, candefacēre
bleak *adj* desertus; immitis
blear-eyed *adj* lippus; **to be — lip**pire
bleat *vi* balare
bleating *s* balat·us –ūs *m*
bleed *vi* sanguinem fundēre
bleeding *adj* crudus, sanguineus
bleeding *s* (*bloodletting*) sanguinis missio *f*; (*flowing of blood*) sanguinis profusio *f*
blemish *s* macula *f*, vitium *n*; labes *f*
blemish *vt* maculare, foedare
blend *vt* commiscēre, immiscēre
bless *vt* beare; (*eccl*) benedicēre; (*consecrate*) consecrare; (*with success*) secundare
blessed *adj* beatus; pius; fortunatus; (*of emperors*) divus
blessing *s* (*thing*) bonum, commodum *n*; (*eccl*) benedictio *f*
blight *s* robigo, uredo *f*
blight *vt* urēre; robigine afficēre; (*fig*) nocēre (*with dat*)
blind *adj* caecus; obscurus; (*fig*) ignarus; **—ly** (*rashly*) temere
blind *vt* caecare, occaecare; (*fig*) occaecare, fallēre
blindfold *vt* oculos obligare (*with dat*)
blindfolded *adj* obligatis oculis
blindness *s* caecitas *f*; (*fig*) temeritas *f*; stultitia *f*
blink *vi* connivēre
bliss *s* beatitudo *f*
blissful *adj* beatus; **—ly** beate
blister *s* pustula *f*
blister *vt & vi* pustulare
blithe *adj* hilaris, hilarus
bloated *adj* tumidus, turgidus
block *s* truncus, stipes *m*; (*of stone*) massa *f*; (*of houses*) insula *f*
block *vt* claudēre; (*to impede*) obstare (*with dat*); **to — up** obstruēre
blockade *s* obsidio *f*; **to raise a —** obsidionem solvēre
blockade *vt* obsidēre, claudēre
blockhead *s* caudex *m*
blood *s* sanguis *m*; (*gore*) cruor *m*, sanies *f*; (*fig*) (*slaughter*) caedes *f*; (*lineage*) genus *n*; **bad —** simultas *f*; **to staunch —** sanguinem supprimēre
bloodless *adj* exsanguis; (*without bloodshed*) incruentus
blood-red *adj* cruentus; sanguineus, sanguinolentus

bloodshed *s* caedes *f*
bloodshot *adj* cruore suffusus
bloodstained *adj* cruentus, cruentatus, sanguinolentus
bloodsucker *s* sanguisuga *f*; hirudo *f*
bloodthirsty *adj* sanguinarius; sanguinolentus
blood vessel *s* vena *f*
bloody *adj* cruentus
bloom *s* flos *m*
bloom *vi* florēre, florescēre; vigēre
blooming *adj* florens; floridus; nitidus
blossom *s* flos *m*
blot *s* macula, litura *f*; (*fig*) labes *f*, dedecus *n*
blot *vt* maculare; conspurcare; **to — out** delēre; (*to erase*) obliterare
blotch *s* macula *f*; pustula *f*
blotched *adj* maculosus
blow *s* (*stroke*) plaga *f*, ict·us –ūs *m*; (*with the fist*) colaphus *m*; (*fig*) plaga *f*; calamitas *f*
blow *vt* (*instrument*) canēre; (*breath*) anhelare; **to — out** extinguēre; **to — the nose** emungēre; **to — up** inflare; *vi* flare; (*of a flower*) efflorescēre; **to — over** (*of a storm*) cadēre; (*fig*) abire
blowing *s* sufflatio *f*; flat·us –ūs *m*; (*of the nose*) emunctio *f*
blowup *s* scandalum *n*; (*scolding*) objurgatio *f*
blubber *s* adeps balaenarum *m*
blubber *vi* lacrimas effundēre
blue *adj* caeruleus
blueness *s* caeruleum *n*
blues *s* melancholia *f*
bluff *s* rupes *f*; promunturium *n*
bluff *adj* rusticus; declivis; ventosus
bluff *vt* fallēre, decipēre; *vi* ampullari, gloriari
blunder *s* (*in writing*) mendum *n*; error *m*, erratum *n*
blunder *vi* offendēre, errare
blunderer *s* homo ineptus *m*
blunt *adj* hebes; obtusus; (*fig*) inurbanus, rusticus; **—ly** plane, liberius
blunt *vt* hebetare, obtundēre, retundēre
bluntness *s* hebetudo *f*; (*fig*) candor *m*
blur *s* macula *f*
blur *vt* obscurare
blurt *vt* **to — out** inconsultum projicēre
blush *s* rubor *m*
blush *vi* erubescēre
bluster *vi* declamitare; fremēre, strepēre
bluster *s* jactatio, declamatio *f*; fremit·us –ūs, strepit·us –ūs *m*
boar *s* aper *m*; verres *m*
board *s* (*plank*) tabula *f*; (*table*) mensa *f*; (*food*) vict·us –ūs *m*; (*council, etc.*) collegium *n*; consilium *n*; concilium *n*; (*judicial*) quaestio *f*; (*for games*) abacus, alveus *m*
board *vt* **to — a ship** navem conscendēre; **to — up** contabulare; *vi* **to — with** devertēre ad (*with acc*)
boarder *s* convictor, hospes *m*

boardinghouse s contubernium n

boast vi se jactare, gloriari

boast s jactantia, jactatio, gloriatio, vanitas f

boastful adj gloriosus; —ly gloriose

boasting s gloriatio f

boat s linter f; cymba f; scapha f; navicula f

boatman s nauta, lintrarius m

bode vt portendĕre, praesagire

bodiless adj incorporalis

bodily adj corporeus; corporalis; in persona

bodily adv corporaliter

body s corpus n; (corpse) cadaver n; truncus m; (person) homo m; (of troops) man·us -ūs, caterva f; (of cavalry) turma f; (of people) numerus m, multitudo f; (heavenly) as-trum n

bodyguard s stipatores, satellites m pl; cohors praetoria f

bog s palus f

boil vt fervefacĕre, coquĕre; to — down decoquĕre; vi fervēre, effervescĕre; (fig) aestuare

boil s furunculus m, ulcus n

boiler s (vessel) ahenum, caldarium n; (kettle) lebes m

boisterous adj procellosus; violentus, turbidus; —ly turbide, turbulente

bold adj audax; impavidus; (rash) temerarius; (saucy) insolens, protervus, impudens; (language) liber; (stout) intrepidus; —ly audacter; temere; fortiter; insolenter

boldness s audacia, fidentia f; (in speech) libertas, impudentia f

bolster s pulvinar n; (of a bed) cervical n

bolster vt supportare, adjuvare; to — up suffulcire

bolt s (of a door) pessulus m; (of thunder) fulmen n; (pin) clavus m; (missile) sagitta f, telum n

bolt vt obserare, oppessulare, claudĕre, occludĕre

bomb s pyrobolus m

bombard vt tormentis verberare; (fig) lacessĕre

bombardment s tormentis verberatio f

bombast s ampulla f pl

bombastic adj inflatus, tumidus; to be — ampullari

bond s vinculum n; nodus m; copula, catena f, jugum n; (document) syngrapha f

bondage s servitus f, servitium n; captivitas f

bondsman s servus m; verna m; addictus m

bone s os n; (of fish) spina f

boneless adj exos

bonfire s ignes festi m pl

bonnet s redimiculum n

bony adj osseus

book s liber m; volumen n; codex m;

bookcase s foruli m pl; librarium n; pegma n

bookish adj libris deditus

bookkeeper s calculator m; actuarius m

bookshelf s pluteus m

bookstore s bibliopolum n, libraria taberna f

bookworm s tinea f; (fig) librorum helluo m

boom s (of a ship) longurius m; (of a harbor) obex m & f, repagulum n

boom vi resonare

boon s bonum, donum n

boor s rusticus m

boorish adj agrestis, rusticus; —ly rustice

boost vt efferre

boot s calceus m; caliga f; (peasant's) pero m; (tragic) cothurnus m; to — insuper

boot vi prodesse; **what boots it?** cui bono?

booth s taberna f, tabernaculum n

booty s praeda f; spolia n pl

border s (edge) margo m & f; (seam) limbus m, fimbria f; (boundary) finis, terminus m

border vt tangĕre, attingĕre; circumjacēre; vi to — on adjacēre (with dat), attingĕre; imminēre (with dat)

bordering adj affinis, finitimus

bore vt terebrare, perforare; excavare; (fig) (to weary) obtundĕre, fatigare

bore s (tool) terebra f; (hole) foramen n; (fig) importunus, molestus m

borer s terebra f

born adj natus; genitus; to be — nasci; (fig) oriri

borough s municipium n

borrow vt mutuari; (fig) imitari

borrowed adj mutuatus, mutuus; alienus

borrowing s mutuatio f

bosom s (breast) pectus n; sin·us -ūs m; (of female) mammillae f pl; (fig) gremium n

Bosphorus s Bosporus m

boss s bulla f; (of a shield) umbo m; (of a book) umbilicus m

boss vt (to order about) dominari in (with acc)

botanical adj botanicus

botanist s herbarius m

botany s herbaria f

botch s bubo, carbunculus m; (bungling work) scruta n pl

botch vt male sarcire; male gerĕre

both adj ambo; uterque

both pron ambo; uterque

both conj — ...and et ...et; cum ...tum; vel ...vel

bother vt vexare, sollicitare; molestus esse (with dat); vi to — about operam dare (with dat)

bother s negotium n; vexatio f; sollicitudo f

bottle s ampulla f; lagoena f

bottle vt in ampullas infundĕre

bottom s fundus m; (of a ship) carina f; (dregs) faex f, sedimentum n; (of a mountain) radix f; **the —** of imus; **the — of the sea** imum mare n

bottom adj imus, infimus

bottomless *adj* fundo carens, immensus; profundus

bough *s* ramus *m*

boulder *s* saxum *n*

bounce *vi* resilire, resultare

bound *adj* alligatus, obligatus, obstrictus; **it is — to happen** necesse est accidat; **to be — for** tendēre ad (*with acc*)

bound *s* salt·us -us *m*; (*limit*) modus, terminus *m*; **to set —s** modum facēre

bound *vt* finire, definire, terminare; *vi* (*to leap*) salire

boundary *s* finis, terminus *m*; (*fortified*) limes *m*

boundless *adj* infinitus, immensus; profundus

bountiful *adj* largus, benignus; **—ly** benigne, large

bounty *s* largitas, benignitas, liberalitas *f*; copia *f*

bouquet *s* corollarium *n*; (*of wine*) flos *m*

bow *s* arc·us -ūs *m*

bow *s* (*of a ship*) prora *f*; (*greeting*) summissio capitis *f*

bow *vt* flectēre, inclinare; (*one's head*) demittēre; *vi* flecti; (*fig*) **to — to** (*to accede to*) obtemperare (*with dat*), obsequi

bowels *s* intestina, viscera *n pl*

bower *s* trichila *f*, umbraculum *n*

bowl *s* cratera, patera *f*; (*for cooking*) catina *f*

bowlegged *adj* valgus

bowman *s* sagittarius *m*

bowstring *s* nervus *m*

box *s* arca, cista *f*; scrinium *n*; (*for medicine*) pyxis *f*; (*tree*) buxus *f*

box *vt* includēre; pugnis certare cum (*with dat*); **to — the ears of** alapam adhibēre (*with dat*)

boxer *s* pugil *m*

boxing glove *s* caest·us -ūs *m*

boxing match *s* pugilatio *f*

boy *s* puer, puerulus *m*

boyhood *s* pueritia *f*; aetas puerilis *f*

boyish *adj* puerilis; **—ly** pueriliter

brace *s* (*strap*) fascia *f*; (*couple*) par *n*; copula *f*; (*in architecture*) fibula *f*

brace *vt* ligare, alligare; (*to strengthen*) firmare

bracelet *s* armilla *f*

bracket *s* mutulus *m*; **—s** (*in writing*) unci *m pl*

brag *vi* se jactare, gloriari

braggart *s* jactator, salaco *m*

bragging *s* jactantia *f*

braid *s* limbus *m*; (*of hair*) cincinnus *m*

braid *vt* plectēre, plicare

brain *s* cerebrum *n*; ingenium *n*

brainless *adj* stolidus, inconsultus, socors

brake *s* (*fern*) filix *f*; (*thicket*) dumetum *n*; (*on wheel*) sufflamen *n*

bramble *s* rubus *m*; (*thicket*) rubetum *n*; (*thorny bush*) sentis, vepris *m*

branch *s* (*of tree*) ramus *m*; (*of pedigree*) stemma *n*; (*division*) pars *f*

branch *vi* (*of trees*) germinare; **to**

— out ramos porrigēre; (*fig*) dividi, scindi, diffundi

brand *s* (*mark*) stigma *n*, nota *f*; (*of fire*) fax *f*, torris *m*; (*type*) genus *n*

brand *vt* inurēre, notare

branding iron *s* cauter *m*

brandish *vt* vibrare

brandy *s* aqua vitae *f*; vini spirit·us -ūs *m*; spirit·us -ūs gallicus *m*

brass *s* orichalcum, aes *n*

brat *s* infans *m & f*

brave *adj* fortis, animosus, strenuus; **—ly** fortiter, strenue

brave *vt* sustinēre

bravery *s* fortitudo *f*; virtus *f*

bravo *interj* eu!, euge!, bene!, macte!

brawl *s* rixa *f*, jurgium *n*

brawl *vi* rixari, jurgare

brawler *s* rixator, rabula *m*

brawling *adj* contentiosus, jurgans

brawn *s* callum aprugnum *n*; (*muscle*) lacertus, torus *m*

brawny *adj* lacertosus, robustus

bray *vi* (*of asses*) rudēre; (*of elephants*) barrire; (*to cry out*) emugire

braying *s* tritura *f*; barrit·us -ūs *m*; rugit·us -ūs *m*

brazen *adj* aēnus; (*fig*) impudens

brazier *s* foculus *m*

breach *s* ruptura, ruina *f*; (*of treaty*) violatio *f*; dissidium *n*

bread *s* panis *m*; (*fig*) vict·us -ūs *m*

breadth *s* latitudo *f*

break *vt* frangēre; rumpēre; **to — apart** diffringēre; **to — down** demoliri, destruēre; **to — in** (*to tame*) domare, subigēre; **to — in pieces** dirumpēre; **to — off** abrumpēre; (*friendship or action*) dirumpēre; (*a meeting*) interrumpēre; **to — open** effringēre; **to — up** interrumpēre, dissolvēre; *vi* frangi; rumpi; (*of day*) illucescēre; (*of strength*) deficēre; **to — forth** erumpēre; **to — into** irrumpēre; invadēre; **to — off** desinēre; **to — out** erumpēre; (*of trouble*) exardescēre; (*of war*) exoriri; (*of fire*) grassari; **to — through** perrumpēre; **to — up** dissolvi, dilabi; (*of a meeting*) dimitti; **to — with** dissidēre ab (*with abl*)

break *s* interruptio *f*, intervallum *n*; interstitium *n*

breakage *s* fractura *f*

breakdown *s* calamitas *f*; frustratio *f*; (*of health*) debilitas *f*; (*of a machine*) defect·us -ūs *m*

breaker *s* fluct·us -ūs *m*

breakfast *s* prandium *n*

breakfast *vi* prandēre

breakup *s* dissolutio *f*

breast *s* pectus *n*; (*of a woman*) mamma *f*; (*fig*) praecordia *n pl*; **to make a clean — of** confitēri

breastbone *s* sternum *n*; os pectorale *n*

breastplate *s* lorica *f*; thorax *m*

breath *s* spirit·us -ūs *m*, anima *f*; halit·us -ūs *m*; **— of air** aura *f*; **deep —** anhelit·us -ūs *m*; **to catch one's —** obstipescēre; **to hold**

one's **breath** animam continēre; to take one's — away exanimare; to waste one's — operam perdĕre
breathe vt ducĕre; spirare; (to whisper) susurrare; to — out exspirare; vi spirare, respirare; to — upon inspirare (with dat)
breathing s respiratio f; halit·us -ūs m; (gram) spirit·us -ūs m
breathless adj exanimis, exanimus; exanimatus
breeches s bracae f pl
breed s genus n
breed vt parĕre, gignĕre; (to cause) producĕre; (to engender) procreare, educare; (to raise) alĕre; (horses) pascĕre
breeder s (man) generator m; (stallion) admissarius m; (animal) matrix; (fig) nutrix f
breeding s fetura f; educatio f; good — urbanitas, humanitas f
breeze s aura f
breezy adj ventosus
brethren s fratres m pl
brevity s brevitas, breviloquentia f
brew vt coquĕre; vi excitari, concitari
bribe s pretium n, merces f
bribe vt corrumpĕre, largiri
briber s corruptor, largitor m
bribery s corruptio, corruptela, largitio f; ambit·us -ūs m
brick s later m
brick adj latericius
bricklayer s laterum structor m
bridal adj nuptialis
bride s nupta f
bridegroom s maritus m
bridesmaid s pronuba f
bridge s pons m
bridge vt pontem imponĕre (with dat)
bridle s frenum n
brief adj brevis, concisus; —ly breviter, paucis verbis
brief s diploma n; sententiola f; summarium n
brigade s (infantry) legio f; (cavalry) turma f
brigadier s tribunus militum m
brigand s latro, latrunculus m
bright adj clarus; lucidus, splendidus; nitidus, candidus; (flashing) fulgidus; (smart) argutus; —ly lucide, clare, splendide
brighten vt illustrare, illuminare; vi lucescĕre; splendescĕre; clarescĕre; (of a person) in hilaritatem solvi
brightness s nitor, splendor, fulgor, candor m; (of the sky) serenitas f
brilliance s splendor m; fulgor m; (of style) nitor m, lumen n
brilliant adj splendidus; nitens; (fig) praeclarus, insignis, luculentus; —ly splendide, praeclare, luculenter
brim s ora, margo f, labrum n; to fill to the — explēre
brimful adj ad summum plenus
brimstone s sulfur n
brine s muria f, salsamentum n; (sea) salum n
bring vt ferre, afferre, inferre; (by

carriage, etc.) advehĕre; to — about efficĕre, perducĕre; to — back referre, reducĕre; reportare; (fig) revocare; (by force) redigĕre; dejicĕre; to — forth prodĕre, depromĕre; parĕre; (to yield) ferre, efferre; to — forward proferre, efferre, agĕre; to — in inferre; invehĕre; inducĕre; (as a farm, etc.) reddĕre; to — off dissuadĕre; to — on afferre; adducĕre; (fig) objicĕre; to — out efferre; producĕre; excire; to — over perducĕre, traducĕre; (fig) perducĕre, trahĕre; conciliare; to — to adducĕre; appellĕre; (fig) persuadēre; to — together conferre; (to assemble) contrahĕre; (fig) conciliare; to — to pass efficĕre; to — under subigĕre; to — up subducĕre; (children) educare; (to vomit) evomĕre
brink s margo f; ora f; (fig) extremitas f
brisk adj alacer, agilis, vividus; laetus; to be — vigēre; —ly alacriter, agiliter
briskness s alacritas f, vigor m
bristle s seta f
bristle vi horrēre
bristly adj setiger, setosus; hirsutus; horridus
Britain s Britannia f
British adj Britannicus
brittle adj fragilis
broach vt in medium proferre
broad adj latus, largus, amplus; (fig) manifestus, apertus; —ly late
broadcast vt divulgare, disseminare
broaden vt dilatare
broadsword s gladius m
brocade s Attalica n pl
broccoli s brassica oleracea Botrytis f
brochure s libellus m
broil s rixa, turba f
broil vt torrēre
broken adj fractus; intermissus; diruptus; (fig) confectus; (of speech) refractus, infractus, corrupte pronuntiatus
brokenhearted adj abjectus, dejectus
broker s transactor, institor m
bronze s aes n
bronze adj aeneus, a(h)enus, aeratus
brooch s fibula f
brood s proles f; (chicks) pullities f
brood vi (as a hen) incubare; (fig) to — over agitare, meditari
brook vt ferre, tolerare
broom s genista f; scopae f pl
broth s jus n
brothel s lupanar n, ganea f
brother s frater m
brotherhood s germanitas, fraternitas f; (fig) sodalitium n
brother-in-law s levir m; sororis maritus m
brotherly adj fraternus
brow s supercilium n; frons f; (of a hill) dorsum n
browbeat vt terrēre, deprimĕre, exagitare, objurgare

brown *adj* fulvus, fuscus, spadix; (*of skin*) adustus

browse *vi* depasci

bruise *vt* contundĕre, sugillare; infringĕre

bruise *s* contusio *f*, contusum *n*, sugillatio *f*

brunette *s* puella subfusca *f*

brunt *s* impet·us -ūs *m*; vehementia *f*

brush *s* scopula *f*; (*painter's*) penicillus *m*; (*bushy tail*) muscarium *n*; (*skirmish*) aggressio *f*

brush *vt* verrĕre, purgare; **to — aside** neglegĕre, spernĕre; **to — away** amovēre

brutal *adj* atrox, immanis, inhumanus; **—ly** atrociter, immaniter, inhumane

brutality *s* atrocitas, ferocitas, saevitia, immanitas *f*

brute *adj* brutus; stupidus

brute *s* belua, bestia *f*

brutish *adj* ferinus; stupidus

bubble *s* bulla *f*

bubble *vi* bullire; (*to gush up*) scatēre

bubbling *s* bullit·us -ūs *m*; scatebra *f*

buccaneer *s* pirata *m*

buck *s* cervus *m*; (*he-goat*) hircus *m*; (*male rabbit*) cuniculus *m*

bucket *s* hama, situla, fidelia *f*

buckle *vt* fibulā nectĕre; *vi* flectĕre

buckle *s* fibula *f*, spinther *m*

buckler *s* parma *f*

bucolic *adj* bucolicus, agrestis

bud *s* gemma *f*, germen *n*; (*of a flower*) flosculus *m*

bud *vi* gemmare, germinare

budding *s* germinatio *f*; emplastratio *f*

budge *vt* ciēre, movēre; *vi* movēri, cedĕre

budget *s* saccus *m*; publicae pecuniae ratio *f*

buffalo *s* urus *m*

buffet *s* (*sideboard*) abacus *m*; (*slap*) alapa *f*; (*fig*) plaga *f*

buffet *vt* jactare

buffoon *s* scurra *m*; sannio, balatro *m*; **to play the —** scurrari

bug *s* cimex *m & f*

bugle *s* buccina *f*

build *vt* aedificare; struĕre, condĕre; (*road*) munire; (*hopes*) ponĕre; **to — up** exstruĕre

builder *s* aedificator, structor *m*

building *s* (*act*) aedificatio *f*; exstructio *f*; (*structure*) aedificium *n*

bulb *s* bulbus *m*

bulge *vi* tumēre, tumescĕre; prominēre

bulk *s* amplitudo, magnitudo *f*; (*mass*) moles *f*; (*greater part*) major pars *f*

bulkiness *s* magnitudo *f*

bulky *adj* crassus; ingens; corpulentus; onerosus

bull *s* taurus *m*

bulldog *s* canis Molossus *m*

bullet *s* glans *f*

bulletin *s* libellus *m*

bullfrog *s* rana ocellata *f*

bullion *s* aurum infectum *n*; argentum infectum *n*; massa *f*

bully *s* salaco, thraso *m*

bully *vt* procaciter lacessĕre

bulwark *s* agger *m*; propugnaculum *n*; moenia *n pl*

bump *s* (*swelling*) tuber *n*; (*thump*) plaga *f*

bump *vt* pulsare, pellĕre; *vi* **to — against** offendĕre

bun *s* libum *n*, placenta *f*

bunch *s* fasciculus *m*; (*of grapes*) racemus *m*

bundle *s* fascis, fasciculus *m*; vesiculus *m*

bundle *vt* consarcinare

bungle *vt* inscite gerĕre; inscite agĕre; *vi* errare

bungler *s* homo rudis *m*

buoy *s* cortex *m*

buoy *vt* **to — up** attollĕre, sublevare

buoyancy *s* levitas *f*; (*fig*) hilaritas *f*

buoyant *adj* levis; (*fig*) hilaris

burden *s* onus *n*; (*fig*) scrupulus *m*

burden *vt* onerare; opprimĕre

burdensome *adj* onerosus, gravis, molestus

bureau *s* armarium, scrinium *n*

burglar *s* fur *m*

burglary *s* (*domūs*) effractura *f*

burial *s* (*act*) sepultura *f*; (*ceremony*) funus *n*

burial place *s* sepulturae locus *m*; sepulcrum *n*

burlesque *s* ridicula imitatio *f*

burly *adj* corpulentus

burn *vt* urĕre, cremare; (*to set on fire*) incendĕre; **to — down** deurĕre; **to — out** exurĕre; **to — up** amburĕre, comburĕre; *vi* flagrare; ardēre; **to — out** extingui; **to — up** conflagrare

burn *s* adustio *f*; combustum *n*

burning *s* ustio, adustio *f*; deflagratio *f*

burning *adj* ardens; fervens

burrow *s* cuniculus *m*

burrow *vi* defodĕre

bursar *s* dispensator *m*

burst *s* impet·us -ūs *m*; eruptio *f*; (*noise*) fragor *m*

burst *vt* rumpĕre, dirumpĕre; **to — open** effrangĕre; *vi* dirumpi; **to — forth** prorumpĕre; (*of tears*) prosilire; **to — in** irrumpĕre; **to — out** erumpĕre; **to — out laughing** cachinnum tollĕre

bury *vt* sepelire; (*to hide*) abdĕre, condĕre

bush *s* dumetum *n*, frutex *m*; (*of hair*) caesaries *f*

bushel *s* medimnus, modius *m*

bushy *adj* (*full of bushes*) dumosus; (*bush-like*) fruticosus

busily *adv* industrie, sedulo, impigre

business *s* negotium *n*; (*trade, calling*) ars *f*; (*employment*) occupatio *f*; (*matter*) res *f*; **to mind one's own —** negotium suum agĕre

businessman *s* negotiator *m*

buskin *s* cothurnus *m*

bust *s* imago *f*; effigies *f*

bustle *s* festinatio *f*; trepidatio *f*

bustle *vi* festinare; trepidare; **to —
about** discurrĕre
busy *adj* occupatus; negotiosus; operosus, impiger; (*meddling*) molestus
busybody *s* ardelio *m*
but *prep* praeter (*with acc*)
but *adv* modo, tantum
but *conj* sed; ast, at; atqui; ceterum;
vero, verum; autem; — **if** quodsi;
sin, sin autem; — **if not** sin aliter, sin minus
butcher *s* lanius *m*; (*fig*) carnifex *m*
butcher *vt* (*animals*) caedĕre; (*people*) trucidare
butcher shop *s* macellum *n*
butchery *s* caedes, trucidatio *f*
butler *s* promus *m*
butt *s* (*mark*) meta *f*; (*cask*) dolium
n; (*mound*) agger *m*; — **of ridicule** ludibrium *n*
butt *vt* arietare; *vi* **to — in** interpellare
butter *s* butyrum *n*
butter *vt* butyro inducĕre
buttercup *s* ranunculus tuberosus *m*
butterfly *s* papilio *m*
buttermilk *s* lactis serum *n*
buttock *s* clunis *m & f*

button *s* bulla *f*
button *vt* nectĕre, confibulare
buttress *s* anterides *f pl*; fulcrum *n*
buttress *vt* suffulcire
buxom *adj* alacer, hilaris, laetus
buy *vt* emĕre, mercari; **to — back**
or **off** redimĕre; **to — up** coemĕre
buyer *s* emptor *m*
buying *s* emptio *f*
buzz *s* bombus *m*; murmur *n*
buzz *vi* bombilare; (*in the ear*) insusurrare
buzzard *s* buteo *m*
by *prep* (*agency*) a, ab (*with abl*);
(*of place*) ad (*with acc*), apud (*with
acc*), juxta (*with acc*), prope (*with
acc*); (*along*) secundum (*with acc*);
(*past*) praeter (*with acc*); (*of time*)
ante (*with acc*); (*in oaths*) per (*with
acc*); — and — mox; — **means of**
per (*with acc*); — **oneself** solus
bygone *adj* praeteritus; priscus
bylaw *s* praescriptum *n*; regula *f*
bystander *s* arbiter *m*
byway *s* trames *m*, semita *f*, dever-
ticulum *n*
byword *s* adagium *n*

C

cabal *s* factio *f*; societas clandestina
f
cabbage *s* brassica *f*, caulis *m*
cabin *s* (*cottage*) tugurium *n*; (*on a
ship*) stega *f*
cabinet *s* armarium *n*; scrinium *n*;
cistula *f*; (*in government*) principis
consilium *n*
cable *s* funis, rudens *m*; (*anchor*) an-
corale *n*
cackle *vi* gracillare; (*fig*) deblaterare
cackle *s* glocitatio *f*; (*fig*) gerrae
f pl; clangor *m*
cacophony *s* dissonae voces *f pl*
cactus *s* cactus *f*
cadaver *s* cadaver *n*
cadence *s* numerus *m*
cadet *s* tiro *m*; discipulus militaris *m*
cage *s* cavea *f*, aviarium *n*; septum *n*
cage *vt* includĕre
cajole *vt* inescare, lactare, blandiri
cake *s* libum *n*, placenta *f*
calamitous *adj* calamitosus; funestus; exitiosus
calamity *s* calamitas *f*; clades *f*; malum *n*; res adversae *f pl*
calculate *vt* computare; (*fig*) aestimare, existimare
calculated *adj* aptus, accommodatus
calculation *s* computatio, ratio *f*;
(*fig*) ratiocinatio *f*
calculator *s* computator *m*; ratio-
cinator *m*
caldron *s* ahenum *n*, lebes *m*
calendar *s* fasti *m pl*; calendarium *n*
calends *s* Kalendae *f pl*
calf *s* vitulus *m*; (*of the leg*) sura *f*

caliber *s* (*fig*) ingenium *n*, indoles *f*
call *vt* vocare; (*to name*) appellare;
to — aside sevocare; **to — away**
avocare; (*fig*) devocare; **to — back**
revocare; **to — down** devocare; **to
— forth** evocare, provocare; (*fig*)
exciĕre, elicĕre; **to — in** advocare;
(*money*) cogĕre; **to — off** avocare,
revocare; **to — together** convocare; **to — to mind** recordari; **to
— to witness** testari; **to — up**
excitare, suscitare, elicĕre; *vi* **to —
on** *or* **upon** (*for help*) implorare;
(*to visit*) visĕre
call *s* vocatio *f*; clamor *m*; (*visit*) salutatio *f*; (*requisition*) postulatio *f*;
(*whistle*) fistula *f*
calling *s* (*profession*) ars *f*, artificium *n*
callous *adj* callosus; (*fig*) durus; expers sensūs; **to become —** occal-
lescĕre; obdurescĕre
calm *adj* tranquillus, placidus, sedatus, quietus; (*mentally*) aequus;
—ly tranquille, aequo animo, placide
calm *s* tranquillitas *f*, tranquillum *n*
calm *vt* pacare, placare, sedare, mulcēre; *vi* **to — down** defervescĕre
calmness *s* tranquillitas *f*; serenitas
f
calumny *s* maledictum *n*, obtrectatio
f, opprobria *n pl*
camel *s* camelus *m*
cameo *s* imago ectypa *f*
camouflage *s* dissimulatio *f*
camouflage *vt* dissimulare

camp *s* castra *n pl*; **summer** — aestiva *n pl*; **to strike** — castra movēre; **winter** — hiberna *n pl*
camp *adj* castrensis
camp *vi* castra ponēre
campaign *s* aestiva *n pl*; stipendium *n*; expeditio *f*
campaign *vi* stipendium merēre; expeditioni interesse
campaigner *s* veteranus *m*
camphor *s* camphora *f*
can *s* hirnea *f*
can *vi* posse; scire; **I** — **not** nequeo; nescio
canal *s* fossa navigabilis *f*
canary *s* fringilla Canaria *f*
cancel *vt* delēre, expungēre; abrogare, tollēre
cancellation *s* deletio, abolitio *f*
cancer *s* cancer *m*
cancerous *adj* cancerosus, canceraticus
candid *adj* candidus, apertus, liber, simplex; —**ly** candide
candidacy *s* petitio *f*
candidate *s* petitor *m*; candidatus *m*
candied *adj* saccharo conditus
candle *s* candela *f*; (*taper*) cera *f*
candlelight *s* lucerna *f*; **to study by** — lucubrare
candlestick *s* candelabrum *n*
candor *s* candor *m*, simplicitas, ingenuitas *f*
candy *s* saccharum crystallinum *n*
cane *s* baculus *m*; virga *f*; (*reed*) harundo *f*
cane *vt* baculo *or* virgā ferire; verberare
canine *adj* caninus
canister *s* canistrum *n*, pyxis *f*
canker *s* (*of plants*) rubigo, robigo *f*; (*fig*) aerugo *f*
cannibal *s* anthropophagus *m*
cannon *s* tormentum *n*
cannon shot *s* tormenti ict·us -ūs *m*
canoe *s* linter *m*
canon *s* regula, norma *f*; canon *m*
canonical *adj* canonicus
canopy *s* canopeum *n*; aulaea *n pl*
cant *s* fucus *m*
cantata *s* carmen *n*
canteen *s* caupona castrensis *f*
canter *s* lenis atque quadrupedans grad·us -ūs *m*
canter *vi* leniter quadrupedare
canticle *s* canticum *n*
canto *s* liber *m*
canton *s* pagus *m*
canvas *s* linteum crassum *n*, carbasus *f*, carbasa *n pl*
canvass *s* (*legal*) ambitio *f*; (*illegal*) ambit·us -ūs *m*
canvass *vt* circumire, prensare; *vi* ambire
cap *s* pileus *m*; calyptra *f*; (*in rituals*) galerus *m*
capability *s* facultas, habilitas *f*
capable *adj* capax; idoneus, potens, doctus
capably *adv* bene, docte
capacity *s* capacitas, mensura *f*; modus *m*; ingenium *n*
cape *s* promontorium *n*; (*garment*)

humerale *n*, chlamys *f*
caper *vi* saltare, tripudire, assilire; (*of animals*) lascivire
caper *s* salt·us -ūs *m*, exsultatio *f*
capital *adj* praecipuus, princeps; (*law*) capitalis; (*of letters*) uncialis; (*outstanding*) insignis, eximius
capital *s* (*architecture*) capitulum *n*; (*chief city*) caput *n*; (*com*) sors *f*, caput *n*; faenus *n*
capitalist *s* faenerator *m*
capitol *s* capitolium *n*
capitulate *vi* ex pacto urbem tradēre; se dedēre
capitulation *s* deditio *f*
capon *s* capus, capo *m*
caprice *s* libido, inconstantia *f*
capricious *adj* levis, inconstans; ventosus, mobilis; —**ly** leviter, inconstanter, ex libidine
capricorn *s* capricornus *m*
capsize *vt* evertēre; *vi* everti
capsule *s* capsula *f*
captain *s* (*in infantry*) centurio *m*; (*in cavalry*) praefectus *m*; (*in navy*) navarchus *m*, (*in merchant marine*) magister *m*
caption *s* caput *n*
captious *adj* argutus; morosus; fallax; —**ly** captiose, morose
captivate *vt* captare, delenire, mulcēre
captive *adj* captivus
captive *s* captivus *m*
captivity *s* captivitas *f*
captor *s* captor *m*; expugnator *m*; victor *m*
capture *s* captura, comprehensio *f*
capture *vt* capēre, excipēre
car *s* carrus *m*
carat *s* unciae triens *m*
caravan *s* commeat·us -ūs, comitat·us -ūs *m*
carbon *s* carbonium *n*
carbuncle *s* carbunculus, furunculus *m*
carcass *s* cadaver *n*
card *s* charta *f*; (*ticket*) tessera *f*; (*for combing wool*) pecten *n*
card *vt* pectēre
cardboard *s* charta crassior *f*
cardinal *adj* principalis, praecipuus
cardinal *s* (*eccl*) cardinalis *m*
care *s* cura, sollicitudo *f*; (*diligence*) diligentia *f*; (*charge*) tutela, curatio, custodia *f*; **to take** — **of** curare
care *vi* curare; **to** — **for** (*to look after*) curare; (*to be fond of*) amare
career *s* curriculum *n*; decurs·us -ūs *m*; (*pol*) curs·us -ūs honorum *m*
carefree *adj* securus
careful *adj* (*attentive*) attentus, diligens; (*cautious*) cautus; (*of work*) accuratus; —**ly** diligenter; caute; accurate, exquisite
careless *adj* neglegens, incautus; (*loose*) dissolutus; —**ly** neglegenter; incuriose; (*loosely*) solute
carelessness *s* incuria, neglegentia *f*
caress *s* blanditiae *f pl*; complex·us -ūs *m*
caress *vt* blandiri, fovēre

cargo s onus n
caricature s imago in pejus detor-
ta f
caricature vt in pejus fingĕre
carnage s caedes, strages f
carnal adj sensualis, carnalis
carnival s feriae f pl
carnivorous adj carnivorus
carol s cant·us -ūs m; carmen n;
Christmas — hymnus de Christi
natu m
carol vi cantare, cantillare
carouse vi comissari, perpotare, per-
bacchari
carp s cyprinus m
carp vi to — at carpĕre, mordēre,
vellicare
carpenter s faber tignarius m
carpentry s ars fabrilis f
carpet s tapes m, tapeta f
carriage s (act) vectura f; (vehicle)
vehiculum n; raeda f, petorritum n;
(bearing, posture) habit·us -ūs, gest·us -ūs, incess·us -ūs m
carrier s portitor, vector, bajulus m;
(of letters) tabularius m
carrion s caro morticina f
carrot s carota f; pastinaca f
carry vt portare, ferre; (by vehicle)
vehĕre; gerĕre; (law) perferre; to
— away auferre; evehĕre; (fig) rapĕre; to — back referre; revehĕre;
to — in importare; invehĕre; to
— off auferre; rapĕre; to — on
promovēre; perducĕre; (fig) exercēre; gerĕre; to — out efferre, exportare; evehĕre; (fig) exsequi; to
— over transferre; to — round
circumferre; to — through perferre; vi (of sound) audiri; to — on
pergĕre; se gerĕre
cart s plaustrum n; curr·us -ūs m;
curriculum m; to put the — before the horse praeposteris consi-
liis uti
cart vt plaustro vehĕre; to — away
auferre
carve vt sculpĕre; caelare, incidĕre;
(at table) secare
carver s caelator m; (at table) carp-
tor m; (knife) cultellus m
carving s caelatura f
cascade s praeceps aquae laps·us
-ūs m
case s (law) causa, actio f; (matter)
res f; (instance) exemplum n; (container) involucrum n; theca f; capsula f; (state) stat·us -ūs m; conditio f; (gram) cas·us -ūs m; in —
si; in that — ergo; since that is
the — quae cum ita sint
cash s pecunia numerata f; nummi
m pl; praesens pecunia f
cashier s dispensator m
cash payment s repraesentatio f
cask s cadus m, dolium n
casket s arcula f; pyxis f
cast s (throw) jact·us -ūs m; (mold)
typus m; forma f
cast vt jacĕre; (metal) fundĕre; to —
about circumjacĕre; to — away
abjicĕre; dejicĕre; to — down dejicĕre; (fig) affligĕre; to — in in-

jicĕre; to — in one's teeth repro-
brare; to — off (the skin) exuĕre;
(fig) amovēre, ponĕre; repudiare;
to — out ejicĕre, expellĕre; to —
over trajicĕre; to — upon super-
injicĕre; (fig) aspergĕre; conferre;
vi to — off ancoram tollĕre
castaway s perditus m; ejectus m
caste s ordo m; to lose — degenerare
castigate vt castigare
castigation s castigatio f
castle s castellum n; arx f
castor oil s cicinum oleum n
castrate vt castrare
castration s castratio, castratura f
casual adj fortuitus; (person) neglegens; —ly fortuito, forte, casu
casualty s cas·us -ūs m; occisus m
cat s feles f
cataclysm s cataclysmos m
catacombs s puticuli m pl; catacum-
bae f pl
catalogue s catalogus m; index m
cataract s cataracta f, cataractes m;
(of the eye) glaucoma n
catastrophe s calamitas f; ruina f;
exit·us -ūs m
catch vt capĕre, captare; (by surprise) comprehendĕre; (falling object) suscipĕre; (in a net) illaquĕre;
(with bait) inescare; (fire) concipĕre;
(disease) contrahĕre; vi to — at
arripĕre; (fig) captare; to — up
with consequi
catching adj contagiosus; (fig) gratus
categorical adj categoricus; —ly
categorice, sine exceptione
category s categoria f; numerus m
cater vi obsonari; cibos suppeditare
caterer s obsonator m
caterpillar s eruca f
cathedral s ecclesia cathedralis f
catholic adj catholicus, generalis
cattle s pecus n
cauliflower s brassica oleracea bo-
tryitis f
cause s causa, res, materia f; (pol)
partes f pl
cause vt facĕre, efficĕre; (feelings)
excīre, movēre
causeless adj sine causa; vanus
causeway s agger m
caustic adj causticus; (fig) mordax,
acerbus
caution s cautio f; cura f; prudentia
f; monitio f, monitum n
caution vt (ad)monēre
cautious adj cautus, consideratus;
circumspectus; providus; —ly caute, prudenter; depetentim
cavalcade s pompa f
cavalier s eques m
cavalry s equitat·us -ūs m; equites
m pl; copiae equestres f pl
cave s spec·us -ūs m; spelunca f;
caverna f; antrum n
cavern s caverna f
cavernous adj cavernosus
caviar s ova acipenseris n pl
cavity s cavum n; caverna f
caw vi crocire, crocitare

cease *vi* desinĕre, desistĕre

ceaseless *adj* assiduus, perpetuus; —ly continenter, assidue, perpetuo

ceasing *s* cessatio, intermissio *f*

cedar *s* cedrus *f*

cedar *adj* cedreus, cedrinus

cede *vt* cedĕre, concedĕre

ceiling *s* laquear, lacunar *n*

celebrate *vt* celebrare; laudare, dicĕre

celebrated *adj* celeber; nobilis, notus, praeclarus

celebration *s* celebratio *f*; (*of rites*) sollemne *n*

celebrity *s* celebritas *f*; fama *f*; (*person*) vir illustris *m*

celery *s* heleoselinum *n*

celestial *adj* caelestis, divinus

celibacy *s* caelibat·us -ūs *m*, caelebs vita *f*

celibate *s* caelebs *m*

cell *s* cella *f*

cellar *s* cella *f*, cellarium *n*

cement *s* ferrumen *n*; caementum *n*; (*glue*) gluten *n*

cement *vt* conglutinare; ferruminare; *vi* coalescĕre

cemetery *s* sepulcretum *n*

censer *s* turibulum *n*

censor *s* censor *m*

censorship *s* censura *f*; magisterium morum *n*

censurable *adj* reprehensione dignus; culpandus

censure *s* vituperatio *f*

censure *vt* animadvertĕre, vituperare

census *s* cens·us -ūs *m*; civium enumeratio *f*

centaur *s* centaurus *m*

centenary *adj* centenarius

centenary *s* centesimus annus *m*

center *s* medium *n*; in the — of the plain in medio campo

center *vt* in centrum ponĕre; *vi* to — on niti (*with abl*)

central *adj* medius, centralis

centralize *vt* (*authority*) ad unum deferre

centurion *s* centurio *m*

century *s* (*pol*) centuria *f*; saeculum *f*

cereal *s* frumentum *n*

ceremonial *adj* caerimonialis, sollemnis; —ly sollemniter, rite

ceremonial *s* rit·us -ūs *m*

ceremonious *adj* sollemnis; (*person*) officiosus; —ly sollemniter; officiose

ceremony *s* caerimonia *f*, rit·us -ūs *m*; (*pomp*) apparat·us -ūs *m*

certain *adj* (*sure*) certus; (*indefinite*) quidam, nonnulus; for — certe, pro certo; it is — constat; —ly certe; profecto

certainty *s* certum *n*; (*belief*) fides *f*

certificate *s* testimonium *n*

certify *vt* recognoscĕre, confirmare

cessation *s* cessatio, intermissio *f*; — of hostilities indutiae *f pl*

chafe *vt* urĕre; (*with the hand*) fricare; (*to excoriate*) atterĕre; (*to vex*) irritare, succensĕre; *vi* stomachari

chaff *s* palea *f*; (*fig*) quisquiliae *f pl*

chagrin *s* dolor *m*; stomachus *m*

chain *s* catena *f*; (*necklace*) troques *m & f*; (*fig*) series *f*

chain *vt* catenis constringĕre; catenas injicĕre (*with dat*)

chair *s* sella, cathedra *f*

chairman *s* praeses *m*

chalice *s* calix *m*

chalk *s* creta *f*; calx *f*

chalk *vt* cretā notare; cretā illinĕre; to — out designare

chalky *adj* (*chalk-like*) cretaceus; (*full of chalk*) cretosus

challenge *s* provocatio *f*; (*law*) recusatio *f*

challenge *vt* provocare, lacessĕre; (*law*) rejicĕre; (*to reclaim*) arrogare

challenger *s* provocator *m*

chamber *s* cubiculum *n*, camera *f*, thalamus *m*; pars interior *f*

champ *vt & vi* mandĕre, mordĕre

champion *s* propugnator, defensor *m*; (*of a party*) antesignanus *m*

chance *s* (*accident*) cas·us -ūs, event·us -ūs *m*; fortuna *f*; (*fig*) alea *f*; (*probability*) spes *f*; by — casu, forte, fortuito

chance *vt* periclitari; *vi* accidĕre, contingĕre

chance *adj* fortuitus; inexpectatus

chancel *s* cancellus *m*

chancellor *s* cancellarius *m*

change *s* mutatio, commutatio, permutatio *f*; (*variety*) varietas *f*; (*pol*) res novae *f pl*; small — nummi *m pl*

change *vt* mutare, commutare, permutare; *vi* mutari, variare; (*of the moon*) renovari

changeable *adj* mutabilis; inconstans; (*of color*) versicolor

changeless *adj* immutabilis

changeling *s* subditus, suppositus *m*

channel *s* canalis *m*; (*of rivers*) alveus *m*; (*arm of the sea*) fretum *n*; (*in architecture*) stria *f*; (*fig*) curs·us -ūs *m*

channel *vt* sulcare, excavare; (*to guide*) ducĕre

chant *s* cant·us -ūs *m*

chant *vt* cantare

chaos *s* chaos *n*; (*fig*) confusio *f*

chaotic *adj* confusus; indigestus

chap *s* fissura *f*; (*person*) homo *m*

chap *vt* scindĕre, diffindĕre; *vi* scindi

chapel *s* aedicula *f*, sacellum *n*

chapter *s* caput *n*

char *vt* amburĕre

character *s* character *m*; mores *m pl*; (*inborn*) indoles, natura *f*; ingenium *n*; (*repute*) existimatio *f*; (*type*) genus *n*; (*letter*) littera *f*; (*in drama*) persona *f*

characteristic *adj* proprius; —ally proprie

characteristic *s* proprium *n*, proprietas *f*

characterize *vt* describĕre, notare, designare

charade *s* aenigma syllabicum *n*

charcoal *s* carbo *m*

charge s (*law*) crimen n; accusatio f; (*mil*) impet·us -ūs, incurs·us -ūs m; (*command*) mandatum n; (*trust*) cura, custodia f; (*office*) munus n; (*cost*) impensa f, sumpt·us -ūs m; **to be in — of** praeesse (*with dat*); **to bring a — against** litem intendĕre (*with dat*); **to put in — of** praeficĕre (*with dat*)

charger s equus bellator m

chariot s curr·us -ūs m; curriculum n; (*mil*) essedarium n

charioteer s auriga m

charitable adj benignus, beneficus; (*fig*) mitis

charitably adv benigne; miti animo

charity s caritas f; liberalitas f

charlatan s pharmacopola m; ostentator, jactator m

charm s incantamentum n; (*fig*) illecebra, gratia f; (*amulet*) amuletum n

charm vt incantare; (*to delight*) capĕre, captare, delectare; **to — away** recantare

charmer s fascinator m; (*thing*) deliciae f pl

charming adj suavis, lepidus, venustus; **—ly** lepide, suaviter, blande, venuste

chart s tabula f

charter s charta f, diploma n

charter vt conducĕre

chase s venatio f, venat·us -ūs m

chase vt (*to hunt*) persequi, venari; (*to engrave*) caelare; **to — away** abigĕre, pellĕre

chasing s caelatura f

chasm s chasma n, hiat·us -ūs m

chaste adj castus, pudicus; (*of language*) purus; **—ly** caste, pudice; pure

chasten vt purificare, castigare

chastise vt castigare

chastisement s castigatio, animadversio f

chastiser s castigator m

chastity s pudicitia, castitas f, pudor m

chat s familiaris sermo m; **to have a —** fabulari, garrire

chat vi fabulari, garrire, colloqui

chattel s bona n pl

chatter s clangor m; (*idle talk*) garrulitas f, loquacitas f; (*of the teeth*) crepit·us -ūs m

chatter vi balbutire; (*to talk nonsense*) garrire, effutire; (*of teeth*) crepitare

cheap adj vilis; **— as dirt** pervilis; **—ly** bene, vili; viliter

cheapen vt pretium minuĕre (*with genit*)

cheapness s vilitas f

cheat vt decipĕre, fraudare

cheat s fraus f; dolus m; (*cheater*) fraudator m

check vt (*to restrain*) cohibĕre, inhibĕre; (*to stop*) retardare; (*to bridle*) refrenare; (*accounts*) dispungĕre; (*to verify*) comprobare

check s (*hindrance*) coercitio, suppressio f; impedimentum n; (*reprimand*) reprehensio f; (*bridle*) fre-

num n; (*disadvantage*) detrimentum n; (*admission ticket*) tessera f

checkered adj varius

cheek s gena f

cheekbone s maxilla f

cheer s (*shout*) clamor, plaus·us -ūs m; hilaritas f

cheer vt hortari, hilarare, exhilarare; (*to console*) solari

cheerful adj hilaris, alacer, laetus; **—ly** hilare, laete; libenter

cheerfulness s hilaritas f

cheering s acclamatio f; plaus·us -ūs m

cheerless adj maestus, tristis, illaetabilis

cheese s caseus m

chemical adj chemicus

chemical s chemicum n

chemise s indusium n

chemist s chemicus, chemiae peritus m

chemistry s chemia, chymia f

cherish vt (*to nourish*) alĕre; (*to treat tenderly*) fovēre; (*fig*) colĕre

cherry s cerasum n

cherry tree s cerasus f

chest s (*of the body*) pectus n; (*box*) cista, arca f; (*for clothes*) vestiarium n; scrinium n

chestnut s castanea f

chew vt mandĕre, manducare; **to — the cud** ruminare; (*fig*) meditari

chewing s manducatio, ruminatio f

chicanery s calumnia, praevaricatio f

chick s pullus m; (*term of endearment*) pulla f

chicken s gallina f

chicken-hearted adj timidus, ignavus

chicory s cichoreum n

chide vt objurgare; corripĕre

chief adj primus; praecipuus, summus; supremus; **—ly** praecipue, imprimis

chief s princeps, procer, dux, auctor m; caput n

chieftain s dux m

child s infans m & f; puer, filius m, puella, filia f; (*in the womb*) embryo m; **to bear a —** parturire; **with —** gravida

childbearing s part·us -ūs m

childbirth s part·us -ūs m; Lucinae labores m pl

childhood s infantia f; pueritia f; **from —** a puero or pueris; a primo tempore aetatis, a parvo

childish adj puerilis; **—ly** pueriliter

childless adj orbus

childlike adj puerilis

chill s frigusculum, frigus n

chill adj frigidulus

chill vt refrigerare

chilling adj algificus; frigidus, gelidus

chilly adj alsiosus; frigidulus

chime s sonus m

chime vi canĕre, sonare; **to — in** interpellare

chimera s chimaera f; figmentum n

chimney s caminus m

chin s mentum n

china s fictilia n pl

chink s rima f; (sound) tinnit·us -ūs m

chink vi tinnire

chip s segmen n, assula f; (for lighting fire) fomes m

chip vt ascio dedolare

chirp s (of birds) pipat·us -ūs m; (of crickets) stridor m

chirp vi (of birds) minurire, pipilare; (of crickets) stridēre

chisel s scalprum, caelum n

chisel vt scalpro caedēre, sculpēre; (fig) decipēre, fraudare

chivalrous adj magnanimus, nobilis

chivalry s equestris dignitas f; (class) equites m pl

chocolate s chocolatum n

choice s electio f, delect·us -ūs m; (power of choosing) optio f; (diversity) varietas f

choice adj electus, exquisitus

choir s chorus m

choke vt suffocare; strangulare; vi suffocari; strangulari

choking s suffocatio f; strangulatio f

choose vt eligěre, optare; to — to (to prefer) malle (with inf)

choosing s electio f

chop s frustum n; (of meat) ofella f

chop vt concidēre; truncare; to — off detruncare; abscidēre; to — up minutatim concidēre

choral adj symphoniacus

chord s chorda f, nervus m

chorus s chorus m; symphonia f

Christ s Christus m

christen vt baptizare

Christendom s cuncti Christiani m pl

Christian adj Christianus

Christianity s Christianismus m

Christian name s praenomen in baptismo inditum n

Christmas s festum nativitatis Christi n

chronic adj diuturnus, perpetuus; inveteratus

chronicle s annales m pl; acta publica n pl

chronological adj in — order ordinem temporum respiciens

chronology s temporum ordo m, temporum ratio f

chubby adj crassus, pinguis

chuckle vi cachinnare

church s ecclesia f; templum n

churl s homo rusticus m

churlish adj agrestis, importunus; —ly rustice

cider s hydromelum n

cinder s cinis m, favilla f

cinnamon s cinnamomum n

cipher s (code) nota f; (a nobody) numerus m; (zero) nihil n

circle s circulus, orbis, gyrus m; (around the moon) halo m; vicious — circulus vitiosus m

circle vt circumdare, cingěre; vi circumire

circuit s circuit·us -ūs, circulus m; to make a — circumire

circuitous adj devius

circular adj orbicus, rotundus

circulate vt spargěre; (news) disseminare, divulgare; vi circulari

circulation s ambit·us -ūs m; (of blood) circulatio f

circumcise vt circumciděre

circumcision s circumcisio f

circumference s peripheria f, ambit·us -ūs, circulus m

circumflex s circumflex·us -ūs m

circumlocution s circumlocutio, periphrasis f; ambages f pl

circumscribe vt finire, terminare, circumscriběre

circumspect adj prudens, cautus, providus

circumspection s cautio, prudentia f

circumstance s res, conditio f; tempus n; sit·us -ūs m; under the —s quae cum ita sint

circumstantial adj adventicius, fortuitus; enumeratus; (of evidence) conjecturalis; —ly subtiliter

circumvent vt circumvenire, fallěre, circumscriběre

circumvention s circumscriptio, fraus f

circus s circus m

cistern s cisterna f, lac·us -ūs m; puteus m

citadel s arx f

citation s citatio, prolatio f; (law) vocatio f

cite vt (law) citare, evocare; (to quote) proferre, memorare

citizen s civis m & f; (of a municipality) municeps m

citizen adj civicus

citizenship s civitas f

city adj urbanus; urbicus

city s urbs f

civic adj civilis, civicus

civil adj civilis; (polite) comis, urbanus; (of war) civilis, intestinus, domesticus

civilian s togatus m; privatus m

civility s urbanitas, comitas f

civilization s cult·us -ūs m; humanitas f

civilize vt excolēre; expolire

clad adj indutus, vestitus, amictus

claim s postulatio, vindicatio f, postulatum n

claim vt postulare, poscěre, vindicare, arrogare

claimant s petitor, vindicator m

clam s chama f

clamber vi scanděre, conscenděre

clammy adj umidus, viscidus, lentus

clamor s clamor m, vociferatio f

clamor vi exclamare, vociferari; — for flagitare

clamp s confibula f; uncus m

clamp vt constringěre

clan s gens f

clandestine adj clandestinus, furtivus; —ly clam, furtim

clang s clangor m

clang vi clangěre, strepěre

clank s strepit·us -ūs m

clank vi crepare

clap s (of hand) plaus·us -ūs m; (of thunder) fragor m
clap vi plaudēre, applaudēre
claptrap s apparat·us -ūs m
clarification s explicatio f, explanatio f
clarify vt deliquare, explanare, explicare
clarion s lituus m
clarity s claritas f; perspicuitas f
clash s concurs·us -ūs m; (sound) crepit·us -ūs m; (fig) dissonantia f
clash vi concurrēre; increpare, increpitare; (fig) dissidēre, discrepare
clasp s fibula f; (embrace) amplex·us -ūs m
clasp vt (to embrace) amplecti, complecti; (to grasp) comprehendēre
class s (pol) classis f, ordo m; (kind) genus n
class vt in classes distribuĕre; **to — as** in numero habēre
classical adj classicus
classics s scriptores classici m pl
classification s in classes distributio, in genera distributio f
classify vt describĕre, in classes distribuĕre, in genera distribuĕre
clatter s strepit·us -ūs, crepit·us -ūs m
clatter vi crepare, crepitare, strepĕre
clause s (gram) membrum, incisum n, articulus m, clausula f; (law) caput n
claw s unguis m
claw vt lacerare
clay s argilla, creta f; **made of —** fictilis
clean adj mundus, purus; (fig) purus, castus; **—ly** munde, pure
clean vt mundare, purgare
cleanliness s munditia f
cleanly adj mundus, nitidus
cleanse vt purgare, depurgare, abluĕre, detergĕre
clear adj clarus; (of weather) serenus; (bright) lucidus; (of liquids) limpidus; (transparent) liquidus; (of voice) candidus, acutus, argutus; (manifest) conspicuus, manifestus; (of space) apertus, patens; (of language) dilucidus; (of conscience) rectus; (of the mind) sagax; **— of** expers (with genit); **it is —** apparet, liquet; **to keep — of** evitare; **—ly** clare; plane, aperte, haud dubie
clear vt purgare; (to acquit) absolvĕre; (a doubt) explanare; (land, forests) extricare; (profit) lucrari; **to — away** detergĕre, amovēre, tollĕre; **to — out** emundare; **to — up** enodare, explanare, explicare; vi **to — up** (of weather) disserenascĕre, disserenare
clearance s purgatio f; (space) intervallum n
clearness s claritas f; (of sky) serenitas f; (of style) perspicuitas f
cleavage s discidium n
cleave vt findĕre; vi **to — to** adhaerēre (with dat)
cleaver s dolabra f

cleft s rima, fissura f, hiat·us -ūs m
clemency s clementia f
clement adj clemens, mitis
clench vt comprimĕre
clerk s scriba m
clever adj sollers, ingeniosus, callidus, astutus, versutus; **—ly** sollerter, callide, ingeniose, astute
cleverness s dexteritas, sollertia, astutia f
click s crepit·us -ūs m
click vi crepitare
client s cliens m & f; consultor m
cliff s cautes f, scopulus m, rupes f
climate s caelum n
climax s gradatio f
climb vt & vi ascendĕre, conscendĕre, scandĕre
climb s ascens·us -ūs m
clinch vt confirmare
cling vi adhaerēre; **to — together** cohaerēre
clink s tinnit·us -ūs m
clink vi tinnire
clip s fibula f
clip vt tondĕre, praecidĕre; (words) mutilare
clipping s tonsura f; **—s** resegmina n pl
cloak s pallium n; (for travel) paenula f; (in rain) lacerna f; (mil) sagum, paludamentum n
cloak vt dissimulare, praetendĕre, tegĕre
clock s horologium n; (sundial) solarium n
clod s glaeba f
clog s (shoe) sculponea f; (fig) impedimentum n
clog vt impedire
cloister s portic·us -ūs f; monasterium n
close adj (dense) densus, spissus; (tight) artus, angustus; (shut) occlusus, clausus; (fast) firmus; (near) propinquus; (secret) arcanus, obscurus; (niggardly) avarus, tenax, parcus; **at — quarters** comminus; **— together** confertus, refertus, densus, continuus; **to be — at hand** adesse, instare; **to keep — to** adhaerēre (with dat); **—ly** prope; (attentively) attente, exacte
close vt claudĕre, operire; (to end) finire, terminare; **to — a bargain** pacisci; vi coire; claudi, concludi, terminari; (in a speech) perorare
close s finis, terminus m, terminatio, conclusio f; **to bring to a —** finire; **to draw to a —** terminari
close adv prope, promime, juxta; **— to** prope (with acc), juxta (with acc)
closet s conclave n, cella f; (for clothes) vestiarium n
closing adj ultimus
closing s conclusio f, finis m
clot s (of blood) cruor, concretus sanguis m
clot vi concrescĕre
cloth s pannus m; (linen) linteum n
clothe vt vestire, induĕre; velare

clothes s vestit·us -ūs m, vestimenta n pl, vestis f
clothing s vestit·us -ūs m, vestimenta n pl, vestis f
cloud s nubes f
cloud vt nubibus velare; (fig) obscurare; vi nubilare
cloudiness s nubilum n
cloudless adj serenus, purus
cloudy adj nubilus; **to grow —** nubilare
clout s ict·us -ūs m; alapa f
cloven adj bisulcus, bifidus
clown s (boor) rusticus m; (buffoon, jester) scurra m
clown vi scurrari
clownish adj rusticus; scurrilis
cloy vt satiare, exsaturare
cloying adj putidus
club s (cudgel) clava f, fustis m; (society) sodalitas f, collegium n
club vt fuste dolare
cluck vi glocire; singultire
clue s indicium n
clump s massa f; (of trees) arbustum n, globus m
clumsily adv rustice, inscite, ineleganter, male, inepte
clumsiness s rusticitas, inscitia f
clumsy adj ineptus, inscitus, rusticus, agrestis; (of things) inhabilis
cluster s (of grapes, etc.) racemus m; (of flowers) corymbus m; (of people) corona f
cluster vi congregari; **to — around** stipare
clutch s unguis m; comprehensio f; **from one's —es** e manibus; **in one's —es** in sua potestate
clutch vt arripĕre, prehendĕre
coach s curr·us -ūs m, raeda f; (trainer) magister m
coagulate vt coagulare; vi concrescĕre
coagulation s coagulatio, concretio f
coal s carbo m
coalesce vi coalescĕre, coire
coalition s conjunctio, coitio, conspiratio f
coal mine s fodina carbonaria f
coarse adj (of material) crassus, rudis; (of manners) incultus, inurbanus, rusticus; **—ly** crasse; inurbane
coarseness s crassitudo f; rusticitas f
coast s ora f, litus n
coast vi praetervehi
coastal adj maritimus, litoralis
coat s tunica, toga f; (of fur) pellis f
coat vt illinĕre, inducĕre, obducĕre
coating s corium n
coat of arms s insignia n pl
coat of mail s lorica f; (skin) pellis f
coax vt cogĕre, mulcĕre, blandiri
coaxing s blandimenta n pl, blanditiae f pl
coaxingly adv blande
cobbler s sutor m
cobweb s aranea f, araneum n
cock s gallus m
cockroach s blatta f

cocoa s faba Cacao f
cocoanut s nux palmae indicae f
cocoon s globulus m
coddle vt indulgēre (with dat)
code s notae f pl
codify vt digerĕre
coerce vt coercĕre, refrenare, cogĕre
coercion s coercitio, vis f
coeval adj coaevus, aequalis
coexist vi simul existĕre
coffee s coffea Arabica f
coffer s arca, cista f
coffin s arca f, sarcophagus m
cog s dens m
cogency s vis f
cogent adj cogens, efficax, gravis
cognate adj cognatus
cognizance s cognitio f
cognizant adj conscius, gnarus
cohabit vi coire, consuescĕre
cohabitation s consuetudo f, convict·us -ūs m
coheir s coheres m & f
cohere vi cohaerēre; (fig) congruĕre
coherence s context·us -ūs m, convenientia f
coherent adj cohaerens, congruens; **—ly** constanter
cohesion s cohaerentia f
cohesive adj tenax
cohort s cohors f
coil s spira f
coil vt glomerare; vi glomerari
coin s nummus m
coin vt cudĕre, signare; (fig) fingĕre
coinage s res nummaria, moneta f
coincide vi congruĕre, convenire, concurrĕre; eodem tempore fieri
coincidence s concursatio f, concurs·us -ūs m; (fig) consens·us -ūs m; **by —** casu
coincidental adj fortuitus
cold adj frigidus, gelidus; **to be —** algēre, frigēre; **to become —** frigescĕre, algescĕre; **—ly** (fig) frigide, gelide, lente
cold s frigus n, algor m, gelu n; (sickness) gravedo f; **to catch a —** gravedinem contrahĕre; **to have a —** gravedine dolēre
coldness s frigus n, algor m
colic s tormina n pl
collapse s labes, ruina f
collapse vi collabi, concidĕre, in se corruĕre
collar s (of garment) collare n; (for dogs) millus m; jugum n
collar vt collo comprehendĕre
collarbone s jugulum n
collate vt conferre
collateral adj transversus; adjunctus, consentaneus
colleague s collega, consors m
collect vt conferre, colligĕre; (to assemble) convocare; (money) exigĕre; **to — oneself** mentem colligĕre, animum colligĕre; vi colligi, aggregari
collected adj praesens
collection s collectio, conquisitio, collecta, congeries f; (out of authors) collectanea n pl

collective *adj* communis, collectivus; —ly una, simul, communiter

college *s* collegium *n*

collegiate *adj* collegialis, collegiarius

collide *vi* confligĕre, concurrĕre

collision *s* concursio, conflictio *f*, concurs·us -ūs *m*

colloquial *adj* quotidianus

collusion *s* collusio, praevaricatio *f*, dolus *m*

colon *s* colon *n*

colonel *s* legatus *m*

colonial *adj* colonicus

colonist *s* colonus *m*

colonize *vt* coloniam constituĕre in (*with abl*)

colonnade *s* portic·us -ūs *f*

colony *s* colonia *f*

color *s* color *m*, pigmentum *n*; —*s* vexillum *n*

color *vt* colorare; (*to dye*) tingĕre, inficĕre; (*fig*) obtegĕre; *vi* erubescĕre

colossal *adj* ingens, immanis

colossus *s* colossus *m*

colt *s* equulus, pullus equinus *m*

column *s* columna *f*; (*mil*) agmen *n*

comb *s* pecten *m*

comb *vt* pectĕre, comĕre

combat *s* pugna *f*, proelium, certamen *n*

combat *vt* pugnare cum (*with abl*); *vi* pugnare, proeliari

combination *s* conjunctio, junctura *f*; (*of persons*) conspiratio, conjuratio *f*

combine *vt* conjungĕre, miscĕre; temperare; *vi* coire; conspirare

combustible *adj* igni obnoxius

combustion *s* concrematio, ustio *f*

come *vi* venire; (*to arrive*) pervenire; (*to happen*) fieri; **to — about** evenire; **to — after** sequi; **to — again** revenire; **to — along** procedĕre; **to — away** abscedĕre; **to — back** revenire, redire; **to — before** praevenire; **to — by** praeterire; (*to get*) acquirĕre; **to — down** descendĕre; (*to fall down*) decidĕre; **to — forth** exire; (*fig*) exoriri; **to — forward** procedĕre; **to — in** introire; **to — near** appropinquare, accedĕre; **to — off** recedĕre, discedĕre; **to — on** pergĕre; **to — out** (*to be published*) edi, emitti; **to — over** supervenire; (*the face*) obire; **to — round** (*fig*) transgredi; **to — to** advenire; (*to come to one's senses*) ad se redire; **to — to pass** evenire, fieri; **to — together** convenire, coire; **to — up** subvenire; (*to occur*) accidĕre, provenire; **to — upon** (*to find*) invenire; (*to attack*) ingruĕre

comedian *s* comoedus *m*; (*playwright*) comicus *m*

comedy *s* comoedia *f*

comely *adj* decens, venustus

comet *s* cometes *m*, stella crinita *f*

comfort *s* consolatio *f*, solatium *n*

comfort *vt* consolari, solari

comfortable *adj* commodus, amoenus

comfortably *adv* commode

comforter *s* consolator *m*

comfortless *adj* solatii expers, incommodus

comic *adj* comicus, facetus

comic *s* scurra *m*

comical *adj* comicus, ridiculus; —ly comice, ridicule

coming *adj* venturus

coming *s* advent·us -ūs *m*

comma *s* comma *n*

command *vt* imperare (*with dat*), jubēre; (*view*) prospectare, despectare

command *s* (*order*) jussum, mandatum, praeceptum *n*, juss·us -ūs *m*; (*mil*) imperium *n*; (*jurisdiction*) provincia *f*; — **of language** copia dicendi *f*; **to be in — of** praeesse (*with dat*); **to put someone in — of** aliquem praeficĕre (*with dat*)

commander *s* dux, praefectus *m*

commander in chief *s* imperator *m*

commandment *s* mandatum *n*

commemorate *vt* celebrare

commemoration *s* celebratio *f*

commence *vt* incipere, inchoare

commencement *s* initium, exordium, principium *n*

commend *vt* approbare, laudare; (*to recommend*) commendare; (*to entrust*) committĕre, mandare

commendable *adj* commendabilis, probabilis, laudabilis

commendation *s* commendatio *f*

commensurate *adj* adaequans, conveniens

comment *vi* commentari; **to — on** explicare, enarrare, interpretari

comment *s* sententia *f*, dictum *n*

commentary *s* commentarius *m*, commentarium *n*

commentator *s* interpres *m*

commerce *s* commercium *n*, mercat·us -ūs *m*, mercatura *f*; **to engage in —** negotiari

commercial *adj* negotialis

commiserate *vi* **to — with** miserēri

commiseration *s* misericordia *f*

commissariat *s* commeat·us -ūs *m*, res frumentaria *f*

commissary *s* procurator, curator *m*

commission *s* mandatum *n*; (*mil*) legatio *f*

commission *vt* delegare, mandare

commissioner *s* delegatus *m*

commit *vt* (*crime*) admittĕre, patrare, perpetrare; (*to entrust*) committĕre; **to — to memory** ediscĕre

commitment *s* (*obligation*) munus, officium *n*; (*to jail*) incarceratio *f*

committee *s* consilium *n*

commodity *s* res venalis, merx *f*

common *adj* communis, publicus; (*ordinary*) vulgaris, quotidianus; (*well known*) pervulgatus; (*repeated*) creber; (*inferior*) mediocris; (*gram*) promiscuus; —ly vulgo, fere, plerumque

commoner *s* plebeius *m*; —*s* plebs *f*

commonplace *adj* vulgaris, pervulgatus, tritus

commonwealth *s* respublica *f*

commotion s commotio, agitatio f, tumult·us -ūs m

commune vi confabulari

communicate vt communicare; (information) impertire, nuntiare; vi **to — with** communicare (with dat), agĕre cum (with abl)

communication s communicatio f; commercium n; (information) nuntius m

communicative adj affabilis, facilis

communion s communio, societas f

community s civitas f

commutation s mutatio, permutatio f

commute vt commutare

compact adj densus, spissus; (of style) pressus; **—ly** dense, spisse, confertim

compact s pactum, foedus n, pactio f

compact vt densare

companion s comes, socius, sodalis; (mil) contubernalis, commilito m

companionable adj affabilis, facilis

companionship s societas, sodalitas, consuetudo f; (mil) contubernium n

company s societas, consuetudo f; (gathering) convent·us -ūs m; (guests) convivium n; (com) societas f; (mil) manipulus m; (theatrical) grex f

comparable adj comparabilis

comparative adj comparatus, relativus; **—ly** comparate

comparative s grad·us -ūs comparativus m

compare vt comparare, conferre; **compared with** ad (with acc), adversus (with acc)

comparison s comparatio, collatio f; **in — with** prae (with abl), adversus (with acc)

compartment s loculus m, cella, pars f

compass s ambit·us -ūs m; (limits) fines m pl; (instrument) circinus m; (magnetic) ac·us -ūs magnetica f

compass vt circumvallare, cingĕre, circumdare; (to attain) consequi, patrare

compassion s misericordia f

compassionate adj misericors; **—ly** misericorditer

compatibility s congruentia, convenientia f

compatible adj congruus, conveniens

compatriot s civis, popularis m

compeer s par, aequalis m

compel vt cogĕre, compellĕre

compendium s summarium n

compensate vt compensare, renumerare; satisfacĕre (with dat)

compensation s compensatio f; poena f

compete vi contendĕre, petĕre, certare

competence s facultas f; (legal capacity) jus n

competent adj congruens, idoneus, peritus, capax; (of authorities) locuples; **—ly** satis, idonee

competition s contentio, aemulatio f, certamen n

competitor s petitor, rivalis, aemulus m

compilation s collectio f, collectanea n pl

compile vt colligĕre, componĕre

compiler s collector, scriptor m

complacency s amor sui m

complacent adj qui sibi placet

complain vi queri

complaint s querela, querimonia f; (law) crimen n; (med) morbus m

complaisance s comitas, accommodatio f, obsequium n

complaisant adj comis, officiosus; **—ly** comiter

complement s complementum, supplementum n

complete adj perfectus, integer, absolutus, plenus; **—ly** plane, prorsus, omnino, abolute, funditus

complete vt complēre; (to accomplish) perficĕre, conficĕre, peragĕre

completion s completio f; (accomplishment) perfectio f; (end) finis m

complex adj multiplex, implicatus, complicatus

complexion s color m

complexity s implicatio, multiplex natura f

compliance s obtemperatio f, obsequium n

compliant adj obsequens

complicate vt impedire

complicated adj impeditus, implicatus, complicatus, nodosus

complication s implicatio f

complicity s conscientia f

compliment s blandimentum n, verba honorifica n pl; **to pay one's —s** to salutare

compliment vt gratulari (with dat); laudare, blandiri

complimentary adj blandus, honorificus

comply vi **to — with** concedĕre (with dat), cedĕre (with dat), parēre (with dat), obsequi (with dat), morigerari (with dat)

component s pars f, elementum n

compose vt componĕre; (verses) condĕre, pangĕre; (to calm) sedare; (quarrel) componĕre; **to — oneself** tranquillari

composed adj tranquillus, quietus, placidus

composer s scriptor, auctor m

composite adj compositus, multiplex

composition s compositio, scriptura f; opus n

composure s tranquillitas f, animus aequus m

compound vt componĕre, miscēre; (words) jungĕre

compound adj compositus

compound s compositio f; (word) junctum verbum n

compound interest s anatocismus m

comprehend vt continēre, amplectari; (to understand) capĕre, percipĕre, comprehendĕre, intellegĕre

comprehensible adj perspicuus

comprehension s intellect·us -ūs m, intellegentia f

comprehensive *adj* plenus, capax; —ly funditus, omnino

compress *vt* comprimĕre

compression *s* compressio *f*, compress·us -ūs *m*

comprise *vt* continēre

compromise *s* (*unilateral*) accommodatio *f*; (*bilateral*) compromissum *n*

compromise *vt* compromittĕre, implicāre; *vi* pacisci

compulsion *s* compulsio, vis, necessitas *f*

compulsory *adj* necessarius, debitus

compunction *s* paenitentia, compunctio *f*

computation *s* ratio, computatio *f*

compute *vt* computāre

comrade *s* socius, sodalis *m*; (*mil*) contubernalis *m*

conceal *vt* celāre, occultāre, abdĕre, dissimulāre

concealment *s* occultatio, dissimulatio *f*; (*place*) latebrae *f pl*; **to be in** — latēre

concede *vt* concedĕre

conceit *s* (*haughtiness*) arrogantia, superbia *f*; (*idea*) notio *f*

conceited *adj* arrogans, superbiā tumens

conceive *vt* concipĕre, percipĕre, intellegĕre

concentrate *vt* in unum locum contrahĕre; *vi* **to** — **on** animum intendĕre in (*with acc*)

concentration *s* in unum locum contractio *f*; (*fig*) animi intentio *f*

conception *s* (*in womb*) concept·us -ūs *m*; (*idea*) imago, notio *f*

concern *s* (*affair*) res *f*, negotium *n*; (*importance*) momentum *n*; (*worry*) sollicitudo, cura *f*

concern *vt* pertinēre ad (*with acc*), attinēre ad (*with acc*); (*to worry*) sollicitāre; **it** —**s me** meā interest, meā refert

concerned *adj* sollictus, anxius

concerning *prep* de (*with abl*)

concert *s* (*music*) concent·us -ūs *m*, symphonia *f*; **in** — uno animo, ex composito

concert *vt* (*plan*) inire

concession *s* concessio *f*; (*thing*) concessum *n*; **to make** —**s** concedĕre

conch *s* concha *f*

conciliate *vt* conciliāre

conciliation *s* conciliatio *f*

concise *adj* brevis, concisus; (*style*) densus; —ly breviter, concise

conciseness *s* brevitas *f*

conclave *s* conclave, consilium *n*

conclude *vt* (*to end*) conficĕre, perficĕre, termināre, finire; (*to infer*) concludĕre, colligĕre

conclusion *s* (*end*) conclusio *f*; (*decision*) determinatio, sententia *f*; (*of speech*) peroratio *f*; (*of action*) exit·us -ūs *m*; (*inference*) conjectura *f*

conclusive *adj* certus, gravis

concoct *vt* concoquĕre; (*to contrive*) excogitāre, conflāre

concoction *s* pot·us -ūs *m*; (*fig*) ma-

chinatio *f*

concomitant *adj* adjunctus, conjunctus

concord *s* concordia, harmonia *f*; (*mus*) concent·us -ūs *m*

concordat *s* pactum *n*

concourse *s* concurs·us -ūs *m*, concursio *f*

concrete *adj* concretus

concrete *s* concretum *n*, concret·us -ūs *m*

concubinage *s* concubinat·us -ūs *m*

concubine *s* concubina *f*

concupiscence *s* libido *f*

concur *vi* congruĕre, consentire

concurrence *s* consens·us -ūs *m*, consensio *f*

concussion *s* concussio *f*

condemn *vt* damnāre; condemnāre; **to** — **to death** capitis damnāre

condemnation *s* damnatio, condemnatio *f*

condensation *s* densatio, spissatio *f*

condense *vt* (con)densāre, spissāre; (*words*) premĕre

condescend *vi* dignāri, descendĕre, concedĕre, se submittĕre

condescending *adj* comis; —ly comiter

condescension *s* comitas *f*

condition *s* (*state*) stat·us -ūs *m*, condicio, res *f*; (*stipulation*) condicio, lex *f*; **on** — **that** ea lege ut

condition *vt* formāre, informāre

conditional *adj* conditionalis; —ly (*law*) conditionaliter; sub condicione

condole *vi* **to** — **with** dolēre cum (*with abl*)

condone *vt* veniam dare (*with dat*), condonāre

conducive *adj* utilis, accommodatus

conduct *s* mores *m pl*, vita *f*; (*management*) administratio *f*

conduct *vt* (*to lead*) adducĕre, deducĕre, perducĕre; (*to manage*) gerĕre, administrāre

conductor *s* dux, ductor *m*

conduit *s* canalis, aquaeduct·us -ūs *m*

cone *s* conus *m*

confection *s* conditura, cuppedo *f*

confectionery *s* cuppedia *n pl*, conditura *f*

confederacy *s* (*alliance*) foedus *n*, societas *f*

confederate *adj* foederatus

confederate *s* socius, conjuratus *m*

confederate *vi* foedus facĕre

confederation *s* societas *f*

confer *vt* conferre, tribuĕre; *vi* colloqui

conference *s* colloquium *n*

confess *vt* fatēri, confitēri; agnoscĕre, concedĕre

confessedly *adv* ex confesso; manifesto, aperte

confession *s* confessio *f*

confidant *s* familiaris *m & f*, conscius *m*, conscia *f*

confide *vt* committĕre, credĕre, mandāre; *vi* **to** — **in** (con)fidĕre (*with dat*)

confidence *s* fides, confidentia, fiducia *f*; **to have** — **in** confidĕre (*with* *dat*); **to inspire — in** fidem facĕre (*with dat*)

confident *adj* confidens, fidens; **—ly** confidenter

confidential *adj* fidus; (*secret*) arcanus

configuration *s* forma, figura *f*

confine *s* finis *m*

confine *vt* includĕre; (*to restrain*) coercēre, cohibēre; (*to limit*) circumscribĕre; **to be confined to bed** lecto tenēri

confinement *s* inclusio *f*; (*imprisonment*) incarceratio, custodia *f*; (*of women*) puerperium *n*

confirm *vt* confirmare; (*to prove*) comprobare; (*to ratify*) sancire

confirmation *s* confirmatio, affirmatio *f*

confiscate *vt* proscribĕre, publicare

confiscation *s* proscriptio, publicatio *f*

conflagration *s* incendium *n*

conflict *s* conflict·us -ūs *m*, contentio, pugna *f*, certamen *n*

conflict *vi* contendĕre; (*differ*) dissentire, discrepare

conflicting *adj* contrarius, adversus

confluence *s* confluens *m*

conform *vt* accommodare; *vi* obsequi, obtemperare

conformation *s* conformatio, figura, forma *f*

conformity *s* convenientia, congruentia *f*; **in — with** secundum (*with acc*)

confound *vt* confundĕre, permiscēre, perturbare; (*to frustrate*) frustrari

confounded *adj* miser, nefandus

confront *vt* obviam ire (*with dat*), se oppōnĕre (*with dat*)

confrontation *s* comparatio *f*

confuse *vt* confundĕre, perturbare, permiscēre

confused *adj* confusus, perplexus; **—ly** confuse, perplexe

confusion *s* confusio, perturbatio *f*; (*shame*) pudor *m*

congeal *vt* congelare, glaciare; *vi* consistĕre, concrescĕre

congenial *adj* consentaneus, concors

congenital *adj* nativus

congested *adj* refertus, densus; frequentissimus

congestion *s* congeries, frequentia *f*

congratulate *vt* gratulari (*with dat*)

congratulation *s* gratulatio *f*

congratulatory *adj* gratulans, gratulabundus

congregate *vt* congregare, colligĕre; *vi* congregari, convenire

congregation *s* coet·us -ūs *m*, auditores *m pl*

conical *adj* conicus

conjectural *adj* conjecturalis, opinabilis; **—ly** ex conjectura

conjecture *s* conjectura *f*

conjecture *vt* conjectare, conjicĕre

conjugal *adj* conjugalis

conjugate *vt* declinare

conjugation *s* conjugatio *f*

conjunction *s* unio *f*, concurs·us -ūs *m*; (*gram*) conjunctio *f*

conjure *vt* obtestari, incantare, fascinare; *vi* praestigiis uti

conjurer *s* magus, praestigiator *m*

conjuring *s* praestigiae *f pl*

connect *vt* connectĕre, jungĕre, copulare; (*in a series*) serĕre

connected *adj* conjunctus; continuus, continens; (*by marriage*) affinis; **to be closely connected with** inhaerēre (*with dat*); **to be connected with** contingĕre

connection *s* conjunctio, colligatio *f*, nex·us -ūs, context·us -ūs *m*; (*kin*) necessitudo *f*; (*by marriage*) affinitas *f*

connivance *s* indulgentia, dissimulatio *f*

connive *vi* connivēre

connoisseur *s* doctus, peritus, intellegens *m*

conquer *vt* vincĕre, superare; domare

conqueror *s* victor *m*, victrix *f*; domitor *m*

conquest *s* victoria *f*

consanguinity *s* consanguinitas *f*

conscience *s* conscientia *f*; **guilty —** mala conscientia; **to have no —** nullam religionem habēre

conscientious *adj* integer, pius, religiosus, diligens; **—ly** diligenter

conscious *adj* conscius, gnarus; **—ly** scienter

consciousness *s* conscientia *f*

conscript *s* tiro *m*

conscript *vt* conscribĕre

conscription *s* delect·us -ūs *m*

consecrate *vt* sacrare, consecrare, dedicare, devovēre

consecration *s* consecratio, dedicatio *f*

consecutive *adj* continuus; **—ly** deinceps, continenter

consent *vi* assentire, consentire

consent *s* consens·us -ūs *m*, consensio *f*; **without my —** me invito

consequence *s* consequentia, consecutio *f*, event·us -ūs, exit·us -ūs *m*; (*logical*) conclusio *f*; (*importance*) momentum *n*

consequent *adj* consequens, consectarius; **—ly** ergo, igitur, itaque

consequential *adj* consentaneus

conservation *s* conservatio *f*

conservative *adj* reipublicae status conservandi studiosus; **— party** optimates *m pl*

conserve *vt* conservare, servare

consider *vt* considerare, animo agitare, revolvĕre; (*to deem*) aestimare, ducĕre, habēre; (*to respect*) respicĕre

considerable *adj* aliquantus; (*of persons*) eximius, illustris; (*of size*) amplus

considerably *adv* aliquantum; multum; (*with comp*) multo, aliquanto

considerate *adj* prudens, humanus, benignus

consideration *s* consideratio, contemplatio, deliberatio *f*; (*regard*) respect·us -ūs *m*; (*ground, motive*)

ratio f; (*importance*) momentum n;
without — inconsulte, temere
considering *prep* pro (*with abl*)
consign *vt* committĕre, mandare,
consignare, tradĕre
consignment *s* consignatio f
consist *vi* consistĕre; **to — of** constare ex (*with abl*)
consistency *s* congruentia, constantia f
consistent *adj* constans; consentaneus; **—ly** constanter, congruenter
consolable *adj* consolabilis
consolation *s* consolatio f; (*thing*)
solacium n
console *vt* consolari
consolidate *vt* corroborare, firmare,
consolidare, stabilire; *vi* solidescĕre
consonant *adj* consonus, consentaneus
consonant *s* consonans littera f
consort *s* consors m & f; (*married*)
conjux *or* conjunx m & f
consort *vi* **to — with** familiariter
uti (*with abl*), se associare cum
(*with abl*)
conspicuous *adj* conspicuus; insignis, manifestus; **—ly** manifeste,
palam
conspiracy *s* conjuratio, conspiratio f
conspirator *s* conjuratus m
conspire *vi* conjurare, conspirare
constable *s* lictor m
constancy *s* constantia, firmitas,
perseverantia f
constant *adj* constans, firmus; perpetuus; fidelis; **—ly** constanter,
crebro
constellation *s* sidus, astrum n
consternation *s* consternatio, trepidatio f, pavor m; **to throw into
—** perterrēre
constituent *s* elector, suffragator m;
(*part*) elementum n
constitute *vt* constituĕre, creare
constitution *s* (*of body*) habit·us -ūs
m, constitutio f; (*pol*) civitatis sta-
t·us -ūs m, reipublicae leges f pl
constitutional *adj* legitimus; (*natural*) naturā insitus; **—ly** legitime
constrain *vt* cogĕre, compellĕre, detinēre
constraint *s* vis, coercitio, necessitas f
construct *vt* construĕre
construction *s* constructio, aedificatio f; figura, forma f; (*meaning*)
sens·us -ūs m, interpretatio f
constructor *s* structor, fabricator m
construe *vt* interpretari; (*gram*) construĕre
consul *s* consul m; **— elect** consul
designatus m
consular *adj* consularis
consulship *s* consulat·us -ūs m; **to
run for the —** consulatum petĕre;
during my — me consule
consult *vt* consulĕre, consultare; *vi*
deliberare
consultation *s* consultatio, deliberatio f
consume *vt* consumĕre, absumĕre;

(*food*) edĕre
consumer *s* consumptor m
consummate *adj* summus, perfectus
consummate *vt* consummare
consummation *s* consummatio f;
(*end*) finis m
consumption *s* consumptio f; (*disease*) tabes f
consumptive *adj* pulmonarius
contact *s* contact·us -ūs m, contagio
f; **to come in — with** contingĕre
contagion *s* contagium n, contagio f
contagious *adj* contagiosus, tabificus
contain *vt* continēre; (*to restrain*)
cohibēre
container *s* vas n
contaminate *vt* contaminare
contamination *s* contaminatio, labes f
contemplate *vt* contemplari, intuēri
contemplation *s* contemplatio, meditatio f
contemporaneous *adj* aequalis;
—ly simul
contemporary *s* aequalis, aequaevus
m
contempt *s* contemptio f, contempt·
us -ūs m
contemptible *adj* contemnendus,
abjectus, vilis
contemptibly *adv* contemptim, abjecte
contemptuous *adj* fastidiosus, superbus; **—ly** fastidiose
contend *vt* (*to aver*) affirmare, asseverare; *vi* contendĕre, certare; (*to
struggle*) luctari; (*to dispute*) verbis
certare; **to — against** repugnare,
adversari
contending *adj* aversus, contrarius
content *adj* contentus
content *vt* satisfacĕre (*with dat*), placēre (*with dat*), mulcēre
contented *adj* contentus; **—ly** aequo
animo, leniter
contention *s* contentio f; certamen
n; controversia f
contentious *adj* litigiosus; pugnax
contentment *s* aequus animus m
contents *s* quod inest, quae insunt;
(*of book*) argumentum n
contest *s* certamen n, contentio, certatio f
contest *vt* (*to dispute*) resistĕre (*with
dat*), repugnare (*with dat*); (*law*)
lege agĕre de (*with abl*)
contestant *s* petitor, aemulus m
context *s* context·us -ūs, sens·us
-ūs m
contiguous *adj* contiguus, conterminus, adjunctus
continence *s* continentia, abstinentia f
continent *adj* abstinens, continens;
—ly abstinenter, continenter
continent *s* continens f
continental *adj* in continenti positus; ad continentem pertinens
contingent *s* (*of troops*) numerus m,
man·us -ūs f
continual *adj* continuus; perpetuus,
assiduus; **—ly** assidue, semper

continuance *s* continuatio, perpetuitas, assiduitas *f*

continuation *s* continuatio *f*

continue *vt* continuare, producĕre; *vi* pergĕre; (*to last*) durare, persistĕre, perstare, (re)manēre

continuity *s* continuitas *f*; (*of speech*) perpetuitas *f*

continuous *adj* continuus, continens, perpetuus; —**ly** continenter

contortion *s* contortio, distortio *f*

contour *s* forma, figura *f*; lineamenta *n pl*

contraband *adj* interdictus, vetitus, illicitus

contract *vt* contrahĕre, astringĕre; (*to shorten*) deminuĕre; (*sickness*) contrahĕre; (*to undertake*) redimĕre; *vi* pacisci; (*to shrink*) contrahi

contract *s* pactum, conventum *n*; (*pol*) foedus *n*

contraction *s* contractio *f*; (*of word*) compendium *n*

contractor *s* redemptor, susceptor *m*

contradict *vt* contradicĕre (*with dat*), obloqui (*with dat*)

contradiction *s* contradictio *f*; (*of things*) repugnantia *f*

contradictory *adj* contrarius, repugnans

contrary *adj* (*opposite*) contrarius, diversus, (*fig*) aversus, repugnans; — **to contra** (*with acc*)

contrary *s* contrarium *n*, contraria pars *f*; **on the** — contra, e contrario

contrast *s* diversitas, dissimilitudo *f*

contrast *vt* comparare, opponĕre; *vi* discrepare

contribute *vt* contribuĕre, conferre; *vi* **to** — **towards** conferre ad (*with acc*)

contribution *s* contributio, collatio *f*; (*money*) stips *f*

contributory *adj* contribuens, adjunctus

contrite *adj* paenitens

contrition *s* paenitentia *f*

contrivance *s* inventio, machinatio *f*; (*thing contrived*) inventum, artificium *n*, machina *f*

contrive *vt* (*to invent*) fingĕre; excogitare, machinari, efficĕre

control *s* (*restraint*) continentia *f*; (*power*) potestas, moderatio, dictio *f*, imperium *n*; **to have** — **over** praeesse (*with dat*)

control *vt* moderari (*with dat*), continēre, regĕre, coercēre

controller *s* moderator *m*

controversial *adj* concertatorius

controversy *s* controversia, disceptatio, concertatio *f*

contusion *s* contusio *f*, contusum *n*

conundrum *s* aenigma *n*; (*quibble*) cavillum *n*

convalesce *vi* convalescĕre

convalescence *s* conditio convalescendi *f*

convalescent *adj* convalescens

convene *vt* convocare

convenience *s* commoditas, opportunitas, convenientia *f*; (*thing*) commodum *n*

convenient *adj* commodus, idoneus, opportunus; —**ly** commode, apte, opportune

convention *s* convent·us -ūs *m*; (*custom*) mos *m*

conventional *adj* usitatus, tralaticius, solitus

converge *vi* vergĕre, coire

conversant *adj* peritus, exercitatus; **to be** — **with** versari in (*with abl*)

conversation *s* colloquium *n*, sermo *m*

conversational *adj* in colloquio usitatus

converse *vi* colloqui

converse *s* contrarium *n*, convers·us -ūs *m*

conversely *adv* e contrario, e converso

conversion *s* conversio *f*

convert *vt* convertĕre, commutare; deducĕre

convert *s* neophytus, discipulus *m*

convertible *adj* commutabilis

convex *adj* convexus

convey *vt* portare, vehĕre, convehĕre; (*property*) abalienare; (*fig*) significare

conveyance *s* (*act*) advectio, vectura *f*; (*vehicle*) vehiculum *n*; (*law*) abalienatio, transcriptio *f*

convict *s* convictus, evictus, reus *m*

convict *vt* convincĕre

conviction *s* (*law*) damnatio *f*; (*certainty*) persuasio, fides *f*

convince *vt* persuadēre (*with dat*)

convivial *adj* hilaris, laetus

convocation *s* convocatio *f*

convoke *vt* convocare

convoy *s* praesidium *n*, deductor *m*

convoy *vt* deducĕre

convulse *vt* concutĕre, convellĕre

convulsion *s* convulsio *f*, spasmus *m*

convulsive *adj* spasticus

cook *s* coquus *m*, coqua *f*

cook *vt* & *vi* coquĕre

cool *adj* frigidulus; (*fearless*) sedatus, immotus, impavidus; (*indifferent*) lentus, frigidus; —**ly** frigide; sedate; lente

cool *vt* refrigerare; *vi* refrigerari; (*fig*) defervescĕre

coolness *s* frigus *n*; (*fig*) lentitudo, cautela *f*; animus aequus *m*

coop *s* (*for chickens*) cavea *f*

coop *vt* **to** — **up** includĕre

cooperate *vi* unā agĕre; **to** — **with** adjuvare

cooperation *s* adjumentum *n*, consociatio, opera *f*

cope *vi* **to** — **with** certare cum (*with abl*); **able to** — **with** par (*with dat*)

copious *adj* copiosus, abundans; —**ly** copiose, abundanter

copper *s* aes, cuprum *n*

copper *adj* aëneus, cuprinus

copse *s* dumetum, fruticetum *n*

copy *s* exemplar *n*, imitatio, imago *f*

copy *vt* imitari; (*writing*) transcribĕre, exscribĕre

coquette *s* lupa, lasciva *f*
coquettish *adj* lascivus
coral *adj* coralinus
coral *s* coralium *n*
cord *s* funis, restis *m*
cordial *adj* benignus, comis; **—ly** benigne, comiter, ex animo
cordiality *s* comitas *f*
cordon *s* corona *f*
core *s* (*of fruit*) volva *f*; (*fig*) nucleus *m*
Corinthian *adj* Corinthiacus, Corinthius
cork *s* cortex *m*; (*stopper*) obturamentum *n*
corn *s* (*grain*) frumentum *n*; (*on toes*) callus *m*
corner *s* angulus *m*; (*of house*) versura *f*; (*of street*) compitum *n*
cornice *s* corona *f*
corollary *s* corollarium *n*
coronation *s* coronae impositio *f*
coronet *s* diadema *n*
corporal *adj* corporeus, corporalis
corporal *s* decurio *m*
corporate *adj* corporatus
corporation *s* collegium *n*; municipium *n*
corporeal *adj* corporeus
corps *s* legio *f*
corpse *s* cadaver *n*
corpulent *adj* corpulentus
corpuscle *s* corpusculum *n*
correct *adj* correctus, rectus, accuratus; **—ly** recte, bene
correct *vt* corrigĕre, emendare; (*to punish*) animadvertĕre, castigare
correction *s* correctio, emendatio *f*; (*punishment*) animadversio, castigatio *f*
correctness *s* puritas, accuratio *f*
correlation *s* reciprocitas, mutua ratio *f*
correspond *vi* congruĕre; (*by letter*) litteras mutuas scribĕre
correspondence *s* congruentia, convenientia *f*; epistolae *f pl*
correspondent *s* epistolarum scriptor *m*
corridor *s* portic·us -ūs *f*, andron, xystus *m*
corroborate *vt* confirmare
corrode *vt* erodĕre, edĕre
corrosion *s* rosio *f*
corrosive *adj* corrosivus; (*fig*) mordax
corrupt *vt* corrumpĕre, depravare; (*a girl*) stuprare
corrupt *adj* corruptus, putridus; (*fig*) pravus, impurus; venalis; **—ly** corrupte; inceste, turpiter
corrupter *s* corruptor *m*, corruptrix *f*, perditor *m*, perditrix *f*
corruption *s* corruptio, putredo *f*; (*fig*) depravatio, pravitas *f*
corselet *s* lorica *f*
corvette *s* celox *f*
cosily *adv* commode
cosmetic *s* medicamen *n*
cost *s* pretium *n*, impensa *f*; **— of living** anona *f*
cost *vi* (con)stare, venire
costliness *s* caritas *f*

costly *adj* carus; (*extravagant*) sumptuosus, lautus
costume *s* habit·us -ūs, vestit·us -ūs *m*
cosy *adj* commodus, gratus
cot *s* lectulus *m*; (*mil*) grabatus *m*
cottage *s* casa *f*, tugurium *n*
cotton *s* xylinum *n*
cotton *adj* gossipinus
couch *s* cubile, pulvinar *n*; lectus *m*
cough *s* tussis *f*; **to have a bad —** male tussire
cough *vi* tussire
council *s* concilium *n*
councilor *s* consiliarius *m*
counsel *s* (*advice*) consilium *n*; (*person*) advocatus *m*
counsel *vt* consulĕre, monēre
counselor *s* consiliarius, consiliator *m*
count *s* computatio, ratio *f*; (*of indictment*) caput *n*
count *vt* numerare, computare; (*to regard as*) ducĕre, habēre; **to — up** enumerare; *vi* aestimari, habēri; **to — upon** confidĕre (*with dat*)
countenance *s* facies *f*, vult·us -ūs, aspect·us -ūs *m*; **to put out of —** confundĕre, perturbare
countenance *vt* favēre (*with dat*), indulgēre (*with dat*), adjuvare
counter *s* (*of shop*) abacus *m*; (*in games*) calculus *m*
counteract *vt* obsistĕre (*with dat*); (*a sickness*) medēri (*with dat*)
counteraction *s* oppositio *f*
counterfeit *vt* imitari, simulare, fingĕre, adulterare
counterfeit *adj* simulatus, spurius, ficticius, adulterinus
counterfeit *s* (*money*) nummus adulterinus *m*; simulatio, imitatio *f*
counterfeiter *s* imitator, falsarius *m*
countermand *vt* renuntiare
counterpart *s* res gemella *f*; par *m*, *f & n*
countersign *vt* contrascribĕre
countless *adj* innumerabilis, innumerus
country *s* terra, regio *f*; (*territory*) fines *m pl*; (*not city*) rus *n*; (*native*) patria *f*
country house *s* villa *f*
countryman *s* civis, popularis *m*
countryside *s* rus *n*, agri *m pl*
couple *s* par *n*; mariti *m pl*; **a — of** duo
couple *vt* copulare, unire; *vi* (*of animals*) coire
courage *s* virtus *f*, animus *m*, fortitudo *f*; **to lose —** animos dimittĕre; **to take —** bono animo esse
courageous *adj* fortis, animosus, acer; **—ly** fortiter, acriter
courier *s* cursor, nuntius, tabellarius *m*
course *s* (*movement*) curs·us -ūs *m*; (*of life*) ratio *f*; (*of water*) duct·us -ūs *m*; (*route*) iter *n*; (*at table*) ferculum *n*; (*order*) series *f*; (*for racing*) circus *m*, stadium *n*; **in due —** mox; **in the —** of inter (*with acc*); **of —** certe, scilicet
court *s* (*law*) forum, tribunal, judi-

cium *n*, judices *m pl*; *(open area)* area *f*; *(of house)* atrium *n*; *(palace)* aula *f*; *(retinue)* comitat·us -ūs *m*

court *vt* colère, ambire; *(woman)* pe- tère; *(danger)* se offerre *(with dat)*

courteous *adj* comis, urbanus; **—ly** comiter, urbane

courtesan *s* meretrix *f*

courtesy *s* comitas, urbanitas *f*; *(act)* officium *n*

courtier *s* aulicus *m*

courtly *adj* aulicus; officiosus

court-martial *s* judicium castrense *n*

courtship *s* amor *m*, ambitio *f*

courtyard *s* aula *f*

cousin *s* consobrinus *m*, consobrina *f*, patruelis *m & f*

cove *s* sin·us -ūs *m*

covenant *s* pactum *n*, pactio *f*

covenant *vi* pacisci, stipulari

cover *s* tegmen, integumentum *n*; *(lid)* operculum *n*; *(shelter)* tectum *n*, *(mil)* praesidium *n*; *(pretense)* species *f*; **under — of** sub *(with abl)*, sub specie *(with genit)*

cover *vt* tegère, operire; *(to hide)* celare, velare; **to — up** obtegère

ooverlet *s* lodix *f*

covet *vt* concupiscère, cupère, appe- tère

covetous *adj* avidus, appetens, cu- pidus; **—ly** avide, avare, appeten- ter

covey *s* grex *m*

cow *vt* domare

coward *s* homo *or* miles ignavus *m*

cowardice *s* ignavia *f*

cowardly *adj* ignavus

cower *vi* sudsidēre

cowherd *s* bubulcus *m*

cowl *s* cucullus *m*

coy *adj* verecundus, pudens; **—ly** ve- recunde, pudenter

coyness *s* verecundia *f*, pudor *m*

cozily *adv* commode, jucunde

cozy *adj* commodus, jucundus

crab *s* cancer *m*

crabbed *adj* morosus, difficilis

crack *s* fissura, rima *f*; *(noise)* cre- pit·us -ūs *m*; **at — of dawn** prima luce

cracked *adj* rimosus; *(fig)* cerritus, delirus

cracker *s* crustulum *n*

crackle *vi* crepitare

crackling *s* crepit·us -ūs *m*

cradle *s* cunae *f pl*, cunabula *n pl*

craft *s* *(cunning)* astutia *f*, artes *f pl*, dolus *m*; *(skill)* ars *f*; *(trade)* ars *f*; *(boat)* scapha, cymba *f*, navigium *n*

craftily *adv* callide, astute; dolose

crafty *adj* astutus, callidus, subdolus

craftsman *s* artifex, faber *m*

craftsmanship *s* artificium *n*, ma- n·us -ūs *f*

cram *vt* farcire; **to — together** constipare

cramp *s* spasmus *m*

cramp *vt* comprimère, coartare

crane *s* *(bird)* grus *m & f*; *(machine)* tolleno *f*; machina *f*

crank *s* *(machine)* uncus *m*; *(person)* morosus *m*

crash *s* fragor, strepit·us -ūs *m*, rui- na *f*

crash *vi* strepère, frangorem dare

crater *s* crater *m*

crave *vt* efflagitare, appetère, concu- piscère, desiderare

craven *adj* ignavus atque abjectus

craving *s* desiderium *n*, appetitio *f*

crawl *vi* repère, serpère

crayfish *s* commarus *m*

crayon *s* creta *f*

craze *s* libido *f*

craziness *s* imbecillitas, mens aliena- ta *f*, furor *m*

crazy *adj* imbecillus, demens, cerri- tus; **to drive —** mentem alienare *(with genit)*

creak *vi* stridère, crepitare

creaking *s* stridor, crepit·us -ūs *m*

creaking *adj* stridulus

cream *s* flos lactis *m*; *(fig)* flos *m*

crease *s* plica, ruga *f*

crease *vt* corrugare, rugare

create *vt* creare; *(fig)* fingère

creation *s* *(act)* creatio *f*; *(world)* summa rerum *f*, mundus *m*; *(fig)* opus *n*

creative *adj* creatrix, effectrix

creator *s* creator, opifex, auctor *m*

creature *s* animal *n*; homo *m*; *(lackey)* minister *m*

credence *s* fides *f*; **to give — to** credère *(with dat)*

credentials *s* litterae commendati- ciae *f pl*; testimonia *n pl*

credibility *s* fides, auctoritas *f*

credible *adj* credibilis; *(of persons)* locuples

credit *s* *(authority)* auctoritas *f*; *(faith)* fides *f*; *(reputation)* existima- tio, fama *f*; *(com)* fides *f*; *(recogni- tion)* laus *f*

credit *vt* credère *(with dat)*; *(com)* ac- ceptum referre *(with dat)*

creditable *adj* honorificus, honestus, laudabilis

creditor *s* creditor *m*

credulity *s* credulitas *f*

credulous *adj* credulus; **—ly** credens

creed *s* fides, religio *f*, dogma *n*

creek *s* aestuarium *n*; fluvius *m*

creep *vi* repère, serpère; *(of flesh)* horrère

crescent *s* luna crescens *f*

crescent-shaped *adj* lunatus

crest *s* crista *f*

crested *adj* cristatus

crestfallen *adj* dejectus, demissus

crevice *s* rima, rimula *f*

crew *s* grex *m*; *(of ship)* remiges, nautae *m pl*

crib *s* *(manger)* praesepe *n*; *(small bed)* lectulus *m*

cricket *s* gryllus *m*, cicada *f*

crier *s* praeco *m*

crime *s* scelus, delictum, maleficium, flagitium *n*

Crimea *s* Tauria *f*

criminal *adj* criminosus, scelestus, flagitiosus; **—ly** nefarie, improbe; *(law)* criminaliter

criminal *s* reus, sceleratus *m*

crimp *vt* crispare

crimson *adj* coccineus
crimson *s* coccum *n*
cringe *vi* adulari, assentari
cringing *s* adulatio abjecta *f*
cripple *s* claudus *m*
cripple *vt* claudum facĕre, mutilare, debilitare; (*fig*) frangĕre
crippled *adj* mancus, claudus
crisis *s* discrimen *n*
crisp *adj* crispus, fragilis; (*fig*) alacer
criterion *s* norma *f*, indicium *n*, index *m*
critic *s* judex, censor, existimator *m*; (*literary*) criticus, grammaticus *m*
critical *adj* criticus, intellegens; (*careful*) accuratus; (*blaming*) fastidiosus, censorius; (*crucial*) anceps, periculosus; **—ly** accurate; periculose
criticism *s* ars critica *f*; censura, reprehensio *f*, judicium *n*
criticize *vt* judicare; carpĕre, reprehendĕre, agitare, castigare
croak *vi* coaxare; (*of raven*) crocitare, crocire; (*fig*) queritari
croaking *s* crocitatio *f*; (*fig*) querimonia *f*
croaking *adj* raucus
crock *s* olla *f*
crocodile *s* crocodilus *m*
crook *s* pedum *n*
crook *vt* curvare, flectĕre
crooked *adj* curvatus, flexus; (*fig*) pravus, dolosus; **—ly** prave
crop *s* (*of grain*) messis, seges *f*; (*of bird*) ingluvies *f*
crop *vt* abscidĕre, tondĕre; (*to harvest*) metĕre; (*to browse*) carpĕre
cross *s* crux *f*; (*figure*) quincunx *m*, decussis *f*; (*fig*) molestia *f*, cruciatus *m*
cross *adj* transversus; (*contrary*) adversus; (*peevish*) acerbus, morosus
cross *vt* transire, transgredi; (*river*) trajicĕre; (*mountain*) transcendĕre; (*to thwart*) frustrari, adversari; **to — out** expungĕre, delĕre
cross-examination *s* percontatio, interrogatio *f*
cross-examine *vt* percontari, interrogare
crossing *s* transitus -ūs, trajectus -ūs *m*; (*of roads*) bivium *n*; (*of three roads*) trivium *n*; (*of four roads*) quadrivium *n*
cross-roads *s* quadrivium *n*
crouch *vi* se submittĕre, subsidĕre
crow *s* (*bird*) cornix *f*; (*of cock*) cantus -ūs *m*, gallicinium *n*
crow *vi* (*of cocks*) canĕre, cucurire; (*to boast*) jactare, gestire
crowbar *s* vectis *f*
crowd *s* turba, frequentia *f*, concursus -ūs *m*; **in —s** gregatim
crowd *vt* arctare, stipare, premĕre; *vi* frequentare; **to — around** stipare, circumfundi
crowded *adj* confertus, frequens, spissus
crowing *s* gallicinium *n*, cantus -ūs *m*
crown *s* corona *f*, diadema *n*; (*top*)

vertex *m*; (*fig*) apex *m*
crown *vt* coronare; (*with garlands, etc.*) cingĕre; (*fig*) cumulare
crucifix *s* imago Christi cruci affixi *f*
crucifixion *s* crucis supplicium *n*
crucify *vt* in cruce suffigĕre
crude *adj* crudus; rudis, incultus, informis; **—ly** imperfecte; inculte
cruel *adj* crudelis, atrox, saevus; **—ly** crudeliter, saeve, dure
cruelty *s* crudelitas, atrocitas, saevitia *f*
cruet *s* guttus *m*, acetabulum *n*
cruise *vi* circumvectari, navigare
cruise *s* navigatio *f*
crumb *s* mica *f*
crumble *vt* friare, putrefacĕre, comminuĕre, conterĕre; *vi* collabi, friari, corruĕre
crumbling *adj* puter, friabilis
crumple *vt* corrugare, duplicare
crunch *vt* dentibus frangĕre
crush *vt* contundĕre, conterĕre; (*fig*) opprimĕre, affligĕre
crush *s* contusio *f*; (*crowd*) turba, frequentia *f*
crust *s* crusta *f*, crustum *n*
crusty *adj* crustosus; (*fig*) cerebrosus, stomachosus
crutch *s* fulcrum *n*
cry *vt* clamare, clamitare; **to — out** exclamare, vociferari; *vi* (*to shout*) clamare, clamitare; (*to weep*) lacrimare, flēre; (*of infant*) vagire; **to — out** exclamare; **to — out against** objurgare
cry *s* clamor *m*; (*of infant*) vagitus -ūs *m*; (*weeping*) ploratus -ūs *m*
crying *s* fletus -ūs, ploratus -ūs *m*
crypt *s* crypta *f*
crystal *adj* crystallinus, vitreus
crystal *s* crystallum *n*
crystal-clear *adj* pellucidus
cub *s* catulus *m*
cube *s* cubus *m*
cubic *adj* cubicus
cubit *s* cubitum *n*, ulna *f*
cuckoo *s* coccyx, cuculus *m*
cucumber *s* cucumis *m*
cud *s* ruma *f*, rumen *n*; **to chew the — ** ruminare
cudgel *s* fustis *m*
cue *s* (*hint*) nutus -ūs *m*, signum, indicium *n*
cuff *s* (*blow*) colaphus *m*; (*of sleeves*) extrema manica *f*
cull *vt* carpĕre, legĕre, decerpĕre
culminate *vi* ad summum fastigium venire
culpable *adj* culpandus, nocens
culprit *s* reus *m*, rea *f*
cultivate *vt* colĕre; (*the mind*) excolĕre; (*friends*) fovēre
cultivation *s* cultura *f*, cultus -ūs *m*
cultivator *s* cultor, colonus *m*
culture *s* cultura *f*, cultus -ūs *m*
cumbersome *adj* onerosus, impediens
cunning *adj* sollers, callidus, doctus, peritus; (*in bad sense*) astutus
cunning *s* calliditas, peritia; astutia *f*
cup *s* poculum *n*, calix *m*; (*of flower*) calyx *m*

cupbearer *s* pocillator *m*
cupboard *s* armarium *n*
Cupid *s* Cupido, Amor *m*
cupidity *s* cupiditas *f*
cupola *s* tholus *m*; turricula rotunda *f*
cur *s* canis *m*; (*fig*) scelestus *m*
curable *adj* medicabilis, sanabilis
curative *adj* medicabilis
curator *s* curator *m*
curb *s* frenum *n*; (*fig*) coercitio *f*, frenum *n*
curb *vt* frenare, infrenare; (*fig*) coercēre, cohibēre
curdle *vt* coagulare; *vi* coagulare, concrescēre
cure *s* (*remedy*) remedium *n*; (*process*) sanatio *f*
cure *vt* medēri (*with dat*), sanare; (*to pickle*) salire
curiosity *s* curiositas *f*; (*thing*) miraculum *n*
curious *adj* curiosus; (*strange*) mirus, novus, insolitus; —ly curiose; mirabiliter, mirum in modum
curl *vt* (*hair*) crispare; torquēre; *vi* crispari; (*of smoke*) volvi
curl *s* (*natural*) cirrus *m*; (*artificial*) cincinnus *m*
curly *adj* crispus
currency *s* (*money*) moneta *f*; (*use*) us·us -ūs *m*
current *adj* vulgaris, usitatus; —ly vulgo
current *s* flumen *n*; (*of air*) afflat·us -ūs *m*, aura *f*; **against the** — adverso flumine; **with the** — secundo flumine
curse *s* exsecratio, maledictio *f*, maledictum *n*; (*fig*) pestis *f*
curse *vt* maledicĕre (*with dat*), exsecrari; *vi* exsecratione uti
cursed *adj* exsecrabilis
corsorily *adv* breviter, summatim
cursory *adj* levis, brevis
ourt *adj* abruptus; —ly breviter
curtail *vt* minuĕre, coartare; decurtare
curtain *s* velum, aulaeum *n*
curvature *s* curvatura *f*
curve *s* curvamen *n*, flex·us -ūs *m*, curvatura *f*

curve *vt* incurvare, flectĕre, inflectĕre, arcuare
curved *adj* curvatus, curvus; (*as a sickle*) falcatus
cushion *s* pulvinar *n*; (*on a seat*) sedularia *n pl*
custard *s* artolaganus *m*
custody *s* custodia, tutela *f*; (*imprisonment*) carcer *m*; **to keep in** — custodire
custom *s* mos, us·us -ūs *m*, consuetudo *f*, institutum, praescriptum *n*; (*duty*) portorium, vectigal *n*
customary *adj* usitatus, consuetus, tralaticius
customer *s* emptor *m*
customs officer *s* portitor *m*
cut *vt* secare; (*to fell*) caedĕre; (*to mow*) succidĕre; **to** — **apart** intercidĕre, dissecare; **to** — **away** recidĕre, abscindĕre; (*to amputate*) amputare; **to** — **down** caedĕre; (*to kill*) occidĕre; **to** — **in pieces** concidĕre; **to** — **off** praecidĕre, abscindĕre; (*the head*) detruncare; (*to intercept*) intercludĕre, prohibēre; (*to destroy*) exstinguĕre; **to** — **open** incidĕre; **to** — **out** exsecare; (*out of rock, etc.*) excidĕre; **to** — **short** intercidĕre; (*to abridge*) praecidĕre; (*fig*) (*to interrupt*) interpellare; **to** — **up** minutatim concidĕre; (*enemy*) trucidare
cutlass *s* ensis, gladius *m*
cutlery *s* cultri *m pl*
cutlet *s* offa *f*, frustum *n*
cutthroat *s* sicarius *m*
cutting *adj* (*sharp*) acutus; (*fig*) mordax
cutting *s* (*act*) sectio, consectio, exsectio *f*; (*thing*) segmen *n*
cuttlefish *s* loligo, sepia *f*
cycle *s* orbis *m*
cylinder *s* cylindrus *m*
cylindrical *adj* cylindratus
cymbal *s* cymbalum *n*
cynic *adj* cynicus
cynic *s* cynicus *m*
cynical *adj* mordax, difficilis; —ly mordaciter
cynicism *s* acerbitas *f*
cypress *s* cupressus *f*

D

dab *vt* illidĕre
dab *s* massula *f*
dabble *vi* to — **in** gustare
dactyl *s* dactylus *m*
dactylic *adj* dactylicus
daffodil *s* asphodelus, narcissus *m*
dagger *s* pugio *m*, sica *f*
daily *adj* diurnus, quotidianus *or* cottidianus
daily *adv* quotidie *or* cottidie, in dies
dainty *adj* (*of persons*) fastidiosus, mollis, elegans; (*of things*) delicatus, exquisitus

dairy *s* cella lactaria *f*
daisy *s* bellis *f*
dale *s* vallis *f*
dalliance *s* lus·us -ūs *m*, lascivia *f*
dally *vi* morari; (*to trifle*) nugari, ludificari
dam *s* moles *f*, agger *m*; (*of animals*) mater *f*
damage *s* damnum, incommodum, detrimentum *n*; (*injury*) injuria, noxa *f*
damage *vt* nocēre (*with dat*), laedĕre; (*reputation*) violare

dame *s* domina, hera, matrona *f*

damn *vt* damnare, exsecrari

damnable *adj* damnabilis, destestabilis

damnably *adv* damnabiliter, improbe

damnation *s* damnatio *f*

damp *adj* (h)umidus

dampen *vt* humectare; *(fig)* infringĕre, restinguĕre

dampness *s* uligo *f*

damsel *s* puella, virgo *f*

dance *s* saltat·us -ūs *m*, saltatio *f*

dance *vi* saltare

dancer *s* saltator *m*

dancing *s* saltatio *f*, saltat·us -ūs *m*

dandelion *s* taraxacum *n*

dandruff *s* porrigo *f*

dandy *s* homo bellus et lepidus *m*

danger *s* periculum *n*

dangerous *adj* periculosus; **—ly** periculose, graviter

dangle *vi* pendēre, dependēre

dangling *adj* pendulus

dank *adj* (h)umidus, uvidus, udus

dappled *adj* variatus, variegatus

dare *vt* provocare; *vi* audēre

daring *adj* audax; **—ly** audacter

daring *s* audacia, audentia *f*

dark *adj* obscurus, opacus; *(in color)* ater, fuscus; *(fig)* obscurus, ambiguus; atrox; **—ly** obscure

dark *s* tenebrae *f pl*; obscurum *n*; **to keep in the —** celare

darken *vt* obscurare, occaecare; *(of colors)* infuscare

darkness *s* obscuritas, opacitas *f*, tenebrae *f pl*

darling *adj* suavis, mellitus, carus, dilectus

darling *s* deliciae *f pl*, corculum *n*

darn *vt* resarcire

dart *s* jaculum, spiculum *n*

dart *vt* jaculari, jacēre; *vi* provolare, emicare, se conjicĕre

dash *vt* *(to splash)* aspergĕre; *(hopes)* frustrari, frangĕre; **to — against** illidĕre, incutĕre, offendĕre; **to — off** *(to write hurriedly)* scriptitare; **to — to pieces** discutĕre; **to — to the ground** prosternĕre; *vi (to rush)* ruĕre, ferri

dash *s* impet·us -ūs *m*; curs·us -ūs *m*; *(animation)* alacritas *f*; *(small amount)* admixtio *f*

dashing *adj* acer, alacer, fulgidus, splendidus

data *s* facta *n pl*

date *s* *(time)* dies *m & f*, tempus *n*; *(fruit)* palmula *f*; **to become out of —** exolescĕre; **to — adhuc;** **out of —** obsoletus

date *vt* diem ascribĕre *(with dat)*; *vi* **to — from** oriri ab *(with abl)*, originem trahĕre ab *(with abl)*

date palm *s* phoenix, palma *f*

dative *s* dativus *m*

daub *vt* oblinĕre, illinĕre

daughter *s* filia *f*

daughter-in-law *s* nurus *f*

daunt *vt* pavefacĕre, perterrēre

dauntless *adj* impavidus, intrepidus; **—ly** impavide, intrepide

dawdle *vi* morari, cessare, cunctari

dawn *s* aurora, prima lux *f*, diluculum *n*; **at —** prima luce

dawn *vi* illucescĕre, dilucescĕre; *(fig)* **to — on** occurrĕre *(with dat)*

day *s* dies *m & f*; lux *f*, sol *m*; **by —** interdiu; **— by —** in dies; **every — quotidie, cottidie; from — to — in dies; next —** postridie; **some — olim; the — after to-morrow** perendie; **the — before** pridie

day *adj* diurnus, dialis

daybreak *s* lux prima *f*; **before —** antelucio

daylight *s* lux *f*, dies *m & f*

daystar *s* Lucifer, Phosphorus *m*

daytime *s* dies *m*, tempus diurnum *n*; **in the —** interdiu

daze *s* stupor *m*

daze *vt* obstupefacĕre

dazzle *vt* obcaecare, praestringĕre

dazzling *adj* fulgidus, splendidus

deacon *s* diaconus *m*

dead *adj* mortuus; defunctus; *(fig)* torpidus, segnis, iners

dead *s* manes *m pl*; **— of night** media nox *f*; **— of winter** summa hiems *f*

dead *adv* omnino, totaliter, prorsus

deaden *vt* hebetare, obtundĕre; *vi* hebetari, obtundi

deadly *adj* mortifer, letalis; *(fig)* capitalis, implacabilis

deaf *adj* surdus; **to be — to** non audire

deafen *vt* exsurdare, obtundĕre

deaf-mute *adj* surdus idemque mutus

deafness *s* surditas *f*

deal *s* *(quantity)* numerus *m*, copia *f*; *(com)* negotium *n*; **a good — longer** multo diutius; **a good — of** aliquantus

deal *vt* partiri, dividĕre, distribuĕre; *vi (com)* mercari, negotiari; **to — with** *(to treat of)* agĕre de *(with abl)*, tractare

dealer *s* mercator, negotiator, distributor *m*

dealing *s* negotiatio, mercatura *f*; *(doing)* facta *n pl*

dean *s* decanus *m*

dear *adj* carus, dulcis, gratus; *(costly)* carus, preciosus; **—ly** valde, ardenter; *(at high cost)* magni, magno

dear *interj* *(dismay)* hei!; *(surprise)* ahem!

dearness *s* caritas *f*

dearth *s* inopia, penuria, fames *f*

death *s* mors *f*, obit·us -ūs, interit·us -ūs *m*; *(in violent form)* nex *f*

deathbed *s* **on the —** moriens, moribundus

deathless *adj* immortalis

deathlike *adj* cadaverosus, luridus

deathly *adj* pallidus

debase *vt* depravare, corrumpĕre; *(coinage)* adulterare; **to — oneself** se demittĕre, se prosternĕre

debasement *s* adulteratio *f*; ignominia *f*, dedecus *n*

debatable *adj* disputabilis, controversiosus, ambiguus

debate *vt* disputare, disceptare; *vi* argumentari, disserĕre

debate *s* disceptatio, controversia, altercatio *f*; (*law*) actio *f*

debater *s* disputator *m*

debauch *vt* stuprare, corrumpĕre, vitiare; *vi* (*to revel*) debacchari

debauchery *s* ganea *f*, stuprum *n*

debilitate *vt* debilitare

debit *s* expensum *n*

debit *vt* in expensum referre

debt *s* aes alienum *n*; (*fig*) debitum *n*; **to pay off a** — aes alienum persolvĕre; **to run up a** — aes alienum contrahĕre

debtor *s* debitor *m*

decade *s* decem anni *m pl*

decadence *s* occas·us -ūs *m*

decadent *adj* degener

decalogue *s* decalogus *m*

decamp *vi* (*mil*) castra movēre; (*fig*) aufugĕre, discedĕre

decant *vt* diffundĕre

decanter *s* lagoena *f*

decapitate *vt* detruncare

decay *s* tabes, ruina *f*, laps·us -ūs *m*; (*fig*) defectio *f*

decay *vi* putrescĕre, tabescĕre, senescĕre

decease *s* mors *f*, obit·us -ūs *m*, dcess·us -ūs *m*

deceased *adj* mortuus, defunctus

deceit *s* fraus *f*, dolus *m*

deceitful *adj* fallax, dolosus, fraudulentus; —**ly** fallaciter, dolose

deceive *vt* decipĕre, fallĕre, fraudare

December *s* (mensis) December *m*

decency *s* decorum *n*, honestas *f*

decent *adj* honestus, pudicus; —**ly** honeste, pudenter

deception *s* deceptio, fallacia, fraus *f*

deceptive *adj* fallax, fraudulentus, vanus, falsus

decide *vt & vi* (*dispute*) disceptare, dijudicare, decernĕre; **to** — **to constituĕre** (*with inf*), statuĕre (*with inf*); **the senate decided** placuit senatui; visum est senatui

decided *adj* firmus, constans; (*of things*) certus; —**ly** certe, plane

deciduous *adj* caducus

decimate *vt* decimare; (*fig*) depopulari

decipher *vt* explicare, expedire, enodare

decision *s* sententia *f*; judicium, arbitrium, decretum *n*; (*of senate*) auctoritas *f*

decisive *adj* certus, firmus; —**ly** praecise

deck *vt* exornare, ornare; (*table*) sternĕre

deck *s* pons *m*

declamatory *adj* declamatorius; (*fig*) inflatus

declaration *s* declaratio, professio, affirmatio *f*; (*of war*) denuntiatio *f*

declare *vt* declarare, affirmare, aperire, profitēri; (*war*) denuntiare, indicĕre; (*proclamation*) edicĕre; *vi* **to** — **for** favēre (*with dat*)

declension *s* declinatio *f*

declinable *adj* declinabilis, casualis

declination *s* declinatio *f*; (*decay*) defectio *f*

decline *s* (*slope*) declive *n*; (*of strength*) defectio, diminutio *f*

decline *vt* (*to refuse*) recusare, renuĕre, abnuĕre; (*gram*) declinare, flectĕre; (*battle*) detrectare; *vi* vergĕre, inclinare; (*to decay, fail*) deficĕre, minui, decrescĕre; (*of prices*) laxare

decode *vt* enodare

decompose *vt* dissolvĕre, resolvĕre; *vi* tabescĕre, putescĕre, dissolvi

decomposition *s* dissolutio *f*

decorate *vt* ornare, decorare

decoration *s* ornatio *f*; (*ornament*) ornamentum *n*; (*distinction*) decus *n*

decorator *s* exornator *m*

decorous *adj* decorus, modestus, pudens; —**ly** decore, modeste, pudenter

decorum *s* decorum, honestum *n*, pudor *m*

decoy *s* illecebra *f*, illicium *n*

decoy *vt* allicĕre, inescare; (*fig*) illicĕre

decrease *s* deminutio, imminutio *f*

decrease *vt* (de)minuĕre, imminuĕre, extenuare; *vi* decrescĕre, (de)minui

decree *s* decretum, edictum *n*; (*of senate*) consultum *n*, auctoritas *f*; (*of assembly*) scitum *n*

decree *vt* decernĕre, edicĕre; (*of assembly*) jubēre, sciscĕre; **the senate** — **s senatui placet, senatui videtur**

decrepit *adj* decrepitus, debilis

decry *vt* detrectare, obtrectare, vituperare

dedicate *vt* dedicare, consecrare, devovēre

dedication *s* dedicatio, devotio *f*; (*of a book*) nuncupatio *f*

deduce *vt* deducĕre, concludĕre

deducible *adj* consectarius

deduct *vt* detrahĕre, subtrahĕre, demĕre

deduction *s* deductio, deminutio *f*; (*inference*) conclusio *f*, consequens *n*

deed *s* factum, facinus *n*; (*law*) syngrapha *f*, instrumentum *n*

deem *vt* judicare, existimare, ducĕre, habēre

deep *adj* altus, profundus; (*of sounds*) gravis; (*of color*) satur; (*fig*) abstrusus, gravis; —**ly** alte, profunde; (*inwardly*) penitus; (*fig*) valde, graviter, vehementer

deep *s* profundum, altum *n*

deepen *vt* defodĕre; (*fig*) augēre; *vi* altior fieri; (*fig*) crescĕre, densare

deer *s* cervus *m*, cerva *f*; (*fallow deer*) dama *f*

deface *vt* deformare, turpare, foedare

defaced *adj* deformis

defacement *s* deformitas *f*

defamation *s* calumnia *f*, opprobrium *n*

defamatory *adj* probrosus, contumeliosus

defame *vt* diffamare, infamare, calumniari

default s culpa f, delictum n, defect·us -ūs m

defeat s clades f; (at polls) repulsa f

defeat vt vincĕre, superare; (to baffle) frustrari

defect s vitium, mendum n; (lack) defect·us -ūs m

defect vi (to desert) deficĕre

defection s defectio f

defective adj vitiosus, imperfectus, mancus; (gram) defectivus

defend vt defendĕre, custodire, tuēri; (in court) patrocinari

defendant s reus m, rea f

defender s defensor, propugnator m; (law) patronus m

defense s (act) defensio f; praesidium, munimentum n, tutela f; (law) patrocinium n; (speech) defensio f

defenseless adj inermis, infensus; defensoribus nudatus

defensible adj excusabilis, justus; inexpugnabilis

defensive adj defendens; — weapons arma n pl

defer vt differre; vi obsequi

deference s observantia, reverentia f, obsequium n; out of — reverenter

defiance s provocatio, ferocia f

defiant adj minax, insolens; —ly insolenter

deficiency s defectio, inopia, penuria f, defect·us -ūs m

deficient adj inops, mancus; to be — deficĕre, deesse

deficit s lacuna f

defile s fauces f pl

defile vt contaminare, inquinare; (fig) foedare

define vt (meaning) explicare; (limits) (de)finire, circumscribĕre, terminare

definite adj definitus, certus; —ly certe, certo, prorsus; definite

definition s definitio f

definitive adj definitivus; —ly definite, distincte

deflect vt deflectĕre, declinare; vi deflectĕre, errare

deflection s deflexio, declinatio f, flex·us -ūs m

deflower vt stuprare

deform vt deformare

deformed adj deformatus, deformis, distortus, pravus

deformity s deformitas, pravitas f

defraud vt fraudare, defraudare

defray vt praebēre, suppeditare

defunct adj defunctus, mortuus

defy vt provocare, contemnĕre, spernēre

degeneracy s mores corrupti m pl

degenerate adj degener

degenerate vi degenerare

degradation s dedecus n, ignominia, infamia f

degrade vt dejicĕre, abdicare; ex loco movēre

degrading adj indignus

degree s grad·us -ūs, ordo m

deification s apotheosis f

deify vt divum habēre, inter deos re-

ferre, consecrare

deign vt dignari, curare

deism s deismus m

deity s numen n; deus m, dea f

dejected adj afflictus, demissus; —ly maeste

dejection s animi abjectio, maestitia f

delay s mora, cunctatio f

delay vt detinēre, tardare, remorari; vi morari, cunctari

delectable adj amoenus, jucundus

delegate s legatus m

delegate vt delegare, mandare, committĕre

delegation s delegatio, legatio f

delete vt delēre

deletion s litura f

deliberate adj deliberatus, consideratus, cautus, prudens; (speech) lentus; —ly deliberate, de industria; lente

deliberate vi deliberare, considerare, consulĕre

deliberation s deliberatio, consultatio f

delicacy s subtilitas, tenuitas f; elegantia f; (manner) lux·us -ūs m; (health) suavitas f; (food) cuppedia f

delicate adj (tender) delicatus, tener, mollis, exquisitus; (of texture) subtilis; (in taste) elegans, fastidiosus; (in health) infirmus; —ly delicate; eleganter; subtiliter

delicious adj suavis, dulcis

delight s delectatio f, gaudium n, voluptas f

delight vt delectare, oblectare; vi to — in delectari (with abl)

delightful adj suavis, jucundus; —ly suaviter, jucunde

delineate vt delineare, describĕre, adumbrare

delineation s designatio, descriptio f

delinquency s delictum n

delinquent s nocens m & f, noxius m

delirious adj delirus, phreneticus

delirium s delirium n, phrenesis f

deliver vt (to hand over) tradĕre, dare; (to free) liberare, eripĕre; (to surrender) prodĕre; (speech) habēre; (sentence) dicĕre; (message) referre; (blow) intendĕre; (child) obstetricari

deliverance s liberatio f

deliverer s liberator m; nuntius m

delivery s liberatio f; (of goods) traditio f; (of speech) actio, pronuntiatio f; (of child) part·us -ūs m

delude vt decipĕre, deludĕre

deluge s diluvium n, inundatio f

deluge vt inundare, obruĕre

delusion s delusio f, error m

demagogue s plebicola m

demand s postulatio, petitio f, postulatum n

demand vt postulare, flagitare, poscĕre; exigĕre

demarcation s confinium n

demean vt to — oneself se demittĕre

demeanor s gest·us -ūs m, mores m pl

demerit *s* culpa *f*, delictum *n*

demigod *s* heros *m*

demise *s* decess·us -ūs, obit·us -ūs *m*

democracy *s* civitas popularis *f*, liber populus *m*

democrat *s* homo popularis *m*

democratic *adj* popularis; **—ally** populi voluntate

demolish *vt* demoliri, disjicĕre, diruĕre, destruĕre

demolition *s* demolitio, destructio *f*

demon *s* dæmon *m*

demonstrable *adj* demonstrabilis

demonstrably *adv* clare, manifeste

demonstrate *vt* (*to show*) monstrare, ostendĕre; (*to prove*) demonstrare

demonstration *s* demonstratio *f*

demonstrative *adj* demonstrativus; **—ly** demonstrative

demoralization *s* depravatio *f*

demoralize *vt* depravare, labefactare

demote *vt* loco movēre

demure *adj* taciturnus, modestus; **—ly** modeste, pudice

den *s* latibulum *n*

deniable *adj* infitiandus

denial *s* negatio, repudiatio *f*

denomination *s* nominatio *f*, nomen *n*; secta *f*

denote *vt* significare

denounce *vt* denuntiare, deferre

dense *adj* densus, spissus, confertus; **—ly** dense, crebro

density *s* densitas, crassitudo *f*; (*crowd*) frequentia *f*

dent *s* nota *f*

dentist *s* dentium medicus *m*

denude *vt* nudare, denudare

denunciation *s* denuntiatio, accusatio *f*

deny *vt* negare,ʼ abnegare; (*to renounce*) renuntiare

depart *vi* abire, discedĕre, proficisci; (*to die*) obire

departed *adj* mortuus, defunctus

department *s* pars, provincia *f*

departure *s* abit·us -ūs, discess·us -ūs, digress·us -ūs *m*; (*deviation*) digressio *f*; (*death*) obit·us -ūs *m*

depend *vi* to — on pendēre ex (*with abl*), niti (*with abl*); (*to rely on*) fidēre (*with dat or abl*)

dependable *adj* fidus

dependence *s* clientela *f*; (*reliance*) fiducia *f*

dependency *s* provincia *f*

dependent *adj* subjectus, obediens, obnoxius

depict *vt* (de)pingĕre; describĕre, exprimĕre

deplete *vt* deminuĕre

depletion *s* deminutio *f*

deplorable *adj* miserabilis, flebilis, plorabilis

deplorably *adv* misere, pessime

deplore *vt* deplorare, deflere

deploy *vt* (*mil*) explicare, expedire

deponent *adj* (*gram*) deponens

deportment *s* gest·us -ūs, habit·us -ūs *m*

depose *vt* (de)movēre

deposit *vt* deponĕre

deposit *s* depositum *n*, fiducia *f*

deposition *s* depositio *f*, testimonium *n*

depositor *s* depositor *m*

depot *s* (*com*) emporium *n*; (*for military supplies*) armamentarium *n*

deprave *vt* depravare

depravity *s* depravatio, turpitudo, pravitas *f*

deprecate *vt* deprecari

deprecation *s* deprecatio *f*

depreciate *vt* detrectare, obtrectare

depreciation *s* detrectatio, obrectatio *f*; (*of price*) vilitas *f*

depredation *s* spoliatio, direptio *f*

depress *vt* deprimĕre; (*fig*) infringĕre, affligĕre

depressed *adj* depressus, afflictus; (*flat*) planus; (*hollow*) cavus

depression *s* depressio, imminutio *f*; (*fig*) tristitia *f*

depressive *adj* tristis, affligens

deprivation *s* privatio, orbatio *f*; (*state*) inopia *f*

deprive *vt* privare, spoliare

depth *s* altitudo, profunditas *f*, profundum *n*; (*bottom*) fundus *m*

deputation *s* legatio *f*, legati *m pl*

deputy *s* legatus, vicarius *m*

derange *vt* (per)turbare, conturbare

deranged *adj* mente captus

derangement *s* perturbatio, confusio *f*; (*of mind*) mentis alienatio *f*

dereliction *s* derelictio, destitutio *f*

deride *vt* deridēre, irridēre

derision *s* ris·us -ūs *m*, irrisio *f*

derisive *adj* irridens

derivation *s* derivatio, origo *f*

derivative *adj* derivativus, derivatus

derive *vt* derivare, deducĕre; *vi* procedĕre, oriri

derogatory *adj* inhonestus, indignus

descend *vi* descendĕre, delabi; to — upon (*to attack*) irrumpĕre in (*with acc*)

descendant *s* progenies *f*; **—s** posteri *m pl*

descent *s* descens·us -ūs *m*; (*slope*) declivitas *f*, clivus *m*; (*lineage*) genus *n*

describe *vt* describĕre, perscribĕre; depingĕre; narrare

description *s* descriptio *f*; narratio *f*

desecrate *vt* profanare, polluĕre

desecration *s* profanatio, violatio *f*

desert *s* (*wilderness*) loca deserta *n pl*, solitudo *f*

desert *s* (*merit*) meritum *n*, dignitas *f*

desert *vt* deserĕre, relinquĕre; *vi* transfugĕre, deficĕre

deserter *s* desertor *m*; (*mil*) transfuga *m*

desertion *s* desertio, defectio *f*; transfugium *n*

deserve *vt* merēre, merēri

deserving *adj* meritus, dignus

design *s* (*drawing*) adumbratio *f*; (*plan*) consilium, propositum *n*

design *vt* designare; (*to sketch*) adumbrare; (*fig*) machinari

designate *vt* designare, nominare, appellare

designation *s* designatio *f*; vocabulum, nomen *n*, titulus *m*

designer *s* inventor, auctor, fabricator, machinator *m*

designing *adj* callidus

desirable *adj* optabilis, desiderabilis

desire *s* appetitio, cupiditas, cupido *f*; (*request*) rogat·us -ūs *m*

desire *vt* cupĕre, optare, expetĕre; (*to request*) orare, petĕre

desirous *adj* cupidus, appetens

desist *vi* desistĕre; (*to cease*) desinĕre

desk *s* scrinium, pulpitum *n*, mensa scriptoria *f*

desolate *adj* desolatus, solitarius; (*of persons*) afflictus

desolate *vt* devastare

desolation *s* vastatio *f*; (*state*) solitudo, vastitas *f*

despair *s* desperatio *f*

despair *vi* desperare

desperado *s* sicarius *m*

desperate *adj* desperatus; (*dangerous*) periculosus; —**ly** desperanter; **to be** —**ly in love** perdite amare

desperation *s* desperatio *f*

despicable *adj* abjectus, vilis, turpis

despise *vt* despicĕre, spernĕre, contemnĕre

despite *prep* contra (*with acc*)

despite *s* malevolentia *f*, odium *n*

despoil *vt* nudare, spoliare

despondency *s* animi abjectio *f*

despondent *adj* abjectus, demissus; —**ly** animo demisso

despot *s* dominus, tyrannus *m*

despotic *adj* tyrannicus; —**ally** tyrannice

despotism *s* dominatio *f*

dessert *s* secunda mensa *f*, bellaria *n pl*

destination *s* destinatio *f*, propositum *n*

destine *vt* destinare, designare

destiny *s* fatum *n*, sors *f*

destitute *adj* egens, inops, destitutus; — **of** expers (*with genit*)

destitution *s* inopia, mendicitas *f*

destroy *vt* destruĕre, subvertĕre, abolēre, delēre, vastare; **to be destroyed** interire

destroyer *s* deletor, vastator *m*

destruction *s* eversio, clades *f*, exitium *n*

destructive *adj* exitialis, perniciosus; —**ly** perniciose

desultory *adj* inconstans

detach *vt* sejungĕre, separare, amovēre

detached *adj* sejunctus; (*of houses*) solus

detachment *s* separatio *f*; (*mil*) man·us -ūs *f*; (*aloofness*) secess·us -ūs *m*

detail *s* singula *n pl*, singulae res *f pl*

detail *vt* enumerare

detain *vt* detinēre, retinēre, retardare

detect *vt* detegĕre, comperire, patefacĕre

detection *s* patefacio *f*, indicium *n*

detective *s* inquisitor *m*

detention *s* retentio *f*; (*law*) mora *f*

deter *vt* deterrēre, avertĕre

detergent *s* smegma *n*

deterioration *s* depravatio, corruptio *f*

determination *s* constantia, obstinatio *f*; (*intention*) propositum *n*

determine *vt* (*to decide*) statuĕre, constituĕre, discernĕre; (*to fix*) determinare, definire

determined *adj* certus; (*resolute*) firmus, obstinatus

detest *vt* abominari, detestari

detestable *adj* detestabilis, foedus

dethrone *vt* regno depellĕre

detonate *vi* crepare

detonation *s* fragor *m*

detour *s* circuit·us -ūs *m*

detour *vi* iter flectĕre, circumagi

detract *vt* detrahĕre; *vi* **to** — **from** detrectare, obtrectare

detraction *s* obtrectatio *f*

detractor *s* obtrectator *m*

detriment *s* detrimentum, damnum *n*

detrimental *adj* injuriosus, damnosus; **to be** — **to** detrimento esse (*with dat*)

devastate *vt* vastare, depopulari

devastation *s* (*act*) vastatio, populatio *f*; (*state*) vastitas *f*

develop *vt* evolvĕre, explicare; (*person*) alĕre; *vi* crescĕre; **to** — **into** evadĕre in (*with acc*)

development *s* explicatio *f*, progress·us -ūs *m*

deviate *vi* aberrare, degredi, decedĕre

deviation *s* aberratio, declinatio, digressio *f*

device *s* (*contrivance*) artificium *n*, machina *f*; (*plan*) consilium *n*; (*emblem*) insigne *n*

devil *s* diabolus, daemon *m*; **go to the** —! abi in malam crucem!

devilish *adj* diabolicus, daemonicus; (*fig*) nefandus

devious *adj* devius; vagus, erraticus

devise *vt* fingĕre, excogitare, concoquĕre

devoid *adj* inanis, vacuus, expers; **to be** — **of** carēre (*with abl*)

devolve *vi* **to** — **upon** obtingĕre, pervenire ad (*with acc*)

devote *vt* devovēre, consecrare; **to** — **oneself to** studēre (*with dat*), se dedĕre (*with dat*)

devoted *adj* deditus, studiosus; — **to** studiosus (*with genit*)

devotee *s* cultor *m*

devotion *s* devotio, addictio *f*, studium *n*

devour *vt* devorare; (*fig*) haurire

devout *adj* pius, religiosus; —**ly** pie, religiose

dew *s* ros *m*

dewdrop *s* gutta roscida *f*

dewy *adj* roscidus, roridus

dexterity *s* sollertia, calliditas *f*

dexterous *adj* sollers, callidus, habilis; —**ly** sollerter, callide, habiliter

diabolical *adj* nefarius, nefandus

diagnose *vt* dijudicare, discernĕre

diagnosis s judicium n
diagonal adj diagonalis; **—ly** in transversum
diagram s forma, descriptio f
dial s solarium n
dialect s dialectus f, sermo m
dialectic adj dialecticus
dialogue s sermo m, colloquium n; (written discussion) dialogus m
diameter s diametros f
diamond s adamas m
diaper s striatura f
diaphragm s praecordia n pl
diarrhea s alvi profluvium n
diary s diarium n, commentarii diurni m pl
diatribe s convicium n
dice s tali m pl; (game) alea f
dictate vt dictare, praescribĕre
dictate s praescriptum, praeceptum, jussum n
dictation s dictatio f; dictatum n
dictator s dictator m
dictatorial adj imperiosus, dictatorius
dictatorship s dictatura f
diction s dictio, elocutio f
dictionary s lexicon n, thesaurus linguae m
didactic adj didascalicus
die s alea f
die vi mori, obire, perire; **to — off** demori; **to — out** emori
diet s (food) vict·us -ūs m; (med) diaeta f
diet vi secundum diaetam vivĕre
dietary adj diaeteticus
differ vi differre, discrepare, distare; (in opinion) dissentire
difference s differentia, diversitas, dissimilitudo f; (of opinion) discrepantia, dissensio f
different adj diversus, dissimilis, dispar; alius; **—ly** diverse, aliter
difficult adj difficilis, arduus
difficulty s difficultas f, labor m, negotium n; **with —** aegre
diffidence s diffidentia, verecundia f
diffident adj diffidens, verecundus, modestus; **—ly** diffidenter
diffuse adj diffusus; (fig) verbosus; **—ly** effuse, latius
diffuse vt diffundĕre
diffusion s diffusio f
dig vt fodĕre
digest s summarium n
digest vt (to arrange) digerĕre; (food) concoquĕre
digestion s concoctio f
digestive adj pepticus
digging s fossio, fossura f
digit s numerus m
dignified adj gravis, augustus
dignify vt honestare, honorare
dignitary s vir amplissimus m
dignity s dignitas f, honor m
digress vi digredi, aberrare, abire
digression s digressio f, digress·us -ūs m
dike s agger m
dilapidated adj ruinosus, obsoletus
dilate vt dilatare; vi dilatari

dilatory adj cunctabundus, lentus, segnis
dilemma s dilemma n; nodus m, angustiae f pl
diligence s diligentia f
diligent adj diligens, sedulus; **—ly** diligenter, sedulo
dilute vt diluĕre, miscēre
dilution s temperatio, mixtura f
dim adj hebes, obscurus; **to become —** hebescĕre; **—ly** obscure, obtuse
dim vt hebetare, obscurare; vi hebescēre
dimension s dimensio, mensura f
diminish vt minuĕre, deminuĕre, extenuare; vi decrescĕre, minui
diminutive adj exiguus, parvulus; (gram) deminutivus
diminutive s (nomen) deminutivum n
dimness s hebetudo, obscuritas, caligo f
dimple s lacuna f, gelasinus m
din s strepit·us -ūs, sonit·us -ūs, fragor m; **to make a —** strepere
dine vi cenare
diner s conviva m
dingy adj fuscus, squalidus
dining room s cenatio f, triclinium n
dinner s cena f
dinner party s convivium n
dint s ict·us -ūs m; **by — of** per (with acc)
dip vt immergĕre, ting(u)ĕre; vi mergi, tingi; (to sink) premi, declinare
dip s devexitas, declinatio f
diploma s diploma n
diplomacy s (function) officium legationis m; (tact) dexteritas f
diplomat s legatus m
diplomatic adj sagax, callidus, astutus
dire adj dirus
direct adj rectus, directus; **—ly** directe, rectā; (immediately) statim
direct vt dirigĕre; (to administer) administrare; (to rule) gubernare; (to order) jubēre; imperare (with dat); (weapon) intendĕre; (letter) inscribĕre; (attention) admovēre
direction s (act) directio f; (quarter) pars, regio f; (management) administratio f; (instruction) mandatum n; (order) praeceptum n
director s rector, magister, gubernator, curator m
directory s (office of director) curatio f, magisterium n; (body of directors) magistri, curatores m pl
dirge s nenia f
dirt s sordes f; (mud) lutum n, limus m
dirtiness s spurcitia f; (fig) obscenitas f
dirty adj spurcus, sordidus; (fig) obscenus
dirty vt foedare, spurcare
disability s impotentia f
disable vt debilitare, enervare
disabled adj inhabilis, debilis, mancus

disabuse *vt* errorem eripĕre (*with dat*)

disadvantage *s* incommodum, detrimentum *n*

disadvantageous *adj* incommodus, iniquus

disagree *vi* discrepare, dissidēre, dissentire

disagreeable *adj* injucundus, molestus, insuavis, gravis; (*of smells*) graveolens; (*of persons*) difficilis, morosus

disagreeably *adv* moleste, graviter, ingrate

disagreement *s* dissensio, discordia *f*, dissidium *n*

disappear *vi* vanescĕre, fugĕre, diffugĕre, abire, perire

disappearance *s* fuga *f*, exit·us -ūs *m*

disappoint *vt* fallĕre, frustrari

disappointment *s* frustratio *f*; incommodum, malum *n*

disapproval *s* reprehensio, improbatio *f*

disapprove *vt* reprehendĕre, improbare

disarm *vt* exarmare

disarrange *vt* (per)turbare, confundĕre

disarray *s* perturbatio *f*

disaster *s* calamitas *f*, incommodum *n*

disastrous *adj* calamitosus, funestus, exitiosus; **—ly** calamitose

disavow *vt* diffitēri, infitiari

disavowal *s* infitiatio *f*

disband *vt* dimittĕre; *vi* dimitti

disbelief *s* diffidentia, incredulitas *f*

disbeliever *s* incredulus *m*

disburse *vt* erogare, expendĕre

disbursement *s* erogatio, solutio *f*

disc *s* orbis *m*

discard *vt* ponĕre, mittĕre; repudiare

discern *vt* discernĕre, distinguĕre

discernible *adj* dignoscendus

discerning *adj* perspicax, sagax, prudens

discernment *s* (*act*) perspicientia *f*; (*faculty*) discrimen, judicium *n*

discharge *vt* (*to unload*) exonerare; (*to dismiss*) dimittĕre; (*to perform*) perfungi (*with abl*); (*debt*) exsolvĕre; (*weapon*) immittĕre, jacĕre, jaculari; (*defendant*) absolvĕre

discharge *s* (*unloading*) exoneratio *f*; (*shooting*) emissio, conjectio *f*; (*dismissal*) missio *f*; (*payment*) solutio *f*; (*bodily*) defluxio *f*

disciple *s* discipulus *m*; (*fig*) sectator *m*

discipline *s* disciplina *f*

discipline *vt* assuefacĕre, coercēre

disclaim *vt* infitiari, diffitēri, negare

disclaimer *s* infitiatio *f*

disclose *vt* aperire, detegĕre, enuntiare

disclosure *s* patefactio *f*

discomfit *vt* fundĕre

discomfort *s* incommoda *n pl*, molestiae *f pl*

disconcerting *adj* molestus

disconnect *vt* sejungĕre, disjungĕre

disconsolate *adj* tristis, afflictus; **—ly** insolabiliter, triste

discontent *s* taedium *n*, molestia, offensio *f*

discontented *adj* parum contentus; **—ly** animo iniquo

discontinue *vt* intermittĕre; *vi* desinĕre, desistĕre

discord *s* discordia, dissensio *f*; (*mus*) dissonantia *f*

discordant *adj* discors, discrepans; (*mus*) dissonus

discount *vt* deducĕre; (*to disregard*) praetermittĕre

discount *s* (*com*) decessio *f*

discourage *vt* deterrēre, examinare; **to be discouraged** animum demittĕre

discouragement *s* animi abjectio *or* infractio *f*

discouraging *adj* adversus, incommodus

discourse *s* sermo *m*, colloquium *n*; (*written*) libellus *m*

discourse *vi* disserĕre, colloqui, verba facĕre

discourteous *adj* inurbanus; **—ly** inurbane

discourtesy *s* inurbanitas *f*

discover *vt* invenire, reperire; (*to find out*) explorare; (*to disclose*) patefacĕre

discoverable *adj* indagabilis, visibilis

discoverer *s* inventor, repertor *m*

discovery *s* inventio *f*; (*things discovered*) inventum *n*

discredit *s* dedecus *n*, ignominia *f*

discredit *vt* notare, infamare

discreet *adj* cautus, prudens; **—ly** consulto, prudenter

discrepancy *s* discrepantia *f*

discretion *s* pudentia, circumspectio *f*; (*tact*) judicium *n*

discretionary *adj* interminatus, liber

discriminate *vt* distinguĕre, dijudicare, discernĕre

discriminating *adj* sagax, discernens

discrimination *s* distinctio *f*; judicium, discrimen *n*

discuss *vt* agĕre, disputare, disserĕre

discussion *s* disputatio, disceptatio *f*

disdain *vt* fastidire, despicĕre, aspernari

disdain *s* fastidium *n*, despect·us -ūs *m*, contempt·us -ūs *m*

disdainful *adj* fastidiosus, superciliosus; **—ly** fastidiose, contemptim

disease *s* morbus *m*, malum *n*

diseased *adj* aegrotus

disembark *vt* e navi exponĕre; *vi* e navi conscendĕre

disenchant *vt* errorem demĕre (*with dat*)

disengage *vt* expedire, eximĕre, avocare

disentangle *vt* expedire, extricare, explicare

disfavor *s* invidia *f*

disfigure *vt* deformare, turpare, mutilare

disfranchise *vt* civitatem adimĕre (*with dat*)

disgorge *vt* revomĕre, evomĕre

disgrace *s* dedecus *n*, infamia *f*; (*thing*) flagitium *n*

disgrace *vt* dedecorare

disgraceful *adj* dedecorus, turpis, flagitiosus; —ly turpiter, flagitiose

disguise *s* (*mask*) persona *f*; simulatio *f*; (*pretense*) praetext·us -ūs *m*

disguise *vt* obtegĕre; (*fig*) celare, dissimulare

disgust *s* (*loathing*) fastidium, taedium *n*, nausea *f*

disgust *vt* fastidium movēre (*with dat*); **I am disgusted with me** taedet (*with genit*), me piget (*with genit*)

disgusting *adj* taeter, foedus; —ly foede

dish *s* (*flat*) patina *f*; (*large*) lanx *f*; (*course*) ferculum *n*, dapes *f pl*

dishearten *vt* exanimare, percellĕre; **to be disheartened** animum demittĕre

disheveled *adj* passus, effusus

dishonest *adj* improbus, perfidus; —ly improbe, dolo malo

dishonesty *s* improbitas *f*, dolus malus *m*, fraus, perfidia *f*

dishonor *s* dedecus *n*, infamia, ignominia *f*

dishonor *vt* dedecorare

dishonorable *adj* inhonestus, turpis

disillusion *vt* errorem adimĕre (*with dat*)

disinfect *vt* purgare

disinherit *vt* exheredare

disintegrate *vi* dilabi

disinter *vt* effodĕre

disinterested *adj* integer; (*of judge*) severus; —ly integre, gratuito

disjoin *vt* segregare, disjungĕre

disjointed *adj* incompositus; —ly incomposite

disk *s* orbis *m*

dislike *s* odium, fastidium *n*, aversatio *f*

dislike *vt* aversari, odisse; fastidire

dislocate *vt* extorquēre, luxare

dislocation *s* luxatura *f*

dislodge *vt* movēre, depellĕre

disloyal *adj* perfidus; —ly perfide

disloyalty *s* infidelitas, perfidia *f*

dismal *adj* maestus, funestus, miser; —ly maeste, misere

dismantle *vt* diruĕre, spoliare, nudare

dismay *s* pavor *m*, consternatio *f*

dismay *vt* terrēre, perterrefacĕre, territare

dismember *vt* membratim dividĕre, lacerare, discerpĕre

dismemberment *s* mutilatio *f*

dismiss *vt* dimittĕre; (*fear*) mittĕre; (*to discharge, to cashier*) exauctorare

dismissal *s* missio, dimissio *f*

dismount *vi* ex equo desilire

disobedience *s* inobedientia, contumacia *f*

disobedient *adj* contumax

disobey *vt* non obedire (*with dat*), non parēre (*with dat*)

disorder *s* confusio *f*; (*med*) aegrotatio *f*; (*of mind*) perturbatio *f*; (*pol*) tumult·us -ūs *m*

disordered *adj* turbatus; (*fig*) dissolutus

disorderly *adj* inordinatus, incompositus, (per)turbatus; (*insubordinate*) turbulentus

disorganization *s* dissolutio *f*

disorganize *vt* conturbare, confundĕre; **to be disorganized** dilabi

disown *vt* (*statement*) diffiteri, infitiari; (*heir*) abdicare; (*thing*) repudiare

disparage *vt* obtrectare, detrectare

disparagement *s* obtrectatio *f*

disparaging *adj* obtrectans

disparate *adj* dispar

disparity *s* inaequalitas, discrepantia *f*

dispassionate *adj* sedatus, tranquillus, frigidus; —ly sedate, frigide

dispatch *vt* mittĕre, dimittĕre, legare; (*to finish*) absolvĕre, perficĕre; (*to kill*) interficĕre

dispel *vt* dispellĕre; (*worries*) ponĕre

dispensary *s* medicamentaria taberna *f*

dispensation *s* distributio, partitio *f*; (*exemption*) immunitas, exemptio *f*

dispense *vt* distribuĕre, dispertiri; (*to release*) solvĕre; *vi* **to — with** indulgēre (*with dat*), omittĕre, praetermittĕre

dispenser *s* dispensator *m*

disperse *vt* spargĕre, dispergĕre, dissipare; *vi* dilabi, diffugēre

dispersion *s* dispersio, dissipatio *f*

dispirited *adj* abjectus, demissus, animo fractus

displace *vt* summovēre; exauctorare

displacement *s* amotio *f*

display *s* (*exhibit*) ostent·us -ūs *m*; (*ostentation*) ostentatio, jactatio *f*

display *vt* ostendĕre, ostentare, exhibēre

displease *vt* displicēre (*with dat*)

displeased *adj* offensus; **to be — at** aegre ferre

displeasing *adj* odiosus, ingratus

displeasure *s* offensa, offensio *f*

disposable *adj* in promptu

disposal *s* dispositio *f*; arbitrium *n*; **at the — of** penes (*with acc*)

dispose *vt* disponĕre, ordinare; (*to incline*) parare, praeparare; *vi* **to — of** abalienare, vendĕre; (*to get rid of*) tollĕre

disposed *adj* inclinatus; (*in bad sense*) pronus

disposition *s* (*arrangement*) dispositio *f*; (*character*) natura, mens *f*, ingenium *n*, animus *m*

dispossess *vt* ejicĕre, detrudĕre, pellĕre

disproportion *s* inaequalitas, inconcinnitas *f*

disproportionate *adj* inaequalis, impar, inconcinnus; **—ly** impariter, inaequaliter

disprove vt refutare, confutare, redarguĕre

disputable adj disputabilis, ambiguus

dispute s (debate) disputatio f; (quarreling) altercatio, controversia f; **beyond —** indisputabilis

dispute vt & vi disputare, contendĕre

disqualification s impedimentum n

disqualify vt inhabilem reddĕre, impedire

disquiet vt inquietare, vexare

disregard s incuria, negligentia f

disregard vt negligĕre, omittĕre

disreputable adj infamis

disrepute s infamia f

disrespect s negligentia, insolentia f

disrespectful adj irreverens, insolens; **—ly** insolenter, irreverenter

disrupt vt dirumpĕre

disruption s dirumptio f; (fig) discidium n

dissatisfaction s molestia, offensio f

dissatisfied adj parum contentus

dissatisfy vt parum satisfacĕre

dissect vt dissecare

dissection s incisio f

dissemble vt & vi dissimulare

disseminate vt dissiminare, divulgare

dissension s dissensio f, dissidium n

dissent vi dissentire, dissidēre

dissent s dissensio f

dissertation s disputatio, dissertatio f

dissimilar adj dissimilis, dispar

dissimilarity s dissimilitudo f

dissipate vt dissipare, diffundĕre; vi dissipari, diffundi

dissipation s dissipatio f

dissolute adj dissolutus, corruptus, perditus; **—ly** immoderate, prodige

dissolution s dissolutio f

dissolve vt dissolvĕre; (to melt) liquefacĕre; (meeting) dimittĕre; vi liquescĕre; (to break up) dissolvi

dissonance s dissonantia f

dissonant adj dissonus

dissuade vt dissuadēre (with dat), dehortari

dissuasion s dissuasio f

distaff s colus f

distance s distantia f, intervallum n; (fig) frigus n; (long way) longinquitas f; **at a —** procul, longe

distant adj distans, disjunctus, longinquus; (fig) parum familiaris; **to be —** abesse

distaste s fastidium n

distasteful adj (of taste) teter; (fig) molestus, odiosus

distemper s morbus m

distend vt distendĕre

distil vt & vi stillare, destillare

distillation s destillatio f

distinct adj (different) diversus, alius; (clear) distinctus; **—ly** clare, distincte, certe

distinction s distinctio, discrepantia f, discrimen n; (status) amplitudo f;

(honor) honos m; **there is no —** nil interest

distinctive adj proprius; **—ly** proprie

distinguish vt distinguĕre, discernĕre; **to — oneself** enitēre

distinguished adj insignis, clarus, notus, eximius

distort vt distorquēre; (fig) depravare

distortion s distortio f; (fig) depravatio f

distract vt distrahĕre, avocare; (to madden) furiare

distracted adj amens, insanus; **—ly** amens, mente alienatus

distraction s (cause) invitamentum n; (state) negligentia f; **to — effictim**

distress s afflictio, aegrimonia, aerumna f, dolor, labor m

distress vt afflictare, angēre

distressed adj anxius, afflictus, sollicitus

distressing adj tristis, gravis, acerbus

distribute vt distribuĕre

distributer s distributor m

distribution s distributio f

district s regio f

distrust s diffidentia f

distrust vt diffidēre (with dat)

distrustful adj diffidens; **—ly** diffidenter

disturb vt perturbare; sollicitare, inquietare

disturbance s perturbatio f; confusio f; (pol) mot·us ‑ūs, tumult·us ‑ūs m

disturber s turbator, concitator m

disuse s desuetudo f

ditch s fossa f

ditty s cantilena f, canticum n

divan s lectulus m

dive vi mergi

diver s urinator m

diverge vi deflectĕre, declinare, devertĕre; (of views) discrepare

diverse adj alius, varius, diversus

diversification s variatio f

diversify vt variare

diversion s (recreation) oblectamentum n; (of thought) avocatio f; (of river, etc.) derivatio f

diversity s diversitas, varietas f

divert vt avertĕre, divertĕre; (attention) avocare; (to amuse) oblectare

divest vt exuĕre, nudare, privare; **to — oneself of** exuĕre, ponĕre

divide vt dividĕre, partiri, distribuĕre; vi discedĕre, se scindĕre

divination s divinatio, vaticinatio f

divine adj divinus; **—ly** divine

divine s theologus m

divine vt divinare, augurari, vaticinari; (to guess) conjicĕre

diviner s augur, haruspex m

divinity s divinitas f; (god) numen n; divus m, diva f

divisible adj dividuus, divisibilis

division s divisio, partitio f; (part) pars f; (mil) legio f; **— of opinion** dissensio f

divorce *s* divortium *n*

divorce *vt* repudiare, dimittĕre

divulge *vt* vulgare, palam facĕre, aperire, patefacĕre

dizziness *s* vertigo *f*

dizzy *adj* vertiginosus

do *vt* agĕre, facĕre, efficĕre; *vi* agĕre; how **do** you —? quid agis?; **to** — **away with** tollĕre, perdĕre

docile *adj* docilis, tractabilis

dock *s* navale *n*; *(law)* cancelli *m pl*

dock *vt* subducĕre

docket *s* lemniscus *m*

dockyard *s* navalia *n pl*

doctor *s* medicus *m*; *(teacher)* doctor *m*

doctor *vt* medicari, curare

doctorate *s* doctoris grad·us -ūs *m*

doctrine *s* doctrina *f*, dogma *n*

document *s* documentum, instrumentum *n*

dodge *s* dolus *m*

dodge *vt* eludĕre; *vi* tergiversari

doe *s* cerva *f*

dog *s* canis *m & f*

dogged *adj* pervicax, pertinax; —**ly** pertinaciter

doggedness *s* pervicacia *f*

doggerel *s* versus inepti *m pl*

dog kennel *s* canis cubile *n*

dogma *s* dogma, placitum, praeceptum *n*

dogmatic *adj* dogmaticus; arrogans; —**ally** arroganter

dogmatism *s* arrogantia doctrinae *f*

dog star *s* canicula *f*, Sirius *m*

doing *s* factum, facinus *n*

dole *s* sportula *f*; donatio *f*

dole *vt* **to** — **out** parce dare

doleful *adj* lugubris, maestus, flebilis; —**ly** maeste, flebiliter

doll *s* pupa *f*

dollar *s* thalerus *m*

dolphin *s* delphinus, delphin *m*

dolt *s* caudex, stipes *m*

domain *s* *(estate)* possessio *f*; *(kingdom)* regnum *n*

dome *s* tholus *m*

domestic *adj* domesticus, familiaris; intestinus

domestic *s* famulus, servus, verna *m*, famula, serva *f*

domesticate *vt* domare, assuefacĕre

domicile *s* domicilium *n*, dom·us -ūs *f*

dominant *adj* praevalens

domination *s* dominium *n*

domineer *vi* dominari

domineering *adj* imperiosus

dominion *s* imperium, regnum *n*

don *vt* induĕre

donation *s* donum *n*, stips *f*

donkey *s* asinus, asellus *m*

donor *s* donator *m*, donatrix *f*

doom *s* fatum, exitium *n*

doom *vt* damnare, condemnare

door *s* janua *f*, ostium *n*, fores *f pl*

doorkeeper *s* janitor *m*, janitrix *f*

doorpost *s* postis *f*

doorway *s* ostium *n*

Doric *adj* Doricus

dormant *adj* sopitus; *(hidden)* latens; **to lie** — jacēre

dormitory *s* cubiculum, dormitorium *n*

dorsal *adj* dorsualis

dose *s* potio *f*

dot *s* punctum *n*

dot *vt* punctum imponĕre *(with dat)*

dotage *s* senium *n*

dotard *s* senex delirus *m*

dote *vi* **to** — **upon** deamare, deperire

doting *adj* deamans, desipiens; —**ly** perdite amans

double *adj* duplex; *(of pairs)* geminus; *(as much again)* duplus; *(meaning)* ambiguus

double *s* duplum *n*; **to march on the** — currĕre

double *vt* duplicare; *(cape)* praetervehi; *vi* duplicari; *(to run)* currĕre

doubly *adv* bis, dupliciter

doubt *s* dubitatio *f*, dubium *n*; *(distrust)* suspicio *f*

doubt *vt* dubitare; suspicari

doubtful *adj* *(of persons)* dubius; *(of things)* incertus, ambiguus, anceps; —**ly** dubie; *(hesitatingly)* dubitanter

doubtless *adv* scilicet, haud dubie, sine dubio

dough *s* farina *f*

doughty *adj* strenuus, fortis

douse *vt* *(to put out)* exstinguĕre; *(to drench)* madefacĕre

dove *s* columba *f*

dowdy *adj* inconcinnus

down *s* pluma *f*; *(of hair)* lanugo *f*; *(of plants)* pappus *m*

down *adv* deorsum; — **from** de *(with abl)*; — **to** usque ad *(with acc)*

down *prep* de *(with abl)*

down *adj* declivis; tristis; **ad inopiam redactus**

downcast *adj* *(of eyes or head)* dejectus, demissus; *(fig)* afflictus, maestus

downfall *s* occas·us -ūs *m*, ruina *f*

downhill *adj* declivis

downright *adj* directus, sincerus

downright *adv* prorsus, plane

downstream *adv* secundo flumine

downward *adj* declivis; pronus

downwards *adv* deorsum

downy *adj* plumeus; lanuginosus

dowry *s* dos *f*

doze *vi* dormitare

dozen *s* duodecim

drab *adj* cinereus

draft *s* *(act of drawing)* lineatio *f*; *(drink)* haust·us -ūs *m*; *(of ship)* immersio *f*; *(first copy)* exemplar *n*; *(of air)* aura *f*; *(mil)* dilect·us -ūs *m*; *(money)* syngrapha *f*; *(of net)* jact·us -ūs *m*

draft *vt* conscribĕre

draft horse *s* equus rhedarius *m*

drag *vt* trahĕre, rapĕre; *vi* trahi

drag *s* *(fig)* impedimentum *n*

dragnet *s* tragula *f*

dragon *s* draco, anguis *m*

drain *s* cloaca *f*

drain *vt* siccare; derivare; *(to drink)*

exhaurire, ebibĕre; (*strength*) exhaurire
drainage *s* derivatio, exsiccatio *f*;
colluvies cloacarum *f*
draining *s* exsiccatio *f*
drake *s* anas *m*
drama *s* drama *n*, fabula *f*
dramatic *adj* dramaticus, scaenicus
dramatist *s* poeta scaenicus, scriptor fabularum *m*
dramatize *vt* ad scaenam componĕre
drape *vt* induĕre, amicire, velare
drapery *s* aulaeum *n*
drastic *adj* vehemens
draw *vt* (*to pull*) trahĕre, ducĕre;
(*picture*) scribĕre, delineare;
(*sword*) destringĕre; (*bow*) adducĕre;
(*inference*) colligĕre; **to — aside**
abducĕre, seducĕre; **to — away**
avertĕre, distrahĕre; **to — back**
retrahĕre; **to — off** detrahĕre, abducĕre; (*wine*) depromĕre; **to —
out** extrahĕre; (*sword, etc.*) educĕre; (*fig*) elicĕre; **to — together**
contrahĕre; **to — up** subducĕre;
scribĕre; (*troops*) instruĕre, constituĕre; *vi* **to — back** pedem referre,
cedĕre; (*fig*) recedĕre; **to — near**
appropinquare; **to — off** cedĕre;
to — up to (*of ships*) appetĕre
drawback *s* impedimentum, incommodum *n*, retardatio *f*
drawbridge *s* pons *m*
drawer *s* (*sliding compartment*) loculus *m*; (*chest*) armarium *n*
drawing *s* descriptio *f*; (*art*) gra-
phice *f*
drawing room *s* exedra *f*
drawl *vi* lentius loqui
dray *s* plaustrum *n*
dread *s* terror, pavor *m*, formido *f*
dread *adj* terribilis, dirus
dread *vt* expavescĕre, formidare
dreadful *adj* terribilis, horribilis,
atrox; **—ly** horrendum in modum,
atrociter
dream *s* somnium *n*; **in a —** in
somno
dream *vt & vi* somniare; (*fig*) dormitare
dreamer *s* (*fig*) nugator *m*
dreamy *adj* somniculosus
drearily *adv* triste, misere
dreariness *s* (*place*) solitudo, vastitas *f*; (*mind*) tristitia *f*
dreary *adj* (*place*) vastus, solus, incultus; (*person*) tristis, miser
dredge *s* everriculum *n*
dregs *s* faex *f*; (*fig*) sentina *f*
drench *vt* madefacĕre, perfundĕre
dress *s* habit·us -ūs, vestit·us -ūs *m*,
vestis *f*, vestimenta *n pl*
dress *vt* vestire, induĕre; (*to deck
out*) (ex)ornare; (*wounds*) curare;
(*to bind up*) obligare; *vi* se induĕre
dressing *s* ornatio *f*; (*of foods*) coc-
tio, coctura *f*; (*med*) fomentum *n*
dressing room *s* procoeton *m*
dribble *vi* stillare
drift *s* propositum *n*; (*purpose*) scopus *m*; (*of sand*) cumulus *m*; (*of
snow*) vis *f*

drift *vi* ferri, fluitare
drill *s* (*tool*) terebra *f*; (*mil*) exercitatio *f*
drill *vt* (*to bore*) terebrare; (*mil*) ex-
ercĕre; (*pupil*) instituĕre
drink *vt* bibĕre, potare; **to — in**
absorbĕre, haurire; **to — up** epo-
tare; *vi* bibĕre, potare; **to — to**
propinare (*with dat*)
drink *s* pot·us -ūs *m*, potio *f*
drinkable *adj* potabilis
drinker *s* potor, potator *m*; (*drunkard*) bibax *m*
drinking *adj* (*given to drink*) bibo-
sus
drinking cup *s* poculum *n*
drip *s* stillicidium *n*
drip *vi* stillare
drive *vt* agĕre, pellĕre, impellĕre; (*to
force*) compellĕre, cogĕre; (*a nail,
etc.*) infigĕre; **to — away** abigĕre;
(*fig*) depellĕre; (*to dislodge*) dejicĕre; **to — back** repellĕre; **to —
in** (*sheep, etc.*) cogĕre; (*fig*) compellĕre; **to — off** abigĕre; **to —
on** impellĕre; **to — out** expellĕre;
to — out of one's senses infuriare; **to — up** subigĕre; *vi* (*in
carriage*) vehi; **to — off** avehi; **to
— on** praetervehi; **to — past**
praetervehi
drive *s* (*in carriage*) vectio *f*; (*energy*) impigritas *f*
drivel *s* saliva *f*, sputum *n*; (*nonsense*) ineptiae, nugae *f pl*
drivel *vi* (*fig*) delirare
driver *s* agitator *m*; (*of carriage*) auriga *m*
drizzle *vi* leniter pluĕre
drizzle *s* lenis pluvia *f*
dromedary *s* dromas *m*
drone *s* (*bee*) fucus *m*; (*person*) nebulo *m*; (*buzz*) bombus *m*
drone *vi* fremĕre
droop *vt* demittĕre; *vi* languĕre; (*of
flowers*) languescĕre, tabescĕre
drooping *adj* languidus
drop *s* gutta, stilla *f*; (*a little bit*)
paululum *n*; **— by —** guttatim
drop *vt* stillare; (*to let slip*) omittĕre;
(*to lay low*) sternĕre; (*hint*) emittĕre; (*anchor*) jacĕre; (*work*) desistĕre ab (*with abl*); *vi* destillare; (*to
fall*) cadĕre; **to — behind** cessare;
to — off to sleep obdormire; **to
— out** excidĕre
drought *s* siccitas, ariditas *f*
drove *s* grex *m*
drown *vt* immergĕre, demergĕre;
(*fig*) opprimĕre; **to — out** obscurare; *vi* in aqua perire
drowsily *adv* somniculose
drowsy *adj* somniculosus, somnolen-
tus; (*fig*) ignavus
drudge *s* (*slave*) mediastinus *m*; (*fig*)
plagiger *m*
drudgery *s* opera servilis *f*
drug *s* medicamentum *n*
drug *vt* medicare
druggist *s* medicamentarius *m*
drugstore *s* taberna medicina, apotheca *f*

Druids s Druidae m pl
drum s typanum n
drum vi tympanum pulsare
drummer s tympanista m
drunk adj ebrius
drunkard s ebriosus, temulentus m
drunken adj ebrius, ebriosus
drunkenness s ebrietas, temulentia f
dry adj aridus, siccus; (thirsty) siti-
  culosus; (fig) jejunus; insulsus
dry vt siccare, desiccare, arefacĕre;
  (in the sun) insolare; vi arescĕre
dryad s dryas f
dryly adv (fig) insulse; (of jokes)
  facete
dryness s ariditas, siccitas f; (fig)
  aridum sermonis genus n
dual adj duplex
dub vt supernominare
dubious adj dubius; —ly dubie
duck s anas f
duck vt submergĕre, demergĕre; (an
  issue) evitare; vi (under water) uri-
  nari
duckling s anaticula f
due adj debitus, justus, meritus; **to
  be — to** fieri (with abl)
due adv rectā; **due east** rectā ad
  orientem
due s debitum n
duel s certamen n
duet s bicinium n
duke s dux m
dull adj hebes; (of mind) tardus, seg-
  nes, insulsus; (of style) frigidus
dull vt hebetare, obtundĕre; stupefacĕre
dullness s stupiditas, tarditas f
duly adv rite; recte
dumb adj mutus; **to be —** obmu-
  tescĕre
dumbfound vt obstupefacĕre
dumb show s mimus m
dumpling s farinae subactae globulus m
dumpy adj brevis atque obesus

dun adj fuscus, furvus
dun vt flagitare, exposcĕre
dunce s homo stupidus m
dung s stercus n, fimus m; (of birds)
  merda f
dungeon s carcer m, ergastulum n
dupe s homo credulus, homo stolidus m
dupe vt decipĕre
duplicate adj duplex
duplicate s duplicitas, fallacia f
duplicate vt duplicare
duplicity s duplicitas f
durability s firmitudo, stabilitas f
durable adj firmus, durabilis, stabilis
duration s spatium temporis n, diuturnitas, perpetuitas f
during prep per (with acc), inter
  (with acc)
dusk s crepusculum, obscurum n
dusky adj obscurus, tenebrosus; fuscus
dust s pulvis m
dust vt detergĕre
dusty adj pulverulentus, pulvereus
dutiful adj pius, officiosus; —ly pie,
  officiose
duty s (social or moral) officium n;
  (task) munus n; (tax) vectigal n; to
  be on — (mil) stationem agĕre
dwarf s nanus, pumilio m
dwarfish adj pumilus
dwell vi habitare, inhabitare; **to —
  upon** commorari in (with abl)
dweller s incola m & f, habitator m
dwelling place s domicilium n, sedes, habitatio f
dwindle vi decrescĕre, imminui
dye vt ting(u)ĕre, colorare, inficĕre,
  fucare
dye s tinctura f, color m
dying adj moriens, moribundus;
  (last) ultimus, extremus
dynamics s dynamica f
dynasty s dynastia, dom·us -ūs f
dysentery s dysenteria f

E

each adj & pron quisque; (of two)
  uterque; **— other** inter se, invicem
eager adj cupidus, avidus, acer, vehemens; —ly cupide, avide, acriter,
  vehementer
eagerness s aviditas, cupiditas, alacritas f, studium n
eagle s aquila f
ear s auris f; (of corn) spica f; **to
  give —** aurem praebēre
earache s aurium dolor m
earl s comes m
early adj (in morning) matutinus;
  (in season) maturus; (of early date)
  antiquus; (beginning) primus, novus
early adv (in morning) mane; (too
  soon) praemature; (quickly, soon)
  cito
earn vt lucrari, merēre or merēri,

consequi
earnest adj intentus, serius, impen-
  sus, vehemens; **in —** serio, sedulo,
  bona fide; —ly intente, impense,
  acriter, graviter
earnestness s assiduitas, gravitas f,
  ardor m
earnings s quaest·us -ūs m, lucrum n
earring s elenchus m
earth s terra, tellus f; (soil) solum n;
  (globe) orbis (terrarum) m
earthen adj terrenus; fictilis
earthenware s fictilia n pl
earthly adj terrenus; terrestris; humanus
earthquake s terrae mot·us -ūs m
earthwork s opus terrenum n, agger m
earthy adj terrenus

ease *s* (*leisure*) otium *n*, quies *f*; (*grace*) lepor *m*, facilitas *f*; (*pleasure*) voluptas *f*; **at —** otiosus, vacuus; securus

ease *vt* levare, exonerare, expedire; (*fig*) lenire, mitigare

east *adj* orientalis

east *s* oriens *m*

Easter *s* pascha *f*, sollemnia paschalia *n pl*

eastern *adj* orientalis

eastward *adv* ad orientem

east wind *s* Eurus *m*

easy *adj* facilis; expeditus; (*manner*) facilis, affabilis; (*graceful*) lepidus

eat *vi* vesci (*with abl*), esse; (*fig*) rodĕre; **to — away** peredĕre; (*fig*) corrodĕre; **to — up** comesse, devorare, exesse

eating *s* es·us -ūs *m*

eaves *s* suggrundia *n pl*

eavesdropper *s* auceps, auricularius *m*

ebb *s* recess·us -ūs *m*; **to be at a low —** jacēre

ebb *vi* recedĕre; (*fig*) decrescĕre

eccentric *adj* insolens, inusitatus, abnormis

ecclesiastic *adj* ecclesiasticus

echo *s* echo, imago *f*

echo *vt* repercutĕre, resonare; (*fig*) subsequi; *vi* resonare, resultare

eclipse *s* (*of sun or moon*) obscuratio solis *or* lunae *f*, defect·us -ūs *m*

eclipse *vt* obscurare, obumbrare

eclogue *s* ecloga *f*

economic *adj* economicus

economical *adj* frugi (*indecl*), parcus; **—ly** parce

economics *s* publicarum opum scientia *f*

economize *vi* parcĕre

economy *s* parsimonia, frugalitas *f*; rei familiaris administratio *f*

ecstasy *s* ecstasis, insania *f*, furor *m*

eddy *s* vortex *m*

eddy *vi* voltari

edge *s* (*brink*) margo *m* & *f*; (*of knife, etc.*) acies *f*; (*of forest*) ora *f*

edge *vt* (*garment*) praetexĕre; (*to sharpen*) acuĕre; *vi* **to — closer** appropinquare

edged *adj* acutus

edging *s* limbus *m*

edible *adj* esculentus, edulis

edict *s* edictum, decretum *n*

edification *s* eruditio *f*

edify *vt* docēre

edit *vt* edĕre, recensēre

edition *s* editio *f*

editor *s* editor *m*

educate *vt* educare, erudire

education *s* educatio, eruditio *f*

educator *s* praeceptor, magister *m*

eel *s* anguilla *f*

efface *vt* delēre, oblitterare, tollĕre

effect *s* effectum *n*, effect·us -ūs; (*show*) jactatio *f*; **—s** bona *n pl*; **in — re** vera; **without —** irritus

effect *vt* efficĕre, exsequi, facĕre

effective *adj* efficiens, efficax, valens; **—ly** valide, graviter

effectual *adj* efficax, valens, potens,

—ly efficaciter, potenter

effeminacy *s* mollities *f*

effeminate *adj* effeminatus, mollis, muliebris; **—ly** effeminate, muliebriter

effete *adj* effetus

efficacious *adj* efficax; **—ly** efficaciter

efficacy *s* efficacia, vis *f*

efficiency *s* virtus, peritia *f*

efficient *adj* efficiens, aptus, idoneus; efficax; **—ly** perite, bene

effigy *s* effigies *f*

effort *s* labor, conat·us -ūs, nis·us -ūs *m*, opera *f*; **to make an — eniti

effrontery *s* audacia, impudentia *f*

effusion *s* effusio *f*

effusive *adj* officiosus

egg *s* ovum *n*; **to lay —s** ova parēre

egotism *s* amor sui *m*

egotist *s* sui amator *m*

egotistical *adj* sibi soli consulens

egress *s* egress·us -ūs, exit·us -ūs *m*

eight *adj* octo; **— times** octies

eighteen *adj* duodeviginti, decem et octo

eighteenth *adj* decimus octavus, duodevicesimus

eighth *adj* octavus

eighth *s* octava pars *f*

eightieth *adj* octogesimus

eighty *adj* octoginta

either *pron* alteruter; uter; alter

either *conj* **— . . . or** aut . . . aut; vel . . . vel

ejaculate *vt* emittĕre

ejaculation *s* clamor *m*

eject *vt* ejicĕre

ejection *s* dejectio *f*

eke *vt* **to eke out a livelihood** victum aegre parare

elaborate *adj* elaboratus; **—ly** elaborate

elaborate *vt* elaborare

elaboration *s* nimia diligentia *f*

elapse *vi* praeterire, abire, labi

elastic *adj* resiliens; (*fig*) mobilis

elate *vt* inflare, superbum reddĕre; **to be elated** efferri

elation *s* gaudium *n*, laetitia *f*, animus elatus *m*

elbow *s* ulna *f*, cubitus *m*

elbow *vt* cubitis depulsare, cubitis trudĕre

elder *adj* major natu

elderly *adj* aetate provectior

eldest *adj* maximus natu

elect *vt* eligĕre, deligĕre, creare

elect *adj* designatus; (*elite*) lectus

election *s* electio *f*, delect·us -ūs *m*; (*pol*) comitia *n pl*

electioneering *s* ambitio *f*

elective *adj* suffragatorius

elector *s* suffragator *m*

electrical *adj* electricus

electricity *s* vis electrica *f*

electrify *vt* electricâ vi afficĕre; (*fig*) percellĕre

elegance *s* elegantia *f*

elegant *adj* elegans, concinnus; **—ly** eleganter, cum elegantia

elegiac *adj* elegiacus; — **verse** elegi *m pl*

elegy *s* elegia *f*

element *s* elementum *n*; —**s** principia, initia *n pl*; (*fig*) rudimenta *n pl*

elementary *adj* elementarius

elephant *s* elephantus, elephas *m*

elevate *vt* levare, attollĕre; (*fig*) efferre, inflare

elevated *adj* editus

elevation *s* elatio *f*; (*height*) altitudo *f*; (*hill*) locus superior *m*

eleven *adj* undecim; — **times** undecies

eleventh *adj* undecimus

elf *s* larva *f*, numen pumilum *n*

elicit *vt* elicĕre

eligible *adj* eligibilis, idoneus

eliminate *vt* amovēre, tollĕre

elision *s* elisio *f*

elite *adj* lectus

elite *s* flos *m*, lecti *m pl*

elk *s* alces *f*

ellipsis *s* ellipsis *f*

elliptical *adj* ellipticus; —**ly** per defectionem

elm *s* ulmus *f*

elocution *s* pronuntiatio *f*

elongate *vt* producĕre

elope *vi* clam fugĕre, aufugĕre

elopement *s* fuga clandestina *f*

eloquence *s* eloquentia *f*; (*natural*) facundia *f*

eloquent *adj* eloquens, disertus; —**ly** diserte, eloquenter, graviter

else *adj* alius; **no one** — nemo alius; **who** — quis alius

else *adv* (*besides*) praeterea; (*otherwise*) aliter

elsewhere *adv* alibi; (*motion*) alio

elucidate *vt* illustrare, explicare

elucidation *s* explicatio *f*

elude *vt* eludĕre, frustrari, evitare

Elysian *adj* Elysius

Elysian fields *s* Elysii campi *m pl*

emaciate *vt* emaciare, macerare

emaciated *adj* macer, macilentus

emaciation *s* macies, tabes *f*

emanate *vi* emanare, oriri

emanation *s* emanatio, exhalatio *f*

emancipate *vt* emancipare, manumittĕre; (*fig*) liberare

emancipation *s* (*of slave*) manumissio *f*; (*of son*) emancipatio *f*; (*fig*) liberatio *f*

emasculate *vt* castrare, emasculare; (*fig*) enervare

embalm *vt* condire, pollingĕre

embalming *s* pollinctura *f*

embankment *s* agger *m*, moles *f*

embargo *s* retentio navium *f*, interdictum *n*; **to lay an** — **upon a ship** navem retinēre

embark *vt* imponĕre; *vi* conscendĕre; **to** — **upon** (*fig*) ingredi

embarkation *s* conscensio *f*

embarrass *vt* perturbare, confundĕre, impedire

embarrassing *adj* incommodus, difficilis

embarrassment *s* conturbatio, implicatio *f*; (*financial*) angustiae *f pl*

embassy *s* legatio *f*, legati *m pl*

embellish *vt* ornare, exornare

embellishment *s* ornamentum, decus *n*, exornatio *f*

embers *s* cinis *m*, favilla *f n pl*

embezzle *vt* peculari

embezzlement *s* peculat·us -ūs *m*

embezzler *s* peculator *m*

embitter *vt* exacerbare

emblazon *vt* insignire

emblem *s* emblema, insigne, signum *n*

emblematic *adj* symbolicus

embody *vt* includĕre, repraesentare

emboss *vt* caelare

embrace *s* amplex·us -ūs, complex·us -ūs *m*

embrace *vt* amplecti, complecti; comprehendĕre

embroider *vt* acu pingĕre

embroidery *s* vestis picta *f*

embroil *vt* permiscēre, implicare

embroilment *s* implicatio *f*

embryo *s* immaturus part·us -ūs *m*

emend *vt* emendare, corrigĕre

emendation *s* correctio, emendatio *f*

emerald *s* smaragdus *m*

emerge *vi* emergĕre; (*to arise*) exsistĕre

emergency *s* tempus, discrimen *n*, cas·us -ūs *m*

emigrant *s* emigrans *m*

emigrate *vi* emigrare

emigration *s* migratio *f*

eminence *s* praestantia, amplitudo *f*; (*rise of ground*) locus editus *m*

eminent *adj* eminens, egregius, praestans; —**ly** eximie, insigniter

emissary *s* emissarius, legatus *m*

emit *vt* emittĕre; exhalare

emotion *s* animi mot·us -ūs *m*, commotio *f*

emotional *adj* mobilis

emperor *s* imperator, princeps *m*

emphasis *s* energia, vis *f*, pondus *n*; impressio *f*

emphasize *vt* exprimĕre

emphatic *adj* emphaticus, gravis; —**ally** emphatice, graviter

empire *s* imperium, regnum *n*

empirical *adj* empiricus; —**ly** ex experimentis

empiricism *s* empirice *f*

employ *vt* uti (*with abl*), adhibēre, exercēre, occupare

employer *s* conductor, dominus *m*

employment *s* (*act*) us·us -ūs *m*; (*occupation*) quaest·us -ūs *m*; (*business*) negotium *n*

empower *vt* potestatem facĕre (*with dat*)

empress *s* imperatrix *f*

emptiness *s* inanitas *f*; (*fig*) vanitas *f*

empty *adj* vacuus, inanis; (*of street*) desertus; (*fig*) vanus

empty *vt* evacuare; exhaurire; *vi* (*of river*) influĕre

empyrean *s* aether *m*

emulate *vt* aemulari, imitari

emulation *s* aemulatio *f*

enable *vt* facultatem facĕre (*with dat*)

enact *vt* decernĕre, sancire

enactment *s* lex, sanctio *f*, decretum *n*

enamel *s* smaltum, vitrum metallicum *n*

enamel *adj* smaltinus

enamoured *adj* amans; **to be — of** amare, deamare

encamp *vi* castra ponĕre

encampment *s* castra *n pl*

encase *vt* includĕre

enchant *vt* fascinare; (*fig*) capĕre, captare, delectare

enchanter *s* incantator *m*

enchanting *adj* (*fig*) venustus, suavissimus

enchantment *s* incantamentum *n*; (*fig*) illecebrae *f pl*

enchantress *s* maga, cantatrix *f*; venefica *f*

encircle *vt* cingĕre, circumdare, circumplecti

enclose *vt* includĕre, saepire

enclosure *s* saeptum *n*

encompass *vt* complecti

encounter *s* (*meeting*) congress·us -ūs *m*; (*fight*) certamen *n*, pugna *f*

encounter *vt* congredi cum (*with abl*), obviam ire (*with dat*), occurrĕre (*with dat*); (*in battle*) concurrĕre cum (*with abl*)

encourage *vt* cohortari, confirmare; favēre (*with dat*)

encouragement *s* hortat·us -ūs *m*, confirmatio *f*, favor *m*

encroach *vi* invadĕre; **to — upon** usurpare, occupare, invadĕre

encroachment *s* usurpatio *f*

encumber *vt* impedire, onerare, praegravare

encumbrance *s* impedimentum, onus *n*

encyclopedia *s* encyclopaedia *f*

end *s* finis, terminus, exit·us -ūs *m*; (*aim*) propositum *n*; (*of a speech*) peroratio *f*; **in the — denique**; **to put an — to** finem imponĕre (*with dat*); **to what —?** quo?, quorsum?

end *vt* finire, terminare, conficĕre; *vi* desinĕre; (*of time*) exire; (*of events*) evadĕre

endanger *vt* periclitari

endear *vt* carum reddĕre, devincire

endearing *adj* carus, blandus

endearment *s* blanditiae *f pl*, blandimenta *n pl*

endeavor *s* conat·us -ūs, nis·us -ūs *m*

endeavor *vi* conari, eniti, laborare, contendĕre

ending *s* finis, exit·us -ūs *m*

endless *adj* infinitus; perpetuus; **—ly** sine fine, perpetuo

endorse *vt* ratum facĕre

endow *vt* dotare, donare, instruĕre

endowed *adj* praeditus

endowment *s* dotatio, dos *f*, donum *n*

endurable *adj* tolerabilis

endurance *s* tolerantia, patientia *f*; (*duration*) duratio *f*

endure *vt* tolerare, pati; *vi* durare; permanēre

enduring *adj* tolerans; durabilis

enemy *s* (*public*) hostis *m*; (*private*) inimicus, adversarius *m*

energetic *adj* impiger, acer, strenuus, navus; **—ally** acriter, impigre, strenuo

energy *s* vis, vehementia, efficacia *f*, impet·us -ūs *m*

enervate *vt* enervare, debilitare

enforce *vt* exsequi, cogĕre; (*arguments*) confirmare

enforcement *s* coactio, sanctio *f*

enfranchise *vt* (*slave*) manumittĕre; civitate donare

enfranchisement *s* (*of slave*) manumissio *f*; civitatis donatio *f*

engage *vt* (*to employ*) adhibēre; (*to reserve*) conducĕre; (*attention*) occupare; (*to involve*) implicare; (*enemy*) proelium facĕre cum (*with abl*); *vi* **to — in** suscipĕre, ingredi; **to engage in battle** proeliari, manum or manus conserĕre

engaged *adj* (*to marry*) sponsus; **to be — in** versari in (*with abl*)

engagement *s* (*to marry*) pactio nuptialis *f*; (*business*) negotium *n*, occupatio *f*; (*mil*) proelium *n*, pugna *f*; (*promise*) pactum *n*, pactio *f*, promissum *n*

engaging *adj* suavis, blandus, amabilis

engender *vt* ingenerare, gignĕre

engine *s* machina, machinatio *f*

engineer *s* machinator, faber *m*

engineering *s* machinalis scientia *f*; **civil —** architectura *f*

England *s* Anglia, Britannia *f*

English *adj* Anglicus, Britannicus

Englishman *s* Anglus, Britannus, Britannicus *m*

engrave *vt* incidĕre, caelare, insculpĕre, scalpĕre

engraver *s* sculptor, caelator *m*

engraving *s* sculptura, caelatura *f*

engross *vt* occupare; **to be engrossed in** totus esse in (*with abl*)

enhance *vt* augēre, amplificare, ornare

enigma *s* aenigma *n*, ambages *f pl*

enigmatic *adj* ambiguus, obscurus; **—ally** ambigue

enjoin *vt* jubēre, injungĕre

enjoy *vt* frui (*with abl*); uti (*with abl*)

enjoyment *s* fruct·us -ūs *m*, voluptas *f*, gaudium *n*; possessio *f*

enlarge *vt* amplificare, augēre, dilatare; *vi* **to — upon** amplificare, prosequi

enlargement *s* amplificatio, dilatio *f*, auct·us -ūs *m*

enlighten *vt* illustrare, illuminare; erudire

enlightenment *s* eruditio, humanitas *f*

enlist *vt* (*support*) conciliare; (*mil*) conscribĕre; *vi* sacramentum dicĕre

enlistment *s* conscriptio *f*

enliven *vt* animare, incitare; exhilarare

enmity *s* inimicitia *f*, odium *n*

ennoble *vt* honestare

ennui *s* taedium *n*

enormity *s* immanitas *f*; atrocitas *f*

enormous adj ingens, enormis, immanis; **—ly** immensum, praeter modum

enough adj satis; **— trouble** satis laboris

enough adv satis; **more than —** satis superque

enrage vt infuriare, exasperare, incendēre

enrapture vt rapēre, captare

enrich vt locupletare, ditare

enroll vt adscribēre, inscribēre; vi nomen dare

enshrine vt consecrare, dedicare

enshroud vt involvēre, amicire

ensign s (flag) vexillum n; (officer) signifer m

enslave vt in servitutem redigēre

enslavement s servitus f

ensnare vt illaquēre, irretire; (fig) illicēre

ensue vi sequi, insequi

ensuing adj insequens, posterus, proximus

entail vt afferre, inferre

entangle vt illaquēre, irretire, impedire, implicare

entanglement s implicatio f

enter vt intrare, inire, ingredi; introire in or ad (with acc); **to — politics** ad rem publicam accedēre; vi intrare, inire, ingredi, introire; **to — upon** (to undertake) suscipēre, ingredi

enterprise s (undertaking) inceptum, ausum n; (in bad sense) facinus n; (quality) animus alacer, animus promptus m

enterprising adj acer, promptus

entertain vt (guest) excipēre, invitare, adhibēre; (idea) admittēre, habēre; (to amuse) oblectare, delectare

entertainer s hospes m

entertainment s (amusement) oblectatio f, oblectamentum n; (cultural) acroama n; (by guest) hospitium n

enthrall vt captare

enthusiasm s studium n, fervor, ardor m

enthusiastic adj fanaticus, ardens, fervidus; **—ally** fanatice, ardenter

entice vt allicēre, elicēre

enticement s illecebra f

enticing adj blandus

entire adj totus, integer, solidus; **—ly** omnino, plane, penitus

entirety s integritas, universitas f

entitle vt (to name) appellare, nominare; inscribēre; (to give title to) potestatem dare (with dat)

entity s ens n, res f

entomologist s entomologicus m

entomology s entomologia f

entrails s viscera, exta, intestina n pl

entrance s adit·us -ūs, introit·us -ūs m; ostium n; (act) introit·us -ūs m, ingressio f

entrance vt rapēre, consopire, capēre

entrance hall s vestibulum n

entrap vt illaquēre, inescare; capēre

entreat vt obsecrare, orare, deprecari

entreaty s rogatio, obsecratio f, preces f pl

entrust vt credēre, mandare, committēre

entry s (act) introit·us -ūs m, ingressio f; (of house) vestibulum n; adit·us -ūs m; (in accounts) nomen n

entwine vt implicare, nectēre

enumerate vt enumerare

enumeration s enumeratio, recensio f

enunciate vt enuntiare, pronuntiare, exprimēre

enunciation s enuntiatio f

envelop vt involvēre, amicire, implicare

envelope s involucrum n

enviable adj invidiosus

envious adj invidus, lividus

envoy s nuntius, legatus, orator m

envy s invidia f

envy vt invidēre (with dat)

ephemeral adj brevis; caducus

epic adj epicus, heroicus

epic s epos n

epicure s helluo, homo voluptarius m

Epicurean adj Epicureus

Epicurean s Epicureus m; (hedonist) voluptarius m

epidemic adj epidemus, contagiosus

epidemic s pestilentia f

epidermis s summa cutis, epidermis f

epigram s epigramma n

epilepsy s morbus comitialis m, epilepsia f

epilogue s epilogus m

epiphany s epiphania f

episode s embolium, eventum n, excurs·us -ūs m

epistle s epistola f

epistolary adj epistolaris

epitaph s epitaphium n, titulus m

epithet s epitheton n

epitome s epitome, epitoma f

epoch s epocha f, saeculum n

equal adj aequalis, aequus, par; **—ly** aeque, aequaliter, pariter

equal s par m, f & n

equal vt aequare, adaequare

equality s aequalitas f, aequum n

equalization s (act) aequatio, exaequatio f; (state) aequalitas f

equalize vt adaequare, exaequare

equanimity s aequus animus m

equation s aequatio f

equator s aequinoctialis circulus m

equatorial adj aequinoctialis

equestrian adj equestris

equestrian s eques m

equidistant adj to be **— aequo intervallo inter se distare**

equilibrium s aequilibrium n

equinox s aequinoctium n

equip vt armare, ornare, instruēre

equipment s arma, instrumenta, armamenta n pl, armatura f, apparat·us -ūs m

equitable adj aequus, justus

equitably adv aeque, juste

equity s aequitas f, aequum n

equivalent *adj* aequus, par

equivocal *adj* ambiguus, anceps; —ly ambigue

equivocate *vi* tergiversari

era *s* tempus, saeculum *n*

eradicate *vt* eruĕre, exstirpare, eradicare

eradication *s* exstirpatio *f*

erase *vt* delēre, eradēre

erasure *s* litura *f*

ere *conj* priusquam

ere *prep* ante (*with acc*); — long brevi, mox; — now ante hoc tempus

erect *adj* erectus, arrectus

erect *vt* (*to raise*) erigĕre; (*to build*) exstruĕre; (*statue*) ponĕre

erection *s* erectio, aedificatio, exstructio *f*

erotic *adj* amatorius, eroticus

err *vi* (ab)errare, peccare

errand *s* mandatum *n*

erratic *adj* inconstans

erroneous *adj* falsus, errore implicitus; —ly falso, perperam

error *s* error *m*; vitium *n*; delictum, peccatum *n*; (*in writing*) mendum *n*

erudite *adj* eruditus, doctus

erudition *s* eruditio *f*

erupt *vi* erumpĕre

eruption *s* eruptio *f*

escape *s* fuga *f*, effugium *n*

escape *vt* fugĕre, evitare; to — the notice of fallĕre; *vi* effugĕre, evadĕre, elabi; (*secretly*) subterfugĕre

escort *s* comitat·us -ūs *m*; (*protection*) praesidium *n*

escort *vt* comitari, deducĕre

especially *adv* praecipue, praesertim, maxime, in primis

essay *s* experimentum *n*, conat·us -ūs *m*; (*treatise*) libellus *m*

essay *vt* conari, tentare

essence *s* essentia, natura *f*

essential *adj* necessarius, propius; —ly natura, necessario

establish *vt* constituĕre, statuĕre; (*firmly*) stabilire, confirmare; (*to prove*) probare, arguĕre

establishment *s* (*act*) constitutio *f*; (*com*) negotium *n*

estate *s* (*state*) stat·us -ūs *m*, conditio *f*; (*property*) fundus *m*, praedium *n*; (*pol*) ordo *m*, dignitas *f*

esteem *s* aestimatio *f*, honor *m*

esteem *vt* aestimare, putare; (*to respect*) magni facĕre

estimable *adj* aestimandus

estimate *vt* aestimare, censēre

estimate *s* aestimatio *f*, judicium *n*

estimation *s* aestimatio, opinio, sententia *f*, judicium *n*

estimator *s* aestimator, calculator *m*

estrange *vt* abalienare

estrangement *s* alienatio *f*, discidium *n*

estuary *s* aestuarium *n*

eternal *adj* aeternus, sempiternus; —ly in aeternum, semper

eternity *s* aeternitas *f*

ether *s* aether *m*

ethereal *adj* aethereus

ethical *adj* moralis

ethics *s* mores *m pl*, ethice *f*; philosophia moralis *f*

etymology *s* etymologia, verborum notatio *f*

eulogize *vt* collaudare

eulogy *s* laudatio *f*, panegyricus *m*

eunuch *s* eunuchus *m*; (*in contempt*) spado *m*

euphony *s* euphonia *f*, sonus dulcis *m*

European *adj* Europaeus

Euxine *s* Euxinus pontus *m*

evacuate *vt* vacuare, vacuefacĕre; (*people*) deducĕre

evacuation *s* discessio *f*; (*of bowels*) egestio *f*

evade *vt* subterfugĕre, eludĕre, devitare

evaporate *vt* exhalare, evaporare; *vi* exhalari

evaporation *s* exhalatio *f*

evasion *s* effugium *n*, tergiversatio *f*

evasive *adj* ambiguus; —ly ambigue

eve *s* vesper *m*; (*of feast*) vigiliae *f pl*; on the — of sub (*with acc*)

even *adj* aequalis, aequus; (*level*) planus; (*of numbers*) par; —ly aequaliter

even *adv* et, etiam, vel; — if etsi, etiamsi; not — ne ... quidem

evening *s* vesper *m*; in the — vespere, vesperi

evening *adj* vespertinus

evening star *s* Hesperus, Vesper *m*

evenness *s* aequalitas, aequabilitas *f*

event *s* cas·us -ūs *m*, factum *n*; (*outcome*) event·us -ūs, exit·us -ūs *m*; in any — saltem

eventful *adj* memorabilis

eventual *adj* ultimus; —ly aliquando, olim, denique

ever *adv* (*always*) semper; (*at any time*) umquam; (*after* si, nisi, num, ne) quando; for — in aeternum

evergreen *adj* sempervivus

everlasting *adj* sempiternus; —ly in aeternum

evermore *adv* semper, in aeternum

every *adj* quisque, omnis; — now and then interdum; — other day alternis diebus

everybody *pron* quisque, nemo non; omnes *m pl*

everyday *adj* quotidianus *or* cottidianus; usitatus

everything *pron* omnia *n pl*

everywhere *adv* ubique, ubivis

evict *vt* expellĕre, dejicĕre, detrudĕre

evidence *s* testimonium, indicium, argumentum *n*; (*witness*) testis *m & f*

evidence *vt* testari

evident *adj* apertus, manifestus; it is — apparet; —ly aperte, manifesto

evil *adj* malus, pravus, improbus

evil *s* malum *n*, improbitas *f*

evildoer *s* maleficus, malefactor *m*

evil-minded *adj* malevolus, malignus

evoke *vt* evocare, excitare, elicĕre

evolution *s* progress·us -ūs *m*, progressio *f*

evolve *vt* evolvĕre, explicare

exact *adj* exactus, subtilis, diligens;

—ly accurate, subtiliter, diligenter; **—ly as** sic ut

exact *vt* exigère

exaction *s* exactio *f*

exactitude *s* diligentia *f*

exaggerate *vt* exaggerare, augēre, in majus extollĕre

exaggeration *s* trajectio, superlatio *f*

exalt *vt* extollĕre, amplificare, evehĕre

exaltation *s* elatio *f*

examination *s* investigatio *f*; (*in school*) probatio *f*; (*of witnesses*) interrogatio *f*

examine *vt* investigare, inquirĕre, scrutari; (*witnesses*) interrogare

examiner *s* scrutator, investigator *m*

example *s* exemplum, exemplar, documentum *n*; **for —** exempli gratiā, verbi gratiā

exasperate *vt* exasperare, exacerbare, irritare

exasperation *s* ira *f*

excavate *vt* excavare, effodĕre

excavation *s* fossio, excavatio *f*, cavum *n*

exceed *vt* superare, excedĕre

exceedingly *adv* valde, magnopere

excel *vt* superare, praestare (*with dat*); *vi* excellĕre

excellence *s* excellentia, praestantia *f*

Excellency *s* illustrissimus *m*

excellent *adj* praestans, egregius, optimus; **—ly** egregie, optime

except *vt* excipĕre

except *prep* praeter (*with acc*); nisi (*followed by appropriate case*); **— that** nisi quod

exception *s* exceptio *f*; **with the — of** praeter (*with acc*)

exceptional *adj* egregius, praestans, singularis; **—ly** praeter modum

excess *s* excess·us -ūs *m*, intemperantia *f*

excessive *adj* immodicus, nimius; **—ly** immodice, nimis

exchange *s* (*barter*) commutatio *f*; (*of money*) collybus *m*

exchange *vt* mutare, permutare

excise *vt* excidĕre

excision *s* excisio *f*

excitable *adj* irritabilis, fervidus

excite *vt* excitare, stimulare; (*to inflame*) incendĕre

excitement *s* commotio *f*; perturbatio *f*; incitamentum *n*

exclaim *vt* exclamare; (*as a group*) conclamare; *vi* **to — against** acclamare (*with dat*); declamitare in (*with acc*)

exclamation *s* exclamatio *f*, clamor *m*

exclude *vt* excludĕre, prohibēre

exclusion *s* exclusio *f*

exclusive *adj* proprius; **— of** praeter (*with acc*); **—ly** solum

excommunicate *vt* excommunicare

excommunication *s* excommunicatio *f*

excrement *s* excrementum, stercus *n*

excretion *s* excrementum *n*, excretio *f*

excruciating *adj* acerbissimus

exculpate *vt* (ex)purgare, excusare, absolvĕre

excursion *s* excursio *f*, iter *n*

excusable *adj* excusabilis

excuse *vt* excusare; ignoscĕre (*with dat*), veniam dare (*with dat*)

excuse *s* excusatio *f*; (*pretense*) pretext·us -ūs *m*, species *f*

execute *vt* (*to perform*) exsequi, efficĕre; (*to punish*) necare, securi ferire

execution *s* effect·us -ūs *m*, effectio *f*; (*capital punishment*) supplicium *n*

executioner *s* carnifex *m*

executive *adj* ad administrationem pertinens

executive *s* administrator *m*

executor *s* curator testamenti *m*

exemplary *adj* egregius, eximius

exemplification *s* expositio *f*

exemplify *vt* explicare

exempt *vt* eximĕre, liberare

exempt *adj* exemptus, immunis, liber

exemption *s* exemptio, immunitas, liberatio *f*

exercise *s* exercitatio *f*, us·us -ūs *m*; (*mil*) exercitium *n*; (*literary*) thema *n*

exercise *vt* exercēre; uti (*with abl*)

exert *vt* adhibēre; **to — oneself** viribus eniti

exertion *s* contentio *f*, nis·us -ūs *m*

exhalation *s* exhalatio *f*, vapor *m*

exhale *vt* exhalare, spargĕre; *vi* exspirare

exhaust *vt* exhaurire; (*to tire*) defatigare, conficĕre, debilitare

exhaustion *s* defatigatio, defectio virium *f*

exhibit *vt* exhibēre, exponĕre, ostendĕre

exhibition *s* exhibitio, propositio *f*; spectaculum *n*

exhilarate *vt* exhilarare

exhilaration *s* hilaritas *f*

exhort *vt* hortari

exhortation *s* hortatio *f*, hortamen *n*

exhume *vt* exhumare, eruĕre

exigency *s* necessitas *f*, angustiae *f pl*

exile *s* (*banishment*) ex(s)ilium *n*; (*person*) exsul, profugus *m*

exile *vt* relegare, in exilium pellĕre, deportare

exist *vi* esse, exsistĕre; vivĕre

existence *s* existentia *f*; vita *f*

exit *s* exit·us -ūs *m*; ostium *n*

exonerate *vt* absolvĕre

exorbitant *adj* nimius, immodicus

exotic *adj* externus, peregrinus

expand *vt* expandĕre, extendĕre, dilatare; *vi* expandi, extendi, dilatari

expanse *s* spatium, expansum *n*

expansion *s* expansio *f*, spatium *n*

expatriate *vt* expellĕre

expect *vt* exspectare, sperare

expectancy *s* spes *f*

expectation *s* exspectatio, spes *f*

expectorate *vt* exspuĕre, exscreare

expediency *s* utilitas *f*

expedient *adj* utilis, commodus; **—ly** apte, commode

expedient *s* modus *m*, ratio *f*
expedite *vt* expedire, maturare
expedition *s* (*mil*) expeditio *f*; (*speed*) celeritas *f*
expeditious *adj* celer, promptus; —ly celeriter, mature
expel *vt* expellĕre, ejicĕre
expend *vt* expendĕre, impendĕre
expenditure *s* sumpt·us -ūs *m*, impensa *f*
expense *s* impensa *f*, sumpt·us -ūs *m*
expensive *adj* carus, pretiosus; sumptuosus, lautus; —ly sumptuose
experience *s* experientia, peritia *f*, us·us -ūs *m*
experience *vt* experiri, cognoscĕre, pati
experienced *adj* peritus, expertus
experiment *s* experimentum *n*
experiment *vi* to — with experiri
experimental *adj* usu comparatus
expert *adj* sciens, peritus, callidus; —ly callide, scienter
expertness *s* calliditas, sollertia *f*
expiate *vt* expiāre, luĕre
expiation *s* expiatio *f*; piaculum *n*
expiration *s* exspiratio *f*, finis, exit·us -ūs *m*
expire *vi* exspirare; (*of time*) exire
explain *vt* explanare, explicare, exponĕre
explanation *s* explanatio, explicatio, enodatio, interpretatio *f*
explicit *adj* apertus, expressus; —ly aperte, plane
explode *vt* displodĕre, discutĕre; *vi* displodi, dirumpi
exploit *s* res gesta *f*, factum, facinus *n*
exploit *vt* uti (*with abl*), abuti (*with abl*)
exploration *s* indagatio, investigatio *f*
explore *vt* explorare, scrutari, perscrutari
explorer *s* explorator *m*
explosion *s* fragor *m*
exponent *s* interpres *m*
export *vt* exportare, evehĕre
exporter *s* exportator *m*
exports *s* merces quae exportantur *f pl*
expose *vt* exponĕre; nudare, detegĕre, patefacĕre; (*to danger*) objicĕre, offerre
exposition *s* explicatio, expositio, interpretatio *f*; (*show*) spectaculum *n*
expostulation *s* expostulatio, querela *f*
exposure *s* (*of guilt*) deprehensio *f*; (*to cold*) expositio *f*
expound *vt* exponĕre, interpretari
express *adj* clarus, expressus; —ly plane
express *vt* exprimĕre, eloqui, dicĕre; significare
expression *s* vox *f*, verbum *n*; (*of face*) vult·us -ūs *m*
expressive *adj* significans; (*fig*) loquax; — of index (*with genit*)

expulsion *s* exactio, ejectio, expulsio *f*
expunge *vt* delēre, oblitterare
expurgate *vt* expurgare
exquisite *adj* exquisitus, elegans; —ly eleganter, exquisite
extant *adj* superstes, exsistens; to be — exstare
extempore *adv* ex tempore, subito
extemporize *vi* subito dicĕre, subita dicĕre
extend *vt* extendĕre, producĕre, propagare; *vi* extendĕre, porrigi
extension *s* extensio *f*; (*space*) spatium *n*; (*of boundaries*) prolatio *f*
extensive *adj* amplus, latus; —ly late
extent *s* spatium *n*; (*of a country*) tract·us -ūs *m*, fines *m pl*; to a great — magna ex parte; to some — aliqua ex parte; to this — hactenus
extenuate *vt* mitigare, minuĕre
extenuation *s* imminutio *f*
exterior *adj* externus, exterior
exterior *s* species *f*
exterminate *vt* exstirpare, exterminare, eradicare
extermination *s* exstirpatio *f*; internecio, occidio *f*
external *adj* externus, extraneus; —ly extrinsecus
extinct *adj* exstinctus, obsoletus; to become — obsolescĕre
extinction *s* exstinctio *f*, interit·us -ūs *m*
extinguish *vt* exstinguĕre, restinguĕre
extol *vt* laudibus efferre
extort *vt* extorquēre, diripĕre, exprimĕre
extortion *s* res repetundae *f pl*
extortioner *s* exactor, extortor *m*
extra *adj* additus
extra *adv* insuper, praeterea
extract *vt* extrahĕre, excerpĕre; (*teeth, etc.*) evellĕre
extract *s* (*chemical*) expressio *f*; (*literary*) excerptum *n*; (*synopsis*) compendium *n*
extraction *s* (*act*) evulsio *f*; (*birth, origin*) stirps, origo *f*, genus *n*
extraneous *adj* extraneus, alienus, adventicius
extraordinarily *adv* mire, praeter solitum, extra modum
extraordinary *adj* extraordinarius, insolitus; (*outstanding*) eximius, mirus
extravagance *s* intemperantia *f*; sumpt·us -ūs *m*
extravagant *adj* immodicus, nimius; profusus, luxuriosus; (*spending*) prodigus; —ly immodice, absurde; prodige
extreme *adj* extremus, ultimus; —ly valde, summe
extreme *s* extremum, summum *n*
extremity *s* extremitas *f*, extremum *n*, finis *m*; (*distress*) miseria *f*
extricate *vt* expedire, extrahĕre, liberare

exuberance *s* ubertas, luxuria, redundantia *f*

exuberant *adj* uber, luxuriosus; **—ly** ubertim

exude *vt* exudare; *vi* emanare

exult *vi* exsultare, gestire

exultant *adj* laetabundus, laetus; **—ly** laete

exultation *s* laetitia *f*

eye *s* oculus *m*; (*of needle*) foramen *n*; (*of plant*) gemma *f*; **to keep one's —s on** oculos defigĕre in (*with abl*)

eye *vt* aspicĕre, intuēri

eyebrow *s* supercilium *n*

eyelash *s* palebrarum pilus *m*

eyelid *s* palpebra *f*

eyesight *s* acies, acies oculi *f*

eyewitness *s* arbiter *m*

F

fable *s* fabula, narratio commenticia *f*

fabric *s* fabrica *f*; (*piece of cloth*) textile *n*

fabricate *vt* fabricare, struĕre; (*fig*) fingĕre

fabrication *s* fabricatio *f*; (*fig*) mendacium *n*

fabulous *adj* fictus, commenticius; **—ly** ficte

face *s* facies *f*, os *n*, vult·us -ūs *m*; **— to —** coram

face *vt* aspicĕre, intuēri; se opponĕre (*with dat*), obviam ire (*with dat*); obire; *vi* spectare, vergĕre; **to — about** (*mil*) signa convertĕre

facet *s* pars *f*

facetious *adj* facetus; **—ly** facete

facilitate *vt* facilius reddĕre

facility *s* facilitas *f*; opportunitas *f*

facing *adj* adversus, spectans

facsimile *s* imago *f*, exemplar *n*

fact *s* factum, verum *n*, res *f*; **as a matter of —** enimvero; **in —** vero, re ipsa; enim, etenim; **the — that** quod

faction *s* factio *f*

factory *s* officina, fabrica *f*

faculty *s* facultas, vis *f*; (*of university*) ordo *m*

fade *vi* marcescĕre, deflorescĕre, palescĕre

fail *vt* (*to disappoint*) relinquĕre, deserĕre, deficĕre; *vi* succumbĕre, concidĕre, cadĕre; (*com*) decoquĕre, foro cedĕre

fail *s* **without —** certo, plane, omnino

failing *s* (*deficiency*) defect·us ūs *m*; (*fault*) culpa *f*, delictum, vitium *n*; (*disappointment*) frustratio *f*; (*ceasing*) remissio *f*

failure *s* defectio *f*, defect·us -ūs *m*; (*fault*) culpa *f*, delictum *n*

faint *adj* (*weary*) defessus; (*drooping*) languidus; (*of sight, smell, etc.*) hebes; (*of sound*) surdus; (*of color*) pallidus; (*of courage*) timidus; **—ly** languide; timide

faint *vi* collabi, intermori, (animo) linqui

fainthearted *adj* timidus, imbellis, ignavus

faintness *s* (*of impression*) levitas *f*; (*of body*) languor *m*

fair *adj* (*in appearance*) formosus,

pulcher; (*of complexion*) candidus; (*of hair*) flavus; (*of weather*) serenus; (*of wind*) secundus; (*impartial*) aequus; (*of ability*) mediocris; **— and square** sine fuco ac fallaciis; **—ly** aeque, juste; (*moderately*) mediocriter

fair *s* nundinae *f pl*

fairness *s* (*of complexion*) candor *m*; (*justice*) aequitas *f*

fairy *s* nympha *f*

faith *s* (*trust*) fides *f*; religio *f*; **to have — in** credĕre (*with dat*), confidĕre (*with dat*)

faithful *adj* fidelis, fidus; **—ly** fideliter

faithfulness *s* fidelitas, integritas *f*

faithless *adj* infidus, infidelis, perfidus; **—ly** perfide

falcon *s* falco *m*

fall *s* cas·us -ūs, laps·us -ūs *m*; (*season*) autumnus *m*

fall *vi* cadĕre, concidĕre, labi; (*to die*) occidĕre; (*to abate*) decrescĕre; (*violently*) corruĕre; **to — apart** dilabi; **to — at** accidĕre ad (*with acc*); **to — back** recidĕre; (*to retreat*) pedem referre; **to — down** decidĕre; concidĕre; **to — forwards** procidĕre, prolabi; **to — foul of** incurrĕre; **to — in(to)** incidĕre; **to — in with** (*to meet*) incidĕre; (*to agree*) congruĕre; **to — in love with** amare, adamare; **to — off** (*fig*) in deterius mutari; **to — out with** (*to have a disagreement with*) dissedĕre; dissentire ab (*with abl*); **to — short of** non contingĕre; **to — sick** in morbum incidĕre; **to — to** (*of inheritances, etc.*) obvenire (*with dat*); **to — under** succumbĕre; (*to be reckoned*) pertinēre; (*to become subjected to*) pati; **to — upon** incidĕre ad (*with acc*); (*to assail*) incidĕre in (*with acc*), ingruĕre in (*with acc*)

fallacious *adj* fallax, captiosus; **—ly** fallaciter

fallacy *s* captio *f*

fallible *adj* errori obnoxius

fallow *adj* (*of land*) novalis; **to lie — cessare**

false *adj* falsus, fictus; **—ly** falso

falsehood *s* mendacium *n*

falsify *vt* supponĕre, corrumpĕre; (*documents*) vitiare, interlinĕre

falter *vi (to stammer)* haesitare; *(to totter)* titubare

fame *s* fama *f*, nomen *n*

famed *adj* clarus, illustris

familiar *adj* familiaris, notus; intimus; **—ly** familiariter

familiarity *s* familiaritas, consuetudo *f*, us·us ·ūs *m*

familiarize *vt* assuefacěre

family *s* familia, dom·us ·ūs, gens *f*, genus *n*

family *adj* familiaris; *(of home)* domesticus; *(relating to race)* gentilicus

famine *s* fames *f*

famished *adj* famelicus; fame confectus

famous *adj* clarus, celeber, inclitus; **—ly** praeclare, insigniter

fan *s* flabellum *n*; *(admirer)* fautor *m*; *(winnowing)* vannus *f*

fan *vt* ventilare; *(fire)* accenděre; *(fig)* excitare, inflammare

fanatic *adj* fanaticus; **—ly** fanatice

fanaticism *s* furor religiosus *m*

fancied *adj* opinatus

fanciful *adj (capricious)* inconstans, levis; *(imagined)* commenticius

fancy *s* opinio, imaginatio *f*; *(caprice)* libido *f*; *(liking)* prolubium *n*; *(faculty)* phantasia *f*

fancy *vt* imaginari

fang *s* dens *m*

fantastic *adj* vanus; monstruosus

far *adj* longinquus, remotus

far *adv* procul, longe; **as — as** quantum, quatenus; tenus *(with abl)*; **by — longe, multo; — and near** longe lateque; **— be it from me to say** equidem dicěre nolim; **— off** procul; **so — hactenus; thus — hactenus**

farce *s* mimus *m*

farcical *adj* mimicus; **—ly** mimice

fare *s (food)* cibus, vict·us ·ūs *m*; *(money)* vectura *f*, portorium *n*

fare *vi* agěre, se habere

farewell *interj* vale!; salve!

farm *s* fundus *m*, praedium *n*

farm *vt (to till)* arare, colěre; *(taxes)* rediměre; **to — out** locare

farmer *s* agricola, colonus *m*; *(of revenues)* publicanus *m*

farming *s* agricultura *f*; res rustica *f*

farsighted *adj* providus

farther *adj* ulterior

farther *adv* longius, ulterius, ultra

farthermost *adj* remotissimus, ultimus

farthest *adj* ultimus, extremus

fasces *n* fasces *m pl*

fascinate *vt* fascinare

fascination *s* fascinatio *f*, fascinum *n*

fashion *s (form)* forma, figura *f*; *(manner)* mos, modus, rit·us ·ūs *m*; *(custom)* consuetudo *f*, us·us ·ūs *m*

fashion *vt* formare, fabricare, effingěre

fashionable *adj* elegans, concinnus; **it is — in usu est**

fashionably *adv* ad morem; eleganter

fast *adj (swift)* celer; *(firm)* firmus, stabilis; *(tight)* astrictus; *(shut)* occlusus

fast *adv* celeriter; firmiter

fast *s* jejunium *n*

fast *vi* jejunare, cibo abstinēre

fasten *vt* affigěre, astringěre; **to — down** defigěre; **to — to** annectěre, impingěre; **to — together** configěre, colligare; **vi to — upon** arripěre

fastening *s* colligatio *f*, vinculum *n*

fastidious *adj* fastidiosus, delicatus, elegans, morosus; **—ly** fastidiose, morose

fasting *s* jejunium *n*, abstinentia *f*

fat *adj* pinguis, obsesus; *(productive)* fertilis

fat *s* adeps *m & f*, lardum *n*

fatal *adj* fatalis; exitialis, funebris; **—ly** fataliter; funeste

fatality *s* fatum *n*; *(misfortune)* infortunium *n*

fate *s* fatum *n*, sors *f*

fated *adj* fatalis

Fates *s* Parcae *f pl*

father *s* pater *m*; **— of the family** paterfamilias *m*

fatherhood *s* paternitas *f*

father-in-law *s* socer *m*

fatherless *adj* orbus

fatherly *adj* paternus, patrius

fathom *s* ulna *f*

fathom *vt* exputare

fathomless *adj* profundissimus

fatigue *s* (de)fatigatio, lassitudo *f*

fatigue *vt* (de)fatigare, delassare

fatigued *adj* (de)fatigatus, (de)fessus

fatten *vt* saginare, farcire; *vi* pinguescěre

fattening *s* saginatio *f*

fatty *adj* pinguis

fatuous *adj* fatuus, insulsus

fault *s* culpa *f*, delictum, vitium *n*, error *m*; *(in writing)* mendum *n*; **to find — with** vituperare, carpěre, incusare

faultless *adj* integer, perfectus; *(corrected)* emendatus

faulty *adj* vitiosus; mendosus

faun *s* faunus *m*

favor *s* favor *m*, gratia *f*; *(goodwill)* benevolentia *f*; *(good turn)* beneficium *n*; *(present)* munus *n*

favor *vt* favěre *(with dat)*, secundare

favorable *adj* prosperus, secundus; commodus, idoneus; benignus, propitius

favorably *adv* fauste, feliciter, benigne; opportune

favorite *adj* dilectus, gratus

favorite *s* deliciae *f pl*

favoritism *s* indulgentia *f*; iniquitas *f*

fawn *s* hinnuleus *m*

fawn *vi* **to — on** *or* **upon** adulari

fawning *adj* blandus, adulatorius; **—ly** blande, adulatorie

fawning *s* adulatio *f*

fear *s* timor, met·us ·ūs *m*, formido *f*

fear *vt & vi* timēre, metuěre, verēri

fearful *adj* timidus, pavidus; *(terrible)* dirus, terribilis; **—ly** timide

fearless *adj* impavidus, intrepidus; **—ly** impavide, intrepide

feasibility *s* possibilitas *f*

feasible *adj* efficiendus, possibilis

feast *s* (*banquet*) convivium *n*, epulae *f pl*; *(holy day)* dies festus *m*

feast *vt* pascĕre; *vi* epulari, convivari

feat *s* facinus, factum *n*

feather *s* penna *f*; *(downy)* pluma *f*

feather *vt* to **— one's nest** opes accumulare

feathered *adj* pennatus; plumosus

feathery *adj* plumeus, plumosus

feature *s* lineamentum *n*; *(fig)* proprietas *f*, proprium *n*

February *s* (mensis) Februarius *m*

federal *adj* foederatus; rei publicae (*genit*)

federalize *vt* confoederare

federation *s* confoederatio *f*

fee *s* merces *f*

feeble *adj* infirmus, debilis; **to grow —** languescĕre

feebly *adv* infirme, languide

feed *vt* (*animals*) pascĕre; *(to nourish)* alĕre; *(fig)* (*of streams, etc.*) servire (*with dat*); *vi* pasci; **to — on** vesci (*with abl*)

feed *s* pabulum *n*

feel *vt* sentire; (*with hand*) tangĕre, tractare; **to — pain** dolore affici; **to — pity for** misereri (*with genit*); *vi* to **— happy** gaudĕre; **to — sad** maestus esse

feel *s* tact·us -ūs *m*

feeling *s* (*touch*) tact·us -ūs *m*; (*sensibility*) sens·us -ūs *m*; (*emotion*) affect·us -ūs *m*; (*taste*) judicium *n*; (*pity*) miseratio *f*

feign *vt* fingĕre, dissimulare, mentiri

feint *s* simulatio *f*

felicitation *s* congratulatio *f*

felicitous *adj* felix; **—ly** feliciter

felicity *s* felicitas *f*

feline *adj* fele(e)us

fell *adj* atrox, saevus, crudelis

fell *vt* (*trees*) caedĕre; (*person*) sternĕre

fellow *s* socius, aequalis *m*

felon *s* scelestus, sceleratus *m*

felonious *adj* scelestus, sceleratus

felony *s* scelus *n*

felt *s* coacta *n pl*

female *adj* muliebris

female *s* femina *f*

feminine *adj* muliebris, femineus; (*gram*) femininus

fence *s* saepes *f*, saepimentum *n*

fence *vt* saepire; **to — off** intersaepire; *vi* batuĕre

fencing *s* ludus gladiatorius *m*

fend *vt* to **— off** arcĕre; *vi* to **— for oneself** sibi providĕre, sibi consulĕre

ferment *s* fermentum *n*; (*fig*) aest·us -ūs *m*

ferment *vt* fermentare; excitare; *vi* fermentari; (*fig*) fervēre

fermentation *s* fermentatio *f*

fern *s* filix *f*

ferocious *adj* ferox, truculentus, saevus, atrox; **—ly** truculente

ferocity *s* ferocitas, saevitia *f*

ferret *vt* to **— out** eruĕre

ferry *s* traject·us -ūs *m*

ferry *vt* trajicĕre, transvehĕre

ferryboat *s* scapha, cymba *f*

ferryman *s* portitor *m*

fertile *adj* fertilis, fecundus

fertility *s* fertilitas, ubertas *f*

fertilize *vt* fecundare

fervent *adj* fervidus, ardens; **—ly** ardenter, vehementer

fervid *adj* fervidus; **—ly** fervide

fervor *s* fervor, ardor *m*

fester *vi* suppurare, ulcerari

festival *s* dies festus *m*, sollemne *n*

festive *adj* festus

festivity *s* sollemnia *n pl*; (*gaiety*) festivitas *f*

fetch *vt* adducĕre, afferre, arcessĕre

fetid *adj* foetidus, graveolens

feud *s* simultas, inimicitia, lis *f*

fever *s* febris *f*; **to have a — be**brire

feverish *adj* febriculosus

few *adj* pauci; **a — aliquot**; **in a — words** paucis, breviter

fiasco *s* calamitas *f*

fiber *s* fibra *f*

fibrous *adj* fibratus

fickle *adj* inconstans, mobilis, instabilis

fiction *s* fictio *f*, commentum *n*; fabula *f*

fictitious *adj* fictus, commenticius; **—ly** ficte

fiddle *s* fides *f*

fiddle *vi* fide ludĕre

fiddler *s* fidicen *m*

fidelity *s* fidelitas, constantia *f*

fidget *vi* trepidare

fidgety *adj* inquietus

field *s* ager *m*; (*plowed*) arvum *n*; (*mil*) acies *f*, campus *m*; (*grassy*) pratum *n*; (*of grain*) seges *f*; (*sphere*) area *f*, locus, campus *m*

fieldpiece *s* tormentum *n*

fiend *s* inimicus *m*; diabolus *m*

fiendish *adj* diabolicus

fierce *adj* atrox, saevus, vehemens; **—ly** atrociter, saeve, vehementer

fierceness *s* atrocitas, saevitia, ferocitas *f*

fiery *adj* igneus; (*fig*) ardens, fervidus

fife *s* tibia *f*

fifteen *adj* quindecim; **— times** quindecies

fifteenth *adj* quintus decimus

fifth *adj* quintus; **for the — time** quintum, quinto

fifth *s* quinta pars *f*

fiftieth *adj* quinquagesimus

fifty *adj* quinquaginta

fig *s* ficus *f*

fight *s* pugna *f*, proelium *n*; (*struggle*) contentio, luctatio *f*

fight *vt* pugnare cum (*with abl*); **to — it out** decernĕre, depugnare; *vi* pugnare, dimicare; (*in battle*) proeliari; (*with sword*) digladiari; **to — hand to hand** cominus pugnare

figment *s* commentum *n*

figurative *adj* translatus, assumptus; **—ly** per translationem, tropice

figure *s* figura, forma, imago *f*; (*of speech*) tropus *m*, translatio *f*; (*in art*) signum *n*

figure *vt* figurare, formare; putare, opinari

figured *adj* sigillatus

filament *s* filum *n*, fibra *f*

filbert *s* nux avellana *f*

file *s* (*tool*) lima *f*; (*for papers*) scapus *m*; (*row*) ordo *m*, agmen *n*

file *vt* limare; (*papers*) in scapo condēre; *vi* to — **off** (*mil*) decurrēre

filial *adj* pius

filigree *s* diatreta *n pl*

filings *s* scobis *f*

fill *vt* complēre, implēre; (*office*) fungi (*with abl*); to — **out** implēre; to — **up** explēre, complēre, supplēre

fill *s* satietas *f*

fillip *s* talitrum *n*

filly *s* equula *f*

film *s* membranula *f*

filmy *adj* membranaceus; (*fig*) caliginosus

filter *s* colum *n*

filter *vt* percolare; *vi* percolari

filtering *s* percolatio *f*

filth *s* sordes, colluvies *f*, squalor *m*

filthiness *s* foeditas *f*, squalor *m*; (*fig*) obscenitas *f*

filthy *adj* sordidus, spurcus; (*fig*) obscenus

filtration *s* percolatio *f*

fin *s* pinna *f*

final *adj* ultimus, postremus, extremus; **—ly** denique, tandem; postremo

finance *s* (*private*) res familiaris *f*; (*public*) aerarium *n*, ratio aeraria *f*, vectigalia *n pl*

financial *adj* aerarius

find *vt* invenire, reperire; (*to hit upon*) offendēre; to — **out** comperire, cognoscēre

fine *adj* (*thin*) subtilis, tenuis; (*of gold*) purus; (*handsome*) bellus, elegans; (*of weather*) serenus; **—ly** subtiliter

fine *s* mul(c)ta *f*, damnum *n*

fine *vt* mul(c)tare

finery *s* ornat·us -ūs *m*

finesse *s* astutia *f*, argutiae *f pl*

finger *s* digitus *m*; (*of glove*) digitale *n*

finger *vt* tractare

finish *vt* conficēre, perficēre; (*to put an end to*) terminare; to — **off** conficēre; peragēre; *vi* desinēre

finish *s* finis *m*; (*in art*) perfectio *f*

finite *adj* finitus, circumscriptus

fire *s* ignis *m*; (*conflagration*) incendium *n*; (*of artillery*) conject·us -ūs *m*; (*fig*) fervor, ardor, impet·us -ūs *m*; **by — and sword** ferro ignique; **to be on —** flagrare; to catch — flammam concipēre; to set on — incendēre

fire *vt* accendēre, incendēre; (*fig*) in-

flammare; (*missile*) jaculari; (*to dismiss*) dimittēre

firefly *s* elater noctilucus *m*

fireplace *s* focus, caminus *m*

fireproof *adj* ignibus impervius

fireside *s* focus *m*

firewood *s* lignum *n*

firm *adj* firmus, solidus; constans; **to be — persevere; to stand —** perstare; **—ly** firme, firmiter; solide; constanter

firm *s* societas *f*

firmament *s* firmamentum *n*

firmness *s* firmitas, constantia *f*

first *adj* primus; (*of two*) prior

first *adv* primum; **at —** primo; **— of all** imprimis

firstborn *adj* primogenitus

firstfruits *s* primitiae *f pl*

fiscal *adj* aerarius, fiscalis

fish *s* piscis *m*

fish *vi* piscari; (*fig*) expiscari

fisherman *s* piscator *m*

fishing *s* piscat·us -ūs *m*, piscatio *f*

fish market *s* forum piscarium *n*

fish pond *s* piscina *f*

fishy *adj* piscosus

fissure *s* fissura, rima *f*

fist *s* pugnus *m*

fit *s* (*of anger, etc.*) impet·us -ūs *m*; (*med*) access·us -ūs *m*; convulsio *f*; (*whim*) libido *f*; **by —s and starts** carptim

fit *adj* aptus, idoneus; habilis; (*becoming*) decens; (*ready*) paratus

fit *vt* accommodare; (*to apply*) applicare; (*to furnish*) instruēre; *vi* (*fig*) convenire

fitful *adj* mutabilis, inconstans

fitness *s* convenientia *f*; (*of persons*) habilitas *f*

fitting *adj* decens, idoneus; **it is —** convenit, decet

five *adj* quinque; **— times** quinquies

fix *vt* (*to repair*) reficēre; resarcire; (*to fasten*) figēre, firmare; (*the eyes*) intendēre; (*time*) dicēre; *vi* **to — upon** inhaerēre (*with dat*)

fixed *adj* firmus, fixus; certus; **— on** (*intent upon*) intentus (*with dat*)

fixture *s* affixum *n*

fizz *vi* sibilare

flabbiness *s* mollitia *f*

flabby *adj* flaccidus, flaccus; (*drooping*) marcidus

flaccid *adj* flaccidus

flag *s* vexillum *n*

flagrant *adj* impudens, apparens, nefarius

flail *s* pertica, tribula *f*

flake *s* squama *f*; (*of snow*) nix *f*

flaky *adj* squameus

flame *s* flamma *f*

flame *vi* flammare, flagrare; **to — up** scintillare; (*fig*) exardescēre

flank *s* (*of animal*) ilia *n pl*; (*mil*) lat·us *n*; **on the — a latere**

flank *vt* tegēre latus (*with genit*)

flap *s* (*of dress*) lacinia *f*

flap *vt* plaudēre (*with abl*); *vi* (*to hang loosely*) fluitare

flare *s* flamma *f*, fulgor *m*

flare *vi* flagrare, exardescēre

flash *s* fulgor *m*; (*of fire*) coruscatio *f*; (*of lightning*) fulmen *n*; — of wit sales *m pl*

flash *vi* fulgēre, coruscare, micare

flask *s* ampulla, laguncula *f*

flat *adj* (*level*) planus, aequus; (*not mountainous*) campester; (*on back*) supinus; (*on face*) pronus; (*insipid*) vapidus; (*fig*) frigidus, insulsus; to fall — (*fig*) frīgēre

flatness *s* planities *f*

flatten *vt* complanare, planum reddēre

flatter *vt* adulari (*with dat*), blandiri (*with dat*), assentari (*with dat*)

flatterer *s* adulator, assentator *m*

flattering *adj* adulans, blandus, adulatorius

flattery *s* adulatio *f*, blanditiae *f pl*

flaunt *vt* jactare; *vi* tumēre, gloriari

flaunting *adj* lautus, gloriosus

flaunting *s* jactatio *f*

flavor *s* sapor, gustat·us -ūs *m*

flavor *vt* imbuēre, condire

flaw *s* (*defect*) vitium *n*; (*chink*) rimula *f*

flawless *adj* emendatus

flax *s* linum *n*

flaxen *adj* lineus

flay *vt* deglubare

flea *s* pulex *m*

fleck *s* macula *f*

fledged *adj* plumatus

flee *vi* fugēre; to — away aufugēre; to — back refugēre; to — to confugēre ad *or* in (*with acc*)

fleece *s* vellus *n*

fleece *vt* tondēre; (*fig*) spoliare

fleecy *adj* laniger

fleet *s* classis *f*

fleet *adj* celer; (*winged*) volucer; (*fig*) fugax

fleeting *adj* fugax; (*flowing*) fluxus

flesh *s* caro *f*; in the — vivus

fleshy *adj* carnosus

flexibility *s* flexibilitas *f*; (*fig*) mollitia *f*

flexible *adj* flexibilis, lentus; (*fig*) exorabilis

flicker *vi* coruscare

flickering *adj* tremulus

flight *s* (*flying*) volat·us -ūs *m*; (*escape*) fuga *f*, effugium *n*; (*covey*) grex *m*; (*of stairs*) scala *f*; to put to — fugare; to take to — aufugēre, terga vertēre

flighty *adj* levis

flimsy *adj* nimis subtilis, praetenuis; (*fig*) frivolus

flinch *vi* retrocedēre, tergiversari; (*to start*) absilire

fling *vt* jacēre, conjicēre; to — away abjicēre; to — down dejicēre; to — off rejicēre; to — open vehementer aperire

fling *s* jact·us -ūs *m*

flint *s* silex *m & f*

flinty *adj* siliceus

flippancy *s* petulantia *f*

flippant *adj* petulans; temere loquens; —ly temere ac leviter

flirt *s* lupus *m*, lupa *f*

flirt *vi* ludēre, lascivire

flirtation *s* amores *m pl*

flit *vi* volitare

float *s* (*raft*) rates *f*; (*on fishing line*) cortex *m*

float *vt* (*to launch*) demittēre; *vi* fluitare, (in)natare; (*in air*) volitare

flock *s* grex *m*; in —s gregatim

flock *vi* concurrēre, convenire, coire

floe *s* fragmentum glaciei *n*

flog *vt* verberare

flogging *s* verberatio *f*, verbera *n pl*

flood *s* (*deluge*) diluvies *f*; (*of river*) torrens *m*; (*tide*) access·us -ūs *m*; (*fig*) flumen *n*

floor *s* (*story of building*) tabulatum *n*; (*on the ground*) solum; (*paved*) pavimentum *n*

floor *vt* (*to throw down*) sternēre

flooring *s* contabulatio *f*

floral *adj* floreus

florid *adj* floridus

flotilla *s* classicula *f*

flounce *s* fimbria *f*

flounder *vi* volutari; (*in speech*) haesitare

flour *s* farina *f*; (*finest*) pollen *m*

flourish *vt* vibrare; (*to sound*) canēre; *vi* florēre, virēre; (*mus*) praeludēre

flourish *s* ornamentum *n*; (*of style*) calamistri *m pl*; (*mus*) praelusio *f*; (*of trumpet*) cant·us -ūs *m*

flout *vt* deridēre, contumeliis afficēre, aspernari

flow *vi* fluēre; (*of tide*) affluēre, accedēre

flow *s* fluxio *f*, laps·us -ūs *m*; (*of tide*) access·us -ūs *m*

flower *s* flos *m*; (*fig*) (*the best*) flos *m*; (*of army*) robur *n*; (*of age*) adulescentia *f*

flower *vi* florescēre

flowery *adj* floreus; floridus

fluctuate *vi* fluctuari; (*fig*) jactare

fluctuation *s* fluctuatio *f*; (*fig*) mutatio *f*

flue *s* cuniculus fornacis *m*

fluency *s* copia verborum, volubilitas linguae *f*

fluent *adj* volubilis; (*eloquent*) disertus; —ly volubiliter

fluid *adj* fluidus, liquidus

fluid *s* fluidum *n*, fluor *m*

fluke *s* (*of anchor*) dens *m*; (*luck*) fortuitum *n*

flurry *s* commotio *f*, tumult·us -ūs *m*

flurry *vt* perturbare, inquietare

flush *s* rubor *m*

flush *vi* erubescēre

fluster *vt* turbare, inquietare

flute *s* tibia *f*; (*in architecture*) stria *f*

flutist *s* tibicen *m*

flutter *s* volitatio *f*, tremor *m*; (*fig*) trepidatio *f*

flutter *vi* (*of the heart*) palpitare; (*of bird*) volitare; (*with alarm*) trepidare

flux *s* flux·us -ūs *m*; to be in a state of — fluēre

fly *s* musca *f*

fly *vi* volare; (*to flee*) fugēre; to — apart dissilire; to — off avolare;

to — open dissilire; to — out provolare; to — up subvolare

flying adj volatilis, volucer

foal s pullus m; (of asses) asellus m; (of horses) equulus m

foal vi parĕre

foam s spuma f

foam vi spumare; (to boil) exaestuare

foamy adj spumans; spumeus, spumosus

focus vt (the mind) intendĕre

fodder s pabulum n

fodder vt pabulum praebĕre (with dat)

foe s (public) hostis m; (private) inimicus m

fog s caligo, nebula f

foggy adj caliginosus, nebulosus

foible s vitium n, error m

foil s (for fencing) rudis f; (leaf of metal) lamina f; (very thin) bractea f; (contrast) repulsa f

foil vt eludĕre; repellĕre

fold s sin·us -ūs m, plica f; (wrinkle) ruga f; (for sheep) ovile n; (for cattle) stabulum n

fold vt plicare, complicare

foliage s frons f, folia n pl

folio s liber maximae formae m

folk s homines m pl

follow vt sequi; (close) instare (with dat), assectari; (a calling) facĕre; (instructions) parēre (with dat); (road) pergĕre; (to understand) intellegĕre; to — out exsequi, prosequi; to — up subsequi

follower s sector m; (of teacher) auditor m

following adj sequens; posterus, proximus

folly s stultitia, insipientia f

foment vt fovēre

fond adj amans, studiosus; ineptus; to be — of amare; —ly amanter; (foolishly) inepte

fondle vt mulcēre, fovēre

fondness s caritas f, studium n

food s cibus m

fool s stultus, fatuus m; to make a — of ludificari; to play the — ineptire

fool vt ludificari

foolhardy adj temerarius

foolish adj stultus, fatuus, ineptus, stolidus; —ly stulte, inepte

foot s pes m; (of mountain) radix f; (of pillar) basis f; on — pedester

football s pila pedalis f

footing s locus m; (condition) stat·us -ūs m

footprint s vestigium n

foot soldier s pedes m

footstool s scabellum, scamnum n

fop s bellus homo m

foppish adj nitidus, delicatus

for prep (extent of time or space) render by acc; (price) render by genit or abl; (on behalf of) pro (with abl); (cause) causā (with genit), ob (with acc), propter (with acc); (after negatives) prae (with abl); (toward) erga (with acc)

for conj nam; enim

forage s pabulum n

forage vi pabulari, frumentari

foray s incursio f

forbear vi parcĕre (with dat), desistĕre

forbearance s patientia, indulgentia f

forbid vt vetare, prohibēre, interdicĕre

forbidding adj insuavis, odiosus

force s vis f; (law) man·us -ūs f; (mil) copiae f pl, impet·us -ūs m; in — validus

force vt cogĕre, impellĕre; (door, etc.) rumpĕre; to — down detrudĕre; to — out extrudĕre, extorquēre

forced adj (unnatural) arcessitus, quaesitus

forced march s magnum or maximum iter n

forceps s forceps m & f

forcible adj per vim factus; (of force) validus; (violent) vehemens; (weighty) gravis

forcibly adv per vim, vi; violenter; graviter

ford s vadum n

ford vt vado transire

fore adj anterior, prior

forearm s bracchium n

forearm vt praemunire; to be forearmed praecavēre

forebode vt (to foretell) portendĕre; (to be prescient of) praesagire

foreboding s portentum, praesagium n; (feeling) praesensio f

foreboding adj praesagus

forecast vt providēre, prospicĕre; praedicĕre

forecast s praedictio f

forecastle s prora f

foredoom vt praedestinare

forefather s atavus m; —s majores m pl

forefinger s digitus index m

forego vt abdicare, dimittĕre

foregoing adj prior, proximus

forehead s frons f

foreign adj externus, alienus, peregrinus

foreigner s peregrinus, advena m

foreknowledge s providentia f

foreman s procurator, villicus m

foremost adj primus, princeps

forenoon s antemeridianum tempus n; in the — ante meridiem

forensic adj forensis

fore part s prior pars f

forerunner s praenuntius, antecursor m

foresee vt providēre, praevidēre, prospicĕre

foreseeing adj providus

foresight s providentia, prudentia f; (precaution) provisio f

forest adj silvestris

forest s silva f

forestall vt occupare, anticipare

foretell vt praedicĕre, vaticinari

forethought s providentia f

forewarn vt praemonēre

forewarning s praemonit·us -ūs m

forfeit s multa, poena f, damnum n

forfeit *vt* mul(c)tari (*with abl*), amittĕre, perdĕre

forfeiture *s* damnum *n*, amissio *f*

forge *vt* fabricari, excudĕre; (*document*) subjicĕre; (*signature*) imitari; **to — money** adulterinos nummos cudĕre

forge *s* furnus fabrilis *m*

forged *adj* falsus, adulterinus

forger *s* fabricator *m*; (*of writings*) falsarius *m*; (*of money*) qui adulterinos nummos cudit

forgery *s* falsum *n*

forget *vt* oblivisci (*with genit*)

forgetful *adj* immemor, obliviosus

forgetfulness *s* oblivio *f*

forgive *vt* ignoscĕre (*with dat*), veniam dare (*with dat*); condonare

forgiveness *s* venia *f*

forgiving *adj* clemens

fork *s* furca *f*; (*of roads*) bivium *n*

forked *adj* bifurcus, bicornis

forlorn *adj* destitutus, derelictus

form *s* forma, figura *f*; **in due — rite**

form *vt* formare, fingĕre; (*to produce*) efficĕre

formal *adj* justus; nimis accuratus; **—ly** frigide ac nimis accurate

formality *s* rit·us -ūs *m*; **with due — rite**

formation *s* conformatio, forma, figura *f*; **in — (** *mil*) instructus

former *adj* prior; (*immediately preceding*) superior; antiquus, priscus; **the — ille; —ly** antehac, olim, quondam

formidable *adj* formidabilis

formidably *adv* formidolose

formless *adj* informis, rudis

formula *s* formula *f*, exemplar *n*

forsake *vt* deserĕre, derelinquĕre

forswear *vt* abjurare, repudiare

fort *s* castellum *n*

forth *adv* foras; (*of time*) inde; **and so —** et cetera

forthwith *adv* protinus, statim, extemplo

fortieth *adj* quadragesimus

fortification *s* munitio *f*, munimentum *n*

fortify *vt* munire

fortitude *s* fortitudo *f*

fortress *s* arx *f*, castellum *n*

fortuitous *adj* fortuitus; **—ly** fortuito

fortunate *adj* fortunatus, felix, prosperus; **—ly** feliciter

fortune *s* fortuna, felicitas *f*; (*estate*) opes *f pl*, res *f*, divitiae *f pl*; **to tell —s** hariolari

fortune-teller *s* fatidicus, sortilegus, astrologus *m*

forty *adj* quadraginta

forum *s* forum *n*

forward *adv* porro, prorsus, prorsum

forward *adj* (*person*) audax, protervus; anterior

forward *vt* (*letter*) perferre; (*cause*) adjuvare, promovēre

foster *vt* alĕre, fovēre, nutrire

foster brother *s* collacteus *m*

foster child *s* alumnus *m*, alumna *f*

foster father *s* altor, nutritor, educator *m*

foster mother *s* altrix, nutrix, educatrix *f*

foul *adj* (*dirty*) foedus, lutulentus, squalidus; (*ugly*) deformis; (*of language*) obscenus; (*of weather*) turbidus; **to fall —** of incurrēre in (*with acc*), inruēre in (*with acc*); **—ly** foede

foul *vt* foedare, inquinare

found *vt* condĕre, fundare, constituēre, instituēre

foundation *s* fundamentum *n*, substructio *f*

founder *s* conditor, fundator, auctor *m*

founder *vi* titubare, submergi

foundling *s* expositicius *m*, exposititia *f*

fountain *s* fons *m*

fountainhead *s* caput fontis *n*

four *adj* quattuor; **— each** quaterni; **— times** quater; **— years** quadriennium *n*; **on all —s** repens

fourfold *adj* quadruplex, quadruplus

fourscore *adj* octoginta

fourteen *adj* quattuordecim

fourteenth *adj* quartus decimus

fourth *adj* quartus; **—ly** quarto

fourth *s* quadrans *n*, quarta pars *f*; **three —s** tres partes *f pl*

fowl *s* avis, volucris *f*; (*domestic*) gallina *f*

fox *s* vulpes *f*; **an old — (** *fig*) veterator *m*

fraction *s* pars exigua *f*

fracture *s* fractura *f*

fracture *vt* frangĕre

fragile *adj* fragilis; (*fig*) caducus

fragility *s* fragilitas *f*

fragment *s* fragmentum *n*

fragrance *s* odor *m*

fragrant *adj* suaveolens, odorus; **—ly** suavi odore

frail *adj* fragilis; caducus, infirmus

frailty *s* fragilitas, debilitas *f*; (*moral*) error *m*

frame *s* (*of buildings, etc.*) compages *f*; (*of body*) figura *f*; (*of bed*) sponda *f*; (*of mind*) habit·us -ūs *m*

frame *vt* fabricari; (*to contrive*) moliri; (*a picture*) in forma includĕre; (*a document*) componĕre

France *s* Gallia *f*

franchise *s* civitas *f*, suffragium *n*

frank *adj* candidus, sincerus, simplex; **—ly** candide, aperte

frankness *s* libertas, simplicitas, ingenuitas *f*

frantic *adj* amens, furiosus, furens; **—ally** furenter

fraternal *adj* fraternus; **—ly** fraterne

fraternity *s* fraternitas *f*; (*association*) sodalitas *f*

fratricide *s* (*doer*) fratricida *m*; (*deed*) fratris parricidium *n*

fraud *s* fraus *f*, dolus *m*; (*person*) dolus malus *m*

fraudulence *s* fraus *f*

fraudulent *adj* fraudulentus, dolosus; **—ly** fraudulenter, dolo malo

fraught *adj* plenus

fray *s* pugna *f*; (*brawl*) rixa *f*

freak *s* (*whim*) libido *f*; monstrum *n*

freckle *s* lentigo *f*

freckled *adj* lentiginosus

free *adj* liber; (*disengaged*) vacuus, otiosus; (*generous*) liberalis; (*from duty*) immunis; (*unencumbered*) expeditus; (*in speech*) liber, candidus; **—ly** libere; (*of one's own accord*) sponte, ultro; (*frankly*) aperte; (*generously*) large, copiose

free *vt* liberare; (*slave*) manumittĕre; (*son*) emancipare

freeborn *adj* ingenuus

freedman *s* libertus *m*

freedom *s* libertas *f*; (*from duty*) immunitas *f*

freehold *s* praedium liberum *n*

freeholder *s* dominus *m*

freeman *s* liber *m*

free will *s* voluntas *f*, liberum arbitrium *n*; **of one's own** — suā sponte, ultro, arbitrio suo

freeze *vt* congelare, glaciare; *vi* consistĕre, rigescĕre; **it is freezing** gelat

freezing *adj* gelidus

freight *s* onus *n*, vectura *f*

freight *vt* onerare

French *adj* Gallicus; **in** — Gallice; **the** — Galli *m pl*

Frenchman *s* Gallus *m*

frenzied *adj* furens, lymphatus

frenzy *s* furor *m*, insania *f*

frequency *s* crebritas, assiduitas *f*

frequent *adj* creber, frequens; **—ly** crebro, frequenter, saepe

frequent *vt* frequentare

frequenter *s* frequentator *m*

fresco *s* opus tectorium *n*

fresh *adj* (*new*) recens, novus; (*cool*) frigidulus; (*not tired*) integer; (*forward*) protervus; (*green*) viridis; **—ly** recenter

freshen *vt* recreare, renovare; *vi* (*of wind*) increbrescĕre

freshman *s* tiro *m*

freshman *adj* novicius

freshness *s* novitas, viriditas *f*

fret *vi* dolēre, angi

fretful *adj* morosus, stomachosus; **—ly** morose, stomachose

fretted *adj* laqueatus

friction *s* frictio *f*, attrit·us -ūs *m*

friend *s* amicus *m*, amica *f*, familiaris *m & f*; (*of a thing*) amator *m*

friendless *adj* amicorum inops, desertus

friendliness *s* benevolentia, comitas, affabilitas *f*

friendly *adj* amicus, benevolus, comis; **in a** — **manner** amice

friendship *s* amicitia *f*

frieze *s* zoophorus *m*

fright *s* pavor, terror *m*

frighten *vt* (per)terrēre; **to** — **away** absterrēre

frightful *adj* terribilis, terrificus; **—ly** foede

frigid *adj* frigidus; **—ly** frigide

frigidity *s* frigiditas *f*

frills *s* segmenta *n pl*; (*rhet*) calamistri *m pl*

fringe *s* fimbria *f*, cirrus *m*; (*fig*) limbus *m*

frisk *vt* scrutari; *vi* lascivire, exsilire

fritter *vt* **to** — **away** conterĕre, comminuĕre, dissipare

frivolity *s* levitas *f*, nugae *f pl*

frivolous *adj* levis, frivolus, inanis; **—ly** inaniter

fro *adv* **to and** — huc illuc, ultro citroque

frock *s* palla, stola *f*

frog *s* rana *f*

frolic *s* lascivia *f*, ludus *m*

frolic *vi* exsultare, hilarescĕre

from *prep* a *or* ab (*with abl*); de (*with abl*); e *or* ex (*with abl*); (*cause*) ob (*with acc*); — **above** desuper; — **abroad** peregre; — **day to day** de die in diem; — **time to time** interdum, passim; — **within** intus; — **without** extrinsecus

front *s* frons *f*; (*mil*) acies *f*, primum agmen *n*; (*fig*) impudentia *f*; **in** — a fronte, adversus; **in** — **of** pro (*with abl*)

front *adj* prior

frontier *s* limes *m*, confinia *n pl*

frost *s* gelu *n*, pruina *f*

frostbitten *adj* praeustus, adustus

frosty *adj* gelidus, glacialis

froth *s* spuma *f*

froth *vi* spumare, spumas agĕre

frothy *adj* spumeus, spumosus

frown *s* contractio frontis *f*

frown *vi* frontem contrahĕre *or* adducĕre

frozen *adj* conglaciatus, gelatus, gelu rigens

frugal *adj* parcus, frugi (*indecl*); **—ly** frugaliter, parce

frugality *s* parsimonia, frugalitas *f*

fruit *s* fruct·us -ūs *m*, frux *f*; (*of tree*) mala *n pl*; **—s of the earth** fruges *f pl*

fruitful *adj* fructuosus, fecundus, fertilis; **—ly** fecunde, feraciter

fruitfulness *s* fecunditas, fertilitas, ubertas *f*

fruitless *adj* sterilis; (*fig*) irritus; **—ly** frustra

fruit tree *s* pomus *f*

frustrate *vt* frustrari; (*to baffle*) decipĕre

frustration *s* frustratio *f*

fry *s* (*dish of things fried*) frixa *f*

fry *vt* frigĕre

frying pan *s* sartago *f*

fuel *s* fomes *m*, materia *f*

fugitive *adj* fugitivus

fugitive *s* profugus, transfuga, fugitivus *m*; (*from abroad*) extorris *m*

fulcrum *s* (*of a lever*) pressio *f*

fulfil *vt* explēre, exsequi, perficĕre

fulfilment *s* exsecutio, peractio, perfectio *f*

full *adj* plenus; (*filled up*) expletus; (*entire*) integer, solidus; (*satiated*) satur; (*of dress*) fusus; **—ly** plene, funditus, penitus

full moon *s* plenilunium *n*

fumble *vi* haesitare
fume *s* fumus, vapor, halit·us -ūs *m*
fume *vi* irasci
fumigate *vt* fumigare, suffire
fumigation *s* suffit·us -ūs *m*
fun *s* jocus *m*, ludibrium *n*
function *s* munus, officium *n*
function *vi* munus implēre
functionary *s* magistrat·us -ūs *m*
fund *s* copia *f*, pecuniae *f pl*
fundamental *adj* fundamentalis, primus; **—ly** penitus, funditus
funeral *s* funus *n*, exsequiae *f pl*
funeral *adj* funebris
funereal *adj* funereus, lugubris
fungus *s* fungus *m*
funnel *s* infundibulum *n*
funny *adj* ridiculus, jocularis
fur *s* villi *m pl*, pellis *m*
furious *adj* furiosus, furens; **—ly** furiose, furenter
furl *vt* complicare; (*sail*) legēre
furlough *s* commeat·us -ūs *m*; **on —** in commeatu
furnace *s* fornax *f*
furnish *vt* suppeditare, ministrare; ornare, exornare, instruēre

furniture *s* supellex *f*
furrow *s* sulcus *m*
furry *adj* pelle insutus
further *adj* ulterior
further *adv* ultra, longius, ulterius
further *vt* promovēre, provehēre; (*to aid*) adjuvare
furtherance *s* progress·us -ūs *m*
furthermore *adv* insuper, porro, praeterea
furthest *adj* ultimus, extremus
furthest *adv* longissime
furtive *adj* furtivus; **—ly** furtim, furtive
fury *s* furor *m*
fuse *vt* fundēre; *vi* coalescēre
fusion *s* fusura *f*
fuss *s* strepit·us -ūs, tumult·us -ūs *m*
fuss *vi* sollicitari
fussy *adj* fastidiosus, importunus
futile *adj* futilis, inanis
futility *s* futilitas *f*
future *adj* futurus, posterus
future *s* futura *n pl*, posterum tempus *n*; **in the —** posthac
futurity *s* posteritas *f*

G

gab *s* garrulitas *f*
gab *vi* garrire
gable *s* fastigium *n*
gadfly *s* tabanus, oestrus *m*
gag *s* jocus *m*
gag *vt* os obstruēre (*with dat*)
gaiety *s* hilaritas *f*; nitor, splendor *m*
gaily *adv* hilare, festive
gain *s* quaest·us -ūs *m*, lucrum *n*
gain *vt* consequi, acquirēre, capēre; (*profit*) lucrari; (*victory*) reportare; (*case*) vincēre; **to — possession of** potiri (*with abl*)
gainful *adj* quaestuosus, lucrosus
gainsay *vt* contradicēre (*with dat*)
gait *s* incess·us -ūs *m*
gala *s* dies festus *m*
galaxy *s* orbis lacteus *m*
gale *s* ventus *m*
gall *s* fel *n*, bilis *f*
gall *vt* urēre
gallant *adj* fortis, animosus; (*to ladies*) officiosus; **—ly** fortiter
gallant *s* amator *m*
gallantry *s* virtus, fortitudo *f*; (*to ladies*) urbanitas *f*
galleon *s* navis oneraria *f*
gallery *s* portic·us -ūs *f*; (*open*) peristylium *n*; (*for pictures*) pinacotheca *f*
galley *s* navis longa, triremis *f*; (*kitchen*) culina *f*
Gallic *adj* Gallicus, Gallicanus
galling *adj* mordax
gallon *s* congius *m*
gallop *s* citatissimus curs·us -ūs *m*; **at a —** citato equo, admisso equo
gallop *vi* quadrupedare

gallows *s* patibulum *n*
gamble *vt* **to — away** ludēre, amittēre; *vi* aleā ludēre
gambler *s* aleator, lusor *m*
gambling *s* alea *f*
gambol *s* salt·us -ūs *m*
gambol *vi* lasciviēre, ludēre
game *s* ludus *m*; (*with dice*) alea *f*; (*quarry*) praeda *f*, ferae *f pl*; **to make — of** ludificari
gander *s* anser *m*
gang *s* grex *m*, caterva *f*
gangster *s* grassator *m*
gangway *s* forus *m*
gap *s* apertura, fissura, lacuna *f*, hiat·us -ūs *m*
gape *vi* hiare, dehiscēre
gaping *adj* hians, hiulcus, oscitans; (*fig*) stupidus
garb *s* vestit·us -ūs, habit·us -ūs *m*
garbage *s* quisquiliae *f pl*
garble *vt* vitiare, corrumpēre
garden *s* hortus *m*
gardener *s* hortulanus, olitor *m*
gardening *s* hortorum cult·us -ūs *m*
gargle *vi* gargarizare
gargling *s* gargarizatio *f*
garland *s* sertum *n*, corona *f*
garlic *s* alium *n*
garment *s* vestimentum *n*, vestit·us -ūs *m*
garner *s* horreum *n*
garnish *vt* decorare, ornare
garret *s* cenaculum *n*
garrison *s* praesidium *n*
garrison *vt* praesidio munire, praesidium collocare in (*with abl*), praesidium imponēre (*with dat*)

garrulity *s* garrulitas *f*

garrulous *adj* garrulus, loquax

garter *s* periscelis *f*

gas *s* spiritūs naturales *m pl*

gash *s* patens plaga *f*

gash *vt* caesim ferire

gasp *s* anhelit·us -ūs, singult·us -ūs *m*

gasp *vi* anhelare, singultare

gastric *adj* ad stomachum pertinens

gastronomy *s* gula *f*

gate *s* janua *f*, ostium *n*; (*of town*) porta *f*

gatekeeper *s* janitor *m*

gateway *s* porta *f*, postis *m*

gather *vt* (*to assemble*) congregare, colligĕre; (*fruit, etc.*) legĕre; (*to pluck*) decerpĕre, carpĕre; (*in logic*) concludĕre; (*to suspect*) suspicare; *vi* convenire, concurrĕre

gathering *s* convent·us -ūs *m*, congregatio *f*; collectio *f*

gaudily *adv* laute

gaudiness *s* lautitia *f*, ornat·us -ūs, nitor *m*

gaudy *adj* lautus, speciosus, splendidus

gauge *s* modulus *m*

gauge *vt* metiri

gaunt *adj* macer

gauntlet *s* manica *f*

gauze *s* coa *n pl*

gawky *adj* ineptus, stolidus

gay *adj* laetus, hilaris, festivus

gaze *s* conspect·us -ūs *m*; (*fixed look*) obtut·us -ūs *m*

gaze *vi* intuēri; **to —at** intuēri, adspectare, contemplari

gazelle *s* dorcas *f*

gazette *s* acta diurna *n pl*

gazetteer *s* itinerarium *n*

gear *s* instrumenta *n pl*, apparat·us -ūs *m*

gelatin *s* glutinum *n*

gelding *s* (*horse*) canterius *m*

gem *s* gemma *f*

gender *s* genus *n*

genealogical *adj* genealogicus

genealogy *s* genealogia *f*

general *adj* generalis; vulgaris, publicus, universus; **in — omnino**; **—ly** plerumque, fere; generatim

general *s* dux, imperator *m*

generalize *vi* in summam loqui

generalship *s* duct·us -ūs *m*; (*skill*) consilium *n*

generate *vt* generare, gignĕre

generation *s* generatio *f*; (*age*) aetas *f*, saeculum *n*

generic *adj* generalis

generosity *s* liberalitas, largitas *f*

generous *adj* liberalis, largus; **—ly** large, liberaliter

genesis *s* origo *f*

genial *adj* comis, benignus; **—ly** comiter, benigne

geniality *s* comitas, benignitas *f*

genitals *s* genitalia *n pl*, veretrum *n*

genitive *s* genitivus *m*

genius *s* ingenium *n*, indoles *f*; vir ingeniosus *m*; **of —** ingeniosus

genteel *adj* elegans, urbanus; **—ly** eleganter

gentile *adj* gentilicus, gentilis

gentile *s* gentilis *m*

gentility *s* nobilitas, elegantia *f*

gentle *adj* lenis, mitis, clemens; (*gradual*) mollis; (*thing*) lenis

gentleman *s* vir honestus, homo liberalis *m*

gentleness *s* lenitas, clementia *f*; (*tameness*) mansuetudo *f*

gently *adv* leniter, clementer, placide; (*gradually*) sensim

gentry *s* optimates *m pl*

genuine *adj* sincerus, purus, verus; **—ly** sincere, vere

genus *s* genus *n*

geographer *s* geographus *m*

geographical *adj* geographicus

geography *s* geographia *f*

geological *adj* geologicus

geologist *s* geologus *m*

geology *s* geologia *f*

geometrical *adj* geometricus

geometry *s* geometria *f*

germ *s* germen *n*

German *adj* Germanus

germane *adj* affinis

Germanic *adj* Germanicus

Germany *s* Germania *f*

germinate *vi* germinare

germination *s* germinat·us -ūs *m*

gesticulate *vi* gestus agĕre, gestu uti

gesture *s* gest·us -ūs, mot·us -ūs *m*

get *vt* nancisci, adipisci, consequi, acquirĕre; (*by entreaty*) impetrare; **to — back** recuperare; **to — down** depromĕre; **to — hold of** prehendĕre, occupare; **to — out** delēre, oblitterare; **to — rid of** amovēre, tollĕre; **to — the better of** superare; **to — together** colligĕre, cogĕre, congregare; *vi* (*to become*) fieri; (*to arrive at*) pervenire; **to — abroad** (*to spread*) palam fieri, emanare; **to — along** procedĕre; **to — away** aufugĕre; **to — back** revertĕre or reverti; **to — down** descendĕre; **to — in** pervenire; **to — off** aufugĕre, dimitti; **to — on** procedĕre, proficisci; (*to succeed*) bene succedĕre; **to — out** exire; (*e curru*) descendĕre; **to — over** transgredi; **to — together** congregari; **to — up** surgĕre; (*from sleep*) expergisci

ghastly *adj* luridus; (*shocking*) foedus

ghost *s* larva *f*, phantasma *n*; umbra *f*

ghostly *adj* spiritualis

giant *s* gigas *m*

gibberish *s* barbaricus sermo *m*

gibbet *s* furca *f*, patibulum *n*

gibe *s* sanna *f*

gibe *vt* illudĕre, subsannare

giblets *s* gigeria *n pl*, anseris trunculi *m pl*

giddiness *s* vertigo *f*

giddy *adj* vertiginosus; (*fig*) levis, inconsultus

gift *s* donum *n*; (*talent*) ingenium *n*

gifted *adj* (*endowed*) praeditus; ingeniosus

gig *s* (*carriage*) cisium *n*

gigantic *adj* ingens, immanis, prae-grandis

giggle *vi* summissim cachinnare

gild *vt* inaurare

gilding *s* (*art*) auratura *f*; (*gilded work*) aurum inductum *n*

gill *s* branchia *f*

gilt *adj* auratus

gin *s* junipero infectus spirit·us -ūs *m*

ginger *s* zinziberi *n* (*indecl*)

gingerly *adv* pedetemptim

giraffe *s* camelopardalis *f*

gird *vt* cingĕre; **to — oneself** cingi

girder *s* tignum *n*

girdle *s* cingulum *n*, zona *f*

girdle *vt* cingĕre

girl *s* puella, virgo *f*

girlhood *s* puellaris aetas *f*

girlish *adj* puellaris, virginalis

girth *s* (*of horse*) cingula *f*; amplitudo *f*, ambit·us -ūs *m*

gist *s* cardo *m*

give *vt* dare, donare; (*to deliver*) tradĕre; **to — away** donare; **to — back** reddĕre; **to — forth** emittĕre; **to — oneself up to** se addicĕre (*with dat*); **to — out** edĕre, emittĕre; nuntiare, proclamare; distribuĕre; **to — over** transferre; relinquere; **to — up** tradĕre; (*to betray*) prodĕre; (*to abandon*) dimittĕre; *vi* **to — in** (*to yield*) cedĕre; **to — way** (*mil*) pedem referre; (*to yield*) cedĕre; (*to comply*) obsequi

giver *s* donator *m*

giving *s* datio, largitio *f*

glacial *adj* glacialis

glacier *s* moles conglaciata *f*

glad *adj* laetus, contentus; **to be —** gaudēre; **—ly** libenter

gladden *vt* laetificare

glade *s* salt·us -ūs *m*

gladiator *s* gladiator *m*

gladness *s* gaudium *n*, laetitia *f*

glamorous *adj* venustus, nitidus; **to be —** nitēre

glamour *s* venustas *f*, nitor *m*

glance *s* aspect·us -ūs *m*

glance *vi* aspicĕre; **to — at** aspicĕre; **to — off** stringĕre

gland *s* glandula *f*

glare *s* fulgor *m*

glare *vi* fulgēre; torvis oculis aspicĕre; **to — at** torvis oculis aspicĕre *or* intuēri

glaring *adj* fulgens; manifestus

glass *s* vitrum *n*; (*for drinking*) calix vitreus *m*

glass *adj* vitreus

glassmaker *s* vitrarius *m*

glassware *s* vitrea *n pl*

glaze *vt* vitrum illinĕre (*with dat*), polire

gleam *s* fulgor *m*, jubar *n*; (*fig*) aura *f*

gleam *vi* coruscare, micare, fulgēre

gleaming *adj* coruscus, renidens

glean *vt* colligĕre, legĕre

gleaning *s* spicilegium *n*

glee *s* laetitia, hilaritas *f*

gleeful *adj* laetus, hilaris; **—ly** laete, hilare

glen *s* vallis *f*

glib *adj* lubricus, volubilis; **—ly** volubiliter

glide *vi* labi

glimmer *s* lux dubia *f*; **— of hope** specula *f*

glimmer *vi* sublucēre

glimpse *s* aspect·us -ūs *m*; **to have a — of** despicĕre

glisten *vi* nitēre

glitter *s* fulgor *m*

glitter *vi* fulgēre, micare, coruscare

gloat *vi* oculos pascĕre; **to — over** inhiare (*with abl*), oculos pascĕre (*with abl*)

globe *s* globus *m*; orbis terrarum *m*

globular *adj* globosus

globule *s* globulus *m*, pilula *f*

gloom *s* tenebrae *f pl*; (*fig*) tristitia *f*

gloomily *adv* maeste

gloomy *adj* tenebrosus, furvus; (*fig*) maestus, tristis

glorification *s* laudatio, glorificatio *f*

glorify *vt* celebrare, glorificare, extollĕre

glorious *adj* gloriosus, illustris; **—ly** glorie

glory *s* gloria, laus *f*

glory *vi* gloriari, se jactare

gloss *s* interpretatio *f*; (*sheen*) nitor *m*

gloss *vt* annotare; **to — over** extenuare, dissimulare

glossary *s* glossarium *n*

glossy *adj* nitidus, expolitus

glove *s* chirotheca *f*

glow *s* ardor, fervor, calor *m*

glow *vi* candēre, ardēre, calēre

glowing *adj* candens, fervens; (*fig*) fervidus

glue *s* gluten, glutinum *n*

glue *vt* glutinare

glum *adj* maestus, tristis

glut *s* satietas *f*

glut *vt* satiare, saturare

glutton *s* helluo, homo gulosus, ganeo *m*

gluttonous *adj* gulosus, edax; **—ly** gulose

gnarled *adj* nodosus

gnash *vt* **to — one's teeth** dentibus frendĕre

gnat *s* culex *m*

gnaw *vt & vi* rodĕre

gnawing *adj* mordax

go *vi* ire, incedĕre, proficisci; **to — about** circumire, perambulari; (*fig*) aggredi; **to — abroad** peregrinari; **to — after** sequi, petĕre; **to — aside** discedĕre; **to — astray** aberrare, vagari; **to — away** abire; **to — back** reverti; **to — before** praeire, antecedĕre; **to — between** intervenire; **to — beyond** egredi; (*fig*) excedĕre; **to — by** praeterire; (*fig*) (*to follow*) sequi; **to — down** descendĕre; (*of sun*) occidĕre; **to — for** petĕre; **to — forth** exire; **to — in** introire; **to — into** inire; **to — off** abire; (*as gun*) displodi; **to — on** (*to continue*) pergĕre; (*to happen*)

fieri; (*to succeed, thrive*) succedĕre;
to — out-exire; (*of fire*) extingui;
to — over transgredi; (*fig*) (*a subject*) percurrĕre; **to — round** circumire; **to — through** obire, pertendĕre; **to — to** adire, accedĕre;
to — towards petĕre; **to — under** subire; submergi; **to — up** ascendĕre; **to let —** dimittĕre; (*to let fall*) omittĕre

goad *s* pertica *f*, stimulus *m*
goad *vt* instigare; (*fig*) stimulare; (*to exasperate*) exasperare
goal *s* finis *m*; (*at racetrack*) calx *f*
goat *s* caper *m*, capra *f*
gobble *vt* devorare, deglutire
gobbler *s* helluo *m*
goblet *s* poculum *n*, scyphus *m*
goblin *s* larva *f*
god *s* deus, divus *m*
God *s* Deus *m*
goddess *s* dea, diva *f*
godhead *s* deitas *f*, numen *n*
godless *adj* atheus; improbus
godlike *adj* divinus
godliness *s* pietas *f*
gold *adj* aureus
gold *s* aurum *n*
golden *adj* aureus
goldfish *s* hippurus *m*
gold leaf *s* auri breactea *f*
gold mine *s* aurifodina *f*
goldsmith *s* aurifex *m*
good *adj* bonus, probus; (*beneficial*) salutaris; (*kindhearted*) benevolus; (*fit*) aptus, idoneus; **— for nothing** nequam (*indecl*); **to do —** prodesse; **to make —** compensare, restituĕre; **to seem —** vidēri
good *s* bonum *n*; (*profit*) commodum, lucrum *n*, utilitas *f*; **to be — for** prodesse (*with dat*); **—s** bona *n pl*, res *f*; (*for sale*) merx *f*
good *interj* bene!; euge!
good-by *interj* vale!; (*to more than one*) valete!; **to say —** valēre jubēre
goodly *adj* pulcher; (*quantity*) amplus; **a — number of** nonnulli
good-natured *adj* comis, benignus, facilis
goodness *s* bonitas *f*; (*moral*) probitas, virtus *f*; (*generosity*) benignitas *f*
goose *s* anser *m*
gooseberry *s* acinus grossulae *m*
gore *s* cruor *m*
gore *vt* cornu perforare, cornu ferire
gorge *s* fauces *f pl*; (*defile*) angustiae *f pl*
gorge *vt* **to — oneself** se ingurgitare
gorgeous *adj* splendidus, lautus; **—ly** splendide, laute
gory *adj* cruentus, cruentatus
gospel *s* evangelium *n*
gossamer *s* aranea *f*
gossip *s* (*talk*) nugae, gerrae *f pl*; (*person*) garrulus *m*, garrula *f*, loquax *m & f*, lingulaca *f*
gossip *vi* garrire
gouge *vt* evellĕre, eruĕre
gourd *s* cucurbita *f*

gourmand *s* helluo, popino *m*
gout *s* morbus articularis *m*, arthritis *f*; (*in the legs*) podagra *f*; (*in hands*) chiragra *f*
govern *vt* imperare (*with dat*), regēre, administrare, gubernare
governable *adj* tractabilis
governess *s* magistra, educatrix *f*
government *s* gubernatio, administratio, res publica *f*
governor *s* gubernator, moderator, praefectus *m*; (*of province*) proconsul, legatus *m*; procurator *m*
governorship *s* praefectura *f*
gown *s* (*of Roman citizen*) toga *f*; (*of women*) stola *f*
grace *s* gratia *f*; (*elegance, etc.*) venustas *f*, lepos *m*; (*pardon*) venia *f*; **to say —** gratias agĕre
grace *vt* exornare; honestare
graceful *adj* gratiosus, venustus, lepidus; **—ly** venuste, lepide
gracefulness *s* venustas *f*
graceless *adj* deformis, illepidus
Graces *s* Gratiae *f pl*
gracious *adj* benignus, misericors; **—ly** benigne, humane
gradation *s* grad·us -ūs *m*; (*in speech*) gradatio *f*
grade *s* grad·us -ūs *m*
gradient *s* proclivitas *f*
gradual *adj* lenis, mollis; per gradus; **—ly** gradatim, pedetentim
graduate *vt* gradibus distinguĕre; *vi* gradum suscipĕre
graduate *s* qui gradum academicum adeptus est
graft *s* surculus *m*; (*pol*) ambit·us -ūs *m*
graft *vt* inserĕre
grain *s* granum *n*; (*fig*) particula *f*; **against the —** (*fig*) Minervā invitā
grammar *s* grammatica *f*
grammarian *s* grammaticus *m*
grammatical *adj* grammaticus
granary *s* horreum *n*, granaria *n pl*
grand *adj* grandis
grandchild *s* nepos *m*, neptis *m & f*
granddaughter *s* neptis *f*
grandeur *s* magnificentia, majestas *f*
grandfather *s* avus *m*
grandiloquent *adj* magniloquus
grandmother *s* avia *f*
grandson *s* nepos *m*
granite *s* granites lapis *m*
grant *vt* concedĕre, permittĕre; (*to acknowledge*) fatēri; dare, praebēre
grant *s* concessio *f*
grape *s* uva *f*, acinus *m*
grapevine *s* vitis *f*
graphic *adj* expressus, significans, manifestus; **—ally** expresse
grapple *vt* compleci; *vi* luctari
grasp *s* complex·us -ūs *m*, comprehensio *f*; pugillum *n*; (*power*) potestas *f*; (*of the hand*) man·us -ūs *f*
grasp *vt* prehendĕre, tenēre, arripĕre;(*fig*) appetĕre, percipĕre, intellegĕre; *vi* **to — at** captare, appetĕre
grasping *adj* avidus, cupidus
grass *s* gramen *n*, herba *f*

grasshopper s grillus m

grassy adj graminosus, herbosus, herbidus

grate s clathri m pl; (hearth) caminus m

grate vt radĕre, conterĕre; vi stridĕre; to — upon offendĕre

grateful adj gratus, juncundus; —ly grate

gratification s gratificatio f; (pleasure, delight) voluptas, oblectatio f

gratify vt gratificari (with dat), morigerari (with dat)

gratifying adj gratus

grating s clathri, cancelli m pl; (sound) stridor m

gratis adv gratuito, gratis

gratitude s gratitudo f, gratus animus m

gratuitous adj gratuitus; —ly gratuito

gratuity s stips f, munus, praemium n

grave adj gravis, serius; (stern) severus; —ly graviter; severe

grave s sepulcrum n, tumulus m

gravedigger s tumulorum fossor m

gravel s glarea f

gravelly adj glareosus

gravestone s monumentum n

gravitate vi vergĕre

gravitation s ponderatio f

gravity s gravitas f, pondus n; (personal) severitas, dignitas f; momentum n

gravy s (broth) jus n; (juice) sucus m

gray adj canus; to become — canescĕre

gray-eyed adj caesius

gray-headed adj canus

grayish adj canescens

grayness s canities f

graze vt (cattle) pascĕre; (to touch lightly) perstringĕre, radĕre; vi pasci

grease s adeps m, pinguitudo, arvina f

grease vt ung(u)ĕre

greasy adj pinguis; unctus; (dirty) squalidus

great adj magnus; ingens, amplus, grandis; as — as tantus quantus; —ly magnopere, valde

great-grandfather s proavus m

greatness s magnitudo f

greaves s ocreae f pl

Grecian adj Graecus

greed s aviditas, avaritia f; voracitas f

greedily adv avide, cupide

greedy adj avarus, cupidus; vorax

Greek adj Graecus

Greek s Graecus m

green adj viridis; (fig) recens; (unripe) crudus, immaturus; to become — virescĕre

green s color viridis m; (lawn) locus herbidus m; —s olera n pl

greenhouse s viridarium hibernum n

greenish adj subviridis

greenness s viriditas f; (fig) cruditas, immaturitas f

greet vt salutem dicĕre (with dat), salutare

greeting s salutatio f

gregarious adj gregalis

grenade s pyrobolus m

greyhound s vertagus m

gridiron s craticula f

grief s maeror, dolor, luct·us -ūs m; to come to — perire

grievance s injuria, querimonia, querela f

grieve vt dolore afficĕre; vi maerēre, dolēre, lugēre

grievous adj gravis, durus, atrox; —ly graviter, aegre

griffin s gryps m

grill vt torrēre

grim adj torvus, atrox, truculentus; —ly torve, truculente, atrociter

grimace s distortus vult·us -ūs m, oris depravatio f

grimace vi os ducĕre

grimy adj niger, squalidus

grin vi distorto vultu ridēre

grin s ris·us -ūs m

grind vt (grain) molĕre; (in mortar) contundĕre; (on whetstone) exacuĕre; to — the teeth dentibus frendĕre

grindstone s cos f

grip s pugillum n, comprehensio f

grip vt arripĕre, comprehendĕre

grisly adj horrendus, horridus

grist s farina f

gristle s cartilago f

gristly adj cartilagineus, cartilaginosus

grit s harena f

gritty adj harenosus, sabulosus

grizzly adj canus

groan s gemit·us -ūs m

groan vi gemĕre

groin s inguen n

groom s agaso, equiso m

groom vt curare

groove s canalis m, stria f

groove vt striare

grope vi praetentare

gropingly adv pedetentim

gross adj crassus, pinguis; turpis; foedus; nimius; —ly nimium, valde

grotesque adj distortus

grotto s antrum n

ground s solum n, terra, humus f; (reason) causa, ratio f; (place) locus m; on the — humi; to give — cedĕre

ground vt fundare; (to teach) instruĕre; (a ship) subducĕre

groundless adj vanus, falsus, fictus; —ly temere, de nihilo

group s corona, turba f, globus m

group vt disponĕre; vi to — around circulari, stipari

grouse s (bird) tetrao m

grove s lucus m, nemus n

grovel vi serpĕre, se prosternĕre

grow vt colĕre, serĕre; vi crescĕre, augēri; (to become) fieri; to — out of (fig) oriri ex (with abl); to — up adolescĕre, pubescĕre

grower s cultor m

growl s fremit·us -ūs m

growl vi fremĕre

grown-up *adj* adultus; puber
growth *s* incrementum *n*, auct·us -ūs *m*
grub *s* vermiculus, lombricus *m*
grub *vi* effodĕre
grudge *s* odium *n*, invidia *f*; **to hold a — against** succensēre (*with dat*)
grudgingly *adv* invitus, aegre
gruesome *adj* taeter
gruff *adj* torvus, asper; **—ly** torve, aspere
gruffness *s* asperitas *f*
grumble *vi* murmurare, mussitare
grunt *s* grunnit·us -ūs *m*
grunt *vi* grunnire; (*fig*) fremĕre
guarantee *s* fides *f*; (*money*) sponsio *f*; (*person*) praes, vas, sponsor *m*; (*bail money*) vadimonium *n*
guarantee *vt* praestare, spondēre
guarantor *s* sponsor *m*
guard *s* custodia, tutela *f*; (*mil*) praesidium *n*; (*person*) custos *m* & *f*; **to be on one's —** cavēre
guard *vt* custodire, defendĕre; *vi* **to — against** cavēre
guarded *adj* cautus, circumspectus; **—ly** caute
guardian *s* custos, praeses *m* & *f*, defensor *m*; (*of minor or orphan*) tutor *m*
guardianship *s* custodia, tutela, curatio *f*
guerdon *s* merces *f*
guess *s* conjectura *f*
guess *vt* & *vi* conjicĕre, divinare, opinari
guest *s* hospes *m*; advena *m*; (*at dinner*) conviva *m*
guidance *s* duct·us -ūs *m*, curatio, moderatio *f*
guide *s* dux, ductor *m*
guide *vt* ducĕre, regĕre; (*to control*) moderari
guidebook *s* itinerarium *n*
guild *s* collegium, corpus *n*, sodalitas *f*

guile *s* dolus *m*
guileful *adj* dolosus
guileless *adj* simplex, sincerus
guilt *s* culpa *f*, crimen, vitium *n*
guiltless *adj* innocens, insons
guilty *adj* sons, noxius, nocens, sceleratus
guinea hen *s* meleagris *f*
guise *s* species *f*
guitar *s* cithara Hispanica *f*; fides *f pl*; **to play the —** fidibus canēre
gulf *s* sin·us -ūs *m*; (*abyss*) abyssus *f*, gurges *m*
gull *s* larus marinus, mergus *m*
gullet *s* gula *f*, guttur *n*
gullible *adj* credulus
gulp *vt* absorbēre, glutire, haurire; *vi* singultare
gulp *s* haust·us -ūs, singult·us -ūs *m*
gum *s* (*of mouth*) gingiva *f*; gummi *n* (*indecl*)
gumption *s* alacritas *f*
gun *s* sclopetum *n*; tormentum *n*
gunner *s* tormentarius *m*
gurgle *vi* singultare; (*of stream*) murmurare
gurgling *s* singult·us -ūs *m*; (*of stream*) murmur *n*, murmuratio *f*
gush *vi* micare, scaturire
gush *s* scaturigines *f pl*
gust *s* impet·us -ūs *m*, flamen *n*
gusty *adj* ventosus, procellosus
gut *s* intestinum *n*
gut *vt* exenterare; (*fig*) diripĕre, amburĕre
gutted *adj* (*by fire*) ambustus
gutter *s* canalis *m*; (*rain gutter*) compluvium *n*; (*in fields or upon roofs*) colliciae *f pl*
guttural *adj* gutturalis
guzzle *vi* potare
guzzler *s* potor *m*
gymnasium *s* gymnasium *n*, palaestra *f*
gymnastic *adj* gymnicus
gymnastics *s* palaestra, palaestrica *f*

H

haberdasher *s* linteo *m*
habit *s* consuetudo *f*, mos *m*; (*dress*) habit·us -ūs, vestit·us -ūs *m*
habitation *s* habitatio, dom·us -ūs *f*
habitual *adj* usitatus, inveteratus; **—ly** de more, ex more
habituate *vt* insuescĕre, assuefacĕre
hack *vt* caedĕre; **to — to pieces** concidĕre
hack *s* (*horse*) caballus *m*
hackneyed *adj* tritus, pervulgatus
haddock *s* gadus morhua *m*
hag *f* an·us -ūs *f*
haggard *adj* macer; ferus
haggle *vi* cavillari, licitare
haggler *s* licitator *m*
hail *s* grando *f*
hail *vt* salutare, appellare

hail *vi* **it is hailing** grandinat
hail *interj* salve!; (*to several*) salvete!
hailstone *s* saxea grando *f*
hair *s* capillus, crinis *m*; (*single*) pilus *m*; (*of animals*) saeta *f*, villus *m*
haircloth *s* cilicium *n*
hairdresser *s* concinnator, tonsor *m*
hairless *adj* (*of head*) calvus; (*of body*) glaber, depilis
hairpin *s* crinale *n*
hairy *adj* pilosus, crinitus; (*shaggy*) hirsutus
halberd *s* bipennis *f*
halcyon *s* alcedo, alcyon *f*
halcyon days *s* alcedonia *n pl*
hale *adj* robustus, validus
hale *vt* rapĕre, trahĕre
half *s* dimidia pars *f*, dimidium *n*

half *adj* dimidius, dimidiatus

half-hour *s* semihora *f*

half-moon *s* luna dimidiata *f*; (*shape*) lunula *f*

half-open *adj* semiapertus

half year *s* semestrium *n*

hall *s* atrium *n*; (*entrance*) vestibulum *n*

hallo *interj* heus!, ohe!

hallow *vt* consecrare

hallucination *s* error *m*, somnium *n*, alucinatio *f*

halo *s* corona *f*

halt *vt* sistĕre; *vi* consistĕre; (*fig*) haesitare; (*to limp*) claudicare

halt *s* pausa, mora *f*; **to come to a — consistĕre

halter *s* capistrum *n*

halting *adj* claudus

halve *vt* ex aequo dividĕre

ham *s* poples *m*; (*smoked, etc.*) perna *f*

hamlet *s* vicus, viculus *m*

hammer *s* malleus *m*

hammer *vt* tundĕre, cudĕre

hamper *s* corbis *f*

hamper *vt* impedire, implicare

hamstring *s* poplitis nervus *m*

hamstring *vt* poplitem succidĕre (*with dat*)

hand *s* man·us -ūs *f*; (*handwriting*) chirographum *n*; (*of dial*) gnomon *m*; **at —** ad manum, praesto, prae manibus, prope; **by —** manu; **in —** junctis manibus; **— to —** cominus; **on the other —** altera parte; **on the right —** a dextra; **to have a —** in interesse (*with dat*); **to take in —** suscipĕre

hand *vt* tradĕre, porrigĕre; **to — down** tradĕre; **to — over** referre; (*to betray*) prodĕre; **to — round** circumferre

handbill *s* libellus *m*

handbook *s* enchiridion *n*

handcuffs *s* manicae *f pl*

handful *s* manipulus *m*

handicraft *s* artificium *n*

handiwork *s* opus, opificium *n*

handkerchief *s* sudarium *n*

handle *s* manubrium *n*; (*of cup*) ansa, ansula *f*

handle *vt* tractare

handling *s* tractatio *f*

handsome *adj* pulcher, formosus; **—ly** pulchre; (*liberally*) liberaliter

handsomeness *s* pulchritudo, forma, venustas *f*

handwriting *s* man·us -ūs *f*, chirographum *n*

handy *adj* (*of things*) habilis; (*of person*) sollers; (*at hand*) praesto

hang *vt* suspendĕre; (*by a line*) appendĕre; (*head*) demittĕre; *vi* pendĕre; **hanging down** demissus; **hanging loose** fluens; **to — down** dependĕre; **to — on** to haerēre (*with dat*); **to — over** imminēre (*with dat*)

hanging *adj* pensilis

hanging *s* (*execution*) suspendium, *n*; **—s** aulaea *n pl*

hangman *s* carnifex *m*

haphazard *adj* fortuitus

happen *vi* accidĕre, fieri, evenire, contingĕre; **to — upon** incidĕre in (*with acc*)

happily *adv* beate, feliciter

happiness *s* felicitas *f*

happy *adj* beatus, felix, fortunatus, faustus

harangue *s* contio *f*

harangue *vt & vi* contionari

harass *vt* vexare, inquietare, exagitare, fatigare

harassing *adj* molestus

harassment *s* vexatio *f*

harbinger *s* praenuntius, antecursor *m*

harbor *s* port·us -ūs *m*

harbor *vt* excipĕre

hard *adj* durus; (*difficult*) difficilis, arduus; (*severe*) acer, rigidus, asper; **to become —** durescĕre

hard *adv* valde, sedulo, summa vi

harden *vt* durare; (*fig*) indurare; *vi* durescĕre; (*fig*) obdurescĕre

hardhearted *adj* durus, crudelis, inhumanus

hardihood *s* audacia *f*

hardiness *s* robur *n*

hardly *adv* vix, aegre; **— any** nullus fere

hardness *s* duritia *f*; (*fig*) iniquitas, acerbitas *f*; (*difficulty*) difficultas *f*

hardship *s* labor *m*, difficultas, aerumna *f*

hardware *s* ferramenta *n pl*

hardy *adj* robustus, durus

hare *s* lepus *m*

harem *s* gynaeceum *n*

hark *interj* heus!

harken *vi* audire; **to — to** auscultare (*with dat*)

harlot *s* meretrix *f*

harm *s* injuria *f*, damnum *n*; **to come to —** detrimentum accipĕre

harm *vt* nocēre (*with dat*), laedĕre

harmful *adj* noxius, nocivus, damnosus

harmless *adj* (*person*) innocens; (*thing*) innocuus; **—ly** innocenter, incolumis

harmonious *adj* canorus, consonus; (*fig*) concors, consentiens; **—ly** consonanter; (*fig*) concorditer, convenienter

harmonize *vt* componĕre; *vi* concinĕre; (*fig*) consentire

harmony *s* harmonia *f*, concent·us -ūs *m*; (*fig*) concordia *f*

harness *s* equi ornamenta *n pl*

harness *vt* ornare, insternĕre

harp *s* lyra *f*

harpist *s* psaltes *m*

harpoon *s* jaculum hamatum *n*

harpoon *vt* jaculo hamato transfigĕre

harpy *s* harpyia *f*

harrow *s* rastrum *n*, irpex *m*

harrow *vt* occare

harsh *adj* asper, raucus, discors, stridulus; (*in taste*) acer; (*fig*) durus, severus, inclemens; **—ly** aspere, acerbe, severe

harshness *s* asperitas, acerbitas, severitas *f*

harvest *s* messis, seges *f*
harvest *vt* metĕre
hash *vt* comminuĕre
hash *s* minutal *n*
haste *s* festinatio, celeritas *f*; **in —** propere; **to make —** properare
hasten *vt* accelerare, properare, praecipitare; *vi* properare, festinare
hastily *adv* propere, raptim; (*without reflection*) temere, inconsulte
hastiness *s* celeritas, temeritas *f*
hasty *adj* properus, praeceps, temerarius, inconsultus
hat *s* pileus, galerus, petasus *m*
hatch *vt* (*fig*) coquĕre, machinari; (*of chickens*) ex ovis excludĕre
hatchet *s* ascia, securis, dolabra *f*
hate *s* odium *n*, invidia *f*
hate *vt* odisse
hateful *adj* odiosus, invisus; **to be — to** odio esse (*with dat*); **—ly** odiose
hatred *s* odium *n*, invidia *f*
haughtily *adv* superbe, arroganter, insolenter
haughtiness *s* superbia, arrogantia *f*, fastidium *n*
haughty *adj* superbus, arrogans, insolens
haul *s* bolus *m*
haul *vt* trahĕre; **to — up** subducĕre
haunch *s* clunis, coxa *f*
haunt *vt* frequentare; (*fig*) agitare, inquietare
haunt *s* locus *m*; (*of animals*) lustra *n pl*, latebrae *f pl*
have *vt* habēre, possidēre, tenēre
haven *s* port·us -ūs *m*
havoc *s* strages *f*
hawk *s* accipiter *m & f*
hawk *vt* venditare
hawser *s* retinaculum *n*
hawthorn *s* crataegus oxyacantha *f*
hay *s* faenum *n*
hayloft *s* faenilia *n pl*
haystack *s* faeni meta *f*
hazard *s* periculum *n*
hazard *vt* periclitari
hazardous *adj* periculosus, anceps; **—ly** periculose
haze *s* nebula *f*
hazy *adj* caliginosus, nebulosus
he *pron* hic, is, ille; (*male*) mas *m*
head *s* caput *s*; (*mental faculty*) ingenium *n*; (*fig*) princeps; **— first** praeceps
head *adj* primus, principalis, capitalis
head *vt* praeesse (*with dat*), ducĕre; *vi* **to — for** petĕre
headache *s* capitis dolor *m*
heading *s* caput *n*, titulus *m*
headland *s* promuntorium *n*
headless *adj* truncus
headlong *adv* praeceps
headquarters *s* praetorium *n*
headstrong *adj* pervicax, contumax
headway *s* profect·us -ūs *m*; **to make —** proficĕre
headwind *s* ventus adversus *m*
heady *adj* (*of drinks*) fervidus, vehemens
heal *vt* medēri (*with dat*), sanare; *vi* sanescĕre; (*of wounds*) coalescĕre

healer *s* medicus *m*
healing *adj* salubris, salutaris
health *s* valetudo, salus *f*; **to be in good —** valēre; **to drink to the — of** propinare (*with dat*)
healthful *adj* salutaris, salubris
healthily *adv* salubriter
healthy *adj* sanus, integer; (*places*) salubris
heap *s* acervus, cumulus *m*, congeries *f*
heap *vt* acervare; **to — up** accumulare, exstruĕre
hear *vt* audire, exaudire; (*to learn*) certior fieri, accipĕre, cognoscĕre
hearing *s* (*act*) auditio *f*; (*sense*) audit·us -ūs *m*; (*law*) cognitio *f*; **hard of —** surdaster
hearken *vi* auscultare
hearsay *s* fama *f*, rumor *m*
heart *s* cor *n*; (*fig*) pectus *n*; (*courage*) animus *m*; **to learn by —** ediscĕre
heartache *s* cura *f*, angor *m*
heartbreak *s* angor *m*
heartbroken *adj* aeger
hearth *s* focus *m*
heartily *adv* sincere, vehementer, valde
heartiness *s* studium *n*, alacritas *f*
heartless *adj* crudelis, inhumanus; **—ly** crudeliter, inhumane
heartlessness *s* inhumanitas *f*
hearty *adj* sincerus, vehemens, alacer
heat *s* calor, ardor *m*; (*fig*) fervor *m*
heat *vt* calefacĕre; *vi* calescĕre
heath *s* (*plant*) erice *f*; (*place*) loca inculta *n pl*
heathen *adj* paganus
heathen *s* paganus *m*
heather *s* erice *f*
heating *s* calefactio *f*
heave *vt* attollĕre, levare; **to — a sigh** gemitum ducĕre; *vi* tumēre, aestuare, fluctuare
heaven *s* caelum *n*; (*fig*) dii, superi *m pl*
heavenly *adj* caelestis, divinus
heavily *adv* graviter; (*slowly*) tarde
heaviness *s* gravitas *f*; (*slowness*) tarditas *f*
heavy *adj* gravis, ponderosus; (*fig*) tardus, segnis, iners; (*sad*) maestus
Hebraic *adj* Hebraicus
Hebrew *s* Hebraeus *m*; (*language*) Hebraea lingua *f*
hecatomb *s* hecatombe *f*
hectic *adj* fervidus, febriculosus
hedge *s* saepes *f*
hedge *vt* **to — in** saepire; **to — off** intersaepire; *vi* tergiversari
hedgehog *s* ericius *m*
heed *s* cura, opera *f*; **to take — ** cavēre, curare
heed *vt* curare, observare, respicĕre; (*to obey*) parēre (*with dat*)
heedless *adj* incautus, temerarius; **— of** immemor (*with genit*)
heedlessness *s* neglegentia *f*
heel *s* calx *m & f*
heifer *s* bucula, juvenca *f*
height *s* altitudo *f*; (*of person*) pro-

ceritas *f;* (*top*) culmen *n;* (*fig*) fastigium *n*

heighten *vt* amplificare, exaggerare, augēre

heinous *adj* atrox, nefarius, foedus; —ly atrociter

heir *s* heres *m;* **sole** *or* **universal —** heres ex asse

heiress *s* heres *f*

heirloom *s* res hereditaria *f*

hell *s* Tartarus *m*, inferi *m pl*

Hellenic *adj* Hellenicus, Graecus

Hellenism *s* Hellenismus *m*

hellish *adj* infernus, diabolicus, nefarius

helm *s* gubernaculum *n*

helmet *s* cassis, galea *f*

helmsman *s* gubernator, rector *m*

help *s* auxilium, subsidium *n*

help *vt* adjuvare (*with acc*), auxiliari (*with dat*), succurrēre (*with dat*), opem ferre (*with dat*)

helper *s* adjutor *m*, adjutrix *f*

helpful *adj* utilis

helpless *adj* inops

helplessness *s* inopia *f*

hem *s* ora *f*, limbus *m*

hem *vt* (*to sew*) suēre; **to — in** circumsidēre, obsidēre

hem *interj* hem!, ehem!

hemisphere *s* hemisphaerium *n*

hemlock *s* cicuta *f*

hemp *s* cannabis *f*

hempen *adj* cannabinus

hen *s* gallina *f*

hence *adv* hinc; (*consequently*) igitur, ideo

henceforth *adv* posthac, dehinc

henpecked *adj* uxorius

her *pron* eam, illam, hanc

her *adj* ejus, illius, hujus; **— own** suus, proprius

herald *s* fetialis *m;* (*crier*) praeco *m*

herald *vt* nuntiare, praenuntiare

herb *s* herba *f;* **—s** herbae *f pl*, olus *n*

herd *s* grex *m;* armentum *n;* (*in contempt*) vulgus *n*

herd *vt* **to — together** congregare, cogēre; *vi* congregari

herdsman *s* pastor, armentarius *m*

here *adv* hic; **— and there** passim

hereafter *adv* posthac, in reliquum tempus

hereby *adv* ex hoc, ex hac re, hinc

hereditary *adj* hereditarius, patrius

heredity *s* genus *n;* **by —** jure hereditario, per successiones

herein *adv* in hoc, in hac re, hic

heresy *s* haeresis *f*

heretical *adj* haereticus; falsus, pravus

hereupon *adv* hic

herewith *adv* una cum hac re

heritage *s* hereditas *f*

hermaphrodite *s* androgynus, Hermaphroditus *m*

hermit *s* eremita *m*

hermitage *s* eremitae cella *f*

hernia *s* hernia *f*

hero *s* vir *m;* (*demigod*) heros *m*

heroic *adj* fortissimus, magnanimus, heroicus; **—ally** fortissime

heroine *s* virago *f*

heroism *s* virtus, fortitudo *f*

heron *s* ardea *f*

herring *s* harenga *f*

hers *pron* ejus, illius

herself *pron* (*refl*) se; (*intensive*) ipsa; **to —** sibi; **with —** secum

hesitant *adj* dubius, incertus; **—ly** cunctanter, dubitanter

hesitate *vi* dubitare, haesitare

hesitation *s* dubitatio, haesitatio, cunctatio *f*

Hesperian *adj* Hesperius

heterogeneous *adj* diversus

hew *vt* dolare, caedere

hey *interj* ohe!

hiatus *s* hiat·us -ūs *m*

hiccup *s* singult·us -ūs *m*

hiccup *vi* singultare

hide *s* pellis *f*, corium *n*

hide *vt* abdēre, abscondēre, celare, occultare; (*to flog*) verberare; *vi* latēre, se abdēre

hideous *adj* foedus, perhorridus, turpis; **—ly** foede, turpiter

hideousness *s* foeditas *f*, horror *m*

hiding *s* occultatio *f;* (*whipping*) verberatio *f*

hiding place *s* latebra *f*

hierarchy *s* hierarchia *f*

high *adj* altus, excelsus, sublimis; (*tall*) procerus; (*of price*) pretiosus, carus; (*of ground*) editus; (*of rank*) amplus; **—ly** (*value*) magni; (*intensity*) vehementer, valde

high *adv* alte, sublimiter; **to aim —** magnas res appetēre

highborn *adj* generosus, ingenuus, nobilis

high-flown *adj* inflatus, tumidus

highhanded *adj* insolens, superbus; **—ly** insolenter, superbe

highland *s* regio montuosa *f*

highlander *s* montanus *m*

high-minded *adj* (*noble*) magnanimus; (*arrogant*) arrogans, insolens

high priest *s* pontifex maximus *m*

highway *s* via *f*

highwayman *s* latro, grassator *m*

hilarity *s* hilaritas *f*

hill *s* collis, tumulus *m;* (*slope*) clivus *m*

hillock *s* tumulus *m*

hilly *adj* montuosus, clivosus

hilt *s* capulus *m*

him *pron* eum, hunc, illum; **of —** ejus, hujus, illius; de eo, de hoc, de illo

himself *pron* (*refl*) se; (*intensive*) ipse; **to —** sibi; **with —** secum

hind *s* cerva *f*

hind *adj* posterior

hinder *vt* obstare (*with dat*); impedire, morari

hindmost *adj* postremus, ultimus, novissimus

hindrance *s* impedimentum *n*

hinge *s* cardo *m*

hinge *vi* **to — on** (*fig*) niti (*with abl*)

hint *s* indicium *n*, significatio *f*

hint *s* & *vi* significare, innuēre, suggerēre

hip *s* coxendix *f*

hippodrome s hippodromos m

hire s conductio, locatio f; (wages) merces f

hire vt conducĕre; **to — out** locare; vi **to — out** operam suam locare

hired adj conductus, conducticius, mercenarius

hireling s mercenarius m

his adj ejus, illius, hujus; **— own** suus, proprius

his pron ejus, illius, hujus

hiss vt & vi sibilare

hissing s sibilus m

historian s historicus, rerum gestarum scriptor m

historical adj historicus

history s historia, memoria rerum gestarum f; **ancient —** antiquitas f; **modern —** memoria recentioris aetatis f

histrionic adj histrionalis

hit s ict·us -ūs m, plaga f; **to be a — bene** succedĕre

hit vt icĕre, ferire, percutĕre; vi **to — upon** invenire

hitch s impedimentum n, mora f

hitch vt (ad)jungĕre

hither adv huc

hither adj citerior

hitherto adv (of time) adhuc; (of place) huc usque

hive s alvus m, alvearium n

hoard s acervus m

hoard vt coacervare, recondĕre

hoarder s accumulator m

hoarse adj raucus; **to get —** irraucescĕre; **—ly** raucā voce

hoary adj canus

hoax s fraus, ludificatio f

hoax vt fallĕre, decipĕre, ludificari

hobble vi claudicare

hobby s avocamentum n

hock s poples m

hoe s sarculum n

hoe vt sarculare; (weeds) pectĕre

hog s porcus, sus m

hoist vt sublevare, tollĕre

hold vt tenēre, possidēre, habēre; (to contain) capĕre; (to think) habēre, existimare, censēre; **to — back** retinēre; **to — forth** porrigĕre, extendĕre; (to offer) praebēre; **to — in** inhibēre, cohibēre; **to — off** abstinēre, arcēre; **to — up** (to lift up) attollĕre, sustinēre; vi **to — back** cunctari; **to — out** (to last) durare, permanēre

holder s possessor m; (handle) manubrium n

holding s possessio f

hole s foramen n; (fig) latebra f; (of mice) cavum n

holiday s dies festus m; **—s feriae** f pl

holiness s sanctitas f

hollow adj cavus; (fig) vanus, inanis

hollow s caverna f, cavum n; (depression) lacuna f

hollow vt **to — out** cavare, excavare

holly s ilex aquifolium n

holocaust s holocaustum n

holy adj sanctus

homage s obsequium n, cult·us -ūs m; **to pay — to** colere

home s domicilium n, dom·us -ūs f; **at —** domi; **from —** domo

home adv (motion) domum; (place where) domi

home adj domesticus

homeless adj tecto carens, profugus

homeliness s rusticitas f

homely adj rusticus, simplex

homemade adj domesticus, vernaculus, domi factus

homesickness s tecti sui desiderium n, nostalgia f

homestead s sedes f, fundus m

homeward adv domum

homicidal adj cruentus, sanguinolentus

homicide s (person) homicida m; (deed) homicidium n

homily s sermo, tractat·us -ūs m

homogeneous adj pari naturā praeditus

hone vt acuĕre

honest adj probus, sincerus; **—ly** probe, sincere

honesty s probitas, sinceritas f

honey s mel n

honeybee s apis mellifera or mellifica f

honeycomb s favus m

honeysuckle s clymenus m

honor s honos m; (repute) fama f; (trust) fides f; (award) decus n; (official distinction) dignitas f; **sense of —** pudor m

honor vt honorare; (to respect) colēre

honorable adj honestus

honorably adv honeste

honorary adj honorarius

hood s cucullus m

hoof s ungula f

hook s hamus, uncus m; **by — or by crook** quocumque modo

hook vt inuncare, confibulare; (fig) capĕre

hooked adj hamatus; (crooked) curvatus, aduncus

hoop s circulus m; (toy) trochus m; (shout) clamor m

hoop vi exclamare

hoot vt explodĕre; vi obstrepĕre; (of owls) canēre

hop s salt·us -ūs m

hop vi salire, subsultare

hope s spes f

hope vt sperare; **to — for** exspectare

hopeful adj bonae spei; **—ly magna cum spe**

hopeless adj exspes, desperatus; **—ly** desperanter

hopelessness s desperatio f

horde s turba, caterva f, grex m

horizon s orbis finiens m

horizontal adj libratus; **—ly ad libram**

horn s cornu n; (as trumpet) buccina f

horned adj cornutus, corniger

hornet s crabo m

horoscope s horoscopus m

horrible *adj* horribilis, foedus; *(excessive)* immoderatus

horribly *adv* horribili modo, foede

horrid *adj* horridus, horrens; **—ly** horride

horrify *vt* horrificare, perterrēre

horror *s* horror *m*; *(deep hatred)* odium *n*

horse *s* equus *m*, equa *f*

horseback *s* **on —** in equo; ex equo; **to fight on —** ex equo pugnare; **to ride on —** in equo vehi

horsehair *s* pilus equinus *m*

horseman *s* eques *m*

horse race *s* curriculum equorum *n*, certatio equestris *f*

horseradish *s* armoracia *f*

horseshoe *s* solea *f*

horsewhip *s* flagellum *n*, scutica *f*

horsewhip *vt* verberare

horticultural *adj* ad hortorum cultum pertinens

horticulture *s* hortorum cult·us -ūs *m*

hose *s* *(stocking)* tibiale *n*; *(tube)* tubulus *m*

hosiery *s* feminalia *n pl*

hospitable *adj* hospitalis

hospitably *adv* hospitaliter

hospital *s* valetudinarium *n*

hospitality *s* hospitalitas *f*

host *s* *(entertainer)* hospes *m*; *(army)* copiae *f pl*, exercit·us -ūs *m*; *(crowd)* multitudo *f*; *(wafer)* hostia *f*

hostage *s* obses *m & f*

hostess *s* hospita *f*; *(at inn)* caupona *f*

hostile *adj* hostilis, infensus, inimicus; **in a — manner** hostiliter, infense

hot *adj* calidus *or* caldus; fervidus; *(boiling)* fervens; *(seething)* aestuosus; *(of spices)* acer; *(fig)* ardens; **to be —** calēre; **to become —** calescēre; **—ly** acriter, ardenter

hotel *s* hospitium *n*, caupona *f*

hound *s* catulus *m*

hound *vt* instare *(with dat)*

hour *s* hora *f*

hourglass *s* horarium *n*

hourly *adv* in horas

house *s* dom·us -ūs *f*, aedes *f pl*, tectum *n*; *(family)* dom·us -ūs, gens *f*; *(in country)* villa *f*; **at the — of** apud *(with acc)*

house *vt* domo excipĕre; *(things)* condĕre

housebreaker *s* fur, effractarius *m*

housebreaking *s* domūs effractura *f*

household *adj* familiaris, domesticus

household *s* familia, dom·us -ūs *f*

householder *s* paterfamilias *m*

household gods *s* Lares *m pl*; Penates *m pl*

housekeeper *s* promus *m*

housekeeping *s* rei familiaris cura *f*

housemaid *s* ancilla, vernacula *f*

housewife *s* materfamilias *f*

hovel *s* tugurium, gurgustium *n*

hover *vi* pendēre, volitare; **to — over** impendēre *(with dat)*

how *adv* quomodo, quo pacto, qui; *(to what degree)* quam; **— many** quot;

— much quantum; **— often** quotiens

however *adv* tamen, nihilominus, autem; quamvis, quamlibet; **— great** quantuscunque; **— many** quotquot; **— often** quotiescunque

howl *s* ululat·us -ūs *m*

howl *vi* ululare, fremēre

hub *s* axis *m*

huckster *s* propola, institor *m*

huddle *vi* congregari

huddle *s* corona *f*

huddled *adj* confertus

hue *s* color *m*

hue and cry *s* conclamatio *f*

huff *s* offensio *f*; **in a —** offensus

huff *vi* stomachari

hug *s* complex·us -ūs *m*

hug *vt* complecti, amplecti

huge *adj* ingens, immensus, vastus, immanis

hulk *s* alveus *m*; navis oneraria *f*

hull *s* alveus *m*

hum *s* murmur *n*, murmuratio *f*; *(of bees)* bombus *m*

hum *vi* murmurare; *(of bees)* bombilare

human *adj* humanus; **— feelings** humanitas *f*; **—ly** humane, humaniter, humanitus

human being *s* homo *m & f*

humane *adj* humanus, misericors; **—ly** humaniter, misericorditer, humanitus

humanity *s* humanitas *f*; homines *m pl*

humanize *vt* excolĕre

humble *adj* *(obscure)* humilis, obscurus; *(modest)* summissus, modestus; **—ly** summisse

humble *vt* deprimĕre, infringĕre; **to — oneself** se summittĕre

humid *adj* humidus

humidity *s* humor *m*

humiliate *vt* humiliare, deprimĕre

humiliation *s* humiliatio *f*, dedecus *n*

humility *s* animus summissus *m*, modestia, humilitas *f*

humor *s* *(disposition)* ingenium *n*, natura *f*; *(whim)* libido *f*; **sense of —** facetiae *f pl*, festivitas *f*

humor *vt* obsequi *(with dat)*, morigerari *(with dat)*, indulgēre *(with dat)*

humorous *adj* facetus, ridiculus, jocularis; **—ly** facete

hump *s* gibber, gibbus *m*

humpbacked *adj* gibber

hunch *s* opinio *f*; **to have a — **opinari

hundred *adj* centum; **— times** centie(n)s

hundredfold *adj* centuplex

hundredfold *s* centuplum *n*

hundredth *adj* centesimus

hunger *s* fames *f*

hunger *vi* esurire

hungrily *adv* avide, voraciter, rabide; jejune

hungry *s* esuriens, jejunus; *(fig)* avide; **to be —** esurire

hunt *s* venatio *f*, venat·us -ūs *m*

hunt *vt* venari, indagare; *vi* **to —
for** quaerĕre, exquirĕre
hunter *s* venator *m*; *(horse)* equus
venaticus *m*
hunting *s* venatio *f*, venat·us -ūs *m*
hunting *adj* venaticus
huntress *s* venatrix *f*
huntsman *s* venator *m*
hurdle *s* crates *f*; *(obstacle)* obex *m*
& *f*
hurl *vt* jacĕre, conjicĕre, jaculari
hurray *interj* io!, evax!
hurricane *s* procella *f*
hurriedly *adv* raptim, festinanter;
(carelessly) negligenter
hurry *vt* rapĕre, accelerare, maturare; *vi* festinare, properare, maturare
hurry *s* festinatio *f*; **in a —** festinanter
hurt *vt* nocēre *(with dat)*, laedĕre;
(fig) offendĕre; *vi* dolēre
hurt *s* vulnus *n*; damnum *n*, injuria *f*
hurt *adj* saucius; *(emotionally)* saucius, offensus
husband *s* maritus, vir *m*
husbandry *s* agricultura, res rustica *f*
hush *s* silentium *n*

hush *vt* comprimĕre, pacare; *(a secret)* celare; *vi* tacēre
hush *interj* st!, tace!; *(to several)* tacete!
husk *s* folliculus *m*; *(of beans, etc.)*
siliqua *f*; *(of grain)* gluma *f*
husky *adj* robustus; *(of voice)* raucus
hustle *vt* trudĕre, pulsare; *vi* festinare
hut *s* tugurium *n*, casa *f*
hyacinth *s* hyacinthus *m*
hydra *s* hydra *f*
hyena *s* hyaena *f*
hymen *s* Hymenaeus *m*
hymn *s* carmen *n*, hymnus *m*
hyperbole *s* superlatio *f*
hypercritical *adj* nimis severus
hyphen *s* hyphen *n* *(indecl)*
hypochondriac *s* melancholicus *m*
hypocrisy *s* simulatio, dissimulatio *f*
hypocrite *s* simulator, dissimulator
m
hypocritical *adj* simulatus, fictus
hypothesis *s* hypothesis, sumptio,
conjectura *f*
hypothetical *adj* hypotheticus, sumptus
hysteria *s* deliratio *f*
hysterical *adj* hystericus

I

I *pron* ego; **— myself** egomet, ego
ipse
iambic *adj* iambeus
ice *s* glacies *f*
icicle *s* stiria *f*
icy *adj* glacialis
idea *s* notio, notitia, imago, conceptio *f*
ideal *adj* perfectus, summus, optimus; *(as mere mental image)* mente conceptus, idealis
ideal *s* exemplar *n*
identical *adj* idem
identify *vt* agnoscĕre
idiocy *s* fatuitas, animi imbecillitas *f*
idiom *s* proprietas linguae, consuetudo *f*
idiomatic *adj* proprius linguae
idiosyncrasy *s* proprium *n*
idiot *s* fatuus, excors *m*
idiotic *adj* fatuus, stultus, ineptus
idle *adj* otiosus, vacuus; *(pointless)*
vanus, inanis; *(lazy)* ignavus, iners,
deses; **to be —** cessare
idle *vt* **to — away** terĕre; *vi* cessare
idleness *s* otium *n*; ignavia, inertia,
desidia *f*
idler *s* cessator, homo ignavus *m*
idle talk *s* nugae *f pl*
idly *adv* otiose; ignave, segniter; *(in
vain)* vane, frustra
idol *s* simulacrum *n*; *(eccl)* idolum *n*;
(person) deliciae *f pl*
idolater *s* simulacrorum cultor *m*
idolatrous *adj* idololatricus
idolatry *s* simulacrorum cult·us -ūs *m*

idolize *vt* venerari
idyl *s* idyllium *n*
if *conj* si; **as —** quasi, tamquam;
and — quodsi; **but —** sin; quodsi;
even — etiamsi; **— not** ni, nisi, si
non; **— only** si modo, dummodo
igneous *adj* igneus
ignite *vt* accendĕre, incendĕre; *vi* ex-
ardescĕre, flammam concipĕre
ignoble *adj* ignobilis, obscurus; *(base)*
turpis
ignobly *adv* turpiter
ignominious *adj* ignominiosus, turpis; **—ly** ignominiose, turpiter
ignominy *s* ignominia *f*
ignoramus *s* idiota *m*
ignorance *s* ignoratio, ignorantia *f*
ignorant *adj* ignarus, nescius; *(un-
learned)* indoctus; **to be — of** ignorare, nescire; **—ly** inscienter, inscite, indocte
ignore *vt* praetermittĕre, neglegĕre
Iliad *s* Ilias *f*
ill *adj* aegrotus, aeger; *(evil)* malus;
to be — aegrotare; **to fall — in**
morbum incidĕre
ill *adv* male, prave
ill *s* malum *n*
ill-bred *adj* inurbanus, agrestis
illegal *adj* vetitus, illicitus; **—ly** contra leges, illicite
illegitimate *adj* haud legitimus; *(of
birth)* spurius, nothus
illiberal *adj* illiberalis; **—ly** illibera-
liter
illicit *adj* illicitus; **—ly** illicite

illiterate *adj* illitteratus, indoctus, ineruditus

illness *s* morbus *m*, aegritudo, aegrotatio, valetudo *f*

illogical *adj* absurdus; **—ly** absurde

ill-starred *adj* infelix

ill-tempered *adj* iracundus, stomachosus, difficilis

illuminate *vt* illustrare, illuminare

illumination *s* illuminatio *f*, lumina *n pl*

illusion *s* error *m*

illusive *adj* falsus, vanus

illusory *adj* fallax

illustrate *vt* illustrare; (*fig*) explanare

illustration *s* illustratio *f*; (*fig*) exemplum *n*

illustrative *adj* exemplaris

illustrious *adj* illustris, insignis, praeclarus; **—ly** praeclare

image *s* signum, simulacrum *n*; (*likeness*) effigies, imago *f*

imagery *s* figurae *f pl*

imaginary *adj* fictus, commenticius

imagination *s* cogitatio *f*

imaginative *adj* ingeniosus

imagine *vt* imaginari, fingĕre; (*to suppose*) opinari

imbecile *adj* (*weak*) imbecillus; (*of mind*) animo imbecillus, fatuus

imbecile *s* fatuus *m*

imbibe *vt* imbibĕre

imbue *vt* imbuĕre, tingĕre

imitate *vt* imitari

imitation *s* imitatio *f*; (*copy*) imago *f*

imitative *adj* ad imitandum aptus

imitator *s* imitator *m*, imitatrix *f*, aemulator *m*

immaculate *adj* integer, castus

immaterial *adj* incorporalis; (*unimportant*) nullius momenti

immeasurable *adj* immensus, infinitus

immeasurably *adv* infinito

immediate *adj* praesens, proximus; **—ly** statim, confestim, extemplo; **—ly after** sub (*with acc*)

immemorial *adj* antiquissimus; **from time —** ex omni memoria aetatum

immense *adj* immensus; **—ly** vehementer

immensity *s* immensitas *f*

immerge *vt* mergĕre, immergĕre

immersion *s* immersio *f*

imminent *adj* imminens, impendens

immobility *s* immobilitas *f*

immoderate *adj* immodicus; **—ly** immoderate, nimie

immodest *adj* immodestus, impudicus; **—ly** immodeste, inverecunde

immodesty *s* immodestia *f*

immolate *vt* immolare

immolation *s* immolatio *f*

immoral *adj* pravus, improbus, corruptus; **—ly** prave

immorality *s* mores mali *m pl*, turpitudo, improbitas *f*

immortal *adj* immortalis

immortality *s* immortalitas *f*

immortalize *vt* aeternare, ad deos evehĕre

immovable *adj* immobilis, immotus

immunity *s* immunitas, vacatio *f*

immure *vt* includĕre

immutability *s* immutabilitas *f*

immutable *adj* immutabilis

imp *s* larva *f*; (*child*) puer lascivus *m*

impair *vt* imminuĕre, atterĕre, debilitare

impale *vt* infigĕre

impart *vt* impertire, communicare

impartial *adj* aequus, aequabilis, severus; **—ly** severe

impartiality *s* aequitas, aequabilitas *f*

impassable *adj* insuperabilis, impervius

impassive *adj* impassibilis, frigidus, lentus

impatient *adj* impatiens, trepidus; **—ly** impatienter, aegre

impeach *vt* accusare

impeachment *s* accusatio *f*

impede *vt* obstare (*with dat*), impedire, retardare

impediment *s* impedimentum *n*; (*in speech*) haesitatio *f*

impel *vt* impellĕre

impenetrable *adj* impenetrabilis; (*fig*) occultus

impenitence *s* impaenitentia *f*

imperative *adj* necessarius; (*gram*) imperativus

imperceptible *adj* tenuissimus, obscurus

imperceptibly *adv* sensim

imperfect *adj* imperfectus, mancus, vitiosus; **—ly** imperfecte, vitiose

imperfection *s* vitium *n*, defect·us -ūs *m*

imperial *adj* imperatorius, regius; **—ly** regie

imperil *vt* in periculum adducĕre

imperishable *adj* perennis, aeternus, immortalis

impermeable *adj* impervius

impersonal *adj* impersonalis; **—ly** impersonaliter

impersonate *vt* sustinēre partes (*with genit*), imitari

impertinence *s* insolentia, protervitas *f*

impertinent *adj* (*rude*) insolens, protervus; (*not to the point*) ineptus, nihil ad rem; **—ly** insolenter, proterve; inepte

impervious *adj* impervius, impenetrabilis

impetuosity *s* impet·us -ūs *m*, vehementia, violentia *f*

impetuous *adj* vehemens, fervidus, violentus; **—ly** vehementer, fervide, violenter

impetus *s* impet·us -ūs *m*, vis *f*

impiety *s* impietas *f*

impinge *vi* incidĕre

impious *adj* impius, nefarius; **—ly** impie, nefarie

implacable *adj* implacabilis, inexorabilis, durus

implacably *adv* implacabiliter, dure

implant *vt* ingignĕre, inserĕre, ingenerare

implement *s* instrumentum *n*

implement vt exsequi

implicate vt implicare, impedire

implication s indicium n; **by —** ta+ cite

implicit adj tacitus, totus; **—ly** ta+cite, omnino

implore vt implorare, obsecrari

imply vt significare; **to be implied in** inesse in (with abl)

impolite adj inurbanus; **—ly** inur+bane

impoliteness s inurbanitas f

impolitic adj inconsultus

imponderable adj ponderis expers

import vt importare, invehěre; (to mean) significare, velle

import s significatio f; **—s** impor+taticia n pl

importance s momentum n, gravi+tas f

important adj magnus, magni mo+menti, gravis

importunate adj importunus; **—ly** importune

importune vt fatigare, efflagitare, sollicitare

impose vt imponěre; (to enjoin) in+jungěre; **to — upon** abuti (with abl)

imposition s (tax) vectigal, tribu+tum n; (excessive burden) impor+tunitas f

impossibility s impossibilitas f

impossible adj impossibilis

imposter s fraudator m

imposture s fraus f

impotence s imbecillitas, infirmitas f

impotent adj imbecillus, infirmus

impound vt publicare; (animals) in+cluděre

impoverish vt in egestatem redigěre

impractical adj inutilis

imprecate vt imprecari, exsecrari

imprecation s exsecratio f, dirae f pl

impregnable adj inexpugnabilis

impregnate vt imbuěre, gravidam facěre

impregnation s fecundatio f

impress vt impriměre; (person) mo+věre; **to — something on** incul+care aliquid (with dat); (e.g., some+one's mind) infigěre aliquid (with dat)

impression s impressio f; (copy) exemplar n; (mark) vestigium n; (idea) opinio, opinatio f; **to make an — on** commověre

impressive adj gravis; **—ly** graviter

imprint s impressio f

imprint vt impriměre, infigěre

imprison vt in vincula conjicěre

imprisonment s custodia f

improbable adj haud credibilis, pa+rum verisimilis

impromptu adv ex tempore

improper adj indecorus; **—ly** inde+core, perperam

impropriety s indecorum n

improve vt emendare, corrigěre, ex+colěre; vi melior fieri, proficěre

improvement s emendatio, correc+tio f, profect·us -ūs m

improvident adj improvidus, impru+dens; **—ly** improvide

improvise vt ex tempore dicěre or componěre

imprudence s imprudentia f

imprudent adj imprudens, inconsul+tus, temerarius; **—ly** imprudenter, inconsulte, temere

impugn vt impugnare, in dubium vo+care

impulse s impuls·us -ūs m

impulsive adj vehemens, violentus; **—ly** impulsu

impunity s impunitas f; **with —** impune

impure adj impurus, obscenus, inces+tus; contaminatus; **—ly** impure, obscene, inceste

impurity s impuritas, obscenitas, impudicitia f

in prep in (with abl); (in the writings of) apud (with acc); (of time) ren+der by abl

in adv (motion) intro; (rest) intra, intus

inability s impotentia f

inaccessible adj inaccessus

inaccuracy s neglegentia f

inaccurate adj neglegens, parum accuratus, minime exactus; **—ly** parum accurate

inactive adj iners, quietus, ignavus

inactivity s inertia, socordia, cessa+tio f

inadequate adj impar; **—ly** parum

inadmissible adj illicitus

inadvertence s imprudentia f

inadvertent adj imprudens; **—ly** imprudenter

inalienable adj proprius

inane adj inanis

inanimate adj inanimus, inanimatus

inapplicable adj **to be —** non va+lěre

inappropriate adj haud idoneus, pa+rum aptus; **—ly** parum apte

inarticulate adj indistinctus

inartistic adj durus

inasmuch as conj quandoquidem

inattentive adj haud attentus, ne+glegens; **—ly** neglegenter

inaudible adj **to be —** audiri non posse

inaugurate vt inaugurare, conse+crare

inauguration s inauguratio, conse+cratio f

inauspicious adj infaustus; **—ly** malo omine

inborn adj ingenitus, innatus

incalculable adj inaestimabilis; (fig) immensus, incredibilis

incantation s carmen, incantamen+tum n

incapable adj incapax, inhabilis; **to be — of** non posse (with inf)

incapacitate vt debilitare

incarcerate vt in vincula conjicěre

incarnate adj incarnatus

incarnation s incarnatio f

incautious adj incautus; **—ly** in+caute

incendiary adj incendiarius

incense s tus n
incense vt ture fumigare; (to anger) irritare, exasperare
incentive s incitamentum n
incessant adj continuus, assiduus; —ly assidue
incest s incest·us -ūs m
incestuous adj incestus
inch s uncia f; — by — unciatim
incident s cas·us -ūs, event·us -ūs m
incidental adj fortuitus; —ly fortuito, casu, forte
incipient adj nascens, primus
incision s incis·us -ūs m, incisura f
incisive adj acer
incite vt incitare, stimulare
incitement s incitamentum n, incitatio f
incivility s rusticitas f
inclemency s inclementia f; (of weather) asperitas f
inclination s (act) inclinatio f; (slope) proclivitas f; (propensity) libido, inclinatio f
incline vt inclinare; vi propendēre
incline s acclivitas f
inclined adj inclinatus, propensus, pronus
include vt includēre, comprehendēre
inclusive adj comprehendens
incognito adv clam
incoherent adj interruptus; —ly interrupte
income s redit·us -ūs, fruct·us -ūs m, merces f
incomparable adj incomparabilis, singularis, unicus, eximius
incomparably adv eximie, unice
incompatibility s repugnantia, diversitas f
incompatible adj repugnans, discors
incompetence s jurisdictionis defect·us -ūs m; inscitia f
incompetent adj inscitus, inhabilis
incomplete adj imperfectus
incomprehensible adj haud comprehensibilis
inconceivable adj incredibilis
inconclusive adj anceps
incongruous adj inconveniens, male congruens; —ly parum apte
inconsiderable adj levis, exiguus
inconsiderate adj inconsultus
inconsistency s inconstantia, discrepantia f
inconsistent adj inconstans, absonus, contrarius; to be — with abhorrēre ab (with abl); —ly inconstanter
inconsolable adj inconsolabilis
inconstancy s inconstantia, levitas f
inconstant adj inconstans, levis
incontestable adj non contentendus
incontinence s incontinentia, impudicitia f
incontinent adj incontinens, intemperans, impudicus; —ly incontinenter
incontrovertible adj quod refutari non potest
inconvenience s incommodum n
inconvenience vt incommodare
inconvenient adj incommodus; —ly

incommode
incorporate vt concorporare, inserēre
incorporation s coagmentatio, co-optatio f
incorporeal adj incorporalis
incorrect adj mendosus, vitiosus, falsus; —ly mendose, falso, perperam
incorrigible adj incorrigibilis; (fig) perditus
incorrupt adj incorruptus, integer
incorruptibility s incorruptibilitas f, incorrupti mores m pl
incorruptible adj incorruptibilis, integer
increase s (act) accretio f; incrementum, additamentum n
increase vt augēre, ampliare; vi augēri, crescĕre
incredible adj incredibilis
incredibly adv incredibiliter, ultra fidem
incredulity s incredulitas f
incredulous adj incredulus
increment s incrementum n
incriminate vt criminari
incubation s incubatio f
inculcate vt inculcare
inculcation s inculcatio f
incumbent adj it is — on oportet (with acc)
incur vt contrahĕre, subire; (guilt) admittĕre
incurable adj insanabilis
incursion s incursio f
indebted adj obaeratus; (obliged) obligatus, devinctus, obnoxius
indecency s indecorum n, obscenitas f
indecent adj indecorus, obscenus; —ly indecore, obscene
indecision s haesitatio, dubitatio f
indecisive adj anceps, dubius, incertus
indeclinable adj indeclinabilis
indeed adv vere, profecto, sane; (concessive) quidem; (reply) certe, vero; (interr) itane?, verone?
indefatigable adj indefatigabilis, indefessus
indefensible adj non excusandus; to be — defendi non posse; (mil) tenēri non posse
indefinite adj infinitus, incertus, anceps, obscurus; —ly indefinite
indelible adj indelebilis
indelicacy s indecorum n
indelicate adj putidus, indecorus
indemnify vt compensare; damnum restituĕre (with dat)
indemnity s indemnitas f
independence s libertas f
independent adj sui potens, sui juris, liber; —ly libere, suo arbitrio
indescribable adj inenarrabilis; —ly inenarrabiliter
indestructible adj perennis, perpetuus
indeterminate adj indefinitus
index s index, elenchus m; (of dial) gnomon m
Indian adj Indicus
Indian s Indus m

indicate vt indicare, significare
indication s indicatio f, signum, indicium n
indicative adj indicativus
indict vt accusare; diem dicĕre (with dat)
indictment s libellus m, accusatio f
indifference s neglegentia, incuria, lentitudo f
indifferent adj (apathetic) remissus, neglegens, lentus; (mediocre) mediocris; **—ly** neglegenter, lente; (without discrimination) promiscue
indigenous adj indigena
indigent adj egens, inops
indigestible adj crudus
indigestion s cruditas f
indignant adj indignans, indignabundus, iratus; **to be —** indignari; **—ly** indignanter
indignation s indignatio f, dolor m
indignity s indignitas, contumelia f
indirect adj indirectus, obliquus; **—ly** indirecte, oblique
indiscreet adj inconsultus; **—ly** inconsulte, temere
indiscretion s immodestia f; (act) culpa f
indiscriminate adj promiscuus; **—ly** promiscue, sine discrimine
indispensable adj omnino necessarius
indisposed adj aversus; (in health) aegrotus; **to be —** aegrotare
indisputable adj manifestus, certus
indissoluble adj indissolubilis
indistinct adj indistinctus, parum clarus, obscurus; **—ly** indistincte
individual adj proprius, singularis, singuli; **—ly** singulatim
individual s homo m & f; **—s** singuli m pl
individuality s proprium ingenium n
indivisible adj indivisibilis, individuus
indolence s inertia, desidia f
indolent adj iners, ignavus; **—ly** ignave, segniter
indomitable adj indomitus
indorse vt ratum facĕre
indubitable adj indubitabilis
indubitably adv sine dubio
induce vt persuadēre (with dat), inducĕre
inducement s incitamentum n, illecebra f
indulge vt indulgēre (with dat), servire (with dat)
indulgence s indulgentia, venia f
indulgent adj indulgens, benignus; **—ly** indulgenter, benigne
industrious adj industrius, sedulus, strenuus; **—ly** industrie
industry s industria, assiduitas f
inebriated adj ebrius, madidus
ineffable adj ineffabilis
ineffective adj irritus, inutilis; **to be —** effectu carēre
ineffectual adj inefficax; **—ly** frustra, nequiquam
inefficiency s inutilitas f
inefficient adj inscitus, inhabilis
ineligible adj non eligibilis

inept adj ineptus
inequality s inaequalitas f
inert adj iners, segnis, socors
inertia s inertia f
inevitable adj necessarius
inexact adj haud accuratus; (of persons) indiligens
inexcusable adj inexcusabilis
inexhaustible adj inexhaustus
inexorable adj inexorabilis, durus
inexperience s imperitia, inscitia f
inexperienced adj imperitus, inexpertus
inexplicable adj inexplicabilis, inenodabilis
inexpressible adj inenarrabilis
inextricable adj inexplicabilis, inextricabilis
infallible adj certus, erroris expers
infamous adj infamis, turpis, flagitiosus; **—ly** flagitiose
infamy s infamia f, probrum n
infancy s infantia f
infant adj infans; puerilis
infant s infans m & f
infanticide s (person) infanticida m; (deed) infanticidium n
infantile adj infantilis
infantry s peditat·us -ūs m, pedites m pl
infatuate vt infatuare
infatuation s amentia, dementia f
infect vt inficĕre; (fig) contaminare
infection s contagium n, contagio f
infectious adj contagiosus
infer vt inferre, conjicĕre
inference s conjectura, conclusio f
inferior adj inferior, deterior, minor
infernal adj infernus
infertility s sterilitas f
infest vt infestare, frequentare
infidel s infidelis m & f
infidelity s infidelitas, perfidia f
infiltrate vi se insinuare
infinite adj infinitus, immensus; **—ly** infinite; (very greatly) infinito
infinitive s infinitivus modus m
infinity s infinitas, infinitio f
infirm adj infirmus, debilis
infirmary s valetudinarium n
infirmity s infirmitas, imbecillitas f
inflame vt inflammare, incendĕre, accendĕre
inflammable adj ad exardescendum facilis
inflammation s inflammatio f
inflammatory adj turbulentus, ardens
inflate vt inflare; **to be inflated** tumēre
inflation s inflatio f
inflect vt inflectĕre, curvare
inflection s flex·us -ūs m, declinatio f
inflexible adj rigidus; (fig) obstinatus, pertinax
inflexibly adv obstinate
inflict vt infligĕre, imponĕre
infliction s malum n, poena f
influence s gratia, auctoritas f, momentum n; **to have — on** valēre apud (with acc)
influence vt movēre, impellĕre
influential adj gravis, potens

influenza *s* catarrh·us -ūs *m*, gravedo *f*

influx *s* influxio *f*

inform *vt* (*to teach*) instruĕre; certiorem facĕre; *vi* **to — against** deferre de (*with abl*)

informant *s* index, delator *m*

information *s* informatio *f*, indicium *n*, nuntius *m*

informer *s* delator *m*

infraction *s* infractio *f*

infrequency *s* raritas *f*

infrequent *adj* rarus

infringe *vt* infringĕre, violare; *vi* **to — upon** occupare, usurpare

infringement *s* violatio, usurpatio *f*

infuriate *vt* efferare

infuse *vt* infundĕre; (*fig*) injicĕre

infusion *s* infusio *f*

ingenious *adj* sollers, callidus, ingeniosus; (*of thing*) artificiosus; **—ly** callide, artificiose

ingenuity *s* ars, sollertia *f*

ingenuous *adj* simplex

inglorious *adj* inglorius, inhonestus; **—ly** sine gloria, in honeste

ingrained *adj* insitus, inveteratus

ingratiate *vt* **to — oneself with** gratiam inire ab (*with abl*)

ingratitude *s* ingratus animus *m*

ingredient *s* pars *f*

inhabit *vt* incolĕre, habitare

inhabitable *adj* habitabilis

inhabitant *s* incola *m* & *f*

inhale *vt* haurire; *vi* spiritum ducĕre

inharmonious *adj* dissonus, absonus

inherent *adj* inhaerens, insitus; **to be — in** inesse (*with dat*)

inherit *vt* excipĕre

inheritance *s* hereditas, successio *f*, patrimonium *n*; **to come into an — hereditatem adire**

inheritor *s* heres *m* & *f*

inhospitable *adj* inhospitalis

inhospitably *adv* minime hospitaliter

inhospitality *s* inhospitalitas *f*

inhuman *adj* inhumanus; **—ly** inhumane

inhumanity *s* inhumanitas *f*

inimical *adj* inimicus

inimitable *adj* inimitabilis

iniquitous *adj* iniquus, improbus

iniquity *s* iniquitas, injustitia *f*

initial *adj* primus

initiate *vt* initiare, instituĕre

initiation *s* initiatio *f*

initiative *s* initium *n*

inject *vt* injicĕre, infundĕre, immittĕre

injection *s* injectio *f*

injudicious *adj* inconsultus; **—ly** inconsulte, temere

injunction *s* mandatum, imperatum *n*

injure *vt* nocēre (*with dat*), laedĕre

injurious *adj* noxius, damnosus, gravis; **—ly** male

injury *s* injuria *f*, damnum, detrimentum, malum *n*

injustice *s* injustitia *f*; (*act*) injuria *f*

ink *s* atramentum *n*

inkling *s* (*hint*) rumusculus *m*, obscura significatio *f*

inland *adj* mediterraneus

inlay *vt* inserĕre; (*with mosaic*) tessellare

inlet *s* sin·us -ūs *m*, aestuarium *n*

inmate *s* incola, inquilinus *m*

inmost *adj* intimus, imus

inn *s* caupona *f*, deversorium *n*

innate *adj* innatus, insitus

inner *adj* interior

innermost *adj* intimus, imus

innkeeper *s* caupo *m*

innocence *s* innocentia *f*; castitas *f*

innocent *adj* insons, innocens, integer, castus; **—ly** innocenter, integre, caste

innocuous *adj* innocuus; **—ly** innocue

innovation *s* novum *n*, res nova *f*

innovator *s* rerum novarum auctor *m*

innumerable *adj* innumerabilis

inoffensive *adj* innocens, innoxius

inopportune *adj* inopportunus; **—ly** parum in tempore

inordinate *adj* immoderatus; **—ly** immoderate

inquest *s* inquisitio *f*; (*law*) quaestio *f*; **to hold an —** quaerĕre

inquire *vi* inquirĕre, rogare; **to — into** investigare

inquiry *s* quaestio, investigatio *f*

inquisition *s* inquisitio *f*

inquisitive *adj* curiosus; **—ly** curiose

inquisitor *s* quaesitor *m*

inroad *s* incursio, irruptio *f*

insane *adj* insanus, vecors; **—ly** insane

insanity *s* insania, dementia *f*

insatiable *adj* insatiabilis, inexplebilis

inscribe *vt* inscribĕre, insculpĕre, incidĕre

inscription *s* inscriptio *f*, titulus *m*

inscrutable *adj* occultus, obscurus

insect *s* insectum *n*, bestiola *f*

insecure *adj* incertus, intutus, instabilis

insecurity *s* periculum *n*

insensible *adj* insensilis; (*fig*) durus

inseparable *adj* inseparabilis

insert *vt* inserĕre; (*in writing*) ascribĕre

insertion *s* insertio, interpositio *f*

inside *adj* interior

inside *adv* intrinsecus

inside *s* interior pars *f*, interiora *n pl*

inside *prep* intro (*with acc*)

insidious *adj* insidiosus, subdolus; **—ly** insidiose, subdole

insight *s* (*knowledge*) cognitio, intellegentia *f*; (*intelligence*) consilium, judicium *n*

insignia *s* insignia *n pl*

insignificance *s* exiguitas, levitas *f*

insignificant *adj* exiguus, levis, nullius momenti; (*rank*) humilis

insincere *adj* insincerus, simulatus, fucosus; **—ly** haud sincere, simulate

insincerity *s* simulatio, fallacia *f*

insinuate vt insinuare; (to hint) significare

insinuation s significatio f

insipid adj insulsus, hebes, frigidus; —ly insulse

insist vt flagitare, exposcěre; vi instare; to — on urgěre, postulare

insistence s pertinacia f

insolence s insolentia, arrogantia f

insolent adj insolens, arrogans; —ly insolenter

insoluble adj insolubilis; (fig) inexplicabilis

insolvent adj to be — solvendo non esse

inspect vt inspicěre, introspicěre, intuēri; (mil) recensēre

inspection s inspectio, cura f; (mil) recensio f

inspector s curator m

inspiration s (divine) afflat·us -ūs m; instinct·us -ūs m; (prophetic) furor m

inspire vt inspirare, incendĕre, injicĕre

instability s instabilitas f

install vt inaugurare, constituĕre

installation s inauguratio f

instalment s pensio, portio f

instance s exemplum n; at my — me auctore; for — exempli gratiā

instance vt memorare

instant adj instans, praesens; —ly extemplo, statim

instant s momentum n; this — statim, actutum

instantaneous adj praesens; —ly continuo

instead adv potius, magis

instead of prep pro (with abl), loco (with genit)

instigate vt instigare

instigation s incitatio f, stimulus m

instigator s instigator m, instigatrix f

instill vt instillare, imbuĕre, injicĕre

instinct s instinct·us -ūs m, natura f

instinctive adj naturalis; —ly instinctu

institute vt instituĕre, constituĕre, condĕre

institute s institutum n

institution s (act) institutio f; (thing instituted) institutum n

instruct vt (to teach) docēre, instituĕre; (to order) praecipĕre (with dat), mandare

instruction s institutio, eruditio, doctrina f; —s mandata n pl

instructive adj ad docendum aptus

instructor s praeceptor, magister, doctor m, magistra f

instrument s instrumentum n; (mus) organum n; (law) tabula, syngrapha f

instrumental adj aptus, utilis

insubordinate adj seditiosus, male parens

insubordination s inobedientia, intemperantia f

insufferable adj intolerandus, intolerabilis

insufficiency s defect·us -ūs m, inopia f

insufficient adj impar, parum sufficiens; —ly haud satis

insular adj insulanus

insulate vt segregare

insult s probrum n, injuria, contumelia f

insult vt insultare; contumeliam imponĕre (with dat), contumeliā afficĕre

insultingly adv contumeliose

insure vt tutum praestare

insurgent adj rebellis

insurgent s rebellis m

insurmountable adj inexsuperabilis

insurrection s rebellio, seditio f

intact adj integer, intactus, incolumis

intangible adj intactilis

integral adj necessarius

integrity s integritas, innocentia, fides f

intellect s intellect·us -ūs, animus m, mens f, ingenium n

intellectual adj ingeniosus

intelligence s ingenium n, intellegentia f; (information) nuntius m

intelligent adj sapiens, argutus, prudens; —ly intellegenter, sapienter, prudenter

intelligible adj intellegibilis, perspicuus

intelligibly adv intellegibiliter, perspicue

intemperance s intemperantia f

intemperate adj immodicus, intemperatus; —ly intemperanter

intend vt (with inf) intendĕre, in animo habēre; (with object) destinare

intended adj destinatus; (of future spouse) sponsus

intense adj acer, fervidus; (of heat) rapidus; (excessive) nimius; —ly vehementer, valde, nimium

intensify vt augēre

intensity s vehmentia, vis f; (of winter, etc.) rigor m

intent adj intentus, attentus; to be — on animum intendĕre in (with acc); —ly intente

intention s propositum, consilium n; (meaning) significatio f

intentionally adv de industria

inter vt inhumare, sepelire

intercede vi intercedĕre, deprecari, se interponĕre

intercept vt excipĕre, intercipĕre, intercludĕre

intercession s deprecatio f; (of tribune) intercessio f

intercessor s deprecator m

interchange vt permutare, commutare

interchange s permutatio, vicissitudo f

intercourse s commercium n; (social) consuetudo f; (sexual) congress·us -ūs, coit·us -ūs m

interdict vt interdicĕre, prohibēre

interdiction s interdictio f, interdictum n

interest s (attention) studium n; (advantage) utilitas f, us·us -ūs m, commodum *n*; (*money*) faenus *n*, usura *f*; **it is of — to me** meā interest, meā refert

interested *adj* **— in** studiosus (*with genit*), attentus (*with dat*)

interfere *vi* intercedĕre, intervenire, interpellare

interference *s* intercessio *f*, dissidium *n*, intervent·us -ūs *m*

interim *s* intervallum *n*; **in the —** interim, interea

interior *adj* interior

interior *s* interior pars *f*

interjection *s* interjectio *f*

interlinear *adj* interscriptus

interlude *s* embolium *n*

intermarriage *s* connubium *n*

intermarry *vi* matrimonio inter se conjungi

intermediary *s* internuntius *m*

intermediate *adj* medius

interment *s* sepultura, humatio *f*

interminable *adj* infinitus

intermission *s* intermissio, intercapedo *f*

intermittent *adj* intermittens, interruptus; **—ly** interdum, aliquando

internal *adj* intestinus, domesticus; **—ly** intus, interne; domi

international *adj* inter gentes

interpolate *vt* interpolare

interpolation *s* interpolatio *f*

interpret *vt* interpretari

interpretation *s* interpretatio *f*

interpreter *s* interpres *m*

interrogate *vt* interrogare, percontari

interrogation *s* interrogatio, percontatio *f*

interrogative *adj* interrogativus

interrupt *vt* interrumpĕre, interpellare

interruption *s* interruptio, interpellatio *f*

intersect *vt* intersecare

intersection *s* quadrivium *n*

intersperse *vt* inmiscēre

intertwine *vt* intertexĕre

interval *s* intervallum, spatium *n*

intervene *vi* (*to be between*) interjacēre; (*to come between*) intercedĕre, intervenire

intervening *adj* medius

intervention *s* intercessio *f*, intervent·us -ūs *m*

interview *s* colloquium *n*, congress·us -ūs *m*

interview *vt* percontari

interweave *vt* intertexĕre, intexĕre

intestinal *adj* ad intestina pertinens

intestine *adj* intestinus; (*pol*) domesticus, civicus

intestines *s* intestina *n pl*; (*of victim*) exta *n pl*

intimacy *s* familiaritas, consuetudo *f*

intimate *adj* familiaris; intimus; **—ly** familiariter; intime

intimate *vt* indicare, innuĕre, denuntiare

intimation *s* indicium *n*, denuntiatio *f*

intimidate *vt* minari (*with dat*), metum injicĕre (*with dat*), terrēre

intimidation *s* minae *f pl*

into *prep* in (*with acc*)

intolerable *adj* intolerabilis, intolerandus

intolerably *adv* intoleranter

intolerance *s* intolerantia *f*; superbia *f*

intolerant *adj* intolerans, impatiens

intonation *s* accent·us -ūs *m*

intone *vt* cantare

intoxicate *vt* ebrium reddĕre

intoxicated *adj* ebrius

intoxication *s* ebrietas *f*

intractable *adj* intractabilis, indocilis

intrepid *adj* intrepidus, impavidus; **—ly** intrepide

intricacy *s* perplexitas, implicatio *f*

intricate *adj* contortus, implicatus, perplexus; **—ly** contorte, perplexe

intrigue *s* conspiratio *f*, dolus *m*, artificia *n pl*

intrigue *vt* fascinare; *vi* machinari, dolis contendĕre

intrinsic *adj* innatus, verus; **—ally** vere, per se

introduce *vt* introducĕre, inducĕre

introduction *s* (*preface*) praefatio *f*, exordium, prooemium *n*; (*to person*) introductio *f*, adit·us -ūs *m*

intrude *vi* se interponĕre, se inculcare, intervenire

intruder *s* interpellator, advena *m*; homo molestus *m*

intrusion *s* interpellatio, usurpatio *f*

intuition *s* intuit·us -ūs *m*, cognitio *f*, acumen *n*

intuitive *adj* intuitivus; **—ly** mentis propriā vi ac naturā

inundate *vt* inundare

inundation *s* inundatio *f*, diluvium *n*

invade *vt* incurrĕre in (*with acc*), invadĕre

invader *s* invasor *m*

invalid *adj* infirmus, vitiosus; (*sick*) aeger, aegrotus

invalid *s* aegrotus *m*

invalidate *vt* irritum facĕre, rescindĕre

invaluable *adj* inaestimabilis

invariable *adj* constans, immutabilis

invariably *adv* semper

invasion *s* incursio, irruptio *f*

invective *s* convicium, probrum *n*

inveigh *vi* **to — against** invehi in (*with acc*), insectari

invent *vt* invenire, reperire; (*to contrive*) excogitare, fingĕre

invention *s* (*act*) inventio *f*; (*thing invented*) inventum *n*

inventive *adj* sollers, ingeniosus

inventor *s* inventor, auctor *m*

inventory *s* bonorum index *m*

inverse *adj* inversus, conversus; **—ly** inverso ordine

inversion *s* inversio, conversio *f*

invert *vt* invertĕre

invest *vt* (*money*) collocare, ponĕre; (*to besiege*) obsidēre

investigate *vt* investigare, indagare; (*law*) quaerĕre, cognoscĕre

investigation *s* investigatio *f*; (*law*) cognitio *f*

investigator *s* investigator, indaga-
tor *m*; (*law*) quaesitor *m*

investment *s* (*of money*) collocatio
f; (*money invested*) locata pecunia
f; (*mil*) obsessio *f*

inveterate *adj* inveteratus

invigorate *vt* corroborare, recreare

invincible *adj* invictus, insuperabilis

inviolable *adj* inviolatus, sacrosanctus

inviolate *adj* inviolatus, intactus

invisible *adj* invisibilis, caecus

invitation *s* invitatio *f*

invite *vt* invitare, adhibēre

inviting *adj* suavis, gratus, blandus;
—**ly** blande

invocation *s* invocatio, testatio *f*

invoice *s* libellus *m*

invoke *vt* vocare, invocare, obtestari

involuntarily *adv* invite, coacte

involuntary *adj* non voluntarius,
coactus

involve *vt* implicare, involvĕre; (*to
comprise*) continēre

involved *adj* **to be** — illigari; **to
be** — **in debt** aere alieno laborare

invulnerable *adj* invulnerabilis

inward *adj* interior; —**ly** intus, intrinsecus

inwards *adv* introrsus

Ionian *adj* Ionicus

irascible *adj* iracundus

ire *s* ira *f*

Ireland *s* Hibernia *f*

iris *s* iris *f*

Irish *adj* Hibernicus

irk *vt* incommodare; **I am irked**
taedet me, piget me

irksome *adj* molestus, odiosus

iron *s* ferrum *n*

iron *adj* ferreus

ironical *adj* ironicus, deridens; —**ly**
per ironiam

irony *s* ironia, dissimulatio *f*

irradiate *vt* illustrare; *vi* effulgēre

irrational *adj* rationis expers, irra-
tionalis, absurdus; —**ly** absurde

irreconcilable *adj* implacabilis; (*incompatible*) repugnans, insociabilis

irrecoverable *adj* irreparabilis

irrefutable *adj* certus, invictus

irregular *adj* irregularis, abnormis;
(*disorderly*) tumultuarius; (*gram*)
anomalus; —**ly** irregulariter

irregularity *s* irregularitas *f*; (*of
conduct*) luxuries, pravitas *f*; (*gram*)
anomalia *f*

irrelevant *adj* non pertinens, alienus; **it is** — nil ad rem pertinet

irreligious *adj* impius

irremediable *adj* insanabilis

irreparable *adj* irreparabilis, irrevocabilis

irreproachable *adj* irreprehensus,
integer

irresistible *adj* inexsuperabilis, invictus

irresolute *adj* dubius, incertus animi; (*permanent characteristic*) parum firmus; —**ly** dubitanter

irresolution *s* dubitatio *f*; animus
parum firmus *m*

irresponsibility *s* incuria *f*

irresponsible *adj* incuriosus

irretrievable *adj* irreparabilis, irrevocabilis

irreverence *s* impietas *f*

irreverent *adj* impius, inverecundus;
—**ly** impie

irrevocable *adj* irrevocabilis

irrigate *vt* irrigare

irrigation *s* irrigatio, inductio aquae
f

irritability *s* iracundia *f*

irritable *adj* irritabilis, iracundus,
difficilis

irritate *vt* irritare; (*wound*) inflammare

irritation *s* irritatio, iracundia *f*,
stomachus *m*

island *s* insula *f*

islander *s* insulanus *m*

islet *s* parva insula *f*

isolate *vt* sejungĕre, secernĕre

issue *s* (*result*) event·us -ūs, exit·us
-ūs *m*; (*question*) res *f*; (*offspring*)
proles *f*; (*of book*) editio *f*; (*of
money*) emissio *f*

issue *vt* (*to distribute*) distribuĕre;
(*orders, etc.*) edĕre, proponĕre, promulgare; (*money*) erogare; (*book*)
edĕre; *vi* emanare, egredi; (*to turn
out, result*) evenire, evadĕre

isthmus *s* isthmus *m*

it *pron* id, hoc

itch *s* prurigo *f*, prurit·us -ūs *m*;
(*disease*) scabies *f*

itch *vi* prurire; (*fig*) gestire

item *s* res *f*

itinerant *adj* circumforaneus, vagus

itinerary *s* itinerarium *n*

its *pron* ejus; — **own** suus

itself *pron* (*refl*) se, sese; (*intensive*)
ipsum

ivory *s* ebur *n*

ivory *adj* eburneus

ivy *s* hedera *f*

J

jabber *vi* blaterare

jackass *s* asinus *m*; (*fig*) stultus *m*

jacket *s* tunica *f*

jaded *adj* defessus

jagged *adj* serratus; (*of rocks*) praeruptus

jail *s* carcer *m*

jailer *s* carcerarius *m*

jam *s* baccarum conditura *f*

jam *vt* frequentare, stipare; (*to obstruct*) impedire, obstruĕre

jamb *s* postis *m*

jangle *vi* crepitare

January *s* (*mensis*) Januarius *m*

jar *s* olla, amphora *f*; urceus, cadus *m*

jar *vt* vibrare; offendĕre; *vi* discrepare

jargon *s* confusae voces *f pl*

jarring *adj* dissonus, discors

jaundice *s* morbus regius *m*

jaundiced *adj* ictericus, felle suffusus; (*fig*) lividus, morosus

jaunt *s* excursio *f*; **to take a —** excurrĕre

javelin *s* pilum, jaculum *n*; **to hurl a —** jaculari

jaw *s* mala, maxilla *f*; **—s** (*fig*) fauces *f pl*

jawbone *s* maxilla *f*

jay *s* graculus *m*

jealous *adj* invidus, lividus; **to be — of** invidēre (*with dat*)

jealousy *s* invidia, aemulatio *f*

jeer *s* irrisio *f*, irris·us ·ūs *m*

jeer *vt* deridēre, explodĕre; *vi* **to — at** irridēre, alludĕre

jelly *s* cylon, quilon *n*

jellyfish *s* pulmo, halipleumon *m*

jeopardize *vt* periclitari, in periculum adducĕre

jeopardy *s* periculum *n*

jerk *s* verber, ict·us ·ūs, impet·us ·ūs *m*

jerk *vt* calcitrare, icĕre

jerky *adj* (*of style*) salebrosus

jest *s* jocus *m*; **in —** joco, jocose

jest *vi* jocari, ludĕre

jester *s* joculator *m*; (*buffoon*) scurra *m*

jestingly *adv* per jocum

Jesus *s* Jesus *m*

jet *s* scatebra *f*

jetty *s* moles *f*

Jew *s* Judaeus *m*

jewel *s* gemma *f*

jeweled *adj* gemmeus, gemmifer

jeweler *s* gemmarius *m*

jewelry *s* gemmae *f pl*

Jewish *adj* Judaicus

jig *s* tripudium *n*

jilt *vt* repudiare

jingle *vi* tinnire

jingle *s* tinnit·us ·ūs *m*

job *s* negotiolum, opus *n*

jockey *s* agaso *m*

jocose *adj* jocosus; **—ly** jocose

jocular *adj* jocularis, facetus

jog *vi* **to — along** lente progredi

join *vt* (*to connect*) jungĕre, conjungĕre; (*to come into the company of*) se jungĕre (*with dat*), se jungĕre cum (*with abl*); *vi* conjungi, adjungi, cohaerēre; **to — in** particeps esse (*with genit*), interesse (*with dat*); **to — together** inter se conjungi

joint *adj* communis; **—ly** una, conjunctim, communiter

joint *s* (*of body*) articulus *m*, commissura *f*; (*of plant*) geniculum *n*; (*of any structure*) compages *f*

jointed *adj* geniculatus

joist *s* tignum *n*

joke *s* jocus *m*

joke *vi* jocari, ludĕre

joker *s* joculator *m*

joking *s* jocus *m*; **all — aside** joco remoto; **—ly** per jocum

jolly *adj* hilaris, festivus

jolt *vt* jactare, concutĕre; (*fig*) percellĕre; *vi* jactari

jolting *s* jactatio *f*

jostle *vt* pulsare, agitare, fodicare

jot *s* hilum *n*; **not a — minime**; **to care not a —** non flocci facĕre

jot *vt* **to — down** notare, subscribĕre

journal *s* ephemeris *f*, acta diurna *n pl*

journey *s* iter *n*

journey *vi* iter facĕre; **to — abroad** peregrinari

journeyman *s* opifex *m*

Jove *s* Jupiter *m*

jovial *adj* hilaris

jowl *s* bucca *f*

joy *s* gaudium *n*, laetitia *f*

joyful *adj* laetus; **—ly** laete, libenter

joyless *adj* illaetabilis

joyous *adj* hilaris, festivus

jubilant *adj* laetus, gaudio exsultans, gaudio triumphans

jubilation *s* exsultatio *f*

jubilee *s* dies anniversarius *m*, solemne *n*

Judaic *adj* Judaicus

Judaism *s* Judaismus *m*

judge *s* judex, quaesitor, arbiter *m*

judge *vt* judicare; (*to think*) existimare, censēre; (*to value*) aestimare; (*to decide between*) dijudicare

judgment *s* judicium, arbitrium *n*; (*opinion*) sententia *f*, judicium *n*; **to pass — on** statuĕre de (*with abl*); **to pronounce —** jus dicĕre

judgment seat *s* tribunal *n*

judicial *adj* judicialis, judicarius; **—ly** jure, lege

judicious *adj* sapiens, sagax, prudens; **—ly** sapienter, sagaciter, prudenter

jug *s* urceus *m*

juggle *vi* praestigias agĕre

juggler *s* praestigiator *m*

juice *s* sucus, liquor *m*

juicy *adj* sucidus

July *s* (*mensis*) Quintilis *or* Julius *m*

jumble *s* congeries, confusio *f*

jumble *vt* confundĕre, permiscēre

jump *s* salt·us ·ūs *m*

jump *vt* transilire; *vi* salire; **to — at** (*opportunity*) captare; **to — for joy** exsultare

junction *s* conjunctio *f*

juncture *s* tempus *n*; **at this —** hic

June *s* (*mensis*) Junius *m*

jungle *s* salt·us ·ūs *m*

junior *adj* junior, minor natu

juniper *s* juniperus *m*

jurisdiction *s* jurisdictio *f*

jurisprudence *s* jurisprudentia *f*

jurist *s* jurisconsultus *m*

juror *s* judex *m*

jury *s* judices *m pl*

just *adj* justus, aequus; (*deserved*) meritus; **—ly** juste; jure, merito

just *adv* (*only*) modo; (*exactly*) prorsus; (*with adv*) demum, denique; **— after** sub (*with acc*); **— as** aeque ac, perinde ac, sic ut, haud secus ac; — **before** sub (*with acc*); — now modo; — **so it** prorsus

justice s justitia, aequitas f; (*just treatment*) jus n; (*person*) praetor m

justifiable adj justus, legitimus, excusatus

justifiably adv jure

justification s purgatio, excusatio f

justify vt purgare, excusare, approbare

jut vi prominēre; **to — out** prominēre, eminēre, procurrēre

juvenile adj juvenilis, puerilis

K

kale s crambe f

keel s carina f

keen adj acer, sagax; **—ly** acute, acriter; sagaciter

keenness s (*of scent*) sagacitas f; (*of sight*) acies f; (*of pain*) acerbitas f; (*enthusiasm*) studium n

keep vt tenēre, habēre; (*to preserve*) servare; (*to celebrate*) agĕre, celebrare; (*to guard*) custodire; (*to obey*) observare; (*to support*) alĕre; (*animals*) pascĕre; (*to store*) condĕre; **to — apart** distinēre; **to — away** arcēre; **to — back** retinēre, cohibēre; (*to conceal*) celare; **to — company** comitari; **to — from** prohibēre; **to — in** cohibēre, claudĕre; **to — off** arcēre, defendĕre; **to — secret** celare; **to — together** continēre; **to — under** compescĕre, supprimĕre; **to — up** sustinēre; vi remanēre, durare; **to — away** abstinēre; **to — up with** subsequi

keep s custodia, cura f

keeper s custos m

keeping s tutela, custodia, cura f; **in — with** pro (*with abl*)

keepsake s monumentum, pignus n

keg s cadus m, testa f

ken s conspect·us -ūs m

kennel s stabulum n

kernel s nucleus m; (*fig*) medulla f

kettle s lebes f

kettledrum s tympanum aeneum n

key s clavis f; (*of a position*) claustra n pl

keyhole s foramen n

kick vt calce ferire; vi calcitrare

kid s haedus m

kidnap vt surripĕre

kidnapper s plagiarius m

kidney s ren m

kill vt interficĕre, caedĕre, occidĕre, necare; (*time*) perdĕre

killer s interfector, necator m

kiln s fornax f

kin s cognati, consanguinei, necessarii m pl

kind adj amicus, benignus, benevolus; **—ly** benigne, clementer

kind s genus n; **what — of** qualis

kindhearted adj benignus

kindle vt incendĕre, accendĕre, inflammare

kindly adj benignus

kindness s benignitas, benevolentia f; (*deed*) beneficium, officium n

kindred adj consanguineus, cognatus

kindred s consanguinitas, cognatio f; cognati, propinqui m pl

king s rex m

kingdom s regnum n

kingfisher s alcedo f

kingly adj regius, regalis

kinsman s necessarius, cognatus, propinquus m

kinswoman s necessaria, cognata, propinqua f

kiss s osculum, basium n

kiss vt osculari

kissing s osculatio f

kitchen s culina f

kite s (*bird*) milvus m

kitten s catulus felinus m

knack s sollertia, calliditas f

knapsack s sarcina f

knave s nebulo, veterator m

knavish adj nefarius, improbus; (*mischievous*) malitiosus

knead vt subigĕre

knee s genu n

kneel vi genibus niti

knell s campana funebris f

knife s culter m; (*for surgery*) scalprum n

knight s eques m

knighthood s equestris dignitas f

knightly adj equester

knit vt texĕre; **to — the brow** frontem contrahĕre

knob s tuber n, nodus m; (*of door*) bulla f

knock vt **to — down** dejicĕre, sternĕre; (*fig*) (*at auction*) addicĕre; **to — in** impellĕre, infigĕre; **to — off** excutĕre, decidĕre; **to — out** excutĕre; vi **to — about** (*to ramble*) vagari; **to — at** pulsare

knock s pulsatio f, puls·us -ūs m

knoll s tumulus m

knot s nodus m, geniculum n; (*of people*) corona f

knot vt nodare, nectĕre

knotty adj nodosus; (*fig*) spinosus

know vt scire; (*person*) novisse; **not to — ignorare**, nescire; **to — how to** scire (*with inf*)

knowing adj callidus, prudens; **—ly** sciens, de industria, consulto

knowledge s scientia, doctrina f; (*of something*) cognitio f; (*skill*) peritia f; (*learning*) eruditio f

known adj notus; (*common*) tritus; **to become —** enotescĕre; **to make — divulgare**, declarare

knuckle s articulus, condylus m

kowtow vi adulari

L

label *s* titulus *m*
labor *s* labor *m*; (*manual*) opera *f*; (*work done*) opus *n*; **to be in —** laborare utero; **woman in —** puerpera *f*
labor *vi* laborare, eniti; **to — under** laborare (*with abl*)
laboratory *s* officina *f*
labored *adj* affectatus
laborer *s* operarius *m*
labyrinth *s* labyrinthus *m*
labyrinthine *adj* labyrinthicus; (*fig*) inextricabilis
lace *s* opus reticulatum *n*
lace *vt* (*to tie*) nectĕre, astringĕre; (*to beat*) verberare
lacerate *vt* lacerare, laniare
laceration *s* laceratio *f*
lack *s* inopia *f*, defect·us -ūs *m*, defectio *f*
lack *vt* carēre (*with abl*), egēre (*with abl*)
lackey *s* pedisequus, servus a pedibus *m*
laconic *adj* brevis, astrictus; **—ally** breviter, paucis
lad *s* puer, adulescens *m*
ladder *s* scala *f*
ladle *s* ligula, spatha *f*, cochlear *n*
lady *s* domina, matrona *f*
lag *vi* cessare, morari, cunctari
lagoon *s* lacuna *f*, stagnum *n*
lair *s* cubile, latibulum *n*
laity *s* laici *m pl*
lake *s* lac·us -ūs *m*
lamb *s* agnus *m*, agna *f*; (*meat*) agnina *f*
lame *adj* claudus; **to walk —** claudicare; **—ly** (*fig*) inconcinne
lameness *s* clauditas *f*
lament *s* lamentum *n*, lamentatio *f*
lament *vt* lamentari, deplorare; *vi* flēre
lamentable *adj* lamentabilis, miserabilis
lamentably *adv* miserabiliter
lamentation *s* lamentatio *f*
lamp *s* lucerna *f*, lynchnus *m*
lampoon *s* satira *f*, libellus *m*
lampoon *vt* famosis carminibus lacessĕre
lance *s* lancea, hasta *f*
lance *vt* incidĕre
land *s* (*soil*) terra, tellus *f*; (*country*) regio *f*; (*estate*) fundus *m*, praedium *n*
land *vt* in terram exponĕre; *vi* egredi, appellĕre
landing place *s* egress·us -ūs *m*
landlord *s* (*of inn*) caupo *m*; (*of land*) dominus *m*
landmark *s* lapis, terminus *m*
landscape *s* regionis sit·us -ūs *m*
landslide *s* terrae lap·us -ūs *m*
land tax *s* vectigal *n*
lane *s* semita *f*
language *s* lingua *f*; (*style or manner of verbal expression*) oratio *f*, sermo *m*, verba *n pl*

languid *adj* languidus; **—ly** languide
languish *vi* languēre, languescĕre
languishing *adj* languidus, tabescens
languor *s* languor *m*
lanky *adj* prolixus, exilis
lantern *s* la(n)terna *f*
lap *s* sin·us -ūs *m*; (*fig*) gremium *n*; (*in racing*) spatium *n*
lap *vt* lambĕre
lapse *s* laps·us -ūs *m*; (*error*) erratum, peccatum *n*, error *m*
lapse *vi* labi; (*of agreement*) irritus fieri; (*to err*) peccare
larceny *s* furtum *n*
lard *s* laridum, lardum *n*, adeps *m & f*
large *adj* magnus, amplus, grandis; **to a — extent** magna ex parte; **—ly** plerumque
largess *s* donativum *n*, largitio *f*; **to give a —** largiri
lark *s* alauda *f*
larynx *s* guttur *n*
lascivious *adj* lascivus, salax, libidinosus; **—ly** lascive, libidinose
lash *s* verber, flagellum *n*, scutica *f*; (*mark*) vibex *m*
lash *vt* (*to whip*) flagellare; (*to fasten*) alligare; (*fig*) castigare
lashing *s* verberatio *f*
lass *s* puella, virgo *f*
lassitude *s* lassitudo *f*
last *adj* postremus, ultimus; (*in line*) novissimus; (*preceding*) proximus; **at —** demum, tandem; **for the — time** postremo
last *vi* durare, perdurare
lasting *adj* diuturnus, perennis
lastly *adv* denique, postremo
latch *s* obex *m & f*
latch *vt* oppessulare
late *adj* serus, tardus; (*new*) recens; (*deceased*) demortuus; (*said of deceased emperor*) divus
late *adv* sero; **too —** sero, serius
lately *adv* modo, recens, nuper
latent *adj* latens, latitans, occultus
lateral *adj* lateralis
lather *s* spuma *f*
Latin *adj* Latinus; **to speak —** Latine loqui; **to translate into —** Latine reddĕre; **to understand —** Latine scire
Latinity *s* Latinitas *f*
latitude *s* latitudo *f*; (*liberty*) licentia *f*
latter *adj* posterior; **the —** hic
lattice *s* cancelli *m pl*
laudable *adj* laudabilis
laudably *adv* laudabiliter
laudatory *adj* laudativus, honorificus
laugh *s* ris·us -ūs *m*
laugh *vi* ridēre; **to — at** deridēre; **to — with** arridēre (*with dat*)
laughingstock *s* ludibrium *n*

laughter s ris·us -ūs m; (loud) cachinnus m, cachinnatio f
launch vt deducěre; (to hurl) jaculari, contorquēre; vi to — forth or out proficisci
laundress s lotrix f
laundry s lavatorium n
laureate adj laureatus
laurel adj laureus
laurel tree s laurus f
lava s liquefacta massa f
lavish adj prodigus; —ly prodige
lavish vt prodigěre, profunděre
lavishness s prodigalitas, profusio f
law s lex f; (right) jus n; (rule) norma f; (divine) fas n; to break the — leges violare; to pass a — legem perferre
law-abiding adj bene moratus
law court s judicium n; (building) basilica f
lawful adj legitimus, licitus, fas; —ly legitime, lege
lawless adj exlex, illegitimus; —ly illegitime, licenter
lawlessness s licentia f
lawn s pratulum n
lawsuit s lis, causa f
lawyer s jurisconsultus, causidicus m
lax adj remissus; (fig) neglegens; —ly remisse; neglegens
laxity s remissio f
lay vt poněre; (eggs) parěre; (foundations) jacěre; (hands) injicěre; (plans) capěre, inire; to — an ambush insidiari; to — aside poněre, amověre; to — before proponěre; to — claim to arrogare, vindicare; to — down (office) resignare; (rules) statuěre; to — down arms ab armis disceděre; to — hold of prehenděre, arripěre; to — open patefacěre; to — out (money) expenděre; (plans) designare; to — up conděre, reponěre; to — waste vastare
lay s cantilena f
layer s (stratum) corium n; (of a plant) propago f
lazily adv ignave, pigre
laziness s segnities, pigritia f
lazy adv ignavus, piger, iners
lead s plumbum n
lead vt ducěre; (life) agěre; to — about circumducěre; to — away abducěre; to — off divertěre; to — on conducěre; vi to — up to tenděre ad (with acc)
leaden adj plumbeus
leader s dux, ductor m; (fig) auctor m
leadership s duct·us -ūs m
leading adj princeps, primus, praecipuus
leaf s folium n; (of vine) pampinus m; (of paper) pagina, scheda f; (of metal) bractea f
leafless adj fronde nudatus
leafy adj frondosus, frondeus
league s foedus n, societas f
leak s rima f, hiat·us -ūs m
leak vi perfluěre, rimas agěre

leaky adj rimosus
lean adj macer, macilentus
lean vt inclinare; vi inclinare, niti; to — back se reclinare; to — on inniti in (with abl), incumběre (with dat)
leap s salt·us -ūs m
leap vi salire; to — for joy exsultare
leap year s bisextilis annus m
learn vt discěre, cognoscěre; (news) accipěre, audire; to — by heart ediscěre
learned adj eruditus, doctus; —ly docte
learning s (act) discěre; (knowledge) eruditio f
lease s conductio, locatio f
lease vt conducěre; to — out locare
leash s lorum n
least adj minimus
least adv minime; at — saltem; not in the — ne minimum quidem
leather s corium n; (tanned) aluta f
leather adj scorteus
leathery adj lentus
leave vt relinquěre, deserěre, destituěre; (to entrust) mandare, traděre; (legacy) legare; to — behind relinquěre; to — out omittěre, praetermittěre; vi (to depart) disceděre, proficisci, abire; to — off desiněre, desistěre
leave s permissio f; — of absence commeat·us -ūs m; to ask — veniam petěre; to obtain — impetrare; to take — of valēre jubēre; with your — pace tua
leaven s fermentum n
leaven vt fermentare
lecherous adj libidinosus, salax
lecture s lectio, praelectio, acroasis f
lecture vi (to reprove) objurgare; vi praelegěre
lecturer s lector, praelector m
ledge s projectura f, limen, dorsum n
ledger s codex (accepti et expensi) m
leech s sanguisuga, hirudo f
leer vi limis oculis spectare
leering adj limus, lascivus
left adj laevus, sinister; on the — a sinistra; to the — ad sinistram, sinistrorsum
leftover adj reliquus
leftovers s reliquiae f pl
leg s crus n; (of table, etc.) pes m
legacy s legatum n
legal adj legalis, legitimus; judicialis; —ly legitime, lege
legalize vt sancire
legate s legatus m
legation s legatio f
legend s fabula f; (inscription) titulus m
legendary adj commenticius, fabulosus
legging s ocrea f
legible adj clarus
legion s legio f
legislate vi leges facěre

legislation *s* leges *f pl*

legislator *s* legum lator *m*

legitimate *adj* legitimus; **—ly** legitime

leisure *s* otium *n;* **at —** otiosus, vacuus

leisure *adj* otiosus, vacuus; **—ly** otiose

leisurely *adj* lentus

lemon *s* pomum citreum *n*

lemonade *s* aqua limonata *f*

lend *vt* commodare; **to — money** pecuniam mutuam dare; (*at interest*) pecuniam faenerare *or* faenerari; **to — one's ear** aures praebēre

length *s* longitudo *f;* (*of time*) longinquitas, diuturnitas *f;* **at —** tandem

lengthen *vt* extendēre, protrahēre, producēre

lengthwise *adv* in longitudinem

lengthy *adj* longus, prolixus

leniency *s* lenitas, clementia, mansuetudo *f*

lenient *adj* lenis, mitis, clemens; **—ly** leniter, clementer

lentil *s* lens *f*

leopard *s* leopardus, pardus *m*

leper *s* leprosus *m*

leprosy *s* leprae *f pl*

less *adj* minor

less *adv* minus

lessee *s* conductor *m*

lessen *vt* minuēre; *vi* decrescēre, minui

lesson *s* documentum *n;* **to give —s in** docēre

lessor *s* locator *m*

lest *conj* ne

let *vt* (*to allow*) sinēre, pati, permittēre; (*to lease*) locare; **to — alone** omittēre, **to — down** (*to disappoint*) deesse (*with dat*), destituēre; **to — fall** a manibus mittēre; **to — fly** emittēre, contorquēre; **to — go** (di)mittēre; **to — in** admittēre; **to — off** absolvēre; **to — out** emittēre; **to — pass** omittēre; **to — slip** omittēre

lethargic *adj* lethargicus

lethargy *s* lethargus *m;* (*fig*) veternus *m*

letter *s* (*of alphabet*) littera *f;* (*epistle*) litterae *f pl,* epistula *f;* **by — per litteras; to the —** ad verbum

letter carrier *s* tabellarius *m*

lettered *adj* litteratus

lettering *s* titulus *m*

lettuce *s* lactuca *f*

level *adj* planus, aequus

level *s* planities *f;* (*tool*) libra, libella *f*

level *vt* aequare, adaequare; (*to the ground*) solo aequare, sternēre

lever *s* vectis *m*

levity *s* levitas *f*

levy *s* delect·us -ūs *m*

levy *vt* (*troops*) conscribēre; (*tax*) exigēre

lewd *adj* impudicus, incestus

lewdness *s* impudicitia *f*

liable *adj* obnoxius

liar *s* mendax *m & f*

libation *s* libatio *f;* **to pour a —** libare

libel *s* calumnia *f*

libel *vt* calumniari

libelous *adj* famosus, probrosus

liberal *adj* liberalis, munificus; (*fig*) ingenuus; **—ly** liberaliter

liberality *s* liberalitas, munificentia *f*

liberate *vt* liberare; (*slave*) manumittēre

liberation *s* liberatio *f*

liberator *s* liberator *m*

libertine *s* homo dissolutus *m*

liberty *s* libertas *f;* licentia *f;* **at —** liber

librarian *s* librarius *m*

library *s* bibliotheca *f*

license *s* (*permission*) copia, potestas *f;* (*freedom*) licentia *f*

license *vt* potestatem dare (*with dat*)

licentious *adj* dissolutus, impudicus; **—ly** dissolute, impudice

lick *vt* lambēre; (*daintily*) liqurrire

lictor *s* lictor *m*

lid *s* operculum, operimentum *n*

lie *s* mendacium *n;* **to give the — to** redarguēre; **to tell a —** mentiri

lie *vi* (*to tell a lie or lies*) mentiri; (*to be lying down*) jacēre, cubare; (*to be situated*) situs esse; **to — down** jacēre; **to — in wait** insidiari; **to — on** *or* **upon** incubare (*with dat*), incumbēre (*with dat*)

lieu *s* **in — of** loco (*with genit*), pro (*with abl*)

lieutenant *s* legatus, praefectus *m*

life *s* vita, anima *f;* (*fig*) vigor *m,* alacritas *f*

lifeblood *s* sanguis *m*

life history *s* vita *f*

lifeless *adj* inanimus, exanimis; (*fig*) exsanguis, frigidus; **—ly** (*fig*) frigide

lifetime *s* aetas *f*

lift *vt* tollēre, attollēre, sublevare; **to — up** attollēre, efferre

ligament *s* ligamentum, ligamen *n*

ligature *s* ligatura *f*

light *s* lux *f,* lumen *n;* (*lamp*) lucerna *f;* **to bring to — in** lucem proferre; **to throw — on** lumen adhibēre (*with dat*)

light *adj* (*bright*) lucidus, fulgens; (*in weight*) levis; (*of colors*) candidus, dilutus; (*easy*) facilis; (*nimble*) agilis; **—ly** leviter

light *vt* accendēre, incendēre; (*to illuminate*) illuminare; *vi* flammam concipēre; **to — on** *or* **upon** incidēre (*with dat*), offendēre; **to — up** (*fig*) hilaris fieri

lighten *vt* (*to illumine*) illustrare; (*weight*) allevare, exonerare; *vi* (*in sky*) fulgurare

lighthouse *s* pharus *f*

lightness *s* levitas, agilitas *f*

lightning *s* fulmen, fulgur *n;* **struck by —** fulmine ictus, de caelo tactus

like *adj* similis (*with dat*); (*equal*) par (*with dat*), aequus (*with dat*)

like *prep* instar (*with genit*); tamquam, ut, velut

like *vt* amare, diligĕre; **I — this** hoc mihi placet; **I — to do this** me juvat hoc facĕre

likelihood *s* verisimilitudo *f*

likely *adj* verisimilis, probabilis

likely *adv* probabiliter

liken *vt* comparare

likeness *s* similitudo *f*; (*portrait*) imago, effigies *f*

likewise *adv* pariter, similiter, item

liking *s* amor *m*; (*fancy*) libido *f*

lilac *s* syringa vulgaris *f*

lily *s* lilium *n*

lily of the valley *s* convallaria majalis *f*

limb *s* art·us -ūs *m*, membrum *n*

limber *adj* flexilis

lime *s* calx *f*

limestone *s* calx *f*

lime tree *s* tilia *f*

limit *s* finis, terminus, modus *m*

limit *vt* terminare, finire, definire; (*to restrict*) circumscribĕre

limitation *s* determinatio *f*; (*exception*) exceptio *f*

limp *s* claudicatio *f*

limp *vi* claudicare

limp *adj* flaccidus, languidus

limpid *adj* limpidus

linden tree *s* tilia *f*

line *s* (*drawn*) linea *f*; (*row*) series *f*, ordo *m*; (*lineage*) stirps *f*, genus *n*; (*mil*) acies *f*; (*of poetry*) vers·us -ūs *m*; (*cord*) funis *m*

line *vt* (*streets*) saepire

lineage *s* stirps *f*, genus *n*

lineal *adj* linearis; **—ly** rectā lineā

lineament *s* lineamentum *n*

linear *adj* linearis

linen *adj* linteus, lineus

linen *s* linteum, linum *n*

linger *vi* morari, cunctari, cessare

lingering *adj* cunctabundus, tardus; **—ly** cunctanter

lingering *s* cunctatio *f*

linguist *s* linguarum peritus *m*

liniment *s* unguentum *n*, linit·us -ūs *m*

link *s* (*of chain*) anulus *m*; (*bond*) vinculum *n*, nex·us -ūs *m*

link *vt* connectĕre, conjungĕre

linseed *s* lini semen *n*

lint *s* linamentum *n*

lintel *s* limen superum *n*

lion *s* leo *m*

lioness *s* lea, leaena *f*

lip *s* labrum *n*; (*edge*) ora *f*

liquefy *vt* liquefacĕre

liquid *adj* liquidus

liquid *s* liquidum *n*, liquor *m*; **to become** — liquescĕre

liquidate *vt* solvĕre, persolvĕre

liquor *s* liquor *m*

lisp *vi* balbutire

lisping *adj* blaesus

list *s* index *m*, tabula *f*; (*of ship*) inclinatio *f*

list *vt* enumerare; *vi* inclinare

listen *vi* auscultare, audire; **to — to** auscultare, audire

listless *adj* remissus, languidus; **—ly** languide

litany *s* litania *f*

literal *adj* litteralis; **—ly** ad litteram, ad verbum

literary *adj* (*person*) litteratus; **— style** scribendi genus *n*

literature *s* litterae *f pl*

litigant *s* litigator *m*

litigate *vi* litigare

litigation *s* lis *f*

litter *s* (*vehicle*) lectica *f*; (*of straw, etc.*) stramentum *n*; (*brood*) fet·us -ūs, part·us -ūs *m*

litter *vt* sternĕre

little *adj* parvus, exiguus

little *adv* parum, paulum; **a — pau**lum, aliquantulum; **— by — pau**latim

little *s* paulum, aliquantulum *n*

live *vi* vivĕre, vitam agĕre; (*to reside*) habitare; **to — on** vesci (*with abl*)

live *adj* vivus; (*of colors*) vegetus

livelihood *s* vict·us -ūs *m*

lively *adj* vivus, vividus, alacer; (*of colors*) vegetus

liver *s* jecur *n*

livid *adj* lividus; **to be — livē**re

living *adj* vivus, vivens

living *s* (*livelihood, food*) vict·us -ūs *m*

lizard *s* lacerta *f*

load *s* onus *n*

load *vt* onerare

loaf *s* panis *m*

loaf *vi* grassari

loafer *s* grassator *m*

loam *s* lutum *n*

loan *s* mutuum *n*, pecunia mutua *f*

loathe *vt* fastidire

loathing *s* fastidium *n*

loathsome *adj* foedus, taeter

lobby *s* vestibulum *n*

lobe *s* lobus *m*

lobster *s* astacus *m*

local *adj* indigena; loci (*genit*), regionis (*genit*)

locality *s* locus *m*, natura loci *f*

lock *s* (*of hair*) cinnus, floccus *m*; (*of door*) sera *f*

lock *vt* obserare, oppessulare; **to — in** includĕre; **to — out** exludĕre; **to — up** concludĕre

locker *s* loculamentum, armarium *n*

lockjaw *s* tetanus *m*

locust *s* locusta *f*

lodge *s* casa *f*

lodge *vt* (*complaint*) deferre; *vi* (*to stay*) deversari; (*to stick*) inhaerēre

lodger *s* inquilinus *m*

lodging *s* hospitium, deversorium *n*

loft *s* tabulatum, cenaculum *n*

lofty *adj* (*ex*)celsus, sublimis; (*fig*) sublimis, superbus

log *s* tignum *n*, stipes *m*

logic *s* dialectica *n pl*

logical *adj* logicus, dialecticus; **—ly** dialectice, ex ratione

loin *s* lumbus *m*

loiter *vi* cessare, cunctari, grassari

loiterer *s* cessator, grassator *m*

loll *vi* recumbĕre
lone *adj* solus
loneliness *s* solitudo *f*
lonely *adj* solitarius; desolatus
long *adj* longus; (*of time*) diuturnus; (*lengthened*) productus
long *adv* diu; — **after** multo post; — **ago** jamdudum, jampridem; — **before** multo ante
long *vi* avēre; **to — for** desiderare
longevity *s* longaevitas *f*
longing *s* desiderium *n*
longing *adj* avidus; **—ly** avide
longitude *s* longitudo *f*
long-lived *adj* vivax
long-suffering *adj* patiens
long-winded *adj* longus
look *s* aspect·us -ūs, vult·us -ūs *m*; (*appearance*) facies, species *f*
look *vi* vidēre; (*to seem*) vidēri; **to — about** circumspicĕre; **to — after** curare; **to — at** intuēri, aspicĕre; **to — back** respicĕre; **to — for** quaerĕre; **to — forward to** exspectare; **to — into** inspicĕre, introspicĕre; (*to examine*) perscrutari; **to — on** intuēri; **to — out** prospicĕre; **to — out for** quaerĕre; **to — towards** spectare; **to — up** suspicĕre; **to — upon** habēre, aestimare
loom *s* tela *f*
loom *vi* in conspectum prodire
loop *s* sin·us -ūs *m*
loophole *s* fenestra *f*; (*fig*) effugium *n*
loose *adj* laxus, solutus, remissus; (*morally*) dissolutus; **—ly** laxe; dissolute
loosen *vt* solvĕre, laxare; *vi* solvi
loquacious *adj* loquax, garrulus
lord *s* dominus *m*
Lord *s* Dominus *m*
lord *vi* **to — it over** dominari in (*with acc*)
lordly *adj* imperiosus
lordship *s* dominatio *f*, imperium *n*
lore *s* doctrina *f*
lose *vt* amittĕre, perdĕre; **to — one's way** aberrare
loss *s* (*act*) amissio *f*; damnum, detrimentum *n*; (*mil*) repulsa *f*
lost *adj* perditus; **to be —** perire
lot *s* pars, portio, sors *f*; **casting of —s** sortitio *f*, sortit·us -ūs *m*; **to draw —s** for sortiri
lotion *s* lotio *f*
lottery *s* sortitio *f*
loud *adj* magnus; **—ly** magnā voce
lounge *vi* cessare, otiari
lounge *s* lectulus *m*
louse *s* pediculus *m*
lousy *adj* pediculosus; (*fig*) vilis
lout *s* rusticus *m*
loutish *adj* agrestis, rusticus
love *s* amor *m*; **to fall in —** amare, adamare
love *vt* amare, diligĕre
love affair *s* amores *m pl*
lovely *adj* venustus, amabilis
love potion *s* philtrum *n*
lover *s* amator, amans *m*

lovesick *adj* amore aeger
loving *adj* amans; **—ly** amanter
low *adj* humilis; (*of price*) vilis; (*of birth*) obscurus; (*of voice*) summissus; (*vile*) turpis; (*downcast*) abjectus
low *adv* humiliter; summissā voce
low *vi* mugire
lowborn *adj* obscurus, degener
lower *vt* demittĕre, deprimĕre; (*price*) imminuĕre; *vi* (*of sky*) obscurari
lower *adj* inferior; **of the — world** infernus; **the — world** inferi *m pl*
lowermost *adj* infimus
lowing *s* mugit·us -ūs *m*
lowlands *s* loca plana, campestria *n pl*, campi *m pl*
lowly *adj* humilis, obscurus
loyal *adj* fidelis, fidus; **—ly** fideliter
loyalty *s* fidelitas, fides *f*
lubricate *vt* unguĕre
lucid *adj* lucidus, clarus, perspicuus; (*transparent*) pellucidus
Lucifer *s* Lucifer *m*
luck *s* fortuna *f*; **bad —** fortuna *f*, infortunium *n*; **good —** fortuna *f*, felicitas *f*
luckily *adv* feliciter, fauste
luckless *adj* infelix
lucky *adj* felix, faustus
lucrative *adj* quaestuosus
lucre *s* lucrum *n*, quaest·us -ūs *m*
ludicrous *adj* ridiculus; **—ly** ridicule
luggage *s* sarcinae *f pl*, impedimenta *n pl*
lukewarm *adj* tepidus; (*fig*) segnis, frigidus; **—ly** (*fig*) segniter
lull *s* quies, intermissio *f*
lull *vt* sopire; (*to calm, as a storm*) sedare; (*fig*) demulcēre
lumber *s* scruta *n pl*
luminary *s* lumen *n*
luminous *adj* lucidus, illustris; (*fig*) dilucidus
lump *s* glaeba, massa, congeries *f*; (*on body*) tuber *n*
lump *vt* **to — together** coacervare
lumpy *adj* glaebosus, crassus
lunacy *s* alienatio mentis *f*
lunar *adj* lunaris
lunatic *s* insanus *m*
lunch *s* merenda *f*, prandium *n*
lunch *vi* prandēre
luncheon *s* prandium *n*
lung *s* pulmo *m*
lunge *s* ict·us -ūs *m*, plaga *f*
lunge *vi* prosilire
lurch *s* impedimentum *n*; **to leave in the —** deserĕre, destituĕre
lurch *vi* titubare
lure *s* illecebra, esca *f*
lure *vt* illicĕre, inescare
lurk *vi* latēre, latitare
luscious *adj* suavis, praedulcis
lush *adj* luxuriosus
lust *s* libido *f*
lust *vi* concupiscĕre
luster *s* splendor, nitor *m*
lustful *adj* libidinosus, salax; **—ly** libidinose, lascive

lustily adv valide, strenue
lusty adj validus, robustus
lute s cithara f, fides f pl
luxuriance s luxuries, ubertas f
luxuriant adj luxuriosus; (fig) luxurians
luxuriate vi luxuriare, luxuriari
luxurious adj sumptuosus, lautus; —ly sumptuose, laute

luxury s luxuria f, lux·us -ūs m
lye s lixivia f
lying adj mendax, fallax
lying s mendacium n
lymph s lympha f
lynx s lynx m & f
lyre s lyra f, fides f pl, barbitos m
lyric adj lyricus
lyric s carmen n

M

macaroni s collyra f
mace s fasces m pl
mace bearer s lictor m
macerate vt macerare
machination s dolus m
machine s machina f
machinery s machinamentum n, machinatio f
mackerel s scomber m
mad adj insanus, vesanus, demens, furiosus; to be — furēre, insanire; —ly insane, dementer
madam s domina f
madden vt mentem alienare (with dat); (fig) furiare
maddening adj furiosus
madman s homo furiosus m, demens m
madness s insania, dementia f, furor m
magazine s (journal) ephemeris f; (storehouse) horreum, armamentarium n
maggot s vermis, vermiculus m
magic adj magicus
magic s ars magica f
magically adv velut magica quadam arte
magician s magus m
magisterial adj ad magistratum pertinens
magistracy s magistrat·us -ūs m
magistrate s magistrat·us -ūs m
magnanimity s magnanimitas f
magnanimous adj magnanimus
magnet s magnes m
magnetic adj magneticus
magnetism s vis magnetica f
magnetize vt magnetica vi afficēre
magnificence s magnificentia f, splendor m
magnificent adj magnificus, splendidus; —ly magnifice, splendide
magnify vt amplificare, exaggerare
magnitude s magnitudo f
maid s ancilla f
maiden s virgo, puella f
maidenhood s virginitas f
maidenly adj puellaris, virginalis
mail s (letters) epistulae f pl; (armor) lorica f
maim vt mutilare
maimed adj mancus
main adj primus, praecipuus, princeps; — point caput n; —ly praecipue, maxime
main s (sea) altum n, pelagus m

mainland s continens f
maintain vt (to keep) tenēre; (to keep alive) nutrire, alēre, sustentare; (to defend) tuēri, sustinēre; (to argue) affirmare
maintenance s (support) defensio, sustentatio f; (means of living) vict·us -ūs m, alimentum n
majestic adj augustus, imperatorius; —ally auguste
majesty s majestas, dignitas f
major adj major
major s (mil) tribunus militum m; (in logic) major praemissa f
majority s major pars f
make vt facēre; (to form) fingēre; (to render) reddēre, facēre; (to appoint) creare, facēre, instituēre; to — amends corrigēre; to — good resarcire, reparare; to — haste accelerare, festinare; to — much of magni facēre; to — over transferre; to — ready praeparare; to — up (story) fingēre; (to compensate) resarcire; (one's mind) decernēre; to — way cedēre; vi to — away with tollēre, amovēre; to — for petēre
make s forma, figura, formatio f
maker s fabricator m; auctor m
maladministration s administratio mala f
malady s morbus m
male adj mas, masculinus
male s mas, masculus m
malediction s dirae f pl, exsecratio f
malefactor s homo maleficus, reus m
malevolence s malevolentia f
malevolent adj malevolus
malice s malevolentia, invidia f
malicious adj malevolus, invidiosus, malignus; —ly malevolo animo
malign vt obtrectare, vexare
malign adj malignus, invidiosus
malignant adj malevolus
malleable adj ductilis
mallet s malleus m
malpractice s delicta n pl
maltreat vt vexare, mulcare
man s (human being) homo m; (male human being) vir m
man vt (ship) complēre; (walls) praesidio firmare
manacle s manica f, compes m
manacle vt manicas injicēre (with dat)
manage vt administrare, curare

manageable adj tractabilis

management s administratio, cura f

manager s curator m; (steward) procurator m; (of estate) villicus m

mandate s mandatum n

mandrake s mandragora f

mane s juba f

maneuver s (mil) decurs·us -ūs m, decursio f; (trick) dolus m, artificium n

maneuver vi (mil) decurrĕre; (fig) machinari

mange s scabies f

manger s praesepe n

mangle vt lacerare, laniare

mangy adj scaber

manhood s pubertas f; virilitas, fortitudo f

mania s insania f

maniac s furiosus m

manifest adj manifestus, apertus; —ly manifeste, aperte

manifest vt declarare, ostendĕre, aperire

manifestation s patefactio f

manifesto s edictum n

manifold adj multiplex, varius

manipulate vt tractare

manipulation s tractatio f

mankind s genus humanum n

manliness s virtus, fortitudo f

manly adj virilis

manner s modus m, ratio f; (custom) consuetudo f, mos m; **after the —of** ritu (with genit), more (with genit); **bad —s** rusticitas f; **good —s** urbanitas f

mannerism s affectatio f

mannerly adj urbanus

mannikin s homunculus, homuncio m

man-of-war s navis longa f

manor s praedium n, fundus m

man servant s servus, famulus m

mansion s dom·us -ūs, sedes f

manslaughter s homicidium n

mantle s penula, palla f

mantle vt celare, tegĕre, dissimulare

manual adj manualis

manual s enchiridion n

manufacture s fabrica f

manufacture vt fabricari, fabrefacĕre

manufacturer s fabricator, opifex m

manure s stercus n, fimus m

manure vt stercorare

manuscript s codex, liber m

many adj multi, plerique, complures; **a good —** nonnulli; **as — . . . as** quot . . . tot; **how —** quot; **—ways** multifariam; **so —** tot

many-colored adj multicolor

map s tabula geographica f

map vt **to — out** designare, describěre

maple adj acernus

maple tree s acer n

mar vt foedare, vitiare, corrumpĕre

marauder s praedator, latro m

marauding s praedatio f, latrocinium n

marble adj marmoreus

marble s marmor n

March s (mensis) Martius m

march s iter n

march vt ducĕre; vi iter facĕre, incedĕre, gradi; **to — on** signa procferre; **to — on a town** oppidum aggredi

mare s equa f

margin s margo m & f

marginal adj margini ascriptus

marigold s caltha f

marine adj marinus

marine s miles classicus, miles classiarius m

mariner s nauta m

maritime adj maritimus

mark s nota f, signum n; (brand) stigma n; (impression) vestigium n; (target) scopus m; (of wound) cicatrix f; (fig) indicium n

mark vt notare, signare; (to observe) animadvertĕre; (with pencil, etc.) designare; **to — out** metari

marker s index m

market s macellum n, mercat·us -ūs m

marketable adj venalis

market day s nundinae f pl

marketing s emptio f

market place s forum n

market town s emporium n

marksman s jaculandi peritus m

marmalade s quilon ex aurantiis confectum n

marquee s tabernaculum n

marriage s matrimonium n, nuptiae f pl

marriageable adj nubilis

marriage contract s pactio nuptialis f

married adj (of woman) nupta; (of man) maritus

marrow s medulla f

marry vt (said of man) in matrimonium ducĕre, uxorem ducĕre (with acc); (said of woman) nubĕre (with dat); **to get married** matrimonio or nuptiis conjungi

marsh s palus f

marshal s dux, imperator m

marshal vt disponĕre

marshy adj paluster

mart s forum, emporium n

martial adj bellicosus, ferox, militaris

martyr s martyr m & f

martyrdom s martyrium n

marvel s res mira f, mirum n

marvel vi **to — at** mirari, admirari

marvelous adj mirus, mirabilis; —ly mire

masculine adj masculus, virilis; (gram) masculinus

mash s mixtura f; (for cattle) farrago f

mash vt commiscĕre; (to bruise) contundĕre

mask s persona, larva f; (fig) praetext·us -ūs m

mask vt (fig) dissimulare

mason s lapicida, caementarius m

masonry s opus caementicium n

mass s moles f; (of people) turba f; (eccl) missa f; **the —es** vulgus n

mass vt congerĕre, coacervare

massacre s caedes, trucidatio f

massacre vt trucidare

massive adj solidus, ingens

mast s (of ship) malus m; (for cattle) glans f, balanus m

master s dominus, herus m; (teacher) magister, praeceptor m; (controller) arbiter m; **to be — of** potens esse (with genit), compos esse (with genit); **not to be — of** impotens esse (with genit)

master vt superare, vincĕre; (to learn) perdiscĕre; (passion) continēre

masterly adj (artist) artificiosus; imperiosus

masterpiece s magnum opus n

mastery s dominatio f, imperium, arbitrium n

masticate vt mandĕre

mastiff s Molossus m

mat s teges, storea, matta f

match s (marriage) nuptiae f pl; (contest) certamen n; (an equal) par, compar m & f; **a — for** par (with dat); **not a — for** impar (with dat)

match vt adaequare, exaequare; vi quadrare

matchless adj incomparabilis

mate s socius, collega m; conju(n)x m & f

mate vi conjungi

material adj corporeus; (significant) haud levis, magni momenti; **—ly** magnopere

material s materia, materies f

maternal adj maternus

maternity s conditio matris f

mathematical adj mathematicus

mathematician s mathematicus m

mathematics s mathematica f, numeri m pl

matricide s (murder) matricidium n; (murderer) matricida m & f

matrimony s matrimonium n

matrix s forma f

matron s matrona f

matronly adj matronalis

matter s (substance) materia f; (affair) res f, negotium n; pus n; **no — nihil interest**

matter v impers **it does not — nihil interest, nihil refert**

matting s tegetes f pl

mattress s culcita f

mature adj maturus, adultus; **—ly** mature

mature vi maturescĕre

maturity s maturitas, aetas matura f

maudlin adj flebilis

maul vt mulcare, delaniare

mausoleum s mausoleum n

maw s ingluvies f

mawkish adj putidus; **—ly** putide

maxim s axioma, praeceptum n, sententia f

maximum adj quam maximus, quam plurimus

May s (mensis) Maius m

may vi posse; **I —** licet mihi

maybe adv forsitan

mayor s praefectus urbi m

maze s labyrinthus m

me pron me; **by — a** me; **to — mihi**; **with — mecum**

mead s (drink) mulsum n

meadow s pratum n

meager adj macer, exilis, jejunus; **—ly** exiliter, jejune

meagerness s macies f; (of soil) exilitas f; exigua copia f

meal s farina f; (food) cibus m; (dinner) epulae f pl

mean adj (middle) medius; (low) humilis; (cruel) crudelis, vilis

mean s medium n, mediocritas f

mean vt dicĕre, significare; (to intend) velle, cogitare, in animo habēre; (to refer to) significare, intellegĕre

meander vi sinuoso cursu labi

meaning s significatio, vis f, sens·us ·ūs m

meanness s humilitas f; (cruelty) crudelitas f

means s (way, method) ratio, via f, consilium n; (wealth) opes f pl; **by all —** maxime, omnino; **by — of** render by abl or per (with acc); **by no —** nullo modo, haudquaquam

meanwhile adv interea, interim

measles s morbilli m pl

measurable adj mensurabilis

measure s mensura f, modus m; (course of action) ratio f, consilium n; (law) rogatio, lex f; **in some — aliqua ex parte**

measure vt metiri; (land) metari; **to — out** admetiri, dimetiri

measurement s mensura f

meat s caro f; (food) cibus m

mechanic s opifex, faber m

mechanical adj mechanicus, machinalis; **—ly** mechanica quadam arte

mechanics s mechanica ars, machinalis scientia f

mechanism s machinatio f

medal s insigne n

medallion s numisma sollemne n

meddle vi se interponĕre

meddler s ardelio m

mediate vi intercedĕre

mediation s intercessio f

mediator s intercessor, conciliator m

medical adj medicus, medicinalis

medicate vt medicare

medicinal adj medicus, salutaris

medicine s (science) medicina f; (remedy) medicamentum n

medieval adj medii aevi (genit, used as adj)

mediocre adj mediocris

mediocrity s mediocritas f

meditate vi meditari, cogitare

meditation s meditatio, cogitatio f

meditative adj cogitabundus

Mediterranean s mare internum or medium, mare nostrum n

medium s (middle) medium n; (expedient) modus m, ratio f; (agency) conciliator m

medium *adj* mediocris
medley *s* farrago *f*
meek *adj* mitis, demissus; **—ly** summisse
meekness *s* animus demissus *m*
meet *adj* aptus, idoneus; **it is — con-**
venit
meet *vt* obviam ire (*with dat*), occurrěre (*with dat*); (*fig*) obire; *vi* convenire; **to — with** offenděre, excipěre
meeting *s* congressio *f*; (*assembly*) convent·us -ūs *m*
melancholy *s* tristitia, maestitia *f*
melancholy *adj* tristis, maestus
mellow *adj* maturus, mitis; (*from drinking*) temulentus
mellow *vt* maturare, coquěre; *vi* maturescěre
melodious *adj* canorus; **—ly** canore, modulate
melody *s* melos *n*, modus *m*
melt *vt* liquefacěre, dissolvěre; *vi* liquescěre, tabescěre
member *s* membrum *n*; (*fig*) sodalis *m*
membrane *s* membrana *f*
memento *s* monumentum *n*
memoirs *s* commentarii *m pl*
memorable *adj* memorabilis, memoriā dignus
memorandum *s* nota *f*
memorial *s* monumentum *n*
memory *s* memoria *f*; **from —** ex memoria, memoriter; **in the — of man** post hominum memoriam; **to commit to —** ediscěre, memoriae mandare
menace *s* minae *f pl*
menace *vt* minari, minitari; (*of things*) imminēre (*with dat*)
menacing *adj* minax; (*only of persons*) minitabundus
mend *vt* emendare, corrigěre, restaurare, reparare; (*clothes*) sarcire; *vi* melior fieri
mendicant *s* mendicus *m*, mendica *f*
menial *adj* servilis, sordidus
menial *s* servus, famulus *m*
mental *adj* mente conceptus; **—ly** mente
mention *s* mentio, commemoratio *f*; **to make — of** mentionem facěre (*with genit*)
mention *vt* commemorare, nominare; **to not — silentio praeterire**
mercantile *adj* mercatorius
mercenary *adj* mercenarius, venalis
mercenary *s* miles mercenarius *m*
merchandise *s* merces *f pl*
merchant *s* mercator, negotiator *m*
merciful *adj* misericors, clemens; **—ly** misericorditer, clementer
merciless *adj* immisericors, inclemens; **—ly** duriter, inhumane
mercurial *adj* vividus, acer, levis
Mercury *s* Mercurius *m*
mercury *s* argentum vivum *n*
mercy *s* misericordia *f*
mere *adj* merus; **—ly** tantummodo, solum, modo
meretricious *adj* meretricius, fucatus

merge *vt* confunděre; *vi* confundi
meridian *s* meridianus circulus *m*; meridies *m*
merit *s* meritum *n*
merit *vt* merēre, merēri
meritorious *adj* laudabilis
mermaid *s* nympha *f*
merrily *adv* hilare, festive
merry *adj* hilaris, festivus
mesh *s* (*of net*) macula *f*
mess *s* (*dirt*) squalor *m*; (*confusion*) turba, rerum perturbatio *f*
messenger *s* nuntius *m*
metal *adj* metallicus, ferreus, aereus
metal *s* metallum *n*
metallurgy *s* metallurgia, scientia metallorum *f*
metamorphosis *s* transfiguratio *f*
metaphor *s* translatio *f*
metaphorical *adj* translatus; **—ly** per translationem
mete *vt* metiri
meteor *s* fax caelestis *f*
meteorology *s* prognostica *n pl*
meter *s* metrum *n*, numerus *m*
method *s* ratio *f*, modus *m*
methodical *adj* dispositus; (*person*) diligens; **—ly** ratione et viā
meticulous *adj* accuratus; **—ly** accurate
metonymy *s* immutatio *f*
metrical *adj* metricus, numerosus
metropolis *s* caput *n*
mettle *s* animus *m*, virtus, magnanimitas *f*
miasma *s* halit·us -ūs *m*
microscope *s* microscopium *n*
mid *adj* medius
midday *adj* meridianus
midday *s* meridies *m*, meridianum tempus *n*
middle *adj* medius
middle *s* medium *n*; **in the — of the road** in media via
midget *s* pumilio *m* & *f*
midnight *s* media nox *f*
midriff *s* diaphragma *n*, praecordia *n pl*
midst *s* medium *n*; **in the — of** inter (*with acc*)
midsummer *s* summa aestas *f*
midway *adv* medius; **he stood — between the lines** stabat medius inter acies
midwife *s* obstetrix *f*
midwinter *s* bruma *f*
midwinter *adj* brumalis
mien *s* vult·us -ūs *m*
might *s* vis, potestas, potentia *f*; **with all one's — summa ope**
might *vi* render by imperfect subjunctive
mightily *adv* valde, magnopere
mighty *adj* potens, validus
migrate *vi* migrare, abire
migration *s* peregrinatio *f*
migratory *adj* advena, migrans
mild *adj* mitis, lenis; (*person*) placidus, clemens; **—ly** leniter, clementer
mildew *s* robigo *f*, mucor, sit·us -ūs *m*
mildness *s* clementia, lenitas, mansuetudo *f*

mile *s* mille passuum, milliare *n*
milestone *s* milliarium *n*
militant *adj* ferox
military *adj* militaris
militia *s* milites *m pl*
milk *s* lac *n*
milk *vt* mulgēre
milky *adj* lacteus
Milky Way *s* orbis lacteus *m*, via lactea *f*
mill *s* mola *f*, pistrinum *n*
millennium *s* mille anni *m pl*
miller *s* molitor, pistor *m*
million *adj* decies centena milia (*with genit*)
millionaire *s* homo praedives *m*
millionth *s* pars una ex decies centenis milibus partium *f*
millstone *s* mola *f*
mime *s* mimus *m*
mimic *s* mimus *m*
mimic *vt* imitari
mimicry *s* imitatio *f*
mince *vt* concidĕre; **not to — words** plane aperteque loqui
mind *s* mens *f*, animus *m*, ingenium *n*; (*opinion*) sens·us -ūs *m*, sententia *f*; **to call to —** recordari; **to make up one's —** animum inducĕre, statuĕre, constituĕre; **to show presence of —** praesenti animo uti
mind *vt* (*to look after*) curare; (*to regard*) respicĕre; (*to object to*) aegre ferre; **to — one's own business** suum negotium agĕre
mindful *adj* attentus, diligens; memor
mine *s* fodina *f*, metallum *n*; (*mil*) cuniculus *m*; (*fig*) thesaurus *m*
mine *vt* effodĕre
mine *pron* meus
miner *s* (*of metals*) metallicus *m*; fossor *m*
mineral *s* metallum *n*
mineral *adj* metallicus, fossilis
mineralogist *s* metallorum peritus *m*
mineralogy *s* metallorum scientia *f*
mingle *vt* commiscēre, confundĕre; *vi* commiscēri, se immiscēre
miniature *s* pictura minuta *f*
minimum *adj* quam minimus
minimum *s* minimum *n*
minion *s* cliens *m & f*
minister *s* minister, administer *m*
minister *vi* ministrare, servire
ministry *s* ministratio *f*, munus, officium *n*
minor *s* pupillus *m*, pupilla *f*
minor *adj* minor
minority *s* minor pars *f*
minstrel *s* fidicen *m*
mint *s* (*plant*) mentha *f*; (*for making money*) moneta *f*
mint *vt* cudĕre
minute *s* temporis momentum *n*
minute *adj* (*small*) minutus, exiguus, pusillus; (*exact*) accuratus, subtilis; **—ly** accurate, subtiliter
minx *s* puella procax *f*
miracle *s* miraculum, monstrum *n*
miraculous *adj* miraculosus; **—ly** divinitus

mirage *s* falsa species *f*
mire *s* lutum *n*
mirror *s* speculum *n*
mirth *s* hilaritas, laetitia *f*
mirthful *adj* hilaris
misadventure *s* infortunium *n*
misalliance *s* matrimonium impar *n*
misapply *vt* abuti (*with abl*)
misapprehend *vt* male intellegĕre
misapprehension *s* falsa conceptio *f*
misbehave *vi* indecore se gerĕre
misbehavior *s* morum pravitas *f*
misbelief *s* fides prava *f*
miscalculate *vi* errare
miscalculation *s* error *m*
miscarriage *s* abort·us -ūs *m*; (*fig*) malus success·us -ūs *m*
miscarry *vi* abortum facĕre; (*fig*) male succedĕre
miscellaneous *adj* promiscuus
miscellany *s* conjectanea, miscellanea *n pl*
mischance *s* infortunium *n*
mischief *s* incommodum, maleficium *n*; (*of children*) lascivia *f*
mischievous *adj* maleficus, noxius; (*playful*) lascivus
misconceive *vt* male intellegĕre
misconception *s* falsa conceptio, falsa opinio *f*
misconduct *s* delictum, peccatum *n*
misconstruction *s* sinistra interpretatio *f*
misconstrue *vt* male interpretari; perverse interpretari
misdeed *s* delictum, peccatum *n*
misdemeanor *s* levius delictum *n*
misdirect *vt* fallĕre
miser *s* avarus, sordidus *m*
miserable *adj* miser, infelix, aerumnosus
miserably *adv* misere
miserly *adj* avarus, sordidus
misery *s* miseria, aerumna *f*
misfortune *s* infortunium, incommodum *n*
misgiving *s* sollicitudo *f*
misgovern *vt* male regĕre
misguide *vt* seducĕre, fallĕre
misguided *adj* (*fig*) demens
mishap *s* incommodum *n*
misinform *vt* falsa docēre (*with acc*)
misinterpret *vt* male interpretari
misinterpretation *s* prava interpretatio *f*
misjudge *vt* male judicare
mislay *vt* amittĕre
mislead *vt* seducĕre, decipĕre
mismanage *vt* male gerĕre
mismanagement *s* mala administratio *f*
misnomer *s* falsum nomen *n*
misplace *vt* alieno loco ponĕre
misprint *s* erratum typographicum, mendum *n*
misquote *vt* falso citare, falso proferre
misquotation *s* falsa prolatio *f*
misrepresent *vt* calumniari
misrepresentation *s* calumnia *f*; falsa descriptio *f*

misrule *s* prava administratio *f*

miss *s* adulescentula, virgo *f*; error *m*

miss *vt (to overlook)* omittĕre, praetermittĕre; *(one's aim)* non ferire,
non attingĕre; *(to feel the want of)*
desiderare; *(to fail to find)* requirĕre; *vi (to fall short)* errare

misshapen *adj* pravus, deformis

missile *s* telum, missile, tormentum *n*

missing *adj* absens; **to be —** deesse

mission *s* legatio, missio *f*

misspell *vt* perperam scribĕre

misspend *vt* prodigĕre, perdĕre, dissipare

misstate *vt* parum accurate memorare

misstatement *s* falsum, mendacium
n

mist *s* nebula, caligo *f*

mistake *s* error *m*, erratum *n*; *(written)* mendum *n*; **to make a —** errare, peccare

mistake *vt* habēre pro *(with abl)*

mistaken *adj* falsus; **to be —** falli;
unless I am — ni fallor

mistletoe *s* viscum *n*

mistress *s* domina, hera *f*; *(sweetheart)* amica *f*; *(paramour)* concubina *f*; *(teacher)* magistra *f*

mistrust *s* diffidentia, suspicio *f*

mistrust *vt* diffidĕre *(with dat)*

mistrustful *adj* diffidens; **—ly** diffidenter

misty *adj* nebulosus, caliginosus;
(fig) obscurus

misunderstand *vt* perperam intellegĕre

misunderstanding *s* error *m*; *(disagreement)* offensio *f*, dissidium *n*

misuse *s* abus·us ·ūs *m*; *(ill treatment)* injuria *f*

misuse *vt* abuti *(with abl)*; *(to revile)*
conviciari

mite *s (bit)* parvulus *m*; *(coin)* sextans *m*

miter *s* mitra *f*

mitigate *vt* mitigare, lenire

mitigation *s* mitigatio *f*

mix *vt* miscēre; **to — in** admiscēre;
to — up commiscēre; *(fig)* confundĕre

mixed *adj* promiscuus, confusus

mixture *s* mixtura, farrago *f*

moan *vi* gemĕre, ingemiscĕre

moan *s* gemit·us ·ūs *m*

moat *s* fossa *f*

mob *s* turba *f*, vulgus *n*

mob *vt* conviciis insectari, stipare

mobile *adj* mobilis

mobility *s* mobilitas *f*

mock *s* irrisio, derisio *f*

mock *vt* ludĕre, ludificari, irridēre

mock *adj* fictus, fucatus

mockery *s* irrisio *f*, irris·us ·ūs *m*

mode *s* modus *m*, ratio *f*; *(fashion)*
us·us ·ūs *m*

model *s* exemplar, exemplum *n*

model *vt* formare, delineare, fingĕre

moderate *adj* moderatus, mediocris,
modicus; **—ly** moderate, mediocriter, modice

moderate *vt* moderari, temperare,
coercēre

moderation *s* moderatio, temperantia *f*, modus *m*

moderator *s* praeses *m*

modern *adj* recens, hodiernus, novus

modest *adj (restrained)* modestus,
pudens, verecundus; *(sight)* modicus,
mediocris; **—ly** pudenter, verecunde

modesty *s* modestia, pudicitia, verecundia *f*

modification *s* modificatio, mutatio *f*

modify *vt* (im)mutare

modulate *vt (voice)* flectĕre; modulari

modulation *s* flexio *f*, flex·us ·ūs *m*

moist *adj* humidus, uvidus, madidus

moisten *vt* (h)umectare, rigare

moisture *s* humor *m*

molar *s* dens genuinus *m*

molasses *s* sacchari faex *f*

mold *s (form)* forma, matrix *f*; *(mustiness)* mucor *m*

mold *vt* formare, fingĕre; *(to knead)*
subigĕre; *vi* mucescĕre

molder *vi* putrescĕre, dilabi

moldiness *s* mucor, sit·us ·ūs *m*

moldy *adj* mucidus, situ corruptus

mole *s (animal)* talpa *f*; *(sea wall)*
moles *f*, agger *m*; *(on skin)* naevus *m*

molecule *s* particula *f*

molehill *s* **to make a mountain
out of a —** e rivo flumina magna
facĕre

molest *vt* vexare, sollicitare

molt *vi* plumas ponĕre

molten *adj* liquefactus

moment *s (of time)* punctum tem-
joris *n*; *(importance)* momentum *n*;
in a — statim; **of great —** magni
ponderis; **this —** ad tempus

momentarily *adv* statim, confestim

momentary *adj* brevis

momentous *adj* gravis, magni momenti *(genit, used adjectively)*

monarch *s* rex, princeps, dominus *m*

monarchical *adj* regius

monarchy *s* regnum *n*

monastery *s* monasterium *n*

monetary *adj* pecuniarius, argentarius, nummarius

money *s* pecunia *f*, nummi *m pl*;
for — mercede

moneychanger *s* nummularius *m*

moneylender *s* faenerator *m*

mongrel *s* hybrida *f*

monitor *s* admonitor *m*

monk *s* monachus *m*

monkey *s* simia *f*

monogram *s* monogramma *n*

monologue *s* oratio *f*

monopolize *vt* monopolium exercēre
in *(with acc)*

monopoly *s* monopolium *n*

monosyllabic *adj* monosyllabus

monosyllable *s* monosyllabum *n*

monotonous *adj* semper idem; *(singsong)* canorus

monotony *s* taedium *n*

monster *s* monstrum, portentum *n*,
belua *f*

monstrosity *s* monstrum *n*

monstrous *adj* monstrosus, porten-
tosus, prodigiosus; **—ly** monstrose

month s mensis m
monthly adj menstruus
monthly adv singulis mensibus
monument s monumentum n
monumental adj (important) gravis, magnus; (huge) ingens
mood s animi affect·us -ūs, habit·us -ūs m; (gram) modus m
moodiness s morositas f
moody adj morosus, maestus
moon s luna f
moonlight s lunae lumen n; **by —** per lunam
moonstruck adj lunaticus
Moor s Maurus m
moor vt religare, anchoris retinēre
moor s tesca n pl
mop s peniculus m
mop vt detergēre
mope vi maerēre
moral adj (relating to morals) moralis, ethicus; (morally proper) honestus; **—ly** moraliter; honeste
moral s (of story) documentum n
morale s animus m, animi m pl; **— is low** animus jacet, animi deficiunt
morality s boni mores m pl
moralize vi de moribus disserēre
morals s mores m pl
morass s palus f
morbid adj morbidus, morbosus
more adj plus (with genit); plures
more adv plus, magis, amplius; ultra; **— and — magis** magisque; **— than** plus quam; **— than enough** plus satis; **no — non** diutius
moreover adv praeterea, ultro, etenim vero
morning s mane n (indecl); tempus matutinum n; **early in the —** multo mane, bene mane, prima luce; **in the — mane**, matutino tempore; **this — hodie** mane
morning adj matutinus
morning star s Lucifer, phosphorus m
morose adj morosus; **—ly** morose
moroseness s morositas f
morsel s offa f, frustulum n
mortal adj mortalis; (deadly) mortifer, letalis; **—ly** letaliter
mortal s mortalis m & f, homo m & f
mortality s mortalitas f
mortar s mortarium n
mortgage s hypotheca f, pignus n
mortgage vt obligare
mortification s dolor m
mortify vt mortificare, coercēre; (to vex) offendēre
mosaic s tessellatum opus n
mosaic adj tesselatus
mosquito s culex m
moss s muscus m
mossy adj muscosus
most adj plurimus, maximus, plerusque; **for the — part** maximam partem
most adv maxime, plurimum
mostly adv plerumque, fere
mote s corpusculum n
moth s blatta f
mother s mater f

motherhood s matris conditio f
mother-in-law s socr·us -ūs f
motherless adj matre orbus
motherly adj maternus
motion s motio f, mot·us -ūs m; (proposal of bill) rogatio f; **to make a — ferre; to set in — ciēre**
motion vi significare, innuēre
motionless adj immotus, immobilis
motive s causa, ratio f, incitamentum n
motive adj movens, agens
motley adj varius, versicolor
mottled adj maculosus
motto s sententia f, praeceptum n
mound s tumulus, agger m, moles f
mount s mons m; (horse) equus m
mount vt scandēre, ascendēre, conscendēre; vi ascendēre, conscendēre, sublime ferri; subvolare
mountain s mons m
mountaineer s montanus m
mountainous adj montuosus, montanus
mounted adj (on horseback) inscensus
mourn vt lugēre, deflēre; vi lugēre, maerēre
mourner s plorator m
mournful adj lugubris, luctuosus, tristis, flebilis, maestus; **—ly** maeste, flebiliter
mourning s luct·us -ūs, maeror m; (dress) vestis lugubris f; **in — pullatus**, sorditatus; **to go into — vestitum** mutare
mouse s mus m
mousetrap s muscipulum n
mouth s os n; (of beast) faux f; (of river) ostium n; (of bottle) lura f
mouthful s buccella f
mouth piece s interpres m
movable adj mobilis
movables s res f pl, supellex f
move vt movēre; (emotionally) commovēre; (to propose) ferre; vi movēri, se movēre; (to change residence) migrare; **to — on** progredi
movement s mot·us -ūs m
moving adj flebilis, miserabilis
mow vt demetēre, secare
mower s faenisex m & f
mowing s faenisicium n
much adj multus; **as — ... as** tantus . . . quantus; **how — quantus; so — tantus; too — nimius; very — plurimus**
much adv multum, valde; (with comparatives) multo; **too — nimium; nimis; very — plurimum**
muck s stercus n
mucous adj mucosus
mud s lutum n, limus m
muddle vt turbare; (fig) perturbare
muddle s confusio, turba f
muddy adj lutosus, lutulentus; (troubled) turbidus
muffle vt involvēre; **to — up** obvolvēre
muffled adj surdus
mug s poculum n
muggy adj humidus
mulberry s morum n

mulberry tree s morus f

mule s mulus m

muleteer s mulio m

mulish adj obstinatus

multifarious adj varius, multiplex

multiplication s multiplicatio f

multiply vt multiplicare; vi augēri, crescēre

multitude s multitudo, turba f

multitudinous adj creberrimus

mumble vt opprimēre; vi murmurare

munch vt manducare, mandēre

mundane adj mundanus

municipal adj municipalis

municipality s municipium n

munificence s munificentia, largitas f

munificent adj munificus, liberalis; —ly munifice

munitions s belli apparat·us -ūs m

mural adj muralis

murder s caedes, nex f, homicidium n

murder vt necare, trucidare, obtruncare

murderer s homicida m & f, sicarius m

murderous adj (fig) sanguinarius, cruentus

murky adj caliginosus, tenebrosus

murmur s murmur n, fremit·us -ūs m

murmuring s admurmuratio f

muscle s musculus, lacertus, torus m

muscular adj lacertosus, robustus

Muse s Musa f

muse vi meditari, secum agitare

mushroom s fungus, boletus m

music s musica f; (of instruments and voices) cant·us -ūs, concent·us -ūs m

musical adj (of person) musicus; (of sound) canorus

musician s musicus m; (of stringed instrument) fidicen m; (of wind instrument) tibicen m

muslin s sidon f

must s mustum n

must vi I — go mihi eundum est, me oportet ire, debeo ire, necesse est (ut) eam

mustard s sinapi n

muster vt lustrare; (fig) cogēre, convocare; to — up courage animum sumēre; vi convenire, coire

muster s copiarum lustratio f, recens·us -ūs m

musty adj mucidus

mutable adj mutabilis

mute adj mutus

mutilate vt mutilare, truncare

mutilated adj mutilus, truncus

mutilation s mutilatio, laceratio f

mutineer s seditiosus m

mutinous adj seditiosus

mutiny s seditio f, mot·us -ūs m

mutiny vi tumultuari, seditionem facēre

mutter vi murmurare, mussitare

mutter s murmuratio f

mutton s ovilla f

mutual adj mutuus; —ly mutuo, inter se

muzzle s capistrum n

muzzle vt capistrare

my adj meus; — own proprius

myriad adj decem milia (with genit); (innumerable) sescenti

myrrh s myrrha, murrha f

myrtle s myrtus f

myself pron (reflexive) me; to — mihi; (intensive) ipse, egomet

mysterious adj arcanus, occultus; —ly arcane, occulte

mystery s mysterium, arcanum n; (fig) res occultissima f

mystical adj mysticus; —ly mystice

mystification s ambages f pl

mystify vt confundēre, fallēre

myth s mythos m, fabula f

mythical adj fabulosus

mythology s fabulae f pl, mythologia f

N

nab vt prehendēre

nadir s fundus m

nag s caballus m

nag vt objurgitare

naiad s naias f

nail s clavus m; (of finger) unguis m

nail vt defigēre

naive adj simplex; —ly simpliciter

naked adj nudus, apertus; —ly aperte

name s nomen n, appellatio f; (reputation) fama, celebritas f; (term) vocabulum n; by — nominatim

name vt nominare, appellare; (to appoint) dicēre

nameless adj nominis expers

namely adv scilicet, videlicet

nap s brevis somnus m; (of cloth) villus m; to take a — meridiari, ja-

cēre

nape s — of the neck cervix f

napkin s mappa f, mantele n

narcotic adj somnificus

narcotic s medicamentum somnificum n

nard s nardus f, nardum n

narrate vt narrare

narration s narratio, expositio f

narrative s fabula f

narrator s narrator m

narrow adj angustus; (fig) arctus; —ly vix, aegre

narrow vt coarctare; vi coarctari

narrow-minded adj animi angusti or parvi (genit, used adjectively)

narrowness s angustiae f pl

nasty adj (foul) foedus; (mean) amarus

natal *adj* natalis

nation *s* gens, natio *f*; (*as political body*) populus *m*; (*state*) res publica *f*

national *adj* publicus, civilis; rei publicae (*genit, used adjectively*)

nationality *s* civitas *f*

native *adj* indigena

native *s* indigena *m & f*

native land *s* patria *f*

native tongue *s* patrius sermo *m*

nativity *s* ort·us -ūs *m*

natural *adj* naturalis; (*innate*) nativus, innatus, insitus; (*fig*) sincerus, simplex; —**ly** naturā; (*unaffectedly*) simpliciter; (*of its own accord*) sponte

naturalization *s* civitatis donatio *f*

naturalize *vt* civitate donare

nature *s* natura, rerum natura *f*; (*character*) ingenium *n*, indoles *f*

naught *pron* nihil; **to set at** — parvi facĕre

naughty *adj* improbus, malus

nausea *s* nausea *f*; (*fig*) fastidium *n*

nauseate *vt* fastidium movēre (*with dat*); **to be nauseated** nauseare, fastidire

nautical *adj* nauticus

naval *adj* navalis, maritimus

nave *s* (*of church*) navis *f*

navel *s* umbilicus *m*

navigable *adj* navigabilis, navium patiens

navigate *vt* gubernare; *vi* navigare

navigation *s* navigatio *f*, res nauticae *f pl*

navigator *s* nauta, gubernator *m*

navy *s* classis *f*, copiae navales *f pl*

nay *adv* non ita

near *prep* prope (*with acc*), ad (*with acc*)

near *adj* propinquus, vicinus; (*of relation*) proximus; — **at hand** propinquus, in promptu

near *adv* prope, juxta

near *vt* appropinquare (*with dat*)

nearly *adv* prope, paene, fere, ferme

nearness *s* propinquitas *f*

nearsighted *adj* myops

neat *adj* mundus, nitidus, concinnus; —**ly** munde, concinne

neatness *s* munditia, concinnitas *f*

nebulous *adj* nebulosus

necessarily *adv* necessario

necessary *adj* necessarius; **it is** — opus est

necessitate *vt* cogĕre

necessity *s* necessitas *f*; (*want*) egestas, necessitudo *f*; (*thing*) res necessaria *f*

neck *s* collum *n*, cervix *f*

necklace *s* monile *n*, torques *m*

necktie *s* collare *n*

nectar *s* nectar *n*

need *s* (*necessity*) opus *n*, necessitas *f*; (*want*) inopia, egestas, penuria *f*; **there is** — **of** opus est (*with abl*)

need *vt* egēre (*with abl*), indigēre (*with abl*); (*to require*) requirēre

needle *s* ac·us -ūs *f*

needless inutilis, minime necessarius, vanus; —**ly** sine causa

needy *adj* egens, indigens, inops

nefarious *adj* nefarius

negation *s* negatio *f*

negative *adj* negans, negativus; —**ly** negando

negative *s* negatio *f*; **to answer in the** — negare

neglect *vt* neglegĕre, omittĕre; deserĕre

neglect *s* neglegentia, incuria *f*, neglect·us -ūs *m*

neglectful *adj* neglegens

negligence *s* neglegentia, incuria *f*

negligent *adj* neglegens; —**ly** negleganter

negligible *adj* levis, tenuis

negotiable *adj* mercabilis

negotiate *vt* (*a deal*) agĕre; agĕre de (*with abl*); *vi* negotiari

negotiation *s* transactio, actio *f*, pactum *n*

negotiator *s* conciliator, orator *m*

Negro *s* Aethiops *m*

neigh *vi* hinnire

neigh *s* hinnit·us -ūs *m*

neighbor *s* vicinus, finitimus *m*

neighborhood *s* vicinia, vicinitas *f*; proximitas *f*

neighboring *adj* vicinus, finitimus

neighborly *adj* familiaris, comis, benignus

neither *pron* neuter

neither *conj* nec, neque, neve, neu; **neither . . . nor** neque . . . neque

neophyte *s* tiro *m*

nephew *s* fratris filius, sororis filius *m*

Nereid *s* Nereis *f*

nerve *s* nervus *m*; (*fig*) temeritas, audacia *f*

nervous *adj* trepidus; —**ly** trepide

nervousness *s* diffidentia, sollicitudo *f*

nest *s* nidus *m*

nest *vi* nidificare

nestle *vi* recubare

net *s* rete *n*

net *vt* irretire

netting *s* reticulum *n*

nettle *s* urtica *f*

nettle *vt* (*fig*) vexare

network *s* reticulum, opus reticulatum *n*

neuter *adj* neuter, neutralis

neutral *adj* medius, neuter

neutrality *s* nullam in partem propensio *f*

neutralize *vt* aequare

never *adv* nunquam

nevermore *adv* nunquam posthac

nevertheless *adv* nihilominus, attamen

new *s* novus, recens, integer; —**ly** nuper, modo

newcomer *s* advena *m & f*

news *s* fama *f*, rumor, nuntius *m*

newspaper *s* acta diurna *n pl*

next *adj* proximus; (*of time*) insequens; — **day** postridie

next *adv* dein, deinde, deinceps

nibble *vt* arrodĕre; (*fig*) carpĕre; *vi* rodĕre

nice *adj* (*dainty*) delicatus; (*choice*)

exquisitus; (*exact*) accuratus; (*fine*) bellus; (*effeminate*) mollis; (*amiable*) suavis; (*of weather*) serenus; —**ly** delicate, exquisite, belle; accurate

nicety *s* accuratio, subtilitas, elegantia *f*

niche *s* aedicula *f*

nick *s* incisura *f*; **in the very — of time** in ipso articulo temporis

nick *vt* incidĕre

nickname *s* agnomen *n*

niece *s* fratris filia, sororis filia *f*

niggardly *adj* parcus, avarus

nigh *adj* propinquus

night *s* nox *f*; **by — —,** nocte, noctu; **to spend the —** pernoctare

nightfall *s* primae tenebrae *f pl*; **at — sub noctem**

nightingale *s* luscinia *f*

nightly *adj* nocturnus

nightly *adv* noctu, de nocte

nightmare *s* incubus *m*

night watch *s* vigilia *f*; (*guard*) vigil *m*

nimble *adj* pernix, agilis

nine *adj* novem; **— times** noviens

nineteen *adj* undeviginti, decem et novem

nineteenth *adj* undevicesimus

ninetieth *adj* nonagesimus

ninety *adj* nonaginta

ninth *adj* nonus

nip *vt* vellicare; (*of frost*) urĕre; **to — off** desecare

nippers *s* forceps *m*

nipple *s* papilla *f*

no *adj* nullus; **— one** nemo *m*

no *adv* non, minime; **to say —** negare

nobility *s* nobilitas *f*; nobiles, optimates *m pl*; (*moral excellence*) honestas *f*

noble *adj* nobilis, generosus; (*morally*) ingenuus, honestus, liberalis

noble *s* optimas *m*

nobleman *s* vir nobilis *m*

nobly *adv* nobiliter, praeclare, generose

nobody *pron* nemo *m*

nocturnal *adj* nocturnus

nod *s* nut·us -ūs *m*

nod *vi* nutare; (*to doze*) dormitare; (*in assent*) annuĕre

noise *s* strepit·us -ūs *m*; (*high-pitched*) stridor *m*; (*loud*) fragor *m*; **to make —** strepĕre, strepitare, increpare

noise *vt* **to — abroad** promulgare, divulgare

noiseless *adj* tacitus; —**ly** tacite

noisily *adv* cum strepitu

noisome *adj* noxius, foedus, taeter

noisy *adj* clamosus

nomad *s* nomas *m & f*

nomadic *adj* vagus, vagabundus

nominal *adj* nominalis; —**ly** nomine, verbo

nominate *vt* nominare, designare

nomination *s* nominatio, designatio *f*; (*of heir*) nuncupatio *f*

nominative *adj* nominativus

nominee *s* nominatus, designatus *m*

none *pron* nemo *m*

nonentity *s* nihilum *n*

nones *s* Nonae *f pl*

nonplus *vt* (*to puzzle*) ad incitas redigĕre

nonsense *s* ineptiae, nugae *f pl*; **to talk —** absurde loqui, garrire

nonsense *interj* gerrae!

nonsensical *adj* ineptus, absurdus

nook *s* angulus *m*

noon *s* meridies *m*; **before —** ante meridiem

noonday *adj* meridianus

no one *pron* nemo *m*

noose *s* laqueus *m*

nor *conj* nec, neque, neve, neu

norm *s* norma *f*

normal *adj* solitus; —**ly** plerumque

north *s* septentriones *m pl*

north *adj* septentrionalis

northern *adj* septentrionalis

northern lights *s* aurora Borealis *f*

north pole *s* arctos *f*

northwards *adv* septentriones versus

north wind *s* aquilo *m*

nose *s* nas·us -ūs *m*, nares *f pl*; **to blow the —** emungĕre

nostril *s* naris *f*

not *adv* non, haud; **— at all** nullo modo, haudquaquam; **— even** ne . . . quidem

notable *adj* notabilis, insignis, insignitus

notably *adv* insignite

notary *s* scriba *m*

notation *s* notatio *f*, signum *n*

notch *s* incisura *f*

notch *vt* incidĕre

note *s* (*mark*) nota *f*; (*comment*) adnotatio *f*; (*mus*) sonus *m*, vox *f*; (*com*) chirographum *n*; (*letter*) litterulae *f pl*

note *vt* notare; (*to notice*) animadvertĕre

notebook *s* commentarius *m*, tabulae *f pl*, pugillares *m pl*

noted *adj* insignis, insignitus, notus, praeclarus

noteworthy *adj* notabilis, memorabilis

nothing *pron* nihil, nil, nihilum; **for — (free)** gratis, gratuito; (*in vain*) frustra; **good for — nequam**; **— but** nihil nisi; **to think — of** nihili facĕre

notice *s* (*act of noticing*) notatio, animadversio *f*; (*announcement*) denuntiatio *f*; (*sign*) proscriptio *f*, titulus, libellus *m*; **to escape — latēre**; **to escape the — of** fallĕre; **to give — of** denuntiare

notice *vt* animadvertĕre, observare

noticeable *adj* insignis, conspicuus

noticeably *adv* insigniter

notification *s* denuntiatio, declaratio *f*

notify *vt* certiorem facĕre

notion *s* notio, suspicio *f*

notoriety *s* infamia *f*

notorious *adj* famosus, infamis, notus, manifestus; —**ly** manifeste

notwithstanding *adv* nihilominus

nought *pron* nihil; **to set at —** parvi facĕre

noun *s* nomen *n*

nourish *vt* alĕre, nutrire

nourishment *s* (*act*) alimentum *n*, cibus *m*

novel *adj* novus, inauditus

novel *s* fabula *f*

novelty *s* res nova *f*; novitas *f*

November *s* (*mensis*) November *m*

novice *s* tiro *m*

now *adv* nunc; (*past*) jam; **— and then** interdum, nonnunquam; **— ... — modo ... modo**

nowhere *adv* nusquam

noxious *adj* noxius

nozzle *s* ansa *f*

nude *adj* nudus

nudge *vt* fodicare

nudity *s* nudatio *f*

nugget *s* massa *f*

nuisance *s* incommodum *n*, molestia *f*

null *adj* irritus

nullify *vt* irritum facĕre

numb *adj* torpidus, torpens; **to become — torpescĕre**; **to be — torpēre**

numb *vt* torpefacĕre; (*fig*) obstupefacĕre

number *s* numerus *m*; **a — of** aliquot; **without — innumerabilis**

number *vt* numerare, enumerare, dinumerare

numberless *adj* innumerus, innumerabilis

numbness *s* torpor *m*; (*fig*) stupor *m*

numerical *adj* numeralis; **—ly** numero, ad numerum

numerous *adj* frequens, creber, multus

numismatics *s* doctrina nummorum *f*

nuptial *adj* nuptialis, conjugalis

nuptials *s* nuptiae *f pl*

nurse *s* nutrix *f*

nurse *vt* (*a baby*) nutrire; (*fig*) fovēre; (*the sick*) ancillari (*with dat*), curare

nursery *s* (*for children*) infantium cubiculum *n*; (*for plants*) plantarium, seminarium *n*

nurture *vt* nutrire, educare

nut *s* nux *f*; **a hard — to crack** (*fig*) quaestio nodosa *f*

nutriment *s* nutrimentum, alimentum *n*

nutrition *s* nutritio *f*, nutrimentum *n*

nutritious *adj* alibilis, salubris

nutshell *s* putamen *n*; **in a — (*fig*)** paucis verbis

nymph *s* nympha *f*

O

oaf *s* stultus, hebes *m*

oak *adj* querceus, quernus

oak *s* querc·us -ūs *f*; (*evergreen*) ilex *f*; (*timber*) robur *n*

oakum *s* stuppa *f*

oar *s* remus *m*; **to pull the —s** remos ducĕre

oarsman *s* remex *m*

oath *s* jusjurandum *n*; (*mil*) sacramentum *n*; **false — perjurium *n*; **to take an — jurare**; (*mil*) sacramentum dicĕre

oats *s* avena *f*

obdurate *adj* obstinatus, pertinax; **—ly** obstinate, pertinaciter

obedience *s* obedientia *f*, obsequium *n*

obedient *adj* obediens, obsequens; **—ly** obedienter

obeisance *s* obsequium *n*, capitis summissio *f*; **to make — to flectĕre ante (*with acc*); (*fig*) obsequi (*with dat*)

obelisk *s* obeliscus *m*

obese *adj* obesus

obesity *s* obesitas *f*

obey *vt* parēre (*with dat*), obedire (*with dat*), obtemperare (*with dat*), obsequi (*with dat*)

obituary *s* Libitinae index *m*

object *s* objectum *n*, res *f*; (*aim*) finis *m*, propositum *n*

object *vi* (*to feel annoyance*) gravari;

(*to make objections*) recusare; **to — to aegre ferre**

objection *s* objectio *f*; impedimentum *n*, mora *f*

objectionable *adj* injucundus, improbabilis

objective *s* finis *m*, propositum *n*

objective *adj* externus, objectivus, verus

oblation *s* donum *n*

obligation *s* debitum, officium *n*; **under — noxius**

obligatory *adj* necessarius, debitus

oblige *vt* (*to force*) cogĕre, impellĕre; (*to put under obligation*) obligare, obstringĕre; (*to do a favor for*) morigerari (*with dat*); **to be obliged to** debēre (*with inf*); (*to feel gratitude toward*) gratiam habēre (*with ddt*)

obliging *adj* officiosus, comis, blandus; **—ly** officiose, comiter

oblique *adj* obliquus; **—ly** oblique

obliterate *vt* delēre, oblitterare

oblivion *s* oblivio *f*

oblivious *adj* obliviosus, immemor

oblong *adj* oblongus

obloquy *s* vituperatio *f*, maledictum *n*

obnoxious *adj* invisus, noxius

obscene *adj* obscenus; **—ly** obscene

obscenity *s* obscenitas *f*

obscure *adj* obscurus; **—ly** obscure

obscure *vt* obscurare

obscurity *s* obscuritas *f*, tenebrae *f pl*; (*of birth*) humilitas *f*

obsequies *s* exsequiae *f pl*

obsequious *adj* officiosus, morigerus, nimis obsequens

obsequiousness *s* obsequium *n*, assentatio *f*

observable *adj* notabilis

observance *s* observantia *f*; (*rite*) rit·us -ūs *m*

observant *adj* attentus; — **of** diligens (*with genit*)

observation *s* observatio, animadversio *f*; (*remark*) notatio *f*, dictum *n*

observe *vt* (*to watch*) observare, contemplari, animadvertĕre; (*to keep*) conservare, observare; (*to remark*) dicĕre

observer *s* spectator *m*

obsess *vt* occupare

obsession *s* studium *n*

obsolescent *adj* **to be —** obsolescĕre

obsolete *adj* obsoletus, antiquatus; **to become —** exolescĕre

obstacle *s* impedimentum *n*; (*barrier*) obex *m*

obstinacy *s* obstinatio *f*, animus obstinatus *m*

obstinate *adj* obstinatus, pertinax; **—ly** obstinate

obstreperous *adj* tumultuosus, clamosus

obstruct *vt* obstare (*with dat*), obstruĕre, impedire

obstruction *s* obstructio *f*, impedimentum *n*; (*pol*) intercessio *f*

obtain *vt* nancisci, adipisci, consequi; (*by entreaty*) impetrare; *vi* valēre

obtainable *adj* impetrabilis

obtrusive *adj* molestus, importunus

obtuse *adj* obtusus, hebes, stolidus

obviate *vt* praevertĕre

obvious *adj* apertus, manifestus, perspicuus; **—ly** aperte, manifesto

occasion *s* occasio *f*, locus *m*; (*reason*) causa *f*; (*time*) tempus *n*

occasion *vt* locum dare (*with dat*), movēre

occasionally *adv* interdum

occidental *adj* occidentalis

occult *adj* occultus, arcanus

occupant *s* possessor *m*

occupation *s* possessio *f*; (*engagement*) occupatio *f*; (*employment*) negotium *n*, quaest·us -ūs *m*

occupy *vt* occupare, tenēre; (*to possess*) possidēre; (*space*) complēre

occur *vi* accidĕre, evenire; (*to the mind*) occurrĕre, in mentem venire

occurrence *s* cas·us -ūs, event·us -ūs *m*

ocean *s* oceanus *m*, mare oceanum *n*

oceanic *adj* oceanus, oceanensis

October *s* (*mensis*) October *m*

ocular *adj* ocularis

oculist *s* ocularius medicus *m*

odd *adj* (*of number*) impar; (*quaint*) insolitus, novus; **—ly** mirum in modum

oddity *s* raritas *f*, ridiculum *n*

odds *s* **the — are against us** impares summus; **to be at — with** dissidēre ab (*with abl*)

odious *adj* odiosus, invisus

odium *s* invidia *f*

odor *s* odor *m*

odorous *adj* odoratus

Odyssey *s* Odyssea *f*

of *prep* (*possession*) *rendered by genit*; (*origin*) de (*with abl*), ex (*with abl*)

off *adv* procul; **far —** longe, procul; **well —** bene nummatus

off *prep* de (*with abl*)

offend *vt* offendĕre, laedĕre; *vi* **to — against** violare

offender *s* peccator, reus *m*

offense *s* (*fault*) offensa, culpa *f*; (*insult*) injuria *f*; (*displeasure*) offensio *f*

offensive *adj* injuriosus; (*odors, etc.*) odiosus, foedus, gravis; (*language*) malignus, contumeliosus; (*aggressive*) bellum inferens; **—ly** injuriose; odiose

offer *vt* offerre, donare, praebēre; (*violence*) adferre; (*help*) ferre

offer *s* conditio *f*

offhand *adj* incuriosus

offhand *adv* confestim, illico

office *s* (*place of work*) officina *f*; (*pol*) honos, magistrat·us -ūs *m*; (*duty*) munus, officium *n*

officer *s* magistrat·us -ūs *m*; (*mil*) praefectus *m*

official *adj* publicus

official *s* minister, magistrat·us -ūs *m*

officiate *vi* officio *or* munere fungi, interesse; (*of clergyman*) rem divinam facĕre

officious *adj* officiosus, molestus; **—ly** officiose, moleste

offing *s* **in the —** procul

offset *vt* compensare

offspring *s* proles, progenies *f*

often *adv* saepe; **very — ** persaepe

ogre *s* larva *f*, monstrum *n*

oh *interj* ohl, ohel

oil *s* oleum *n*

oil *vt* ung(u)ĕre

oily *adj* oleosus; (*like oil*) oleaceus

ointment *s* unguentum *n*

old *adj* (*aged*) senex; (*out of use*) obsoletus; (*worn*) exesus, tritus; (*ancient*) antiquus, priscus; **of —** olim, quondam; **to grow —** senescĕre

old age *s* senectus *f*

old-fashioned *adj* priscus, antiquus

old man *s* senex *m*

old woman *s* an·us -ūs *f*

oligarchy *s* optimates *m pl*

olive *s* olea *f*

olive grove *s* olivetum *n*

Olympiad *s* Olympias *f*

Olympic *adj* Olympicus

omelet *s* laganum de ovis confectum *n*

omen *s* omen, auspicium *n*

ominous *adj* infaustus; **—ly** malis ominibus

omission *s* praetermissio, neglegentia *f*

omit *vt* omittĕre, mittĕre, praetermittĕre

omnipotence *s* omnipotentia, infinita potentia *f*

omnipotent *adj* omnipotens

omnivorous *adj* omnivorus

on *prep* (*place*) in (*with abl*); (*time*) render by abl; (*about, concerning*) de (*with abl*); (*ranged with*) a(b) (*with abl*); (*depending, hanging on*) de (*with abl*); (*near*) ad (*with acc*)

on *adv* porro; (*continually*) usque; **and so** — et cetera, ac deinceps; **to go** — pergĕre

once *adv* (*one time*) semel; (*formerly*) olim, quondam; **at** — statim, illico, ex templo; **for** — aliquando; **— and for all** semel in perpetuum; **— more** iterum; **— upon a time** olim

one *adj* unus

one *pron* unus; unicus; (*a certain person or thing*) quidam; **it is all** — perinde est; **— after another** alternus; **— another** inter se, alius alium; **— by** — singulatim; **— or the other** alteruter; **— or two** unus et alter

one-eyed *adj* luscus

onerous *adj* onerosus, gravis

oneself *pron* (*refl*) se; **to** — sibi; **with** — secum; (*intensive*) ipse

one-sided *adj* inaequalis, iniquus, impar

onion *s* caepa *f*

only *adj* unicus, unus, solus

only *adv* solum, tantum, modo; **not — ... but also** non solum ... sed etiam

only-begotten *adj* unigenitus

onset *s* impet·us -ūs *m*

onslaught *s* incurs·us -ūs *m*

onward *adv* porro

ooze *vi* manare, (de)stillare

opaque *adj* densus, opacus

open *adj* (*not shut*) apertus, patens; (*evident*) manifestus; (*sincere*) candidus, ingenuus; (*public*) publicus, communis; (*of space*) apertus; (*of question, undecided*) integer; **in the — air** sub divo; **to lie** — patēre; **—ly** aperte, palam

open *vt* aperire, patefacĕre; (*to uncover*) retegĕre; (*letter*) resignare; (*book*) evolvēre; (*to begin*) exordiri; (*with ceremony*) inaugurare; *vi* patescĕre, se pandĕre; (*to gape*) dehiscĕre; (*of wound*) recrudescĕre

open-handed *adj* liberalis, largus

open-hearted *adj* simplex, ingenuus

opening *s* (*act*) apertio *f*; (*aperture*) foramen *n*, hiat·us -ūs *m*; (*opportunity*) locus *m*, occasio *f*

open-minded *adj* docilis

operate *vt* agĕre, gerĕre; *vi* operari

operation *s* effectio *f*; (*business*) negotium *n*; (*med*) sectio *f*

operative *adj* efficax, activus

operator *s* opifex *m*

opiate *s* mendicamentum somnificum *n*

opinion *s* opinio, sententia, mens *f*; (*esteem*) existimatio *f*; **public —**

fama *f*

opium *s* opion *n*

opponent *s* adversarius *m*

opportune *adj* opportunus, idoneus, commodus; **—ly** opportune, in tempore

opportunity *s* copia, occasio, opportunitas *f*

oppose *vt* opponĕre, objicĕre; *vi* repugnare, resistĕre, adversari

opposite *adj* adversus, contrarius, diversus

opposite *prep* contra (*with acc*)

opposite *adv* contra, ex adverso

opposition *s* oppositio, repugnantia, discrepantia *f*; (*obstacle*) impedimentum *n*; (*party*) adversa factio *f*

oppress *vt* opprimĕre, vexare, gravare, onerare

oppression *s* gravatio, injuria *f*

oppressive *adj* praegravis, acerbus, molestus; **to become** — ingravescĕre

oppressor *s* tyrannus *m*

opprobrious *adj* turpis, probrosus

opprobrium *s* dedecus, probrum *n*

optical *adj* opticus

option *s* optio *f*

opulence *s* opulentia *f*

opulent *adj* opulens, opulentus

or *conj* vel, aut, —ve; (*in questions*) an; **— else** aut, alioquin; **— not** annon; (*in indirect questions*) necne

oracle *s* oraculum *n*

oracular *adj* fatidicus

oral *adj* verbalis, verbo traditus; **—ly** voce, verbis

orange *s* malum aurantium *n*

oration *s* oratio *f*

orator *s* orator *m*

oratorical *adj* oratorius

oratory *s* ars oratoria, eloquentia, rhetorice *f*

orb *s* orbis, gyrus *m*

orbit *s* orbis *m*; (*in astronomy*) ambit·us -ūs *m*

orchard *s* pomarium *n*

orchestra *s* symphoniaci *m pl*

ordain *vt* (*to appoint*) edicĕre

ordeal *s* discrimen *n*, labor *m*

order *s* (*class, arrangement*) ordo *m*; (*command*) mandatum, jussum, imperatum *n*; (*fraternity*) collegium *n*; **by — of** jussu (*with genit*); **in — dispositus; in — that so; in — that not** ne; **out of —** incompositus; **to put in —** ordinare, disponĕre

order *vt* (*to command*) imperare (*with dat*), jubēre; (*to demand*) imperare (*with acc*); (*to put in order*) ordinare, disponĕre, digerĕre

orderly *adj* compositus, ordinatus; (*well-behaved*) modestus

orderly *s* accensus *m*; (*mil*) tesserarius *m*

ordinal *adj* ordinalis

ordinance *s* edictum, rescriptum *n*

ordinarily *adv* fere, plerumque

ordinary *adj* usitatus, vulgaris, solitus, quottidianus

ordnance *s* tormenta *n pl*

ore *s* aes *n*

organ s (*of body*) membrum n; (*musical*) organum n

organic adj organicus

organism s compages f

organization s ordinatio f, structura f

organize vt ordinare, instituĕre

orgy s comissatio f

Orient s oriens m

oriental adj Asiaticus

orifice s foramen, os n

origin s origo f, principium n; (*birth*) genus n; (*source*) fons m

original adj pristinus, primitivus, primus; (*one's own*) proprius; (*new*) novus, inauditus; **—ly** primum, principio, initio

original s archetypum, exemplar n; (*writing*) autographum n

originality s proprietas ingenii f

originate vt instituĕre; vi oriri

originator s auctor m

ornament s ornamentum n, ornat·us -ūs m

ornament vt ornare, decorare

ornamental adj decorus

ornate adj ornatus; **—ly** ornate

orphan s orbus m, orba f

orphaned adj orbatus

orphanage s orphanotrophium n

oscillate vi agitari; (*fig*) dubitare

oscillation s agitatio f; (*fig*) dubitatio f

ostensible adj simulatus, fictus

ostensibly adv specie, per speciem

ostentation s ostentatio, jactatio f

ostentatious adj ambitiosus, gloriosus, jactans; **—ly** ambitiose, jactanter

ostracism s ostracismus m

ostrich s struthiocamelus m

other adj (*different*) alius, diversus; (*remaining*) ceterus; **every — day** tertio quoque die; **on the — hand** contra, autem; **the — alter**

otherwise adv aliter

otter s lutra f

ought vi **I —** debeo, oportet me

ounce s uncia f

our adj noster

ours pron noster

ourselves pron (*reflex*) nos, nosmet; **to —** nobis; (*intensive*) nosmet ipsi

oust vt ejicĕre

out adv (*outside*) foris; (*motion*) foras; **— of** de (*with abl*), e(x) (*with abl*); (*on account of*) propter (*with acc*); **— of the way** devius

outbreak s eruptio f; (*fig*) seditio f

outburst s eruptio f

outcast s exsul, extorris, profugus m

outcome s event·us -ūs m

outcry s clamor m, acclamatio f, convicium n

outdo vt superare

outdoors adv foris, sub divo

outer adj exterior

outermost adj extremus

outfit s apparat·us -ūs m; (*costume*) vestimenta n pl

outflank vt circumire, circumvenire

outgrow vt excedĕre ex (*with abl*), staturā superare

outing s excursio f

outlandish adj externus, barbarus

outlast vt diutius durare (*with abl*)

outlaw s proscriptus m

outlaw vt aquā et igni interdicĕre (*with dat*), proscribĕre

outlay s sumpt·us -ūs m, impensa f

outlet s exit·us -ūs m

outline vt describĕre, adumbrare

outline s adumbratio f

outlive vt supervivĕre (*with dat*), superesse (*with dat*)

outlook s prospect·us -ūs m

outlying adj externus; (*distant*) remotus

outnumber vt multitudine superare

outpost s statio f

outpouring s effusio f

output s fruct·us -ūs m

outrage s injuria f, flagitium n

outrage vt flagitio afficĕre, violare

outrageous adj flagitiosus, atrox; (*excessive*) immodicus; **—ly** flagitiose; immodice

outright adv (*at once*) statim; (*completely*) prorsus, penitus

outrun vt praevertĕre, linquĕre

outset s initium, inceptum n

outshine vt praelucĕre (*with dat*)

outside s pars exterior, superficies f; (*appearance*) species f; **on the — extrinsecus**

outside adj externus

outside adv foris, extra; (*motion*) foras; **from — extrinsecus**

outside prep extra (*with acc*)

outskirts s suburbium n, ager suburbanus m

outspoken adj candidus, liber

outspread adj patulus

outstanding adj praestans; (*of debts*) residuus

outstretched adj extentus, porrectus, passus

outstrip vt praevertĕre, cursu superare

outward adj externus

outward adv extra, extrinsecus

outweigh vt praevertĕre (*with dat*), praeponderare

outwit vt deludĕre, decipĕre

oval adj ovatus

ovation s plaus·us -ūs m; (*triumph*) ovatio f

oven s furnus m, fornax f

over prep (*across*) super (*with acc*), trans (*with acc*), per (*with acc*); (*above*) super (*with abl*), supra (*with acc*); (*with numbers*) plus quam

over adv supra; (*excess*) nimis; **all — ** ubique, passim; **— and above** insuper; **— and — again** iterum ac saepius, identidem

overall adj totus

overawe vt (de)terrēre

overbalance vt praeponderare

overbearing adj superbus, insolens

overboard adv ex nave; **to jump — ** ex nave desilire

overburden vt nimis onerare

overcast adj obnubilus

overcharge *vt* plus aequo exigĕre ab (*with abl*)

overcoat *s* paenula, lacerna *f*

overdo *vt* exaggerare, in majus extollĕre

overdue *adj* (*money*) residuus

overestimate *vt* majoris aestimare

overflow *s* inundatio *f*

overflow *vt* inundare; *vi* abundare, redundare

overgrown *adj* obductus, obsitus; (*too big*) praegrandis

overhang *vt* impendĕre

overhaul *vt* reficĕre

overhead *adv* desuper, insuper

overhear *vt* excipĕre, auscultare

overjoyed *adj* to be — nimio gaudio exsultare

overladen *adj* praegravatus

overland *adj* per terram

overlay *vt* inducĕre, illinĕre

overload *vt* nimis onerare

overlook *vt* (*not to notice*) praetermittĕre; (*to pardon*) ignoscĕre (*with dat*); (*a view*) despectare

overlord *s* dominus *m*

overpower *vt* exsuperare, opprimĕre

overrate *vt* nimis aestimare

overreach *vt* circumvenire

overriding *adj* praecipuus

overripe *adj* praematurus

overrun *vt* (per)vagari; (*fig*) obsidēre

overseas *adj* transmarinus

oversee *vt* praeesse (*with dat*)

overseer *s* curator, praeses, custos *m*

overshadow *vt* obumbrare; (*fig*) obscurare

overshoot *vt* excedĕre, transgredi

oversight *s* incuria, neglegentia *f*, error *m*

oversleep *vi* diutius dormire

overspread *vt* obducĕre

overstate *vt* in majus extollĕre

overstep *vt* excedĕre, transgredi

overt *adj* apertus; —ly palam

overtake *vt* consequi

overtax *vt* (*fig*) abuti (*with abl*)

overthrow *s* eversio, ruina *f*, excidium *n*

overthrow *vt* subvertĕre, evertĕre, dejicĕre

overture *s* (*mus*) exordium *n*; (*proposal*) conditio *f*; to make —s to agĕre cum (*with abl*)

overturn *vt* evertĕre, subvertĕre

overweening *adj* superbus, insolens, arrogans

overwhelm *vt* obruĕre, opprimĕre

overwork *vt* to — oneself plus aequo laborare

owe *vt* debēre

owing to *prep* propter (*with acc*)

owl *s* bubo *m*, strix *f*

own *adj* proprius; one's — suus, proprius

own *vt* possidēre, tenēre; (*to acknowledge*) fatēri, confitēri

owner *s* dominus, possessor *m*

ownership *s* possessio *f*, mancipium, dominium *n*

ox *s* bos *m*

oyster *s* ostrea *f*

oyster shell *s* ostreae testa *f*

P

pace *s* (*step*) pass·us -ūs, grad·us -ūs *m*; (*measure*) pass·us -ūs *m*; (*speed*) velocitas *f*, grad·us -ūs *m*

pace *vi* incedĕre, gradi; to — up and down spatiari

pacific *adj* pacificus, tranquillus

pacification *s* pacificatio *f*

pacify *vt* pacare, placare, sedare

pack *s* (*bundle*) sarcina *f*, fasciculus *m*; (*of animals*) grex *m*; (*of people*) turba *f*, grex *m*

pack *vt* (*items of luggage*) colligĕre, componĕre; (*to fill completely*) frequentare, complēre; (*to compress*) stipare; (*of vasa*) colligĕre

package *s* sarcina *f*, fasciculus *m*

packet *s* fasciculus *m*

pack horse *s* equus clitellarius *m*

packsaddle *s* clitellae *f pl*

pact *s* pactum *n*, pactio *f*; to make a — pacisci

pad *s* pulvinus, pulvillus *m*

pad *vt* suffarcinare

padding *s* fartura *f*

paddle *s* remus *m*

paddle *vi* remigare

paddock *s* saeptum *n*

pagan *s* paganus *m*

page *s* (*of book*) pagina, scheda *f*; puer *m*

pageant *s* pompa *f*, spectaculum *n*

pail *s* hama, situla *f*

pain *s* dolor *m*; (*fig*) angor *m*; to be in — dolēre; to take — s operam dare

pain *vt* dolore afficĕre, excruciare; *vi* dolēre

painful *adj* gravis, acerbus, molestus; —ly graviter, magno cum dolore

painless *adj* doloris expers

painstaking *adj* operosus

paint *s* pigmentum *n*; (*for face*) fucus *m*

paint *vt* pingĕre, depingĕre

paintbrush *s* penicillus *m*

painter *s* pictor *m*

painting *s* pictura *f*

pair *s* par *n*; (*of oxen*) jugum *n*

pair *vt* conjungĕre, componĕre

palace *s* regia *f*, palatium *n*

palatable *adj* jucundus, suavis, sapidus

palate *s* palatum *n*

palatial *adj* regius

pale *adj* pallidus; **to be —** pallēre; **to grow —** pallescēre

pale *s* palus *m*

paling *s* saepes *f*

palisade *s* vallum *n*

pall *s* pallium *n*

pall *vi* satiare; *vi* vapescēre

pallet *s* grabat·us -ūs *m*

palliative *s* lenimentum *n*

pallid *adj* pallidus

pallor *s* pallor *m*

palm *s* (*of hand*) palma *f*; (*tree*) palma *f*

palpable *adj* tractabilis; (*fig*) apertus, manifestus

palpitate *vi* palpitare

palsied *adj* paralyticus

palsy *s* paralysis *f*

paltry *adj* vilis, minutus

pamper *vt* indulgēre (*with dat*)

pamphlet *s* libellus *m*

pan *s* patina, patella *f*; (*for frying*) sartago *f*

pancake *s* laganum *n*

pander *s* leno *m*

pander *vi* lenocinari

panegyric *s* laudatio *f*

panel *s* (*of wall*) abacus *m*; (*of ceiling*) lacunar *n*; (*of jury*) decurio *m*; (*of door*) tympanum *n*

paneled *adj* laqueatus

pang *s* dolor *m*

panic *s* pavor *m*

panic-stricken *adj* pavidus

panoply *s* arma *n pl*

panorama *s* conspect·us -ūs *m*

pant *vi* palpitare, anhelare; **to — after** (*fig*) gestire

pantheism *s* pantheismus *m*

pantheist *s* pantheista *m*

pantheon *s* Pantheon *n*

panther *s* pantera *f*

panting *adj* anhelus

panting *s* anhelit·us -ūs *m*

pantomime *s* (*play and actor*) mimus *m*

pantry *s* cella penaria *f*

pap *s* papilla, mamilla *f*

paper *s* (*stationery*) charta *f*; (*newspaper*) acta diurna *n pl*; **—s** scripta *n pl*

paper *adj* chartaceus, charteus

papyrus *s* papyrus *f*

par *s* **to be on a — with** par esse (*with dat*)

parable *s* parabole *f*

parade *s* (*mil*) decurs·us -ūs *m*; pompa *f*; (*display*) apparat·us -ūs *m*, pompa *f*

parade *vt* (*fig*) ostentare, jactare; *vi* (*mil*) decurrēre

paradise *s* paradisus *m*

paradox *s* oxymora verba *n pl*

paragon *s* specimen, exemplar *n*

paragraph *s* caput *n*

parallel *adj* parallelus; (*fig*) consimilis

parallel *vt* exaequare

paralysis *s* paralysis *f*; (*fig*) torpedo *f*

paralytic *adj* paralyticus

paralyze *vt* debilitare, enervare, percellēre

paramount *adj* supremus

paramour *s* (*man*) moechus, adulter *m*; (*woman*) meretrix, pellex *f*

parapet *s* pluteus *m*

paraphernalia *s* apparat·us -ūs *m*

paraphrase *s* paraphrasis *f*

paraphrase *vt* vertēre, interpretari

parasite *s* parasitus *m*

parasol *s* umbella *f*, umbraculum *n*

parcel *s* fasciculus *m*; (*plot of land*) agellus *m*

parcel *vt* **to — out** partire, dispertire

parch *vt* torrēre

parched *adj* torridus, aridus; **to be — arēre**

parchment *s* membrana *f*

pardon *s* venia *f*

pardon *vt* ignoscēre (*with dat*); (*an offense*) condonare

pardonable *adj* ignoscendus, condonandus

pare *vt* (*vegetables*) deglubēre; (*the nails*) resecare

parent *s* parens *m & f*

parentage *s* genus *n*, stirps *f*

parental *adj* patrius

parenthesis *s* interpositio, interclusio *f*

parity *s* paritas, aequalitas *f*

park *s* horti *m pl*

parlance *s* sermo *m*

parley *s* colloquium *n*

parley *vi* colloqui

parliament *s* senat·us -ūs *m*

parliamentary *adj* senatorius

parlor *s* exedrium *n*

parody *s* ridicula imitatio *f*

parole *s* fides *f*

paroxysm *s* access·us -ūs *m*

parricide *s* (*murder*) parricidium *n*; (*murderer*) parricida *m & f*

parrot *s* psittacus *m*

parry *vt* avertēre, defendēre

parse *vt* flectēre

parsimonious *adj* parcus; **—ly** parce

parsing *s* partium orationis flexio *f*

parsley *s* apium *n*

part *s* pars *f*; (*in play*) partes *f pl*; (*duty*) officium *n*; **for the most — maximam partem; in —** partim; **on the — of** ab (*with abl*); **to act the — of** sustinēre partes (*with genit*); **to take — in** interesse (*with dat*), particeps esse (*with genit*)

part *vt* separare, dividēre; **to — company** discedēre; *vi* discedēre, abire; (*to go open*) dehiscēre; **to — with** dimittēre

partial *adj* iniquus; (*incomplete*) mancus; **to be —** favēre (*with dat*); **—ly** aliqua ex parte

partiality *s* iniquitas *f*

participant *s* particeps *m & f*

participate *vi* interesse; **to — in** interesse (*with dat*), particeps esse (*with genit*)

participation *s* participatio, societas *f*

participle *s* participium *n*

particle *s* particula *f*

particular *adj* (*own*) proprius; (*special*) peculiaris, singularis, praecipuus; (*fussy*) fastidiosus; **—ly** praecipue, praesertim

particularize *vt* exsequi

particulars *s* singula *n pl*

parting *s* discess·us -ūs, digress·us -ūs *m*

partisan *s* fautor *m*

partition *s* partitio *f*; (*between rooms*) paries *m*; (*enclosure*) saeptum *n*

partly *adv* partim, ex parte

partner *s* socius *m*, socia *f*, particeps *m* & *f*; (*in office*) collega *m*; (*in marriage*) conju(n)x, consors *m* & *f*

partnership *s* consociatio, societas, consortio *f*

partridge *s* perdix *m* & *f*

party *s* (*entertainment*) convivium *n*; (*pol*) factio *f*, partes *f pl*; (*detachment*) man·us -ūs *f*; **to join a —** partes sequi

pass *s* angustiae *f pl*

pass *vt* (*to go by*) praeterire, transire, transgredi; (*to exceed*) excedēre; (*to approve*) probare; (*time*) agēre, degēre; (*a law*) perferre; **to — around** circumferre, tradēre; **to — down** tradēre; **to — sentence** jus dicēre; **to — the test** approbari; *vi* (*of time*) transire, abire, praeterire; **to come to —** evenire, fieri; **to let —** praetermittēre, dimittēre; **to — away** (*to die*) perire, abire; **to — for** habēri, vidēri; **to — on** (*to go forward*) pergēre; (*to die*) perire; **to — out** collabi, intermori; **to — over** transire

passable *adj* (*of road*) pervius; (*fig*) mediocris, tolerabilis

passably *adv* mediocriter, tolerabiliter

passage *s* (*act*) transit·us -ūs *m*; (*by water*) transmissio, trajectio *f*; (*of book*) locus *m*

passenger *s* viator *m*; (*on ship*) vector *m*

passer-by *s* praeteriens *m*

passing *s* obit·us -ūs *m*

passion *s* cupiditas, permotio *f*, fervor *m*; (*anger*) ira *f*; (*lust*) libido *f*

passionate *adj* fervidus, ardens; iracundus; **—ly** ardenter, iracunde

passive *adj* passivus; **—ly** passive

passport *s* diploma *n*

password *s* tessera *f*

past *adj* praeteritus; (*immediately preceding*) proximus, superior

past *s* tempus praeteritum *n*

past *prep* praeter (*with acc*), post (*with acc*)

paste *s* gluten *n*

paste *vt* agglutinare, conglutinare

pasteboard *s* charta crassa *f*

pastime *s* oblectamentum *n*, ludus *m*

pastoral *adj* pastoralis, bucolicus

pastoral *s* poema bucolicum *n*

pastry *s* crustum *n*

pasture *s* past·us -ūs *m*, pascuum *n*, pastio *f*

pasture *vt* pascēre; *vi* (*to graze*) pasci

pat *adj* idoneus

pat *vt* permulcēre, demulcēre

patch *s* assumentum *n*, pannus *m*

patch *vt* resarcire, assuēre

patchwork *s* cento *m*

patent *adj* apertus, manifestus; **—ly** manifesto

patent *s* privilegium *n*

paternal *adj* paternus

paternity *s* paternitas *f*

path *s* semita *f*, trames, callis *m*; (*fig*) via *f*

pathetic *adj* maestus; **—ally** maeste

pathless *adj* invius

pathos *s* pathos *n*, dolor *m*

pathway *s* semita *f*, callis, trames *m*

patience *s* patientia *f*

patient *adj* patiens, tolerans; **—ly** patienter, aequo animo

patient *s* aegrotus *m*, aegrota *f*

patriarch *s* patriarcha *m*

patriarchal *adj* patriarchicus

patrician *adj* patricius

patrician *s* patricius *m*

patrimony *s* patrimonium *n*

patriot *s* amans patriae *m*

patriotic *adj* amans patriae

patriotism *s* amor patriae, amor in patriam *m*

patrol *s* excubiae *f pl*

patrol *vt* circumire; *vi* excubias agēre

patron *s* patronus *m*

patronage *s* patrocinium, praesidium *n*

patroness *s* patrona *f*

patronize *vt* favēre (*with dat*), fovēre

patronymic *s* patronymicum nomen *n*

pattern *s* exemplar, exemplum, specimen *n*

paucity *s* paucitas *f*

paunch *s* ingluvies *f*

pauper *s* pauper *m*

pause *s* pausa, mora *f*; (*mus*) intermissio *f*, intervallum *n*

pause *vi* insistēre, intermittēre

pave *vt* sternēre

pavement *s* pavimentum *n*, stratura *f*

pavilion *s* tentorium *n*

paving stone *s* saxum quadratum *n*

paw *s* ungula *f*, pes *m*

paw *vt* pedibus pulsare

pawn *s* pignus *n*

pawn *vt* pignerare

pawnbroker *s* pignerator *m*

pay *s* merces *f*; (*mil*) stipendium *n*

pay *vt* solvēre; (*in full*) persolvēre, pendēre; (*mil*) stipendium numerare (*with dat*); **to — a compliment** to laudare; **to — for** solvēre (*with acc of thing and dat of person*); **to — respects** to salutare; **to — the penalty** poenam dare, poenam luēre; *vi* **it pays** operae pretium est, prodest, lucro est

payable *adj* solvendus

paymaster *s* dispensator *m*; (*mil*) tribunus aerarius *m*

payment *s* (*act*) solutio *f*; (*sum of money*) pensio *f*

pea *s* pisum, cicer *n*
peace *s* pax *f*; quies *f*, otium *n*
peaceful *adj* tranquillus, placidus, pacatus; —**ly** tranquille, placide, cum bona pace
peacemaker *s* pacificator *m*
peace offering *s* placamen, placamentum, piaculum *n*
peacetime *s* otium *n*
peach *s* malum Persicum *n*
peacock *s* pavo *m*
peak *s* (*of mountain*) cacumen *n*; vertex, apex *m*
peal *s* (*of thunder*) fragor *m*; (*of bells*) concent·us -ūs *m*
peal *vi* resonare
pear *s* pirum *n*
pearl *s* margarita *f*
pearly *adj* gemmeus
peasant *s* agricola, colonus *m*
peasantry *s* agricolae, agrestes *m pl*
pebble *s* lapillus, calculus *m*
peck *s* modius *m*
peck *vt* rostro impetĕre, vellicare
peculation *s* pecul·at·us -ūs *m*
peculiar *adj* proprius, peculiaris, praecipuus, singularis; —**ly** praecipue
peculiarity *s* proprietas *f*
pecuniary *adj* pecuniarius
pedagogue *s* paedagogus *m*; (*schoolmaster*) magister *m*
pedant *s* scholasticus *m*
pedantic *adj* putidus, nimis diligens; —**ally** nimis diligenter
pedantry *s* eruditio insulsa *f*
peddle *vt* venditare, circumferre
peddler *s* venditor, institor *m*
pedestal *s* basis *f*
pedestrian *adj* pedester
pedestrian *s* pedes *m*
pedigree *s* stemma *n*, stirps *f*
pediment *s* fastigium *n*
peel *s* cortex *m*
peel *vt* decorticare, glubĕre
peep *s* aspect·us -ūs, tuit·us -ūs *m*
peep *vi* inspicĕre
peephole *s* conspicilium *n*
peer *s* par *m*; (*of peerage*) patricius *m*
peer *vi* to — at intuĕri
peerless *adj* unicus, incomparabilis
peevish *adj* stomachosus, morosus, difficilis; —**ly** stomachose, morose
peg *s* clavus, paxillus *m*
pelican *s* pelicanus, onocrotalus *m*
pellet *s* globulus *m*
pelt *s* pellis *f*
pelt *vt* (*to hurl*) jacĕre; (*to beat*) verberare, petĕre
pen *s* (*to write with*) calamus, stylus *m*; (*enclosure*) saeptum *n*; (*for sheep*) ovile *n*; (*for pigs*) suile *n*
pen *vt* scribĕre, componĕre; to — in includĕre
penal *adj* poenalis
penalize *vt* poenā afficĕre, mul(c)tare
penalty *s* poena, mul(c)ta *f*
penance *s* satisfactio *f*
pencil *s* stilus *m*, graphis *f*
pending *adj* suspensus; (*law*) sub judice
pending *prep* inter (*with acc*)

pendulum *s* libramentum *n*
penetrate *vt* penetrare
penetrating *adj* acer, perspicax
penetration *s* acies mentis *f*, acumen *n*
peninsula *s* paeninsula *f*
penitence *s* paenitentia *f*
penitent *adj* paenitens; —**ly** paenitenter
penitentiary *s* carcer *m*
penknife *s* scalpellum *n*
penmanship *s* man·us -ūs *f*
pennant *s* vexillum *n*
penniless *adj* inops
penny *s* quadrans *m*
pension *s* annua *n pl*
pensive *adj* meditabundus
penultimate *s* paenultima syllaba *f*
penurious *adj* parcus, sordidus
penury *s* egestas, inopia *f*
people *s* (*nation*) populus *m*; homines *m pl*; (*common people*) plebs *f*; — say dicunt
people *vt* frequentare
pepper *s* piper *n*
pepper *vt* pipere condire; (*fig*) (*with blows*) verberare
peppermint *s* mentha *f*
perceive *vt* percipĕre, sentire, vidēre, intellegĕre
percentage *s* portio *f*
perceptible *adj* percipiendus, manifestus
perceptibly *adv* sensim
perception *s* perceptio *f*, sens·us -ūs *m*
perch *s* (*for birds*) pertica *f*; (*type of fish*) perca *f*
perch *vi* insidēre
perchance *adv* forte
percolate *vt* percolare; *vi* permanare
percussion *s* ict·us -ūs, concuss·us -ūs *m*
perdition *s* interit·us -ūs *m*; exitium *n*
peremptory *adj* arrogans
perennial *adj* perennis
perfect *adj* perfectus, absolutus; (*gram*) praeteritus; —**ly** perfecte, absolute; (*entirely*) plane
perfect *vt* perficĕre, absolvĕre
perfection *s* perfectio, absolutio *f*
perfidious *adj* perfidus, perfidiosus; —**ly** perfidiose
perfidy *s* perfidia *f*
perforate *vt* perforare, terebrare
perforation *s* foramen *n*
perform *vt* perficĕre, peragĕre; (*duty*) fungi (*with abl*); (*to play*)
performance *s* perfunctio, executio *f*; (*work*) opus *n*; (*of a play*) actio *f*; (*play, drama*) fabula *f*
performer *s* actor *m*; (*in play*) histrio *m*
perfume *s* odor *m*, unguentum *n*
perfume *vt* odoribus imbuĕre
perhaps *adv* forte, forsitan, fortasse
peril *s* periculum *n*
perilous *adj* periculosus; —**ly** periculose
period *s* (*gram*) periodus *f*; tempus, spatium *n*, aetas *f*; (*rhet*) circuit·us -ūs *m*

periodic *adj* certus; (*style*) periodicus; **—ally** certis temporibus
periphery *s* peripheria *f*, ambit·us
-ūs *m*
periphrastic *adj* per periphrasin
dictus
perish *vi* perire, interire
perishable *adj* fragilis, caducus,
mortalis
peristyle *s* peristyl(i)um *n*
perjure *vt* to — **oneself** pejerare,
perjurare
perjured *adj* perjurus
perjury *s* perjurium *n*; **to commit**
— pejerare, perjurare
permanence *s* stabilitas, constantia *f*
permanent *adj* diuturnus, perpetuus, mansurus; **—ly** perpetuo
permeable *adj* pervius
permeate *vt* penetrare; *vi* permanare
permission *s* permissio, venia, potestas *f*
permit *vt* permittĕre (*with dat*), sinĕre
permutation *s* permutatio *f*
pernicious *adj* perniciosus; **—ly**
perniciose
peroration *s* peroratio *f*
perpendicular *adj* perpendicularis,
directus
perpendicular *s* linea perpendicularis *f*
perpetrate *vt* facĕre, perficĕre
perpetrator *s* auctor, reus *m*
perpetual *adj* perpetuus, perennis,
sempiternus; **—ly** perpetuo
perpetuate *vt* perpetuare, continuare
perpetuity *s* perpetuitas *f*
perplex *vt* turbare, confundĕre
perplexing *adj* perplexus, ambiguus
perplexity *s* perturbatio, dubitatio *f*
persecute *vt* persequi, insequi, vexare
persecution *s* insectatio *f*
persecutor *s* insectator *m*
perseverance *s* perseverantia, constantia *f*
persevere *vi* perseverare, perstare,
constare
persevering *adj* perseverans, constans, tenax; **—ly** perseverante,
constanter
persist *vi* perstare, perseverare
persistence *s* permansio, pertinacia,
perseverantia *f*
persistent *adj* pertinax; **—ly** pertinaciter
person *s* homo *m & f*, quidam *m*;
(*body*) côrpus *n*; **in** — ipse
personage *s* persona *f*
personal *adj* privatus, suus; (*gram*)
personalis; **—ly** ipse, per se, coram
personality *s* persona, natura *f*, ingenium *n*
personification *s* prosopopoeia *f*
personify *vt* personā induĕre
personnel *s* membra *n pl*, socii *m pl*
perspective *s* scaenographia *f*
perspicacious *adj* perspicax
perspicacity *s* perspicacitas *f*
perspiration *s* sudatio *f*, sudor *m*
perspire *vi* sudare

persuade *vt* persuadēre (*with dat*)
persuasion *s* persuasio *f*
persuasive *adj* suasorius; **—ly** persuasibiliter
pert *adj* procax; **—ly** procaciter
pertain *vi* pertinēre, attinēre
pertinent *adj* appositus; **to be** —
ad rem pertinēre; **—ly** apposite
perturb *vt* turbare, perturbare
perturbation *s* perturbatio *f*
perusal *s* perlectio *f*
peruse *vt* perlegĕre, evolvĕre
pervade *vt* invadĕre, permanare, perfundĕre
perverse *adj* perversus, pravus; **—ly**
perverse
perversion *s* depravatio *f*
perversity *s* perversitas, pravitas *f*
pervert *vt* (*words*) detorquēre; depravare, corrumpĕre
pest *s* pestis *f*
pester *vt* vexare, infestare, sollicitare
pestilence *s* pestilentia *f*
pestle *s* pilum *n*
pet *s* corculum *n*, deliciae *f pl*
pet *vt* fovēre, in deliciis habēre
petal *s* floris folium *n*
petition *s* petitio *f*, preces *f pl*; (*pol*)
libellus *m*
petition *vt* supplicare, orare
petitioner *s* supplex *m*
petrify *vt* in lapidem convertĕre; *vi*
lapidescĕre
petticoat *s* subucula *f*
pettiness *s* animus angustus *m*
petty *adj* minutus, angustus, levis
petulance *s* petulantia, protervitas *f*
petulant *adj* protervus
phalanx *s* phalanx *f*
phantom *s* simulacrum, phantasma
n, species *f*
pharmacy *s* ars medicamentaria *f*;
(*drugstore*) taberna medicina, apotheca *f*
phase *s* (*of moon*) lunae facies *f*; (*fig*)
vices *f pl*
pheasant *s* phasianus *m*, phasiana *f*
phenomenal *adj* singularis
phenomenon *s* res *f*; (*remarkable
event*) portentum, prodigium *n*
philanthropic *adj* humanus
philanthropy *s* humanitas *f*
philologist *s* philologus, grammaticus *m*
philology *s* philologia *f*
philosopher *s* philosophus, sapiens *m*
philosophical *adj* philosophicus;
—ly philosophice, sapienter; (*calmly*) aequo animo
philosophize *vi* philosophari
philosophy *s* philosophia, sapientia
f; (*theory*) ratio *f*
philter *s* philtrum *n*
phlegm *s* pituita *f*, phelgma *n*
phlegmatic *adj* (*fig*) lentus
phosphorus *s* phosphorus *m*
phrase *s* locutio *f*; (*gram*) incisum *n*
phraseology *s* locutio, loquendi ratio *f*
physical *adj* physicus; (*natural*) corporis (*genit, used adjectively*); **—ly**
naturā

physician *s* medicus *m*
physicist *s* physicus *m*
physics *s* physica *n pl*
physiognomy *s* oris habit·us -ūs *m*
physique *s* vires *f pl*
pick *vt* (*to choose*) eligĕre; (*to pluck*) carpĕre; (*to gather*) decerpĕre; **to — off** avellĕre; **to — out** eligĕre; **to — up** tollĕre
pick *s* (*tool*) dolabra *f*; (*best part*) flos *m*, lecti *m pl*
pickax *s* dolabra *f*
picked *adj* electus, delectus
picket *s* (*mil*) statio *f*
pickle *s* muria *f*
pickle *vt* in aceto condire, in muriā condire
pickled *adj* muriā conditus
picture *s* tabula picta, pictura *f*; (*fig*) descriptio *f*
picture *vt* (*to imagine*) fingĕre, ante oculos ponĕre
picture gallery *s* pinacotheca *f*
picturesque *adj* venustus, amoenus
pie *s* crustum *n*
piece *s* pars, portio *f*; (*of food*) frustum *n*; (*of cloth*) pannus *m*; (*broken off*) fragmentum *n*; (*coin*) nummus *m*; (*drama*) fabula *f*; **to fall to —s** dilabi; **to tear to —s** dilaniare, lacerare
piece *vt* resarcire; **to — together** fabricari, consuĕre
piecemeal *adv* frustatim, membratim
pier *s* moles *f*, agger *m*
pierce *vt* perforare; (*with sword, etc.*) transfigĕre, perfodĕre; (*fig*) pungĕre
piercing *adj* acutus, stridulus
piety *s* pietas, religio *f*
pig *s* porcus *m*, sus *m & f*
pigeon *s* columba *f*
pigment *s* pigmentum *n*
pigsty *s* hara *f*, suile *n*
pike *s* (*weapon*) hasta *f*; (*fish*) lupus *m*
pilaster *s* parasta, columella *f*
pile *s* (*heap*) acervus, cumulus *m*; (*for cremation*) rogus *m*; (*for building*) moles *f*; (*nap of cloth*) villus *m*
pile *vt* coacervare, congerĕre; **to — up** exstruĕre
pilgrim *s* peregrinator *m*
pilgrimage *s* peregrinatio *f*
pill *s* pilula *f*
pillage *s* vastatio, direptio, expilatio, rapina *f*
pillage *vt* vastare, diripĕre, depopulari, expilare, praedari
pillar *s* columna, pila *f*, columen *n*
pillow *s* pulvinus *m*, culcita *f*, cervical *n*
pillowcase *s* cervicalis integumentum *n*
pilot *s* gubernator *m*
pilot *vt* gubernare
pimp *s* leno *m*
pimple *s* pustula *f*
pimply *adj* pustulosus
pin *s* ac·us -ūs, acicula *f*; (*peg*) clavus *m*
pin *vt* acu figĕre; affigĕre
pincers *s* forceps *m & f*

pinch *vt* vellicare; (*as cold*) (ad)urĕre; (*to squeeze*) coartare; (*of shoe*) urĕre
pine *s* pinus *f*
pine *vi* **to — away** tabescĕre, languĕre; **to — for** desiderare
pineapple *s* (nux) pinea *f*
pink *adj* rosaceus, rubicundus
pinnacle *s* fastigium *n*, summus grad·us -ūs *m*
pint *s* sextarius *m*
pioneer *s* praecursor *m*
pious *adj* pius; (*scrupulous*) religiosus; (*saintly*) sanctus; **—ly** pie, religiose, sancte
pipe *s* (*tube*) tubus *m*; (*mus*) fistula *f*
pipe *vt* fistulā canĕre
piper *s* tibicen *m*
piquant *adj* salsus, facetus; **—ly** salse
pique *s* offensio *f*
pique *vt* offendĕre
piracy *s* latrocinium *n*
pirate *s* pirata, praedo *m*
piratical *adj* praedatorius
pit *s* fossa, fovea *f*, puteus *m*; (*in theater*) cavea *f*; (*quarry*) fodina *f*
pitch *s* pix *f*; (*sound*) sonus *m*; (*degree*) grad·us -ūs *m*, fastigium *n*; (*slope*) fastigium *n*; **to such a —** of eo (*with genit*)
pitch *vt* (*to fling*) conjicĕre; (*camp*) ponĕre; (*tent*) tendĕre
pitcher *s* urceus *m*
pitchfork *s* furca *f*
piteous *adj* miserabilis; **—ly** miserabiliter, misere
pitfall *s* fovea *f*
pith *s* medulla *f*
pithy *adj* (*fig*) sententiosus
pitiable *adj* miserandus
pitiful *adj* misericors; (*pitiable*) miserabilis, miserandus; **—ly** misere
pitiless *adj* immisericors, durus; **—ly** immisericorditer
pittance *s* (*allowance for food*) demensum *n*; (*trifling sum*) mercedula *f*
pity *s* misericordia, miseratio *f*
pity *vt* miserēri (*with genit*); **I — him** miseret me ejus
pivot *s* axis, paxillus *m*; (*fig*) cardo *m*
placard *s* titulus, libellus *m*
place *s* locus *m*, **in —** of pro (*with abl*), loco (*with genit*); **in the first —** primum, primo; **out of —** intempestivus; **to take —** fieri, accidĕre
place *vt* ponĕre, locare, collocare
placid *adj* placidus, tranquillus; **—ly** placide, tranquille
plagiarism *s* furtum litterarium *n*
plagiarist *s* fur litterarius *m*
plagiarize *vt* furari
plague *s* pestilentia *f*; (*fig*) pestis *f*
plague *vt* vexare, exagitare
plain *s* campus *m*, planities *f*; **of the —** campester
plain *adj* (*clear*) apertus, manifestus, perspicuus; (*unadorned*) inornatus, simplex; (*of one color*) unicolor; (*frank*) sincerus; (*homely*)

invenustus; —ly aperte, manifeste; simpliciter; sincere

plaintiff s petitor m

plaintive adj querulus, flebilis; —ly fiebiliter

plan s consilium, propositum n; (drawing) descriptio f; (layout) forma f

plan vt (to scheme) excogitare, meditari; (to intend to) in animo habēre (with inf); (to draw) designare, describēre

plane s (tool) runcina f; (level surface) planities f

plane vt runcinare

planet s planeta, stella errans or vaga f

plank s assis m, tabula f

plant s planta, herba f

plant vt serĕre, conserĕre; (feet) ponĕre

plantation s plantarium n

planter s sator m

planting s sat·us -ūs m, consitura f

plaster s tectorium, gypsum n; (med) emplastrum n

plaster vt gypsare, dealbare

plastic adj plasticus, ductilis

plate s (dish) patella f, catillus m; (coating) lamina f; (silver) argentum n

plated adj bracteatus

platform s suggest·us -ūs m, suggestum n

platitude s trita sententia f

Platonic adj Platonis (genit, used adjectively)

platter s patella, lanx f

plausible adj verisimilis

play s ludus m; (drama) fabula f

play vt ludĕre; (instrument) canĕre (with abl); (game) ludĕre (with abl) (role) agĕre; to — a trick on ludificari

player s (in game) lusor m; (on stage) histrio, actor m; (on wind instrument) tibicen m; (on string instrument) fidicen m

playful adj lascivus, jocosus, ludibundus; (words) facetus; —ly per ludum, per jocum

playmate s collusor m

plaything s ludibrium n

playwright s fabularum scriptor m

plea s (law) petitio, exceptio, defensio f; (excuse) excusatio f

plead vi (in court) causam agĕre; (to beg) obsecrare, implorare, orare; to — against causam dicĕre contra (with acc); to — for defendĕre

pleasant adj amoenus, gratus, jucundus, suavis; —ly jucunde, suaviter

pleasantry s jocosa dicacitas f, facetiae f pl

please vt placēre (with dat), delectare; if you — si placet; please! obsecro!; sis!, amabo! (colloquial)

pleasing adj gratus, jucundus

pleasurable adj jucundus

pleasure s voluptas f; it is my —libet; to derive — voluptatem capĕre

plebeian adj plebeius

plebeians s plebs f

pledge s pignus n; (proof) testimonium n

pledge vt (op)pignerare, obligare; to — one's word fidem obligare

Pleiads s Pleiades f pl

plenary adj plenus, perfectus

plenipotentiary s legatus m

plentiful adj largus, affluens, uber; —ly large, ubertim

plenty s copia, abundantia f

plethora s pletura f

pleurisy s pleuritis f

pliable adj flexibilis, tractabilis, mansuetus

pliant adj lentus

plight s conditio f, stat·us -ūs m, discrimen n

plod vi assidue laborare

plodder s sedulus homo m

plodding adj laboriosus, assiduus, sedulus

plot s (conspiracy) conjuratio f, insidiae f pl; (of drama) argumentum n; (of ground) agellus m

plot vi conjurare, moliri

plow s aratrum n

plow vt arare; to — up exarare

plowing s aratio f

plowman s bubulcus, arator m

plowshare s vomer m

pluck s animus m

pluck vt carpĕre; to — off avellĕre, decerpĕre; to — out evellĕre, eripĕre; to — up eruĕre; to — up courage animo esse

plug s obturamentum n

plug vt obturare

plum s prunum n

plumage s plumae, pennae f pl

plumber s plumbarius m

plume s crista f

plummet s perpendiculum n

plump adj pinguis, obesus

plum tree s prunus f

plunder s (act) rapina f; (booty) praeda f

plunder vt praedari

plunderer s praedator m

plundering s rapina, praedatio f

plundering adj praedatorius, praedabundus

plunge vt mergĕre, submergĕre; (sword, etc.) condĕre; vi immergi, se mergĕre

pluperfect s plus quam perfectum tempus n

plural adj pluralis

plurality s multitudo f, numerus major m

plush adj lautus

ply vt exercēre, urgēre

poach vt (eggs) frigĕre; vi illicita venatione uti

poacher s fur m

pocket s sin·us -ūs, sacculus m

pocket vt in sacculis condĕre

pocket book s pugillaria n pl

pockmark s cicatrix f

pod s siliqua f

poem s poema, carmen n

poet s poeta, vates m

poetess *s* poetria, poetris *f*
poetic *adj* poeticus; **—ly** poetice
poetics *s* ars poetica *f*
poetry *s* (*art*) poetice *f*; (*poems*) poemata, carmina *n pl*, poesis *f*
poignancy *s* acerbitas *f*
poignant *adj* acerbus, pungens
point *s* punctum *n*; (*pointed end*) acumen *n*, acies *f*; (*of swords, etc.*) mucro *m*; (*fig*) quaestio, res *f*, stat·us -ūs *m*, argumentum *n*; **beside the — ab re**; **from this — on** posthac, hinc; **— of view** sententia *f*; **to the — ad rem**; **up to this —** adhuc, hactenus
point *vt* (*to sharpen*) acuěre; **to — out** monstrare, indicare
pointed *adj* acutus; (*fig*) salsus; (*stinging*) aculeatus; **—ly** acute, aperte
pointer *s* index *m & f*
pointless *adj* (*fig*) insulsus, frigidus; **—ly** insulse
poise *s* (*fig*) urbanitas *f*
poise *vt* ponderare, penděre, librare
poison *s* venenum, virus *n*
poison *vt* venenare, veneno necare; (*fig*) vitiare
poisoning *s* veneficium *n*
poisonous *adj* venenatus, venenosus
poke *vt* (*to jab*) cubito pulsare, fodicare; (*fire*) foděre
polar *adj* arcticus
polarity *s* polaritas *f*
pole *s* asser, contus *m*, pertica *f*; (*of earth*) polus *m*
polemic *s* controversiae *f pl*
pole star *s* stella polaris *f*
police *s* vigiles, custodes *m pl*
policeman *s* vigil *m*
policy *s* ratio *f*, consilium *n*
polish *vt* polire; **to — up** expolire
polish *s* nitor, levor *m*; (*refined manners*) urbanitas *f*; (*literary*) lima *f*
polite *adj* comis, urbanus; **—ly** comiter, urbane
politeness *s* urbanitas, comitas *f*
politic *adj* prudens, astutus
political *adj* civilis, publicus
politician *s* magistrat·us -ūs *m*
politics *s* res publica *f*; **to enter —** ad rem publicam acceděre
poll *s* caput *n*; **—s** comitia *n pl*
poll *vt* suffragiis petěre
polling booth *s* saeptum *n*
poll tax *s* capitum exactio *f*
pollute *vt* polluěre, inquinare, contaminare
pollution *s* (*act*) contaminatio *f*; (*filth*) colluvio, impuritas *f*
polygamy *s* polygamia *f*
polysyllabic *adj* polysyllabus
polytheism *s* multorum deorum cult·us -ūs *m*
pomegranate *s* malum Punicum *n*
pommel *vt* pulsare, verberare
pomp *s* pompa *f*, apparat·us -ūs *m*
pomposity *s* magnificentia *f*
pompous *adj* magnificus, gloriosus; **—ly** magnifice, gloriose
pond *s* stagnum *n*
ponder *vt* in mente agitare, considerare, ponderare

ponderous *adj* ponderosus, praegravis
pontiff *s* pontifex *m*
pontifical *adj* pontificalis
pontificate *s* pontificat·us -ūs *m*
pontoon *s* ponto *m*
pony *s* mannulus, equulus *m*
pool *s* lacuna *f*, stagnum *n*
pool *vt* conferre
poor *adj* (*needy*) pauper, inops, egens; (*inferior*) tenuis, mediocris; (*of soil*) macer; (*pitiable*) miser; (*meager*) exilis; **—ly** parum, mediocriter, misere, tenuiter
pop *s* crepit·us -ūs *m*
pop *vi* crepare; **to — out** exsilire
poplar *s* populus *f*
poppy *s* papaver *n*
populace *s* vulgus *n*, plebs *f*
popular *adj* popularis; **—ly** populariter
popularity *s* populi favor *m*, populi studium *n*
populate *vt* frequentare
population *s* civium numerus, incolarum numerus *m*
populous *adj* frequens
porcelain *s* fictilia *n pl*
porch *s* vestibulum *n*, portic·us -ūs *f*
porcupine *s* hystrix *f*
pore *s* foramen *n*
pore *vi* **to — over** assidue considerare, scrutari
pork *s* porcina *f*
porous *adj* rarus
porpoise *s* porculus marinus *m*
porridge *s* puls *f*
port *s* port·us -ūs *m*
portal *s* porta *f*
portend *vt* praesagire, portenděre, significare
portent *s* monstrum, portentum, prodigium *n*
portentous *adj* monstruosus, prodigiosus
porter *s* janitor, ostiarius *m*; (*carrier*) bajulus *m*
portfolio *s* scrinium *n*
portico *s* portic·us -ūs *f*
portion *s* portio, pars *f*
portion *vt* partire
portly *adj* amplus, opimus
portrait *s* imago, effigies *f*
portray *vt* depingěre, expriměre
pose *s* stat·us -ūs, habit·us -ūs *m*
pose *vi* habitum *or* statum suměre
position *s* positio *f*, sit·us -ūs *m*; (*of body*) gest·us -ūs *m*; (*office*) honos *m*; (*state*) conditio *f*, stat·us -ūs *m*; (*rank*) amplitudo, dignitas *f*
positive *adj* certus; (*gram*) positivus; (*fig*) confidens; **—ly** praecise, certo
possess *vt* possiděre, teněre
possession *s* possessio *f*; (*estate*) bona *n pl*; **in the — of** penes (*with acc*); **to gain — of** potiri (*with abl*), occupare
possessive *adj* quaestuosus, avarus; (*gram*) possessivus
possessor *s* possessor, dominus *m*
possibility *s* facultas *f*
possible *adj* **as quickly as —** quam celerrime; **it is —** fieri po-

test; it is — for me to possum (*with inf*)
possibly *adv* fortasse
post *s* (*stake*) postis, cippus *m*; (*station*) statio, sedes stativa *f*; (*position*) munus *n*
post *vt* collocare, ponĕre, constituĕre; to — a letter tabellario litteras dare
postage *s* vectura (epistulae) *f*
postdate *vt* diem seriorem scribĕre (*with dat*)
poster *s* libellus *m*
posterior *adj* posterior
posterity *s* posteri, minores *m pl*, posteritas *f*
posthaste *adv* quam celerrime
posthumous *adj* postumus
postman *s* tabellarius *m*
postpone *vt* differre, prorogare
postscript *s* ascriptio *f*
posture *s* stat·us -ūs, habit·us -ūs, gest·us -ūs *m*
pot *s* olla *f*, ahenum *n*
potato *s* solanum tuberosum *n*
potentate *s* tyrannus *m*
potential *adj* futurus
potion *s* potio *f*
potter *s* figulus *m*
pottery *s* fictilia *n pl*
pouch *s* sacculus *m*, pera *f*
poultry *s* aves cohortales *f pl*
pounce *vi* to — on insilire (*with dat or in* + *acc*)
pound *s* libra *f*
pound *vt* contundĕre, conterĕre
pour *vt* fundĕre; to — in infundĕre; to — out effundĕre; *vi* fundi, fluĕre; to — down (*of rain*) ruĕre
pouring *adj* (*of rain*) effusus
pout *vi* stomachari
poverty *s* paupertas, pauperies *f*
powder *s* pulvis *m*
powder *vt* pulvere conspergĕre
power *s* vis, potestas *f*; (*pol*) imperium *n*; (*mil*) copiae *f pl*; (*excessive*) potentia *f*; (*divine*) numen *n*; to have great — multum posse, multum valēre
powerful *adj* validus, potens; (*effectual*) efficax; —ly valde
powerless *adj* invalidus, impotens; (*vain*) irritus; to be — nil valēre
practical *adj* utilis, habilis; —ly fere, paene
practice *s* us·us -ūs *m*, experientia, exercitatio *f*; (*custom*) mos *m*, consuetudo *f*
practice *vt* (*to engage in*) exercēre, tractare; (*to rehearse*) meditari
practitioner *s* exercitator *m*; (*medical*) medicus *m*
pragmatic *adj* pragmaticus
prairie *s* campus *m*
praise *s* laus *f*
praise *vt* laudare
praiseworthy *adj* laudabilis, laudandus
prance *vi* exsultare, subsultare; (*of persons*) jactare
prank *s* ludus *m*; (*trick*) jocus, dolus *m*
pray *vt* precari, orare; *vi* precari, orare; to — for petĕre, precari;

to — to adorare, supplicare
prayer *s* preces *f pl*
preach *vt & vi* praedicare
preamble *s* prooemium, exordium *n*
precarious *adj* precarius, periculosus, incertus; —ly precario
precaution *s* cautio, provisio *f*; to take — cavēre, praecavēre
precede *vt* praeire (*with dat*), antecedĕre
precedence *s* prior locus *m*; to take — over antecedĕre
precedent *s* exemplum *n*
preceding *adj* prior, superior
precept *s* praeceptum *n*
preceptor *s* praeceptor, magister *m*
precinct *s* termini, limites *m pl*, templum *n*; (*ward*) regio *f*
precious *adj* pretiosus, carus; — stone gemma *f*
precipice *s* praeceps *n*; down a — in praeceps
precipitate *vt* praecipitare
precipitous *adj* praeceps, praeruptus, declivis
precise *adj* certus, definitus; (*exact*) accuratus, exactus; —ly subtiliter, accurate
precision *s* accuratio, cura *f*
preclude *vt* praecludĕre, excludĕre
precocious *adj* praecox
preconceive *vt* praecipĕre, praesentire; **preconceived idea** praejudicium *n*
preconception *s* praeceptio, praejudicata opinio *f*
precursor *s* praenuntius *m*
predatory *adj* praedatorius, praedabundus
predecessor *s* antecessor, decessor *m*
predestine *vt* praedestinare
predicament *s* discrimen *n*, angustiae *f pl*
predicate *vt* praedicare
predicate *s* praedicatum *n*
predict *vt* praedicĕre, augurari
prediction *s* praedictio *f*, praedictum, vaticinium *n*
predilection *s* studium *n*
predispose *vt* inclinare
predisposition *s* inclinatio *f*
predominant *adj* praevalens
predominate *vi* praevalēre
preeminence *s* praestantia, excellentia *f*
preeminent *adj* praecipuus, praestans, excellens; —ly praecipue, excellenter
preexist *vi* antea exstare *or* esse
preface *s* praefatio *f*
prefatory *adj* to make a few — remarks pauca praefari
prefect *s* praefectus *m*
prefecture *s* praefectura *f*
prefer *vt* praeponĕre, anteponĕre; (*charges*) deferre; to — to (*would rather*) malle (*with inf*)
preferable *adj* potior, praestantior
preference *s* favor *m*; in — to potius quam; to give — to anteponĕre
preferment *s* honos *m*
prefix *s* syllaba praeposita *f*

prefix vt praefigĕre, praeponĕre

pregnancy s graviditas f

pregnant adj gravida; (of language) pressus

prejudge vt praejudicare

prejudice s praejudicata opinio f, praejudicium n

prejudice vt **to be prejudiced against** praejudicatam opinionem habēre in (with acc), invidēre (with dat); **to — the people against** studia hominum inclinare in (with acc)

prejudicial adj noxius

preliminary adj praevius; **to make a few — remarks** pauca praefari

prelude s (mus) prooemium n, praelusio f

prelude vt praeludĕre

premature adj praematurus, immaturus, praeproperus; **—ly** ante tempus

premeditate vt praemeditari

premier s princeps m

premise s (major) propositio f; (minor) assumptio f; **—s** fundus m, praedium n

premium s praemium n; **at a —** carus

premonition s monit·us -ūs m, monitum n

preoccupation s praeoccupatio f

preoccupy vt praeoccupare

preparation s comparatio, praeparatio f, apparat·us -ūs m; (rehearsal) meditatio f

prepare vt parare, comparare, apparare; (to rehearse) meditari; **to — to** parare (with inf)

preponderance s praestantia f

preposition s praepositio f

preposterous adj praeposterus; **—ly** praepostere, absurde

prerogative s jus n

presage s praesagium n

presage vt praesagire, portendĕre, significare

prescience s providentia f

prescient adj providus, sagax

prescribe vt praescribĕre, proponĕre

prescription s praescriptum n; (of physician) medicamenti formula f

presence s praesentia f; (look) aspect·us -ūs m; **in my —** me praesente; **in the — of** coram (with abl)

present adj praesens, hic; **for the — in praesens tempus; to be — adesse; —ly** mox, illico, statim

present s donum, munus n

present vt donare, offerre; introducĕre; (in court) sistĕre; (to bring forward) praebēre, offerre; **to — itself or oneself** occurrĕre, obvenire

presentation s donatio f; (on stage) fabula f

presentiment s praesagitio f, praesagium n

preservation s conservatio f

preserve vt conservare; (fruits) condire

preserver s conservator m

preside vi praesidēre, praeesse; **to — over** praesidēre (with dat), praeesse (with dat)

presidency s praefectura f

president s praeses, praefectus m

press s (for wine) prelum n; (of people) turba f

press vt premĕre, comprimĕre; (fig) urgēre; **to — down** deprimĕre; vi **to — forward** anniti; **to — on** pergĕre, contendĕre

pressing adj gravis, urgens

pressure s pressio, pressura f, press·us -ūs m

pressure vt urgēre

prestige s auctoritas f

presumably adv sane

presume vt sumĕre, credĕre, conjicĕre; (to take liberties) sibi arrogare

presumption s (conjecture) conjectura f; (arrogance) arrogantia f

presumptuous adj arrogans, insolens, audax; **—ly** insolenter, arroganter

presuppose vt praesumĕre

pretend vt simulare, dissimulare, fingĕre

pretender s simulator, captator m

pretense s simulatio, species f; **under — of** per speciem (with genit); **without —** sine fuco

pretension s (claim) postulatio f; (display) ostentatio f; **to make —s** to affectare

preterite s tempus praeteritum n

preternatural adj praeter naturam

pretext s species f, praetextum n; **under the — of** specie (with genit), sub specie (with genit), sub praetextu (with genit)

pretor s praetor m

pretorian adj praetorianus

pretorship s praetura f

prettily adv belle, concinne

pretty adj bellus, venustus, lepidus

pretty adv satis, admodum; **— well** mediocriter

prevail vi (to be prevalent) esse, obtinēre; (to win) vincĕre; **to — upon** persuadēre (with dat)

prevalent adj (per)vulgatus; **to become —** increbrescĕre

prevaricate vi tergiversari

prevarication s praevaricatio, tergiversatio f

prevaricator s praevaricator, mendax m

prevent vt impedire, prohibēre

prevention s anticipatio, impeditio f

preventive adj prohibens, anticipans

previous adj prior, superior; **—ly** antea, antehac

prey s praeda f

prey vi **to — on** praedari, rapĕre; (fig) vexare, consumĕre

price s pretium n; **at a high — magni; at a low —** parvi

priceless adj inaestimabilis

prick vt pungĕre; (fig) stimulare; **to — up the ears** aures arrigĕre

prickle s aculeus m

prickly adj spinosus

pride s superbia f; (*source of pride*) decus n

pride vt to — oneself on jactare

priest s sacerdos m; (*of particular god*) flamen m

priestess s sacerdos f

priesthood s (*office*) sacerdotium n; (*collectively*) sacerdotes m pl

priestly adj sacerdotalis

prig s homo fastidiosus m

prim adj (nimis) diligens

primarily adv praecipue

primary adj primus, principalis; (*chief*) praecipuus

prime s flos m; to be in one's — florēre, vigēre

prime adj primus, egregius, optimus, exquisitus

primeval adj pristinus, priscus

primitive adj priscus, antiquus, incultus

primordial adj priscus

primrose s primula vulgaris f

prince s regulus, regis filius m; (*king*) rex, princeps m

princely adj regius, regalis

princess s regia puella, regis filia f

principal adj principalis, praecipuus; —ly praecipue, maxime

principal s caput n, praeses, praefectus, princeps m; (*money*) caput n, sors f

principality s principat·us -ūs m

principle s principium n; (*in philosophy*) axioma n; (*maxim*) institutum n

print s nota impressa f; (*of foot*) vestigium n

print vt imprimĕre

prior adj prior, potior

priority s primat·us -ūs m

prism s prisma n

prison s carcer m, vincula n pl

prisoner s reus m, rea f; (*for debt*) nex·us -ūs m

prisoner of war s captivus m

pristine adj pristinus

privacy s solitudo f, secretum n

private adj (*secluded*) secretus; (*person*) privatus; (*home*) domesticus; (*one's own*) proprius; (*mil*) gregarius; —ly clam, secreto; (*in a private capacity*) privatim

private s miles, miles gregarius m

privation s egestas, inopia f

privilege s privilegium n, immunitas f

privy adj privatus, secretus; — to conscius (*with genit*)

privy s forica, latrina f

prize s (*reward*) praemium n, palma f; (*prey*) praeda f

prize vt magni aestimare, magni facēre

prize fighter s pugil m

probability s veri similitudo, probabilitas f

probable adj verisimilis, probabilis

probably adv probabiliter

probation s probatio f

probe vt scrutari, inspicēre

probity s probitas, honestas f

problem s quaestio f; to have —s laborare

problematical adj anceps, incertus

procedure s progress·us -ūs, modus m, ratio f

proceed vi (*to go on*) pergĕre, procedĕre, incedĕre; to — against persequi; to — from oriri ex (*with abl*)

proceedings s acta n pl; (*law*) lis, actio f

proceeds s redit·us -ūs m

process s ratio f; (*law*) lis, actio f

proclaim vt promulgare, edicĕre, pronuntiare, declarare

proclamation s pronuntiatio f, edictum n

proconsul s proconsul m

proconsular adj proconsularis

proconsulship s proconsulat·us -ūs m

procrastinate vi cunctari, procrastinare

procrastination s procrastinatio f

procreate vt procreare, generare

procreation s procreatio f

proctor s procurator m

procurable adj procurandus

procurator s procurator m

procure vt parare, acquirĕre, nancisci, adipisci

procurement s comparatio f

procurer s leno m

prodigal adj prodigus

prodigal s ganeo m

prodigality s dissipatio, effusio f

prodigious adj prodigiosus, immanis, ingens

prodigy s prodigium, monstrum, portentum m; (*fig*) miraculum n

produce s fruct·us -ūs m; (*of earth*) fruges f pl; (*in money*) redit·us -ūs m

produce vt (*to bring forward*) proferre, producĕre; (*to bring into existence*) parēre, procreare, gignĕre; (*to cause*) efficĕre, facĕre; (*to put on, as a play*) docēre; (*crops*) ferre

product s (*of earth*) fruges f pl; opus n

production s productio f

productive adj ferax, fecundus, uber

productivity s feracitas, ubertas f

profanation s violatio f

profane adj profanus, impius; —ly impie

profane vt vilare, profanare, polluĕre

profanity s impietas f, nefas n

profess vt profitēri

professed adj apertus, manifestus

profession s professio f

professional adj ad professionem pertinens; (*expert*) peritus

professor s doctor m

professorship s doctoris munus n

proffer vt offerre, promittĕre, proponĕre

proficiency s progress·us -ūs m, peritia f

proficient adj habilis, peritus

profile s facies obliqua f; (*portrait*) imago obliqua f

profit s quaest·us -ūs, redit·us -ūs m, lucrum n

profit vt prodesse (with dat); vi proficěre; **to — by** uti (with abl), frui (with abl)

profitable adj fructuosus, quaestuosus, utilis; **to be —** prodesse

profitably adv utiliter

profitless adj inutilis, vanus

profligacy s nequitia f, perditi mores m pl

profligate adj perditus, flagitiosus, nequam (indecl)

profligate s nepos, ganeo m

profound adj altus, subtilis, abstrusus; **—ly** penitus

profundity s altitudo f

profuse adj profusus, effusus; **—ly** effuse

profusion s effusio, profusio, abundantia f

progeny s progenies, proles f

prognosticate vt praedicěre

prognostication s praedictio f, praedictum n

program s libellus m

progress s progress·us -ūs m; **to make —** proficěre

progress vi progredi

progression s progress·us -ūs m

progressive adj proficiens; **—ly** gradatim

prohibit vt interdicěre (with dat), vetare

prohibition s interdictum n

project s propositum, consilium n

project vt projicěre; vi prominěre, exstare; (of land) excurrěre

projectile s missile n

projecting adj eminens, prominens

projection s projectura, eminentia f

proletarian adj proletarius

proletariat s plebs f

prolific adj fecundus

prolix adj longus, verbosus

prolixity s verbositas f

prologue s prologus m

prolong vt producěre, prorogare, extenděre

prolongation s proragatio, dilatio f

promenade s (walk) ambulatio f; (place) xystus m

promenade vi spatiari, ambulare

prominence s eminentia f

prominent adj prominens, insignis

promiscuous adj promiscuus; **—ly** promiscue, sine ullo discrimine

promise s promissio f, promissum n; **to break a —** fidem fallěre; **to make a —** fidem dare

promise vt promittěre, pollicěri; (in marriage) desponděre

promising adj bonā spe (abl used adjectively)

promissory note s chirographum n

promontory s promontorium n

promote vt (in rank) producěre, provehěre; (a cause, etc.) favěre (with dat), adjuvare

promoter s adjutor, fautor m

promotion s amplior grad·us -ūs m, dignitas f

prompt adj promptus, paratus; **—ly**

statim, extemplo

prompt vt subjicěre, suggerěre; (to incite) impellěre, commověre

promulgate vt promulgare

promulgation s promulgatio f

prone adj pronus, propensus

prong s dens m

pronominal adj pronominalis

pronoun s pronomen n

pronounce vt (to declare) pronuntiare; (to articulate) enuntiare, eloqui; (sentence) dicěre, pronuntiare

pronunciation s appellatio, elocutio, locutio f

proof s documentum, argumentum, indicium, signum n

proof adj tutus, securus; **— against** invictus ab (with abl), adversus (with acc)

prop s tibicen m, fulcrum n; (for vines) adminiculum n

prop vt fulcire, sustiněre

propaganda s divulgatio f

propagate vt propagare, vulgare, disseminare

propagation s propagatio f

propel vt impellěre, propellěre

propeller s impulsor m

propensity s propensio, inclinatio f

proper adj (becoming) decorus, decens; (suitable) aptus, idoneus; **it is —** decet; **—ly** decore; apte

property s (characteristic) proprium n, proprietas f; (things owned) res f, bona n pl, fortuna f; **private —** res familiaris f

prophecy s praedictum n, praedictio, vaticinatio f

prophesy vt vaticinari, praedicěre

prophet s vates m & f, fatidicus m; (Biblical) propheta f

prophetess s vates, fatiloqua f

prophetic adj fatidicus, divinus, vaticinus; **—ally** divinitus

propitiate vt propitiare, placare

propitiation s propitiatio f, placamentum n

propitious adj felix, faustus; **—ly** fauste

proportion s ratio, proportio f; **in —** pro ratā parte; **in — to** pro (with abl)

proportionately adv pro portione

proposal s propositio, conditio f; (of senate) rogatio f

propose vt ferre, rogare; **to — a toast** to propinare (with dat)

proposition s (offer) condicio f; (logic) propositio f, pronuntiatum n

propound vt proponěre, exponěre

proprietor s possessor, dominus m

propriety s decorum n, convenientia f

propulsion s propulsio f

prosaic adj aridus, jejunus

proscribe vt proscriběre

proscription s proscriptio f

prose s prosa f

prosecute vt (to carry out) exsequi; (law) litem intenděre (with dat), accusare

prosecution s exsecutio f; (law) accusatio f

prosecutor s accusator, actor m

prospect s prospect·us -ūs m; (hope) spes f
prospective adj futurus
prosper vt prosperare, secundare; vi prosperā fortunā uti, florēre, vigēre
prosperity s res secundae f pl
prosperous adj prosperus, secundus; —ly prospere, bene
prostitute s scortum n, meretrix f
prostitute vt prostituĕre
prostrate vt sternĕre, projicĕre; (fig) affligĕre
prostrate adj prostratus, projectus; (fig) afflictus, fractus; to fall — se projicĕre
prostration s (act) prostratio f; (state) animus fractus m
protect vt tuēri, protegĕre, defendĕre, custodire
protection s praesidium n, tutela f
protector s defensor, patronus m
protest s obtestatio, denuntiatio f
protest vt affirmare; vi obtestari, reclamare; (pol) intercedĕre
protestation s affirmatio f
prototype s exemplar n
protract vt protrahĕre, differre
protrude vt protrudĕre; vi prominēre
protuberance s tuber n, tumor, gibbus m
proud adj superbus, arrogans; to be — superbire; —ly superbe, arroganter
prove vt probare, confirmare, evincĕre, arguĕre; vi (of person) se praebēre, se praestare; (of thing, event, etc.) evadĕre, fieri, exire
proverb s proverbium n
proverbial adj proverbialis, tritus, notus
provide vt (to furnish) suppeditare, (com)parare, praebēre; vi to — for providēre (with dat), consulĕre (with dat); (of laws) jubēre
provided that conj dum, modo, dummodo, eā condicione ut
providence s providentia f
provident adj providus, cautus; —ly caute
providential adj divinus; —ly divinitus
province s provincia f
provincial adj provincialis; (countrified) inurbanus, rusticus; (narrow) angusti animi (genit, used adjectively)
provincialism s dialectos f
provision s (stipulation) condicio f; —s cibus, vict·us -ūs m, alimentum n; (mil) commeat·us -ūs m, res frumentaria f
provisional adj temporarius; —ly ad tempus
proviso s condicio f; with the — that eā lege ut
provocation s provocatio, offensio f
provoke vt provocare, irritare, stimulare
provoking adj molestus, odiosus
prow s prora f
prowess s virtus f
prowl vi vagari, grassari
prowler s praedator m

proximity s propinquitas f
proxy s vicarius m
prude s fastidiosa f
prudence s prudentia f
prudent adj prudens; —ly prudenter
prudish adj tetricus
prune s prunum conditum n
prune vt (am)putare, resecare, recidĕre
pruning s putatio f
pry vi perscrutor; to — into investigare, explorare
prying adj curiosus
pseudonym s falsum nomen n
puberty s pubertas f
public adj publicus, communis; (known) vulgatus; —ly palam, aperte
public s homines m, pl, vulgus n
publican s publicanus m
publication s publicatio, promulgatio f; (of book) editio f; (book) liber m
publicity s celebritas, lux f
publish vt publicare, divulgare, patefacĕre; (book) edĕre
publisher s editor m
pucker vt corrugare
pudding s placenta f
puddle s lacuna f, stagnum n
puerile adj puerilis
puerility s puerilitas f
puff s aura f, flamen n
puff vt inflare, sufflare; vi anhelare
puffy adj sufflatus, tumens
pugilist s pugil m
pugnacious adj pugnax
pull vt (to drag) trahĕre, tractare; to — apart distrahĕre; to — away avellĕre; to — down detrahĕre; (buildings) demoliri, destruĕre, evertĕre; to — off avellĕre; to — out extrahĕre; (hair, etc.) evellĕre; vi to — at vellicare; to — through pervincĕre; (illness) convalescĕre
pull s (act) tract·us -ūs m; (effort) nis·us -ūs m; (influence) gratia f
pulley s trochlea f
pulmonary adj pulmoneus, pulmonaceus, pulmonarius
pulp s pulpa, caro f
pulpit s suggest·us -ūs m, rostra n pl
pulsate vi palpitare
pulse s puls·us -ūs m; (plant) legumen n; to feel the — venas temptare
pulverization s pulveratio f
pulverize vt pulverare, contundĕre
pumice s pumex m
pump s antlia f
pump vt haurire, exantlare; to — with questions percontari
pumpkin s pepo, melopepo m
pun s verborum lus·us -ūs m, agnominatio f
punch s (tool) veruculum n; (blow) pugnus, ict·us -ūs m
punch vt pugnum ducĕre (with dat)
punctilious adj scrupulosus, religiosus
punctual adj promptus, accuratus, diligens; —ly ad tempus, ad horam

punctuality s diligentia f
punctuate vt interpungĕre
punctuation s interpunctio f
punctuation mark s interpunctum n
puncture s punctio f, punctum n
pungent adj pungens, acutus; (caustic, as speech) mordax, aculeatus
Punic adj Punicus
punish vt punire
punishable adj puniendus, poenā dignus
punishment s (act) punitio, castigatio f; (penalty) poena f, supplicium n; **without —** impune
punster s argutator m
puny adj pusillus
pup s catulus m
pupil s pupillus, discipulus m, pupilla, discipula f; (of eye) pupilla, pupula f
puppet s pupa f
puppy s catulus m
purchase s (act) emptio f; (merchandise) merx f
purchase vt emĕre
purchase price s pretium n; (of grain) annona f
purchaser s emptor m
pure adj mundus, purus; (unmixed) merus; (morally) castus, integer; **—ly** pure, integre; (quite) omnino; (solely) solum
purgation s purgatio f
purge vt purgare, mundare
purge s purgatio f; (pol) proscriptio f
purification s purificatio, purgatio f
purify vt purgare; (fig) expiare
purity s puritas, munditia f; (moral) castitas, integritas f
purple s purpura f; **dressed in —** purpuratus
purple adj purpureus
purport s significatio, sententia, vis f
purport vt significare, spectare ad (with acc)
purpose s propositum, consilium n, animus m; (end, aim) finis m; (wish) mens f; **on —** consulto; **to good — ad rem; to no —** frustra, nequaquam; **to what —** quo, quorsum
purpose vt in animo habēre, velle
purposely adv consulto, de industria
purr s murmur n
purr vi mumurare

purring s murmuratio f
purse s crumena f, marsupium n
purse vt corrugare, contrahĕre
pursuance s continuatio f; **in — of** ex (with abl), secundum (with acc)
pursuant adj **— to** ex (with abl), secundum (with acc)
pursue vt (per)sequi, insequi, insectari; (plan, course) insistĕre
pursuit s persecutio, insectatio f; (occupation) studium, artificium n, occupatio f
pus s pus n, sanies f
push vt trudĕre, urgēre, impellĕre; **vi to — on** contendĕre, iter facĕre
push s ict-us -ūs, puls-us -ūs, impuls-us -ūs f; (fig) conat-us -ūs m
pushing adj audax, confidens; (energetic) strenuus
pusillanimous adj timidus
put vt ponĕre, collocare; **to — an end to** finem facĕre (with dat); **to — aside** ponĕre; **to — away** seponĕre, abdĕre, amovēre; (in safety) recondĕre; **to — back** reponĕre; **to — down** deponĕre; (to suppress) supponĕre, sedare; (in writing) scribĕre; **to — in** inserĕre; **to — in order** ordinare; **to — off** (to postpone) differre; **to — on** imponĕre; (clothes) se induĕre (with abl); (to add) addĕre; **to — out** ejicĕre, extrudĕre; (fire) extinguĕre; (money) ponĕre; **to — out of the way** demovēre; **to — together** componĕre, conferre; **to — up** erigĕre, statuĕre; **to — up for sale** proponĕre, venum dare; **vi to — in** (of ships) portum petĕre, appellĕre; **to — out to sea** solvĕre; **to — up with** tolerare
putrefaction s putredo f
putrefy vi putrescĕre, putrefieri
putrid adj puter or putris, putridus
puzzle s quaestio abstrusa f, nodus m, aenigma n
puzzle vt confundĕre, perturbare; **to be puzzled** haerēre, dubitare
puzzling adj perplexus, ambiguus
pygmy s nanus, pumilio, pumilus m
pyramid s pyramis f
pyre s rogus m
Pythagorean adj Pythagoraeus
Pythian adj Pythius

Q

quack s (charlatan) circulator, pharmacopola m
quack vi tetrinnire
quadrangle s area f
quadruped s quadrupes m & f
quadruple adj quadruplex, quadruplus
quadruple vt quadruplicare
quaestor s quaestor m
quaestorship s quaestura f

quaff vt ducĕre, haurire
quagmire s palus f
quail s coturnix f
quail vi pavēre
quaint adj rarus, insolitus, novus
quake vi tremēre
qualification s (endowment) indoles f; (limitation) exceptio, condicio f
qualified adj (suited) aptus, idoneus, dignus; (competent) peritus, doctus

qualify vt aptum or idoneum red- děre, instruěre; (to limit) temperare, mitigare, extenuare

quality s proprietas, qualitas f; —s ingenium n, indoles f

qualm s fastidium n; — of con- science religio f, scrupulus m

quandry s confusio f, angustiae f pl

quantity s numerus m, multitudo, vis, copia f; (in scansion) quantitas, mensura f

quarrel s jurgium n; (dispute) alter- catio, controversia f; (violent) rixa f

quarrel vi altercari, jurgare, rixari

quarrelsome adj jurgiosus, rixosus, pugnax

quarry s lapicidinae, lautumiae f pl; (prey) praeda f

quart s duo sextarii m pl

quarter s quarta pars f, quadrans m; (side, direction) pars, regio f; (district) regio f; at close —s com- minus; —s (dwelling) tectum n, ha- bitatio f; (temporary abode) hospi- tium n; (mil) castra, contubernia stativa n pl; (of moon) lunae phases f pl; to give — to parcěre (with dat)

quarter vt in quattuor partes divi- děre; (to receive in one's house) hospitium praebēre (with dat)

quarterly adj trimestris

quarterly adv quadrifariam, tertio quoque mense

quartermaster s castrorum prae- fectus m

quash vt (to subdue) oppriměre; (law) rescinděre, abolēre

quatrain s tetrastichon n

queasy adj fastidiosus; to feel — nauseare

queen s regina f

queen bee s rex m

queer adj novus, insolitus, rarus, in- eptus

quell vt oppriměre, sedare, domare

quench vt exstinguěre; to — the thirst sitim sedare

querulous adj querulus, queribundus

query s quaestio, interrogatio f

query vt dubitare; vi quaerěre, quae- ritare

quest s inquisitio f; to be in — of quaerěre, requirěre; to go in — of investigare

question s interrogatio f; (doubt) dubitatio f, dubium n; (matter) res, causa f; there is no — that non

dubium est quin; to ask a — quae- rěre, rogare; to call in — dubi- tare; without — sine dubio, haud dubie

question vt interrogare, percontari; (to doubt) dubitare, in dubium vo- care; (to examine) scrutari

questionable adj dubius, incertus

questioning s interrogatio, inquisi- tio f

questor s quaestor m

questorship s quaestura f

quibble s captio, argutiola f

quibble vi cavillari

quibbler s cavillator, sophista m

quibbling s cavillatio, captio f

quick adj (swift) celer, velox; (nim- ble) agilis; (mentally) sagax, astu- tus, acutus; (with hands) facilis; (of wit) argutus; —ly cito, velociter; (with haste) propere, festinanter

quicken vt accelerare; (to enliven) vivificare, animare; (to rouse) exci- tare

quicksand s syrtis f

quicksilver s argentum vivum n

quiet adj quietus, tranquillus, placi- dus; (silent) tacitus, taciturnus; to keep — quiescěre; (to refrain from talking) silēre, tacēre; —ly quiete, tranquille; tacite, per silentium

quiet s quies, tranquillitas f; (lei- sure) otium n; (silence) silentium n

quiet vt tranquillare, pacare, sedare

quill s penna f, calamus m

quilt s culcita f

quince s cydonium n

quince tree s cydonia f

quintessence s vis, medulla f, flos m

quip s dictum n, facetiae f pl

quirk s cavillatio, proprium n

quit vt relinquěre, deserěre

quite adv omnino, penitus, prorsus, magnopere; not — minus, parum; (not yet) nondum

quiver s pharetra f; wearing a — pharetratus

quiver vi treměre, contremiscěre, trepidare

quivering s tremor m, trepidatio f

Quixotic adj ridiculus

quoit s discus m

quota s portio, pars, rata pars f

quotation s (act) prolatio f; (pas- sage) locus m

quote vt adducěre, proferre, com- memorare

R

rabbit s cuniculus m

rabble s plebecula, faex populi f; (crowd) turba f

rabid adj rabidus; —ly rabide

race s (lineage) genus n, stirps f; (nation) gens f; (contest) certamen n; curs·us -ūs m, curriculum n

race vi certare, cursu contenděre

race horse s equus cursor m

racer s (person) cursor m; (horse) equus cursor m

racetrack s circus m, curriculum n

rack s (shelf) pluteus m; (for punish- ment) equuleus m, tormentum n

racket s (noise) strepit·us -ūs m

radiance s fulgor, splendor m

radiant adj radians, fulgidus, splendidus

radiate vt emittĕre; vi radiare, fulgēre, nitēre

radiation s radiatio f

radical adj insitus, innatus; (thorough) totus; —**ly** penitus, omnino

radical s rerum novarum cupidus m

radish s raphanus m

radius s radius m

raffle s alea f

raffle vt to — off aleā vendĕre

raft s ratis f

rafter s trabs f

rag s panniculus, pannus m

rage s furor m, rabies f

rage vi furĕre, saevire

ragged adj pannosus

raid s incursio, invasio f, latrocinium n

raider s praedator, latro m

raid vt praedari

rail s palus, asser transversus, longurius m

rail vt to — off consaepire; vi to — at insectari, conviciari

railing s (fence) saepimentum n; (abuse) convicium, maledictum n

raiment s vestis f, vestit·us -ūs m

rain s pluvia f, imber m

rain vi pluĕre; **it is raining** pluit

rainbow s pluvius arc·us -ūs m

rain cloud s imber m

rainy adj pluvius, pluvialis; pluviosus

raise vt tollĕre, elevare; (to erect) erigĕre; (to build) exstruĕre; (money) cogĕre; (army) conscribĕre; (siege) solvĕre; (to stir up) excitare; (children) educare; (to promote) provehĕre, producĕre; (price) augĕre; (crops) colĕre; (beard) demittĕre; **to — up** sublevare

raisin s astaphis f

rake s rastellus, irpex m; (person) nebulo, nepos m

rake vt radĕre; **to — together** corradĕre

rally s convent·us -ūs m, contio f

rally vt in aciem revocare; vi ex fuga convenire; (from sickness) convalescĕre

ram s aries m

ram vt fistucare, paviare; (to cram) infercire

ramble s vagatio f

ramble vi vagari, errare; **to — on** (in speech) garrire

rambling adj errans; (fig) vagus

ramification s ramus m

rampage vi saevire

rampant adj ferox

rampart s vallum, propugnaculum n

rancid adj rancidus

rancor s simultas f, dolor m

random adj fortuitus; **at —** temere

range s series f, ordo m; (of mountains) jugum n; (reach) jact·us -ūs m

range vt ordinare, disponĕre; vi pervagari

rank s series f, ordo, grad·us -ūs m, dignitas f

rank vt in numero habēri; vi in numero habēri

rank adj luxuriosus; (extreme) summus, maximus; (of smell) foetidus, gravis, graveolens

rankle vi suppurare, exulcerare

ransack vt diripĕre, spoliare; (to search thoroughly) exquirĕre

ransom s (act) redemptio f; pretium n

ransom vt redimĕre

rant vi ampullari; **to — and rave** debacchari

rap s (slap) alapa f; (blow) ict·us -ūs m; (at door) pulsatio f; (with knuckles) talitrum n

rap vt (to criticize) exagitare; vi **to — at** pulsare, ferire

rapacious adj rapax, avidus

rapacity s rapacitas, aviditas f

rape s stuprum n; (act of carrying away) rapt·us -ūs m

rape vt violare, per vim stuprare

rapid adj rapidus, celer, velox; —**ly** rapide, cito, velociter

rapidity s rapiditas, velocitas f

rapier s verutum n

rapine s rapina f

rapture s exsultatio f, animus exsultans m

rapturous adj mirificus

rare adj rarus, inusitatus; (fig) eximius, singularis; (thin) tenuis; —**ly** raro

rarefy vt extenuare, rarefacĕre

rarity s raritas, paucitas f; (thing) res rara, res singularis f

rascal s homo nequam, scelestus m

rascally adj scelestus, flagitiosus; nequam (indecl)

rash adj praeceps, temerarius; —**ly** temere, inconsulte

rash s eruptio pustulae f

rashness s temeritas f

raspberry s morum idaeum n

raspberry bush s rubus idaeus m

rat s sorex, mus m; (person) transfuga m

rate s proportio f; (price) pretium n; (scale) norma f; (tax) vectigal n; **— of interest** faenus n, usura f

rate vt aestimare

rather adv potius, prius, libentius; (somewhat) aliquantum, paulo, or render by comparative of adjective

ratification s sanctio f

ratify vt ratum facĕre, sancire

rating s aestimatio f

ratio s proportio f

ration s (portion) demensum n; (mil) cibaria n pl

ration vt demetiri

rational adj ratione praeditus, intellegens; —**ly** ratione, sapienter

rationalize vi ratiocinari

rattle s crepit·us -ūs, strepit·us -ūs m; (toy) crepitaculum n

rattle vt crepitare, crepitare (with abl); vi increpare, crepitare; **to — on** inepte garrire

raucous adj raucus

ravage vt vastare, spoliare, populari

ravages s vastatio, direptio f

rave vi furĕre, saevire, bacchari

ravel vt involvěre, implicare

raven s corvus m, cornix f

ravenous adj rapax, vorax; **—ly** voraciter

ravine s fauces f pl

raving adj furiosus, furens, insanus

ravish vt consturpare

raw adj crudus, incoctus; (of person) rudis, imperitus; (of weather) asper

rawboned adj strigosus

ray s radius m

raze vt solo aequare, excidĕre

razor s novacula f

reach s (grasp, capacity) capt·us -ūs m; (of weapon) ict·us -ūs, jact·us -ūs m; **out of my —** extra ictum meum

reach vt attingĕre; (of space) pertinēre ad (with acc), extendi ad (with acc); (to come up to) assequi; (to arrive at) pervenire ad (with acc); (to hand) tradĕre

react vi affici; **to — to** ferre

read vt & vi legĕre; **to — aloud** recitare

readable adj lectu facilis

reader s lector m; (lecturer) praelector m

readily adv (willingly) libenter; (easily) facile

readiness s facilitas f; **in —** in promptu

ready adj paratus, promptus, expeditus; (easy) facilis; **— money** praesens pecunia f; **to be —** praesto esse

real adj verus, sincerus; **—ly** re vera; (surely) sane, certe

real estate s fundus m

realistic adj verisimilis

reality s veritas, res ipsa f, verum n

realization s effectio f; (of ideas) cognitio, comprehensio f

realize vt (to understand) intellegĕre, vidēre, comprehendĕre; (to effect) efficĕre, ad exitum perducĕre; (to convert into money) redigĕre

realm s regnum n

ream s (of paper) scapus m

reap vt metĕre, desecare; (fig) percipĕre, capĕre

reaper s messor m

reappear vi redire, revenire, resurgĕre

rear vt educare, alĕre; vi (of horses) arrectum se tollĕre

rear s tergum n; (mil) novissimum agmen n, novissima acies f; **on the — a tergo; to bring up the —** agmen cogĕre

rearing s educatio f

reascend vt & vi denuo ascendĕre

reason s (faculty) mens, ratio, intellegentia f; (cause) causa f; (moderation) modus m; **by — of** ob (with acc), propter (with acc), a(b) (with abl); **there is no — why** non est cur

reason vi ratiocinari; **to — with** disceptare cum (with abl)

reasonable adj (fair) aequus, justus; (moderate) modicus; (judicious) prudens

reasonably adv ratione, juste; modice

reasoning s ratiocinatio, ratio f; (discussing) disceptatio f

reassemble vt recolligĕre, cogĕre

reassert vt iterare

reassume vt resumĕre

reassure vt confirmare, redintegrare

rebel s rebellis m

rebel vi rebellare, desciscĕre, seditionem commovēre

rebellion s rebellio, seditio f, rebellium n

rebellious adj rebellis, seditiosus; (disobedient) contumax

rebound s result·us -ūs m

rebound vi resilire, resultare

rebuff s repulsa f

rebuff vt repellĕre, rejicĕre

rebuild vt reparare, reficĕre

rebuke s reprehensio f

rebuke vt reprehendĕre, vituperare

rebuttal s refutatio f

recall s revocatio f

recall vt revocare; **to — to mind** in memoriam redigĕre

recant vt retractare, revocare

recantation s recept·us -ūs m

recapitulate vt repetĕre, summatim colligĕre

recapitulation s repetitio, enumeratio f

recapture s recuperatio f

recapture vt recipĕre, recuperare

recede vi recedĕre, refugĕre

receipt s (act) acceptio f; (note of acceptance) apocha f; (money) acceptum n

receive vt recipĕre, capĕre, excipĕre

receiver s receptor m

recent adj recens; **—ly** nuper

receptacle s receptaculum n

reception s adit·us -ūs m, admissio f; (of guest) hospitium n

recess s (place) recess·us -ūs m; (in wall) adytum n, angulus m; (intermission) intermissio f; (vacation) feriae f pl

recipe s praescriptum, compositio f

recipient s acceptor m

reciprocal adj mutuus; **—ly** mutuo, vicissim, inter se

reciprocate vt referre

reciprocity s reciprocatio f

recital s narratio, enumeratio, recitatio f

recitation s recitatio, lectio f

reckless adj temerarius; **—ly** temere

reckon vt numerare, computare, aestimare; vi **to — on** confidĕre (with dat)

reckoning s numeratio f; (account to be given) ratio f

reclaim vt reposcĕre, repetĕre

recline vi recubare, recumbĕre; (at table) accumbĕre

recluse s homo solitarius m

recognition s cognitio, agnitio f

recognize vt agnoscĕre, recognoscĕre; (to acknowledge) noscĕre; (to admit) fatēri

recoil vi resilire; **to — from** receděre ab (with abl), refugěre ab (with abl)

recoil s recessio f

recollect vt recordari

recollection s memoria, recordatio f

recommence vt redintegrare, renovare

recommend vt commendare

recommendation s commendatio, laudatio f; **letter of —** litterae commendaticiae f pl

recompense s remuneratio f

recompense vt remunerare; (to indemnify) compensare

reconcilable adj placabilis; (of things) conveniens

reconcile vt reconciliare, componěre; **to be reconciled** in gratiam restitui

reconciliation s reconciliatio f, in gratiam redit·us -ūs m

reconnoiter vt explorare

reconquer vt revincěre, recuperare

reconsider vt revolvěre, retractare

reconstruct vt restituěre, renovare

reconstruction s renovatio f

record s monumentum n, historia f; **—s** annales m pl, tabulae f pl

recorder s procurator ab actis m

recount vt referre, enarrare, commemorare

recoup vt recuperare

recourse s refugium n; **to have — to** (for safety) fugěre ad (with acc); (to resort to) descenděre ad (with acc)

recover vt recuperare, recipěre; vi (from illness) convalescěre; (to come to one's senses) ad se redire

recoverable adj reparabilis, recuperandus; (of persons) sanabilis

recovery s recuperatio, reparatio f; (from illness) recreatio f

recreate vt recreare

recreation s oblectatio, remissio f, lus·us -ūs m

recriminate vi invicem accusare

recrimination s mutua accusatio f

recruit vt (mil) conscriběre; (strength) reficěre

recruit s tiro m

recruiting s delect·us -ūs m

recruiting officer s conquisitor m

rectification s correctio f

rectify vt corrigěre, emendare

rectitude s probitas f

recumbent adj resupinus

recur vi recurrěre, redire

recurrence s redit·us -ūs m

recurrent adj assiduus

red adj ruber; (ruddy) rubicundus; **to be —** ruběre; **to grow —** rubescěre

redden vt rubefacěre, rutilare; vi rubescěre; (to blush) erubescěre

reddish adj subrufus, subruber, rubicundulus

redeem vt rediměre, liberare

redeemer s liberator m

Redeemer s Redemptor m

redemption s redemptio f

redhead s rufus m

red-hot adj candens

redness s rubor m

redolence s fragrantia f

redolent adj fragrans, redolens; **to be —** redolēre

redouble vt ingeminare

redoubt s propugnaculum n

redoubtable adj formidolosus

redound vi redundare

redress vt restituěre

redress s satisfactio f; **to demand —** res repetěre

reduce vt minuěre, deminuěre; (to a condition) redigěre; (mil) vincěre, expugnare

reduction s deminutio f; (mil) expugnatio f

redundancy s redundantia f

redundant adj redundans, superfluus

reed s harundo f, calamus m

reef s scopulus m, saxa n pl

reek s fumus, vapor m

reek vi fumare; **to — of** olēre

reel s fusus m

reel vi (to stagger) titubare

reestablish vt restituěre

reestablishment s restitutio f

refer vt referre, remittěre; vi **to — to** perstringěre, attingěre

referee s arbiter m

reference s ratio f; (in book) locus m

refine vt purgare, excolěre, expolire; (metals) excoquěre

refined adj politus; (fig) elegans, urbanus, humanus

refinement s (of liquids) purgatio f; (fig) urbanitas, humanitas, elegantia f

reflect vt repercutěre, reverberare; (fig) afferre; vi **to — on** considerare, revolvěre

reflection s repercussio f, repercuss·us -ūs m; (thing reflected) imago f; (fig) consideratio, meditatio, cogitatio f; **without —** inconsulte

reflective adj cogitabundus

reflexive adj reciprocus

reform vt reficěre, refingěre; (to amend) corrigěre, emendare; vi se corrigěre

reform s correctio, emendatio f

reformation s correctio f

reformer s corrector, emendator m

refract vt refringěre

refraction s refractio f

refractory adj contumax, indocilis

refrain s vers·us -ūs intercalaris m

refrain vi **to — from** abstinēre ab (with abl), parcěre (with dat); **I — from speaking** abstineo quin dicam

refresh vt recreare, reficěre; (the memory) redintegrare

refreshing adj jucundus, dulcis

refreshment s (food) cibus m; (drink) pot·us -ūs m

refuge s refugium, perfugium, asylum n; **to take — with** confugěre in (with acc)

refugee s profugus m, ex(s)ul m & f

refulgence s fulgor m

refulgent adj fulgidus

refund vt refunděre, rependěre

refusal s recusatio, repulsa f
refuse vt recusare, negare; (scornfully) repudire, renuĕre
refutation s refutatio, confutatio f
refute vt refutare, refellĕre, redarguĕre
regain vt recipĕre, recuperare
regal adj regalis, regius; **—ly** regaliter
regale vt excipĕre
regalia s insignia regia n pl
regard s respect·us -ūs m, ratio f; (care) cura f; (esteem) gratia f
regard vt (to look at) respicĕre, intuĕri; (to concern) spectare ad (with acc); (to esteem) aestimare; (to consider) habēre
regarding prep de (with abl)
regardless adj neglegens, incuriosus
regency s procuratio regni f, interregnum m
regenerate vt regenerare
regeneration s regeneratio f
regent s interrex m
regicide s (murderer) regis occisor m; (murder) caedes regis f
regime s administratio f
regimen f vict·us -ūs m
regiment s cohors, caterva f
region s regio, plaga f, tract·us -ūs m
register s tabulae f pl, catalogus m, album n
register vt in tabulas referre; (emotion) ostendĕre; vi profitēri, nomen dare
registrar s tabularius, actuarius m
registration s perscriptio, in tabulas relatio f
registry s tabularium n
regret s indignatio, paenitentia f, dolor m
regret vt dolēre; **I —** paenitet me (with genit), piget me (with genit)
regretful adj paenitens
regular adj (common) usitatus; (proper) justus, rectus; (consistent) constans, certus; **—ly** ordine, constanter; juste, recte
regularity s symmetria f; (consistency) constantia f
regulate vt ordinare, disponĕre, dirigĕre; (to control) moderari
regulation s ordinatio, temperatio, moderatio f; (rule) lex f, jussum n
rehabilitate vt restituĕre
rehearsal s meditatio f
rehearse vt meditari
reign s regnum n
reign vi regnare, dominari
reimburse vt rependĕre
reimbursement s pecuniae restitutio f
rein s habena f; **to give full — to** habenas immittĕre (with dat); **to loosen the —s** frenos dare; **to tighten the —s** habenas adducĕre
reindeer s reno m
reinforce vt firmare, supplĕre
reinforcement s supplementum, subsidium n; **—s** (mil) novae copiae f pl
reinstate vt restituĕre

reinstatement s restitutio f
reinvest vt iterum locare
reiterate vt iterare
reiteration s iteratio f
reject vt rejicĕre, repudiare, repellĕre, respuĕre
rejection s rejectio, repulsa f
rejoice vi gaudēre, exsultare
rejoin vt redire ad (with acc); vi respondēre
rejoinder s responsum n
rekindle vt resuscitare
relapse s novus laps·us -ūs m
relate vt referre, memorare, narrare; (to compare) conferre; vi **to — to** pertinēre ad (with acc)
related adj propinquus, conjunctus; (by blood) consanguineus, cognatus; (by marriage) affinis
relation s narratio f; (reference) ratio f; (relationship) cognatio f; (relative) cognatus m, cognata f
relationship s (by blood) consanguinitas, cognatio f; (by marriage) affinitas f; (connection) necessitudo, vicinitas, conjunctio f
relative adj attinens; cum ceteris comparatus; **—ly** pro ratione, ex comparatione
relative s cognatus, propinquus m, cognata, propinqua f
relax vt remittĕre, laxare; vi languescĕre
relaxation s remissio, relaxatio, requies f
relaxing adj remissivus
release s liberatio, absolutio, missio f
release vt (prisoner) liberare; solvĕre, resolvĕre
relegate vt relegare
relent vi mitescĕre, mollescĕre, flecti
relentless adj immisericors, inexorabilis, atrox; **—ly** atrociter
relevant adj **to be —** ad rem attinēre
reliance s fiducia, fides f
reliant adj fretus
relic s reliquiae f pl
relief s (alleviation) levatio f, levamentum n; (comfort) solatium, lenimen n; (help) auxilium n; (in sculpture) toreuma n; (of sentries) mutatio f
relieve vt levare, allevare, mitigare; (to aid) succurrĕre (with dat); (a guard) succedĕre (with dat), excipĕre
religion s religio f, deorum cult·us -ūs m
religious adj religiosus, pius; **—ly** religiose
relinquish vt relinquĕre; (office) se abdicare ab (with abl)
relish s (flavor) sapor m; (enthusiasm) studium n; (seasoning) condimentum n
relish vt gustare
reluctance s aversatio f; **with —** invite
reluctant adj invitus; **—ly** invite
rely vi **to — on** confidĕre (with dat), niti (with abl)
remain vi manēre, permanēre; (of things) restare

remainder s reliquum n

remains s reliquiae f pl

remark vt dicĕre

remark s dictum n

remarkable adj insignis, memorabilis, mirus, egregius

remarkably adv insignite, mire, egregie

remediable adj sanabilis

remedial adj medicabilis; emendatorius

remedy s remedium n; (law) regress·us -ūs m

remedy vt medēri (with dat), sanare, corrigĕre

remember vt meminisse (with genit); reminisci (with genit); recordari

remembrance s memoria, commemoratio f

remind vt admonēre, commonefacĕre

reminder s admonitio f, admonitum n

reminisce vi meditari; to — about recordari

reminiscence s recordatio f

remiss adj neglegens

remission s venia, remissio f

remit vt remittĕre, condonare

remittance s remissio f

remnant s reliquum, residuum n; —s reliquiae f pl

remodel vt reformare, transfigurare

remonstrance s objurgatio f

remonstrate vi reclamare, reclamitare; to — with objurgare

remorse s paenitentia f

remorseless adj immisericors

remote adj remotus, longinquus, reconditus; —ly procul

remoteness s longinquitas, distantia f

removable adj mobilis

removal s amotio f; (banishment) amandatio f; (change of residence) migratio f

remove vt amovēre, tollĕre, auferre; vi migrare

remunerate vt remunerari

remuneration s remuneratio f

rend vt lacerare, scindĕre; (to split) findĕre

render vt reddĕre, tradĕre; (to translate) vertĕre; (thanks) referre

rendering s (translation) conversio f; (interpretation) interpretatio f

rendezvous s constitutum n

renegade s desertor, transfuga m

renew vt renovare, instaurare, redintegrare

renewal s renovatio, instauratio, repetitio f

renounce vt renuntiare, repudiare, abdicare; (an office) se abdicare (with abl)

renovate vt renovare, reficĕre

renovation s renovatio, reparatio f

renown s fama, gloria f

renowned adj praeclarus, insignis, celebris

rent s (of lands) vectigal n; (of houses) merces, pensio f; (tear: fissure) scissura f

rent vt (to let out) locare; (to hire) conducĕre

renunciation s repudiatio, cessio, abdicatio f

reopen vt iterum aperire

repair vt reparare, reficĕre, restituĕre; (clothes) resarcire

repair s refectio f; in bad — ruinosus

reparation s satisfactio f

repartee s sales m pl

repast s cena f

repay vt remunerari; (money) reponĕre, retribuĕre

repayment s solutio, remuneratio f

repeal vt abrogare, rescindĕre, tollĕre

repeal s abrogatio f

repeat vt iterare, repetĕre; (ceremony) instaurare

repeatedly adv iterum atque iterum, identidem

repel vt repellĕre; (fig) aspernari

repent vi I — paenitet me

repentance s paenitentia f

repentant adj paenitens

repercussion s repercuss·us -ūs m

repetition s iteratio, repetitio f

repine vi conquĕri

replace vt reponĕre, restituĕre

replant vt reserĕre

replenish vt replēre

replete adj repletus, plenus

repletion s satietas f

reply vi respondĕre

reply s responsum n

report vt referre, narrare, nuntiare; (officially) renuntiare

report s (rumor) fama f, rumor m; (official) renuntiatio f; (noise) fragor m

repose vt ponĕre, reponĕre; vi quiescĕre

repose s quies, requies f

repository s receptaculum n

reprehend vt reprehendĕre, vituperare

reprehensible adj culpā dignus, improbus

represent vt repraesentare, exprimĕre, describĕre, proponĕre; (a character) partes agĕre (with genit)

representation s (act) repraesentatio f; (likeness) imago f

representative s legatus, vicarius m

repress vt reprimĕre, coercĕre, cohibēre

repression s coercitio, cohibitio f

reprieve s supplicii dilatio, mora, venia f; to grant a — supplicium differre, veniam dare

reprieve vt veniam dare (with dat)

reprimand s reprehensio f

reprimand vt reprehendĕre

reprint vt denuo imprimĕre

reprisal s ultio f; to make —s on ulcisci

reproach s exprobratio, vituperatio f, probrum n; (cause for reproach) opprobrium n

reproach vt opprobrare, vituperare, increpitare

reproachful adj objurgatorius, contumeliosus; —ly contumeliose

reprobate s perditus m

reproduce *vt* regenerare, propagare; (*likeness*) referre

reproduction *s* regeneratio, propagatio *f*; (*likeness*) effigies *f*

reproof *s* reprehensio, vituperatio, objuratio *f*

reprove *vt* reprehendĕre, objurgare

reptile *s* serpens, bestia serpens *f*

republic *s* civitas popularis, libera civitas *f*

republican *adj* popularis

repudiate *vt* repudiare

repudiation *s* repudiatio *f*

repugnance *s* fastidium *n*, aversatio *f*

repugnant *adj* aversus, repugnans, alienus

repulse *s* depulsio *f*; (*political defeat*) repulsa *f*

repulse *vt* repellĕre

repulsion *s* repulsio *f*

repulsive *adj* odiosus, foedus

reputable *adj* honestus

reputation *s* fama *f*, nomen *n*

repute *s* fama, opinio *f*, nomen *n*

request *s* petitio, rogatio *f*; **to obtain a —** impetrare

request *vt* rogare, petĕre

require *vt* postulare, poscĕre; (*to need*) egēre (*with abl*); (*to call for*) requirĕre

requirement *s* necessarium *n*

requisite *adj* necessarius

requisition *s* postulatio *f*, postulatum *n*

requital *s* retributio, merces *f*; (*return for a service*) gratia *f*

requite *vt* compensare, retribuĕre; (*for a favor*) remunerari

rescind *vt* rescindĕre, tollĕre

rescue *s* liberatio, salus *f*; **to come to the —** of subvenire (*with dat*)

rescue *vt* liberare, servare, eripĕre

research *s* investigatio *f*

resemblance *s* similitudo, imago *f*, instar *n* (*indecl*)

resemble *vt* similis esse (*with genit, esp. of persons, or with dat*)

resembling *adj* similis (*with genit, esp. of persons, or with dat*)

resent *vt* aegre ferre

resentful *adj* iracundus, indignans

resentment *s* indignatio *f*, dolor *m*

reservation *s* retentio *f*; (*mental*) exceptio *f*; (*proviso*) condicio *f*

reserve *s* (*restraint*) pudor *m*, taciturnitas *f*; (*stock*) copia *f*; (*mil*) subsidium *n*; **in —** subsidiarius; **without —** aperte

reserve *vt* servare, reservare, reponĕre

reserved *adj* (*of seat*) assignatus; (*of disposition*) taciturnus

reservoir *s* cisterna *f*, lac·us -ūs *m*

reset *vt* reponĕre

reside *vi* habitare, commorari; **to — in** inhabitare

residence *s* habitatio, sedes *f*, domicilium *n*

resident *s* incola *m* & *f*

residue *s* residuum *n*

resign *vt* cedĕre, remittĕre; se abdicare a(b) (*with abl*); **to — oneself** animum summittĕre (*with dat*); *vi* se abdicare

resignation *s* (*act*) abdicatio *f*; (*fig*) aequus animus *m*

resigned *adj* summissus; **to be —** aequo animo esse; **to be — to** aequo animo ferre

resilience *s* mollitia *f*

resilient *adj* resultans, mollis

resin *s* resina *f*

resist *vt* resistĕre (*with dat*), obstare (*with dat*), repugnare (*with dat*)

resistance *s* repugnantia *f*; **to offer — to** obsistĕre (*with dat*), repugnare (*with dat*)

resolute *adj* firmus, constans, fortis; **—ly** constanter, fortiter

resolution *s* (*determination*) constantia *f*; (*decision, decree*) decretum *n*; (*of senate*) consultum *n*

resolve *s* constantia *f*

resolve *vt* decernĕre, statuĕre, constituĕre; (*to reduce, convert*) resolvĕre, dissolvĕre

resonance *s* resonantia *f*

resonant *adj* resonus

resort *s* locus celeber *m*; (*refuge*) refugium *n*

resort *vi* **to — to** (*to frequent*) frequentare, celebrare; (*to have recourse to*) confugĕre ad (*with acc*)

resource *s* subsidium *n*; **—s** facultates, opes, copiae *f pl*

respect *s* (*regard*) respect·us -ūs *m*; (*reference*) ratio *f*; **in every —** ex omni parte

respect *vt* (re)verēri, observare

respectability *s* honestas *f*

respectable *adj* honestus, bonus

respectably *adv* honeste

respectful *adj* observans, reverens; **—ly** reverenter

respecting *prep* de (*with abl*)

respective *adj* proprius, suus; **—ly** mutuo

respiration *s* spirit·us -ūs *m*

respite *s* intermissio, cessatio, requies *f*

resplendence *s* nitor, splendor *m*

resplendent *adj* resplendens, splendidus; **—ly** splendide

respond *vi* respondēre

respondent *s* (*law*) reus *m*

response *s* responsum *n*

responsibility *s* cura *f*; **it is my —** est mihi curae

responsible *adj* obnoxius, reus

rest *s* quies, requies *f*; (*support*) fulcrum, statumen *n*; (*remainder*) reliqua pars *f*, reliquum *n*; **the — of the men** ceteri *m pl*

rest *vt* (*to lean*) reclinare; *vi* (re)quiescĕre; (*to pause*) cessare; **to — on** inniti in (*with abl*), niti (*with abl*)

restitution *s* restitutio *f*; (*restoration*) refectio *f*

restive *adj* (*balky, unruly*) contumax; (*impatient*) impatiens

restless *adj* inquietus, turbidus, tumultuosus; (*agitated*) sollicitus; **—ly** inquiete, turbulenter

restoration *s* restauratio, refectio, renovatio *f*

restore *vt* restituĕre, reddĕre; (*to re-*

build) restaurare, reficĕre; (*to health*) recurare, recreare; **to — to order** in integrum reducĕre

restrain *vt* cohibēre, coercēre, continēre; (*to prevent*) impedire

restraint *s* temperantia, moderatio *f*

restrict *vt* cohibēre, restringĕre, circumscribĕre, (de)finire

restriction *s* modus, finis *m*, limitatio *f*

result *s* exit·us -ūs, event·us -ūs *m*; eventum *n*; **without —** nequiquam

result *vi* evenire, fieri, evadĕre

resume *vt* resumĕre, repetĕre

resumption *s* resumptio, continuatio *f*

resurrection *s* resurrectio *f*

resuscitate *vt* resuscitare

retail *vt* divendĕre

retailer *s* caupo, propola *m*

retain *vt* retinēre, obtinēre, conservare

retainer *s* (*adherent*) cliens, asectator, satelles *m*; (*fee*) arrabo *m*

retake *vt* recipĕre, recuperare

retaliate *vi* ulcisci

retaliation *s* ultio *f*

retard *vt* retardare

retch *vi* nauseare

retention *s* retentio, conservatio *f*

retentive *adj* tenax

reticence *s* taciturnitas *f*

reticent *adj* taciturnus

retinue *s* comitat·us -ūs *m*

retire *vi* recedĕre, regredi; (*from office*) abire; (*for the night*) dormitum ire

retired *adj* (*of place*) remotus, solitarius; (*from work*) emeritus

retirement *s* (*act*) recess·us -ūs *m*, abdicatio *f*; (*state*) otium *n*, solitudo *f*

retiring *adj* modestus

retort *s* responsum *n*

retort *vt* respondēre

retrace *vt* repetĕre, iterare

retract *vt* revocare, recantare, renuntiare

retraction *s* retractatio *f*

retreat *vi* recedĕre, refugĕre, se recipĕre, pedem referre

retreat *s* (*act*) recess·us -ūs *m*, fuga *f*; (*place*) recess·us -ūs *m*, refugium *n*; (*mil*) recept·us -ūs *m*

retrench *vt* recidĕre

retrenchment *s* recisio *f*

retribution *s* compensatio, poena *f*

retrieve *vt* recuperare, recipĕre

retrogression *s* regress·us -ūs, retrogress·us -ūs *m*

retrospect *s* retrospect·us -ūs *m*; **in — respiciendi**

retrospective *adj* respiciens; **—ly** retro

return *s* (*coming back*) redit·us -ūs *m*; (*repayment*) remuneratio *f*; (*income, profit*) fruct·us -ūs *m*

return *vt* (*to give back*) reddĕre, restituĕre, referre; *vi* (*to go back*) redire; (*to come back*) revenire, reverti

reunion *s* readunatio *f*, convivium *n*

reunite *vt* iterum conjungĕre; recon-

ciliare; *vi* reconciliari

reveal *vt* retegĕre, recludĕre, aperire; (*to unveil*) revelare

revel *s* comissatio, bacchatio *f*; **—s** orgia *n pl*

revel *vi* comissari, debacchari, luxuriare *or* luxuriari

revelation *s* patefactio, revelatio *f*

reveler *s* comissator *m*

revelry *s* comissatio *f*, orgia *n pl*

revenge *vt* ulcisci

revenge *s* ultio, vindicta *f*; **to take — on** se vindicare in (*with acc*)

revengeful *adj* ulciscendi cupidus

revenue *s* redit·us -ūs, fruct·us -ūs *m*, vectigal *n*

reverberate *vi* resonare

reverberation *s* repercuss·us -ūs *m*, resonantia *f*

revere *vt* reverēri, venerari

reverence *s* reverentia, veneratio, religio, pietas *f*

reverend *adj* reverendus

reverent *adj* reverens, pius, religiosus; **—ly** reverenter, religiose

reverential *adj* venerabundus

reverie *s* cogitatio, meditatio *f*

reversal *s* infirmatio *f*

reverse *s* contrarium *m*; (*change*) conversio, commutatio *f*; (*defeat*) clades *f*

reverse *vt* invertĕre, (com)mutare; (*decision*) rescindĕre, abrogare

revert *vi* redire, reverti

review *s* recognitio *f*; (*critique*) censura *f*; (*mil*) recensio, lustratio *f*

review *vt* recensēre, inspicĕre; (*mil*) recensēre, lustrare

reviewer *s* censor, editor *m*

revile *vt* maledicĕre (*with dat*), insectari

revise *vt* corrigĕre, recognoscĕre

revision *s* emendatio *f*; (*of literary work*) recensio, lima *f*

revisit *vt* revisĕre, revisitare

revival *s* redanimatio *f*; (*fig*) renovatio *f*

revive *vt* resuscitare; (*to renew*) renovare; (*to encourage*) animare, instigare, excitare; *vi* reviviscĕre

revocation *s* revocatio *f*

revoke *vt* revocare, renuntiare; (*a law*) rescindĕre

revolt *vt* offendĕre; *vi* rebellare, desciscĕre, deficĕre

revolt *s* rebellio, seditio, defectio *f*

revolting *adj* taeter, foedus

revolution *s* conversio *f*; (*change*) commutatio *f*; (*of planets*) ambit·us -ūs *m*; (*pol*) res novae *f pl*, mot·us -ūs *m*

revolutionary *adj* seditiosus, novarum rerum cupidus

revolutionize *vt* novare

revolve *vt* (*in mind*) meditari, volutare; *vi* revolvi, se (re)volvĕre

revulsion *s* taedium, fastidium *n*; **to cause — fastidium movēre**

reward *s* praemium *n*

reward *vt* remunerare, compensare

rewrite *vt* rescribĕre

rhapsody *s* rhapsodia *f*

rhetoric *s* rhetorica *n pl or f*

rhetorical *adj* rhetoricus, oratorius; **to practice** — declamare
rhetorician *s* rhetor *m*
rheumatism *s* dolor artuum *m*
rhinoceros *s* rhinoceros *m*
rhubarb *s* radix Pontica *f*
rhyme *s* homoeteleuton *n*
rhythm *s* numerus, rhythmus *m*
rhythmical *adj* numerosus
rib *s* costa *f*
ribald *adj* obscenus, spurcus
ribaldry *s* obscenitas *f*
ribbed *adj* costatus, striatus
ribbon *s* infula *f*
rice *s* oryza *f*
rich *adj* dives, locuples; (*of soil*) fertilis, uber, opimus; (*food*) pinguis; (*costly*) pretiosus, lautus; **—ly** copiose, pretiose, laute
riches *s* divitiae, opes *f pl*
rickety *adj* instabilis
rid *vt* liberare; **to get — of** dimittere, deponere, exuere
riddle *s* aenigma *n*
ride *vi* **to — a horse** equo vehi; *vi* equitare; vehi; **to — away** *or* **off** avehi
ride *s* (*on horseback*) equitatio *f*; (*in carriage*) vectio *f*
rider *s* eques *m*; (*in carriage*) vector *m*; (*attached to documents*) adjectio *f*
ridge *s* jugum, dorsum *n*
ridicule *s* ridiculum, ludibrium *n*, irris·us -ūs *m*
ridicule *vt* irridēre
ridiculous *adj* ridiculus; **—ly** ridicule
riding *s* equitatio *f*
rife *adj* frequens
riffraff *s* plebecula, faex populi *f*
rifle *vt* despoliare, diripere
rig *vt* adornare; (*ship*) armare, ornare
rigging *s* armamenta *n pl*, rudentes *m pl*
right *adj* rectus; (*just*) aequus, justus; (*opposed to left*) dexter; (*suitable*) idoneus, aptus; (*true*) verus, rectus; **—ly** recte, rite, juste, vere
right *s* (*hand*) dextra *f*; (*law*) jus, fas, aequum *n*; **on the — a** dextra
right *vt* emendare, corrigēre; (*to replace*) restituēre; (*to avenge*) vindicare, ulcisci
righteous *adj* justus, pius; **—ly** juste, pie
righteousness *s* justitia, pietas, probitas *f*
rightful *adj* legitimus, justus; **—ly** juste
rigid *adj* rigidus; **—ly** rigide
rigidity *s* rigiditas *f*
rigor *s* severitas, duritia *f*
rigorous *adj* severus, asper; (*hardy*) durus
rill *s* rivulus *m*
rim *s* ora, margo *f*, labrum *n*
rind *s* crusta *f*
ring *s* anulus *m*; (*of people*) corona *f*; (*for fighting*) arena *f*; (*sound*) sonit·us -ūs *m*; (*of bells*) tinnit·us -ūs *m*
ring *vt* **to — a bell** tintinnabulum

tractare; *vi* tinnire, resonare
ringing *s* tinnit·us -ūs *m*
ringleader *s* auctor, dux *m*
rinse *vt* colluēre, eluēre
rinsing *s* colluvies *f*
riot *s* tumult·us -ūs, mot·us -ūs *m*; **to run** — luxuriari
riot *vi* seditionem movēre, tumultuari
rioter *s* seditiosus *m*
riotous *adj* seditiosus, tumultuosus; **— living** luxuria *f*
rip *vt* scindēre; **to — apart** discindēre, diffindēre; (*fig*) discerpēre
ripe *adj* mitis, maturus, tempestivus
ripen *vt* maturare; *vi* maturescēre
ripple *s* flucticulus *m*
ripple *vi* trepidare
rise *vi* oriri, surgēre; (*from sleep*) expergisci; (*to mount*) ascendēre; (*to increase*) crescēre; (*of rioters*) consurgēre; (*of passion*) tumescēre; **to — again** resurgēre, reviviscēre; **to — up** exsurgēre
rise *s* (*ascent*) ascens·us -ūs *m*; (*origin*) origo *f*, ort·us -ūs *m*; (*increase*) incrementum *n*; (*slope*) clivus *m*; **to give — to** parēre
rising *s* (*of sun*) ort·us -ūs *m*; (*insurrection*) mot·us -ūs, tumult·us -ūs *m*
risk *s* periculum *n*; **to run a —** periculum subire, periclitari
risk *vt* in periculum vocare, periclitari
rite *s* rit·us -ūs *m*
ritual *s* rit·us -ūs *m*, caeremonia *f*
rival *s* rivalis, aemulus, competitor *m*
rival *vt* aemulari
rivalry *s* aemulatio *f*, certamen *n*; (*in love*) rivalitas *f*
river *s* flumen *n*, amnis *m*
rivet *s* clavus *m*
rivet *vt* (*eyes, attention*) defigēre
rivulet *s* rivus, rivulus *m*
road *s* via *f*, iter *n*; **on the — in** itinere; **to build a — viam** munire
roam *vi* errare, vagari
roar *s* fremit·us -ūs, rugit·us -ūs, strepit·us -ūs *m*
roar *vi* fremēre, rudēre, rugire
roast *vt* torrēre; (*in a pan*) frigēre, assare, coquēre
roast *adj* assus
roast *s* assum *n*
rob *vt* spoliare, compilare, latrocinari
robber *s* latro, fur *m*
robbery *s* latrocinium *n*, spoliatio *f*
robe *s* vestis, palla *f*
robe *vt* vestire
robin *s* sylvia rubecula, rubisca *f*
robust *adj* robustus, validus, lacertosus
rock *s* saxum *n*; (*cliff*) scopulus *m*, rupes *f*
rock *vt* jactare; **to — a cradle** cunas agitare; *vi* vibrare, vacillare
rocket *s* missile *n*
rocky *adj* saxosus, scopulosus
rod *s* virga, ferula *f*
roe *s* caprea *f*; (*of fish*) ova *n pl*
roebuck *s* capreolus *m*
rogue *s* nequam (homo), furcifer *m*
roguish *adj* malus, improbus

roll *vt* volvĕre, versare; *vi* volvi; *(of tears)* labi

roll *s (book)* volumen *n*; *(of names)* catalogus *m*, album *n*; *(of bread)* collyra *f*

roller *s* cylindrus *m*

Roman *adj* Romanus

Roman *s* Romanus, Quiris *m*

romance *s* fabula, narratio ficta *f*; *(affair)* amores *m pl*

romantic *adj* fabulosus, commenticius, amatorius

roof *s* tectum, fastigium *n*; *(of mouth)* palatum *n*

roof *vt* contegĕre, integĕre

room *s (space)* spatium *n*, locus *m*; *(of house)* conclave *n*

roomy *adj* laxus, spatiosus

roost *s* pertica *f*

roost *vi* cubitare, insidēre

root *s* radix *f*; *(fig)* fons *m*, origo *f*; **to take —** coalescĕre

root *vt* **to become rooted** *(fig)* inveterascĕre; **to be rooted** inhaerēre; **to — out** eradicare, exstirpare; *vi* radices agĕre; *(fig)* inveterascĕre

rope *s* funis *m*, restis *f*

rose *s* rosa *f*

roseate *adj* roseus

rosy *adj* roseus, rosaceus

rot *vi* putrescĕre, tabescĕre

rot *s* putredo, tabes, caries *f*

rotate *vi* volvi, se convertĕre

rotation *s* ambit·us -ūs *m*, conversio *f*; *(succession)* vicissitudo *f*; **in — ordine**

rote *s* **by — memoriter**

rotten *adj* putridus, tabidus, cariosus

rotunda *s* tholus *m*

rouge *s* fucus *m*

rough *adj* asper; *(of character)* agrestis, durus; *(of weather)* inclemens; *(shaggy)* hirsutus; **—ly** aspere, duriter

roughen *vt* asperare

roughness *s* asperitas *f*; *(brutality)* feritas *f*

round *adj* rotundus, globosus; **—ly** aperte, plane, praecise

round *s* orbis, circulus *m*; *(series)* ambit·us -ūs *m*

round *vt (a corner)* circumire, flectĕre; *(a cape)* superare; **to — off** concludĕre, complēre

rouse *vt* excitare, animare

rout *s* fuga *f*; *(defeat)* clades *f*; *(crowd)* turba *f*

rout *vt* fugare, fundĕre

route *s* via *f*, iter *n*

routine *s* consuetudo *f*, ordo, us·us -ūs *m*

rove *vi* vagari, errare

rover *s* ambulator *m*

row *s* series *f*, ordo *m*; *(quarrel)* rixa *f*

row *vt* remis propellĕre; *vi* remigare

rower *s* remex *m*

rowing *s* remigatio *f*, remigium *n*

royal *adj* regalis, regius; **—ly** regaliter, regie

royalty *s* regia potestas *f*, regnum *n*

rub *vt* fricare; **to — away** *or* **off** detergĕre

rub *s* fricatio *f*; *(fig)* difficultas *f*

rubbing *s* attrit·us -ūs, affrict·us -ūs *m*, fricatio, frictio *f*

rubbish *s* rudus *n*; *(fig)* quisquiliae *f pl*

rubble *s* rudus *n*

rubric *s* rubrica *f*

ruby *s* rubinus, carbunculus *m*

rudder *s* gubernaculum *n*

ruddy *adj* rubicundus, rubens, rutilus

rude *adj* rudis, rusticus, inurbanus; *(impertinent)* impudicus; **—ly** rustice, incondite

rudeness *s* rusticitas, inhumanitas, insolentia *f*

rudiment *s* elementum, initium, rudimentum, principium *n*

rudimentary *adj* inchoatus, elementarius

rue *vt* **I — me paenitet** *(with genit)*

rueful *adj* maestus, luctuosus

ruffian *s* sicarius, grassator *m*

ruffle *vt* agitare, turbare; *(to irritate)* commovēre

ruffle *s* limbus *m*

rug *s* stragulum *n*

rugged *adj* asper, praeruptus

ruin *s* pernicies *f*, exitium *n*; ruina *f*; **—s ruinae** *f pl*

ruin *vt* perdĕre, corrumpĕre; *(morally)* depravare

ruination *s* vastatio *f*

ruinous *adj* damnosus, exitiosus

rule *s (regulation)* praeceptum *n*, lex *f*; *(government)* regimen, imperium *n*, dominatio *f*; *(instrument)* regula, norma *f*

rule *vt* regĕre, moderari; *vi* regĕre, dominari

ruler *s (person)* rector, dominus, rex *m*; *(instrument)* regula *f*

ruling *s* edictum *n*

rum *s* sicera *f*

rumble *s* murmur *n*

rumble *vi* murmurare, crepitare, mugire

rumbling *s* murmur *n*, mugit·us -ūs *m*

ruminate *vi* ruminare

rumination *s* ruminatio *f*

rummage *vi* **to — through rimari**

rumor *s* rumor *m*, fama *f*

rump *s* clunis *f*

rumple *s (in garment)* plica, ruga *f*

rumple *vt* corrugare

run *vt (to manage)* gerĕre, administrare; *(to aground)* impingĕre; **to — up** *(an account)* augēre; *vi* currĕre; *(to flow)* fluĕre; **to — about** discurrĕre, cursare; **to — after** sequi, petĕre, sectari; **to — aground** offendĕre; **to — away** aufugĕre; **to — away from** defugĕre; **to — down** decurrĕre; *(as water)* defluĕre; **to — for** conquirĕre; **to — foul of** collidi; **to — into** *(to meet)* incidĕre in *(with acc)*; **to — off** aufugĕre; *(as water)* defluĕre; **to — on** percurrĕre, continuare; **to — out** excurrĕre; *(of time)* exire; *(of supplies)* deficĕre; **to — over** *(details)* percurrĕre; *(of fluids)* superfluĕre; **to — short** deficĕre; **to — through** *(to dissipate)* dissipare; **to — together** concurrĕre; **to — up** accurrĕre; **to — up against** incurrĕre in (with acc)

runaway s transfuga m

runner s cursor m

running s curs·us -ūs m; (flowing) flux·us -ūs m

rupture s hernia f; seditio, dissensio f

rupture vt rumpĕre, abrumpĕre; vi rumpi

rural adj agrestis, rusticus

ruse s dolus m, fraus f

rush s (plant) juncus m; (charge) impet·us -ūs m

rush vt rapĕre; vi ruĕre, ferri; **to — forward** prorumpĕre, se proripĕre;

to — in inruĕre, incurrĕre; **to — out** erumpĕre, evolare

russet adj russus, rufus, ravus

rust s rubigo, aerugo f; (of iron) ferrugo f

rust vi rubiginem contrahĕre

rustic adj rusticus, agrestis

rustic s rusticus m, ruricola m & f

rustle vi crepitare, increpare

rustle s crepit·us -ūs m

rusty adj rubiginosus, aeruginosus; **to become —** rubigine obduci; (fig) desuescĕre

rut s (of wheel) orbita f

ruthless adj immisericors, inexorabilis, crudelis; **—ly** incrudeliter

rye s secale n

S

Sabbath s sabbata n pl

saber s acinaces m

sable adj pullus, ater, niger

sable s (fur) pellis zibellina f

sack s saccus m; (mil) direptio f

sack vt (mil) vastare, diripĕre

sackcloth s cilicium n

sacred adj sacer, sanctus, sacrosanctus

sacrifice s (act) sacrificium n, immolatio f; (victim) hostia, victima f; (fig) jactura f

sacrifice vt immolare, mactare, sacrificare; (fig) devovēre

sacrilege s sacrilegium n

sacrilegious adj sacrilegus

sad adj tristis, maestus, miserabilis; **—ly** maeste

sadden vt contristare, dolore afficĕre

saddle s ephippium n

saddle vt imponĕre (with acc of thing and dat of person); **to — a horse** equum sternĕre

saddlebags s clitellae f pl

sadness s tristitia, maestitia f

safe adj tutus; (without hurt) incolumis; **— and sound** salvus; **—ly** tute

safe-conduct s tutela f, commeat·us -ūs m

safeguard s praesidium n, tutela f

safety s salus, incolumitas f; **in —** tuto

saffron adj croceus

sagacious adj sagax; **—ly** sagaciter

sagacity s sagacitas f

sage s (wise man) sapiens m

sage adj sapiens, prudens; **—ly** sapienter

sail s velum n; **to set —** vela dare

sail vi nave vehi, vela facĕre, navigare

sailing s navigatio f

sailor s nauta m

saint s vir sanctus m, femina sancta f

saintly adj sanctus, pius

sake s for the **— of** gratiā (with genit), causā (with genit), pro (with abl)

salad s acetaria n pl, moretum n

salamander s salamandra f

salary s salarium n, merces f

sale s venditio f; for **— venalis; to put up for —** venum dare

salesman s venditor m

salient adj prominens, saliens

saline adj salsus

saliva s saliva f, sputum n

sallow adj pallidus, luridus

sally s eruptio f, impet·us -ūs m

sally vi eruptionem facĕre, erumpĕre

salmon s salmo m

saloon s caupona f

salt s sal m

salt vt salire, sale condire

salting s salsura f

saltless adj insulsus

salt mine s salifodina f

salt shaker s salinum n

salt water s aqua marina f

salubrious adj salubris

salutary adj salutaris, utilis

salutation s salutatio, salus f

salute s salus, salutatio f

salute vt salutare

salvage vt servare, eripĕre

salvation s salus f

salve s unguentum n

same adj idem; **at the — time** eodem tempore, simul; **the very —** ipsissimus

sameness s identitas f

sample s exemplum, specimen n

sample vt libare

sanctify vt sanctificare, consecrare

sanctimonious adj sanctitatem affectans

sanction s comprobatio, auctoritas, confirmatio f

sanction vt ratum facĕre, sancire

sanctity s sanctitas, sanctimonia f

sanctuary s sanctuarium n; (refuge) asylum n

sand s (h)arena f

sandal s solea, crepida f

sandstone s tofus, tophus m

sandy adj (h)arenosus, sabulosus, (h)arenaceus; (in color) rufus

sane *adj* sanus

sanguinary *adj* sanguinarius, cruentus

sanguine *adj* sanguineus, alacer

sanitary *adj* salubris

sanity *s* sanitas, mens sana *f*

sap *s* sucus *m*

sap *vt* subruĕre, haurire

sapling *s* surculus *m*

Sapphic *adj* Sapphicus

sapphire *s* sapphirus *f*

sarcasm *s* dicacitas *f*

sarcastic *adj* acerbus, mordax; —ally acerbe, amare

sarcophagus *s* sarcophagus *m*

sardine *s* sarda *f*

sardonic *adj* amarus

sash *s* cingillum *n*, zona *f*

Satan *s* Satanas, Satan *m*

satchel *s* sacculus *m*, pera *f*

satellite *s* satelles *m & f*

satiate *vt* satiare, saturare

satire *s* satura *f*

satirical *adj* acerbus, satiricus

satirist *s* derisor, saturarum scriptor *m*

satirize *vt* notare, perstringĕre

satisfaction *s* compensatio *f*; (feeling) voluptas *f*

satisfactorily *adv* ex sententia (meā, tuā, etc.)

satisfactory *adj* idoneus, jucundus, gratus

satisfied *adj* contentus

satisfy *vt* satisfacĕre (with dat); (to indemnify) compensare; (desires) explēre

satrap *s* satrapes *m*

saturate *vt* saturare, imbuĕre

satyr *s* satyrus *m*

sauce *s* condimentum *n*; (of meat) eliquamen *n*

saucer *s* patella, scutella *f*

saucily *adv* petulanter

saucy *adj* petulans, procax, protervus

saunter *vi* vagari, ambulari

sausage *s* farcimen *n*

savage *adj* ferus, efferatus; (cruel) saevus, atrox, immanis; —ly crudeliter, immaniter

save *vt* servare, conservare; (from danger) liberare, eripĕre; to — up reservare

save *prep* praeter (with acc)

saving *s* conservatio *f*; —s peculium *n*

savior *s* servator, liberator *m*

Saviour *s* Salvator (mundi) *m*

savor *s* sapor, gust·us -ūs *m*

savor *vi* sapĕre

savory *adj* sapidus

saw *s* (tool) serra *f*; (saying) proverbium *n*

saw *vt* serrā secare; *vi* serram ducĕre

sawdust *s* scobis *f*

say *vt* dicĕre; **that is to** — scilicet; **to** — **that . . . not** negare

saying *s* dictum, proverbium *n*

scab *s* crusta *f*

scabbard *s* vagina *f*

scaffold *s* tabulatum *n*, fala *f*

scald *vt* urĕre

scale *s* (of fish) squama *f*; (for weighing) libra, trutina *f*; (mus) diagramma *n*; (gradation) grad·us -ūs *m*

scale *vt* (fish) desquamare; **to** — **a wall** murum per scalas ascendĕre

scallop *s* pecten *m*

scalp *s* pericranium *n*

scaly *adj* squamosus, squameus

scamp *s* furcifer *m*

scamper *vi* cursare; **to** — **about** discurrĕre, cursitare; **to** — **away** aufugĕre

scan *vt* examinare, explorare; (verses) scandĕre

scandal *s* ignominia *f*, opprobrium *n*

scandalize *vt* offendĕre

scandalous *adj* probrosus, flagitiosus

scantily *adv* exigue, anguste

scanty *adj* tenuis, exiguus, exilis

scapegoat *s* piaculum *n*

scar *s* cicatrix *f*

scarce *adj* rarus; —ly vix, aegre

scarcity *s* paucitas, inopia *f*

scare *vt* terrēre, territare

scarecrow *s* terriculum *n*

scarf *s* fascia *f*, focale *n*

scarlet *s* coccum *n*

scarlet *adj* coccinus, coccineus

scathing *adj* acerbus, aculeatus

scatter *vt* spargĕre, dispergĕre, dissipare; *vi* dilabi, diffugĕre

scavenger *s* cloacarius *m*

scene *s* prospect·us -ūs *m*, spectaculum *n*; (on stage) scaena *f*; (place) locus *m*

scenery *s* (in theater) scaenae apparat·us -ūs *m*; (of nature) species regionis *f*

scent *s* (sense) odorat·us -ūs *m*; (of dogs) sagacitas *f*; (fragrance) odor *m*

scent *vt* odorari

scented *adj* odoratus

scepter *s* sceptrum *n*

sceptic *s* scepticus *m*

sceptical *adj* dubitans, incredulus

schedule *s* ratio *f*

scheme *s* consilium *n*

scheme *vt & vi* moliri, machinari

schism *s* schisma, discidium *n*

scholar *s* litteratus *m*

scholarly *adj* litteratus, doctus

scholarship *s* litterae *f pl*, eruditio *f*

scholastic *adj* scholasticus

scholiast *s* scholiastes, interpres *m*

school *s* ludus *m*, schola *f*; (group holding like opinions) secta *f*

schoolboy *s* discipulus *m*

schoolmaster *s* magister *m*

schoolroom *s* schola *f*

science *s* scientia, doctrina, disciplina, ars *f*

scientific *adj* physicus; —ally physice; (systematically) ratione

scientist *s* physicus *m*

scimitar *s* acinaces *m*

scion *s* edit·us -ūs *m*, progenies *f*

scissors *s* forfex *f*

scoff *s* irrisio, derisio, cavillatio *f*

scoff *vi* cavillari; **to** — **at** irridēre, deridēre

scoffer *s* derisor, irrisor *m*

scold *vt* objurgare, increpare; *vi* desaevire

scolding *s* objurgatio *f*

scoop *s* trulla *f*

scoop *vt* to — out excavare

scope *s* campus *m*, spatium *n*

scorch *vt* adurēre, torrēre

score *s* nota *f*; (*total*) summa *f*; (*twenty*) viginti; (*reckoning*) ratio *f*

score *vt* notare

scorn *s* contemptio *f*

scorn *vt* contemnēre, spernēre, aspernari

scornful *adj* fastidiosus; **—ly** fastidiose, contemptim

scorpion *s* scorpio, scorpius *m*

Scot *adj* Scoticus

Scotchman *s* Scotus *m*

Scotland *s* Scotia *f*

Scottish *adj* Scoticus

scoundrel *s* nebulo, furcifer *m*

scour *vt* (*to rub clean*) (de)tergēre; (*to range over*) pervagari, percurrēre

scourge *s* flagellum *n*; (*fig*) pestis *f*

scourge *vt* verberare

scourging *s* verberatio *f*, verbera *n pl*

scout *s* explorator, speculator *m*

scout *vt* speculari, explorare

scowl *vi* frontem contrahēre

scowlingly *adv* fronte contractā

scramble *vi* to — up scandēre, escendēre

scrap *s* fragmentum, frustum *n*

scrape *vt* radēre, scabēre; to — together corradēre

scrape *s* difficultas *f*; (*quarrel*) rixa *f*

scraper *s* radula *f*

scraping *s* rasura *f*; **—s** ramenta *n pl*

scratch *s* levis incisura *f*

scratch *vt* radēre, scalpēre

scrawl *s* scriptio mala *f*

scrawl *vt* & *vi* male scribēre

scream *s* ululat·us -ūs, clamor *m*; (*of an infant*) vagit·us -ūs *m*

scream *vi* ululare, clamitare

screech *s* stridor *m*

screech *vi* stridēre

screen *s* umbraculum *n*, obex *m*

screen *vt* protegēre

screw *s* cochlea *f*

screw *vt* torquēre

scribble *vt* & *vi* scriptitare

scribe *s* scriba *m*

script *s* scriptum *n*; (*hand*) man·us -ūs *f*

scrofulous *adj* strumosus

scroll *s* volumen *n*, schedula *f*

scrub *vt* defricare, detergēre

scruple *s* scrupulus *m*, religio, dubitatio *f*

scrupulous *adj* religiosus, anxius; **—ly** religiose

scrutinize *vt* scrutari, perscrutari

scrutiny *s* scrutatio, perscrutatio *f*

scud *vi* celeriter aufugēre

scuffle *s* rixa *f*

scuffle *vi* rixari

sculptor *s* sculptor, scalptor *m*

sculpture *s* (*art*) sculptura *f*; (*work*) opus, signum *n*

sculpture *vt* sculpēre

scum *s* spuma *f*; (*fig*) sentina *f*

scurrilous *adj* scurrilis

scurvy *s* scorbutus *m*

scutcheon *s* scutum *n*

scythe *s* falx *f*

sea *s* mare, aequor *n*, pontus *m*

sea captain *s* navarchus *m*

seacoast *s* ora maritima *f*

seafaring *adj* maritimus, nauticus

sea gull *s* larus *m*

seal *s* sigillum, signum *n*; (*animal*) phoca *f*

seal *vt* signare; (*fig*) sancire; **to — up** obsignare

seam *s* sutura *f*

seaman *s* nauta *m*

seamanship *s* nauticarum rerum us·us -ūs *m*, ars navigandi *f*

sear *vt* adurēre

search *s* investigatio, scrutatio *f*

search *vt* investigare, explorare; (*a person*) excutēre; *vi* to — for quaerēre, exquirēre; **to — out** explorare

seasick *adj* nauseabundus; **to be —** nauseare

season *s* tempestas *f*, anni tempus *n*; (*proper time*) opportunitas *f*, tempus *n*; **in —** tempestive

season *vt* condire; (*fig*) assuefacēre, durare

seasonable *adj* tempestivus, opportunus

seasoning *s* condimentum *n*

seat *s* sedes, sella *f*; (*dwelling*) sedes *f*, domicilium *n*

seat *vt* sede locare; **to — oneself** considēre

seaweed *s* alga *f*

secede *vi* secedēre

secession *s* secessio *f*

seclude *vt* secludēre, removēre, abdēre

secluded *adj* remotus, solitarius

seclusion *s* solitudo *f*, locus remotus *m*

second *adj* secundus, alter; **a — time** iterum; **—ly** deinde, tum

second *s* (*person*) adjutor *m*; (*of time*) punctum temporis *n*

second *vt* adesse (*with dat*), favēre (*with dat*), adjuvare

secondary *adj* secundarius, inferior

secondhand *adj* alienus, tritus

second-rate *adj* inferior

secrecy *s* secretum *n*; (*keeping secret*) silentium *n*

secret *adj* secretus, occultus, arcanus; **to keep —** celare; **—ly** clam

secret *s* secretum *n*, res arcana *f*; **in —** clam

secretary *s* scriba, amanuensis *m*

secrete *vt* celare, occultare, abdēre

secretion *s* secretio *f*

sect *s* secta *f*

section *s* pars, sectio *f*

sector *s* sector *m*, regio *f*

secular *adj* profanus

secure *adj* tutus; **—ly** tuto

secure *vt* confirmare, munire; (*to obtain*) parare, nancisci; (*to fasten*) religare

security s salus, incolumitas f; (*pledge*) satisdatio f, pignus n
sedan s lectica f
sedate adj gravis, sedatus; —**ly** graviter, sedate
sedentary adj sedentarius
sedge s ulva, carex f
sediment s sedimentum n, faex f
sedition s seditio, rebellio f
seditious adj seditiosus, turbulentus; —**ly** seditiose
seduce vt seducĕre, corrumpĕre, depravare
seducer s corruptor m
seduction s corruptela f
seductive adj blandus; —**ly** blande
see vt & vi vidēre, cernĕre, conspicĕre; (*to understand*) vidēre, intellegĕre, sentire; **to go to** — visĕre; **to** — **to** curare
seed s semen n; (*offspring*) progenies f; (*of fruit*) acinum n
seedling s surculus m
seek vt quaerĕre, petĕre; **to** — **to** conari (*with inf*), laborare (*with inf*)
seem vi vidēri
seeming adj speciosus; —**ly** in speciem, ut videtur
seemly adj decens, decorus
seep vi manare
seer s vates m
seethe vi fervēre, aestuare
segment s segmentum n
segregate vt segregare, secernĕre
segregation s separatio f
seize vt prehendĕre, arripĕre, rapĕre; (*mil*) occupare; (*fig*) afficĕre
seizure s comprehensio, occupatio f
seldom adv raro
select vt seligĕre, eligĕre, deligĕre
select adj electus, lectus, exquisitus
selection s (*act*) selectio f; (*things chosen*) electa n pl
self-confident adj sibi fidens, confidens
self-conscious adj pudibundus
self-control s continentia, temperantia f
self-denial s abstinentia f
self-evident adj manifestus
self-indulgent adj intemperans
selfish adj avarus
selfishness s avaritia f
self-respect s pudor m
sell vt vendĕre; vi venire
seller s venditor m
semblance s species, similitudo f
semicircle s hemicyclium n
semicircular adj semicirculus
senate s senat·us -ūs m; (*building*) curia f
senator s senator m
senatorial adj senatorius
send vt mittĕre; (*on public business*) legare; **to** — **away** dimittĕre; **to** — **for** accessĕre; **to** — **forward** praemittĕre
senile adj senilis, aetate provectus
senior adj natu major
seniority s aetatis praerogativa f
sensation s sens·us -ūs m; (*fig*) mirum n
sense s (*faculty; meaning*) sens·us

-ūs m; (*understanding*) prudentia f; (*meaning*) vis, significatio f
sense vt sentire
senseless adj absurdus, ineptus; (*unconscious*) omni sensu carens
sensible adj sapiens, prudens
sensibly adv prudenter, sapienter
sensitive adj sensilis, patibilis; (*touchy*) mollis
sensual adj voluptarius, libidinosus; —**ly** libidinose
sensualist s homo voluptarius m
sensuality s libido f
sentence s (*gram*) sententia f; (*law*) judicium n; **to pass** — judicare
sentence vt damnare, condemnare
sententious adj sententiosus; —**ly** sententiose
sentiment s (*opinion*) sententia, opinio f; (*feeling*) sens·us -ūs m
sentimental adj mollis, effeminatus
sentimentality s mollities animi f
sentinel s custos, vigil m
sentry s custos, vigil m; **sentries** excubiae, stationes, vigiliae f pl
separable adj separabilis
separate adj separatus, disjunctus; —**ly** separatim
separate vt separare, disjungĕre, dividĕre; vi separari, disjungi
separation s separatio, disjunctio f
September s (*mensis*) September m
sepulcher s sepulcrum n
sepulchral adj sepulcralis
sequel s exit·us -ūs m
sequence s ordo m, series f
seraph s seraphus m
serenade vt occentare
serene adj serenus, tranquillus; —**ly** serene
serenity s serenitas, tranquillitas f
serf s servus m
serfdom s servitium n, servitus f
sergeant s optio m
series s series f, ordo m
serious adj serius, gravis; —**ly** serio
seriousness s gravitas f, serium n
sermon s oratio sacra f
serpent s serpens f, anguis m & f
servant s famulus m, famula f, servus m, serva f; (*public servant*) minister m
serve vt servire (*with dat*); (*food*) apponĕre; (*to be useful to*) prodesse (*with dat*); **to** — **a sentence** poenam subire; vi (*mil*) merēre, militare; (*to suffice*) sufficĕre
service s (*favor*) officium n; (*mil*) militia f, stipendia n pl; (*work*) ministerium n; **to be of** — **to** prodesse (*with dat*), bene merēri de (*with abl*)
serviceable adj utilis
servile adj servilis, humilis
servility s humilitas f, animus abjectus m
servitude s servitus f
session s sessio f, convent·us -ūs m
set vt ponĕre, sistĕre, collocare; (*course*) dirigĕre; (*example*) dare; (*limit*) imponĕre; (*sail*) dare; (*table*) instruĕre; **to** — **apart** secernĕre, seponĕre; **to** — **aside** ponĕre; (*fig*)

rescindĕre; **to — down** deponĕre; (in writing) perscribĕre; **to — forth** exponĕre; **to — free** liberare; **to — in motion** ciēre; **to — in order** componĕre; **to — off** (to adorn) adornare; **to — on fire** incendĕre, accendĕre; **to — someone over** aliquem praeficĕre (with dat); **to — up** statuĕre; vi (of stars, etc.) occidĕre; **to — in** (to begin) incipĕre; **to — out** proficisci

set adj (fixed) certus, praescriptus

set s congeries f

setting s occas·us -ūs m

settle vt statuĕre; (business) transigĕre; (colony) deducĕre; (argument) componĕre; (debts) solvĕre, expedire; vi (to take up residence) considĕre; (to sink) subsidĕre

settlement s constitutio f; (agreement) pactum n; (colony) colonia f; (of liquids) sedimentum n

settler s colonus m

seven adj septem; **— times** septies

sevenfold adj septemplex

seventeen adj septemdecim, decem et septem

seventeenth adj septimus decimus

seventh adj septimus; **the — time** septimum

seventieth adj septuagesimus

seventy adj septuaginta

sever vt separare; vi disjungi

several adj aliquot, complures; **—ly** singulatim

severe adj severus, gravis, durus; (of weather) asper; **—ly** severe, graviter

severity s severitas, gravitas f

sew vt suĕre; **to — up** consuĕre

sewer s cloaca f

sewing s sutura f

sex s sex·us -ūs m

sextant s sextans m

sexton s aedituus m

sexual adj sexualis

shabbily adv sordide, obsolete

shabbiness s sordes f pl

shabby adj sordidus, obsoletus

shackle vt compedibus constringĕre

shackles s vincula n pl, compedes f pl

shade s umbra f; **—s** (of the dead) manes m pl

shade vt opacare, adumbrare

shadow s umbra f

shadowy adj umbrosus, opacus; (fig) inanis, vanus

shady adj umbrosus, opacus

shaft s (arrow) sagitta f; (of spear) hastile n; (of mine) puteus m

shaggy adj hirsutus, villosus

shake vt quatĕre, concutĕre; (head) nutare; vi tremĕre; (to totter) vacillare

shaking s quassatio f; (with cold, fear, etc.) tremor, horror m

shaky adj instabilis

shallow adj brevis, vadosus; (fig) insulsus, levis

sham s dolus m, simulatio, species f

sham adj fictus, simulatus

shambles s laniena f, laniarium n

shame s pudor m; (disgrace) dedecus n, infamia, ignominia f

shame vt ruborem incutĕre (with dat)

shamefaced adj pudens, verecundus

shameful adj probrosus, turpis; **—ly** probrose, turpiter

shameless adj impudens; **—ly** impudenter

shamrock s trifolium n

shank s crus n

shanty s tugurium n

shape s forma, figura, facies f

shape vt formare, fingĕre

shapeless adj informis, deformis

shapely adj formosus

share s pars, portio f; (of plow) vomer m

share vt partire, impertire; particeps esse (with genit)

shark s p(r)istix m

sharp acutus; (bitter) acer, acerbus; (keen) acutus, acer, sagax; **—ly** acriter, acute; (bitterly) acerbe

sharpen vt acuĕre

shatter vt quassare, confringĕre; (fig) frangĕre

shave vt radĕre

shavings s ramenta n pl

shawl s amiculum n

she pron ea, illa, haec

sheaf s manipulus, fascis m

shear vt tondēre

shearing s tonsura f

shears s forfices f pl

sheath s vagina f

sheathe vt in vaginam recondĕre

shed vt fundĕre, effundĕre

shed s tugurium n; (mil) vinea f

sheep s ovis f

sheepfold s ovile n

sheephook s pedum, baculum pastorale n

sheepish adj pudibundus; **—ly** pudenter

sheepskin s pellis ovilla f

sheer adj merus

sheet s linteum n; (of paper) plagula, scheda f; (of metal) lamina f

shelf s pluteus m, tabula f, pegma n

shell s concha, crusta f; (husk) folliculus m; (of nuts, etc.) putamen n

shell vt decorticare

shellfish s concha f

shelter s tegmen n; (refuge) refugium n; (lodgings) hospitium n

shelter vt tegĕre, defendĕre; (refugee) excipĕre

shepherd s pastor, opilio, pecorum custos m

shield s scutum n, parma f

shield vt tegĕre, protegĕre

shield bearer s scutigerulus, armiger m

shift vt mutare, amovēre; vi (as the wind) vertĕre; (to change position) se movēre, mutari

shift s (change) mutatio f

shifty adj varius, mobilis

shin s tibia f, crus n

shine s nitor m

shine vi lucēre, fulgēre, nitēre; **to — forth** elucēre, enitēre, exsplendescēre; **to — on** *or* **upon** affulgēre (*with dat*)

shiny *adj* lucidus, fulgidus, nitidus

ship *s* navis *f*, navigium *n*

ship *vt* navi invehēre

shipbuilder *s* naupegus *m*

shipbuilding *s* architectura navalis *f*

shipmaster *s* navicularius *m*

shipwreck *s* naufragium *n*; **to suffer — naufragium facēre**

shipwrecked *adj* naufragus

shirk *vt* defugēre, detrectare

shirt *s* subucla, camisia *f*

shiver *vi* contremiscēre, horrēre

shoal *s* caterva *f*, grex *m*; (*shallow*) brevia *n pl*

shock *vt* percutēre, percellēre; (*fig*) offendēre

shock *s* concussio *f*, impet·us -ūs *m*; (*fig*) offensio *f*

shocking *adj* flagitiosus, atrox

shoe *s* calceus *m*

shoemaker *s* sutor *m*

shoot *vt* (*missile*) conjicēre, jaculari; (*person*) transfigēre; *vi* volare

shoot *s* surculus *m*

shooting star *s* fax caelestis *f*

shop *s* taberna, officina *f*

shopkeeper *s* tabernarius *m*

shore *s* litus *n*, ora *f*

short *adj* brevis; **to run — deficēre; —ly brevi, mox**

shortage *s* inopia *f*

shortcoming *s* defect·us -ūs *m*, delictum *n*

shorten *vt* coarctare, contrahēre; *vi* contrahi, minui

shorthand *s* notae breviores *f pl*

shortness *s* brevitas, exiguitas *f*; **— of breath** asthma *n*

short-sighted *adj* myops; (*fig*) improvidus, imprudens

short-winded *adj* anhelus

shot *s* ict·us -ūs *m*; (*reach, range*) jact·us -ūs *m*

should *vi* debēre; **I — go** mihi eundum est

shoulder *s* (h)umerus *m*; (*of animal*) armus *m*

shoulder *vt* suscipēre

shout *s* clamor *m*, acclamatio *f*

shout *vt & vi* clamare, acclamare, vociferari

shove *vt* trudēre, pulsare

shovel *s* pala *f*, rutrum *n*

shovel *vt* pala tollēre

show *vt* monstrare; (*to display*) exhibēre; (*to teach*) docēre; **to — off** ostendēre; *vi* **to — off** se jactare

show *s* (*appearance*) species *f*; (*display*) ostentatio *f*; (*pretense*) simulatio *f*; (*entertainment*) spectaculum *n*

shower *s* imber *m*

shower *vt* fundēre, effundēre

showy *adj* speciosus

shred *s* segmentum panni *n*; (*scrap*) frustum *n*

shrew *s* mulier jurgiosa *f*

shrewd *adj* acutus, astutus, callidus, sagax; **—ly** acute, callide, sagaciter

shrewdness *s* calliditas, astutia, sagacitas *f*

shriek *s* ululat·us -ūs *m*, ejulatio *f*

shriek *vi* ululare, ejulare

shrill *adj* peracutus, stridulus

shrimp *s* cancer pagurus *m*; (*person*) pumilio, homulus *m*

shrine *s* fanum, delubrum *n*

shrink *vt* contrahēre; *vi* contrahi; (*to withdraw*) refugēre; **to — from** abhorrēre ab (*with abl*), refugēre ab (*with abl*)

shrivel *vt* corrugare, torrefacēre; *vi* corrugari, torrescēre

shroud *s* integumentum *n*; (*of ship*) rudentes *m pl*

shroud *vt* involvēre, obducēre

shrub *s* frutex *m*

shrubbery *s* fruticetum *n*

shrug *s* (h)umerorum allevatio *f*

shrug *vt* **to — the shoulders** (h)umeros contrahēre *or* allevare

shudder *vi* horrēre; **to — at** horrēre

shuffle *vt* miscēre; *vi* claudicare

shun *vt* vitare, devitare, fugēre

shut *vt* claudēre, occludēre; **to — out** excludēre; **to — up** concludēre; *vi* **to — up** conticescēre

shutter *s* claustrum *n*, foricula *f*

shy *adj* timidus, pudibundus; **—ly** timide

shyness *s* timiditas, verecundia *f*

sibyl *s* sibylla *f*

sick *adj* (*mentally or physically*) aeger; (*physically*) aegrotus; **I am — of me** taedet (*with genit*), fastidio; **to be — aegrotare**

sicken *vt* fastidium movēre (*with dat*); *vi* in morbum incidēre, nauseare

sickle *s* falx *f*

sickly *adj* infirmus

sickness *s* morbus *m*, aegrotatio *f*

side *s* latus *n*; (*direction*) pars *f*; (*district*) regio *f*; (*faction*) partes *f pl*; (*kinship*) genus *n*; **at the — of a latere** (*with genit*); **on all —s** utrimque; **on both —s** utrimque; **on one — unā ex parte; on that — illinc; on the mother's — materno genere; on this — hinc; on this — of cis** (*with acc*), citra (*with acc*); **to be on the — of stare ab** (*with abl*), sentire cum (*with abl*)

side *adj* lateralis, obliquus

side *vi* **to — with partes sequi** (*with genit*), stare ab (*with abl*), sentire cum (*with abl*)

sideboard *s* abacus *m*

sidelong *adj* obliquus, transversus

sideways *adv* in obliquum, oblique

siege *s* obsessio, oppugnatio, obsidio *f*; **to lay — to obsidēre**

siesta *s* meridiatio *f*; **to take a — meridiare**

sieve *s* cribrum *n*; (*little sieve*) cribellum *n*

sift *vt* cribrare; (*fig*) scrutari

sigh *s* suspirium *n*

sigh *vi* suspirare; **to — for desiderare**

sight *s* (*sense*) vis·us -ūs *m*; (*act of seeing*) aspect·us -ūs *m*; (*range*) conspect·us -ūs *m*; (*appearance*) species *f*; (*show*) spectaculum *n*; **at**

first — primo aspectu; **to catch — of** conspicĕre; **to lose — of e** conspectu amittĕre

sight vt conspicari

sightless adj caecus

sightly adj decorus, decens

sign s signum, indicium n; (*mark*) nota f; (*distinction*) insigne n; omen, portentum n

sign vt (*e.g., a document*) subscribĕre, signare, consignare

signal vi signum dare; (*by a nod*) annuĕre

signal s signum n; (*mil*) classicum n

signal adj insignis, egregius

signature s signatura f, nomen n

signer s signator m

signet s sigillum n

significance s (*meaning*) significatio, vis f, sens·us -ūs m; (*importance*) momentum n

significant adj gravis, magnus, magni momenti (*genit*)

signify vt significare, portendĕre

silence s silentium n

silence interj tace!; (*to more than one person*) tacete!

silence vt comprimĕre; (*by argument*) refutare

silent adj tacitus, taciturnus; **to become** — conticescĕre; **to be —** tacēre; **—ly** tacite

silk s sericum n, bombyx m & f

silk adj sericus, bombycinus

silkworm s bombyx m & f

sill s limen inferum n

silly adj stultus, ineptus

silver s argentum n

silver adj argenteus

silversmith s faber argentarius m

silvery adj argenteus; (*of hair*) canus

similar adj similis; **—ly** similiter, pariter

similarity s similitudo f

simile s translatio, similitudo f

simmer vi lente fervēre

simper vi inepte ridēre

simple adj simplex; (*easy*) facilis; (*frank*) sincerus; (*silly*) stultus

simpleton s stultus, ineptus m

simplicity s simplicitas f

simplify vt faciliorem reddĕre

simply adv simpliciter; solum, tantummodo

simulate vt simulare

simulation s simulatio f

simultaneous adj eodem tempore; **—ly** simul, unā, eodem tempore

sin s peccatum, delictum n

sin vi peccare

since prep ex (*with abl*), ab (*with abl*), post (*with acc*); **ever —** usque ab (*with abl*)

since adv abhinc; **long —** jamdudum, jampridem

since conj (*temporal*) ex quo tempore, postquam, cum; (*causal*) quod, quia, quoniam, cum

sincere adj sincerus, candidus; **—ly** sincere, vere

sinew s nervus, lacertus m

sinewy adj nervosus, lacertosus

sinful adj impius, pravus; **—ly** im-

pie, improbe

sing vt & vi canĕre, cantare

singe vt adurĕre, amburĕre

singer s cantator m, cantatrix f

singing s cant·us -ūs m

single adj solus, unicus, unus, singularis; (*unmarried*) caelebs; **not a — one** ne unus quidem

single vt **to — out** eligĕre

singly adv singulatim, viritim

singsong s canticum n

singsong adj canorus

singular adj unicus, singularis; (*outstanding*) egregius, eximius; **—ly** singulariter, unice, egregie

sinister adj infaustus, malevolus, iniquus

sink vt submergĕre, demergĕre, deprimĕre; (*money*) collocare; vi considĕre, subsidĕre; (*in water*) mergi; (*of morale, etc.*) cadĕre

sink s sentina f

sinless adj peccati expers

sinner s peccator m, peccatrix f

sinuous adj sinuosus

sip vt libare, sorbillare, degustare

siphon s sipho m

sir s (*title*) eques m

sir interj (*to a master*) ere!; (*to an equal*) bone viri, vir clarissimi!

sire s genitor m

siren s siren f

sister s soror f

sister-in-law s glos f

sisterly adj sororius

sit vi sedēre; **to — beside** assidēre (*with dat*); **to — down** considĕre; **to — on** insidēre (*with dat*); **to — up** (*to be awake at night*) vigilare

site s sit·us -ūs m

situated adj situs, positus

situation s sit·us -ūs m; (*circumstances*) res, conditio f

six adj sex; **— times** sexies

sixfold adj sextuplus

sixteen adj sedecim

sixteenth adj sextus decimus

sixth s sexta pars f

sixtieth adj sexagesimus

sixty adj sexaginta

size s magnitudo, mensura f

skein s glomus m

skeleton s sceletos m, ossa n pl

sketch s adumbratio, lineatio f

sketch vt adumbrare, delineare; (*fig*) describĕre

skiff s scapha f

skilful adj dexter, peritus, scitus; (*with hands*) habilis; **—ly** perite, scite

skill s sollertia, calliditas, peritia f

skilled adj peritus, doctus

skillet s cucumella f

skim vt despumare; (*fig*) percurrĕre, stringĕre

skin s (*of men*) cutis f; (*of animals*) pellis f; (*prepared*) corium n

skin vt pellem exuĕre (*with abl*)

skinny adj macilentus

skip vt praeterire; vi subsultare; **to — over** transilire

skirmish s concursatio, velitatio f

skirmish vi velitari

skirmisher *s* veles *m*
skirt *s* instita *f*; (*border*) fimbria *f*
skirt *vt* tangĕre, legĕre
skull *s* cranium, caput *n*
sky *s* caelum *n*, aether *m*; **under the open — sub divo**
slab *s* tabula, tessera *f*
slack *adj* remissus, laxus; (*fig*) piger, neglegens
slacken *vt* remittĕre, laxare, minuĕre; *vi* minui, remitti
slag *s* scoria *f*
slain *adj* occisus
slake *vt* exstinguĕre, sedare
slander *s* calumnia, obtrectatio *f*
slander *vt* obtrectare (*with dat*), calumniari
slanderer *s* obtrectator *m*
slanderous *adj* calumniosus, maledicus
slang *s* vulgaria verba *n pl*
slant *vt* acclinare; (*fig*) detorquĕre
slanting *adj* obliquus
slap *s* alapa *f*
slap *vt* alapam dare (*with dat*), palmā ferire
slash *s* (*cut*) caesura *f*; (*blow*) ict·us -ūs *m*; (*wound*) vulnus *n*
slash *vt* caedĕre, incidĕre
slaughter *s* caedes, trucidatio *f*
slaughter *vt* mactare, trucidare
slaughterhouse *s* laniena *f*
slave *s* servus *m*, serva *f*
slave dealer *s* venalicius, mancipiorum negotiator *m*
slavery *s* servitus *f*, servitium *n*
slave trade *s* venalicium *n*
slavish *adj* servilis; **—ly** serviliter
slay *vt* interficĕre, occidĕre, necare
slayer *s* necator, homicida *m*
sledge *s* traha, trahea *f*
sleek *adj* levis, politus, nitidus, pinguis
sleep *s* somnus *m*
sleep *vi* dormire
sleepless *adj* insomnis, pervigil
sleepy *adj* somniculosus, semisomnis; (*fig*) iners
sleet *s* nivosa grando *f*
sleeve *s* manica *f*
slender *adj* gracilis, tenuis
slice *s* segmentum, frustum *n*, offula *f*
slice *vt* secare
slide *vi* labi
slight *adj* levis, exiguus, tenuis; **—ly** leviter, paululum
slight *s* neglegentia, contemptio *f*
slight *vt* neglegĕre, contemnĕre
slily *adv* astute, callide, vafre
slim *adj* gracilis
slime *s* limus *m*
slimy *adj* limosus, mucosus, viscosus
sling *s* funda *f*; (*for arm*) fascia *f*
sling *vt* jaculari
slink *vi* **to — away** furtim se subducĕre
slip *s* laps·us -ūs *m*; (*of paper*) scheda *f*; (*in grafting*) surculus *m*; (*error*) peccatum *n*, culpa *f*
slip *vt* (*to give furtively*) furtim dare; *vi* labi; **to let — omittĕre; to — away elabi**
slipper *s* solea, crepida *f*

slippery *adj* lubricus; (*deceitful*) subdolus
slit *s* incisura *f*
slit *vt* incidĕre, discidĕre
slop *s* vilis pot·us -ūs *m*
slope *s* declivitas *f*, clivus *m*
slope *vi* proclinari, vergĕre
sloping *adj* declivis, pronus; (*upward*) acclivis
sloppy *adj* lutulentus, sordidus
slot *s* rima *f*
sloth *s* ignavia, pigritia, inertia *f*
slothful *adj* piger, segnis, iners; **—ly** pigre, segniter, ignave
slouch *vi* languide incedĕre
slough *s* (*of snake*) exuviae *f pl*; (*mire*) caenum *n*
slovenly *adj* sordidus, ignavus
slow *adj* tardus, lentus; (*gentle*) lenis; **—ly** tarde, lente, sensim
sluggard *s* homo piger *m*
sluggish *adj* piger, ignavus, segnis; **—ly** pigre, segniter
sluice *s* cataracta *f*
slumber *s* somnus, sopor *m*
slumber *vi* obdormiscĕre, dormitare
slur *s* macula *f*
slur *vt* inquinare; *vi* **to — over extenuare**, leviter attingĕre
slut *s* meretrix *f*
sly *adj* astutus, vafer, callidus; **on the — clam; —ly astute, callide, vafre**
smack *s* (*flavor*) sapor *m*; (*blow*) alapa *f*
smack *vt* (*to strike*) ferire; *vi* **to — of sapĕre**
small *adj* parvus, exiguus, tenuis
smart *adj* (*clever*) sollers, callidus; (*elegant*) lautus, nitidus; (*of pace*) velox; **—ly callide; nitide**
smart *s* dolor *m*
smart *vi* dolēre
smash *s* concussio, fractura *f*
smash *vt* confringĕre
smattering *s* cognitio manca, levis scientia *f*
smear *vt* illinĕre, oblinĕre
smell *s* (*sense*) odorat·us -ūs *m*; (*odor*) odor *m*
smell *vt* olfacĕre, odorari; *vi* olēre; **to — of olēre, redolēre**
smelly *adj* olidus, graveolens
smelt *vt* (ex)coquĕre, fundĕre
smile *s* ris·us -ūs *m*; **with a — subridens**
smile *vi* subridēre; **to — at arridēre** (*with dat*)
smirk *vi* subridēre
smite *vt* ferire, percutĕre
smith *s* faber *m*
smithy *s* ferramentorum fabrica *f*
smock *s* tunica *f*
smoke *s* fumus *m*
smoke *vt* (*to cure by smoking*) infumare; *vi* fumare
smoky *adj* fumeus, fumidus, fumosus
smooth *adj* levis; (*of skin*) glaber; (*polished*) teres; (*calm*) placidus; (*of talk*) blandus; **—ly leviter; blande**
smooth *vt* polire, limare
smother *vt* suffocare, opprimĕre
smudge *s* sordes *f*

smudge *vt* inquinare, conspurcare

smug *adj* lautus, nitidus, sui contentus

smuggle *vt* furtim importare, sine portorio importare

smut *s* fuligo *f*

smutty *adj* obscenus; *(blackened)* fumosus

snack *s* portio, morsiuncula *f*

snail *s* cochlea *f*, limax *m & f*

snake *s* anguis *m & f*, serpens *f*

snap *vt (to break)* frangĕre; **to — the fingers** digitis concrepare; **to — up** corripĕre; *vi* disilire, frangi; **to — at** mordēre

snap *s* crepit·us -ūs *m*

snare *s* laqueus *m*, pedica *f*; *(fig)* insidiae *f pl*

snare *vt* illaquēre, irretire

snarl *vi (as a dog)* ringĕre, hirrire

snatch *vt* rapĕre, corripĕre; **to — away** eripĕre; **to — up** surripĕre

sneak *s* perfidus *m*

sneak *vi* repĕre, serpĕre, latitare

sneer *s* rhonchus *m*, irrisio *f*

sneer *vi* irridēre, deridēre

sneeringly *adv* cum irrisione

sneeze *s* sternutamentum *n*

sneeze *vi* sternuĕre

sniff *vt* odorari, naribus captare

snip *vi* amputare; **to — off** decerpĕre, praecidĕre

snivel *s* mucus *m*

snivel *vi* mucum resorbēre

snob *s* homo arrogans *m*, homo fastidiosus *m*

snobbish *adj* fastidiosus

snore *s* rhonchus *m*

snore *vi* stertĕre

snort *s* fermit·us -ūs *m*

snort *vi* fremĕre

snout *s* rostrum *n*

snow *s* nix *f*

snow *vi* ningĕre; **it is snowing** ningit

snowball *s* glebula nivis *f*

snowdrift *s* niveus agger *m*

snowstorm *s* ningor *m*

snowy *adj* niveus, nivalis; *(full of snow)* nivosus

snub *vt* reprehendĕre, neglegĕre

snub *s* repulsa *f*

snuff *vt* **to — out** exstinguĕre

snug *adj* commodus; **—ly** commode

so *adv* sic, ita, *(before adjectives)* tam; **— far** eatenus, adhuc; **— much** tantum; **— so** mediocriter; **— that** ita ut; **— that not** ne; **— then** quare, quapropter

soak *vt* madefacĕre, macerare; *vi* madēre

soap *s* sapo *m*

soar *vi* in sublime ferri; *(of birds)* subvolare

sob *s* singult·us -ūs *m*

sob *vi* singultare

sober *adj* sobrius; *(fig)* moderatus, modestus; **—ly** sobrie; moderate

sobriety *s* sobrietas *f*; *(fig)* continentia *f*

sociable *adj* sociabilis, facilis, affabilis

social *adj* socialis, civilis, communis

society *s* societas *f*; **high —** optimates *m pl*; **secret —** sodalitas *f*

sock *s* pedale *n*, udo *m*

socket *s (in anatomy)* cavum *n*

sod *s* caespes *m*, glaeba *f*

soda *s (in natural state)* nitrum *n*; *(prepared)* soda *f*

sofa *s* lectulus, grabatus *m*

soft *adj* mollis, tener; *(fig)* delicatus, effeminatus; **—ly** molliter, leniter

soften *vt* mollire, mitigare; *(fig)* lenire, placare; *vi* mollescĕre; *(of fruits)* mitescĕre; *(fig)* mansuescĕre, mitescĕre

softness *s* mollitia, teneritas, lenitas *f*; *(effeminacy)* mollities *f*

soil *s* solum *n*, terra *f*

soil *vt* inquinare, contaminare

sojourn *s* commoratio, mansio *f*

sojourn *vi* commorari

solace *s* solatium *n*

solace *vt* consolari

solar *adj* solaris; solis *(genit)*

soldier *s* miles *m*

soldierly *adj* militaris

soldiery *s* miles *m*

sole *adj* solitarius; **—ly** solum, modo, tantum

sole *s (of foot)* planta *f*; *(of shoe)* solea *f*; *(fish)* solea *f*

solemn *adj* sollemnis; gravis; **—ly** sollemniter; graviter

solemnity *s* sollemne *n*, sollemnitas *f*; gravitas *f*

solemnization *s* celebratio *f*

solemnize *vt* celebrare

solicit *vt* rogare, flagitare

solicitation *s* flagitatio *f*

solicitor *s* flagitator *m*; *(law)* advocatus *m*

solicitous *adj* anxius, trepidus; **—ly** anxie, trepide

solicitude *s* sollicitudo, anxietas *f*

solid *adj* solidus; purus; *(fig)* verus, firmus; **—ly** solide

soliloquize *vi* secum loqui

soliloquy *s* soliloquium *n*

solitary *adj* solitarius; *(of places)* desertus

solitude *s* solitudo *f*

solstice *s* solstitium *n*

soluble *adj* dissolubilis

solution *s* dilutum *n*; *(fig)* solutio, explicatio *f*

solve *vt* solvĕre, explicare

solvency *s* facultas solvendi *f*

some *adj* aliqui; *(a certain)* quidam; nonnulli, aliquot

some *pron* aliqui; nonnulli; *(certain people)* quidam

somebody *pron* aliquis; **— or other** nescio quis

someday *adv* olim

somehow *adv* quodammodo, nescio quomodo, aliquā (viā)

someone *pron* aliquis; **— else** alius

something *pron* aliquid; **— else** aliud; **— or other** nescio quid

sometime *adv* aliquando

sometimes *adv* interdum, nonnumquam; **sometimes . . . sometimes** modo . . . modo

somewhat *adv* aliquantum; *(with comparatives)* aliquanto, paulo
somewhere *adv* alicubi; *(with motion)* aliquo; **— else** alibi; *(with motion)* alio
somnolence *s* somni cupiditas *f*
somnolent *adj* semisomnus
son *s* filius *m*
song *s* cant·us -ūs *m*; *(tune)* melos *n*
son-in-law *s* gener *m*
sonorous *adj* sonorus, canorus; **—ly** sonore, canore
soon *adv* brevi tempore, mox; **as — as** simul, simulac, simulatque; **as — as possible** quamprimum; **— after** paulo post
sooner *adv* prius; *(preference)* potius; **— or later** serius ocius
soot *s* fuligo *f*
soothe *vt* permulcēre, mitigare, delenire
soothsayer *s* hariolus, sortilegus *m*
soothsaying *s* vaticinatio *f*
sooty *adj* fumosus
sop *s* offa, offula *f*
sophism *s* sophisma *n* cavillatio *f*
sophist *s* sophistes *m*
sophisticated *adj* urbanus, lepidus
sophistry *s* cavillatio captiosa *f*
soporific *adj* soporifer
sorcerer *s* magus *m*
sorceress *s* maga, saga *f*
sorcery *s* veneficium *n*
sordid *adj* sordidus, foedus; **—ly** sordide
sore *adj* *(aching)* tener; *(grievous)* atrox, durus; **—ly** graviter, vehementer
sore *s* ulcus *n*
sorrow *s* dolor, maeror, luct·us -ūs *m*
sorrow *vi* dolēre, lugēre
sorrowful *adj* luctuosus, tristis, maestus; **—ly** maeste
sorry *adj* *(pitiable)* miser; **I am — about** me paenitet *(with genit)*; **I feel — for** me miseret *(with genit)*, misereo *(with genit)*
sort *s* genus *n*, species *f*; **of that —** ejusmodi
sort *vt* digerere, ordinare
sot *s* fatuus *m*; *(drunkard)* ebrius, potator *m*
sottish *adj* ebriosus
soul *s* *(principle of life)* anima *f*; *(principle of intellection and sensation)* animus *m*; *(person)* caput *n*
sound *adj* *(healthy)* validus, sanus; *(strong)* robustus; *(entire)* integer; *(in mind)* mentis compos; *(true, genuine)* verus; *(of sleep)* artus; *(valid)* ratus; **—ly** *(of beating)* vehementer, egregie; *(of sleeping)* arte
sound *s* sonus *m*; *(noise)* strepit·us -ūs, sonit·us -ūs *m*; *(of trumpet)* clangor *m*; *(strait)* fretum *n*
sound *vt* *(trumpet)* canēre; *vi* canēre, sonare; *(to seem)* vidēri
soundness *s* sanitas, integritas *f*
soup *s* jus *n*
sour *adj* acidus, acerbus; *(fig)* amarus, morosus; **to turn —** acescēre; *(fig)* coacescēre
source *s* fons *m*; *(of stream)* caput *n*;

(fig) origo *f*, fons *m*
South *s* meridies, auster *m*
southern *adj* australis, meridionalis
southward *adv* in meridiem, meridiem versus
south wind *s* auster, notus *m*
souvenir *s* monumentum *n*
sovereign *adj* supremus
sovereign *s* princeps, rex, regnator *m*
sovereignty *s* dominatio *f*, princip·at·us -ūs *m*
sow *s* sus *m* & *f*
sow *vt* serēre, seminare; *(a field)* conserēre
space *s* spatium *n*; *(of time)* intervallum *n*
spacious *adj* spatiosus, amplus
spade *s* ligo *m*, pala *f*
span *s* *(extent)* spatium *n*; *(measure)* palmus *m*
spangle *s* bractea *f*
spangle *vt* bracteis ornare
Spaniard *s* Hispanus *m*
Spanish *adj* Hispanicus, Hispaniensis
spar *s* tignum *n*
spar *vi* dimicare; *(fig)* digladiari
spare *vt* parcēre *(with dat)*, parce uti *(with abl)*
spare *adj* parcus, frugalis, exilis
sparing *adj* parcus; **—ly** parce
spark *s* scintilla *f*; *(fig)* igniculus *m*
sparkle *vi* scintillare; *(as wine)* subsilire
sparkling *adj* coruscans
sparrow *s* passer *m*
Spartan *adj* Laconicus, Spartanus
spasm *s* spasmus *m*, convulsio *f*
spasmodically *adv* interdum
spatter *vt* aspergēre, inquinare
spatula *s* spatha *f*
spawn *s* ova *f pl*
spawn *vi* ova gignēre
speak *vt* & *vi* loqui, fari, dicēre; **to — of** dicēre de *(with abl)*; **to — to** alloqui *(with acc)*; **to — with** colloqui cum *(with abl)*
speaker *s* orator *m*
spear *s* hasta *f*
spear *vt* hastā transfigēre
special *adj* specialis, praecipuus; **—ly** specialiter, praecipue
specialty *s* proprietas *f*
species *s* species *f*, genus *n*
specific *adj* certus
specify *vt* enumerare, designare
specimen *s* specimen, exemplum *n*
specious *adj* speciosus
speck *s* macula *f*
speckle *vt* maculis variare
spectacle *s* spectaculum *n*
spectator *s* spectator *m*
specter *s* larva *f*, phantasma *n*
spectral *adj* larvalis
spectrum *s* spectrum *n*
speculate *vi* cogitare, conjecturam facēre; *(com)* foro uti
speculation *s* cogitatio, conjectura *f*; *(com)* alea *f*
speculative *adj* conjecturalis
speculator *s* contemplator *m*; *(com)* aleator *m*

speech s oratio f, sermo m; (*faculty*) lingua f

speechless adj mutus, elinguis; (*fig*) obstupefactus

speed s celeritas, velocitas f

speed vt accelerare, maturare; vi properare, festinare

speedily adv cito, celeriter

speedy adj citus, velox, celer

spell s incantamentum, carmen n

spelling s orthographia f

spelt s far n

spend vt impendĕre, consumĕre; (*to exhaust*) effundĕre; (*time*) agĕre

spendthrift s nepos, prodigus m

spew vt vomĕre

sphere s sphaera f, globus m; (*fig*) provincia f

spherical adj sphaericus, sphaeralis, globosus

sphinx s sphinx f

spice s condimentum n

spice vt condire

spicy adj conditus, aromaticus

spider s aranea f

spider web s araneum n

spigot s epistomium n

spike s clavus m

spill vt effundĕre, profundĕre

spin vt (*thread*) nēre; to — round versare, circumagĕre; vi versari

spinach s spinacea oleracea f

spinal adj dorsalis

spine s spina f

spinster s innupta f

spiral adj intortus

spiral s spira, involutio f

spirit s spirit·us -ūs m, anima f; (*character*) ingenium n; (*ghost*) anima f; —s (*of the dead*) manes m pl

spirited adj animosus, alacer

spiritless adj piger, ignavus

spiritual adj animi (*genit*)

spit s veru n; (*spittle*) sputum n

spit vt & vi sputare, spuĕre

spite s livor m, malevolentia f, odium n

spite vt offendĕre

spiteful adj lividus, malevolus; —ly malevole

spittle s sputum n

splash vt aspergĕre

splash s fragor s

splendid adj splendidus; —ly splendide

splendor s splendor m

splint s ferula f

splinter s assula f

splinter vt assulatim findĕre

split s fissura f

split vt findĕre; vi findi

spoil vt spoliare; (*to mar*) corrumpĕre; (*to ruin*) perdĕre, depravare, vitiare

spoils s spolia n pl, praeda f

spoke s radius m

spokesman s orator m

spondee s spondeus m

sponge s spongia f

spongy adj spongiosus

sponsor s sponsor m

spontaneity s impuls·us -ūs m

spontaneous adj voluntarius; —ly

sponte, ultro

spool s fusus m

spoon s cochleare n

spoonful s cochleare n

sport s ludus, lus·us -ūs m; (*mockery*) ludibrium n, irrisio f

sport vi ludĕre, lascivire

sportive adj jocosus; —ly jocose

sportsman s venator m

spot s macula f; (*stain*) macula, labes f; (*place*) locus m

spot vt (*to speckle*) maculis notare; (*to stain*) inquinare, maculare

spotless adj integer, purus, castus

spotted adj maculosus, maculis distinctus

spouse s conju(n)x m & f

spout s (*pipe*) canalis m; (*of jug*) os n; (*of water*) torrens m

spout vt ejaculare; (*speeches*) declamare; vi emicare

sprain vt intorquēre, convellĕre

sprawl vi se fundĕre, prostratus jacēre

spray s aspergo f

spray vt aspergĕre

spread vt pandĕre, distendĕre, extendĕre; diffundĕre; (*to make known*) divulgare; vi patēre; (*of news*) manare, divulgari; (*of disease*) evagari

sprig s ramusculus m, virgula f

sprightly adj alacer, vegetus

spring s (*season*) ver n; (*leap*) salt·us -ūs m; (*of water*) fons m, scaturgo f

spring adj vernus

spring vi (*to come from*) oriri, enasci; (*as rivers, etc.*) scatēre, effluĕre; (*to leap*) salire, exsilire

springtime s vernum tempus n

sprinkle vt spargĕre, aspergĕre; vi rorare

sprite s spectrum n

sprout s pullus, surculus m

sprout vi pullulare

spruce adj lautus, nitidus, comptus; —ly nitide

spur s calcar n; (*fig*) incitamentum n

spur vt calcaribus concitare; (*fig*) urgēre

spurious adj fictus, fucosus, spurius

spurn vt spernĕre, aspernari

spurt vi emicare

sputter vi balbutire

spy s explorator, speculator m

spy vt conspicĕre; vi speculari

squabble s jurgium n, rixa f

squabble vi rixari

squad s manipulus m, decuria f

squadron s (*of cavalry*) ala, turma f; (*of ships*) classis f

squalid adj squalidus, sordidus

squall s procella f

squalor s squalor m, sordes f

squander vt dissipare, effundĕre

squanderer s prodigus m

square adj quadratus; (*fig*) honestus, probus

square s quadratum n, quadra f; (*tool*) norma f

square vt quadrare; vi convenire, congruĕre

squash vt conterĕre, contundĕre

squat *vi* succumbĕre, recumbĕre, subsidĕre
squat *adj* parvus atque obesus
squeak *vi* stridēre; (*as a mouse*) dintrire
squeak *s* stridor *m*
squeamish *adj* fastidiosus; **to feel —** fastidire
squeeze *vt* comprimĕre, premĕre; **to — out** exprimĕre
squint *vi* strabo esse
squint-eyed *adj* paetus
squire *s* armiger *m*; (*landowner*) dominus *m*
squirrel *s* sciurus *m*
squirt *vt* projicĕre; *vi* emicare
stab *s* ict·us -ūs *m*, puncta *f*
stab *vt* fodĕre, perforare
stability *s* stabilitas *f*
stabilize *vt* stabilire, firmare
stable *adj* stabilis, solidus
stable *s* stabulum *n*; (*for horses*) equile *n*; (*for cows, oxen*) bubile *n*
stack *s* acervus *m*, strues *f*
stack *vt* coacervare, cumulare
staff *s* baculum *n*, scipio *m*, virga *f*; (*of a magistrate*) consilium *n*; (*mil*) contubernales *m pl*
staff officer *s* contubernalis *m*
stag *s* cervus *m*
stage *s* (*in theater*) scaena *f*; (*degree*) grad·us -ūs *m*; (*on journey*) iter *n*
stagger *vt* obstupefacĕre; *vi* titubare
stagnant *adj* stagnans, torpens; (*fig*) iners
stagnate *vi* stagnare; (*fig*) refrigescĕre
stagnation *s* cessatio *f*, torpor *m*
staid *adj* gravis
stain *s* macula, labes *f*
stain *vt* maculare, contaminare; (*to dye*) tingĕre
stainless *adj* immaculatus, purus, integer
stair *s* scala *f*, grad·us -ūs *m*
staircase *s* scalae *f pl*
stake *s* palus *m*; (*wager*) depositum *n*; **to be at — agi**
stake *vt* deponĕre, appignerare
stale *adj* vetus, obsoletus; (*of bread*) secundus; (*of wine*) vapidus
stalk *s* (*of plant*) caulis, stipes *m*; (*of grain*) calamus *m*
stalk *vt* venari; *vi* incedĕre
stall *s* stabulum *n*
stall *vt* sistĕre; *vi* consistĕre
stallion *s* admissarius *m*
stamina *s* patientia *f*
stammer *vi* balbutire, linguā haesitare
stammering *adj* balbus
stammering *s* balbuties *f*
stamp *s* (*mark*) nota *f*; (*with the foot*) vestigium *n*; (*impression made*) impressio *f*
stamp *vt* imprimĕre, notare; (*money*) cudĕre; (*feet*) supplodĕre
stand *s* locus *m*, statio *f*; (*halt*) mora *f*; (*platform*) suggest·us -ūs *m*
stand *vt* (*to set upright*) statuĕre, constituĕre; (*to tolerate*) tolerare, perferre, sustinēre; *vi* stare; **to —**

aloof abstare; **to — by** adesse (*with dat*); **to — fast** consistĕre; **to — for office** petĕre; **to — in awe of** in metu habēre; **to — in need of** indigēre (*with abl*); **to — on end** horrēre; **to — out** exstare, eminēre, prominēre; **to — still** consistĕre, subsistĕre
standard *adj* solitus
standard *s* (*mil*) vexillum, signum *n*; (*measure*) norma, mensura *f*
standard-bearer *s* vexillarius, signifer *m*
standing *s* stat·us -ūs, ordo *m*, conditio *f*; **of long —** vetus
standing *adj* perpetuus
standstill *s* **to be at a —** haerēre
stanza *s* tetrastichon *n*
staple *adj* praecipuus
star *s* stella *f*, sidus *n*; (*fig*) lumen *n*
starch *s* amylum *n*
starch *vt* amylare
stare *s* obtut·us -ūs *m*, oculorum intentio *f*
stare *vi* stupēre; **to — at** intuēri
stark *adj* rigidus
stark *adv* omnino, penitus
starlight *s* siderum lumen *n*
starling *s* sturnus *m*
starry *adj* sidereus, stellatus
start *s* initium *n*; (*sudden movement*) salt·us -ūs *m*; (*of journey*) profectio *f*
start *vt* incipĕre, instituĕre; (*game*) excitare; *vi* (*to begin*) incipĕre, (ex)ordiri; (*to take fright*) resilire
starting gate *s* carceres *m pl*
startle *vt* terrēre, territare
starvation *s* fames *f*
starve *vt* fame interficĕre; *vi* fame confici
state *s* stat·us -ūs, locus *m*; (*pol*) civitas, respublica *f*; (*pomp*) magnificentia *f*
state *vt* declarare, dicĕre, affirmare
state *adj* publicus
stately *adj* grandis, lautus, splendidus
statement *s* affirmatio *f*, dictum *n*; testimonium *n*
statesman *s* vir reipublicae regendae peritus *m*
statesmanship *s* reipublicae regendae ars *f*
station *s* statio *f*, locus *m*
station *vt* locare, disponĕre
stationary *adj* stabilis, statarius, immotus
stationery *s* res scriptoriae *f pl*
statistics *s* cens·us -ūs *m*
statue *s* statua *f*, signum *n*
stature *s* statura *f*
statute *s* institutum, decretum *n*, lex *f*
staunch *adj* certus, firmus, fidus
staunch *vt* (*blood*) sistĕre
stave *vt* perrumpĕre; **to — off** arcēre
stay *vt* detinēre, sistĕre; (*to curb*) coercēre; *vi* manēre, commorari
stay *s* (*sojourn*) commoratio, mansio *f*; (*delay*) mora *f*; (*prop*) fulcrum *n*
steadfast *adj* constans, firmus, stabilis; **—ly** constanter

steadily *adv* constanter, firme, magis magisque

steadiness *s* stabilitas, constantia *f*

steady *adj* stabilis, firmus; (*fig*) constans, gravis

steak *s* offa, offula *f*

steal *vt* furari; *vi* furari; **to — away** se subducĕre

stealing *s* furtum *n*

stealthily *adv* furtim

steam *s* vapor *m*

steam *vi* fumare

steed *s* equus bellator *m*

steel *s* chalybs *m*

steep *adj* arduus, praeceps, praeruptus

steep *vt* imbuĕre, madefacĕre

steeple *s* turris *f*

steepness *s* acclivitas, declivitas *f*

steer *s* juvencus *m*

steer *vt* gubernare, dirigĕre

steering *s* gubernatio *f*

stem *s* stipes *m*; (*of ship*) prora *f*

stem *vt* obsistĕre (*with dat*), cohibĕre, reprimĕre

stench *s* foetor *m*

step *s* pass·us -ūs, grad·us -ūs *m*; (*plan, measure*) ratio *f*; **flight of —s** scalae *f pl*; **— by —** gradatim, pededentim

step *vi* gradi

stepbrother *s* (*on father's side*) vitrici filius *m*; (*on mother's side*) novercae filius *m*

stepdaughter *s* privigna *f*

stepfather *s* vitricus *m*

stepmother *s* noverca *f*

stepson *s* privignus *m*

sterile *adj* sterilis

sterility *s* sterilitas *f*

sterling *adj* verus, bonus

stern *adj* durus, severus, torvus; **—ly** dure, severe, torve

stern *s* puppis *f*

sternness *s* severitas *f*

stew *s* carnes cum condimentis elixae *f pl*

stew *vt* lento igne coquĕre

steward *s* procurator *m*; (*of estate*) vilicus *m*

stewardship *s* procuratio *f*

stick *s* fustis *m*; (*cane*) baculum *n*

stick *vt* affigĕre; *vi* haerēre, haesitare

sticky *adj* viscosus, viscidus

stiff *adj* rigidus; (*fig*) severus, frigidus; **—ly** rigide

stiffen *vt* rigidum facĕre; (*with starch*) amylare; *vi* obdurescĕre

stifle *vt* suffocare; (*fig*) restinguĕre

stigma *n* stigma *n*, nota *f*

stigmatize *vt* notare

still *adj* quietus, immotus, tranquillus

still *adv* (*adversative*) tamen, nihilominus; (*yet*) adhuc, etiamnum; (*with comparatives*) etiam

still *vt* pacare, sedare

stillborn *adj* abortivus

stillness *s* silentium *n*, taciturnitas *f*

stilts *s* grallae *f pl*

stimulant *s* irritamentum *n*, stimulus *m*

stimulate *vt* stimulare, excitare

stimulus *s* stimulus *m*

sting *s* aculeus *m*; (*fig*) (*of conscience*) angor *m*

sting *vt* pungĕre, mordēre

stinginess *s* avaritia *f*, sordes *f pl*

stingy *adj* avarus, sordidus

stink *s* foetor *m*

stink *vi* foetēre; **to — of** olēre (*with acc*)

stint *s* modus *m*

stint *vt* coercēre

stipend *s* salarium *n*, merces *f*

stipulate *vt* stipulari

stipulation *s* stipulatio, conditio, lex *f*

stir *vt* excitare; *vi* se movēre

stir *s* tumult·us -ūs *m*

stirring *adj* (*of a speech*) ardens

stitch *s* suĕre

stock *s* (*supply*) copia *f*; (*race*) stirps *f*, genus *n*; (*handle*) lignum *n*

stock *vt* instruĕre; suppeditare

stockade *s* vallum *n*

stockbroker *s* argentarius *m*

stocking *s* tibiale *n*

Stoic *s* Stoicus *m*

stoical *adj* patiens, durus; **—ly** patienter

Stoicism *s* Stoica disciplina *f*

stole *s* stola *f*

stolen *adj* furtivus

stomach *s* stomachus *m*

stomach *vt* tolerare, perferre, pati

stone *s* lapis *m*, saxum *n*

stone *vt* lapidare

stonecutter *s* lapicida, lapidarius *m*

stone quarry *s* lapidicina *f*

stony *adj* (*full of stones*) lapidosus; (*of stone*) saxeus; (*fig*) durus

stool *s* scabellum *n*

stoop *vi* proclinare; (*fig*) se summittĕre

stop *vt* sistĕre, obturare, prohibēre; *vi* subsistĕre; (*to cease*) desistĕre

stop *s* mora, pausa *f*

stopgap *s* tibicen *m*

stoppage *s* obstructio *f*, impedimentum *n*

stopper *s* obturamentum *n*

store *s* (*supply*) copia *f*; (*shop*) taberna *f*

store *vt* condĕre, reponĕre

storehouse *s* promptuarium *n*; (*for grain*) horreum *n*; (*fig*) thesaurus *m*

stork *s* ciconia *f*

storm *s* tempestas, procella *f*

storm *vt* (*mil*) expugnare; *vi* desaevire

stormy *adj* turbidus, procellosus; (*fig*) tumultuosus

story *s* narratio, fabula *f*; (*lie*) mendacium *n*; (*of house*) tabulatum *n*

storyteller *s* narrator *m*; (*liar*) mendax *m*

stout *adj* corpulentus; (*brave*) fortis; (*strong*) firmus, validus; **—ly** fortiter

stove *s* focus, caminus *m*

stow *vt* condĕre, recondĕre; *vi* **to — away** in navi delitescĕre

straddle *vi* varicare

straggle *vi* palari

straggler *s* palans *m*

straight *adj* rectus, directus

straight *adv* directo, rectā

straighten vt rectum facĕre; **to —
out** corrigĕre

straightforward adj apertus, simplex, directus

straightway adv statim

strain vt contendĕre; (muscle) luxare;
(to filter) percolare; vi eniti

strain s contentio f; (effort) labor m;
(mus) modus m

strained adj (style) arcessitus

strainer s colum n

strait adj angustus, artus

strait s fretum n; **—s** (fig) angustiae f pl

straiten vt contrahĕre, artare

strand s litus n; (of hair) floccus m

strand vt vadis illidĕre; vi impingi

strange adj insolitus, novus; mirus;
(foreign) peregrinus; **— to say** mi-
rabile dictu; **—ly** mirum in modum

strangeness s novitas f

stranger s advena, peregrinus m

strangle vt strangulare

strap s lorum n, strupus m

strapping adj robustus

stratagem s stratagema n; (trickery)
dolus m

strategic adj idoneus

strategy s consilium n

straw adj stramineus

straw s stramentum n; (for thatch)
stipula f

strawberry s fragum n

stray vi errare, aberrare

streak s linea f; (of character) vena f

streak vt lineis distinguĕre

stream s flumen n, amnis m

stream vi fluĕre, currĕre

streamer s vexillum n

street s via f; (narrow) vicus m

strength s robur n, vires f pl, nervi
m pl

strengthen vt roborare, confirmare;
munire

strenuous adj strenuus, sedulus;
—ly strenue

stress s (accent) ict·us -ūs m; (meaning) vis f, pondus n; (effort) labor m

stress vt exprimĕre

stretch vt tendĕre, extendĕre, distendĕre; **to — oneself** pandiculari;
to — out (hands) porrigĕre; (to
lengthen) producĕre; vi extendi, dis-
tendi; produci; patescĕre

stretch s spatium n

stretcher s lecticula f

strew vt spargĕre, sternĕre

stricken adj saucius, vulneratus

strict adj (severe) severus, rigidus;
(accurate) accuratus, exactus, diligens; **—ly** severe, diligenter; **—ly
speaking** immo

stricture s vituperatio f

stride s grad·us -ūs, pass·us -ūs m

stride vi varicare

strife s jurgium n, lis, pugna, discordia f

strike vt ferire, pulsare, percutĕre;
to — fear into incutĕre in (with
acc)

strike s cessatio operis f; (blow)
ict·us -ūs m

strikingly adv mirum in modum

string s filum n; (for bow) nervus m;
(for musical instrument) chorda f;
(fig) series f

string vt (bow) intendĕre

stringent adj severus

stringy adj fibratus

strip vt spoliare; denudare; (clothes)
exuĕre

strip s (of cloth) lacinia f; (of paper)
scheda f; (of land) spatium n

stripe s linea f; (blow) ict·us -ūs m;
(mark of blow) vibex f; (on toga)
clavus m

strive vi (e)niti, moliri, conari, laborare; **to — for** anniti, sectari

striving s contentio f, nis·us -ūs m

stroke s ict·us -ūs m, plaga f; (with
pen) pennae duct·us -ūs f; (of oar)
puls·us -ūs m

stroke vt (per)mulcēre

stroll s ambulatio f

stroll vi perambulare, spatiari

strong adj robustus, firmus, validus;
(smell) gravis; (powerful) potens;
(feeling) acer; (language) vehemens;
—ly valide, graviter, vehementer,
acriter

stronghold s arx f, castellum n

structure s structura f; (building)
aedificium n

struggle s certamen n, pugna f;
(fig) luctatio f

struggle vi contendĕre, (ob)niti, luctari

strumpet s scortum n, meretrix f

strut s incess·us -ūs m

strut vi turgēre, tumēre

stubble s stipula f

stubborn adj obstinatus, contumax,
pervicax; **—ly** obstinate, pervica-
citer

stubbornness s obstinatus animus
m, obstinatio, pertinacia f

stud s clavus m; equus admissarius m

student s discipulus m

studied adj meditatus; (style) exquisitus

studious adj studiosus discendi;
(careful) attentus

study s studium n; (room) bibliotheca f

study vt studēre (with dat); (to scrutinize) perscrutari

stuff s materia, materies f

stuff vt farcire; (with food) saginare

stuffing s (in cooking) fartum n; (in
upholstery) tomentum n

stultify vt ad irritum redigĕre

stumble vi offendĕre; **to — upon**
incidĕre in (with acc)

stumbling block s offensio f

stump s truncus, caudex m

stun vt stupefacĕre; (fig) confundĕre,
obstupefacĕre

stunted adj curtus

stupefy vt obstupefacĕre, perturbare

stupendous adj mirus, admirabilis

stupid adj stupidus, fatuus; **—ly**
stupide

stupidity s stupiditas, fatuitas f

stupor s stupor, torpor m

sturdiness s robur n, firmitas f

sturdy adj robustus, validus, firmus

sturgeon s acipenser m
stutter vi balbutire
sty s suile n, hara f
style s (literary) scribendi genus n; (rhetorical) dicendi genus n; (architectural) rit·us -ūs m; (of dress) habit·us -ūs m
style vt appellare, nominare
stylish adj speciosus, affectatus, elegans
suave adj suavis, urbanus
subdivide vt iterum dividĕre
subdivision s pars f
subdue vt subjicĕre, domare, vincĕre
subject adj — to obnoxius (with dat), subjectus (with dat)
subject s homo subditus m; civis m; (topic) materia f, argumentum n; (matter) res f; (gram) subjectum n
subject vt subjicĕre, subigĕre
subjection s servitus f; patientia f
subjective adj proprius
subjugate vt subigĕre, domare
subjunctive s subjunctivus modus m
sublime adj sublimis, excelsus; —ly excelse
sublimity s elatio, sublimitas f
submerge vt demergĕre, inundare; vi se demergĕre
submission s obsequium, servitium n, reverentia f
submissive adj summissus, obsequiosus; —ly summisse
submit vt (e.g., a proposal) referre; vi se dedĕre; to — to obtemperare (with dat)
subordinate vt subjicĕre, supponĕre
subordinate adj secundus, subjectus, inferior
suborn vt subornare
subscribe vt (to contribute) conferre; vi to — to assentiri (with dat)
subscriber s subscriptor m
subscription s collatio f
subsequent adj sequens, posterior, serior; —ly postea, deinde
subserve vt subvenire (with dat)
subservient adj obsequiosus
subside vi desidĕre; (of wind) cadĕre; (of passion) defervescĕre
subsidiary adj secundus
subsidy s subsidium n, collatio f, vectigal n
subsist vi subsistĕre
subsistence s vict·us -ūs m
substance s substantia f; res f; (gist) summa f; (wealth) opes f pl
substantial adj solidus, firmus; (real) verus; (rich) opulentus; (important) magnus; —ly magnā ex parte, re
substantiate vt confirmare
substantive s nomen, substantivum n
substitute s vicarius m
substitute vt supponĕre
substitution s substitutio f
subterfuge s effugium n, praetext·us -ūs m
subterranean adj subterraneus
subtle adj subtilis, tenuis; (shrewd) acutus, vafer
subtlety s subtilitas, tenuitas f;

(cleverness) astutia f
subtract vt subtrahĕre, detrahĕre, deducĕre
subtraction s detractio, deductio f
suburb s suburbium n
suburban adj suburbanus
subversion s eversio f
subversive adj seditiosus
subvert vt evertĕre
succeed vt succedĕre (with dat), insequi, excipĕre; vi (of persons) rem bene gerĕre; (of activities) prospere evenire, succedĕre
success s success·us -ūs, bonus event·us -ūs m, res secundae f pl
successful adj fortunatus, prosper; —ly fortunate, prospere
succession s successio f; (series) series f
successive adj continuus; —ly in ordine, continenter
successor s successor m
succinct adj succinctus, brevis, pressus; —ly presse
succor s subsidium, auxilium n
succor vt succurrĕre (with dat), subvenire (with dat)
succulence s sucus m
succulent adj sucosus, suculentus
succumb vi succumbĕre
such adj talis; — ... as talis ... qualis
suck vt sugĕre; to — in sorbĕre; to — up exsorbĕre, ebibĕre; vi ubera ducĕre
suckle vt nutricari
suction s suct·us -ūs m
sudden adj subitus, repentinus, inexpectatus; —ly subito, repente
sue vt litem intendĕre (with dat); vi to — for orare, rogare, petĕre
suffer vt pati, tolerare, sustinĕre; vi dolēre, affici
sufferable adj tolerabilis, tolerandus
suffering s dolor m
suffice vi sufficĕre, satis esse
sufficient adj satis (with genit); —ly satis
suffocate vt suffocare
suffocation s suffocatio f
suffrage s suffragium n
suffuse vt suffundĕre
suffusion s suffusio f
sugar s saccharum n
sugar vt saccharo condire
sugar cane s arundo sacchari f
suggest vt suggerĕre, subjicĕre, admonēre
suggestion s suggestio, admonitio f
suicide s suicidium n; to commit — sibi mortem consciscĕre
suit s lis, causa f; (clothes) vestit·us -ūs m
suit vt accommodare; convenire (with dat), congruĕre (with dat)
suitable adj aptus, idoneus, congruus
suite s comitat·us -ūs m; (apartment) conclave n
suitor s procus m
sulfur s sulfur n
sulk vi aegre ferre
sulky adj morosus

sullen *adj* torvus, tetricus, morosus;
—**ly** morose

sully *vt* inquinare, contaminare

sultry *adj* aestuosus, torridus

sum *s* summa *f*

sum *vt* to — up computare; (*to summarize*) summatim describĕre, breviter repetĕre

summarily *adj* breviter, summatim

summarize *vt* summatim describĕre

summary *adj* subitus, brevis

summary *s* epitome *f*, summarium *n*

summer *adj* aestivus

summer *s* aestas *f*

summit *s* culmen *n*; (*fig*) fastigium *n*

summon *vt* arcessĕre; (*a meeting*) convocare; to — up courage animum erigĕre, animum colligĕre

summons *s* vocatio *f*

sumptuary *adj* sumptuarius

sumptuous *adj* sumptuosus, lautus; —**ly** sumptuose

sun *s* sol *m*

sunbeam *s* radius *m*

sunburnt *adj* adustus

Sunday *s* Dominica *f*

sunder *vt* separare, sejungĕre

sundial *s* solarium *n*

sundry *adj* diversi, varii

sunlight *s* sol *m*

sunny *adj* apricus

sunrise *s* solis ort·us -ūs *m*

sunset *s* solis occas·us -ūs *m*

sunshine *s* sol *m*

sup *vi* cenare

superabundant *adj* nimius; —**ly** satis superque

superannuated *adj* emeritus

superb *adj* magnificus; —**ly** magnifice

supercilious *adj* superbus, arrogans

superficial *adj* levis; —**ly** leviter

superfluity *s* redundantia *f*

superfluous *adj* superfluus, supervacaneus

superhuman *adj* divinus, major quam humanus

superintend *vt* praeesse (*with dat*), administrare

superintendence *s* cura, curatio *f*

superintendent *s* praefectus, curator *m*

superior *adj* superior, melior; to be — to praestare (*with dat*)

superior *s* praepositus *m*

superiority *s* praestantia *f*

superlative *adj* eximius; (*gram*) superlativus

supernatural *adj* divinus

supernumerary *adj* ascripticius, accensus

supersede *vt* succedĕre (*with dat*)

superstition *s* superstitio *f*

superstitious *adj* superstitiosus

supervise *vt* procurare

supervision *s* cura, curatio *f*

supine *adj* supinus; —**ly** supine

supper *s* cena *f*; after — cenatus

supple *adj* flexibilis, flexilis

supplement *s* supplementum *n*, appendix *f*

supplement *vt* amplificare

suppliant *s* supplex *m & f*

supplicate *vt* supplicare

supplication *s* supplicatio, obsecratio *f*

supply *s* copia *f*; **supplies** (*mil*) commeat·us -ūs *m*

supply *vt* praebēre, suppeditare

support *s* (*prop*) fulcrum *n*; (*help*) subsidium *n*; (*maintenance*) alimentum *n*

support *vt* (*to hold up*) fulcire, sustinēre; (*to help*) adjuvare; (*to maintain*) alĕre

supportable *adj* tolerabilis

supporter *s* adjutor, fautor *m*

suppose *vt* opinari, putare, credĕre

supposition *s* opinio *f*

supremacy *s* dominat·us -ūs, principat·us -ūs *m*, imperium *n*

supreme *adj* supremus, summus; —**ly** unice, maxime

sure *adj* certus; (*faithful*) fidus; (*safe*) tutus; —**ly** certe, scilicet, profecto

surety *s* vas *n*; (*person*) sponsor *m*

surf *s* aest·us -ūs *m*

surface *s* superficies *f*; the — of the sea summum mare *n*

surfeit *s* satietas *f*; (*fig*) taedium *n*

surfeit *vt* saturare; (*fig*) satiare

surge *s* fluct·us -ūs, aest·us -ūs *m*

surge *vi* tumescĕre, surgĕre; to — forward proruĕre

surgeon *s* chirurgus *m*

surgery *s* chirurgia *f*

surgical *adj* chirurgicus

surly *adj* morosus, difficilis

surmise *s* conjectura *f*

surmise *vt* conjicĕre, suspicari

surmount *vt* superare, vincĕre

surmountable *adj* superabilis

surname *s* cognomen *n*

surpass *vt* superare, excedĕre, antecedĕre

surplus *s* reliquum, residuum *n*

surprise *s* (ad)miratio *f*; to take by — deprehendĕre

surprise *vt* admirationem movēre (*with dat*); (*mil*) opprimĕre; to be surprised at mirari, admirari

surprising *adj* mirus, mirabilis; inexpectatus; —**ly** mire, mirabiliter

surrender *s* (*mil*) deditio *f*; (*law*) cessio *f*

surrender *vt* dedĕre, tradĕre, cedĕre; *vi* se tradĕre, se dedĕre

surreptitious *adj* furtivus, clandestinus; —**ly** furtim, clam

surround *vt* circumdare, circumvenire, cingĕre

surroundings *s* vicinia *f*

survey *s* inspectio, contemplatio *f*; (*of land*) mensura *f*

survey *vt* inspicĕre, contemplari; (*land*) permetiri

surveyor *s* agrimensor, metator *m*

survival *s* salus *f*

survive *vt* supervivĕre (*with dat*); *vi* superstes esse

survivor *s* superstes *m & f*

susceptible *adj* mollis

suspect *vt* suspicari, suspicĕre; to be suspected of in suspicionem venire quasi (*with verb in subjunctive*)

suspend *vt* suspendĕre, intermittĕre, differre

suspense *s* dubitatio *f*; **in —** suspensus

suspension *s* suspensio, dilatio *f*

suspicion *s* suspicio *f*; **to throw — on** suspicionem adjungĕre ad (*with acc*)

suspicious *adj* suspicax; (*suspected*) suspectus; **—ly** suspiciose

sustain *vt* sustinēre, sustentare; (*hardships, etc.*) ferre

sustenance *s* vict·us -ūs *m*

swab *s* peniculus *m*

swab *vt* detergēre

swaddling clothes *s* fasciae *f pl*, incunabula *n pl*

swagger *vi* se jactare

swaggerer *s* homo gloriosus *m*

swallow *s* (*bird*) hirundo *f*

swallow *vt* vorare, sorbēre; **to — up** devorare, absorbēre

swamp *s* palus *f*

swamp *vt* demergĕre

swampy *adj* paludosus

swan *s* cygnus *m*

swank *adj* lautus

swarm *s* examen *n*

swarm *vi* congregari

swarthy *adj* fuscus

swathe *s* fascia *f*

sway *s* dicio, dominatio *f*, imperium *n*

sway *vt* regĕre, movēre; *vi* vacillare

swear *vt* jurare; **to — in** sacramento adigĕre, sacramento rogare; *vi* jurare

sweat *s* sudor *m*

sweat *vi* sudare

sweep *vt* verrĕre; **to — out** everrĕre; *vi* **to — by** (*to dash by*) praetervolare; **to — over** (*to move quickly over*) percurrĕre

sweet *adj* dulcis, suavis; (*fig*) blandus, jucundus; **—ly** suaviter

sweeten *vt* dulcem facĕre; (*fig*) lenire, mulcēre

sweetheart *s* deliciae *f pl*, amica *f*

sweetness *s* dulcedo, suavitas *f*

sweets *s* cuppedia *n pl*

swell *s* aest·us -ūs *m*, unda *f*

swell *vt* inflare, tumefacĕre; *vi* tumēre

swelling *s* tumor *m*

swelter *vi* aestu laborare

swerve *vi* aberrare, vagari

swift *adj* celer, velox; **—ly** celeriter, velociter

swiftness *s* celeritas, velocitas *f*

swim *vi* natare, nare

swimmer *s* natator *m*

swimming *s* natatio *f*; (*of head*) vertigo *f*

swimming pool *s* piscina *f*

swindle *vt* fraudare, circumvenire

swindle *s* fraus *f*

swindler *s* fraudator *m*

swine *s* sus *m & f*

swineherd *s* suarius *m*

swing *s* oscillatio *f*

swing *vt* librare; *vi* oscillare

switch *s* (*stick*) virga, virgula *f*; (*change*) commutatio *f*

switch *vt* (*to flog*) flagellare; (*to change*) (com)mutare

swoon *vi* intermori, collabi

swoop *s* impet·us -ūs *m*

swoop *vi* incurrĕre; **to — down on** involare in (*with acc*)

sword *s* gladius, ensis *m*, ferrum *n*; **with fire and —** ferro ignique

sycamore *s* sycomorus *f*

sycophant *s* sycophanta, assentator *m*

syllable *s* syllaba *f*

syllogism *s* syllogismus *m*, ratiocinatio *f*

symbol *s* signum, symbolum *n*

symbolical *adj* symbolicus; **—ly** symbolice

symmetrical *adj* congruens, concinnus

symmetry *s* symmetria, concinnitas *f*

sympathetic *adj* concors, misericors

sympathize *vi* consentire; **to — with** miserēri (*with genit*)

sympathy *s* consens·us -ūs *m*, misericordia, concordia *f*

symphony *s* symphonia *f*, concent·us -ūs *m*

symptom *s* indicium, signum *n*

synagogue *s* synagoga *f*

syndicate *s* societas *f*

synonym *s* verbum idem declarans *n*

synonymous *adj* idem declarans, idem valens

synopsis *s* breviarium *n*, epitome *f*

syntax *s* syntaxis *f*

system *s* ratio, disciplina *f*

systematic *adj* ordinatus; **—ally** ratione, ordine

T

tab *vt* designare, notare

tabernacle *s* tabernaculum *n*

table *s* mensa *f*; (*list*) index *m*, tabula *f*

tablecloth *s* mantele *n*

table napkin *s* mappa *f*

tablet *s* tabula, tabella *f*, album *n*

tacit *adj* tacitus; **—ly** tacite

taciturn *adj* taciturnus

tack *s* clavulus *m*

tack *vt* **to — on** assuĕre, affigĕre; *vi* (*of ships*) reciprocari

tact *s* judicium *n*, dexteritas *f*

tactful *adj* prudens, dexter; **—ly** prudenter, dextere

tactician *s* rei militaris peritus *m*

tactics *s* res militaris, belli ratio *f*

tadpole *s* ranunculus *m*

tag *s* appendicula *f*

tail *s* cauda *f*

tailor *s* vestitor, textor *m*

taint *s* contagio *f*, vitium *n*

taint *vt* inficĕre, contaminare; (*fig*) corrumpĕre

take *vt* capĕre, sumĕre, accipĕre; to — away demĕre, auferre, adimĕre; to — down (*in writing*) exscribĕre; to — for habēre pro (*with abl*); to — hold of prehendĕre; to — in (*e.g., a guest*) recipĕre; (*through deception*) decipĕre; to — in hand suscipĕre; to — off exuĕre; to — out eximĕre; (*from storage*) promĕre; to — up suscipĕre; to — upon oneself sibi sumĕre; *vi* to — after similis esse (*with genit or dat*); to — off (*to depart*) abire; to — to amare, diligĕre

tale *s* fabula, narratio *f*

talent *s* talentum *n*; (*fig*) ingenium *n*

talented *adj* ingeniosus

talk *s* sermo *m*, colloquium *n*; idle — nugae *f pl*

talk *vi* loqui; to — with colloqui cum (*with abl*)

talkative *adj* loquax, garrulus

talker *s* (*idle*) gerro *m*

tall *adj* altus, celsus, procerus

tallow *s* sebum *n*

tally *s* tessera *f*

tally *vi* convenire

talon *s* unguis *m*

tambourine *s* tympanum *n*

tame *adj* cicur, mansuetus, domitus; —ly mansuete, leniter

tame *vt* domare, mansuefacĕre

tamer *s* domitor *m*

tamper *vi* to — with (*persons*) sollicitare; (*writings*) depravare

tan *vt* (*by sun*) adurĕre; (*hides*) perficĕre

tangible *adj* tractabilis

tangle *s* implicatio *f*, nodus *m*

tangle *vt* implicare

tank *s* lac·us -ūs *m*

tankard *s* cantharus *m*

tantalize *vt* vexare

tantamount *adj* par

tap *s* levis ict·us -ūs *m*

tap *vt* leviter ferire; (*wine, etc.*) relinĕre

tape *s* taenia *f*

taper *s* cereus *m*

taper *vt* fastigare; *vi* fastigari

tapestry *s* aulaeum, tapete *n*

taproom *s* taberna *f*

tar *s* pix *f*

tardily *adv* tarde, lente

tardiness *s* tarditas, segnitia *f*

tardy *adj* tardus, lentus

target *s* scopus *m*

tariff *s* portorium *n*

tarnish *vt* infuscare; *vi* infuscari

tarry *vi* commorari, cunctari

tart *adj* acerbus, amarus

tart *s* scriblita *f*, crustulum *n*

task *s* pensum, opus *n*; to take to — objurgare

taste *s* (*sense*) gustat·us -ūs *m*; (*flavor*) sapor *m*; (*fig*) judicium *n*

taste *vt* (de)gustare; *vi* sapĕre

tasteful *adj* elegans; —ly eleganter

tasteless *adj* insipidus; (*fig*) insulsus, inelegans; —ly insulse

tasty *adj* sapidus, dulcis

tattered *adj* pannosus

tatters *s* panni *m pl*

taunt *s* convicium *n*

taunt *vt* exprobrare

taut *adj* intentus

tavern *s* taberna, caupona *f*

tavern keeper *s* caupo *m*

tawdry *adj* fucatus, vilis

tawny *adj* fulvus

tax *s* vectigal, tributum *n*

tax *vt* vectigal imponĕre (*with dat*)

taxable *adj* vectigalis, stipendiarius

taxation *s* vectigalia *n pl*

tax collector *s* exactor *m*

teach *vt* docēre, instituĕre, erudire

teachable *adj* docilis

teacher *s* magister, praeceptor *m*; (*of primary school*) litterator *m*; (*of secondary school*) grammaticus *m*; (*of rhetoric*) rhetor *m*

teaching *s* institutio, eruditio *f*

team *s* jugales *m pl*; (*of animals*) jugum *n*

tear *s* lacrima *f*, flet·us -ūs *m*; (*a rent*) scissura *f*

tear *vt* scindĕre; to — apart discindĕre; to — in pieces dilacerare, dilaniare; to — off abscindĕre; to — open rescindĕre; to — out evellĕre; to — up convellĕre

tease *vt* vexare, ludĕre

teat *s* mamma *f*

technical *adj* (*term*) proprius; technicus, artificialis

technique *s* ars *f*

technology *s* officinarum artes *f pl*

tedious *adj* molestus; —ly moleste

tedium *s* taedium *n*

teem *vi* scatēre, redundare

teethe *vi* dentire

teething *s* dentitio *f*

tell *vt* narrare, memorare, referre; (*to order*) imperare (*with dat*), jubēre; — me the truth dic mihi verum

teller *s* numerator *m*

temerity *s* temeritas *f*

temper *s* temperatio *f*, animus *m*, ingenium *n*; (*bad*) iracundia *f*

temper *vt* temperare; (*fig*) lenire

temperament *s* animus *m*

temperance *s* temperantia *f*

temperate *adj* temperatus, moderatus, sobrius; —ly temperanter, sobrie

temperature *s* calor *m*, caloris grad·us -ūs *m*

tempest *s* tempestas *f*

tempestuous *adj* turbulentus, procellosus

temple *s* templum *n*, aedes *f*; (*of forehead*) tempus *n*

temporal *adj* humanus; profanus

temporarily *adv* ad tempus

temporary *adj* brevis

temporize *vi* tergiversari

tempt *vt* temptare, illicĕre

temptation *s* illecebra *f*

ten *adj* decem; — times decies

tenable *adj* defensibilis, stabilis

tenacious *adj* tenax, pertinax; **—ly** tenaciter, pertinaciter

tenacity *s* tenacitas, pertinacia *f*

tenancy *s* conductio *f*

tenant *s* conductor, colonus, incola *m*

tend *vt* curare; *vi* tendĕre, spectare

tendency *s* inclinatio *f*

tender *adj* tener, mollis; **—ly** tenere, indulgenter

tender *vt* offerre

tenderness *s* mollitia *f*; (*affection*) indulgentia *f*

tendon *s* nervus *m*

tendril *s* (*of vine*) pampinus *m*; (*of plants*) claviculus *m*

tenement *s* conductum *n*

tenement house *s* insula *f*

tenet *s* dogma *n*

tenfold *adj* decemplex, decuplus

tennis *s* to play **—** pilā ludĕre

tennis court *s* sphaeristerium *n*

tenor *s* tenor, sensus·us -ūs *m*

tense *adj* intentus, attentus

tense *s* tempus *n*

tension *s* intentio *f*

tent *s* tentorium, tabernaculum *n*

tentative *adj* tentans

tenth *adj* decimus

tenth *s* decima pars *f*

tenuous *adj* tenuis, rarus

tenure *s* possessio *f*

tepid *adj* tepidus

term *s* (*word*) verbum *n*; (*limit*) terminus *m*; (*condition*) condicio, lex *f*

terminate *vt* terminare, finire; *vi* terminari, desinĕre; (*of words*) cadĕre

termination *s* terminatio *f*, finis, exit·us -ūs *m*

terrace *s* ambulatio *f*

terrestrial *adj* terrestris, terrenus

terrible *adj* terribilis

terribly *adv* horrendum in modum

terrific *adj* terrificus, terrens, formidabilis

terrify *vt* terrēre, perterrēre

territory *s* regio *f*, ager *m*, fines *m pl*

terror *s* terror *m*, formido *f*

terse *adj* brevis, pressus; **—ly** presse

test *s* probatio *f*, experimentum *n*

test *vt* probare, experiri

testament *s* testamentum *n*

testamentary *adj* testamentarius

testator *s* testator *m*

testify *vt* testificari, testari

testimonial *s* laudatio *f*

testimony *s* testimonium *n*

testy *adj* stomachosus, obstinatus, morosus

tether *s* retinaculum *n*

tether *vt* religare

text *s* verba *n pl*

textbook *s* enchiridion *n*

textile *adj* textilis

texture *s* textura *f*

than *adv* quam; atque, ac

thank *vt* gratias agĕre (*with dat*)

thankful *adj* gratus; **—ly** grate

thankless *adj* ingratus; **—ly** ingrate

thanks *s* gratiae, grates *f pl*

thanks *interj* gratias!

thanksgiving *s* grates *f pl*, gratula-

tio *f*; (*public act*) supplicatio *f*

that *adj* ille, is, iste

that *pron demonstrative* ille, is, iste; *pron rel* qui

that *conj* (*purpose, result, command*) ut; (*after verbs of fearing*) ne

thatch *s* stramentum *n*

thatch *vt* stramento tegĕre

thaw *vt* (dis)solvĕre; *vi* tabescĕre

the *article, not expressed in Latin*

the *adv* (*with comparatives*) **the . . .** the quo . . . eo

theater *s* theatrum *n*

theatrical *adj* scenicus, theatralis

thee *pron* te; **of —** de te; **to — tibi**; **with —** tecum

theft *s* furtum *n*

their *adj* illorum, eorum, istorum; **— own** suus

them *pron* eos, illos, istos; **to — eis,** illis, istis

theme *s* thema, argumentum *n*

themselves *pron reflex* se; **to — sibi**; **with —** secum; *pron intensive* ipsi

then *adv* (*at that time*) tum, tunc; (*after that*) deinde, inde; (*therefore*) igitur, ergo; **now and —** interdum, nonnumquam

thence *adv* inde, illinc; (*therefore*) ex eo, exinde

thenceforth *adv* ex eo tempore, dehinc

theologian *s* theologus *m*

theological *adj* theologicus

theology *s* theologia *f*

theoretical *adj* contemplativus

theory *s* ratio *f*

there *adv* ibi, illic; (*thither*) illuc; **— are** sunt; **— is** est

thereabouts *adv* circa, circiter, fere

thereafter *adv* deinde, postea

thereby *adv* eā re, eo

therefore *adv* itaque, igitur, idcirco, ergo

therefrom *adv* exinde, ex eo

therein *adv* in eo, in ea re

thereupon *adv* exinde, subinde

thesis *s* thesis *f*, propositum *n*

they *pron* ii, illi, isti

thick *adj* densus, spissus; **—ly** dense

thicken *vt* densare, spissare; *vi* concrescĕre

thicket *s* dumetum, fruticetum *n*

thickness *s* crassitudo *f*

thief *s* fur *m*

thievery *s* furtum *n*

thigh *s* femur *n*

thin *adj* tenuis, exilis, rarus; (*lean*) macer; **—ly** tenuiter, rare

thin *vt* attenuare; **to — out** rarefacĕre

thine *adj* tuus

thine *pron* tuus

thing *s* res *f*; **—s** (*possessions*) bona *n pl*; (*clothes*) vestimenta *n pl*

think *vt* cogitare; (*to believe, imagine, etc.*) putare, credĕre, opinari; **to — over** in mente agitare; *vi* **to — highly of** magni habēre

thinker *s* philosophus *m*

thinking *s* cogitatio *f*

thinness *s* tenuitas, raritudo *f*; (*of person*) macies *f*

third *adj* tertius; **—ly** tertio
third *s* tertia pars *f*
thirst *s* sitis *f*
thirst *vi* sitire; **to — for** sitire
thirstily *adv* sitienter
thirsty *adj* sitiens
thirteen *adj* tredecim, decem et tres
thirteenth *adj* tertius decimus
thirtieth *adj* tricesimus
thirty *adj* triginta
this *adj* hic
thistle *s* carduus *m*
thither *adv* illuc, istuc, eo
thong *s* lorum *n*
thorn *s* spina *f*, aculeus *m*
thorny *adj* spinosus; (*fig*) nodosus
thorough *adj* germanus, perfectus;
—ly penitus, funditus
thoroughbred *adj* generosus, genuinus
thoroughfare *s* pervium *n*, via pervia *f*
though *conj* quamquam, quamvis
thought *s* (*act and faculty*) cogitatio
f; (*product of thinking*) cogitatum *n*
thoughtful *adj* cogitabundus; providus; **—ly** anxie, provide
thoughtless *adj* inconsultus, improvidus; **—ly** temere, inconsulte
thousand *adj* mille; **a — times** millies
thousandth *adj* millesimus
thraldom *s* servitus *f*
thrall *s* servus *m*
thrash *vt* terēre; (*fig*) verberare
thrashing *s* verbera *n pl*
thread *s* filum *n*
thread *vt* inserĕre
threadbare *adj* tritus, obsoletus
threat *s* minae *f pl*, minatio *f*
threaten *vt* minari (*with dat of person*); *vi* impendĕre, imminēre
three *adj* tres; **— times** ter
threefold *adj* triplex, triplus
three-legged *adj* tripes
thresh *vt* terēre
threshing floor *s* area *f*
threshold *s* limen *n*
thrice *adv* ter
thrift *s* frugalitas, parsimonia *f*
thriftily *adv* frugaliter
thrifty *adj* parcus, frugalis
thrill *s* gaudium *n*, voluptas *f*; (*of fear*) horror *m*
thrill *vt* commovēre, percellĕre
thrilling *adj* mirus, mirabilis
thrive *vi* virēre, vigēre, valēre
thriving *adj* vegetus, prosperus
throat *s* jugulum, guttur *n*, fauces *f pl*
throb *s* palpitatio *f*, puls·us ·ūs *m*
throb *vi* palpitare
throes *s* dolor *m*
throne *s* solium *n*; (*fig*) regia dignitas *f*
throng *s* multitudo, turba, frequentia *f*
throng *vi* **to — around** stipare
throttle *vt* strangulare
through *prep* per (*with acc*); (*on account of*) ob (*with acc*), propter (*with acc*)
through *adv* *render by compound verb with* trans- *or* per-, *e.g.*, **to**

read — perlegĕre; **— and —** penitus, omnino
throughout *adv* prorsus, penitus
throughout *prep* per (*with acc*)
throw *vt* jacĕre, conjicĕre; (*esp. weapons*) mittĕre, jaculari; **to — away** abjicĕre; **to — back** rejicĕre; **to — down** dejicĕre; **to — open** patefacĕre; **to — out** ejicĕre; **to — together** conjicĕre in unum; *vi* **to — up** vomĕre
throw *s* jact·us ·ūs *m*
thrush *s* turdus *m*
thrust *s* impet·us ·ūs, ict·us ·ūs *m*
thrust *vt* trudĕre, impellĕre; (*with sword*) perfodĕre
thumb *s* pollex *m*
thump *s* percussio *f*
thump *vt* tundĕre
thunder *s* tonitr·us ·ūs *m*
thunder *vi* tonare
thunderbolt *s* fulmen *n*
thunderstruck *adj* attonitus, obstupefactus
thus *adv* ita, sic; **and —** itaque
thwart *vt* obstare (*with dat*), frustrari
thy *adj* tuus
tiara *s* diadema *n*
tick *s* (*insect*) ricinus *m*; (*clicking*) levis ict·us ·ūs *m*
ticket *s* tessera *f*
tickle *vt & vi* titillare
tickling *s* titillatio *f*
ticklish *adj* periculosus
tide *s* aest·us ·ūs *m*
tidings *s* nuntius *m*
tie *s* vinculum *n*; (*relationship*) necessitudo *f*
tie *vt* (al)ligare; (*in a knot*) nodare, nectĕre
tier *s* ordo *m*
tiger *s* tigris *m*
tight *adj* strictus, astrictus, artus; **—ly** arte
tighten *vt* astringĕre, adducĕre, contendĕre
tile *s* tegula, imbrex *f*
till *conj* dum, donec
till *prep* usque ad (*with acc*)
till *vt* colĕre
tillage *s* agricultura *f*
tiller *s* (*person*) agricola *m*; (*helm*) gubernaculum *n*
tilt *vt* proclinare
timber *s* materia *f*, lignum *n*
time *s* tempus *n*, dies *f*; (*age, period*) aetas *f*; (*leisure*) otium *n*; (*opportunity*) occasio *f*; (*interval*) intervallum, spatium *n*; (*of day*) hora *f*; **another —** alias; **at the same —** simul; **for a —** parumper; **for a long —** diu; **for some —** aliquamdiu; **from — to —** interdum; **in a short —** brevi; **in — ad tempus**; **on —** tempestive; **what — is it?** quota hora est?
timely *adj* tempestivus, opportunus
timepiece *s* horarium, horologium *n*
timid *adj* timidus
timidity *s* timiditas *f*
timorous *adj* pavidus
tin *s* stannum, plumbum album *n*
tin *adj* stanneus

tincture *s* color *m*
tinder *s* fomes *m*
tinge *vt* tingĕre, imbuĕre
tingle *vi* formicare, verminare
tinkle *vi* tinnire
tinsel *s* bractea, bracteola *f*
tip *s* cacumen, acumen *n*, apex *m*
tip *vt* praefigĕre; (*to incline*) invertĕre
tipple *vi* potare
tippler *s* potor *m*
tipsy *adj* ebriolus, temulentus
tiptoe *adv* in digitos erectus
tire *vt* fatigare, lassare; *vi* defatigari
tired *adj* fessus, lassus; **I am — of** me taedet (*with genit*); **— out** defessus
tiresome *adj* laboriosus; molestus
tissue *s* text·us -ūs *m*
titanic *adj* ingens
tithe *s* decuma *f*
title *s* titulus *m*; (*of book*) inscriptio *f*; (*of person*) appellatio, dignitas *f*; (*claim*) jus *n*
title page *s* index *m*
titter *s* ris·us -ūs *m*
to *prep commonly rendered by the dative; (motion, except with names of towns, small islands and* rus) ad (*with acc*), in (*with acc*); **— and fro** huc illuc
toad *s* bufo *m*
toast *s* (*bread*) panis tosti offula *f*; (*health*) propinatio *f*; **to drink a — to** propinare (*with dat*)
toast *vt* torrēre; (*in drinking*) propinare (*with dat*)
today *adv* hodie
today *s* hodiernus dies *m*
toe *s* digitus *m*
together *adv* simul, unā
toil *s* labor *m*, opera *f*
toil *vi* laborare
toilsome *adj* laboriosus, operosus
token *s* signum, pignus, indicium *n*
tolerable *adj* tolerabilis; mediocris
tolerably *adv* tolerabiliter; mediocriter
tolerance *s* patientia *f*
tolerant *adj* tolerans, indulgens, patiens; **—ly** indulgenter
tolerate *vt* tolerare, ferre
toleration *s* toleratio, indulgentia, patientia *f*
toll *s* vectigal *n*; (*at ports*) portorium *n*
toll collector *s* exactor, portitor *m*
tomb *s* sepulcrum *n*
tombstone *s* lapis, cippus *m*
tomorrow *adv* cras
tomorrow *s* crastinus dies *m*; **the day after —** perendie
tone *s* sonus *m*, vox *f*; (*in painting*) color *m*
tongs *s* forceps *m* & *f*
tongue *s* lingua *f*; (*of shoe*) ligula *f*; (*pole of carriage*) temo *m*
tonsils *s* tonsillae *f pl*
too *adv* nimis, nimium; (*also*) quoque, insuper
tool *s* instrumentum *n*; (*dupe*) minister *m*
tooth *s* dens *m*; **— and nail** totis viribus
toothache *s* dentium dolor *m*
toothless *adj* edentulus

toothpick *s* dentiscalpium *n*
tooth powder *s* dentifricium *n*
top *adj* summus
top *s* vertex, apex *m*; (*of tree*) cacumen *n*; (*of house*) fastigium *n*; (*toy*) turbo *m*; **the — of the mountain** summus mons *m*
top *vt* superare
topic *s* res *f*, argumentum *n*
topmost *adj* summus
topography *s* regionum descriptio *f*
topple *vt* evertĕre; *vi* titubare
torch *s* fax *f*
torment *s* tormentum *n*, cruciat·us -ūs *m*
torment *vt* (ex)cruciare, torquēre
tormenter *s* tortor *m*
torpid *adj* torpens; **to be —** torpēre
torpor *s* torpor *m*
torrent *s* torrens *m*
torrid *adj* torridus
tortoise *s* testudo *f*
tortoise shell *s* testudo *f*
torture *s* tormentum *n*, cruciat·us -ūs *m*
torture *vt* torquēre, (ex)cruciare
torturer *s* cruciator, tortor *m*
toss *s* jact·us -ūs *m*
toss *vt* jactare; *vi* jactari
total *adj* totus, universus; **—ly** omnino, prorsus
totality *s* summa, universitas *f*
totter *vi* vacillare, titubare
touch *vt* tangĕre, attingĕre; (*to stir emotionally*) movēre, commovēre, afficĕre; *vi* inter se contingĕre; **to — on** attingĕre
touch *s* (con)tact·us -ūs *m*, tactio *f*
touching *adj* mollis, flexanimus
touchstone *s* (*fig*) obrussa *f*
touchy *adj* stomachosus
tough *adj* durus, lentus; (*fig*) strenuus; difficilis
tour *s* (*rounds*) circuit·us -ūs *m*; (*abroad*) peregrinatio *f*
tourist *s* peregrinator *m*
tournament *s* certamen *n*
tow *s* stuppa *f*
tow *vt* remulco trahĕre
toward *prep* versus (*with acc*), ad (*with acc*); (*of feelings*) erga (*with acc*), in (*with acc*); (*of time*) sub (*with acc*)
towel *s* mantele *n*; sudarium *n*
tower *s* turris *f*
tower *vi* **to — over** imminēre (*with dat*)
towering *adj* excelsus, arduus
towline *s* remulcum *n*
town *s* urbs *f*; (*fortified*) oppidum *n*
town hall *s* curia *f*
townsman *s* oppidanus *m*
toy *s* crepundia *n pl*, oblectamentum *n*
trace *s* vestigium *n*; (*for horse*) helcium *n*
trace *vt* delinēre, describĕre; indagare, investigare; **to — back** repetĕre
track *s* vestigium *n*; (*path*) semita *f*, calles *m*
track *vt* investigare
trackless *adj* avius, invius

tract s (*of land*) tract·us -ūs *m*, regio *f*; (*treatise*) tract·us -ūs *m*

tractable *adj* tractabilis, docilis, obsequiosus

trade s mercatura *f*, commercium *n*; (*calling*) ars *f*, quaest·us -ūs *m*

trade *vt* commutare; *vi* negotiari, mercaturas facĕre

trader s mercator *m*

tradesman s opifex *m*

tradition s traditio, fama, memoria *f*, mos majorum *m*

traditional *adj* patrius, a majoribus traditus

traduce *vt* calumniari, infamare

traffic s commercium *n*; (*on street*) vehicula *n pl*

tragedian s (*playwright*) tragoedus, tragicus poeta *m*; (*actor*) tragicus actor *m*

tragedy s tragoedia *f*

tragic *adj* tragicus; (*fig*) tristis, miserabilis; **—ally** tragice; miserabiliter

trail *vt* investigare; (*to drag*) trahĕre; *vi* trahi, verrēre

trail s vestigium *n*; (*path*) calles *m*

train s (*line*) series *f*, ordo *m*; (*of robe*) instita *f*; (*retinue*) comitat·us -ūs *m*; (*of army*) impedimenta *n pl*

train *vt* educare, instruĕre, assuefacĕre

trainer s lanista, aliptes *m*

training s disciplina, institutio *f*; (*practice*) exercitatio *f*

trait s mos *m*

traitor s proditor *m*

traitorous *adj* perfidus; **—ly** perfide

trammel *vt* impedire, vincire, irretire

tramp s vagabundus, homo vagus *m*; (*of feet*) puls·us -ūs *m*

tramp *vi* gradi

trample *vt* calcare, conculcare; *vi* to **— on** obterĕre, proterĕre, opprimĕre

trance s stupor *m*, ecstasis *f*

tranquil *adj* tranquillus; **—ly** tranquille

tranquility s tranquillitas *f*, tranquillus animus *m*

tranquilize *vt* tranquillare

transact *vt* transigĕre, gerēre

transaction s negotium *n*, res *f*

transcend *vt* superare, vincĕre

transcendental *adj* sublimis, divinus

transcribe *vt* transcribĕre

transcription s transcriptio *f*

transfer s translatio *f*; (*of property*) alienatio *f*

transfer *vt* transferre; (*property*) abalienare

transference s translatio *f*

transfigure *vt* tranfigurare

transform *vt* vertĕre, commutare

transformation s commutatio *f*

transgress *vt* violare, perfringĕre; *vi* peccare, delinquĕre

transgression s violatio *f*, delictum *n*

transgressor s violator, maleficus *m*

transient *adj* transitorius, brevis, fluxus

transition s transitio *f*, transit·us -ūs *m*

transitive *adj* transitivus; **—ly** transitive

transitory *adj* transitorius, brevis, fluxus

translate *vt* vertĕre, transferre

translation s translata *n pl*

translator s interpres *m*

transmission s transmissio *f*

transmit *vt* transmittĕre

transmutation s transmutatio *f*

transparent *adj* pellucidus; (*fig*) perspicuus

transpire *vi* perspirare, emanare; (*to happen*) evenire

transplant *vt* transferre

transport *vt* transportare, transvehĕre

transport s vectura *f*; (*ship*) navigium vectorium *n*, navis oneraria *f*; (*rapture*) sublimitas *f*

transportation s vectura *f*

transpose *vt* transponĕre

transposition s transpositio, trajectio *f*

trap s laqueus *m*, pedica *f*; (*fig*) insidiae *f pl*; **to lay a —** insidiari

trap *vt* (*to snare*) irretire; (*fig*) inlaqueare

trappings s ornamenta *n pl*, apparat·us -ūs *m*; (*of horse*) phalerae *f pl*

trash s scruta *n pl*; (*fig*) nugae *f pl*

trashy *adj* vilis; obscenus

travel *vi* iter facĕre; **to — abroad** peregrinari

traveler s viator, peregrinator *m*

traverse *vt* transire, peragrare, lustrare

travesty s perversa imitatio *f*

tray s ferculum *n*, trulla *f*

treacherous *adj* perfidus, dolosus; **—ly** perfidiose

treachery s perfidia *f*

tread *vt* calcare; *vi* incedĕre

tread s grad·us -ūs, incess·us -ūs *m*, vestigium *n*

treason s perduellio, proditio *f*

treasonable *adj* perfidus, proditorius

treasure s thesaurus *m*

treasure *vt* fovēre, magni aestimare

treasurer s aerarii praefectus *m*

treasury s aerarium *n*, fiscus *m*

treat *vt* uti (*with abl*), tractare; (*patient*) curare; (*topic*) tractare; (*to entertain*) invitare

treatise s libellus *m*, dissertatio *f*

treatment s tractatio *f*; (*by doctor*) curatio *f*

treaty s foedus, pactum *n*; **to make a —** foedus icĕre

treble *adj* triplex, triplus; (*of sound*) acutus

treble *vt* triplicare

tree s arbor *f*

trellis s clathrus *m*

tremble *vi* tremĕre, tremiscĕre

trembling *adj* tremulus

trembling s trepidatio *f*

tremendous *adj* immanis, ingens, vastus; **—ly** valde, maxime

tremulous *adj* tremulus, vacillans

trench s fossa *f*

trespass *vt* violare, offendĕre; *vi* delinquĕre

trespass *s* violatio, culpa *f*

tress *s* crinis, cirrus *m*

trestle *s* fulcimentum *n*

trial *s* tentatio, experientia *f*; *(test)* probatio *f*; *(trouble)* labor *m*; *(law)* judicium *n*, quaestio *f*

triangle *s* triangulum *n*

triangular *adj* triangulus, triquetrus

tribe *s* trib·us ·ūs *f*

tribulation *s* tribulatio, afflictio *f*

tribunal *s* *(raised platform)* tribunal *n*; *(court)* judicium *n*

tribune *s* tribunus *m*

tribuneship *s* tribunat·us ·ūs *m*

tributary *adj* vectigalis, stipendiarius

tributary *s* amnis in alium influens *m*

tribute *s* tributum, vectigal *n*

trick *s* dolus *m*, artificium *n*, fraus, ars *f*

trick *vt* fallĕre, decipĕre

trickle *s* guttae *f pl*

trickle *vi* stillare, manare

trickster *s* veterator, fraudator *m*

trident *s* tridens *m*

triennial *adj* triennis

trifle *s* res parvi momenti *f*, nugae *f pl*

trifle *vi* nugari

trifling *adj* levis, exiguus, frivolus

trill *s* sonus modulatus *m*

trill *vt* vibrare

trim *adj* nitidus, comptus, bellus

trim *vt* adornare; *(to prune)* putare, tondēre

trinket *s* tricae *f pl*

trip *s* iter *n*

trip *vt* supplantare; *vi* titubare; *(fig)* errare

tripartite *adj* tripartitus

tripe *s* omasum *n*

triple *adj* triplex

triple *vt* triplicare

tripod *s* tripus *m*

trireme *s* triremis *f*

trite *adj* tritus

triumph *s* *(entry of victorious Roman general)* triumphus *m*; *(victory)* victoria *f*

triumph *vi* triumphare; vincĕre; **to — over** devincĕre

triumphal *adj* triumphalis

triumphant *adj* victor; elatus, laetus

trivial *adj* levis, tenuis

triviality *s* nugae *f pl*

troop *s* turma, caterva *f*, grex, globus *m*; **—s** *(mil)* copiae *f pl*

trooper *s* eques *m*

trope *s* tropus *m*

trophy *s* tropaeum *n*

tropical *adj* tropicus

tropics *s* loca fervida *n pl*

trot *vi* tolutim ire

trouble *s* labor, dolor *m*, incommodum *n*, aerumna, molestia *f*

trouble *vt* turbare, vexare, angĕre

troublesome *adj* molestus, operosus

trough *s* alveus *m*

trounce *vt* *(to punish)* castigare; *(to defeat decisively)* devincĕre

troupe *s* grex *m*

trousers *s* bracae *f pl*

trout *s* tru(c)ta *f*

trowel *s* trulla *f*

truant *s* cessator *m*

truce *s* indutiae *f pl*

truck *s* carrus *m*

truculent *adj* truculentus

trudge *vi* repĕre

true *adj* verus; *(genuine)* germanus; *(faithful)* fidus; *(exact)* rectus, justus

truism *s* verbum tritum *n*

truly *adv* vere, profecto

trump *vt* **to — up** effingĕre, ementiri

trumpet *s* tuba, bucina *f*

trumpeter *s* tubicen, bucinator *m*

truncheon *s* fustis *m*

trundle *vt* volvĕre

trunk *s* truncus *m*; *(for luggage)* cista *f*; *(of elephant)* proboscis *f*

trust *s* fiducia, fides *f*

trust *vt* fidĕre *(with dat)*, credĕre *(with dat)*; *(to entrust)* committĕre

trustee *s* fiduciarius, tutor *m*

trusteeship *s* tutela *f*

trustful *adj* credulus

trusting *adj* fidens; **—ly** fidenter

trustworthiness *s* integritas, fides *f*

trustworthy *adj* fidus; *(of witness)* locuples; *(of an authority)* bonus

trusty *adj* fidus

truth *s* veritas *f*, verum *n*; **in —** vero

truthful *adj* verax; **—ly** veraciter, vere

try *vt* tentare, probare, experiri; *(law)* cognoscĕre; *(to endeavor)* laborare; **to — one's patience** patientiā abuti

trying *adj* molestus, incommodus, gravis

tub *s* labrum, dolium *n*

tube *s* fistula *f*

tuck *vt* **to — up** succingĕre

tuft *s* floccus, cirrus *m*, crista *f*

tug *s* conat·us ·ūs, nis·us ·ūs *m*; *(ship)* navis tractoria *f*

tug *vt* trahĕre

tuition *s* tutela *f*

tumble *vi* corruĕre, collabi, volvi

tumbler *s* poculum vitreum *n*

tumor *s* tumor, tuber *m*

tumult *s* tumult·us ·ūs *m*

tumultuous *adj* tumultuosus, turbulentus; **—ly** tumultuose

tune *s* tonus *m*, moduli *m pl*

tuneful *adj* canorus

tunic *s* tunica *f*

tunnel *s* canalis, cuniculus *m*

turban *s* mitra, tiara *f*

turbid *adj* turbidus, turbulentus

turbulence *s* tumult·us ·ūs *m*

turbulent *adj* turbulentus; **—ly** turbulente

turf *s* caespes *m*

turgid *adj* turgidus

turkey *s* meleagris gallopavo *f*

turmoil *s* turba, perturbatio *f*, tumult·us ·ūs *m*

turn *s* *(circuit)* circuit·us ·ūs *m*; *(revolution)* conversio *f*, circumact·us ·ūs *m*; *(change, course)* vicissitudo *f*; *(inclination of mind)* inclinatio *f*, ingenium *n*; **a good —** officium, beneficium *n*; **in —** invicem

turn *vt* vertĕre, convertĕre; (*to twist*) torquĕre; (*to bend*) flectĕre; **to — aside** deflectĕre; **to — away** avertĕre; **to — down** (*refuse*) recusare, denegare, respuĕre; **to — into** mutare in (*with acc*), vertĕre in (*with acc*); **to — over** (*to hand over*) tradĕre, transferre; (*property*) alienare; (*in mind*) agitare; **to — one's attention to** animadvertĕre; **to — out** ejicĕre, expellĕre; **to — round** volvĕre, circumagĕre, rotare; **to — up** (*with hoe*) invertĕre; **to — up the nose** nares corrugare; *vi* verti, converti, versari; **to — against** disciscĕre ab (*with abl*), alienari ab (*with abl*); **to — aside** devertĕre, se declinare; **to — away** discedĕre, aversari; **to — back** reverti; **to — into** (*to be changed into*) vertĕre in (*with acc*), mutari in (*with acc*); **to — out** cadĕre, evadĕre, contingĕre, evenire; **to — round** converti; **to — up** intervenire, adesse

turnip *s* rapum *n*

turpitude *s* turpitudo *f*

turret *s* turricula *f*

turtle *s* testudo *f*

turtledove *s* turtur *m*

tusk *s* dens *m*

tutelage *s* tutela *f*

tutor *s* praeceptor, magister *m*

tutor *vt* edocēre

tweezers *s* volsella *f*

twelfth *adj* duodecimus

twelve *adj* duodecim; **— times** duodecies

twentieth *adj* vicesimus

twenty *adj* viginti; **— times** vicies

twice *adv* bis

twig *s* surculus, ramulus *m*, virga, virgula *f*

twilight *s* crepusculum *n*; (*dawn*) diluculum *n*

twin *adj* geminus

twin *s* geminus, gemellus *m*

twine *s* filum *n*, resticula *f*

twine *vt* circumplicare, contorquēre; *vi* circumplecti

twinge *s* dolor *m*

twinkle *vi* micare, coruscare

twinkling *s* (*of eye*) nict·us -ūs *m*

twirl *vt* versare, circumagēre; *vi* versari

twist *vt* torquēre; *vi* flecti

twit *vt* exprobrare, objurgare

twitch *s* vellicatio *f*

twitch *vt* vellicare; *vi* micare

twitter *vi* minurire

two *adj* duo; **— at a time** bini; **— times** bis

twofold *adj* duplex, duplus

type *s* (*model*) exemplum, exemplar *n*; (*class*) genus *n*, forma, figura *f*

typhoon *s* turbo *m*

typical *adj* solitus, proprius

tyrannical *adj* tyrannicus, superbus; **—ly** tyrannice, superbe

tyrannicide *s* (*act*) tyrannicidium *n*; (*person*) tyranni interfector, tyrannicida *m*

tyrannize *vi* dominari

tyranny *s* tyrannis, dominatio *f*

tyrant *s* tyrannus, dominus superbus *m*

tyro *s* tiro *m*

U

udder *s* uber *n*

ugliness *s* deformitas, foeditas *f*

ugly *adj* deformis, turpis, foedus

ulcer *s* ulcus *n*

ulcerous *adj* ulcerosus

ultimate *adj* ultimus, extremus; **—ly** tandem

umbrage *s* offensio *f*; **to take — at** aegre ferre

umbrella *s* umbella *f*

umpire *s* arbiter, disceptator *m*

unabashed *adj* intrepidus

unabated *adj* integer

unable *adj* impotens, invalidus; **to be —** to non posse, nequire

unaccented *adj* accentu carens

unacceptable *adj* ingratus, odiosus

unaccompanied *adj* incomitatus, solus

unaccomplished *adj* infectus, imperfectus

unaccountable *adj* inexplicabilis, inenodabilis

unaccountably *adv* praeter opinionem, sine causa

unaccustomed *adj* insolitus, insuetus, inexpertus

unacquainted *adj* **— with** ignarus (*with genit*), expers (*with genit*)

unadorned *adj* inornatus, incomptus, simplex

unadulterated *adj* merus, integer

unaffected *adj* simplex, candidus

unafraid *adj* impavidus

unaided *adj* non adjutus, sine ope

unalterable *adj* immutabilis

unaltered *adj* immutatus

unanimous *adj* unanimus, concors; **—ly** concorditer, consensu omnium

unanswerable *adj* irrefragabilis

unappeased *adj* implacatus

unapproachable *adj* inaccessus

unarmed *adj* inermis

unasked *adj* injussus, non vocatus

unassailable *adj* inexpugnabilis

unassuming *adj* modestus, moderatus, demissus

unattached *adj* liber, vacuus

unattainable *adj* arduus

unattempted *adj* inexpertus, inausus, intentatus

unattended *adj* incomitatus, sine comitibus

unattractive *adj* invenustus
unauthorized *adj* illicitus
unavailing *adj* inutilis, irritus
unavenged *adj* inultus
unavoidable *adj* inevitabilis
unaware *adj* inscius, nescius, ignarus
unbearable *adj* intolerabilis
unbeaten *adj* invictus
unbecoming *adj* indecorus, indecens; **it is —** dedecet
unbefitting *adj* indecorus
unbend *vi* animum remittĕre
unbending *adj* inflexibilis, inexorabilis
unbiased *adj* incorruptus, integer
unbidden *adj* injussus, ultro
unbleached *adj* crudus
unblemished *adj* integer, intactus
unblest *adj* infortunatus
unborn *adj* nondum natus
unbroken *adj* irruptus; integer; (*of horses*) indomitus
unbuckle *vt* refibulare
unburden *vt* exonerare
unbutton *vt* refibulare
unceasing *adj* constans, assiduus; **—ly** assidue
uncertain *adj* incertus, dubius; **—ly** incerte, dubie
uncertainty *s* dubium *n*, dubitatio *f*
unchangeable *adj* immutabilis
unchanged *adj* immutatus
unchanging *adj* integer, idem
uncharitable *adj* immisericors
unchaste *adj* impudicus, obscenus; **—ly** impudice, impure
uncivil *adj* inurbanus
uncivilized *adj* incultus
unclasp *vt* defibulare
uncle *s* (*father's brother*) patruus *m*; (*mother's brother*) avunculus *m*
unclean *adj* immundus
uncomfortable *adj* incommodus, molestus
uncommon *adj* rarus, insolitus, inusitatus; **—ly** raro, praeter solitum
unconcerned *adj* securus, incuriosus
unconditional *adj* absolutus, sine exceptione; **—ly** nullā condicione
unconnected *adj* disjunctus
unconquerable *adj* invictus
unconscionable *adj* iniquus, injustus, absurdus
unconscious *adj* omni sensu carens; **— of** ignarus (*with genit*), inscius (*with genit*)
unconstitutional *adj* illicitus; **—ly** contra leges
uncontrollable *adj* impotens
unconventional *adj* insolitus
unconvinced *adj* non persuasus
unconvincing *adj* non verisimilis
uncooked *adj* rudus
uncorrupted *adj* incorruptus
uncouth *adj* inurbanus, agrestis
uncover *vt* detegĕre, reclūdĕre, nudare
uncritical *adj* credulus
uncultivated *adj* incultus; indoctus
uncut *adj* intonsus
undamaged *adj* integer, inviolatus
undaunted *adj* impavidus, intrepidus

undecided *adj* incertus, dubius, anceps
undefended *adj* indefensus, nudus
undefiled *adj* purus, incontaminatus
undefined *adj* infinitus
undeniable *adj* haud dubius
under *adv* subter, infra
under *prep* (*position*) sub (*with abl*); (*motion*) sub (*with acc*); (*less than*) intra (*with acc*), infra (*with acc*)
underage *adj* impubes
underestimate *vt* minoris aestimare
undergarment *s* subucula *f*
undergo *vt* subire, pati
underground *adj* subterraneus
undergrowth *s* virgulta *n pl*
underhanded *adj* clandestinus, furtivus; **—ly** clam, furtive
underline *vt* subnotare
underling *s* minister, assecla *m*
undermine *vt* subruĕre, suffodĕre; (*fig*) labefacĕre, labefactare
underneath *adv* infra, subter
underneath *prep* (*position*) infra (*with acc*), sub (*with abl*); (*motion*) sub (*with acc*)
underrate *vt* minoris aestimare
understand *vt* intellegĕre, comprehendĕre
understanding *adj* prudens, sapiens
understanding *s* mens *f*, intellectus -ūs *m*; (*agreement*) consensus -ūs *m*; (*condition*) condicio *f*
undertake *vt* adire ad (*with acc*), suscipĕre; (*to begin*) incipĕre
undertaker *s* vespillo, libitinarius *m*
undertaking *s* inceptum, coeptum *n*
undervalue *vt* minoris aestimare
underworld *s* inferi *m pl*
undeserved *adj* immeritus, injustus; **—ly** immerito
undeserving *adj* indignus
undiminished *adj* imminutus
undiscernible *adj* imperceptus, invisus
undisciplined *adj* immoderatus; (*mil*) inexercitatus
undisguised *adj* apertus
undismayed *adj* impavidus, intrepidus
undisputed *adj* certus
undistinguished *adj* ignobilis, inglorius
undisturbed *adj* imperturbatus, immotus
undivided *adj* indivisus
undo *vt* (*knot*) expedire; (*fig*) infectum reddĕre; (*to ruin*) perdĕre
undone *adj* (*not completed*) infectus, imperfectus; (*ruined*) perditus
undoubted *adj* certus, haud dubius; **—ly** haud dubie
undress *vt* exuĕre; *vi* vestes exuĕre
undressed *adj* nudus; (*fig*) rudis
undue *adj* nimius, iniquus
undulate *vi* undare, fluctuare
undulation *s* undarum agitatio *f*
unduly *adv* nimis, plus aequo
undying *adj* aeternus, sempiternus
unearth *vt* detegĕre, effodĕre
unearthly *adj* humano major, divinus
uneasiness *s* sollicitudo, anxietas *f*

uneasy adj sollicitus, anxius

uneducated adj indoctus, illiteratus

unemployed adj vacuus, otiosus

unemployment s otium n, cessatio f

unencumbered adj expeditus

unending adj infinitus, perpetuus

unendurable adj intolerandus

unenjoyable adj injucundus

unenlightened adj ineruditus

unenviable adj non invidendus, miser

unequal adj inaequalis, dispar, impar; —ly inaequaliter, impariter, inique

unequaled adj singularis, eximius

unerring adj certus; —ly certe

uneven adj inaequalis, iniquus; (rough) asper

unexpected adj inopinatus, insperatus, improvisus; —ly de improviso

unexplored adj inexploratus

unfading adj semper recens

unfailing adj certus, perpetuus; —ly semper

unfair adj iniquus; —ly inique

unfaithful adj infidus, perfidus, infidelis; —ly perfide

unfamiliar adj ignotus, alienus

unfashionable adj obsoletus

unfasten vt laxare, resolvĕre

unfavorable adj adversus, iniquus, inopportunus

unfavorably adv male, inique

unfed adj impastus

unfeeling adj durus, crudelis; —ly dure, crudeliter

unfetter vt vincula demĕre (with dat)

unfinished adj imperfectus; (crude) rudis, impolitus

unfit adj inhabilis, ineptus, inutilis

unfold vt explicare, evolvĕre; (story) enarrare; vi dehiscĕre, patescĕre

unforeseeing adj imprudens, improvidus

unforeseen adj improvisus, insperatus

unforgiving adj inexorabilis

unfortified adj immunitus, nudus

unfortunate adj infelix, infortunatus, nefastus; —ly infeliciter

unfounded adj vanus, fictus

unfriendly adj parum amicus, inimicus, alienus

unfruitful adj infructuosus, sterilis, infecundus

unfulfilled adj infectus

unfurl vt pandĕre, solvĕre

unfurnished adj imparatus

ungainly adj ineptus, inhabilis

ungenerous adj illiberalis

ungentlemanly adj inurbanus, illepidus

ungird vt discingĕre

ungodly adj impius

ungovernable adj indomabilis, intractabilis

ungracious adj iniquus, asper

ungrateful adj ingratus; —ly ingrate

ungrudging adj non invitus; —ly sine invidia

unguarded adj incustoditus, indefensus; (of words) inconsultus

unhandy adj inhabilis

unhappily adv infeliciter, misere

unhappiness s tristitia, miseria, maestitia f

unhappy adj infelix, infortunatus, miser

unharness vt disjungĕre

unhealthiness s valetudo, gravitas f

unhealthy adj infirmus, morbosus; (unwholesome) gravis, insalubris

unheard-of adj inauditus

unheeded adj neglectus

unhelpful adj invitus, difficilis

unhesitating adj promptus, confidens; —ly confidenter

unhinge vt de cardine detrahĕre; (fig) perturbare

unholy adj impius, profanus

unhoped-for adj insperatus

unhurt adj incolumis, salvus

unicorn s monoceros m

uniform adj constans, aequabilis; —ly constanter, aequabiliter

uniform s vestit·us -ūs m; (mil) sagum n

uniformity s constantia, aequabilitas f

unify vt conjungĕre

unilateral adj unilaterus

unimaginative adj hebes

unimpaired adj integer, intactus

unimpeachable adj probatissimus

unimportant adj nullius momenti (genit), levis

uninformed adj indoctus

uninhabitable adj non habitabilis, inhabitabilis

uninhabited adj desertus

uninjured adj incolumis

uninspired adj hebes

unintelligible adj obscurus

uninteresting adj frigidus, jejunus

uninterrupted adj continuus, perpetuus

uninviting adj injucundus, non alliciens

union s (act) conjunctio f; (social) consociatio, societas f; (agreement) consens·us -ūs m; (marriage) conjugium n

unique adj unicus, singularis

unison s concent·us -ūs m

unit s monas f, unio m

unite vt conjungĕre, consociare; vi coalescĕre, coire; conjurare

unity s concordia f

universal adj universus, universalis; —ly universe, ubique

universe s mundus m, summa rerum f

university s academia, universitas f

unjust adj injustus, iniquus; —ly injuste, inique

unjustifiable adj indignus

unkempt adj incomptus, neglectus

unkind adj inhumanus; —ly inhumane

unknowingly adv insciens

unknown adj ignotus, incognitus

unlawful adj illegitimus, illicitus; —ly contra legem or leges

unless conj nisi

unlike adj dissimilis, dispar, diversus

unlikely adj parum verisimilis

unlimited adj infinitus, immensus

unload vt exonerare

unluckily adv infeliciter

unlucky adj infelix, infaustus

unmanageable adj intractabilis, contumax

unmanly adj mollis

unmannerly adj male moratus, inurbanus

unmarried adj (man) caelebs; (woman) innupta

unmask vt detegĕre

unmatched adj unicus, singularis

unmerciful adj immisericors; —ly immisericorditer

unmindful adj immemor

unmistakable adj certissimus

unmistakably adv sine dubio

unmoved adj immotus

unnatural adj (event) monstruosus; (deed) immanis, crudelis; —ly contra naturam

unnecessarily adv ex supervacuo, nimis

unnecessary adj haud necessarius, supervacaneus

unnerve vt debilitare

unnoticed adj praetermissus; to go — latēre

unobjectionable adj culpae expers, honestus

unoccupied adj vacuus; otiosus; (of land) apertus

unofficial adj privatus

unpack vt e cistis eximĕre

unpaid adj (of money) debitus; (of a service) gratuitus

unpalatable adj amarus, insuavis

unparalleled adj unicus, singularis

unpardonable adj inexcusabilis

unpatriotic adj immemor patriae

unpitying adj immisericors, inexorabilis

unpleasant adj injucundus, incommodus; —ly injucunde, incommode

unpolluted adj impollutus; (fig) integer, intactus

unpopular adj invisus, invidiosus

unpracticed adj inexpertus, imperitus

unprecedented adj novus, inauditus

unprejudiced adj aequus

unpremeditated adj subitus, ex tempore

unprepared adj imparatus

unprincipled adj improbus

unproductive adj infecundus, infructuosus, sterilis

unprofitable adj vanus, inutilis

unprofitably adv inutiliter, frustra

unprotected adj indefensus

unprovoked adj non lacessitus, ultro

unpunished adj inpunitus, inultus

unqualified adj haud idoneus, inhabilis

unquenchable adj inexstinctus

unquestionable adj haud dubius, certissimus

unquestionably adv certe

unquestioning adj credulus

unravel vt retexĕre; (fig) enodare, explicare

unreasonable adj rationis expers, absurdus; iniquus

unreasonably adv absurde, inique

unrefined adj rudis, crudus, incultus

unrelenting adj implacabilis, inexorabilis

unremitting adj assiduus, continuus

unrepentant adj impaenitens

unrestrained adj effrenatus, indomitus, effusus

unrighteous adj injustus, iniquus; —ly injuste

unripe adj immaturus, crudus

unroll vt evolvĕre, explicare

unruliness s petulantia f

unruly adj effrenatus, turbulentus

unsafe adj intutus, periculosus

unsatisfactory adj non idoneus, malus

unsavory adj insipidus, insulsus, insuavis

unseasonable adj intempestivus, immaturis; incommodus, importunus

unseemly adj indecorus, indecens

unseen adj invisus

unselfish adj suae utilitatis immemor, liberalis; —ly liberaliter

unsettle vt turbare, sollicitare

unsettled adj incertus, inconstans; (of mind) sollicitus

unshaken adj immotus

unshaved adj intonsus

unsheathe vt destringĕre, e vagina educĕre

unsightly adj turpis, foedus

unskilful adj imperitus, inscitus; —ly imperite, inscite

unskilled adj imperitus, indoctus

unsophisticated adj simplex

unsound adj infirmus; (mentally) insanus; (ill-founded) vanus

unsparing adj inclemens; (lavish) prodigus, largus; —ly inclementer; prodige, large

unspeakable adj ineffabilis, inenarrabilis

unstable adj instabilis; (fig) levis, inconstans

unstained adj incontaminatus, purus

unsteadily adv inconstanter, instabiliter

unsteady adj inconstans, instabilis

unsuccessful adj infelix, infaustus; —ly infeliciter

unsuitable adj inhabilis, incommodus, alienus

unsuited adj haud idoneus

unsullied adj incorruptus

unsuspected adj non suspectus

untamed adj indomitus, ferus

untasted adj ingustatus

untaught adj indoctus, rudis

unteachable adj indocilis

untenable adj infirmus, inanis

unthankful adj ingratus

untie vt solvĕre

until conj dum, donec, quoad

until prep usque ad (with acc), in (with acc); — now adhuc

untimely adj intempestivus, importunus, immaturus

untiring adj assiduus, indefessus

untold adj innumerus

untouched adj intactus, integer; (fig) immotus

untrained adj inexercitatus

untried *adj* inexpertus, intemptatus

untrodden *adj* non tritus, avius

untroubled *adj* placidus, tranquillus; (*of sleep*) levis

untrue *adj* falsus, mendax; (*disloyal*) infidus

untrustworthy *adj* infidus

unusual *adj* inusitatus, insolitus, insuetus; —**ly** praeter solitum, raro

unutterable *adj* infandus, inenarrabilis

unvarnished *adj* (*fig*) nudus, simplex

unveil *vt* detegěre, patefacěre

unversed *adj* imperitus

unwarranted *adj* injustus, iniquus

unwary *adj* imprudens, incautus

unwearied *adj* indefessus, impiger

unwelcome *adj* ingratus, injucundus

unwholesome *adj* insalubris

unwieldy *adj* inhabilis

unwilling *adj* invitus; —**ly** invite

unwind *vt* revolvěre, retexěre

unwise *adj* imprudens, insipiens; —**ly** imprudenter, insipienter

unworthy *adj* indignus

unwrap *vt* explicare, evolvěre

unwritten *adj* non scriptus

unyielding *adj* inflexibilis, obstinatus

unyoke *vt* disjungěre

up *adv* sursum; — **and down** sursum deorsum

upbringing *s* educatio *f*

upheaval *s* eversio *f*

uphold *vt* servare, sustiněre, sustentare

upkeep *s* impensa *f*

uplift *vt* sublevare

upon *prep* (*position*) super (*with abl*), in (*with abl*); (*motion*) super (*with acc*), in (*with acc*); (*directly after*) e(x) (*with abl*); (*dependence*) e(x) (*with abl*)

upper *adj* superus, superior

uppermost *adj* summus, supremus

upright *adj* erectus; (*of character*) honestus, integer; —**ly** recte; integre

uproar *s* tumult·us -ūs *m*, turba *f*

uproot *vt* eradicare, eruěre

upset *vt* evertěre, subvertěre, percellěre

upset *adj* perculsus

upstream *adv* adverso flumine

up to *prep* usque ad (*with acc*), ad (*with acc*), tenus (*postpositive, with abl or genit*)

upwards *adv* sursum, sublime; — **of** (*of number*) plus quam

urban *adj* urbanus, oppidanus

urge *vt* urgēre, impellěre, hortari; **to** — **on** stimulare

urge *s* impuls·us -ūs *m*

urgency *s* gravitas, necessitas *f*

urgent *adj* gravis, instans, vehemens; **to be** — instare; —**ly** vehementer, magnopere, graviter

urn *s* urna *f*

us *pron* nos; **to** — nobis; **with** — nobiscum

usage *s* mos *m*, consuetudo *f*

use *s* us·us -ūs, mos *m*, consuetudo, usura *f*; **no** —! frustra!; **to be of** — usui esse, prodesse; **to make** — **of** uti (*with abl*)

use *vt* uti (*with abl*); (*to take advantage of*) abuti (*with abl*); **to** — **something for** aliquid adhiběre (*with dat*); **to** — **up** consuměre, exhaurire; *vi* **I used to** solebam (*with inf*)

used *adj* usitatus; — **to** (*accustomed to*) assuetus (*with dat*)

useful *adj* utilis, commodus, aptus; —**ly** utiliter, commode, apte

useless *adj* inutilis, inhabilis; (*of things*) inanis; —**ly** inutiliter, frustra

usual *adj* usitatus, solitus, consuetus; —**ly** plerumque, fere, ferme; **I** — **go** soleo ire

usurp *vt* usurpare, occupare

usurper *s* usurpator *m*

usury *s* usura *f*; **to practice** — faenerari

utensils *s* utensilia, vasa *n pl*, supellex *f*

utility *s* utilitas *f*

utilize *vt* uti (*with abl*), adhiběre

utmost *adj* extremus, ultimus, summus; **to do one's** — omnibus viribus contenděre

utter *adj* totus, extremus, summus; —**ly** omnino, funditus

utter *vt* eloqui, proferre, pronuntiare, eděre

utterance *s* elocutio, pronuntiatio *f*, dictum *n*

uttermost *adj* extremus, ultimus

V

vacant *adj* vacuus, inanis; **to be** — vacare

vacation *s* vacatio *f*, feriae *f pl*

vacillate *vi* vacillare

vacuum *s* inane *n*

vagabond *s* vagabundus, grassator *m*

vagrant *adj* vagabundus, vagus

vague *adj* vagus, dubius, ambiguus; —**ly** incerte, ambigue

vain *adj* vanus, futilis; superbus, arrogans; **in** — frustra; —**ly** frustra

valet *s* cubicularius *m*

valiant *adj* fortis; —**ly** fortiter

valid *adj* validus, legitimus, ratus; (*argument*) gravis

valley *s* vallis *f*

valor *s* fortitudo *f*

valuable *adj* pretiosus

valuation *s* aestimatio *f*

value *s* pretium *n*, aestimatio *f*

value *vt* aestimare, ducěre; **to** — **highly** magni aestimare, magni haběre

valueless *adj* vilis, inutilis

vanguard *s* (*mil*) primum agmen *n*

vanish *vi* vanescĕre, diffugĕre

vanity *s* gloria, ostentatio *f*

vanquish *vt* vincĕre, superare

vapor *s* vapor *m*, exhalatio *f*

variable *adj* commutabilis, varius

variation *s* varietas, commutatio, vicissitudo *f*

variety *s* varietas, diversitas, multitudo *f*

various *adj* varii, diversi; **—ly** varie, diverse

vary *vt* variare, mutare; *vi* mutari

vase *s* amphora *f*, vas *n*

vast *adj* vastus, ingens, immensus; **—ly** valde

vastness *s* immensitas *f*

vault *s* fornix, camera *f*; (*leap*) salt·us -ūs *m*

vault *vi* salire

vaunt *vt* jactare; *vi* se jactare

veal *s* caro vitulina *f*

vegetable *s* holus *n*

vegetable *adj* holitarius

vehemence *s* vehementia, vis *f*, impet·us -ūs *m*

vehement *adj* vehemens, violentus, fervidus; **—ly** vehementer, valde

vehicle *s* vehiculum *n*

veil *s* velamen *n*, rica *f*; (*bridal*) flammeum *n*; (*fig*) integumentum *n*

veil *vt* velare, tegĕre

vein *s* vena *f*

velocity *s* velocitas, celeritas *f*

velvet *s* velvetum *n*

vend *vt* vendĕre

veneer *s* ligni bractea *f*; (*fig*) species *f*

venerable *adj* venerabilis

venerate *vt* venerari, colĕre

veneration *s* adoratio *f*, cult·us -ūs *m*

vengeance *s* ultio, poena *f*; **to take — on** vindicare in (*with acc*), ulcisci

venom *s* venenum, virus *n*

vent *s* spiramentum, foramen *n*

vent *vt* aperire; **to — one's wrath on** iram erumpere in (*with acc*)

ventilate *vt* ventilare

venture *s* ausum *f*

venture *vt* periclitari; audēre

veracious *adj* verax

veracity *s* veracitas *f*

verb *s* verbum *n*

verbal *adj* verbalis; **—ly** verbo tenus

verbatim *adv* ad verbum

verbose *adj* verbosus; **—ly** verbose

verdict *s* sententia *f*; **to deliver a — sententiam pronuntiare

verge *s* margo, ora *f*; **to be on the — of** non procul abesse ut

verge *vi* vergĕre

verification *s* affirmatio *f*

verify *vt* ratum facĕre, confirmare

vermin *s* bestiolae *f pl*

versatile *adj* varius, agilis, versatilis

verse *s* vers·us -ūs *m*

versed *adj* peritus, exercitatus

version *s* forma, translatio *f*

vertex *s* vertex, vortex *m*

vertical *adj* rectus, directus; **—ly** ad lineam, ad perpendiculum

very *adj* ipse

very *adv* valde, admodum

vessel *s* vas *n*; (*ship*) navigium *n*

vest *s* subucula *f*

vestal *s* virgo vestalis *f*

vestige *s* vestigium, indicium *n*

vestment *s* vestimentum *n*

veteran *s* (*mil*) veteranus, vexillarius, emeritus *m*; (*fig*) veterator *m*

veterinarian *s* veterinarius *m*

veto *s* intercessio *f*, interdictum *n*

veto *vt* interdicĕre (*with dat*); (*as tribune*) intercedĕre (*with dat*)

vex *vt* vexare, sollicitare

vexation *s* vexatio, offensio *f*, stomachus *m*

via *prep* per (*with acc*)

vial *s* phiala *f*

vibrate *vi* tremĕre, vibrare

vibration *s* tremor *m*

vicar *s* vicarius *m*

vice *s* vitium *n*, turpitudo *f*

vicinity *s* vicinitas, vicinia *f*

vicious *adj* vitiosus, perditus; (*of temper*) ferox; **—ly** ferociter

vicissitude *s* vicissitudo *f*

victim *s* victima, hostia *f*; (*exploited*) praeda *f*

victimize *vt* circumvenire

victor *s* victor *m*, victrix *f*

victorious *adj* victor; (*of woman*) victrix; **to be —** vincĕre

victory *s* victoria *f*; **to win a —** victoriam reportare

vie *vi* certare, contendĕre; **to — with** aemulari (*with dat*)

view *s* aspect·us -ūs, conspect·us -ūs *m*; (*from above*) despect·us -ūs *m*; (*opinion*) opinio, sententia *f*, judicium *n*; **in my —** me judice; **to have in —** praevidēre

view *vt* visĕre, conspicĕre, intuēri, inspicĕre

vigil *s* pervigilatio *f*, pervigilium *n*

vigilance *s* vigilantia, diligentia *f*

vigilant *adj* vigilans, diligens, intentus; **—ly** vigilanter, diligenter

vigor *s* vigor, impet·us -ūs *m*, robur *n*

vigorous *adj* strenuus, acer, vegetus; **—ly** strenue, acriter

vile *adj* vilis, abjectus, perditus, flagitiosus

vilify *vt* infamare, calumniari

villa *s* villa *f*

village *s* vicus, pagus *m*

villager *s* vicanus, paganus *m*

villain *s* scelestus, nequam (*indecl*) *m*

villany *s* scelus *n*, improbitas, nequitia *f*

vindicate *vt* vindicare; (*to justify*) purgare; (*person*) defendĕre

vindictive *adj* ultionis cupidus

vine *s* vitis *f*

vinegar *s* acetum *n*

vineyard *s* vinea *f*, vinetum *n*

violate *vt* violare

violation *s* violatio *f*

violator *s* violator *m*

violence *s* violentia, vis *f*, impet·us -ūs *m*; (*cruelty*) saevitia *f*

violent *adj* violentus, vehemens; **—ly** violenter, vehementer

virgin *adj* virginalis

virgin *s* virgo *f*

virile *adj* virilis

virility *s* virilitas *f*

virtually *adv* fere

virtue *s* virtus, probitas *f*; *(power)* vis *f*; **by — of** per *(with acc)*, ex *(with abl)*

virtuous *adj* probus, honestus; *(chaste)* castus, pudicus; **—ly** honeste, caste

virulence *s* vis *f*, virus *n*; *(fig)* acerbitas *f*

visage *s* facies *f*, os *n*

viscous *adj* viscosus, lentus

visible *adj* aspectabilis, conspicuus, manifestus; **to be —** apparēre

visibly *adv* manifesto

vision *s* *(sense)* vis·us -ūs *m*; *(apparition)* visum *n*, visio *f*

visionary *adj* vanus, fictus, inanis

visit *s* salutatio *f*

visit *vt* visēre, visitare

visitor *s* salutator *m*, salutatrix *f*; advena, hospes *m*

visor *s* buccula *f*

vista *s* prospect·us -ūs *m*

visual *adj* oculorum *(genit)*

vital *adj* vitalis; *(essential)* necessarius; **—ly** praecipue

vitality *s* vis *f*, animus *m*

vitiate *vt* vitiare, corrumpěre

vituperate *vt* vituperare, reprehendēre

vituperative *adj* maledicus

vivacious *adj* vividus, alacer, hilaris; **—ly** acriter

vivacity *s* alacritas *f*

vivid *adj* vividus, acer; **—ly** acriter

vivify *vt* animare, vivificare

vocabulary *s* verborum copia *f*

vocal *adj* vocalis, canorus

vocation *s* officium, munus *n*

vociferous *adj* clamosus

vogue *s* mos *m*; **to be in — in** honore esse

voice *s* vox *f*, sonus *m*; *(vote)* suffragium *n*

void *s* inane, vacuum *n*

volatile *adj* levis, volaticus

volcanic *adj* flammas eructans

volcano *s* mons ignivomus *m*

volition *s* voluntas *f*

volley *s* conject·us -ūs *m*

voluble *adj* volubilis

volume *s* *(book)* volumen *n*; *(quantity)* copia, multitudo *f*; *(size)* amplitudo *f*

voluminous *adj* copiosus, amplus, magnus

voluntary *adj* voluntarius; *(unpaid)* gratuitus

volunteer *s* voluntarius *m*; *(mil)* miles voluntarius, evocatus *m*

volunteer *vi* sponte nomen dare

voluptuous *adj* voluptarius, voluptuosus, delicatus

vomit *vt* vomēre, evomēre

voracious *adj* vorax; **—ly** voraciter

voracity *s* voracitas *f*

vortex *s* vortex *m*

vote *s* suffragium *n*; *(fig)* *(judgment)* sententia *f*

vote *vi* suffragium ferre, suffragium inire; *(of judge)* sententiam ferre; *(of senator)* censēre; **to — against** antiquare; **to — for** suffragari *(with dat)*

votive *adj* votivus

vouch *vi* spondēre; **to — for** testificari, asseverare

voucher *s* *(person)* auctor *m*; *(document)* testimonium *n*

vow *s* votum *n*

vow *vt* *(to promise)* (de)vovēre, spondēre, promittēre

vowel *s* vocalis littera *f*

voyage *s* navigatio *f*

voyage *vi* navigare

voyager *s* navigator *m*

vulgar *adj* vulgaris, communis; *(low)* plebeius, vilis

vulgarity *s* insulsitas *f*

vulnerable *adj* obnoxius

vulture *s* vultur *m*

W

wade *vi* per vada ire; **to — across** vado transire

wag *vt* vibrare, agitare

wage *vt* **to — war** bellum gerēre

wager *vt* deponěre; *vi* sponsionem facěre

wages *s* merces *f*, stipendium *n*

wagon *s* carrus *m*, plaustrum *n*

wail *vi* plorare, plangěre, ululare

wailing *s* plorat·us -ūs, planct·us -ūs *m*

waist *s* medium corpus *n*

wait *vi* manēre; **to — for** exspectare; **to — on** servire *(with dat)*

wait *s* mora *f*; **to lie in — for** insidiari *(with dat)*

waive *vt* decedēre de *(with abl)*, remittēre

wake *vt* exsuscitare, excitare; *vi* expergisci

wake *s* vestigia *n pl*; **in the — of** post *(with acc)*

wakeful *adj* insomnis, vigil

waken *vt* exsuscitare, excitare; *vi* expergisci

walk *s* *(act)* ambulatio *f*; *(place)* ambulacrum *n*, xystus *m*; *(covered)* portic·us -ūs *m*; *(gait)* incess·us -ūs *m*

walk *vi* inceděre, ambulare, gradi

wall *s* *(of house)* paries *f*; *(of town)* moenia *n pl*, murus *m*

wall *vt* muro cingěre, moenibus munire

wallow *vi* volutari

walnut *s* juglans *f*

wan *adj* pallidus, exsanguis

wander *vi* vagari, errare; **to — about** pervagari; **to — over** pererrare

wanderer *s* erro, vagus *m*

wandering *s* erratio *f*

wane *vi* decrescěre, minui, tabescěre

want s egestas, inopia, indigentia, defectio f

want vt (to wish) velle; (to lack) egēre (with abl), indigēre (with abl), carēre (with abl); (to miss) desiderare

wanting adj (defective) vitiosus; (missing) absens; **to be —** deficĕre, deesse

wanton adj protervus, lascivus, petulans; **—ly** lascive, petulanter

war s bellum n; **to declare —** bellum indicĕre; **to declare — on** bellum indicĕre (with dat); **to enter —** bellum suscipĕre; **to wage — bellum** gerĕre

war vi bellare

war cry s ululat·us -ūs m

ward s (of town) regio f; (guard) custodia f; (minor) pupillus m, pupilla f

ward vt **to — off** arcēre, avertēre, defendĕre

warden s custos m; (of prison) carcerarius m

warehouse s apotheca f

wares s merx f

warfare s bellum n, res bellica f

war horse s equus bellator m

warlike adj militaris, bellicosus

warm adj calidus, (fig) acer; **to be — calēre; —ly** ardenter, acriter

warm vt calefacĕre, tepefacĕre

warmth s calor, fervor m

warn vt monēre, praemonēre

warning s monitio f, monit·us -ūs m; (object lesson) exemplum n

warrant s auctoritas f, mandatum n

warrant vt praestare, promittĕre

warranty s satisdatio f

warrior s bellator, miles m, bellatrix f

wart s verruca f

wary adj cautus, providus, circumspectus

wash vt lavare; **to — away** abluĕre, diluĕre; **to — out** eluĕre; vi lavari

wash s (clothes) lintea lavanda n pl

washing s lavatio f, lotura f

wasp s vespa f

waste s detrimentum n, effusio, dissipatio f; (of time) jactura f

waste adj vastus, desertus; **to lay — vastare, (de)populari**

waste vt consumĕre, perdĕre, dissipare; (time) absumĕre, terĕre; vi **to — away** tabescĕre, intabescĕre

wasteful adj profusus, prodigus; **—ly** prodige

wasteland s solitudo, vastitas f

watch s (guard) vigilia f; (sentry) excubiae f pl; **to keep —** excubare; **to keep — over** invigilare (with dat), custodire

watch vt (to observe) observare, spectare, intuēri; (to guard) custodire; vi **to — out** for exspectare

watchful adj vigilans; **—ly** vigilanter

watchman s vigil, excubitor m

watchtower s specula f

watchword s tessera f, signum n

water s aqua f

water vt irrigare; (animals) adaquare

waterfall s cataracta f

watering place s aquarium n

watery adj aquaticus, aquosus

wave s unda f, fluct·us -ūs m

wave vt agitare, vibrare, jactare; vi undare, fluctuare

waver vi fluctuare, labare, dubitare

wavering adj dubius, incertus

wavy adj undans, undosus; (of hair) crispus

wax s cera f

wax vt incerare; vi crescĕre, augēri

waxen adj cereus

way s via f, iter n; (manner) ratio f, modus m; (habit) mos m; **all the — from** usque ab (with abl); **all the — to** usque ad (with acc); **to get in the — of** intervenire (with dat); **to give — (of a structure)** labare; (mil) pedem referre; **to give — to** indulgēre (with dat); **to stand in the — of** obstare (with dat)

wayfarer s viator m

waylay vt insidiari (with dat)

wayward adj inconstans, levis, mutabilis

we pron nos; **— ourselves** nosmet ipsi

weak adj infirmus, debilis, imbecillus; (argument) tenuis; (senses) hebes; **—ly** infirme

weaken vt infirmare, debilitare, enervare; vi labare, hebescĕre, infirmus fieri

weakness s infirmitas, debilitas f; (of mind) imbecillitas f; (flaw) vitium n; (of arguments) levitas f

wealth s divitiae, opes f pl; copia, abundantia f

wealthy adj dives, opulentus; abundans

wean vt ab ubere depellĕre; (fig) desuefacĕre

weapon s telum n

wear vt (clothes) gerĕre; **to — out** terĕre, exedĕre; vi durare

weariness s lassitudo f

wearisome adj molestus

weary adj lassus, fessus, fatigatus

weather s caelum n, tempestas f

weather vt **to — a storm** procellam superare

weave vt texĕre

web s (on loom) tela, textura f; (spider's) araneum n

wed vt (a woman) ducĕre; (a man) nubĕre (with dat); vi (of husband) uxorem ducĕre; (of bride) nubĕre

wedge s cuneus m

wedlock s matrimonium n

weed s herba inutilis f

weed vt eruncare

week s hebdomas f

weekly adj hebdomadalis

weep vi flēre, lacrimare; **to — for** deplorare

weeping s plorat·us -ūs m, lacrimae f pl

weigh vt pendĕre, ponderare, trutinari; (fig) meditari; **to — down** degravare; (fig) opprimĕre; vi **to — much** magni ponderis esse

weight s pondus n, gravitas f; (influence) (fig) auctoritas f; (importance) momentum n
weighty adj ponderosus, gravis
welcome s gratulatio, salutatio f
welcome vt salvēre jubēre, excipēre
welcome interj salve!; (to several) salvēte!
weld vt (con)ferruminare
welfare s salus f
well s puteus, fons m
well adj sanus, validus, salvus
well adv bene, recte, probe; **very —** optime
well interj heia!
well-bred adj generosus, liberalis
well-known adj pervulgatus; notus, nobilis
welter s congeries, turba f
west s occidens, occas·us -ūs m
western adj occidentalis
westward adv in occasum, occasum versus
west wind s Zephyrus, Favonius m
wet adj humidus, uvidus, madidus
wet vt madefacĕre, rigare
whale s balaena f, cetus m
wharf s navale n, crepido f
what pron interrog quid, quidnam, ecquid
what adj interrog qui; **— sort of** qualis
whatever pron quisquis
whatever adj quicumque
wheat s triticum n
wheedle vt blandiri, delenire
wheedling adj blandus
wheel s rota f
wheelbarrow s pabo m
whelp s catulus m
when adv quando
when conj cum, ubi, ut
whence adv unde
whenever conj quandocumque, utcumque, quotiens
where adv ubi
where conj quā, ubi
whereas conj quandoquidem
whereby adv re, quā viā, quo, per quod
wherefore adv quare, quamobrem, quapropter
wherein adv in quo, in quibus, ubi
whereof adv cujus, quorum; de quo, de quibus
whereto adv quo, quorsum
whereupon adv quo facto, post quae
wherever conj quacumque, ubicumque
whet vt acuĕre; (fig) exacuĕre
whether conj (in single indirect question) num, -ne, an; **whether . . . or** (in multiple indirect questions) utrum . . . an, -ne . . . an, . . . an; (in disjunctive conditions) sive . . . sive, seu . . . seu; **whether . . . or not** utrum . . . necne
whetstone s cos f
which pron interrog quis; (of two) uter; pron rel qui
which adj interrog qui; (of two) uter; adj rel qui
whichever pron quisquis, quicum-

que; (of two) untercumque
while s tempus, spatium n; **a little — ** paulisper; **a long — ** diu; **it is worth —** operae pretium est; **once in a —** interdum
while conj dum, quoad, donec
whim s libido f
whimper vi vagire
whimper s vagit·us -ūs m
whimsical adj levis, mobilis
whine vi miserabiliter vagire
whip s flagellum n, scutica f
whip vt flagellare, verberare
whirl vt torquēre, rotare; vi torquēri, rotari
whirlpool s vertex, gurges m
whirlwind s turbo, typhon m
whisper s susurrus m
whisper vt & vi susurrare
whistle s (pipe) fistula f; (sound) sibilus m; (of wind) stridor m
whistle vi sibilare
white adj albus; (brilliant) candidus; (of hair) canus
whiten vt dealbare, candefacĕre; vi albescĕre, canescĕre
who pron interrog quis; pron rel qui
whoever pron quicumque, quisquis
whole adj totus, cunctus; integer
whole s totum n, summa f; **on the —** plerumque
wholesome adj saluber, salutaris
wholly adv omnino, prorsus
whose pron cujus; quorum
why adv cur, quare, quamobrem
wicked adj improbus, nefarius, impius; **—ly** improbe, nefarie
wickedness s nequitia, improbitas, impietas f, scelus n
wicker adj vimineus
wide adj latus, amplus; **—ly** late
widen vt dilatare, laxare, extendĕre; vi patescĕre, dilatari, laxari
widow s vidua f
widower s viduus m
widowhood s viduitas f
width s latitudo, amplitudo f
wield vt tractare, vibrare
wife s uxor, conju(n)x f
wifely adj uxorius
wig s capillamentum n
wild adj ferus; (of trees, plants, etc.) silvestris; (of land) vastus, incultus; (of disposition) saevus, amens, ferox; **—ly** saeve, ferociter
wilderness s vastitas, solitudo f, loca deserta n pl
wile s fraus f, dolus m
wilful adj pervicax, consultus; **—ly** de industria
will s voluntas f, animus m; (intent) propositum, consilium n; (document) testimonium n; (of gods) nut·us -ūs m; **at —** ad libidinem
will vt velle; (legacy) legare, relinquēre
willing adj libens, promptus; **to be —** velle; **—ly** libenter
willow s salix f
wily adj vafer, astutus
win vt adipisci, nancisci, consequi, (victory) reportare; (friends) sibi

conciliare; **to — over** conciliare;
vi vincĕre, superare

wind *s* ventus *m*

wind *vt* circumvolvĕre, circumver-
tĕre, glomerare, torquēre; **to — up**
(*to bring to an end*) conclūdĕre; *vi*
sinuare

windfall *s* (*fig*) lucrum insperatum *n*

winding *adj* sinuosus, flexuosus

windmill *s* venti mola *f*

window *s* fenestra *f*

windpipe *s* aspera arteria *f*

windy *adj* ventosus

wine *s* vinum *n*; (*undiluted*) merum
n; (*sour or cheap*) vappa *f*; (*new*)
mustum *n*

wing *s* ala *f*; (*mil*) cornu *n*

winged *adj* alatus, volucer

wink *vi* nictare, connivēre

winner *s* victor *m*

winning *adj* (*fig*) blandus, amoenus

winnings *s* lucrum *n*

winnow *vt* ventilare

winter *s* hiems *f*; **in the dead of —**
media hieme; **to spend the —** hiemare

winter *vi* hiemare, hibernare

winter *adj* hibernus

winter quarters *s* hiberna *n pl*

wintry *adj* hiemalis, hibernus

wipe *vt* detergēre; **to — away** ab-
stergēre; **to — out** delēre, abolēre,
expungēre

wire *s* filum aeneum *n*

wisdom *s* sapientia, prudentia *f*

wise *adj* sapiens, prudens; **—ly** sapienter, prudenter

wise *s* modus *m*; **in no —** nequaquam

wish *s* optatum, votum *n*; **best —es**
salus *f*

wish *vt* optare, velle, cupĕre; *vi* **to
— for** exoptare, expetĕre

wisp *s* manipulus *m*

wistful *adj* desiderii plenus; **—ly**
oculis intentis

wit *s* (*intellect*) ingenium *n*, argutiae
f pl; (*humor*) sales *m pl*, facetiae *f
pl*; (*person*) homo facetus *m*; **to be
at one's —s' end** delirare; **to —**
scilicet

witch *s* venefica, saga *f*

witchcraft *s* ars magica *f*, veneficium *n*

with *prep* cum (*with abl*); apud (*with
acc*)

withdraw *vt* seducĕre, avocare;
(*words*) revocare; *vi* recedĕre, discedĕre

wither *vt* torrēre, corrumpĕre; *vi*
marcēre, arescēre

withered *adj* marcidus

withhold *vt* retinēre, abstinēre, cohibēre

within *adv* intus, intra; (*motion*) intro

within *prep* intro (*with acc*), in
(*with abl*); **— a few days** paucis
diebus

without *adv* extra, foris; **from —**
extrinsecus

without *prep* sine (*with abl*), absque (*with abl*), expers (*with genit*);

to be — carēre (*with abl*)

withstand *vt* obsistĕre (*with dat*),
resistĕre (*with dat*)

witness *s* testis *m* & *f*; (*to a signature*) obsignator *m*; **to call to —** testari,
testificari; **to call to —** testari,
antestari

witness *vt* testificari; (*to see*) intuēri, vidēre

witticism *s* sales *m pl*

witty *adj* facetus, salsus, acutus

wizard *s* magus, veneficus *m*

woe *s* dolor, luct·us -ūs *m*; **—s** mala
n pl

woeful *adj* tristis, luctuosus, miser;
—ly triste, misere

wolf *s* lupus *m*, lupa *f*

woman *s* mulier, femina *f*

womanhood *s* muliebris stat·us -ūs *m*

womanly *adj* muliebris

womb *s* uterus *m*

wonder *s* admiratio *f*; (*astonishing
object*) miraculum, mirum *n*

wonder *vi* (ad)mirari; **to — at** admirari

wonderful *adj* mirabilis, admirandus; **—ly** mirabiliter, mirifice

wont *adj* **to be — to** solēre (*with inf*)

woo *vt* petĕre

wood *s* lignum *n*; (*forest*) silva *f*, nemus *n*

wooded *adj* lignosus, silvestris

wooden *adj* ligneus

woodland *s* silvae *f pl*

woodman *s* lignator *m*

wood nymph *s* Dryas *f*

wooer *s* procus, amator *m*

wool *s* lana *f*

woolen *adj* laneus

word *s* verbum, vocabulum *n*; (*spoken*) vox *f*; (*promise*) fides *f*; (*news*)
nuntius *m*; **in a — denique**; **to
break one's —** fidem fallĕre; **to
give one's —** fidem dare; **to keep
one's —** fidem praestare; **— for —**
ad verbum

wordy *adj* verbosus

work *s* opera *f*, opus *n*; (*trouble*) labor *m*; (*task*) pensum *n*

work *vt* (*to exercise*) exercēre; (*to till*)
colĕre; *vi* laborare, operari

workman *s* (*unskilled*) operarius *m*;
(*skilled*) faber, opifex *m*

workmanship *s* opus *n*, ars *f*

workshop *s* officina *f*

world *s* (*universe*) mundus *m*, summa rerum *f*; (*earth*) orbis terrarum
m; (*nature*) rerum natura *f*; (*mankind*) homines *m pl*

worldly *adj* profanus

worm *s* vermis, vermiculus *m*, tinea *f*

worm-eaten *adj* vermiculosus

worry *s* sollicitudo, cura *f*

worry *vt* vexare, sollicitare; *vi* sollicitari

worse *adj* pejor, deterior; **to grow
—** ingravescĕre

worsen *vi* ingravescĕre

worship *s* veneratio *f*, cult·us -ūs *m*

worship *vt* venerari, adorare, colĕre

worshiper *s* cultor, venerator *m*

worst *adj* pessimus, deterrimus

worst *vt* vincĕre

worth s (*value*) pretium n; (*merit*) dignitas, virtus f; **to be —** valēre

worthless adj vilis, inutilis; (*of person*) nequam (*indecl*)

worthy adj dignus

wound s vulnus n

wound vt vulnerare; (*fig*) offendēre, laedēre

wounded adj saucius

wrap vt involvēre; **to — up** complicare

wrath s ira, iracundia f

wrathful adj iratus, iracundus; **—ly** iracunde

wreak vt **to — vengeance on** ulcisci, vindicare

wreath s sertum n, corona f

wreathe vt (*to twist*) torquēre; (*to adorn with wreaths*) coronare, nectēre

wreck s naufragium n

wreck vt frangēre; (*fig*) perdēre

wren s regulus m

wrench vt detorquēre, luxare

wrest vt extorquēre, eripēre

wrestle vi luctari

wrestler s luctator, athleta m

wretch s miser, perditus, nequam (*indecl*) m

wretched adj miser, infelix, abjectus; **—ly** misere, abjecte

wretchedness s miseria, aerumna f

wring vt contorquēre, stringēre; **to — the neck** gulam frangēre

wrinkle s ruga f

wrinkle vt corrugare; **to — the forehead** frontem contrahēre

wrinkled adj rugosus

writ s (*law*) mandatum n

write vt scribēre, perscribēre; (*poetry*) componēre; (*history*) perscribēre

writer s scriptor, auctor m

writhe vi torquēri

writing s (*act*) scriptio f; (*result*) scriptum n, scriptura f; (*hand*) man·us -ūs f

wrong adj pravus, perversus, falsus; (*unjust*) injustus, iniquus; **—ly** falso, male, perperam; **to be —** errare, falli

wrong s nefas n, injuria f, malum n; **to do —** peccare

wrong vt nocēre (*with dat*), injuriam inferre (*with dat*), laedēre

wrought adj factus, confectus, fabricatus

wry adj distortus, obliquus

Y

yard s (*court*) area f; (*measure*) tres pedes m pl; **a — long** tripedalis

yawn vi oscitare, hiare; (*to gape open*) dehiscēre

year s annus m; **every —** quotannis; **five —s** quinquennium n; **four —s** quadriennium n; **three —s** triennium n; **two —** biennium n

yearly adj annuus, anniversarius

yearly adv quotannis

yearn vi **to — for** desiderare

yeast s fermentum n

yell s ululat·us -ūs m, ejulatio f

yell vi ululare, ejulare

yellow adj flavus, luteus, gilvus, croceus

yelp vt gannire

yes adv ita, immo, sane

yesterday adv heri

yet adv (*contrast, after adversative clause*) tamen, nihilominus; (*time*) adhuc; (*with comparatives*) etiam; **as —** adhuc; **not —** nondum

yield vt (*to produce*) ferre, parēre,

praebēre; (*to surrender*) dedēre, concedēre; vi cedēre

yoke s jugum n; (*fig*) servitus f

yoke vt jugum imponēre (*with dat*), conjungēre

yonder adv illic

you pron (*thou*) tu; (*ye*) vos; **— yourself** tu ipse

young adj juvenis, adulescens; (*of child*) parvus; (*fig*) novus

younger adj junior, minor natu

youngster s adulescentulus m

your adj tuus; vester

yours pron tuus; vester

yourself pron reflex te; **to — tibi; with — tecum;** *intensive* tu ipse

yourselves pron reflex vos; **to — vobis; with — vobiscum;** *intensive* vos ipsi, vosmet ipsi

youth s (*age*) adulescentia f; (*collectively*) juventus f; (*young man*) juvenis, adulescens m

youthful adj juvenalis, puerilis; **—ly** juveniliter, pueriliter

Z

zeal s studium n, ardor, fervor m

zealous adj studiosus, ardens; **—ly** studiose, ardenter m

zenith s vertex m

zephyr s Zephyrus, Favonius m

zero s nihil, nihilum n

zest s (*taste*) sapor, gust·us -ūs m;

(*fig*) gustat·us -ūs, impet·us -ūs m

zigzag adj tortuosus

zodiac s signifer orbis m

zone s zona, regio f

zoology s zoologia, animantium descriptio f